ANCIENT WRITERS

Greece and Rome

ANCIENT WRITERS

Greece and Rome

T. JAMES LUCE

EDITOR IN CHIEF

Volume II

LUCRETIUS

TO

AMMIANUS MARCELLINUS

CHARLES SCRIBNER'S SONS / *New York*

Copyright © 1982 Charles Scribner's Sons

Library of Congress Cataloging in Publication Data
Main entry under title:

Ancient writers.

    Includes bibliographies and index.
    Contents: v. 1. Homer to Caesar—v. 2.
Lucretius to Ammianus Marcellinus.
    1. Classical literature—History and
criticism. I. Luce, T. James (Torrey James),
1932-
PA3002.A5 1982   880'.09   82–50612
ISBN 0-684-16595-3 Set   AACR2
ISBN 0-684-17814-1 Volume I
ISBN 0-684-17815-X Volume II

3 5 7 9 11 13 15 17 19 Q/C 20 18 16 14 12 10 8 6 4 2

PRINTED IN THE UNITED STATES OF AMERICA.

The paper in this book meets the guidelines for permanence and durability of
the Committee on Production Guidelines for Book Longevity of the Council
on Library Resources.

ANCIENT WRITERS
Greece and Rome

LUCRETIUS

(94?–50? B.C.)

THE EPICUREAN SLOGAN, "Go through life without being noticed," was fulfilled almost to the letter by Lucretius. Cicero—who incidentally made every effort to apply the opposite principle in his own life—left the only contemporary reference to Lucretius in a letter to his brother, Quintus, written in February 54 B.C. (*Ad Quintum fratrem* 2.9.3): "The *poemata* of Lucretius are as you write: much brilliance of genius, much art too. But when you come. . . ." At least this is proof that in 54 Marcus and Quintus Cicero had both read some of Lucretius' work, although the unusual word *poemata*, properly applied to poems or short passages of poetry rather than to a monumental epic, makes it doubtful whether Cicero was speaking of *De rerum natura* as we have it. A generation later, Vergil was echoing some of the phrases he found in Lucretius' epic and writing what is generally taken to be a complimentary reference to him: "Happy the man who was able to grasp the causes of things" (*Georgics* 2.490). His name is mentioned in the first century A.D. by Ovid, Vitruvius, and Velleius. But of his life, we know nothing from those who might have been acquainted with him and very little from any ancient authors at all. Further, some of the few scraps of information that we have are sufficiently sensational to be suspicious. But this needs some explanation.

Lucretius was an Epicurean. That means he was an "outsider" in a sense that will become clearer in the next two sections of this essay. He defended the materialism of the old Greek Atomists, including the thesis that our world, and every one of its inhabitants, is no more than a temporary assembly of atoms, fated to crumble away, after a shorter or longer interval, into what we might today call interstellar dust. To make our world, as he did, into an unremarkable member of a host of worlds—past, present, and future—scattered through the infinite void, and to give the human soul a life no longer than that of the mortal heart and lungs, was to fly in the face of the philosophical consensus both of Roman paganism and of early Christianity. During the centuries when the Christians formed all the centers of learning in the western world, Lucretius' poem was little read and only just survived. The earliest centuries of Christianity seem to have created and handed on a sketchy and unflattering portrait of the poet. In 94 B.C., "the poet Titus Lucretius is born; he was driven mad by an aphrodisiac draft, later in the intervals between madness wrote several books, which Cicero afterwards edited [*emendavit*: the exact sense of the verb is uncertain], and died by his own hand in his forty-fourth year." This is from St. Jerome's additions to Eusebius' *Chronicle*, written after he had renounced the reading of pagan classical authors because it distracted him from thoughts of God. The story of the poet's madness induced by an aphrodisiac and of his suicide is repeated in the preface, written during the Renaissance, to one of the early Venetian editions of the poem (the so-called Borgia Life). It may be true; it may be a mistake; or it may be a malicious fabrication based on certain ideas found in the poem itself, especially the unsympathetic account of sex in book 4 and the satire on those who are afraid to die at the end of book 3.

There is still much disagreement about the exact dates of Lucretius' birth and death, but the dates given by Jerome are approximately confirmed by the Borgia Life and by Donatus in his commentary on Vergil. It is clear that Lucretius lived from the nineties to the second half of the fifties in the first century B.C.; and that tells us something about the circumstances of his life, even though we know nothing for certain about his family and home, or about the conditions of his education and his philosophical and literary development.

He was a child when Marius returned to power in Rome, with Cinna, and began the sequence of cruel retaliations that characterized Roman political history in the first century B.C. He was perhaps in his teens when Sulla came back from the east and became dictator in Rome, with the notorious proscriptions of Romans who had opposed him. His youth was spent during the complicated struggle for power between Pompey, Crassus, and Julius Caesar, and he died before Caesar's victory offered the hope of a kind of stability. It was a half century of frequent civil strife, which involved not only the Romans but much of the population of rural Italy as well.

This last point may perhaps have some significance, since it is not quite certain that Lucretius was Roman or that he lived in Rome: some have believed that he was a country man, perhaps from Campania. External sources tell us nothing. Nor is there any direct and unmistakable statement in *De rerum natura*; as we shall see, Lucretius' interest in nature is of the theoretical kind, not dependent on close observation and description of the sights and sounds

of his own environment. What we learn from the poem about his literary milieu is that he was closely associated with Memmius, to whom his work is dedicated; and this Memmius is probably to be identified with the Gaius Memmius who was praetor in Rome in 58 B.C. and then governor of Bythinia. He was plainly familiar with earlier Roman poets such as Ennius and Pacuvius. Most significant of all, he is a master of Latin and calls it his mother tongue (if that is an acceptable translation of *patrius sermo*), and this seems to tell heavily against the theory that he was a Celtic freedman, and perhaps also against the theory that he belonged to the predominantly Greek-speaking circle of Epicureans in Campania. Against the latter theory we may also mention the fact that no word about Lucretius has yet been found among the fragments in the Epicurean library at Herculaneum. The balance of such evidence as there is suggests that he was a Roman, well-educated, and of good family.

THE EPICUREAN WAY OF LIFE

How and where Lucretius became persuaded of the truth of the philosophy of Epicurus is unknown, but there is no doubt that he was an Epicurean. He himself writes in glowing terms of Epicurus and the benefits he brought to mankind by his moral teaching.

> Great Memmius, admit: he was a God,
> Who first discovered that philosophy
> That we call Wisdom; who by art
> Rescued our life from darkness and rough
>   seas
> And rested it in the unclouded light of peace.
>   (*De rerum natura* 5.8–12)

If we are to understand Lucretius, we must know something of the founding of the Epicurean school and its early history.

Epicurus was the son of Athenian parents who lived, at the time of his birth in 341 B.C., on the island of Samos. Shortly before 300, he established a school of philosophy in Athens, in a house with a garden attached to it; the school was known in antiquity as "the Garden," in token of its search for peace and retreat from the busy world. (At about the same time, Zeno of Citium in Cyprus founded a rival school in Athens, which took its name from the porch or *stoa* where it usually met.) The word "school" is commonly used in connection with the Epicureans, and with some justice, since they engaged in the systematic teaching of the young; but throughout their history Epicurus and his followers created communities of friends, rather than schools, in which groups of like-minded people lived together studying the philosophy of Epicurus and applying his moral principles to the conduct of their lives. These communities, remarkable in antiquity for including among their members women and slaves, somewhat resembled the early Christian communities. They were not confined to Athens, but had branches or offshoots in various cities of the Greek world, especially in the east, where Epicurus had lived as a young man. Epicurus communicated with them by open letter, rather in the manner of St. Paul. Three such letters survive, addressed to Herodotus, Pythocles, and Menoeceus; they were fortunately transcribed and so preserved by Diogenes Laertius in the tenth book of his *Lives and Opinions of the Philosophers*.

The cornerstone of Epicurus' philosophy of life, at least so far as Lucretius is concerned, is the connection between cosmology and morality. Epicurus claimed that in order to live one's life according to sound moral principles, it was necessary to study the natural world. Not only that, but one must be persuaded of a particular theory about the natural world, namely, the atomic theory first created in the fifth century B.C. by Leucippus and Democritus.

"All men by nature desire to know." So Aristotle, a generation before Epicurus, began his *Metaphysics*. Epicurus, by contrast, claimed a strictly practical motive for theoretical studies:

If we were not disturbed by suspicions of the phenomena of the sky and about death, fearing that it concerns us, and also by our failure to grasp the limits of pains and desires, we should have no need of natural science [*physiologia*].

(*Principal Doctrines* 11)

For Epicurus the motive is not pure intellectual curiosity, as it was for Aristotle; it is psychotherapy. This change of emphasis has been epigrammatically and accurately described in a much quoted sentence by C. F. Angus, writing in the *Cambridge Ancient History*: "Philosophy is no longer the pillar of fire going before a few intrepid seekers after truth; it is rather an ambulance following in the wake of the struggle for existence and picking up the weak and wounded." This is as true of the Stoic school as it is of the Epicureans. The emphasis falls on philosophy as a cure for anxieties. Consequently it changes its tone and its manner of speaking: it turns away from metaphysical theories such as Plato's theory of Forms and Aristotle's inquiries into the nature of substance, and widens its audience by staying closer to the experience and concerns of the ordinary human being.

It is easy, however, to overstate this contrast. The truth is that Plato and Aristotle were themselves vitally concerned with the bearing of philosophical study on the conduct of life, and that Epicurus was far from being a stranger to disinterested intellectual curiosity. What we observe is a change of emphasis in philosophy, not a change from philosophy to counseling. Epicurus, and Lucretius too, were engaged in the same enterprise as Plato in the *Timaeus* and Aristotle in his writings about the physical world, and it is with these rivals that we must compare Lucretius' picture of the world, in the next section of this essay.

But first we must fill out in a little more detail our account of the connection that Epicurus made between his science and his morality.

The first principles of the Epicurean philosophy of life are summed up in a formula composed in the school and labeled "the Fourfold Remedy" (*tetrapharmakon*): "God unterrifying; death unworrying; the good accessible; the bad

603

endurable." These were lessons to be learned from the study of nature, and they were to be learned from the following considerations.

What is meant by "god" is a living being who is deathless and perfectly happy; this is asserted by Epicurus apparently as a proposition with which every sensible person will agree. It follows that we must not attribute to gods any emotions or anxieties that might disturb this perfect tranquillity. But they could not fail to be thrown into unbecoming turmoil if they were in any way concerned with our world and its inhabitants, and especially if they were offended by crimes and sins of omission, or jealous of human power and achievement. A consistent picture of gods, therefore, will place them in a region remote from this turbulent world, in the "interworld" spaces, living a life of such happiness together that it is unthinkable that they could have any motive for interference in the affairs of men. The Epicureans were not atheists, as their enemies claimed: they offered to the gods an idealized version of their own philosophical garden. Their residence is imagined by Lucretius in some famous lines, addressing Epicurus and modeled on Homer's *Odyssey* (6.42–46):

> When your philosophy, your godlike mind,
> Reveal the nature of the universe,
> My mind's fears fade; the ramparts of the world
> Recede; now nothing's hid through all the void.
> The gods' majesty I see, and their quiet home,
> Which no winds shake, no clouds soak with their
>   showers,
> No snow compacted hard with sharp frost spoils
> With its white fall: a cloudless sky forever
> Mantles it, joyful, with a radiant light.
> Nature supplies their needs: through all of time
> No single thing lessens their peace of mind.
>
> (*De rerum natura* 3.14–24)

The appropriate attitude for humans to adopt with regard to such gods is not one of fear or anxious observance of traditional rites, but rather one of simple admiration.

This positive view of the gods is reinforced by a critique of those theologies that gave the gods an active role in the world. Epicurus had to show that he had no need of the hypothesis of gods in order to explain the world. He had to produce, from his *physiologia*, an explanation that could be seen to be a better alternative to the idea of divine creation, as described in Plato's *Timaeus*, and to the elaborate system of heavenly spheres eternally activated by desire for god that had been worked out by Aristotle. This, as we shall see, is the motive of much of the argument of Lucretius' *De rerum natura*. But always, as we read Lucretius' poem, we cannot help realizing that this is not merely a negative motive; it is not constituted merely by a desire to demolish the theologies of others. The construction of an alternative was an inspiration to him. The atomic theory of the universe "haunted him like a passion"; Wordsworth's phrase in "Tintern Abbey" captures better than any other the strangely powerful force of this theory on Lucretius' imagination.

Death, the second major source of anxiety in Epicurus' standard list, was to be rendered harmless by a total acceptance of man's mortality:

> Accustom yourself to the belief that death is nothing to us. For every good and evil lies in sensation; but death is absence of sensation. From this consideration, right knowledge that death is nothing to us makes the mortality of life enjoyable, not by prolonging life to eternal duration, but by taking away the desire for immortality.
>
> (*Letter to Menoeceus* 124)

This argument, like the first of the Fourfold Remedy, is reinforced from natural philosophy. The soul is a material thing, a compound of atoms, and like every compound it gets its character from the fact that atoms of certain kinds are assembled together in a certain limited space. But at death, the soul is manifestly no longer assembled together as it was during the life of the body; being released from the body that protected it in life, it must be dispersed. Being dispersed, it cannot function in any way as it did before; it cannot constitute a personality, an "I." Death is therefore not a painful or distressing state of the personality: there *is* no personality in death.

The buttressing given by physical theory to the remaining two items of the Fourfold Remedy is rather more complex, and it will not be possible here to do more than sketch the outline. The foundation of the whole scheme is the assertion that pleasure is a natural standard by which we determine what is good. The atomic theory thus rules out, for example, Plato's thesis that the good life is achieved by freeing the soul so far as possible from the body. Pleasure is not a criterion that depends on a theory; it does not have to be argued for. It is, Epicurus says, *syngenikon* or *symphyton*—congenital or cognate. But although we do not have to learn how to feel pleasure, we can and must learn how to feel pleasure at the right things. This sounds at first as though pleasure is not after all the ultimate criterion of what is good; but that is not so. What we aim at, in Epicurus' view, is simply the maximum of pleasure, rather than every immediate pleasure. Some experiences give pleasure at the time, only to be followed by much greater pains—pains of remorse, for example, or punishment by society, or nausea and a headache. We have to learn not to be attracted by such pleasures. And similarly we have to learn to tolerate pain if it is necessary for future pleasure: we pay bills, visit the dentist, frustrate some of our children's wishes, all in the interest of future pleasure.

The optimism of the last two items in the Fourfold Remedy—"the good accessible; the bad endurable"—is achieved with the help of an analysis of desires. Some desires are natural and necessary: that is to say, we cannot avoid them, and their satisfaction is in some way necessary for the good life. (The desire for enough food and drink to satisfy hunger and thirst is an instance.) But Epicurus claims that these are easy to satisfy; no one in the civilized Greek world need go without the bare minimum of food, drink, clothing, and housing. A second group of desires consists of those that are natural but unnecessary: sexual desire is the primary example. Such desires must be recog-

nized as natural; but no one dies directly from unfulfilled sexual desire, and, according to Epicurus, once one has recognized its unnecessary nature one will not allow it a place in one's life beyond what is easily accommodated. The third class of desires is unnatural and unnecessary. This class contains all desires for food and drink beyond what is necessary, for luxuries, for political honors, or power, or wealth. The lack of these things can cause the utmost misery—but only in those who have failed to realize that their desire, and hence their misery, is unnecessary. Although in the main Lucretius turns his attention to the physical rather than the moral doctrine, he often returns (especially at the end of books 3 and 4) to this cardinal doctrine of the Epicurean way of life, that desires must be limited.

So in the name of pleasure Epicurus recommends the simplest way of life: a quiet, retired life in the Garden, content with little. How could such an unambitious ideal attract a man of such ardent intensity as Lucretius? This is one of the paradoxes in the character of this strange poet. But we must guess that he found it appealing just because it was difficult for him to achieve. He is honest enough to admit his own un-Epicurean desire for fame: a great hope has smitten his heart with the sharp spur of praise—praise for being the first to compose an epic poem in Latin on nature (1.920–30). "Fame is the spur," as Milton wrote, "that the clear spirit doth raise . . . To scorn delights, and live laborious days." Scorning delights and undergoing hardships for the sake of a great reputation as a poet: this is hardly consistent with Epicurus' principles. Yet this is only one instance among many where Lucretius reveals an emotional force that must be thought of as hostile to Epicurean tranquillity. His most famous lines seem to convey a sense that his own appreciation of Epicurean peace was precisely the result of his personal knowledge of turmoil and distress:

> How sweet to watch, from land, while winds
> enrage

The great sea's waves, another man in trouble!
—Not taking pleasure in another's pain,
But seeing what evils you yourself are spared.

(2.1–4)

Peace is to be achieved, then, by understanding the true nature of the universe and man's place in it. That means that the reader must be won over from allegiance to other cosmological theories current at the time. We must see what these were.

THE RIVAL WORLD PICTURES

Plato and Aristotle had persuaded much of the intellectual world of Greece of a particular view of the cosmos and man's place in it. According to this view, the world in which we live is a unique being, exhausting the whole of physical reality. It is spherical in shape: the circumference of the sphere is the region of the fixed stars that we see from earth. Inside this outer shell, according to the elaborate theory handed down by Aristotle, other hollow spheres carry the planets and the sun and moon. The spheres themselves are made of a pure and transparent substance (Aristotle's followers gave it the name *ether*); each of them rotates on its own axis at a constant speed, and the poles of the axis of each inner sphere are fixed in the sphere immediately next to it on the outside. With the help of this model, worked out by astronomers, Aristotle could give an account of the observed motions of the heavenly bodies, as seen from the earth. The whole complex system was composed of motions at uniform speed in circular orbits.

The earth is a sphere, situated at the center of the heavenly spheres. If its surface were entirely even, it would be completely surrounded by a thin layer of water; being uneven, it protrudes in many places through the water. The combined sphere of earth and water is surrounded by air and fiery substance, which occupy all of the space between the earth and the innermost sphere of the heavens. There is no empty space anywhere in the world (or outside it); matter fills the whole of space as a continuous mass of varying density. So everything that moves, moves in the manner of a fish: it makes its way through some medium by parting it, except in the case of the heavenly spheres, which move as a whole.

There is an irreducible difference, in Aristotle's theory of matter and motion, between the heavens and everything inside the heavens. The matter of the heavens is incorruptible and changeless, and it moves naturally in circular orbits. The matter of the world under the moon—consisting of fire, air, water, earth, and their compounds—is perpetually changing its form and moves naturally in straight lines. Earth and water have a natural tendency to seek the center of the world and to rest there when they arrive; air and fire naturally tend to seek the circumference of the world and to rest there. But the action of heat and cold, caused ultimately by the movement of the sun, changes these elements into each other and thus brings about the restless motion of the elements in the region near the surface of the earth.

This cosmos, according to both Plato and Aristotle, is everlasting: the motions of the heavens continue eternally, and by their eternal, regular motion they guarantee the eternal cyclical changes in the world underneath the moon. But Plato and Aristotle appear to have differed about the origin of the cosmos: Plato attributed it to the creative activity of an unnamed god whom he calls the Craftsman (*demiourgos*), whereas Aristotle denied that it had any beginning at all. Some in antiquity thought Plato's Craftsman was merely an expository device, and that when expressed in literal terms, his cosmology was not different from Aristotle's in this respect. In any case, what is important for assessing the position of the Atomists' alternative cosmology is that Plato and Aristotle both envisaged an *ordered* world, organized on rational principles, in such a way that its life might be maintained forever.

It is worth dwelling a little on the question of the relation of god or gods to the world in this cosmology. Plato, as we have mentioned, wrote in the *Timaeus* of a Craftsman god who made the world and everything in it. To those who were brought up in the Judaeo-Christian tradition, these words have misleading implications. So it should be stated, first, that Plato's Craftsman is described as having made the world according to certain eternal patterns that he did *not* make. His work was to impose a certain order, which he found already laid out for him, so to speak, in the eternal Forms or Ideas of Plato's theory, onto a preexistent material that lacked all shape or order. Secondly, we should remember that some of the things created by the Craftsman were themselves called "gods" by Plato, namely, the stars, planets, sun, moon, and the whole world itself. There is no sharp distinction, as in Christian theology, between the creator and the creation. Plato does, however, describe the Craftsman as a benign and provident deity, wishing what is best for the world; and what is best for it is eternity and good order.

In the surviving works of Aristotle, the relation between god and the world is still less like the Christian model. Since there is no creation, there is no creator: the good order and eternity of the world are in no sense imposed by an act of god. But if they are not imposed, they are at least maintained by gods. The whole complex of the heavenly spheres was spoken of by Aristotle as divine, but there is a supreme divinity in his system: the Prime Mover of the first sphere of the heavens, which carries the fixed stars. It was his belief that each of the spheres must have an eternal and immaterial mover to account for its eternal rotation, and at the top of the hierarchy was the mover of the first sphere. Since the eternal rotation of the heavens is the guarantee of the eternal cycles of the seasons and of birth and death in the sublunary world, the whole world thus depends for its life and being upon the Prime Mover of the cosmos. But this remote divinity is no personal, benign father figure; he does not *plan* the orderly working of the cosmos or oversee its operations for the benefit of its inhabitants. He is an imper-

sonal symbol of eternity and rationality, an ideal to which the world aims and without which it would collapse into disorder and death.

It is clear that when these austere, philosophical theologies penetrated to the ordinary cultured Greeks, they did so in modified form; even Aristotle himself, in works like his dialogue *On Philosophy* (now lost), seems to have spoken of the providence of the gods and to have allowed a more direct connection between the good order of the world and the thoughts of god. Xenophon in his *Memoirs of Socrates* had long ago put into Socrates' mouth an "argument from design," according to which features of the natural world that appear to be well designed constitute evidence that they were in fact designed by a benign, providential god (*Memorabilia* 1.4). The cosmology we have been describing seems to have entered the public consciousness—and indeed to have won the approbation of the majority—in a form that attributed the features of good order and permanence to the direct action of the gods.

In this form, the same world picture was picked up and developed by the Stoic school, starting at the same time as Epicurus framed his attack on it and continuing in opposition to Epicurus in later years. Since the Stoic school was the dominant philosophy in the Rome of the Republic, it is often claimed that Lucretius' polemical writing was directed especially at the Stoics. But this is not so. There were certain features that the Stoics added by way of modification to Aristotle's cosmology, and these are ignored by Lucretius. For example (it is an important example), the Stoics denied one of Aristotle's major tenets: the eternity of the world. They held instead that the world is periodically consumed by fire and then reborn from the fire in the same shape as before. This is not the version at which Lucretius directs his attacks; his target is the Aristotelian world picture or that version of it against which Epicurus himself matched his own philosophy of nature.

This Aristotelian world picture was opposed at almost all points by Lucretius and the Epicureans. They agreed on one point: they too accepted the astronomers' judgment that the earth is stationary and the stars, planets, sun, and moon move around it. Instead of supposing this world to be unique, however, they claimed that it is merely one among an innumerable multitude of worlds scattered through the infinite universe. Thus they made an important distinction, which we shall maintain throughout this essay despite twentieth-century usage, between the concepts of the universe and the world. The *universe* is everything that exists; it includes many worlds and has no boundaries. A *world* is a finite system, with a boundary formed by its stars. Lucretius thinks of our world as a walled city and mentions "the flaming ramparts of the world" (a richly alliterative phrase in Latin: *flammantia moenia mundi*).

Like all material compounds, except the gods themselves, all worlds have a limited life span. Each world comes into existence at some time, out of a random swirl of matter in the void, and will ultimately crumble away into its component particles once more. Not only the world as a whole, but everything in it, similarly, has a beginning and an end, not just in the sense that each individual mortal thing has a birth and a death, but in the much more profound sense that each *species* or *kind* of thing that exists in the world has an origin and an end in time, in each world. This marks perhaps the most far-reaching difference between the two cosmologies, and the one with the most fateful consequences in history. Plato and Aristotle could assume that the *kinds* of things are a given fact of nature: they are there to be discovered and explored and charted by the philosopher, but he is not required to explain their origin out of simpler elements. Plato's Craftsman, as has been said, did not invent the Forms, but rather created images, in a given material, of preexistent Forms. Aristotle, although he abandoned the Platonic theory of separately existing Forms, claimed that immanent forms are an irreducible feature of the eternal cosmos. The Epicureans, on the other hand, had to show

how the forms that we observe around us (the specific form of man, horse, bee, oyster, oak, and so on) might be supposed to have *grown* naturally from material elements in random motion. The enormity of this task, given the primitive scientific models available in classical times, goes far to explain the tone and structure of Lucretius' poem, as we shall see.

Instead of the Aristotelian material continuum, the Epicureans posited atoms and void. They presented a number of arguments to show that the observed qualities of physical objects can best be explained by the supposition that, when broken down into their ultimate constituents, all things are composed of the *same* material, totally invariant in quality everywhere and at all times but existing in particles of different shapes and sizes and differently distributed in space. They claimed that the Aristotelian idea of motion as swimming through a continuous elastic medium was incoherent; there must be empty space *somewhere* if things are to move at all: elasticity itself presupposes that there is space into which the collapse takes place. There are no other irreducible beings in their cosmology, neither elements such as earth, water, air, and fire (these are simply aggregates of differently shaped atoms), nor qualities such as hot and cold, dry and wet (these are derived from the different shapes of atoms and their different distribution or motion in space).

It is important to observe that by this theory the Epicureans eliminated the dualism of the Aristotelian cosmos; they made no distinction between the matter of the heavens and the matter of the sublunary world. Their stars and sun and moon were not made of a special divine material of surpassing purity and incorruptibility, but of the same sort of matter as the fire that heats the cooking pot. In their theory there is no matter that naturally moves in circles and so ensures the unlimited duration of the cycle of the seasons; the circular motion of their heavenly bodies is a derived and secondary phenomenon, like the motion of a whirlpool or a tornado. This conflict between the two systems rose to great prominence and fame in the seventeenth century, after the newly discovered telescope first gave men a view of the rugged and "earthy" surface of the moon. The incorruptibility of the heavens, which had been adopted as a dogma by the church, was dangerously challenged by this unexpected sight. It was an important stage in the fall of Aristotelianism and the rise of the old atomic theory in a new guise.

Most passionately, Lucretius opposes the idea that the cosmos is divine and that it is created, organized, or maintained by the gods. Such an idea conflicted with the first principle of the Fourfold Remedy, as we have seen: fear of the intervention of the gods was held by Epicurus to be a prime source of anxiety, and the remedy for it was to understand that the world can be better explained by the supposition that the gods *never* take action in the world and have nothing to do with it. Lucretius' opposition has two prongs: negatively, he criticizes the argument from design and other parts of his opponents' case; positively, he shows that the atomic theory can explain those features of the natural world that had been taken as evidence of design. We shall now look at this—the kernel of Lucretius' philosophical position—in more detail.

BOOKS 1 AND 2: THE FUNDAMENTALS OF ATOMISM

An epic poem on nature: it had been attempted before, although not in Latin, as Lucretius points out with pride. Sometime around 450 B.C., the Sicilian Greek poet Empedocles had written such a poem. To judge from the surviving fragments, it was probably not nearly as long as Lucretius' seven thousand lines, but it was written in the meter and idiom of the Homeric epics. Lucretius begins with a veiled compliment to Empedocles, who had attributed the motive power of the cosmos to two opposed forces, which he called Love and Strife, sometimes also giving them the personal names of Aphrodite and Ares. Lucretius begins his epic with an invocation to the Roman goddess of love, Venus, and prays that she will woo the god of war into the ways of peace. He invokes Venus as the power that tames the cosmic elements and brings them into a productive harmony—as the goddess of spring and natural generation. There is a striking paradox in his invocation of a divinity in this role, since the main force of his argument is to be that the world grows and lives *without* any intervention by the gods; but such an invocation was conventional, and Lucretius evidently assumed that his personification of this cosmic force of generation would not be misunderstood.

Generation is indeed the theme at the opening of the poem. The first subject he describes as "generative bodies" (genitalia corpora) and "seeds of things" (semina rerum) (1.58–59). These are the *atoms*, but the argument begins before atoms have been introduced into the picture. The first move is to establish what may be called a principle of conservation. Although all the objects around us have an origin and an end—a birth and a death, in the case of living things—they do not originate from or pass away into *nothing*. They come into being out of elements that existed before them, and they pass away into elements that continue to exist. For the elements to produce new compounds, they must be able to change place: and if that is to be possible, there must be empty space to give room for movement. These arguments, then—Lucretius calls up many illustrations from ordinary perceptual experience—establish the two fundamental ingredients of the physical universe: indestructible matter and void space.

The next step is to establish some facts about the nature of matter. It exists in the form of particles that are totally solid and absolutely without void intervals in them, and so hard that to split one is an impossibility. "Unsplittable" is the root meaning of the Greek term *a-tomos* used by Epicurus. Cicero converted it into

Latin, *atomus,* but Lucretius never uses it; he prefers words that refer to the function of the atoms as the elements or primary units out of which things are made *(primordia, principia).*

The indivisibility of the elements and their eternal immutability are characteristics that taken together separate the Epicurean theory from most other Greek theories of matter; and Lucretius takes the opportunity, after setting out the essentials of his own view, of lambasting some others. His language suggests a certain hard relish, as he demolishes first a representative monistic theory—that of Heraclitus, who is said to have held that fire is the single element from which all other things grow—and then the pluralistic theories of Empedocles and Anaxagoras. He is kindest, in his criticism, to Empedocles:

> Indeed, his godlike mind cries and declares
> In song such notable discoveries,
> He seems created of no human stock.
>
> (1.731–733)

All the same, he was wrong. The four elements—earth, water, air, and fire, without void—cannot account for motion and do not provide a satisfactory explanation of the great variety of objects in the world. Lucretius must, of course, dispose of this theory, since it was adopted in essentials by Aristotle.

At the end of each book of his poem, Lucretius elevates the tone of his verse in a splendid set piece. He always chooses a new subject, not a summary of what has been said before, but one that has a clear relevance to the rest of the book. So he ends book 1 with the grandest of all subjects—the infinity of the universe. He sets out his own arguments and incorporates some sardonic objections to the geocentric, closed world of the Aristotelians. For the modern reader there is a sad paradox in these lines. We want to applaud his bold imagination in rejecting the earth-centered vision that otherwise dominated the ancient world, but we have to listen also to his rebuttal of a spherical earth and his misplaced laughter at the idea of an an-

tipodean people walking upside down on the other side.

The second book on the fundamentals deals with two subjects: the motion of atoms and the ways in which they produce, in compounds, different perceptible qualities.

This book is our major source for the most notorious proposition of Epicurean physics: the swerve *(clinamen)* of atoms. The whole theory is based on two observations, one of them in fact mistaken. The first is that heavy objects, when unsupported, fall downward in straight lines; the mistake is the belief that the lines of natural fall of all bodies, anywhere on earth, are *parallel* to each other. The Epicureans were so determined that the earth is not the center of the infinite universe that they would not allow it to be any kind of center at all. The fall of heavy bodies on earth, they maintained, is simply a small sample of what would be observed anywhere in the universe. The infinite void has no center and no boundaries, but it has *direction:* the direction of natural fall in parallel lines is simply a fact of nature that is constant everywhere.

The second observation is just that there are compounds of atoms, and it is inferred that the binding together of atoms into compounds entails that the atoms sometimes collide. But if the natural tendency of atoms is to fall eternally in parallel straight lines, it seems there would be no explanation of collisions; the atoms would always fall like the drops in a heavy rainstorm. Observation seems to demand another explanatory postulate: that at least occasionally atoms do *not* fall precisely in a straight line. Occasionally they "swerve" and so collide. Nothing causes an atom to swerve: we are already at the most basic level, and nothing more primary can be invoked to explain it. Nothing that falls naturally is ever seen to swerve, so we must postulate that all swerves are too small to be perceived. And statistically swerves must be so rare that they do not upset the general predictability of the behavior of matter.

But there is another observation, says Lucretius, that demands the postulate of swerving atoms:

> Whence comes this *will*, I ask, wrested from Fate,
> By which we go wherever pleasure leads?
>
> (2.257–258)

If we examine our own (or other people's) actions, it seems clear that they are not to be explained simply as the predetermined outcome of the fall and collision of atoms. If it were the case that all events in the universe were due to the straight-line fall of atoms modified only by their collisions with others (supposing for a moment that collisions could be explained without postulating some third cause), then in principle every event would be predetermined from infinite time past. But experience shows that we want to make a distinction: some events appear to satisfy those conditions (for example, the cycle of the seasons or the succession of day and night), but others, such as human actions, do not. We choose our actions, in a way that the earth does not choose to freeze in winter. This distinction, Lucretius claims, demands a third cause of motion, in addition to downward fall due to weight and collisions:

> A minute swerve of atoms causes this,
> At neither certain place nor certain time.
>
> (2.291–292)

But *how* exactly does the swerve save this distinction? Lucretius offers virtually no help in answering this, and the relevant texts of Epicurus himself (always supposing this is an original doctrine of Epicurus—some have doubted it) are lost.

The last of the fundamentals remaining to be discussed is the *shape* of atoms and its effects on the perceptible qualities of compounds. Lucretius begins with the claim that there must be a vast amount of variation in atomic shapes, because there is so much variation at the perceptible level. The characteristic fusion of science and poetry can be seen here at its clearest. The scientific argument requires a statement of the

degree of variation in the physical world. The poet presents an unforgettable image of this variation: a cow robbed of its calf noisily searches the fields for that unique calf and no other. Each calf has its own peculiar differences. It is a passage that was imitated by later Latin poets, including Ovid (*Fasti* 4. 459ff.), but Lucretius' verse has a quality here that is worth a special comment. The language of the passage is full of careful alliteration and rich in "poetic" adjectives until the last line, which is made of the ordinary words of everyday speech in a normal order:

> The tender willows, grass refreshed with
>   dew,
> Familiar rivers filling high their banks—
> None can please her mind nor soothe her
>   care,
> Nor the sight of other calves in the glad fields
> Can mollify her or distract her mind:
> So much she needs her own, the one she
>   knows.
>
> (2.361–366)

(usque adeo quiddam proprium notumque requirit)

In the earlier lines, we are in a familiar and comfortable poetic landscape: the last line makes it an uncomfortable and disconcerting matter of fact.

After establishing that there must be variation, Lucretius shows how variation in the shapes of atoms can account for all the perceptible varieties of things, for different tastes, sounds, smells, colors, temperatures, and textures, and then the different species of plants and animals. Atoms themselves have none of the perceptible qualities. Even life itself, like color or texture, is a derivative property, a function of the shapes and numbers of the atoms that constitute the living creature.

The book ends with another richly orchestrated finale. We have been shown that the universe is infinite and contains an infinite supply of matter. It is to be expected, then, that the same conditions that produced our world exist elsewhere in the universe and produce the same effects, that there are other worlds beyond the "flaming ramparts" of our world. Moreover, as worlds come into being by the natural processes brought about by collisions of atoms, so they perish, too. There is a time of growth and a time of decay. This applies no less to our own world than to any other compound, and if we pause to consider the matter, we can see that whereas our earth must once have produced abundant forms of life spontaneously, in its youth, it is now already sinking into the barrenness of old age.

> Grimly the planter of the worn-out vine
> Rails at the flow of time, curses his age;
> And grumbling that his pious forebears once
> Sustained life easily on a small estate,
> When less land was allotted to each man,
> Forgets that all must age, and fade, and make
> The universal march toward the grave.
>
> (2.1168–1174)

The book ends with death. This pair of books began with a hymn to life and generation, in the person of Venus. It is a pattern that Lucretius repeats in later books, and one cannot doubt that in this, his poem symbolizes the first principle of the atomic universe: the cycle of birth and death, both brought about by the same elements.

BOOKS 3 AND 4: ON THE SOUL

The introduction to the fourth book of De rerum natura, as it has been transmitted by the manuscript tradition, is clearly an undesigned amalgam of two different prologues, one of them meant to follow book 3 and the other to follow book 2. The likeliest explanation is that book 3 was placed in its position later than the other books, and a new prologue to book 4 was then written and untidily juxtaposed, at some time, to the earlier one. Book 3 is in fact recognizably different from the others; it covers a narrower range. It has a single topic: mortality. Most of the book is taken up with arguments to show that the psyche is a compound of atoms and subject to dissolution, as all other compounds are. (So the book follows rationally upon the finale of book 2.) Then follows a long passage of fine satirical writing, in which Lucretius points to the folly of those who are afraid of death.

We need not delay longer over the first and longer part of book 3. The argument is naive and unrewarding; Epicurean theory in this area must strike any reader of Aristotle's On the Soul as intensely disappointing. (It is regrettable that book 3 is often taken to be the most suitable introduction to Lucretius for young readers.) The last quarter of the book, however, is splendidly challenging. We need not suppose that Lucretius' readers (or those who read Epicurus himself) were especially prone to live in dread of punishment in the afterlife. The point is that in Epicurean psychological theory other fears and anxieties are traced back to an origin in fear of death, often an unacknowledged and hidden fear. The cure is to persuade oneself of the slogan, "Death is nothing to us." To be dead is to be no feeling organism at all; and what we cannot feel when it is present should not concern us when it is imminent. We felt nothing in the time before our own existence, and it does not concern us now that we did not exist then; similarly we must be unconcerned about our nonexistence in the future. If we have enjoyed life, then we should get up and go, when the time comes, like one leaving after a good dinner. If we have not enjoyed it, then we should reflect that nature has nothing different to offer from what we have already had.

The famous myths about Hades are nothing but allegories of the torments of unnecessary anxieties in life: Tantalus, cowering under the rock poised above him, is the man who lives in fear of the gods. Tityos, whose liver was torn in Hell by vultures, is the frustrated lover. Sisyphus, whose punishment was to roll a rock to the top of a hill and see it roll to the bottom again each time, is the ambitious politician vainly wooing the people for election. And so on.

Here, on the earth, is Hell—the life of fools!
(3.1023)

Satire is a genre that particularly inspired the Roman mind, and in this section Lucretius shows his mastery of the form in a rapidly changing sequence of narrative and conversation, of scornful denunciation and compassionate solace, of pity and anger.

After this satire, we return to the atomic theory. Book 4 is a strange work, often misunderstood. Perhaps the key to grasping its unity is to realize that it handles those topics that might seem most difficult for the atomic theory of the mind and soul. In other words it answers or anticipates a challenge to the Epicurean theory in this area: "But how can your theory account for *these* phenomena? For perception? Illusions? Dreams? Memory? Imagination? Love?"

For the history of philosophy, the most important contribution of the book is the theory of *simulacra* or "images" (*eidola* is the Greek word used by Epicurus). The theory is involved in a dilemma. Its purpose is to provide an account of how the observer obtains knowledge of his physical environment, such that he can be confident that he is not deluded. He must have this confidence, if the Epicurean "therapy by natural philosophy" is to be able to free him from anxiety. Yet it is plain—and a much-discussed topic in earlier philosophy—that the world is not always as it seems to be. This must be explained too. But the stronger the theory was in defending the reliability of perception, the harder it was to account for the differences between appearance and reality.

The fundamental principle of the theory is that all physical objects, being compounded of atoms, constantly give off from their surface a superfine skin, of minimal thickness but otherwise preserving the shape of the exterior. These simulacra are the causes of all our perceptions, by the gross process of colliding with our sense organs, where they stimulate the atoms of the soul. This stimulation modifies the motions of the soul atoms in such a way that they somehow capture the form of the object from which the simulacra came. All perception is thus a kind of touching: in a literal sense, we are in touch with the external world.

How can it ever happen, then, that when we stand in front of a mirror we seem to see ourselves, standing a few feet away? How can it happen that if we walk a mile outside the city walls and look back at the square gate tower, it seems at that distance to be round? How can our shadow seem to follow us around and imitate our movements? This is the kind of problem the theory has to face. With considerable care, and a wealth of pleasant detail, Lucretius shows how the mechanism of the simulacra can account for these phenomena.

The theory is stretched to its limits—beyond them, perhaps—in explaining imagination and other activities of the mind. Some simulacra are of such fine texture that they escape the coarser filters of the sense organs and impinge directly upon the atoms of the soul. Dream images, visions, the pictures of the imagination, and all such things are to be explained by these simulacra. The essential difference between this operation and the working of the senses is that in normal sense perception the image is produced by a close array of simulacra proceeding from an object that is near at hand, whereas the simulacra that produce imagination are rare and infrequent, and they stimulate only a mind that is somehow sensitized or attuned to a particular kind of experience.

Book 4 ends with another long set piece, in which satire and sardonic humor are mingled with atomic theory. The subject is sex. In part, Lucretius' purpose is to explain the reproductive process, but this is combined, in a manner quite typical of him, with a moral message:

Without love, yet you'll have the joys of Venus—
The benefits without the penalties.
In this the healthy win a purer pleasure
Than the unhappy.

(4.1073–1076)

By "healthy" (*sani*) he means those who avoid passionate involvement with a lover—for passion leads to agonies of mind that a good Epicurean must avoid. Lucretius' message is the same as that of the girl in the old English folk song "The Sally Garden": "She bade me take love easy/As the leaves grow on the tree." To be in love with a single sexual partner is to risk the pangs of jealousy and the torture of rejection: better to remain heart-whole, and to take sexual pleasure where you find it.

This extraordinarily bleak moral attitude to love is relieved only by the high value that Epicureans placed on friendship. This relationship is not given any place in the passage we are considering, but elsewhere in Lucretius—and frequently in classical descriptions of Epicureanism by outsiders—it receives proper emphasis. To have many friends is to have greater security against the external world: such is the rationale set out by Epicurus. But the fact that he offered such utilitarian reasoning for making friends evidently did not diminish the value placed on his friendship by others. The ancient biographer Diogenes Laertius, after repeating some malicious stories of Epicurus' bad temper to others, remarks: "But those who tell these stories are crazy. There are sufficient witnesses to this man's unsurpassed goodwill towards everyone—his city which honored him with bronze statues, and his friends, numbering so many that they cannot even be measured in whole cities!" (10.9).

BOOKS 5 AND 6: THE NATURE OF OUR WORLD

In the standard English edition of Lucretius, by Cyril Bailey, it is said that books 5 and 6 are "of the nature of an appendix." There could not be a greater mistake! On the contrary, book 5, at least, is the culmination of the enterprise. We have now read the arguments that are to persuade us of the true nature of matter and its motion and of the human soul and its interaction with the external world. Now the whole theory must be put into action, so to speak, to demonstrate what Lucretius set himself to show: that

from these principles he can explain our world and can explain it better than his rivals. This is where we shall see how our familiar environment can be as it is without having been created or maintained by divine beings of a different order from ourselves and other mortal compounds.

The crux of the matter was to explain the regularity and order of the world. Even the words themselves—the Greek word *cosmos* and the Latin *mundus*—draw attention to this feature in their etymologies. There is a regular cycle of seasons, year by year; the motions of the sun and the other heavenly bodies are a paradigm of orderly movement. All of life on earth depends, in some way or another, upon this regularity, and living species are manifestly shaped in such a way that they can profit from it. Such observations were the keystone of the cosmology of Plato, Aristotle, and the Stoics.

But how could regularity, order, and adaptiveness come from the random jostlings of innumerable atoms in illimitable space? That was the central problem for the atomic theory, and it is the subject of book 5 of *De rerum natura*. After a prologue in praise of Epicurus, Lucretius writes a long passage—partly hot denunciation, partly scientific reasoning—in criticism of the rival theory of the divine nature of cosmic order, summed up in the famous lines:

> But even not knowing our first principles,
> This from the workings of the heavens
>   themselves
> And many other things I dare maintain:
> In no way is the universe arranged
> For us by gods—it has so many flaws!
> (5.195–199)

The rest of the book is devoted to the proof that the world order is the product of nothing but nature—of atoms in motion in the void.

It is essential to the plausibility of Lucretius' account of the origin of the world (as we have seen, it was an *origin* that was in question) that we keep in our minds some notion of what we would call the laws of chance. Without this idea the whole atomic theory would collapse or need some new support. It was at precisely this point, in its first revival in the seventeenth century, that it was radically changed and based on a different principle. Walter Charleton, for example, in his *Physiologia Epicuro-Gassendo-Charletoniana* of 1645 (the subtitle is *A Fabrick of Science Natural upon the Hypothesis of Atoms, founded by Epicurus, repaired by Petrus Gassendus, augmented by Walter Charleton*), substituted creation by God for the accident of random collisions in his account of the origin of the world. Lucretius, however, must do the best he can to bridge the gap between the random and the regular while staying strictly within the bounds of his materialism. The attempt is worth quoting at length:

> In what ways this concourse of matter laid
> The fundaments of earth and sky and sea,
> The sun's course and the moon's, I'll now set out.
> It's sure that atoms did not take up posts,
> Each at its purposed station, wittingly,
> Or skillfully coordinate their moves.
> But multitudinous atoms in uncounted
> Ways, from infinite time moved on by blows
> And by their own weight influenced, have come
> To try out every mode of union,
> To element all things they *can* create.
> Hence, for a vast age randomly dispersed,
> Attempting every move and confluence,
> At last they come together in such sets
> That all at once the seeds of mighty things
> Are made—of earth, sea, sky, and living things.
>
> (5.416–431)

If we accept the arguments of books 1 and 2, we know that atoms, with their various shapes and sizes, can produce all the varied compounds that we see in the world around us. But if they can produce these things, then we must accept that random conjunctions repeated an unlimited number of times *will* ultimately produce all of them, including things as vast and complex as a world. If you start tossing coins now and you immediately get a series of ten heads in a row, this is surprising; but if you go on tossing coins forever, it is not surprising that ultimately there comes a set of ten heads in a row. Our world is indeed a remarkable and untypical set of atoms; but even such remarkable sets must be expected to turn up occasionally in an unlimited series of randomly formed sets.

This is the basis of the theory. It does not say, of course, that our world came into existence all at once, exactly as we see it now, out of a colliding mass of atoms. The growth of the world is a gradual process, and it is described in book 5 step by step. The first step, as Lucretius puts it in the passage we have just quoted, is the formation of "seeds," that is to say, groups of atoms that because of their shapes and the way they move have the power to adhere together and to retain others as they collide, gathering mass like a snowball. There is first a "storm" (*tempestas*: 436); a host of atoms meet in confused motion; and as the motion continues, atoms of similar shape and size are sorted into different regions, thus separating the sky, the earth, and the sea. The old fifth-century B.C. Atomist, Democritus, had suggested as an analogy to this process the way in which the waves of the sea, as they break, sort out the pebbles by size on the shore (frag. 164).

The earth, made of large and heavy atoms, sinks to the bottom of the conglomeration, squeezing out the lighter and more mobile atoms to the periphery. There they spread out and encircle the whole mass, to form "the flaming ramparts of the world." They acquire a circular motion, according to Lucretius (5.509–533), by being blown around by currents of air, or in the manner of animals seeking food, or in some other way. It is characteristic of the Epicureans to offer a choice of explanations in these matters where observation can give no certain answer. In this they differed from the fifth-century B.C. Atomists, who committed themselves to a single explanation of the motions of the heavenly bodies: namely, that they are the residue of the "whirl" or "vortex" from which the cosmos grew in the first place.

The rest of the argument in book 5 has its high and low points. The Epicurean theory is at its least convincing in its account of the motions of the heavenly bodies. Greek astronomy, building on the achievements of earlier civilizations in this field, had reached a high level of mathematical precision by the time Epicurus lived: it was hardly enough to offer suggestions that the sun and moon are blown this way and that by currents of air. He and Lucretius could do little better by way of explaining the regularity of the natural cycles than to assert, hopefully, that similar causes always produce similar effects. We observe regularity, for example, in the blossoming of trees and the growth of beards, and we do not habitually invoke the action of gods or other unnatural causes to explain it. So with the motions of the heavenly bodies: their regularity can be attributed to nature and not to divinity. For the Epicurean program, this was enough: the goal was to eliminate the action of gods by showing that it was an unnecessary hypothesis.

Book 5 is unlike the others in that its finale is several hundred lines long, amounting to half of the book. It contains a marvelously imaginative description, step by step, of the growth of living forms from the earth, and the progress of human civilization from primitive men who lived in the woods and caves and ate whatever they could pick or catch, to sophisticated peoples who created cities, agriculture, music—and war. In each stage of this brilliant and exciting sequence (why do we not prescribe this as an introduction to Lucretius, instead of book 3?), his concern is to show how necessity coupled with human ingenuity can reasonably be supposed to have produced the next step in the progression. There is a melancholy strain in his story: so many false steps are taken, leading to fear and anxiety. But this is of course what we should expect from Lucretius here, where he is telling the story of human development *before* Epicurus. In pointed and deliberate contrast, he begins book 6 with a short hymn of praise to Athens—the home of the man who showed the way to salvation from the anguish of contemporary life.

One point in the story of the development of living forms from the earth deserves special mention, because it is an important part of the defense of atomism against its opponents. Since Aristotle's time—perhaps before—the purposiveness of the structure of animals had been a well-documented phenomenon: the arrangement of teeth in the mouth, the usefulness of eyelids, the different kinds of beaks in birds with different habitats, such things had been listed by Aristotle and summed up in a slogan, "Nature does nothing in vain." But Epicureanism had to maintain that nature does indeed do many things in vain; there are a million atomic collisions that produce no result, as against the very few that "make the seeds of mighty things." So what account could the Epicureans give of these well-known instances of purposiveness in animal structure? Were they all just the result of coincidence?

The answer was provided by a theory of the survival of the fittest. The earth produced, spontaneously, not only the ancestors of all the well-adapted creatures that we see around us but also, at the same time, a host of ill-adapted monsters that could not make a living:

> The androgyne, not one thing nor another,
> Remote from both; the footless and the handless;
> The dumb without a mouth, the faceless blind;
> The stuck together limb-locked holomorph—
> All such that could not act nor move at all
> To flee from harm or seek for sustenance.
> And many other prodigies earth made—
> In vain, since nature stopped them from increase:
> They could not pluck maturity's sweet flower,
> Nor capture food, nor mate in Venus' way.
>
> (5.839–848)

Thus all the inefficient creatures perished. The earth, once fertile enough to generate all kinds of beings spontaneously, is now old and produces nothing more than a few grubs and worms (it was a common belief of Greek biologists that grubs were spontaneously generated in warm, moist, earthy matter). Hence, all the animals that we see are those that are efficient at getting a living and reproducing themselves. This is a theory that the Epicureans borrowed from Empedocles, and it is the nearest the

Greeks or Romans came to a theory of evolution. It will be observed that although it includes a well-marked theory of natural selection, it says nothing at all about inheritance or the progressive differentiation of species.

The last book of the poem provides not a climax but a filling out of some selected topics. Many of them fall into the range of what the Greeks called *meteorologica*, the phenomena of the region between the earth and the sky. We are given a theory of the nature of thunder and lightning, clouds, rain, and rainbows. Then the range widens to include earthquakes, the flooding of the Nile, magnetism: these are conventional topics in the collections of *problemata physica*. Lucretius shows how these problems can be handled by the atomic theory. But the book ends in a surprising way, with a description of the great plague in Athens at the beginning of the Peloponnesian War, the same subject that Thucydides handled in a famous section of his *History* (2.47–52). There has been much discussion about whether this is the intended end of Lucretius' epic or whether he was somehow prevented from finishing it according to his plan. There are, indeed, some indications here and there in the text that the poem we have is not exactly as the poet would have wished; the clearest is at 5.155, where he promises to discuss the nature of the gods and their abode at greater length, a promise that is not fulfilled. However, it is by no means clear that the plague is *not* the intended end. As we have seen, Lucretius tends to conclude each book with a finale characterized by a tone different from the rest of the book, often including some satire and a more obvious moral message than the rest. And this description is satisfied by the account of the plague. Moreover, this ending makes a significant "ring form" with the beginning of the book: the prologue speaks of Athens at the peak of fertility, both in its agriculture and in its literature; the end shows the same city in the grip of disease, demoralization, and death. From generation to death: this is the same cycle that we observed in the beginning and end of the first pair of books, and

it is repeated elsewhere. Strange and forbidding though it may seem, this is probably the intended end of the epic.

But perhaps it is not so strange. It reminds us of the true and ultimate fact of the world and the human condition: our world, with all its inhabitants, must die. The poem is, after all, a declaration of faith that in spite of suffering and in the face of death, we *can* learn to live and enjoy a happy life. If we have been persuaded by the rest of the poem, we shall not find its conclusion forbidding. We shall have the strength to face death—even death by plague—with equanimity.

THE GODLIKE PLEASURE

But why, after all, an epic poem? Epicurus advised the wise man not to write poetry (Diogenes Laertius, 10.121) and expounded his own philosophy in tough and stringy prose. Lucretius in fact suggests three reasons for his choice of verse. One of them has been mentioned already: it is the hope of winning praise for himself. Second, he stresses the sheer pleasure of attempting something new, a poem on such an important theme and with so lofty a motive as "loosening religion's choking knots" (1.924–932). Third, he explains that the subject matter may seem so grim (*tristior*: 1.944) to those encountering it for the first time that they need all the charm of the Muses to help them to swallow it, just as children must have their medicine disguised by a touch of honey on the rim of the cup.

Now this third reason has an implication that is thoroughly misleading: it is that there are two distinct and separable elements in Lucretius' poem—nasty science and pleasant poetry. Commentators and editors have sometimes suggested that one could mark off certain passages as containing all the "poetry" and put all the rest into a package labeled "exegesis in verse." It is strange that Lucretius himself should have gone so far toward licensing this simplistic and imperceptive assessment of his creation. We shall return to the theme of its inadequacy at the end, but first we must observe one more paradox in the story of this unique book: it was just this impoverished view of *De rerum natura* that preserved it from oblivion.

Christian scholars rejected Epicureanism with particular emphasis, as we have mentioned before, because of its theses that God had no part in the creation and maintenance of the world order and that the human soul is a mortal and material compound. Lactantius at the end of the third century A.D. wrote a powerful and passionate denunciation of Epicureanism in his *Divine Institutes,* an attack founded on detailed knowledge of Lucretius' text. It seems to have been thoroughly effective, no doubt in conjunction with other similar criticisms, since by the time of Augustine, Epicureanism had virtually disappeared: in one of his letters (*Epistles* 2.118c) Augustine claims that the Epicureans have become so silent that the schools hardly remember what their doctrines were.

Lucretius was still studied and quoted by those interested in language. He had chosen, deliberately, to enliven his verse with interesting archaisms, words and word forms that had already passed out of normal usage in his time. Some of them were quoted, in contexts of a verse or two, by grammarians of the early Christian period. The quotations give some evidence of the state of the text at the time, and they show that the text was still available; but the grammarians had no time for the subject matter. Lucretius was soon little more than a name attached to a few quotations. It is typical, and revealing, that he was of no significance to Dante or Petrarch, both of whom were, of course, devoted readers of Vergil. For some centuries, there is little or no evidence that anyone had direct acquaintance with the text of *De rerum natura.* A very few manuscript copies lurked, unread, in monastery libraries, but it would have required a minimum of unlucky accident to bring about the total loss of the poem.

The great revival in its fortunes began in the early fifteenth century A.D., when Poggio Bracciolini, acting as apostolic secretary for the pope at the Council of Constance in 1414–1418, conducted some forays upon remote monastic libraries that could be reached from Constance and found a manuscript of Lucretius in one of them, probably at Murbach in the Vosges. He had a copy made and lent it to Niccolò de' Niccoli of Florence, who made his own copy, in his own hand, a copy still preserved in the Laurentian Library. Other copies were made from this.

Fifteenth-century Italy was fine soil for the growth of an appreciation of Lucretius' poetry. The splendid rhetoric of his diatribes against fear of death and against extravagant sexual desire made an immediate appeal. The adventurous imagination of book 5 led Jovianus Pontanus, in Naples, to try a similar account of the evolutionary growth of mankind in his *Urania sive de stellis.* The rich pictorial imagery of *De rerum natura* delighted and stimulated the contemporaries of Benozzo Gozzoli, Andrea del Castagno, and Pollaiuolo. The famous opening invocation to Venus, the goddess of generation, is often referred to, most notably in one of the best known of all Florentine paintings, Botticelli's *Primavera.* That sensuous, rich, glowing work is not, of course, a simple illustration of Lucretius—its imagery has a much more complicated ancestry—but there can be little doubt that the words of Lucretius played a part in Botticelli's inspiration.

But it was first the honey on the cup, not the pill, that Renaissance Italy swallowed. The theory of the infinite universe, the atomic explanation of matter, and the denial of creation and providence were rejected and ignored. The Italian humanists and scholars remained loyal to Christian doctrine and to the Aristotelian world picture. The atomic theory began its dramatic rise to a dominant position for the first time in the seventeenth century A.D. The overthrow of the "closed world" cosmology of Aristotle was not, of course, caused by a rediscovery of the merits of the ancient Atomists. The causation worked rather in the opposite direction: the new science of Galileo, Johannes Kepler, and Sir Isaac Newton kindled a new interest in the ancient alternative to Aristotelianism, first in the work of Epicurus himself and even in the fragmentary remains of Democritus, rather than Lucretius. The new followers of Epicurus found a way of combining atomism with creation and the providence of God. Newton puts it typically in a famous sentence of his *Opticks:*

> It seems probable to me that God in the beginning formed matter in solid massy hard impenetrable moveable particles, of such sizes and figures and with such other properties and in such proportion to space, as most conduced to the end for which he formed them.
>
> (book 3, part 1, question 31)

After the scientific revolution there was no danger that the ancient Atomists would be forgotten again.

It was for the sake of its language and poetry, then, that the text of *De rerum natura* was kept alive through a long period of neglect into the era of the printed book, in spite of its doctrines. But now, in the late twentieth century, the doctrines are no longer shocking. We are all Atomists; we accept that our solar system is an unremarkable part of an unimaginably vast universe of matter and void; we subscribe to an evolutionary theory of the growth of living forms; and even if we do not individually deny that there is a God who cares for the world and will bring our souls to judgment after death, we are no longer appalled by those who do deny it. In this environment, we can look at Lucretius' achievement as a whole: we have no compelling need to filter out the "poetry" from the "exegesis in verse." We can see and appreciate the ardent excitement that informs, not just particular passages but the whole structure of the epic, and creates a kind of beauty even in a theory of the qualities of liquids or the magnet.

In spite of Lucretius' own words, the simile of the honey and the pill seems almost as far from representing the truth about the creation of his poem as the more extravagant theories of

later times—from Jerome's idea of a madness brought on by an aphrodisiac, to a post-Freudian suggestion of a psychic trauma caused by thwarted cannibalism when the poet was a baby. Why should we not rather take at its face value the second of the three motives suggested by Lucretius in the passage quoted at the beginning of this section: the pleasure of creating something new on this grand and serious theme? This is something far more important than the utilitarian view of natural science put forward by Epicurus, but it is still consistent with Epicurus' view of the good life. Lucretius takes pleasure in his understanding of the universe and in the poetic genius that enables him to communicate it. He sums up the feeling that pervades the whole poem in words addressed to Epicurus:

> When your philosophy, your godlike mind
> Reveal the nature of the universe,
> My mind's fears fade; the ramparts of the world
> Recede; now nothing's hid through all the void.
>
> . . .
>
> And then a godlike pleasure seizes me,
> A shudder of awe, and wonder that your power
> Makes nature everywhere so plain and clear.
>
> (3.14–17; 28–30)

Selected Bibliography

TEXTS AND CONCORDANCE

Roberts, Louis. *A Concordance to Lucretius.* Supplement to *Agon.* Berkeley, Calif., 1968. Invaluable.

De Rerum Natura, edited and translated by Cyril Bailey. Oxford, 1947. The best text. Vol. 1 has introductory essays, and English translation; vols. 2 and 3 contain an extensive commentary, useful on linguistic matters but unreliable on the history of science and philosophy. The translation is artificial.

De Rerum Natura Book 3, edited by E. J. Kenney. Cambridge, 1971. Has English commentary.

TRANSLATIONS

De Rerum Natura, translated by R. E. Latham. Harmondsworth, 1951. Penguin edition. Reliable prose version.

De Rerum Natura, translated by Alban D. Winspear. New York, 1956.

De Rerum Natura, translated by Palmer Bovie. New York, 1974.

Humphries, Rolfe. *The Way Things Are: the "De Rerum Natura" of Lucretius*. Bloomington, Ind., 1968. An exciting verse translation, deplorably titled.

INTERPRETATION AND CRITICISM

Bignone, E. *L'Aristotele perduto e la formazione filosofica de Epicuro*. 2 vols. Florence, 1936.

Boyancé, P. *Lucrèce et l'Epicurisme*. Paris, 1963.

Ernout, A., and L. Robin. *Lucrèce, De rerum natura: Commentaire exégétique et critique*. 3 vols. Paris, 1925–1928. Commentary without text or translation.

Kenney, E. J. "The Historical Imagination of Lucretius." *Greece and Rome* 19:12–24 (1972).

Logre, J. B. *L'anxieté de Lucrèce*. Paris, 1946. Psychological and dubious.

Long, A. A. *Hellenistic Philosophy*. London, 1974. Philosophical background.

Rist, J. M. *Epicurus: an Introduction*. Cambridge, 1972.

Santayana, G. *Three Philosophical Poets: Lucretius, Dante, Goethe*. Cambridge, Mass., 1910.

Schrijvers, P. H. *Horror ac divina voluptas: Études sur la poétique et la poésie de Lucrèce*. Amsterdam, 1970.

West, David. *The Imagery and Poetry of Lucretius*. Edinburgh, 1969.

COLLECTIONS OF CRITICAL ESSAYS

Dudley, D. R., ed. *Lucretius*. London, 1965.

Reverdin, O., and B. Grange, eds. *Lucrèce*. Vandoeuvres-Genève, 1978.

STUDIES OF PARTICULAR PROBLEMS

Amory, Anne. "*Obscura de re lucida carmina:* Science and Poetry in *De rerum natura*." *Yale Classical Studies* 21:145–168 (1969).

Bollack, Mayotte. *La raison de Lucrèce*. Paris, 1978. Contains an extended study of book 4.

Cox, A. S. "Lucretius and His Message: A Study in the Prologues of the *De rerum natura*." *Greece and Rome* 18:1–16 (1971).

Furley, David J. "Lucretius and the Stoics." *Bulletin of the Institute of Classical Studies* 13:13–33 (1966).

——. *Two Studies in the Greek Atomists*. Princeton, N.J., 1967. Study 2 is on the *clinamen*.

LATER HISTORY

Hadzsits, George Depue. *Lucretius and His Influence*. New York, 1935.

Koyré, Alexander. *From the Closed World to the Infinite Universe*. Baltimore and London, 1957. Reprinted 1968.

BIBLIOGRAPHY

Dalzell, A. "A Bibliography of Work on Lucretius, 1945–72." *The Classical World* 66:389–427 (1973) and 67:65–112 (1973).

DAVID J. FURLEY

SALLUST

(86–35 B.C.)

C. SALLUSTIUS CRISPUS was born, according to Jerome's *Chronicle,* in 86 B.C. Not all Jerome's dates are unimpeachable, but the date he gives for Sallust's birth accords well enough with the few secure facts we possess about the historian's later career. He was thus significantly younger than the great figures who dominated the last generation of the Roman Republic: Julius Caesar (born 100 B.C.); Caesar's associates Pompey the Great (born 106) and Marcus Licinius Crassus (born 115?); Caesar's most implacable opponent, the younger Cato (born 95); and Marcus Tullius Cicero (born 106), who more than most in that turbulent and destructive period glimpsed a concept of politics and the republic that meant more than the ruthless pursuit of personal ambition.

Sallust, or his family, came not from Rome itself but from Amiternum, near the modern Aquila in the Abruzzi, the Sabine territory. We may assume that Sallust's family belonged to the local nobility of office in their native town. In the towns of Italy such local aristocracies, engrossing political power and social position, mirrored the senatorial nobility of Rome and formed the hinge upon which Roman control of the whole of Italy turned. It had been through their connections with the leading men not only of the Roman but also the Latin and allied towns that the Roman nobility had maintained its control of Italy before the Social War—in which the allied communities rose in 91 B.C. to demand the full Roman citizenship from the re-luctant Romans—and the connections did not lapse when as a result of that war the Roman citizenship had been granted to the whole peninsula south of the Po Valley. Moreover, it had always been from the Roman townships of Italy, of which Amiternum had been one since, it would appear, some time in the second century B.C., that the nobility of Rome, ever on the lookout for young men of talent and promise, had drawn its new recruits to be introduced, under patronage, into public life in the imperial capital. It is a subject beset with misconceptions, for which Sallust himself, as much as anyone, must be held responsible. Writing of Marius' candidature for the consulship, he said, "even then . . . the nobles passed the consulship from hand to hand among themselves. No new man was so famous or of so great achievements that he was not considered unworthy of that office and the office itself, as it were, polluted" (*Jugurtha* 63.6).

This statement, widely repeated in modern works, needs critical examination. Any ruling class that becomes totally exclusive, a completely closed caste, is doomed to progressive debilitation or speedy extinction at the hands of a strong outsider. The Roman nobility, on the contrary, was from first to last of vigorous vitality and ever in search of new talent. Its attitude was not one of rigorous exclusion of outsiders but of carefully controlled inclusion. Not many new men would reach the consulship. That is neither sinister nor surprising. The consulate conferred supreme power and access to it was more strictly controlled than to the lower offices—and there were only two consuls a year. Yet the records show that in the century and a half that followed the defeat of Hannibal, between one in six and one in eight of the consuls came from families new to the office. These are minimum figures, based on the appearance of new names in the consular lists, and exactly how many were from families not merely nonconsular but nonsenatorial (as Sallust's was) is difficult to determine, perhaps nearly half the total. It is clear that far from being rigorously exclusive of all new men at all costs, the Roman oligarchy was in a state of continuous recruitment and regeneration. Many of the new men, advanced for personal talent or the convenience of their noble patrons, remained isolated examples: their descendants, though sometimes detected in the lower reaches of the Senate, lapse from eminence. Others, however, founded powerful political families that took places only little inferior to aristocratic houses of fabulous antiquity. By Sallust's day the Roman oligarchy was a heterogeneous body. Families of vast antiquity vied with those of much more recent origin. The most extreme and efficient faction of the oligarchy was led and animated by the younger M. Porcius Cato. His great-grandfather had been a farmer in the Sabine country, introduced to Rome by the patrician L. Valerius Flaccus.

In this revolutionary age the significance of Italian origin is undeniably difficult to determine. It is impossible, however, to overestimate the importance of the leading men in the towns of Italy, the class from which Sallust came. By the middle of the first century B.C., men of Italian origin may already have approached half the membership of the Senate, as they certainly did in the Senate as enlarged by Caesar. It was with them that Rome's future lay. Most came, as would be expected, from communities near to Rome that had possessed the Roman citizenship for many generations. Yet before Caesar's death P. Vatinius was consul, in 47 B.C. He was of the Marsi, enfranchised only after the Social War. Then came the phenomenal P. Ventidius, consul in 43 B.C. He was from Asculum, the stronghold of the allied rebellion, and as an infant had been captured when the fortress was taken and had been led in the triumph celebrated by Cn. Pompeius Strabo, father of Pompey the Great. C. Asinius Pollio was consul in 40 B.C. He came from Teate, and only fifty years before, his grandfather, Herius Asinius, had led the Marrucini against Rome and had died fighting for Italia. All three reached their consular eminence well before Sallust's death. Before long, the men of Italy were to establish first equality with and then superiority over the old Roman nobility in the government of Rome and of its empire.

Nor was it merely soldiers and politicians who came from Italy. The Italian communities gave to Rome many of the most famous names in Roman literature: Cicero from Arpinum, the hometown of the general Marius; M. Terentius Varro, the most learned man of his age, from Sabine Reate, in the same territory as Sallust's Amiternum; Asinius Pollio from Teate; Propertius from Assisium in Umbria; Ovid from Paelignian Sulmo; Horace from Venusia on the border of Apulia and Lucania; and from outside Roman Italy, from Cisalpine Gaul, the Po Valley, a notable triad: Catullus from Verona, Livy from Patavium, Vergil from Andes near Mantua. Such names highlight the problem of the significance of Italian origin. It may be safest to regard Sallust as a Roman in all but the accident of his *patria*. That his ancestral home was Amiternum does not necessarily imply that he was in actual fact born there.

Many motives not scrutable to us might impel a young man from Italy to embark on the perilous course of a public career at Rome. Much later, in a passage of self-justificatory special pleading (*Catiline* 3.3), Sallust was to state that he early desired a political career, became corrupted and held prisoner in his youthful weakness by ambition, and suffered ill-repute and jealousy because of his passion for office. Apart from this passage, we know absolutely nothing of Sallust's life between his birth and his candidature for the office of plebeian tribune thirty-three years later, in the summer of 53 B.C. But the passage allows a guess. Sallust describes himself as a youth (adulescentulus) at that time, and this would put him in his late teens or early twenties. If Sallust has told the truth about his early ambition and if he used the term adulescentulus accurately, then, on the basis of what we know of his contemporaries a decade before his tribunate, when he would have been in his early twenties, he ought to have been in military service.

There is no direct evidence, but two indications are suggestive. Later, Sallust was employed by Caesar in a military capacity. In 49 B.C., he commanded a legion for Caesar in Illyricum. In 47 B.C., as praetor designate, he was sent to settle a mutiny in Campania. In Caesar's African campaign, Sallust had charge of a supply fleet and ended as governor of Africa. The assumption that Sallust had never seen an army before 49 B.C. is quite inexplicable. Caesar's power and prospects depended on his army. Loyalty is precarious in civil war; mutiny, infectious. Caesar could have won the war against Pompey and his enemies only to lose his victory to his own army. The trouble in Campania was not an isolated outbreak: the Sicilian legions were also disaffected. Sallust was unsuccessful, but lucky. The mutinous army killed two other envoys of praetorian standing and marched on Rome. Military experience and skill in handling troops are the first essentials in dealing with such a situation. For Caesar to employ Sallust, especially after his lack of success in 49 B.C. in Illyricum, suggests that he was thought to possess these attributes. Previous military service must surely be predicated. If comparison with such of his contemporaries as we have adequate information about is any guide, he should have been in military service from the age of eighteen to twenty onward.

Here the second suggestive indication finds its place. In retirement after Caesar's assassination, Sallust wrote an account of Catiline's conspiracy of 63 B.C. That work gives no evidence of personal observation, no indication

that Sallust was in Rome when Catiline conspired, and that is curious. In 63 B.C., Sallust was some twenty-three years old, of full age to observe and remember. The Conspiracy of Catiline was Sallust's first work, and the historian, frustrated and bitter at the wreck of his early ambition, might have been expected to set the record straight from personal knowledge. He does not. Instead we have timeless reflections on general conditions, introductory or resumptive formulas, reports of rumor and speculation (which are as much literary devices as genuine records of historical fact), and occasional personal reminiscences about individuals. Sallust is not writing from personal knowledge gained at the time of the events themselves. His main source is Cicero's four speeches against Catiline. The one piece of information for which he is prepared to vouch explicitly and personally is expressly said to have been acquired after the event (postea: Catiline 48.9). If not in Rome and if already intent on a political career, Sallust ought to have been abroad in military service. And if truly ambitious, he should have been with the greatest man of the age, Pompey, connection with whom in these years was profitable not merely to new men or personal adherents but even to nobles seeking profit and advancement in their careers.

Be that as it may, it is as tribune of the plebs in 52 B.C. that Sallust emerges into history. By that year the republic was moving tumultuously to its close. Pompey was inching away from his alliance with Caesar, which he had never really desired and with which he had never been comfortable. Tribunes had prevented the election of consuls and praetors for 53 B.C. until July. Agitation for the appointment of a dictator mounted. The year 52 B.C. opened without consuls either: only the ten tribunes, including Sallust, were in office. P. Clodius Pulcher, standing for the praetorship, supported Pompey's candidates for the vacant consulate. On 18 January, Clodius was killed on the Via Appia by the band of his rival political gangster, T. Annius Milo. His body, brought to Rome and exhibited in the Forum, was cremated while tribunes inveighed against Milo. The mob rioted; the Senate house burned. One of the orating tribunes was Sallust; later, when Pompey, now sole consul, held Milo's trial under virtual martial law, Sallust verbally attacked Milo's defender, Cicero, as a bandit and assassin. Later in the year the whole college of tribunes united to pass a bill allowing Caesar to stand for the consulship in absentia, and a banquet was given in honor of Q. Caecilius Metellus Pius Scipio (whose daughter Pompey married and whom he had had elected as his colleague in the consulship for the final months of the year) and the ten tribunes, at which entertainment in the form of a *lupanar* Munia and Flavia, both ladies glorious in their fathers and their husbands, and a boy of noble family, Saturninus, were prostituted.

The sequel to Sallust's tribunate is perplexing. At the close of their year of office, his two closest associates among his colleagues were tried and condemned. Sallust escaped prosecution. He may have been less compromised than his two associates and thus still useful to Pompey. It may be that the part he played in the events of 52 B.C. was of minimal importance, of interest only in the light of his subsequent literary activity and high moral tone. Certainly he is nowhere named as an instigator, always as supporting action started by his two colleagues. Sallust's tribunate left no mark on the historical record proper. Only the learned Asconius, commenting on Cicero's speeches, records it. Sallust may have escaped because he was beneath notice. It may have been that the other side was satisfied with the condemnation of T. Munatius Plancus and Q. Pompeius Rufus—especially if a bargain had been struck with Pompey the Great as proof of his intentions to abandon Caesar—or that Caesar intervened. Unconsciously we tend to adopt simple formulas: Senate and people; optimates and populares; Caesarians and Pompeians. The polarities obscure a fluid situation. Caesar and Pompey will be found in cooperation when their interests coincide, in opposition when their aims and ambitions conflict. Similarly with minor figures. Constant al-

legiance was not to be relied upon in this age. The tribunician college of 52, bitterly divided over Milo, united to promote the bill allowing Caesar to stand for the consulship in absentia and to attend Metellus' banquet. Sallust and his like would serve their ambitions where they could. Like Britain in the nineteenth century, they had neither lasting allies nor enemies, only interests. But they were exposed to an added hazard: they were liable to be used and discarded. T. Munatius Plancus, abandoned by Pompey and prosecuted by M. Caelius Rufus, betook himself to Caesar in Gaul. Two years later Sallust followed, ejected from the Senate by the censor Ap. Claudius Pulcher, with misleading results for the evaluation of both his political career and his literary works.

Caesar had been in Gaul since 58 B.C. There he had consolidated a following that his enemies characterized as a ghastly crew. Caesar was not fussy. As he himself put it: if he had used muggers and bandits in defense of his *dignitas* (prestige), he would give such men, too, comparable reward. Throughout his career he had appealed to the dispossessed and disaffected; above all, to the followers of Marius and their descendants, those who had been disadvantaged by the settlement of Sulla, Marius' enemy, the proscribed, and the partisans of Catiline and Clodius. Early in 49 B.C., Caesar crossed the Rubicon, invaded Italy, and began the civil war against Pompey and his other enemies. Sallust finds no mention in Caesar's *Civil War*. Yet, as we have seen, he found employment, the praetorship of 46, and the governorship of Africa, a province of the first rank, and the command of its garrison and three legions. On his return he was accused of extortion. It is said he escaped condemnation at his trial by bribing Caesar. More probably his malversations, if they existed, were hushed up. At all events, Caesar did not consider him for the consulship of 43, for which he would have been eligible. Decimus Junius Brutus was to hold the office in 42, Marcus Junius Brutus and Cassius in 41. Caesar, meanwhile, would go to the East to defeat the Parthians. However, on the Ides of March 44 B.C., the conspirators, prominent among them D. and M. Brutus and Cassius, murdered Caesar at the foot of Pompey's statue.

HISTORICAL THEMES AND METHODS

From this milieu emerged Sallust the historian. Exactly when and under what conditions he retired from political life, we do not know. It may have been in 45 B.C., when he was accused of extortion, or immediately after the Ides of March, or later, in the autumn of 44. It may have been that disappointment and frustration in 45 hardened into disillusion and distaste under the pressure of events rapidly developing after Caesar's murder. But, although Sallust's retirement may have resulted from no single happening or from no specific decision, it was genuine. In the turbulent and violent sequel to the assassination of Julius Caesar, he seems to have been unmolested; had ambition and passion for office remained, he could have satisfied them with Antony or Octavian, as many like him did. Yet his political failure rankled, and he felt compelled to justify his withdrawal from public life:

> Therefore when my mind found peace after many miseries and dangers and I determined that the rest of my life must be passed far away from public life, it was not my intention to waste the blessings of leisure in indolence and idleness nor to lead a life devoted to slavish pursuits by farming or hunting; but I resolved to return to an early interest from which evil ambition had kept me and to write the history of the Roman people by topics, as each subject seemed worthy of record.
>
> (Catiline 4.1-2)

The curious outburst against hunting and agriculture ("slavish pursuits") relates both to the debased condition of such activities among the Roman upper class and to Sallust's deep-seated belief that it was in intellectual activity that man's proper function was to be found. Sallust conducts his self-justification in terms of a tradition that prescribed public life as the only fit occupation for a free man of appropriate status. Social standing and position, influence, and fame (dignitas, auctoritas, gloria) were attainable only through the service of the respublica. Terms such as "leisure," "indolence," and "idleness" (otium, socordia, desidia) have in this tradition a sharp and hostile connotation: refusal to play a part in politics. The attacks on men like Lucullus who withdrew to their estates and the opulent contemplation of their fishponds were directed not mainly at their wealth and luxury, in which they were no different from those who attacked them, but at their willful noninvolvement in public affairs. Hunting and agriculture might be honorable pastimes: they ought not to engross the whole of a man's attention. Nor, even, should history. A senator might write history for pleasure or political profit: but he wrote in the intervals of a vigorous public career.

It was not fitting for a public man completely to withdraw from public life to devote himself to writing history at an age when office was still attainable. Sallust felt keenly the necessity to justify both his retirement and its occupation. The theme recurs. Public service is the greatest and most important activity by which the highest distinction may be won.

> But of the other activities that are carried on by the intellect, the recording of past achievements [memoria rerum gestarum] is especially of great service.... For I have often heard that Q. Maximus, P. Scipio, and other famous men of our state were accustomed to say that whenever they gazed upon the masks of their ancestors their minds were violently inflamed to the pursuit of manliness [virtus]. Of course they did not mean that the mere wax of the effigy had such great power over them but that through the recollection of great achievements that flame grows in the breasts of outstanding men and is not quenched until their own manliness has equaled the fame and glory of their ancestors.
>
> (Jugurtha 4.1; 5-6)

Neither to Sallust nor to any other Roman historian was history a detached and scientific inquiry into what had happened in the past. It was a public activity, morally and politically committed, with a strong didactic purpose, setting forth examples both to imitate and to avoid.

From Sallust's retirement came three works: a monograph on the conspiracy of Catiline in 63 B.C.; another on Rome's involvement with Jugurtha of Numidia in the later years of the second century B.C.; and the *Histories*. Unfortunately, this last, Sallust's longest and most mature work, has almost entirely perished. Four speeches and two letters excerpted from the work in antiquity survive as well as a number of shorter fragments, many of which owe their preservation to their enshrining some linguistic oddity. The known fragments, from five books, deal with events from the years 78 to 67. The latter year seems to provide no suitable terminus for the work: the *Histories* may have been left incomplete on Sallust's death in 35 B.C.

Before Sallust wrote, the historical monograph had been domesticated at Rome by L. Coelius Antipater, who toward the end of the second century B.C. had written on the Hannibalic War. Coelius had been a conscious stylist, and Cicero admitted that his work was epoch making. Coelius' work has perished. Sallust's remains as the leading example of the genre in Latin.

Both *Catiline* and *Jugurtha* begin with short introductions or prologues. Both show a basic similarity of structure and subject. Quintilian later remarked that these prologues had nothing to do with *historia*. By this he meant not that they had no relation to or relevance for the following narratives, but that Sallust, intending to write works of history, began with prologues that belong in style to a different literary genre. Long before Sallust a strict convention had become established: the function of the first sentence in a literary work in prose was to establish, if not the specific topic to be treated, at least the literary genre to which the work belonged. If in classical antiquity you set yourself to write history, then your very first sentence

must make that quite clear to the reader. Sallust is the unique exception. Both *Catiline* and *Jugurtha* begin with large reflections on human nature: "All men who desire to excel the other animals must strive with all their power not to pass through life in silence like beasts" (*Catiline* 1.1); and "Falsely the human race complains of its nature, that it is weak and short-lived and ruled by chance rather than by *virtus*" (*Jugurtha* 1.1). What these openings announce, according to the ancient convention, are not historical monographs, but philosophic treatises. Why? Perversity and a desire to shock, unique among our remains of classical literature? That, given Sallust's character as it emerges from his works, is not remote from all possibility. Alternatively these opening sentences may be taken at their face value as seriously meant. Then Sallust was announcing that what follows was not straight history but a philosophical disquisition on politics and public affairs of which the historical facts were, so to speak, extended examples.

From their large initial propositions both prologues go on to argue the obligation to seek fame and glory, to leave as long-lasting a memory as possible. But true glory can be won only by the use of the intellect in appropriate spheres and according to proper standards. The highest sphere is the service of the *respublica*. This leads Sallust to the justifications of his withdrawal from public life, which he describes as wholly corrupt and corrupting in his own day, and of the worth of history. Thus we arrive at those statements of subject that, according to convention, should have stood at the head of the two works: "I shall treat of Catiline's conspiracy as truthfully as I can in a short compass; for I believe that event is especially noteworthy because of the uniqueness of the crime and its danger" (*Catiline* 4.4); "I intend to write the history of the war which the Roman people waged with Jugurtha, king of Numidia; first because it was long and savage and now one side, now the other was victorious; secondly because then for the first time opposition was made to the arrogance of the nobility" (*Jugurtha* 5.1).

The whole discussion in the prologues is conducted in terms of a group of concepts centering on that of *virtus* ("worth," "manliness"—the Latin word denotes the peculiar quality of a man, *vir*) as the use of *ingenium* ("intellect," "innate quality") to achieve great deeds, especially in the service of the *respublica*, and thus to win glory according to proper moral standards. This is itself a restatement or redefinition of the Roman aristocratic ideal of *virtus* as the pursuit of glory through the service of the commonwealth to suit the radically changed conditions of the late republic, in which the new men claimed that it was individual ability and individual achievement, not birth and the inherited position and advantages of the nobility, that formed the title to office and power. This cluster of concepts forms the basis of all Sallust's historical analysis, his criterion for judging the worth of individuals and events, and the mechanism he sees working in human affairs. The fundamental purpose of *Catiline*, *Jugurtha*, and, so far as we can judge from the surviving fragments, the *Histories* is to analyze the collapse of the Roman Republic in terms of the collapse of this tradition of *virtus*.

We may distinguish two levels of application of this analysis: to the general course of Roman history and to the particular events of the individual works. Early in *Catiline* (6-13) Sallust sets out at length his view of the development of Roman history, and the picture there presented is repeated more briefly elsewhere in the monographs and in the fragments of the *Histories* (for example, *Jugurtha* 41; *Histories* 1.11 ff.). In both *Catiline* and *Jugurtha*, Sallust consistently represents the whole history of the Roman Republic down to 146 B.C. as one of unbroken *concordia* (social harmony), *virtus*, and the highest moral standards. After the foundation of the city, in which a diverse and wandering mob was made into a community *(civitas)* by the action of *concordia*, Rome was first governed by kings who, however, fell prey to arrogance and tyranny *(superbia dominatioque)*. The kings were then expelled and the republic, with its system of annual magistracies, was established, traditionally in 509 B.C. Then followed a long period of excellent morality and greatest concord, when *virtus* reigned supreme and directed all the actions of the citizens. All this was ended in 146 B.C. when Carthage, "the rival of Roman power," was destroyed. The removal of the external threat caused the rise of *ambitio* (or, *cupido imperii*, the lust for power) and *avaritia* (or, *cupido pecuniae*, the lust for wealth) until, under the domination of Sulla, *luxuria* (extravagance) gave the final impetus to Rome's descent to utter ruin—moral, social, and political.

In *Jugurtha* 41-42, Sallust begins by referring to the original concord of the republic: "The people and Senate of Rome peacefully and with restraint shared the government of the Republic." Then came the destruction of Carthage, relief from the external threat, peace, and a superfluity of good things. The result was that men's minds were seized by desire *(lubido or cupido)*, and both nobles and people turned to a struggle for glory and domination while the *respublica*, which lay in the middle, was torn to pieces. According to Sallust's principles, both parties were originally equally guilty, but because of their superior strength and resources, the nobles were able to oppress the people. Then, together with this lust for power, greed burst in without restraint or moderation, polluted and devastated everything, and held nothing important, nothing sacred until it hurled itself to destruction. Finally, in putting down the Gracchi, who were themselves not untouched by the lust for victory, the nobles compromised themselves utterly. "For a good man it is better to be overcome than to overcome injustice by evil means" (*Jugurtha* 42.3): it it is a judgment no less on the nobles than on the Gracchi. Good men, men of *virtus* who respected the concord of the commonwealth, would not have acted as they had done.

That Sallust's picture of the history of Rome

to 146 B.C. is highly idealized needs little demonstration. For the earlier part of the second century B.C. alone, our sources contain numerous references to trouble with the armies, misconduct by provincial governors and commanders in the field, the growth of wealth and luxury, demoralization and unrest at home. In the *Histories* Sallust modified his view. The turning point is still the removal of the external threat with the destruction of Carthage. But before this, Sallust distinguishes a period of discord with the expulsion of the kings, the external threat from the Etruscans, a further period of discord representing the struggle of the plebeians for equal rights and opportunities with the patricians, and finally, between the Second and Third Punic Wars, a period of excellent morality and greatest concord under the influence of the fear of Carthage. This has been taken as showing increased pessimism or deeper insight. It seems more likely that the modifications were forced on Sallust by criticism of the earlier versions in the monographs with their total idealization of the period before 146. But both the idealization (although the time span is limited) and the lack of convincing motivation for the decline after the destruction of Carthage remain in the *Histories*.

In choosing the destruction of Carthage as his turning point, Sallust set a fashion that lasted to St. Augustine and beyond. As we have seen, it appears in all three works, allied with the theory of the external threat (*metus hostilis*), relief from which led to the breakdown of *virtus* and thus of social harmony. That theory was a commonplace in ancient thought and indicates no special philosophical interest on Sallust's part. In the famous debate between the elder Cato and Scipio Nasica on the proposed destruction, Nasica is said to have urged the preservation of Rome's great enemy precisely on the ground that the maintenance of Roman discipline depended on the existence of an external threat. It seems probable that this is the immediate source of Sallust's account of the effects of the destruction of Carthage. The debate between Cato and Nasica was famous, the theory a commonplace that seems to have been urged on other occasions by other Roman politicians, including Cato himself. But it would seem that Nasica advocated the preservation of Carthage to check a degeneration of which the signs were already apparent. The general tradition of the moral crisis of the second century B.C. and the many extant fragments of Cato's speeches attacking the growing luxury and corruption at Rome suggest that this was, indeed, Nasica's purpose. For Sallust, however, 146 B.C. marked not an intensification of an already existing corruption, but the very beginning of it, the moment when "fortune began to rage and throw everything into confusion" (*Catiline* 10.1).

By the time Sallust wrote, there existed a strong and well-established tradition that by the middle of the second century B.C., Rome had undergone a crisis from which it never recovered and that the processes that eventually destroyed the republic had already begun to work. Different authorities chose different moments of crisis when change became obvious and irreversible. But two points deserve to be made: the tradition on the moral crisis of the second century B.C. goes back to contemporary sources, and there is remarkable unanimity on the mechanism of the change. The acquisition of an overseas empire and the influx into Rome in the late third and early second centuries B.C. of Greek culture and Asiatic luxury led to the abandonment of the traditional moral restraints of the old Roman peasant society. Abandonment of the traditional value system undermined the basis of the personal relationships upon which the structure of society and politics rested, and this led, in turn, to the destruction of political and social stability and, ultimately, to the disintegration of the republic.

This case Sallust, although proposing his own date for the turning point in Rome's fortunes, accepts. Central to both his and other Roman analyses is the concept of social harmony. Sallust describes the time between the Second and Third Punic Wars as that when the Romans lived with the most excellent morality and the greatest concord. It was social harmony that united the motley collection of foreigners and aboriginal tribes into the original community of Rome. It was harmony especially between Senate and people that was the particular characteristic of the republic when *virtus* held everything under control. It was harmony that was destroyed by the rise of political strife after the destruction of Carthage, when men, basing their actions not on *virtus* but on desire expressed in the lust for power and wealth, tore the *respublica* asunder in pursuit of their selfish ends. It is a principle of government that "by concord small states grow great, by discord the greatest are destroyed" (*Jugurtha* 10.6).

The Romans perceived the proper ordering of a stable society as a clearly defined and structured hierarchy of statuses, in which all persons knew their place, stayed in it, and performed in it according to the traditional moral code, discharging the obligations appropriate to their place. That is what the Romans meant by *concordia,* the cardinal principle in Roman political thought. The discharge of appropriate obligations enjoined by the traditional moral code ensured social harmony, and it was this that in turn assured the stability, strength, and well-being of the *respublica*. Destroy the traditional moral restraints and you destroy social harmony; destroy social harmony and the *respublica* itself will disintegrate. It was not a foolish or unsupportable view, given the structure and organization of Roman society and politics.

Sallust cannot have been unaware of the second-century tradition of decline before 146 B.C. The extent of his debt to the elder Cato was much remarked in antiquity. This debt is usually represented as one of language, but an acquaintance with the language of the elder Cato implies a knowledge of content also. Sallust's remarks in all three works on the demoralization that tends to follow prosperity can be paralleled in the fragments of Cato. Cato also seems to have been the chief source for the account of the foundation and early history of Rome that appears in *Catiline*. Much of the tradition of the moral crisis of the second century

B.C. goes back to the elder Cato, who was chiefly responsible, under the assault of Greek culture and wealth, for codifying the Roman value system in coherent form. His censorship in 184 B.C. had been directed particularly against luxury and moral decline and was commemorated by a statue set up in his honor with an inscription recording how he had restored the tottering republic.

Sallust is thus concerned with a particular concept of *virtus*, which imposed the obligation to acquire glory by the commission of great and meritorious deeds in the service of the commonwealth. It is valid to analyze the breakdown of the republic in terms of the perversion of this ideal, whereby personal power and preeminence were pursued at the expense, and ultimately to the destruction, of the *respublica;* and if Sallust retrojected, as he did, a concept of *virtus* belonging to the political polemic of his own time (though it may have derived finally from Cato the Censor), that is venial. It is when Sallust applies his theory to events that doubt begins. His general view of the course of Roman history exposes real deficiencies. The idealization of the period before 146 B.C. (the modification in the *Histories* only underlines the dubiousness of the method), the destruction of Carthage and the removal of the external threat, the descent through lust for power to lust for wealth, extravagance, and all things vile—the scheme is artificial and mechanical. Sallust rejected one tradition of Rome's decline only to reproduce its essential features in his own, even to the arrival of extravagance with an army from the East—Sulla's from 88 B.C. (*Catiline* 11. 5-6) rather than Manlius Vulso's in 187 B.C., as in the tradition represented by Livy (39.6-7). Quite apart from gross discrepancy between theory and historical fact, the theory itself raises unanswered questions. Do true *virtus* and harmony exist only under external threat, and collapse immediately when that pressure is removed? Why did the removal of the rival to Roman power cause headlong descent into utter corruption? Vague references to fortune and to "peace and the abundance of those things which mortals consider of first importance" do not provide an intellectually compelling explanation.

CATILINE

Sallust's concept of *virtus* and its schematic application to the course of Roman history form the foundations on which he erects his narratives of the events of the Catilinarian Conspiracy and the Jugurthine War and the bases of his interpretation of those events. In *Catiline* the personality and character of the archconspirator and the particular events of the narrative are from the beginning closely tied to Sallust's view of the development of Roman history and the forces he sees working in it. Immediately before the long digression on the previous history of Rome, after the prologue, Catiline is formally introduced: "L. Catilina, born of a noble family, possessed great force both of mind and of body, but an evil and depraved disposition" (*Catiline* 5.1). This at once relates Catiline's character to Sallust's concept of *virtus*. His great mental and bodily force might have fitted him for great achievements, but all was vitiated by his evil and depraved disposition (*ingenium*) as a result of which he was given over to *cupido*. From his youth he reveled in civil war, murder, plunder, and discord (*discordia*). After the domination of Sulla, his *cupido* so increased that he became possessed of a powerful desire to seize control of the commonwealth. Nor did he care how he achieved it, as long as he made himself tyrant. He was driven on by poverty, a sense of guilt, and the corruption of public morals, which was aggravated by the two worst evils, extravagance (*luxuria*) and greed (*avaritia*). It is this statement that forms the occasion for the long disquisition showing how from the noblest and best of cities Rome had become the worst and most vicious. Not only does this digression expand on a theoretical level Sallust's application of his scheme (the decline of *virtus*) to the history of the Roman Republic, but it also puts Catiline in context as the child of his age, the typical product of the process of degeneration that began with the destruction of Carthage. At the end of the digression, the connection is again made clear: "In so great and so corrupt a city, Catiline, as it was very easy to do, kept about him, like a bodyguard, crowds of the debauched and criminal of every kind" (*Catiline* 14.1).

It is, however, quite clear that Sallust's dating of Catiline's revolutionary designs to the dictatorship of Sulla is, as a matter of historical fact, quite wrong. As late as 65 B.C., Cicero could contemplate the defense of Catiline and the collusion of the prosecutor, leading to an electoral alliance between Cicero and Catiline. But Sulla's dictatorship is exactly the point in Sallust's general scheme at which extravagance was added to the lust for power and the lust for wealth as a disruptive and degenerating force. What Sallust has done is violently to antedate Catiline's revolutionary designs in order to establish clearly at the outset the relationship between the general effects and the particular case he is about to describe.

Later Sallust employed the same technique on a larger scale in *Jugurtha*. There, a summary of the previous relationships between Numidia and Rome and of the early life of Jugurtha serve the same purpose as the character sketch of Catiline. The two passages are even introduced by similar formulas (*Jugurtha* 5.3 ff.). Jugurtha's *virtus* and its degeneration play the same part in the Jugurthine War as Catiline's character and its causes in the history of his conspiracy. Moreover, in *Jugurtha* we meet the same chronological dislocation. Jugurtha's corruption is traced to conversations with "many new men and nobles, to whom riches were preferable to morality and honor; men engaged in political intrigue at home, powerful among Rome's allies, famous rather than honorable," whom he met while serving with the Roman army at Numantia in Spain. They inflamed his ambition and told him that everything at Rome was for sale. The Roman commander, Scipio, on the other hand, advised Jugurtha to cultivate the friendship of the Roman people and not to engage in bribery, since it was dangerous to buy from the few what belonged to the many. Power would come, if only Jugurtha continued as he had begun, but too hasty action would bring ruin through his own money (*Jugurtha* 8). The composition and choice of phrase are artfully designed to suggest that it was the recollection of what he had heard at Numantia that led Jugurtha, after the murder of Hiempsal and the defeat of Adherbal, to place his hopes in "the avarice of the nobility and his own money" (*Jugurtha* 13.5). And through the later chapters "at Rome everything is for sale" runs like a leitmotif.

Sallust had already pointed out in *Catiline* that one of the characteristics of avarice, the lust for money, was to teach that everything was for sale (*Catiline* 10.4). Nor is it a matter of composition only. The destruction of Numantia took place in 133 B.C. Micipsa, king of Numidia, died in 118 B.C. Fifteen years, therefore, elapsed between the two events. Yet Sallust says that Micipsa died "a few years" after Jugurtha's return (*Jugurtha* 9 4) and that when Micipsa read the letter that Jugurtha had brought from Scipio in Spain, he "immediately" adopted him (*Jugurtha* 9.3). A little later we learn that the adoption took place not more than three years before Micipsa's death (*Jugurtha* 11.6). Sallust has again manipulated the chronology to give the impression that the interval between Jugurtha's service in Spain and the discord that arose after the death of Micipsa was little more than three years, not about sixteen as was in fact the case. The purpose is clear: to suggest that Jugurtha's conduct to Adherbal and Hiempsal was directly conditioned by his conversation with the corrupt and corrupting nobles at Numantia, to bring the particular facts into close and causal relationship with the general scheme. Moreover, the fragments of the first book of the *Histories* allow the suspicion that there too Sallust employed similar techniques to relate his narrative to his general historical scheme: a digression summarizes the history of the previous fifty years, and when the narrative proper opens in 78 B.C., the incautious reader, as Sir Ronald Syme has pointed out, might suppose that Sulla

was still in full enjoyment of dictatorial power. In fact, he was in retirement and soon to die.

Sallust seems to have been quite incapable of conceiving a slowly developing situation or character. His general historical scheme proceeds in a series of distinct stages introduced by sudden turning points—the destruction of Carthage, the dictatorship of Sulla; so too with his chief characters, Catiline, Jugurtha, Marius. Parallel to Sallust's antedating of Catiline's general revolutionary disposition to Sulla's dictatorship is his treatment of the formation of the actual conspiracy. We are told that this began about 1 June 64 B.C., that the plans were betrayed by Curius and his mistress Fulvia, and that this betrayal was the cause of Cicero's election to the consulship for 63 (*Catiline* 17; 23). This cannot be, for several reasons. It is incredible that such a leakage would have gone unnoticed by Catiline for some seventeen months; yet Sallust has Fulvia still informing in November 63 (*Catiline* 28.2). It is clear that Cicero as consul, so far from having such a source of information from the beginning of his consulate, was able to proceed vigorously only after the capture of the Allobroges (*Catiline* 41 ff.). It is clear, too, that Catiline's great ambition was to be elected to the consulship. He had been debarred from standing in 66 as being under notice of prosecution for misgovernment in his propraetorian province of Africa. The trial was held in 65, and Catiline was acquitted, but too late to stand at the elections for 64. In that year, running for the consulship of 63, he stood with C. Antonius, but Cicero was elected in his stead. Again Catiline was prosecuted, this time for murder during Sulla's regime, and again he was acquitted. But in the summer of 63 he again stood for the consulship and again failed.

Whatever Catiline's character, his persistence for the consulate suggests other ambitions than the destruction of the republic. Even Sallust implies more than once that the success of the conspiracy was felt to depend on success at the elections. Furthermore, the plans of which Cicero was informed "from the beginning of his consulship" were merely Catiline's intention of standing once more in the hope of having the support of Antonius if he became consul elect (*Catiline* 26). It was with this knowledge that Cicero detached Antonius by assigning to him the province of Macedonia. The meeting on about 1 June 64, if it took place, can only have been intended to explore the ground and estimate what support could be expected at the consular elections. That as early as June 64 Catiline was associated with men who, after the consular elections in 63, took part in the conspiracy proper is possible, if not probable. Sallust's antedating of the stage at which revolutionary plans became explicit and dominant is typical of his mind and method; typical, too, is the way his interpretation of events is belied by his own narrative.

"In so great and so corrupt a city," Sallust describes in detail how Catiline gathered around him all the most debauched and criminal, and corrupted any innocent man who became his friend (*Catiline* 14). Then we pass to the enormities of Catiline's youth: seduction of a noble virgin and of a Vestal (who, we happen to know, was tried and acquitted) and other unlawful and impious acts of the same kind. The culmination is Catiline's passion for Aurelia Orestilla, "whom no good man ever praised except for her beauty." Because she hesitated to marry Catiline from fear of having a grown-up stepson, Catiline was firmly believed to have killed him to expedite the marriage. There is sufficient evidence to show that Sallust is here repeating contemporary charges against Catiline, some of which were true. But once more Sallust has his own purposes. He might have mentioned Catiline's acts of murder as Sulla's henchman and his incest with his own daughter. Sallust's choice is a deliberate literary device for psychological analysis and, once more, illicit linking of events (*Catiline* 15). Sallust returns to Catiline's effects on the young men, describing how he involved them in his own crimes and incited them to commit others of their own. Trusting to these associates, he resolved to put into action his long-standing passion to gain control of the state. His reasons are given as the enormity of his debts in all parts of the world, the squandering of their property by most of Sulla's veterans, who remembered their earlier plunder and victories and longed for civil war, the lack of any army in Italy, the absence of Pompey, his own desire for the consulship, and the Senate's unalertness. The prevalent safety and peace offered Catiline a golden opportunity (*Catiline* 16).

The effect of this lengthy introduction is to stress Sallust's concept of the real nature of the conspiracy. Catiline himself is presented as wholly corrupt, given over to lust, greed, and extravagance, and, after the murder of his son, as not a little mad, which Sallust thought was his special reason for hastening the conspiracy:

> His guilty mind, at peace with neither gods nor men, could find no rest either awake or sleeping: so completely did conscience ravage his tortured mind. His complexion was pallid, his eyes bloodshot, his walk now quick, now slow; in short, in his face and expression madness sat.
>
> (*Catiline* 15.4–5)

His associates are presented as being or as soon becoming under his influence so many lesser Catilines. The whole picture of the corrupt and debauched youth is expressly related to the general theme of the total depravity of Roman social and political life after Sulla's dictatorship.

Throughout the rest of the monograph this remains the picture of Catiline's following. When he made his first definite moves, about 1 June 64 B.C. according to Sallust, he gathered the most desperate and reckless men, who are carefully named, as well as many who were prominent in the colonies and the towns of Italy. In addition, there was a more mysterious class of supporters among the nobles, inspired more by the hope of absolute power than poverty or other necessity. Sallust also reports that there were those who believed Crassus to be party to the plot. He gives the alleged reasons, but he himself neither confirms nor denies. This technique of indirect reporting is a favorite with Sallust, and it is here the more effective since at this point he breaks off to describe the supposed conspiracy of two years earlier when, whatever did or did not happen, Crassus seems certainly to have been instrumental in having Piso sent to Spain. As for that supposed conspiracy, the truth about certain political intrigues of the year 66 will now never be known. What can be said about Sallust's apparently highly circumstantial account (*Catiline* 18) is that it is a piece of research into political polemic and propaganda libel, advertised as such by careful dating and the listing of names—and it is wrong in principle and erroneous in detail. But in Sallust's hands it further inflates the enormity of Catiline and again places his revolutionary designs in a wider political context (compare *Catiline* 17.7 and 19 on Crassus and Pompey).

According to Sallust, the election of Cicero and Antonius in 64 B.C. to the consulship for 63, although it alarmed the other conspirators, did not abate Catiline's furious madness. The scope of the conspiracy was widened and gained the support of men of all conditions and some women, who had at first financed their monstrous extravagance by prostitution but had later fallen deeply into debt when age had put an end to their income but not their prodigality. Through them Catiline hoped to tamper with the city slaves, set fire to Rome, and either win over or kill their husbands. As an example Sempronia is described at length. She plays no part in the action and the reader may well wonder why she was chosen. In part she forms a female counterpart to Catiline, type and pattern of the prevailing lust and extravagance, and once again this presentation reinforces Sallust's view of the essential nature of the conspiracy. Yet she is not a monster, mechanically constructed, but the one believable character in all Sallust's works. The historian, one is tempted to feel, had known the lady and experienced her wide literary culture, her stimulating conversation, and the wit and charm he acknowledges that she possessed (*Catiline* 24–25).

From the elections in 64 B.C., Sallust passes rapidly (too rapidly—what was Catiline, already on the brink of a murderous and incendiary revolution, doing in that year?) to those of 63, another defeat for Catiline. From that point Catiline's plans were detected and baffled by Cicero. Hurling himself from the Senate house with the words "Since I am surrounded by enemies and driven to desperation, I will extinguish the fire that burns me by general ruin," Catiline left the city to join C. Manlius and his army in Etruria. Both men were declared public enemies (*Catiline* 26–36.3).

Sallust writes:

> At that time the power of the Roman people seemed to me to be in a uniquely pitiable state. Although from the rising to the setting of the sun the whole world, conquered by her arms, was in subjection to Rome, although at home peace and riches, which men consider of first importance, were in abundance, yet there existed citizens who with perverse obstinacy were determined to ruin both themselves and the commonwealth.

(*Catiline* 37.4)

These sentiments introduce a long digression on the social and political background to the conspiracy (*Catiline* 37–39.5). Sallust begins with the urban mob that supported Catiline not so much because it approved his intentions as from a general desire for revolution typical of those who have nothing. There were the vicious and criminal, who had consumed their substance in riotous living or had been forced to leave home because of some disgrace and had all flowed into Rome "as if into a cesspit." There were those who remembered the results of Sulla's victory with its rapid promotion of common soldiers to high rank and enormous wealth. There were young men, tired of the labor of the countryside, who came to Rome to live in idleness on private and public largess. Those whose parents had been proscribed by Sulla, had lost their property, and had had their civil rights curtailed are also mentioned, as are those whose political stance was opposed to the Senate and who preferred the commonwealth to be convulsed to the diminution of their own power.

This is a remarkable statement from an author who has often been claimed as an anti-senatorial propagandist. Even more remarkable is his dating of the return of this evil to the restoration of the powers of the tribunes of the plebs, those touchstones of antisenatorial agitation, by Pompey and Crassus in 70 B.C. According to Sallust, young men, who were naturally aggressive, gained great power through the tribunate and began to inflame the plebs by attacks on the Senate and to excite them still more by largess and promises. The majority of the nobility opposed them, ostensibly on the Senate's behalf, but really for their own self-aggrandizement.

> After that time all who undermined the stability of the commonwealth used honorable pretexts, some as though they were defending the rights of the people, others that the authority of the Senate should be supreme; but under the pretext of the public good each strove for personal power. They showed neither restraint nor moderation in their struggle; each side used their victories mercilessly.

(*Catiline* 38.3–4)

Sallust echoes the Greek historian Thucydides (3.82), but his words are totally applicable to his own age. That the struggles in which the republic perished were for power, naked and unadorned, was early apparent to Cicero. Although Pompey's departure to the East, to fight the pirates and Mithridates, allowed the nobility to regain some measure of control, an extremely dangerous situation remained, liable to erupt into open conflict at the slightest provocation. For Sallust, here lay the real political significance of the conspiracy. In itself a desperate undertaking of the corrupt and disaffected under a half-mad leader that had little chance of success, it could easily have supplied the spark that sent the republic up in flames. Had Catiline been victorious in the first battle or even held his own, great bloodshed and disaster might have overwhelmed the common-

wealth. Nor would he long have enjoyed his victory: when his followers had been worn down and exhausted, one more powerful would have come and wrested from them power and liberty. It is clear that Pompey hoped that just such a situation would arise and that he would be recalled to deal with it. The danger must have been plain to Sallust as he contemplated the result of another conspiracy, the assassination of Julius Caesar, in the alignment of Antony and Octavian for the final struggle over the corpse of the republic.

This digression puts the conspiracy in its social setting, points the real danger, and lays bare the true nature of Roman politics as a struggle for power disguised under fair and honorable names. The corruption of the political vocabulary is a constant theme in Sallust. In his scheme it is inherent in the lust for power (see *Catiline* 10.5). From first to last, from his early speech to the conspirators (*Catiline* 20.2–17) to his last exhortation to his forces before the battle of Pistoria (*Catiline* 58), the perversion and debasement of noble sentiments, which Sallust sees as typical of the age, remain the keynotes of Catiline's propaganda. And Sallust preserves a precious document, a letter of Catiline himself to Q. Lutatius Catulus (*Catiline* 35). It is probable that Sallust, in conformity to ancient convention, has made the style more literary but has reported the content with substantial accuracy. He claims it as an exact copy. Catiline writes that, aroused by slights and insults because he had not obtained a position of prestige (*dignitas*) and had been deprived of the fruits of his toil and industry, he had after his usual custom taken up the general cause of the unfortunate; not because he could not have paid his personal debts, but because he saw unworthy men honored by office and realized that he was rejected on false suspicion. For this reason he had pursued the hope, honorable in his circumstances, of preserving what was left of his prestige. Just so was Caesar to make the defense of the commonwealth and his own *dignitas* (which he himself said he valued more than his life) his excuse for crossing the Rubicon. Catiline and Caesar together document the ruin of the republic.

After the digression the story moves, with the capture of the Allobroges and the first solid documentary evidence against Catiline and his accomplices, to its denouement, interrupted only by the great set piece of the debate in the Senate on 5 December 63 B.C. and the comparison of Caesar and Cato. That Sallust gives speeches from only Caesar and Cato has been held to be part of a systematic defamation of Cicero, the presiding consul. In truth Sallust could do no more. The verbatim inclusion of Cicero's speech would have grossly unbalanced the work and was precluded by the conventions of ancient historiography; to write his own version would be difficult when the original had long been published and well known. Further, in sober fact, the decisive interventions were those of Caesar and Cato, the former urging reflection and at least a temporary leniency to the captured conspirators; the latter, speaking as tribune-elect low in the hierarchical order of senatorial debate, rallying the senators to the death penalty that the consul desired. Sallust's procedure both here and elsewhere is very far from a denigration of Cicero. On Sallust's showing and in Sallust's terms, Cicero acquitted himself nobly and served the commonwealth well.

Like all speeches in ancient historiography, those of Caesar and Cato are Sallust's own composition. As far as we can judge from the meager reference elsewhere to what was actually said, he has preserved something of the general tenor and argument. But he has his own purposes, too. Many passages of both speeches, but especially that of Cato, show close resemblance to views elsewhere put forward as Sallust's own. In other words, Sallust uses the debate as an occasion to reiterate his view of the sources of Rome's strength and the reasons for its decline, to bring his particular narrative once more into the perspective of his general theme.

Indeed, immediately after the debate the general theme is restated. So closely, in fact, is this passage connected with what precedes it that it can hardly be termed a digression in any real sense. The form is personal, giving the result of what Sallust himself had heard, read, and thought on the greatness of Rome. After long reflection he came to the conclusion that it was the outstanding *virtus* of a few citizens that had accomplished everything, that had made poverty superior to riches and smallness of numbers to a multitude. But after the community had become corrupted, the commonwealth had by its own strength supported the vices of its generals and magistrates instead of their making it great by *virtus*. It was as though the *respublica* had become barren, and for a long time no one at all was produced at Rome who was great in *virtus*. Nevertheless, in his own memory there had been two men of enormous *virtus*, but different character, Cato and Caesar. In the ensuing comparison Sallust first establishes that the two men were really comparable and that neither possessed any significant advantage of birth, age, or natural endowment over the other. Then he contrasts the different ways they attained glory. Bribery and appeal to the disaffected lurk behind the picture of Caesar. His notorious *clementia* is hidden under synonyms and periphrases, with good reason: *clementia* was the arbitrary mercy, bound by no law, shown by a superior to an inferior who is entirely in his power. It is the quality of the tyrant; in the free republic it properly belonged to the Roman people in their historic role of pardoning the defeated. Cato, on the other hand, is presented as a man out of his time, typical of the uncorrupted commonwealth before the destruction of Carthage. There can be no doubt that in the comparison Cato is the winner, and Sallust's terminology and treatment make it quite clear that this was his intention.

Thereafter, the story moves rapidly to its climax with the execution of the captured conspirators and the final defeat of Catiline's forces. According to Sallust they died well: each fell where he had stood in the battle and all had their wounds in front. "Catiline himself was found far in advance of his own men, among the corpses of his enemies, still breathing slightly and still showing in his expression the fierceness of spirit he had possessed when alive" (*Catiline* 61.4).

JUGURTHA

After *Catiline*, Sallust went back in time to the involvement with Jugurtha of Numidia that occupied Rome, in diplomacy and warfare, from 118 to 105 B.C. Two aspects, he tells us, attracted him to the subject: first, it was a great and hazardous war, the outcome of which was long in doubt; second, the war brought the first effective challenge to the arrogance of the Roman nobility, a challenge that evoked such extremity of passion that it led in the end to civil war and the devastation of Italy (*Jugurtha* 5.1–2). It formed, that is, a decisive stage in Sallust's analysis of the disintegration of the commonwealth.

The main body of the narrative after the prologue is divided by three digressions, marked by their opening and closing formulas: the geography and ethnography of Africa (*Jugurtha* 17–19), the origins of political conflict at Rome (41–42), and the city of Lepcis (78–79). In an ancient historian a digression may serve to amplify or explain the text itself, afford variety and relief for the reader, provide the author with an opportunity to display his erudition. Its purpose may also be structural, to mark a climax or stage in the progress of argument or narrative. So here *Jugurtha* is divided by the digressions into four acts, and within these acts Sallust is concerned with working out the interaction of his main themes, the progress of the war and the state of politics at Rome. Thus the first act is introductory, setting out three main strands: the antecedents to the war, the corruption of the nobility, and, binding the two together, the corruption of Jugurtha. At the outset Jugurtha is presented as a man of Sallustian *virtus*, using his innate ability (*ingenium*) to achieve great deeds and thus win glory. In many ways Sallust's description recalls that of Roman youth

before the destruction of Carthage, when *virtus* held all else under control (*Catiline* 7–8). Jugurtha's corruption, as we have seen, comes with his exposure to the Romans at Numantia, who convince the Numidian that at Rome everything is for sale. The digression on Africa stands at the point when Jugurtha is finally convinced that so long as he has money to distribute in bribes at Rome, he can indulge his ambition to become sole ruler. The frequent references to the avarice of the Roman nobility both explain how Jugurtha's actions and success were possible and also prepare the way for the political strife described in the next section.

This section takes up the situation as it was at the end of the first. Rome had achieved a settlement by the Opimian commission without military intervention. That military intervention became necessary was the result of the interaction of Jugurtha's corruption with the already corrupt Roman nobility. Jugurtha, in fact, shows the typically Sallustian pattern of decline from *virtus*. It was because his intellect was avid for power, because he was blinded by desire, because he had fallen prey to lust for power that he precipitated Rome's intervention by again attacking Adherbal after the partition of Numidia. The three themes set out in the first act are woven so closely together that it is impossible in this section to discuss the history of the war without reference, on the one hand, to Jugurtha's character and, on the other hand, to the avarice of the Roman nobility. Jugurtha's ambition finds its purpose served by their avarice, which, in turn, dictates the course of the war. Military events are described in the bare minimum of words, except when, as in the defeat of A. Postumius Albinus, they are relevant to the theme of avarice, which appears as the sole motivation of the nobility.

It has often been pointed out that this picture of the nobility is something less than credible. The particular case of M. Aemilius Scaurus, much stressed by Sallust, is quite unbelievable. Sallust shows him as a man who at first refused to be bribed because he hoped thus better to further his secret political ambitions, but then changed his attitude just as public opinion was being aroused by Memmius against the nobility's management of the war and, moreover, then not only escaped punishment but actually was elected a member of the Mamilian commission, which, in Sallust's words, was set up "more out of hatred of the nobility than from concern for the commonwealth" (*Jugurtha* 40.4).

In fact, it can be argued that the Senate's conduct of the early stages of the war was traditional and realistic. The year 112 B.C. was no time to involve Rome in a full-scale war overseas: the northern frontier of Italy itself was threatened by the Cimbri, who had in the previous year defeated Cn. Papirius Carbo with the loss of nearly his whole army. Hence the reluctance to declare war and the preference for a peaceful settlement imposed by Roman commissions. When this proved impossible, war was begun with the limited objective of suppressing Jugurtha himself, which was all that was necessary. In fact, Calpurnius and Scaurus persuaded him to come to Rome with little trouble and could have prevented Rome from becoming embroiled in an unnecessary war had it not been for the fundamentally irresponsible agitation of the tribunes of the plebs. If members of the nobility saw in Numidia the opportunity for booty and military glory, that was traditional. If Jugurtha was able to call on the support and patronage of prominent senators, that was in accordance with normal Roman procedure in international affairs.

Yet in presenting this picture of the nobility, Sallust himself has no partisan purpose. The establishment of the Mamilian commission marks the culmination of the theme of challenge to the arrogance of the nobility. Yet that body conducted its investigation harshly and violently on the basis of hearsay evidence and popular caprice. On that occasion the plebs fell captive to insolence arising from success as the nobility had often done in the past (*Jugurtha* 40.5). If Sallust writes much against the nobility, it is because the nobility was usually in control of policy, power, and position. When their opponents usurp power and succeed to this position, they are condemned no less heartily (for example, *Catiline* 36.4–39.4; *Jugurtha* 40.3–5, 41–42; and the general portrayal of Marius throughout). The nobility succeeded in its domination only because of its superior resources and its control of the machinery of state. When, as with the establishment of the Mamilian commission, the plebs asserted its liberty, they did so only to turn it into caprice and political license. The political disintegration of the commonwealth was complete.

In fact, it would seem that Sallust is once again subordinating the complex facts of history to his simplified theory of decline both in individual Romans and in the Roman state. In this theory the period between the destruction of Carthage and the dictatorship of Sulla is marked by lust for power (*ambitio*) and for wealth (*avaritia*), for it is not until Sulla that extravagance (*luxuria*) becomes an important factor. If Sallust, having described in *Catiline* Rome in complete degeneration, then went back to analyze in *Jugurtha* an earlier pre-Sullan stage according to his generalized historical scheme, his insistence in the latter work on the all-pervading and all-corrupting avarice of the nobility becomes intelligible, although it remains in detail unhistorical.

The theme of the challenge to noble arrogance reaches its climax in the setting up of the Mamilian commission and is marked by the digression on Roman politics (*Jugurtha* 41–42), which also concludes a stage in the war itself, the end of mismanagement, and the beginning of its successful and wholehearted prosecution under Q. Caecilius Metellus. Now attention is focused sharply on the war. Unlike the previous section, the scene rarely changes from Numidia to Rome. Political conflict is mentioned only toward the end, in connection with Marius' candidature for the consulship. For Sallust, the progress of the war was determined exactly by the *virtus*, or lack of it, of the men in charge. Metellus, though a noble and even opposed to the popular party, was (to Sallust) that rare phenomenon at Rome after 146 B.C., a man of *virtus*. Nevertheless Sallust is led to the qualification demanded by the general scheme—that Metellus had a contemptuous and arrogant spirit ("the common disease of the nobility")—and designed to prepare the reader for Metellus' insult to Marius. The result of Metellus' appointment was the restoration of *concordia*. In preparing a new force for Numidia, the whole Roman state, the Latins, allies, and client kings strove with the greatest zeal. Metellus restored the army in Africa, undisciplined, demoralized, and debauched, to ancient and ancestral discipline. Faced with such an opponent, Jugurtha at once attempted "to make a genuine surrender."

Metellus' campaign is described at length, and the part played in it by Marius repeatedly pointed out. Marius' formal introduction, however, is delayed until the end of the season's fighting, when he comes forward to play a more important part with the prophecy of the soothsayer at Utica, who portended great and marvelous things: let him trust in the gods, carry out what he had in mind, and put his fortune to the test as often as possible. This Marius interpreted in the light of his enormous lust for the consulship. When Metellus refused him leave to run for consul, Marius became totally given over to ambition, intriguing against Metellus and undermining his authority.

Sallust's treatment of Marius provides an illuminating example of his historical method. On Marius' formal introduction, Sallust deliberately suggests that his rise to that point had been swift and easy, office following office in almost unbroken succession (*Jugurtha* 63.2–6). It is beyond doubt that the suggestion is false and that Sallust knew it to be so: in reality, Marius' career had been slow and undistinguished. But Sallust is here not much concerned with the historical Marius. His business is with an abstraction, a type: the new man of unspoiled character and brilliant attainments opposed by the arrogance of the nobility. Marius here forms the particular example of Sallust's general statement about the attitude of the nobles to the consulship and their considering

it polluted if held by a new man (*Jugurtha* 63; see also *Catiline* 23.6).

The whole episode of Marius and Metellus derives from a propaganda cliché, just as Marius' speech on his election, a Sallustian composition, is a repository of the clichés of antinoble polemic (*Jugurtha* 85). What is interesting is that Sallust, operating with the clichés of propaganda, has again no partisan motive. The balance is held between Metellus and Marius, with the latter, if anything, depreciated. Treacherous toward his commander, Marius won the consulship by a combination of intrigue, blatant demagogy, and luck. He was able to cash in on a situation created by others. Metellus' success in the war had sprung from his *virtus*, which restored *concordia* and ancient standards; when Marius took over the command, he was already given up to ambition. His success, therefore, had to be explained away. Sallust invokes Fortune, not prominent elsewhere in his work. His preferred machinery of explanation and motivation is psychological. Fortune is solicited when all else fails, particularly to explain why the destruction of Carthage caused Rome's descent into corruption and discord. Fortune is irrational, basing her operations on the evil principle of desire and caprice (*lubido*). Her benefits, though desirable and open to the man of *virtus*, are evanescent (*Catiline* 8.1; *Jugurtha* 1.3). The part played by Fortune, under various guises, in the account of Marius' campaigns is the more remarkable. Remarkable, too, is the disproportion of that account.

Metellus' campaigning had been treated at length. The whole of Marius', apart from two incidents, is dismissed in no more than ten sentences, but those two incidents, the capture of Capsa and the fortress on the Muluccha, are elaborately described, and throughout the descriptions the part played by chance is insisted on again and again. By thus continually recalling the prediction of the soothsayer at Utica, by ignoring most of the campaign, including the extremely difficult march westward from Capsa to the Muluccha, a distance of some 700 miles, and by describing at disproportionate length two operations in which chance played an important, if not decisive, part, Sallust suggests that Marius owed all his success to the caprice of Fortune. It is the same process as that by which Sallust treated Marius' early career, operating this time in reverse. There Sallust suppressed facts to build Marius into a man of *virtus*, a new man of brilliant achievement and promise. Here Marius has declined into ambition. Success attends only *virtus*. Fact is again twisted, and Marius' military talent depreciated.

The end of Metellus' active campaigning and the virtual end of his command are marked by the digression on Lepcis, which stands also at the point at which Sallust introduces a new element, the alliance of Jugurtha with Bocchus of Mauretania, who was finally to betray him. Sallust attributes Metellus' inaction to chagrin at the news that Marius was to supersede him. But Metellus' inaction is intelligible without invoking typical noble arrogance. His vigorous campaigning must have exhausted his army and caused considerable losses. Moreover, it was reasonable to wait to recruit the strength of the army until the significance of the new alliance became apparent. The explanation of Metellus' inaction forms an easy transition to affairs at Rome.

Sallust recalls that Marius had been made consul with the greatest eagerness on the part of the plebs and had obtained the command in Numidia. His obtaining the command in Numidia had further increased his hatred of the nobility. Meanwhile he pursued his preparations, the Senate being powerless to prevent him in face of the general "passion to go with Marius," which he encouraged in a public harangue. As already noted, this speech is a repository of the propaganda themes of the new men of the late republic. It is difficult to believe that the historical Marius stood for a career open to personal talent or that he at any time supported a program of radical reform such as this speech suggests. Marius again appears here as a type of the new men of the last years of the republic, and, although Marius' claim that the nobles were degenerate and no longer fit to rule may represent his general propaganda line, the formulation of the speech is Sallust's own. As such it embodies the logical outcome of the historian's concept of *virtus* in the idea of a personal, not inherited, nobility acquired by individual achievement. But in Sallust's view, Marius is now irredeemably given over to ambition, the lust for personal power. Metellus had succeeded in his preparations for the war because, being a man of *virtus*, his appointment restored for a brief moment the concord and unity of the commonwealth. Marius' success in the same operation sprang merely from the victory of the plebs that prevented interference from the Senate and served his own ambition. He proceeded not, like Metellus, according to ancestral tradition, but on the basis of desire and caprice.

The odd features of Sallust's account of Marius' campaign have already been noted. Its end is marked by the formal introduction of L. Cornelius Sulla, the future dictator, which looks forward to the growing part he is to play in the negotiations leading to the capture of Jugurtha (*Jugurtha* 95–96). Considering the part played by Sulla in the demonology of late republican propaganda and in Sallust's own historical scheme, the portrait is remarkably even-handed. In one important respect, Sallust judges Sulla superior to Marius. On his arrival at the Roman army, Sulla ingratiated himself with all ranks but did not try to harm the reputation of the consul or of any good man, "as is the habit of depraved ambition." The contrast with Marius' behavior to Metellus is clear and pointed.

Thereafter, the narrative concentrates on the closing stages of the war. Sallust pays tribute to Marius' vigilance and personal interest in his troops, whom he controlled by appealing to their sense of shame rather than by punishment. But immediately the technique of indirect reporting is employed: many said that Marius acted thus through ambition and that accustomed to hardship from childhood he now took pleasure in it and in other things usually considered afflictions. At all events, the commonwealth was as well served as it would have been with the fiercest discipline. The device is an obvious and favorite one to suggest motive and the real significance of events to the reader. Attention is then fixed on Sulla and his negotiations with Bocchus, which end with the betrayal of Jugurtha. The work ends with a short epilogue that refers to the defeat of Q. Caepio and Cn. Manlius by the Cimbri, the reelection of Marius to the consulship in absentia, his appointment to the province of Gaul, and his triumphal entry into Rome "with great glory" on 1 January 104 B.C. The final sentence is full of foreboding for the future: "At that time the hopes and welfare of the community were placed in him."

It is not until St. Augustine, who found Sallust's morose moralizing much to his taste, that the historian is praised for accuracy and veracity. What struck earlier critics and imitators was his style. The style commands attention, remote alike from the artful and artificial simplicity of Caesar and the opulent periods of Cicero. For Seneca it was characterized by truncated phrases, words coming before expected, and obscure brevity (*Epistulae* 114; 117). Brevity, too, and an abrupt type of speech, delightful to a cultivated reader at leisure but useless for forensic speeches, are noted by Quintilian (4.2.45; 10.1.32), who also praises Sallust's "immortal swiftness" of utterance (10.1.102). Capable on occasion of writing a smooth and regular period, Sallust more commonly strained for concision and concentration, for rapidity of expression. We may note also the use of archaisms, both in vocabulary and in syntax, and of Greek constructions. New words are coined and new meanings for old words. Where synonyms or near synonyms were available, it was Sallust's practice to avoid the normal and contemporary, to embrace the elevated and recondite. Similarly, consecrated phrases, which by Sallust's time had become single semantic units, are subjected to studious variation or turned back to front.

In vocabulary, syntax, and sentence structure Sallust waged continual warfare against expectation, balance, and harmony. The continual search for contrast and antithesis in the use of words and in the structure of sentences seems to reflect the quality of Sallust's own mind, abrupt and rapid, alert for the reality behind the appearance, and cynical. The speed, restlessness, and discordancy of the writing match well the violence and disharmony in Sallust's chosen theme, the distintegration of the Roman Republic. And the style is uniform, whether in narration or speeches, though in the speeches concision, abruptness, and disharmony are appropriately abated. But Catiline, Caesar, Cato, Adherbal, Memmius, and Marius all speak in the words and expressions of Sallust. It is a powerful style, harsh, willful, idiosyncratic. How much, one may wonder, of Sallust's idiosyncrasy and innovation in language is to be assigned to sheer perversity and frustrated ambition, to satisfying the ambition and lust for glory he had so signally failed to fulfill as a politician by forcing attention through willful eccentricity of style?

Yet the style admirably suits the theme. As a historian Sallust exhibits disquieting features. Accuracy in recording facts, carefulness in chronology, ability in delineating individual character, insight into the complexity of general trends—these are some of the chief requirements for a historian. In all of them Sallust is seriously defective. Yet behind his defects, indeed, the cause of his defects, is a single purpose: "to describe the institutions of our ancestors in peace and war, how they managed the commonwealth and how powerful they left it; and how, by gradual alteration it has become from the finest and the best the worst and most depraved" (*Catiline* 5.9). The formula is one of digression, introducing the long disquisition on the history of Rome: the sentiment and purpose underlie all Sallust's work. Sallust's preferred mechanism of analysis and explanation is moral: the disintegration of the republic was consequent on the disintegration of the tradition of *virtus*. That is neither strange nor remarkable: all Romans saw social, political, economic change in moral terms—and, given the nature of their society and its structure, they were right to do so. Whatever Sallust's inadequacies, and they are many, his analysis of the destabilization and disintegration of the Roman Republic is, I would claim, fundamentally correct and not without relevance to the present day.

Selected Bibliography

TEXTS

Bennett, Alva. *Index Verborum Sallustianus.* New York and Hildesheim, 1970.

Catilina, Iugurtha, Fragmenta Ampliora, edited by A. Kurfess. Leipzig, 1976. Teubner edition. The standard text; includes the speeches and letters from the *Histories.*

Historiarum Reliquiae. Collected and edited by B. Maurenbrecher. Stuttgart, 1967. Teubner edition in one volume. Reprinted from the first, two-volume edition of 1891–1893. The standard collection of the fragments of the *Histories.*

TRANSLATIONS

The most accessible English translations are those by J. C. Rolfe in the Loeb Classical Library, which also include on the facing page the Latin text of *Catiline, Jugurtha,* and the speeches and letters from the *Histories* as well as the spurious works; and by S. A. Hanford in the Penguin Classics series.

Sallust. Translated by John C. Rolfe. Cambridge, Mass., 1965. Loeb Classical Library.

Sallust, Jugurthine War, Conspiracy of Catiline. Translated with an introduction by S. A. Handford. Harmondsworth, 1963. Penguin Classics.

COMMENTARIES

McGushin, P. *C. Sallustius Crispus, Bellum Catilinae, A Commentary.* Mnemosyne Suppl. 16. Leiden, 1977. For *Catiline.*

Watkiss, L. *Gaii Sallusti Crispus Bellum Iugurthinum.* London, 1971. For *Jugurtha.*

CRITICAL STUDIES

Bolaffi, E. *Sallustio e la sua fortuna nei secoli.* Rome, 1949.

Buchner, K. *Sallust.* Heidelberg, 1960.

Earl, D. C. *The Political Thought of Sallust.* Cambridge, 1961.

La Penna, A. *Sallustio e la Rivoluzione Romana.* Milan, 1968.

Latte, K. "Sallust." *Neue Wege zur Antike* 2, no. 4 (1935).

Paladini, V. *Sallustio.* Florence, 1945.

Schur, W. *Sallust als Historiker.* Stuttgart, 1934.

Steidle, W. *Sallusts historische Monographien.* Historia, Einzelschriften, Heft 3. Wiesbaden, 1958.

Syme, R. *Sallust.* Berkeley and Los Angeles, 1964. The best discussion of all aspects of Sallust's work.

Tiffou, Etienne. *Essai sur la pensée morale de Salluste.* Paris, 1974.

BIBLIOGRAPHY

Catiline, Jugurtha, and the surviving fragments of the *Histories* together make a fairly slim volume. The bibliography that Sallust's works have attracted is enormous, most of it in the languages of continental Europe and much of it devoted to the bogus *Letters to Caesar* and *Invective Against Cicero* and its alleged reply, which are here ignored.

Leeman, A. D. *A Systematical Bibliography of Sallust (1879–1964).* Mnemosyne Suppl. 4. Leiden, 1965. Full bibliography to 1964.

DONALD C. EARL

CATULLUS

(84–54 B.C.)

IT IS ONLY to be expected that the interpretation of an ancient author should be as much the result of the reader's preconceptions as of the author's intent, and in that respect Catullus' fate has been no different from that of every ancient poet. It is currently the fashion to concentrate on the more learned aspects of his poetry—the technical mastery of his verse, his use of literary allusion, his debt to the scholar-poets of third-century-B.C. Alexandria. Not long ago, a more romantic interpretation predominated. Catullus was a lyric genius or the passionate and wretched poet whose deepest feeling was expressed in the poignant epigram:

> I hate and love. Perhaps you ask why I do so?
> I do not know, but I feel it happen and I am
>   tortured.*

(poem 85)

> *Odi et amo. Quare id faciam, fortasse requiris?*
> *Nescio, sed fieri sentio et excrucior.*

In the Renaissance, however, Catullus had yet another character, as a poet of sometimes cynical wit. When Ben Jonson adapted poem 5 in his song to Celia in *Volpone*, he turned Catullus' wish to conceal the number of kisses Lesbia had given him "so that we won't know how

many, and so no enemy can cast an evil eye" into a more general defense of surreptitious love:

> Why should we deferre our joyes?
> Fame, and rumor are but toyes.
> Can we not delude the eyes
> Of a few poore houshold spyes? . . .
> 'Tis no sinne, loves fruit to steale,
> But the sweet theft to reveale:
> To be taken, to be seene,
> These have crimes accounted beene.

The theme of the brevity of life found in Catullus' poem and Jonson's is a commonplace in the Renaissance, but few critics now would read Catullus' poem as cynically as did those poets.

Whether one reads Catullus as a cavalier or as a romantic, however, there is certainly good cause to think of him primarily as a love poet, and much precedent for it. Ancient critics tend to group him with the Augustan elegists Propertius and Ovid, and those poets in turn name him as a precursor. Their poems, however, are rarely read as autobiographical, as Catullus' often are; but that is perhaps because such a total concentration on erotic subjects is difficult to take as literal truth. But since Catullus' love poems to and about Lesbia appear as discrete moments scattered over a considerably larger body of poetry, the lack of an obviously premeditated arrangement lends them an apparent spontaneity; and that, in turn, encourages re-

---

*The translations given here, which are my own, are intended to be fairly literal; I have kept the line divisions of the original as much as possible for convenience of reference, not because these versions are meant to be verse.

construction of a narrative account of Catullus' relations with Lesbia. It would, however, be equally wrong to think of Catullus purely as a poet of passion as to think of him as a dispassionate scholar-poet: if Propertius refers to Catullus as *lascivus* (wanton), Ovid calls him *doctus* (learned). Any full appreciation of Catullus' true genius requires keeping both aspects in mind; both are right, and neither is a full description.

CATULLUS' LIFE AND HIS BOOK

Because it is so easy to fall into biographical interpretation, it is worth stressing how little objective evidence we have for the life of the real Gaius Valerius Catullus. The *Chronicle* of St. Jerome records (with a few chronological errors) his dates and place of origin: he was born in Verona in 84 B.C. and died in 54. That he was Veronese his poems amply attest, and from both the poems and other evidence it is clear that he was a member of a family of Roman citizens, of some substance and local importance; his father was an acquaintance of Julius Caesar. As the promising son of an affluent provincial family, Catullus undoubtedly received a good basic education in Verona (as Vergil, some fifteen years later, did in Mantua and Milan), and was then sent on to finish his training in the capital. As was the case with Ovid, who tells us himself, Catullus was probably destined by his family for a career in public life and (perhaps) political office: we know from several poems, notably 10 and 28, that he went out to Bithynia as a *contubernalis* (staff aide) to Gaius Memmius, the governor of that province, in 57–56 B.C. That would be a logical activity for a young man aspiring to a political career. But Catullus, as far as we know, went no further in that direction. It is not easy to tell why he gave it up—although Ovid's description of his own distaste for a forensic career may well apply to his predecessor—but the disgust evinced for Memmius, for provincial gover-

nors, and for political life at Rome in general in many of Catullus' poems may be personal as well as serving a poetic function.

Aside from his one excursion into an administrative career, only Catullus' private and emotional life is at all known to us, and that through his poetry alone. The major themes of his poems undoubtedly reflect real events and experiences, and two of those are of singular importance. One of these, to which we shall return later, was the death of his brother, whose grave at Troy Catullus seems to have visited on his voyage to Bithynia. The other, the subject of many of his poems, was his love for the woman he called Lesbia.

Like all Roman love poets, Catullus addressed his mistress by a pseudonym that was metrically equivalent to her real name; and we know from Apuleius that the real name of Lesbia was Clodia. That much is made almost explicit by one of Catullus' own poems: *Lesbius est pulcer* ("Lesbius is pretty") is the beginning of poem 79, which goes on to accuse Lesbia of incestuous relations with Lesbius, her equally pseudonymous brother. But by calling him *pulcer* (pretty), Catullus puns on the real name of Lesbia's brother, P. Clodius Pulcer, who was notorious at Rome not only for his violent political activity (he was killed in a street brawl in 52 B.C.) and for having profaned the all-female ritual of the Good Goddess in 61, but also for having indulged in incest with one or more of his sisters. The only problem is that Clodius had three sisters, all suspected of incest with him, all known to have been less than strict in their morals, all witty, elegant, and cultivated women. It is customary to identify Lesbia with Clodia the wife of Metellus, the woman whose character Cicero assassinated in his defense of Caelius in 56; but although that identification is satisfying and economical, there is no proof. It does not really matter; the sisters shared a strong family resemblance.

The Lesbia poems do not offer much chance to establish even a fictional chronology of Catullus' relationship with her, but one or another poem seems to describe the basic stages of a love affair. At least one poem (68) describes their early meetings in the house of Allius; several are poems of courtship or erotic banter. In other poems there are indications of a quarrel and reconciliation (36, 107); of attempts of other men to win her affections away from Catullus (77, 82); of Catullus' feelings when she is with other men, possibly including her husband (51, 83). Finally, there are a great many that concern her infidelity to and final rejection of Catullus, and his resulting misery.

Aside from the general impropriety of taking poems as literal truth, there are several reasons for not believing the Lesbia poems to be a strictly accurate reflection of Catullus' relationship with her. One is the fact that, as will be seen below, several of the poems that are usually taken as belonging to the beginning (51) and end (11, 76) of the relationship seem to have been composed as a group; the same is true of the epigrams (70, 72, 73, 75) that reflect successive stages of Catullus' disillusionment with her. A reasonable inference from this is that the Lesbia poems are to be taken as, at best, composed as a unit after the end of the affair. A second and related feature, which concerns not only the Lesbia poems but the entire corpus of Catullus, is that there is no poem that can be assigned to a historical date earlier than the trip to Bithynia (57–56 B.C.) or later than 54, the usually accepted date for Catullus' death, which was probably deduced from the absence of any later references. Again, the very speed of composition suggests that the poems are a unit, not occasional verses that are an immediate reflection of events in Catullus' life. A final argument concerns the relationship between the Lesbia poems and others in the collection: there is no doubt, as will be seen below, that poem 51 to Lesbia is designed to be read in conjunction with poem 50 to Licinius Calvus. It is also clear that poem 36 to Lesbia, which is also an oblique literary attack on the *Annals* of Volusius, is connected to poem 35, a poem about Catullus' fellow poet Caecilius, and that poems to Lesbia involving other people, such as Furius and Aurelius in poem 11, make far more sense when read in conjunction with the other poems concerning the same characters.

All three reasons given in the preceding paragraph for reading the Lesbia poems less in the context of Catullus' life than in the context of his poetry bear on a more general problem, that of the arrangement of Catullus' works. The idea that the Lesbia poems were composed as a group, that they are supposed to be read in conjunction with other poems in the corpus, is not entirely supported by the shape of the extant collection. The single copy of the poet's works that survived the Dark Ages aligns the 116 poems in three distinct sections. The first sixty poems (generally referred to as polymetrics) are all short, and are all written in Greek lyric meters, of which the most common is the phalaecean verse, also called hendecasyllable (eleven-syllable), which was used occasionally by Hellenistic Greek poets but was never, except for Catullus, a popular meter with Roman poets. The next eight poems (61–68) share one particular formal characteristic, their length: except for the twenty-four-line epistle to Hortensius (65), which is really a preface to Catullus' translation of Callimachus' *Lock of Berenice* (66), they range from 48 to 408 verses, and as a whole are longer than the rest of the collection put together. They are followed in turn by a set of short poems (69–116) written in elegiac couplets (generally referred to as epigrams).

There is no way to tell for certain whether Catullus intended all 116 poems to constitute a single book, and there are strong arguments either way. On the one hand, it is, in its present form, totally unlike any of the poetic books composed by the Augustan poets, where there are clear structural designs involving all the poems. More important than that, however, is that Catullus' book has no clear unity of style or subject. The longer poems are extremely learned; they include a translation of Callimachus (66), two wedding hymns (61, 62), a poem on the legend of Attis, the eunuch priest of Cybele (63), written in an extremely difficult and recondite Greek meter, the galliambic, and, above all, an epyllion (short epic poem), "The Wedding of Peleus and Thetis" (64).

The longer poems share a sophistication of style and subject that reveals Catullus' immense debt to the Alexandrian poets, and these features are not to be found to anything like the same degree in either the polymetrics or the epigrams. While the polymetrics do share some techniques with the longer poems, they are, unlike them, apparently occasional verses on personal, not mythological, subjects. They also have a vocabulary of their own, usually referred to as "the vocabulary of *urbanitas*": that is, they are filled, particularly the Lesbia poems, with words like *urbanus* (urbane), *lepidus* (light or witty), *venustus* (charming), and they abound in the use of diminutives. The subject matter, also, is generally treated with wit and elegance. The final section of the book, the epigrams, displays for the most part neither the learning of the long poems nor the wit of the polymetrics. Their narrative technique and vocabulary show little influence of Greek poetry, the obscenity of some of them is crude in comparison with that of the polymetrics, and the emotion expressed in some of the Lesbia epigrams and in the poem on the death of Catullus' brother (101) is painfully direct in comparison with the distanced and learned grief of comparable polymetrics.

None of these categorizations is absolute; there are elegant epigrams and polymetrics that appear, except for their meter, to belong in the last section of the book. But on the whole, the impression of three collections of poems remains strong. At the same time, however, it is hard not to see all the poems as a single group. Not only are there patterns encompassing sections of the book, and even some correspondences between polymetrics and epigrams, but, as will become evident, the apparently impersonal longer poems share themes with some of the shorter ones, and the mutual illumination of the various parts of the collection is not inconsiderable. And finally, when we consider that there is no poem that can be dated outside the short span of two years, it is tempting to see the collection as a unit. Whether or not the final arrangement was due to the poet himself or to an executor, the various poems share a single poetic impulse and a single, if complex, persona. In the corpus as a whole, even though its arrangement is in certain respects awkward and possibly unfinished, we can see an attempt to create a single poetic voice, a desire to integrate learning and experience, myth and reality, poetic technique and personal emotion. Catullus was the first Roman poet to try to bring the poetics of Alexandria to bear on both the traditions of Rome and his own life; and if his book is not as graceful as later ones, that is merely an indication of the difficulty of the task.

THE NEW POETRY

We have already had occasion to refer to Catullus' interest in Hellenistic poetry, and in this context it is necessary to say something about the third-century B.C. poet-scholar Callimachus, the greatest genius of Alexandrian literature. He set out his credo of the proper nature of poetry in a passage that was known to all Roman poets (although lost to modern readers until rediscovered in this century on a papyrus). In the preface to his last work, the *Aetia* ("Causes"), a collection of elegies recounting, for the most part, the origins of obscure cults and rituals, Callimachus included an apologia for his own poetry and an attack on his critics. They criticized him, he tells us, because he had not written an epic poem, and he replied by a denunciation of bulky works. According to Callimachus—whose language is highly metaphorical—the true poet should aim at polish, elegance, and learning; he should be brief and allusive, not tediously copious. Epic themes (kings and battles) were not his subject, nor was the tone of epic suitable to his voice. The true poet, according to Callimachean theory, should drink from a pure spring and seek a new and untrodden path; he should avoid the public well or the muddy river and the road worn by wagons. A few of his dicta illustrate the manner: "It is Zeus's part to thunder, not mine"; "measure a poem by its craft, not by a surveyor's rope"; "I hate everything public."

Callimachean poetry had a significant and, for a while, salutary effect on Greek poetry; in its own time, it was a welcome criticism of the stale repetition of worn-out forms, and a declaration that poetry was now the province of the scholar rather than the bard. As time went on, however, it led to excessive obscurity and preciosity, and there is remarkably little Greek poetry worth the name after the third century B.C. In Rome, however, Callimachus played quite a different role, and a far more important one, not merely for Catullus, but from almost the beginning of Roman literature.

When the Romans first began to write poetry, in the third century B.C., they turned for models to Greece, and, not surprisingly, the poets that they first encountered were their contemporaries, not the classical poets. In the middle of the second century, when Quintus Ennius wrote his *Annals*, an epic poem on Roman history, he not only introduced a Greek meter, the hexameter, in place of the native Saturnian meter used by his predecessors, he also felt obliged to justify the very fact of writing an epic by refuting the poetic theory of Callimachus' proem, introducing into his *Annals* an account of a dream in which Homer himself gave Ennius permission to write epic. Later in the century, when the satirist Lucilius discoursed in verse on the theory of poetry and the ideals of both literature and life, it was again Callimachus to whom he turned for the substance and methods of his argument. And when Roman gentlemen of the late Republic turned their hands in idle hours to writing verse, it was Hellenistic epigrams, including some by Callimachus, that they naturally took as their models. What is more, when any Roman—schoolboy, poet, or educated gentleman—read the Greek classics, it was through the medium of commentaries and interpretations written by these same Alexandrian scholar-poets. It was Alexandria that transmitted Greek culture to Rome.

In a real sense, therefore, when aspiring poets of Catullus' generation turned to Callimachus for their inspiration, they were doing only what every Roman had done for more than a century. Although Catullus and his friends were far more skilled than their predecessors in the use of Alexandrian techniques, even the first Roman poet, Livius Andronicus, had been aware of some of these two hundred years before. It had been the delight of Callimachus and his contemporaries to show their scorn for all that was commonplace by the use of obscure words of Homeric and archaic diction, often demonstrating by its placement that they were renewing or redefining an obsolete word. So too, apparently, did Livius Andronicus and Ennius as well as Catullus. Catullus' generation, of course, go rather further in this direction: not only do they employ such archaic glosses using early Latin words, they also transliterate Greek words and endings; they adopt Hellenistic metrical techniques; they write on obscure subjects in strange meters.

But stylistic technique, though important, matters far less for understanding the difference between Catullus and his predecessors at Rome than does poetic theory. Ennius may have used Alexandrian methods and may have been a scholar-poet like Callimachus, but he still adapted the proem of the *Aetia* only to refute it. At Rome, before the time of Catullus, serious poetry was expected to serve a public function. While various poets or politicians might write short or light verse in their idle hours—and even Cicero, in his youth, translated the lengthy didactic poem on astronomy by the Hellenistic poet Aratus—it was not their major work. Poetry at Rome before Catullus existed primarily in two genres: drama and epic. The first of these, like Athenian drama, was written to be performed at religious festivals and thus had a public use; epic was written on historical themes, to glorify the deeds of the Roman people. Poetry was not valued at Rome for its art or for its wit, but for its edifying social worth.

Nothing could be further from this than the attitude toward poetry taken, in adherence to Callimachean poetics, by Catullus and his friends, particularly two men, C. Helvius Cinna and C. Licinius Calvus. Callimachus had expressed his scorn for common or public themes in no uncertain terms, comparing epic poetry to a common whore; not one of this group wrote an epic. And while, in their public lives, these poets may have taken the same interest in politics or law as did their nonpoetic contemporaries (certainly Calvus and Cinna had significant political careers, and Calvus was one of the greatest orators of his day), their poetry does not share such an attitude. In the poetry of Catullus, public affairs, politics, and even political language are seen as corrupt and debased; it is poetry alone that matters, and it is poetry on personal and private themes, or on mythological subjects, that is to be taken seriously, not epic or drama. Poetry turns into a society in its own right, and it is a society whose values are diametrically opposed to those of Rome. It is scarcely surprising that Cicero did not approve of their poetic views, and that (a few years after Catullus' death) he gave them the name by which they are commonly known: *neoterics* (new poets). It should not be forgotten that, in the traditional and conservative society of Rome, there could be no more pejorative term than "new."

Probably no poem demonstrates the values espoused by the neoterics as well as a short poem, unfortunately somewhat damaged, that Catullus wrote to celebrate the completion of an epyllion (short epic) by his friend Cinna, a poem on the story of Zmryna (Myrrha), who had tricked her father into incest with her because of her uncontrollable passion and had been driven from her city and turned into the myrrh tree (which only after this metamorphosis gave birth to her son, Adonis).

My friend Cinna's *Zmyrna* has been published, nine summers and winters after it was begun; meanwhile, Hortensius in one [month? year?] [has composed] five hundred thousand.

. . .

The *Zmyrna* will be sent all the way to the clear
   waters of the Satrachus;
the centuries grown old will read the *Zmyrna*.
But the *Annals* of Volusius will die by the Po,
and will provide copious wrappings for fish.
The memorials of my [friend] are dear to my heart;
but let the people delight in bloated Antimachus.

(poem 95)

Zmyrna mei Cinnae nonam post denique messem
   quam coepta est nonamque edita post hiemem,
milia cum interea quingenta Hortensius uno

. . .

Zmyrna cavas Satrachi penitus mittetur ad undas,
   Zmyrnam cana diu saecula peruoluent.
at Volusi annales Paduam morientur ad ipsam
   et laxas scombris saepe dabunt tunicas.
parva mei mihi sint cordi monimenta . . .
   at populus tumido gaudeat Antimacho.

In this oblique, elegant, and polemical poem, whose style is marked by the careful balancing of numbers, rivers, and proper names, Catullus sets forth precisely what is good about Cinna's poem by comparing it in three successive sections to three other works. In the first, Cinna is compared to Hortensius, who was primarily an orator known for his overblown style. Cinna's poem was labored over carefully, while Hortensius spews forth his stuff (which may be a poem or his speeches) with immense rapidity. Secondly, Cinna is compared to Volusius (whose poem is also attacked in Catullus' poem 36). Cinna's work will be read all over the world, even next to the obscure river in Cyprus that had been mentioned in his poem, and it will be read forever; but Volusius' poem will never get out of his hometown, except as fish-wrappings. It should be noted that it is significant that Volusius (who is unknown) wrote *Annals*, historical epic: Catullus is here extolling the value of mythological learning over historical fact or panegyric. And finally, in the last couplet, Catullus turns back to the Greek polemics that lie behind his own poem. Antimachus had written an epic, the *Thebaid*, and was one of the poets most violently attacked by Callimachus. Here he is called *tumidus* (swollen)— one of the greatest terms of abuse in neoteric vocabulary—and it is made evident that Catullus is scorning the judgment of the people in favor of the elect, learned readers and poets for whom this kind of poetry was designed. Thus from this poem one can get a strong sense of the values of Catullan and neoteric verse: care, learning to the point of obscurity, and brevity are qualities to be sought; length and public approbation are to be avoided; and the approval of posterity, not mere temporary fame, is the result. And it is no coincidence that Catullus' own poem is difficult to understand without commentary; in that it is an accurate reflection of neoteric ideals.

In the poems that Catullus wrote to poets or about poetry, it is clear that he is deeply concerned with the power of language and the ways in which language, and poetry in particular, is in some ways more real than events themselves. Just as in the poem on the *Zmyrna* it is care and craft with words that are the true source of immortality, so in one of the poems to Licinius Calvus it is the passion inherent in poetic composition that holds the poet spellbound:

> Yesterday, Licinius, when we were at
>   leisure,
> we played a great deal on my writing tablets,
> since we had agreed to be gay:
> each of us wrote verses,
> playing now with one meter, now with
>   another,
> capping each other through jokes and wine.
> And I went home from there, Licinius,
> warmed by your wit and charm,
> so much that food did not relieve my
>   suffering,
> nor would sleep cover my eyes in peace,
> but overcome with passion I tossed

> over the whole bed, waiting for the dawn,
> so that I could speak with you and be with
>   you together.
> But when my half-dead limbs collapsed
> on the bed, exhausted from effort,
> I wrote this poem to you, sweet man,
> to show you clearly how I suffered.
> So now beware of being rash, and please,
> dear man, do not reject my prayers,
> lest Fate exact from you some punishment.
> She is a fierce goddess: beware of offending
>   her.

(poem 50)

It is not possible, even with the most literal translation, to catch the nuances of this poem. Catullus and Calvus have spent an evening together writing poetry, and it has so excited Catullus that he cannot sleep. That is the basic plot of the poem, but the language conveys something quite different. In the first lines, the activity of the poets is described as *ludere* (play), and they are described as *delicati* (gay), a word that suggests both sexual play (heterosexual or homosexual) and the writing of not-quite-proper verse (*deliciae*, a related word, is one of the terms that Catullus uses to describe Lesbia's sparrow). The opening lines thus set up an implicit equation, found also in other poems of Catullus, between the writing of light verse and sexual activity, between delight in the words and delight in the act. And Catullus' description of his night alone carries this even further. He is *incensus* (on fire) as a result of Calvus' wit; the same image is a standard one of love poetry. He can neither eat nor sleep—typical symptoms of a lover—and he tosses alone on his bed. Thus the writing of poetry is made totally equivalent to the act of love; and the poem emerges as a love poem to Calvus and, in particular, to Calvus' poetic genius. The progression in the poem from poetry as sport and wit to poetry as erotic passion is also reflected in the progression of names that Catullus calls Calvus: from Licinius, his proper name, he progresses to *iucunde* (sweet man), to *ocelle*, translated here as "dear man" but literally "little eye," a term of affection that Catullus elsewhere applies to Lesbia.

Poem 50 is by no means the only one in which poetry is seen to have a more profound effect on Catullus than real events. In poem 44, he writes (in a poem that is a parody of a hymn) to his farm, thanking it for curing him of a cold (*gravedo frigida*) that he got from reading an icy (*frigida*)—that is to say, sterile and academic—oration by Sestius. Literary quality, here reflected in a bad pun, again affects him in the appropriate manner. Likewise, in poem 14 he writes to Calvus, complaining that Calvus had sent him as a present for the Saturnalia a book of poems so poisonous that they nearly killed him. On a more positive note, Catullus writes to another neoteric poet, Caecilius, urging him to finish his epyllion on Cybele, the Great Goddess; but Caecilius is in love and cannot write. Ever since his mistress read the beginning of this poem, she loves him desperately:

> For ever since she read the beginning of "the mistress of Dindymus," the poor girl's marrow is consumed by fire. I pardon you, a girl more learned than Sappho's Muse; the beginning of Caecilius' "Great Mother" is indeed entrancing.
>
> (poem 35, lines 13–18)

The word translated here as "entrancing" is *venuste*, a word that Catullus often applies to Lesbia, to her sparrow, or to anything else he wishes to praise for its elegance and refinement. But here, as elsewhere, he is playing on the etymology of the word, which is derived from Venus. Caecilius' mistress has read the beginning of the poem, which is *venustus*, and has, quite logically, been smitten by the goddess in question. Again, for a neoteric poet, poetry is more real and compelling than reality itself.

One other poem, also to Calvus, deserves to be examined in this context, because it demonstrates to an astonishing degree both how far this poetry is from the immediate expression of personal emotions and how deeply these poets believed in the seriousness of their poetic stance:

> If anything to please the silent dead,
> Calvus, can come from our pain,
> from the longing by which we renew old loves,
> and weep for friendships long ago dismissed,
> then it is certain that Quintilia's early death
> brings her less pain than your love brings her joy.
>
> (poem 96)

At first sight, this appears to be a gracious and moving poem of condolence to Calvus on the death of his wife, Quintilia; but what we know about Calvus' own poetry gives quite a different view of it. In the first place, the middle couplet of the poem refers to friendships that we have *dismissed*, not lost; and this coincides with what we know of one of Calvus' elegies, that it used the death of his wife as the occasion for writing about his love affairs:

> This [i.e., love poetry] was what the poems of learned Calvus confessed, when he sang of the death of poor Quintilia.
>
> (Propertius 2.34.89–90)

Although this may seem an odd occasion to write of poetic infidelities, we may assume that Calvus in this poem rejected as unimportant the other loves that he mentioned in comparison with that for Quintilia. Secondly, two fragments of this poem survive: "When I shall have become gray ash . . ." is one; presumably this was a quotation from Quintilia herself, summoned up as a ghost addressing the poet. The other is more striking:

> Perhaps even the ashes will rejoice in this.
>
> *Forsitan hoc etiam gaudeat ipsa cinis.*

Comparison of this line with Catullus' final couplet—the repetition of *gaudere* (to rejoice), and the contrast between Calvus' *forsitan* (perhaps) and Catullus' *certe* (certainly)—makes it clear that Catullus is not writing a poem of condolence immediately after Quintilia's death, but rather a reply to Calvus' poem on Quintilia's death, and it is a profound compliment. Where Calvus had merely hoped that his poem might please the dead Quintilia, Catullus is certain that it will, and Quintilia after death is moved, like Eurydice, by the poetic power of her husband's voice, by the transmutation of feeling into verse which, in turn, is capable of giving both joy and, through the skill of the poet, a real kind of immortality. It is not love that conquers death; it is love poetry.

To interpret Catullus' poetry as being in some sense "about poetry" is to fall into what has become a commonplace of the interpretation of modern poetry, but it nonetheless has a certain truth. What Catullus is really concerned with in these poems, however, is establishing the fact that all poetry, not merely verse on weighty public themes, has a serious aspect, that the *ludus*, the play of poetry, has an important role not only as the interpreter of experience but as a means of making individual experience universal. Catullus, like Callimachus, is also deeply concerned about demonstrating the regenerative powers of language itself. He would almost certainly have agreed with one of his greatest modern admirers, Robert Frost, that "the whole function of poetry is the renewal of words, is the making of words mean again what they meant." And Catullus, like Frost, deals not only with the use of language to make private feelings and events universal, but with the public use of language, the necessity for clarity, brevity, and simplicity in public life as well as private.

In no poem is Catullus' concern with public language more clear than in a little poem to the great orator Cicero himself:

> Most eloquent of the descendants of Romulus,
> Marcus Tullius, as many as now are, as many as
>   have been,
> as many as will come to be in the future;
> Catullus thanks you greatly,

Catullus the worst poet of all,
by so much the worst poet of all,
as you are the greatest advocate of all.
(poem 49)

> *Disertissime Romuli nepotum,*
> *quot sunt quotque fuere, Marce Tulli,*
> *quotque post aliis erunt in annis,*
> *gratias tibi maximas Catullus*
> *agit pessimus omnium poeta,*
> *tanto pessimus omnium poeta,*
> *quanto tu optimus omnium patronus.*

What the occasion for this poem was is uncertain; that it reflects serious gratitude is highly unlikely. As in the case of the poem that follows this one, poem 50 to Calvus, it is not a private poem addressed to one person, but a poem in the guise of a private letter, in reality designed for a larger audience. It is, in the first place, most improbable that Catullus, whose sense of dedication to his craft we have already seen, seriously meant us to believe that he thought of himself as the "worst poet of all." It is a hyperbolic statement, obviously ironic, and that irony casts doubt on the sincerity of the rest of the poem. If Cicero is as much the best orator as Catullus is the worst poet, and if Catullus by "worst" means "best," then he is being less than flattering to Cicero.

More remarkable is the care that has gone into the structure and language of the poem. As it is a poem on oratory, it begins with a word, "most eloquent," that deals with that subject, and ends with another, "advocate." It falls into clear divisions: in the first half of the poem, the word *quot* (as many) is used three times; in the second, *omnium* (of all) is. Lines 2 and 3 begin with the same word, the second and third lines from the end close with the same word. The main clause of the sentence falls in the exact middle, "Catullus thanks you greatly," between the first half, describing Cicero, and the second, describing Catullus. In fact, the form of this poem is highly untypical of Catullus; it is a bombastic sentence, filled with superlatives

CATULLUS

(which Catullus generally avoids), repetitive, with parallel phrases and periodic structure. It is a Ciceronian sentence, not a Catullan one, and there are clear parallels for several phrases in Cicero's speeches. In short, not only is the compliment ironic, but the poem as a whole is a parody of Cicero. The apparent poem of thanks emerges as an oblique statement of the proper use of language: by uttering a sentiment that is not his own in a style that is not his own, Catullus draws attention to the relationship between words and meaning, and he criticizes the overly orotund and meaningless verbiage of Ciceronian style. It is concerned, to use Frost's phrase again, with "the renewal of words" and by implication with the inflated rhetoric of public life. In very Roman terms, it is an adaptation of Callimachus' "It is Zeus's part to thunder, not mine."

It must have taken a certain amount of brashness for a young man from the provinces to address a poem like 49 to one of the most important men in Rome; and it is perhaps that fact that has led so many readers to take it as a serious, not ironic, compliment. It is, of course, possible that it was meant to be read in two ways: Catullus' friends, who knew his beliefs about language and poetry, were to take it as ironic, whereas Cicero, a man by no means averse to accepting extravagant compliments at face value, was meant to take it at its surface meaning. A similar doubt must shadow the interpretation of a poem that is in many ways like the poem to Cicero, but with an important difference: it is the first poem in the collection, the dedication of Catullus' little book:

> To whom shall I give my clever, new little book,
> just now smoothed with dry pumice?
> To you, Cornelius, for you used to think
> that my little trifles had some worth,
> even at the time when you, alone of the Italians,
> dared to unroll all time in three volumes,
> learned volumes, by Jupiter, and full of toil.
> Therefore take as your own this little book,
> whatever it's worth; and, patroness Muse,
> may it last through more than one generation.
>
> (poem 1)

> *Cui dono lepidum novum libellum*
> *arida modo pumice expolitum?*
> *Corneli, tibi: namque tu solebas*
> *meas esse aliquid putare nugas*
> *iam tum, cum ausus es unus Italorum*
> *omne aevum tribus explicare cartis*
> *doctis, Iuppiter, et laboriosis.*
> *quare habe tibi quidquid hoc libelli*
> *qualecumque; quod, o patrona virgo,*
> *plus uno maneat perenne saeclo.*

Because this poem refers to the collection that it introduces as a *libellus*, a little book, it was probably not written to be the preface to the collection as we have it, which is too large and diverse for such a term. But whatever book it began, it is a dedicatory epistle, and as such it should be expected to tell the reader something about the style, contents, and purpose of the collection. And several questions arise. Why did Catullus dedicate it to Cornelius Nepos the historian? What did Catullus think of Nepos' book? And what did Nepos think of Catullus' *nugae* (trifles)? Finally, why does Catullus switch addressees at the end of the poem and turn to a Muse instead of Nepos? We know a certain amount about Nepos, and it is puzzling to find him here. He was, indeed, from the same region as Catullus; he was an older man, a historian, who had come to Rome before Catullus and was a friend of various eminent figures in the capital, not least of them being Atticus, Cicero's rich friend and correspondent, whose biography by Nepos survives. He was not, however, a person whom we might expect to look favorably on the new poetry of Catullus. His own writings are dry compilations, written in a remarkably awkward style, and his poetic tastes, as revealed by comments in his extant works, were both catholic and unimaginative. He is not likely to have encouraged Catullus to write the kind of verse that we have.

A hint of Nepos' attitude to Catullus' poetry is found in this poem. "You used to think that my *nugae* had some worth," says Catullus, and it is quite likely that *nugae*, a highly patronizing word, is a quotation from Nepos himself. In other words, he probably thought of Catullus' poetry as light and entertaining, but by no means an important contribution to Latin letters. And Catullus' view of Nepos' work, this poem suggests, was also less than flattering. Nepos "dared" to enclose all history in three volumes, his *Chronicle,* a work that was probably no more than an extended chronological table with brief descriptions of significant events. Catullus is not altogether uncomplimentary about this work: he describes it as *doctus* (learned), a word that was clearly laudatory in the neoteric vocabulary. But what he gives with one hand he seems to take away with the other: it was *laboriosus,* full of toil. If by that Catullus meant merely that Nepos had worked hard at it, the word is one of praise; but if, as is more than likely, he also meant that it took a great deal of effort to read, it is rather less complimentary. Nepos, then, had the learning that was required for good writing, but somehow failed to have the wit or elegance to make his book readable.

Catullus' little poem also contains implicit contrasts between his own work and Nepos' that seem less than flattering. He has written one little book, and it is both witty *(lepidum)* and well-polished—the pumice stone refers literally to the physical book, but clearly applies to its contents as well. Nepos has written three volumes, and they are *laboriosi,* not *lepidi.* Nepos' work, moreover, is concerned with all past time, while Catullus has ignored history, and Rome, but claims from his Muse eternal life for his book. One may well suspect that that is Catullus' reason for abandoning Nepos in favor of the Muse: he may know the past, but Catullus is aiming at the future. The ponderous material of Nepos' work is, both in its manner and in its matter, dead, a chronicle of wasted time; Catullus' book is designed for all eternity. And by invoking the patronage of the Muse, Catullus makes it quite clear that he does not regard his poetry as mere "trifles"—or rather, he shows that his trifles are intended to be as worthy of serious consideration as the epic poems that the Muses are usually requested to assist.

As in the poem to Cicero, the dedication to Nepos is a highly ironic poem, perhaps intended to mean one thing to the addressee, another to the attentive reader. It establishes the tone of Catullus' book perfectly; the self-deprecating surface covers a high seriousness about trifles that Catullus does not really believe to be trifles; it conveys a belief that words are to be used with great attention to their tone and meaning. Just as the poems to Catullus' fellow poets suggest that poetry is more significant than reality, so this poem suggests that style is substance. The book that is polished on the outside is polished on the inside, and the irony of Catullus' tone in speaking of Nepos is the subject of this poem as well as its main technique. It is a poem that teaches its audience how to read it.

LESBIA

It is customary to think of Catullus' poems to and about Lesbia as being primarily concerned with emotion rather than language, and it is certainly true that there is a degree of intensity in those poems that prohibits their being read as some sort of academic exercise. But that is scarcely surprising, since the central point of Catullus' poetic theory is that poetry is not supposed to be merely academic but is to be taken seriously as both a subject and a means of expression. And in fact the Lesbia poems, while they convey deep feeling, do so in large part through reflections, often implicit, on the ability of language, poetry in particular, to convey feeling, and through the manipulation of the vocabularies of two very different semantic fields: the language of politics and Roman public life and the vocabulary of *urbanitas,* the learned, witty, and distanced speech that is a part of Catullus' inheritance from Alexandrian poetics.

Although the poems of *urbanitas* are for the most part those found in the opening section of Catullus' book, it is just as well to begin with one from the second half that offers a brief characterization of the qualities this concept involves:

Quintia is beautiful [*formosa*] to many people; to
  me she is fair, tall
and straight. But if I accept these things one at a
  time,
I still deny the entire "beautiful," for there is no
  grace [*venustas*],
no grain of wit in so large a body.
Lesbia is beautiful, and she is not only totally
  dazzling,
but she has stolen every charm from everyone else.

(poem 86)

"Charm" is a weak translation of an untranslatable word: *veneres*. All the attributes of Venus belong to Lesbia; she is *venusta*, and she is beautiful not because she is merely physically attractive but because she is animated by wit, literally *mica salis* (grain of salt).

The type of wit that was appreciated by such women (and poets) is nowhere more clearly illustrated than in the first poem in the book that concerns Lesbia (who is in fact not named in it), poem 2. Coming right after the dedication to Nepos with its obliquely programmatic defense of trifles, nothing could demonstrate more clearly just what Catullus meant than his poem to Lesbia's sparrow:

Sparrow, the delight of my love,
with whom she plays, whom she holds in her lap,
to whom she gives her finger-tip to fight
and stirs it up to violent bites,
whenever it pleases my love to play some little
  game,
some solace for her pain, I suppose,
to ease the heat of her passion—
I wish that like her I could play with you
and lighten the sad passion of my heart.
It pleases me as much as people say
the golden apple did that swift girl
because it undid her long-knotted girdle.

Despite certain obscurities of syntax and sequence, the techniques of the poem are clear and indicate as well as any poem the complex relationship of Catullus to the poetic traditions of Alexandria and the poetic use to which he puts his relationship to Lesbia. The poem begins as pure "trifle": it is addressed not even to a person, but to a bird, and it is written as a parody of a hymn to a god. So far, it is purely in the Alexandrian tradition, and similar Greek mock-hymns exist. But the distance and coolness of Alexandrian parody are soon given quite another sense; at first Lesbia plays with the bird as a game (and it should be noticed that *ludere*, "play," is also, as in poem 50, the word for Catullus' writing of his own poetry). It then emerges that there is a reason for playing with the bird: it relieves the pain and suffering of love. Catullus then addresses his prayer to the bird, an unfulfilled wish that he had some similar relief from his love for Lesbia. The poem thus moves from the ironic distance of parody to the immediacy of emotion, and somehow suggests that mere games and learning are not adequate either for the expression or the satisfaction of emotion. In the last three lines, however, the poem takes a different twist, turning back to Alexandrian learning, but with a difference. Although the style of these verses is typical of Callimachean poetry, with its learned allusion to the legend of Atalanta's footrace with Hippomenes (both of whom are unnamed) and its use of *ferunt* (they say) to indicate knowledge of poetic tradition, its substance is used in a highly personal way. Catullus not only equates himself, not Lesbia, with Atalanta, taking the typical elegiac stance of the hapless and passionate male lover facing a cool and obdurate mistress, but he also alters the story to suggest that Atalanta wanted to be beaten, possibly expressing in the most circumspect and allusive way the hope that the sparrow will have the same effect on Lesbia that the apple did on Atalanta. Thus, by moving from distanced learning to direct emotion and then stepping back to a complex fusion of the two, Catullus demonstrates his own alteration of the genre of poetry that he is writing, and he shows beyond all doubt that his *nugae* are more than mere trifles.

Catullus' poems to Lesbia should not, however, be seen as being as pompously programmatic as this discussion might suggest; the next poem in the book is a sequel to the hymn to the sparrow, and it reverses the direction of that poem. Like 2, poem 3 is a parody, but of a dirge not a hymn. Lesbia's bird has died, and Catullus gives it an epitaph:

Mourn, you Venuses and Cupids,
and whatever men have any share of Venus
  [venustiorum]:
my love's sparrow has died,
sparrow, the delight of my love,
whom she loved more than her very eyes.
It was, indeed, a sweet thing, and knew its mistress
as well as any girl knows her own mother,
and never used to budge from her lap,
but hopping now this way, now that,
kept chirping to its mistress.
But now it goes along that shadowy path
to that place whence no traveller e'er returns.
A plague on you, you evil shades of Hell,
who eat up all that's pretty:
so pretty was the sparrow you stole from me.
O evil deed, poor sparrow, by your act
my love's eyes are puffed and red from tears.

In this poem, in contrast to poem 2, Catullus begins with witty parody and degenerates into deliberate bathos. Only after the description of the chirping creature stumbling along the path to an almost epic underworld do we learn the real reason for Catullus' grief and anger at the sparrow's death: Lesbia has been weeping, and Catullus is annoyed that it has made her face blotchy. In a sense, the two poems are companion pieces in more than the shared sparrow: in each of them, Catullus makes it clear that he resents Lesbia's being more interested in the bird than in him, but in the first he ennobles his own passion by the mythological comparison at the end, while in the second he seems to take revenge on Lesbia by making her seem ridiculous.

Poems 2 and 3, the sparrow poems, create between them a dramatic progression—the sparrow has, after all, died in the interval—but they are clearly composed as a unit, the product of the same conceit and the same view of the relationship between Catullus and Lesbia. The tension exhibited in them between the urbane wit, which both the character of Lesbia (at least as created by Catullus) and the style of composition demand, and the emotional intensity that cannot fully be expressed in such a style is also to be found in the other famous pair of poems that follows, poems 5 and 7. The first of these is a carefully wrought plea to Lesbia to abandon her detachment:

Let us live, my Lesbia, and let us love;
let us value all the mutterings of stern old men
as worth about a nickel all together.
Suns can fall and rise again:
but once our short light has set
we have a single, permanent night to sleep.
Give me a thousand kisses, then a hundred,
then another thousand, then another hundred,
then still another thousand, then a hundred.
Then, when we have counted many thousands,
we'll mix them up, so we won't know how many,
and so no enemy can cast an evil eye
when he knows the precise account of kisses.

One element in this poem, of course, is the plea that Lesbia should give him an infinite number of kisses now, to make up for the single, but eternal, night of death that is to come; this contrast is made emphatic by the juxtaposition of the monosyllabic words *lux* and *nox* (light and night) at the end of line 5 and the beginning of line 6. The basic conceit of this poem, as of the poem to Nepos, is one of number, beginning from the collocation of *omnes unius* (all rumors, one nickel) in line 3, continuing with *semel* (once), *perpetua* (eternal), and *una* (one) in lines 5 and 6, the hundreds and thousands of lines 7–9, and the metaphor from account books in the final lines. There is another element that contributes to the wit and neoteric stance of the poem: by only indulging in kissing while ignoring the values of old men, and by using a serious and Roman practice, accounting, in tallying kisses, the poem expresses an attitude of opposition to standard Roman values.

Poem 5 seems to maintain an almost perfect balance between its elegant style and the direct simplicity of its message; its sequel shows just how delicate that balance is. Poem 7 begins by addressing Lesbia: "You ask how many of your kissings are enough for me." Catullus thus seems to make the reader reconstruct the scene that dramatically contains the two poems. Catullus, in this fiction, has delivered himself of the eloquent poem 5, and Lesbia has asked for more precision. The reply that poem 7 embodies starts with mock-learning and wit: just as in poem 5 the word for "kiss," *basium*, was probably native to Catullus' own northern Italy and first appears in Latin in this text, so in poem 7, Catullus starts by coining a new word, *basiatio*, a formal-sounding abstract noun based on his own new word of the previous poem. He then goes on to answer Lesbia's question with two comparisons:

> As great as the number of Libyan sands
> that lie in Cyrene of the silphium plants
> between the oracle of steamy Jove
> and the sacred grave of ancient Battus;
> or as many as the stars, in the silence of night,
> that look on the stealthy loves of men:
> to kiss you so many kisses is enough
> for your insane Catullus,
> so many that the nosy cannot number them
> nor bewitch us with an evil tongue.

Once again, the poem develops from distant wit to present passion. The first comparison continues the learned tone of *basiatio*: although the basic idea, "as many as the sands in the desert," was probably as trite then as now, Catullus adorns it with obscure references, making up a pompous-sounding new compound, *lasarpiciferis*, to describe the main cash crop of Cyrene, alluding to the famous monuments of the region (the oracle of Zeus Ammon and the shrine of Battus, the mythical founder of Cyrene), using a Greek form for Libyan, *Libyssae*, instead of the Latin *Libycae*. And an ancient reader would also be aware of the oblique nod to the poetic idol of the neoterics, Callimachus, who came from Cyrene and claimed descent from Battus.

But the mock-pedantry of the first comparison gives way to something more immediate in the second, "as many as the stars in the sky." Catullus ends a verse with the monosyllable *nox* (night), recalling the night of death in poem 5; and by displaying the stars looking down on the loves of men he reminds the reader (and Lesbia) that Catullus himself is one of those enchained by passion. The last four lines of the poem return more clearly to the language of poem 5 and seem to sum up the pair; but it is significant that Catullus gives himself a new epithet, *vesanus* (insane).

The progression within these poems lends itself to a number of interpretations, and perhaps the most appealing is a biographical one. The poems, at least, give a portrait of a passionate and direct poet coping with a sophisticated and detached woman; she deals in wit and play, always remaining somehow aloof behind the screen of urbanity, while he attempts to write in her mode of speech but somehow always turns eventually to more direct expression. In other words, the exhibition of poetic skill and wit in an Alexandrian manner appears to be less than satisfying as a means either of expressing or of controlling deep emotion. But the poems to Catullus' fellow poets discussed above, particularly poem 50 to Calvus, lead to a different interpretation: somehow, within the development of each of these poems, the act of writing love poetry, however much it may begin as an exercise in poetic versatility, makes the poet believe what he is writing. Just as *ludere*, the play of words in poem 50, brought Catullus to such a degree of passion that he experienced all the symptoms of a man truly in love, so in the Lesbia poems that begin his book, Catullus is led by the expression to the reality, from love poetry to love.

Such an interpretation seems to be encouraged by the very next poem in the book, one whose dramatic setting is the failure of Catullus' relationship with Lesbia:

Poor Catullus, stop playing the fool,
and what you have seen die accept as dead.
Once the suns shone bright for you,
when you tagged along where your mistress led
    you,
loved by you more than any woman will be.
And then, when many pleasant games took place,
which you desired, and she did not refuse,
truly the suns shone bright for you.
Now she refuses: and since you have no power, so
    should you,
don't chase a girl who runs, don't live a wretch,
but with a stubborn mind hold on, be stern.
Good-bye, my lady. Now Catullus has grown stern;
he won't ask for you, won't plead with your
    unwillingness.
But you will suffer, when you aren't asked for at
    all.
What life remains for such a criminal as you?
Who will now approach you? To whom will you
    seem pretty?
Whom will you love now? Whose will you be said
    to be?
Whom will you kiss? On whose lips will you
    nibble?
But you, Catullus, be fixed, be stern.

(poem 8)

Miser Catulle, desinas ineptire,
et quod vides perisse perditum ducas.
fulsere quondam candidi tibi soles,
cum ventitabas quo puella ducebat,
amata nobis quantum amabitur nulla.
ibi illa multa cum iocosa fiebant,
quae tu volebas nec puella nolebat,
fulsere vere candidi tibi soles.
nunc iam illa non vult: tu quoque impotens noli,
nec quae fugit sectare, nec miser vive,
sed obstinata mente perfer, obdura.
vale puella. iam Catullus obdurat,
nec te requiret nec rogabit invitam.
at tu dolebis, cum rogaberis nulla.
scelesta, vae te, quae tibi manet vita?
quis nunc te adibit? cui videberis bella?
quem nunc amabis? cuius esse diceris?
quem basiabis? cui labella mordebis?
at tu, Catulle, destinatus obdura.

Not a small part of the effect of this powerful poem is derived from reading it in its sequence in the book. From the impassioned, but by no means unhappy, poems on kisses, we are suddenly dropped into a poem in which all is misery. From insane Catullus, we meet *miser* (wretched) Catullus; from the suns that can rise and set again in poem 5, we come to the repeated line of this poem, the suns that once shone bright. Just as the sun of life comes to an end, so the repeated suns of Catullus' happiness have set, and forever. The major techniques used in the poem itself are equally striking. For one thing, the meter: limping iambics, a meter of satire or anger. For another, the sound patterns: the repeated *l* sounds of Catu*ll*us, pue*ll*a, nu*ll*a, be*ll*a, labe*ll*a; the long, open vowels, especially *a*; the repetition of words and the repetition of verses in such a way as to constitute a near refrain. This is true not only of lines 3 and 8 but also of the last line of the poem, *at tu, Catulle, destinatus obdura*, which is composed of fragments of the preceding verses: *at tu* (14), *Catulle* (1), *destinatus* recalling *desinas* (1), *obdura* (11). The articulation of the poem is also artful: after two lines of introduction, there are six verses (3–8) on the past, when he was happy with Lesbia, beginning with *quondam* (once). There follow three lines on the present (9–11), introduced by *nunc* (now), and seven lines on the future, of which three (12–14) are on his future and four (15–18) are on hers, while the last verse (19) sums up the entire poem.

Above all, however, it is the internal monologue and its effect on the poet as he speaks it that most create the sense of barely restrained emotion. The repetition of words has an almost incantatory effect, while the poet's addresses to himself seem to recall him from imagined and recollected joys to present needs. And in particular, his images of what Lesbia will do in the last few lines, verses of increasing eroticism that progress from "what life awaits you" through "whom will you love" to "whose lips will you bite," demonstrate with more intensity the same effect that is employed in poems 2 and

7: it is the poem's own words that arouse the poet's emotions, which he is then forced to restrain. In Catullus' poetic world, clearly, it is love poetry that causes love, words that create emotion.

In no poem is this sense of the real power of poetry to create feeling clearer than in poem 51. Most of this poem is a translation of a famous poem of Sappho, and biographical interpreters have long taken it as the "first" Lesbia poem, because it supplies an explanation for her pseudonym: Lesbia, the woman of Lesbos, is Sappho.

> That man seems to me to equal a god,
> that man (if one may say it) surpasses the gods
> who, sitting opposite, over and over
>   sees you and hears you
> sweetly laughing, something which, as I suffer,
> snatches all my senses away; for, Lesbia,
> once I see you, I have no more
>   [voice left to me].
> But my tongue grows heavy, a subtle flame
> trickles down my limbs, my ears ring
> with their own sound, my eyes are covered
>   by double night.
> Leisure, Catullus, is a burden to you:
> leisure makes you run riot and get too eager;
> leisure long before has destroyed kings
>   and prosperous cities.

While the first three stanzas of this poem are a fairly close rendition of the first four stanzas of Sappho, fragment 31 (omitting some of the symptoms that Sappho had given), the fourth has no equivalent in the model, and that has led many readers to believe that it is a separate poem. But that is both unlikely on technical grounds (Catullus used the Sapphic meter in only two, closely related poems) and improbable when the poem is read as a whole and in conjunction with the poem that immediately precedes it in the book, poem 50 to Calvus. Why should Catullus, after giving his translation of Sappho, suddenly break off and talk about the perils of leisure? Once again, the interior drama of the poem explains it: as in poem 8,

Catullus is moved by his own words, even if they are a translation of someone else's words, to true rather than literary passion. As he describes the scene, as the symptoms become more vivid, he becomes the prey of the emotion he describes; and, as in the same place in poem 7, it is night, symbolic of both love and death, that is the final straw. It is, in fact, worth noticing that Sappho's phrase for blindness does not use the word "night"; she merely says "there is no more sight in my eyes."

In the final stanza of poem 51, then, Catullus recalls himself from the passion aroused by his own words. But why *otium* (leisure)? It is highly significant that the word is also found in the first line of the preceding poem in the collection, poem 50:

> Yesterday, Licinius, when we were at leisure.

> *Hesterno, Licini, die otiosi.*

Otium, the time free from the normal concerns of life and business, is the time in which Catullus and his friends write poetry. And just as the *otium* in which he and Calvus wrote verses together led him to experience the symptoms of love, so the *otium* in which he translates Sappho's description of love causes the real thing. The great irony, however, is that love-poetry, which is supposed to cause love in the receiver, in Catullus' case seems only to affect the writer.

Although it comes near the end of the first part of Catullus' collection of poems, poem 51 provides a basis for reconstructing the fictional narrative of Catullus' love affair with Lesbia as it is implied by the poems. For poem 51, by its Sapphic allusion, and by its indication of the power of poetry to affect the writer's sensibilities, states more clearly than the poems discussed above the basic tension in the poetry between presence and distance, between feeling and writing. And the one other poem in the same meter, poem 11, by its direct correspondences with 51, somehow seems to close the cycle:

Furius and Aurelius, companions of Catullus,
if he goes to the furthest Indies
where the shore is pounded by the long-resounding
     Eastern wave,
or if he goes to Hyrcania, or to the soft Arabs,
the Sacae or the arrow-bearing Parthians,
or to the plains that are colored
     by the seven-mouthed Nile,
or if he goes across the lofty Alps,
to visit the memorials of great Caesar,
the Gallic Rhine, the bristling sea,
     the utmost Britons,
all these things, whatever the will of the gods
shall bring, ready to bear together,
take a short, unpleasant message
     to my mistress.
Let her live and fare well with all her lovers,
whom she grips three hundred at once,
loving truly none, but over and over
     busting their groins;
let her take no heed, as she used to, of my love,
which, by her fault, has fallen like a flower
at the edge of a meadow, after it is touched by
     a passing plough.

Three features of this poem make its relationship to poem 51 evident. The two share a meter, the Sapphic stanza, which Catullus uses nowhere else; the word *identidem* (over and over) appears in only these two poems, and nowhere else in Catullus, and is in the same metrical position; and, just as poem 51 begins with a version of Sappho, so the last stanza of this poem is based on a fragment of one of Sappho's wedding hymns.

Poem 11, however, does not involve the meditation on the effect of poetry that we have found in poem 51 and others; rather, it leads toward a final group of poems to Lesbia, most of them found in the collection of epigrams at the end of the book. In this poem, the structure is built not so much around the contrary attitudes of Catullus and Lesbia to their relationship as around the contrast between public and private life, between war and love. Not only is this found in the poignant last stanza, where Catullus, as a flower in a meadow, is destroyed by a plough, the instrument of agriculture and society, but it is central to the long geographical introduction. Furius and Aurelius (who, we know from other poems of Catullus, were no friends of his) are said to be willing to go to the ends of the known world—India or Egypt, Scythia or Britain. Instead, they are asked to do something that is apparently simpler, but in Catullus' eyes is far more dangerous: to mount an expedition to Lesbia. As is to a certain extent the case with poem 1, we have here a contrast between Roman deeds of history and Catullan trifles, between the concerns of the state and the concerns of the individual. And just as in poem 1 the trifles were in fact more serious than the histories of Nepos, so here the visit to Lesbia is far more significant than the conquests of Caesar.

It is, finally, by placing his love for Lesbia not only in the context of urbane and sophisticated society but also in the context of Roman history and political life that Catullus achieves his most powerful effects; indeed, as will be seen later, it is the amalgamation of personal feeling, Roman traditional values, and Greek mythological learning in his longer poems that is Catullus' most original poetic contribution. Most of the "political" poems to Lesbia are found in the last part of the collection, but one other lyric besides poem 11 seems to strive for similar effects:

Caelius, my Lesbia, that Lesbia,
the Lesbia whom alone Catullus
loved more than himself and all his family,
now in the crossroads and the alleyways
shucks the descendants of great-hearted Remus.
     (poem 58)

Caeli, Lesbia nostra, Lesbia illa,
illa Lesbia, quam Catullus unam
plus quam se atque suos amavit omnes,
nunc in quadriviis et angiportis
glubit magnanimi Remi nepotes.

It is difficult to capture in any translation the shocking effect intended by the last verse. After elaborating, again with effective use of repetition, the depth of his love for Lesbia, Catullus uses an agricultural obscenity (*glubit:* literally the act of peeling the bark from a tree) in juxtaposition with the epic diction of *magnanimi* (great-souled). But the verse has repercussions not only for one's sense of how Catullus' vision of Lesbia has changed, but for the reader's understanding of the degeneration of Roman society that Lesbia's corruption reflects. Remus (and Romulus) would not have submitted to Lesbia's advances; they were heroes, truly great-souled men. But their descendants have become as evil as Lesbia herself, and by expressing his disgust with her in these terms, Catullus brings his private emotions into the context of his more strictly political poems, his attacks on Caesar and his minions, on Memmius and the corruption of provincial government, and on the meaningless language of politics and history. It should not be forgotten that Cicero too, in poem 49, is described as a "descendant of Romulus."

The complex interrelationships between Lesbia as the emblem of *urbanitas,* with all its faults, and Lesbia as the symbol of all that has gone wrong with Roman public life emerges nowhere more clearly than in a series of five poems (70, 72, 73, 75, 76) that come at the beginning of the last section of Catullus' book, and that seem to chronicle the realization that Lesbia is, in fact, totally corrupt. The sequence begins with relative detachment:

> My lady says she wishes to marry no one
> more than me, not if Jupiter himself should ask.
> So she says, but what a woman says to a greedy
>   lover,
> should be written on wind and running water.
>
> (poem 70)

The poem is modeled on the beginning of Callimachus' epigram 25:

Kallignotos swore to Ionis that he would never have anyone dearer than her.
He swore: but they say truly that the oaths of lovers never reach the ears of the gods.

The effect of Catullus' adaptation of Callimachus in this poem makes explicit what is only implicit in poems like 7: where Callimachus' epigram was a narrative about others, Catullus' concerns himself; where Callimachus talks only of love, Catullus speaks of marriage, and he refers to Lesbia not (as he does in the opening poems of the book) as *puella* (my girl), but as *mulier* (my wife).

The location of his relationship to Lesbia in the context of society and marriage is continued in the succeeding poems, where the vocabulary becomes more explicitly Roman:

> Once you said that you knew Catullus alone,
> Lesbia, and that you would rather hold me than
>   Jupiter.
> Then I loved you not as the crowd loves its women,
> but as a father loves his sons and sons-in-law.
> Now I know you: and so, even if I burn the more,
> still you are much cheaper and less valued to me.
> How can that be, you ask? Because such an injury
>   causes a lover
> to love more, but to have less good will.
>
> (poem 72)

As in poem 8, Catullus progresses from past, *quondam* (once), to present, *nunc* (now). But instead of erotic language, Catullus expresses his feelings in terms of politics. It may strike a reader oddly that Catullus compares his love to that of a father for his sons and sons-in-law, but both relationships were basic to the Roman system of familial politics, based on marriage bonds and *amicitia* (which means not only "friendship" but "political alliance"). In one of the few hopeful epigrams to Lesbia (109), Catullus prays that their relationship may be permanent, and calls it an *aeternum sanctae foedus amicitiae,* "an eternal bond of sacred friendship"—referring not to marriage, but to the sacred bonds of Roman society that linked men to one another in loyalty and political life. The last line of poem 72 stresses the same opposition between public and private worlds, not between "love" and "like," but between "love" and "feel well disposed toward," *bene velle*. It was *benevolentia*, a sense of shared respect and mutual responsibility, that led one politician to help another.

Just as poem 72 begins where 70 left off, so poem 73 begins "cease to wish to deserve well of anyone," *bene velle mereri*, and goes on to say that *pietas*, that most Roman concept of proper respect and subservience to family, gods, and state, can no longer exist, that *gratia*, another form of political tie, is now meaningless. So too in poem 75, there is not only the opposition between "love" and "have good will," but the uselessness of *officium*, doing a service for someone, is also stressed. The full corruption of the language of public life and of his relationship to Lesbia is expressed in poem 76, the longest of the Lesbia cycle. It begins by repeating that Catullus has remained true to the Roman code of public values:

If there is any pleasure for a man in remembering
   former good deeds [*benefacta*],
when he thinks how he was honorable [*pium*],
how he violated no trust [*fidem*], how in no bond
   [*foedere*]
did he abuse the name of the gods to deceive men,
then many pleasures in advancing age, Catullus,
await you from this ungrateful love of yours.

As in poem 8, he goes on to urge himself to remain firm, to give up his love for Lesbia, but he then breaks out in impassioned prayer to the gods:

O gods, if it is in you to take pity, or if ever
you have brought aid at the edge of death itself,
look on me in my misery and, if I have led a pure
   life,
snatch from me this destructive plague
which steals like lethargy deep in my limbs
and has driven all happiness from my heart.
I no longer seek that she should love me in return,

or, something impossible, that she should be
   chaste:
I wish to be healthy myself, to shed this vile
   disease.
O gods, give me this in return for honest conduct.

O di, reddite mi hoc pro pietate mea.

Not only has the slender flame of love in poem 51 (to which the language of 76 clearly alludes) become a destructive plague, but Catullus, in his private relationship to Lesbia, has become the bearer of true Roman values, the upholder of *fides* and *pietas*. In the corrupt world of Roman politics in the late Republic, the sacred concepts of Roman society had become perverted; lip service was paid to *pietas* and *amicitia* while the real values that lay beneath them seemed as long lost as the world of Romulus and Remus. By rejecting the current world of Rome in favor of his poetic values, and by remaining true to the words he used, Catullus has paradoxically become the one true Roman in a society where both words and history have lost their value. It is through his integrity in a most un-Roman way of life that Catullus renews the language and the morals of Rome.

"THE WEDDING OF PELEUS AND THETIS"

The poems examined so far reveal a number of themes that tend to appear also in Catullus' longer poems. Both the poems to public figures and the Lesbia epigrams reveal a sense of despair aroused by the lack of honesty and honor and by the sense that Rome has degenerated from its past values. What is more, many of the poems seem to reflect a sense that the ability to rouse or to convey emotion is no longer to be found in the large patriotic or epic forms of annals or oratory, which have lost whatever immediacy they once had, but in the small, personal forms, which embody meaning that is no longer conveyed in the traditional ways.

Even though Catullus' masterpiece (and his longest poem), "The Wedding of Peleus and Thetis" (64), speaks neither of Rome past or present, nor of the personal concerns of Catullus, it embodies in a complex and oblique manner a number of the concerns just enumerated. By putting them into a mythic context, moreover, Catullus seems to provide a longer perspective on personal concerns. Just as the simile at the end of poem 2, in which Catullus compared himself to Atalanta, elevated a specific event to the level of myth and at the same time altered myth to make it more immediate, so poem 64, on a far larger scale, seems to renew the mythic and epic past, to make it more vivid; and at the same time, its clear connections to his shorter and more personal poems seem to confer on them an objectivity and universality that they might not, on their own, possess.

The form of poem 64 was invented by the Alexandrians and is peculiar to them and their Roman imitators. It is a short epic poem—given the convenient label epyllion by modern critics—and it has the clear poetic intention of criticizing and revising the themes and values of traditional epic poetry. Where Homeric epic is vast and emphasizes narrative, reducing the author's intrusion into his creation to a minimum, epyllion does the opposite. Not only is it brief, but it eclipses narrative almost entirely in favor of psychological description (particularly of emotions of love, doubt, fear, and anger) and reported speeches. It also tends to stress precisely those events or scenes that traditional epic avoids: wars and battles are shunned in favor of romantic interludes, the great deeds of heroes are neglected in favor of their infancy or minor actions. It is somehow a hybrid form: the most personal of narrative forms, the most epic of personal lyrics. Catullus' subject in poem 64 is the wedding of Peleus and Thetis, the parents of Achilles. Within a framing introduction and conclusion that tell of the meeting of the couple and extol the glories of that mythic age in comparison with the present, the entire poem describes the wedding itself. Most of that description, however, is taken up with apparent digressions: more than half the poem is a description of the embroidery on the coverlet of the wedding couch, which depicts Ariadne, standing deserted on the beach of Dia and cursing the departed Theseus. And after the wedding proper, Catullus quotes the wedding song sung by the Parcae (Fates), which reveals the future history of Achilles, offspring of this marriage.

Both the beginning and the end of the poem create the expectation that it is to be a work of escapism and nostalgia for the heroic age that is gone. Near the end of the proem, Catullus apostrophizes the crew of the *Argo*:

> You heroes who were born at the most enviable
> time in history,
> hail, race of the gods! Noble children of your
> mothers,
> hail once more . . .
>
> (64.22–24)

And at the end of the poem he draws explicit comparison between the glorious age of which he is writing and the corrupt present. After listing occasions in the heroic age when gods appeared to men, since *pietas* had not been abandoned, he compares it to the present:

> But after the earth was steeped in unspeakable
> crime
> and all men had chased justice from their greedy
> minds,
> brothers drenched their hands in brothers' blood.
> . . .
> The mixing of all things speakable and
> unspeakable in madness
> turned the just mind of the gods away from us.
>
> (64.397–399; 405–406)

In order to make his mythic age more golden, moreover, Catullus deliberately altered the story of the marriage. According to the traditional version of the tale, Thetis had married Peleus against her will and at the command of Jupiter, because it was fated that she should give birth to a son stronger than his father. The marriage, moreover, was short-lived: Thetis gave birth to Achilles and then took him and abandoned Peleus. Catullus' version is very different: in poem 64, Thetis falls in love with Peleus at first sight, when she and the other sea-nymphs look up from the ocean at the *Argo*, the first boat, in which Peleus was sailing.

Fairy-tale romantic nostalgia, however, is by no means all that the poem contains, and it would be trivial if that were so. Even the manner in which Catullus tells of the meeting of Peleus and Thetis shows that he is aware of the violence that he is doing to tradition, and the fact that he opens his poem with the sailing of the *Argo* is designed to instill a certain uneasiness in the reader:

> Pines once sprung from Pelion's peak are said
> to have swum through Neptune's liquid waves
> to the waters of the Phasis and the land of
> Aeetes. . . .
>
> (64.1–3)

Not only is the first sea-voyage traditionally an emblem of the fall of man from the golden age through transgressing the limits of land and sea set by the gods, but the opening words are intended to recall the opening of Euripides' *Medea*:

> If only Argo's ship had never flown through
> the Clashing Rocks to the land of Colchis,
> and the pine tree cut in the groves of Pelion
> had never fallen, nor heroes taken oars in their
> hands,
> who went to get the golden fleece for Pelias.

The result of the voyage of the *Argo* in that context is not the happy wedding of Peleus and Thetis, but the tragic meeting of Jason and Medea, a subject never explicitly mentioned but always present in poem 64.

How far any sense of foreboding is meant consciously to be in the reader's mind in reading the opening lines is not clear; but that the heroic age is not all sweetness and light is made abundantly evident in the course of the poem,

in both its general themes and in the details of the narrative. The two digressions in particular seem strangely inappropriate both to the dramatic context of the wedding and to the tone of happiness that the poet seems to proclaim. Most important is the coverlet, which we see through the eyes of the wedding guests who throng the palace and admire it. The poet tells us what the embroidery is supposed to signify:

> This garment, embroidered with the figures of
> ancient men,
> points out with wondrous skill the great deeds of
> the heroes.
>
> (64.50–51)

"Great deeds" is a translation of *virtutes*, a highly Roman concept that includes both moral and physical characteristics. But the *virtutes* shown on the coverlet are peculiar. We see in the center the figure of the deserted Ariadne on the beach, hurling curses at the absent Theseus. In his description of the coverlet, Catullus digresses further to summarize the story of Theseus and the Minotaur, and after quoting Ariadne's lament and her curse of forgetfulness on Theseus, he tells of the arrival of the absentminded hero in Athens, the consequent death of his father, Aegeus, and the rescue of Ariadne by Dionysus, all of which was, he says, shown on the coverlet. But the abandonment of his savior by Theseus, and his unintentional destruction of his father, are scarcely deeds of manly virtue. Even more, it is made quite clear that Catullus both sympathizes with Ariadne rather than Theseus and somehow equates Theseus' desertion of Ariadne with Lesbia's of him. In particular, the language used by Ariadne in describing Theseus and their relationship is the same language of politics and trust used by Catullus in the epigrams: she speaks of their marriage, of Theseus' lack of *fides*, of false oaths, of promises that, like Lesbia's words to Catullus in poem 70, are snatched away by the winds.

Even without the personal resonances of Ariadne's lament, a scene of male perfidy and the failure of a marriage is scarcely an appropriate subject for a marriage bed. It is, however, consonant with the other set piece in the wedding, the song of the Parcae. That too is a departure from traditional descriptions of Thetis' wedding, where the Muses are usually said to have provided the entertainment. The Parcae are aged, weird sisters, and the joy that they predict for the marriage in the opening of their song turns into a grisly prediction of Achilles' life and deeds. Starting from the traditional hymeneal blessings on bride and groom, they turn to Achilles' birth and greatness. At first it is said that he will be fearless, that he will outrun the deer (338–341). Then we learn that no Trojan will stand against him "when the Phrygian fields will drip with Trojan blood" (344), that bereaved mothers will speak of his "exceptional deeds [virtutes] and great acts" as they tear their hair and beat their breasts (348–351). The description of Achilles' virtus becomes increasingly bloodcurdling, reaching an awful climax with the sacrifice of Polyxena, Priam's last daughter, on Achilles' tomb:

> his lofty grave will grow wet with Polyxena's
>   blood;
> like a victim falling to the double axe
> she will bend her knee and throw down her
>   headless trunk.
>
> (64.368–370)

Again, this is scarcely appropriate to such a happy occasion, but the Parcae go on to draw the somewhat illogical conclusion from their prophecy that Peleus and Thetis should consummate this long-desired match. Once again, the idea of virtus seems to be contradicted by the actions that are said to embody it: Achilles' demand for the sacrifice of a virgin, the filling of a river with corpses, the wailing of bereaved parents. Even in the heroic age, heroism seems tainted.

If the announced argument of poem 64 is the glory and the virtue of the heroic age, the happiness of marriage in that unsullied time, it is totally undercut by the narrative of events. It is worthwhile comparing the opening and the manner of this poem with that of poem 8. Poem 64 begins, in a manner typical of this type of poetry, with *quondam*, a word whose closest English equivalent in this context is the fairy-tale phrase,

> Once upon a time, in a far away kingdom . . .
>
> *Peliaco quondam prognatae vertice pinus . . .*

In poem 8, when Catullus is reminiscing about past happiness in the face of present misery, he uses the sentence

> Once the suns shone bright for you.
>
> *Fulsere quondam candidi tibi soles.*

In each case, the context requires that we revise the poet's own evaluation of the past by the evidence that he supplies. The past in each case seems, or rather Catullus wishes it to have been, golden. In each case he ends by showing that the past is in reality no different from the present. Ariadne was betrayed as Catullus was, *virtus* is a mere word, empty of meaning then as now. The shining glory of past time exists only in the faulty or willful reconstructions of later men: when the past was present, it was the same as the present is now.

CATULLUS AND TROY

Catullus' reevaluation of the significance of Peleus, Thetis, and Achilles is not merely a reflection on the changing meaning of the past; it can also be seen as a criticism of Homeric epic. Given the fact that the epyllion form itself was an implicit criticism of epic, that is not surprising, but in poem 64 as well as some of the other longer poems Catullus seems to see Troy and the Trojan War in a more personal context. His reduction of heroic warfare to the grisly slaughter of innocents seems, indeed, far more intense than a poetic polemic need be. And in fact there is a personal connection between Catullus and Troy: his brother, as we learn in poem 68, was buried there, and in poem 101 Catullus records his visit to the grave:

Traveling through many peoples, over many seas,
I come, brother, to these sad rites,
to give you the final gifts of death,
to speak in vain to your silent ashes. . . .

The poem is intense, and its language adds complexity to it by associating it with Catullus' other poems concerning Troy. The opening words of the poem are not a literal description of Catullus' voyage to Bithynia with Memmius, the occasion for this visit, but an adaptation of the opening words of the *Odyssey* (translated by Lattimore):

Tell me, Muse, of the man of many ways, who was
    driven
far journeys, after he had sacked Troy's sacred
    citadel.
Many were those whose cities he saw, whose
    minds he learned of,
many the pains he suffered in his spirit on the wide
    sea. . . .

Catullus' repetition of "many," his use of "peoples" and "seas," come from Homer. But the context is totally reversed. Odysseus' travels are on his voyage home from Troy, after the city had been destroyed; Catullus' voyage is to Troy, to visit the grave of one dead there. It is an epic voyage backward to the Trojan War, to death and to the past.

It is in poem 68b, a long and complex elegy, that the fullest chain of associations with Troy is formed, and it is evident that the connections are associative, not logical. The poem is not entirely clear (nor is it even clear whether poem 68 is one, two, or even three poems), but that may well be because it was not intended to be. It is a highly experimental poem, unlike any other in Latin literature. The poem begins as an expression of gratitude to Catullus' friend Allius, who had apparently supplied a house in which Catullus and Lesbia might meet. He offers Allius, in return for his past help, the poem itself, which carries with it the gift of immortality:

I cannot keep silent, Muses, the matter in which
Allius helped me, or in how many ways he helped
    me,
lest fleeing time with its forgetful ages
should cover his aid with unseeing night:
but I will tell you, and you tell many thousands,
and make this page still speak when it grows old.
                                        (68b.41–46)

In a series of involved similes, Catullus first compares his passion to the fires of Aetna or Thermopylae, and then Allius' aid to a cool stream refreshing a traveler or a favoring breeze helping sailors at sea. It is only when he turns to recalling Lesbia's arrival at the house that the Homeric connections appear:

(the house) where my shining goddess came on her
    soft feet . . .
just as once, on fire with love for her husband,
Laodamia came to the house of Protesilaus . . .
(an ill-omened marriage) . . .
as Laodamia learned when she lost her husband,
forced to give up the embrace of her new groom
before one winter or two had sated her love with
    long nights,
so that she could live with her marriage ended—
which the Fates knew was not far off,
if he went as a soldier to the walls of Troy.
                                (68b.74–75; 80–86)

For Catullus to compare his relationship to Lesbia to that of Protesilaus and Laodamia is scarcely designed to encourage belief in its permanence: Protesilaus' marriage lasted only one day before he went to Troy and was the first person killed there.

The thought of death at Troy leads Catullus inevitably to the thought of his brother, in vehement language that evokes Andromache's lament for Hector in the *Iliad*:

For then, by stealing Helen, Troy had begun
to call the leading men of Greece to it,

Troy (shame!) the common grave of Asia and
   Europe,
Troy, the bitter ash of all men and virtues,
which brought wretched death even to my brother.
Alas, brother snatched from me in my pain,
alas, sweet light snatched from your brother in
   pain,
along with you our whole house was buried,
along with you all my joys perished,
the joys which your sweet love nourished in life.
Whom now, so far away, not among familiar tombs
nor buried with the ashes of his family,
but buried in obscene Troy, barren Troy,
a foreign land holds him in its furthest soil.

                (68b.87–100)

After this Catullus returns to the story of Protesilaus, who was restored for a year to life through Laodamia's love, and then to his own relationship with Lesbia, whose infidelities, he says, he has learned to live with.

This is a strange poem in more ways than one, but the central section on Troy is remarkable for its associative logic. He begins by thinking of himself as Protesilaus receiving Lesbia as Laodamia into the house; he then proceeds to the story of Protesilaus at Troy, in which he, suddenly, seems to have taken the role of Laodamia, and his brother is the dead Protesilaus. Troy, which killed both Protesilaus and Catullus' brother, is described as obscene and barren, the bitter ash of all men and virtues (*Troia virum et virtutum omnium acerba cinis*). Although it is not clear why, except for its obvious poetic power, there is a clear connection in Catullus' poem between the failure of his love for Lesbia and the death of his brother; in some ways, it almost appears as if he is suggesting that, in loving Lesbia, he was responsible for his brother's death.

Seen in either poetic or personal terms, therefore, the Trojan War is a crucial element in Catullus' poetry. In Catullus' descriptions, Troy is less the scene of epic heroism than of the destruction of heroism, and above all of the destruction of domestic and married life. Certainly Catullus' Troy lends itself to such an interpretation: the Trojan War is caused by the adultery of Helen and proceeds, through meaningless and unheroic slaughter, to the perversion of marriage that is the sacrifice of Polyxena. It is no coincidence that all Catullus' longer poems deal, in one way or another, with the topics of marriage and fidelity, nor is it surprising that in poem 63, which tells the story of Attis, who sails from Greece to Phrygia to worship Cybele and there castrates himself in her service, the scene takes place on Mount Ida and on the neighboring seashore—which is Troy. When Propertius (2.34.88) praised Catullus for having made Lesbia more famous than Helen, he was very close to the mythic core of Catullus' thought.

To say that Catullus' poetry is about the two great losses of his life, about the proper functions of language and poetry, or about the reinterpretation of either the Roman or the Homeric past would be to enforce clarity at the expense of truth. All these themes are interwoven in his poetry, and it would do neither the poet nor the reader any service to try to label one as dominant or to suggest that Catullus was writing in the service of an idea rather than composing serious, complex, and beautiful poetry. It is, however, possible to say something about Catullus' contribution to the creation of Latin poetry. From the poetic and political traditions of Rome, which in Catullus' day seemed both empty and irrelevant, the poet turned to the utterly different poetic world of Alexandria. There he found a tradition that emphasized skill in expression rather than grandeur of theme, that showed how a poet could take the materials of previous literature and put his own stamp on them, creating new and personal interpretations from the familiar materials of Greek myth.

But despite all the bravado of his antipolitical stance, Catullus was far too much a Roman to abandon the concerns, even if he rejected the attitudes, of his own society. Rather than ape the Alexandrians in a poetry that paid far less attention to content than to style, he used their techniques to fashion a personal voice, to fuse Greek myth with Roman politics, to find a depth for private sorrows in the perspective of public life, to show that traditional themes, of Greek epic or of Roman history, could be mastered and transmuted through the poetic voice. That the love poetry of the Augustan elegists owed its existence to Catullus is obvious; but without Catullus' Troy we also would not have Vergil's Rome.

Selected Bibliography

TEXTS AND COMMENTARIES

Catullus, edited by C. J. Fordyce. Oxford, 1961. Expurgated text and commentary.

Catullus: The Poems, edited by Kenneth Quinn. London, 1970. Text and commentary.

C. Valerii Catulli Carmina, edited by R. A. B. Mynors. Oxford, 1958. Oxford Classical Text; text only.

Ellis, R. *A Commentary on Catullus*. Oxford, 1876.

TRANSLATIONS

Copley, F. O. *Catullus: The Complete Poetry*. Ann Arbor, Mich., 1957.

Gregory, H. *The Poems of Catullus*. New York, 1933.

Michie, James. *The Poems of Catullus*. New York, 1971.

Whigham, P. *The Poems of Catullus*. Baltimore, 1966. Penguin edition.

There is no one standard translation.

CRITICAL STUDIES

Bacon, H. "Dialogue of Poets: *Mens Animi* and the Renewal of Words." *Massachusetts Review* 19: 319–334 (1978). Primarily on Frost, but also on his use of Catullus.

Bramble, J. C. "Structure and Ambiguity in Catullus 64." *Proceedings of the Cambridge Philological Society* 16:22–41 (1970).

Bright, D. F. "*Confectum Carmine Munus*: Catullus 68." *Illinois Classical Studies* 1:86–112 (1976).

Clausen, W. "Callimachus and Latin Poetry." *Greek, Roman and Byzantine Studies* 5:181–196 (1964). Reprinted in Quinn, *Approaches* (see below).

———. "The New Poetry and Catullus." Forthcoming in *Cambridge History of Classical Literature*.

Commager, S. "Notes on Some Poems of Catullus."

Harvard Studies in Classical Philology 70:83–110 (1965).

Curran, L. C. "Catullus 64 and the Heroic Age." *Yale Classical Studies* 21:171–192 (1969).

Elder, J. P. "Catullus' *Attis*." *American Journal of Philology* 68:394–403 (1947). Reprinted in Quinn, *Approaches*.

———. "Notes on Some Conscious and Unconscious Elements in Catullus' Poetry." *Harvard Studies in Classical Philology* 60:101–136 (1951). Reprinted in Quinn, *Approaches*.

———. "Catullus 1, his Poetic Creed, and Nepos." *Harvard Studies in Classical Philology* 71:143–149 (1966).

Fraenkel, E. "Catullus Trostgedicht für Calvus." *Wiener Studien* 69:279–286 (1956). Reprinted in Quinn, *Approaches*.

Havelock, E. A. *The Lyric Genius of Catullus*. Oxford, 1929. Reprinted New York, 1967.

Khan, H. A. "Catullus 35, and the Things Poetry Can Do to You." *Hermes* 102:475–490 (1974).

Kinsey, T. E. "Irony and Structure in Catullus 64." *Latomus* 24:911–931 (1965).

Konstan, D. *Catullus' Indictment of Rome: The Meaning of Catullus 64*. Amsterdam, 1977.

Putnam, M. C. J. "The Art of Catullus 64." *Harvard Studies in Classical Philology* 65:165–205 (1961). Reprinted in Quinn, *Approaches*.

———. "Catullus' Journey." *Classical Philology* 57:10–19 (1962). Reprinted in Quinn, *Approaches*.

———. "Catullus 11: The Ironies of Integrity." *Ramus* 3:70–86 (1974).

Quinn, Kenneth. *The Catullan Revolution*. Melbourne, 1959.

———, ed. *Approaches to Catullus*. Cambridge, 1972. Extremely valuable collection of articles.

Ross, D. O., Jr. *Style and Tradition in Catullus*. Cambridge, Mass., 1969.

———. *Backgrounds to Augustan Poetry*. Cambridge, 1975.

Segal, C. P. "Catullan *Otiosi*: The Lover and the Poet." *Greece and Rome* 17:25–31 (1970).

Wheeler, A. L. *Catullus and the Traditions of Ancient Poetry*. Berkeley, 1934.

Williams, G. *Tradition and Originality in Roman Poetry*. Oxford, 1968.

Wills, G. "Sappho 31 and Catullus 51." *Greek, Roman and Byzantine Studies* 8:193–197 (1967).

Wiseman, T. P. *Catullan Questions*. Leicester, 1969.

———. *Cinna the Poet*. Leicester, 1974.

———. *Clio's Cosmetics*. Leicester, 1979.

JAMES E. G. ZETZEL

VERGIL

(70–19 B.C.)

LIFE AND POETIC CAREER

Mantua me genuit, Calabri rapuere, tenet nunc
Parthenope; cecini pascua, rura, duces.

Mantua produced me,
Calabria ravished me,
Naples keeps me now.
I have sung of pastures, fields, leaders.

PUBLIUS VERGILIUS MARO died in 19 B.C., at the age of fifty-one, during his return to Italy from a trip to Greece. He is said to have composed the above epitaph for himself on his deathbed. In it he mentions the place of his birth, Mantua; the place of his death, Calabria; and the place where he was to be buried, Naples. He does not mention Rome, although he was, and is, Rome's greatest poet.

Mantua lies in the rich agricultural region of the Po Valley, settled successively by Etruscans and Celts and—in Vergil's own time—discharged Roman soldiers; the poet's father is said to have lost his farm to one such veteran. Naples, with its neighbors Cumae and Puteoli, was a Greek city founded centuries before, which still preserved its Hellenic associations and culture. Rome was the center of political and military power that dominated Mantua far to the north, as it dominated Naples to the south.

In order to get from Mantua to Naples one had to pass through Rome. Vergil's schooling followed this route: elementary education in Mantua, advanced rhetoric in Rome, and Greek philosophy in Naples. While in Rome, he met other poets on the rise, some of the great men who were their patrons, and finally Maecenas, the friend of the young man Octavian, who was engaged in a bloody struggle to become sole heir to the power of Julius Caesar and who would eventually succeed and be named Augustus. Vergil did not stay in the capital city, but only moved through it on his way toward the older culture around Naples, which became his spiritual home. In the only explicit autobiographical statement in his works, he says that "sweet Naples provided him with sustenance" while he was composing the *Georgics* (4.563–564).

He could choose not to live in Rome, but he could not escape its influence. Rome dominated and troubled the poet's imagination as it dominated and troubled the Italy of his birth and the Greece of his yearning. On the first page of his first published book of poetry, the *Eclogues*, the city's towering buildings loom almost grotesquely over the poem's pastoral landscape:

The city they call Rome, Meliboeus—
I thought in my folly
it was like this town of ours
where we shepherds often drive our young lambs.
I knew that puppies were like dogs
and kids like their mothers:
that's the way I compared big things to small.

But that city has reared its head as high among the others
as a cypress-tree among pliant hedge-roses.

(*Eclogues* 1.19–25)

Although Vergil could escape from the city for the most part in the world of the *Georgics*, "the walls of towering Rome" appear again to block his way in the first sentence of the *Aeneid*, and there he must confront them head on.

By the time of Vergil's birth, Rome had grown into a monster whose strength seemed bent upon self-destruction. The question then was whether that strength could be turned toward constructive ends, to ensure enough peace and stability within the civilized world for man to continue to enjoy his humanity. We are accustomed to viewing this question with the privilege of historical hindsight, knowing that Vergil's lifetime was followed by 300 years of relatively undisturbed peace in the Roman Empire, including the century during which Edward Gibbon has told us that "the condition of the human race was most happy and prosperous"; the New Rome of Christianity; the Renaissance with its rediscovery of classical culture; the Age of Reason; and all the subsequent ages down to our own time, however we may wish to designate them. We can still understand and appreciate the philosophical and literary values of Greek culture that Vergil cherished. And it is because of Rome that we can do so. Vergil himself had no such grounds for optimism. To him the great city remained more of a threat than a promise: a threat both to the values of a remembered or imagined simpler rural life and to Greek refinement. He seemed to resent and to struggle against the fact that all roads did lead through Rome, even his own new path of poetry: for Vergil's great literary achievement was to create a new and truly Roman poetry out of all the past strands of both the Greek and Italian traditions.

The Romans had long felt a sense of artistic inferiority to the Greeks. Vergil's contemporary Horace epigrammatically expressed their feeling as cultural latecomers:

Captured Greece took its savage victor captive
and imported the arts to rustic Latium.

(*Epistles* 2.1.156–157)

Vergil himself helped to perpetuate the myth of the Romans as pragmatists and philistines in Anchises' often-quoted statement of his descendants' mission:

Others will shape breathing bronze statues
    with a softer touch
(so I believe),
they will draw living faces out of marble,
plead cases better,
describe the motions of the sky with a compass,
and name the rising stars.
You, Roman, must remember to rule nations with
    authority
(these will be your arts),
impose tradition on peace,
spare the conquered,
and crush the haughty.

(*Aeneid* 6.847–853)

Although poetry is omitted from this list of non-Roman achievements, poets must have felt the burden of the Greeks more than any other group of artists when they attempted to shape a poem in Latin, for the very meters in which they had to sing had been borrowed from Greek verse and imposed artificially onto their own language. Accompanying this was the feeling among the Greeks themselves that many poetic genres—epic, tragedy, lyric—had already been developed, reached their prime, been exploited, and then were exhausted: a feeling that produced the learned and decorative Alexandrianism typical of Greek poetics in the third and second centuries B.C., when the Romans first began to look to Greece for help in creating Latin poetry. In imitation, Vergil's contemporaries had even developed a special Roman brand of Alexandrianism that included a pointed refusal to write about the political and military accomplishments of the leaders who were their real or potential patrons, on the ground that their poetic talents were far too slim for such important subjects. In pretended embarrassment they would invoke a jocose or erotic Muse while they created exquisite patterns of verse and elaborate formal structures of great beauty. They argued among themselves about the proper function and possible importance of poetry; they read and parroted and parodied each other, as well as their Greek predecessors; but for the most part they avoided dealing with the reality of Rome. They might promise, like Ovid, that some day they would write a proper epic on a proper Roman theme, but they never seriously intended to do so. Except for Vergil.

In other respects Vergil shares his contemporaries' Alexandrian qualities. His poetry is extremely learned. In addition to Homer, Hesiod, and Theocritus, his primary models, the Greek writers whom he knew and used include Appollonius of Rhodes, Aratus, Callimachus, Eratosthenes, Euripides, Nicander, and Sophocles. He read learned commentaries on Homer and Hesiod, antiquarian treatises about Italic institutions and religious rites, and etymological dictionaries. He likes to startle—and please—his readers with quotations from earlier works: some of his most famous and moving passages turn out upon examination to be elaborate cross-references to other poets. In *Aeneid* 9, for example, he thus describes the death of a young Trojan warrior:

Euryalus rolls down in death:
along his beautiful body blood comes,
his neck relaxes,
his head sinks upon his shoulders:
as when a dark red flower is cut down by a plow
and grows limp as it dies;
as poppies droop their heads with wearied necks
when a heavy rainstorm weighs them down.

(433–437)

This compressed double simile, which translates the visual image of a boy's slumping head and red blood into drooping red flowers, is compounded from two sources. Vergil took the poppies, appropriately enough, from Homer's description of the death of a young Trojan in the *Iliad*:

He bent, drooping his head to one side, as a garden poppy
bends beneath the weight of its yield and the rains of springtime;
so his head bent slack beneath the helm's weight.

(8.306–308)

But the flower nicked by the plow comes from a different literary environment, the love poetry of Vergil's predecessor Catullus, who had compared his lost love for his mistress to "a flower on the edge of the meadow after it had been touched by a passing plow" (11.21–24). Vergil's literary tour de force here serves a larger end than the mere recognition of cleverness: it enhances the significance of the particular event for the reader, who observes the collocation in adjacent lines of two different genres of poetry, heroic and lyric; two different contexts, military and erotic; as well as two different cultures, archaic Greek and recent Roman—all at the moment of the unnecessary death of a young boy in pursuit of glory.

Vergil also delights in creating intricate, artificial patterns of sounds, words, and verses. The lines in which he describes Orpheus' song of lamentation for Eurydice are nearly abstract musical sound:

Te, *dulcis coniunx,* **te** *solo in litore secum*
Te *ve-nien-***te** *die* **te** *de-ce-den-***te** *canebat.*
(*Georgics* 4.465–466)

You, sweet wife, you, he sang alone on the lonely shore,
You at dawning day, you at departing day.

On every page we find verses in which the formal patterns of repeated letters, syllables, and word shapes seem to dominate the sense; for example:

Ardet inexcita Ausonia atque immobilis ante;
Pars pedes ire parat campis, pars arduus altis....

(*Aeneid* 7.623–624)

Ausonia, once unaroused and immobile,
prepares in part to go on foot over the fields,
in part high on lofty horses....

Vergil shared with his contemporaries the love of manipulating word order to achieve symmetrical patterns and startling collocations. "I shall practice rustic music on a delicate reed," in normal Latin prose (if a normal Roman would ever dream of saying it) would be

Musam agrestem harundine tenui meditabor

but is translated into Augustan poetry as

agrestem tenui meditabor harundine Musam

Rustic delicate I shall practice on reed music

creating a pattern in which the verb in the center of the line is symmetrically enclosed by the two adjectives at the beginning and the two corresponding nouns at the end.

Nor is such self-conscious pattern making restricted to single lines. Vergil inserts the name of his patron Maecenas into the four books of the *Georgics* with mathematical precision: at line 2 in books 1 and 4, and at line 41 in books 2 and 3. In the nearly 13,000 verses of the *Aeneid*, the half-line *solvuntur frigore membra* ("his body comes apart shivering") occurs twice. Vergil uses it first to describe Aeneas at his initial appearance in the poem, when a storm has attacked the Trojan fleet:

Immediately Aeneas' body comes apart shivering.
He groans and stretches both palms toward the stars.

(*Aeneid* 1.92–93)

The phrase reappears in the last two lines of the epic, this time to describe the final appearance of Aeneas' enemy, Turnus:

His body comes apart shivering,
and with a groan his life flees plaintively beneath the shadows.

(12.951–952)

Artistic symmetry in Vergil's hands here serves a deadly serious purpose, revealing to us how Aeneas and his enemy are mirror images of one another as the Trojan lifts up his hands to the stars and as the Italian flees down into the darkness.

In addition to his desire for polished craft, Vergil shared his contemporaries' concerns about the role of poetry itself. He understood their commonplace refusal to treat serious and possibly dangerous subjects under the pretense of insufficient talent. He introduces this pose himself into his sixth eclogue.

While I was singing of kings and battles,
Apollo tweaked my ear and admonished me:
"Tityrus,
it behooves a shepherd to graze fat sheep
but write delicate verse."
So for now, since there will be plenty of others
eager to sing your praises, Varus,
and lay up gloomy wars,
I shall practice rustic music on a delicate reed.

(6.3–8)

But already in the *Eclogues* the pose is highly ironic, for Vergil is trying to expand, while he explores, the possibilities of the pastoral genre. So, too, in the *Georgics* he claims that he must pursue for now "the forests and the meadows" of his chosen rural theme, but that he will soon "gird up his loins to sing of the hot battles of Augustus" (3.40–48). We cannot know how much pressure may have come from his patron Maecenas, although Augustus surely would have been pleased to have a first-rate epic written about himself. But Vergil seems to have been peculiarly self-driven to stretch the limits of his poetic talent, to move into larger forms and explore more difficult issues. His epitaph encapsulates his poetic career in the words *cecini pascua, rura, duces* ("I have sung of pastures, fields, leaders"): his works mirror the history of culture from pastoral to agricultural to urban, as he moves steadily closer to the center of civilization, toward a confrontation with history.

THE BOOK OF PASTORAL

The *Eclogues*, finished about 36 B.C., is a book of ten pastoral poems—also known as bucolics—varying in length from 63 to 111 lines. Vergil's Greek model was the Hellenistic poet Theocritus, who created that most urbane of genres, the pastoral, with its artificial landscape peopled by goatherds and shepherds who spend the intervals of leisure between their simple tasks jesting with one another about their loves and engaging in contests of music and highly patterned song. Vergil borrowed Theocritus' trappings openly: the simple plots of some of the poems, the kinds of prizes for which the singers compete, the names like Tityrus and Menalcas, Daphnis and Thyrsis, Amaryllis and Galatea. Some of the eclogues in isolation—2, 3, 7, and 8—are in fact Theocritean idylls composed in Latin, beautifully elegant formal compositions, but little more than imitations. Unlike Theocritus in his collection of pastoral poems, Vergil organized his eclogues into a book that, when read as a whole, has an overall structure and meaning—a "plot" in which the elegant Theocritean idylls are only chapters.

The book begins with a shepherd piping.

Tityrus, there you are,
lying under cover of a spreading beech tree,
practicing your woodland music on a slender oaten
    straw.

                                        (1.1–2)

If the species of tree has changed, there is still no mistaking the Theocritean woods, since the Greek poet's first idyll had begun, "Sweetly that pine tree there by the springs is whispering its music, goatherd, and sweetly you are piping too." But in the third line, Vergil's speaker contrasts his own lot with that of the Theocritean shepherd.

We are leaving our homeland and sweet fields.
We are leaving our homeland for exile.

                                        (1.3–4)

In the course of the ensuing conversation it emerges that the speaker, Meliboeus, has lost his land to a soldier and that he and some others like him are about to be scattered to the far corners of the Roman Empire, while some "barbarian" lives on his carefully cultivated farm. His older companion Tityrus, on the other hand, although he had been a slave and had not previously been able to save enough money to buy his freedom, had recently been to the city of Rome and returned with a guarantee that he could remain on his small plot of land. His benefactor in Rome was a young man whom he calls "a god."

Meliboeus, a god gave us this leisurely life:
for he will always be a god to me,
and a young lamb from our sheepfold
will always stain his altar.
He has allowed my oxen to roam,
as you can see,
and me to play what I will on my rustic reed.

                                        (1.6–10)

Meliboeus envies Tityrus' lot and laments his own, and the eclogue ends as Tityrus invites his fellow shepherd to stop with him for the night.

Meliboeus:
Go on, my little goats,
go on, once happy flock.
Never again will I lie stretched out in a grassy cave
and watch you hanging from a bush-covered rock
    far away.

I will sing no more songs.
I will not be your shepherd, little goats,
as you graze on the flowering shrubs
and bitter willows.
Tityrus:
But at least you could rest here with me for tonight
on green leaves.
We have ripe apples, soft chestnuts, and plenty of
  cheese.
Smoke is rising now from the rooftops of the
  houses far away,
and longer shadows are falling from the high
  mountains.

(1.74–83)

From the very beginning Vergil's pastoral world is under a threat. Of its two inhabitants whom we meet, the older can continue to enjoy its values, but only through the intervention of the godlike youth from the city. The younger is being driven out and his source of poetry cut off ("I will sing no more songs"), as this landscape, like Vergil's text, is literally invaded by the Roman army and the Roman Empire. There is only one evening left in which the two can share the food, and perhaps the song, typical of this idyllic world, before the lengthening shadows overwhelm it in darkness.

Meanwhile its other inhabitants can indulge their fantasy—and we ours—by remembering the love song of the frustrated shepherd Corydon for handsome, spoiled Alexis (eclogue 2), or engaging in a meaningless game of invective and verse capping, while Tityrus tends their flocks (eclogue 3). In those two poems Rome is nearly forgotten. The only intrusion of contemporary reality into Arcadia is Pollio, who may have been Vergil's patron at the time; but he poses no threat, since he is himself a poet, and besides "he likes our music, even if it is rustic" (3.84). The only negative force here is passion, Amor, who has set Corydon on fire and is blamed by Damoetas for the leanness of his stud bull; but the poetry successfully controls the passion with its carefully balanced structure, and the two poems end at moments of cheerful equilibrium.

You'll find another Alexis,
If this one disdains you.

(2.73)

Close the sluice-gates now, boys;
the fields have drunk enough.

(3.111)

The pastoral voice that opens the fourth eclogue, however, is apparently dissatisfied with the light play of the preceding poems.

Sicilian Muses,
let us sing something
a little more substantial!
Not everyone likes trees and lowly tamarisks.
If we sing about woods,
let them be woods fit for a Roman consul.

(4.1–3)

This is followed by a heavy, prophetic proclamation in lofty oracular tone.

The last era of the Cumaean oracle has now
  arrived.
The great progression of ages is born anew.
Now the Virgin is coming back, Saturn's rule is
  about to return.
Now a new offspring is being sent down from
  heaven on high.
Favor the boy-child being born,
with whom the iron age first will cease to be
and a golden people rise throughout the world,
O chaste goddess of childbirth;
now your Apollo reigns.

(4.4–10)

Vergil's ponderous pronouncement of the arrival of a new golden age is indeed far more substantial than anything that had previously appeared in the world of pastoral poetry, although some of the descriptive details that follow are couched in terms appropriate to shepherds.

She-goats will bring the milk home by themselves
in swollen udders,
nor will the cattle fear the mighty lions.

Your very crib will shower you with sweet
blossoms.

(4.21–23)

But the prophecy grows confusing when the reader discovers that this age of innocence will almost immediately begin to deteriorate as the child grows up.

Some few vestiges of ancient crime will linger,
urging men to attack the sea with ships,
encircle cities with walls,
and split the earth with furrows.
Another pilot Tiphys will arise
and another Argo to transport choice heroes,
and even a new series of wars:
Great Achilles will be sent to Troy a second time.

(4.31–36)

There follows a promise that things will right themselves again when the child reaches adulthood, and commerce and agriculture will cease once more. The Romans, however, need not fear the loss of imported luxury items, such as colorful dyed cloth from the Orient.

Wool will not learn to deceive us by switching
    colors:
the ram by himself in the meadow will change his
    fleece,
now sweetly blushing crimson,
now saffron yellow,
and spontaneous vermilion
will clothe the grazing lambs.

(4.42–45)

Whoever the baby may have been who is supposed to usher in this golden age, his parents were surely expected to be laughing as Vergil's pastoral Muse ends his prophetic vision with this picture of varicolored sheep safely grazing.

"Whose child did you have in mind?" was perhaps the first question asked by the friends to whom Vergil read this poem. His reply is not known. In his later years, if the *Georgics* and the *Aeneid* may be taken to reflect their author's mood, the poet grew more and more mel-

ancholy. But in his grave he must be heartily amused by the thousands of pages of scholarly speculation debating the identity of the baby in this fourth eclogue. There are at least a half-dozen "logical" candidates for the expected infant, including hoped-for children of Augustus, Pollio, Mark Antony, and Octavia. But the success of Vergil's messianic riddle—and I assume that it was intended as a riddle—was most strongly demonstrated by his early Christian readers, who saw the prophecy as alluding to the birth of Jesus, thus ensuring Vergil a special position among pagan poets.

At any event, by introducing a Roman consul into his pastoral forest, and by putting messianic imagery into the mouth of his Arcadian singer, Vergil created a strange new poem whose influence was far greater than the request in its first line for "something a little more substantial."

As if the experiment had been a failure, in the fifth eclogue the pretentious manner of the prophetic voice gives way to the more traditional pastoral dialogue between two herdsmen, Mopsus and Menalcas, who leave Tityrus to tend their sheep while they share bits of song with each other. Yet the way in which their paired songs are framed suggests that pastoral poetry is still undergoing a change. Menalcas asks Mopsus to begin first with one of his old songs, if he remembers them: "The Loves of Phyllis" or "The Praises of Alcon" or "Insults for Codrus." Menalcas replies:

No, I shall try these verses.
Recently, on living beech-bark,
I wrote them down
and marked their alternating tunes.

(5.13–14)

After the singing, when the two shepherds exchange gifts, Menalcas gives Mopsus a "fragile reed-pipe" that had taught him to sing "Mopsus Loved Fair Alexis" and "Whose Flock Is This?"—namely, Vergil's own eclogues 2 and 3.

The new song within this dialogue, which is

meant to take the place of the older pastoral, treats of the death of the shepherd-poet Daphnis, at which all nature mourned and turned hostile, followed by his deification among the stars, at which all nature rejoiced and peace returned.

> Star-white Daphnis marvels
> at the new sight of Olympus' threshold,
> as he sees beneath his feet the clouds and stars.
> Thus the woods and all the countryside,
> Pan and the shepherds and the forest nymphs,
> are possessed by livening joy.
> The wolf designs no ambush for the flock,
> the net no treachery against the deer:
> good Daphnis loves the peaceful life.
>
> (5.56–61)

Eclogue 5 looks back to a golden age of poetry, as the fourth looked ahead to a golden age of careless plenty. Where eclogue 4 spoke of a child who would come down from the sky, the fifth raises a dead shepherd-poet, Daphnis, to the stars. Thus in the last two poems in this half of the book of eclogues, singers of pastoral have attempted to expand their subject matter by speculations on time and history, by fantasizing on a golden age that would interrupt the deteriorating course of civilization and allow humans to begin again in a world at harmony with nature.

It is with some confidence, then, that the singer of the sixth eclogue, who calls himself Tityrus, attempts an even more spectacular tour de force, abandoning Theocritean shepherds completely for a poem—or rather a poem about a poem—on cosmogony and mythological metamorphosis. The poem's author is supposed to have been Silenus, the old companion of the god Dionysus. Some rustics find him asleep one day and tie him up, in the hope of hearing some of his enchanting poetry. He abundantly obliges them.

> He sang how through the great void the seeds
> of earth and air and sea had been assembled,
> and of pure fire too,
> and how from these four elements

> all things had grown together,
> even the young circle of the world;
> and how the ground began to harden,
> closing off Nereus in the sea,
> and gradually assumed the shapes of objects.
> And the lands are amazed at the light of the new-
>   formed sun;
> and rains fall as the clouds move higher.
> Then for the first time woods begin to grow,
> and scattered animals roam the hills that do not
>   know them.
> Then he sang of Pyrrha throwing the stones,
> of Saturn's reign,
> of the Caucasian birds and Prometheus' theft.
>
> (6.31–42)

This table of contents continues with the stories of Hylas, Pasiphaë, the daughters of Proetus, Atalanta, Phaethon's sisters, Scylla, and Tereus and Philomela. The treatment varies from one line for Atalanta's tale—"He sang of the girl who marveled at the apples of the Hesperides"(6.61)—to sixteen lines for Pasiphaë, whose story of erotic desire for a bull encloses a cleverly contrasted allusion to Proetus' daughters, who, driven mad by Juno in punishment for their pride, imagined themselves to be cows. Along with all these unfortunate mythological victims of passion appears the figure of an important contemporary Roman poet and politician, Gallus, being initiated into the rites of the Muses. Apparently Silenus would have gone on endlessly except for the approach of nightfall, which abruptly ends the eclogue while reminding the reader of the pastoral context that has long been abandoned.

> Until the Evening Star bade us gather the sheep in
>   their folds
> and count them, as he moved through an unwilling
>   sky.
>
> (6.85–86)

Vergil rehearses, in this difficult and allusive poem, the poetic accomplishments and values of his immediate predecessors and contemporaries. The cosmogony suggests didactic, philosophical poetry, and specifically reflects the

676

concerns, and even the vocabulary, of Lucretius. The mythology, especially the tale of Pasiphaë, suggests the learned epyllion (little epic) and alludes specifically to a now lost poem by Calvus on the myth of Io, a victim of Jupiter's passion who was actually transformed into a cow and pursued by a jealous Juno. The real Roman, Gallus, who wrote books of elegiac love poetry as well as learned verse, serves here as a symbol for the best hopes of Roman Alexandrianism. He reappears in Vergil's last eclogue.

Pastoral, it seems, has been stretched beyond its conceivable limits into something like a general literary manifesto. It now turns back inward with eclogues 7 and 8, which repeat, in reverse order, the Theocritean motifs of eclogues 2 and 3, the singing contest and the love song. Eclogue 9 closes the circle and returns us to the dramatic situation at the opening of the book:

Lycidas:
Where are you walking, Moeris?
Taking the road all the way to the city?
Moeris:
Lycidas, we have lived too long!
An outsider
(I never thought it would come to this)
has taken possession of our little field and said,
"This is mine, now.
You old settlers must move away."
We are beaten and sad.
Since all is ruled by chance,
we are sending these kids to him,
and may his luck be bad!
Lycidas:
But surely I had heard how,
where the hills begin to lower and release the
    gently sloping ridge,
all the way to the water and those old beech trees
with their broken tops,
your companion Menalcas had saved all that
with poetry.
Moeris:
You may have heard it: that was the story.
But our poetry has as much effect amid war's
    weapons
as "oracular doves at the eagle's coming."

(9.1–13)

The older shepherd, whose counterpart in the first eclogue had been allowed to stay on the land and sing under the beech tree's shade, has now been driven out; and with him Menalcas and his poetry. Eclogue 5 had identified Menalcas as the singer of eclogues 2 and 3, and now, as Lycidas and Moeris lament the lost solace of Menalcas' song and recall snatches of his poetry, which suggest earlier eclogues, they lead us back through the whole range of Vergil's experiments in the pastoral genre.

He wrote of shepherds' work and imitated shepherds' rough banter:

Tityrus, till I return—
it's a short trip—
tend the goats and lead them to drink when
    they've grazed,
and while you're driving them watch out,
don't run into that buck—
he butts with his horns.

(9.23–25)

He put beautiful verse into the mouths of lovesick herdsmen.

Come hither, Galatea. What sport can there be in
    the waves?
Here the spring is crimson;
here the ground pours forth so many sorts
of flowers round the river banks;
here a white poplar hangs over a grotto
and pliant vines weave charming shadows.
Come hither, and let the mad waves beat against
    the shore.

(9.39–43)

He addressed consuls and spoke of the realities of contemporary Italy:

Varus, if only our Mantua may survive—
Mantua, too near to poor Cremona—
singing swans will carry your name aloft to the
    stars.

(9.27–29)

He fantasized about a rising new star that would inaugurate a golden age of peace and prosperity.

Daphnis, why gaze up
to see the ancient constellations as they rise?
Look, the star of Venus-born Caesar has come
    forth:
under its sign grainfields may rejoice in their
    fruits,
and the grape ripen purple on the sunny hillside.
Graft your pear trees, Daphnis:
your grandchildren will gather your fruit.

                        (9.46–50)

But it has all been to no avail, as the shepherd-singers' last remembered line makes bitterly clear in this poem's present context of dispossession and flight. Worse, as Moeris further remarks:

Age steals everything, even the mind.
I remember how, as a boy,
I would often sing the sun underground on long
    summer evenings.
Now I have forgotten so many poems.
Moeris has even lost his voice.

                        (9.51–54)

But if poetry is ineffective in the political sphere, and if in addition it is short-lived, surely it can still provide pleasure in itself and offer personal consolation to lighten our grief. The ending of the ninth eclogue calls even this value into question. As the shepherds walk together toward the city, the younger Lycidas wants to continue their singing.

Lycidas:
We can sing all the way there:
the journey will be less painful.
So that we may sing as we walk
I will lighten you of that basket.
Moeris:
Stop, that's enough, boy!
Let's just do what we have to.
It will be better to sing songs whenever he comes.

                        (9.64–67)

The plot that began with the threat to the pastoral world in eclogue 1 has now reached its conclusion with the cessation of singing and the journey to the city.

The tenth poem serves as epilogue, further exploring the question left in suspense at the end of eclogue 9, the value of poetry in the face of human suffering. Vergil's "one last effort" (10.1) in the genre is a poem dedicated to his poet-friend Gallus, the distraught lover who is the subject of the eclogue and a major speaker in it. He is also, not incidentally, an upper-class Roman with a political and military career. Vergil imagines Gallus—as Gallus had no doubt portrayed himself in his own love poetry—as dying from passion for his mistress Lycoris, who had run off with a rival soldier. In his misery the poet wants to run away to Vergil's Arcadia, where he wishfully foresees two possible remedies for his pain.

Yet you will sing of these sufferings,
Arcadians, on your mountains;
only Arcadians are skilled in song.
Oh, how softly would my bones rest then,
if only some day your reed pipe should tell my
    loves. . . .
I will go and take those poems I composed in
    Chalcidic verse,
and play them on a Sicilian shepherd's oaten
    straw.
No! I would rather suffer in the woods amid wild
    beasts' lairs,
and carve my "Loves" upon young trees:
the trees will grow, and you will grow, my loves.

                (10.31–34; 50–54)

Vergil's tone here may be playful, as he mocks the conventional lover's pose of dying from rejected love and quotes his own "oaten straw" and the writing down of verses upon trees. But behind the playfulness lies the question of poetry's power to represent reality or to substitute for it. We doubt Gallus' naive assumption that his word "love" on the tree is identical with, or indeed can have any effect on, his experience of love. And Gallus himself doubts a few lines later.

As if this could be a remedy for our madness!
As if that god could ever learn gentleness
toward men's suffering!

I have no more liking now for wood nymphs,
or even song.
Let the woods themselves go back where they
came from! . . . Passion overcomes everything
[*omnia vincit amor*],
so let us surrender to passion.

(10.60–63; 69)

Then Vergil in his mask as shepherd-singer stands up and begins to drive his well-fed goats homeward, as evening comes.

THE POEM OF THE LAND

Vergil around 36 B.C. turned to work on the *Georgics*, a poem in four books on "matters related to farming" (the English translation of its Greek title). The opening lines announce it as a didactic treatise on agriculture.

What makes grainfields fertile,
under what sign it is right to turn the soil,
Maecenas,
and to attach the vines to the elms,
how to care for oxen and tend a flock,
and whatever knowledge is needful for thrifty
bees—
from this point I will begin my poem.

(1.1–5)

The division into four books corresponds to the announced table of contents:

1. Grain production
2. Arboriculture and viticulture
3. Animal husbandry
4. Apiculture

Vergil indeed incorporates a great deal of technical material into the poem: how to make a plow, for example, or methods of testing soil, or remedies for sheep mange. One of the pleasures for the reader, as it was surely one of the purposes of the author, is the display of artistic magic by which even such recalcitrantly prosaic matter as this can be transmuted into poetry of great formal beauty.

But a mere agricultural manual, no matter how finely versified, would scarcely fulfill the promise of eclogues 4 and 6 or justify the expenditure of seven years' effort by the sensitive and philosophically inclined Vergil in his thirties. Nor does the dedication to Maecenas or the reference to that patron's "rather pressing entreaties" (3.41) allow us to interpret the *Georgics* as a propaganda effort on behalf of Augustus' back-to-the-farm movement. Any Roman who might have been thinking of leaving the urban mob for a healthy, leisurely life in the country would have immediately rejected that idea on even a cursory reading of Vergil's description of harsh and unremitting toil, weeds, insects, blight, rodents, poisonous snakes, drought, flash floods, various diseases, and plague.

Vergil characterizes his poem as "a Hesiodic song for Roman cities" (2.176). Hesiod's *Works and Days* provides some of the material and structure for book 1, but its formal influence is far less detailed and thoroughgoing than was the case with Theocritus' *Idylls* as a model for the *Eclogues*. Hesiod, however, was the founder of didactic poetry, in which the poet speaks frankly as teacher and adviser. His *Works and Days* not only provides a farmer's almanac of lucky and unlucky days for specific tasks, but offers maxims like "Do not get base profits, for base profits are as bad as ruin." Furthermore, Hesiod sets his practical and ethical teaching within a larger view of human history, the myth of the successive debasement of mankind from an original generation of gold, who lived during the age of Saturn, down to a fifth generation of iron, who live in the poet's own time:

Would that I were not among the men of the fifth generation, but either had died before or been born afterward. For now truly is a race of iron, and men never rest from toil and grief by day, nor from destruction by night. And the gods will give them difficult suffering.

(*Works and Days* 174–178)

It is in this sense that Vergil's *Georgics* is most Hesiodic: it attempts to translate the harsh realism of Hesiod's world view into Roman terms, as this clashes with the Augustan promise of a new generation of gold.

In the golden age of the fourth eclogue, "Every land will produce all crops" (*Eclogues* 4.39); but in the *Georgics*, "Not every land can produce all crops" (2.109). That statement occurs in a technical section discussing the varieties of trees and the varied conditions favorable to their production, but it leads Vergil into a long description of the peculiar qualities of his own land, Italy:

> But neither the forests of the Medes, richest of
>   lands,
> nor the beautiful Ganges and the Hermus turbid
>   with gold,
> may vie with the praises of Italy;
> not Bactria nor India,
> nor all of sleek Arabia with incense-bearing
>   sands.
>   . . . Here spring hangs on, and summer, in
>   months not their own;
> flocks are twice pregnant,
> trees twice useful with their fruit.
> Yet there are no rabid tigers
> or savage seed of lions.
>
> (2.136–151)

Vergil continues his catalog of Italy's virtues with its cities and towns, and then turns to its native peoples:

> She brought forth a fierce race of men:
> Marsians and Sabine youths,
> the Ligurian accustomed to troubles,
> and Volscian dartmen;
> men like Decius and Marius and great Camillus,
> the Scipios hardened in war,
> and you, mighty Caesar, who now,
> already victorious in Asia's farthest reaches,
> fend off the unwarlike Indian from the citadel of
>   Rome.
> Hail, great mother of crops, Saturnian land,
> great mother of men.
>
> (2.167–174)

Vergil here juxtaposes the soft and nourishing imagery of a mythically exaggerated Mother Italy with the hard and threatening picture of her historical human children. It is at the end of this troubled and troubling "hymn of praise" that Vergil identifies himself as the Roman Hesiod.

Each book of the *Georgics* is a self-contained poem over 500 lines long, beginning with an author's preface in the first person and ending with a long poetic set piece. The preface to book 1 introduces the entire work, and a short eight-line epilogue concludes it. The prefaces alternate between forty-two and eight lines in length, and there are other formal patterns indicating Vergil's careful planning of the whole within a single conceptual framework. The rural subject matter progresses from lower to higher, more sophisticated forms of life: from grain to grape, from oxen and horses to bees. At the end, in the story of Aristaeus and Orpheus, we reach the human being as shepherd-beekeeper, prophet, lover, and poet.

Throughout the progression runs the dominating theme of *labor* ("toil"), which Vergil introduces in a full statement early in the first book, after a section of technical advice about plowing:

> Although toiling men and oxen
> have followed my precepts as they turned the soil,
> nevertheless the wicked goose,
> the Strymonian cranes,
> and chicory weeds with bitter fibers
> thwart their efforts,
> or the shade causes destruction.
> The Father himself begrudged an easy way to
>   farm,
> as he first introduced the science of turning the
>   soil,
> sharpening mortal minds with troubles,
> not letting his realm grow sluggish
> under the heavy weight of lethargy.
> Before Jupiter no farmers subjugated fields.
> Even marking the ground or dividing the plain
>   with boundaries
> was not thought right.
> Folks gathered things in common,
> and the Earth herself in generosity
> brought forth every crop unasked.

He added the harmful venom to black snakes.
He taught wolves to prey and the sea to stir.
He shook the honey out of the leaves and removed
  fire,
and checked the streams that ran with wine
  everywhere,
so that practical experience and thought
could hammer out various skills,
a little at a time,
and hunt for grain in furrows;
so that man could strike out the fire
god had hidden away in the veins of flint.

(1.118–135)

Vergil's version of a Heavenly Father who drives mankind out of the garden of paradise seems extraordinarily cruel and heartless, especially since Jupiter was not motivated by any sin on mankind's part, but apparently merely by some abstract interest in technology accompanied by the belief that "necessity is the mother of invention." That theodicy is summed up near the end of this cheerless passage:

tum variae venere artes. Labor omnia vincit
improbus et duris urgens in rebus egestas.

(1.145–146)

Then came other sorts of crafts. Toil overcame
  everything,
wicked toil and poverty pressing in hard
  circumstances.

Civilization and suffering stand confronting each other at the center of the first line. Artes includes everything from mining to metaphysics, from building ships to composing verses. Labor has none of the constructive, dignified associations of English "work," but connotes "toil, drudgery, pain, and hardship." The problem posed by the juxtaposition of the two words can be stated in various forms: Is there a necessary connection between technical progress and human suffering? Does the result, which may include poetry like the Georgics, justify the means? How capable is art itself of comprehending, if not coping with, suffering? This cluster of questions permeates all Vergil's poetry, from the beginning of the Eclogues to the end of the Aeneid. In the end it remains unresolved, except by the greatness of his own accomplishment. Here in these lines at the beginning of the Georgics, however, the weight of labor tips the balance against artes and overwhelms everything else, just as at the end of Gallus' song in the tenth eclogue everything was overcome by passion (omnia vincit amor: 10.69).

Vergil's dominant image for farming in book 1 is that of warfare. Enemies "lay ambush," "invade," and "attack" the crops, and the farmer must maintain constant "sentry-duty." His tools are "weapons" with which to conquer the earth, and his chores are acts of violence: he "rends," "bursts," "harasses," and "tries to subdue" the soil. In the end he is still at the mercy of great armies beyond his control.

Often an immense column of waters marches
  through the sky,
clouds massed from the sea roll up ranks
into an ugly storm of black rain;
heaven rushes down from on high
and washes away in its mighty flood
the fertile seedlings and the oxen's labors. . . . The
  Father himself in the darkness of the rainclouds
wields flashing bolts in his strong right arm;
he moves and the great earth trembles,
beasts flee,
and the mortal hearts of humble folk are prostrate
  with fear.

(1.322–331)

The Roman Hesiod's Works and Days have assumed the harsh military character of the Roman world that Vergil knew, and so we may be better prepared for the devastating picture of the Roman Empire with which Vergil ends the first book of his agricultural poem:

So many wars throughout the world!
So many faces of wickedness!
Nowhere does the plow have its just honor.
Fields lie overgrown, their farmers marched away.
Curved sickles are melted into an unbending
  sword.

The Euphrates to the east
and Germany to the north
are starting wars.
Neighbor cities break treaties
and take arms against each other.
Mars rages irresponsibly through all the world.
See how chariots rush from the starting gate and
    move into the course:
the driver vainly holds the bridle,
but is swept along by his horses,
and the chariot does not heed the reins.

                           (1.505–514)

Book 2 is more cheerful, as befits the subject of vineyards, although even now there is plenty of toil, and "Jupiter is still to be feared when the grapes are ripe" (2.419). In marked contrast to the reality of contemporary Rome with which he ended the first book, Vergil ends *Georgics* 2 with some imaginary versions of a peaceful life, whether for farmer or poet. The wealth and ambition of the city are far removed, as are the sounds of warfare. There is still work to be done all year round, but the poet now dwells on the resulting fertility and birth.

The farmer has moved aside the earth with his
    curved plow.
That is the year's labor:
with it he sustains homeland and little
    grandchildren,
herds of oxen and deserving bullocks.
And without rest the year abounds in fruits
or the young of flocks
or sheaves of harvest grain,
and loads the furrows and overwhelms the barns
    with produce.
Winter is here:
Sicilian olives are pressed in the mill,
the pigs come home happy with their acorns,
the forests give berries.
Autumn too gives birth to its manifold children,
and vineyards ripen high upon the sunny rocks.
Meantime sweet children hang on their father's
    kisses,
a chaste house preserves its virtue,
cows lower their milk-filled udders,
and on the rich grass
fat kids wrestle each other with butting horns.

                           (2.513–526)

But even as he lulls us with these images of fertility and peace, Vergil jarringly reminds us that they are fantasies from another time.

This was life on the earth in golden Saturn's reign,
when men had not yet heard war trumpets blare,
nor yet swords clatter upon hard anvils.

                           (2.538–540)

When the poet then turns to the animal kingdom for the second half of the *Georgics*, he promises in a grandiose preface that he will someday depict the historical clash of Roman arms in an epic voice; but meanwhile he will write for those who wish to raise prize horses or cattle.

The major forces that oppose men's efforts in these next two books are lust and death. The militant violence with which Vergil portrayed man's struggle against the earth in the first book is now transferred to his description of the competitiveness of animals in rut:

One after the other they mix in battle with great
    violence.
Wound follows wound, dark blood bathes their
    bodies,
as they aim their horns and lunge against straining
    opponents.
Their endless moans are bellowed back
by the woods and far-off Olympus.

                           (3.220–223)

The poet enlarges his picture of sexual desire with fearsome details unrelated to the practical concerns of animal husbandry.

Every kind of man and beast on land,
every sea-creature, flock animal, and painted bird,
all rush alike into madness and fire.
Passion is the same for them all.
No other time does the lioness forget her cubs
to range savagely through the fields;
brutish bears kill randomly,
wreaking mayhem through the forests;
the boar is savage then,
the tigress at her worst.

                           (3.242–248)

Even if we could control this destructive force that is loosed during the mating season, we are completely defenseless against the long and gruesome plague with which Vergil chooses to end book 3. As his predecessor Lucretius had ended his philosophical poem *De Rerum Natura* with a detailed description of the plague that attacked Athens early in the Peloponnesian War, so Vergil closes his account of the breeding and care of livestock with a hundred lines describing a disease that does not merely attack individual animals, but "wipes out, at one stroke, the flock, the whole stock from its origin, and all hope for the future" (3.472–473).

We have reached the lowest point in the *Georgics'* alternation between fertility and toil, hope and despair. The bees of book 4 provide some much-needed comic relief, as well as some hope of salvation.

Vergil promises Maecenas and us "a look at less weighty matters" (*levium spectacula rerum*: 4.3), in a short preface that, unlike the grandiloquent introduction to book 3, seems to forecast a return to the Alexandrian playfulness of the *Eclogues*. The inimical toil of the first book appears now as the poet's "work on his slender subject" (*in tenui labor*: 4.6), and the beekeeper's hoped-for honey is described in terms that seem appropriate to a new golden age—"a gift from the sky" (*caelestia dona*: 4.1).

Vergil then treats us to 250 lines of the most openly playful, as well as superbly crafted, poetry of his career—from which the poet's early biographers deduced that his father must have been a beekeeper. He magnifies the tiny bee (with a parenthetical request for the reader's permission to "compare small things to large") into a mock-epic Roman soldier, a hard-working citizen of a Platonic ideal state, a giant Cyclops, an oriental monarch, and a part of the Stoic "divine mind." There is of course a satirical edge to this entertaining apiarian utopia: Vergil's anthropomorphic bees are rather too human in their proneness to warfare, and there is too much enforced business in their ideal community. But the primary purpose of all this regulated activity is to gather honey from flowers—a metaphor for the poet's own creative activity—and Vergil's overall tone remains correspondingly optimistic.

Bees, furthermore, escape the two major threats to the animals of book 3, sexual desire and death.

You will be amazed at the following system
adopted by the bees:
they neither indulge in coitus,
nor lazily weaken their bodies in sexual pleasure,
nor labor to bring forth children;
but gather offspring in their mouths from leaves
    and sweet grasses,
spontaneously replenishing king and little citizens,
remaking their halls and waxen realms.
Often in roaming they crush their wings against
    hard rocks,
and voluntarily surrender their life beneath their
    burdens:
so great is their passion for flowers,
their ambition to beget honey.
Therefore, though each life span is cut short by a
    narrow limit,
never extends beyond seven summers,
yet the breed remains deathless,
for many years the fortune of the house stands
    firm,
and they count their fathers' fathers.

                    (4.197–209)

Bees, then, have sublimated their sexual desire in their work and have overcome their individual fear of death to achieve immortality for the group. Even if a plague should strike and wipe out the whole breed, the beekeeper need not despair, because a new hive can be produced by spontaneous generation from a slain calf. Vergil gives detailed instructions for this process, and his description of new bees gradually moving within a rotting bovine carcass and then flying out into the spring air seems a wholly fitting end to the *Georgics*, reversing the image of death and decay with which the previous book had ended.

But as if dissatisfied with the descriptive and philosophical conclusion that his poem has reached, Vergil turns to the Muses and asks them for help in going further.

What god, Muses, hammered out this art for us?
From what source did this strange new experience
enter men's lives?

(4.315–316)

In his answer he leaves the "scientific" view of
the *Georgics* behind and enters the world of
pure poetic fiction, in order to reexamine, in
mythic terms, the phenomenon of dead cattle
producing live bees.

Once upon a time there was an Arcadian
shepherd named Aristaeus, son of Apollo and
the water nymph Cyrene. He had lost all his
bees from disease and starvation, and complained bitterly to his mother. Pitying him, she
brought him down to visit her, deep under the
earth at the source of all waters. There she told
him that he must go for knowledge to the old
man of the sea, Proteus, "a prophet who knows
all things that are, that have been, and that soon
will be." It is difficult to obtain an answer from
him, since he must first be caught and bound
fast, despite his ability to change his shape at
will, into a snake or a lion, or into fire or water.
Aristaeus succeeds in capturing the elusive
Proteus, who tells him that the cause of his misfortune was the ghost of Orpheus, the singer
who won his dead wife's resurrection by his
song, but lost her again as he turned to look at
her with love. After listening to Proteus tell the
story of Orpheus and Eurydice, Aristaeus returns to his mother, who prescribes a sacrifice
of bulls and heifers to placate the spirits of the
poet and his bride. He obeys, and when he returns to the site of the sacrifice nine days later,

> they behold a sudden marvelous apparition.
> Among the liquified entrails of the cattle
> bees were buzzing all through their bellies
> and seething out between the broken ribs;
> great clouds of them rose up
> swarming together in a treetop,
> and lowered their grape cluster from the
>   pliant branches.

(4.554–558)

This "second ending" is in itself a masterful
poem, an epyllion framing one myth inside another and incorporating reminiscences of Homer's *Iliad* and *Odyssey* magically transformed
to fit new environments. Coming as the finale
to the *Georgics*, it enables Vergil to transcend
the limits of his subject matter, whether that be
regarded as the ostensible business of husbandry, or contemporary politics, or even the
broad sweep of human civilization. Under the
guise of the beekeeper the reader now goes
deeper inside the world to the wellsprings of
feeling and ritual. He grasps for certain knowledge and hears a song about a great poet whose
human failings resulted in personal tragedy. In
the end he experiences the triumph of poetry
itself over the threatening and constantly
changing plagues of reality.

THE AENEID: HOMER AND HISTORY

Vergil finished the *Georgics* about 29 B.C. in
the nourishing peace of Naples, "while great
Caesar was thundering in war beside the Euphrates" (*Georgics* 4.560–561). But his distance
from actual warfare was of little avail to the
poet as he began the epic task that was to occupy him for the rest of his life and soon came
to haunt his poetic peace: for the *Aeneid's* first
word is "War."

Arma virumque cano: the subject is warfare
and the individual hero, military conquest and
the man on whose shoulders lies the responsibility for that conquest. Vergil's verb, "I sing,"
accepts the poet's personal responsibility for
turning to epic subjects, as it asserts the highly
individual talent he needed to create a successful epic poem in his own times.

To write an epic was to compete with
Homer. This was as true for the Romans as for
the Greeks: the first work of Greek literature
translated into Latin had been the *Odyssey*, and
the educated audience for whom Vergil was
writing would know both Homeric poems well
and assume them as the standard by which any
epic must be measured. Yet the conventions of
Homeric epic were outdated. Homeric gods
and heroes seemed out of place amid the real-

ities of Roman civilization: Julius Caesar could scarcely have his hair pulled by the goddess Minerva to restrain him from striking Pompey, nor Cleopatra argue with Venus about her affair with Mark Antony. To avoid such incongruity, most poets before Vergil had either written of historical subjects without using the traditional epic conventions or treated non-Homeric but mythical Greek heroes who were safely distanced in time. Their poems often succeeded as versified chronicle or entertaining narrative—but the next great epic after Homer had not yet been written.

Vergil's bold solution to the problem enabled him to utilize fully both Homer and Roman history.

There was a tradition that the Roman people were descended in part from a group of Trojans who had emigrated to Italy after the Trojan War under the leadership of Aeneas. A few details, some in variant versions, had been manufactured about the Trojans' route to Italy and their reception by the natives after they arrived. Vergil chose this Trojan, Aeneas, as his hero and took the following events as the basic action for the poem.

During the final hours when Troy was being sacked by the Greeks, Aeneas escaped from the conflagration with his father, young son, and a small band of followers. They sailed westward to find a site in which to resettle. After several false starts, Aeneas became convinced that he must found his new city near the mouth of the Tiber River on the west coast of Italy. Despite the dangers of a protracted liaison with Dido, the queen of Carthage, he reached his destination, and the Trojans were welcomed by the local king, Latinus. Opposition arose, however, from inhabitants who saw the Trojans as a threat, and a war broke out, with tragic casualties on both sides. In the end the fighting resolved itself into single combat between Aeneas and Turnus, the intended husband of the king's daughter. Aeneas was the victor.

In order to expand this bare and somewhat unpromising material into a narrative of epic proportions, Vergil turned directly to Homer,

not merely to borrow Homeric conventions, but to transform and fill out his plot as a reenactment of both the *Iliad* and the *Odyssey* with a new cast of characters. Then he superimposed his own historic world onto this fictional screen, both literally—with the author's privilege of prophecy—and allegorically. The result is a text that unfolds, and must be read, simultaneously in more than one chronological dimension. This is already revealed in the epic's first sentence.

> Warfare and a man are the subject of my poem:
> from Troy he came, fate's exile,
> to Italy and the Lavinian coast,
> much harassed on land and sea by god-forces
> for savage Juno's unforgetting wrath;
> enduring many troubles in war too,
> until he could found a city
> and import his gods to Latium:
> whence the Latin people,
> the Alban nobility,
> and the walls of towering Rome.
>
> (1.1–7)

The sentence, like the *Aeneid* as a whole, moves from Troy to imperial Rome, although the plot itself only reaches the events in the middle of the sentence ("troubles in war too"), and the man Aeneas will die 333 years before the city is even founded.

The historical Rome that Aeneas foreshadows and symbolizes appears undisguised at several critical moments in the epic, as a seeming answer or consolation for the questioning and suffering characters in the poem's narrative present. The first such view into the future occurs early in book 1, when Jupiter tries to soothe Aeneas' distraught mother, Venus, and to answer her question: "What end do you grant, great king, to their sufferings?" (1.240). The god responds with a prophecy extending a thousand years beyond those sufferings to a direct descendant, Julius Caesar, and his adopted son Augustus, who is to close the gates of war. A second prophetic vision occurs during Aeneas' visit to the world of the dead in book 6. There, after he has witnessed the carefree life of bards and former warriors in the Elysian fields, Aeneas sees a crowd of souls clamoring to cross back over the river into life. In dismay he exclaims to his father, Anchises:

"Father, I can't believe it!
Do some of these exalted souls leave this place,
ascend, go back to slow, dull bodies?
Poor wretches! What is this fearsome desire for life?"

(6.719–721)

His father, by means of the fiction of the transmigration of souls, tries to answer his son's troubled question by pointing to the yet-unborn souls of the great leaders of Roman history, naming them and telling of their future achievements.

Finally, after Aeneas has reached Italy but has been drawn unwillingly into a war against the Latin people, Vulcan makes Aeneas a great shield to wear into combat. On the model of Homer's *Iliad*, Vergil describes the decoration of the shield at length. But unlike Homer's timeless scenes that draw the reader out of the specific battlefield in which Achilles fights into a universal vision of normal human life, Aeneas' shield is engraved with particular dated events from Roman history, ending in Vergil's own time with a huge central panel depicting the battle of Actium (in which Augustus defeated Antony and Cleopatra) and the victor's triumphant celebration in Rome. In his description, moreover, the poet uses verbal parallels to link Aeneas specifically to Augustus, whose job it was, after his victory, to restore peace and confidence to a war-torn and disheartened world. When he picks up the shield, Aeneas must bear the weight of all subsequent history: "Hoisting to his shoulder the reputation and fate of his descendants" (8.731). Unlike the reader, however, the poem's hero cannot comprehend this reality that he must project, because he is still living in a world long past, the mythical world of the Bronze Age hero and the literary world of Homer, and his actions are shaped to follow his Homeric models.

Like Odysseus, Aeneas is introduced near the end of a period of hardship and wandering, a few years after the Greeks had razed Troy. Like Odysseus, Aeneas is driven by a storm onto the shore of an unknown country, where he is hospitably received by the ruling queen and narrates, at a night-long banquet, the tale of his previous adventures. He shares with his literary predecessor the mysterious experience of visiting the world of the dead, where both heroes receive visions of their past and their future. At the midpoints of their respective epics, both Aeneas and Odysseus arrive at their destinations, but they are faced by strong local opposition that they eventually overcome, defeating their rivals in armed combat at the epic's end.

In addition to this Odyssean outline, the *Aeneid*'s epic warriors also must reenact the *Iliad*. Aeneas mirrors Achilles when he presides over athletic contests among his men during the ritual celebration of a funeral (book 5); when he receives, at his mother's request, a divinely made and elaborately decorated shield before entering the field (book 8); when he is driven into a brutal, merciless rage at the death of a friend (book 10); and when he kills the enemies' champion in single combat after a long chase outside the walls of the besieged town (book 12). Vergil frequently complicates his allusions to Iliadic material by changing the literary equations between characters, with the result, for example, that Aeneas may suddenly switch from the role of Achilles to that of Achilles' enemy Hector. Or the Roman poet may pointedly reverse the Homeric order of events: Vergil's funeral games, for example, come before slaughter on the battlefield, not after it, as in Homer.

This thoroughgoing and complex use of Homer is not literary gamesmanship. True, Vergil demands a skillful and sophisticated reader who will recognize his allusions and appreciate his subtle manipulations of those allusions. But more importantly, with Homer's text always in the background, Vergil has a concise means for defining his own characters' actions and motives, without the poet's editorial comment, either by revealing their deviation from the Homeric norm or by showing their adherence to a Homeric model in the face of the pressures of a non-Homeric Roman reality. Homer's Odysseus, Achilles, Hector, and Diomedes serve Vergil as models by which to study the heroism of his own time, and it is precisely when he most closely reflects the older Greek epic that Vergil most forcefully reveals his image of that new heroism.

We see the *Aeneid*'s hero for the first time as his fleet has been caught in a terrible storm off the coast of Sicily.

> Immediately Aeneas' body comes apart shivering.
> He groans,
> stretches both palms toward the stars,
> and cries out:
> "They were lucky three and four times over:
> their fathers were looking on from Troy's tall
>   ramparts
> when they got the chance to die.
> Diomedes, bravest of the Greeks,
> why could I not have lain down upon the plain of
>   Ilium
> and spilled this life from your hand's wound,
> where savage Hector lies dead from Achilles'
>   spear,
> and mighty Sarpedon,
> where the Simois River caught up in its waves
> so many heroes' shields and helmets and strong
>   bodies,
> and rolled them under?
>
> (1.92–101)

Aeneas' lament to the heavens echoes the words of Homer's Odysseus when he was caught in a storm at sea:

> Three times and four times happy those Danaans
>   were who died then
> in wide Troy land, bringing favor to the sons of
>   Atreus,
> as I wish I too had died at that time and met my
>   destiny
> on the day when the greatest number of Trojans
>   threw their bronze-headed

weapons upon me, over the body of perished
  Achilleus,
and I would have had my rites and the Achaians
  given me glory.
Now it is by a dismal death that I must be taken.

> (*Odyssey* 5.306–312)

It is remarkable that Aeneas' first words in his own epic are virtually a direct quotation from Homer. In addition to the suggestion that this poem's hero may feel more comfortable with artistic representation than with reality, more at home in the past than in the present, his use of a well-known Homeric tag in this crisis forces the reader to compare Aeneas with Odysseus, and to consider the appropriateness of the quotation to the changed circumstances of the Roman poem. Despite the surface similarities imposed by the literary shape that Vergil has given Aeneas' adventures, the two heroes' "Odysseys" are quite different. Odysseus was a leader on the winning side of the military expedition against Troy, trying to return home after his victory and reestablish an earlier, known life. Aeneas was a leader on the losing side, his home has been destroyed, and he is struggling to leave the known and move outward toward some distant goal that lies beyond his experience. At the moment of the storm, Odysseus is alone on a raft, whereas Aeneas is in command of a fleet of seven ships, leading a whole people to a new, god-promised home. But while he rails at the heavens (Odysseus speaks only "to his own heart"), Aeneas says nothing of his mission, nor even of his own lost glory in missing an honorable soldier's burial. His mind dissolves, instead, into a wistful vision of arms and men being swept away under the water.

We begin to be aware that such a hero as Aeneas will not fit easily into the role demanded of him. He shows none of the cleverness and self-possession of his Greek predecessor. He would not go on now to swim for two days and two nights to reach land, as Odysseus did. Nor, if he had, would he charm his way into the heart of a young princess with a speech full of grace and wit. Vergil chose to withhold from Aeneas the Odyssean traits of self-confidence, intelligence, and charm, making him an unsatisfying hero to most of the millions of schoolchildren who have met him as their first epic prince.

During Troy's last hours—as Aeneas himself relates the story in book 2—he was an ineffective military leader, when he was not being a raging, suicidal fool. According to one version of the events current in Vergil's time, Aeneas had been the model of intelligent generalship, maintaining the defenses on the citadel in a holding action while systematically planning the retreat of the remaining civilian population. Vergil's Aeneas, however, describes his activities differently.

Out of my mind, I arm myself.
There's no plan or purpose in fighting.
But gathering a band for war
and running up into the citadel with companions—
that enflames our hearts.
Rage and anger overwhelm my sense;
I think how beautiful it is to die in battle.

(2.314–317)

He learns then from the priest of Apollo that the situation is hopeless, that the gods have deserted Troy and the city is already dead, but he continues his mindless activity, collects a small group of like-minded madmen, and encourages them with this piece of battlefield rhetoric.

Young valiant hearts
purposelessly brave,
this is my last bold effort.
If you yearn to follow me,
here is how things stand:
all gods have abandoned their temples and altars
and left the realm they helped to be powerful
  once.
You are trying to help a city in flames.
Let us die and rush into battle.
The one hope for the defeated is to have no hope.

(2.348–354)

The core of the exhortation is "Let us die and rush into battle" (moriamur et in media arma ruamus), which commentators are quick to point out as an example of the rhetorical figure called "hysteron proteron," an illogical reversal of events. But here the illogical reversal clearly reveals the priorities in Aeneas' mind. He wants to die and be done with it. He does not succeed, however, although most of his brave young band is killed off around him. Again and again during that last night of Troy's existence, he tries to lose himself in the black hell of the burning city, only to be driven out finally by his father's vision of future glory for his family and by the admonition of his dead wife's ghost. At the end of the book he finds himself outside the city, where a band of people have gathered waiting to be led. He wonders where they came from, and, as the sun rises over the mountains, he shrugs, hoists his crippled father onto his shoulders, and starts walking uphill.

This unwilling hero with his tired resignation to life is vastly different from his Homeric prototypes, and Vergil uses Homer to remind us of this throughout the epic. In the last book, as Aeneas sets out to fight Turnus, he speaks to his son Ascanius for the only time in the poem.

Battle eager
he had already encased his shins in gold—left,
  right—
he despises delay and brandishes his spear.
After shield and breastplate are fitted to his torso
he embraces Ascanius with armor strewn around
and skims off the top of a kiss
through his helmet:
"My boy," he said,
"Learn courage from me, and the true meaning of
  toil;
learn about luck from others.
For now my right arm will defend you in the fray
and lead you amid great prizes.
But see to it—
you will be grown up soon—
that you always remember,
and when you search your mind for models from
  your family,

be stirred by your father Aeneas
and don't forget your uncle Hector."
The speech over,
he rushed in his might through the gate,
shaking his monstrous spear.

(12.430–442)

As Aeneas is about to attack his Italian enemies' champion in his hopes to finish the war,
he unexpectedly recalls Hector, the defeated
Trojan champion of the *Iliad*, and thus helps us
to recall and compare one of the most famous
scenes in Homer, Hector's own farewell to his
son Astyanax:

So speaking glorious Hektor held out his arms to
    his baby,
who shrank back to his fair-girdled nurse's bosom
screaming, and frightened at the aspect of his own
    father,
terrified as he saw the bronze and the crest with its
    horse-hair,
nodding dreadfully, as he thought, from the peak of
    the helmet.
Then his beloved father laughed out, and his
    honoured mother,
and at once glorious Hektor lifted from his head
    the helmet
and laid it in all its shining upon the ground. Then
    taking
up his dear son he tossed him about in his arms,
    and kissed him,
and lifted his voice in prayer to Zeus and the other
    immortals:
"Zeus, and you other immortals, grant that this boy,
    who is my son,
may be as I am, preeminent among the Trojans,
great in strength, as I am, and rule strongly over
    Ilion;
and some day let them say of him: 'He is better by
    far than his father,'
as he comes in from the fighting; and let him kill
    his enemy
and bring home the blooded spoils, and delight the
    heart of his mother."

(*Iliad* 6.466–481, R. Lattimore ed.)

Homer's scene is justly admired for the directness and warmth of the human emotions portrayed: the child's fright, the parents' loving
laughter, the father's affection for his family
and ambition for his son. Vergil has twisted and
stripped the scene to the point of cruel parody.
As there is no woman present (Vergil left Ascanius' mother behind at Troy and killed off
Aeneas' nurse when the Trojans reached Italy
at the beginning of book 7), so there is no laughter or fear or love. The only emotion left is
Aeneas' impatient desire to get back to the battlefield. Hector's helmet was a part of him: one
of his stock epithets is "Hector of the shining
helm." But when he saw that it frightened his
child he took it off, disarming himself so that he
could kiss the boy. Vergil inverts the actions,
making Aeneas arm himself totally before approaching his son, so that the embrace is the
feel of leather and metal, and the kiss only as
close as the breathing-hole of a battle helmet
will allow. The Roman hero is obliged to enclose himself against the intrusion, and the
expression, of emotion. The only things in his
speech that reveal the intensity of his inner
feelings are the mention of Hector—one of
those Trojans whom Aeneas thought were
"three times and four times happy" because
they had died at Troy—and the injunction to
his son to look elsewhere to learn about luck.
Once Aeneas had received his mission to found
a new nation, and certainly once he had put on
the armor of Roman history at the end of book
8, he no longer had the luxury to experience
fortune, to take his chances on the field of battle
to kill or be killed, to win or lose individual
glory for himself. Luck had to be rejected in
favor of toil, courage, and responsibility.

The determinant characteristic of Aeneas'
heroism is represented by his famous epithet
pius, "responsible." It is an epithet that he
wears around his neck like a stone, much as he
carries his father with him from Troy to Sicily,
and his history-graven shield on the battlefields
of Latium. When he has landed in Carthage
and his mother in disguise asks him his identity,
he replies: " I am Aeneas the responsible" (*sum
pius Aeneas*: 1.378), as he complains about his

tribulations between the fall of Troy and his forced landing at Carthage. And it is an epithet that can stun the reader at moments of intense emotion. The last time Dido and Aeneas are together, the queen breaks out into a passionate speech of frustration and hatred, and then faints. The poet describes his hero's reaction:

> But responsible Aeneas,
> although his desire was to console her,
> soothe her pain and turn aside her cares with
> words,
> although he moaned long
> and his spirit was shaken by the force of passion,
> nevertheless
> he followed the gods' orders and returned to the
> fleet.
>
> (4.393–396)

THE BLOCKING FORCE

Why, if the foundation of Rome is divinely ordained and guided, must there be so much suffering along the way, both by the poem's hero and by so many of those whom he touches? What, in other terms, is the evil force blocking the epic's drive toward order and civilization? Vergil concentrates that force in one major symbolic figure, whom he announces in the poem's first sentence: between Troy and Rome stands "savage Juno's unforgetting wrath" (1.4).

> Muse, tell me the reasons.
> How had her godhead been injured?
> What was her heart-grief?
> Why did the queen of gods compel
> a man distinguished in responsibility
> to endure so much misfortune,
> undertake so much toil?
> Do heavenly minds harbor such great anger?
>
> (1.8–11)

Even the Muse cannot answer the last question, which hangs like a shadow over the entire poem; but she reveals the proximate and particular causes of Juno's hatred of the Trojans. The goddess was resentful because one of her favorite cities, Carthage, would be overthrown by Rome about 800 years after Aeneas' death; she was jealous because of her husband's preference for Ganymede, a young Trojan boy; and she was angry because the Trojan Paris had not awarded her first prize in the famous beauty contest with Minerva and Venus. Paris accepted Venus' bribe of the most beautiful woman in the world, Helen, whom he seduced away from her Spartan husband, Menelaus, thus inciting the Greek retaliatory expedition against Troy.

Her fears for Carthage lead us to understand Juno's anger historically as well as mythologically. During the third and second centuries B.C. Rome fought two long and difficult wars with Carthage, coming close to defeat at the hands of Hannibal. Then, on flimsy grounds, the Romans declared a third war, at the end of which they razed the city and plowed the land with salt. That was the year (146 B.C.) in which they also sacked Corinth in Greece, a year that many of Vergil's contemporaries saw as a turning point, marking the beginning of Rome's moral decline because of her loss of formidable and worthy opponents.

But Juno is more than the historical protectress of Carthage and the mythological jealous wife of Jupiter. In Roman cult, both public and private, she was the guardian of marriage and the family, the religious projection of every Roman woman's position within the home—a function that accounts meaningfully for her wrath over Jupiter's homosexual affair and the home-wrecking adultery that resulted from the judgment of Paris. In short, Aeneas' chief opponent, and the major destructive force in the *Aeneid*, is woman as wife and mother.

The first manifestation of her enmity is the storm with which the epic's action begins. Vergil makes Juno bribe Aeolus to release his storm winds against Aeneas' fleet, in terms that underscore her function as marriage goddess. She promises him a beautiful nymph,

> whom I will join and bind to you in stable
> wedlock;

as thanks for your great services
she will spend her life with you
and make you father of fair offspring.

(1.73–75)

Juno's disorderly passions are imaged by the winds, which at first "rage with indignation all around their cages" (1.55–56) and then break loose with violence, stirring up the sea and turning it into an undifferentiated confusion of night and day, land and water, fire and sky. This tumultuous chaos threatens to overwhelm the Trojans before they can reach Italy, but a male takes the reins.

Neptune tempers the sea,
gliding over the wavetops on light wheels.
Often in a populous city sedition will arise
and the nameless mob grows savage;
firebrands and stones begin to fly
as their madness finds weapons.
Then if by chance they catch sight of some man,
stern and responsible,
who has earned their respect,
they hush and stand waiting attentively.
He speaks.
His words govern their passions and calm their
   minds.
Just so the sea's crashing subsided utterly
when father Neptune looked out upon the waves
and rode through the clear sky.

(1.146–155)

In this, the poem's first simile, Vergil extends the symbol of Juno's disordering passion into yet another area: the storm of her personal emotions is not only projected onto nature, but also onto the body politic. It is represented as rebellion and anarchy on the social level, disturbing the well-ordered male hierarchy of stable government as guided by the idealized father-ruler.

Juno's next intervention also takes the form of a storm. Although the Trojans had been driven off their course to Italy, they were hospitably received at Carthage, where they were promised assistance by that young city's just and beneficent queen, Dido. She was, like Aeneas, an exile founding a new city, and her first husband was dead. She fell in love with her Trojan counterpart, and Juno, in her role as marriage goddess, decided that Dido must have a wedding. When the two rulers were out hunting on the hills outside Carthage,

The heavens rumbled in loud confusion.
Then came a cloudburst mixed with hail.
Their Tyrian followers
and the young Trojans
and Venus' Dardan grandson
scattered through the fields,
seeking shelter in their fright.
Rivers are rushing down the hillsides.
Dido and the Trojan leader reach the same cave.
First Mother Earth and Juno Brideswoman
give the signal:
fires flashed and the upper air witnessed the
   nuptials.
Nymphs screamed from the mountaintop.

(4.160–168)

This perversion of a traditional Roman wedding ceremony, with lightning bolts for marriage torches, Juno as matron-of-honor, and bridesmaids behaving like mourners at a funeral, graphically foreshadows the results for the bride and groom. The marriage was barren, although Dido pleaded in vain for Aeneas at least to leave her with a child when he departed. Further, it caused her death and the death of her city, because before she killed herself, Dido called down a curse of eternal enmity upon their two nations.

Dido's book (book 4) is probably the best-known part of the *Aeneid*. Augustine in the *Confessions* recalls weeping over the story of Dido's love when he read Vergil as a schoolboy, and countless readers after him have been moved by her story, often to despise Aeneas as a heartless, spineless cad. She is the only woman with whom Aeneas interacts after the fall of Troy. Creusa, his first wife, is abandoned within the lost city, and Vergil does not even let Aeneas see Lavinia, the princess whom he is destined to marry in Italy. Unlike Odysseus, Aeneas has no Penelope, and the delaying roles played by the other women of the *Odyssey*—Circe, Calypso, Nausicaa, Arete—are all compressed into the role of Dido.

Our first picture of her, in book 1, is far different from that of the raging, lovesick woman who commits suicide at the end of book 4. On the day after coming to shore near Carthage, Aeneas, wrapped in a cloud of invisibility to protect him from the eyes of the curious, reconnoiters the city. He finds himself at a temple dedicated to Juno and is surprised to see its doors decorated with scenes from the Trojan War. While he is avidly reading this story of his own past, he is interrupted by Dido's arrival.

There, mixed among the Achaean chieftains,
he recognized himself,
and the battalions from the East,
and black Memnon's weapons.
There, leading the ranks of crescent-shielded
  Amazons,
was Penthesilea,
burning with rage among the thousands,
a golden band circling beneath her exposed
  breast—
a warrior-maiden bold enough to battle men.
Dardan Aeneas finds these pictures marvelous.
He is in a trance, fixed dumbly in an unbroken
  stare,
when the queen entered the temple,
beautiful Dido,
pressed by a great throng of young men.
Just as on the banks of the Eurotas
or over the slopes of Mount Cynthus
Diana rouses her dancers
and a thousand mountain nymphs follow pressing
  on every side;
a quiver hangs from her shoulders;
striding she towers above all other goddesses;
her mother Latona's heart is assaulted with joy—
Dido was like that:
so happily did she walk among them,
busy with building for her kingdoms to be.
Now she was at the goddess' doorway,
now beneath the temple roof;
fenced about with arms, she took her seat high
  upon a throne.
She was dispensing justice and making laws for
  men,

and allotting the work of construction in fair
  shares.

                    (1.487–508)

Vergil has surrounded Dido with the images of Penthesilea and Diana, virgin-warrior and virgin-huntress. Her paradigm is the woman who rejects the role of mother and wife but is man's equal on the battlefield or in the hunt; and Dido has succeeded in transferring this equality to the field of governing a city. The joyfulness of the dance continues beyond the simile into Dido's present life among her people, and the reader almost forgets that all this is taking place within the sacred precinct and under the watchful eyes of Juno, who would not be able to tolerate these incompleted images of womanhood. The goddess' intervention, this time with the connivance of Aeneas' own mother, Venus, transforms Dido into Juno's image and makes her in effect a surrogate for the goddess as Aeneas' divine enemy, storming with irrationality, rage, and violence. In the process the happiness that lighted this entrance scene is obliterated: before the end of the first book, Vergil's epithet for the queen is *infelix*, "tragic" (1.712; 749), and she will never again be at peace.

Juno's other intrusions into the narrative are of the same order. Whenever events seem to be moving toward some happy, peaceful resolution, she introduces violence and irrationality. In book 5, when the Trojan men have nearly reached Italy once more and are relaxing from their labors to play games that look forward to future days of Roman peace, Juno makes their women set fire to the Trojan ships. Once they reach Italy, Aeneas sends ambassadors to request a treaty from the local king, while he and his men begin laying out a city near the shore. Everything goes according to plan.

With these impressive gifts and words from King
  Latinus
Aeneas' men ride back, seated high on horseback.
They are carrying peace.

Suddenly, in her journey home from Inachian
  Argos,
Jupiter's savage wife,
riding the winds in her course,
looked out and saw Aeneas happy. . . . She sees
  them building houses now,
trusting the land now, their ships deserted.
She stopped short,
pierced with sharp pain.

                       (7.284–291)

This time Juno uses an even more terrifying agent to destroy the Trojans' happiness: the Fury Allecto, a primeval monster from below the earth, a daughter-of-night whose hair is venomous serpents. Allecto does her work well; so well, in fact, that the peace and city building with which the last half of the epic begins is never seen again in the *Aeneid*, except as prophecy.

Jupiter had indeed foretold to Venus in the first book that someday the gates of war would be closed, but Juno herself tears them open in book 7, when King Latinus refuses to do so, and they are still open at the end. Jupiter also promised that Juno would begin to think constructively (*consilia in melius referet*: 1.281). Thus Vergil holds out from the beginning the hope of a reconciliation in which the forces of irrational disorder would yield to order and rationality. Such a reconciliation ostensibly occurs just before the conclusion of the *Aeneid* (12.791–842). Jupiter there demands that Juno finally stop harassing the Trojans, and she agrees on condition that the Trojans give up their own name and language as they settle in Italy. Jupiter accepts her terms and adds the promise that the resulting mixed people of Italy will honor her more than any other nation. It is her last appearance in the epic, and she departs in a happy state of mind.

What happens next may well be a deeper reason for her happiness than Jupiter's bribe of future glory. The king of the gods, her own brother as well as husband, sends for an agent to end the battle that still continues in the human world below. He chooses a Fury, a ser-
pent-haired daughter-of-night, sister of that Allecto whom Juno had employed to wreck the peace. Vergil now reveals to us that these Furies

stand before the throne of Jupiter
and keep attendance at the threshold of that savage
  king,
to whet the fear in sickly mortals
when the king of gods devises frightful death and
  plagues
or terrifies deserving cities with war.

                       (12.849–852)

If this be heaven, then how are we to choose between heaven and hell?

THE GOLDEN AGE

With its burdened, often incapacitated hero, with its preferment, at the end, of the forces of darkness over the forces of light, the *Aeneid* is not an optimistic poem, although those with an overwhelming faith in Western man's ability to achieve moral progress through reason may read it as one.

> In closing my work on the Twelfth Aeneid, I cannot but look back over the two years in which Virgil, with his large and liberal humanity, has been my constant and helpful companion. It has been a time of great anxiety and sorrow; but the dark days are now passing away. As I write, it is becoming daily more certain that *violentia*, with its delusions and pretenses, is not to prevail, and that *iustitia* and *fides* are still to be the foundation-stones of our civilization. I have all along not only hoped but believed that this would be so. I now not only hope but believe that justice and good faith will also be our guides through all the difficulties and dangers that may be yet to come.

So wrote the learned and sensitive British classicist W. W. Fowler (*The Death of Turnus*, 1919) on 18 October 1918, less than a month before the armistice that ended World War I and a scarce two decades before the beginning of World War II.

After the last act of violence in the *Iliad*, Homer returns his hearers to a world of balance and normalcy in a long concluding section in which men compete freely without destruction, and in which the victorious hero sits face to face with his slain victim's father while the two men weep over shared mortality, and talk, and eat. Vergil stops the *Aeneid* abruptly at the instant of Aeneas' blow and Turnus' death. What lies beyond is hidden, within the earlier fabric of the poem's time or within the reader's imaginings.

In addition to the fictional time that the hero Aeneas plays out and the real time of Rome's history, which that fictional time allegorically represents, there is yet a third kind of time in Vergil's epic, more difficult to fix. We see it clearest in those transitional books (5–8) between the Trojan past of books 1–4 and the Roman present of books 9–12: for the internecine warfare of those last four books, which ravaged Italy and killed many of the fairest of her youth, was a fearful reality for every listener to Vergil's words. The war between Antony and Augustus, the last great civil war in a series of conflicts that lasted for two generations, had ended only a year or two before Vergil began work on the *Aeneid*, and there were few Roman readers of his epic who had not lost at least one member of their immediate families in those civil wars. When Juno says of the war she is about to incite between Aeneas and the Latins,

> Let this be their people's cost
> when son-in-law and father-in-law unite:
> maiden, your dowry will be Trojan and Rutulian blood,
>
> (7.317–318)

the Romans automatically thought of the costly conflict between Pompey and his father-in-law, Julius Caesar, a bitter period that was part of the readers' recent history, despite Anchises' plea to the unborn souls of those two future Roman leaders in the previous book.

> Oh, what an immense war between them,
> if ever they see life.
> What long battle lines and awful destruction they will cause,
> father-in-law descending from his Alpine fortifications and the citadel of Monaco,
> son-in-law drawn up against him with his Eastern troops.
> Don't, my boys!
> Don't school your hearts to warfare of such magnitude.
> Don't turn your mighty strength against your own land's bowels.
> You first be merciful,
> you who are descended from Olympus.
> Throw your weapons down,
> O my own blood!
>
> (6.828–835)

Anchises begs in book 6 for the power to stop time, for, as he has just remarked, "These two souls are in harmony now, and as long as they are restrained by night" (6.827).

In book 6, Vergil removes his hero from the world of light into the world of darkness, beneath the earth. There, as in a dream, Aeneas is freed from the normal constraints of time so that he can converse with people long dead and experience events that have not yet happened. In miniature his dream experience mirrors the outer form of the *Aeneid* as a whole, as it moves from images of Aeneas' Trojan past to images of his Roman future. Vergil signals with unusual explicitness the precise moment at which Aeneas and the reader have reached the center of the dream and of the poem. Aeneas is listening to a Trojan, Deiphobus, tell the story of Helen's treachery during Troy's last hours.

> During this exchange of conversation
> Aurora in her rose-red chariot
> had passed the midpoint in her journey through the sky.
> Perhaps they would have spent the whole allotted time
> in such rememberings,
> had not his companion the Sibyl admonished them with no waste of words:

"Night is rushing onward, Aeneas;
We are spending the hours weeping.
This is the place where the road splits in two."
(6.535–540)

During the next 130 lines Aeneas, under the Sibyl's guidance, is permitted a glimpse of an eternal world, where humans have completely escaped the limitations of time. Here, if anywhere, is Vergil's "Divine Comedy," wherein he can mold a moral universe to fit his epic's deepest needs.

Violence, to be sure, exists in this universe. It is here that Vergil first describes those female monsters covered with snakes, the Furies, whom he finds such a ready symbol for the world's evil. Yet in this eternal world they are confined within a fortified city girt with a river of fire, and their function is to mete out punishment to those who have broken fundamental bonds of human relationships, or betrayed their country, or manipulated the law for money. The suffering in this city is in the service of *fides* (trust) and *iustitia* (justice), as even the sufferers understand; *discite iustitiam moniti* ("Be warned and learn justice!": 6.618–620) comes a loud cry through the darkness from the most wretched of all.

Protected from the contamination of this city, and separated from it by a giant wall, lies Elysium, the dwelling place of the happy:

No one has a fixed house:
we live in shady groves
and along the banks of streams in the fresh
meadows.

(6.673–675)

Warriors of past generations are there, but they enjoy looking at their now functionless chariots as their horses graze scattered over the field. They race and wrestle for sport. Above all, deserving citizens and incorrupt priests alike have time to listen to the great poets of the past, Orpheus and Musaeus and "all the bards who had been responsible and spoken words worthy of Apollo" (6.662).

Unlike the Judaeo-Christian tradition, in which heaven is imaged as a city, New Jerusalem, foursquare and paved in gold, Vergil rejects the city altogether in his paradise, but chooses it instead for his model of hell. That he would do so in either the *Eclogues* or the *Georgics* would be scarcely surprising, but that he does so in an epic devoted to the founding of Rome is a startling indication of the poet's profound doubts about the capacity of his own civilization to nurture the moral and aesthetic values that he feels are of primary importance to mankind. And the poet projects these doubts onto his hero, who questions why anyone would wish to give up this pastoral ideal and move back into the mainstream of time. Neither bard nor Sibyl answers Aeneas, but his past, in the form of his father, reveals his future in the form of his sons' sons, and "kindles in his heart a passion for the history that lies ahead" (6.889).

Whether humans as we know them can live at peace with one another and with nature in a rationally organized political system is perhaps the overriding question of the *Aeneid*. There are a few moments outside the timeless center of the epic when the reader glimpses the possibility of such a "Golden Age." The first is at the end of Jupiter's prophecy in book 1:

In those days
harsh generations will lay aside war, turn gentle;
venerable Trust and the Hearth-Goddess,
Romulus with his brother Remus,
will dispense justice.
The frightful Gates of War will be locked tight with
iron chains.
Irresponsible Fury will sit inside upon his savage
weapons,
bound with a hundred brazen knots behind his
back,
horribly roaring through bloody jaws.

(1.291–296)

Here, as in the underworld, violence is restrained behind closed doors. Here justice is so far restored that even the primal act of fratricide that occurred at the moment of Rome's actual founding by Romulus is erased, as the murdered brother sits beside his murderer on the magistrates' bench. Furthermore the Roman reader, if he wished, could identify the fulfillment of this prophecy with a specific event in recent Roman history, for in 29 B.C., after the battle of Actium, the Roman Senate voted that, for the first time in more than two hundred years, the Gates of War should be ceremonially closed, thus indicating that no Roman army was engaged in combat anywhere in the world. That same reader might have noted, however, that the door of violence did not stay shut for long, because the Senate had to repeal its vote only four years later, in 25 B.C. Vergil had begun to write the *Aeneid* in the interim.

Aeneas does not hear Jupiter's prophecy, which refers at any event to a time a thousand years after his death. When he lands in Italy, however, he comes in contact with another golden age:

> There Latinus was king over fields and cities;
> now old, he ruled them in the calm of a long
>   peace.
> Tradition tells that he was son of Faunus
> and a Laurentian nymph, Marica.
> Faunus' sire was Picus,
> who calls you his parent, Saturn:
> you are the founder of their bloodline.
>
> (7.45–49)

There are already cities here, but they are in harmony with the land, and Vergil uses Latinus' genealogy to show the close bond between man and nature: Faunus is a shepherd's god like the Greek Pan, Picus is a woodpecker, and Saturn is the Italic agricultural deity of sowing. The Romans also associated Saturn with the Greek Kronos, father of Zeus and his predecessor as ruler of the gods; and so the age of Saturn was also a golden age, before Jupiter took over control and—as Vergil himself described in the *Georgics* (1.121–159)—made life bitterly difficult for the men who must live in the hard age of iron. Only three generations re-

moved from Saturn, Latinus can still say to the Trojan ambassadors:

> Do not flee our hospitality;
> know that the Latins are Saturn's people
> and practice justice not because of chains or laws,
> but in free and willing continuance of the old god's
>   ways.
>
> (7.202–204)

But, as we have seen, the peace that Latinus proffers cannot withstand the forces of violence that Juno helps to unleash, and before the end of book 7, Vergil dramatically portrays the end of the age of Saturn, as he tells with savage irony how Latinus retired in revulsion into the darkness while Juno, "Saturn's daughter, broke down the iron-clad doors of war" (7.622).

When Aeneas himself reaches the site of the future city of Rome, seeking help from the Arcadian king Evander, who had settled on the hill where one day Augustus would live, he is directly informed about the current status of the golden age:

> These woods were once inhabited by native fauns
>   and nymphs,
> and a race of men born from tree trunks and hard
>   oak,
> with no civilization, no culture;
> they had not learned to yoke oxen or gather wealth
> or save what they acquired,
> but got their food from trees and troublesome
>   hunting.
> Then Saturn came down from Olympus in the
>   skies,
> fleeing Jupiter's weapons,
> an exile who had lost his kingdom.
> He gathered the untaught folk scattered high in the
>   hills,
> gave them laws,
> and chose Latium [hiding-place] for a name—
> he had hidden safely in this region.
> The age men call golden existed in his reign,
> for he ruled the people in the calm of peace,
> until gradually a worse and faded age succeeded,
> with the madness of war, the passion for
>   possessions.
>
> (8.314–327)

Immediately after describing this downward course of civilization, Evander takes Aeneas on a tour of his small settlement on the banks of the Tiber, while Vergil's reader superimposes his own picture of the huge marble buildings and vast wealth that covered that site in his own day. As Aeneas assumes his first major responsibility that will enable Rome to grow, as he collects allies for a war that he does not want to fight, he must do so with the conviction that the age of Saturn is somehow recoverable in time. Otherwise his own suffering and the tragic loss he witnesses around him on both sides of the war would be intolerable. Yet Vergil has made it very difficult for him—and us—to maintain that conviction, by constructing his epic in such a way that the vision of a peaceable kingdom recedes farther into the distance as Aeneas moves away from the dream center of the sixth book.

STRUCTURE AND IMAGE

Like the *Eclogues* and the *Georgics*, the *Aeneid* reveals a careful plan with intricate formal patterns. Each book is not only conceived as an artistic unit with its own internal structure but is also connected to other books by verbal and thematic parallels. Vergil is said to have begun by writing a fairly detailed outline of the whole work in prose, and then composing or polishing whatever segments of verse he wished, knowing where they were to fit in the overall pattern. The resulting text is so complex and highly organized that the full meaning of a passage is often realized only in conjunction with parallel passages that may be separated from it by several thousand lines.

The basic organization of the whole is concentric, with the twelve books envisioned as simultaneously forming two halves of six each and three thirds of four each. Seen in halves, the epic divides into an "Odyssey" and an "Iliad," a man at sea and a war on land, the past of Troy and the present of Italy. In its tripartite

division the emphasis changes. The first tetrad (books 1-4) is framed by the figure of Dido triumphant and Dido destroyed, while its middle two books recall the death of old Troy. Similarly the last tetrad (9-12) is framed by the figure of Turnus triumphant and Turnus destroyed, while its middle two books reveal the death of young Italy in Pallas, Lausus, Camilla, and others. The central third of the epic escapes the limitations of the individual tragedies of Dido and Turnus and explores the larger dimensions of Roman history, as well as the relationships among art, myth, dream, and reality.

Vergil both outlines this overall structure and connects the different parts into a coherent whole by his careful use of verbal echoes and recurrent images, joining single passages in a nexus that often extends backward and forward over many books.

At the beginning of book 12, Turnus is aware that the time has come for him to fight Aeneas in single combat, and he is eager for the battle to begin. Vergil comments on his situation with a simile:

> Poenorum qualis in arvis
> saucius ille gravi venantum vulnere pectus
> tum demum movet arma leo, gaudetque
>   comantis
> excutiens cervice toros fixumque latronis
> impavidus frangit telum et fremit ore cruento.
>   (12.4–8)

As when in Punic fields,
wounded in the chest by a grievous blow from
   hunters,
a lion finally advances into battle,
rejoicing as he shakes the hairy muscles on his
   neck.
Fearlessly he breaks the shaft of the bandit's
   embedded spear,
roaring through bloody jaws.

The violence and danger of the lust for battle, once aroused, are appropriately transferred to the image of a lion about to turn on its hunters. The last phrase is especially vivid, projecting as it does both the sound of the lion's roar and the sight of its open mouth and long teeth dripping with red blood. But the last phrase does more than add pictorial detail to this image of Turnus; it recalls an earlier image:

> As when a starving lion wreaks havoc in the
>   crowded folds.
> Maddening hunger drives him on.
> He eats and drags away the soft lambs mute with
>   fear,
> as he *roars through bloody jaws*.
>   (9.339–341; emphasis added)

The soldier-lion in the earlier simile was Euryalus, a handsome young Trojan who volunteered with his lover for a night mission through the enemy lines. Because he could not control his lust for blood and plunder in this, his first taste of military action, he and his lover were caught, killed, and beheaded. By the allusion Vergil not only takes us back into book 9, underscoring the formal unity of the last four books, but also reminds us that the animal violence unleashed in war is not particular to Turnus, although at this moment in the poem he may appear to be the central focus of the opposition to Aeneas and hence to Rome. In fact, both the innocent young Trojan and the Italian prince are suddenly revealed as temporary manifestations of the universal beast Fury, who, as Jupiter prophesied in book 1, will someday be bound up, "horridly *roaring through bloody jaws*" (1.296; emphasis added). With this one short but vivid phrase, which he uses nowhere else in the poem, Vergil has taken his reader back through the entire epic to its beginning, and forcefully underscored the distance still separating us from the poem's—or at least Jupiter's—promise of peace.

The particular qualities of the lion who is Turnus also lead us elsewhere in the *Aeneid*. The first word of Vergil's simile locates him in Punic territory, and the startling appearance of a Punic lion in Italy makes us think of that part of the epic that took place in Punic Carthage. Once we make the connection, we must recall

the image of Dido just after she had fallen in love with Aeneas:

> All this time a flame is eating at her soft marrow,
> a silent wound is living under her breast.
> Poor Dido is on fire.
> She roams the whole city in her madness,
> like a doe hit by an arrow:
> far away and heedless of danger in the Cretan
>   woods,
> the creature was pierced by a shepherd
> exercising his weapons,
> abandoning the flying steel unaware;
> in flight she roams the forests and pastures of
>   Mount Dicte
> with the lethal shaft stuck in her flank.
>   (4.66–73)

Vergil represents Dido at the beginning of book 4, like Turnus at the beginning of 12, as a wounded animal with the point of a weapon still lodged in its body. She never recovers from her metaphorical wound, but grows more and more feverish and rabid throughout the book, until she actualizes the simile by falling on Aeneas' sword. As she dies, "there is a hiss from the wound still lodged deep under her breast" (4.689).

Aeneas, the wielder of the weapon in both cases, is portrayed quite differently in the two images. With Dido he is like a shepherd who means no harm and is not responsible for the results of his random shooting. Typically, Vergil uses the details within such apparently decorative and objective similes to reveal inner thoughts and feelings of his characters. At this early stage in their relationship Dido can still look on Aeneas as he likes to think of himself, despite all the indications that he has had to the contrary of his mission to guide his people to found a city: namely, a shepherd living in an age of innocence. Turnus the lion, however, could scarcely be expected to view his enemy in the same light. His harassers, the Trojans, are seen as hunters who deliberately set out to kill him, while their leader is insultingly named a "bandit."

As surely as the doe's wound is repeated by

the stroke of Aeneas' sword "under her breast" (sub pectore: 4.689), and Dido dies in the last line of her book,

> all the warmth slipped away
> and her life dispersed into the winds;
>
> (4.704–705)

so surely is the lion's wound repeated by the stroke of Aeneas' sword "under his breast" (sub pectore: 12.950), and when Turnus dies in the last line of book 12, and of the epic,

> his body comes apart shivering,
> and with a groan his life flees plaintively beneath the shadows.
>
> (12.951–952)

The metaphor of hunting that connects Turnus and Dido is itself only part of a larger series of hunts within the *Aeneid*, both figurative and literal. Vergil marks three major turning points in the narrative with hunting scenes. Aeneas' first act in the poem, after the Trojans have come safely to land near Carthage, is to shoot down seven tall stags (1.184–194). Later, the storm with which Juno drives Dido and Aeneas into a cave to mate comes while the two leaders are out hunting together with their companions:

> Dislodged from their rocky heights,
> wild goats ran down the hillsides;
> coursing across the open fields from the other direction,
> deer raised dust as they fled in crowded formation, abandoning the mountains.
> But the child Ascanius in the valley below enjoys his spirited horse,
> passing now one group, now another,
> eagerly hoping for a foaming boar to appear among the harmless flocks,
> or a tawny lion to come down from the mountain.
>
> (4.152–159)

After the Trojans have reached Italy and are still at peace with the Italians, Ascanius gets his wish for more significant prey. While he is out hunting with other young Trojans, his dogs start a tall, handsome stag. The lad, "aflame with passion for special praise" (7.496), shoots and fatally wounds the creature. Since the deer was the tame pet of the daughter of the king's chief herdsman, which she had raised from a fawn, her family and their neighbors take offense at the young Trojans' sporting and attack them. The first blow in the war in Italy is struck because Aeneas' son wounds a stag while hunting.

This, in book 7, is the last literal hunt in the epic, since hunting is a peacetime activity. But as the deathblow in the war is about to be struck at the end of book 12, the image of the hunted animal with which Vergil introduced Turnus at the beginning of that book reappears in strikingly changed form. Aeneas is chasing Turnus on foot.

> As when a deer is cut off by a river,
> or hemmed in by a frightening rope hung with feathers of Punic scarlet;
> the hunter-hound has caught up with him and presses at his heels, barking.
> Terrified at the rope's ambush and the steep bank,
> he flees in a hundred different directions,
> but the untiring Umbrian sticks to him openmouthed.
> Now he has him and now he seems to have him and as the jaws snap shut
> he bites on empty air.
>
> (12.749–755)

The joyous strength of a wounded but threatening lion has turned into the hopeless terror of a trapped deer; the hunter has himself become a beast, a carnivore, of a kind bred and trained to kill. As there are no humans present, so there are no motives: neither hunger, nor glory, nor revenge. There remains, as the epic is about to end, only the fear of the hunted and the frustration of the hunter.

CONCLUSION

Throughout most of the two thousand years after his death, Vergil has been both a school text and a classic. If this has added to his renown, it has detracted considerably from a proper appreciation of his poetry. Schoolchildren assume, if they are not taught, that Vergil's Latin must be normal: his usage correct, his syntax regular, and his verse canonical. For the most part this misapprehension is perpetuated by commentators and translators alike, who shut their eyes to the unprecedented word, explain away the syntactic riddles, and reduce the boldly experimental variety of his rhythms to "the stateliest measure/ever molded by the lips of man."

As a classic, Vergil has been assumed to represent and defend the ideals of Roman civilization, as these were understood by later times. He was seen as the poet of the order and stability of the City of Man, and even somehow as the precursor of the City of God. The ambiguity and doubt, the passion and violence with which his poetry abounds were reduced to nothing more than gentle melancholy. Vergil's work has ceased to be a school text now, and his position as author of a Roman classic no longer assures him of a pedestal. We are free to read him as a highly imaginative poet struggling with language and disturbed by conflicting visions.

Vergil died before he had finished revising the *Aeneid* to his own satisfaction. On his deathbed he is said to have given orders to burn the manuscript. We are not told why he considered the poem a failure, but we may trust his judgment that it was. Vergil's epic fails finally to reconcile the forces that it sets in opposition to one another: Juno and Jupiter, city and country, passion and heroism, war and man. It fails because, unlike the *Georgics*, in which poetry at the end subsumes and defeats the death-filled pessimism threatening to overwhelm that poem, the *Aeneid* ends with a plunge down into the violent blackness it has attempted to conquer. It ends suicidally where it began, without resolving the conflicts it so forcefully portrays. It ends in ambiguity, driving its readers back into the poem again and again, to find their own hope or despair mirrored in the powerful and disturbing images of Vergil's poetry.

Selected Bibliography

TEXTS

The Aeneid of Virgil, edited by R. D. Williams. 2 vols. London, 1972–1973. Text and commentary.

P. Vergili Maronis Bucolica et Georgica, edited by T. E. Page. London, 1898. Text and commentary to *Eclogues* and *Georgics*.

P. Vergili Maronis Opera, edited by R. A. B. Mynors. Oxford, 1969. Oxford Classical Text. Latin text; the standard.

Vergil, Eclogues, edited by R. Coleman. Cambridge, 1977. Cambridge Greek and Latin Classics. Text and commentary.

Virgil, Aeneid Book VIII, edited by K. W. Gransden. Cambridge, 1976. Cambridge Greek and Latin Classics. Text and commentary.

Virgil. 2 vols. Cambridge, Mass., and London, 1916. Loeb Classical Library. Latin text with an English translation by H. R. Fairclough.

TRANSLATIONS

The Aeneid of Virgil. Translated by A. Mandelbaum. New York, 1971. The best modern verse translation.

The Georgics of Vergil. Translated by S. Palmer Bovie. Chicago, 1956.

The Georgics of Virgil. Translated by C. Day Lewis. London, 1940.

Vergil, The Aeneid. Translated by F. O. Copley. 2nd ed. Indianapolis, 1975. Line-for-line verse translation.

Virgil. Translated by H. R. Fairclough. 2 vols. Cambridge, Mass., and London, 1916. Loeb Classical Library.

Virgil: The Aeneid. Translated by W. F. Jackson Knight. London, 1956. Excellent prose translation.

Virgil's Works. Translated by J. W. Mackail. New York, 1934.

COMMENTARIES WITH TEXT

Commentaries on individual books of the *Aeneid*:
Austin, R. G., ed. Book 1. Oxford, 1971.
———. Book 2. Oxford, 1964.
———. Book 4. Oxford, 1955.
———. Book 6. Oxford, 1977.
Fletcher, F., ed. Book 6. Oxford, 1941.

Fordyce, C. J., ed. Books 7–8. Oxford, 1977.

Williams, R. D., ed. Book 3. Oxford, 1962.

———. Book 5. Oxford, 1960.

Conington, J., and H. Nettleship. *The Works of Virgil with a Commentary.* 5th ed. revised by F. Haverfield. London, 1898. Reprinted 1963.

CONCORDANCE

Warwick, H. H. *A Vergil Concordance.* Minneapolis, 1975.

CRITICAL STUDIES

Alpers, Paul. *The Singer of the Eclogues: A Study of Virgilian Pastoral.* Berkeley, 1979. Includes text and translation.

Anderson, W. S. *The Art of Aeneid.* Englewood Cliffs, N. J., 1969.

Broch, Hermann. *The Death of Virgil.* Translated from the German by J. S. Untermeyer. New York, 1945. Fiction, based on a sensitive study of Vergil's poetry and times.

Camps, W. A. *An Introduction to Virgil's Aeneid.* Oxford, 1969.

Commager, S., ed. *Virgil: A Collection of Critical Essays.* Englewood Cliffs, N. J., 1966.

Comparetti, D. *Vergil in the Middle Ages.* Translated from the Italian by E. F. M. Benecke. London, 1895.

Johnson, W. R. *Darkness Visible.* Berkeley, 1976.

Knight, W. F. Jackson. *Roman Virgil.* London, 1944; rev. ed., 1966.

Otis, Brooks. *Virgil: A Study in Civilized Poetry.* Oxford, 1963.

Poschl, V. *The Art of Vergil: Image and Symbol in the Aeneid.* Translated from the German by G. Seligson. Ann Arbor, Mich., 1962.

Putnam, M. C. J. *Virgil's Pastoral Art: Studies in the Eclogues.* Princeton, N. J., 1970.

———. *Virgil's Poem of the Earth: Studies in the Georgics.* Princeton, N. J., 1979.

Rieu, E. V. *Virgil, the Pastoral Poems.* London, 1954. Prose translations and short essays on each eclogue.

Wilkinson, L. P. *The Georgics of Virgil: A Critical Survey.* Cambridge, 1969.

BIBLIOGRAPHY

Thousands of pages are published on Vergil each year. *Vergilius,* the journal of the Vergilian Society, prints an annual bibliography.

JOHN ARTHUR HANSON

HORACE

(65–8 B.C.)

INTRODUCTION

QUINTUS HORATIUS FLACCUS, the poet we know as Horace, was born in Venusia (modern Venosa), in southern Italy, on 8 December 65 B.C. His father was a freedman (that is, a former slave) who made a modest living as an auctioneer; of his mother we know nothing. Horace's father apparently recognized his son's talent early and realized the need for better education than could be found in Venusia. Horace himself, in a justly famous passage, tells us how his father took him to Rome, arranged for his education, and himself served as escort and protector (*Satires* I.6.71 ff.). For his higher education Horace went to Athens, where the focus of his studies was philosophy but where he no doubt also gained close acquaintance with the Greek poets whose works were so to influence his own later poetry.

Following the assassination of Julius Caesar in 44 B.C., Horace, along with other young Romans in Athens, was swept into the maelstrom of civil war on the Republican side. He apparently followed Brutus to Asia Minor in 43–42 B.C., rising to the rank of tribune in the Republican army. His military career came to an abrupt and ignominious end, however, in the defeat of Brutus and his forces at Philippi in November 42 B.C. In the years following, "with wings clipped and stripped of paternal hearth and home" (*Epistles* II.2.50–51), Horace returned to Rome to rebuild his life. He obtained a position of some importance in the Roman equivalent of the treasury, a post he continued to hold for a number of years. More important, he began to write poetry, and his early efforts soon attracted the attention of Vergil and other Roman poets. These in turn introduced him to Maecenas, Augustus' confidential adviser and an important patron of the arts, and around 37 B.C., Maecenas invited Horace into his circle. Some time between 35 and 30 B.C., Maecenas gave Horace a modest estate in the Sabine hills, a place whose beauties Horace never tired of singing. From this time until his death on 27 November 8 B.C., Horace devoted himself largely to poetry, either in Rome or at this well-loved retreat.

Horace's life thus spans the critical period from the Catilinarian conspiracy in 63 B.C. to the establishment of the Augustan principate in the 20's and teens, and Horace himself moves from active support of the Republican cause in 44–42 B.C. to active support of Augustus in later years. One of the most fascinating aspects of his poetry is the way it reflects the events of this turbulent period and Horace's own change of sentiments, moving from two deeply pessimistic poems that focus on the civil wars through several poems that revolve around the campaign against Antony and Cleopatra (in 31–30 B.C.) down to numerous later poems that respond, not always without ambivalence, to Augustus and his new regime.

Horace's writings, with approximate dates of

publication, consist of *Satires* I and II (35 and 30 B.C.), *Epodes* (30 B.C.), *Odes* I–III (23 B.C.), *Epistles* I (20 B.C.), *Odes* IV (13 B.C.), and the three literary epistles in *Epistles* II—the Letter to Augustus (13 B.C.), the Letter to Florus (19–18 B.C.), and the *Ars Poetica* (19–17 B.C.). To cover in depth such a range of works (*Odes* I-III alone contains 88 poems) in an essay of this length is obviously impossible. In what follows I place greatest emphasis on the two collections that are most frequently read, *Satires* I and *Odes* I–III. In addition, I single out for at least brief mention the most important individual poems from the entire corpus; but a number of works, most notably the three epistles of *Epistles* II, receive admittedly short shrift. My strategy is to approach different collections from different perspectives, focusing on Horace the man in the section on the *Satires* and *Epistles,* on Horatian "play" in the section on *Odes* I–III, on larger structural and thematic concerns in the section on the *Epodes* and *Odes* IV. My intent is not to suggest that there is any one best approach for any particular collection; one could just as well, for instance, study Horace the man in *Odes* I–III, Horatian play in *Epodes* and *Odes* IV, overall structure and theme in the *Satires* and *Epistles*. I wish rather to suggest some of the many ways in which one can approach Horace, and my hope is that readers will experiment with these and other approaches in ways I have not done. Horace, as we shall see, is a poet addicted to play, and he yields his delights most fully to readers who bring to his poetry a similar spirit of serious play.

Before we turn to the individual collections, we should speak briefly about their literary background. Horace, like virtually all poets of his day, works always within a literary tradition established by earlier poets. His genres and meters, many of his themes, and occasionally even his words come from earlier poets; his originality finds expression in the ways he makes these earlier materials his own. His *Satires*, for instance, falls within a tradition that stretches back at least as far as the great Roman poet Ennius (239–169 B.C.), a tradition whose purely Roman provenance Quintilian emphasizes but that in fact owes much to Greek Old Comedy and to the popular diatribes of post-Socratic Greek philosophy. Horace's particular debt, as he readily admits, is to the works of the prolific Roman satirist Lucilius (died 102/101 B.C.), but he regularly adapts Lucilius' models to his own needs. Thus, to mention one example, Horace transforms a satire in which Lucilius tells of a journey from Rome to Sicily into an account of an actual journey Horace and friends made to Brundisium in the spring of 37 B.C. (*Satires* I.5). The *Epodes* and *Odes* contain even more direct imitations, in this case of Greek poets. Epodes 4, 6, 8, 10, and 12 owe much to the iambic lampoons of the early Greek poets Archilochus (seventh century B.C.) and Hipponax (sixth century B.C.). Other epodes—such as, 5, 11, 13, 14, 15—are similarly influenced by models from the Hellenistic period. A number of odes are versions of specific Greek poems. Thus, to mention some of the most striking examples: I.9, I.14, and I.37 are closely related to lyric poems by Alcaeus (sixth century B.C.); I.23 to a lyric by Anacreon (sixth century B.C.); I.15 to a choral dithyramb by Bacchylides (fifth century B.C.); I.12, III.4, and IV.6 to choral poems by Pindar (518–438 B.C.). Here too, however, Horace consistently reshapes the originals to his own needs. An Alcaeus poem on the death of the tyrant Myrtilus provides the starting point for Horace's ode on Cleopatra (I.37); another Alcaeus poem, one dealing with the "ship of state," is adapted to reflect Horace's changing attitudes toward Augustan Rome (I.14); and two Pindaric odes to Sicilian tyrants (*Olympian* 2 and *Pythian* 1) provide starting points for two odes to Augustus (I.12 and III.4). Characteristic also is the fact that Horace's *Odes*, despite the numerous debts to these early Greek models, also display throughout—especially in the emphasis on refinement and on quality rather than quantity—the influence of the Alexandrian poets and especially of Callimachus (third century B.C.). Horace's blend of early and late, of Greek and Roman, has, of course, a close counterpart in the work of his friend Vergil, whose *Aeneid,* for instance, mixes Homer with Apollonius, pre-classical with Hellenistic, reshaping these Greek sources into a poem that focuses on Augustan Rome.[1]

HIS WHOLE LIFE PICTURED: THE SATIRES AND EPISTLES

Horace's first published work, *Satires* I, is remarkable both for its mature artistry and for its inexhaustible variety. The artistry, as we shall see, is well concealed though thoroughly conscious. The variety is immediately apparent.

On the most obvious level, there is the variety of subject matter among the ten satires themselves. The book begins with three satires whose thrust is general, the first focusing on ambition and dissatisfaction with one's lot, the second on sex, particularly adultery, and the third on the need for consistency and balance in assessing one's own and others' faults. The second triad, *Satires* I.4–6, brings Horace himself more into center stage. *Satires* I.4 deals primarily with Horace's own satiric principles and purposes; I.5 recounts the trip Horace and friends took from Rome to Brundisium; and I.6 focuses on the contrasting poles of Horace's life—a freedman father on the one hand, acceptance into Maecenas' literary circle on the other. *Satires* I.7 through I.9 tell three humorous stories: I.7 recounts the tale of a certain Persius who questions why Brutus, the great slayer of kings, did not polish off an obnoxious provincial official by the name of Rex ("King"); I.8 tells how an exploding statue of Priapus sent the witches Canidia and Sagana scuttering off

from a graveyard where they had been practicing their foul trade; I.9, often referred to as "The Bore," is Horace's justly famous account of his encounter with a pushy social and literary climber; I.10 closes the collection by focusing again on the writing of satire and, in particular, on Horace's relation to Lucilius, his acknowledged model in the genre.

Scarcely less striking is the variety of styles encountered in these ten poems. The overall tone is colloquial, to be sure, in keeping with Horace's own title *Sermones,* "talks." The meter throughout is the dactylic hexameter. But what variations there are within these bounds! Philosophical language follows close upon a list of homely examples (I.3.80–106). Epic parody sets the stage for the rough-and-ready language of longshoremen and the verbal sparrings of two buffoons (I.5.9 ff. and 53 ff.). Oracular obscurities and a divine rescue, Homeric style, interrupt the colloquial jabber of Horace's encounter with the bore (I.9.29–34 and 78). And, with typical irony, Horace builds to perorations of considerable eloquence only to burst the bubble at the end (I.1.120–121 and I.4.138–143).

Above all, however, there is in *Satires* I an exuberant variety of character and situation, for Horace drives home his points less by argument than by example, a practice he traces back to his father (I.4.105 ff.). *Satires* I, for instance, opens with a brisk catalog of human types, diverse in occupation but united in dissatisfaction with their present lives. There follows the vivid picture of Jupiter puffing his cheeks in disgust at these fickle humans who at one moment desperately wish to exchange lots, at the next refuse to do so when offered the chance (lines 15–22). The remainder of this satire contains a veritable gallery of misers—the miser who gazes on his piles of lucre as if they were works of art or sacred objects (lines 70–72); the miser, a certain Ummidius, so rich that he measures rather than counts his money—and whom a freedwoman, "bravest of Clytemnestras," dispatches with an axe (lines 95–100); the miser whose assumption that his money will assure him the best of medical care is set

[1]On Horace and Vergil, see G. E. Duckworth, "Animae Dimidium Meae: Two Poets of Rome," *Transactions of the American Philological Association* 87:281–316 (1956). The scope of the present chapter does not permit discussion of Horace's influence on post-classical authors. For good introductions to some aspects of this vast topic, see C. D. N. Costa, ed., *Horace* 135–159; K. J. Reckford, *Horace* 146–152; L. P. Wilkinson, *Horace and his Lyric Poetry* 159–176; and P. F. Saintonge, L. G. Burgevin, and H. Griffith, *Horace: Three Phases of his Influence* (Chicago, 1936). All contain useful bibliographies.

against the fact that no one—wife, son, neighbor, acquaintance—wishes him healthy (lines 80–85). *Satires* I.2 contains an even more zesty array, largely adulterers and lechers: Maltinus with tunic dragging around his ankles, his unnamed opposite with tunic hitched up to his loins (lines 25–26); Rufillus smelling of perfumed lozenges and Gargonius of a goat (line 27); Cupiennus ("Lusty"), who will only look at noble *cunni,* and Sallustius, insane over freedwomen (lines 36, 48–49); Villius shut out while his wife cavorts with Longarenus (lines 64–67). And, as corollaries to this noble assembly, there are the vivid accounts of what awaits those caught in the act (lines 41–46 and 127–134).

One could go on endlessly: the singers who never sing when asked, never stop singing when asked not to, and the philosopher who, "king" that he is, gets his beard pulled by mischievous boys (I.3.1 ff. and 129 ff.); Lucilius, dictating two hundred verses per hour, standing on one foot; and Crispinus, in vain challenging Horace to a speed-writing contest (I.4.9 ff.); the eager host who in his zest to cook a splendid dinner almost burns the house down, and the lying wench who stands Horace up (I.5.71 ff.); Natta, robbing the lamps for his olive oil, and Tillus, praetor though he be, followed by his slaves carrying the cook-out kit as he makes his way to Tibur (I.6.124 and 107 ff.). The profusion of pointed tales in I.1 through I.6 leads naturally, of course, to I.7–9, which are all story. Of a piece with Horace's penchant for the vivid vignette is his ability to come up with the telling image, be it the little ant of I.1.32 ff.; the stubborn donkey of I.9.20 ff.; the frantic race of ambition in I.1.111 ff.; or ambition dragging all behind its gleaming chariot in I.6.23 ff. Not all the examples and images are Horace's own, of course, and his general use of examples owes much not only to his father but also to the tradition of the philosophical diatribe (see II.3 for a good example of this genre); but the vigor, the terseness, and the eye for detail are Horace's own, and they are characteristic strengths not only of the *Satires* but of all his writings.

Two passages deserve particular emphasis.

The first is Horace's account of his introduction to Maecenas, followed by his reminiscences of his father.

Here I return to myself, born of a freedman father, whom all snap at as born of a freedman father—now, Maecenas, because I am your close friend, but formerly because a Roman legion obeyed me as a tribune. The two situations are, however, different, since, while anyone might perhaps justly envy me that office, he could not similarly envy me you as friend, you who are so careful to take to yourself only those who are worthy, and free of base ambition. I could not call myself "lucky" in this, that by some good fortune I drew you as my friend: for no mere chance offered you to me. Some time back that best of men, Vergil, and after him Varius, told you what I was. When I came into your presence, speaking few words haltingly, for tongue-tied bashfulness kept me from saying more, I told you not that I was from a distinguished father, not that I was carried about my estates on a Saturneian nag—I told you what I was. You answered, as was your custom, but a few words; I went off. Nine months later you called me back and bade me count myself among your friends. I consider it a great thing that I pleased you, you who separate the honorable from the shameful not by the distinction of one's father but by the purity of one's life and one's soul.

And yet, if my character is flawed by faults that are minor and few but is otherwise sound—as if you should censure a few moles sprinkled on an otherwise splendid body; if no one can justly charge me with greed, miserliness, or debauchery; if, to praise myself, I live pure and guiltless and dear to my friends, the cause of all these things was my father who, a poor man on a poor farm, nonetheless was unwilling to send me to Flavius' school, where the big boys, born of big centurions, used to go, slinging their book bags and tablets from their left shoulders, each bringing his monthly pittance on the Ides. But he dared to take his son to Rome, to be taught those subjects that any knight or senator might teach his son. If anyone saw my clothes and the servants in attendance, as was the custom in the great city, he would naturally have assumed that these expenses were furnished me from an ancestral estate. My father himself, the most incorruptible of guardians, went around with me to my teachers. Why say more? He kept me clean—and that is the first flower of virtue—not only from any shameful deed but even from any suspicion of shame. Nor did he fear that he might be criticized if someday, like him, I should end up pursuing petty trade as an auctioneer or collector of monies; nor, had that happened, would I have complained. As it is, however, I owe him the greater praise and the greater gratitude.

(*Satires* I.6.45–88)

The second, coming at the conclusion of the same poem, is Horace's description of how he spends a typical day in Rome.

I go wherever I please, alone. I ask the price of vegetables and flour; I wander around the tricky Circus and, in the evening, often the Forum; I stop by the fortune tellers; then I take myself home to a plate of leeks and peas and pancakes. Three slaves serve dinner; a marble slab supports the two goblets and the ladle, the cheap saltcellar and an oil flask and saucer, of Campanian ware, stand near by. Then I go to sleep, without worry that I must rise early in the morning to obey Marsyas in the Forum—Marsyas who says he can no longer stand the face of the younger Novius. I lie in bed until mid-morning. After that I wander about or, after I've read or written something to please me for a quiet moment, I rub myself down with oil (with something better than what dirty Natta uses after he's robbed the lamps). But when I'm tired and the midday sun warns me to bathe, I flee the Campus and the game of ball. After a light lunch—just enough to keep me from spending the day on an empty stomach, I take my ease at home. This is the life of those free of the sorrow and burden of ambition; with joys such as these I console myself that I shall live a better life than if my grandfather, father, and uncle had all been quaestors.

(*Satires* I.6.111–131)

These two passages exemplify Horace's ability to create character and setting with a few deft strokes. Horace's father, limned in this short passage and one other of comparable scope (I.4.103–126), is as vividly evoked as many a character from a full-length novel. More important, however, is what these and similar passages tell us about Horace himself. For of all the portraits we get in *Satires* I, the most important, and by far the most fascinating, is of the poet himself. In II.1.30–34, Horace praises Lucilius because "he used to entrust all his secrets to his books as if to faithful companions. . . . Thus it happens that the whole life of the old man is laid open, as if pictured on a votive tablet." Perhaps Horace's most significant debt to Lucilius is that the same words well describe the way Horace's personality comes across in his satires. It is this quality of *Satires* I, even more than its chronological precedence, that makes it the ideal starting point for reading Horace.

A striking feature of the Horace we encounter in *Satires* I is his emphasis on simplicity. The theme runs throughout Horace's verse, and again one suspects the influence of his father. One meets this theme in the contrast between Horace's simple, satisfied life in I.6.111 ff. and the frantic, complex, unsatisfied lives of most other denizens of *Satires* I; one meets the same theme in many of the subsequent poems to Maecenas, where a contrast between Horace's and Maecenas' differing life-styles becomes almost a commonplace; and one meets it especially in the many poems where Horace celebrates the simple, satisfying joys of his Sabine farm.

A corollary to Horace's emphasis on simplicity is his emphasis on distinguishing what is important from what is not. Addressing those who seem unable to use or to enjoy their wealth, Horace writes, "Don't you know what money's for, what end it serves? One can buy bread, greens, a spot of wine . . ." (I.1.73–74). A bit later he adds, "Finally, let there be an end of seeking, and when you have more, may you fear poverty less and begin to end your labors, having attained what you desired" (I.1.92–94). The description of his introduction to Maecenas again stresses what is important as against what is not: what Maecenas values, and what both Horace and his supporters emphasize, is what a person is, not how much he possesses or who his parents are (I.6.54–64).

A second corollary to the basic thrust toward simplicity is a reliance on solid common sense, and it is this same common sense, perhaps more than any philosophical stance, that leads Horace to another central emphasis—avoidance of extremes (again one suspects the influence of his father, whose terse injunctions, quoted toward the end of I.4, tend to focus on extreme instances). Horace writes at I.1.106–107, "There is measure in things; there are, finally, certain boundaries beyond or this side of which the right cannot stand." The same sense of balance and proportion, the same avoidance of extremes (see his familiar phrase, *aurea mediocritas*, "the golden mean": *Odes* II.10.5), are evident also in Horace's life-style as described in I.6.111 ff. His simplicity has place for style and elegance and lacks any suspicion of stinginess or of cynic shabbiness. His daily regimen has a certain rhythm but is devoid of rigidity; there is room for the play of fancy, for leisure as well as for work.

The same balance shapes Horace's attitude toward human foibles. For one thing, he is able to see his own flaws as clearly as he can those of others. His encounter with the bore, for instance, pokes as much fun at himself as it does at his adversary; in I.3.63 ff. he refers with charming candor to his habit of troubling Maecenas with trivia at the most inopportune moments; and in I.4.138 ff. he mentions his penchant for dabbling at verse as one of several minor flaws that good friends will perhaps pardon! Moreover, the Horace who expects this forbearance from his friends is ready to tolerate the foibles of others. The whole of I.3 is, in fact, a deeply felt, if thoroughly amusing, essay on the importance of balancing one's own faults against those of others, of matching censure to flaw and punishment to crime in a reasonable fashion, of putting others' failings into the best, rather than the worst, possible light.

Horace's balanced tolerance determines, in turn, the type of satire he writes. He has a keen eye for human folly and an infallible instinct for holding it up, in its manifold guises, to the ridicule it deserves; but his satiric wit always, at least implicitly, includes himself among its targets. Horace characteristically laughs with the world rather than at it. This is satire lacking in bitterness or malice, thoroughly different in tone from the satire of a Juvenal or a Swift. The same difference in tone separates Horatian from Lucilian satire. Of Lucilius, Horace writes, "He rubbed down the city with much salt" (I.10.3–4), and the substantial remains of Lucilius seem fully to justify the phrase. Horace, even at his most Lucilian, as in I.2, writes satire that is milder, more controlled, more compassionate.

Behind the gentle, tolerant irony of the *Satires* lies another quality that sets Horace apart from most other satirists—his ever-present humanity. Horace, as the *Satires* abundantly document, is a people watcher, a person who, like his father, enjoys observing others, noting their distinctive traits, becoming acquainted with the limitless variety of the human species, searching out the inner forces that make people act the way they do. Horace's absorbing interest in people finds expression both in the entrancing cast that appears in the *Satires* and also in the depth of affection that radiates from these poems—affection for his father, for instance, for Vergil and Varius and other literary friends, for his patron Maecenas. Strong attachment to his friends (and they were apparently many) is, like the emphasis on simplicity, a thread that runs throughout Horace's poetry, further evidence of Horace's ability to distinguish what is really important; the same capacity for friendship is yet another quality that sets Horace apart from the misanthropic thrust of much satire.

If *Satires* I is the ideal place to meet Horace the man, it is also a good place to meet Horace the artist. Like all the Augustan writers, Horace is a highly self-conscious artist, and his poems, like theirs, frequently focus on poetry. *Satires* I.4 and I.10 deal primarily with his conception of satire, and Horace the writer seems implicit also in those other poems where Horace the man is on stage: for instance, I.5, I.6, and I.9. Already very much present in his statements on satire is the characteristic emphasis on craftsmanship, that theme which is so basic to his two collections of odes, and which finds explicit and extended expression in the literary essays of *Epistles* II. This theme emerges especially in Horace's comparison of himself with Lucilius, a comparison in which he balances his own superior craft against Lucilius' superior passion and sweep, applying to Lucilius the same image of a powerful but uncontrolled torrent (I.4.11; see also I.10.50 and 62) that many years later he will use in comparing himself to Pindar (*Odes* IV.4.2.5–12).

The artistry that Horace so stresses in I.4 and I.10 is abundantly present in the collection itself. Indeed, one of the many remarkable features of *Satires* I is that this collection, Horace's first published work, already displays the same immaculate artistry that will mold his later works. One of the most characteristic features of this artistry is its unobtrusiveness: this is art that hides art. The colloquial, seemingly improvisatory flow of these "chats" is such that one scarcely notices, for instance, the virtuosity with which Horace manipulates the hexameter, giving it epic sweep at one moment, oracular pomposity at another, conversational choppiness at yet another, often in rapid alternation. One is still less likely to notice the larger structures that undergird these seemingly rambling poems. In I.6, for instance, the opening forty-four lines balance the concluding forty-three (lines 89–131), with Horace in both sections contrasting his attitudes and concerns with those of the masses; in between these outside panels is the core of the poem, the passage, discussed earlier, in which Horace speaks first of his introduction to Maecenas, then of his father (lines 45–88), with the transition between these two key topics coming at the precise center of the poem (lines 65 ff.). The structure might seem the result of chance were it not that numerous details support it (for example, the Latin phrase *quas tibi, Tilli,* twenty-five lines from the end, finds a close counterpart in *quo tibi, Tilli,*

twenty-four lines from the beginning), and were it not that a similar structure—with variations, to be sure—shapes several other satires in the book. Furthermore, the shape of the book as a whole, with its opening triad of general satires, its central triad of poems focusing on Horace, and its third triad of story-satires, displays in macrocosm the same general pattern, with I.10, like the closing portions of several satires, recapitulating earlier themes. One even wonders if there may not be some parallel between Horace's ability to avoid extremes, to find the central issue, and his persistent tendency to place key themes and key works at central locations.[2]

Satires II, published some five years after *Satires* I, has a similarly tight structure, with the first four poems standing roughly parallel to the last four. Thus II.1, where Horace consults the lawyer Trebatius, balances II.5, where Horace consults the seer Tiresias; II.2, Ofellus' discourse on the virtues of plain living, finds realization in II.6, where Horace praises the joys of the simple life at his country estate; in II.3 Damasippus, a bankrupt merchant, repeats a Stoic sermon to Horace, whereas in II.7 Davus, one of Horace's slaves, makes the most of Saturnalian freedom of speech to deliver his own sermon to his master; and the gastronomic advice reported by Catius in II.4 balances Fundanius' account of a disastrous dinner party in II.8. As with *Satires* I, delights abound: the lighthearted banter of II.1 as Horace, apparently in more confident spirits than in I.4 and I.10, returns to the subject of satire; the many-directioned parody of II.3, the longest by far of Horace's satires, which not only pokes fun at Damasippus and Horace but also, in the very act of repeating the sermon of the Stoic philosopher Stertinius, aims numerous jabs at the philosopher himself; the profusion of detail and the virtuosity of treatment that make II.2, II.4, and II.8 endlessly amusing despite their seem-

---

[2]Horace places similar emphasis on central locations in the *Odes* and *Epodes*. For a fascinating discussion, see L. A. Moritz, "Some 'Central' Thoughts on Horace's *Odes*," *Classical Quarterly* 18:116–131 (1968).

ingly limited gastronomic focus; the stunning anachronisms of II.5, where Tiresias, in a strange sequel to the *Odyssey* (book 11), instructs Ulysses on how to rebuild his fortune through the Roman art of legacy hunting; the sharp jabs Horace aims at himself via Damasippus in II.3, Davus in II.7, leading at the end of both poems to the poet's wrath toward his outspoken interlocutor. Above all there is II.6, one of the loveliest poems in all of Horace, a truly perfect piece, which juxtaposes the simple joys of country life with the complex frustrations of life at Rome and which drives its point home with the tale of the country mouse and the city mouse. Typically Horatian is the fact that in the very next poem Davus ridicules as insincere his master's longing for the country (II.7.28–29), an ironic touch that in no way sullies the pure beauty of II.6 but that does confirm our suspicion that Horace, whose delight in wandering around Rome is manifest from many poems, is not all country mouse.

The twenty poems of *Epistles* I, published in or shortly after 20 B.C., resemble the *Satires* in form and character. There is somewhat less colloquial exuberance than in the *Satires*, but there is the same diversity of character and incident, the same vividness of description, the same keenness of humor (see, for example, *Epistles* I.1 and I.6, both among Horace's finest poems, and both bearing numerous resemblances to the *Satires*—including the characteristic humorous twist at their conclusions).

If the *Epistles* lack some of the raw energy of the *Satires*, they more than make up for this lack by their increased sense of personal involvement. Perhaps more than any other collection, *Epistles* I lets us into the heart of Horace. The Horace we find has the same love of simplicity, the same common sense, the same balanced tolerance, the same wide range of close friends as the Horace of the *Satires*, but the passage of time has brought a new melancholy. Horace sounds this note early in the book: "My age is not the same, nor is my mind" (I.1.4). The book ends with a reference to his age (I.20.26–28—note also the delightful self-

portrait that precedes these lines); and there are hints of the same preoccupation in a number of other poems (most notably, perhaps, at I.7.25–28 and I.14.32–36). Accompanying this melancholy are a new urgency and a heightened concern to set his spiritual house in order, notes that again are sounded early in the first poem (I.1.10–12, 20–26). Poem after poem finds Horace searching for answers to basic personal and moral questions. In I.2, for instance, he explores the moral lessons implicit in the *Iliad* and the *Odyssey*; in I.10 and I.14, two poems contrasting city with country life, and in I.11, I.12, and I.15, three letters to friends away from Rome, he consistently mingles discussion of external, physical matters with concern for the inner, spiritual realm. There is, accordingly, a philosophic cast to much of *Epistles* I. As in the *Satires*, however, Horace makes his points more by specifics than by generalities, and though he draws freely on many philosophic schools (even to the point of calling himself "a pig from Epicurus' herd" in I.4.16), he makes it clear that he is a disciple of no one school: "And lest you should ask under what leader, what hearth I find refuge, bound to the oaths of no one master, I am borne as guest wherever the storm takes me" (I.1.13–15).

The resolute independence that breathes from this last passage finds even fuller expression in what is perhaps the finest of all the *Epistles*, I. 7. In this poem Horace, with tact and humor but with absolute firmness, asserts his independence from Maecenas. He warmly expresses his gratitude toward his patron, but, with equal weight, he stresses that he must be his own man, even if this should mean giving up all he has received from Maecenas (see especially line 34). We do not know what called forth this remarkable poem. Problems of the client-patron relationship are clearly on Horace's mind also in I.17 and I.18, and it may well be that some actual tensions between Horace and Maecenas lie behind these poems and I.7. Whatever the motivation, I.7 remains a key document for understanding Horace. The poem is quintessentially Horatian in its indirection and delicacy and in its use of stories to make its point (four stories in ninety-eight lines—lines 14 ff., 29 ff., 40 ff., 46 ff., of which the last occupies most of the second half of the poem). The poem also suggests a strength of character, a firmness of resolve, a clarity of purpose that are often obscured by Horace's characteristic irony and self-depreciation. Above all, I.7 underscores a side of Horace that is easily overlooked—Horace the loner. Whether Horace is wandering around Rome (as in *Satires* I.6 and I.9), writing and rewriting at home (as in many passages of the *Satires* and *Epistles*), or confronting the sources of his inspiration (as in several odes—for instance, *Odes* II.19, III.4, III.25), he tends to be alone. Many and close friends he has, and he constantly turns to them; but he knows that as poet he is and must be alone. In *Epistles* I.7 Horace in effect confronts the necessity of this artistic independence. That somehow Maecenas understood and accepted Horace's pleas is evident from *Odes* IV.11, a later poem in which Horace expresses his abiding and deep friendship for his patron and does so without the references, so frequent in other Maecenas poems, to distinctions of wealth and class.[3]

Epistles I.7 is not alone in suggesting that the period of *Epistles* I was a time of inner turmoil for Horace. Beneath its humor, I.19 reflects Horace's considerable disappointment over the reception of *Odes* I–III, a disappointment that apparently led to Horace's temporary abandonment of lyric poetry in the years 23–17 B.C. We have already mentioned the melancholy awareness of time's passing that suffuses so much of the collection. A passage in I.8 suggests an even greater agitation of spirit:

> If he asks how I am doing, say that while threatening many and fine things I live neither rightly nor well—not because hail has bruised my vines or the summer heat has blighted my olives, nor because my cattle are sickening in the distant fields, but because, less healthy in mind than in body, I am willing to hear nothing, to learn nothing that might lighten my malady; I am offended by my faithful doctors, I am angry with my friends, because they try to protect me from my fatal lethargy; I pursue those things that have harmed me, I flee those that I believe will help me; fickle as the wind, I love Tibur when in Rome, Rome when in Tibur.
>
> (*Epistles* I.8.3–12)

The straightforward candor of passages like this, combined with a perfection of workmanship throughout that surpasses even what we find in the *Satires*, make *Epistles* I, perhaps Horace's least-known collection, one of his most affecting creations. It is, in addition, the work that comes chronologically between *Odes* I–III and *Odes* IV, and as such it is of the first importance to our understanding of Horace's artistic development.

It is clearly impossible to deal here with the intricacies of the lengthy epistles of *Epistles* II in more than the most cursory fashion. These three poems may lack Horace's characteristic terseness, but they are exceptionally rich in other characteristic Horatian qualities. All three abound in delightful anecdotes, pointed examples, and telling imagery, and all three have much to tell us of Horace the man as well as of Horace the poet. In II.1, to Augustus, we find not only Horace's fascinating discussion of the Roman prejudice against the New Literature (line 18 ff.), not only his noble account of the poet's contribution to society (line 124 ff.), not only his perceptive survey of Roman literary history (line 139 ff.), but also important glimpses into his relations with Augustus near the end of his life. *Epistles* II.2, addressed to the Florus of I.3 in response to Florus' complaint that Horace has failed to send some promised poetry, is another of Horace's fine, but littleknown works. Again there are shrewd comments on literature, most notably the description of the poet's calling, which begins at the center of the poem—line 109 (see also the central position accorded to the poet's role in the letter to Augustus). Above all, however, there

---

[3]Horace also at some point turned down, presumably for similar reasons, an invitation to become Augustus' private secretary; see Fraenkel, *Horace* 17–19.

are in II.2 a congenial informality, a directness and intimacy of tone. These qualities are apparent in every aspect of the poem, whether in its unusually rich fund of stories, its delightful and ironic account of how Horace first came to write poetry (line 49 ff.), or its similarly exaggerated explanation of why Horace, surrounded by the noisy helter-skelter of Rome, is unable to compose the promised poems. This peculiarly personal character finds its most affecting outlet in the final third of the poem, where Horace, with a seriousness that surprises after what has preceded and in a mood reminiscent of *Epistles* I, turns from literary to moral concerns.

In contrast to the Letter to Florus, the Letter to the Pisones (II.3), known since the time of Quintilian as the *Ars Poetica,* is among Horace's most familiar works. Its familiarity owes much, of course, to its great impact on authors from antiquity to the present, authors as diverse as St. Augustine, Peter Abelard, Dante, Ben Jonson, Nicolas Boileau-Despréaux, and Alexander Pope. (It caught the fancy even of Elizabeth I, who translated a portion of it into English.) The work itself comes across not as a formal treatise on poetry but as a series of jottings, colloquial in tone and seemingly digressive in character. One suspects that Horace might be amused to find that his rather pragmatic suggestions have so often been treated as rigid prescription. The letter is filled with important information, keen insights, and wise advice on various literary matters. It has contributed a remarkable number of familiar phrases to the language of literary criticism: *purpureus . . . pannus* ("purple patch": lines 15–16), *lucidus ordo* ("clear arrangement": line 41), *callida . . . iunctura* ("clever joining": lines 47–48), *in medias res* ("into the middle of things": line 148), *laudator temporis acti* ("praiser of time past": line 173), *bonus dormitat Homerus* ("good Homer nods": line 359), *ut pictura poesis* ("a poem is like a painting": line 361)—all come from the *Ars Poetica,* as do several equally familiar longer phrases (see lines 23, 309, 343).

In the end, however, the most memorable qualities of the poem may well lie on a more personal level. There are, for one thing, the characteristic Horatian vignettes, such as the thumbnail sketch of the successive stages of human life (line 158 ff.), the vivid evocation of the business-oriented education of a Roman youth (line 325 ff.), the exaggerated portrait of the mad poet (line 453 ff.). There are unforgettable images: the hybrid monster with human head, equine neck, diverse feathers and limbs, woman above and fish below, which Horace conjures up in his opening salvo against art that lacks unity; or, at the other end of the scale, the *ridiculus mus* whose monosyllabic, anticlimactic appearance at the end of a grandiloquent line parodies poems that open grandly but continue lamely: *parturient montes, nascetur ridiculus mus* ("the mountains will bring forth, there will be born a ridiculous mouse," line 139). Above all, in the *Ars Poetica,* as in all of the *Satires* and *Epistles,* there is Horace himself, for the characteristic emphases of this poem are precisely those that govern Horace's own poetry: appropriateness (the meter appropriate to the material, the matter appropriate to a particular writer, the words appropriate to a particular character); poetry as the fruit of both native talent and art (line 408 ff.); the necessary mixing of the pleasing *(dulce)* and the useful *(utile)* in poetry (line 343); good sense, wisdom *(sapere)* as the fountainhead of good writing (line 309); careful choice of subject matter, skillful arrangement, clever joining as keys to the art (line 38 ff.); hard work, candid criticism from impartial critics, ample time for revision and reconsideration (line 292 ff.; line 386 ff.); recognition that in art there is no place for mediocrity (line 372 ff.). These are the themes and principles that animate Horace's own poetry, and the ultimate fascination of the *Ars Poetica* is that it tells us as much about Horace the poet as it does about poetry in general. And what we find in the artist are the same qualities we found in the man: balanced judgment, keen sense of proportion and of what is really important, an understanding of the value of good friends, and an ability to laugh about even the most serious matters.[4]

HORATIAN PLAY: ODES I–III

Horace frequently speaks of his poetry in terms of play. Thus he writes of his *Satires*, "I play at these things" (*haec ego ludo:* I.10.37) and "I play with papers" (*illudo chartis:* I.4.139). He uses the same verb, *ludo,* of his lyric poetry in *Odes* I.32.1–2 when he says to his lyre, "If, in an idle moment under the shade, I've played anything with you . . ." (*si quid vacui sub umbra lusimus tecum*), and he uses the cognate words *ludus* and *ludicra* when he speaks in *Epistles* I.1.3 and 10 of giving up the frivolous play of lyric poetry.

Along the same lines he describes his poetry as *levis,* "light" (both in weight and in character, as in English *levity*), and as *tenuis,* "slender," "delicate," "refined"—perhaps "fine" with its connotations both of slimness and of excellence comes closest to capturing the meaning of the Latin. Both words suggest Horace's adherence to the ideal of a poetry that is slight in compass but exquisite in workmanship, an ideal associated especially with the Alexandrian poet Callimachus. Horace also speaks of composing poetry when he is "fancy-free," *vacuus* (as in the passage cited from *Odes* I.32); he describes his lyre as "jocose" (*iocosa: Odes* III.3.69) and his poetry as "trifles" (*nugae: Satires* I.9.2).

Why is it that a poet who obviously takes his art very seriously, and whose poems often deal with private and public themes of the utmost gravity, so characteristically associates his poetry with words that suggest lightness, unconcern, inconsequence, idle play? In part the an-

swer lies in the influence on Horace, as on so many Augustan poets, of the Callimachean tradition. In part also we must allow for Horace's characteristic irony: occasionally, for instance, he will mention the lightweight character of his verse only to contradict himself at the next moment (see, for example, the final stanza of *Odes* III.3, where his rejection of large themes immediately precedes the longest of all his odes). More significant, however, is the simple fact that, on one level, at least, Horace *does* approach poetry as play, as something to toy with, to toss about in one's idle moments, as an all-absorbing game.

Nowhere is this spirit more manifest than in the great lyric collection *Odes* I–III, eighty-eight poems in all, which Horace published in 23 B.C. One sees Horace's playfulness at every level of this collection, be it verbal, metrical, structural, or thematic. He loves, for one thing, to play with word order. In I.6.9, for instance, he juxtaposes at the precise center of the line the two words that suggest on the one hand the lightness of his poetry and on the other the grandeur of epic subject matter (which Horace is rejecting for himself): *tenues grandia.* Similar oxymora abound: *simplex munditiis* ("simple in elegance," I.5.5) and *splendide mendax* ("splendidly untruthful," III.11.35) are only the most famous examples. Another typical, but more complex, example of Horace's verbal play, again almost impossible to reproduce in English, is the opening line of Horace's famous ode to Pyrrha, where the very word order mirrors the situation:

> *quis multa gracilis te puer in rosa* (. . . *urget*)
> "What slender boy, amidst many a rose (presses upon) you?"
>
> (*Odes* I.5)

Both in the scene and in the language, the girl (*te*) is enclosed by the slender boy (*gracilis . . . puer*) and he, in turn, by the many roses (*multa . . . rosa*). Characteristic also is Horace's sheer virtuosity with sounds: thus a profusion of liq-

---

[4]Several scholars have persuasively suggested that the *Ars Poetica* comes at the end of Horace's life, ca. 10–8 B.C., at a time when he is no longer writing lyric poetry (see line 306, *nil scribens ipse*—"writing nothing myself"). If so, it represents in effect a retrospective summary that draws on a lifetime of poetic activity.

uid sounds suggests the plash of water at the end of III.13; sibilants mimic the buzz of whispered nighttime conversations in I.9.18–20; and harsh guttural sounds, reinforced by alliteration and anaphora, underscore the bitter message of II.14.13–16.

Equally evident is Horace's delight in playing with different Greek meters. One of his proudest claims, made explicit in the final lines of *Odes* I–III and implicit in several other poems (see especially *Epistles* I.19.21–33), is that he first adapted Greek lyric meters to Latin poetry. The boast needs qualification, of course: Catullus had written two poems in the Sapphic stanza. But in its broad outlines it is justified: no previous Latin poet had handled so many Greek lyric meters with such dexterity. In *Odes* I–III alone, Horace uses twelve different meters, though seven—the Alcaic stanza, the Sapphic stanza, and the five forms of Asclepiad meter—account for the great majority of the eighty-eight poems. Horace's delight in his metrical prowess is everywhere apparent, whether in the parade of different meters with which *Odes* I opens (ten different meters in the first eleven poems); in the alternation of Alcaic and Sapphic in the first eleven poems of *Odes* II (an alternation set up by the last two poems of *Odes* I and broken by the change to an Asclepiad meter in II.12); in the exclusive use of Alcaics for the six great national poems (the Roman Odes) that begin *Odes* III (a pattern again set up by the last two poems of the previous book and broken by the Asclepiad meter of III.7); or in the use of the first Asclepiad for only two poems, the first and the last of the collection, both dealing with Horace's own poetry.[5]

If Horace's metrical play, like much of his verbal play, is largely lost in translation, his grouping of poems by metrical considerations suggests a type of *structural* play that can survive translation. Horace begins each of his three books of the *Odes* with a major group of poems. *Odes* I opens with the so-called Parade Odes, twelve poems[6] that parade not only the characteristic meters but also the characteristic themes and genres of the collection. *Odes* III opens with the Roman Odes, six long and serious poems all in the same meter, a phenomenon unique in the collection. And *Odes* II opens with a group of twelve poems not only thematically related to each other in a complex symmetrical pattern but that also alternate Alcaic and Sapphic meter in II.1 through II.11, and have similar lengths (twenty-four or twenty-eight lines) in II.2 through II.12 (phenomena again without parallel in the collection). Complementing the internal symmetry of II.1–12, and emphasizing their thematic centrality in the collection, is the fact that this group comes at the precise center of the three books, with thirty-eight poems on either side (the thirty-eight of *Odes* I on one side, the eight remaining of *Odes* II plus the thirty of *Odes* III on the other). Along the same lines, I.1 and III.30, the outside poems of the collection, balance each other in various ways, as do I.2 and III.29, the poems standing second from the beginning and second from the end, respectively.

A concern for structure is equally apparent in Horace's shaping of individual poems, as one brief example will suggest. *Odes* I.17 is one of Horace's loveliest poems, a celebration alike of rural peace, of gentle love, and of poetry. The following translation merely renders the literal meaning.

> Often swift Faunus leaves [Arcadian] Lycaeus for [Sabine] Lucretilis, and ever he protects my goats from the fiery summer and the rainy winds.
> Without harm through the safe groves the wandering mates of the smelly lord seek the hiding arbutus and the thyme, and the kids fear neither green snakes
> nor the wolves of Mars, whenever, Tyndaris, the valleys and the smooth rocks of the sloping Sabine hills have sounded with his sweet panpipes.
> The gods protect me; my piety and my Muse are close to their hearts. Here for you will pour forth

---

[5]The only other poem in this meter is IV.8, the central poem of *Odes* IV and, like I.1 and III.30, on the theme of poetry.

[6]The Parade Odes are often referred to as the first *eleven* poems, but the set is really rounded off by I.12.

from the horn of plenty a rich abundance of the blessings of the land.

Here in a hidden valley you will avoid the heat of the Dog Star, and on Teian lyre you will tell of Penelope and glittering Circe striving for the same man.

Here you will drink cups of harmless Lesbian wine under the shade, nor will Semele's son Bacchus join battle with Mars nor, suspected, will you fear headstrong

Cyrus, lest he cast incontinent hands on you, scarcely his equal, and tear your undeserving dress and the crown that clings to your hair.

(*Odes* I.17)

In form this poem is an invitation to Tyndaris to come to Horace's farm. The first three stanzas (lines 1-12) describe how the rural divinity Faunus visits the locale each year, bringing relief from the heat, safety from wolves and snakes, and the sweet music of his pipe. The final three stanzas (lines 17-28) closely parallel this opening section: at Horace's villa Tyndaris will find relief from the heat, refuge from violence and danger, and music. The correspondences go beyond a mere thematic balance: thus Faunus warding off the fiery summer (*aestatem:* line 3) parallels Tyndaris avoiding the heat (*aestus:* line 18); the goats feeding without danger in the groves (lines 5-7) balance Tyndaris' drinking harmless wine in the shade (lines 21-22); and *nec . . . metuunt* ("nor do they fear," line 8) precisely parallels *nec metues* ("nor will you fear," line 24). In the central stanza, lines 13-16, Horace focuses on poetry. It is song that binds Faunus, Tyndaris, and Horace together, song that offers the real haven from the heat and violence of the world. It is accordingly fitting that poetry occupies the central, innermost place in the poem, that music is first introduced as we approach this "inner sanctum" (lines 10-12), and that the theme of song flows out from this central core into the first stanza to Tyndaris (lines 17-20). Horace's real invitation is to the land of poetry, and I.17 is but one of many poems in which the real landscape of his Sabine farm merges with the ideal landscape associated with poetry.

The same type of structure shapes many other poems also, with a central theme often occupying a central position and the outside portions balancing each other (for good examples, see I.6 and I.22; on a larger scale, III.4 and III.29). The similarity of this form to the larger structure of the whole collection, in which balancing outside sections of thirty-eight poems each enclose a central core, itself concentrically organized (II.1-12), is obvious; and we have already seen in *Satires* I a foreshadowing of this same sort of structural play. This is not to suggest, of course, that all of Horace's poems follow this one pattern; other patterns abound, and one of the delights of reading Horace, whether in Latin or in translation, lies in discovering how consistently, but with what variety, he unites form and content.

Also capable of surviving translation is the play of image and motif, as brief reference to four of Horace's most famous odes will suggest. We have already mentioned the verbal acrobatics with which I.5, the ode to Pyrrha, begins. Equally dazzling is the poem's *ludus* of imagery and motifs. There is, on the most obvious level, the sustained comparison of Pyrrha to the sea, a comparison that certainly lends her a touch of Venus, the sea-born goddess. But if Pyrrha is the sea—dark, glooming, harsh—she is also fire: her very name is etymologically connected with fire, and she herself is blond, golden, glittering. The whole poem can, in fact, be seen as an extended interplay of dark moisture on the one side, glittering brightness on the other, an interplay perhaps foreshadowed in the contrast of the bright roses with the dark grotto in stanza one. Above all hovers Pyrrha herself, mediator of opposites, *simplex munditiis, tenuis,* an incarnation of Horatian play.

Liquid imagery is central also in the famous ode to Postumus, *Eheu fugaces* (II.14). The image, introduced indirectly in the *labuntur* (slip by) of line 2, becomes explicit in the second and third stanzas in the underworld waters that all must sail. The motif is picked up in the fourth stanza by the broken waves of the Adriatic and again in the fifth by the waters of the underworld (along with a glancing reference to the Danaids, whose punishment was forever to carry water in leaky vessels). The motif is absent from the sixth stanza but returns, in a striking metamorphosis, in the final stanza: the wine that the previous owner has preserved under lock and key will be spilled recklessly on the pavement by his profligate heir.

Yet another famous ode, *O fons Bandusiae* (III.13), works further variations on liquid imagery as we move from the clear spring and sweet wine of the first stanza through the warm blood staining the waters in the second to the chattering waters of the final lines. As in the Pyrrha ode, Horace plays effectively also with various binary oppositions: the clear, glassy waters of the spring against the dark, pulsing blood of the kid; the burgeoning, lusty life of the young animal against the impersonal immortality afforded by poetry; cold versus hot, animate versus inanimate, life versus death.

Similar oppositions shape also the familiar Soracte ode, *Vides ut alta* (I.9). If again we consider only the most obvious examples, we find, both in nature and in human existence, death against life, white against green,[7] cold against warmth, rigidity against movement, constraint against freedom. The wintry images of the first stanza, bright, distant, frozen, find their response not only in the warm fire of the second stanza but also in the summertime scenes of the final lines—dark, intimate, supple; and the poem itself, slight in compass but vivid, taut, vigorous, is as much Horace's response to the human condition as is the explicit message that begins at line 9.

Nor is Horace's playfulness in *Odes* I–III limited to the technical areas—language, meter, structure, imagery—so far discussed. A similar instinct is manifest also in the collection's virtuosic profusion of themes and genres, a variety scarcely surprising coming as it does from the author of the *Satires*. The collection

begins and ends with poems about poetry, and a number of the intervening poems also focus on Horace's own art. We have already mentioned I.6 and I.32, two poems that articulate Horace's artistic credo. Of great interest also are II.19 and III.25, which associate Horace and his verse with the awesome power of Dionysus, and II.20, which describes Horace's poetic immortality in grotesquely literal (and no doubt ironic) terms of his transformation into a swan. The collection contains also a number of odes addressed to divinities: I.10 and III.11 to Mercury; I.21 to Apollo and Diana; I.30 to Venus; I.31 to Apollo; I.35 to Fortune. Several such odes to divinities touch more or less directly upon Augustus and his regime, thus complementing and extending another major group of poems, those dealing with national themes. Thus I.21 appeals to Apollo, and I.35 to Fortune for protection of Augustus and his people; I.31 celebrates Augustus' dedication of a splendid new temple to Apollo; and Horace's prayers to various divinities in I.2 climax in Augustus himself. Other poems focusing on national themes include an impressive Pindaric ode on Augustus, I.12; the famous "ship of state" and Cleopatra odes, I.14 and I.37; a charming ode celebrating Augustus' return from Spain, III.14; and above all, the Roman Odes, III.1–6, a magnificent set that explores the soul of Rome in the early years of Augustus' principate by means of a complex weave of past and present, myth and reality, public and personal.

A far larger group of poems deals with more private themes. Several focus squarely on human mortality (for example, I.4, I.24, I.28, and especially II.13 and II.14), and death looms large in a surprising number of other poems. Horace, however, not only stresses our mortality; he also articulates in poem after poem his response to human limitations. Several odes urge a course familiar from the *Satires* and *Epistles*: moderation, simplicity, satisfaction with what one has or is (for example, I.38, II.2, II.10, II.16, II.18, III.23, III.29). An even more characteristic response is *carpe diem*, "pluck the day"—make the most of today for who

[7]Note especially the oxymoron *virenti canities* of line 17, where the green *(virenti)* and white *(canities)* of nature are applied to human existence.

knows what tomorrow will bring. The famous phrase itself comes from I.11, and the theme is focal in numerous other odes (for example, I.9, II.3, II.11, III.28) and implicit in many others. "Plucking the day" almost invariably entails wine and love, and the *carpe diem* poems thus overlap at many points with two other large groups of personal poems—drinking songs and love songs (examples of both types are ubiquitous). Even here our catalog is not complete: we have said nothing of the two extended mythological pieces (I.15 and III.27), nothing of the numerous personal poems that spring from some particular occasion—the return, departure, death of some friend (as in, respectively, I.36, I.3, I.24). And we have but suggested the huge cast of characters—real and fictitious—that Horace brings on stage in *Odes* I–III and have but alluded in passing to the charming and endlessly varied pictures of the natural world that provide the backdrop for so many poems.

The Parade Odes of *Odes* I nicely exemplify these last sorts of variety. The addressees in the first six odes are, respectively, Maecenas, Augustus, Vergil, Sestius (consul in the year of the collection's publication), Pyrrha (!), and Agrippa; and among the vivid natural scenes painted in these same odes are flood and storm in I.2, sea in I.3 and I.5, winter and spring in I.4. These same Parade Odes, which proclaim the metrical variety of the collection, also foreshadow virtually all of its many thematic foci: thus I.1 and I.6 introduce the poems on poetry, I.2 and I.10 the poems to divinities, I.2 and I.12 the national poems; I.4 foreshadows the many poems focusing on death, I.3 the many recommending moderation (and, simultaneously, the many poems to close friends), I.9 and I.11 the many *carpe diem* poems; I.5 and I.8 are the first of many love poems, I.7 the first of many drinking songs.

Equally striking is Horace's playful manipulation of these varied materials. Genres that might seem mutually exclusive interpenetrate: national poems receive a highly personal twist, private poems a public touch; a seemingly light poem suddenly darkens, a poem that starts out as lofty praise of moral integrity turns into a light and somewhat ironic love poem. In addition, Horace imbues each of his recurrent types with infinite variety. Thus one drinking song urges moderation (I.27), another drunken abandon (III.19); one poem sets human mortality against a backdrop of spring (I.4), another of winter (I.9); national odes view Augustan Rome now with joy (I.37), now with alarm (III.6); and the collection's assortment of love poems explores the entire range of the genre: rivalry (III.20), separation (III.7), jealousy (I.13), the excluded lover (III.10), the bereaved lover (II.9), the infatuated girl (III.12), the infatuated man (I.19), girls too young (I.23 and II.5), women too old (I.25 and III.15), quarrel and reconciliation (III.9), escape and reentry (III.26). Horace seems unable to touch a familiar theme or genre without playing with it; even a tree that nearly killed him by its fall becomes the excuse for variation (see II.13.1 ff., II.17.27 ff., III.4.27, III.8.6 ff.). One is reminded of the comment of the composer Anton Webern, another master of the *tenuis*, on the Parthenon frieze: "Always the same, but in a thousand different manifestations."[8]

Moreover, the same instinct toward constant variation leads Horace to arrange his poems in such a way that love poems rub elbows with national odes, hymns to gods and goddesses with drinking songs, slight, light poems with lengthy mythological excursions, joyful poems celebrating life with sorrowful poems lamenting mortality, humorous poems to unknown or fictitious acquaintances with serious poems to the heads of state.

Our focus thus far has been on various forms of Horatian play. Three points need to be stressed at this time. First, the Horace who composes this Pyrrha-like collection of diverse materials is obviously akin to the Horace we met in the *Satires*: a man fascinated with the complexities of the human race, its variety of types, its gamut of pleasures and pastimes and pas-

[8]A. Webern, *Briefe an Hildegarde Jone und Josef Humplik*, edited by J. Polnauer (Vienna, 1959), p. 21.

sions; a man also with an uncanny sense of balance, a persistent inclination to see issues and persons from both sides, and an ironic tendency to stand back and laugh at anyone, himself included, who takes himself too seriously. Second, just as the colloquial, improvisatory character of the *Satires* masks a tight structure underneath, so the seemingly random collocations of *Odes* I-III are in fact carefully controlled. *Odes* I-III combine many contrasting themes and genres, often in striking juxtaposition, but the play is purposeful, the end result in no way similar to the hybrid creatures, the products of caprice and desperation, that Horace castigates at the start of the *Ars Poetica*. Third, common to these several varieties of Horatian play is an inclination to match opposites, be it in the oxymoron so common in the language, in the counterpoint of contrasting motifs, or in the juxtaposing of poems of differing character. This fascination with the play of opposites becomes almost a controlling principle in the construction of Horace's verse, a type of play that can be deeply serious and expressive in effect and that often provides the means of shaping both individual poems and groups of poems.

A striking early example is epode 2. The first sixty-six lines describe the joys of country life vividly and in great detail, and one naturally assumes that the poem is another expression of Horace's own love of simple, rural life. The final four lines reveal, however, that this whole opening section has been a speech and that the speaker all along has been not Horace but a Roman moneylender named Alfius. Moreover, Alfius' rural idyll proves to be but words, words, words: having taken in his loans on the Ides in preparation for a move to the country, by the following Kalends (a couple of weeks later) Alfius has decided to remain in Rome and is engaged in lending his money out again.

This conclusion is more than a clever surprise ending. Not only is the praise of the country undercut and the true speaker revealed, but the whole poem suddenly takes on a satiric cast.

Looking back over the first sixty-six lines we now see things we missed the first time through: we notice, for instance, that Alfius, moneylender that he is, speaks of freedom from moncylending as among the first advantages of country life (line 4); and we now perceive that Alfius' whole picture of country life is slightly overdone, an idealized daydream that betrays a city-bound misunderstanding of what farm life is all about. The effect is kaleidoscopic: a quick shake makes us see the same materials in a new configuration, from an entirely different perspective.

This technique, common throughout Horace, is especially characteristic of *Odes* I-III. Horace's famous ode to Cleopatra (I.37) is a splendid example. From an opening filled with nigh-ecstatic joy over the final defeat of the queen and her diabolical, demented schemes (lines 1–17), Horace moves, via two somewhat ambivalent similes (lines 17–20), to a concluding three-stanza description of the queen's death. These final stanzas, filled with appreciation and even admiration for Cleopatra's courage in defeat, pull strongly against the opening seventeen lines, and this sharp tension is what makes the poem so powerful. Our reaction to each section is colored by our reaction to the other, and the total emotional impact, itself largely the product of this very tension of opposites, far exceeds the mere sum of the emotional contents of the component parts. Typically Horatian also is the perfect balance between this *thematic* disjunction, which pushes these two sections apart, and the poem's *artistic* unity, which holds them together, largely through a series of motifs sounded in the first section and picked up in the last (especially the motif of drinking, emphasized throughout the first half of the poem and effectively recalled in the queen's drinking of the poison in lines 27–28).

Similar in construction is I.2, which opens with the omens that signal Rome's agony—lightning, storm, hail, flood (lines 1–20)—but concludes with the divinities who have the power to rescue the state (lines 30–52, with 21–

30 serving as transition). Again, much of the impact resides in the balanced tension between contrasting masses: the dark, unnatural, twisted portents of lines 1–20 against the radiant Apollo, Venus, Mercury, and Augustus of lines 30–52; revenge turned inward in the first part, outward in the second; a universe in chaos in the first part, in order in the second. Again, either part would be effective in itself, but typically Horatian is the creation of the poem out of the balanced opposition of the two.

Similar balances characterize many other poems in *Odes* I–III. In I.4, for instance, the ever-recurring springtime of nature (lines 1–8) is set against the one springtime of human life (lines 13–20, with lines 9–12, the center of the poem, serving as pivot or fulcrum). In II.14 the sarcasm of the final stanza provides a jarring perspective on the melancholy of the first twenty-four lines. In III.9 boy is set against girl, new love against old, flirtatious play against true affection, with the antiphonal structure of the poem perfectly articulating the play of opposites. And in I.22, the famous *Integer vitae*, the first eight lines, a high-sounding assertion of the inviolability of moral virtue, prove to be but the prelude to a love song about Lalage ("Chatterbox"); the true source of the speaker's inviolability is his song, and the poem, like the Tyndaris and Bandusia odes (I.17 and III.13), turns out to be concerned above all with poetry.

The complexities of *Integer vitae* lead us to those poems where Horace shakes the kaleidoscope not once but several times. *Odes* I.3, for instance, opens as an impassioned prayer for the safety of Vergil, who is setting out on a sea voyage (lines 1–8), moves abruptly to twelve lines expressing admiration for those courageous enough to brave the seas (lines 9–20), and concludes with twenty lines that place seamanship in a very different light, as one of the many activities through which man, by pushing beyond his natural bounds, brings on himself the wrath of the gods (with, however, the hint of admiration in lines 34–37). The poem's rapid, jerky progression from love and concern for

Vergil to pride in human courage to despair over *hybris* is admittedly puzzling, especially on a first reading; but this very progression by its jagged contradictions projects Horace's ambivalent reaction to Vergil's departure, an ambivalence that remains unaffected whether we view Vergil's voyage as an actual trip, as symbolic of human striving in general, or, as some have suggested, as Vergil's embarkation on the new and dangerous waters of the *Aeneid*.

Odes II.1, addressed to another author, Pollio, contains a similarly complex array of moods. Pollio is at the time writing a history of the Roman civil wars, and Horace begins his ode by praising the skill, courage, and knowledge that Pollio brings to this task (lines 1–8) and by mentioning Pollio's accomplishments in other areas (lines 9–16). Praise of Pollio's ability to evoke the sights and sounds of war (lines 17–24; again, the central stanzas serve as fulcrum) leads, however, to a very different mood as Horace recalls the horrors of civil war, the lust for revenge, the fields enriched with Latin blood, the rivers and seas discolored by carnage (lines 25–36). Then, as if to reject scenes he no longer can bear, Horace concludes with a jaunty rejection of all such weighty subjects, a typically playful appeal to his Muse to seek measures of lighter (*leviore*) character (lines 37–40). The poem is one of Horace's most powerful, and its power comes in large part from those very shifts that on one level are instances of Horatian play: thus mention of Pollio's descriptive powers suddenly, mysteriously unlocks a whole well of deep feelings, and the light ending underlines the dark horror of the lines that precede it and suggests Horace's depth of revulsion.

Equally meteoric in its shifts is II.13, in which Horace, by turns, recalls with mock rage his narrow escape from the infamous falling tree (lines 1–12), reflects more seriously on the fragility of human life (lines 13–20), and comments on how narrowly he himself missed going to Hades (lines 21–40). In this final section, however, Horace's initial horror rapidly shifts to something approaching fascination as he imagines, almost as if he wishes he were there, what he would have seen in the underworld—Sappho and Alcaeus singing their poetry.

As we have mentioned, Horace's arrangement of poems frequently displays a similarly mercurial play of opposites. Thus the delicate and minuscule I.38 stands between the emotionally complex and profound Cleopatra ode (I.37) and the Pollio ode (II.1). The grandiose I.12 celebrating Augustus is enclosed by two short, highly personal poems, an arrangement echoed in the enclosing of I.35, the long ode to Fortune, by the shorter personal poems I.34 and I.36. And the frivolous ode to Asterie (III.7) follows the six Roman Odes, a placement rendered the more jarring by the fact that the final Roman Ode, III.6, is the darkest of the set.[9] *Odes* II.13, Horace's whimsical, half-humorous musings on his near-death, immediately precedes II.14, one of his most serious poems on death; and III.29, in which Horace emphasizes his lowly estate and his human limitations, immediately precedes III.30, in which he praises the almost regal power of his own poetry and predicts his own immortality.

Furthermore, just as individual poems frequently involve the interplay of not just two but several contrasting themes, so the larger groupings also progress far beyond simply binary oppositions. *Odes* II.1–12, for instance, the group that stands at the precise center of the whole collection, is clearly organized by symmetrically balanced pairs, but the thematic links and contrasts between the balanced members point in many different directions: II.1 balances II.12, the former a highly serious poem to Pollio (who, as mentioned, is composing a history of the devastating civil wars), the latter a light poem to Maecenas (who is composing a history of Au-

gustus' recent triumphs); in II.1 Horace progresses from Pollio's history to the actual agonies of the wars, whereas in II.12 he progresses from Maecenas' history to the flirtatious delights awaiting Maecenas in the arms of Licymnia. *Odes* II.2 and II.10 urge philosophic control and acceptance, but II.3 and II.11, their paired (and motivically related) companion pieces, present more anguished, active, and even rebellious responses to human limitations (see especially II.3.9 ff.; II.11.13 ff.). *Odes* II.4–5 and 8–9 are all love poems, but whereas 4 and 5 look ahead to future joys, 8 and 9 recall past frustration and loss. *Odes* II.4 deals with a lovely and naive girl who is wrongly suspected on grounds of lowly birth; II.8, with a girl, far from naive, who somehow escapes the retribution she so deserves. *Odes* II.5 predicts ripening love and future union; II.9 deals with the anguish of lost love. The same chiaroscuro of joy and sorrow, of past and future, that animates these other pairs of II.1–12 is present also in II.6–7, the pair at the midpoint of both the set and the collection. Both poems deal with deeply felt friendship; the fact that both end with the word *amicus*, "friend," further underscores the centrality of friendship in Horace's poetry and his life. But whereas II.6 looks ahead to the future and to the hope of a peaceful old age, and ends in the separation of death, II.7 looks back to the past and to escape miraculously won in wartime, and ends in the pleasures of shared drinking.

What must again be emphasized about II.1–12 is that this ubiquitous play of opposites is not merely art for art's sake: the impact and significance both of the set as a whole and of the individual poems owe much to that very play. Thus, II.8 is more than just a poem to a hussy precisely because, like I.5, it evokes both the danger and the infuriating, irresistible charm of the girl; II.6 derives much of its power from the tension between anticipation of peaceful old age and anticipation of death; II.3 moves us because of its powerful juxtaposition of the ecstasy of life and the bleakness of death. Similarly the philosophical poems II.2–3 and II.10–

[9]Typically, however, Horace balances the *tonal* gulf between III.6 and III.7 by various motivic ties, of which the theme of sexual fidelity (and infidelity) is only the most obvious. Compare the way the motif of drinking binds the slight I.38 to the weighty I.37, with the last word of I.38, *bibentem*, "drinking," picking up the *nunc est bibendum*, "now is the time to drink," with which I. 37 begins.

11 gain in gravity by their juxtaposition with the erotic poems II.4–5 and II.8–9; the moderation urged in II.2 and 10 and the *carpe diem* course urged in II.3 and 11 set each other off; the seriousness of II.1 is underscored not only by the levity of its own final lines but also by that of its structural counterpart in the set, II.12; and, via a typically Horatian counterpoint, we move from the public themes of II.1 to the intimacy of the central pair, II.6–7, and thence back to the public themes of II.12.9 ff.

Similar, and similarly complex, thematic oppositions also characterize Horace's great set of national poems, the Roman Odes of *Odes* III. For one thing, Horace again constantly interweaves private and public themes. Thus III.1 moves from its hieratic opening, all-inclusive in compass, to a highly personal close; III.2 from public, military *virtus* in the first half to more inner forms of *virtus* in the second (and again to a very personal close). *Odes* III.3 begins with the individual and with inner virtue but broadens out into national concerns with Juno's epic-style speech, only to end in Horace's rejection of all such high-flying themes (compare the end of II.1). The progress of III.4 is similar: the individual and his inviolability at the start, an excursion into national and epic themes in the second half. *Odes* III.5 sings of Regulus, a hero of the First Punic War, but it celebrates less his military achievements than his inner courage and integrity; and again, as in III.1 and III.2, a personal, falling close balances a grandiose opening. *Odes* III.6, with its pessimistic portrayal of moral deterioration in contemporary Rome, throughout mixes public concerns with private, making clear what is everywhere implicit in the set: individual integrity is the presupposition of national success. The Roman Odes represent perhaps the peak of Horace's national poetry, but one of their most memorable features, one that renders them affecting two millennia after Augustan Rome, is this constant weaving of personal, inner themes into a fabric of national celebration.

Another thematic tension in the Roman Odes and the national poems in general arises from Horace's own response to Augustus and his new regime. There is every reason to believe that Horace saw Augustus' principate as a necessary and welcome step toward ending the horrors of a century of civil war, and the gratitude he voices for this accomplishment rings true. There is also reason to believe that Horace saw in Augustus at least the potential for unthinking violence, for unrestrained exercise of power, and that Horace, like Vergil, found this side of Augustus deeply troubling. Something of this concern comes out in the opposition just mentioned, that between personal, inner morality on the one hand and external, military accomplishment on the other.

This central ambivalence comes out even more clearly in what is Horace's longest and perhaps greatest national ode, III.4. The ode, yet another example of Horace's penchant for building a poem around the pull of opposites, not only balances the personal focus of the first half against the public focus of the second half, but also poses the predominantly peaceful thrust of the first half against the prevailing violence of the second. Lines 1–36 give us Horace the poet wandering in sacred groves, the baby Horace wreathed by the Muses while he sleeps, Horace protected from harm (be it snakes, war, or the falling tree), and Horace safe from savagery, no matter where he ventures—all thanks to the Muses. It is, of course, the theme of *Integer vitae* again, here, as there, not without irony and playful exaggeration. Lines 42–80 give us Typhoeus and Mimas, Porphyrion and Rhoetus and Enceladus (the very sound of their names suggests violence), Jupiter striking down the rebellious band with his thunderbolt, the rapists Orion and Tityos and Pirithous, and Mother Earth mourning her fallen children, buried with her.

At the fulcrum between peace and violence Horace places Augustus himself (lines 37–42). He prays that Augustus, like the poet, may find rest from weariness and labor, peace in place of war, and, above all, the gift of gentle counsel (*lene consilium*: line 41). Later in the poem, as if to underline the message of this central passage, Horace explicitly warns against unrestrained violence: "Might devoid of counsel falls of its own weight. The gods themselves prosper *tempered* might, but these same gods abhor the violence that in its soul sets all evil in motion" (lines 65–68, a message set up by the peaceful picture of Apollo in lines 61–64). Horace, with characteristic tact and good sense, makes no explicit reference to Augustus' potential for violence, but the very shape of his poem, in which the *princeps* stands at the crossroads between peace and violence, makes Horace's point clearly and effectively.

The same point emerges also from Horace's handling of the figure of Jupiter throughout the Roman Odes. In III.1.5–8 and III.5.1–4 Horace uses Jupiter as an analogue to Augustus, a symbol of the social and moral order in the universe as Augustus is in the state. Less orderly and less comprehensible, however, is Jupiter's demeanor in III.2.29–30, and his ominous mention in III.3.6 is totally divorced from morality. His major appearance is in III.4, and in that poem he, like Augustus, is poised between two roles. He is, on the one hand, the divine king who brings order out of chaos, who rules justly, who punishes lustful violence. However, what first strikes the reader as he moves from the lines on *lene consilium* (lines 41–42) into the picture of Jupiter is that the god himself is not immune from exercising the very violence against which the poem warns. Horace portrays Jupiter's defeat of the giants as just, but he spares us nothing of its harsh violence.

Another basic opposition in the Roman Odes involves themes of time, different ways of viewing past, present, and future. On the political front the Augustan principate clearly represented a break with the past, new departures that offered hope for a better future. At the same time, Augustus himself, through his words and programs, advocated a return to the purer, simpler mores of early Rome as a means of combating the moral bankruptcy of the present. Numerous passages in the Roman Odes suggest a sense of new birth, new beginnings. Juno's abandonment of her long-held wrath in III.3,

for instance, opens the way for a better future, and her proviso against rebuilding Troy suggests that this is a time for moving ahead, not for looking back. *Odes* III.4 clearly portrays Augustus-Jupiter as the bringer of new hope, and other Roman Odes similarly refer directly or obliquely to the programs and accomplishments of the new regime. Balancing this optimism about the future, however, are despair over the present and memories of a nobler past. *Odes* III.1 deplores the extravagance of contemporary private buildings, their needless incursions into the natural world. *Odes* III.5 contrasts the integrity of a Regulus with the moral weakness of Romans in the first century B.C. *Odes* III.6 moves from a vivid portrayal of the degenerate mores of contemporary Rome into a haunting reminder of a simpler, better time (lines 37–44) and ends on a note of relentless moral decline. If the Roman Odes place Augustus at the crossroads between peace and violence, moral accomplishment and physical might, they also poise Augustan Rome at the crossroads between past and future, the new and the old, hope and despair.

One could move on to examples on an even larger scale, to the interplay among the three great groups of poems, for instance, with II.1–12 focusing on personal concerns but with an undercurrent of national issues, III.1–6 focusing on national concerns but with a strong counterpoint of personal issues, and the Parade Odes of *Odes* I daringly juxtaposing and alternating these two foci. One could probe the links between outer ends of the collection: the hopes for poetic success in I.1, the claims of poetic accomplishment in III.30; national issues in I.2, personal issues in III.29, with I.2 balancing agony against hope, III.29 balancing Maecenas against Horace, and with flood scenes playing major roles in both poems (I.2.1–20; III.29.36–41); a puzzling send-off to Vergil in I.3, an equally puzzling send-off to Galatea in III.27 (a poem not without Vergilian touches).

Readers who come to Horace looking for the epic sweep of a Vergil, the focused intensity of a Catullus, will no doubt feel some disappointment. Those who, however, are willing to "play his game" will find a world of delights, emotional as well as intellectual, serious as well as frivolous. Indeed, play at its best is always potentially more serious, more important, more "real" than life. Think, for instance, of the intensity with which both children and adults play a game, of the emotions an exciting game arouses in the spectator, of the emotional range and depth of a great play.[10] It is the same with Horatian *ludus*. No poet ever took his art more seriously, and Horace had powerful feelings about many subjects and persons; but the ultimate seriousness of his poetry, and its true emotional power, resides not in its expression of any one theme or emotion but in that very play of contrasting moods, themes, and genres which on the surface seems so frivolous.

That most characteristic of Horace's odes, I.5, is again pertinent. It is no accident that Pyrrha finds a place in the parade of important addressees with which *Odes* I begins, or that her poem immediately precedes that ode in which Horace proclaims his devotion to what is *tenuis* (I.6). Critics occasionally criticize I.5 as emotionally shallow, pointing to the ubiquitous irony and the accompanying sense of distance, to the fact that one does not sense behind Pyrrha (or behind many of Horace's women, for that matter) the flesh and blood of a real person, a genuine passion. On one level these criticisms are valid, but they miss the essential points. Pyrrha, whether or not she is based on an actual person, remains one of the most "real" figures in Western poetry, a figure as vivid and as unforgettable, and in her own way as affecting, as a Lesbia or a Cynthia, even though we know these heroines from hundreds of lines of Catullus and Propertius, but Pyrrha from one short poem only. Furthermore, Horace's attitude toward Pyrrha may reveal irony and distance, but his continued fascination with this Venus-like, golden creature also comes through; in a typical Horatian balance, the poem pulls irresistibly toward Pyrrha at the same time as it purports to be pulling away from her. If the poem lacks the single-minded focus on one searing passion that we find in Catullus, it contains instead a rich and varied assortment of human feelings: continued attraction for a lovely but fickle woman; amusement and delight (perhaps even envy) over the plight of Pyrrha's current victim; humor over the poet's own escape, but not without memories of the time when Pyrrha gleamed for him; and, suffusing it all, an immense and sympathetic understanding, as wise as it is ironic, of the human condition.

THE CONSOLATION OF SONG: EPODES AND ODES IV

It is clear from *Odes* I–III that Horace's concern is with the structure not only of an individual poem but also of a collection as a whole, a concern he shares with other Augustan poets. Our focus in *Odes* I–III was largely on static, architectural aspects of the larger structure: the placement of large groups of poems at the start of each book, the symmetrical arrangement of poems within II.1–12, the balances between I.1 and III.30, I.2 and III.29, and so on. One can study larger structure also in terms of the movement and development of themes, ideas, images, or tone from poem to poem: the way I.5 leads into I.6, for instance, with I.5 exemplifying the general stance articulated in I.6; or the way a somewhat lighthearted poem on death (II.13) leads into a much more serious poem on the same subject (II.14). In our analysis of the *Epodes* and of *Odes* IV, two collections of far smaller compass (seventeen and fifteen poems respectively) than *Odes* I–III, we shall focus on these larger structural questions rather than on individual poems.

Central to the architecture of the *Epodes*, published around 30 B.C., are four poems. Two

---

[10]See Horace's own frequent comments on play and humor as means of dealing with serious matters: for example, *Satires* I.1.24 ff., *Epistles* II.1.262–263. See also Horace's comments on Alcaeus' blend of the light and the serious (*Odes* I.32.5 ff.) and his familiar statement on the blending of pleasure with utility (*Ars Poetica* 343–344). On the whole subject of serious play, see J. Huizinga, *Homo Ludens. A Study of the Play-Element in Culture* (Boston, 1955).

poems to Maecenas, comparable in length and both dealing with the campaign against Antony and Cleopatra, open the two halves of the book—epodes 1 and 9. Balancing this pair of Maecenas poems are two epodes, 7 and 16, that focus on the ravages of the civil wars. The balanced opposition between these interlocked pairs, 1 and 9 on the one side, 7 and 16 on the other, provides the focal tensions for the book: 1 and 9 look with hope toward a restoration of Rome, whereas 7 and 16 emphasize Rome's decline and the impossibility of recovery. From the standpoint of mood, the remaining epodes fall somewhere between the polar extremes established by these two pairs; more important, in both halves of the book (1–8, 9–17) we progress from the hope and affection of the Maecenas poem to the despair and alienation of the civil war poem.

This movement is especially marked in the first half of the book. Epode 1 exudes affection, hope, and confidence mixed with concern. Epode 2 maintains this bright mood in its idyllic reverie on country life, its picture of a world of peace and fellowship. There are, however, jarring notes in both poems. Hanging over epode 1 is the fact that Horace and Maecenas must part, that Maecenas is off to the scene of dangerous wars; and the tone of epode 2 changes radically, as we have seen, when we discover at the end that the whole reverie is just that— the idle dream of a man who, whether he likes it or not, is bound to the sordid realities of Rome. Epode 3, again to Maecenas, remains basically cheerful throughout. Horace's exaggerated outrage over some garlic Maecenas has served him at a dinner is obviously in jest, and it is clear that a warm and open friendship of poet for patron lies behind the poem. Epode 3 does, however, introduce a number of motifs that will become more sinister in subsequent poems—interfamily strife, poison, blood, the witches Canidia and Medea, substances that burn and seethe. The tone of epode 4 is both harsher and more unpleasant. The discord (*discordia*, line 2) on which it focuses is elemental, of a piece with that which obtains between

lambs and wolves, and its source is no passing jest. This discord carries overtones of class strife, a contrast to the easy friendship of Horace and Maecenas in 1 and 3, that of the farmer and his slaves in 2; and whereas 3 ends with a smile, 4 ends with a clear reference to recent wars.

Epode 5, the longest of the *Epodes* and the longest of Horace's three poems on Canidia, is on one level merely a splendid example of Horatian play, a virtuoso exercise within a popular genre, the witch poem. Horace works into this poem, however, numerous motifs that are significant elsewhere in the book, and the overall coloration of epode 5 is anything but light. Witches and poisons, introduced in epode 3, become ubiquitous in 5, but whereas in 3 they were touched upon humorously, here the poisons are violent and virulent, the witches a sinister coven worthy of *Macbeth*. And if epode 4 began with a comparison of the human to the animal world, in epode 5 the bestial has taken over the human at every point. This is a world of savage, predatory, destructive creatures, and adding to the terror is the fact that humans are working with, not against, these unleashed animal energies. Discord, hatred, wrath, lust for revenge, unbridled passions are the forces that rule; the fiery garlic of epode 3 has become a host of substances that burn out of control. Above all there is the horror of the basic situation—a young boy all but buried alive, tortured, his body mutilated. The genre in which Horace is working is by nature grotesque, but Horace goes far beyond generic requirements. What remains with us from the poem is not black humor, the fascination of a chilling gothic tale, but the pathos of a young child made victim to such evil forces and, in the end, himself transformed into a curse-mouthing creature like his tormentors.

Epode 6, though briefer than 5, picks up some of the same motifs. Most notable again is the pervasive comparison of humans to predatory animals, once more with a clear hint of the passions that turn humans into beasts. The poem, with its sneers at a cowardly blackmailer and its threat of poetic revenge, is lighter in tone than epode 5, but like epode 4 it has an underlying ugliness of tone; it is a poem with a snarl.

When we come to epode 7, one of Horace's finest poems and a supreme example of his ability to deal with vast subjects, powerful emotions, on the smallest of canvases, we understand where all the previous poems have been leading. Epode 7 throughout deals explicitly with the Roman civil wars, applying to this theme the motifs that have been introduced in the previous epodes. The poison of epodes 3 and 5 now becomes the Roman blood spilled on land and sea, an irrevocable stain on later generations. The hints of internecine strife in epode 3 and the child tortured in 5 lead in 7 to the murder of Remus by his brother, and the cursing motif so common in the previous four poems becomes the everlasting curse born of this fratricide. Like the humans in epodes 4-6, the Romans of epode 7 turn against each other, driven by evil forces beyond their control; terror marks their faces as it did the face of the young boy in epode 5. The animal motif is again present, though here with a cruel twist: even animals, unlike the Romans, do not turn against their own kind. In short, the themes and motifs of the previous epodes, handled there always with at least a touch of humor, return in epode 7 in complete earnest, capping the inevitable march from the hope and harmony of epodes 1 and 2 to the black despair of 7. The hints of separation and war introduced in epode 1 move through a crescendo of antagonism in epodes 3-6 to the all-encompassing civil strife of epode 7; in the same way, Alfius' idyllic vision in 2, a vision revealed as merely utopian by the end of that poem, recedes even farther into the distance as we move in 3-6 increasingly into a world dominated by substances and forces beyond human control and arrive, in 7, in a world where blind madness, ancestral guilt, and the curse of fraternal murder reign supreme.

Epode 8, a skillful poem in a rather unpleasant genre, serves two functions in the larger structure of the collection. By its sheer ugliness and its use of numerous motifs familiar from the previous poems (disease, animal-human comparisons, distaste of one person for another, etc.), it underscores the progression from the fellowship and harmony of 1 and 2 to the separation and violence of 7. It serves also, however, as transition to epode 9, for its vulgarity is so overdone, its conclusion so clever in its very obscenity, that one can scarcely take it seriously. The very ugliness that makes it an appropriate companion to epode 7 thus provokes the laughter that is the necessary antidote to 7 and the needed preparation for 9.

The second half of the book follows a similar progression, though its movement is less regular, the overall tone somewhat less dark. There is no need to chart this progression in detail. Again we begin with Horace and Maecenas, with hope, companionship, joy, with escape from danger and disease and war (though, as in 1, not without occasional off-key notes, such as the mention of recent Roman disgrace in line 10 ff., the reference to *nausea* in line 35). Again we move from here to a deeply pessimistic poem about civil war, epode 16, a poem that picks up many specific motifs from epode 7 (compare *ruit*, "falls to ruin," in line 2 of 16, with *ruitis*, "rush to your ruin," line 1 of 7; the animal motif in 16.10 with similar motifs in 7.11–12). And again the intervening poems mediate between these two poles, effecting a transition, here somewhat jerky, from one to the other. Epode 10 reintroduces various motifs familiar from 3 to 7—rage, separation, thirst for revenge, curses on an antagonist, predatory animals, the pallor of terror, and so on. In 11 and 14, both love poems, Horace treats passion as something that invades the individual, leaving him helpless, burning, tortured, wounded, stricken out of his senses. Epode 12 is an obvious throwback to epode 8 in mood, tone, and theme, with the typical elements—rage, disease, animals—treated with perhaps even greater venom and virtuosity than in 8. Epode 13 begins with a violent, earth-shaking storm and ends with war, separation, death, and, metaphorically, the disease of living; and 15 focuses on unbridled, uncontrolled passions—on anger, threats, separation, revenge. Like its structural counterpart, epode 6, it ends with teeth bared, an effective preparation for 16, as 6 is for 7.

The progression from 9 to 16 is thus clearly less measured than that from 1 to 7. Perhaps more important is the fact that this second half is considerably more optimistic in tone than is the first. For one thing, 1 has as its occasion the departure of Maecenas for the uncertainties of the campaign against Antony and Cleopatra, while 9 celebrates the victory at Actium and looks ahead to Maecenas' return. Epodes 11 and 14 deal with possession by passion, but the passion is love, not the hatred of 4 and 6. And 13, despite the presence of storm, destruction, and death, projects an attractive and typically Horatian *carpe diem* response to these givens of the human condition. Above all, 16, while painting the horrors of civil war almost as vividly as does 7, at least offers a possible solution—mass exodus to the Blessed Isles. This famous and beautiful vision of a better life in a better world picks up and rights many of the motifs we have met earlier in the book: this is a world free from poison, a world where animals normally antagonistic are friends, a world free from human villainy and antagonism, a world of peace and plenty.

It is clear, however, that we are not meant to accept this vision too completely; as always, Horace juggles the kaleidoscope. For one thing, in the architecture of the *Epodes* there is a clear balance between 16 and 2, the one standing second in the collection, the other next to last (compare the complementary relation of I.2 and III.29 in *Odes* I–III). In addition, the poems are of approximately the same length, and both project a lovely but unrealistic vision of a better world—if only one could get there! The ending of 2 makes it clear that Alfius will never attain his vision. Epode 16 stops at line 66, the line parallel to the end of Alfius' speech in 2, but it is clear that here too Horace's vision is a utopia, a "no-place." As if to underline his point, Horace proceeds to end his book with a return to

Canidia. Epode 17 is in form a recantation, Horace pretending to retract the ugly things he has said of Canidia in earlier poems. In keeping with the generally brighter tone of the second half of the *Epodes*, 17 is less ugly than 5, but it nonetheless reinforces some of the darker themes from the rest of the book. Again we are plunged into a world of hatred and wrath, of flame and blood and poison and destructive beasts, of humans confronted with forces and emotions beyond control. Significant also is the fact that Horace's plea is rejected: Canidia's perverted passions are the note on which the *Epodes* end.

The structure of the *Epodes* thus consists of two varied but complementary progressions from order, peace, and harmony to chaos, antagonism, and discord. The rhythms of *Odes* IV, again on several mutually complementary levels, move in precisely the opposite direction. Both books, of course, albeit on a large scale and in progressive as well as static form, exemplify the same sort of thematic tensions, the same focusing on opposites, that we found typical of the poems and groups of poems of *Odes* I–III.

The overall movement of *Odes* IV is most easily approached through the contrast between its outside poems, IV.1 and IV.15. *Odes* IV.1 opens the book with war, separation, and loss. By the time Horace comes to IV.15, he is singing of peace, plentiful sharing, and poetry. The completeness of this about-face becomes fully apparent if we juxtapose key passages from each poem. The opening lines of IV.1 lament the resumption of wars; IV.15.4–9 rejoices in the coming of peace. *Odes* IV.1.29–32 proclaims Horace's separation from others, from the joys of feast and symposium, from poetry and song; IV.15 ends with Horace joining others in symposium and song, joyful concerns that seem far removed from the resumption of wars with which the book began. And in yet one more of the motivic links that tie these poems together and simultaneously underscore the tonal gulf between them, Venus the *mater saeva* ("cruel mother") at the start of IV.1, yields to Venus the *alma mater* ("loving mother") at the end of IV.15; Venus the instigator of new wars yields to Venus the subject of peaceful song.

Contributing to this movement from separation to union, war to peace, silence to song, a movement we shall find at many levels of *Odes* IV, are several actual events. On the political front, the years during which Horace was composing *Odes* IV witnessed a literal movement from war and separation to peace and return. In 16 B.C. Roman forces under Lollius suffered a major defeat on the northern frontier, and in the years immediately following this defeat both Augustus and his stepsons, Drusus and Tiberius, became actively involved in the Germanic campaigns, with Augustus himself not returning to Rome until 13 B.C. Several poems in the book reveal the impact of these events. *Odes* IV.9 is addressed to Lollius, with its second half focusing on those inner qualities that externals cannot touch (though with no specific reference to Lollius' defeat). *Odes* IV.4 and IV.14, two poems apparently commissioned by Augustus, stand equidistant from IV.9 in either direction and celebrate the military victories of Drusus and Tiberius in extravagant, Pindaric terms—not without traces of the distaste that so often accompanies Horace's celebration of military achievement. In contrast, Horace's references in IV.2 and IV.5 to Augustus' absence from Rome breathe sincere concern and genuine warmth, and one suspects that Augustus' return in 13 B.C., a return celebrated by the erection of the Arch of Peace, lies behind the fulfilled joy of IV.15 and its emphasis on union, peace, and return.

Horace in this period experienced separation on the personal front as well. Vergil, the poet whom Horace had called "the half of my soul" in *Odes* I.3 and with whom he had shared a long personal and professional friendship, had died in 19 B.C. Another friend, the elegiac poet Tibullus, to whom Horace had addressed *Odes* I.33 and *Epistles* I.4, had died around the same time. There had in addition been tensions, perhaps even something of a rift, between Horace and Maecenas, as we have seen from *Epistles* I. Finally, Horace alludes in IV.13 to the death of Cinara, a woman mentioned four times, always with feeling, in Horace's late poetry. We know nothing more about Cinara than what these passages tell us, but there is about her a reality lacking in most of the women Horace mentions, and her appearance always carries overtones of melancholy. From these several separations there could be no complete recovery, no literal return that, like Augustus' return to Rome, would fully restore what had been lost. But several poems toward the end of *Odes* IV suggest some sense of healing. Horace's poem on Maecenas, IV.11, certainly bespeaks warm reunion as well as underlying sadness, and his poem to Vergil, IV.12, seems best interpreted as an immortalizing through poetry of the close friendship the poets had once shared. And although IV.15 does not explicitly mention Vergil, it is significant that the song on which *Odes* IV ends is one with decidedly Vergilian overtones and that, almost alone of *Odes* IV, this final poem carries no reference to the ultimate separation of death.

The years preceding the composition of *Odes* IV had, in addition, witnessed Horace's literal return to lyric poetry. As we have seen from *Epistles* I.19, Horace had been disappointed by the reception accorded *Odes* I–III upon their publication in 23 B.C., and this disappointment may well have been what turned him from lyric poetry to the writing of *Epistles* I in the years immediately following. Whatever the reason, *Epistles* I.1 declares Horace's abandonment of the *ludus* of lyric, and we can date no lyric poem surely to the years 23–17 B.C. In 17 B.C., however, Horace was selected to compose the official poem for a major national festival, the *Ludi Saeculares* (Secular Games). The resulting poem, the *Carmen Saeculare*, a heartfelt prayer of praise, thanksgiving, and supplication that stresses the peaceful and moral accomplishments of Augustan Rome, was apparently received with great enthusiasm.[11] Horace refers with obvious pleasure to the *Carmen Saeculare* in *Odes* IV.6, and it seems likely that his selection to compose this national ode and the subsequent success of his composition played a major role in his decision to return to lyric poetry in the years 17–13 B.C., a return that culminates in the publication of *Odes* IV in 13 B.C.

We have seen that IV.1 and IV.15 represent the polar extremes of *Odes* IV. The intervening thirteen poems move between these poles, though in no precisely modulated sequence. By the time we get to IV.8 and IV.9, for instance, the theme of poetry is already sounding loud and clear, and poetic immortality is being held up as an answer to death; similarly, the alienation Horace feels in IV.1 is clearly breaking down by the time we reach IV.5 and IV.6. There is, however, something of a steady progression since not until we reach IV.15 do we complete the movement toward peace, poetry, harmony, life: in all of the intervening poems something remains, albeit in varying degrees, of the wars, the separation, the loss sounded in IV.1.

Odes IV.2, for instance, brings Horace closer to other people, closer to poetry, and it looks forward to Augustus' return and to the joy and peace ("the forum free of lawsuits": lines 43–44) that will attend his return. On the other hand, war, violence, and death still loom large, and Augustus' return is still only a hope; the poem focuses on the gulfs that divide Horace from Pindar and from Antonius, and it ends poignantly in the death of the young animal taken from its mother. *Odes* IV.3 suggests Horace's renewed sense of poetic power and achievement, but there remain many hints of separation: the distinctions, sharply drawn, between

Horace and other men; the reference to envy, diminished but still present; the definition of poetic acceptance in terms of the fingers that now point him out as someone different, a far cry from the communal poetry in which Horace participates at the end of IV.15. *Odes* IV.4 may celebrate the union of god and man, of father and stepson, of new and old, but what dominates the poem is war—war from which Horace stands noticeably apart and which he describes in the most violent terms. The poem may speak of new life out of old, but we retain more its ubiquitous images of death, destruction, and separation. *Odes* IV.5, like IV.15, stresses Augustus' peaceful rather than his military accomplishments, and like IV.15 it ends with Horace joining other Romans in praise of Augustus. It differs from IV.15, however, in that its most memorable passage, the comparison of Rome's longing for Augustus to a mother's longing for her son, emphasizes separation. The joyful union envisioned at the end of IV.5 remains only a vision, a hope shadowed by the pain, the sadness, and the sense of distance evoked by this beautiful image.

Odes IV.6, standing near the center of the collection, is literally split down the middle by the movement that characterizes the book as a whole. In the first twenty lines we have war, violence, death, and separation; in the final twenty, gentleness, new life, and, above all, poetry (the central four lines, 21–24, provide a deft transition between the contrasting outer panels). The Apollo of the second half is similar to the Apollo at the beginning of IV.15; the Horace at the end of IV.6, happily directing his young singers, is similar to the Horace at the end of IV.15. But how different is the violent Apollo at the start of IV.6; and how different from the peaceful world of the final twenty-four lines is the hell that gapes in the first twenty. *Odes* IV.7 sings of springtime and the return of new life in nature, but it emphasizes that for man there is no second springtime, no return, only the final separation; and although it ends on a note of friendship—man for man,

---

[11]For a full discussion of the *Carmen Saeculare*—its occasion, its performance, its importance in Horace's career—see Fraenkel, *Horace* 364–382. The *Carmen Saeculare* was actually sung by a chorus of young girls and boys (see Horace's address to this chorus in *Odes* IV.6), a fact that distinguishes it from Horace's other lyric poems, which were probably intended for recitation and reading rather than for actual singing to the accompaniment of a lyre.

goddess for man—it is friendship that fails to overcome death and separation. *Odes* IV.8 and IV.9 emphasize poetry and its power to confer what IV.7 denies—a second springtime to man; but both poems contain also ample reminders of war, violence, separation, and death. Again in IV.8, as in IV.3, Horace describes his poetic vocation in terms that stress the differences between him and other men, and again he explicitly alludes to the dividing force mentioned in IV.3—envy. This same force reappears in the "malicious oblivions" of IV.9.33–34, and the praise of private morality with which IV.9 ends emphasizes that the man of integrity must face isolation, hostility, even death.

The mixture of separation with union, death with life, in IV.10–13 is readily apparent. *Odes* IV.10 and IV.13 both begin with Horace standing apart from Ligurinus and Lyce, enjoying their suffering, but both move from this separation to a sense of sharing and of sympathy; IV.11 and IV.12 look forward to shared joys, to the renewed springtime of song, but both do so with numerous reminders of separation, death, and violence. And, as we have seen, behind IV.11 may well lie the tensions that had divided Horace from Maecenas; behind IV.12 almost certainly is the fact of Vergil's death. Finally, IV.14, like IV.4, balances its hints of togetherness, peace, and immortality against its explicit mentions of violence, war, division, and death.

The progression that shapes the book as a whole shapes also a number of its component parts. Several poems, for instance, reflect in microcosm the movement of the whole. We have already commented on this feature in IV.6, and something of the same happens in several other poems. *Odes* IV.1 moves from Horace's separation from Venus, from Paulus, from the joys of youth, to the concluding revelation of his love for Ligurinus. *Odes* IV.5 progresses from its early emphasis on Augustus' absence to its concluding pageant of union and reunion; and IV.10 and IV.13 move from vindictive distance at their starts to empathy at their conclusions. Similarly, to speak of progressions between in-

stead of within poems, Horace moves from a focus on war and death in IV.4 and IV.14 to a focus on peace and renewed life in IV.5 and IV.15, from isolation and silence in IV.1 to poetry and acceptance in IV.3 (with IV.2 as midway point), from separation and death in IV.7 to poetry and immortality in IV.8 and IV.9.

There are, in addition, further, more complex ways in which the contrasting pulls of IV.1 on the one side and IV.15 on the other are worked into the fabric of individual poems and groups of poems. *Odes* IV.11, for instance, contains many hints of loss, separation, death: Phyllis' frustration in love, Horace's awareness that she is the last of his loves, the mention of the on-flowing rivers of time in lines 19–20, the dark mythological *exempla* of lines 25–28; even, perhaps, the sacrifice of the second stanza and the dark smoke of the third. On the other side, however, are many balancing motifs of union and joy: the bright, green, fresh preparations for a feast; the affection of Horace for Phyllis and for Maecenas, the latter an affection that has survived the tensions reflected in *Epistles* I.7 and that now speaks as friend to friend, not as client to patron; the promise of comfort and consolation in song—*minuentur atrae carmine curae* ("black cares will be diminished by song": lines 35–36).

A similar tension between the poles represented by IV.1 and IV.15 animates IV.12, Horace's final poem to Vergil.[12] The ostensible mood of the poem is jovial: it opens with a picture of springtime, moves to jocular banter suggesting that Vergil must earn Horace's wine by a contribution of nard, and closes with anticipation of shared pleasures. The brightness is clouded, however, by dark touches—the violence and death of lines 5–8, the bitter cares of lines 19–20, the black fires (of death) of line 26. Above all, there is the simple fact that there can

---

[12]Not everyone agrees that the Vergil addressed in IV.12 is Vergil the poet—see, for example, Fraenkel, *Horace* 418, note 1. It is fair to say, however, that in recent years most criticism on the poem has inclined toward this identification.

never again be a literal reunion of Horace with Vergil: Vergil died six years before the book was published. The best interpretation of IV.12 seems to be that it is Horace's attempt to immortalize in poetry the lively friendship he and Vergil had once shared. The poem thus gives concrete expression to the dichotomy between mortality and loss on the one side, poetry and renewal on the other, a dichotomy that is thematically central throughout the book and that is rendered structurally central by the juxtaposition of IV.7 (loss, death) with IV.8 and IV.9 (poetry, immortality) in the book's central triad. *Odes* IV.12 contains clear indications of Horace's sorrow and his sense of loss, but its strong implication is that through poetry his friendship with Vergil lives on. Even the springtime opening of the poem points in these two contrasting directions. On the one hand, it recalls the opening lines of IV.7, a poem that contrasts the recurrent cycles of the seasons with the linear movement of human life: for humans, there is no return to spring. On the other hand, the landscape of the opening of IV.12 is the poetic landscape of both Horace and Vergil: its quiet streams and gentle fields remind us of scenes Horace associates with his own poetry in IV.2.27–32 and IV.3.10–2, and IV.3.9–12 recalls the landscape of Vergil's *Eclogues*. There may be no literal second springtime for humans, but there is, especially for Vergil and Horace, the eternal springtime of poetry.

Our analyses of these two collections reveal underlying rhythms that are highly contrasting: a persistent downward pull toward war, violence, disintegration in both halves of the *Epodes*, a persistent upward pull toward union, peace, poetry in *Odes* IV. One suspects that the downward drift of the *Epodes* owes much to Horace's experience of the civil wars, to his initial uncertainties about Augustus, and to his own still tenuous position in the literary life of Rome. One feels less hesitation in seeing behind *Odes* IV a poet increasingly at peace with Augustus, with Maecenas, with the fact of Vergil's death, and, above all, with himself and his own advancing years. *Odes* I–III stands mid-

way between the *Epodes* and *Odes* IV both in time and in its thematic emphases. It is clearly the work of a poet more sure of himself, more confident in the Augustan regime, than is the poet of the *Epodes*: at the same time, however, the ambivalences of the Roman Odes and the several powerful recollections of the horrors of the recent civil wars retain something still of the malaise of the *Epodes*.[13] One senses the same malaise also in the fact that whether in the Parade Odes, in II.1–12, in the Roman Odes, or in the balance of I.2 against III.29, Horace in *Odes* I–III constantly sets private values and concerns against public, individual against national. The dichotomy is not absolute, of course: Horace can in III.14 take immense personal pleasure in Augustus' return, and the final poem of the set, III.30, speaks of Horace's poetic immortality in terms drawn from public life (see especially lines 8–9). Nothing in this earlier collection, however, approaches the sense of wholeness, of "at-onement," that we find at the end of IV.15, where Horace, the man and the poet, joins with other citizens in singing of Roman greatness, past and future.

We have stressed the larger rhythms of the *Epodes* and *Odes* IV not only to suggest Horace's personal and artistic development but also to suggest a different way of reading Horace. One tends to read lyric poems one at a time and accordingly to think of a lyric poet primarily as the creator of exquisitely crafted miniatures. Horace *is* that, of course, but he is also the creator of carefully crafted *collections*, and taken as wholes, these collections make total statements that in magnitude and significance far exceed the mere sum of their parts. Horace remains the poet par excellence of the *tenuis*; but we miss an important side of his poetry, as well as a characteristic Horatian irony, if we fail to recognize that in the very act of putting together the slender parts he creates collections that have much of the *grandis* about them.

---

[13]Horace's apostrophe to the "Ship of State" in *Odes* I.14.17–18 aptly suggests the ambivalence apparent elsewhere in *Odes* I–III.

Selected Bibliography

TEXTS

Q. Horati Flacci Opera, edited by F. Klinger. Leipzig, 1970.

Q. Horati Flacci Opera, edited by E. C. Wickham and H. W. Garrod. Oxford, 1912. The standard text in English-speaking countries.

TRANSLATIONS

The following are all readable, modern translations. My own preference is for Rudd or Fuchs in the Satires and Epistles and Michie in the Odes (includes Carmen Saeculare but not the Epodes). A particular advantage of Rudd and Fuchs is that they retain the original line numbers; an advantage of Michie is that he prints the Latin originals opposite his translations.

Bovie, S. P. The Satires and Epistles of Horace. Chicago, 1959.

Clancy, J. P. The Odes and Epodes of Horace. Chicago, 1960.

Fuchs, J. Horace's Satires and Epistles. New York, 1977.

Henze, H. R. The Odes of Horace. Norman, Okla., 1961

Michie, J. The Odes of Horace. Indianapolis, Ind., 1963.

Rudd, N. Horace: Satires and Epistles. Persius: Satires. New York, 1973.

COMMENTARIES

Brink, C. O. Horace on Poetry. Vol. 2: The Ars Poetica. Cambridge, 1971.

Kiessling, A., and R. Heinze. Horaz. Vol. 1: Oden und Epoden, 10th ed. Berlin, 1960. Vol. 2: Satiren, 8th ed. Berlin, 1961. Vol. 3: Briefe, 7th ed. Berlin, 1961. The standard edition of the complete works. Notes are in German.

Nisbet, R. G. M., and M. Hubbard. A Commentary on Horace. Odes 1. Oxford, 1970; Odes 2. Oxford, 1978. Contains excellent introduction to Horace's meters.

Wickham, E. C. The Works of Horace. Vol. 1: The Odes, Carmen Saeculare and Epodes, 3rd ed. Oxford, 1896. Vol. 2: The Satires, Epistles and De arte poetica. Oxford, 1891.

Williams, G. The Third Book of Horace's Odes. Oxford, 1969.

CRITICAL STUDIES

Brink, C. O. Horace on Poetry. Vol. 1: Prolegomena to the Literary Epistles. Cambridge, 1963. Excellent source on all questions relating to the background of the three literary epistles.

Carrubba, R. W. The Epodes of Horace. A Study in Poetic Arrangement. The Hague, 1969.

Commager, S. The Odes of Horace. New Haven, 1962. Excellent critical and interpretative study. Fine chapter on the literary background of Horace's poetry.

Costa, C. D. N., ed. Horace. London, 1973.

Fraenkel, E. Horace. Oxford, 1957. The most important modern study of Horace. Especially useful on Horace's life and the literary background of his poetry.

Lee, M. O. Word, Sound, and Image in the Odes of Horace. Ann Arbor, 1969.

McGann, M. J. Studies in Horace's First Book of Epistles. Brussels, 1969.

Reckford, K. J. Horace. New York, 1969.

Rudd, N. The "Satires" of Horace: A Study. Cambridge, 1966.

West, D. A. Reading Horace. Edinburgh, 1967.

Wilkinson, L. P. Horace and His Lyric Poetry. Cambridge, 1945.

DAVID H. PORTER

LIVY

(ca. 59 B.C.–ca. A.D. 17)

LIVY WAS NOT a man inclined by nature to reveal his own personality. But as his later years stole upon him he drew aside the veil, ever so slightly, to speak of an inner force that compelled him to keep at his work: "I have attained enough personal fame and could lay my pen aside—but my very soul, restless within me, draws sustenance from work."

The historian and the singular devotion with which he pursued his monumental history of Rome were legendary even in his own day. Pliny tells of a man from remotest Spain who traveled to Italy expressly to get a glimpse of him; then, having done so, he turned and went back home. Livy himself referred on a few occasions to the immensity of his task. And well he might, since he undertook to record the history of Rome from its founding; hence its name, the *Ab Urbe Condita Libri*. Issuing his work in installments of five or ten books (called pentads and decades), Livy ultimately wrote 142 books covering 745 years of Roman history (753–9 B.C.). Throughout his long working life—it exceeded forty years—he was to maintain the astonishing average output of three and a half books per year.

Titus Livius was born in 59 B.C. (possibly 64 B.C.) in the prosperous commercial town of Patavium near the Adriatic coast of northern Italy, a place well known for its strict adherence to old-fashioned Roman virtues. Livy's pride in his native district is evident in the opening sentences of the *History*, which stress the ancient and common heritage of his people and Rome. Of his life almost nothing is known. Yet he, along with the rest of his generation, must have been influenced mightily by the horrors of the civil wars fought during the 40's and 30's B.C. He may well have seen his own town expel Antony's legates in 43 B.C. During these years he profited greatly from the standard education with its emphasis on rhetoric, a skill that he would employ to great effect in his *History*. At this point also there are two striking omissions in his life, both inferred rather than attested. He seems not to have taken the customary tour of the East for advanced training in the universities of Athens or Rhodes; both his vagueness on geography and the political disorders of his early manhood point to this conclusion. Nor does he appear to have served in the army, for he shows no knowledge of military life. His whole working life was devoted to literary interests. He is known to have achieved great distinction of style in several works, presumably early in his career: books expressly on philosophical topics and dialogues of a historical and philosophical character.

He traveled to Rome at some time, most likely soon after the Battle of Actium restored peace in 31 B.C. There he began work on the *History*; internal evidence suggests that he wrote book 1 around 27 B.C. What is certain is that he brooked little distraction from his literary pursuits. He never held office. He took little part in the flourishing literary society of Rome. Nor is he mentioned as being in the company of Vergil or Horace, much less the faster set around Ovid. Horace might draw sustenance from retiring to the countryside, or Ovid find his inspiration by mingling with polished urban society. Livy's work celebrates neither country nor city, nor even the Roman people of his day. Livy's subject is historical and more abstract. Beyond understanding particular events, he is interested in the Roman people as they once were and how they changed through time. He is especially interested in those moral values that had once made Rome a tranquil republic at home; feared and respected abroad. To see the historical importance of these values required our historian's private contemplation among the records of history, not the observation of land or people around him. No wonder, then, that he did not consort with literary society. He found his inspiration in the library, poring over the records of the past.

It is altogether likely that Livy was a man of independent means; certainly he never mentions a patron. This too may have contributed to his isolation from the society of other authors. He did, however, enjoy the friendship of Augustus and was familiar enough to encourage the future emperor Claudius to write history. And yet there is every reason to believe that he was not overawed by his proximity to the great. By no means a court historian, he staunchly maintained his pro-Republican views. He considered Brutus and Cassius, the slayers of Julius Caesar, to be men of distinction; his judgment of Pompey was so favorable that Augustus called him a Pompeian. When Augustus cited evidence regarding Cossus' *spolia opima* (spoils of honor, offered by a general who defeats an enemy leader in single combat), Livy only placed his testimony alongside another version (4.20.5–11). It is possible that his relationship with Augustus chilled somewhat in later years. The last twenty-two books of the *History* deal with events after the death of Cicero; that is, the events of Augustus' career. These Livy wrote

with the integrity that marked his earlier work; he therefore deemed it unwise to publish them during Augustus' lifetime.

It is fitting that Livy's one distraction from writing was his family. He had a daughter who married Lucius Magius, a rhetorician of no conspicuous talent. He probably had two sons also. The best reading of the evidence is that the first of these died quite young and that the second was interested in rhetoric and geography.

Livy returned to Patavium before he died in A.D. 17 (perhaps A.D. 12). Even in these last years he may still have been composing the final books of his monumental history.

THE HISTORY

> . . . writing, the sole trustworthy guardian of our memory of the past.
>
> (6.1.2)

Livy's *History* enjoyed great success in antiquity, immediately becoming the standard work on Rome. So favorable was its reception that all previous general histories of Rome were swept away. Of the earlier historical writings in Latin, only specialized studies or commentaries survive: the works of Sallust and Caesar.

His reputation as a historian has not fared so well in modern times, a fact due in large part to two schools of thought that have dominated most, though not all, of recent scholarship. We may call these the poetic and the historical schools. Each has taken a rather specialized interest in certain aspects of the *History*, presenting us with two totally different views of the writer. While each approach has borne some fruit, neither correctly understands the essence of his work, for in neither is there any inkling that Livy functions as a competent historian.

It is the massiveness of Livy's *History*, combined with its overtly literary character, that has caused some scholars to perceive it as Rome's prose epic and Livy as a poet in prose. Scholars of this poetic school have found much to admire: vivid scenarios centering on noble Romans, evocative portraits of the traditional Republican values, lofty, even poetic vocabulary, and an elevated rhetorical style. On a larger scale, however, he wins only vague approval for a fitting—if somewhat loosely organized—overall portrayal of Rome's greatness, a fact that consorts oddly with the supposedly epic nature of his work. Livy emerges in this reading as a kind of songster for Rome's imperial might.

Scholars of the other school, examining his historical views, have found him naive. History, in the eyes of this school, has little to do with the public deeds and values of men; it is "not like Livy." These scholars often wish aloud that he had emphasized, as Tacitus later did, the private deals and secret alliances, the decisions behind closed doors where history was "really" made. Livy is particularly condemned by this school for his failure to grasp and organize his material on a large scale. He is accused of having little skill in perceiving relationships between events and of lacking a personal viewpoint in his writing, two charges that have proved disastrous to his reputation as a historian.

Allied to the viewpoint that Livy has little to say about history is a critical method that I would gladly ignore were it not so common. This method ascribes all of the historical content of the *History* to Livy's sources. If there happen to be ideas or judgments expressed, those too are ascribed to Livy's sources; even lost sources will do if extant ones fail to provide the needed parallels. One study even explains the variety of Livy's prose style in this same way. If he wanted to write an episode in rich and elaborate style, he chose a source that treated the episode in that way; if sparer prose were required, a version written in plainer style would be chosen. One is tempted to observe that our poor historian, stripped of responsibility for content, ideas, and style, is left to decide only the length of his books. But, alas, even this merest shadow of personal contribu-

tion is denied him—we hear that he ended his individual books when he ran out of room on each scroll. To such depths has this scholarship sunk.

Now it is surely true that Livy took most or all of his factual material from the inherited traditions he found in earlier sources. There are uninteresting sections where he does little more than translate. It is even demonstrable in many cases that he owes particular points of interpretation to his predecessors. But to say that he borrowed everything—fact, interpretation, even style—from earlier historians surely raises larger questions. Why did Livy bother to write at all? And why was his work so well received? Fortunately, the grip of such attitudes is loosening. It is possible, without denying Livy's debt to earlier writers, to speak of a historical conception and a literary method that are peculiarly his own.

In the account that follows, I will claim neither that Livy's historical facts are always correct nor that he always interprets them insightfully. It is true that he sometimes commits errors of detail through carelessness or haste. At other times he seems incurious about the fine points of his subject—siegecraft and military tactics, for example. Less frequently he prefers to base his narrative on one source when an obviously superior one was available to him.

Livy's very method of judging historical truth, however, has provoked a deeper dissatisfaction that deserves to be examined. Two points are noteworthy in Livy's approach. First, he did not particularly distrust any of his sources. True, he did recognize that family records were apt to lie outright; he knew also that some historians were given to particular faults—for example, Valerius Antias exaggerated numbers. But he could not seek eyewitness accounts to verify information on Rome's distant past; nor, in all probability, did independent documentary evidence suffice for such a broad task. He had no means, therefore, to reach the conclusion of modern scholars (who have applied modern critical methods) that some of his sources systematically falsified history. When confronted with divergent accounts, his critical reaction was seldom the modern one: "Source A is more to be trusted than Source B." Instead, he impartially applied various tests of inherent probability to the different versions: for example, how closely contemporary a writer was to the events described, or whether the account fit the character of the participants or explained other events that were known to have followed. If (as was often the case) these methods yielded no clear verdict, he had no way of deciding what version to believe. The result is that his account of events is at times demonstrably wrong; but it is easier to note the error than to blame the historian.

Second, for modern scholars it is a complex process to judge what happened in antiquity. The process involves critical examination of all the ancient literary sources and inscriptions. The latest evidence from fields like archaeology and numismatics is brought to bear on the problem, too. From all this evidence is derived a new version of what happened, a synthesis based on some or all of these sources accordingly as they offer likely solutions to the various parts of the problem. This composite method owes much to modern scientific processes of inquiry. It was foreign to Livy and indeed to antiquity in general. Livy saw the task of determining the truth in much simpler terms. His aim was to select, by his various tests of probability, which single version to follow in its entirety; infrequently he would supplement it with additional facts from another source. The idea of creating a new interpretation pieced together from many accounts would have seemed irresponsible: no reliable source attested it.

I shall attempt in these pages to transcend the exclusive presentation of Livy either as a literary or historical writer. He saw himself as a literary historian, for at its best his work uses prose writing of the highest order and a fine sense of dramatic structure to underline genuine historical insight. Chiefly I shall focus on three elements that define his achievement as a historian with literary methods: first, his perceptions of historical trends and of the specific causes behind particular events; second, his general interpretation of the development of the Roman national character throughout history—an avowedly moral theme that is sometimes the direct cause of historical changes; and thirds, the literary technique that he uses to underline and define his historical interpretations to the reader. These are, partly or wholly, new themes, but essential ones to the proper appreciation of Livy's achievement. They are not, of course, the whole story. Those readers interested in a fuller treatment are fortunate to be able to consult P. G. Walsh's excellent book, *Livy, His Historical Aims and Methods*.

A few general observations are in order, however, before we examine the extant books of the *History*. Only thirty-five books now survive of the original work, and these are from the early years: books 1–10 (753–293 B.C.) and books 21–45 (218–167 B.C.). The others (except books 136 and 137) are known from brief summaries called the *Periochae*. The extant books are the ones that presented Livy with the gravest problems in judging the merits of his sources and supplementing them with primary information like speeches. In the period before the Gallic sack in 390 B.C., the problem assumed such magnitude that, as Livy himself knew all too well, the course of events could be perceived only in dim outline. We cannot know exactly how Livy's methods of determining historical truth changed as he began to treat contemporary history with its abundance of available evidence. But it is important to realize that his methods surely did change. The accident that his early, not his late, books survive means that his methods cannot be compared fairly with those of other historians who wrote about events very close to or actually contemporary with their own lifetimes.

Livy set about writing history in annalistic form, committing to paper all the events of one year before proceeding to the next. The method was at once greatly attractive and very dangerous—attractive because it offered a ready-made organization for the massive body of evidence he would handle, and (since it was the traditional format of old Roman records) lent a certain air of antiquity and patriotism; dangerous because he saw that the mere narration of events in chronological order could obscure essential relationships between facts widely separated in time. To clarify these relationships, to illuminate the ongoing *development* between events, was at the very heart of his plan. The central problem facing him, therefore, was to stress the important events and the historical developments they marked as easily discernible threads drawn across his annalistic format.

Livy ordered and interpreted history on a large scale in several ways that transcend the limited view of strictly year-to-year history. Indeed, he was perhaps the most successful of the ancient annalists in this respect. Livy unified books or groups of books around a single topic. This technique allowed him to clarify the large-scale division of material into historical periods or phases. For example, he divided major events among separate pentads or decades. Books 21–30 cover the Second Punic War, while the next three pentads focus respectively on wars with Philip V, Antiochus, and Perseus. The same division could be achieved on a smaller scale as well. Book 36, for example, covers Rome's campaign against Antiochus in Greece while book 37 treats the campaign in Asia. He devised two further means, both thoroughly literary, of indicating historical issues and their development. These he employed according to his growing maturity as a writer and historian and the nature of the material itself. We shall examine Livy's use of these two methods in some detail below, but they deserve brief discussion here. Livy used literary motif to indicate the frequent recurrence of particular historical issues. If, for example, several different events all threatened the freedom of early Rome, then Livy could choose to build a unit of his work—one book, perhaps—around these events, unifying the whole by the recurrent

motif of the danger to liberty. This device, though vivid and arresting at best, tends to be rather static in its conception since it defines an issue rather than showing its development.

A more sophisticated approach was needed if Livy was to explain the ongoing developments of history. From this need he developed, by degrees, a second device: drama. Now instead of building segments of his *History* around static ideas like liberty, he could take a historical development and dramatize it. The Second Punic War, for example, could be assigned distinct dramatic phases: a beginning, middle, and end. The historical incidents that demarcated these phases could be treated as the turning points in the dramatic scheme. The result would be a genuine historical judgment set forth in an exciting and dramatic narrative. We will trace this subject more fully later.

Livy often sees public morality and the improvement or decay of morals as a crucial factor in history. For this view he has been frequently—and often wrongly, I think—condemned by modern critics. His moral concerns, construed at the broadest level, are profoundly penetrating and true. Nowadays the same concept masquerades under a different name. If blacks and whites learn to live together and accept each other in racial harmony; if Israel and Egypt exchange tourists and cultural groups in the hope that fondness and respect may one day supplant hatred—we regard both of these as educational processes. Those who promote these processes we are pleased to call statesmen. But the public enlightenment implied in racial and international peace represents a change within the minds and hearts of men: a moral change. The importance of such changes ultimately far overshadows the decisions of political leaders; Livy perceived this truth more clearly than any other ancient historian. It is true that Livy did not understand the decision-making process as well as other writers. But his concern with the role of morals in history reflects his interest in setting forth statesmanlike policies, not the decision-making process. Indeed, he found an ideal audience immediately in the person of Augustus, for it was the moral outlook of Livy and others that the emperor incorporated as the central feature of his attempt to reform Rome. Augustus' revival of archaic religious practices, his laws fostering the values of marriage and discouraging adultery, and his official encouragement of bearing children—all of these found ready models in Livy's early writings.

Livy, I believe, saw the virtues of his *History* in the fact that, first, it was to be comprehensive and thoroughly researched, the fullest account of Roman history as a whole. Indeed, his broad interest in combing through different sources allowed him to write the definitive version of many major events. By using sources like Polybius (whose excellence Livy perceived) and Coelius, he eclipses all previous Roman versions of the Second Punic War and the later Eastern wars. Second, the *History* is written in an unabashedly literary style, powerful enough to do justice to the grandeur of his subject. Lastly, it contains genuine insight and judgment regarding the key historical developments: the city's early growth, the formation of the Republic, the struggle of the orders, the extension of Roman rule, and (sometimes overshadowing it all) the changes in Rome's national character.

BOOKS 1–5 (753–390 B.C.)

> When each man, by pretending to want equality, raises his lot above that of another; and when men make themselves fearsome in order that they might not live in fear; and when we avert injury from ourselves only to inflict it on others, as if injury had to be inflicted or sustained—then moderation in defending liberty is difficult indeed.
>
> (3.65.11)

The first five books, covering the period before the burning of Rome in 390 B.C., forced Livy at the very outset to declare clearly his historical intentions. Various authors had adopted various attitudes toward this era. At one end of the spectrum Claudius Quadrigarius seems to have omitted it completely from his history, no doubt perceiving that the burning of records in the general conflagration made judgment difficult on this remote period. On the other hand, many of Rome's most famous and patriotic legends belonged to this period. The corpus was large enough to enable Dionysius of Halicarnassus at the other extreme to write thirteen books on the era. Livy chose a middle course: one book for the regal period (Dionysius had written four), four more (versus Dionysius' nine) on the Republican period down to 390 B.C. He explicitly states on various occasions that he is aware of the difficulties involved in recounting the early period. Partly his inclusion of the material was a concession to patriotism and an opportunity for congenial literary exercise: "This license is granted to antiquity: to make the beginnings of cities more majestic by mingling the gods with human affairs" (preface 7). Mostly, however, his decision was motivated by historical reasons. Despite the general unreliability of the evidence, the overall outline of the foreign wars could be made out. Moreover, certain important issues at home really could be discerned. And if the history of the regal period was for the most part palpably invented, still there were some important developments that surely did take place under the kings. So Livy determined his course. He would include the events before the Gallic sack; the history of Rome would be seriously incomplete without it. But he would not accord the period much space. As a result, these first five books cover 364 years. He would ultimately write 137 books to cover the next 381 years.

It is not at all surprising that much of Livy's information in the first pentad has been proved wrong. What is surprising, given the scholarly opinion that he has little to say about history, is his emphasis on the important developments in Rome under the kings and the important social issues of the early republic.

Book 1 rather briefly sets forth the reigns of the seven kings and stresses their several contributions to the new city. Livy believed that the population of early Rome consisted mostly of undesirables: vagabonds, shepherds, and exiles. The Roman state would have fallen apart, Livy says explicitly (2.1.3–6), if the kings had not held these rootless people in check. As it was, they ruled mildly (the last Tarquin excepted) while common ties of family and soil slowly cemented Romans together. The kings prepared Romans for liberty in another way, by shaping the character of the early rabble. Romulus steeled the Roman character for the rigors of war; Numa softened and rounded this character by fostering care for religion. Other kings extended and reinforced these good effects. And Servius Tullius stood out for his constitutional innovations. Livy considers the growth of the city to be particularly important and carefully notes the various additions to the population: rabble gathered indiscriminately from neighboring peoples, the Sabine women who will bear children, later the whole Sabine and Alban peoples, and the populations of several nearby towns. Alongside these developments Livy also takes care to mark the minor changes in the city, and to explain them if he can. Thus he notes, to cite only a few examples, the first spoils of honor, the first temple to be consecrated in Rome, the first Roman Games, even the first bridge spanning the Tiber. He believes the scant evidence actually allows him to explain the building of a prison above the Forum: it was to reduce crime caused by the recent influx of citizens. Livy therefore has attempted to trace and, where possible, to explain the changes in Rome under the kings. His portrayal of the kings is undeniably an oversimplification. But that period is so remote that even modern scholars have reached no very clear idea of the truth. Livy's version has the distinction of being far more sophisticated than the notions commonly held about the early period. Dionysius, Cicero, and possibly the elder Cato all thought that Rome was of Greek origin and a place of high refinement from the start; Sallust too saw no process of development in the early history.

Book 1 also derives a certain superficial literary unity from the occasionally recurring motif of Rome's future greatness. In books 2–5, which take up the history from the birth of the Republic, this literary unity becomes increasingly important as an interpretive device. Livy's literary emphasis upon historical issues may be explained as follows. He sets divisions between individual books to coincide with general changes in historical content. One book covers an era marked particularly by one type of problem; in another book a different problem or issue stands out. Livy knows, of course, that these issues cannot be strictly divided into separate eras; all of them occur to some degree throughout books 2–5. But these issues are especially highlighted and elaborated upon within their proper books. The result is that each individual book acquires a distinctive "flavor." Each gives special definition to a particular issue or problem. Book 2 deals with the nature and problems of freedom, a concern that in fact occupies Livy's attention throughout this pentad. Books 3 and 4 consider particular threats to liberty. In book 3 he stresses the need for *moderatio* (self-control) in the patrician exercise of authority. In book 4 the emphasis is on the need for *modestia* (popular obedience to authority) as an appropriate response to patrician self-control. Finally, book 5 illustrates the importance of *pietas* (religious piety). Through the observance of piety Rome captures the city of Veii; then, after neglecting the gods, Romans suffer the capture and burning of their own city.

An examination of book 2 will suffice to illustrate Livy's method. He announces the book's theme at the outset, saying that since the kings have been expelled, he will be dealing henceforth with a free people. The treatment of events in the book carries out the general theme. Threats to the city from ambitious individuals and foreign armies alike are treated as threats to liberty. Thus, it is for the sake of their freedom that the people require the abdication of the consul Lucius Tarquinius Collatinus, who bore the name of the hated king. Liberty again is said to be threatened by the conspiracy of the noble Aquilii and Vitelii. The attempt of Lars Porsinna, king of Clusium, to restore Tarquin to the throne is portrayed as a royal attempt to stamp out the dangerous idea of liberty. The theme may be easily discerned in other attempts to restore Tarquin's throne, both by the people of Tarquinii and Veii and by the Latins. The suspicion directed against Publius Valerius demonstrates the Romans' perhaps overzealous protectiveness of freedom. At the same time, Livy sees an attempt to protect liberty in the limitation of the consuls' term of office and in the granting of the right of appeal. He stresses also that the awesome power of the dictatorship rests on fear created by the suspension of civil liberties.

After the death of Tarquin at Cumae removes the fear of kingly rule, a new threat to liberty is added: internal discord between patricians and plebeians (21.5–6). Throughout the rest of the book, the threat to liberty emerges as a theme in various internal quarrels and foreign wars. The practice of nexum (enslavement for debt) is regarded by impoverished plebeians as a clear and present danger to their freedom. The practice is seen as especially threatening since patricians rigorously insist on military service even when that will plunge the soldier into debt and ultimately into slavery; here, too, therefore, liberty is the issue. Livy vividly portrays the deep divisions in the state over these issues; repeatedly he shows that those divisions implicitly threaten liberty since they weaken Rome against external threats. Again, while liberty is an incidental theme in the attack of Coriolanus, it is a central one in Spurius Cassius' agrarian proposal. By this general theme Livy imparts to the book a unifying flavor. The various episodes of private ambition, civil strife, and foreign war all help to define the different aspects of the problems of liberty.

Books 3 and 4 portray the domestic struggles of plebeians and patricians with all their terrible strife. Particularly noteworthy is a device that would become one of Livy's favorites. In the middle of book 3—that is, at the center of the whole pentad—he places a story worthy of special emphasis, the tyrannical rule of the decemvirs in the years 451–450 B.C. This episode gives particular expression to the principal dangers of the whole domestic struggle—individual ambition and factional strife.

Wherein did Livy perceive the causes of this terrible struggle, and where did the solution lie? We have already seen that the struggle of the orders began only after the fear of kings had been removed: the opening was signaled not by Tarquin's expulsion from Rome but by his death at Cumae. The kingly master had been forever removed. Romans, released for the first time in history from the fear of a king, immediately fell into class struggle. The causes, however, had long been at hand and the struggle repressed only by the overriding presence of the king. The causes of conflict were the plebeians' desire for agrarian reform and liberation from the crushing burden of usury. Likewise, some of them now aspired to hold political office. The patricians, on the other hand, resolved to assert their traditional prerogatives against all of these aspirations. Books 3 and 4 stress time and again the unyielding attitude of both sides. The patricians do not possess self-control, nor the plebeians obedience. It is the ongoing mastery of these social virtues that will mark the attainment of political maturity. These virtues will secure the heritage of freedom against internal excesses and guarantee Rome's strength against foreign foes. The sad truth, however, is that in this pentad Livy sees no substantial progress toward solving the struggle of the orders. The Romans of 390 B.C. have no more mastered moderatio and modestia than the Romans of 509 B.C.

Another issue complicates and deepens the problem. It touches the most profound questions of humanity and is the philosophical heart of the whole struggle for public office: are plebeians equal in talent and worth to patricians? The tribune Canuleius points out that this issue is crucial to Rome's fortunes (4.3.13), for the city must use all of her talented citizens if she is to prosper. The dispute on this issue emerges most clearly in the debate on two proposals that depend on judgments of innate worth. One, the Canuleian Law, would allow plebeians to marry patricians; the other would allow them to serve as consuls (4.1–6). The patricians oppose both laws, vigorously denying the worth of plebeians. With deadlock on this issue, it is apparent (4.4.1–4) that Rome will not enjoy the fullest help of all her citizens until certain changes are made in the historical roles of the orders. Accommodation to these changes—that is, a recognition of the plebeians' inherent worth—will be important in two ways. It will help to end the struggle of the orders and to guarantee Rome's future prosperity. Throughout the first five books, however, patricians remain unwilling to accept plebeians as their equals.

Livy sees the problems in human terms. Although Rome once enjoyed internal stability under the kings, the reign of Tarquinius Superbus reveals that kingship can too easily become tyranny. Republican liberties are infinitely preferable. But liberty itself contains the seeds of disorder. Without a master, men must build a social order by learning to master themselves. This is the challenge of freedom that Rome has yet to meet. Fortunately, her enervating quarrels did not altogether destroy Rome. Salvation lay in the happy fact that her citizens always united in the face of extraordinary perils. But in the long run more would be required: a reconciliation of individual rights and aspirations based on self-control, obedience, and mutual respect.

Despite the gloomy present, certain rays of hope portend a brighter future. Livy sees in the election of plebeians as quaestors, or minor judges, a step toward their later winning the consulship. When the tribunate is restored after the decemvirs' expulsion, mention is made of a future time when plebeians may wield great power. Greater than these, however, both in its hope and in its challenge for the future is a speech by Camillus. The speech closes the entire pentad and in its way provides the most stirring chapters of these books. The speech is occasioned by a proposal that the Romans, in the wake of the Gallic sack of Rome, should move en masse to Veii. The proposal was linked to the plebeian tribunes, but Livy is of no mind to treat the matter as an internal quarrel.

His mind is on a higher theme—the greatness of Rome. The people's ultimate decision to remain and rebuild is pregnant with implications, unabashedly literary and undeniably powerful. It indicates that Rome is destined not merely to survive but to rule the world:

> Here is the Capitoline. Once a human head was discovered here, and the soothsayers replied that in this place would be the head of the world and the supreme authority of empire. Here, when auguries had been taken and the Capitoline was being cleared, to the great joy of your ancestors, Juventas and Terminus did not allow their shrines to be removed. Here are the fires of Vesta, here the shields were sent down from heaven, here—as long as you shall remain—all the gods will favor you.
>
> (5.54.7)

The tone has been set for books 6–10, in which Rome will begin to achieve her destiny of greatness.

Cicero, writing in the middle of the first century B.C., believed that Rome still lacked a history whose style and content matched the city's greatness. In style no less than in content, Livy's first pentad began to fill the void. His writing is marked by a superb sense of dramatic force. He can relate light, airy stories but is at his best in highly charged scenes of desperation and conflict such as his lively descriptions of bitter political struggles. The soul of his dramatic writing is a vivid historical imagination; his skill is unsurpassed in portraying the emotions and reactions of people caught up in the events of history. He did not, of course, possess every gift. The rape of Lucretia, to choose just one example, is powerfully imagined and vividly drawn (1.57–59), but Livy's narrative has nothing insightful to say about Sextus Tarquinius or the nature of lust; nor does he really explore the nature of the woman's suffering. His enthusiasm is directed toward the moral value of chastity, as upheld by her suicide, and the drama of the moment, for this episode caused the expulsion of Rome's last king. It is generally fair to say that Livy injects emotion primarily to add flavor to an event or crisis; it is not explored for its own sake. He lacks the poet's concern for people and their emotions per se. Livy is, after all, a literary historian. He is not a poet.

The stylistic achievement of these books does not end there, for they show a basic narrative pattern that may well have originated with Livy. As he researched his history he found certain events that were congenial or important, while others were less worthy of his attention. To suit the nature of the different topics, and to keep the narrative from becoming monotonous, he decided to vary his narrative pace and style. For important events he would wax full and elegant. For lesser topics a sparer style would suffice. The result was a basic historical style that fully met Cicero's prescription for excellence. Future historians could emulate Livy's narrative style; they could never improve it.

BOOKS 6–10 (389–293 B.C.)

... that age, the most abundant ever in all good qualities. ...

(9.16.19)

Books 6–10 represent the coming to maturity both of the writer and his subject. For it is in describing Rome's ascent to greatness that Livy comes in control of his fullest, surest powers as a historian. Curiously, these books are little read now; Livy could (and did) write books of far less merit.

Just as Livy created a new historical style in his first pentad, here he extends the achievement by creating a new historical form, a new and avowedly literary vehicle that can do justice to history. History, he realizes, cannot be regarded merely as a list of facts. At its heart lie certain ongoing processes and developments that cause and explain changes in men, institutions, and even nations over a long period of time. The historical changes related in books 1–5 described the Roman people as they developed under the kings to become worthy of liberty. But mostly these books were static in conception, defining the particular values and virtues that Romans needed to learn. He saw, to his sorrow, little historical development toward mastering these social virtues. Now, in books 6–10, major developments are at hand. The old device of having each book individually stress an unchanging virtue gives way to a new dramatic form: his historical narrative accentuates the processes and developments, not only the unchanging problems, of history.

Some of the elements for his new approach lay already at hand, suggested by certain important scenes in the first pentad. In writing of the Canuleian Law, Livy had achieved, with drama and vigor, a clear exposition of the issue at stake: the very worth of the plebeians. In the speech of Camillus and its aftermath, he had achieved, with equal vigor and even greater dramatic mastery, the clear expression of a lesson learned: that the people must not migrate to Veii. The dramatic finality of the latter scene, Livy perceived, was enhanced by its position at the end of its book.

To Livy, the task was to gather the isolated effects of those scenes into a unity, to bring them to bear on a single development in Roman history. If he could take a historical issue and set it forth vigorously, as he had done with the Canuleian Law; if he could draw its later resolution with the decisiveness that marked Camillus' speech; and if, beyond this, he could draw pertinent events of the middle period in some detail, indicating their movement toward the later resolution, then by this method he would have fashioned a progressive dramatic pattern to give effective literary expression to the ongoing developments of history. In his first five books Livy had depended primarily on direct statements to point out developments through time. Literary effects were largely confined to unchanging, static elements, to abiding themes like liberty, obedience, self-control, and piety. But now the correspondence of literary form to historical subject would, for the first time, mirror the historian's more sophisticated judgments of ongoing processes and changes.

The historians of Greece in the Hellenistic period had long cultivated dramatic effects in their writing. Rhetorical or even tragic flavoring had been consciously sought; episodes such as sieges or public debates were carefully constructed along dramatic lines to evoke emotions like pity, fear, or surprise. Structurally, these scenes were composed in accordance with the principles of tragedy; Aristotelian theory held that such writing was to have a clearly defined beginning, middle, and end. These techniques were certainly known to Roman historiography before Livy. Cicero wrote a famous letter to Lucceius (*Ad Familiares* 5.12) in which he urged the historian to devote part of his larger history to Cicero's own life from his consulship down to his return from exile. He specifically counsels Lucceius to treat the work as a literary dramatization of Cicero's life and changing fortunes; the historian, however, never undertook the project.

In all cases, the dramatic structure and emotional effect seem to have been applied to the careers of individuals or to single historical episodes. Livy too had used dramatic techniques to structure individual episodes in books 1–5, and would continue to do so in the future. But his new concept, to make a dramatic narrative underline and define the ongoing process of historical change, represents a breakthrough to a new level, an incomparably important extension of the old techniques. In emphasizing historical developments in books 6–10, Livy at one stroke surpasses both the work of the Hellenistic historians and his own work in the first pentad.

Before examining the long-term historical developments, let us note briefly the formal and dramatic methods by which Livy usually emphasizes important events within his ongoing historical patterns. On a formal level, the important events are frequently treated at substantial length and placed in emphatic positions at the start, middle, or end of individual books. Many literary techniques are also used to impart dramatic force to the narration of these events. A list of just a few techniques will suggest his dramatic method within these major scenes. Livy's dramatic secret is that he aims to heighten and increase his effects as a scene progresses. He is fond of portraying battles in terms of increasing danger; the peril grows as the contest builds to its most crucial and desperate phase. Once that phase has been reached and the dramatic moment has been fully exploited, Livy usually notes the turn of fortune and the victory of Roman troops in just two or three sentences. Similarly, Livy likes to describe speeches and debates in terms of growing emotion. The increased emotion is often signaled by a switch from indirect to direct discourse, or by such techniques as elaborate periodic sentences, vivid series of questions, even the cadence of the sentences themselves. A third device that Livy uses to increase dramatic tension is episodic structure. By this technique he breaks the narrative into segments often separated by internal "dividers"—digressions, silent pauses by characters, and so forth. In the segment following each divider he builds dramatic tension ever higher, perhaps by showing increased emotion, perhaps by showing events mounting inexorably to their final resolution. Through techniques like these Livy clearly distinguishes major events from other incidents that had less influence on the course of history.

The historical changes that Livy sees are worth describing in some detail here. In books 6–10 he deals with two major historical trends: Rome's expansion toward Italian hegemony and the progress toward reconciliation between patricians and plebeians.

The struggle of the orders had taken a back seat to military affairs during book 5; in the middle of book 6 Livy graphically portrays its revival in the sedition of Manlius Capitolinus (11.14–20). The sedition is a particularly fine example of how episodic structure can be used to build up a sense of increasing tension. What results is a vivid picture of the plebeian class financially ruined by patrician policy, ridden by debt, and forced into bondage to pay up—a class that regards the patricians as its oppressors and that is perilously close to violence, if given an adroit demagogue.

The issue that Livy regards as central to the struggle comes to the fore at the close of book 6 during the highly charged debate on the Licinio-Sextian Laws of 367 B.C. (34–42). In this debate, which recalls and extends the discussion of the Canuleian Law, the main issue is whether or not the plebeians are competent to hold curule, or high-ranking, office. Plebeians argue that events have already proved their abilities: they have served the government well as military tribunes and quaestors and will serve well as consuls. Patricians, however, find their spokesman in Appius Claudius, who denies that plebeians are competent to hold office. First, he charges that plebeians simply are not consular timber; their "unworthiness" (41.4) should bar them from high office. Claudius adds a second objection: the strictures of religion disqualify them from the consulship. To put the divine auspices into their hands would be pollution, a mockery of religion. In this climate of hatred—and the hatred is vividly portrayed—the Licinio-Sextian Laws are passed; plebeians will be consuls. But in this debate Livy has defined the main issues and has directed the reader's attention to their future resolution. Will the plebeians prove competent to hold office? Will they be acceptable to the gods? And will they convince the patricians of their worth?

Subsequent books closely follow the changing relationship between the orders as it evolves from the bitter strife of book 6 to harmony in book 10, a harmony all the more enduring as it will be based on mutual respect. The defeat of Lucius Genucius, the first plebeian consul to lead an army into battle, is seen by patricians as proof that they have been right all along: plebeians are unfit for high office (7.6.7–12). Various small quarrels in book 7 underscore the strained relations between the orders: harshly conducted drafts of troops, disagreeably long campaigns imposed on plebeian soldiers, and the burden of debt. More important is the patricians' opinion that the appointment of a plebeian dictator has sullied the majesty of the office; their contempt for the plebs, vigorously expressed, leads them to try to monopolize the consulship in spite of the Licinio-Sextian Laws—and in several years they succeed. The plebeians, however, still insist that they are quite capable of handling high office and point to Marcus Popilius Laenas as an example of an effective leader from their ranks.

But even now Rome is on the verge of a major breakthrough: at the end of book 7 the orders will finally learn obedience and self-control. Patricians will still not accept plebeians as equal partners in high office but will at least learn forbearance. The immediate occasion of this important step is a conspiracy among plebeian soldiers in 342 B.C. (38.5–41.8). Livy describes their anger over poverty and debt, their gathering at Lautulae and their march on Rome, where they are met by an army under Valerius Corvus. At this point Rome is on the verge of civil war; Livy makes it clear that only the adoption of self-control and obedience averts the conflict. First, the patricians' choice of Valerius (whose pro-plebeian sympathies Livy has recently described) is said to be a clear token that they are now at last committed to a policy of self-control. Second, Quinctius, leader of the conspiracy, wins his men's commitment to obedience. We will see at the end of this chapter that Livy must contrive his characterizations of Valerius and Quinctius to a certain degree in order to achieve the desired effect of moral learning: literary contrivance brings out a legitimate historical development. For the present, we will merely note that when Valerius offers peace and some resolution of grievances, the plebeian soldiers respond to his overtures with trust. This adoption of the civic virtues bears fruit in several measures put into effect for the relief of the soldiers.

Why did Livy choose this particular event to

exemplify the learning of self-control and obedience? Might he not have chosen some other incident just as appropriate? The answer is that two factors recommended this particular episode to Livy as the crucial point where the social virtues were finally learned. First, the patricians never again after 343 B.C. usurped the plebeians' right to consulship. Second, Livy saw that after this point there really was an enduring improvement in relations between the orders. The struggle between them was not over, but henceforth its intensity would be much diminished.

Books 8 and 9, chronicling a period of Roman preoccupation with great foreign wars, nevertheless demonstrate the fruits of the social virtues. There are so few incidents of strife that Livy himself remarks upon the fact (9.33.3). In book 10, Livy shows the resolution of the pentad's great domestic issues in two major scenes. There is the debate on the Ogulnian Law of 300 B.C., which seeks to admit plebeians as pontiffs and augurs (6.3–9.2). But Decius Mus, a plebeian who supports the law, transcends the immediate context to address the larger issue of the plebeians' qualifications to be consuls. By this time the plebeians have served as consuls for well over half a century, establishing a record on which they can be judged. Decius is now able to refute decisively both of Claudius' old charges by reviewing the deeds of plebeian magistrates since the institution of the Licinio-Sextian Laws. He cites examples to show that plebeians have proved their religious merits: the gods have accepted their vows and auspices; they have long served as decemvirs in charge of the sacred rites; and the self-sacrifice of the elder Publius Decius Mus showed that plebeians are just as "pure and holy to the gods" as the patricians. Beyond their religious qualifications, Decius cites historical examples to demonstrate that they can also discharge the responsibilities of high office. He names successful plebeians in every magistracy and states that they enjoy an "acknowledged fitness for office" (7.12). He concludes that results have already proved, and will continue to prove, that

they are entitled to hold the magistracies: "Plebeian and patrician leadership have been equally prosperous so far, and so shall they continue to be" (8.10).

The patricians show none of their old fire in resisting the Ogulnian Law and are not surprised by its passage. Indeed, the conflict of the orders has been so unspirited since the end of book 7 that Livy must now "pump up" interest in it. It is characteristic of his writing that he concludes major issues in dramatic fashion. So now he revives interest in the struggle with two lesser episodes before its dramatic conclusion during the consulship of Fabius and Decius Mus. First, he uses a quarrel between Claudius and Volumnius to point out the destructive effects of discord (18.5–19.22). Second, the establishment of the cult of *Pudicitia Plebeia,* or Plebeian Chastity, demonstrates that plebeian women, like their male counterparts, are striving to prove their worth (23.3–10). The consulship of Fabius and Decius Mus in 295 B.C. occasions the last major scene in the struggle between the orders (24–30). Here the patricians finally accept the plebeians as full partners in running the state. Decius is emblematic of all plebeians who aspire to the highest magistracies. His personal quarrel with Fabius over the apportioning of consular provinces is transposed (24.2) into a quarrel between the orders. At issue is whether a plebeian can overcome patrician opposition and share equally in the glory and danger of high office. It is the recognition of Decius' merits by his patrician colleague Fabius that at last signals the rapprochement of the orders on the basis of mutual respect. When Decius personally intervenes to avert disaster in the Battle of Sentinum, his noble death on the battlefield shows clearly that plebeians can indeed share equally in the glory and danger of the magistracies.

This scene virtually ends Livy's record of the struggle of the orders. There is hardly a single rumble of discontent in the last half of book 10. And well might the account rest here, for two major issues have come full circle in the pentad. Domestic strife has turned into harmony.

Patrician contempt for the plebeians has given way to profound respect. These developments constitute the dramatic highlights of the five books.

The second important historical development, the expansion of Rome's military power, receives similarly dramatic treatment, though its structure is rather different. Instead of the single development toward harmony, Livy finds two distinct phases in Rome's military expansion: a series of wars that consolidated her hold on neighboring peoples followed by a concerted effort to widen her domination to the entire peninsula. The pentad is structured largely around this crucial turn of direction in the foreign wars, which is placed in the middle of book 8, at the very center of the pentad. Because of its critical importance in giving definition to Rome's conquests generally, we may best begin by examining this turning point.

After the end of the Latin Rebellion in 338 B.C., Livy indicates by two important speeches (13.11–18; 20.10–21.10) that the period of local conquest has drawn to a close. The first speech deals with the treatment of the Latins; the second, some nine years later, with the treatment of Privernum. Out of these it emerges clearly that local resistance to Rome has been absolutely crushed. More important is the second lesson that Livy draws from these speeches: that Rome can ensure lasting peace with her neighbors and prepare for future expansion by granting citizenship to these defeated peoples. The sentiments of the consul Lucius Furius on the Latins are worth quoting: "Do you wish to follow the old ways and increase the Roman state by receiving the vanquished as citizens? You have at hand the means to expand and achieve glory. Surely that government is much the firmest that people are glad to obey" (13.16). In each case Rome chooses the mild treatment that will ensure her ability to expand still further; Livy records that her conduct did in fact earn the gratitude of the conquered.

These speeches are followed almost immediately by the great scene that governs the pen-

tad's second half, the outbreak of hostilities with Samnium in 327 B.C., a war known to us as the Second Samnite War. Livy sketches the preliminaries to war in detail and with an ever increasing dramatic tension as its outbreak draws near. The tension finally culminates in the actual challenge to war, where Livy dramatically marks this conflict as a new phase in Rome's conquests. Henceforth, the issue at stake in her struggle will not be the dominion of local peoples but the hegemony of Italy. In the words of the Samnite speaker:

> Why do we beat around the bush? It will not be the words of legates nor any arbiter's decision that will decide our struggles, Romans, but the plain of Campania—where we must meet in battle—and force of arms, and the common chance of war. Let us encamp then face to face between Capua and Suessula, and settle the question whether Samnite or Roman is to be master in Italy.
>
> (23.8–9)

The juxtaposition of these two scenes makes it clear that it is the generous policy of granting citizenship that allows Rome to extend her ambitions to all of Italy. Furthermore, the placing of these two scenes together in the middle of book 8 performs a useful organizational function. It divides the unending list of Roman battles into two halves—what we might call the wars for local and for national control. The crucial turn of direction between the one and the other becomes the central event of the entire pentad.

Before we consider the rest of the pentad in its dramatic framework, however, we should note that two other scenes in book 8 illustrate a second factor that Livy considers important for Rome's expansion: a humane form of military discipline. These two scenes are a symmetrical pair placed near the beginning and end of the book (6.14–8.2; 30.1–37.2).

The first portrays the decision of the consul Manlius to behead his son for breaking orders. It epitomizes the brutality of Rome's old-fashioned discipline: Livy calls it a return to the "old ways" (6.14). He does not condone young Manlius' violation of orders—he had killed a foe in single combat in spite of the consul's prohibition of such fights. But our historian stresses the mitigating circumstances surrounding the offense and emphasizes the shocking harshness of the beheading. The soldiers believe the consul's axes have been readied against their own necks, too, and they spare neither tears nor curses when they throng to young Manlius' funeral. Livy himself adds that inflicting punishment of this sort is not discipline but terror.

Livy's horror over the punishment is based on his belief that the citizens of this era are far different from the earliest Romans. The rough and ready types who populated the early city may have needed to be controlled by force, as Livy himself suggested at the beginning of book 2. But this situation no longer applies. Already in book 7 Livy had shown the rise of civic virtues; the state is now more harmonious and civilized than ever before, and this new maturity requires a basic change of approach to military discipline.

In the second scene, a quarrel between the dictator Papirius and Fabius, his master of the horse, Livy shows that Rome has learned a major lesson: a more humane form of discipline now promotes military success far more effectively than the harshness of antiquity. In this quarrel Papirius wishes to behead Fabius for violating orders. Although Livy again concedes that disobedience is wrong, his real interest is in showing that Papirius' idea of discipline is intolerable. Not only does he stress the dictator's immoderate anger, but he goes even further by showing its evil effects: it stifles the initiative of subordinate officers with disastrous results and so alienates the common soldiers that they deliberately obstruct victory. Once the evil effects of severity have been clearly delineated, Livy points out the solution. Papirius realizes that his own relentless discipline created his problems; severity must be mingled with kindness to be effective. He begins to visit the wounded and entrust them by name to their legates, tribunes, and prefects. His change of

heart produces a change of fortune. He crushes the Samnites so thoroughly that they resolve never to engage him again. The superiority of the new discipline, more suited to these civilized times, could hardly be more explicit.

Book 8, then, stands as the center of the military narrative of the entire pentad and not only literally. In it are expressed Livy's most significant historical judgments on the importance of treating allies well and maintaining a military discipline that acknowledges the humanity of the soldier. Moreover, placing the Samnites' challenge to Italian hegemony midway in the book divides the pentad into distinct halves and sets the dramatic framework for the rest of the pentad.

Events in the military sphere have very little dramatic impact in the first half of the pentad. Partly this may be attributed to the fact that these books are also devoted heavily to domestic affairs. More important, however, is the fact that Rome's numerous battles—and victories— never seem to have much relation to each other. Instead, there are scattered campaigns directed now against Volsci, Latins, or Hernici, now against some local combination of foes. While some of these may be impressively narrated, there is little apparent connection between them. Even the First Samnite War in book 7, which represents a major effort against a major foe, is not treated as a thing important in itself. Instead, Livy handles it as an introduction to the Second and Third Samnite Wars to follow. Here he merely shows that the Romans are morally justified in fighting the Samnites and that the enemy is very tenacious in battle.

The pentad's first half, therefore, generates no dramatic sense of Roman momentum and growth toward greater power. The battles do at least give the impression that Rome has recovered from the Gallic sack. Beyond that, we can merely add that heroes like Camillus in book 6 or Valerius Corvus and Manlius Torquatus in book 7 give expression to her confidence and prowess. It is this relatively unexciting era of local conquest that ends with the generous grants of citizenship in book 8.

Subsequent events are quite different: over the pentad's second half they are carefully narrated and carefully placed within books in order to foster the dramatic impression that Rome is on the march, that she, not the Samnites, will be the mistress of Italy. After the onset of the Second Samnite War, Livy describes various Roman successes and hints (8.27.3–4) that Rome's activity is bringing her closer to Italian hegemony. A victory won by Papirius Cursor reduces the Samnites to desperate straits. Finally, a major Roman victory at the end of book 8 (38.1–39.9) reinforces dramatically her growing ascendancy over the Samnites. The battle is contested long and bitterly. But such is the magnitude of the Samnites' defeat that Livy says their power to wage war has been broken. They decide to seek peace from Rome, only to have their advances rebuffed; the war therefore continues into book 9.

Books 9 and 10 each create within themselves a strong impression of Rome's march to victory. Each book, however, is only a part—historically and dramatically—of the larger movement toward Italian hegemony that began in the middle of book 8. That book 9 should achieve this effect is remarkable since its early chapters record the terrible defeat suffered by Rome at Caudium (1.1–12.4). Livy, however, greatly reduces the significance of the defeat. Indeed, it is worth noting that his dramatic method of underlining Roman expansion requires this, for if he dwells on the defeat he must inevitably lose the dramatic impression of Rome's growing power. His decision to play down, though not to deny, the defeat should not be attributed to virulent patriotism; he emphasizes certain Roman defeats elsewhere. Here his intention is merely to preserve a strong dramatic impression of the larger (and genuine) historical trend: the expansion of Roman power. Accordingly, he attributes the setback exclusively to temporary factors: unfavorable terrain, poor generalship, loss of divine favor, and even—a stylized tour de force here—the Romans' sudden and inexplicable loss of char-

acter. Indeed, he constantly stresses the transience of these factors and vividly foreshadows the day when Rome in her turn will humiliate the Samnites. It may be fairly said, therefore, that Rome's military momentum hastens undisturbed right through the Caudine defeat.

The theme of vengeance for Caudium dominates the many Roman victories that follow in book 9. The superiority of the Roman soldiers over the Samnites is frequently stressed; on a fair field they are irresistible. Finally, at the end of the book, the Samnites (40.1–17) and their Etruscan allies (39.5–11) are decisively beaten. Of the Etruscans Livy says that their ancient power was broken in the battle. The Samnites fare no better in their engagement. Livy describes their elaborate preparation of magnificent armies, accoutered in gold and silver, as they prepare to stake everything on one throw of the dice—all to no avail, since Rome wins a complete victory. After these two triumphs, the Etruscans and Samnites must both seek the peace that ends the Second Samnite War. For the moment, the supremacy of Roman arms is unchallenged.

Book 10 carries Rome's military momentum to an appropriate dramatic climax. After the declaration of the Third Samnite War fairly early in the book (11.11–12.3), Livy directs his attention forward to the climax of the campaign, the Battle of Sentinum, where Rome would fight the ultimate battle for supremacy against a great coalition of foes comprising Samnites, Etruscans, Umbrians, and Gauls. Livy indicates the battle's historical importance and builds toward it as a dramatic climax by foreshadowing it several times as a great and difficult struggle. This battle will represent the maximum effort of each side; Rome's dire peril is explicitly and repeatedly stated. The result of these devices is that the early battles of the Third Samnite War seem like mere preliminaries; the great emphasis, both dramatically and historically, is thrown onto the Battle of Sentinum (27.8–29.20). The battle is portrayed as a very "near run" thing; the Roman left wing, cavalry and infantry alike, is thrown into panic before the consul Decius Mus reverses its fortunes. The Romans ultimately rout the enemy on both wings, inflict horrible casualties, and capture the Samnite camp.

This victory, Livy says, breaks the back of Italian resistance. He notes that the Samnites are desperate (31.6) and, although he admires their obstinate courage, calls their situation impossible:

> In the past year the Samnites, operating both on their own and in unison with their allies' forces, had been slaughtered by four Roman armies under four different generals: in the territory of Sentinum, among the Paeligni, at Tifernum, and in the Stellate plains. They had lost their nation's most distinguished commander. They clearly saw their allies, the Etruscans, Umbrians, and Gauls, reduced to the same state as themselves. Neither at home nor abroad could they find any proper strength to resist—and yet they would not give up the fight! They were so set upon defending their freedom—even though their cause was lost—that they would rather be conquered than not try for victory.
>
> (31.12–14)

Livy's tribute is, in effect, the epitaph for serious Italian resistance in the pentad. Thereafter, his overwhelming emphasis is on the ease with which Rome conquers and on the desperation of her foes. Many Roman victories follow; at one point (37.1) Livy says that Samnite resistance is virtually finished. The last major battle in the pentad (38.1–42.7), which portrays the rout of the Linen Legion, is used for much the same purpose as the last scenes of books 8 and 9: it gives expression to the Romans' ascendancy over their enemy. Here again the Samnites are putting their best men into the struggle, again equipping them elaborately; they are said to represent the entire strength of Samnium. Further, they bind their leaders with a gruesome oath to fight to the death rather than flee. The Romans' superiority, however, is clearly shown: they scorn the Samnites' fancy weapons as mere idle display and face the bat-

tle with confidence. The engagement becomes an instant massacre; the Samnites finally break and flee pell-mell, suffering disastrous losses.

With this battle, major operations come to a close; Roman forces continue to display absolute supremacy through the few chapters that remain in the book. The grand triumphs of the consuls Papirius and Carvilius end the account of military affairs on an unmistakable note: Rome is everywhere triumphant over her enemies.

Livy thus brings this historical issue full circle in books 6–10. From her weakness after the Gallic sack, Rome has come forward first to the domination of her neighbors, then to a position of irresistible power in her quest to rule Italy.

In addition to the carefully developed drama of these books, Livy shows a fondness for studied architectural symmetry. Many of the important scenes in books 6–10 are symmetrically balanced with related scenes. The conquest of the Latins in the middle of book 8 ends the pentad's first half and concludes Rome's wars against local enemies. The Second Samnite War immediately launches Rome's peninsular conquests, a topic that dominates the second half of the pentad. The quarrel of Papirius and Fabius late in book 8 thematically and structurally parallels the brutal discipline of Manlius early in the book. The pentad's first and last major events in the struggle of the orders, the Manlian sedition in the middle of book 6 and the quarrel of Decius and Fabius in the middle of book 10, parallel each other. The debates on the plebeians' merits are also symmetrically placed, indicating that the Ogulnian Law at the beginning of book 10 should be seen in relation to the Licinio-Sextian Laws at the end of book 6. Careful architectural design was in Augustan times considered an important ordering device in works of literature. And the evidence of Livy's control of his subject lies in the general structure of his work.

The development of both major historical trends has been clearly and dramatically set forth. What of Livy's perception of historical causation—the forces behind the growing military supremacy and the new domestic harmony? The causes are avowedly moral—as Livy told his readers they would be: "I would have each reader pay special attention to these matters: what our life and character used to be, through what men, and by what conduct at home and abroad, dominion was gained and extended" (preface 8–9). Nowhere in the extant books, in fact, are morals more directly responsible for historical changes. Livy of course gives Rome's great generals full credit for their role in her expansion. But moral qualities are an even more important factor. He sees that expansion required the largeness of mind to extend citizenship to allies. Also essential was a new and humane attitude toward the soldiers; military discipline must be consistent with their dignity as men. Beyond this, there was a certain inherent toughness that made Roman soldiers more than a match even for the Samnites. Above all, it was the struggle of the orders that demanded moral learning. The political maturity that finally made domestic peace a reality was founded on the mastery of self-control, obedience, and mutual respect.

Is this moral view necessarily simplistic, even dull-witted? I think not. Again I would suggest that Livy's vision is profoundly true, even statesmanlike. The respected political observer Carl Rowan offered this commentary about the recent treaty in Zimbabwe (Rhodesia):

> After fifteen agonizing weeks of peace talks, Great Britain's Thatcher government has gotten one point through to whites who have held power so long that they would kill to keep it and blacks who wanted power so badly that they would kill to get it: There can be no viable Rhodesia, or worthwhile future for any Rhodesians, unless whites and blacks learn to share power and live together in mutual respect.
>
> ("From a Bloody River: Driftwood of Reason," *Cincinnati Enquirer*, 26 December 1979)

Livy saw the problems of Rome in similar terms. Deeply felt injury, even hatred, had torn the state into rival camps. Surely he was not wrong to find that, at bottom, the healing of divisions came from the moral learning of men.

Livy's desire to create an overall dramatic pattern to reflect historical developments greatly influenced his treatment of particular characters. Now, much has been written about the finesse and excellence of Livy's characterizations; they are commonly considered one of the finest aspects of the *History*. But, in fact, Livy has little to say about most of his characters. The English historian Thomas Babington Macaulay was quite right when he called Livy's heroes "the most insipid of all beings, real or imaginary, the heroes of Plutarch excepted."

A discussion of the issue must proceed from this premise: the mere fact that Livy records certain people doing certain things is not per se any proof of literary characterization. It is of course proper to view men in the light of their deeds, but characterization calls for more. If, for example, the society page of a newspaper states that Mrs. John Doe gave a garden party on behalf of the local hospital, surely that reveals something of Mrs. Doe's philanthropic nature. It is equally sure that this is not literary characterization, which requires some portrayal of internal consistency in the character. In books 21–30, for example, Quintus Fabius Maximus the Delayer is given a very distinct and consistent personality as an advocate of cautious strategy against Hannibal. This personality is hardly complex, but at least it molds and affects the course of events: it is Fabius, and no other, who advises Paullus against engaging Hannibal in book 22 and who opposes Scipio's invasion of Africa in book 28. Most of Livy's heroes are far different—especially in these first ten books, where the rapid survey of many years leaves little scope for drawing well-developed characters. To be sure, certain virtues do emerge from their conduct before the Senate, in battle, or in their dealings with defeated enemies. It cannot be said of them, however, that their characters mold external events; rather it is the record of events that defines their characters in the simplest fashion. Demonstrating in their various adventures now loyalty, now fairness, now valor, they become simple agglomerates of whatever virtues (or vices) attach to the deeds that history has associated with their names; they acquire no internal consistency.

Manlius Capitolinus exemplifies the insipidity of these characters. In book 5 he is a hero who single-handedly saves the very citadel of Rome from capture by the Gauls. In book 6, however, he plots to overthrow the state. Livy makes little attempt to understand Capitolinus as a character, to portray the internal tensions of his soul as he turns from patriot to traitor. He is simply a one-dimensional figure in whom a glorious deed and a foul one coexist with only the most perfunctory explanation: Manlius was impetuous by nature and envied the honors accorded to Camillus. Other men's deeds may happen to be consistent, yet the men themselves are not any more penetratingly observed.

But if Livy is uninterested in portraying characters for their own sake, he is consummately interested in using them as stage props to clarify the great historical developments of the era. The examples of Valerius and Quinctius will suffice. Just before the military conspiracy that ends book 7, Valerius' character is described in detail (32.10–33.4); special emphasis is given to his love of plebeians. Now, if Livy were concerned with Valerius' character per se, he would have offered further observations on the man during his later career; certainly he reappears many times in later books. Yet Livy has nothing to say about him on any of those occasions. After the early bloom, any trace of personality seems to wilt away completely. It is clear, in fact, that the only reason Livy emphasizes Valerius' character at all is his usefulness as a symbol of self-control (40.7–9) so that the patricians' choosing him to face the military conspiracy can be represented as a conscious adoption of moderate policies by the patrician order in general (40.17–18).

The treatment of Quinctius, leader of the conspiracy, is nothing less than a tour de force

(7.39.11–41.2). It shows unmistakably how unconcerned Livy could be about characterizing men by their deeds. Quinctius' role as the author of obedience requires a certain moral stature of him. If he is tainted with the crime of sedition, he will hardly be a satisfactory symbol of morality. Livy therefore stresses his innocence: he is described as a retired soldier with no political ambitions, on whose help the conspirators cannot rely. They must drag him off by force to be their leader; once in command he is still "stunned" and takes no part in the decision to march on Rome. He is said to be worn out with fighting for his country, let alone against it. Even Valerius is aware of his unwillingness to rebel. In short, Livy assigns Quinctius no role in his own conspiracy other than to help Valerius end it!

BOOKS 21–30 (218–201 B.C.)

> Yet these disasters and the defections of her allies [after Cannae] did not cause even a whisper for peace among the Romans either before the consul's arrival at Rome or after he returned and renewed the bitter thoughts of their defeat. At this critical hour the spirit of the country was so great that men of all stations thronged the consul as he returned from a complete disaster—one chiefly of his own making—and thanked him because he had not given up hope for the republic. If he had been a Carthaginian general returning home, he would have suffered every manner of punishment.
>
> (22.61.13–15)

Books 11–20 have been lost; the first five of these carried the *History* through the defeat of Pyrrhus and the conquest of Italy. The next five books recounted the First Punic War and quickly surveyed events down to the Second.

In writing the history of the Second Punic War in books 21–30, Livy saw three main phases in the conflict. First came a rush of stunning Carthaginian victories, after which Hannibal's army in Italy won over many of Rome's allies and threatened the city with imminent destruction. Roman recovery and a more sporadic positional warfare in Italy marked the second phase. Indeed, as the recovery progressed Rome was able to recover clear strategic superiority. Finally, the third phase saw Rome's invasion of Africa; Scipio's complete victory over Hannibal at Zama crowned the campaign and ended the war.

Livy explicitly sets forth the historical causes that governed the development of the war. In the first phase Hannibal's unrivaled tactical genius ensured victory for Carthage, first in the engagements at the Ticinus and Trebia, then in the great battles of annihilation, Lake Trasimene and Cannae. With the defection of Rome's allies in southern Italy, the war had reached its nadir (22.61.10–15). The bloody defeats at length taught Rome a strategic lesson that brought on the war's "middle" phase. The new strategy was to wear Hannibal down by indirect methods instead of engaging him directly. Even allowing the loss of her southern allies, Rome still possessed a vast reserve of citizens and allies, arms, horses, and supplies. These daily increased her strength while Hannibal, far from his homeland, inevitably grew weaker as time passed (22.39.11–17). Hannibal therefore lacked the manpower to meet Roman threats against all his holdings; towns with small Carthaginian garrisons were attacked in his absence. Through this positional warfare Rome was able to winkle the Carthaginians gradually out of their positions without an open engagement.

Hannibal suffered particularly from the lack of reinforcements. In the war's early years he needed a suitable port to receive supplies by sea (see 23.1.5). In the long run, however, it was Carthage's own internal factions, as well as the preference to defend Spain rather than attack Italy, that denied him the needed supplies (28.12.9; 30.20.2–4). Hannibal saw the handwriting on the wall when Hasdrubal's army, attempting to join him overland, was destroyed at the Metaurus. He could no longer hope to maintain his scattered garrisons against Roman pressure and had to withdraw into the toe of Italy (27.51.11–13), an action that finally eliminated the threat to Rome and central Italy (28.11.8). It was the removal of this danger, along with the successful conclusion of the war in Spain, that in Livy's view justified Rome's decision to invade Africa. Livy therefore sees changes in Rome's strategic policy and situation as the factors moving the war through its various phases. Her new cautionary strategy ends Hannibal's period of success; the growing strength and security derived from this policy finally justify a direct attack on Africa.

Livy's explanation of the course of the war is, in broad outline, still followed today. The historical causation that he perceives here differs markedly from the moral learning that he considered so important an explanation for ending the struggle of the orders and strengthening Rome's military power in books 6–10. But if at one level Rome owes her progress in the war to wise and timely strategies, at another level it is still the excellence of the Roman soldier and the moral strength of the nation that allows her to win. Rome's soldiers are regarded as second to none in the world, equal to Hannibal's best and far superior to those of most nations. As for Rome itself, Livy's repeatedly stresses her determination to resist the foe, without disguising the fact that her moral strength was pressed close to the limit. He especially marvels at the moral strength that bade Rome fight after Cannae: it was, in his judgment, her finest hour (22.61.13–15).

Books 21–30 do not deal with moral development in the specific terms of books 6–10. Nonetheless, it seems fair to say that in his first thirty books Livy has created an unforgettable picture of specifically Roman virtues. To those learned virtues—obedience, self-control, respect among all classes of citizens, discipline based on consideration for a soldier's humanity, generosity to allies—may be added his many individual portraits of other virtues such as courage, loyalty, perseverance, and patriotism. For example, the conduct of Romans during the elections for 210 B.C., during which the leading candidate turned down the consulship and a junior century actually consulted its seniors for advice, seemed to Livy an eloquent proof of the moral soundness of those times (26.22.14–15). Morality is not used as the exclusive explanation for every Roman success; Livy's idea of historical causation is more sober than that. He does, however, in specific cases, acknowledge that moral learning and moral character are the foundations of progress. With the close of the Second Punic War, Rome has reached perhaps the pinnacle of her excellence. The first hints of moral decline are close at hand.

Just as he did in books 6–10, Livy constructs his dramatic narrative around his historical interpretation. The structure of books 21–30 grows out of his interpretation of the war's three phases. Books 21 and 22, covering events through the Battle of Cannae and the defection of Rome's southern Italian allies, correspond to the first phase. The long middle phase of the war, during which Rome avoids open battle with Hannibal, comprises the next six books. Within these six books two subphases are discernible: Carthage still retains the ascendancy in books 23–25 (through 212 B.C.). The midpoint of the decade is the balance point of the war. Rome is ascendant in books 26–28 (211–205 B.C.); her successes in book 26 bring the war back, as it were, to its starting point: neither side holds an advantage (26.37.9). In these books Hannibal's position becomes increasingly untenable, and Rome wins complete control of Spain. Books 29–30 cover the third phase, the period of Roman supremacy, the invasion of Africa and successful conclusion of the war.

This structural scheme is reinforced by the changing dramatic quality of Livy's narrative as the war passes from phase to phase. In books 21–22 Livy may be said to reach the height of his literary achievement. Nowhere else in the extant thirty-five books does he achieve the dramatic tension that marks these two books. The magnitude of the war, the greatness of the enemy, and the extremity of Rome's peril all lend unmatched dramatic power to his narrative of the war's first years. The disasters at Lake Trasimene and Cannae are told forcefully and at length; they are placed emphatically at the start and end of book 22. The characterization of Hannibal as a nearly invincible opponent adds to the effect. It also lends point and even irony to the Romans' debates on strategy. These debates are exploited for dramatic effect. The quarrel of Minucius and Fabius Maximus, for example, centers around their respective preferences for offensive and defensive strategies. The disastrous results of Minucius' policy are powerfully drawn (22.25–30). Strategy is again the subject of disagreement between Varro and Paullus. Again the decision to engage Hannibal is exploited for dramatic effect; it strikingly foreshadows the disaster at Cannae (22.38–45, especially 43.8–9).

If the choice of rash methods creates powerful dramatic effects in books 21–22, the adoption of a temporizing strategy marks both the end of Rome's greatest danger historically and a much reduced dramatic intensity in books 23–28, the middle period when the war was fought on the most even terms. Already at the end of book 22 Rome's recovery was foreshadowed in Maharbal's comment that Hannibal did not know how to deliver a "knockout blow" after Cannae, Scipio's oath, and Rome's refusal to despair. In succeeding books Fabius' strategy of delay clearly checks Hannibal in Italy. Action in the other theaters is regarded as no imminent threat to Rome. Carthage seems in general, however, to retain its advantage through the first half of the decade. As late as book 25, Livy (using a chronology now known to be wrong) found one major Roman success (the capture of Syracuse) far outweighed by two great Carthaginian successes (the capture of Tarentum and the destruction of two Roman armies in Spain).

In book 26, however, all of the major successes belong to Rome: Hannibal's march on Rome fails to lift the siege of Capua, Rome strikes an alliance with the Aetolians, Capua falls, and the important Spanish town of New Carthage is seized. Allusions to Rome's growing ascendancy frame the book and underscore the effect of the major victories. The opening sentences of the book make it clear that the retaking of Capua might well bring many Italian cities back into the Roman camp. The book's last sentence observes that the loss of New Carthage was a serious blow to Punic strength. During the next two books Rome wins the great battle at the Metaurus and completely subdues Spain. Hannibal's decision to withdraw into the toe of Italy closes book 27 in a forceful manner. Book 28 closes with a dramatic flourish to underline Rome's coming offensive. A speech of Scipio (43.2–44.18), refuting Fabius (40.3–42.22), makes it clear that the time for attack has finally arrived. And in the last sentence, Hannibal mounts an inscription of his deeds at the temple of Juno Lacinia, as if to write *finis* to his Italian campaign.

In the war's last phase, it is Rome that enjoys the clear dramatic momentum of books 29 and 30. Major scenes emphasize the invasion of Africa, the success at Utica, and the decisive victory at Zama. Hannibal withdraws from Italy, fully acknowledging defeat; the evil omen that greets him upon sighting Africa (30.25.11–12) contrasts with the good omen that greeted Scipio (29.27.12). In this very brief account I do not wish to suggest that there are no incidents that break the general tone of the war's different phases. There are omens of hope in Rome's hour of trial. Likewise there are doubts expressed about the Romans' ability to endure even during their years of success. These allusions actually lend extra interest to the narrative, for they invite the reader to consider how easily events might have turned out differently.

Characterization is far more vivid in these books than in books 1–10 since Livy now has more information about the personages of his history. To some extent, however, characters are still used for the same purpose: to give historical focus to the action of the narrative. The technique does not necessarily conflict with portraying the genuine traits of individuals, but it can result in rather one-sided personalities. Fabius, for example, is noteworthy only for his

caution: he consistently espouses delaying tactics against Hannibal. Minucius and Varro, on the other hand, emerge as rash proponents of the offensive. Debates involving these three in books 21 and 22 are used to focus on the strategic policy that stands behind Rome's early defeats. Again in book 28, Fabius characteristically warns against the invasion of Africa. He now loses the debate to Scipio, however. Livy, without a word of criticism against the great man, has politely indicated that the time for delaying tactics is past.

The treatment of Hannibal is less one-sided than that of Fabius but also serves a distinct dramatic purpose. He is portrayed as a man of limitless, unscrupulous resource and undying hatred of Rome. This portrayal of unbelievable skill gives dramatic force to Livy's historical judgment that it is Hannibal's army alone that can threaten Rome, and conversely that only by defeating Hannibal can Rome defeat Carthage. If Hannibal is ultimately less one-dimensional than Fabius, it is because of the range of skills that Livy attributes to him. Indeed, as the prospect of defeat stretches more clearly before him, he acquires a certain greatness. Livy is frankly astonished at a personality capable of uniting an army without common laws, customs, or language and maintaining discipline even when the army was unpaid, underfed, and without hope of victory.

Scipio surely receives a more vivid characterization than any other Roman. His military skill, determination, and ambition are all well portrayed. The reader also sees a more personal side of this great man. He is moved by the beauty of a maiden betrothed to Allucius. And when dining with Hasdrubal at the table of King Syphax—was ever a social evening so tense?—he charms both host and foe.

BOOKS 31–45 (201–167 B.C.)

. . . this victory, which has made you masters of the world. You should now lay aside your quarrels against all mortals and, like the gods, should mercifully consider the interests of the entire human race.

(The legates of Antiochus to the Romans, after the Battle of Magnesia: 37.45.8–9)

You, by Hercules, as men of war, must be on guard against the pleasantness of Asia and must hasten from it as soon as possible: such is the power of these foreign pleasures to put out every spark of military spirit in you. Such too is the effect even of contact with the training and ways of the natives.

(Manlius to his troops: 38.17.18)

Various scholars have remarked that Livy's prose becomes somewhat mechanical in the last fifteen books. The historian seems to be tiring of his labors; indeed, he confesses his weariness in the preface to book 31. Along with the prose style, I believe that the dramatic quality of these books also declines. Though Livy has much to say about Roman history in this period, these, of all the extant books, are generally the least effective as literary history.

Two factors in particular contribute to the diminished dramatic impact of books 31–45. First, these pentads contain many events unrelated to their respective wars: with Philip V, Antiochus, and Perseus. The seventh pentad covers events from the middle of 201 through 192 B.C., but the war with Philip lasted only from 200 until 196. The eighth pentad includes the years 191 through 179 B.C., while the war with Antiochus lasted from 191 through 188, with the decisive battle coming as early as 190. In the ninth pentad we have the events of 178 through 167 B.C., but the war with Perseus was fought from 171 to 168. Although Livy devotes extra attention to the war years, they still comprise only about one half of their respective pentads. In the remaining space he covers the years between the wars: a host of unrelated events that largely destroy the unity of the whole pentad. In books 31–35, for example, Livy places the declaration of war against Philip near the very start of book 31; the war, however, is over before the middle of book 33. There are major scenes thereafter—notably the proclamation of Greek freedom in

the middle of the whole pentad (33.32–33)—yet the last two and a half books limp along, merely foreshadowing the upcoming war with Antiochus.

This problem is the result of the increased information available to Livy about these years. In his early books Livy was able to pass very quickly through the periods between major events. In the fourth pentad, for example, he had covered the First Punic War (264–241 B.C.) and subsequent events (241–219 B.C.) down to the eve of the Second Punic War. There he made books 16–19 deal with the war itself, while book 20 encompassed the whole period between the wars—twenty-two and a half years in a single book. Interruption of the main topic was thus minimized. The increasing volume of information available on the later periods has now ruled out the use of that procedure. Never again after book 20 would Livy cover more than seven years in a book; seldom would he cover more than three. The fact that he can no longer pass over uninteresting periods quickly now makes it more difficult to compose pentads tightly unified around single historical topics.

The second factor in the reduced dramatic effect of these pentads is simply that Livy has not even treated the wars with much dramatic force. One change in technique particularly stands out. Much of the overriding sense of direction in books 6–10 and 21–30 came from certain scenes that pointed out historical issues that would be important in the future. Would the plebeians be able to prove their worth as consuls on the secular and religious planes? Would Rome be able to withstand Hannibal's onslaught? These issues, once clearly defined, were carefully and dramatically developed over periods of many books.

The approach in the later pentads is far different. Scenes raising general issues for dramatic development are hardly to be found. One such scene is Philip's speech in book 33, where he says that Macedonia's confidence must be in its phalanx (3.11–4.4). The scene seems to suggest that the reader judge Macedonia's future fortunes according to this yardstick; but the scene does not give a sense of direction to ensuing books, for the phalanx is smashed at Cynoscephalae just five chapters later. Likewise in book 36 Livy emphasizes that Antiochus' hopes of controlling Greece will be dashed if his Aetolian allies surrender to Rome (26.1–6). Again the reader has been directed to follow a future development; but again that development comes almost immediately. The surrender of the Aetolians at Naupactus (34.1–35.6) marks the end of the war with Antiochus in Greece (35.14).

We may observe that neither the phalanx nor the Aetolians could really be used anyway as unifying ideas for those entire wars. They are only small parts of the wars. Perhaps the problem in these pentads is that there exists no readily available person (like Hannibal) or issue (like the plebeians' worth) to give definition to events overall. Lacking clear focal points, they do not lend themselves very well to dramatic presentation. If this interpretation is correct, it may not be true that dramatic tension is lacking here because Livy grew tired. The opposite may in fact be closer to the truth. Livy may have grown tired, even somewhat bored, because his material lacked the potential for dramatic tension that comes from an important overriding issue to unify events and explain their meaning. This tiredness creates, I think, more than a mechanical prose style; it makes his treatment of major events differ substantially from his treatment of important events in earlier books. As before, the major episodes are usually described at length; likewise, Livy continues to put them in emphatic positions at the beginning, middle, or end of books. Gone, however, are the devices that were so important before: the sense of danger, the high emotion, the episodic structure to build exciting effects. There may be good reason for the lack of danger—Livy regarded the Syrian king Antiochus, for example, with utmost contempt—but the fact remains that major events are now seldom treated as dramatic episodes. They miss the

dramatic force that in earlier books so clearly underscored important historical events and often even defined their particular importance. The naval battle off Myonnesus, for example, is fought with hardly any indication of its importance as a preparation for the Roman invasion of Asia (37.26–30). The effect of the battle is merely stated in the aftermath. This scene may be contrasted with the Battle of Sentinum in book 10, where the narrative showed that control of Italy hinged quite directly on the outcome of a desperate battle.

It is to Livy's credit that, having failed to find individual persons or issues to unify these wars, he sought other (and in fact more appropriate) ways to organize and interpret them. With varying success, he did find other means to show how and why these wars developed as they did. The result is hardly ever stirring reading, but it is at its best a rather workmanlike product. We will examine each of the three pentads briefly.

Of the three, books 31–35 seem to have the least to recommend them. The old dramatic technique is virtually absent, and it has not been satisfactorily replaced with other methods to show the importance of major events. In the latter part of book 31, for example, the war against Philip is narrated in the most perfunctory fashion—bare accounts of cities attacked, routes of march, and so on. Nor is there any better indication of the importance of other events, like naval movements or the siege of Atrax. Some indication of the war's progress to date comes in the speech of Aristaenus before the Achaean League (32.21). The defection of Nabis to the Romans at the end of book 32, however, seems to have no discernible importance in Livy. Finally, at the beginning of book 33 a few events indicate the approach of the war's end. Besides Philip's speech about the Macedonian phalanx, the Romans' alliance with the Boeotians is said to secure their rear area and signal the coming end of the war (2.9). And, Philip's weakness is very evident: with Macedonia bled white by generations of warfare, he must conscript both youths and old veterans (3.1–5). These are dramatic strokes of the most modest sort, but at least they underline the significance of those events.

In books 36–40, the war with Antiochus is all but concluded in the first two books. The peace treaty is placed in the middle of book 38. The second half of this pentad, like the previous one, is therefore somewhat loosely organized around the topic of the upcoming war with Perseus. The war with Antiochus in books 36 and 37 is rather more effectively narrated than that with Philip. The important phases of the conflict are clearly marked out; literary touches underline these phases and point out important historical events and decisions. Book 36 recounts the campaign in Greece. Its beginning brings the declaration of war; in the center a major scene shows the rout of Antiochus' army at Thermopylae and the ejection of the king himself from Greece; near the book's end the Aetolian surrender at Naupactus signals the close of hostilities in Greece. These events point up the overall progress of the campaign. One literary device in particular helps to fill out the picture. Hannibal, now present at Antiochus' court, is employed as a prophetic figure. He urgently advises the king to win at any cost the support of Philip V for his Greek campaign, wise counsel that Antiochus ignores to his sorrow and that portends the failure of his expedition. And near the end of the book Hannibal foresees that the Romans will cross over into Asia: the next phase of the war is to be waged in, and for possession of, Asia. Book 36 ends with the Battle of Cyssus, a Roman naval victory that confirms the truth of Hannibal's insight.

Book 37 covers the decisive campaign in Asia. Its first half records the preliminaries to invasion; the second half relates the campaign itself. It is clear from the outset that the Asian campaign will be the subject of the book (2.3; 3.9). A host of small episodes follow: Rome's renewed war with the Aetolians as well as Antiochus' naval warfare against the Rhodians and land battles against the Pergamenians. In the face of the complexity of all this information, Livy focuses rather effectively on the Roman crossing. He stresses Antiochus' foolishness in abandoning Lysimachia, where his garrison would have controlled the embarkation points to Asia (31.1–4); prominent too is the fight to control the sea. The defeat of the king's fleet off Myonnesus is described in a major midbook scene (26–30). After this battle, Antiochus, abandoning all hope of opposing the invasion with his navy, resolves to fight a decisive engagement on land (31.4–6). When the decisive battle does come at Magnesia, the extent of the king's preparation is evident in the description of his order of battle (40.1–41.1). His forces are crushed and his hopes ruined in the actual battle, however (41.2–44.2); he is forced to seek peace (45.4–19).

Livy perceives the special importance of this battle. Rome has now defeated the last great rival power; henceforth she stands alone with the whole world at her feet. The king's legates (45.8) and the Rhodians (54.15) both recognize Rome as master of the world. As if to emphasize the point, delegations pour into the city from all the peoples of Asia (45.21).

The war with Antiochus, then, is clearly set forth. The devices by which Livy shows its development are mostly structural, though the focus is aided by occasional dramatic touches. That these books ultimately lack dramatic force is due partly to the lack of a single controlling personality or idea, partly to the unexciting narration of major episodes. But the reason goes deeper than that. The fact of the matter is that Livy held Antiochus, and Eastern royalty in general, in the deepest contempt. He frequently stresses the empty show inherent in kingship and contrasts Antiochus' extravagant boasts with the weak force that he actually brings to Greece. Livy reserves particular censure for the king's disgraceful conduct in Greece, where he married a lowborn woman and then spent a winter in banquets and drunken sleep. When Antiochus takes up his station at Thermopylae, Livy cannot resist contrasting his soft troops with those Spartans whose heroism immortalized the pass. Given this attitude, Livy could hardly have regarded the war with Antiochus as a dangerous or dramatic episode in Roman history.

The last extant pentad (books 41–45) suffers from several gaps in the text: about half of books 41 and 43 and smaller sections of books 44 and 45 are missing. In spite of these gaps, however, Livy's interpretation of the war with Perseus may be quite clearly discerned. As in books 36–40 he indicates the war's progress by dividing its major phases into different books. War breaks out in the middle of book 42; the Macedonians are clearly ascendant until the end of book 43. The first battle of the war at the end of book 42 marks the start of their success. Through the entire next book the war continues in the same general tenor. Perseus' bold winter campaign secures his kingdom against any flanking attack from Illyria; Rome suffers several reverses; discipline especially has suffered among the Roman forces; the Senate hears a discouraging report on the war. Perseus himself is represented as swift and resourceful in action—until the end of book 43, when his stingy refusal to spend money for the Illyrians' support foreshadows the imminent reversal of fortunes.

Book 44 covers the period of Roman success; the decisive battle at Pydna, which ends the war, closes this book. From the outset of this book the changed fortunes of both sides are evident. The restoration of Roman discipline under Aulus Hostilius is noted at the start. The later arrival of Aemilius Paullus as commander brings the troops to the highest degree of discipline and efficiency. On the other hand, Perseus, once bold and resourceful, now appears to be completely out of his wits, unable to conduct a campaign rationally. His stinginess especially seems to be a fatal flaw, for it costs him the aid of some fine Gallic mercenaries. At the end of the book, Rome's great victory at Pydna decides the war; after the battle the cities of Macedonia surrender. The explanation of the war's outcome, which can be culled from var-

ious passages and deduced from the structural break between books 43 and 44, is compounded of several factors: Paullus' excellence as commander, the fighting efficiency of Rome's legions, Perseus' unwillingness to buy the support of badly needed allies, the Roman victory over his ally Gentius, and Perseus' frankly unexplained failure as a commander in time of crisis.

A parallel development, sometimes overshadowing the history of the three wars, is that Rome's national character begins by slow degrees to show traces of decline—as Livy said it would: "In his mind let the reader follow the way morals at first subsided, as it were, as discipline slipped little by little" (preface 9). This decline is portrayed in occasional incidents spread over many books. We would not in fact expect a process like moral decline to lend itself to treatment over a short period of history or to have well-defined turning points. Indeed, Livy does not attempt to identify particular watersheds for Roman morality here, with one exception—the Battle of Magnesia, the victory that thrusts Rome upward, in a dizzying spiral, to mastery of the world and that makes accessible the temptations of Asia. Prior to the battle there was only one major scene criticizing Roman character or conduct in this era, Cato's speech lamenting the spread of avarice and luxury (34.2–4). Greed, however, has always existed to some degree, as the Licinian Law of 367 B.C. and the Cincian Law of 204 B.C. both attest. The problem was not insufferable at the time of Cato's speech. His concern was primarily for the future, when the wealth of the East, under Roman control, would make greed widespread:

> You have often heard me complaining . . . that the state is vexed by avarice and luxury, the diseases that have overthrown all the great empires. As our country's fortune becomes better and happier daily and as our empire grows—already we have made the crossing into Greece and Asia, places filled with all the enticements of pleasure, and we are even handling the treasures of kings—the

more I dread that those things might capture us instead of our capturing them.

(4.1-3)

We should note that Scipio's words to Antiochus' legates after the Battle of Magnesia perhaps recognize the integrity of the Roman character through that time (37.45.11-12). The conquest of Asia, however, brought two new problems. Wealth was available on an undreamed-of scale, and the way was laid open for foreign practices to pervert traditional Roman values. Livy treats both problems at some length; the theme of incipient moral decline dominates books 38 and 39.

The evil effects of Asian wealth on the Roman people, especially on the Roman soldiers, are almost immediately discernible. The exactions of Manlius' army upon the various cities of Asia are recorded in sad detail. His train, more intent on booty than on battle, can scarcely toil along at five miles per day. The consul Lepidus later says that Manlius performed his duties as if he were another Antiochus: he roamed about Asia threatening its states with war and selling peace at high price to people against whom there was no declaration of war. Poetic justice is served when Manlius' army, still so laden with booty that it cannot maintain proper speed, is itself largely stripped of its plunder in Thrace. It was these soldiers, however, who according to Livy first introduced foreign luxury to Rome: bronze couches, tapestries, and expensive banquets complete with female musicians and professional chefs. Money has another evil effect—the direct or indirect perversion of military discipline. Its direct effect is to encourage soldiers to disobey orders in their quest for wealth: twice they plunder enemy camps in violation of direct orders. Its indirect effect is to encourage commanders like Manlius to relax discipline in their armies. The damage caused by contact with the "soft," rich peoples of the East is underscored in the first chapter of book 39, where Livy offers as a pointed contrast the salutary effect of fighting the poor, warlike Ligurians. On this front the triple difficulties caused by hard terrain, a hardened enemy, and hard labor in the field—a simple life without booty—resharpen Roman discipline in the intervals between the Eastern wars.

Equally disastrous are the effects of Eastern customs. Several cases reveal Livy's belief that peoples become like the lands and neighbors to which they are exposed. Hard lands and hard neighbors produce tough, resilient peoples like the Samnites, Ligurians, and those of the rugged areas of Macedonia. Soft lands, on the other hand, can soften even warlike nations; the Gallogrecians are an example. The conquest of Asia therefore poses a real threat to Roman character; Manlius Volso, quoted earlier in this essay, accordingly urges the Romans to avoid the delights of that land lest it extinguish Roman valor.

Unfortunately for Rome, Eastern customs begin to flood into the city after Magnesia. Book 39 is an unhappy record of the beginning moral decline. Livy portrays in detail a major example of Eastern vice: the Bacchanalian conspiracy (8-19). He stresses the foreign nature of the rites, which spread to thousands in Rome "like a contagious disease" (9.1). He particularly dwells on the Bacchanals' unnatural vices. Although the Senate takes severe action to excise the evil, its growth vividly illustrates the new and increasing assault on traditional Roman values. The account of Cato's censorship (42.5-44.9) also underscores the erosion of old-time values. The idea receives its most explicit formulation in the scene of Hannibal's death:

This day will prove forever how greatly the character of the Roman people has changed. A previous generation once warned King Pyrrhus to beware of being poisoned—and he was an armed foe keeping troops in Italy. Today's Romans have dispatched a legate of consular rank to urge King Prusias to murder his aged guest.

(51.10-11)

In books 42-45 the scope of the moral decline expands. Several examples in books 42 and 43 document a new arrogance even in Rome's treatment of allies. The consul Postumius' demands on Praeneste set an evil precedent for future mistreatment of allied towns. The same spirit is evident in the censor Fulvius Flaccus, who strips the roof of the temple of Juno Lacinia to build another temple at Rome. Allied legations from Spain and Chalcis complain of the depredations of Roman officials. Abdera is sacked without provocation.

These outrages are, if anything, surpassed by Rome's treatment of her enemies. Popilius Laenas' brutal treatment of the Statellate Ligurians sets a terrible precedent that angers the Senate and provokes a general revolt in Liguria. No better is the conduct of Quintus Marcius, an envoy to Perseus who plays on the king's hope for peace in order to give Rome time to prepare for hostilities and deploy her troops in the theater of war. Although the legate is inordinately proud of his duplicity, several older senators, mindful of proper old Roman ways, condemn his conduct as a prime example of the "new and all too crafty wisdom" (42.47.9). In the cases of both the Statellates and Perseus, the old morality dictates that it is better to defeat enemies man to man in open combat than to assail the distressed or deceive the unwary (42.8.8; 47.8). Destruction and perfidy, however, continue to be the order of the day. The town of Haliartus is razed by Gaius Lucretius. The missing portion of book 43 related the continuing misdeeds of Roman officials in Greece—not just Lucretius but Lucius Hortensius and Publius Licinius Crassus too. By the end of book 43, however, the abuses have been curbed; senatorial decrees against official misconduct have taken effect in both Spain (4.5) and Greece (17.2–10).

Military discipline continues to suffer in these books but, like the morality of high officials, is restored. In book 43 sailors quartered in Chalcis behave disgracefully, even selling citizens into slavery and plundering temples. Ambitious commanders frequently curry favor among the troops with the loosest policies on enlistments, discharges, and leaves. Military

discipline is corrected under Hostilius and Paullus in book 44. It is this correction, as well as the suppression of official misconduct in book 43, that directly results in Rome's victory over the Macedonians. These righteous policies maintain Rome's loyal allies and strong fighting armies; Livy's concern with these issues here recalls his concern with them in book 8. The war with Perseus thus provides another clear example of his view that wise and virtuous policies are attended by good fortune: " . . . the gods favor dutiful and faithful conduct: the very qualities that have lifted Rome to her lofty eminence" (44.1.11). The formulation may be moralistic, but it addresses a practical truth. Events in book 45, however, suggest that the days of unquestioned military discipline may already be slipping beyond recall. After the defeat of Perseus, Paullus' soldiers, accustomed by now to indulgent commanders, are all too ready to vote against his triumph. Although the triumph is finally authorized, it is clear that the old-fashioned discipline is shaking under the challenge of the troops.

More impressive in book 45 is its pervasive and deeply felt theme of the mutability of fortune. Perseus, being led in Paullus' triumph, provides a conspicuous example of capricious fortune. The spectacle of the fallen king evokes great pity; Paullus comments with genuine feeling on the changeability of fortune and the spirit in which men must bear their fates. Indeed, Paullus himself is a no less conspicuous example of fate: within days of his triumph he suffers the death of his two sons. He then speaks nobly once more about the blows of fate, adding the prayer that fortune might be content to strike him and spare Rome. Perhaps most striking is the fall of Macedonia itself. Livy briefly but impressively traces the rise and fall of an empire supreme on earth. The plunge from the pinnacle of its fortunes down to its final demise, Livy says, required but 150 years. Is there not contained, in the discussion of fortune, a warning? The city of Rome, now at the zenith of prosperity, may also plunge into the abyss.

It is impossible in this short essay to speculate at length about the ideas that Livy expressed in the lost books. The scant contents of the *Periochae* do not indicate the emphasis and viewpoint of his *History*. We may, however, proceed from his known beliefs about moral health in society to surmise his views on later Roman history.

It is clear that Livy believed good conduct should arise naturally from the moral excellence of men and their societies. In the absence of proper morals, societies could still repress improper conduct in deference to higher or external forces. In early Rome, for example, the fear of kings long suppressed the struggle of the orders; after their expulsion, fear of external foes at times served the same purpose (for example, 2.39.7). There was a belief, espoused by Sallust and widespread in Livy's day, that the destruction of Carthage in 146 B.C. had initiated Rome's moral decline. Did Livy believe that this event was an important landmark in the moral deterioration? Very possibly he did. But there is an important distinction between Sallust's attitude and that which I take to be Livy's on this matter. For Sallust, Roman virtue had existed unspoiled before the destruction of Carthage; afterward Rome had begun to experience avarice and luxury. The absence of a powerful foreign enemy removed a fear that had bound Roman society to right conduct. Unchecked by that fear, evil human nature naturally degenerated toward avarice and luxury. Livy believed decline entered Roman life earlier and by a different process: corruption from the East. Nor was fear essential to check misconduct. Men could learn moral values as a basis for proper conduct. They had done so in Rome before: the domestic quarrels, which early on had been suppressed only by a king or a foreign threat, were ultimately eliminated—even in the absence of kings or foreign threats—when men learned obedience, self-control, and mutual respect. There was no reason why Rome must decline in the absence of foreign foes. If the destruction of Carthage did appear to Livy as a crucial event in Rome's history, it was only because circumstances had again made external pressure necessary to maintain good conduct. The extant books show that Livy already saw an alarming decline in self-restraint and a corresponding rise in arrogance and greed even before 146 B.C. In this situation the destruction of the last great enemy might have been a catalyst that accelerated Rome's decline.

It is certain (preface 9) at any rate that he believed the later period was one of headlong moral degeneration—fights over agrarian laws, flagrantly self-serving magistrates, disgraceful treatment of the allies, political murder, civil war. The idea of headlong moral decline was hardly original with Livy; everybody in his time knew it had taken place. What may be original with Livy in the later books, as in the extant ones, is his specific assessment of the events and causes that marked the moral decline. In a society where good conduct was no longer enforced either by inherent moral excellence or by external forces, what course of correction might have suggested itself to Livy? Return to an authoritarian ruler? Livy the Republican, the supporter of Pompey, could not endure that; it meant discarding centuries of political learning, the long and proud tradition of the world's foremost people. Besides, the external imposition of good conduct was artificial and would break down when the external force was removed. The remedy must lie in morals, then. What was needed—and needed more than ever in a nation that feared no men—was fear of the eternal gods. That, and a rededication to Roman ideals, especially self-restraint.

Livy may even have been optimistic about the prospects for a moral recovery, at least in the early years of Augustus' rule. Temples had been restored; against the tide of Eastern customs Roman traditions were being officially encouraged; the rule of law had been reestablished. With this fair start, proper attitudes toward gods and men needed to be nurtured again in the Roman people. There is no reason to believe Livy thought the task beyond Augustus' ability. The kings had once formed Roman character, even using legislation to do it. During the war with King Perseus, Aemilius Paullus and the Senate had curbed the violations of discipline and official good conduct. Our historian must therefore have been immensely hopeful for the success of Augustus' moral program.

Livy would not have approved, however, of the loss of political freedom, especially Augustus' plans to provide a successor from within his own circle. And as the failure to restore moral values became increasingly apparent—even the two Julias were guilty of scandal—Livy may have become deeply pessimistic for the future. His last years, after the accession of Tiberius, may have been haunted by a double tragedy. Rome had accepted authoritarian rule. There had been, however, no corresponding repression of vice, no return to proper conduct. His sense of tragedy could only have been increased by the belief that events need not have turned out so.

Of all Rome's historians, only Livy rises fully to the sweep and grandeur of events. He gave a new style of utmost variety and polish, a new form of supreme dramatic power, to Roman history. These are massive achievements that rightly place him in the front rank of literary figures.

Beyond this, his *History* was comprehensive. And while particular factual problems of Rome's distant past may have been difficult to solve, still his overall perception of trends and developments was incisive. Indeed, many of his views are, at least in broad outline, accepted even today. A few examples must suffice. The struggle of the orders is a standard feature in modern histories of early Rome. Livy may have been the first to formulate the early social conflicts into a systematic account of the struggle of the orders. His verdict on the critical importance of the Battle of Sentinum is accepted. His outline of the Second Punic War is still followed to a large extent.

Yet excellence of form and expression, even the perceptiveness of his historical interpretation, do not fully explain his instant and enduring popularity. As Augustan Rome pondered a century of civil wars and asked how and when and where it had lost the harmony and discipline of the more distant past, it was Livy who gave the answers that satisfied. He addressed the central questions of his time, accounting for the development and decline of Roman character with a sophistication his rivals could not match. At this level the *History* is perhaps our most important document for ancient thinking on the rise and decline of Rome.

While Livy speaks hardly at all of himself, kind fortune has granted us a singular and revealing document: a tombstone, most probably Livy's, which was found at Patavium. On it there is no mention of Livy's fame as a historian, not one word about his association with the house of Augustus. These recommendations are not the ones with which Livy commends himself to posterity. His inscription suggests to the passerby nothing more than a good Roman life and strong family values. To our historian, in death as in life, these things were the heart of the matter.

> Here lie Titus Livius
> and his sons
> Titus Livius Priscus
> and
> Titus Livius Longus
> and his wife
> Cassia Prima

Selected Bibliography

TEXTS

The *Oxford Classical Texts* series covers books 1–10 and 21–35; these include a full critical apparatus and constitute the standard editions.

Vol. 1: Libri I–V, edited by R. M. Ogilvie. Oxford, 1974.
Vol. 2: Libri VI–X, edited by C. F. Walters and R. S. Conway. 1919.

Vol. 3: Libri XXI–XXV, edited by C. F. Walters and R. S. Conway. 1929.

Vol. 4: Libri XXVI–XXX, edited by S. K. Johnson and R. S. Conway. 1935.

Vol. 5: Libri XXXI–XXXV, edited by A. H. McDonald. 1965.

The older *Teubner Texts* by W. Weissenborn (Leipzig, 1865–1870; later reed., 1887–1908) include all of the extant books. Of special interest to supplement the *Oxford Texts* are volumes 3 (Stuttgart, 1972) and 4 (Stuttgart, 1973), which reprint the W. Weissenborn-M. Müller text of books 31–40 and 41–45. Volume 4 also includes O. Rossbach's edition of the *Periochae*, fragments, and *Obsequens*.

The *Loeb Classical Library* series covers all of the extant books. Each volume includes a text, translation, and maps.

Vol. 1: books 1–2, edited by B. O. Foster. London and Cambridge, Mass., 1919.

Vol. 2: books 3–4, edited by B. O. Foster. 1922.

Vol. 3: books 5–7, edited by B. O. Foster. 1924.

Vol. 4: books 8–10, edited by B. O. Foster. 1926.

Vol. 5: books 21–22, edited by B. O. Foster. 1929.

Vol. 6: books 23–25, edited by F. G. Moore. 1940.

Vol. 7: books 26–27, edited by F. G. Moore. 1943.

Vol. 8: books 28–30, edited by F. G. Moore. 1949.

Vol. 9: books 31–34, edited by E. T. Sage. 1935.

Vol. 10: books 35–37, edited by E. T. Sage. 1935.

Vol. 11: books 38–39, edited by E. T. Sage. 1936.

Vol. 12: books 40–42, edited by E. T. Sage and A. C. Schlesinger. 1938.

Vol. 13: books 43–45, edited by A. C. Schlesinger. 1951.

Vol. 14: *Summaries, Fragments,* and *Obsequens,* edited by A. C. Schlesinger. With a general index to Livy by R. M. Geer. 1959.

TRANSLATIONS

An English translation of all of the extant books is available in the Penguin Classics series.

Livy: The Early History of Rome. Translated by A. de Sélincourt. London, 1971. Books 1–5.

Livy: Rome and Italy. Translated by B. Radice. In progress. Books 6–10.

Livy: The War with Hannibal. Translated by A. de Sélincourt. London, 1965. Books 21–30.

Livy: Rome and the Mediterranean. Translated by H. Bettensen. London, 1976. Books 31–45, slightly abridged.

CONCORDANCE

A full concordance is available, based on the *Oxford Classical Texts* through book 35 and on the Teubner series for books 36–45.

Packard, D. W. *A Concordance to Livy,* 4 vols. Cambridge, Mass., 1968.

COMMENTARIES

Among the commentaries on Livy, the following are especially important.

Briscoe, J. *A Commentary on Livy.* Books 31–33. Oxford, 1973.

Ogilvie, R. M. *A Commentary on Livy.* Books 1–5. Oxford, 1965.

Weissenborn, W., and H. J. Müller. *T. Livi Ab Urbe Condita Libri.* Berlin, 1860–1864. 2nd ed., 1880. Reprinted regularly. Text and commentary for all of the extant books.

CRITICAL STUDIES

Begbie, C. M. "The Epitome of Livy." *Classical Quarterly* 17:332–338 (1967).

Bornecque, H. *Tite-Live.* Paris, 1933.

Briscoe, J. "The First Decade." *Livy,* edited by T. A. Dorey. London and Toronto, 1971. Pp. 1–20.

Bruckmann, H. *Die römischen Niederlagen im Geschichtswerk des T. Livius.* Dissertation. Bochum-Langendreer, 1936.

Burck, E. *Die Erzählungskunst des T. Livius.* Berlin, 1934. Reprinted with a new introduction, Berlin-Zurich, 1964.

———. *Einführung in die dritte Dekade des Livius.* Heidelberg, 1950.

———. "The Third Decade." *Livy,* edited by T. A. Dorey. London and Toronto, 1971. Pp. 21–46.

Carney, T. F. "Formal Elements in Livy." *Proceedings of the African Classical Association* 2:1–9 (1959).

Catin, L. *En lisant Tite-Live.* Paris, 1944.

Dorey, T. A., ed. *Latin Historians.* London, 1966.

———. *Livy.* London and Toronto, 1971.

Gries, K. *Constancy in Livy's Latinity.* New York, 1947.

———. "Livy's Use of Dramatic Speech." *American Journal of Philology* 70:118–141 (1949).

Jumeau, R. "Tite-Live et l'historiographie hellenistique." *Revue des Études Anciennes* 38:63–68 (1936).

———. "Remarques sur la structure de l'exposé livien." *Revue de Philologie* 65:21–43 (1939).

———. "Tite-Live historien." *Latomus* 25:555–563 (1966).

Kajanto, I. *God and Fate in Livy.* Turku, 1957.

———. "Notes on Livy's Conception of History." *Arctos* 2:55–63 (1958).

Laistner, M. L. W. *The Greater Roman Historians.* Berkeley, 1947.

Liebeschuetz, W. "The Religious Position of Livy's History." *Journal of Roman Studies* 57:45–55 (1967).

Lipovsky, J. *A Historiographical Study of Livy: Books 6–10.* New York, 1981.

Luce, T. J. "The Dating of Livy's First Decade." *Transactions and Proceedings of the American Philological Association* 96:209–240 (1965).

———. "Design and Structure in Livy: 5.32–55." *Transactions and Proceedings of the American Philological Association* 102:265–302 (1971).

———. *Livy: The Composition of His History.* Princeton, 1977.

McDonald, A. H. "The Style of Livy." *Journal of Roman Studies* 47:155–172 (1957).

Momigliano, A. "Camillus and Concord." *Classical Quarterly* 36:111–120 (1942).

Ogilvie, R. M. "Livy, Licinius Macer, and the *Libri Lintei.*" *Journal of Roman Studies* 48:40–46 (1958).

Petersen, H. "Livy and Augustus." *Transactions and Proceedings of the American Philological Association* 92:440–452 (1961).

Stadter, P. A. "The Structure of Livy's History." *Historia* 21:287–307 (1972).

Syme, R. "Livy and Augustus." *Harvard Studies in Classical Philology* 64:27–87 (1959).

Taine, H. *Essai sur Tite-Live.* Paris, 1910.

Ullman, B. L. "History and Tragedy." *Transactions and Proceedings of the American Philological Association* 73:25–53 (1942).

Walbank, F. W. "The Fourth and Fifth Decades." *Livy,* edited by T. A. Dorey. London and Toronto, 1971. Pp. 47–72.

Walsh, P. G. "The Literary Techniques of Livy." *Rheinisches Museum* 97:97–114 (1954).

———. "Livy." *Latin Historians,* edited by T. A. Dorey. London, 1966. Pp. 115–142.

———. "Livy and Augustus." *Proceedings of the African Classical Association* 4:26–37 (1961).

———. *Livy, Greece and Rome. New Surveys in the Classics.* No. 8. Oxford, 1974.

———. *Livy, His Historical Aims and Methods.* Cambridge, 1961.

———. "Livy's Preface and the Distortion of History." *American Journal of Philology* 76:369–383 (1955).

———. "The Negligent Historian: 'Howlers' in Livy." *Greece and Rome* 5:83–88 (1958).

Witte, K. "Über die Form der Darstellung in Livius' Geschichtswerk." *Rheinisches Museum* 65:270–305; 359–419 (1910). Reprinted separately Darmstadt, 1969.

JAMES P. LIPOVSKY

TIBULLUS

(54?–18 B.C.)

PROPERTIUS

(50?–15? B.C.)

IN HIS LIST of books that the budding orator should read, Quintilian, the first professor of rhetoric in Rome, enunciated the orthodox view of the Roman elegists: "In elegy also we challenge the Greeks. In this genre Tibullus seems to me to be the most polished and elegant writer. There are some who prefer Propertius. Ovid is more sensual than either, just as Gallus is harsher" (*Institutio oratoria* 10.1.93).[1] The verdict of posterity, however, has been largely in favor of Propertius, to judge from the number of translations and critical works devoted to him; although this may reflect the difficulties of his text as well as his more immediate and varied appeal to modern sensibilities.

Propertius and Tibullus came from similar social and literary backgrounds and were almost equal in age when they were writing. In the conventional view, Albius Tibullus' birth is put between 60 and 48 B.C., his premature death shortly after September in 18 B.C. Sextus Propertius was born between 54 and 47 and died at some date between 15 and 1 B.C., perhaps leaving a family, since another elegiac poet, Passenus Paulus, claimed descent from him.

[1]His view of Tibullus is supported by Ovid, Velleius Paterculus, and Suetonius.

Propertius, however, may well have been the first to publish some of his love poetry: his earliest book, the so-called *Monobiblos* or *Cynthia*, seems to have appeared in 28 B.C. and was extremely well received. According to Martial, it was still a popular present a hundred years later.

The prefatory elegies to their first books sound the same note:

The chains of a beautiful girl hold me shackled and I sit like a doorman in front of her obdurate doors. I don't care for glory, dear Delia: provided I'm with you, I want to be called lazy and unambitious. Let me look on you when my last hour comes, and as I die, let me hold you with my faltering hand.

(Tibullus, 1.1.55–60)

Cynthia was the first woman who trapped me and made me miserable with her eyes, though I had never before been touched by amorous desires. Then Love made me lower my arrogant gaze and he ground my head beneath his feet, till he taught me to hate respectable girls and live without a plan. And this madness has not left me now in a whole year, even though I am still forced to face the hostility of the gods.

(Propertius, *Elegiarum liber* 1.1.1–8)

765

Yet Propertius, by publishing his work earlier, may have established himself thereby as the leading writer of erotic verse and the literary heir of Catullus and Gallus, since we hear of no similar contemporary reaction to the publication of Tibullus' first book, which may be dated tentatively to 26 B.C.

Before we examine their differences and relative literary merits, let us look at some of their similarities. Both belonged to the equestrian order, that is, to the Roman middle class. Tibullus' birthplace was Gabii or Pedum in Latium, the modern Gallicano, just a few miles from Rome; Propertius was apparently from a prominent family in Assisi, a small town in Umbria nearly eighty-seven miles north of the capital. Both attracted the attention of rich Roman patrons for their actual or potential services. Both were heavily indebted to Hellenistic, specifically Alexandrian, influences in their writings and are coupled in literary histories as two central links in the tradition of the Roman love elegy: Catullus, Varro, Calvus, Gallus, Propertius, Tibullus, and Ovid. Although at times they found other subjects for their art, each of them presents himself as hopelessly in love with recalcitrant, often cruel, mistresses, and the core of their poetry is a narration of their past sufferings, present joys, or future hopes.

Consequently, for the modern reader perhaps the most important similarity is that of the psychological portraits they have painted of themselves in their erotic elegies. Both come forward as tormented, if occasionally hopeful, even happy, lovers. Of course, it is vital to remember that under discussion is the persona (mask) of each poet, to use a term popularized by Ezra Pound. The relationship between the poetry and reality is bound to be complex, if indeed it is recoverable at all.

Propertius offers the simpler picture of the beginning and the end—with all the joys and miseries in between—of a long relationship between a younger poet and a disreputable, talented, cruel, and older woman named Cynthia. We read of an intense beginning to the affair when Propertius was eighteen or so; a year's painful rejection by her; then five years' uneasy and jealous devotion, apparently between 29 and 24 B.C., which slowly cooled into the final bitter rejection (3.25), after which Cynthia seems to have died in poverty. Nevertheless she still dominated Propertius' imagination in death, reappearing to him as a plaintive ghost, protesting her past fidelity and his fickleness (4.7).

It could be argued that fidelity is one of the major themes of book 4, culminating in the picture of the devoted wife in elegy 11, which, of course, would be elegy 12 if we accept the idea that the long first elegy of this book is in fact a diptych and meant to be read as two complementary poems (a not uncommon practice with the elegists).

Tibullus' representation of his love life is more complex. We find him in love with Delia, with whom he hopes to retire gracefully to the countryside, away from war's alarms and the pursuit of wealth and fame (1.1). Delia, however, belongs to, or leaves him for, another (1.2). Later he professes his tormented love for a more cruel and rapacious mistress, this time named Nemesis (2.3–6), who is involved with a rich rival. In between these episodes he falls briefly in love with a young boy called Marathus (1.4), who rejects his advances for an older and richer lover, apparently because he himself is in love with a girl, Pholoe, who treats him as cruelly as he had treated the poet (1.8). An assumption of male bisexuality is, of course, common in much of Greek literature and is found in Catullus, the romantic precursor of Tibullus and Propertius, as well as in such other Roman writers as Petronius, Martial, and Juvenal.

Nevertheless, the basic profile of the lover presented by our two poets is much the same. It is much like the picture presented by Catullus of himself, by Vergil in his tenth eclogue of the soldier-elegist Gallus, and, in more ironic vein, by Ovid, the last of the great Roman elegists. Thus it becomes clear that we are dealing with a phenomenon comprising both literature and life. The critical problem is to isolate, as best we can, the different elements.

There can be no question that the first century B.C. in Rome witnessed the emergence of a new type of emancipated woman. The Roman upper class had always included women of strong character and influence, despite the theoretical supremacy of the paterfamilias, or head of the household. But in the final century of the republic and beyond, there grew up women of strong character who did not follow the traditional patterns of dutiful daughter and patriotic wife. There were, as well, women of considerable personal, social, and political power, whose private lives departed considerably from traditional Roman standards of feminine behavior. This phenomenon was accounted for, along with so much else in late republican Rome, by the freedom, moral laxity, and degeneration of the old-fashioned virtues, trends so deplored by censorious authorities of the time as a consequence of the Punic Wars and the resulting wealth that flowed into Roman coffers. The true explanations are a matter for sociologists, but the age-old theme of the corrupting influence of wealth on female affections and constancy is common to both our poets, as is the exaggerated, if traditional, protestation of their own poverty. What is clear from the literary evidence is the high degree of social mobility at this period. The turmoil of the civil wars in the last century of the republic had its compensations for some. One result, certainly, was the growth of a recognizable demimonde that permeated upper- and middle-class social life. This group included ex-slaves, lower-class free women, actresses like Volumnia (the mistress of Gallus and Antony), even women of some family and independent means—all of them women of talent and charm.

Apuleius is a witness to their existence. He claims (*Apology* 10) that the elegists and the other love poets were wont to give their ladies meaningful and usually metrically equivalent pseudonyms. So Catullus' Clodia became Lesbia, in honor of Sappho, the poet's lyric model. Cynthia's true name was Hostia, which might imply a decent background. If we believe Propertius' reference (3.20.8) to her literary grandfather and his praise of her own poetic and musical talents, this *docta puella* may have been the granddaughter of Hostius, author of an epic poem on the Istric War of 129 B.C. Propertius presumably chose Hostia's pseudonym out of deference to Apollo, whose cult name "Cynthius" derives from his birth on Delos, where Mt. Cynthus stands. Tibullus chose the appellation Delia to pun on his inamorata's name, Plania, but the name had also connotations of Apollo, the god of poetry and music. Ovid's Corinna, an imaginative composite if there ever was one, incorporates a tribute to the Boeotian poetess of that name. Volumnia's more euphonious nom de guerre was Lycoris.

These ladies did not have to haunt the Via Sacra and the many archways of the city or lurk in the tiny dens in the slums of the Subura. Their talents admitted them into the society of better-placed Romans, whether as mistresses or for more casual liaisons. Marriage with most of them was, of course, socially unacceptable. Propertius has a poem (2.7) bitterly protesting the punitive Julian legislation of 28 B.C. (later modified) by which Augustus, through economic penalties, would have forced young men like the elegists to marry respectable wives. The poet insists: "No wife, no other mistress, will ever seduce me away; you will always be my mistress, you will always be my wife" (2.6.41–42). Given such women of high and low degree, the standard Roman presupposition of the inferiority of women naturally became somewhat harder to defend. Women became persons rather than things, with characters of their own, not aggregations of ancient virtues or modern vices. The Greek motif of the lover as a slave to his mad passion and to his beloved (whether male or female), best expressed in Plato's *Symposium* and *Phaedrus,* found some grounding in Roman reality.

A social revolution, of course, does not always necessitate a revolution of feeling and sentiment, but it is arguable that a certain sentimental revolution did take place at this period. The first witness is Catullus, as we see in the poetry that emerges from his affair with Lesbia. Her reputation in society, as witness Cicero's attack in his speech in defense of Lesbia's former lover Caelius, put her on the level of the freed women embraced by Propertius, Tibullus, and Ovid. Lesbia, like Messalina, the consort of the emperor Claudius, was a sister under the skin of the more menial mistresses of our elegiac poets.

This new attitude toward male and female relationships cannot be assimilated into the usual classical analysis of passionate love as a simple madness, even though Propertius and Tibullus naturally use this imagery.[2] The trouble lies not in the absurdity of the passion-- which would be the classical attitude—but in the misdeeds and callousness of the objects of these poets' passions, whether Lesbia, Lycoris, Cynthia, Delia, or Nemesis. Tibullus and Propertius both depict themselves as romantic lovers; both defiantly fly in the face of classical attitudes to love and Roman attitudes to civic duty; both profess a hatred of war, even though Tibullus seems to have served creditably on the staff of his patron, Corvinus Messalla, in Gaul around 28 B.C. The hopes and complaints of Tibullus and the admiration and complaisance of Propertius are typical of the romantic overestimation of the love object. Their mistresses (dominae) are their equals, if not, as Propertius sometimes proclaims, their superiors. They are valuable not simply as seductive beauties, but as possible helpmeets, such as Tibullus' Delia, or inspiring intellectual companions, like Propertius' Cynthia. We see in this period an earlier version of the courtly love found in medieval troubadour poetry and the romantic love

so well depicted by nineteenth-century European writers such as Goethe, Keats, and Shelley.

The characteristics of courtly love have been described as humility, courtesy, adultery, and the religion of love; its definition relies heavily on the Roman elegists, as represented by Ovid. Its object is another man's wife or mistress; its despairs spring from the obduracy of the lady or the existence of a rival. Only men of culture and poetic sensitivity are capable of feeling such great passion. But a deeper analysis of the love poetry of the Roman elegists, as well as the poetry written in other relevant literary periods, reveals a significant type of passionate love that helps explain the splendors and miseries of Tibullus and Propertius. It is, incidentally, a type of love that is not difficult to encounter in everyday life. It is for this reason that one may legitimately turn to the social sciences for enlightenment.

Sigmund Freud described a special type of love object chosen by some lovers, enumerating the conditions of love necessary for such men.[3] These lovers are frequent characters in poetry and fiction; a classic example is the Chevalier des Grieux in Prévost's Manon Lescaut. The same type of lover may also be seen in Dumas's La Dame aux Camélias, Proust's Du Côté de chez Swann, Dostoevski's The Eternal Husband, Somerset Maugham's Of Human Bondage, John O'Hara's Butterfield 8, and William Styron's Lie Down in Darkness. Freud's discussion also helps our understanding of Propertius' and Tibullus' feelings toward their mistresses.

Lovers like Propertius and Tibullus (and we can include Catullus and Gallus) fall in love when the following conditions are met. First, there must be an injured third party: a husband or a fiancé or an already established lover who has right of possession. Second, the woman must be one who is more or less sexually discredited, whose fidelity and loyalty admit of some doubt. She may be a married woman

---

[2]The best recent analysis of amorous passion since Stendhal's *L' Amour* is to be found in D. Tennov, *Love and Limerance: The Experience of Being in Love* (New York, 1979), particularly chapters 2 to 4.

[3]See S. Freud, "A Special Type of Choice of Object Made by Men," in *Collected Papers* 4 (London, 1953), p. 192.

around whom some breath of scandal circulates, a *grande amoureuse*, or even a prostitute; hence Freud's characterization of this passion as the love for a harlot *(Dirnenliebe)*. Third, in normal love and in social convention a woman's value is measured by her sexual integrity; but this type of lover shows a striking departure from the norm, for he sets the highest value upon the woman he loves. He does not use her and despise her like an ordinary prostitute, but regards her as the only woman whom it is possible to love. His relationships with her, at least for a time, absorb the whole of his mental energy to the exclusion of everything else. Fourth, this type of lover sets up an ideal of his own fidelity to the beloved, however often it may be shattered in reality. Fifth, feelings of jealousy are a necessity for such a man. Not until he has an occasion for jealousy does his passion reach its height, and he never fails to seize upon some incident whereby this intensity of feeling may be called out. Most often this jealousy is directed against new acquaintances or strangers whom he suspects. And sixth, most astonishing of all to the observer, is a desire to rescue the beloved: Tibullus wants to snatch Delia away to a placid life in the country, away from temptation; Propertius seeks to discourage Cynthia from wearing cosmetics and seductive clothes and to lure her back from the fleshpots of Baiae. Such a man is convinced that his beloved needs him, that without him she would lose all hold on respectability and rapidly sink into degradation. He is saving her from this by not letting her go. This trait is no less plain even when there is no real occasion for it. Freud describes a man who in such relationships devoted endless pains, like Propertius, to composing tracts to keep his beloved on the path of virtue, that is, fidelity to himself.

Naturally the relative strength and prominence of these traits may vary in different cases. Freud even explains the genesis of this character type: a strong unconscious devotion to the maternal image makes it impossible for such a man to fuse affection and respect with sensuality. Passion is therefore only possible with a woman who is the unmistakable opposite of that maternal image.

Here we have a recognizable class of man, common in both literature and life. And this purely descriptive summary is all that need be accepted in examining our two elegists. For the character of the lover that emerges from Tibullus' and Propertius' poetry fits exactly the character type described by Freud, as is seen when the characteristics of the lover's persona in both poets are compared with these general traits.

To begin with the first: although most of the poems probably deal with the period when Propertius was already deeply involved with Cynthia, it is plain that at some point, presumably early in the relationship, the deception of another was necessary. Cynthia's ghost recalls their early meetings: "Had you forgotten already our stolen meetings in the watchful Subura and my window-sill worn by our nocturnal deceptions?" (4.7.15–16). Elsewhere Propertius speaks of the door furtively opened to let him in (2.9.42). Elegy 2.23 is an important document. Love entails slavery (*nullus liber erit, si quis amare volet:* 2.23.24), and this slavery is compounded of dependence on another's whims and the necessity of waiting until the lover or husband of one's mistress is absent before one can see her: "What free man gives presents to another man's slave, so that he will take his promised message to his mistress?" (2.23.3–4). The lover will hear his mistress say, "I'm afraid, hurry and get up now, please; hard luck, today my man is coming back from the country" (2.23.19–20). Cuckolding is one of the didactic themes imposed upon him by Apollo "so that he who will wish to strike an artful blow at respectable husbands may know, through you, how to charm out locked-in young ladies" (3.3.49–50). And the subject of rivals' replacing established lovers is not infrequent: "You are conquered or you conquer: this is the wheel of love" (2.8.8.).

Tibullus sounds the same note in his oeuvre:

For a cruel watch has been set over my girl and the strong door has been closed with a hard bolt.... You too, Delia, you must deceive your guards without fear. You must be bold. Venus herself sides with the brave. She looks kindly on a young man testing new doorways or on a girl unlocking the doors with gritted teeth. She teaches her how to creep stealthily from a soft bed, to step without a sound; how to pass eloquent nods in the very presence of her mate and hide sweet messages in a prearranged code. She does not teach this to everyone, but only to those who are not lumbered by laziness or deterred by fear from rising in the dark night.

(1.2.5–6; 15–24)

Propertius and Tibullus depict Cynthia, Delia, and Nemesis as hard, fickle, and venal, leaving little doubt that the obsessed poets were in the grip of what Freud termed *Dirnenliebe*, the passionate, infatuated, and romantic love for a harlot. In no case are these women portrayed as respectable. During the time of Cynthia's affair with Propertius, at least three rivals are specifically recorded as enjoying her favors, not to mention the frequent references to possible infidelities on her part (1.8; 2.16; 3.8; 2.5.1 ff.; 2.34.11). There are, in addition, various references to Cynthia's avarice, such as: "A praetor has just come from Illyria, Cynthia, a great prize for you, a great worry for me" (2.16.1–2). But in any event Propertius has no illusions about her character. She is flagrantly unfaithful, and he says, "With you or for you against rivals, it will always be war for me: where you are concerned, there are no joys of peace for me" (3.8.33–34). Yet he accepts her for what she is. And this is not because he has no conception of fidelity or chastity—an ancient as well as a modern ideal—nor because he does not value it in the conventional way. Not only does he cite mythological examples of fidelity, such as Penelope, Evadne, and Hypsipyle (1.15.9 ff.) when encouraging Cynthia to be faithful, but he also describes in glowing terms the fidelity of Aelia Galla (3.12).

Tibullus' description of Nemesis is sketchier but amounts to the same thing. "Damn! I see that girls are delighted by rich men. If the goddess of Love wants wealth, now let me have loot, so that my beloved Nemesis may float in luxury and parade through the city adorned with my gifts" (2.3.52–55).

Following Freud's analysis, we find that, despite their portrayals of their mistresses as hardhearted and unfaithful, there is no question of the poets' despising them for their lack of sexual integrity. Propertius exclaims, "What great joys I garnered this past night: I will be a god, if there be such another!" (2.14.9–10). In fact, so far from despising her he can claim, "Yet if I must lay down my life on your body, this will be no dishonorable end for me" (2.26.57–58).

As he calls for unmixed wine to drown his sorrows, Tibullus complains that Delia has been shut away from him by her husband (or established lover) in the carefully crafted second elegy of his first book. The poet will try anything to get to see her. He reassures her about the risks of meeting with him, but, as we might now expect, he cannot resist warning her against other emotional entanglements (*tu tamen abstineas aliis*: 1.2.57). These, he claims, would be far more likely to come to her mate's notice. Despite the suspicions that prompt this injunction, he does not pray to be cured of his passion, but to have it returned in equal measure (1.2.63–64), so that they can lead together a life of happy rural simplicity (71–76). Fears of her infidelity, twice stated, are juxtaposed even with his trust that her prayers on his behalf will help him in his near mortal illness on Corfu. (Compare 81–84 with 9–30.)

Propertius, unlike Tibullus, however, constantly sets up an ideal of his own fidelity to Cynthia, although she herself is notoriously unfaithful to him even in the *Monobiblos*. His vows of fidelity are reiterated throughout the first two books; he sees it almost as a moral matter: "It is not right for me either to love another or leave this girl: Cynthia was first, Cynthia will be the last" (1.12.19–20). He considers their relationship to be as binding as any more conventionally legitimated ties: "No wife, no other mistress, will ever seduce me away; you will always be my mistress, you will always be my wife" (2.6.41–42). Even though she rejects him, still, he says, he will feel bound to remain celibate: "Nor will any mistress leave her traces in my bed: I shall stay alone, since I may not belong to you" (2.9.45–46). Yet no less easy to substantiate is the shattering practice of this ideal: we have a vivid and humorous description in 4.8 of his frustrated attempt to revenge himself for one of Cynthia's presumed infidelities by playing her false with two ladies of easy virtue named Phyllis and Teia. Propertius' sentiments are not those of a lover who sees infidelity as utterly unthinkable, but rather of a lover who sets up an ideal to which he does not always conform. And Cynthia apparently recognizes this in complaining of his possible infidelities (2.20; 3.6.19 ff.; 3.16).

Tibullus, of course, despite his fervent protestations of his deep love for Delia and his desire for the quiet rural life with her by his side, and despite his admonitions to her to shun other lovers, can hardly present himself in his two books as the lifelong lover Propertius professes to be, at least until we come to the end of book 3. As a cynic once remarked, "True love lasts three years: eternal love lasts five."

Jealousy is, of course, everywhere apparent in both poets. Obvious examples are Propertius' tirades against the praetor from Illyria (2.16) and other unnamed rivals (2.9 and 2.18). His general fears of Cynthia's faithlessness, sometimes of a very unreal nature, are constantly in evidence. Looking at Cynthia asleep, Propertius is even afraid that she might be raped in her dreams (1.3.30). He is jealous of Gallus (1.5) and Lynceus (2.34), of the dangers of Baiae (1.11), of the opportunities offered by the games and temples of Rome. He is delighted when she is in the country out of harm's way. "There will be no young seducer in those pure fields, who by his blandishments will not let you be faithful. . . . There no games can corrupt you, no temples, the main cause of your sins" (2.19.3–4; 9–10).

Tibullus' jealousy has already been lightly touched upon, but the theme, however conventional, keeps recurring. He has saved her from death, he claims, but now she is in the arms of a luckier rival, and all his attempts to console himself with drink or other women are useless (1.5.17–18; 37–42). He has taught her how to deceive her established lover or husband; now he fears that she is using her expertise to betray him with yet another (1.6.5 ff.).

The desire to rescue the beloved that Freud found so surprising a feature in lovers of this type takes various forms in our two poets. There is in Propertius, for example, a concern for his mistress' reputation, particularly noticeable as he says, "But it matters less about me: the damage to your good name will be as pitiably great as you deserve" (2.32.21–22).

The elegies for Cynthia's safety in time of illness (2.28 a–c) may be only cautiously cited as further evidence, since these would be compatible with any deep relationship. Still, it is noteworthy that Tibullus makes an identical claim for his solicitude in similar circumstances:

I am the one who is said to have rescued you by my prayers when you were lying in the tiring grip of a painful illness: I myself went round you, purifying you with sulphur, once the old witch had intoned her magic spell. I myself with a woolen band on my head, with my tunic unloosed, prayed nine times in the silent night to Hecate, goddess of the crossroads. I did everything properly: now another man enjoys your love and happily gets the benefits of my prayers.

(1.5.9–18)

Nevertheless Freud's example of the lover who wrote tracts to keep his mistress on the path of virtue prepares us for the subtler forms this instinct can take. A number of Propertius' elegies read like such tracts; their hortatory character distinguishes them from the poems prompted simply by jealousy. There are protests against her ways of dressing and her use of cosmetics, largely because they lead to or imply moral degradation (1.2; 2.18.23–38). He pleads with her to remain faithful to him (2.5; 2.15) and warns her of the possible dangers and penalties (1.8.5–8; 2.5.3–4). He praises her when she avoids the temptations of the town by staying in the country (2.19). This is, of course, reminiscent of Tibullus' desire to get Delia away to the peaceful countryside and the frugal life. But Tibullus also employs sterner threats in the last jealous elegy dedicated to Delia (1.6). Unfaithful mistresses may be subject to the anger of the goddess Bellona as well as the blows of the betrayed poet, and they may end up in poverty, spinning wool on a rented loom, their unscrupulous behavior having left them with no protector.

But there are more complex and subtle ways of expressing this agonizing concern over a wayward mistress. Tibullus, despite the strong Alexandrian influence manifest in his work, decided to eschew the use of mythological examples and, consequently, the polysyllabic Greek names and adjectives so common in Propertius. He thereby deliberately limited himself to the smooth elegance that was to impress Quintilian, but he also deprived himself of the use of much evocative symbolism and simile.

Propertius, however, doubtless following in the footsteps of Gallus and his mentor, Parthenius of Nicaea, uses Greek myth to powerful effect. A case in point is his deployment of the mythological examples that begin elegy 1.3: Ariadne and Andromeda, two famous heroines, the one deserted by Theseus, the lover she had rescued from the Cretan labyrinth; the other abandoned by her parents to the jaws of a sea monster until she was rescued by Perseus. These pathetic heroines symbolize very well the protective feelings felt by the poet as he gazes down on his sleeping mistress. His feelings are later revealed more starkly. He tells his mistress, "and when, now and again, you moved and heaved a sigh, I froze numb, believing it an omen, fearing lest some vision bring you strange fears, or lest someone force you to be his against your will" (1.3.27–30).

All of the traits described so succinctly by Freud and well documented in erotic literature can be paralleled in Propertius, and most of them also in Tibullus. If this is accepted, many aspects of their relationships with their mistresses become clear. It is, for example, easy to

understand why so much of their poetry is openly concerned with the degrading emotion of jealousy: it was a necessary ingredient in the relationship. Sometimes indeed Propertius seems aware of this. The complaisance he shows in 2.32.62—"Forever live free from my judgment" (semper vive meo libera iudicio)—would be otherwise most surprising. He does not, despite his jealousy, find her infidelities as unbearable as Catullus found Lesbia's.

Tibullus also accepts the realities of the relationship with Delia, despite his hopes of rustic domesticity and his pleas for fidelity. When we come to book 2 and his relationship with his next mistress, Nemesis, we find that she is acknowledged from the beginning as greedy and extravagant, seeing in Tibullus' beloved countryside only the profits that come from sheep, vines, and wheat (2.3.41–42; 61–67), not the simple life there (2.3.5–20) that the poet had also envisaged when daydreaming about Delia. Despite this clear-sighted evaluation of the type of woman Nemesis exemplifies, in elegy 2.4 Tibullus accepts his enslavement to her for all her avarice and her taste for jewels and finery. He would drink poison, if only she would look on him with a kindly face:

> Here I see slavery and a dominating mistress awaiting me; so for me, goodbye now to the freedom my father left me. Slavery, but a miserable one, is my lot; I am bound in chains, and love never unfastens the shackles of an unhappy lover. . . . Ah, damnation to whoever collected green emeralds and dyed snowy fleece in Tyrian purple! Fine silks from Cos and shining pearls from the Red Sea are further causes for female greed. . . . Yet if only Nemesis would look at me with a pleased face, though she mix a cup from a thousand other noxious plants, I would drink it.
>
> (2.4.1–4; 27–30; 59–60)

Like Propertius with Cynthia, Tibullus claims to find in her, despite her faults and her cruelty (2.6.11–20; 27–30), a subject and an inspiration for his elegiac verse, and he clings to the vain hope that underneath she has a heart of gold (2.6.44).

The portraits of Cynthia, Delia, and Nemesis (not to mention Marathus), which vary from the highest praise to unflattering reflections on their sexual morality, become now more explicable. These women had to be sexually tarnished for the poets to fall in love with them, yet they are lauded, and, for most modern readers, overpraised for all their other talents and attractions, be they beauty, domesticity, dress, culture, or poetic taste. Whatever the exaggeration and poetic rhetoric, whatever the dependence on earlier Greek or Roman poets to define their feelings, Propertius and Tibullus provide two of the earliest and clearest examples of a certain type of romantic passion. Both use their material to express a coherent attitude to their mistresses and offer us a consistent picture of themselves as a certain type of lover.

Propertius and Tibullus, along with Catullus and perhaps Gallus, represent a revolution in sentiment akin to the rise of courtly love in eleventh-century Languedoc. Ovid, on the other hand, represents a counterrevolution and a return to more conventional classical attitudes. Of course, one could invoke literary fashion rather than amorous passion as the main inspiration of this dramatic rise of one of the most important and impressive genres in Latin literature, but one may reasonably presume that men and women have been falling in love, for good or ill, since the beginning of civilization and they have not always produced great poetry. It must also be remembered that the choice of modes, or indeed models, to channel one's personal poetic interests and concerns is not purely arbitrary. A total cynic about patriotism, or even the Augustan regime, could not write the *Aeneid* or Horace's first three books of *Odes* and the *Carmen saeculare*. A new, emancipated breed of women had emerged in Rome who could attract, indeed torment, talented members of the middle and upper classes. Historical phenomena often underlie the emergence of literary forms. How

else can one account for the rise of the English novel and social realism in the modern age?

I have stressed the primacy of the two poets' emotional attachments because they both made these relationships central to their work, whatever other themes they took up. This is clear from the programmatic elegies introducing their first books. This emphasis on the personal element and the psychological realism of the Roman love elegy allows the reader to avoid the critical trap of seeing such poetry as nothing but pure form, which leads to such a vapid judgment as "Love for a single woman is neither the primary subject of Tibullus' book nor the accepted raison d'être of elegy."

Still, content must be given form; and emotion, however genuine or exaggerated, must be appropriately structured if one is to write serious love poetry. Petrarch and Shakespeare chose the sonnet form. With Roman elegy the question must be: What was the style Propertius and Tibullus adopted or adapted?

It was of course the style and the literary motifs of the famous scholar-poets who flourished mainly between 300 and 230 B.C., and whom we associate with the sophisticated Egyptian metropolis of Alexandria. Even a minimal list of the writers associated with this city must include Zenodotus and Menecrates of Ephesus; Phanocles; Hermesianax and Phoenix of Colophon; Philetas and Herodas of Cos; Simias and Apollonius of Rhodes; Asclepiades and Posidippus of Samos; Euphorion and Lycophron of Chalcis; Aratus of Soli; Theocritus of Syracuse; and above all Callimachus of Cyrene, the most far-ranging and representative of them all. Their influence on their Greek and then their Latin successors was to last well beyond that golden age. Indeed it would be little of an exaggeration to say that Alexandrian poetry and critical theory took literary Rome by storm, a subtle revenge for Rome's brutal conquest of the Greek world. A key figure in opening the gates seems to have been the Callimachean enthusiast Parthenius of Nicaea, a Roman captive freed in Italy about 73 B.C., who strongly influenced Gallus, the elegiac predecessor of our two poets, and possibly Vergil also. His strange erotic stories, which he thought suitable for elegiac treatment, are extant.

"Alexandrian" is a vague but unavoidable critical term, particularly since many of the Greek poets so described did not live in Alexandria or hold posts at the great library there, as did Apollonius and Callimachus. Nor were the recognizable styles and preferred literary genres abandoned after that golden age. The problem is to characterize and identify the literature and writers we now term "Alexandrian." These poets apparently turned away from the old classical genres, such as epic, lyric, and tragedy, to more polished minor forms: elegy, pastoral, and epigram. Callimachus and his near contemporaries regarded the former as too ambitious for the new age and turned instead to the invention of new forms in a desire for innovation and experiment. Epic indeed continued to be written by some Alexandrian poets, not least by Apollonius of Rhodes. Tragedy, too, the second most prestigious genre to come down from the classical age of Greece, still had its practitioners, but it is noticeable that their productions have not come down to posterity. Only lyric poetry of the Pindaric type seems to have had little representation among the many experiments and revivals of old forms in Alexandrian literature. This fact is significant for the study of Horace, who chided his friend Tibullus for writing elegy (miserabiles elegos) and urged on him the composition of more public and less private poetry. There can, on the other hand, be little doubt that Horace was a caustic rival of Propertius and that the hostility was returned. Disapproval of contemporaries, political or poetic, was generally expressed in the ancient world by silence and innuendo rather than by direct attack, which might lead to a rival's literary immortality.

Of the new forms that were prominent or invented in the years after 300 B.C., many were simply developments of forms that had been used in the classical and preclassical periods.

Epic, whether mythological or historical (the distinction was not always as clear to the Greek mind as it is to us), tragedy, and epigram continued. So did didactic poetry, with Hesiod as the great exemplar of the genre, although it flourished in this period as never before. In effect, there are precious few forms that one might accept as truly Alexandrian, and even then their beginnings may be paralleled in one way or another in the archaic and classical ages: narrative elegy, the *epyllion* (a short, oblique poem on an epic theme or motif), hymns, nontragic iambic poetry, and others.

Given this small haul of really innovative forms that we may attribute to the Alexandrian period, can we point to a totally different spirit that distinguished this literary period from the period before 300 B.C.? Alexandrianism is supposedly dominated by a thirst for knowledge and reflects the enormous progress being made in natural science, mathematics, and philology. Historical and literary research, because of its importance in the great libraries, became a dominant mode in poetry as well. Hence the fondness for artificial dialects, archaism, learned and scientific allusion, and metrical experimentation.

It is, however, in the attempt to penetrate the essence of Alexandrianism that we run into difficulty. On the one hand, we find a retreat to the study, or rather the library, to concentrate on mythological, etiological, and lexical research; on the other hand, we find an urban realism in the *Mimes* of Herodas that is reflected in the work of Propertius, as well as escapist pastoralism in the *Eclogues* of Theocritus that is a persistent note in the elegies of Tibullus. On the one hand, we are told of the Alexandrians' interest in the softer side of human life, as seen in Apollonius' treatment of his heroine Medea in the *Argonautica* and in the erotic epigrams of the period; on the other, we are told of their delight in such arid versified treatises as Aratus' *Phaenomena*. The confusion seems to arise from trying to impose on a period of several centuries a set of literary characteristics that may better be used to differentiate that period from the great eras that preceded it. In fact, we find here an attempt to impose scholarly order on what might be regarded, more charitably, as creative chaos. It is better to single out from this chaotic postclassical period some significant themes and poetic modes that directly affected Roman poetry in the long generation of Catullus, Gallus, Tibullus, and Propertius, in particular those motifs that became dominant influences on the art of our two elegists.[4]

What must be stressed, since in the past it was overlooked when contrasting our two major exemplars of Roman love elegy, is that Tibullus, in his own way, is almost as Alexandrian as Propertius. The difference is that Tibullus hides his indebtedness,[5] whereas Propertius openly avows his obligations to the great masters Callimachus and Philitas (3.1) as well as to his Latin forerunners in love poetry, Varro of Atax, Catullus, Calvus, and Gallus. Tibullus, however, is reticent about his Greek and Latin forerunners; their influence is traceable only in his technique and themes. Propertius is avowedly proud of his Greek lineage: "Shades of Callimachus and sacred emblems of Coan Philitas, allow me, please, to enter your grove. . ." (3.1.1–2). Later he will boast of being the Roman Callimachus (4.1.64).

He is just as proud of his pioneering Latin precursors, the Neoterics, whose success in the poetry of love he hopes to emulate:

Varro, too, played with these themes when his translation of the *Argonautica* was completed,

Varro, the great passion of his dear Leucadia; the writings of the lascivious Catullus also have poems of this sort, and through them Lesbia is more famous than Helen herself; the pages of the learned Calvus, too, admit to all this when he writes of the death of luckless Quintilia, and later, from the writings of Gallus about the lovely Lycoris, we know how many heartaches he took beyond the grave with him. And now there is Cynthia, praised in Propertius' poetry, if Fame is willing to put me in the company of these poets.

(2.34.85–94)

Naturally enough, the two poets both chose what was most appealing to them from the Hellenistic traditions they were following. The Alexandrian elements in Tibullus are presented more indirectly: in his narrative technique, in his lightly worn learning, in his antiquarian delight prominent in his first programmatic poem, in the rituals and rhythms of rural life, and even in the geographical catalogs of 1.7. But most striking of all is his concern for finely honed language, which must surely have prompted Quintilian's critical verdict on the polish and elegance of his sixteen elegies. But the similarities between them are almost as striking as the differences.

If the dissimilarities are taken first, we find that Tibullus, like Ovid, chose not to follow Propertius in his earlier imitation of the complex polysyllabic pentameter endings of Greek elegiac verse. Perhaps he felt that they did not suit the genius of the Latin language as it was developing in the Augustan age. Although there are still modern admirers, such as Bertrand Axelson, of the heavier metrical structure of Catullus and the young author of the *Monobiblos*, it was Propertius who gradually conformed to the metrical practice of Tibullus and Ovid, reducing the percentage of polysyllabic endings from 39 percent in book 1 to 2 percent in book 4.[6]

[4]Catullus, although important to his successors, is to be regarded as a protoelegist, despite the strong Alexandrian influence on his many-sided oeuvre. Ovid mockingly furnished—in the second edition of the *Amores* as well as in the *Ars amatoria* and the *Remedia amoris*—the reductio ad absurdum of what the great elegiac tradition of love poetry stood for. He effectively precluded, of course, any further serious developments of the genre, although the writing of elegy by minor poets continued. It was left to Goethe (1749–1832) in his *Römische Elegien* and Ezra Pound (1885–1972) in his *Homage to Sextus Propertius* to provide new directions for elegy.

[5]It was previously the fashion to underrate the Alexandrianism of Tibullus, a view enshrined in Kirby Flower Smith's edition of the Tibullan corpus, but that view has now been corrected by the work of A. Bulloch and F. Cairns (see bibliography).

[6]This is just one obvious example of the metrical differences between Propertius and Tibullus; for further discussion, consult M. Platnauer, *Latin Elegiac Verse* (Cambridge, 1951); and B. Axelson, "Der Mechanismus des ovidischen Pentameterschlusses," in *Ovidiana*, edited by N. I. Herescu (Paris, 1958), p. 121.

The Alexandrianism of Tibullus, however, is less obvious than the flamboyant parade of learning in Propertius. It emerges in his literary reminiscences of older Greek poets, in his antiquarian, but lively, interest in Roman country rituals, in his use of Hellenistic philosophical themes, but, above all, in his contrived, sometimes self-restricting, use of language to produce a patterned tissue of etymological allusions, sound effects, and semantic reverberations.[7]

What is particularly striking is that Tibullus eschews the prominent elements of mythology to be found in the poetry of both Callimachus and Propertius, whether used as ornament, analogy, or illustration. This may have been a deliberate and personal choice, an attempt to make elegy more Roman, even more personal and autobiographical, and thus less indebted to his Greek predecessors, who used mythological motifs to convey indirectly their amorous pangs and passions over rejection and loss of the beloved. The Roman contribution to the elegiac tradition was, after all, the strong infusion of the autobiographical note, a note that may be heard also in their epistolography.

Propertius presumably found rare versions of myths as fascinating as the Alexandrian poets had found them, just as he was later to find some material for his fourth book in applying the Callimachean interest in etiology, the study of origins, to Roman subjects. For example, he offers discussions of the name of the Etruscan god Vertumnus (4.2); why the Tarpeian rock is so called (4.4: the traitorous vestal virgin Tarpeia was flung to her death from it); why women are excluded from the rites of the Ara Maxima (4.9: because Hercules had been denied water by the priestess of the Bona Dea); why Jupiter is given the title "Feretrius" (4.10); and a tendentious account of the *spolia opima*, the spoils taken by Roman generals from enemy leaders killed by them in personal combat (tendentious because Augustus did not wish to award this honor to one of his own generals

who had killed an opposing leader in single combat in the campaigns of 29 B.C.).

This brings us to the vexed question of the elegists' political stance. Now, with these elegists, there is no obvious way of distinguishing entirely between personal predilections and friendships, literary principles and conventions, and politics proper, since they blend with one another. Moreover, the close relationships that existed in the comparatively small city of Rome between the various writers of different persuasions and their patrons further blur the distinctions. Horace disliked Propertius but was friendly toward Tibullus; Vergil was close to Gallus; and Propertius admired both Horace and Vergil, at least overtly. Messalla was a late and somewhat uncomfortable supporter of Augustus; he resigned an important post given him by the emperor because it did not sit well with his notion of civic responsibilities. It is therefore significant that Tibullus, for all his praise of Messalla's military achievements in the imperial cause, never once mentions the emperor himself. Propertius, however, openly criticizes Augustus for his moral reforms that might destroy his relationship with Cynthia (2.7). He was on uneasy terms with Augustus' domestic adviser and propaganda minister, that great, if somewhat self-interested and self-indulgent patron of letters, Maecenas (2.1; 3.9).

Whereas Tibullus chose silence about what displeased or discomforted him on the contemporary literary and political scene, Propertius consistently used the *recusatio* (the refusal to write on a given topic). This literary type was given its classic form in Callimachus' prologue to his masterpiece, the *Aitia* or "Causes," but it could be transferred to many other genres—satire, elegy, odes, epistles, or eclogues. This refusal to write on a certain topic, Augustus' military successes, for instance, could be prompted, supposedly, by the poet's own lack of talent or by the too great importance of the theme itself. The poet might pretend to be dissuaded or influenced by Apollo, by the Muses, by an astrologer, or by his mistress' superior attractions for his pen. Its main purpose, how-

[7]The best account is Cairns, chapter 4 (see bibliography).

776

ever, is to resist unwelcome political pressures and define the true nature of the elegist's art.

It would be a very unaware reader who did not detect an ambiguity in the attitudes of Propertius and Tibullus toward the subject of peace. For example, in one elegy Tibullus attacks war, praises the advantages of peacetime, and ends with this appeal: "Come to us, kindly Peace; bring the ears of grain and let apples pour forth from your white bosom" (1.10.67–68). Yet in the opening elegy of book 2, he compliments Messalla, his friend and patron, on his victories in Gaul. As we have noticed from the evidence of the fragmentary, anonymous life that has come down to us, he served with Messalla in the Aquitanian war of 31 B.C. and was rewarded with military decorations. Of course, when he is at death's door in 30 B.C. and Messalla is sailing off to Cilicia, he has to praise the golden age when all was peaceful: "There were no battle lines, no atrocities, no wars, and the savage armorer had not yet fashioned swords with his grim art" (1.3.47–48). We see then a rejection of war and conquest resting uneasily alongside a very Roman acceptance of these as necessary, indeed glorious, modes of existence. So in proclaiming a preference for making love, not war, the elegist must self-consciously set himself at odds with the assumptions of his militaristic society.

What would reinforce this dubious attitude toward war, the obvious route to a premature end, is the inevitable romantic juxtaposition of love with death.[8] To die for love is an honorable end, but to die in battle? Death is constantly in the wings, menacing either the poet, in Tibullus' case, or the beloved, as with Propertius. The brevity of life, and thus the necessity of enjoying love while we can, is a frequent theme in Alexandrian epigram, and it is a constant motif in our elegists. Tibullus' poignant lines "Meantime, while fate allows, let us unite ourselves in love, for already Death is on his way,

his head shrouded in shadows . . ." (1.1.69–70) echo Propertius' exhortation to Cynthia: "While fate allows us to do it, let us sate our eyes with love: the long night is on its way to you, and the day will never return . . ." (2.15.23–24). This ambivalence about peace and war reveals itself in even more complex forms in Propertius, and it is one of several reasons for the detectable irony running through many of his poems. Quite apart from the conventional elegiac preference for love rather than war, Propertius had his own personal reasons for his antimilitaristic stance. His family had been on the wrong side in the Civil War; the family property had suffered from the confiscations after the war (4.1.129–130); and he had lost at least one relative in the aftermath of the siege of Perusia in 41 B.C. (1.22.7–8). He speaks out bitterly against war and particularly against civil strife. The protestations about the poet's unfitness for military glory (1.6.29) and the lover's devotion to peace, although conventional in their theme, are individual and detailed enough in their expression to convey conviction. The basic problem of the poet, after all, is to express the uniqueness of his poetic persona through often time-worn devices and poetic clichés.

Propertius developed other personal and more subtle ways of expressing his dissent. Tibullus' silence on Augustus' deeds and misdeeds is eloquent, but Propertius has a way of referring adversely to incidents in the Civil War that Augustus would rather have forgotten. In the middle of the opening poem of the second book he claims that were he not a love poet he would be a writer of contemporary epic (like Cornelius Severus) and would celebrate Augustus' wartime exploits; but, most untactfully, he then alludes to the more painful episodes of the Civil War, to Mutina, to Philippi, and, not least and once again, to the Perusine War, when he refers to the overturned hearths of the ancient Etruscan race (*eversosque focos antiquae gentis Etruscae*: 2.1.29). Even Actium, for Horace the theme of a great victory ode, provides Propertius only with an occasion for regretful moralizing. If everyone lived, like Pro-

---

[8]This is most obviously seen in the Japanese practice of *shinjū* (literally, inside the heart) when two lovers go so far as to kill themselves since life has nothing greater to offer them or is placing obstacles in their way.

pertius, a life of wine, women, and song, then there would be none of the disasters of war and Rome would not be in constant mourning:

> If everybody wanted to run through life like this, and lie wallowing in strong wine, there would be no cruel steel, no warships, and the sea off Actium would not be rolling Roman bones. Nor would Rome, assaulted so often by triumphs over her own citizens, be weary of tearing down her hair in mourning.
>
> (2.15.41-46)

Toward imperial conquest and further wars, which were so much in the air at the time of his writing, Propertius' attitude is again quietly but unmistakably critical. Parthian, Persian, Arabic, or even British expeditions were for Horace opportunities for adulation of the new ruler or for jingoistic boasting. At the very least they were adventures that offered a welcome alternative to civil war (*Odes* 1.12.53-56; 1.35.29-32; 37-40; 2.9.18-24; 3.3.42-47; 3.5.2-4). Propertius, however, dismisses such exhortatory or celebratory poetry: "Goodbye to any poet who trammels Apollo in warfare" (3.1.7). He knows that there will be many able to sing Rome's praises in their poetic annals and proclaim that Bactria (roughly modern Afghanistan) will be the boundary of the empire, but he himself claims to offer something one can read in peacetime:

> Many poets will hymn your praises in their chronicles, great Rome, and they will sing of Bactria as the future boundary of your empire. But for something *to read in peace,* my pages have brought down from the mountain of the Muses this work by a road untrodden before.
>
> (3.1.15-18; italics added)

As for that very sore point with the Romans, the standards of Crassus captured by the Parthians in 53 B.C., Propertius is almost flippant about them. His poem on Caesar's proposed expedition to the Indies begins with an impressive description of his possible territorial and financial acquisitions. Propertius offers a hasty

prayer for its success and for Rome's vengeance on its traditional enemy (3.4.9-10). But the patriotic note sounds less impressive when we learn that Propertius will be lolling in his girl friend's embrace and merely watching the triumph and the captive captains from the side of the Sacred Way:

> And reclining in the embrace of my dear lady-love, may I start watching and read off the list of conquered cities, the missiles of the retreating cavalry, the bows of the trousered soldiery and the captured commanders sitting under their weapons. . . . Let all this loot go to them whose labors have earned it: it will be enough for me to be able to applaud along the Sacred Way.
>
> (3.4.15-18; 21-22)

A further proof that his celebration of Augustus' imperialist adventures is not seriously meant is that the next poem in the collection announces "Love is the God of peace; we lovers worship peace" (3.5.1). Moreover, in this poem we find the most poignant general criticism of what Augustus is doing:

> Now we are tossed by the wind against a great sea [because of our passion for wealth]; we even seek out enemies to conquer; and we take on further wars. You'll carry no wealth with you to the river of Acheron; you'll ride, you fool, naked on the infernal ferry. The conqueror is jumbled in with the conquered among the shades: captive Jugurtha sits with the consul Marius who captured him.
>
> (3.5.11-16)

The concluding lines of the poem expressly nullify Propertius' early prayer for Augustus' success. After a life of love and wine, he says, he'll turn to philosophy; this is how his life will end; let those who prefer war bring home the standards of Crassus (3.5.47-48). Anything further removed from Horace's *dulce et decorum est pro patria mori* ("sweet and honorable it is to die for the fatherland") can hardly be imagined.

It is this persistent strain of criticism—expressed in various modes of irony, indirection, humor, pathos, and elegiac complaint throughout the first three books—that casts doubt on the traditional theory of Propertius' conversion in book 4 to Augustan ideals, particularly in the elegiac hymn celebrating the battle of Actium in 32 B.C. (4.6). The features of that puzzling book are, as we shall see, open to a different explanation. Propertius, like Horace and Vergil but unlike Tibullus and Ovid, may have been in a difficult position. He had some tenuous connection at some time with Maecenas' circle since two poems are addressed to Maecenas, but his literary principles and his general social and political views seem radically different. This would have an effect on his poetry and would account partly for its allusive, elliptical, and sometimes difficult and ambiguous character, which contrasts with the artful lucidity of Tibullus. Like Horace in his *Satires* and Vergil throughout his work, Propertius must have been subject to various sorts of social and personal pressure, which have clearly left their mark on his poetry. Tibullus, comfortable in the poetic circle of the powerful Messalla, could afford to ignore such pressures and concentrate on love poetry.

Yet perhaps it was this outside pressure, or lack of it, that explains the considerable difference of range between the two poets. Propertius, in his own way, grappled with political problems; Tibullus, except in his intermittent pacifism, ignored them.

This may explain why time was so unkind to Tibullus' elegant, if meager, collection. The second surviving book may have been published posthumously, but the *corpus Tibullianum*, comprising also the work of the other poets in Messalla's circle (his niece Sulpicia, Lygdamus, the anonymous author of a panegyric on Messalla, and some pieces of unknown authorship), barely survived in manuscript the wreck of antiquity. His survival perhaps depends on a single lost copy from fourteenth-century France. With the revival of classical learning he resurfaced along with Catullus and Propertius in 1472 and was duly honored with various critical editions thereafter. But he suffered from critical comparison with his contemporary.

Even though allusions and references to Propertius in ancient literature are also comparatively few, Martial claims that Cynthia made him a poet (*Cynthia te vatem facit, lascive Properti*: 8.73.5), and the description seems at least to indicate that the *Monobiblos* was the work best known and most circulated after his death. Yet there are Propertian borrowings in the pseudo-Vergilian *Copa*, Manilius, Calpurnius Siculus, Lucan, Petronius, Valerius Flaccus, Statius, Silius Italicus, and even in a graffito found in Pompeii. After Juvenal, who alludes wittily to Propertius' poems, there was a revival of interest in his poetry with Nemesianus and Ausonius, an interest that continued until the time of Venantius Fortunatus. Claudian's poem "On the Rape of Proserpina," in particular, echoes several passages of Propertius. This is the last specific reference to him that we have for some centuries.

Neither Propertius nor Tibullus had much to offer the Middle Ages, as did, for example, both Vergil the magician and, selectively used, Juvenal the moralist. They were known and they survived, but any real understanding of their literary value seems to have vanished in the centuries following the decline of Rome, perhaps because their Alexandrian models fared even worse in the transmission of the literature of classical antiquity. Their successor and imitator, Ovid, because of the very diversity of his work and the simplicity of his Alexandrianism, did far better. Ovid's gift for storytelling, so unlike the oblique and impressionistic narrative lines of Tibullus and Propertius; his blatant vulgarization in the *Ars amatoria* of such elegiac motifs of the poet as the teacher of love (*praeceptor amoris*); these made him an easier author for the late Middle Ages to comprehend—and also to misunderstand. His rhetorical, linear development of traditional themes of elegy made him far more acceptable to those generations than did the subtle craftsmanship of Tibullus and the oblique, allusive, and elliptical art of Propertius. Ovid's rhetorical facility, almost vulgarity, in certain parts of his work, effectively supplanted the work of Propertius and Tibullus even for those readers and imitators who might have had an affinity for Roman love elegy. Perhaps only Catullus, with his directness, stood some chance against the all-pervasiveness of the Ovidian achievement.

Petrarch stands out as the first humanist who went beyond Ovid and took an interest in Propertius, which he expressed in his work. For example, the sonnet "Solo e pensoso" (1.35) is based on Propertius 1.18, an uncharacteristic elegy, which may well have been influenced by Vergil's *Eclogue* 10, where Gallus laments his lost Lycoris amid the inhospitable terrain of Arcadia. Coluccio Salutati, the famous Florentine statesman, who died in 1406, possessed a late-fourteenth-century manuscript of Propertius, the *Codex Laurentianus,* now in Florence, which indicates a similar interest in Propertius. The manuscript was probably copied from Petrarch's.

The great age of Propertian scholarship came in 1816 with Karl Lachmann, who first began the scientific treatment of Propertius' text. Tibullus presented fewer problems. Two main directions of scholarship since then must be noted. One is the belief in wholesale corruption, transposition, and interpolation; the other is a willingness to believe in the obscure, careless, and emotional qualities of Propertius' writings. Tibullus' elegant elegies, although their narrative technique can be slippery, presented no such puzzles. This second hypothesis must be treated with considerable care, since the deliberate artistry of books 1 and 4 is undeniable, and the problems of the excessively lengthy book 2 are probably due to the fusion of two separate books. Although radical redivision of the elegies and radical transpositions of lines have been suggested by such critics as O. L. Richmond, it is probably better to approach the problems pragmatically and cautiously.

The literary criticism and appreciation of Propertius in the nineteenth century tended to center around critical editions and work on the text. There is more merit than is currently allowed in Lachmann's suggestion that Propertius should be credited with five books of poetry rather than four.

In the nineteenth century, as is evident from the obiter dicta of the commentaries and from the translations produced during the period, a real understanding of Propertius' art was difficult to find. True, Propertius found unexpected defenders and admirers in diverse times and places. One such was Vincenzo Padula (1819–1893), who wrote and published in 1871 a dissertation on Propertius entitled *Pauca Quae in Sexto Aurelio Propertio Vincentius Padula Ab Acrio Animadvertebat (A Few Observations of Sextus Aurelius Propertius by Vincenzo Padula).* This offered perhaps an overly enthusiastic and romantic view of Propertius, but some of the defenses Padula offered against the charges of obscurity and insincerity anticipate modern critical positions among classical scholars, who tend to see him as a romantic writer whose poetry was overlaid and whose passion was chilled by a pedantic display of learning: the recondite Alexandrianism seemed oppressive to some.

Some dissident critical voices, outside classical circles, made themselves heard. The litterateur Julien Benda, for example, wrote an interesting, if impressionistic, sketch of Propertius entitled *Properce ou les amants de Tibur,* published in Paris in 1923. Benda's book is interesting because he stresses the Alexandrian artistry of Propertius, playing down the normal assessment of him as a melancholy and obscure love poet. Nevertheless twentieth-century Propertian studies, were it not for one critical event, would have been best characterized by their caution. Scholars tried to purge the text of its errors by emendation and transposition; the explication of individual poems and passages and the analysis of his themes became, and still is, almost an industry.

Sed quod pace legas ("But for something you may read in times of peace"): just as Goethe in his *Römische Elegien* (1793) seems to show more genuine appreciation of Propertius than many professional students of the classics, so Ezra Pound's notorious *Homage to Sextus Propertius,* completed in 1917 (the text of which appears in my *Ezra Pound and Sextus Propertius*), constituted the first genuine critical advance in the study of Propertius. Since that time, in addition to inspiring other translations of Propertius, as well as such imitations as Robert Lowell's "The Ghost," Pound has been largely responsible for stimulating a lively discussion of the nature of Propertius' art. Tibullus must still await a poet or critic of genius who can bring him to life for the modern reader.

Selected Bibliography

TEXTS

PROPERTIUS
Die Elegien des Sextus Propertius, edited by M. Rothenstein. Berlin, 1898.
The Elegies of Propertius, Edited and with an Introduction and Commentary, edited by Harold E. Butler and Eric A. Barber. Oxford, 1933.
Properz und Tibulli: Liebeselegien, edited by Georg Luck. Zurich, 1964.
Sexti Aurelii Propertii carmina, edited by Karl Lachmann. Leipzig, 1816.
Sexti Propertii carmina 2, edited by Eric A. Barber. Oxford, 1960.
Sextus Aurelius Propertius, Elegies, edited by William A. Camps. 4 vols. Cambridge, 1961–1967.
S. Propertii elegiarum, liber 2, edited by Petrus J. Enk. Leiden, 1962.

TIBULLUS
Albii Tibulli aliorumque carminum, libri 3, edited by Friedrich W. Lenz. 2nd ed., Leiden, 1964. 3rd ed., 1971.
The Elegies of Albius Tibullus, edited by Kirby F. Smith. New York, 1913. Reprinted Darmstadt, 1964.
Tibulli aliorumque carminum, libri 3, edited by John P. Postgate. 2nd ed., Oxford, 1915. Rev. ed., 1968.

TRANSLATIONS
Carrier, C. *The Poems of Propertius.* Bloomington, Ind., 1963; 1968.

Creekmore, H., *The Erotic Elegies of Albius Tibullus.* New York, 1966.
Lee, A. G., *The Elegies of Tibullus.* Cambridge, 1979.
Musker, R. *The Poems of Propertius.* London, 1972.

COMMENTARIES
Putnam, Michael C. J. *Tibullus: A Commentary.* Norman, Okla., 1973.
Richardson, Lawrence J. *Sextus Aurelius Propertius, Elegies 1–4: A Commentary.* Norman, Okla., 1977.

CONCORDANCES
O'Neil, Edward N. *A Critical Concordance of the Tibullan Corpus.* London, 1963.
Schmelsser, B. *A Concordance to Propertius.* Hildesheim, 1972.
Sullivan, J. P. *Ezra Pound and Sextus Propertius: A Study in Creative Translation.* Austin, Texas, 1964. London, 1965.

BIOGRAPHICAL AND CRITICAL STUDIES
Allen, A. W. "Sunt qui Propertium malint." In *Critical Essays on Roman Literature,* edited by J. P. Sullivan. London, 1962. Pp. 107 ff.
Baker, R. J. "Laus in amore mori: Love and death in Propertius." *Latomus* 29:670–698 (1970).
Benda, Julien. *Properce ou les amants de Tibur.* Paris, 1923.
Boucher, J.-P. *Études sur Properce: Problèmes d' inspiration et d'art.* Paris, 1965.
Bulloch, A. W. "Tibullus and the Alexandrians." *Proceedings of the Cambridge Philological Society* 199:71 ff. (1973).
Cairns, F. *Generic Composition in Greek and Roman Poetry.* Edinburgh, 1972.
––––––. *Tibullus: A Hellenistic Poet at Rome.* Cambridge, 1979.
Clausen, W. V. "Callimachus and Roman Poetry." *Greek, Roman and Byzantine Studies* 5:193 (1965).
Copley, F. O. *Exclusus Amator. A Study in Latin Love Poetry.* Madison, Wisc., and Oxford, 1956.
––––––. "Servitium Amoris in the Roman Elegists." *Transactions of the American Philological Association* 78:285 (1974).
Day, A. A. *The Origins of Latin Love Elegy.* Oxford, 1938.
Edwards, M. W. "Intensification of Meaning in Propertius and Others." *Transactions of the American Philological Association* 92:128–144 (1961).

Elder, J.-P. "Tibullus: *Tersus atque elegans.*" In *Critical Essays on Roman Literature*, edited by J. P. Sullivan. London, 1962. Pp. 65 ff.

Fontenrose, J. "Propertius and the Roman Career." *University of California Publications in Classical Philology* 13:371-388 (1949).

Fraser, P. M. *Ptolemaic Alexandria.* Oxford, 1972.

Freud, S. "The Most Prevalent Form of Degradation in Erotic Life." In *Collected Papers*, vol. 4. London, 1953. Pp. 203-216.

———. "A Special Type of Choice of Object Made by Men." In *Collected Papers*, vol. 4. London, 1953. Pp. 192-202.

Goold, G. P. "Noctes Propertianae." *Harvard Studies in Classical Philology* 71:59-106 (1966).

Hallett, J. P. "The Role of Women in Roman Elegy: Countercultural Feminism." *Arethusa* 6:103 (1973).

Highet, G. *Poets in a Landscape.* Harmondsworth and Baltimore, 1959.

Hubbard, M. *Propertius.* London, 1974.

Jacoby, F. "Zur Entstehung der römischen Elegie." *Rheinisches Museum* 60:38-105 (1905).

Leach, E. W. "Poetics and Poetic Design in Tibullus' First Elegiac Book." *Arethusa* 13:83 (1980).

Lefèvre, E. *Propertius Ludibundus: Elemente des Humors in seinen Elegien.* Heidelberg, 1966.

Lewis, C. S. *The Allegory of Love.* Oxford, 1936.

Lilja, S. *The Roman Elegists' Attitude to Women.* Helsinki, 1965.

Luck, G. *The Latin Love Elegy.* London, 1969.

Marx, A. "De Sex. Propertii vita et librorum ordine temporibusque." Ph.D. dissertation, Columbia University, 1963.

Michels, A. K. "Death and Two Poets." *Transactions of the American Philological Association* 86:160-179 (1955).

Nethercut, W. R. "Propertius and Augustus." Ph.D. dissertation, Columbia University, 1963.

———. "The Ironic Priest, Propertius' Roman Elegies." *American Journal of Philology* 91:385-407 (1970).

Newman, J. K. *Augustus and the New Poetry.* Brussels, 1967.

Otis, B. "Horace and the Elegists." *Transactions of the American Philological Association* 76:177-190 (1945).

Pillinger, H. E. "Some Callimachean Influences on Propertius, Book 4." *Harvard Studies in Classical Philology* 73:171-199 (1969).

Reitzenstein, E. *Wirklichkeitsbild und Gefühlsentwicklung bei Properz. Philologus Supplementband* 29.2. Leipzig, 1936.

Rostagni, A. "L'influenza greca sulla origini dell' elegia erotica latina." In *L'influence grecque sur la poésie latine de Catulle à Ovide* 2:59-92. *Entretiens Fondation Hardt.* Geneva, 1956.

Schuster, M. *Tibull-Studien.* Vienna, 1930. Reprinted Darmstadt, 1968.

Sellar, W. Y. *The Roman Poets of the Augustan Age: Horace and the Elegiac Poets.* Oxford, 1899.

Shackleton Bailey, D. R. *Propertiana.* Cambridge, 1956.

Skutsch, O. "The Structure of the Propertian Monobiblos." *Classical Philology* 58:238 (1963).

Smyth, W. R. *Thesaurus criticus ad Sexti Propertii textum.* Leiden, 1970.

Solmsen, F. "Propertius and Horace." *Classical Philology* 43:105 ff. (1948).

———. "Tibullus as an Augustan Poet." *Hermes* 90:298-299 (1962).

Stroh, W. *Die römische Liebeselegie als werbende Dichtung.* Amsterdam, 1971.

Syme, R. *The Roman Revolution.* Oxford, 1939; 1960.

Tennov, D. *Love and Limerance: The Experience of Being in Love.* New York, 1979.

Tomaszuk, P. V. *A Romantic Interpretation of Propertius: Vincenzo Padula.* Aquila, 1971.

Tränkle, H. *Die Sprachkunst des Properz und die Tradition der lateinischen Dichtersprache.* Hermes Einzelschrift 15. Wiesbaden, 1960.

Wheeler, A. L. "Propertius as Praeceptor Amoris." *Classical Philology* 5:28-40 (1910).

Williams, G. *Tradition and Originality in Roman Poetry.* Oxford, 1968.

Wimmel, W. *Kallimachos in Rom: Die Nachfolge seines apologetischen Dichtens in der Augusteerzeit.* Hermes Einzelschrift 16. Wiesbaden, 1960.

———. *Der frühe Tibull.* Munich, 1968.

BIBLIOGRAPHIES

Ball, R. J. "Recent Work on Tibullus (1970-1974)." *Eranos* 73:62 ff. (1975).

Cartault, A. *À propos du Corpus Tibullianum: un siècle de philologie latine classique.* Paris, 1906.

Harrauer, H. *A Bibliography to the Corpus Tibullianum.* Hildesheim, 1971.

———. *A Bibliography to Propertius.* Hildesheim, 1973.

J. P. SULLIVAN

OVID

(43 B.C.–A.D. 18)

INTRODUCTION

My father kept telling me over and over: "Even
Homer left little worth leaving to his heirs.
Why do you bother your head with this poetry
　　stuff?"
So I did what my father suggested and stopped
　　writing verse,
And I tried writing prose—
But once the pen was secure between index and
　　thumb,
Then verses, O flawless verses,
Flowed, perfectly flowed from the fluid ink.
　　　　　　　　　　　　　　　(*Tristia* 4.10.21–26)*

THESE VERSES, PART of a fascinating autobiographical poem that Ovid wrote in
exile toward the end of his life, account not a
little for the decline in his reputation that began
in the early nineteenth century and ended only
in the mid-twentieth century. Ovid boasts delicately, wittily of his facility, and his hostile critics have never failed to take hold of the fatal
handle he innocently offered them. Facility
means, we are told by such critics, an inevitable
lack of depth; means a penchant for razzle-
dazzle and fireworks; means an absence of genuine content; means, evil of all evils, insincerity. For romantic critics—and many critics
remain essentially romantic—"facility" is the

dirtiest word in the critical lexicon, and among
ancient writers Ovid is frequently displayed as
a prime example of this dirtiest vice.

It does not, of course, follow that grace, fertile invention, and apparent ease in composition necessarily imply poverty of mind, shal-
lowness of soul, or a heart of glass. Spontaneity
and intensity of feeling are not incompatible
with artistry; nor, for that matter, does sincerity
ensure good art or even artistic honesty. No
doubt Ovid erred grievously in the matter of
rhetorical strategy when he chose to describe
his artistry by underscoring the facility of his
verbal gifts; such a tactic invites hostility as well
as the predictable denigration that Ovid has
suffered since William Wordsworth published
his preface to the *Lyrical Ballads* (1800) and
anathematized fluent artistry in poetry. But
Ovid made the further error of promoting one
of his gifts at the expense of greater, rarer gifts
that truly define his genius. He has elegance,
variety, urbanity; he is capable of an easy radiance, of a style as smooth and iridescent as
watered silk; but his manner—or, rather, his
manners (for he has a wider range of styles than
most other Latin poets)—are rooted in and
flower from his particular vision of life, from a
special, unique content.

Only in bad art is form imposed upon matter.
In good art—in great art—form grows out of
matter, shapes itself to the needs of matter. It is
this precise interdependence of form and content, for Ovid as for other great poets, that al-

---

*Line references are to the Latin text and are the same in
every edition. Published translations, of course, vary in line
numbers.

lows him the freedom and the discipline of imagination that distinguish the highest art. Despite his insistence on his facility, Ovid's technical skill is an effect, not a cause, of his growth and achievement as a poet—in other words, his formal dexterity increases, keeps pace with, the deepening of his moral and spiritual vision. What finally confers greatness on his poetry is the greatness of his vision—that and the tenacity that enabled him to pursue his vision, to enlarge it constantly, and to grow with it.

To define Ovid's vision of the world is difficult because it is complicated and because it kept changing in subtle ways throughout his poetic career. In the pages that follow I shall attempt not so much to define that vision as to describe its surfaces and its depths, its limits and its expanses. For now it is enough to sketch Ovid's vision in this way: Ovid is in essence a storyteller, and the prime strength of his narrative artistry lies in his curiosity about human beings and in his love for human beings. In particular, he has tremendous interest in and tremendous sympathy for people in love, for it is in humankind's capacity to love and to be loved that Ovid finds the basic integrity, freedom, and moral value of the individual. If this emphasis on the erotic origins of identity seems commonplace and obvious to us, who have grown up on fragments of Sigmund Freud, we must remember that in ancient Greece and Rome it was the *polis* (the *civitas*, the city) that defined the human being; that eros, for all its prevalence in ancient life and literature, was generally regarded as an irrational force, as a sickness—as a destructive energy that threatened the personality with disintegration.

But Ovid, although he understood the darker side of eros as well as it has been understood, came gradually to affirm eros as a creative force, to praise the lover's will to love as the core of that person's freedom, integrity, and possible moral beauty. Seen in this light, it is perhaps no coincidence that in a period when the depersonalization of life seems constantly to overwhelm humankind, when the nature and meaning of love become ever vaguer, ever more susceptible of skepticism and trivialization, Ovid should be enthusiastically rediscovered, not as flippant rhetorical machine, not as brazen huckster of sly pornographies, but as authentic master of those who love.

LIFE

We know as much about Ovid's life as we know about the lives of most other Latin poets—that is, not very much. This is unfortunate in some ways, of course, because certain things in his poetry remain mysterious that doubtless would be clarified if we knew more about him. On the other hand, this lack of information is something of a blessing: it is good for poetry to keep some of its mysteries intact and for us to enjoy those mysteries; or, if mystery irritates us, we are free to invent "serious gossip" in order to diminish the mysteries. The former process is called reading; the latter is sometimes confused with genuine scholarship.

Ovid (Publius Ovidius Naso) was born on 20 March 43 B.C. It is perhaps unwise to formulate magical significance for dates, but it is interesting to note that on this day the battle of Mutina (now Modena) took place; and since the consuls Aulus Hirtius and Gaius Vibius Pansa died on this field of battle in their struggle against Marc Antony and Octavian, the heirs of Julius Caesar, there is some justification for regarding this date as marking the death of the Roman Republic. Ovid was born in the town of Sulmo (now Sulmona), a hundred miles to the east of Rome, in a region inhabited by a people called the Paeligni. Although Ovid recalls the beauty of his birthplace with affection, he shows little of the nostalgia for rusticity that marks the Augustan poets who were slightly older than he; for all his mastery of landscape in the *Metamorphoses*, Ovid is essentially a city poet, and what most characterize the visible surface of his poetry are the expressions, the gestures, and, above all, the speech of living human beings. In short, he apparently removed to Rome in his teens, if not before, and it was in the streets of

Rome that he truly learned about the world that was peculiarly his to love and to know.

He went to Rome to go to school, and at Rome he studied rhetoric. Much, indeed too much, has been made of Ovid's study of rhetoric during his adolescence. Ovid came of an upper-middle-class family with old money; therefore, like everyone else in his class, and like everyone who wanted to join his class, he studied rhetoric because through it lay the path to a conventional public career. Indeed, rhetoric was the core of Roman education in Ovid's time, as it had been for almost a century before his birth and as it was to be for centuries after his death. So far as one can tell, Ovid benefited from his study of formal discourse more than most Roman students, and he was far less harmed by it than were other, less gifted, more credulous students. What rhetoric did for Ovid is what it was supposed to do: it refined his talents. To suggest anything else—that, for example, rhetoric corrupted him—is to misunderstand both the nature of talent and the nature of education.

When his formal training was completed, Ovid went off to the obligatory postgraduate year in Athens to dabble in philosophy, to listen to learned teachers disagree, and to have a good time in a foreign, rather decadent country. After Athens there was the standard guided tour of the ruins and survivals of the eastern Mediterranean; then came a leisurely inspection of Sicily; then home to begin the career in earnest.

It did not work. Fathers of poets seem to have a penchant for trying to turn their male offspring into lawyers, doctors, or engineers. Usually this stratagem is effective because most sons are not poets. Most fathers confronted with the problem of a versifying son, therefore, turn out to be right; Ovid's father turned out to be wrong. As we have seen, Ovid strove to satisfy the demands of filial devotion, but he failed to do so. Law studies were abandoned; he drifted off to the bookstalls and to poetry readings; he became acquainted with most of the leading poets of the time (but the reclusive Vergil eluded him; Vergil he only glimpsed). So he began his career in earnest when he was not quite twenty, just when Augustus was completing the consolidation of his power and establishing the monarchy that would set the political patterns of Europe for fifteen hundred years and more. As Augustus began his reign as emperor, Ovid began to write the *Amores*.

In a moment we shall look at Ovid's relationship with Augustus and his banishment in some detail. Until this catastrophe in A.D. 8, when Augustus exiled him to Tomis on the Black Sea, Ovid's life appears to have been uneventful, as the lives of great artists so frequently are. We are told that Ovid married three times, which might suggest domestic turmoil of an unusual sort; but given the social fragmentation of his time, even this apparent disorder may have been merely ordinary. In any case, the third and final marriage seems to have been an extraordinarily good one, and Ovid's devotion to the wife he left in Rome when he went to Tomis is manifest in his poems to her in his final volumes. He was, as his poetry shows everywhere, a man who loved women (and his only child was a daughter). For the rest there is only silence and the poems—except for the collision with Augustus, which is symbolic of the conflicts in Ovid's art and to which we now turn.

OVID AND AUGUSTUS

Ovid discusses his banishment and its causes in a long poem (*Tristia* 2), but though he fastens the blame for his exile directly on himself ("Two offenses, a poem and a mistake, have destroyed me" [2.207]), the precise nature of his wrongdoings eludes us, for what seems an apology to his prince is in fact an elaborate self-defense and self-justification. Through the centuries various speculations have illumined or obscured both the poem and the error responsible for Ovid's removal from Rome to the wilderness, but it is unlikely that the puzzle will ever be completed in a satisfying way. What follows here is also speculation, and readers who are unpersuaded by it should consult the masterly synthesis of these difficulties by John C. Thibault (see bibliography). But before we ponder the crimes of Ovid, a brief sketch of the man who punished those crimes is in order.

The grandnephew of Julius Caesar, Octavian—or, to give him his splendid full name, Gaius Julius Caesar Augustus Octavianus—was born in 63 B.C., and was therefore twenty years Ovid's senior. He came to Rome (not for the first time) a year before Ovid's birth to try to collect the fortune, power, and prestige that his granduncle and adoptive father had bequeathed to him. The next decade and a half of his life were spent in countering those who were interested in seizing the power and glory of Julius Caesar for themselves, or who were interested in destroying the achievement of Julius Caesar and returning Rome to its traditional political and social patterns. The ultimate triumph of Augustus over both groups is the exact index both of his remarkable tenacity and of a political genius that, however one finally judges its morality, had no rivals in the ancient world and has had few serious rivals in medieval or modern times.

By the time Augustus had secured his rule over the city of Rome and over its empire, Ovid had begun to abandon law for poetry (roughly 23 B.C.). It was not inevitable that these two men who differed in age, temperament, and interests should collide as they did, but as one reads through the poems of Ovid, and as one surveys the development of Augustus' statecraft, their final confrontation and its result seem fated— from the moment Ovid took up his pen. The emperor and the poet were natural antagonists. In part this antagonism may be explained by their differences in age and in occupation, but it is at last their fundamental disagreement about the nature of the human being and about the meaning and purpose of human life that set them against one another.

It seems likely that this enmity was slow in developing, was imperceptible both to the antagonists themselves and to the people around them. While Augustus was devoting himself to the reform of a social order that nearly a hundred years of civil war had left in ruins, Ovid devoted himself to the refinement of his craft and of his observation of Roman high society. That Augustus paid much attention to Ovid early in the poet's career seems very unlikely. Ovid, whose eye is on the beautiful people and their foibles, glances at the emperor in these years (23-3 B.C.) occasionally, and his attitude is one of mild flippancy and tolerant good humor. This attitude toward the new majesty, together with his willingness to mingle in elegant, liberated modern society even while keeping a satirist's distance from it, Ovid had learned from his friend and mentor, Sextus Propertius; and he was to spend most of his poetic life reformulating and deepening these strategies. But for the period in question, he was merely the brightest of the poetic spokesmen for all the bright young things who rejoiced in having been born in a new age of leisure, wealth, and fun, and who looked back on the recent dark ages of the vanished Roman Republic—when adultery was almost unthinkable and everyone did his or her duty, and no one smiled or partied or wore interesting clothes— with a charitable mixture of pity and horror.

In these wonderful "Children of the Sun" Ovid had found—better than he first knew— the poetic material that suited his genius precisely; and in Ovid the smart set, as it quickly recognized, had found its perfect celebrant, its giddy, naughty Pindar. In this world Augustus could be taken for granted, the remote daddy who threw the party or at least paid the bills; or, like other fathers, he could be lightly mocked and finally ignored.

What Ovid and his playmates did not understand, what would have appalled them had they been able to grasp it, was that Augustus was utterly, deadly serious in his efforts to purify and revitalize the social patterns of Rome: he disliked the new sexual liberation not because he was a puritan (for he was not) but because he saw a disintegration of the family that threatened, as he thought, the entire social fabric. So he passed laws against various forms of sexual activity among the unmarried, and he encouraged marriage by offering economic rewards to those who were fertile in their marriages and by threatening with economic punishment those who avoided marriage and children.

In short, in the eyes of the beautiful young things, Augustus tried to regulate love. This effort seemed to the smart set at first droll and futile, then inconvenient and irritating. So it seemed to Ovid for a while. But as Ovid's art matured, Augustus' efforts to reform society by constraining men and women to devote their capacities for love to the state and its grand designs began to look to Ovid like a symptom of a larger, more sinister threat to human freedom and human integrity. It was on this issue that the lines of their enmity were drawn.

Another thing about Augustus that Ovid and his admiring first audience failed to notice was a change that began to take place in the emperor during the last decade of the last pre-Christian millennium. In the early years of his climb to power he had been ruthless, sometimes even ferocious. But as his power grew, he took a leaf from his granduncle's book: he became tolerant of criticism, he became suave, detached, generous. That necessary pose—yet it was, for a while, more than a pose—lasted until he entered his mid-fifties. Then, when his worries about his health, about the increasing complexities of power, about his lack of a male heir and the anxieties of the succession began to crowd in on him, he began to behave as aging potentates often behave: he grew irritable and suspicious, became more and more impatient with bad luck and incompetence. The general tone of his closing years is marked by a sense of intolerable frustration, a sense of profound futility that the magnificence of his achievement, far from being able to alleviate, could only mock and magnify.

It is in the light of this alteration in Augustus' condition and character that Ovid's banishment should be viewed. As he worked at *Tristia* 2 in the desolation of Tomis, Ovid may well have wished for simple explanations of the riddle of his incredible misfortune; it may well have comforted him to think that one of his poems (*The Art of Love*), coupled with some minor, mysterious indiscretion (being somehow privy to some misbehavior in the royal family), was the cause of his unmerited suffering. So Ovid may have felt, but this explanation is not adequate. *The Art of Love* was published about A.D. 1 (see Barsby, pp. 4–5; Jacobson, pp. 316–317), and Ovid was not banished until A.D. 8. If that wickedly funny attack on Augustan reform (and, as we shall see, on frivolous sexuality as well) had enraged Augustus, why did he wait seven years before acting on his rage?

The error—what I call the minor indiscretion—is more promising as moving cause for the banishment. In *Tristia* 2.103 ff. Ovid laments having seen something, but refuses to specify what it was for fear of reawakening the imperial wrath (see 2.208–210). When we recall that Augustus' granddaughter, Julia the Younger, was banished in the same year as Ovid, we may be tempted to connect the two events. Such a connection is plausible, though hardly inevitable, provided we refrain from bedding Julia down with Ovid. Suppose, rather, that Ovid was little more than a semi-innocent bystander in the sensational scandal—that is, suppose it was discovered, when the adultery was discovered, that Ovid had been a confidant to Julia or to her lover, had sympathized, and had helped in the concealment. In this version we would have little more than ordinary court intrigue, an intrigue in which Ovid's part, however peripheral, however innocent, cost him his life in Rome and doomed him to humiliation and the loneliness and griefs of Tomis.

In the year that Ovid and Julia the Younger were banished, Augustus was seventy-one years old. Eight years before, his only daughter, Julia the Elder, had been banished for committing adultery with the son of Augustus' archenemy, Marc Antony. In that instance immorality may well have been fused with political intrigue; but whatever the truth about the elder Julia's affair with Iullus Antonius, it symbolized to Augustus the ruin, the hopelessness of his achievement. He had been betrayed by fate, which had systematically killed off all his heirs apparent, and now he was betrayed by his only child. The sense of irremediable loss and of isolation may well have been intolerable when the elder Julia departed for Pandateria, the island of her exile. When the younger Julia repeated her mother's offense, the old, failing emperor may have felt that he lived in a recurring nightmare.

That Ovid had stumbled into that nightmare unaware helped him not at all. The huge indiscretion of the younger Julia was the last of many last straws; and Ovid's small complicity in that business, whatever its nature, was part, in Augustus' eyes, of a wider pattern of destruction. It is not, then, a question of one poem and one mistake, for the effect of Ovid's poems and of his mode of life was cumulative. There had been many flippant and bantering poems, from the *Amores* to the opening books of the *Metamorphoses*, and both the elder and the younger Julia had been part of the appreciative audience for whom Ovid had written: the sensual, sophisticated, irresponsible courtiers who had mocked and defied their emperor and who, harmless at first, now showed themselves to be dangerous, diseased, possibly fatal. At the center of this glittering menace—encouraging it, shaping it, giving it a language and a voice—was Ovid, the last of the Augustan poets.

In this version of the story of his banishment, Ovid is both innocent and guilty; becomes, along with the younger Julia, the scapegoat for the sins and follies of two generations of golden sophisticates who had impeded and jeered at the will of their prince; becomes the symbol for what had finally ruined the prince's grand design; and becomes the target of his pitiful, desperate rage.

This version of the banishment, like other versions, is mere speculation, for the truth of what actually happened to Ovid has been hidden in the secret and lost history of Augustus' reign. But the surface story, what actually happened, is less important to us than what remains to us, what we can see and hear going on in the poetry of Ovid: the confrontation between two irreconcilable visions of human life, the collision of political necessity with poetic freedom, of pragmatism with a humanism that is grounded in religious intuitions, of the contingencies of history with moral imagination.

THE AMORES

> And I would rather have my sweet,
> Though rose-leaves die of grieving
> Than do high deeds in Hungary
> To pass all men's believing.
> (Ezra Pound, "An Immorality," 5–8)

Most readers have little difficulty in responding warmly to the *Amores*: the fresh, clear voice of these poems is as astonishing and as convincing as the voice of the young Dante, or that of William Shakespeare's sonnets, or that of Charles Baudelaire's *Flowers of Pain*. Our problem with reading the *Amores* is to try to decide what happened to the collection between its first appearance in five books (sometime about 16 B.C.) and its revision and reappearance in a second edition of three books (sometime about 3 B.C.). Before we examine the question of this revision, though, we must take a brief look at the poetic tradition that Ovid inherited and at what he did with the conventions that he found in force when he began writing love elegies.

The Latin love elegy is a peculiar fusion of Roman sensibility with the sophisticated, erudite poetry of Alexandria. It is most closely connected with the name of Callimachus (third century B.C.) and has as its special hallmark a delight in extreme elaboration of technical refinement and in subtle shadowing of content—the matter of the poetry deliberately, ironically obscured by the rich variations of its form and its manner. This Callimachean poetics arrived in Rome in the late 70's B.C. and profoundly influenced the young poets of that time (the generation of Catullus). Aside from that of Catullus, most of the poetry of this first "modernist" generation has disappeared; but we guess from the long poems of Catullus that it was essentially lyrical in spirit—that is, despite its narrative modes and highly polished surfaces, it was deeply subjective, concerned chiefly with finding significant visible form for the emotions.

The second generation of Roman Callimacheans altered the poetics of the preceding generation in subtle yet radical ways. In Propertius and Albius Tibullus a sense of the former subjectivity remains, and their poems seem to be about their experiences and feelings (or those of the protagonists they imagine); but the profound subjectivity of the previous generation has been curiously refined in these poems, which show a peculiar distance between the poet and his poem. These poems are less representations of, attempts to describe, the movement of a hidden inwardness than they are meditations upon, analyses of, the nature of such inwardness as it manifests itself in society. To put it another way, Propertius and Tibullus are trying to become novelists, and what interests them is not so much emotion in its pure state as personality, erotic personality, in its relations to the society that shapes it and against which it reacts. Vague though their narrative frames and highly stylized though their narrative modes may be, both poets are principally concerned with psychology and social structures.

Ovid's treatment of Latin love elegy reduces its former inwardness still further. In his hands the narrative frame with which Propertius and Tibullus had experimented is strengthened; the representation of emotional states is now purely a means, not an end, and it now serves chiefly to provide descriptive analyses of the personality in its erotic conflicts with self and with the world outside self. The protagonist of Tibullus is dreamy and rather vague, is largely given to gentle rumination and nostalgia, enchants the reader with a curiously attractive incompetence. The protagonist of Propertius is always mildly crazy and off center, speaks always in fascinating hyperbole and snarled, obsessive syntax (he is a great comic creation). In contrast with these characters, the protagonist of Ovid constantly shows a dazzling self-confidence; his speech is marked by easy elegance; he is never at a loss for witty insights into the frivolous society that he delicately mocks yet hungers to shine in. The tones of Ovid's character range from silken languor and rich effrontery through graceful cynicism to boisterous, macho vitality; beneath all this are a severe clarity of thought, a genuine intellectual discipline, and an inescapable, pitiless eye. He is of the smart set, understands it, even, in a sense, loves it; for being frivolous himself, he relishes the frivolity of others. This constant insouciance gives the *Amores* much of its incomparable verve, its easy momentum. Yet Ovid's hero is also outside the gilded world he thrives in and records. This aspect of the poem, the shift from participation in the beau monde to contemplation of it, can best be accounted for if we ponder the problem of the second edition of the *Amores*.

But before we look at that problem, let us watch and listen to Ovid's thoroughly modern young man-about-town in what I take to be his initial and pure state:

Every lover's a soldier in Love's wars,
And Cupid conducts an Officers' Training Corps.
Atticus, trust me, trust me, when I tell you,
Every lover's a soldier, fighting for love.

I used to be perfectly lazy, spending my days
Lolling about in the shade, but a beautiful girl
Jolted me out of my indolence, made me enlist
Under the standards of Love. Now I'm fit and I'm
    trim,
Prepared at the drop of a hat for nocturnal
    engagements.
If anyone's tired of just sitting around like a stone,
Wants to get back into shape, let him fall right in
    love.

                (*Amores* 1.9.1–4: 41–46)

The radical disenchantment with traditional Roman values—military duty in behalf of the republic, other service in peacetime—that informs this poem is a standard Catullan motif, but Ovid enriches the inherent irony of the motif by turning it against itself. For Catullus the leisure, the purely anti-Roman idleness that

789

good poetry and good loving require, replace patriotism, duty, and hard work for the sake of the common good. Using this transvaluation of Roman values, Catullus suggests a new form of identity: the individual is to be defined not in terms of citizenship and its duties but in terms of dedication to artistry and in terms of the intensity and purity of amorous desire.

This new, un-Roman concept of personality Ovid accepts unconditionally and uses as the basis of his poetry throughout his career. But in this poem, and indeed throughout the *Amores*, he pretends to answer the antiquated critics of the new poetry and new poetic lovers by insisting on the stalwart energies and the high purposes of poetry and love. Had Catullus been subversive and selfish? Had he somehow called into question the worth of traditional Roman social patterns? Had he mocked grizzled veterans, triumphant generals, and energetic magistrates? Surely not! He had meant only, doubtless, that love and poetry, though they may seem subversive and decadent and selfish, are different from traditional Roman pursuits only on the surface; deep down, the Roman poet and the Roman lover possess the same ferocious energy, the same unswerving dedication, that shaped the men who founded and enlarged and maintained the Roman state.

This poem is, as its first critics and admirers doubtless recognized, truly subversive, for Ovid here claims that making poems—and making love, and encouraging making love by making poems about making love—is as strenuous and as meritorious an endeavor as making war and making empires. Other, earlier users of the Catullan motif tended to be (mockingly) apologetic, as if the poet-lovers' leisure, their love, their art, were somehow minor forms of treachery to the state. But when Ovid rejects empire, together with epic and tragedy, its literary counterparts, he often does so with heroic gusto (*Amores* 1.1, 1.15, 2.1, 3.1). The protagonist of the *Amores* comes to us not as a querulous, pale, sickly spokesman of art and love against the claims of life. The world is this man's oyster; and he, as red-blooded a Roman as ever lived, has come to claim it, to devour it

robustly, zestfully. It is amusing to see the embodiment of *virtus*, the old farmer-soldier of history, suddenly appear before us powdered and barbered, clad in delicate garments as befits the poet and lover, lustily bawling for the fulfillment of his desires. This witty creation, this almost impossible fusion of old Rome and new Rome, this merciless flippancy, this powerful yet subtle voice, is the controlling principle of the *Amores*.

Or, rather, it was the controlling principle of the initial edition. In the revised edition, made more than a decade after the first edition appeared, the hungry sensuality and swaggering virility and mindless egotism, the outrageous vitality, are still intact, but—or so it seems likely to me—the book has taken on a radically new shape and, with it, a radically new meaning.

Between the first and second editions of the *Amores*, Ovid had written a tragedy titled *Medea*, now lost, and the *Heroides*. By the time the revision of the *Amores* was completed, Ovid had (probably) begun to sketch, and perhaps even had begun to write, the *Ars amatoria*. The young poet of twenty-five or so who had celebrated unequivocally the joys of sex and other benefits of *la dolce vita* has disappeared into the middle-aged poet who is ready to conceive and execute his mature masterpieces. This is not to say that Ovid in his maturity looked back on his younger self with contempt, that he had lost all affection for that nearly innocent self-esteem, that copious exuberance. But, though he was unwilling and unable to revise his estimate of Augustus—indeed, his sense of the discrepancy between what Augustus says and what Augustus means constantly increases—he has, by the end of his thirties, developed a subtler concept of the erotic personality and deepened his understanding of the nature of love. The young man had gloried in the sweetness and the intensity of desire; and in this delicious, voracious pattern even erotic sorrows, even erotic loss and failure, had their own special excitement, their own pleasures. When the middle-aged poet looked back on this world of unexamined hedonism, his vision of love became complexly dialectical. On the one hand, though he never lost his sympathy for young people in love, he began to see, beyond love's pleasures and satisfying egotism, genuinely destructive forces; on the other hand, he gained a steadier, more experienced, and more profound faith in the capacity of love to perfect the human personality, to help it achieve true humanity. This complex vision is most clearly evident in the *Metamorphoses*, but the foundations for the new seriousness are laid in the revision of the *Amores* and in the composition of the *Ars amatoria.*

As was said above, the protagonist of the *Amores* is immensely likable (even women who denounce the palpable chauvinism of these poems often admire, despite themselves, the menacing charm of Ovid's hero, and like the danger of his guile and appetite). What appeals to us, beyond this hero's unflagging energies, is his frank affirmation of pleasure as the summum bonum of human existence; yet this unqualified hedonism is neither crass nor repulsive: the hero's sweetness and his illusion of innocence seem to vindicate his amorality even as they soften his egotism.

But not finally. As we feel the modulations of tone in the *Amores*, as we approach the hero's erotic failure and the catastrophes of book 3, we begin to apprehend that this man (this grown-up child) lives a lie, and that this lie must inevitably catch up with him, overwhelm him. Propertius' lover is obviously a zany, is obviously in the grip of an obsession the shape and perils of which he cannot recognize. The irony here is that we can watch the amorous clown, not contemptuously, but with amused good humor; we do not, though A.E. Housman did, at a time of different erotic fashion, identify with him.

Ovid's protagonist, in this way as in others, is more insidious and in the end more illuminating than Propertius'. We do identify with Ovid's lover because we judge him, as we tend to judge ourselves, not by his acts but by his intentions, not by his recurrent follies but by the lucidity and sanity of his plans. By the time we have finished book 3, though, we can hear Ovid

saying to us, not explicitly but through the final catastrophic modulations, through the disintegration of the lover and his plans: "Yes, reader, this man, for all his cool deliberations, his mastery of the mechanisms of seduction, his supremacy in the games of love, for all his intellectual and verbal clarity—this man is deeply obsessed, is in fact trapped in the machinery that he claims to manipulate—and you, reader, you who applaud this pathetic creature, are you perhaps in some ways similar to him?"

Doubtless there were purely technical considerations that prompted Ovid's revision of his first collection. The last of the Roman Callimacheans must have found that his first published verses needed polishing and cutting, that some of the poems, beyond polishing and cutting, needed the wastebasket. The aims here were technical perfection, condensation, distillation, a total refinement that ten years of progress in the craft of verse had made possible. But this aspect of the revision was interdependent with the other, more important aspect. The poems now came to be arranged with dramatic force and with strict, tense patterning to show the seducer's progress and the hedonist's decline and fall. The great satirist, now in full control of his powers and fired with his new, hard-won dialectical vision of love, subjected his bright and amorous young man to the same scrutiny that he bestowed on empire and emperor, classical art, and current society. The result was this glittering yet somber portrait of one of love's saddest victims: the lover, richly gifted for love, who is wholly ignorant of what love means and who is therefore destroyed by it.

THE HEROIDES

Still round and round the Ghosts of Beauty glide,
And haunt the places where their Honour dy'd.
(Alexander Pope, *Of the Characters of Women:
An Epistle to a Lady,* 241–242)

In the last poem in the *Amores* 3.15, Ovid bids farewell to the genre of love elegy while claiming poetic immortality for himself and announcing that his genius is turning to higher themes and higher styles. The poem is conventional in its forms and motifs, original in its suave brevity and casual ironies: he had no more intention of abandoning the themes of love than he had of taking up the themes of war and empire. But the claim for greatness is genuine, and so, in a very real way, is his tone of "good-bye to all that." For although love will continue to haunt him throughout his career, the genre that Catullus began and that Propertius and Tibullus developed Ovid has let go of—because, in effect, he has demolished it, has taken it to its farthest limits and beyond them. In classical Latin poetry there would be no more love elegy after Ovid.

If I am correct in assuming a radical revision for the *Amores*, accomplished just before Ovid began *The Art of Love*, the *Heroides* may be considered Ovid's earliest extant work. This collection has, not without reason, begun to enjoy a revival of critical esteem in recent years; but despite its virtues and despite its great influence on later European poetry, the book strikes me as being, with the single exception of the *Ex Ponto*, Ovid's least satisfying work.

The central defect of the *Heroides* does not lie in its conception, for its idea (borrowed from Propertius 4.4) of having a group of famous women from myth and literature—lost, jilted, abandoned—write to their faithless or forgetful lovers had wide poetic possibilities, all of which Ovid discovered and exploited. If there is an inherent monotony in the scheme—querulous voices muttering and shrieking, one after another, "You done me wrong!"—Ovid manages to escape or to lessen such tedium, letter after letter, by ingenious, often breathtaking variations. Nor is it the artificiality of the women's situations—correspondents writing arias to vanished gentlemen, many of whom have thoughtlessly left behind them no forwarding addresses—that gradually unbalances the design of the collection. This artificiality, like the anachronism of letting the mythic ladies think and talk like Ovid's sophisticated contemporaries, is attractive, and invites and promotes a pleasing suspension of disbelief. We can hear these women, we want to listen to them, and we believe in their existence and their suffering—almost.

Almost, because we end up withdrawing our belief from them, imperceptibly losing our interest in them and in this imagination of erotic loss. What is lacking in the scheme is an overarching charity, some sense of genuine sympathy with these women. Given Ovid's later success with the same material in the *Metamorphoses*, his total empathy with Procris or Byblis or Myrrha in that poem, this defect in the *Heroides* is puzzling. Does the deficiency arise from an uncertainty of poetic technique or from an inability to imagine the women in their griefs and anxieties, as they perceive them?

The inadequacies of the *Heroides* can be traced to both imperfect technique and failure of imagination, and these deficiencies are interdependent. The dramatic monologue is one of the most difficult dramatic forms, since the poet who employs it must present his character from the outside while simultaneously representing the character's inwardness, and he must define his own sympathies with his creation unobtrusively, through what the character says. He cannot comment on or evaluate what the character says directly, and therefore cannot intervene to guarantee the authenticity of the character's feelings or utterances—in essence, the character is on his own. A case in point here is Dido's letter to Aeneas (letter 7). The letter is moving and amusing by turns, but the passion and the wit never quite fuse. Dido writes:

When you were hurled to shore by the breakers of
   the sea,
I gathered you into secure shelter;
Having hardly heard your name,
I offered you a share of my kingdom.
I wish now I had stopped with such ministrations,
That the rumor of our dalliance had vanished.
On that day came my destruction,
When sudden rain from the dark blue sky
Drove us together down to the fatal cave.

I thought I heard voices then,
Thought that the nymphs were chanting our
    wedding song—
It was the Furies howling out my doom.

                    (89–96)

Her direct allusions to Vergil's *Aeneid* (see also 77–78, 85, 129) are as witty as they seem inevitable, but *nymphas ululasse putavi* ("I thought I heard the nymphs rejoicing [or keening]") wickedly recalls a crucial irony in Vergil's epic. (Was Dido married to Aeneas or not? See *Aeneid* 4.168.) And this movement outside the poem, which is neither necessary nor helpful to its momentum, causes us to see Ovid's Dido for what she is: a literary contrivance. So far from existing only in her own right, she is available for her creator's extraneous purposes—here, Vergilian parody.

The passion and the wit do not fuse here or in any of the *Heroides* (as they will fuse, magnificently, in the *Metamorphoses*) because the passion, or a shadow of what it should be, is Dido's, while the wit is wholly Ovid's. The charges of flippancy and extreme artifice, of excessive rhetorical ingenuity, that are unjustly brought against Ovid's work as a whole have some truth to them in the case of the *Heroides*. Perhaps Ovid realized that his central design was not yet within his reach, that he could not yet imagine women in love, women in the ruin of their love, with requisite precision and delicacy. Perhaps he even saw that instead of making a consistent effort to look at these women as they looked at themselves, he had in fact been rather patronizing to his characters and to their sufferings. It is sometimes suggested nowadays that male writers never have any business trying to imagine the minds and destinies of women, but that notion seems somehow absurd—as if Homer and Sophocles, Dante and Geoffrey Chaucer, Jean Racine and William Shakespeare, Leo Tolstoy and Henry James were rubbish to be swept away in this new, secular apocalypse.

Nevertheless, in the *Heroides* Ovid does seem to play with his women's sufferings, to exploit them: not, I think, from malice or misogyny, but from inexperience. The young man had not yet learned enough about himself to be able to learn, as he would later learn, about women. Therefore, though he had the idea of trying to portray them sympathetically, he was not yet ready to effect such portrayals. This awkwardness with content led him to choose what turned out to be an intractable form: the static, undramatic recital of past woes. And this combined mistake, which he seems gradually to have guessed at, led him to try to make up for the deficiencies of content and form with brilliance of wit and style. The result is the appearance of frivolity (the superior male manipulating the phenomenon of female hysteria) and a real frivolity (Ovid's inability to grapple with the ambivalence, the genuine sorrow and genuine happiness of love, hidden under fertile technical invention). The world of the *Heroides* is an airless, dusty one in which disembodied voices, whining their futile resentments, reverberate, now feebly, now shrilly, against brittle, gilded surfaces.

Some of these deficiencies Ovid seems to have recognized, for, probably after the completion of the first section composed of fifteen dramatic monologues of lonely women, he wrote three pairs of letters (Paris and Helen, Leander and Hero, Acontius and Cydippe) in which masculine overtures are answered by feminine encouragement. This stratagem provides a certain tension that is missing from the first section of letters and that diminishes the unreal self-melodramatization and the aura of doomed narcissism that haunt the dramatic monologues. But even here the poems cannot take fire; and despite numerous fine moments, the general effect is one of rather frigid elegance, of rich gifts that cannot discover their proper intensities and depths. In sum, the importance of the *Heroides* lies in the opportunity they provided Ovid to refine his art: the severe technical demands of these poems forced the poet to chasten his craft; their intricate and troubling content required him to define for himself the circuit of his imagination and to discover the direction he must follow, the ways in which he needed to deepen his vision of human love.

THE ART OF LOVE; THE CURE OF LOVE

Where uncouth simplicity was
Now Rome is golden,
Sleek with the wealth of the conquered world.
See what the Capitol is, recall what it was. . . .
The Palatine, where Apollo and emperors live,
Glitters and shines—there, where the dumb oxen
    grazed.

. . .

Let the simple-minded groan for those good old
    days;
I'm very glad I was born in modern times.
This Age of Refinement, this elegant, civilized era,
Exactly suits what I am and what I want.

            (*Art of Love* 3.113–115; 119–122)

Self-assured, cultivated, exquisitely modulated, this voice of the Professor of Love recalls something of the voice of the lover of the *Amores*, but the occasional uncertainties of that earlier voice have been abolished. The young man in love with love and with himself had thought he knew what he wanted and where he was going, had pretended to be at home in his skin and in the spacious ease of Augustan society; but, in fact, he was profoundly unsure of himself, and he was deeply, irremediably obsessed by forces that were beyond both his knowledge and his power. The Professor of Love, on the other hand, is so completely in control of himself and his world that he can offer himself as our instructor in the arts of love. For he has mastered not only the physiology and the psychology of love but also its economics and its sociology. The world and Rome have, in his philosophy, been reduced to the stage on which the comedy of love, in all its endless variations, is played; and it is the Professor who directs this comedy, lightly, impeccably.

In the passage quoted above, a double irony operates against the world that Augustus had struggled for four decades to reform and to maintain. On the one hand, Augustus had re-created his Rome after the pattern of the great monarchies of the Hellenistic East; both for its outward splendors and for its new political efficiency, Augustan Rome had been borrowing from the achievements of the successors of Alexander and had thereby become, as it needed to become, the modern center of the Mediterranean world. On the other hand, Augustus was not—could not be—wholehearted in his efforts to convert Rome from the old Italian city to the new, essentially Greek, cosmopolis. Both his temperament and his sure political instinct told him that the process of conversion upon which he had entered could succeed only if he managed to preserve as much of the past as he could while effecting the transformation of Rome from fortunate city-state to effective, stable capital of the known world. History shows that Augustus was remarkably successful in achieving his complex designs, but, such was the ambivalence in those designs, such the conflicts between the values of the old Rome and the new, that Augustus failed even as he succeeded, for the past was finally lost.

It is this ambivalence—though Ovid mistakenly viewed it as hypocrisy—in Augustus' feelings about the past and about the present and the future that engages Ovid's wit in the passage quoted above. Did Augustus not see the hopeless discrepancy between the old Rome he kept trying vainly to retrieve and the new Hellenistic world that he had brilliantly fashioned? In the old Rome one was a soldier and a citizen, and one's identity was rigorously defined by the fact of one's citizenship, by one's duties and one's service to family and to state for the common good. But the growth of empire and the influx of wealth that attended it had gradually weakened this political paradigm of identity. The greater the size of the empire, the less direct and the more limited the individual's involvement in the process of government; moreover, the greater the wealth of empire and the greater the contact with alien cultures, the greater the individual's leisure and the means to enrich and to use the leisure for his or her own purposes. This was the world in which both Ovid and Augustus lived; it was the world that Augustus' genius had perfected.

From the time of Catullus down to that of Ovid, from writers as diverse as Lucretius (who was hostile to any variety of politics) and Cicero (who was fervent in his faith in man's ability to sustain good society even as the republic crumbled around him), we read more and more about the person, the individual human being, who exists both in the state and outside it, the core of whose life is hidden, exempt from the world and its purposes, and known, if at all, only to himself. In the *Epistles* of Horace the idea of the person, the reality of Horace's self and his self-awareness, the values and the meaning of the self, are examined in imagery and in rhetorical modes that can best be called philosophical. In Ovid the poetic concept of the person develops very slowly, and reaches its perfection only in the *Metamorphoses*.

Ovid's starting point—and it is here that he first encounters Augustus' social designs as obstacle and as stimulus—is the person as hedonist, the selfish self in its search for pleasure, in its shifts to avoid restriction of pleasure. As we have already seen, even by the time of the second edition of the *Amores*, Ovid had begun to deepen this concept, to subject both hedonism and the authoritarian law and order that seeks to constrain or destroy it to the scrutiny of satire. Both selfish obsession with pleasure and the obsessions of the state with pragmatism and conformity threaten the person's integrity and dignity. Ovid challenges the impersonality of the Roman ideal (law, empire) and its Augustan manifestation by playing them off against radical hedonism; then radical hedonism is left, in the *Art* as in the *Amores*, to destroy itself through its excesses, which are by turns absurd and pathetic.

This hedonist rejection of Roman impersonality and of Augustan moral reforms echoes throughout the poem, now delicately, now re-

soundingly. At 1.217 ff. this mockery blares out, and the wit is insolent, unconstrained. The Professor has been instructing his pupils in how to go about finding someone to love—that is, a girl or woman to seduce, to trifle with, and to abandon (1.91–92). Attractive and pliable ladies may be encountered at the theater and the racetrack, for instance. That all sounds, given the Professor's questionable premises, innocent enough. But suddenly the Professor begins a patriotic digression, praising Augustus for his plan to revenge Rome on Parthia, which had inflicted on Rome its most humiliating defeat in centuries, and celebrating Gaius Caesar, Augustus' grandson, who is to effect this revenge and who will, on his return, ride through the streets of Rome in triumph. This panegyric is spun out through forty verses with deadpan solemnity—and then explodes. As the heir apparent, Gaius, mounts in glory to the Capitol, says the Professor:

> The young gentlemen (and the young ladies
>   crowded next to them)
> Will gaze with fervor on the victor's progress,
> And on that happy day
> Their souls will flood with joy.

For patriotic reasons? No. The young ladies, ignorant of politics and geography, will ask the young gentlemen to interpret the meaning of certain triumphal insignia. The young gentlemen will, naturally, comply with these requests and explain the insignia, or, if they happen not to understand them, will invent explanations so as not to disappoint the young ladies. Thus the stage for imperial grandeur becomes, along with other public spectacles, along with theaters and banquets, merely another place to pursue and ensnare the prey of love. Augustan society and the grand Augustan reformation have been reduced to the setting for seduction, to means to erotic ends. This is the hedonist's own triumph, which is, in his view, far grander and far more secure than victory over Parthia or the Augustan peace (the Pax Romana). And this is why, at the end of book 2, when the Professor imagines his pupils safely bedded down with their chosen ladies, he can indulge himself in his own panegyric on himself: As great as were the physicians and wise men or the priests and heroes of myth and epic, so great a lover, a master of love, am I (*tantus amator ego*):

> Praise me now as your prophet, O men in love!
> Let the wide earth sound with my praises!
> For as Vulcan gave weapons to Achilles,
> So I have given weapons to you—
> Conquer with these your gifts, as Achilles
>   conquered with his,
> And inscribe on your triumph's trophies:
>   NASO MY MASTER WAS.
>
> (2.733–738)

With this *sphragis* (seal, his name) Ovid completes his transvaluation of all Roman-Augustan values. The world of epic and myth, the world of history and empire, the world of law and public service, have been replaced by the world of selfhood, pleasure, and love.

The first two books of the *Art* are directed to young men who want to win the game of love; after this instruction is completed, the Professor sings the victory song we have just seen, and then, with fiendishly ironic compassion, he turns in the third and final book to instruct girls and women in how to love successfully. Since young men have been so splendidly educated in seduction, the odds are now heavily against the female. Ovid therefore undertakes to help women catch men as he had helped men catch women.

We are not surprised, perhaps, when we quickly observe that the Professor's instructions to women differ markedly from his instructions to men. The master spends most of his time discoursing to his female pupils on niceties of toilette, on posture, deportment, coiffure, ways of tormenting their lovers, ways of deceiving their spouses, and, not least, on the most effective sexual positions. In short, so far from helping women against men, he tries to convince them to turn themselves into the kind of sex objects that men want, thus making the male's

task of seduction easier and more rewarding. If women are fooled by this ironic assistance, it is not they, but their seducers, who will benefit: the master of love is also the complete master of chauvinism. This final portion of the *Art* possesses all the fertile invention that marked the first two books, yet book 3 shows also a deliberate cruelty, a deep, black mockery that illumines the poem as a whole. The Professor of Love is not merely a shallow superhedonist; he is, beyond solipsism and corrupt sensuality, an erotic monster.

The Cure of Love, though marked off from the *Art* by its separate title, must be considered part of the *Art:* the entire poem functions as a kind of dark quartet. Here the monster, claiming to feel pangs of guilt for having aided young men (he is not here concerned with women) to destroy themselves, offers a crash course in modes of falling out of love. Needless to say, the lovers who learn these remedies for love will entangle themselves still deeper in their sufferings. Most of these "remedies" will serve only to focus the lover's mind on his plight without alleviating that plight in any way. And some of the advice is downright rotten. The Professor suggests, for instance, that a lover who is going off to see his mistress should first have intercourse with someone—anyone—in order to take the edge off his appetite (396 ff.); he also suggests that the lover choose sexual positions that will disgust (and, of course, ultimately excite) him, or that show the defects of his mistress' body and thus (not very likely) intensify his disgust. Another remedy to lessen desire is to have two mistresses—or more, if possible—at the same time, and thus let love consume itself if it resists being uprooted.

Above all, the lover must get his mind off his fixation. This means not going to the theater, where there are ladies who will automatically recall the particular lady, and love stories that will recall this fatal love story of his; it means not listening to mood music or watching interpretive dancing, or, a special danger, not reading love poetry, particularly not the poetry of Ovid. And the lover must not think about his rival. He must never, never think of him—that, of course, would be to pour generous oil on the hopeless fire. This discourse ends abruptly, and bathetically, with some limp hints about diet: Don't eat onions; do eat bitter rue; if you drink, drink heavily.

The calm surfaces of the *Art* seldom if ever reveal the tensions that have called it into being and that sustain it. As we listen to the self-assured voice of the Professor, the multiple ironies that haunt him, of which he is totally unaware, remain hidden, unheard—until we close the book. Then come muffled echoes of questions we had been vaguely prompted to ask him but that we left unasked, even unformed, while he entertained us richly, dazzled us with his subtle effronteries. Something is very wrong with the teacher and with his book of instructions. When he was speaking to us, we knew, dimly, that we were being manipulated, but such was the fun of it, such was his charm, that we hardly minded. The suave enchanter who undertook to instruct us in the arts of seduction had seduced us. Well, why shouldn't he? Wasn't he supposed to be our model, wasn't he what we wanted to become?

Yes, and no. We may have thought we wanted to learn what he had to teach; may have found, initially, the syllabus and the exercises delightful. Yet now there is a taste of ashes. We have been duped; we feel small, dirty. We had wanted to be lovers, to love and be loved. We had thought the bright, brittle talk was an amusing, useful pose; we had been certain that under the sophistication was genuine sentiment, fidelity, real love—and there is not. This realization shakes us and rends the poem, and under the bright, broken surfaces we now see the violent disorders of the poem; and we see, too, something about ourselves that we had not wanted to see. And the vanished charlatan who mocked us, what of him? We begin to see that the Professor of Love, so far from being a trickster, was caught hopelessly in his own obsessions, was not so much a cynic who duped us as he was his own helpless dupe.

Love has become too important to Ovid to be treated frivolously or cynically. The prophet of the smart set, the naughty young man who threw idle spitballs at the Establishment, has somehow grown up. The Establishment remains, and will continue to remain, as the prime object of satiric observation; but the poet of love who had revised the *Amores* to reveal the defects of his inadequate lover-hero now, in the *Art,* trains his sights on someone very like himself—on a dead, sad poseur that he has outgrown. In the *Art* and the *Cure* it is the neurotic theoretician of love who is caricatured.

What the Professor teaches—thinks he knows and tries to teach—is the practice of psychological rape. The fears and the angers of Don Juan are precisely adumbrated in this strange, ambivalent poem. Under its wit and sophistication, under its bitter social comment, are criticisms of Augustan politics; and under these rejections of impersonality and empire is a definitive analysis of narcissism, of its sufferings and of its savage, destructive illusions. In the *Art* Ovid does not explicitly show the alternative vision of love and personality toward which he has moved; we gradually sense from this poem what genuine love must be and what human beings should be, as we remember listening to the Professor expound on what he was and what he represented. And we sense too, with a shudder, that if we have ears to hear him, we are somehow akin to him. When these recognitions have been accomplished, Ovid and we are ready to move onward to the alternative vision of love in the *Metamorphoses.*

THE METAMORPHOSES

Whenever the characters of an author suffer, they do so at the behest of their author—the author is responsible for their suffering and must justify his cruelty by the seriousness of his moral imagination.
(Lionel Trilling, "The Morality of Enertia," in *A Gathering of Fugitives*)

By the horns of Isis-Luna, compassion. . . .
(Ezra Pound, *Canto* 93)

OVID

In the 1950's few adults were reading the *Metamorphoses*. This collection of "blithe stories" about the loves of gods for humans, about amazing transformations, about fantastic voyages through the heavens and over the seas, had, suitably abridged, been delivered to the nursery for the entertainment of children and for the easy access it provided them to classical mythology. Children were thought not to be very serious, and Ovid clearly was not serious at all: it was a perfect match.

Some critics still speak of the *Metamorphoses* as being essentially a kind of fun machine, and deny Ovid any serious purpose in it (beyond aesthetic perfections). But this view has been challenged steadily in recent years, and it may, with luck, disappear. This great poem did not seize and hold the imaginations of Chaucer, Shakespeare, John Milton, Pope, John Keats, and Pound merely because of its verbal ingenuities and visual conceits; and it did not, in different ways, haunt the minds and hearts of both medieval and Renaissance readers because it provided a painless entry into classical culture.

It could be argued that no other poem from antiquity has so influenced the literature and art of western Europe as has the *Metamorphoses*. The reason for this influence is partly to be found in its brilliant artistic surface, but essentially the complex vision of the nature of human life in the poem and its profound sense of human personality and human freedom account for its singular attraction for the poets and artists of Europe. Far from being a mindless confection for the mindless, Ovid's poem is, on one level, about rape, about the irresponsibility and cruelty of the Olympian gods, about the ignorance and fatal rage of humankind; on another level it is about a suffering world the suffering of which is, or seems to be, at once meaningless and irremediable; and on yet another level it is about the meaning of love, about the mysterious ways in which suffering may be transcended, the ways in which what seems demonic in gods and men may be seen as terrible illusions that the power and purity of love can disperse.

There is no question that Ovid is playful in this poem, and this lightness of touch and shimmer of wit in a poem about suffering and salvation may account in part for the poem's having been excluded from the attention of adults for almost three decades. Ovid *is* playful in this very serious poem; that is, he is playful in earnest. The tension between the manner of the poem and its matter may puzzle us initially; but only a false, simplistic solution to the problems of this tension would suggest that there is no tension between the smooth, witty surfaces and the troubled depths because there are no depths. The reader who comes to this poem from, say, the fiction of Flannery O'Connor will not be confused by the discordant concord of matter and manner, by the highly organized dynamism of opposites that are fused—wit with tragedy, beauty with terror, apparent levity with genuine gravity. When poets like Ovid and O'Connor move from satire to meditation on human suffering, their art becomes anagogical; and their comedy, far from disturbing decorum, serves it. This art is an art of exaggeration and of surprise. It puts familiar themes in unfamiliar, fantastic lights: through exaggeration and comic modes these artists invite us to see what we can recognize only because of enlargements, dislocations, and paradox. Through the grotesque and the absurd they point the way to the mysteries of the ideal and the real.

Such an artist is Ovid's Arachne, the gifted weaver who challenges Minerva to a contest the outcome of which will show which of the two, mortal or goddess, is the more talented. Minerva, disguised as an old woman, tries to persuade Arachne to learn some humility before it is too late; having failed, she angrily prepares for the contest. The intentions and actions of both Arachne and Minerva are delicately imagined, and the narrative point of view shifts subtly as the story unfolds. By the end of the story our sympathy has moved from Minerva to Arachne. The angry goddess, her vanity and jealousy manifest in her defeat, inflicts a terrifying punishment on her human victim when she transforms her into a spider. The artist's arrogance was terrible, but its punishment is more terrible still; and we finish this story loathing the goddess and feeling an ambivalent, troubled grief for the girl. Many human beings in this poem are destroyed, punished with eternal and humiliating transformations by divine anger and whim: some *may* deserve their punishment, but most clearly do not. It is a fine poetic irony (which Ovid perhaps glimpsed as he wrote this story) that Arachne, the mistress of a fresh, radical, powerful art form, will be destroyed by her own art.

That art, which is carefully contrasted with the official art of Minerva, resembles Ovid's own art in its graceful ease and in its intense focus on divine injustice and on the grotesque and the terrible. Arachne, like her creator, fuses elegant surfaces with violent depths. Her opponent is a representative of classical—or, rather, of neoclassical—academic art. Minerva's tapestry has as its subject her own victory over Neptune when the two of them vied for the possession and the naming of Athens. In the center of her tapestry she depicts the twelve Olympians, with Jupiter in their midst, marveling witnesses to her triumph and to Neptune's defeat. This lifeless advertisement for herself is surrounded at its four corners by representations of divine punishment of human malefactors, the impious "justly" in angry, supernatural hands. The entire square is tightly and decorously framed by Minerva's hallmark, an olive wreath.

Against this feeble exercise in self-aggrandizement Arachne sets her limpid, supple pictures of the gods in their lust and the victims of their lust. The language and rhythm that had described Minerva's artifact were mechanical and stilted. In describing the tapestry of Arachne, Ovid's diction becomes sumptuous and his cadences have the lilt and freshness that only he could devise for Latin. These pictures have enormous speed: where Minerva's images were static and literal, these are rapid, sensual, impressionistic. Arachne's tapestry has no easily discernible shape because its shape (or shapes) has become indistinguishable from its incomparable movement—it is all but impossible to speak of structure here, for in this passage, as in the entire poem, the modulations are so quick and so sure, and the images are so vivid and so compressed, that neither ears nor eyes can dissect the stimuli that propel and enchant them. What surrounds this epiphany of sights, sounds, and moral judgments (for the gods are judged here, accurately, ruthlessly) is not a frame but an aura—at the circumference of her tapestry, Arachne strews blossoms mingled with ivy: wavering fragrance, shifting tints. In the work of Minerva the lie disguised as truth stares glumly out at the viewer from the ruins of dead classicism: this art is didactic in the worst sense. In the work of Arachne the viewer participates in the recognition of truths discovered in the ordered swirl of living artistry: this art is maieutic in the best sense.

Useful as the tapestry of Arachne is as a symbol of Ovid's own artistic methods, it does not fully suggest the purpose of the artistry of the *Metamorphoses*. Arachne is concerned only with the monstrous Olympians and their crimes; but this, though a major theme in the poem, is subordinate to its other major themes. Ovid's stated subject, as outlined in the four verses with which the poem opens, and as the title suggests, is the transformation of living entities, of their shapes and beauties (for *forma*, the crucial word here, means both "shape" and "beauty") into new shapes and beauties. There is nothing peculiar in this emphasis, for many myths deal with transformations. What is peculiar here is that Ovid has decided to treat his theme from the beginning of the world (*prima ab origine mundi*) down to his own times (*ad mea tempora*).

If Ovid's purpose was to retell the old myths of Greco-Roman culture in an amusing way, to offer a lighthearted compendium of entertaining primitive tales of the ways of gods to men (and women), why should he choose so vast a frame? Couldn't he see that by doing so he was, with an arrogance worthy of Arachne herself, challenging comparison with Homer, Hesiod, the pre-Socratics, the Greek tragedians, and the great founding poets of Rome—even with Vergil himself? Yes, he saw all that, but he didn't worry, however high the stakes, because he trusted his inspiration. He had decided to transform epic into mock epic, then mock epic into counterepic. His epic would not tell, in the traditional sense, a story; would not have a plot; nor would it, in the usual way, have a protagonist. Rather, the story (the many, mysterious stories) would consist of a criticism of the classical story, would be a parody of human history, of "large-mannered motions," and of "mythy minds"; and the protagonist (but there is not merely one, and they are many and varied) would be the human spirit as it searches for integrity in an often frightening, always unintelligible world. Ovid *is* an epic poet in this poem if we allow him—and he does not care whether we allow him or not—to reject the idea of epic, to transvalue it and transform it.

Hesiod, in telling the story of the birth of the gods in his *Theogony*, had begun with Chaos. Ovid, who imitates Hesiod and corrects him, also begins with Chaos, but, taking the traditional Olympian deities for granted, quickly passes to the creation of the world by a mysterious god (1.21, 32, 79) who has no place in traditional Greco-Roman myth and whose benevolence and providence recall the demiurge of Plato's *Timaeus*, the Stoic conception of a creator god, and, astonishingly, the God of Genesis. This god is not manifest in the rest of the poem, where the divinities are, for the most part, the violent, amoral Olympians seen without the classicizing rationalism that usually attended them until Euripides. Yet this unknown god, in various oblique manifestations, haunts the poem: it is he—or she, or something beyond gender—who has created human beings from divine seed and has made human beings, alone of his creations, to stand erect and has prompted them to look up at the night sky and contemplate the stars (*os homini sublime dedit caelumque videre/iussit et erectos ad sidera tollere vultus*; 1.85-86).

This emphatic affirmation of human dignity is crucial throughout the poem and resonates throughout Ovid's depiction of humankind's suffering. On one level of his poem, Ovid shows us human beings thwarted in their loves, destroyed by gods or by each other or by themselves; seen from this angle, his poem ought to be somber, even sinister and nihilistic. Yet the affirmation of the unknown god and of his creatures who, despite the ruins of history and despite their own folly, aspire to goodness and wholeness, more than countervails the darkness of the poem. Weak though they may be, corrupted though they seem in their passions as in their reason, Ovid's human beings tend to a certain nobility. If they are tormented and destroyed by psychotic gods, if they flounder through their lives foolishly, some of them show an extraordinary yearning for integrity and for truth. At the heart of Ovid's counterepic is a profound faith in humankind's need and capacity for a moral transfiguration for which the physical transformations are constant and persuasive metaphors.

Nevertheless, the darkness of the poem is real. After he has imagined the creation of human beings, Ovid again borrows from Hesiod, this time from his versions of the myth of the four ages, which he swiftly sketches. Crucial in this sketch is Ovid's emphasis on the identification of Saturn with the Golden Age. When Saturn is sent by his son, Jupiter, into shadowy Tartarus, the Silver Age begins, along with Jupiter's reign (*postquam Saturno tenebrosa in Tartara misso/sub Iove mundus erat*; 113-114); and after this the decline of the world continues, from silver to bronze, from bronze to iron. The Iron Age is presided over by Jupiter, and during the Iron Age and the reign of Jupiter the events of the poem occur; the Iron Age lasts, then, down to Ovid's own times and through (and apparently beyond) the reign of the earthly Jupiter, Augustus Caesar. This configuration (Saturn, Jupiter, Augustus) opens the poem and resounds loudly and wittily at its close, where Julius Caesar, after this apotheosis, views Rome from his new home in heaven and realizes, with pride and pleasure, that the achievements of Augustus, his adopted son, will be greater than his own (15.851-875). So, says Ovid, many of the great fathers of epic were outdone by their greater sons; so even

Saturn was outdone by Jupiter, and Caesar by Augustus. Perhaps the most frequent motif in Augustus' propaganda was his myth of a golden age restored to Rome by his leadership.

This echo of Saturn's Golden Age and Jupiter's Iron Age effectively counters the Augustan myth of the Roman world made new and golden. Indeed, all the traditional myths, all the old gods and heroes of epic, meet with savage irony in this poem. They are all associated with empire and dominion, with tyranny and oppression in their various disguises; and in Ovid's eyes they are all absurd at best, sinister and destructive at worst. They claim to destroy the monsters and to create civilization and to sustain it (recall, in particular, the myths of Apollo and Hercules), but what they actually do in this poem is to indulge their passions indiscriminately, to rape and pillage and murder. Throughout the *Metamorphoses* the heroic world and the world of historical empire are a nightmare for which there is no remedy or solace, to which there is no end—only a further descent into the hells of the Iron Age, only a progressive disintegration of reality.

But this vision of history and the state as vast demonic machines that devour humankind is balanced, and more than balanced, by another vision, at once subtler and more powerful, of human beings who, despite their immense vulnerability, may yet win through to moments of authentic being that transcend the horrors that seem to engulf them.

Central to this vision are deities who have little or no connection with the traditional deities of Greece and Rome, and who derive their meaning from the great mystery religions of the Near East that were coming into their own just as Ovid was writing the *Metamorphoses*. As against the impersonal state cults of the classical world, these religions focused on the relationship between individuals and their gods; these gods—and they were often goddesses—promised release to the individual from the sufferings of this world, promised salvation, a union with themselves in another world after death. At its profoundest level Ovid's counterepic mirrors a radical transition in the ancient world, one from state religion, in which salvation was for the city, to personal religion, in which salvation is for the individual. As Ovid's poem rejects the values of epic and the values of the city, as it everywhere rejects violent heroics and the will to empire and faith in the redemptions of history, so it rejects the old gods of the city in favor of new deities through whose compassion and grace persons, no matter what their class or citizenship, find some solace in the world and powerful hope for good lives in another world.

In book 1, after Jupiter in his self-righteousness has tried to destroy humankind by flood, the lone survivors, Deucalion and Pyrrha, pray to Themis (the Great Mother in one of her manifestations). After their prayers the wrath of Jupiter is mysteriously and quickly stilled, and Themis gives them instructions as to how to renew mankind (by throwing the bones of their mother—that is, of Earth herself—over their shoulders; 1.318–394). In book 2, when the earth is again threatened with destruction, this time from the fire of Phaeton's borrowed sun chariot, it is the prayer of Tellus (again, the Earth Mother) that (again mysteriously) moves Jupiter to save the world. In book 5, the nymph Arethusa (487 ff.) averts the destruction of humankind by famine when she supplicates Ceres, the goddess of harvest; enraged by grief over the loss of her daughter, Persephone, Ceres stops the growth of grain. Arethusa explains to Ceres what has happened to her daughter, and thereby institutes the actions that will assuage the wrath of the stricken goddess. At the end of book 9, having gradually modulated from the world and its sufferings to individuals and their sufferings, Ovid shows Isis as she saves a despondent lover (Iphis) in response to a prayer from the girl's mother. Finally, in book 10, an unknown god grants the incestuous Myrrha her repentant prayer (483–487). Rare as these passages are (to them we should add the prayer of Daphne in book 1 and the transformations of Byblis and Dryope), different as they are in tone, they have in common their insistence on an order of being that is beyond the chaos of history and the malice of dominion, and that is grounded in compassion, in mercy, and in love. If these epiphanies of the Great Mother do not totally expel the darkness of the poem, they move our minds to what is necessary: the alternative vision by means of which the darkness can be transcended.

This alternative vision of human integrity, born of folly and suffering, and of divine grace that proffers redemption, finds its perfection in the figure of Myrrha. Roughly speaking, the lovers in Ovid's poem can be divided into two groups: the Olympians and the human victims of their lust, and the human lovers who victimize each other and themselves. The gods and goddesses in love run the gamut from the sentimental to the ridiculous to the brutal; they have no conception of what love means, and we come gradually, after feeling horror at them, almost to pity them. The human lovers, on the other hand, show extraordinary variety and complexity in their efforts to encounter the mysteries and dangers of love, and in dealing with his human characters, Ovid is almost unfailingly sympathetic. For what all these lovers have in common (as the deities have mindless lust in common) is a deep vulnerability and an equally deep need for love. Thus, throughout the poem the loves of the gods and the loves of human beings create a kind of dialectical harmony, and from this uneasy pattern emerges a strong and wholehearted affirmation of the human personality in all its fragility and all its curious strength, all its potential honesty and goodness. These lovers deceive themselves and each other very often; they fumble, almost always, through their loves to failure or destruction; but they are redeemed, in whole or in part, by the intensity of their passion and by the purity of their will.

The culmination of this motif is in the death and transfiguration of Myrrha. The story of Myrrha's love for her father, of her gradual realization of her forbidden passion, of her complex response to it, of her efforts to deal with it, of its final, terrible consummation, is recounted in Ovid's wittiest style. A deliberate ambiguity of tone treats her now almost mockingly, as a creature of a farcical melodrama, now seriously as a tragic heroine. But under this ambivalent wit the essential seriousness of Myrrha's plight is constantly deepened. When her father discovers the ruse by which she has managed to seduce him, she flees his rage and, after nine months of desperate flight, comes at last to Arabia, exhausted and ready to die. She then offers up, from the depths of her anguish and contrition, a prayer to the gods. She begs that she be allowed neither to live (and thus pollute the living) nor to die (and thus pollute the kingdoms of the dead). At this moment, when she accepts responsibility for what she is and for her love, when she asks for an expiation that later ages will call purgatory (*merui nec triste recuso/supplicium*, "I have deserved it and do not refuse the stern punishment"; 10.484–485), she takes on magnificence and becomes a genuine, a new kind of heroine in this new kind of poem, this counterepic.

The deity who answers her prayer is left unnamed (*numen aliquod*), but it is perhaps not wrong to wonder if this deity is not Isis or the Great Mother, Earth, in another of her aspects. The land of Myrrha's death and transformation is Arabia, after all, and the child to whom she is about to give birth is Adonis, who has a special, central place in the Great Mother's worship. Finally, Myrrha herself is transformed into a myrrh tree, her eternal tears changed into a fragrance that will constantly be used in rites of the mystery religions. In this transformation, the horrors and chaos of the heart made new and beautiful, all the anguished, thwarted lovers of the poem find their salvation. By grace and by nature, lovers, all good lovers, now seen clearly in their weakness and in their strength, have won through.

The poet of love has purified his vision completely, and the human heart, in all its confusion and folly and in all its greatness, has been vindicated. After Myrrha the parodic review of Greco-Roman culture and history is intensified until it seems like a carousel gone out of control. This satire on state and empire, with Aeneas lost hopelessly in the blur of it, spins on dizzily until it crashes abruptly into the absurd apotheosis of Julius Caesar and the imminent, no less absurd apotheosis of Augustus Caesar. These men, these human, political gods, are no match for Myrrha and what she represents. In the counterepic the losers are the winners, and the empire and its glories are well lost for love, for the perfection of the human heart.

THE FASTI
AND THE EXILIC POEMS (TRISTIA *AND* EX PONTO)

> Where you come from is gone, where you thought you were going never was there, and where you are is no good unless you can get away from it. Where is there a place for you to be? No place.
> (Flannery O'Connor, *Wise Blood*)

Part of the *Fasti* was written in Rome; but some of it, like the last two collections, *Tristia* and *Ex Ponto*, was written during Ovid's exile in Tomis. I group these three collections together because, as the products of his last years, they show a uniform range of moods and a general decline in achievement; this decline is occasioned not so much by a failure of talent as by the desperation of his final circumstances.

Whatever the exact date of the *Fasti* (before, during, or after the writing of the *Metamorphoses*), whatever its immediate inspiration (there are indications that it was sometimes and perhaps initially intended to mollify the imperial wrath), the poem is a disturbing, though often magnificent, failure. This poem ought to be, and often tries to be, a description of the Roman religious calendar in which the traditional festivals and rituals are discussed and their origins and meanings are illuminated with vividness and sympathy. If such a book could be written (Ovid seems to have thought), perhaps Augustus could forget and forgive the satirist's wit and the individualist's affirmation of love in its many disguises. Perhaps Ovid

thought this, but if he did, he was not recalled; and in any case he could not keep the design of the *Fasti* steadily before him as he wrote.

From time to time Ovid comes upon a festival that stirs in him a depth of piety that is rare in Augustan literature. At brief moments a veneration for the old minor deities of the countryside, the spirits of fruition and plenty (see here David Malouf's brilliant re-creation), flares up and kindles the poem to extraordinary vibrance. Then, just as suddenly, the moment passes, and the poem reverts to mechanical survey, to bare listings and erudite glosses. At other times, forgetting his new discretion, Ovid offers rich lubricities (Pan, Hercules, and Omphale; Silenus, Priapus, and Lotis; Flora and Juno) or political pasquinade (Anna Perenna, Aeneas, and Lavinia; Janus; Romulus) in which the old, iridescent insolence returns unimpaired. But these diverse modes found none of the poetic coincidence that Ovid had known how to fashion in the *Metamorphoses*, and he seems at last to have despaired both of his efforts to reconcile himself with Augustus and of his attempt to record (when it was too late), to recall, and to renew the rural pieties that had been at the heart of Roman life and that he and his age had rejected. The *Fasti*, then, is a sad fragment with numerous moments of inspiration that serve only to light up the despair of the author, the ruin of his artistry, and the spiritual desolation of his times.

But the desolations of the exile itself, as these are seen in the poems written in exile about exile, are even greater. They go beyond unhappiness and frustration to a genuine tragic sense. This tragic sense, though, does not and cannot, as tragedy always must, point beyond itself to a higher and deeper reality, to a wisdom beyond itself—or, failing that, to a recognition of human limitation. There are lovely poems widely scattered through the first exilic collection, *Tristia* (a poignant recollection of the last night in Rome, 1.3; the energetic, ironic, and angry defense of his poetry, 2; the great spring poem for Tomis, 3.12; the fine prayer for his wife, 5.5.13–26), but no genuine piece of inspiration could be sustained for very long. Ovid knew this was so, and tells us so with chilling clarity:

> I speak with myself,
> Handle once more words that have grown strange
>   to me,
> Grope for the fatal tokens of my craft,
> And in this way drag out
> My spirit and my years,
> In this way push myself from thoughts of pain.
> In verse I seek oblivion from grief,
> And if my craft can win that prize,
> It is enough.
>
> *(Tristia* 5.7.63–68)

It was a prize he would never obtain, as he knew very well. In 4.6.21–22 he says:

> Patience has not been won,
> However long the time I spend
> Searching to grasp it, master it;
> My mind still feels old pains, old griefs,
> As if these wounds were fresh.

Ovid is, while attempting to compose these poems, locked into a rage and a despair that cannot be escaped, forgotten, or transcended. He tries humiliating himself and speaking of his guilt and of Augustus' "gentlest clemency" (*Tristia* 1.2.61; see also *Ex Ponto* 1.2.59, 95–96; 2.2.129); but the sense of outraged innocence and a fury deeper than any resentment, an anger at Augustus and fate and friends who did not (could not) help him, burst out again and again. All we can hear in these poems, and particularly in *Ex Ponto*, is the fading voice of a man who has been crushed by forces that are as effective as they are mysterious and brutal.

Many of these poems are written in letter form, and some of them may have been sent back to Rome as letters. Yet they do not have the vitality of genuine letters, nor do they have the energy of Ovid's immediate models for these poems, the *Epistles* of Horace. Two things precluded Ovid's triumph in the poetic genre that Horace perfected and even, in a sense, invented. First, Horace's "exile" was self-im-

posed and self-sustained (he was, in the modern phrase, "an internal émigré"). Second, when he wrote these poems, and even long before, Horace was a creature of inwardness: he did not need and did not want the stimulus of the city because the authentic motions of his soul were all within him, and it was these he needed to observe and to come to know. Ovid, on the other hand, had been forced into exile; and what his poems breathe is humiliation, confusion, and hopeless passivity—a kind of spiritual slavery to despair and loneliness that can find no freedom, not even from itself; for him, "solitude" is not, cannot be, "the cure of loneliness." In order to live and to write, Ovid needed Rome, its movement, and its people. Ovid was a novelist, and what he needed to know about reality was to be found in the faces and voices of men and women as they moved through the "smoke and glitter and noise" of the Rome that Horace had abandoned; was to be found not in the inwardness of lyric or philosophy, but in many human hearts and their union in society. For him solitude was an unintelligible agony and a long death, of which these bitter, terrible poems (the isolation of which recalls the isolations of the *Heroides*) are the monotonous, imperfect record.

Yet, as Ovid guessed, even in the utmost pitch of misery, it was not and is not the bitterness of exile that matters most about this life and its art. Several things matter, all of them unified in the poetry. First, the verse itself, of which the elegance of syntax and fresh, sharply observed images of the outer world would inspire poets and artists for almost two thousand years (and will probably continue to inspire them: one of the very greatest of modern poets, Ezra Pound, is Ovidian to the core). Powerful and subtle by turns, Ovid's grasp of what the world really looks like, the world through which his people move and in which they live, is mirrored in a language that is vigorous and delicate, that catches in its cadences and in the shape of its sentences the necessary shade, the necessary tone.

It was wonderful luck that for thousands of European artists the first Latin poet they encountered was one who could offer them, as pattern and as inspiration, this refinement of vision, sound, and syntax, and this richness of invention, this limitless hunger for the world and its beauty. For Ovid, unlike Vergil, who offers another pattern and another inspiration, is this-worldly even (and not least) when he praises the truth of Isis; and his peculiar delight in the magnificence of the world and his peculiar capacity for an accurate ordering of that magnificence with seeming ease are permanent and invaluable for the literature of the West.

Next is Ovid's contribution to the art of fiction. It is probably too much to say that he invented the modern story; but when one looks at what Giovanni Boccaccio and Chaucer were to make of what they borrowed from him, and when one looks back from the great modern masters to Ovid's imagination of the erotic temperament in the *Amores* and in the *Art* or to his renderings of the stories of Narcissus, Philomela, Scylla, Procris, Pygmalion, Myrrha, and Alcyone, it is hard not to want to say: "This is the poet who found, beyond the requirements of elegy or epic, the significant form for the imagining of the human personality in its conflicts with self, with others, and with society." In Ovid's handling of psychology are a new precision and a new compassion that enable him to see the complexities of human personality clearly and to record them, to imagine them, with astonishing accuracy and tenderness. As we look at his landscapes and see in them beauty that is at once ideal and real, so in his pictures of the human heart, whether the mood is gentle or grotesque, we see ourselves and our fellow human beings as we actually are and also as we might become. No writer before Ovid had attempted so passionately and so constantly to catch in fictions the inconsistencies and the nearly invisible fluctuations, the flowerings and witherings, of human personality. After Ovid's success, many of his heirs would be able to make similar attempts with similar success.

Finally, this achievement in the art of fiction is grounded in a habit of Ovid's mind that we have constantly returned to in these pages—his sensitivity to human ignorance and self-delusions and the vulnerabilities and radical disorders of the human heart. It is precisely in these disorders that Ovid discovers human freedom and the human need to give love and to receive it; these disorders and their contrary virtues evoke Ovid's incomparable compassion and his steady, gentle affirmation of human experience despite the chaos of that experience. At a peculiar moment in Western history, when humankind's sense of what it was began imperceptibly to change and when the meaning and value of the human being began to emerge and to evolve, Ovid gave powerful and permanent form to the new, amorphous aspirations; he discovered the necessary sights and sounds for the new hungerings for better lives.

Selected Bibliography

TEXTS, COMMENTARIES, AND TRANSLATIONS

Amores I, edited by John A. Barsby. New York, 1973. Translation and commentary.

Amores, Ars amatoria, Remedia amoris, edited by E. J. Kenney. New York, 1961. Revised ed. 1965. Text.

Ars amatoria I, edited by A. S. Hollis. New York, 1977. Text and commentary.

Ars amatoria: Selections, edited by M. J. Griggs. London and New York, 1971. Text and commentary.

The Art of Love, edited by Rolfe Humphries. Bloomington, Ind., 1957. Most widely used translation.

The Fasti, edited by F. Bömer. 2 vols. Heidelberg, 1957. Text, translation, and commentary (in German).

The Fasti, edited by Sir James Frazer. London, 1931. Loeb Library edition, which is the standard text and translation.

Heroides, edited by Grant Showerman. London, 1924. Revised text 1977. Most widely used translation.

Metamorphoses, edited by William S. Anderson. Leipzig, 1977. Text.

OVID

Metamorphoses, edited by F. Bömer. Heidelberg, 1969–1977. Commentary (in German).

Metamorphoses, edited by Horace Gregory. New York, 1958. Translation.

Metamorphoses, edited by Rolfe Humphries. Bloomington, Ind., 1955. Most widely used translation.

Metamorphoses, edited by A. E. Watts. Berkeley, 1954. Translation.

Ovid's Metamorphoses: Books 6–10, edited by William S. Anderson. Norman, Okla., 1972. American Philological Association series of classical texts. Text and commentary.

Tristia, edited by G. Luck. Heidelberg, 1967. Text.

Tristia, Ex Ponto, edited by Arthur L. Wheeler. London, 1924. Loeb Library edition, which is the most widely used text and translation.

CRITICISM

Binns, J. W., ed. *Ovid.* Greek and Latin Studies in Classical Literature and Its Influence. London, 1973. A distinguished collection of essays on various aspects of Ovid's poetry.

Barsby, John A. *Ovid.* Greece and Rome, New Surveys in the Classics, no. 12. Oxford, 1978.

Coleman, R. "Structure and Intention in the *Metamorphoses.*" *Classical Quarterly* 65:461–476 (1971).

Curran, L. "Transformations and Anti-Augustanism in Ovid's *Metamorphoses.*" *Arethusa* 5:71–91 (1972).

———. "Rape and Rape Victims in the *Metamorphoses.*" *Arethusa* 11:213–241 (1978).

Due, O. *Changing Forms: Studies in the Metamorphoses of Ovid.* Copenhagen, 1974.

Elliott, A. G. "Ovid's *Metamorphoses:* A Bibliography, 1968–1978." *Classical World* 73:385–412 (1980).

Fränkel, Hermann. *Ovid: A Poet Between Two Worlds.* Berkeley, 1945.

Fyler, John M. "*Omnia Vincit Amor:* Incongruity and the Limitations of Structure in Ovid's *Amores.*" *Classical Journal* 66:196–202 (1971).

———. *Chaucer and Ovid.* New Haven, 1979.

Galinsky, G. Karl. *Ovid's Metamorphoses: An Introduction to Its Basic Aspects.* Berkeley, 1975.

Holleman, A. W. "Ovid and Politics." *Historia* (Wiesbaden) 20:458–466 (1971).

Jacobson, Howard. *Ovid's Heroides.* Princeton, 1974.

Johnson, W. R. "The Problem of the Counter-classical Sensibility and Its Critics." *California Studies in Classical Antiquity* 3:123–151 (1970).

———. "The Desolations of the *Fasti.*" *Classical Journal* 74, no. 1:7–18 (1978).

Jones, A. H. M. *Augustus.* New York, 1971.

Kenney, E. J. "The Poetry of Ovid's Exile." *Proceedings of the Cambridge Philological Society* 11:37–49 (1965).

Leach, E. W. "Ekphrasis and the Theme of Artistic Failure in Ovid's *Metamorphoses.*" *Ramus* 3, no. 1:102–142 (1974).

Little, D. A. "The Non-Augustanism of Ovid's *Metamorphoses.*" *Mnemosyne* 25:389–401 (1972).

Malouf, David. *An Imaginary Life: A Novel.* New York, 1978. An extraordinary novel about, among other things, Ovid in exile.

Otis, Brooks. *Ovid as an Epic Poet.* 2nd ed. New York, 1971.

Parker, Douglass. "The Ovidian Coda." *Arion* 8, no. 1:80–97 (1969).

Rand, Edward K. *Ovid and His Influence.* Boston, 1925; New York, 1963.

Segal, C. P. *Landscape in Ovid's Metamorphoses: A Study of the Transformation of a Literary Symbol.* Hermes Einzelschriften, no. 23. Wiesbaden, 1969.

———. "Myth and Philosophy in the *Metamorphoses:* Ovid's Augustanism and the Augustan Conclusion of Book XV." *American Journal of Philology* 90:257–292 (1969).

Syme, Sir Ronald. *History in Ovid.* New York, 1979.

Thibault, John C. *The Mystery of Ovid's Exile.* Berkeley, 1964.

Wiedemann, T. "The Political Background of *Tristia* 2." *Classical Quarterly* 25, no. 2:264–271 (1975).

Wilkinson, L. P. *Ovid Recalled.* New York, 1955. Abridged as *Ovid Surveyed.* New York, 1962.

Williams, Gordon. *Change and Decline: Roman Literature in the Early Empire.* Berkeley, 1978.

W. R. JOHNSON

SENECA THE YOUNGER

(4? B.C.–A.D. 65)

I

NO ANCIENT WRITER is more elusive than Seneca. Although we know far more of his life than, for example, of Aeschylus' or Livy's, and although his works are both copious and fluent—even, some have said, exhibitionist—the personality that emerges is so manifold that we seem to be meeting not one individual but at least six.

Seneca was known as a leading intellectual at a time of sophisticated literary and artistic movements encouraged by imperial patronage. He lived in court circles in Rome, was exiled to Corsica on a charge of adultery with Claudius' niece Julia, and was recalled by Agrippina's intervention to be tutor to the future emperor Nero. For eleven years he held a position of unprecedented influence as imperial adviser, in political as well as social and cultural fields; his relation to Nero during this time was by turns that of schoolmaster, trusted administrator, ghost writer for public occasions, cover-up man, even pander. His family in Spain, where he was born, had always been rich, and now he had become one of the wealthiest men in the world. He invested his gains with expertise. From A.D. 62, the eighth year of Nero's reign, Seneca began to lose his influence over the emperor and rapidly fell into a precarious position of disfavor. Three years later, when he was about seventy years old, he died by enforced suicide, an act that he carried out with meek fortitude.

Throughout all his changing experiences Seneca wrote constantly and very diversely. As a professional philosopher, he expounded Stoic doctrine in some eight volumes of *Natural Questions*, meant for the serious student of physics and sometimes of metaphysics, and also in the ten so-called *Dialogues* (*On the Shortness of Life, On Providence*, and so on). These, with the seven volumes of *On Benefits*, make up his formal study of Stoic ethics. More personal in style are the 124 *Moral Letters*, where familiar ideas are presented at undemanding length; the prose is accomplished, epigrammatic, suave. Seneca's official relation to Nero was expressed in the treatise *On Mercy*, an adulatory discourse, originally in three books, written to recommend a policy of lenient rule; and his unofficial relation to Claudius is perhaps expressed in the bizarre medley of malicious satire known as *Apocolocyntosis Divi Claudi* (*The Pumpkinification* [?] *of an Emperor*). Totally unlike any of these works are the tragedies, of which seven and a half authentic ones survive, with two of doubtful authorship. These are brilliant, even lurid, works, handling traditional plots from Greek legend in a rhetorical idiom that is strangely used to express imaginative experience of great intensity. To dramatists of the Renaissance these plays brought an intoxicating challenge that inspired all the "theater of blood," poetic plays of horror and revenge from *The Spanish Tragedy* to *Hamlet*. Seneca's works had been well known throughout the Middle Ages, when, apart from his important influence on Peter Abelard and Roger Bacon, he was widely viewed almost as a martyr, a supposed friend of St. Paul, and the source of numerous anthologies of moral maxims.

Can any single individual be discerned behind these many masks, or any unifying quality be found in these disparate writings?

Seneca left no written *apologia pro vita sua*, though according to Tacitus (*Annals* 15.60–63), his last hours were occupied in delivering a discourse to his wife and friends, on the moral instruction to be derived from his example. This went on, says Tacitus, as long as the power of speech remained to him, and reporters were brought in to make sure it was all put on record and later published. The sneer is customary in Tacitus' references to Seneca, who inevitably played a large part in his account of the reigns of Claudius and Nero (and presumably appeared also in the lost books on Gaius). No consistency can be found in the portrait of Seneca that we have in the *Annals*. The historian seems to treat this chameleon-like figure with some dislike, though forced at times to admire him, and does not at any point attempt to reconcile the ambiguities. Seneca's dying address is not likely to have made any such attempt either. The incongruities of his political career and his philosophic principles were glaring, and in later years many readers—St. Augustine and Petrarch among them—regretted the apparent and unexplained hypocrisy of his conduct over at least twenty years. His personal dilemmas were hardly ever referred to in his work, except in the most indirect and probably unintentional way. When Seneca wrote of his own experiences, it was either in vivid day-to-day reporting (on seasickness, letter 53; on the noise of the baths, letter 56) or in passages expressing emotional responses of a compelling but generalized and static kind (on the joy of sharing knowledge, letter 6; on illness and the fear of death, letter 54). But these experiences are not related to Seneca's actions in the way that Cicero's letters (in some sense Seneca's epistolary models) related his moods and impulses and the steps of his thinking to the events of his ac-

tive life. That kind of self-expression, in Seneca's time and in Seneca's position, was no longer possible.

II

If Seneca said little about his actions and experiences, he was never reticent in expounding his philosophical position. Inconsistency appears here also, but it is conscious and explicit. Seneca's Stoicism was not a rigid orthodoxy, in either its metaphysics or its ethics; ideas from Cynic, Epicurean, and Cyrenaic sources are freely used throughout his prose works. "It is my habit to go over into the enemy's camp—not as a deserter, but on reconnaissance," he remarks (letter 2: the last two words, *tamquam explorator*, used to be inscribed as a motto in books owned by Ben Jonson, one of the most Senecan of English writers in style and often in temper). Seneca here brings the language of war, traditional between Stoics and Epicureans for three centuries, into an informal epistolary context; but the good-humored, even casual, tone that Seneca adopts here should not mislead us. Epicurean ideas in his work are not the spoils of random forays.

Seneca's quotations from Epicurus and other non-Stoic sources are usually concerned with ethics and psychology rather than metaphysics, and they tend to enlarge, rather than to contradict, Stoic views. His Stoicism was indeed wholehearted but unusually broad in its scope: even where he remained clearly within the Stoic tradition, he liked to express his thought in a flexible way, allowing that truth might be many-sided. So one could describe the creator of the universe as "all powerful God—or incorporeal Reason, framer of mighty works—or divine spirit spread through all things in equal intensity—or Fate, and an unchangeable sequence of causes linked with one another" (*Consolation to His Mother, Heluia* 8.3). These varying definitions all have Stoic sources and are incompatible with the Epicurean concept of anthropomorphic deities remote from the life of this world. To a Stoic, however eclectic his temper, the radiant serenity of the Epicurean gods, "careless of mankind," offered nothing. There is no trace of this Lucretian concept of the gods in the imagery of Seneca's tragedies either.

It is when Seneca writes of human affairs that he goes out to reconnoiter in the enemy camp. He uses a different metaphor, perhaps more illuminating, in letter 84: the use of ideas drawn from other authors is compared to the collection of different pollens by bees that produce honey from all of them together. In its new context the borrowed idea takes on a different significance, "so that even though it has been made clear where it was taken from, yet it appears to be something different from its source." Although Seneca's references to Epicurus often have an air of comfortable mockery, there is a serious emphasis on the points of fundamental agreement between the rival schools, as A. L. Motto and J. R. Clark have pointed out. These authors go so far as to call Seneca "the Epicurean Stoic," and a passage in his treatise *On the Shortness of Life* suggests that he might not have objected. In that work Seneca argues that in our brief time on earth we must draw wisdom from any source we can find, taking the founders of all philosophical schools as men who have prepared a way of life for us. In this context, though not when writing of the gods, his language becomes Lucretian:

> We are escorted through the efforts of other men toward glorious rewards which have been drawn forth from darkness into light: we are not cut off from any generation, we are admitted to all things; and if with greatness of spirit we choose to go beyond the confines of human weakness, the extent of time through which we may pass is very great. One may argue, along with Socrates; share in the doubts of Carneades; withdraw from active life with Epicurus; conquer human nature with the Stoics; or with the Cynics transcend it.
>
> (*On the Shortness of Life* 14.1-2)

All these are right approaches to living; and whether we think of God as reason, power, or

fate is less decisive for us as human beings than our steadfast pursuit of the path we choose.

III

Seneca's aim in all his philosophical writing is clear. It is to help those who need spiritual guidance, instruction, or (a favorite metaphor) healing, as they strive toward the practice of virtue. Sometimes he writes of this striving in terms of battle, sometimes of arduous travel or discovery. Because this moral struggle and discovery is an experience that in this life never ends, and because the forms it may assume are endlessly varied, men must have guidance, according to their individual needs.

Unlike the earlier Stoics, Seneca does not divide mankind into the virtuous and the wicked, without intermediate stages, and he does not seek in his hortatory works to impose a condition of *apatheia*—total freedom from pleasure, pain, desire, and fear—as the state that must be attained by all who seek wisdom. The struggle for moral freedom is more human than this:

> What is the principal thing in human life? Not to have filled the seas with ships, to have planted a flag on the shores of the Arabian Gulf, and when our territory is too small to satisfy our grievances, to go wandering over the ocean in search of the unknown: it is to have seen everything within the mind and to have subdued one's vices; there is no victory greater than this. . . .
>
> What is the principal thing? To raise the mind above the threats and promises of fortune. . . . For what does she possess that is worth your coveting? . . .
>
> What is the principal thing? To be able to bear adversity with a joyful heart, and whatever may have happened, to bear it as if this were what you had wished to happen to you. For it would have been your duty to wish it, if you knew that all things take place by God's command; to weep, to complain, to groan, is to be disloyal.
>
> What is the principal thing? A will that is resolute, and invincible, a sworn enemy to luxury; . . .
>
> What is the principal thing? Not to admit evil

purposes into the heart, and to lift up clean hands to heaven. . . .

What is the principal thing? To raise one's courage high above all that depends on chance; to remember what man is, so that if you are fortunate, you may know it will not be for long, or if you are unfortunate, you may be sure you are not so unless you think so.

What is the principal thing? To have life on the very lips, ready to issue forth when summoned. This makes a man free—not by right of Roman citizenship, but by the right of nature.

(*Natural Questions*, book 3, preface, 10–15)

The work that contains this passage is often dismissed as a popularizing and loosely constructed tract of little scientific or literary interest. The "natural questions" are not approached with scientific detachment, and the prose is more traditional—in the Ciceronian tradition—than in Seneca's later works. But in making these judgments we may be seeking the wrong things. What Seneca expresses when he regards the natural universe is not curiosity but awe, and he writes in the style of Ciceronian eloquence because his purpose is to evoke a like awe and to inspire a moral endeavor. Unless we maintain that all rhetorical writing is a kind of affectation, we must recognize that Seneca here is in earnest, and that the details of such a passage deserve consideration. The language, whether literal or figurative, is vigorously physical: *vitia domuisse*, to have gained control over our vices, tamed them like a man who breaks in a horse or an ox; *erigere animum*, to raise up the mind (this verb is repeated throughout the passage, and though a familiar phrase, it was no more a dead metaphor than "lift up your hearts" is in English); *vitam in summis labris habere*, to have your life on your lips, like a man consciously and willingly near sudden death. Although Seneca is asserting that the important experiences of life are inward—acts of resolution, mental endurance, self-control, recollection—all of these are expressed in metaphors drawn from the world of action, from military and political life, and from the ceremonials of public religion. These activities all belong to the outer world, but like the inner life they are under God's command, and all can contribute to the wise man's enlightenment.

The philosopher, then, passes through life not in a condition of *apatheia*, detachment from all feeling, but responding with joy—*laeto animo* (not *sereno* or *tranquillo* merely)—to whatever experience he meets. This joy must be among the rational emotions (*eupatheiai*) that are admitted as valuable by all but the most severely orthodox Stoics. Living in this spirit of joy, the wise man never forgets *what man is*. He has the knowledge of his place in the universe, one might almost say of his own identity, which comes from a consciousness unmarred by egotistic impulses of fear and desire. With this unclouded awareness he can make right moral choices, freely accepting his destiny, and so is able to rise above the capricious Fortuna who threatens and promises by turns. No longer fortune's slave, he is in some sense master of events. "He who gladly runs to meet his own destiny" is the definition of the true king, according to the chorus in Seneca's *Thyestes*, and this kingship can be attained by everyone:

> a king is he who fears nothing,
> a king is he who will desire nothing.
> This kingdom each man gives to himself.
> (388–390)

Each man, this chorus declares, bestows this gift of royal power upon himself; and it is the only gift he can ever bestow, since all external things are outside the realm of human choice, and our actions do not have predictable consequences. Fate will not be in any way modified by our response to events; only we ourselves and our subjective experiences can be affected by our choices. "The Fates lead the willing man, and drag the unwilling." This famous line was apparently Seneca's own, added to his Latin verse translation of some lines from the "Hymn to Zeus" written in Greek by Cleanthes in the third century B.C. "Our own" Cleanthes, Seneca calls him, as the recognized head of the Stoic school after Zeno's death, and the philosopher who introduced a note of religious dedication into the Stoic ethic: the hymn expresses a most fervent personal devotion to the omnipotent Zeus, the "universal Law":

Lead me, O Zeus, and you, my destined lot,
in that direction where I was once appointed by
   you;
so let me follow, unhesitating; and if I do not
   consent,
yet none the less, found worthless, I shall follow.

"Found worthless": the difference between the willing and the unwilling man is not simply that one lives and dies with dignity and the other in an ignominious scramble. In letter 107, in which Seneca quotes this passage, he goes on to speak of the "great soul" who has made an act of self-surrender, contrasted with "the petty and debased character who struggles on, finds fault with the order of the universe, and wants the gods to be set right rather than himself." The two types of person see the whole order of creation differently, and while the "great soul" welcomes whatever the divine will has chosen for him, the impulse of Fate's reluctant victim is to tamper with divine order, to destroy where he can, and to set in motion forces of ruin that he will find he cannot control. This is one of the central themes of Seneca's tragedies.

To attain the royalty of free consent to Fate, a man might be helped by a philosophic discipline, and most of all by personal discipleship under the guidance of a teacher who would also be a friend; for the lessons of philosophy are not learned by a course of abstract study so powerfully or so quickly as they are by example. Letter 6, which contains the maxim "The way is long by instruction, short and effective by examples," goes on to cite Socrates and Epicurus as teachers who imparted wisdom through association more than by doctrine, and also Zeno, who in this way shaped the life of Cleanthes. But exempla may be studied through history or poetry as well as in life. Few critics have followed B. M. Marti in interpreting Seneca's whole dramatic oeuvre in a strictly

didactic sense; but a didactic element is unmistakably present in these strange and compelling works.

The exemplum, of course, whether acted on stage or merely described, makes its impact upon the emotions of the hearer rather than upon the reasoning intellect; it might therefore be thought suspect to a Stoic, but in fact it had become a traditional element in Stoic discourse long before Seneca's time. In the "consolatio" genre, for instance, exempla were a regular element, and were regularly placed after the precepts that the grieving person was asked to study. In the *Consolation to Marcia*, Seneca deliberately transposed these two parts of his work, because he was addressing a woman, and "it is desirable for the usual practice to be changed on this occasion; different people must be approached differently." He therefore begins with exempla and goes on to instruction, though introducing further exempla at several points later in the work.

The three consolations of Seneca that we have, together with two letters, 63 and 96, addressed to friends in time of bereavement, show considerable diversity of treatment. The circumstances were diverse, but it is the individual addressed who demands a particular approach, says Seneca, rather than the situation. What the philosopher-guide most needed was a personal awareness of his pupil's nature, and he had to be willing to use methods that would influence and train the emotions rather than proceeding only by rational argument.

Something was evidently due to Posidonius here, but with our fragmentary knowledge of his work it is impossible to estimate how much. Galen (*On the Opinions of Hippocrates and Plato* 452–453) says that Posidonius attributed the passions to the influence of something "illogical and godless" in the soul, as opposed to the power within us that shares the nature of what governs the universe. These irrational elements in the soul Posidonius considered as innate, and dangerous to psychological health; yet they might be brought into harmony with virtue if they were trained and habituated to accept their own place "according to nature." The irrational elements could be aided or injured only by irrational means, not by reasoning. So music, descriptive literature, and the other arts might be used to stir emotional impulses that would counteract their opposites, the impulses that threatened the spiritual order.

Seneca frequently refers in respectful terms to Posidonius—one of the most influential Stoics of the first century B.C.—but he does not (at least in his extant works) mention this aspect of his teaching. It does seem, however, that his way of regarding human personality, especially in the plays, was influenced by Posidonius' "new psychology." Seneca's acceptance of the rational emotions (*eupatheiai*) as positively valuable in human life leads him to treat the passions traditionally shunned by the Stoics—fear, desire, joy, sorrow—as fit material for the significant conflict and suffering of tragedy. A proper degree of sorrow, for instance, is admitted as part of the wise man's experience, together with the positive joy that we have already seen to be a highly valued rational emotion. Men should seek human fortitude, not the hardness of stone or metal. This is the theme of the essay *On the Steadfastness of the Wise Man*. The same reasonableness and warmth are expressed in Chaucer's paraphrase of part of letter 63 (in the prose "Tale of Meliboeus"): "'When that thy friend is dede,' quod he [Senek], 'let not thyne eyen to moyste ben of teres, nor to much drye; although the teres come to thyne eyen, let hem not falle.'"

The philosopher's state of mind, then, is the emotional control (*metriopatheia*) suggested by Aristotle: a proper degree of fear or desire is to be admitted, as well as joy and grief, in reasonable measure, in appropriate circumstances. A spirit of caution or ambition may be a right response in due measure, and the condition of equanimity is to be reached by a balancing of impulses rather than by the exclusion of all except reason.

No Stoic imagined that this balancing of impulses, this establishing of right order in the soul, could be an easy matter. Human nature is disorderly and rebellious. Chrysippus in the third century B.C. had written of the violent impulses (he uses the word *pathe* in this sense) that arise in the soul to destroy the spiritual order by their excess, "going beyond the proper and natural symmetry of the impulses." This concept seems to lie behind the views of Posidonius. In Stoic psychology all action as well as all emotion resulted from instinctive impulses, and these could not all be regarded as undesirable in themselves, or the wise man would have to be totally inactive, both in mind and body. The difference between the good (or wise) man and the bad one was that the wise man's impulses were ordered by reason, while the bad man's were disordered, excessive, and violent. An example would be what the Stoic called *orexis*, desire for what is a necessary or appropriate object of human striving, and its excess, *epithymia*, a craving going beyond that proper desire and becoming manic or destructive. This concept of a human impulse moving into parody of itself is highly relevant to Senecan tragedy.

The philosopher's task was to bring all impulses under the control of reason, and if we remember that for a Stoic reason and nature were one and the same, we realize that this would mean not so much a process of learning something new as discovering what existed in the soul already. "We seek the way by which the soul may fare forward on an even course, *be kindly to itself, and look upon its own being with joy . . .*" (*On Spiritual Tranquillity* 2.4; italics added). In man as in the universe, the rational order was seen to be the natural one. This correspondence between the ordered personality and the order of the cosmos was an important theme, which again throws light on the treatment of personal and cosmic disorder in the tragedies.

A Stoic then would inevitably be a person given to self-examination; if he wrote an autobiography, it would be a record not of events but of successive states of mind. His whole life was a course of hard spiritual lessons, or (as Seneca often puts it) a term of service under the discipline of a stern commander. "Not what you have to bear, but how you bear it—this is what matters." This is one, at least, of fortune's mysterious purposes; its blows allow or even force men to emerge in their real character, revealed to themselves and to others.

In the tragedies, Phaedra, Hercules, Oedipus, Medea, and others are preoccupied with their own identity, absorbed in watching as well as experiencing their own moral struggles, until at a moment of appalling choice they triumphantly recognize themselves for what they now are:

"Now I am Medea."
(*Medea* 910; after killing Creon and Creusa)

"Do you recognize your wife?"
(*Medea* 1021; Medea addresses Jason, after killing their children)

"Earth is not large enough for Hercules."
(*Hercules Furens* 960; as madness possesses Hercules, he is about to kill his wife and children: "This is the fitting way for Hercules' weapons to be aimed")

"Now summon the complete Ulysses."
(*The Trojan Women* 614; as Ulysses resolves to trick Andromache into betraying her child's presence, and then to kill him)

"O I am loftiest of all the gods, and king of kings."
(*Thyestes* 911; Atreus has tricked his brother into eating his own children)

T. S. Eliot justly observed that if Seneca's heroes had not proclaimed their identity in this way, we should never have heard the cries "This is I, Hamlet the Dane" or "I am Duchess of Malfi still." The Senecan stance of Shakespeare's or Webster's heroes as they face oncoming doom is (as Eliot emphasized) a nobler self-awareness than the Stoic catchwords of many Jacobeans, but it is still less complex and subtle than the dramatic use of self-discovery in Seneca's own plays. For Medea, Hercules, and the rest, the assertion of identity is a kind

of parody or reversal of the ideal Stoic's moment of moral victory, when he steps forward with glad freedom to consent to his fate. For Hercules and Oedipus, this hallucinatory grandeur is not the end; but in most of the tragedies, we leave the hero on the point of final disintegration.

IV

Seneca's plays are generally associated with the theme of revenge, but this is a major motive only in *Thyestes* and *Medea*; what is more striking, when one looks at the stories chosen by Seneca from Greek legend as plots for his tragedies, is the pervasiveness of what Shakespeare called "bloody, shameful, and unnatural acts." Tragedy was likely to include acts of violence, of course; but the particular stress given to enmity within a family, for example, to incest and the killing of children, was by no means inevitable. Literary tradition almost compelled Seneca to take his plots from Greek mythology, but he could have chosen to write an *Achilles* or an *Ion*, for example, or in the plots he did choose he could have avoided the emphasis on the gruesome and the abnormal, which causes his *Oedipus* and his *Hercules Furens*, for instance, to induce a revulsion not inspired by the comparable plays of Sophocles and Euripides. Descriptions of death, disease, and physical afflictions are lengthy and detailed; characters and choruses respond to them with intense horror and dismay, calling upon the gods, but with no expectation that any help will come from them. Sometimes the horrors seem to be enacted upon the stage, unlike the violent acts of Greek tragedy. Medea apparently stabs her children while standing on a rooftop and then flings their bodies at Jason's feet; and Atreus uncovers the heads of Thyestes' children before his face, with the gloating question: "Do you recognize your children?" (But the real coup de theatre is not the exposure of the heads; it is Thyestes' reply, "I recognize my brother.") The practical difficulties in some of these scenes have given support to those who believe that Seneca's plays were never intended for stage performance, but for public or private readings; but the arguments are not conclusive.

There is usually at least one character in a Senecan play who looks forward to and enjoys the infliction of pain and mutilation (occasionally, as in Hercules' case, this is followed by a recoil from what he has done). The acts of incest and other sexual aberrations, however, are not described in any detail or with any expression of pleasure; if Senecan drama has produced the theater of cruelty, it has never been called pornographic.

The disturbing subjects treated in the plays, then, present a complete contrast with the philosophic works, with their emphasis on steadfast moral aspiration and tranquillity of mind. The lurid atmosphere and violent imagery, the extremity of pain and mental anguish that they constantly express, are also quite unlike the cool discursive tone, always poised even in earnest exhortation, of the prose writings. So marked is the difference that some critics in later times have followed Sidonius Apollinaris in supposing that the plays were not written by the philosopher Seneca at all. This subjective judgment, however, is not borne out by analysis of stylistic features (except in the case of *Hercules Oetaeus*, which is not generally thought to be authentic, and of *Octavia*, an experiment in a very different genre where marked differences of style would in any case be inevitable). Seneca's authorship is well attested, and we must look at the works themselves, both drama and prose, to see whether any principle of unity exists between them.

The plays present a combination of gruesome plots, horrific atmosphere, and rhetorical—some critics say "mannerist"—style, with austere moral doctrine often pronounced by the chorus and exemplified by the fate of the characters. Human beings are studied at a moment of choice, when a kind of madness or moral blindness (which Seneca calls *furor*) impels them to choose a course of destruction leading to their own doom. The hero, or heroine, is usually well aware of what the choice means in moral terms, and the choice is a real one, although there is no possibility of an ending that could be considered happy in external terms. Phaedra, for example, cannot possibly win Hippolytus' love, but she could choose to accept this fate with a willing act of renunciation, or—as she does—rage against it, plunging into a fantasy world that leads to havoc around her and to her own destruction: "I shall put off Phaedra, with my life and with my crime." When she says this, Phaedra has lost everything, and she recognizes that the identity asserted by her act of choice must be discarded when death is before her. Similarly Medea, Clytemnestra, and Atreus make a conscious choice of *furor* and release forces of chaos that ultimately destroy them as well as their victims.

These characters may be seen as exempla illustrating, in a different medium, the kind of man described in letter 107, the "petty and debased" man who "finds fault with the order of the universe, and wants the gods to be set right rather than himself." In contrast, a few of the characters in the plays adopt decisively admirable attitudes (in Stoic terms), usually after experiencing tragic guilt or error. These right decisions do not, of course, alter the course of events or exempt the hero from further suffering. So Oedipus, who throughout the play of that name has been filled with fear and sometimes bitterness at the destiny laid on him (even at the beginning he was in a confused way aware that the blight in the air of Thebes derived from himself), goes out at last to begin a stumbling journey along an unknown way, and the play ends with his words:

> Violent Fates, fearful trembling of Disease,
> Starvation, black Plague, and raging Pain,
> Go with me, with me! These are the guides I
>   choose.
>
>   (1059–1061)

The concluding verb *libet*, "I choose, it is my pleasure," recalls *Thyestes* 368: *occurrit suo li-*

bens fato, "with pleasure [the true king] runs to meet his fate." Oedipus here welcomes pain or grief (*dolor:* the unseen character shunned or feared or defied by so many Senecan speakers) not as a *pathos* in the sense of an emotion that destroys judgment and drives men to evil, but as something to be accepted throughout life with tranquil courage.

The figure of Oedipus, blind and aged, groping along in humility and pain, is very different from the Oedipus who solved the Sphinx's riddle by his intelligence and audacity. Seneca began a second play on the Oedipus story, the unfinished *Phoenissae* (*The Phoenician Women*); and here Oedipus is made to recall that distant time:

> As my death is near, I choose to go to the place where the Sphinx sat, on the high rock, twisting up riddles with her half-animal mouth. Guide my steps here, set your father in this place; that the dreadful seat may not be empty, put back a greater prodigy [*monstrum*]. Seated on this rock I will utter the dark story of my destiny, which no one may solve.
>
> (118–124)

To answer "a man" to the Sphinx's old riddle had meant nothing. What is a man? In all Seneca's plays, men and women are tormented by the question of who they are, and what it means to be a human being.

Oedipus is not the only Senecan character who is called a *monstrum;* the word is used also of Medea and of Hercules. These characters are impelled to try to realize their identity by an ascending series of crimes, a megalomania that takes them farther and farther away from the order of nature and the world of reality. Most extraordinary of all perhaps is the figure of Atreus in *Thyestes,* uniquely free from hesitation in his choice of evil, and driven on (like Medea) by his own *dolor* (anguish) to find new forms of atrocity. Against him stands his brother Thyestes, guilty of great sins in the past, but now a penitent who discourses at length on very conventional Stoic themes: the precarious existence of rulers, the security of a simple life,

the deceptions of power, and (at the end) the gods' will to avenge the innocent. But the penitence of Thyestes is swept aside by his brother and is entirely ineffectual. The same is true of Jason's repentance in *Medea;* it comes late, and it could in any case have no power to influence events. Medea says:

> My country gave way to you, my father, brother,
>   my sense of shame.
> With this dowry I married you.
>
> (488)

The choice was irreversible, and now

> my only peace is
> to see all things blotted out with myself in
>   destruction.
> Let all things pass away with me.
>
> (426)

V

The most interesting study of penitence leading to a right choice is found in *Hercules Furens,* a play that was once very popular and is now much less so, even among scholars who do not undervalue the plays as a whole. It contains the most famous mad scene in ancient literature, which gave Bottom (in act 5 of *3 Henry VI*) his phrase "Ercles' vein" to describe a soliloquy of murderous rant; it also includes some of Seneca's most evocative descriptive writing, especially in the account of Hercules' visit to Hades, and some of his most impressive passages of choral lyric, powerfully designed and exquisite in detail. The violent plot is not exploited for sensational theater, but used to develop character in a most subtle and serious way. To examine this play in some detail may lead to a fuller understanding of Seneca's works as a whole.

Hercules does not appear until almost halfway through the play. He has long been absent, pursuing his series of labors and subduing various monsters, including finally Cerberus, the guardian of Hades' gate. He is the object of Juno's jealous hatred and of his own family's pride and anxious hope as they are threatened by the evil tyrant Lycus. The chorus refer apprehensively to Hercules toward the end of their first lyric, the long passage (125–204) that follows Juno's prologue. (Unlike Greek choruses, Seneca's are not identified as male or female, old or young, or in any other way; they are an unspecific human voice.)

This first chorus begins with the sky at dawn; it has been called an *aubade*, a dawn serenade. A few stars twinkle faintly as Phosphoros marshals their glittering line and the sun god looks out from Oeta's height. (Mount Oeta is at least 100 miles away from Thebes, where the play takes place, but there is an obvious association with Hercules' funeral pyre.) With the sun arises hard toil that stirs all kinds of anxiety as men's homes are opened to the day. A series of tiny sketches suggest the multifarious activities of the world's ordinary life: flocks going out to pastures whitened with morning frost; birdsong; sailors and fishermen and all humble people enjoying the little they have. Then follows a short passage of expected contrast, presenting the nervous life of the city and the miser paradoxically destitute amid his heaped-up gold. Fear and anger dominate men here, as they are whirled along to their destined end without awareness of the flight of time or of their own identity. Their actions only serve to speed their way to death: "Of our own choice we seek the waters of Styx" (185). At this point the name of Alcides (Hercules) follows, in lines of forceful severity: "With too much courage in your heart, Alcides, you hurry on to approach the melancholy dead. At a fixed time the Fates come. No man may linger when he is under orders, no man may postpone the recorded day" (186–190). Men must die, in anonymous throngs; the chorus go on to reject fame and ambition in favor of secure and lowly old age: "Spirited valor falls from on high" (201).

This passage strikes a note of mystery as well as moral authority. Can a man be *too* courageous? (The word is *fortis*, not the more equivocal *audax*.) And what does "under orders"

mean? Hercules' journey to Hades has already been described by Juno, in the prologue, with scorn and resentment, as an occasion when he arrogantly seized a forbidden prize and intended to break the natural order by bringing souls of the dead back to earth. Juno is determined to frustrate this ambition. Like the Juno of Vergil's *Aeneid*, book 1, she complains that she is being ousted by lesser deities from her position as supreme goddess; Jupiter's children by other goddesses or women have usurped the honor she should be receiving. Anger and bitter resentment drive her to destroy Hercules. She intends to call up from Hades personified companions for Hercules whom he does not expect: "hated Crime, fierce Impiety, Error, and Madness ever armed against itself. Let this, this, be the servant for my anguish to use" (96–99). *Dolor* may be translated as "anguish," but Seneca's constant use of this word as subject of an active verb suggests a force more destructive than simple grief; it means rather a vindictive agony that impels violence beyond human control. Juno's *dolor* is like that of Atreus in its purposeful activity; Atreus' *dolor* "must find out some greater deed" (*Thyestes* 274) and will use Thyestes himself as its weapon (258); and Medea too experiences an anguish that rises self-moved (*Medea* 49) and demands satisfaction from her: "do not be hasty, anguish . . . I had nothing more to offer you, anguish . . ." (1016–1019). The terrible power of Juno's anguish will cause madness to seize on Hercules, so that after his return from Hades his courage will have led only to self-defeat, and he will long for death. Then, Juno mockingly adds, his father may admit those hands—that famous power of action—to heaven if he likes.

When the chorus, therefore, speak of "too much courage in your heart, Alcides" and "the recorded day which no man may postpone," they are touching on the themes of Juno's threatening speech: "I have found the day when Hercules' hated courage may bring me help" (114–115). The kind of courage Hercules is showing by his journey to Hades is the "spirited valor" that is doomed to fall. This thought

816

is expressed in the gnomic and Horatian style that the chorus have used throughout, except in the few lines of warning addressed personally to Hercules.

In this play the chorus remain almost entirely detached from the action, never taking any part in the dialogue, and their view of Hercules is different therefore from the personal attachment of Megara and Amphitryon, different also from Juno's antagonism. In the first part of the play the chorus seem to regard Hercules as an example of foolhardiness rather than a beneficent hero. Later they express awe at his achievements and also distress that he should be brought so low as to face either continued madness or a burden of dreadful guilt (1094–1099). Immediately before his first entry, the second choral lyric (524–591) expresses apprehension for Hercules (since fortune is malicious toward brave men), but recalling his previous victory over death when Alcestis was freed and the release of Eurydice through Orpheus' song, they conclude that the kingdom of death can be defeated by Hercules' strength and call on him to "burst [the bonds of] Fate by your hand" (566).

Hercules at once enters, in an attitude of humility rather than triumph. He prays to Phoebus, asking pardon for bringing the offensive Cerberus into the light of day; he has done this, he says, "under orders" (596), and "she who ordered it" (604) was Juno. He can now afford to despise death, and his strength is at the disposal of Juno; what else would she like to order? The tone here certainly has an element of irony, at this point very lightly touched, to return more distinctly later, in reference to Juno as well as in the presentation of Hercules. (This more than any other tragedy displays some of the talent for caricature that Seneca shows in the *Apocolocyntosis*.)

If all Hercules' feats of strength have been carried out "under orders," he ought not to be too confident in his own powers, and in fact he never seems to have any distinct sense of purpose in their use. His valor, or strength (of hand), consists of a physical prowess and an ability to survive endurance tests whose aim is vaguely beneficent for mankind. "Do you think valor means being thrown to face wild beasts and monsters?" (434). The question is pertinently asked by the tyrant Lycus, who is not impressed by a hero invariably controlled by another, whether Eurystheus, Juno, or Fate. Hercules' wife replies, "The part of valor is to subdue what terrifies all men." Examples of the things that terrify all men have been produced from land, sea, and air (as Juno said in the prologue), and all have been crushed by Hercules. There really are no monsters left, and it is more trouble for her to hand out orders to Hercules than it is for him to fulfill them; he joyfully "welcomes commands"—like a Stoic or a would-be Stoic, preparing to meet his fate. In his latest expedition to Hades, Hercules is seeking to conquer the last of man's terrors; but as we have seen, the chorus suggest something insecure and perhaps presumptuous about this. The menace conveyed in Juno's prologue and the warning of "too much courage" in the first chorus compel us to take the confident ending of the second chorus with some scepticism:

The Kingdom (of Hades) that could be overcome by song,
That Kingdom will also prove open to conquest by force.

(590–591)

This really is not very convincing at this point in the play, and we need not think that Seneca meant it to be. We have already seen the forlorn Megara and her family threatened with death by Lycus, and we have heard the account from Amphitryon of the chaos and disaster left behind on earth (250–274) when Hercules started on his adventure in Hades. Hercules' exertions for world peace have brought no stable order anywhere, and the suggestion that somehow the journey to Hades would open a way for mortals to return from the dead has led to nothing. The enthusiasm shown by Hercules for more ordeals looks more like ostentatious record-breaking than the true joy of a "great soul" going forward to his destiny.

An element of irony in this play's treatment of the hero-figure has already been suggested (it is seen again in the figure of Pyrrhus in *The Trojan Women*). A ridiculous side is allowed to appear at times; it is hard to believe that Seneca did not realize he was writing most effective comic narrative in the account of the fight with Cerberus (783–827). There is also criticism of a biting kind from Lycus, who suggests that Hercules' real self has been in his off-duty pursuits: the herds of girls carried off and the famous hands applied to effeminate percussion work (465–471). Hercules' courage was put off with his lion-skin, says Lycus, and this blind self-indulgence goes with an insatiable desire for more conquests, for their own sake. The dialogue in this scene deals with Hercules' achievements not in terms of benefits to mankind but as a qualification for the hero-role, and so as an exemption from ordinary human distresses:

> The man you find courageous you may not call wretched.
>
> (463)

But as Amphitryon has just said, distress is the common lot of mankind:

> The man you find wretched you may call human.
> (462)

These epigrammatic ripostes are so polished that they may sound glib, but in them Seneca is saying something of central importance to the play. Why seek to escape all suffering, if this escape also cuts one off from humanity? This question is raised by the same speaker, Amphitryon, in the last scene, when he urges Hercules to go on living after intolerable disaster has struck him, and to "go on enduring this mass of evil" (1239).

There is recurrent ambiguity throughout the play about who Hercules' real father is. In his inflated, lion-skin guise, Hercules claims apotheosis as Jupiter's son; but he also regularly addresses Amphitryon as "father," and a decisive moment comes for him when he resolves to live and calls on his valor to "submit, and go on to endure my father's rule" (1315). Amphitryon speaks throughout the play with the voice of true wisdom and human insight, clearly expressing his own need and refusing to allow Hercules to escape his duty by wallowing in indiscriminate self-reproach when his madness has passed:

> Amphitryon: Who ever gave the name of crime to a delusion?
>
> (1237)

> Hercules: Let me perish!
> Amphitryon: In your father's sight?
> Hercules: I have taught him to look on sin.
> Amphitryon: As you rather look on the deeds all must remember, seek forgiveness of yourself for this one charge.
> Hercules: Can he who gave forgiveness to no other give it to himself? My deeds of glory I performed under orders; this only is my own. . . .
>
> (1263–1268)

> Amphitryon: This weapon Juno put into your hands.
> Hercules: This will I use now. . . .
>
> (1297–1298)

> Amphitryon: See, now you are going to commit a crime willing and knowing it. . . .
> Hercules: Show me: what do you order to be done?
>
> (1300–1301)

The clarity of the moral instruction given by Amphitryon is made more compelling by the alternation of emotionally appealing lines in the same scene:

> By the holy rites of kinship, by both claims of my name—whether you call me foster-father or parent—by my white hairs, which demand respect from the righteous: I pray you, spare my forsaken old age, my weary years. . . .
>
> (1246–1250)

See how my unhappy heart throbs with fear and beats against my troubled breast. . . .

(1298–1299)

This faint soul I hold on my lips—exhausted by old age, exhausted no less by troubles. Does anyone give life so late to a father?

(1308–1311)

As in the passage from *Natural Questions*, quoted previously, the man who holds his life "on the lips" is the ideal Stoic, prepared to meet his fate at any moment, under providence. The emotional appeal here is not divorced from the rational analysis of Amphitryon's more didactic speeches, and both are in close accord with the prose works that deal with suicide and social obligations.

This scene between father and son is remarkable in several further ways, which can be mentioned only briefly here. It gives Hercules' decision to live a different emphasis from the corresponding scene in Euripides, where Heracles rather easily gives up his purpose of suicide in response to Theseus, who reminds him of his reputation. In Seneca, Theseus does mention Hercules' valor, but says that a father's prayers are enough to compel him to live, without this incentive. Seneca adds the idea of a thirteenth labor awaiting Hercules, which he links with the theme of obedience to his father (not to Eurystheus). The language and the emotional relationship between Hercules and Amphitryon in this scene strongly recall those between Aeneas and Anchises in *Aeneid*, book 2. The scene there is the reverse of this one, since in Vergil it is the father who is won over by the son to face the future; but there are echoes both of general atmosphere and of detail, including the image of the hand that has been polluted by bloodshed and yet becomes the means of support for the helpless father and (in Vergil) the young child. This hand image runs through the whole play, standing for Hercules' strength, which is at first a mere tool for Juno's destructive will, then disowned by Hercules, who wants to fling his weapons and hands together

on the fire, and finally submitted to purification in Athens (as were the bloodstained hands of Mars) under the guidance of Theseus, who "loves sinners."

The similarity of the Hercules-Amphitryon relationship and that between Seneca and his own father has to be mentioned with caution, but there was certainly one occasion when an impulse to suicide was checked by the realization of the elder Seneca's love and dependence (letter 78.1–4). This wish for death was caused during Seneca's youth by the torment of persistent illness of an asthmatic kind, not by the social and moral frustration that he discusses elsewhere as grounds for suicide.

In the last scene of *Hercules Furens*, the hero's future after he has decided to live is suggested only in a tentative way. For himself, Hercules only desires obscurity; he would choose to go back to the world of the dead and be subject to the bonds from which he once freed Theseus in Hades. The old desire for apotheosis is thus wholly reversed. Just as Phaedra "puts off" her identity in accepting death, so Hercules says, "I will give back Hercules to the dead" (1218). At this point, he is intending to fling himself on a pyre and burn himself to death. Amphitryon recognizes that his madness is not yet over; this self-destructiveness is a special mark of madness *(furor)*. This is what Juno intended when she threatened in the prologue that he should "wage war against himself" (85), "defeat himself and wish for death" (116). Sanity will mean reconciliation within the divided personality, beginning, if it ever does begin, "on the far side of despair" and accepting life "under orders," not as Juno's tool, but like the Stoic "under God's command."

VI

If this state of reconciliation is no more than a possibility at the end of *Hercules Furens*, in most of the plays it is never glimpsed at all. Mental disintegration is the end for Medea and Phaedra; it is prophesied for Clytemnestra and

Aegisthus in the last line of *Agamemnon*; it is implied for both Thyestes and Atreus; and Eteocles in the incomplete *Phoenissae* seems likely to develop after the same pattern. Pyrrhus in *The Trojan Women* is also possessed by frenzy, although in that play attention is directed rather to its innocent victims than to the destructive madman himself.

Why was this theme of madness so important to Seneca? He has no systematic treatise on the subject, but mentions it frequently in the prose works. He ascribes madness to various causes: fear (*Natural Questions* 6.29); excessive love of possessions (letter 42); excessive desire (letter 82), pleasure (*On the Happy Life* 11.1), or grief (*Consolation to Polybius* 9.2–3). It shows itself in an irrational vehemence, in extremes of self-indulgence such as drunkenness, and in a desire for war or murder (*On Mercy* 2.2). A concordance to Seneca will give us the most frequent associations of madness with the passion of anger, but this may be a distorted picture, since he has left us a treatise *On Anger* but not one *On the Fear of Death* or *On Mental Disturbances*.

In the tragedies, it is usually anguish rather than anger that prompts the soul to the fatal act of choice leading to madness. "Act of choice" implies a voluntary step; can madness be thought culpable? In the prose works Seneca often speaks of the false conceptions that seize the mind of an insane person (*On Tranquillity of Mind* 12.5) and the mistaken value the insane give to things (*On Anger* 3.34); moral judgments thus become perverted (*On the Happy Life* 6.3), and men lose the capacity to see things in their true nature. When Seneca's Hercules slaughters his wife and children in madness, he has reached a state where he is clearly not culpable. Amphitryon declares that this was the work of Juno; but Juno (who takes the role played by Lyssa, personified madness, in Euripides' play) has obtained control of him only by using his megalomaniac valor, his willfully chosen course of insatiable ambition. This Juno can use to spread chaos. For this purpose she invites madness, or frenzy, to envelop herself as well

as Hercules: "We must first be mad. Juno, why do you not rave yet?" (107–108). Hercules' strength, his special gift, becomes the instrument for the forces of evil to work catastrophe. Similarly Medea's esoteric skill is used by Hecate for destructive ends. So in the Stoic view can any man's power to reason—the special human excellence—be perverted to evil purposes when he has made a wrong choice, allowing frenzy to take over direction of his mind and will.

Seneca clearly saw a kind of madness in the acquisitive and callous society he lived in, and he must have seen it with particular horror in the world of cruelty and pretenses surrounding the imperial family. An autocrat (as Tacitus later remarked) tended to rate his success in terms of his power to injure others, and to exact thanks for the injuries he inflicted. For Atreus in *Thyestes*, "this is the greatest good in royal power—the mass of men are forced to praise while they endure their lord's actions" (205–207). Praise, Atreus adds, is even more to be desired if it is insincere; anyone may receive honest admiration, but lying acclaim is given only to the powerful. This evaluation of a ruler's rewards is the reverse of the Stoics' ideal king, whose good is the welfare of his people. Atreus is an autocrat like the wild beast vividly described in *On Mercy*, as a warning to the young Nero. For the tyrant, moral values are a part of his domain, to be adopted or discarded, defined and redefined, as he likes; but this alienates him from the moral order as sane men know it:

> Atreus: Holiness, religious obligation, loyalty are private goods; kings may go by what way they choose.
> Attendant: I think it sin to injure even a wicked brother.
> Atreus: In his case, righteousness is what in a brother's case is sin.
>
> (*Thyestes* 216–219)

Atreus is the most complete example of the tyrant figure deliberately expelling all religious sanctions (*pietas*) from his house and inviting frenzy (attended by Furies and monsters) to take over his personality. The scene recalls Lady Macbeth's invocation to the "murthering ministers" who "wait on Nature's mischief," asked to turn the life-sustaining milk of her breasts to gall. Atreus says, "My heart does not yet glow with madness great enough: my choice is to be filled with a greater monster [than myself]" (252–254). Oedipus similarly calls himself "a greater monster" than the Sphinx (*Phoenissae* 122), as Medea and Hercules also do, when they experience inward division and come to recognize their own alienation from humanity. This recognition does not impel them to attempt any reparation or approach to human relationships. They are impelled only to identify themselves and to accept with this identity a need or obligation to commit further crimes.

This self-identification is what K. Anliker in a notable study has described as arising "from being born thus." He is writing primarily of Aegisthus, who plays a minor but extremely interesting role in *Agamemnon*: Aegisthus associates sin (*nefas*) with his own name and his own identity in the way that Medea associates crime or grief with hers, and Hercules deeds or hardships with his. Sin is imposed upon Aegisthus by the circumstances of his birth and by his own nature. This is what he was born for, as he plainly says (*Agamemnon* 48) in an address to himself, a characteristic example of the "remember who you are" soliloquy found in so many Senecan and Elizabethan plays. Gordon Braden describes this recurrent soliloquy scene: it is the monarch or the man of power who lives under this compulsion and who in responding to it becomes a parody of the Stoic at the moment of joyous consent to his fate. So Atreus goes on to plan the Thyestean banquet:

> Something swells in my heart, something greater and vaster than any familiar thing, beyond the bounds of human custom—it presses on my slow-moving hands—what it is I do not know, but some huge deed. Let it be so! seize on it, my heart. The act is fit for Thyestes and fit for Atreus. . . .
>
> (*Thyestes* 266–277)

At this moment Atreus seems to be possessed by a kind of demonic force: "I am swept along and where I go I know not, but I am swept along." He hears a groaning from below the ground, and thunder peals; the housetops crack, and the statues of his household gods are overturned. Later the messenger and chorus and also Thyestes are aware of earth tremors, sudden darkness, and chaos in the constellations; these cosmic disturbances are not hallucinatory experiences of Atreus, but part of the action of the play. He is aware of what is happening to him; though he has no control over the catastrophe initiated by his choice, he welcomes it when it comes in response to his invitation: "Let this take place! Let the sin be, which you fear, O gods" (264–265). Atreus' perverted ambition demands that he, like Aegisthus, should assert his identity by continually scaling new heights of unnatural crime, reversing the values of sanity and parodying the good man's search for integrity "to live in accordance with one's own nature."

To the moral philosopher in any age, a meretricious society will appear a parody of what life ought to be; but for a man who lived in Caligula's Rome this was not simply a matter of predictable disapproval from a strict moralist surveying a licentious and violent world. The particular association of the atmosphere of terror and unreason in Seneca's tragedies with the events of Caligula's reign was first emphasized by Otto Regenbogen in his article *Schmerz und Tod in den Tragödien Senecas* (1924), a masterly revaluation of the tragedies, which at the time were little understood or even taken seriously except as a literary influence.

Regenbogen regarded Senecan drama as sui generis, a genre whose special quality did not derive at all from its Greek models or from the traditions of rhetoric. These provided a framework and a medium, no more. Seneca's tragedies, Regenbogen says, are concerned with suffering. They are explorations of what the infliction or the experience of grief means for the human individual, for society, and for the cosmos.

Although so unusual in its discerning appreciation, Regenbogen's view of the plays had been foreshadowed (as he acknowledged) by J. R. Klein, who as early as 1865 asked readers of Seneca to remember that he wrote against the background of an expanding Roman empire; the Mediterranean world for a Stoic in the first century A.D. was not a realm of fantasy or travelers' tales merely, but the area of administrative responsibility, the training ground of action and moral duty for a Roman. This awareness enhances the sense of the long geographical choruses, in particular that in *Medea* (369 ff.), which describes with a shiver of dismay the shifting of frontiers and the opening up of lands beyond the ocean, leaving no ultima Thule unrevealed. Travel has become casual, nothing is left in its own place. Seneca and his readers could not fail here to recall Horace's ode on this theme (1.3), which presents the first navigator as both foolhardy and impious, to be classed with Daedalus, who tried to fly "with wings not given to men," and with those like Theseus, who broke through the barriers of Hades. Was Roman empire-building to be seen as another example of such presumption? It might even be that the arbitrary cruelties of Tiberius and Claudius, and the actual insanity Seneca had seen in personal contact with Caligula and Nero, were inevitable consequences and expressions of the nature of world dominion.

The theme of insanity almost always appears as an element in the suffering that Senecan plays present. There is, says Klein, a characteristic quality of nausea in Seneca's treatment of grief and pain. Pain *(dolor)* can destroy the order of nature, as a poison can induce vomiting; the moral and the physical are inextricable, as when Thyestes' appetite revolts at the sight of his children's flesh, though he does not know what the food is. The brutal witticisms of, for example, Thyestes wondering how to bury the children he has eaten, or of Theseus trying to fit together fragments of his son's dismembered body, suggest the intolerable degradation of the well-intentioned man who is trapped in a par-

ody of life, where both morally and physically nature has gone into a kind of reverse sequence. Oedipus addresses himself in the hour of disaster: "Use your wits, wretch; a way must be found for you to wander apart from the dead and yet cut off from the living; die, but not to join your father" (947–949). And again, when blinded: "Go on, outcast—no, stop, or you may fall over your mother" (1051).

Klein and Regenbogen did not dismiss these sick jokes as mere lapses of literary taste. They found them peculiarly Roman, closely related to the bizarre realities of life in imperial circles. It was the grotesque seesaw of power in this world that prompted Tacitus to write of "the trivial absurdity of human affairs." Seneca in *On Anger* relates how Caligula commanded a Roman knight to join him at a banquet immediately after his son's execution: "and the poor man hardened himself to do it, as if it were his son's blood that he drank ... if the guest had not pleased the executioner, his other son had died" (*On Anger*, 2.33.4 and 6). In the same essay Seneca recounts the story of the proconsul who looked on three hundred corpses whose execution he had ordered and exclaimed, *"O rem regiam!"* (O royal sight!). Whether these anecdotes were authenticated or not is, as Regenbogen says, unimportant; they expressed a spiritual truth for their age: that power could turn men into monsters. It is because they are figures of awe-inspiring power that Medea and Oedipus can become monsters; although Oedipus does not deliberately choose to unleash destruction as Medea does, evil spreads uncontrollably from him also, because he is a royal victim, supernaturally chosen to demonstrate this truth of man's condition.

The ambivalent figure of Hercules suggests a profound ambiguity in this theme of destruction. Hercules also is a monster (*Hercules Furens* 1280), although the destruction of monsters has been his lifelong vocation. He is a monster because he slaughters his own wife and children in madness, and also because he has presumed to enter Hades with the intent to usurp divine authority. His purpose was to release mankind from the pain and terror of death; but this was a mission accepted in obedience to Juno, not a spontaneous initiative; it is not a purpose that man can or should entertain. The double character of Hercules' visit to Hades, both heroic and sinful, is implied in Megara's apprehensive speech before he appears and is fully expressed in the first speech Hercules himself gives, on his return from the underworld. He prays for forgiveness, since he has polluted Phoebus' sight by displaying what should be kept unseen in the world of death. Ironically, he also calls on the gods to hide their faces and forsake the sight of earth, leaving it to only Juno and himself. This prayer is of course dramatically fulfilled when madness rules him, and he sees the sun's movement reversed and the stars forsaking their courses. The picture of planetary chaos is closely parallel to that in *Thyestes*, although here it is presented as a delusion experienced by Hercules only.

What is this world of death that Hercules has claimed to conquer, at the indirect cost of his own sanity? The journey to Hades takes place before the action of *Hercules Furens* begins, but it occupies our attention during a long section in the middle of the play. The killing of Lycus had taken place offstage. This is the first use of Hercules' strength in the play, and (unlike those that follow) it is an act of righteous retribution. The time during which this act is carried out is occupied by a strangely slow and detailed account of the visit to Hades given by Theseus in response to Amphitryon's questions.

The picture of Hades here is profoundly Vergilian, echoing the journey of Aeneas in many verbal details as well as in an atmosphere of obscurity, frailty, and often terror. Seneca's underworld, however, includes no ampler light of Elysium such as radiates about the spirits of the blessed in *Aeneid*, book 6. This is a world of negatives: no light of day, no color, no movement, no growing plants, no breezes. Desolation wastes the expanse of hell. Chaos itself is here described as *densum*, "closely packed, impenetrable, thick," an adjective that almost denies the unruly or changing sense of its noun. Hell indeed is not unruly or changing, in spite of Hercules' flailing bravado and the grotesquerie of his fight with Cerberus. Hell is a realm of solemn order, as we see in the chorus that follows Theseus' speech.

This chorus picture the throngs of old and young who are driven on through the silent region, each in the darkness becoming aware that he is dead, "his head sunk below all the earth." Infants alone, by a surprising touch of tenderness, are allowed the ritual torch carried before them to allay their fear. This vast concourse of the dead must claim us all; and if death is slow, we hurry there ourselves, a thought repeated in the play's first chorus, "of our own choice we seek the waters of Styx." The three stanzas that conclude the Hades chorus (875 ff.) change to the short-line glyconic meter and issue an invitation to rejoicing at Hercules' return from the conquest of hell. At this moment, however, the rejoicing sounds like an illusory euphoria, as it soon proves to be; the immensity of death's domain is not assailed by Hercules or any other.

Throughout the tragedies, this theme of death's awful kingdom recurs many times. In many passages, especially choruses, Seneca amplifies Horace's memorable line: "We are all driven in the same direction," expressing human helplessness and sense of dread before the universal power that overrides all individual claims.

But the loss of individuality may also suggest a kind of fellowship in death, and many other passages express a sense that the approach to death is a natural one for man, and one for which "we are being prepared." *Tibi, mors, paramur* ("For you, o death, we are being prepared"): here the Hades chorus of *Hercules Furens* directly address death, almost as a friend or welcoming host. Death can even be chosen as a haven after the anguish of life: "O death, we take refuge in you." It is Phaedra, after her guilt and despair, who speaks at last these words of Stoic consent to providence. Shortly before these lines, Phaedra spoke of Hades as a place of unending torment and madness

(1179–1180). The conversion from frenzied protest to acceptance that takes place before Phaedra meets her death goes with a significant change from singular to plural verb forms. The transition is beautifully conveyed in Studley's translation, published in 1581.

Hell shall not hold me from thy syde. . . .
My selfe I shall in spite of fate my fatall twist
    untwine.
This blade shall rive my bloudy breast, my selfe I
    will dispoile
Of soule, and sinne at once; through floods and
    Tartar gulphes that boyle,
Through Styx and through the burning Lakes I wil
    come after thee. . . .
O death the chiefest joy
Of wounding shame: Death onely ease of stinging
    Loves annoy:
We runne to thee; embrace our sowles within thy
    gladsome breast.

(1175–1190)

The meeting with death can thus be, for Seneca, a fulfillment as well as an end. It is the culmination of the self-discovery that every individual has to pursue throughout life (since every man, said the Stoic teacher Panaetius, has his vocation). True self-discovery also meant the awareness of human kinship; it is vice that separates men from one another; the good life is one of harmony and wholeness. Seneca develops this theme in his essay *On the Happy Life*, and it is implicit throughout the tragedies, where evil men isolate themselves as well as their victims. Death then may be a way of choosing humanity in preference to a life that denies kinship and freedom. "What is the way to freedom?" Seneca puts this question in his essay *On Anger*. Was this passage in Jean-Paul Sartre's mind when he chose the title for his great trilogy of novels, *Les Chemins de la liberté* (1945–1949)? The answer found by Sartre's Mathieu was the same for Seneca: "any vein in your body." Freely chosen death was the answer for Phaedra, and for the chorus in *Agamemnon*: "while an escape from evils lies open, and free death invites the wretched—a harbor tranquil in eternal peace" (591).

This note of wan tranquillity is heard again in the unique *Octavia*, a play whose authorship is disputed and whose rare imaginative quality is often unremarked. *Octavia* deals with events in Seneca's own life, and whether it was written by himself or by someone else who was close to those events, it has a curious and consistent tone of resignation, making death a thing of sorrow but also of peace, as the "quiet grave" was for Edmund Spenser:

Sleepe after toyle, port after stormy seas,
Ease after warre, death after life does greatly
    please.

To welcome death in this way is a spiritual act that perhaps lies "on the other side of despair"; and it recalls another saying of Sartre's: "he who chooses despair chooses himself in his eternal value."

VII

In his prose works Seneca frequently touches on the theme of self-choice, the acceptance of one's own identity through self-knowledge. He thinks of this as a process in human development that must go on throughout life, each age having its own appropriate experience in "the endeavor to persist in one's own being" (*conatus in suo esse perseverandi*). This phrase is used as an equivalent for the Greek term *oikeiosis*, a concept derived from Chrysippus, or possibly from Zeno himself, and variously translated today as "appropriation," "familiarization," or even "endearment."

None of these translations (or any single word in English) conveys the sense of the Greek word as used by Stoics, implying a recognition and acceptance of relationship between the perceiving self and what it encounters. The definition of Diogenes Laertius (7.85) refers to *oikeiosis* as "the prime impulse of every animal toward self-preservation, by which Nature has caused it to repel what is harmful and to welcome everything that is appropriate for itself." This sounds like a biological mechanism resulting in survival, but Diogenes is talking of something more far-reaching: in a human being, *oikeiosis* includes the process of growth in childhood whereby reason develops sufficiently to control impulse, not as its opponent but "as the technician to take charge of it." This relationship between reason and impulse is the natural and proper one that the young human being comes to recognize and accept, so that in adult life *oikeiosis* operates in a consciously reasoning way, making someone aware of his true being and at home in the human world, able to make rational rather than instinctive choices of what is naturally in his true interest. For Cicero, in book 3 of *On Ends* and in his *Priora Academica*, the concept of *oikeiosis* led clearly on to the idea of man as a naturally social being, needing to relate himself to other men and to the "cosmic city." For Seneca, the individual is the focus of attention, and in one of his longer letters (121), he discusses human growth in personal terms and in relation to nature. The theme is pursued also in the shorter, more urgently didactic letter 41, which considers the element of divinity in human personality. Both these letters deserve close attention.

Characteristically, both letters begin with a second-person verb in a simple statement:

> You are doing an excellent thing, and in your own interest, if you are going on, as you say in your letter.
>
> (letter 41.1)

> You will take up the case against me, I see.
>
> (letter 121.1)

The tone and the diction are those of informal conversation, and the opening implies a recent letter from Lucilius, itself part of a continuing interchange: "When I have analyzed today's little question, in which we have stuck long enough . . ." (letter 121).

The situation assumed for the letters—dated within the years 62–64, when Seneca had lost his influence over Nero though he had not been given permission to retire—was that Lucilius had embarked on a serious and exacting course in Stoic philosophy, carried on at a rapid pace and demanding all his energies and time. Miriam Griffin points out the difficulties of regarding this setting for the letters as actuality. She describes the letters as "a highly artificial work," having "an epistolary veneer inspired by Cicero." The veneer consists of colloquial language combined with effortless rhetorical skill, producing an air of spontaneity that most readers have found really winning and a few disagreeably bland. The letters are arranged in dramatic sequence, so that Lucilius (i.e., the reader) is presumed to have studied letter 41 sometime before letter 121. We may find it more useful, however, to look at letter 121 first.

The "little question" mentioned in the first line of letter 121 is not so little. Before he defines it, Seneca imagines his pupil raising objections:

> What has this to do with morality? you will protest. Well, protest! but let me first bring out other opponents for you to meet—Posidonius and Archidemus: these will take the role of judge; and then let me say, not every aspect of human conduct contributes to good moral practice. One thing relates to human nutrition, another to exercise, another to clothing, another to teaching, another to pleasure: yet all these things concern man, even if they do not all improve him morally.
>
> (1–2)

All this is very leisured and detached; but the little question, when it comes, is both forceful and profound:

> When I ask why nature has produced mankind and why she has raised him above other animals, do you maintain that I have moved far away from the subject of morality? That is not true. For how will you know what should be regarded as moral conduct, unless you have found out what is best for man, unless you have looked right into his nature?
>
> (3)

Lucilius may be supposed to have learned his Stoic lesson well in demanding that a philosophical inquiry should contribute to an ethical or psychological end. Otherwise, speculation in the fields of physics and biology could be regarded as merely frivolous. Seneca gives an earnest reply to this call for moral teaching and for a release from desire and fear.

> I will satisfy your longing: I will acclaim virtue and castigate vice; though some critic may judge me too vehement and extreme on this side. I will not give up my harassment of wrongdoing, my suppression of wild emotions, my strict control of pleasures which will issue in grief, my insistent protests and prayers.
>
> (4)

The expression here has become terse and strenuous, and the tone is no longer that of informal conversation; Seneca is alone now, in the hearing of all men or none, and of the gods. This stance is brief. With the interjection *Quidni* ("Of course!") he falls back into the colloquial manner and ends his isolation, in a return to the dialogue setting by means of a sentence in the first-person plural: "Of course! Since we have chosen the greatest of our troubles, and whatever address we make [to the gods] takes its beginning from thanksgiving." The slightly ironical tone here, and the transitional *interim* (meanwhile), allow Seneca to move easily at this point into the main body of the letter: "Allow me to analyze those questions which appear a little too remote. We were enquiring. . . ." He now considers animal behavior, the movements of infants, and the degree of self-awareness that animals and infants can be thought to experience. The writing here is distinguished by its lucidity and discretion. There is no sense of hurry or compression, the illustrations are vivid and detailed (such as the artist expertly glancing as his hand moves from painting to palette, or the tortoise on its back, ceaselessly struggling in a restless longing, precisely defined as *not* agony, for its natural position). There is no self-indulgent elaboration here, no virtuosity; Seneca's interest clearly is in his theme, for itself. The argument proceeds

systematically, each stage marked by a comment or question from an uncharacterized listener. *Inquit* (he says) replaces all reference to "you," that is, Lucilius, the named individual with whom Seneca has a personal relationship, until the last twenty lines of the letter. The remarks introduced by *inquit* are always pertinent and objective, and make no reference to the occasional passages of a more personal and dramatic kind that appear in the course of the exposition. So when Seneca is discussing the process of *oikeiosis* (which he expresses by the verb *conciliari*) in childhood and youth, he speaks of the various stages of human development, first in abstract and then in personal terms:

> The age of infancy is one thing, childhood another, then youth, and old age: but I am the same person who has been infant, boy, young man. So although there are different stages of development for each individual, the experience of relating oneself to each stage is the same. For it is not a boy or a young man or an old man that nature brings me to meet, but myself. . . . I seek pleasure. For whom? for myself; so I am caring for myself. I recoil from pain. For whom? for myself; so I am caring for myself. If everything I do is through care for myself, then care for myself comes before all else. This care exists in all living beings, and it is not implanted but inborn.
>
> Nature brings forth her young, and does not cast them away; and because the surest protection comes from the closest source, each individual is entrusted to himself. So, as I said in previous letters, even frail living creatures, just emerged from the mother's womb or from the egg, instantly know for themselves what is dangerous, and shun what brings death; they even shrink from the shadow of wings flying past, if they are exposed to birds that live on prey. No living being enters into life without the fear of death.
>
> (16–18)

The imaginary questioner intervenes here (but not when Seneca brought his own experience into the discussion) to ask how a newly born creature can have gained any understanding of danger. The Stoic's answer is the expected one: this is a gift of nature. In this concluding paragraph he reverts to the second-person singular: "You see what skill bees have ... you see how a spider's web cannot be imitated ... you will not find self-contempt or self-neglect in any creature." The anonymous interlocutor is discarded and Lucilius returns.

Seneca has thus been able to conduct his philosophic inquiry in a more various and complex style than that of the Platonic dialogues, which have obviously suggested some aspects of the approach and style used in the letters. Letter 121 shows, in addition to the qualities looked for in a prose letter or dialogue, some of the dramatic skill and the expressive use of language found in the tragedies; letter 41 has something of their intensity also.

The theme in letter 41 is human awareness of the divine. God is known as "close to you, with you, within you; so I tell you, Lucilius, a holy spirit dwells in us, the watcher and the guardian of evil and of good in our life; and as he has been treated by us, so does he himself treat us." These solemn words suggest the possibility of a new and profounder kind of *oikeiosis*, the conscious and welcoming establishment of relationship with the "guardian of evil and of good in our life," the giver of all that is beneficial to the self. To realize the possibility of this relationship with God within us is what Seneca very simply calls "right thinking" or "good sense" (*bona mens*, the deified abstraction to which Propertius devoted himself when seeking liberation from his consuming passion for Cynthia). Seneca warns Lucilius that good sense is not reached by wishing, or by conventional religious gestures; it is a state we can claim as our own if we listen to the "grand and lofty counsels" that the god himself gives to us. So far the whole of this letter is written in short authoritative sentences whose verbs are present-tense statements; so too is the line from Vergil (*Aeneid* 8.352) with which Seneca ends this section, applying it to the individual soul: "In every individual among good men 'a god—what god is unknown—has his dwelling.'" In Vergil these words are spoken by Evander as he guides Aeneas over the uncultivated hillocks where Rome is one day to arise and points to the grove that makes passing tribesmen tremble with awe at the undoubted presence of an unnamed god. The appearance of this grove is only hinted in Vergil; it stands on a rocky hill with leafy peak, where often storm clouds gather. One day this will be the gleaming Capitol. The Arcadians believe they have glimpsed the shade of Jupiter here, his darkening shield brandished in his right hand.

This passage in Vergil was too well known for Seneca's readers to miss these numinous associations of majesty and age. When Seneca then continues the letter with a descriptive passage taking the appearance of a forest as sign of God's presence, the awe-inspiring quality of Vergil's grove is evoked without any precise verbal echoes. Seneca has here returned to the personal address: "If you have ever come across a grove...." Other forms of landscape are then described as manifesting the divine: natural caverns, the sources of great rivers, hot springs, deep pools. Most of all, the sense of veneration is stirred by meeting a human being who has realized his true nature by recognizing and living close to the god within him:

a human being who is not alarmed by danger, not moved by cravings, happy in adversity, serene in the midst of storm. . . . Will you not say, "Here is a thing too great, too lofty, to be regarded as similar to this insignificant body in which it exists? Into that body a divine force has descended." So great a thing cannot stand without the support of a deity. Just as the rays of the sun do touch the earth, but remain in the place from which they are sent, so a great and holy soul, sent down for this purpose, that we might come to know the divine more closely, associates with us indeed, but clings to its source; it depends on that source, looks to that source and strives toward it, taking

What then is this soul, which shines with no good quality but its own? For what is more stupid than to praise in a human being things which are not his own? What more crazy than a man who admires things which can be directly handed over to someone else? Golden reins do not make a better horse.

(41.4–6)

Indeed, gilding a lion's mane, Seneca goes on, destroys the peculiar glory of his nature, which is in his wild energy and strength; just as a vine's peculiar virtue is its natural fruitfulness, not the gold grapes and leaves of legend. The parallel with man is drawn in a passage that must have been acutely felt at the time Seneca wrote it, when he was trying, against Nero's will, to relinquish the wealth and social prestige that had become both distasteful and dangerous to him:

> In a human being too, what should be praised is what belongs to his own self. He has a fine household and a beautiful home, he cultivates a large estate, lends large amounts of money; none of these things is in himself, all are around him. Praise in him what cannot be snatched away and cannot be given, what is man's peculiar quality. You ask what this is? His soul, and reason perfected in the soul. For man is a reasoning being. So his good is realized if he has fulfilled the purpose for which he is born. And what is it that his reason demands of him? A very easy matter—to live according to his own nature.
>
> (7–8)

The Stoic ideal was never expressed with more clarity and persuasiveness.

To read these two letters—whose qualities are found in many others also—is to recognize the note of moral assurance, of positive Stoic equanimity, that won for Seneca the postion of moral authority that he held for so long in medieval and modern Europe. There is a natural decorum and coherence in the writing of Seneca the moralist, combined with literary expertise, that enables him to dazzle and then amuse, sometimes going on almost at once to strike a note of intense fervor (though never of fanaticism). Many readers whose lives were harassed or confused have turned to the *Moral Letters* to find serenity and strength; one thinks of Queen Elizabeth I, who "did much admire his wholesome advisings, when the soul's quiet is fled away."

As a literary form these letters are one of the most original in ancient literature. Horace wrote his satirical letters in verse, Cicero his philosophic treatises in fluent prose (sometimes in dialogue form); Cicero's genuine letters also offered a model in their spontaneity and their colloquial vigor. Seneca's *Moral Letters* combine some qualities from each of these, and some from Greek writers also, to create a new genre, the discursive essay, as original and as widely imitated as Senecan tragedy.

VIII

The tragedies and the prose works are in many ways antithetical. Almost all the qualities that have been noted in letters 121 and 41 are lacking in the plays: coherence and decorum, equanimity, the celebration of the natural world, and the sense of moral order; these are replaced by the thrusting forward of grotesque and horrific subjects, often juxtaposed without logical sequence, producing bewilderment and shock. These themes of chaos and terror are presented within a structure of severely classic tradition, which again contrasts with the casual variety of the essay. The strict form of the tragedies seems to be needed to hold the horrific material in check (a chorus cannot be in effect shown as mad, even if, as in Euripides' *Bacchae*, it is made up of individuals subject to a psychic possession or frenzy). Certainly the dramatic power of these plays derives in part from the tension between ordered form and monstrous theme.

One man's work, even if employing diverse forms at different times or for different subjects, usually has the unity of a recognizable single voice. In Seneca's case it is extraordinarily hard to recognize such a unity; the difference between prose and plays is not one of maturing mind or of changes in mood or interests. The profoundest difference is that the assertions made in the philosophical works—nature is good, providence is all-wise and all-powerful, order prevails in the universe beyond the reach of human wrongs and follies—cannot be reconciled with what we see in the tragedies. There, evil spreads in the cosmos as it does in the soul. The gods do not exist in a universe that admits Medea. Nature (and it is the sane choruses who often tell us this) has reversed its order and is hurtling toward destruction.

None of the plays expresses this theme of nature overthrown more powerfully than *Thyestes*, where the response of revulsion (which Greek playwrights generally avoided even in their treatment of gruesome or occult elements in legendary material) is deliberately evoked by every possible means. Atreus, as we have seen, deliberately sets himself outside the order of nature and chooses a vengeance that will make nature itself revolt. When the children are massacred, their fragmented bodies groan in bewildered protest, and the flames themselves recoil, reluctant to take part in the preparations for such a meal. At the beginning of the play, when Tantalus' ghost was drawn unwillingly up from Hades, earth trembled and the sun hesitated to rise; a shudder spread through the house at his unnatural entry. So when the father stretches out his hand for the cup that contains his children's blood, a weight holds back his arm, and the table springs up from the quivering earth. These—like the signs of cosmic disorder that accompany the murders of children by parents in *Medea* and *Hercules Furens*—are not omens in the sense of indications of future events, but expressions of what present events mean in cosmic terms.

The fullest demonstration of this universal meaning comes when the sun reverses its course at midday and brings darkness upon the world at noon. Atreus does not mention this darkness—as if it made no difference to his darkened consciousness—but Thyestes and the messenger are aware of it, and the chorus have a long, strange, complex lyric on the theme of cosmic chaos:

This is the fear, the fear that knocks at the heart,
That the whole world is now to fall in the ruin
Which Fate foretells; that Chaos will come again
To bury the world of gods and men. . . .

That belt of constellations that marks out the
   passage of the years,
The highway of the holy stars that lies oblique
   across the zones,
Will fall away. . . .

And last of the twelve signs, the *Fish*, will
   disappear.
Into the universal deluge will the *Wain* descend,
Which never touched the sea before;
The *Snake*, like a meandering river sliding
Between the *Bears*; and the great *Dragon*'s smaller
   neighbour
The freezing *Cynosura*; and the slow-footed
   watcher
Beside the wagon, *Arctophylax*, will be shaken
And fall into the deep.

And are we chosen out of all earth's children
To perish in the last catastrophe
Of a disjointed universe?
      (*Thyestes* 829–877, E. F. Watling trans.)

A passage in one of Seneca's prose works, the ethical treatise *On Benefits*, suggests that this theme of nature in disorder was not merely a literary figure like the pathetic fallacy. He is referring to the appalling story of the tyrant Phalaris, who was said to have burned his enemies alive inside a brazen bull. Such acts, says Seneca, are monstrosities in nature, like a crack in the earth, or an outbreak of fire in the caverns of the sea. The order of the universe does not admit such actions; yet they happen, and not only in the tales of mythology. Stoic philosophy bases itself on the concept of order in the universe. But if that order does not prevail?

Should one perhaps see Seneca's tragedies as a means of expressing what his philosophy could not find room for, this element of the monstrous in human nature? The human choice of evil spreads chaos and destruction throughout the cosmos, just as does Eve's bite on the apple in Milton's *Paradise Lost:* "Earth felt the wound." The spectator is forced to watch scenes of such cruelty and degradation that they seem to destroy the possibility of meaning in life, to make us think the unthinkable. Several recent films associate such a closed universe of horror with the rise of fascism; we remember again that Seneca's own world was the Rome of Caligula and Nero.

Seneca died by suicide, but he was acting under imperial orders, so his death—courageous though it was—could not be called a voluntary choice. But death is seen in both his prose and plays as having a positive value and meaning. Suicide could mean a chosen withdrawal from the transient chaos of this world to another order of creation, the eternal providence beyond nature. This is accepted Stoic doctrine, and it does not imply a belief in personal immortality. Again and again the choruses in the tragedies (and choruses often know more of moral truth than any characters do) speak of death as the realm of tranquillity and of freedom. Death is ghastly, death is fearful, death is unimaginable; yet when the universe is seen for the meaningless horror it is, death can be seen as offering a positive hope, for death is part of the order of nature, and a part that does not lie within the realm of human corruption. The sense of awe and profound acceptance with which Seneca contemplates the work of nature even in our flawed universe inspires many passages in both tragedies and prose. The third chorus of *Phaedra* memorably expresses this sense of awe:

> O Nature, whence all gods proceed;
> And Thou, King of Olympian light,
> Whose hand makes stars and planets speed
> Round the high axis of the night:
> If thou canst guide with ceaseless care
> The heavenly bodies in their train,
> To make the woods in winter bare

> And in the springtime green again,
> Until the summer's Lion burns
> To bring the ripening seed to birth
> And every force of nature turns
> To gentleness upon the earth—
> Why, if such power is in thy hand
> To balance by an ordered plan
> The mass of things, why dost thou stand
> So far from the affairs of man?
> Thou dost not care to help the good
> Nor punish men of evil mind.
> Man lives by chance, to Fate subdued,
> And evil thrives, for Fate is blind.
> Vile lust has banished purity.
> Vice sits enthroned in royal state;
> Mobs give to knaves authority
> And serve them even while they hate.
> Poor is the prize sour virtue gains,
> Want lies in wait for honesty,
> Sin reigns supreme. What good remains
> In shame, what worth in dignity?
> (*Phaedra* 963–988, E. F. Watling trans.)

Many passages in both *Letters* and *Natural Questions* speak of the inevitable dissolution of the universe that was expected by Stoics, when all things were to be destroyed by fire and returned to their original elements. The never-ending craftsmanship of God, says Seneca in letter 71, is working transformations in all things, bringing a new order out of the old; the present order is not eternal. Sometimes Seneca writes of the new order to come as if it were a further stage of history to succeed the ages of mankind. Elsewhere he suggests something so like the Christian hope of immortality that the esteem, almost veneration, given to him in the Middle Ages is easy to understand:

Some day nature will reveal to you all her secrets; this darkness will be dispelled and glorious light break in upon you. Think of the marvel of that light, in which the light of all the stars is added together—a perfect light, without a shadow of darkness. The whole expanse of heaven will be one pure radiance; the distinction of day and night is only a property of our lower atmosphere. When, totally translated, you look upon the infinite light, which you now perceive only dimly through the slits of your eyes, you will know that life has been to you but darkness. Already, even at a distance, that light is something which you marvel at; what will you think of the divine light when you are in its very presence? This is a thought to banish from one's mind all that is sordid, mean, or cruel; to assure us that the gods watch over everything that happens; to bid us earn their good will, prepare to meet them, and keep the image of eternity before our eyes.

(letter 102.28–29, E. F. Watling trans.)

Selected Bibliography

TEXTS

The following are in the Loeb Classical Library, with full Latin text and English translation on the facing page.

Ad Lucilium Epistulae Morales. Translated by R. M. Gummere. 3 vols. Cambridge, Mass., and London, 1917.

Dialogues (Moral Essays, De Clementia, and De Beneficiis). Translated by J. W. Basore. 3 vols. 1935.

Naturales Quaestiones. Translated by T. H. Corcoran. 2 vols. 1972.

Tragoediae. Translated by F. J. Miller. 2 vols. 1960.

Recent editions of text alone are:

Epistulae Morales, edited by L. D. Reynolds. Oxford, 1965.

Tragedies, edited by G. C. Giardina. Bologna, 1966.

TRANSLATIONS

Campbell, Robin, ed. and trans. *Letters from a Stoic.* Harmondsworth, 1969. Penguin Classics.

Hughes, Ted, adapt. *Oedipus.* London, 1969. With an introduction by Peter Brook.

Newton, Thomas, ed. *Seneca His Tenne Tragedies.* London, 1581. Reprinted Bloomington, Ind., 1966. With an introduction by T. S. Eliot.

Watling, E. F., trans. *Four Tragedies by Seneca, and Octavia.* Harmondsworth, 1966. With an introduction by the editor. The four tragedies are *Thyestes, Phaedra, The Trojan Women,* and *Oedipus.* Penguin Classics.

HISTORICAL BACKGROUND

Dill, S. *Roman Society from Nero to Marcus Aurelius.* London, 1904. The chapter "The Philosophic Director" is especially relevant.

Macmullen, Ramsay. *Enemies of the Roman Order.* Cambridge, Mass., 1967.

Warmington, B. H. *Nero, Reality and Legend.* London, 1969.

STUDIES OF STOICISM AND THE PHILOSOPHY OF SENECA

Coleman, Robert. "The Artful Moralist: A Study of Seneca's Epistolary Style." *Classical Quarterly* 68:276–289 (December 1974).

Edelstein, L. *The Meaning of Stoicism.* Oxford, 1976.

Griffin, Miriam T. *Seneca: A Philosopher in Politics.* Oxford, 1976.

Kerferd, G. B. "The Origin of Evil in Stoic Thought." *John Rylands Bulletin* 60:482–494 (1978).

———. "The Search for Personal Identity in Stoic Thought." *John Rylands Bulletin* 55:177–196 (1972–1973).

Long, A. A., ed. *Problems in Stoicism.* London, 1971.

Motto, A. L., and J. R. Clark. "Paradoxum Senecae: The Epicurean Stoic." *Classical World* 62:6–11 (1968).

Sandbach, Francis H. *The Stoics.* London, 1975.

CRITICAL STUDIES

Anliker, Kurt. *Prologe und Akteinteilung in Senecas Tragödien.* Bern, 1959.

Braden, Gordon. "The Rhetoric and Psychology of Power in Seneca's Tragedies." *Arion* 9:5–41 (1970).

Canter, Howard V. *Rhetorical Elements in the Tragedies of Seneca.* Urbana, Ill., 1925.

Costa, C. D. N., ed. *Seneca.* Boston, 1974. Contains essays on various aspects of Seneca.

Eliot, T. S. "Shakespeare and the Stoicism of Seneca." In Eliot, *Selected Essays.* London, 1948.

Giancotti, F. *Saggio sulle tragedie di Seneca.* Rome, 1953.

Henry, Elisabeth (B. Walker), and Denis Henry. "The Futility of Action: A Study of Seneca's *Hercules Furens*." *Classical Philology* 40:11–22 (1965).

———. "Loss of Identity: *Medea superest*? A Study of Seneca's *Medea*." *Classical Philology* 62:169–181 (July 1967).

———. "Phantasmagoria and Idyll: An Element of

Seneca's *Phaedra." Greece and Rome* 2, no. 13:223–239 (October 1966).

———. "Seneca and the *Agamemnon." Classical Philology* 58:1–10 (January 1963).

Herington, C. J. "Senecan Tragedy." *Arion* 5:422–471 (1966).

Klein, J. L. *Geschichte des Dramas.* Vol. 2. Leipzig, 1865.

Lefevre, Eçkard, ed. *Senecas Tragödien.* Wege der Forschung series. Darmstadt, 1972.

Regenbogen, Otto. "Schmerz und Tod in den Tragödien Senecas." *Vorträge der Bibliothek Warburg* 7:167–218 (1927–1928). Reprinted in Regenbogen, *Kleine Schriften.* Munich, 1961.

Seidensticker, Bernd. *Die Gesprachsverdichtung in den Tragödien Senecas.* Heidelberg, 1969.

Shelton, Jo-Ann. *Seneca's "Hercules Furens": Theme, Structure, and Style.* Göttingen, 1978. Contains a useful, up-to-date bibliography.

ELISABETH HENRY

PETRONIUS

(*d.* A.D. 66)

I

OF THE ENORMOUS literature of Greek and Roman antiquity, only a very small portion, of diverse quality and value, survived the Middle Ages intact. And much that survived—like the poetry of Sappho and Alcman, or the drama of Sophocles, or ancient Latin poetry and satire—did so only in pitifully small fragments. Few literary fragments surviving from antiquity, however, are more impressive or more tantalizing than the remains of Petronius' masterpiece, the *Satyricon*. It is mostly read nowadays as a surreptitious classic—like the *Heptameron* or any number of "bedside" tales belonging to the genre of "picaresque erotic"—for titillation or amusement; or, if read seriously, as one of the earliest examples of the novel. But even in its mutilated condition, the *Satyricon* is one of the most brilliant accomplishments of the Roman imagination, a work whose vigor and electric vividness of colloquial speech, everywhere oddly grafted onto echoes of epic and tragedy and the "high style" of classic eloquence, make it unique in ancient literature. I use the word "unique" advisedly. There is literally nothing like this book; not, at least, in ancient culture. Apparently a cunningly devised potpourri of very different modes and styles, constantly enjambing the comic against the tragic, the colloquial against the aulic, the burlesque against the epic and heroic, the realistic against the poetic, it is nonetheless a distinct composition, stamped with its author's personality and temperament, inviting comparison with the tradition while at the same time again and again subverting or outraging all generic expectations. In short, a work of quite astonishing originality. In some sense it is obviously a satire, in another no satire at all; in some very obvious sense an "entertainment," extending an invitation to the reader's pleasure and delight, in another sense no entertainment at all. Visibly like a novel in its realistic control and narrative pace, it is somehow not a novel at all. What was it intended to be, and what sort of writer wrote it?

II

Unfortunately we know almost nothing of the author of the *Satyricon*, and almost nothing with certainty. Even the name of Petronius is of uncertain attribution, while the date of composition has been the subject of long and inconclusive discussion. (The most thorough and conclusive study of the problems is that of K. F. C. Rose, *The Date and Author of the Satyricon*, 1971.) Despite this, there is, it seems to me, something like a clear consensus among scholars that the author of our book is to be identified with Petronius Arbiter, a Roman consul and intimate of the emperor Nero (reigned A.D. 54–68). The little we know of this Petronius Arbiter comes from the fascinating account given us by the historian Tacitus. The notice deserves to be cited in its entirety:

> Gaius Petronius deserves a brief obituary. He spent his days sleeping, his nights working and enjoying himself. Others achieve fame by energy, Petronius by laziness. Yet he was not, like others who waste their resources, regarded as dissipated or extravagant, but as a refined voluptuary. People liked the apparent freshness of his unconventional and unselfconscious sayings and doings. Nevertheless, as governor of Bithynia and later as consul, he had displayed capacity for business.
>
> Then, reverting to a vicious or ostensibly vicious way of life, he had been admitted into the small circle of Nero's intimates, as Arbiter of Taste: to the *blasé* emperor, smartness and elegance were restricted to what Petronius had approved. So Tigellinus, loathing him as a rival and expert hedonist, denounced him as a friend of Flavius Scaevinus. This appealed to the emperor's outstanding passion—his cruelty. A slave was bribed to incriminate Petronius. No defence was heard. Indeed, most of his household were under arrest.
>
> The emperor happened to be in Campania. Petronius too had reached Cumae; there he was detained. Delay, with its hopes and fears, he refused to endure. He severed his veins. Then, having them bound up again when the fancy took him, he talked with his friends—but not seriously, or so as to gain a name for fortitude. And he listened to them reciting, not discourses about the immortality of the soul or philosophy, but light lyrics and frivolous poems. Some slaves received presents—others were beaten. He appeared at dinner, and dozed, so that his death, if compulsory, might look natural.
>
> Even his will deviated from the routine deathbed flatteries of Nero, Tigellinus, and other leaders. Petronius wrote out a list of Nero's sensualities—giving names of each male and female bed-fellow and details of every lubricious novelty—and sent it under seal to Nero. Then Petronius broke his signet-ring, to prevent its subsequent employment to incriminate others.
>
> (*Annals* 16, 18 ff., M. Grant, trans.)

A remarkable man, as unconventional in his dying as in his living. Great freedom from received opinions and the Stoic cliches of conduct; real appetite for pleasure but obvious discrimination—and perhaps restraint, the restraint that makes of the hedonist a refined voluptuary; obvious distaste for heroics and highfalutin cant; consideration for others; unmistakable courage in the presence of death: if we were forced to imagine for ourselves the likely lineaments of the man who wrote the *Satyricon*, it is surely something along these lines we would have to invent. Which is to say that a sound and reasonable principle of economy supports the claims of Tacitus' Gaius Petronius as the author of the *Satyricon*. Such a man, such a combination of administrative capacity and seriousness (his governorship, his consulship) with voluptuary taste and aesthetic discrimination, would have been a rarity in any age, and those who reject Gaius Petronius' authorship of the *Satyricon* must accept the responsibility for finding a more likely candidate.

III

If we know precious little of Petronius, we know almost as little about the nature of the *Satyricon* as a whole: its theme, its unity, its genre, its size, even its title are matters of scholarly dispute. We have a few facts, but of uncertain value. For instance, appended to the famous manuscript of the work found at Trau, Dalmatia, by Petit in 1663 there is a note informing us that the contents are fragments "from the fifteenth and sixteenth books." But even on the generous assumption that the *Satyricon* consisted of sixteen rather than, say, twenty or the normal epic twenty-four books, the result would be a work of exceptional length (though the emperor Nero planned a poetic work on Troy, we are told, in one hundred books). What we in fact possess is a fragment from a whole of unknown length, and even those parts that we do possess are not continuous but are marred by lacunae of greater or lesser length. But the very length of the *Satyricon* as it has come down to us clearly forbids us to entertain the once-fashionable view that the work is to be identified with the catalog of debaucheries sent by the dying Petronius to Nero.

The title is of uncertain meaning. *Satyricon* appears to be formed from a Greek genitive plural, though it is impossible to decide whether we should read *Satyricon* or *Satiricon*, and perhaps it does not finally matter. For Petronius may have been punning on both *satura* ("satire" in its specifically Roman sense—a farrago or hodgepodge of mixed subjects in a variety of styles) and *satyrika* (concerned with satyrs, which is to say, lecherous matters, randy things). By this interpretation, the *Satyricon* (or *Satiricon*) would mean a book of randy satires, or of satyr-matters treated in the manner of Roman satire, and it is pretty much this that the extant fragments show us.

Formally, the *Satyricon*, like Boethius' *On the Consolation of Philosophy*, belongs to the genre known in antiquity as Menippean satire, a curious blending of prose with verse and philosophy with realism, invented by the Cynic philosopher Menippus of Gadara (in the early third century B.C.) and continued by his Roman disciple, Varro (116–27 B.C.). But this tells us little, for apart from its use of alternating prose and verse, Petronius' work is tonally and perhaps thematically as far removed from the homespun moralizings of Menippus as Shakespeare's histories are from Holinshed. Moreover, though recognizably satirical in some Roman sense, the *Satyricon* generally exhibits very little resemblance to the form of satire that the Romans thought was their distinctive contribution to literature. Compare Petronius with the major Roman satirists and the differences are immediately apparent. The crucial difference is that the *Satyricon* is unmistakably comic, everywhere pervaded by a gusto and verve and grace of humor almost totally absent from the tolerantly good-natured strictures of Horace, the gentle, crabbed austerity of Persius, or the bitter savagery of Juvenal. One *laughs*, after all, with Petronius. The effect of the *Satyricon* is neither scorn nor indignation but the laughter appropriate to satire enlarged by the gaiety of comedy. The comic crowns the work and gives the whole randy fiction that effortless natural gaiety that makes it so improbably wholesome. Trimalchio may well be a satirical portrait of the nouveau riche in the age of Nero, but he is also, like Falstaff and Don Quixote, a comic creation in his own right, vulgarity on such a scale, so vast and vivid, that he easily survives his own function as a satirical butt. And it is this wonderful blending of satire and comedy that, to my mind, makes Petronius unique among Roman satirists and the *Satyricon* a genre of its own: sui generis.

But as a farrago or potpourri, the *Satyricon* amply satisfies at least one sense of ancient satire (*satura*—a medley, a mixed dish, a farrago), for it is literally one huge mélange of genres and styles, incongruously blending verse with prose, the fabulous with the realistic, grafting pompous epic onto doggerel or lyric, setting high speech against low speech in constant profusion of parody and mockery. Variety, the deliberate variety of incongruity, is everywhere, and it needs to be seen for what it is—the source of Petronius' satirical comedy. For if the characters are realistic, they also reach out for the archetypal and even the fabulous; if they mock one another, they are in turn mocked by what they are or by their placing in the narrative situation. And the source of these ironies is the crisscrossing of perspectives and incongruous styles. If we observe how the realistic undercuts the fabulous, we should also observe how the fabulous or generic is precipitated by the realistic. Trimalchio, for instance, is satirized with scathing accuracy and fullness, but the very grossness of his outsize humanity is clearly employed in order to mock and undercut the sophisticated snobbery of the educated Encolpius and his friends. Similarly, we see a wretched old hag suddenly bursting into the high Vergilian hexameters of the literary witch, or the courtesan Circe being set off, in a sudden poetic epiphany, as the figure of "the true Danae." Or again, Encolpius begins a stale rhetorical set piece on the vicissitudes of human fortune only to come upon the unmistakable poetry of passionate conviction. And invariably, when the perverted lovers reach their nadir of anguish or height of happiness, we find them, in their words and sentiments, undercutting themselves, mocking as it were their own narrative position by talking the melodramatic humbug of farce or the sentimental clichés of Greek romance. Petronius, in other words, constantly employs the traditional elements out of which his farrago is constructed in such a way that he transcends the genres he uses, transforming his structural elements and recombining them in a new amalgam. The work in this sense is profoundly literary and presumes real knowledgeability in the audience, which must recognize the transformations and the tensions inherent in language and situations that have been wrenched from their customary setting, violently decontextualized, and thus endowed with fresh meaning.

The *Satyricon*, then, is in some sense a satirical comedy of deeply literary nature based upon a fictional narrative both episodic and recognizably picaresque in nature. It also gaily and freely mixes and parodies half a dozen genres, and these parodied genres, when set against each other in striking ways, are central to the comedy at the same time that they provide the literary satirist with the material—but also the vehicle—of his satire. Thus we find several so-called Milesian tales (the famous story of the widow of Ephesus is a good example of the genre), as well as a continuous running inversion of the sentimental Greek romance with its stereotypical lovers and its melodramatically contrived situations (capture by pirates, shockingly sudden reversals of fortune, and so on). The allusions to mime and farce are everywhere and also overtly insisted upon so that the audience will not miss its cues. Alternatively the whole work could be (and has been) described as a burlesque or mock-epic, an *Odyssey* buffo or satyr's *Aeneid,* in which the narrator Encolpius as antihero or erotic Odysseus suffers the wrath of the god he has outraged— Priapus. And yet the *Satyricon*, by reason of its variety and originality in mingling its compo-

nent genres, is something markedly different from any one of them.

Can we perhaps cut through this scholarly thicket of genres by declaring the *Satyricon* to be a satirical or comic novel and leaving it at that? There is no reason why we should not, though the definition hardly seems helpful. Besides, in at least one important respect the *Satyricon* is quite unlike later satirical comedies or picaresque tales like, say, Lesage's *Gil Blas* or Tobias Smollett's *Roderick Random.* That respect is rhetoric, the fact of *oral* presentation. For unless I am badly mistaken, the *Satyricon* was composed for a listening audience; it was meant to be recited aloud by a trained artist or *rhetor* (perhaps more than one), with the kind of voice and virtuosity that could adequately represent the enormous variety of the work and its typically Roman relish for high sound, but also its abrupt shifts of pace and tone, its nuances of parody and inversion. Indeed the episodic structure of the *Satyricon* is, I believe, largely determined by this fact of oral presentation. Variety is central, and so we see the work again and again separate itself into discrete episodes, each episode bounded by a given subject or style or genre—the erotic stories, the Menippean symposium looming behind Trimalchio's quite unphilosophical dinner party, a stream of virtuoso invective, a lecture on the decline of the arts, a harangue on education or how to write an epic, a showpiece on the vicissitudes of fortune, a rhetorician's shipwreck, and so on. Showpiece upon showpiece, parody upon parody—but particularly parody of those genres that depend upon oral presentation: epic, mime, tragedy, rhetorical "setpieces" *(suasoria).* Wherever one looks, the work suggests, and in suggesting seems to require, the mediation of a skilled interpretive voice.

If we imagine the *Satyricon* being read aloud, it is immediately apparent how the variety and virtuosity of the writing would be sustained and enlarged by the actor's voice; how the prose sections can, without the slightest unnaturalness, suddenly leap into poetry according to the requirements of Menippean satire. We understand, that is, how the voice of the reader by tone and emphasis guides the individual sections and fits them into the overall design, interpreting as he proceeds. In prose that is merely read to oneself, the narrative strategies—the picaresque pervert as narrator, the farrago of genres and styles—are ticklish; the slightest error, either overstatement or understatement, can be fatal. And with Petronius the tone of irony that everywhere attends the lovemaking and lovers' crises of Encolpius, Ascyltus, and the minion Giton is often missed by modern readers precisely because the voice that once sustained and shaped things is no longer audible. But in Latin the *sound* of irony is unmistakable, a melodramatic inflation, a stagey overblown diction that constantly undercuts—now lightly, now heavily—these perverse lovers. Their trials are saturated in the bathos of Greek romance (usually heterosexual) turned inside-out, and this makes them as lovers something less than wholly serious. So, too, elsewhere we *hear* Eumolpus and Agamemnon beautifully hoisted by their own petard, that frigid, thumping rhetoric of theirs. In the dinner scene at the house of Trimalchio, the vividness is doubled and the satire intensified if we can actually manage to hear the actor's voice informing Trimalchio's tantrums or lectures and, by accurate imitation or parody, emphasizing the contrasting styles of the speakers: the correct, sophisticated Latin of Encolpius against the crackling, racy Greek of Trimalchio and his freedmen guests, each style undercutting the other, correctness and sophistication set against ignorance and fatuity, but also warmth and color of humanity exposing the tacitly assumed superiority of the educated narrator.

Reading the *Satyricon* requires, as does almost all ancient literature, but in an even higher degree, the sense of a third dimension, the aural dimension. It is this third aural dimension, for instance, that clearly separates the ancient novel—all of it, not only Petronius and Apuleius, but the Greek romances as well—from the modern novel as a whole. Rhetoric,

the virtuosity of the practiced speaking voice and the virtuosity of ear that appreciates eloquence and can accurately distinguish its degree, is, as the *Satyricon* both reveals and teaches, the great achievement of Latin literature, and also its greatest curse.

IV

The *Satyricon* is a book obsessed by, saturated in, a quality or mode of existence that the Romans called, always pejoratively, *luxuria*. The central idea of *luxuria* is lushness; an exuberance of sensual life in things and animals, whence the idea of voluptuous excess, the rankness of proliferating indulgence, randiness, lechery, wanton profusion. Like *hybris* in Greek (which meant originally lushness, thence wanton excess, a kind of spilling over that, applied to moral life, expresses the idea of trespass, the sort of overfulfillment of one individual at the expense of others), *luxuria* offends the sense of natural economy and restraint, even austerity, which is everywhere encountered, for obvious reasons, in archaic cultures of poverty. This is not to suggest that Petronius' attitude is that of a severe puritanical moralist like the elder Cato—anything but. Yet, for whatever reason, Petronius invokes the idea throughout the whole surviving fragmentary work, not merely in the account of Trimalchio's dinner (*Cena Trimalchionis*). And it is important that we should try to understand why this is so. Nothing is gained by airily asserting that the *Satyricon* has no purpose whatever except to entertain a small circle of Neronian sophisticates; if this were so, we have to ask why Petronius should constantly suggest that he has larger ends in view—ends that may have very little to do with the mainstream of Roman satire, with its Horatian admonishment or savage denunciations à la Lucilius of the life of *luxuria*.

But the *Satyricon* is no less obsessed by *luxuria* than it is by death, and it is the intrication of these two themes that any responsible interpreter of the work is obliged to consider. Trimalchio, to take the chief example, is a man on whom the ideas of *luxuria* and death clearly weigh very heavily. Wealth and death are persistently, obsessively on his mind. And throughout the entire banquet at Trimalchio's, Petronius plays on these fundamental themes—mortality and money, surfeit and sickness, impotence and plenty—constantly intertwining them, with intricate variations, first gently, then insistently, and finally blending them into the blaring brasses of the apocalyptic funeral scene that closes the *Cena*. In technique, the *Cena* seems to be, and has always been regarded as, brilliant realism—a realism as unconventional in Latin literature as it is remarkable in execution. But there is a great deal more here than realism, a fact that has been most inadequately observed by Petronius' interpreters. Petronius' realism is in fact so immediately impressive, so astonishing in the context of Roman literature, that its very virtuosity has concealed the fact that the whole narrative is directed and controlled by extraordinary structural and thematic concentration. It is the structure—and the relation of theme to structure, even theme-*as*-structure—that the reader of Petronius must consider if he is to understand what this very original writer is trying to accomplish.

It is my belief that the *Satyricon*—all of it, not merely the *Cena*—even in its mutilated and fragmentary state, possesses unmistakable coherence and unity; and that, if we understand the structure of the tale and the power of thought expressed by the structure, we shall be forced to revise our estimate of Petronius' value. He has traditionally been regarded as a minor classical writer; it is my contention that Petronius is one of the greatest Latin writers, certainly the finest imaginative writer after Vergil and Ovid, and easily the greatest master of an admittedly odd form of Roman satire.

These are large claims, which many will resist or propose to modify. Any attempt to revise our estimate of a classic inevitably seems an impertinence. A reasonable economy, it may be said, supports the notion that sixty or seventy generations cannot have been wholly mistaken

about a classic. On the other hand, the classics, simply because they are classics, are particularly susceptible to distortion and stultification. They constantly serve, after all, extraliterary purposes, and these other "cultural" uses of the classics frequently interfere with critical judgment, preventing the reassessment, even the assessment, of the works. Many classics—I think of Sophocles—are far more subversive of Christian culture than we suppose, and for this reason interpretations that reveal subversiveness are particularly resisted. This is, oddly enough, also the case with the *Satyricon*, which is traditionally classified—alongside Boccaccio and Rabelais, and even alongside William Burroughs and Vladimir Nabokov—as a bawdy or surreptitious classic. Hence the critic who wants to argue, as I do, that the *Satyricon* is a fundamentally serious work of art, a genuine comedy of ideas, and perhaps a sophisticated Epicurean satire, is apt to sound as implausible as the critic who maintains that *Oedipus Rex* is really a farce. To some small extent the difficulties are compounded by the picture of Petronius that Tacitus has left us (and Hollywood has embellished)—that image of a refined, sybaritic, and corrupt courtier who ministered to Nero's pleasures and committed suicide like an Epicurean fop, languorously and courageously. A second objection is the fragmentary state of Petronius' work; we simply do not know whether the *Satyricon* was a big book or a small one, and this is unsettling. Doubtless the knowledge that the *Satyricon* is fragmentary has deterred critics from looking at it with analytical eyes, since no unity could be conclusively claimed. Certainly all I claim for my own interpretation is that it fits the fragments of the work as we have it, and fits them too well to be dismissed as accidental. Finally, there is the superbly controlled realism of Petronius' narrative, a realism so convincing and colloquial, combined with so fine a satirical eye for detail, that one is tempted to look no further, to suppose that surface is everything.

I myself translated the entire *Satyricon* without ever suspecting the presence of the pattern that now seems to me so incontrovertibly there. The *Satyricon* I tried to translate was in fact the familiar *Satyricon* of literary history: a splendid bawdy novel, told with fine realism and a typically Roman relish for high sound, whose purpose was literary parody and broad comic satire of Neronian Italy. In all this there is, fortunately, nothing radically wrong. It was the underlying pattern, the structure, that was missing from the interpretation.

To observe that structure, the reader should perhaps look first at the *Cena*, the only complete episode of the book and the one in which the pattern is most clearly elaborated in its two central themes.

The setting is the house of Trimalchio, in a Greek community somewhere in the bay of Naples. Invited to dinner are a group of Trimalchio's freedmen friends and that trio of picaresque perverts—the narrator Encolpius, his friend Ascyltos, and his minion Giton—with whose adventures the story is mostly concerned.

Trimalchio, as I noted earlier, is a man obsessed with death. And for that reason I should like to plant here, large as life, the apocalyptic funeral in which the whole episode culminates, and then to show from the beginning how the pattern is developed and sustained. Toward the close of the *Cena*, Trimalchio, thoroughly drunk, reads his will aloud in the presence of those people who are to inherit from him; then, with the entrance of Habinnas, a maker of grave monuments, a maker of tombs, he proceeds to order, in detail, his own tomb. Even this gruesome episode, however, is not enough to placate Trimalchio's obsession with mortality, and he concludes as follows, with full dispassion, his whole being concentrated on death:

"Take my word for it: money makes the man. No money and you're nobody. Big money, big man. That's how it was with yours truly: from mouse to millionaire.

"In the meantime, Stichus," he called to a slave, "go and fetch out the clothes I'm going to be buried in. And while you're at it, bring along some perfume and a sample of that wine I'm having poured on my bones."

Stichus hurried off and promptly returned with a white grave-garment and a very splendid robe with a broad purple stripe. Trimalchio told us to inspect them and see if we approved of the material. Then he added with a smile, "See to it, Stichus, that no mice or moths get into them, or I'll have you burned alive. Yessir, I'm going to be buried in such splendor that everybody in town will go out and pray for me." He then unstoppered a jar of fabulously expensive spikenard and had us all anointed with it. "I hope," he chuckled, "I like this perfume as much after I'm dead as I do now." Finally he ordered the slaves to pour the wine into the bowl and said, "Imagine that you're all present at my funeral feast."

The whole business had by now become absolutely revolting. Trimalchio was obviously completely drunk, but suddenly he had a hankering for funeral music too and ordered a brass band sent into the dining room. Then he propped himself on piles of cushions and stretched out full length along the couch. "Pretend I'm dead," he said, "say something nice about me." The band blared a dead march, but one of the slaves ... blew so loudly that he woke up the entire neighborhood. Immediately the firemen assigned to that quarter of town, thinking that Trimalchio's house was on fire, smashed down the door. ... Utter confusion followed ... and we rushed out of there as though the place were really in flames.
(77.6–78.8)

If this is the note on which the *Cena* closes, it is also the note on which it begins. When we first hear of Trimalchio, we are told that he has "a great big clock in his dining room and a uniformed bugler who blows a horn every hour so the old man won't forget how fast his time is slipping away." Death at the beginning and death at the end: death by bugles. The patterning will be obvious. But as the theme is developed, it begins to attach other themes to it, and then gradually to subsume them into a larger, more comprehensive theme: the satiety of body and spirit that is *luxuria*. Thus, there is almost a cyclical rhythm here of associations between thematic ideas. The thought of death invariably arouses the thought of wealth; wealth brings thoughts of defecation (for wealth is symbolically a satiety that cannot evacuate itself). Defecation in turn brings thoughts of death and money. And so the tropes pursue each other in an endless chain, but also relentlessly forward to the finale: the vision of satiety and *luxuria* as a description of an entire culture—or that version of a culture that one might call, to borrow from Tertullian, *Romanitas*—and its living death.

The note is at first struck gently. Trimalchio orders a silver skeleton brought into the dining room, and the servants flex it into "suggestive" postures, a scene that provides Trimalchio with the opportunity to recite a little poem on the theme of carpe diem—a drunken doggerel meditation on death:

> Nothing but bones, that's what we are,
> Death hustles us humans away.
> Today we're here and tomorrow we're not,
> So live and drink while you may.
>
> (34.10)

Now there is nothing in all this that is, for a Roman banquet, particularly unusual. Trimalchio's skeleton is merely a heightened version of the ancient custom of reminding people, even in the midst of their pleasures, of their mortality, a memento mori. Thus, dining-room mosaics from Pompeii and elsewhere show us reclining skeletons or skeletons with an accompanying Greek inscription ΓΝΩΦΙ ΣΑΥΤΟΝ ("Know thyself"). Trimalchio's only refinement is to confound things further by using a silver skeleton and having it flexed, perhaps into sexual postures. But the innovations themselves serve insensibly to widen the theme—to extend *luxuria* beyond money to sex and death. The one thing Trimalchio does not know is what might be called the mortal modalities; and his whole concept of a feast, based upon satiety to the point of nausea or constipation, bears out his immense lack of knowledge. So terrifying to him is his own habit of memento mori—the skeleton that reminds him of death—that he drives himself toward death by satiety. By eating he proposes to forget death, to "seize the day" and to live; he passionately desires life, but with every mouthful he takes, he tastes death. And this (thoroughly Epicurean) point is made, I think, with extraordinary comic neatness and firm realism as well, in Trimalchio's famous constipation speech at table:

> Well, anyone at table who wants to go has my permission, and the doctors tell us not to hold it in. . . . Take my word for it, friends, the vapors go straight to your brain. Derange your whole system. I know some who've died from being too polite and holding it in.
>
> (47.4–6)

This seems on the surface like simple realism, an exquisite parody of monumental vulgarity, but Petronius' point is also this: food consumed to the point of satiety is an instance, a symbol, of *luxuria*; the end of satiety is constipation; and flatulent vapors "go straight to your brain" and "Derange your whole system," and especially the reason, which should, at least in Epicurean ethics, control the appetites: "I know some who've died from . . . holding it in." That is, *luxuria* is death, extinction of the rational will.

That this is everywhere Petronius' essential symbolism can be seen by a brief glance at the obsessive *sexual* themes of the book. For it is odd, to say the least, that in the *Satyricon*, so commonly regarded as a naughty or orgiastic book, successful sex of any kind is rare, and that the impotence of the hero seems to provide the mainspring of the plot. There is also the fact of perversion, which, it will be remembered, is the subject of explicit condemnation as *unnatural* in Eumolpus' epic effusion on the decay of *Romanitas* (compare 119.19–27). Though it is doubtless true that classical attitudes toward homosexuality were more lenient than our own, they were not entirely permissive, especially in the stern context of Republican morality, and I am inclined to believe that perversion is a theme in this book precisely because Petronius believes that perversion and also impotence are typical symptoms of a luxurious and unnatural society. And in the field of sexual appetite, satiety, indulgence to the point of debility, appears as impotence. As constipation stands to food, so impotence stands to sexuality; both are the products of *luxuria* in a society that has forgotten its cultural modalities and cannot recover life, except by Epicurean *ascesis* (spiritual exercise or discipline)—by rediscovering the sense of true need, or necessary economy, in pleasure. The *pain* of loss is the pain that is suffered by the constipated Trimalchio and the impotent Encolpius, and although their pain is comic to the reader, to them it is total, since it affects the appetites to which their whole lives are in fact devoted. If your name happens to be Encolpius—which means, literally, something like "The Crotch"—and you are stricken with impotence, you are in some clear sense a dead man. Circe makes the point abundantly clear in the mocking letter she sends to Encolpius:

> I have heard doctors say that impotent men are incapable of even standing up straight. So, my dear, you must take good care of yourself, or your paralysis will be total. Never before have I seen a young man in such *infirm* health, or so close to death. One might almost say you were dead already.
>
> (129.5–6)

That this is Petronius' theme—the death that *luxuria* brings in sex, food, and language; that is, in the areas of energetic desire and social community—is made abundantly clear in the *Cena*. The evidence is, in fact, so overwhelming that I can deal with it in only the most schematic way. But those who reread the episode with the connection between satiety and *luxuria* and death firmly in mind will quickly recognize the deliberate symbolic intent beneath the comic realism.

A few examples: After Trimalchio leaves the room, the freedmen's conversation is begun by Seleucus, who, strange to say, has just come from the funeral of a man called Chrysanthus (which means Goldflower). Goldflower's funeral reminds Seleucus of what might be called a drunkard's modalities: "Just goes to show you. What are men anyway but balloons on legs, a lot of blown-up bladders? Flies, that's what we are. No, not even flies. Flies have something inside. But a man's a bubble." And on he goes, establishing the invidious modal verities that eventually appear inverted in the final scene, when the whole feast turns into a funeral.

Even small things assume the size of symbols when the context becomes so death-centered. Thus Trimalchio's famous remark on the Sibyl—"For with my own eyes I saw the Sibyl at Cumae, hanging in a bottle, and when little boys asked her 'Sibyl, what do you want?' she said, 'I want to die'"—begins to loom large, to look, in fact, remarkably like what Joyce called an "epiphany," one of those revelations designed to set before the reader, like an explosion, the "whatness" of a particular event. In a single comprehensive image, it binds together all the diverse thematic strands and reveals the central narrative idea at a higher level. In this case the epiphany is clearly the death of *Romanitas*—*Romanitas* turned inside out and upside down in a slavish Saturnalia—which we witness at Trimalchio's dinner.

There, the linking of death and wealth and food is persistent, overwhelming. One of the freedmen is described by another as follows: "What a life he had! But I don't envy him. And, you know, he had a nice respectable business. *Undertaking*. Ate like a king: boars roasted whole, pastry as tall as buildings, pheasants, chefs, the whole works." (38.14–15, italics added). In short, what might be called the *luxuria* syndrome. When Trimalchio brags about his silver, he confuses not only the minor conventions of taste, jumbling together scenes from mythology with contemporary gladiatorial games, but the major modalities. "I've got a hundred bowls," he says, "all engraved with the story of Cassandra: how she killed her sons, you know, and the kids are lying there dead so naturally that you'd think they were still alive."

Comic confusion, true; but also indicative of Trimalchio's governing inability to distinguish between the modalities.

In answer to Nicero's werewolf story, Trimalchio tells the tale of the slave who tried to fight off the witches, and the theme of death-in-life makes its appearance, introduced by the *luxuria* motif:

> When I was just a little slave with fancy curls— I've lived in the lap of luxury from my boyhood on, as coddled as they come—my master's pet slave happened to die one day. He was a jewel all right, a little pearl of perfection, clever as hell and good as good. Well, while his mother was tearing out her hair and the rest of us were helping out with the funeral, suddenly the witches started to howl. They sounded like a whole pack of hounds on the scent of a hare. Now at that time we had a slave from Cappadocia, a giant of a man, scared of nothing and strong as iron. That boy could have picked up a mad bull with one hand. Well, this fellow whips out his sword and rushes outside with his left arm wrapped in his cloak for a shield. The next thing we knew he had stabbed one of those wild women right through the guts—just about here, heaven preserve the spot! Then we heard groans and when we looked out, so help me, there wasn't a witch to be seen. Well, our big bruiser came stumbling in and collapsed on a bed. He was covered from head to toe with black and blue spots as though he'd been flogged, though we knew it was that evil hand that had touched him. We shut the door and went back to work. But when his mother went to give him a hug, she found there was nothing there but a bundle of straw. No heart, no guts, no anything. As I see it, the witches had made off with the body and left a straw dummy in its place. But it just goes to show you: there are witches and the ghouls go walking at night, turning the whole world upside down. As for our big meathead, after the witches brought him back, he was never the same again, and died raving mad a few days later.
>
> (63.3–10)

No heart, no guts, no anything. Diagnosis: *luxuria.*

At the close of Trimalchio's dinner, the crescendos gather with the kind of obsessive power that makes analysis unnecessary. The decisive turning point is the entrance of Habinnas; he too, like Seleucus, has just come from a funeral. He gives a few meager comments on the funeral, and Trimalchio interrupts him: "But what did they give you to *eat?*" There follows a detailed description of dinner by Habinnas, the real point of whose speech is one more instance of the modalities in confusion. If Trimalchio turns a feast into a funeral, Habinnas turns a funeral into a feast, completely confounding life and death. It is this confusion, and the related theme of the living dead, that fill out the rest of the episode. Thus Habinnas' appearance—and his profession—not only announce the theme but permit Trimalchio to discuss his tomb and then to read his will aloud in public. That will is Trimalchio's only power over the living; nothing else but that knowledge sustains either him or those who depend upon him. "Nobody in this house," he says, alluding to his dog Scylax, "loves me as much as that mutt." And he is right. It is for this reason that he turns the feast into a funeral, in the hope that the pretense of his own death will stimulate the love and gratitude, the immortality of memory, that he covets but does not know he covets. It is a terrible picture, but one done in full realism and charity. No heart, no guts, no anything. This is what has happened to this society. "Never has there been greater lust for life [*major cupido vitae*] or less care taken of it," says Pliny. The *numen*, the radiance in ordinary things, in simple necessities, the natural economy of Epicurean simplicity, has been destroyed by the compulsive insatiability of *luxuria* and the devouring terror of death.

Consider the parallel theme of brutalization. Like the life-in-death theme, it is introduced naturalistically first and then widened in its implications until it reaches its climax at Croton. The distaste with which Petronius' contemporary Seneca viewed the animal games of the Empire is well known. Spectators, gladiators, and animals all exist on a single common level; if anything, the spectators are lower than the animals. The emphasis in Petronius is extremely similar, as the quite Senecan passage in Eumolpus' effusion on the Civil War makes clear:

Rome rampant
on a victim world. . . .
　　　　New shapes of slaughter everywhere,
Peace a pool of blood.
　　　　　　With gold the hunters' snares are set:
driving through Africa, on and on; the hunters at
　　　Hammon,
and the beaters thrashing the thickets where the
　　　flailing tiger screams.
Hunters, hawkers of death. And the market for
　　　murder at Rome:
fangs in demand. At sea sheer hunger prowls the
　　　ships;
on silken feet the sullen tiger pads his gilded cage,
crouches at Rome, and leaps! And the man, gored
　　　and dying,
while the crowd goes wild.

(119.1; 13 ff.)

That the sentiment here is Petronian, however, and not merely a parody of Lucan or Seneca, becomes clear in the remarkably apposite speech of one of Trimalchio's freedmen guests. During Trimalchio's brief absence from the table, the freedmen speak their minds openly. First Ganymede makes a splendidly serio-comic speech on the decay of the times, rounding it off with the standard explanation of Rome's decay, that men have neglected the gods. To this the freedman Echion replies, somewhat irritably, that things are no worse than anywhere else—as though that argument disposed of Ganymede's complaint. As evidence of his contention, he enthusiastically describes some forthcoming gladiatorial games and a public handout. First the gladiatorial games:

And don't forget, there's a big gladiator show coming up the day after tomorrow. Not the same old fighters either; they've got a fresh shipment in and there's not a slave in the batch. You know how old Titus works. Nothing's too good for him when he lets himself go. Whatever it is, it'll be something special. I know the old boy well, and

he'll go whole hog. Just wait. There'll be cold steel for the crowd, no quarter, and the amphitheater will end up looking like a slaughterhouse. He's got what it takes too. When the old man died—and a nasty way to die, I'm telling you—he left Titus a cool million. Even if he spent ten thousand, he'd never feel it, and people won't forget him in a hurry either.

(45.4–6)

The phrase "like a slaughterhouse" catches us up and once again suggests the link between food and death. And the coarse relish of Echion's enthusiasm is ironically concentrated in the remarks about the death of "old Titus'" father; Echion seems utterly unaware that the gladiators' death in the arena might also be a "nasty way of dying." Petronius thereby allows us to see both Echion's callousness to the gladiators and his attitude to Titus' father as governed by a common obsessive hunger for death in all its forms. Death, food, and money: these are Echion's world. And the obsessive theme is thereupon repeated for emphasis, this time in even sharper terms—food and death, interminably:

Well, they say Mammaea's going to put on a spread. Mmmm, I can sniff it already. There'll be a nice little handout all around. And if he does, he'll knock old Norbanus out of the running for good. Beat him hands down. And what's Norbanus ever done anyway, I'd like to know. A lot of two-bit gladiators and half-dead at that: puff at them and they'd fall down dead. Why, I've seen better men tossed to the wild animals. A lot of little clay statues, barnyard strutters, that's what they were. One was an old jade, another was a clubfoot, and the replacement they sent in for him was half-dead and hamstrung to boot. There was one Thracian with some guts, but he fought by the book. And after the fight they had to flog the whole lot of them the way the mob was screaming, "Let 'em have it!" Just a pack of runaway slaves.

(45.10–12)

Now, as stated, Echion's garrulous enthusiasms here are little more than a dramatically vivid and concentrated statement of the moralist's commonplace of "bread and circuses." The mode is seemingly realism, but the irony of Petronius' structure and symbolism again cuts deeper. It reveals, first, what the satirist's denunciation does not, that the man Echion (his name is Greek and means "snake") is literally brutalized by what he sees and what he eats, and this brutality is confirmed in the animal vigor of his language. In the second place, it shows starkly that "bread and circuses" are merely diverse expressions of the same fact—the satiety that is death. Satiety of food kills; satiety of death kills; satiety in the *Satyricon* is to become animal, to become all belly, pig, or hog, wolf, snake, or cannibal.

That this is so the sheer volume of animal metaphors clearly indicates. "Women," says a freedman, "they're a race of kites." The Zodiac dish, as explained by Trimalchio, systematically equates men's fates with their animal equivalents. Trimalchio places nothing on his sign, which is Cancer, because he fears "queering" it, inviting disaster. The meaning he gives his sign is that he, like the crab, is at home on land or sea, because his possessions lie in both elements. The bad omen he tries to avert is death, death by Cancer, the inward crab. His fate is, of course, both: the cancer wealth that kills. "We're big lions at home, and scared foxes in public," comments a freedman on his own political hypocrisy. The centerpiece of the brutalization theme in the *Cena*, however, is Niceros' story of the werewolf, the soldier who turns wolf and slaughters the sheep. "The place looked like a butcher shop, blood all over," says Melissa, and we remember the arena, and how it is that men are turned into animals: by literal metamorphosis, by being eaten alive. And Habinnas promptly makes the echo explicit. Describing the funeral feast he has attended, Habinnas says that the pièce de résistance was bear meat, which is to say strong meat. It was so strong that his wife lost her supper, but Habinnas put down about a pound of it, because, as he says, "it reminds me of wild boar, and besides . . . if bears eat men, why shouldn't men

eat bears?" The transitions are revealing, as is the whole speech. Between wild boar and bear, there is no difference; satiety and savagery both equal death. Habinnas means by bears here precisely the bears of the arena, to whom criminals were fed. That is, Habinnas will be the thing he eats, just as Echion will be the thing he watches. But if bears eat men, what is the word for men who eat man-eating bears? Cannibals, surely.

If it were not for the scene at Croton, all this might perhaps seem merely so much tiresome ingenuity. But at Croton all the themes of brutalization are gathered up with supreme horror in a cannibal apocalypse. That cannibalism is the master metaphor is obvious. Croton itself is described as "a place which is like a countryside ravaged by the plague, a place in which you will see only two things: the bodies of those who are eaten and the carrion crows who eat them" (*oppidum tamquam in pestilentia campos, in quibus nihil aliud est nisi cadavera quae lacerantur aut corvi qui lacerant:* 116.9). And the episode as a whole concludes with the reading of Eumolpus' will, which requires the people of Croton to become in fact what they symbolically are: cannibals. Here realism and symbolism combine to produce an effect of grotesque horror that is, I think, unique in literature prior to Jonathan Swift. Here are Eumolpus' words:

With the exception of my freedmen . . . all those who come into money by the terms of my will shall inherit only upon satisfaction of the following condition: they must slice up my body into little pieces and swallow them down in the presence of the entire city. . . .

We know that in certain countries there exist laws which compel a dead man's relatives to eat his body. So rigorously, in fact, are these laws enforced that men who die of sickness or disease frequently find themselves reproached by their relatives for having made their meat inedible. So I warn my friends not to disregard my last wishes, but to eat my body as heartily as they damned my soul.

I am not in the least disturbed by any fear that your stomachs may turn. They will obey you quite without qualms so long as you promise them years of blessings in exchange for one brief hour of nausea. Just close your eyes and imagine that, instead of human flesh, you're munching a million. If that isn't enough, we'll concoct some gravy that will take the taste away. As you know, no meat is really very tasty anyway; it all has to be sauced and seasoned with great care before the reluctant stomach will keep it down. And if it's precedents you want, there are hundreds of them. The people of Saguntum, for instance, when Hannibal besieged them, took to eating human flesh, and did so, moreover, without the slightest hope of getting an inheritance out of it. And when a terrible famine struck Petelia, the people all became cannibals, and the only thing they gained from their diet was that they weren't hungry anymore. And when Scipio captured Numantia, the Romans found a number of mothers cuddling the half-eaten bodies of their children in their laps.

(141.2 ff.)

Like *hybris, luxuria* affects a man so that he eventually loses his sense of his specific function, his *virtus* or *arete*. He surpasses himself, luxuriating into other things and forms. It is for this reason that the *Satyricon* is so full of luxuriant falsenesses, pretenses, fakes, metamorphoses. Forms of life are jumbled incongruously, transformed, degenerated. If men are bestialized both literally and metaphorically, Trimalchio's chef Daedalus is a wizard of changes, making "pigeons out of bacon, doves from ham, and chicken from pigs' knuckles." Out of a roast boar comes a flock of thrushes; out of another tumble sausages in imitation of intestines. Transvestism is everywhere: Encolpius walks with mincing steps, whorelike; Ascyltos' lips are painted scarlet; Eumolpus complains poetically of "the mincing gait, effeminate, the girl-men, their hair curried to silk, and the clothes, so many and so strange, to mew our manhood up" (119.24–26). If it is not perversion, it is posing, or playacting, or simulation. Thus Giton feigns suicide and castration; Trimalchio apes the equestrian; a painted dog

terrifies a man; Eumolpus plays slave owner. And everywhere the language of mime and rhetorical tragedy take over in situations of love or terror or passion, subverting them, emptying them of meaning. Hypocrisy, by etymology the actor's nature, touches everything. And behind hypocrisy stands *luxuria,* that abundance and satiety that make men lose their sense of human function and turn unnatural or bestial.

Associated with *luxuria* in food and sexuality is *luxuria* in language. In contrast to rhetoric or the *bella figura* of language grown luxuriant, Petronius sets his own ideal of "pure speech" *(sermo purus)* and "verbal candor" *(lingua candida).* The theme opens with Encolpius' splendid tirade against the Fury-haunted language of the schools, continues in the parody of epic poetry put in Eumolpus' mouth, and concludes at Croton. Encolpius' tirade is directed particularly against excess in style, the so-called "Asianic" or "opulent" manner represented by those "twin Atreidae" of fustian, the rhetoricians Agamemnon and Menolaus:

Action or language, it's all the same: great sticky honeyballs of phrases, every sentence looking as though it had been plopped and rolled in poppyseed and sesame. A boy gorged on a diet like this can no more acquire real taste than a cook can stop stinking. What's more, if you'll pardon my bluntness, it was you rhetoricians who more than anyone else strangled true eloquence. By reducing everything to sound you concocted this ridiculous drivel, with the result that eloquence lost its sinew and died.

But in those great days when Sophocles and Euripides invariably found the exact word, talent had not yet been cramped into the mold of these set-speeches of yours. Long before you academic pedants smothered genius with your arrogance, Pindar and the nine lyric poets were still so modest that they declined even to attempt the grand Homeric manner. Nor are my objections based on poetry alone. What about Plato or Demosthenes? I never heard it said of them that they ever submitted to your sort of formal training. No, great language is chaste [*pudica*] language—if you'll let me use a word like "chaste" in this connection—

not turgidity and worked-up purple patches. It soars to life through a natural, simple loveliness. But then, in our own time, that huge flatulent rhetoric [*ventosa istaec et enormis loquacitas*] of yours moved from Asia to Athens. Like a baleful star, it blighted the minds of the young; their talents shriveled at the very moment when they might have taken wing and gone on to greatness. And once the standards of good speech were corrupted, eloquence stopped dead or stuttered into silence. Who, I ask you, has achieved real greatness of style since Thucydides and Hyperides? Poetry herself is sick, her natural glow of color leached away. All the literary arts, in fact, cloyed with this diet of bombast [*omnia quasi eodem cibo pasta*], have become stunted or have died, incapable of whitening naturally into an honest old age. And in painting you see the same decay: on the very day when Egyptian arrogance dared to reduce it to a set of sterile formulas, that great art died.

(1.3–2.9)

What we should notice here is the way in which the terms used to describe *luxuria* in language are skillfully transferred from the related *luxuriae* of food and sex. Language in rhetorical use is like "great sticky honeyballs of phrases." When Encolpius says that "eloquence lost its sinew," he means sexual sinew. Rhetorical language is impotent. For the same reason he tells us that "great language is chaste language" and then, as though to stress the point, adds: "if you'll let me use a word like 'chaste' in this connection." As for poetry, it is "sick," and all the other literary arts, "cloyed with this diet of bombast," have become stunted or have died. In sum, *luxuria* of language is on the same level as *luxuria* in food and sex; all three are symptoms of satiety and excess, and all three culminate in death unless controlled.

It is clearly part of Petronius' design that the section dealing with rhetoric, mostly lost, should be set against the *Cena*, with its pointed display of freedmen speech in all its vulgarity and energy. What is Petronius' attitude toward freedmen speech? It is not easy to say, but there are, I think, reliable hints. That it was genial snobbery, as many scholars seem to think,

strikes me as quite untenable, as a view borrowed from Tacitus' portrait of the fastidious Neronian courtier. Two factors militate against it. First is the fact that Petronius' effort here is unparalleled in Roman literature, and this tells us something about the bent of his mind, that he was not willing simply to indulge in contempt for vulgarity, but described it in minute and loving detail. In a Mandarin literature like Latin, the fact is doubly unusual. Petronius' narrative, that is, deals precisely with those people who have traditionally been regarded, in both Latin and Italian, as "unworthy" of art, their lives too sordid to be redeemed by rhetoric. The second hint is to be found in Encolpius' remarks to Agamemnon, when he inveighs against Sophistic education as artificial and complains that it keeps children "utterly ignorant of real life. The common experience is something they never see or hear" (*nihil ex his, quae in usu habemus, aut audiunt aut vident*). When one speaks in this way, it is clear that one has something like "common culture" in mind, and also a common language—which is the sign of an integrated culture. It is my belief that Petronius views the speech of freedmen with amusement and delight in its energy—is there anything more self-evident in the whole *Satyricon* than the sheer electrical joy of language?—and that he saw in it something like the possibility of renewal, a source of freedom, invigoration, and reform for a language grown artificial, rhetorical, and stale. I cannot, of course, prove such a point, and I realize that such a view is at odds with the older view of Latin literature. But then so is the *Satyricon*. And in no point is it more unusual than in this relish for life in language, however vulgar, and the sympathy that is, despite satire and parody, diffused over all the freedmen alike.

What is Petronius' point, then, in the vulgar Latin of the *Cena*? Is he merely making the point that freedmen's culture is a hit-or-miss affair, compounded of bad mythology, garbled Vergil, vulgar astrology—in short, high-culture-in-caricature? That is, to be sure, one of his points. But he is also telling us, I think, of the failure of a Mandarin culture to diffuse itself, to make itself available. And his point is as much the snobbery and parasitism of the educated as the vulgarity of the freedmen. If Trimalchio is capable of applauding an atrocious recitation of Vergil, Encolpius applies, with shocking effect, Vergil's splendid description of Dido's reception of Aeneas in the underworld—"she turned her head away and gazed upon the ground" (132.11)—to his own impotence. If the freedmen vulgarize, Encolpius, Eumolpus, and Agamemnon *desecrate* the culture they profess. The point is important, I think, since it emphasizes the equality of educated and uneducated in a world whose sole standard is wealth. If the freedmen show that they secretly hate culture, Encolpius and Eumolpus are hypocrites and snobs whose culture is no more than veneer. In practice, they betray it on every possible occasion.

With this in mind, consider Eumolpus' preface to that appalling parody of Lucan that Petronius assigns to him:

> Serious poets, of course, despise this dilettante approach to their art; from hard experience they know that the imagination is utterly incapable of conceiving, let alone producing, a real poem unless the poet's mind has been literally saturated in the poetry of the past. Cliché and cheap language, for instance, must be ruthlessly resisted. No great poetry has ever been founded on colloquial language, language that has been, so to speak, debased and corrupted by popular usage. Its motto is that of Horace: "I loathe the vulgar crowd, and shun it."
>
> (118.3–4)

These words are, I think, an accurate description of traditional upper-class Roman attitudes toward literary culture, and their parody in the poem that Eumolpus claims is based upon such principles makes Petronius' lack of sympathy evident. Needless to say, the poem does not necessarily impugn the principles, but Petronius here suggests, I think, that the luxurious and self-indulgent language that Eumolpus regards as traditional and elegant is in fact more corrupt than the language against which he protests. And its corruption is clear in the luxuriousness it exhibits even while excoriating the death of a culture by general *luxuria*. Typically, Petronius makes any part of his work do double duty, and this epic on the Civil War is no exception. It is not only that Eumolpus' rank and tortured language prove his poetic point—that *luxuria* did destroy Rome—but that Eumolpus elsewhere is a flagrant practicer of the same moral vices he so roundly lashes here, particularly pederasty. He is the hypocrite of a traditional culture, whose values have become words without substance—that is, rhetoric.

This theme of *luxuria* in language is finally rounded off at Croton. Our evidence is fragmentary, a single unfinished sentence, but it makes the point with great effectiveness. Eumolpus, playing the role of a wealthy old man, makes his announcement that the people of Croton must turn cannibal in order to inherit from him; then the text says merely, "Gorgias stood ready to manage the funeral...." Petronius' names are almost always used to carry meaning, either ironic or descriptive. In this case the meaning is descriptive: Gorgias was the actual founder of Sophistic rhetoric, the man who first systematically developed the artificial style—*luxuria*-in-language—and whose style later became a model of the exuberant Asian manner. Gorgias, as Petronius observes, is always professionally willing to assist at a funeral. That is his profession: undertaker of language.

One incident in particular—the speech of the freedman Echion—reveals Petronius' attitude toward culture and class, as well as the extraordinary economy of his narrative. Childlessness is, among the Roman moralists, the typical identifying trait of an unnatural society organized on the principle of *luxuria*. It is also an overt theme in the *Satyricon*, culminating in the cannibalism at Croton, and the final sentence of the book: "When Scipio captured Numantia, the Romans found a number of mothers cuddling the half-eaten bodies of their children in their laps." The Numantine mothers could at least have pleaded necessity, whereas the Roman mother can only plead profit. And, as a general rule, children appear in the *Satyricon* only to be prostituted by their parents or tutors, either literally, as in the story of Philomela, or figuratively in the words of the rhetorician Agamemnon: "As with everything else, even the children are sacrificed on the altar of [their parents'] ambition" (4.2). Typically, these prostituted children are less innocent and more corrupt than their corruptors: one thinks of Giton, or the children of Philomela, or the boy in the Pergamene episode. These are, of course—like Nabokov's Lolita—the children of satire: they exist as exaggerations, meant to make a special shocking point about the toxicity and pervasiveness of *luxuria*. There is, however, one instance—and only one—in the book that deals with something like normal, everyday paternity, and this is the case of the freedman Echion. For these very reasons, its uniqueness and its realism, the account has a particular significance.

Echion's speech begins as a rambling answer to Ganymede's attack on the times, and its relish for gladiators and death is part of the overall theme. Before long Echion's vulgar relish for the games evidently brings a pointed yawn from the "refined" Agamemnon, and Echion replies in some irritation:

> Well, Agamemnon, I can see you're thinking, "What's that bore blabbing about now?" You're the professor here, but I don't catch you opening your mouth. No, you think you're a cut above us, so you just sit there and smirk at the way we poor men talk. Your learning's made you a snob.
>
> (46.1)

One notes parenthetically here that Petronius' genius for dialogue lies partly in his managing to give, simply by warping the speech of the speaker, the sense of the response to the speech. Echion thereupon proceeds to ask Agamemnon to his house, an invitation that must have met with doubtful response from Agamemnon since Echion promptly reassures him,

"Don't you worry, you'll find food." Theme and realism merge; it is only the promise of a good meal that can move Agamemnon, just as Agamemnon adapts his rhetoric to the hunger of his audience. Echion knows his man. He then proceeds:

> You remember that little shaver of mine? Well, he'll be your pupil one of these days. He's already doing division up to four, and if he comes through all right, he'll sit at your feet someday. Every spare minute he has, he buries himself in his books. He's smart all right, and there's good stuff in him. His real trouble is his passion for birds. I killed three of his pet goldfinches the other day and told him the cat had got them. He found some other hobby soon enough. And, you know, he's mad about painting. And he's already started wading into Greek, and he's keen on his Latin.... The older boy now, he's a bit slow.... Every holiday he spends at home, and whatever you give him, he's content. So I bought him some of those big red law books. A smattering of law, you know, is a useful thing around the house. There's money in it too. He's had enough literature, I think. But if he doesn't stick it out in school, I'm going to have him taught a trade. Barbering or auctioneering, or at least a little law. The only thing that can take a man's trade away is death. But every day I keep pounding the same thing into his head: "Son, get all the learning you can. Anything you can learn is money in the bank.... Take my word for it, son, there's a mint of money in books, and learning a trade never killed a man yet."
>
> (46.3–7)

One notices immediately the delicate double viewpoint that Petronius brings to bear upon the monologue. Echion's younger boy is simply a reader, one of those wonderful childlike readers, who read because they are rapt away, quite without motive, for the sheer joy of it, in a state of what one might call free innocence, the condition of all true education. To Echion, however, the innocence is regrettable because impractical. It is on a level with the three goldfinches, and he reveals his gratuitous practical brutality in killing them. And so he rambles on, everywhere advancing his own motives and finally culminating with the practicality that education is good because it makes money. Indeed the whole section is a superb example of Petronius' skill in mingling and reporting double realities. Echion the gladiator enthusiast has a son who reads and keeps pet goldfinches (which his father kills); it is a familiar but subtly observed pattern. The picture of Echion himself is remarkably vivid: an affectionate father, proud of his children, coarse-natured, with a strong streak of practical brutality. He has an awareness of money that is downright Roman, hard-headed and shrewd; he feels ambiguous toward culture—he thinks he admires it, but actually despises it unless it produces money. But it is important to note the *rounded* quality of the portrait—we are being offered not a stock portrait of freedman vulgarity, but a portrait based upon clear, realistic contempt, with some sympathy. There is nothing exaggerated: such, we are meant to think, must have been a middle-class freedman. If Echion does not understand the fineness of his son's nature, the point is that these things go together, that where there is death, there is life; too much brutality creates a reaction of gentleness; coarse fathers often have fine children. It is an important point.

Can we leave the *Satyricon* at that? The moralist Petronius, preoccupied to the point of nausea and despair by the hopelessness of a culture corrupted by *luxuria*; a culture that turns men into the living dead, that degrades, desecrates, and finally annuls; a culture without joy, without hope, without animal faith? This is where the critic Helen Bacon, for instance, leaves him. In Bacon's own words:

> Sweeney, Doris, Mr. Eugenides, Encolpius, Trimalchio, Circe, Giton,
>
> De Bailhache, Fresca, Mrs. Cammel, whirled
> Beyond the circuit of the shuddering Bear in
> fractured atoms . . .
>
> a polyglot society with no realities but money, and frustration. The over-educated Greek and the Syrian freedman are atoms adrift in the heterogeneous world which Rome ruled without uniting. The safe, parochial standards of their individual cultures have been invalidated, by science, by comparison with other cultures, by the sheer brutality of experience in a world of famine, where luxury tries to tease the satiated senses into the appearance of life. The Sibyl is the symbol for this waste land as well as Eliot's. With this difference, perhaps, that to Petronius she does not seem to suggest the possibility of rebirth when the longed-for death has been achieved. . . . The heart is dead. Love is an attitude.
>
> The "Satyricon," like the "Waste Land," contains a series of rapes, seductions, intrigues, and esoteric sexual adventures in high and low life. And here too is sensuality without joy, satiety without fulfillment, degradation without grief or horror.
>
> The traditional comparison to Aristophanes, Rabelais, and Sterne is as inappropriate for Trimalchio and Encolpius as it is for Sweeney and Doris. Real laughter is rare in Petronius. There is little joy. The characters lack just what Eliot's characters lack—the feeling of being alive, the sense of good and evil.[1]

It is all a little depressing. Right up to a point, Miss Bacon sees for the first time that the *Satyricon* is not a symptom of a corrupt society, but a penetrating *description* of it. And she also sees what almost no other scholar has seen—that Petronius' narrative, though realistic on the surface, is controlled with extraordinary symbolic and structural skill. But when she forces the whole book to yield the Christian, almost Manichaean, desolation of Eliot's *Waste Land*, she goes, I think, deeply wrong. And when, in order to support this view, she denies that the *Satyricon* is basically comedy and that the characters are alive, I think she misrepresents her text, its plain comic ambitions, and its extraordinary liveliness in both life and language. Whatever else readers have made of Petronius,

---

[1] "The Sibyl in the Bottle," *Virginia Quarterly Review* 34:262–276 (Spring 1958). Despite my interpretative disagreement with Bacon, her article represents a real breakthrough in our understanding of Petronius, and I am indebted to her for stimulating, in reaction, the reflections that eventually led me to the interpretation presented here.

nobody has ever denied him a fundamental gaiety; the gaiety may seem wicked or innocent, but "gaiety" is the word for the book. Indeed it is this very gaiety that has prevented scholars from seeing what is, I maintain, so obviously there—the searching analysis of the death throes of classical *Romanitas*. Bacon seems to assume that comedy and moral seriousness are incompatible, that gaiety and the description of cultural decay are incompatible. She is, I believe, wrong.

Is it really true that there is little laughter in the *Satyricon*? How, in that case, are we meant to respond to Trimalchio's table conversation on the topic of constipation? That it is vulgar? Nothing more? When Encolpius says, "I don't know whether to be angrier with my mistress for seducing my boy, or with my boy for seducing my mistress," are we to note, with appropriate solemnity, that Petronius is describing the quandary of sexual ambiguity? Is the story of Philomela and her children only satirical description? What Bacon fails to notice is that Petronius' charity is the source of his comic attitude—a charity based upon realism; a resolute cheerfulness in the face of the facts of human nature—and it is this good cheer that represents him best. The good cheer derives from relation to the realities, the modalities, and not from sick indulgence of degeneration like Seneca's, or narrow-minded and heavy-handed denunciation in the manner of Juvenal.

What about the characters? Do they "lack the feeling of being alive, ... of good and evil"? The very words are revealing, with their suggested equation of "life" and "the sense of good and evil." A sense of good and evil is precisely what these characters don't have; life they *do* have. Like children, precisely; what this amounts to is nothing less than an improbable kind of innocence, a *comic* innocence in which immoral actions are incongruously set against a fundamental and rather charming naiveté. Encolpius' deepest trait is innocence; he is either beyond or below good and evil. His love for Giton is pederasty, true, but it is also love. And

what is more, it is unrequited love, as Petronius takes pains to show us. If we recognize Encolpius' deformity and pathos, we are also meant to recognize that he is not a monster, but pathetic. For all his defects, Encolpius has the basic gifts of life: love, generosity—combined with poverty and bad luck. He is a marginal man, like Augie March, or even a dissolute antique Huck Finn, one of those who refuse to turn cannibal, to ape the ape, to brutalize themselves. With the gift of life, he has other traits that belong to death. Eumolpus may be an atrocious poet, a lower-class Lucan, a hypocrite, a pederast, and a thief, but he also has a certain style; he is, like Nikita Khruschev in Robert Frost's description, "a grand old ruffian." And however we may condemn these characters, we need to bear in mind that they are all fictive devices for bringing society to account. Just as Nabokov in *Lolita* shows us that poor old Humbert is an amateur of vice compared to Lolita, that subteenage professional, so Petronius sets his rascals and rogues in sharp contrast to society's greater immoralism, hypocrisy, and vulgarity. Compared to the people of Croton, Eumolpus and Encolpius are likeable and innocent conmen, the bearers of poetic justice.

Another example is the treatment of Lichas, not a character anybody would call sympathetic. Merchant, captain, and pervert par excellence, he is cruel, jealous, proud, and unforgiving—even his very name is an obscenity, though he too has famous forebears. But when he dies in the wreck of his own ship, and his body drifts slowly shoreward, the tone of the narrative suddenly changes. Encolpius feels the tears tugging at his eyes, and reflects: "But drowned! To think our every human hope must someday come to this, this corpse of great ambitions, this poor drowned body our dreams! O gods, and was this once a man, this thing that floats now merely?" (115.10). Then he recognizes that the body is that of Lichas and bursts into tears, weeping openly, unashamedly, at the death of his enemy: "O god, how far he lies from his destination! Why, doom is everywhere, at any time....Why, if you calculate our chances in this life, what do they cry but death? Shipwreck is everywhere" (115.15–16).

Encolpius is given to melodramatic outbursts and to rhetorical *topoi,* or commonplaces, like this one, but the language here is not that of melodrama; it is that of mourning. Petronius crowns the death of the despicable Lichas with a funeral oration, and what gives this oration force and power is precisely the sense that Lichas, for all his crippled life, carries, in his death, the whole tragedy of human existence, helplessness, and futility. We feel what we feel at the funerals of strangers: that our lives and deaths are involved in theirs, that all men are mourned in every funeral. If life refuses us solidarity, death does not. Encolpius' compassion is total, not sentimental. And behind it stands, I think, Petronius' extraordinary charity. Total clarity and ample charity, with nothing missing.

Finally, there is the story—I almost want to say "parable"—of the widow of Ephesus (111 ff.). In context an urbanely cynical Milesian fable on the inconstancy of women, it also immediately and forcibly suggests a wider symbolic meaning. When Christopher Fry based his play *A Phoenix Too Frequent* upon the widow of Ephesus, he did no more, I think, than dramatize the obvious symbolic intent of Petronius' tale. The symbolism itself is still another of Petronius' vivid oxymorons, but one this time weighed on the side of life rather than death: the symbolism of love-in-the-tomb, of life rising phoenix-like from its own ashes. Against Trimalchio, who turns a feast of living men into a funeral, is set the story of the soldier who celebrates his marriage in the tomb. The design could hardly be more schematic, and it is confirmed by the convergence of all the familiar themes of the *Cena,* but this time inverted. Thus, whereas the *Cena* insists that satiety is death, the story of the widow insists upon the stimulus conferred on desire by denial, frugality, *ascesis.* The widow's vigil for her dead husband, we learn, takes her to the point of starvation before she is tempted by the soldier's

food. As for the soldier's supper, it was, we are told, a "little one," "a frugal repast," but evidently it satisfied. At least Petronius immediately proceeds: "Well, you know what temptations are normally aroused on a full stomach. So the soldier, mustering all those blandishments by means of which he had persuaded the lady to live, now laid determined siege to her virtue" (112.1). And the result of his siege is, as we know, the consummation of love in the tomb, love doing its work beside the corpse of the dead husband.

Consummation: the very word itself, set against the pervasive theme of sexual impotence, is revealing. And when to the fact of consummation we add the only instance in the book of satisfied heterosexual love, the force is increased. Here Petronius seems to be saying, I give you an image of the rebirth of human life; here are the hope and energy that everywhere else are baffled by satiety and thereby transformed into death. In place of perversion, natural marriage; in place of impotence, consummation; in place of unappeasable appetite, satisfied desire; in place of death, life. It is the same miracle that occurs elsewhere in the book, but always oppressed by circumstances, or overwhelmed by its context—the flock of thrushes that bursts from the stomach of the roast boar served at Trimalchio's; the gentle goldfinch-and-book-loving son of the coarse freedman Echion. And finally, it is thematically bound up with those splendid bursts of poetry that throughout the book seem to hover over the action like blessings of fertility or shapes of irrecoverable felicity, of lost power and innocence. Thus, when Encolpius and Circe make their first ill-fated attempt at love, the scene is haunted not only by the memory of Odysseus and another Circe, but of the even greater scene that all human love-making imitates, in fertility and naturalness:

Such flowers as once on Ida's peak the fruitful earth in gladness spilled, when Jupiter with Juno lay in lawful love, and all his heart was touched to flame: bursting roses blew, and violets, and rushes, and from the fields, like snow, the sudden lilies laughed. Such earth, it seemed, as summons Venus to the grass: the light spilled brighter, bursting on our hidden love.

(127.9)

Like everything in Petronius, the effect of these miraculous descents of the poetic dove is multiple. They are emblems of lost power, divine memories against which the corruption of the present is measured, but with which the future is also blessed. Eating and sex, sex and food, it is all rehearsal, repetitions designed to recover the old rapture and rediscover the divine presence, the *numen*, with which the world once was filled, the world of the beginnings, *illud tempus*. Every whore, every woman in love, recalls Circe; every Encolpius has the hope of being Odysseus; this is a countryside where, as Quartilla says, "one might more easily meet a god than a man." That is the *hope*, not the *fact*; but it is a hope of which Petronius, even in the midst of so much degradation and death, never loses sight. If society has organized itself around the satiety that brings death, human hope is to rediscover the old pagan landscape, the radiance here and now, in which everything had *numen*, and nobody needed eternal life because life itself was good and had God in it. As a description of cultural crisis, the *Satyricon* is as extraordinary an achievement as Joyce's *Ulysses*, and is as fundamentally bright, cheerful, and gay. But Petronius is also, I believe, the last great witness to the pagan sense of life, and the last classical author in whom we can feel the firmness of moral control that underlies the Greek tragedians.

Selected Bibliography

TEXTS

Petronii Arbitri Satirarum Reliquiae, edited by Franz Bücheler. Berlin, 1862.
Petronii Arbitri Satyricon cum apparatu critico, ed-ited by Konrad Müller. Munich, 1961. The best edition of the text.
Le Satiricon de Pétrone, edited by E. Ernout. 5th ed. Paris, 1962. Text and translation.
Il Satyricon de Petronio, edited by E. Paratore. Florence, 1933. Introduction and commentary.

TRANSLATIONS

Arrowsmith, William, trans. *The Satyricon of Petronius*. New York, 1962. Mentor Classics. With introduction.
Heseltine, Michael, trans. *Petronius*. Cambridge, Mass., and London, 1969. Loeb Classical Library.
Sullivan, John P., trans. *Petronius: The Satyricon and the Fragments*. Baltimore, 1965. With introduction.

CRITICAL STUDIES

Auerbach, E. "Fortunata." In *Mimesis: The Representation of Reality in Western Literature*. Princeton, 1953.
Bacon, Helen. "The Sibyl in the Bottle." *Virginia Quarterly Review* 34:262–276 (Spring 1958). Illuminating and adventurous analysis of the *Satyricon* as an account of the death-wish of Roman culture.
Bagnani, G. *Arbiter of Elegance*. Phoenix, supplement 2. Toronto, 1954.
Fröhlke, Franz. *Petron. Struktur und Wirklichkeit*. Frankfurt, 1977. Frequently brilliant and enlightening analysis of structural implications of traditional literary elements and expressive form in Petronius.
Highet, Gilbert. "Petronius the Moralist." *Transactions of the American Philological Association* 72:176–194 (1941). Pioneering effort to present Petronius as a serious satirist and moralist in the great Roman tradition.
Raith, Oskar. *Petronius: ein Epikureer*. Nurnberg, 1963. Detailed and well-researched study of the Epicurean tradition in which Petronius wrote; indicates that Petronius' Epicureanism was heterodox and syncretic, not doctrinal.
Rankin, H. D. *Petronius the Artist. Essays on the Satyricon and its Author*. The Hague, 1971. Informed, sensible, intelligent discussion; the historical emphasis is particularly rewarding.
Rose, K. F. C. *The Date and Author of the Satyricon.*

Mnemosyne, supplement 16. Leiden, 1971. Most thorough and convincing discussion of this topic to date.

Sullivan, J. P. *The Satyricon of Petronius: A Literary Study.* London, 1968. Basically a philological study, disappointingly conventional in method and conclusion.

Walsh, Patrick G. *The Roman Novel. The "Satyricon" of Petronius and the "Metamorphoses" of Apuleius.* Cambridge, 1970. Sturdily British commonsensical discussion; denies Petronius any artistic aim beyond entertaining his friends. Displays little critical imagination.

————. "Was Petronius a Moralist?" *Greece and Rome* 21:181 (1974).

Zeitlin, Froma. "Petronius as Paradox: Anarchy and Artistic Integrity." *Transactions of the American Philological Association* 102:631–684 (1971). Excellent discussion of the form of the *Satyricon;* attempts to account for the multifariousness of the work; rich in genuinely critical insight.

WILLIAM ARROWSMITH

PERSIUS

(A.D. 34–62)

JUVENAL

(A.D. 60?–140?)

PERSIUS AND JUVENAL are the two poetic satirists who have survived from the period of early imperial Rome (A.D. 1–150), and there is every indication that they were the best. Alike in some respects, they are more striking in their differences. They agree in choosing poetic satire as their literary form and writing nothing but satire. They are similar in their backgrounds: both belonged to respectable middle-class families and were brought up some distance from Rome, to which they came to complete their educations. Both immersed themselves in literature and reacted strongly, they claimed, to the prevailing trends in poetry of their periods, and in part their satire springs from reaction to what they considered outrageously poor poetry on trivial topics. Nobody, however, would ever mistake a satire by Persius for one by Juvenal, and part of my interest in this essay will be in defining and discussing the differences between the two and the flexibility of Roman poetic satire that could embrace two such distinct poetic talents as Persius and Juvenal.

PERSIUS

General Background

Not long after Persius died, a Latin scholar put together a brief biography of him, and we gratefully use its data to place Persius in a context. Born 4 December 34, during the last years of Tiberius, Aules Persius Flaccus passed his first twelve years in the Tuscan town of Volterra, not far from modern Florence. He presumably was too young to be aware of the enormities of Caligula, being happily insulated by distance, and Claudius had brought stability again to Rome and Italy when in 46–47 Persius went to the capital to get the advanced education that his wealth and status demanded. That stability did not long survive, but there is no sign of external disturbance in the apparently quiet life of study and poetic creativity that Persius was able to lead even in Rome and at the estate on the Appian Way just outside the city where he regularly worked and where, not quite twenty-eight, he died on 23 November 62. Claudius had been murdered by his wife in 54, and Nero succeeded him, a promising teenager who became a quixotic tyrant within five years, murderer of his murderess-mother, murderer of rival claimants to the throne, murderer of his young wife, pretender to literary and artistic skills that could not be shared or welcomed by austere Persius. But Persius says nothing of Nero in his satires, and he was one fortunate person whom Nero did not victimize for either his talent or his money. Persius died young, but of natural causes.

The biography gives us some useful information about Persius' family and friends. His father died when he was six; his mother remarried, but that husband also died after a few years. It is quite evident that Persius' mother was left with a comfortable estate and income, and the move to Rome, when Persius was twelve and needed education from the best teachers available, occasioned no financial difficulties. We are told that Persius got on well with his mother, sister, and aunt, and that he had a characteristically gentle and modest manner, from which some scholars have imagined that women dominated his life. However, Persius' writings give no such impression: they are forceful, virile, and addressed exclusively to male interests. In his satire 3, Persius tells us a curious story ostensibly about himself: he casts himself as a typical rebellious student, so opposed to learning the last words of the famous Cato as he committed suicide to avoid surrendering to Julius Caesar that he deliberately dropped olive oil into his eyes so as to appear sick with jaundice or the like (3.44 ff.). None of that is unusual. What is odd is that he adds that his father used to proudly bring his friends to school to hear Persius recite; hence, this malingering also hurt his father. Now, all calculations demonstrate that Persius' real father was long dead when he had reached this stage in school, and it seems likely that his stepfather had also died. Hence, this attractive story is a fiction. It might be interpreted to suggest Persius' longing for a father, but it is probably better construed as evidence of the poet's vigorous imagination.

In satire 5, Persius gives other details in the first person that are confirmed by data in the biography. "When I was old enough to be on my own, free from the routine of school," he says (5.30 ff.), "I put myself under the authority of Cornutus." In other words, he consciously rejected immature freedom for profitable intellectual slavery to this teacher. The next sentence is even more significant: "Cornutus lifted up my tender years into his Socratic bosom." Those strange words, entirely typical of Persius, as we shall see, use good Roman idiom—lifting up in the arms—to suggest that Cornutus treated Persius as a father does a newborn child (hence "tender years"); but they then go on to qualify the bosom as "Socratic" and thus change the notion of "father" from physical to spiritual. If indeed Persius was seeking a father to replace his long-dead parent, then he found one in Cornutus, but one appropriate to the stage in life that he had reached. Annaeus Cornutus was Greek, a former slave in the household of Seneca who had been given his freedom and was a successful teacher of rhetoric and philosophy at that time in Rome. With that background, he obviously could not offer Persius the status and economic comfort that were already his, inherited from his dead father; he could give Persius the companionship, advice, and discipline that an adolescent of sixteen sometimes seeks. He gave point to Persius' rather aimless existence, and he remained Persius' close friend and trusted adviser for the next twelve years—so trusted that Persius remembered Cornutus fondly in his will, and Cornutus exerted considerable influence on the poet's mother in the publishing of his poetry. It is plain from satire 5 that Persius regards Cornutus as his father-confessor both in questions of poetic style and in matters of morality.

Of the other friends who are cited in the biography, Persius himself mentions only the lyric poet Caesius Bassus, in satire 6. But it seems that Persius was well acquainted with the great Seneca and Seneca's nephew Lucan (five years younger than Persius but very precocious, and destined to write more in his short life of twenty-six years than the satirist did in twenty-eight). The biography claims that Persius was not in the least bewitched by Seneca's talent and that Lucan testified to the superiority of the satirist; at least, it is obvious to any reader of the three that Persius strikes out in a very original, independent manner. Although other friends are mentioned, I will name only Paetus Thrasea, a relative in some degree, made famous for us in the pages of Tacitus, where his opposition to Nero and to the general obsequiousness of politicians under Nero eventually earned him death in 66, four years after Persius'. Thrasea's austere political independence seems to have been informed by the same Stoic morality that Persius embraced and used in his satires. Thus, although Persius exhibited no interest in politics in this troubled era, he nevertheless practiced freedom in his own way, under the principal inspiration of Cornutus.

The Stoic Satirist

The biographical information that seems relatively independent from the few facts and names that Persius himself provides in his satires shows us a man who is both poet and moralist, and whose friends are literary men or devotees of philosophy or both, as Cornutus was. Poetry and ethics form the basic material of Persius' satires and constitute one of the traditional aspects of Roman satire from earliest times. The father of Roman satire, Lucilius, who composed his poems at the end of the second century B.C., sometimes attacked prominent politicians and sometimes told personal anecdotes about his early education, travels, or erotic experiences, none of which involves much ethics; but he also often dealt with familiar ethical doctrines and situations, and some of the prominent Greek exponents of particular ideas. Horace continued that interest, indeed expanded it in proportion to the whole collection of his satires, as he at once drastically cut the lampoons and personal attacks, and excessively detailed the confessions.

The blend of poetry and ethics can vary widely from satire to satire and from satirist to satirist. Persius occupies a unique position from the militant way he applies his ethics. Whereas Horace, for all his serious concern for the ethical life, presents morality in a modest, nondoctrinaire way, adopting an eclectic stance closer to Epicureanism than to Stoicism, Persius opts for a Stoic ethics and a special Stoic way of preaching it uncompromisingly. In Horace, the Cynic-Stoic preacher functions as a laughable extremist, a foil to the genial reasonability of the Horatian satirist. Persius says that he admires Horace, but he exploits Horatian phrases to advocate a position that is diametrically opposed to Horace's. In satire 3, for example, he touches on a famous Stoic paradox: none but the wise is sane; every other person is insane. And in satire 5, he frankly defends a second paradox: none but the wise is free; every other person is a slave. Now, Horace had devoted two brilliant poems (satires 2.3 and 7) to exploring the ridiculous perversity of these paradoxes and the wild excesses of the men who advocate them. Persius obviously believes that these paradoxes are neither perverse nor ridiculous, and he takes very seriously the need of men to be sane and free.

Horace presents himself as a tolerant fellow, one who tells the truth with a laugh, without hurting anyone. Juvenal, as we shall see, presents himself as an indignant Roman, one who angrily denounces the criminal vices of his city, toward which he feels a passionate love-hate. Unlike them both, Persius adopts the role of a convinced Stoic who will not tolerate the defective multitude, and he harangues us lost mortals not from anger, certainly not with laughter, but with utter contempt for our failure to achieve Stoic wisdom and the freedom and sanity that go with it. Thus, whereas Horace and Juvenal both get their audience on their side, whether in laughter or in hating others, Persius prides himself on his indifference to popular success, opts for a few sympathetic readers, and declares his intention to offend the majority. He puts his position metaphorically, in a way that we today would find appropriate to either loudspeakers or musicians: he intends to hurt our ears.

Ears mean a lot to this satirist. The tendency to define both his ideal stance and the deficiency of the public in terms of ears shows the poet at work brilliantly supporting the moralist. Satire 1 introduces himself and the assault on ears that Persius obviously wanted to print on our consciousness as his characteristic manner. He has a companion ask him, "What need is there to rasp on the tender ears [of the audience] with biting truth?" (1.106). The companion goes on to suggest that Persius sounds like a snarling watchdog (1.109). Unlike Horace and Lucilius, who resent the charge of biting and vigorously deny it, Persius welcomes the implicit accusation in the companion's query. He sneers at sensitive feelings, then deliberately misrepresents the attitudes of Lucilius and Horace in order to imply their general agreement with himself, and finally he takes on the "ears" by alluding to the famous story of King Midas and his barber (presumably as told by Ovid in *Metamorphoses* 11.174 ff.). Midas had disagreed with the verdict in a singing contest and so offended the god of music and poetry, Apollo, that he was punished and had his human ears replaced with ridiculously long ass's ears. He tried to conceal the embarrassing appendages beneath a hat, but his barber inevitably discovered the truth. Afraid to tell anyone but bursting with his knowledge, the barber unwisely whispered it into a carefully dug hole in the ground. Alas, some reeds grew up in the hole and whispered into the air the awful fact. Neatly exploiting the story, Persius pretends to be the naive barber who is bursting with the truth, not about Midas, but about humanity in general, and he whispers into his book of satires, "Who is there who does not have ass's ears?" (1.121). We are all like Midas, lacking any judgment in poetry, impervious to Stoic wisdom, indeed demanding that our ears be soothed and caressed by melodious, sensuous nonsense, not scraped by the truth. The truth itself hurts, and the poetic techniques in which it comes to us in Persius' satires "hurt" because they are definitely not melodious, not easy to work out as conventional narrative and amatory poetry was then. In violent rejection of the vast majority with their tender, long ass's ears, Persius appeals to the rare reader whose ears have been thoroughly cleaned and are open to the truth (1.126). Such a reader would be totally attentive and attuned to the harsh voice of the satirist who elsewhere talks admiringly of "the Stoic whose ear has been washed out with biting vinegar" (5.86). Ass's ears and cleaned-out ears define in striking poetic terms the extreme ethical position chosen by Persius.

The ethical position is extreme, as I have noted, by contrast with that of traditional satirists such as Lucilius and Horace, who assumed that they were conversing or reminiscing with an intelligent upper-class audience that expected more pleasure than moral edification from poetic satire. It is also extreme by contrast with that of Seneca, who in his *Moral Letters* does advocate a Stoic position, but without the uncompromising harshness that Persius prefers. What Persius most resembles is a preacher, someone who harangued the crowds on Roman street corners, much like the evangelists of modern times with their hell-fire-and-brimstone techniques. The message, then, is denunciation of the world's corruption, contempt for the ass's ears and the utter stupidity of humanity. By itself, that message would be of slight interest except as a variation on the more tolerant eclecticism of Persius' predecessors. It is the manner, the medium by which Persius develops his relatively commonplace message, that makes his satires so unique and that gave them such success with the apparently despised public in their time.

Persius' Poetic Genius

The biography reports that Persius composed infrequently and at a late point in his short life. Since in the satires he made no certain allusions to his own time that would permit us to date them, all we can say is that he left 660 verses, an amount that most talented and careful classical poets could have produced in less than a year. Whenever he did begin writing, it seems evident that he labored long and lovingly on his lines. And he created verse that is like nothing else in the tradition of Roman satire or indeed in the entire Latin poetic tradition. For example, I have discussed what would seem to be a clear and effective metaphorical antithesis in satire 1 between ass's ears and ears cleaned out with vinegar. But consider the way the ears are first introduced, in this passage:

> You have the nerve to read this stuff to the people, all combed, in a new toga, sporting your sardonyx birthstone, white and seated on a lofty chair, after washing out your flexible throat with a liquid modulation, corrupt as you are with your seducing eye. Then you would see in no honorable manner and with no calm voice the grand Tituses tremble as the poetry penetrates their sexual parts and their internal organs are scraped by the pulsing verse. Are you, old man, collecting tidbits for others' ears?
>
> (1.15–22)

The question at issue is what kind of satire Persius intends to write. In this passage, he invents a poet of the type he loathes and imagines that the poet is giving a reading of his verse. As the satirist constructs the scene, we have a short description of the poet's neat appearance, and then we move on to a curious clause about the workings of his throat, another about his eye. Each has its prejudicial effect, the liquid modulation alluding to the flowing sensuousness of his verse, the corrupt seductiveness of his eye to what Persius regards as his criminal homosexuality. What follows, then, is a very obvious allusion to the excitement of an orgasmic experience as sexual penetration occurs—this is Persius' choice analogy for the effect of sensuous poetry on a foolishly receptive audience. After all these references to liquidity and sexual corruption, the satirist ends with a relatively mild mixed metaphor about dainty food for the ears. The cumulative technique of the passage involves piling one prejudicial image

on another, to combine all the organs of sense as the targets and recipients of this perverse poetry, to suggest that the corrupt poet deliberately operates on all the senses, above all on sexual sensations, and totally ignores the mind, himself lacking any rational purpose or rational relation to his material. The ears, at the end of this brilliant description, substitute for eyes, mouth, and genitals as the primary recipient of the sensuous nonsense mouthed by the poets Persius utterly rejects.

This piling up of images and conscious mixing of metaphors constitute a basic technique of the satirist, one that every rhetorical handbook and teacher of writing in Persius' time and thereafter would deplore, if consulted about an abstract case. As we know, when we mix our images, we do it from carelessness, and it was precisely that inattention that the teachers of the time criticized. When Persius piles up seemingly inconsistent metaphors here, he does so deliberately, presumably after careful consideration, and the result is a powerful denunciation of essential vices in the poetry of his day, a result that, we are told, won Persius' satires envious approval from Lucan and great success with the sophisticated reading public of Rome. With his absorbing interest in poetic effects, Persius patently did not intend to deal with his audience by the relatively direct techniques of rhetoric.

Persius' Stoic bias, his fascination with striking combinations of images, and his stance as a satirist work together to emphasize the negative side. It is implicit in the argument of satire 1 that he expects the audience to treat his kind of poetry as ideal, but in fact he concentrates almost exclusively on the faults of other poets and their audiences, so the positive must largely be deduced from the explicit negative attacks. In satire 2, Persius aims at the way people pray. Addressing an admired friend on his birthday, he encourages him to sacrifice to the gods. But immediately he shifts to the negative by saying: "You don't pray with a mercenary plea . . . but most people . . ." (2.3–5). The remainder of the poem, except for two lines at the end (73–74), consists of a vividly sardonic review of corrupt and foolish prayers. Like Jesus in Matthew 6:5–15, Persius urges his audience not to be like the hypocrites, but he has no model Lord's Prayer to offer, to put the stress on the positive.

Of course, most satire is negative. However, other satirists tend to indicate a stance of opposition in a way that implies they expect to win—as they do—our sympathy. Horace makes himself a most genial and convincing ethical antithesis to the fallible people he satirizes. Juvenal, as we shall see, presents himself as an indignant Roman in his early satires, a fearless denouncer of those who debase Roman ideals. Virulent as he may be, Juvenal at least takes a position with which his Roman audience can readily identify. When Persius contemptuously pictures the moral corruption around him, he is powerful and bleak and largely indifferent to his audience. His image clusters are brilliantly contrived, but ugly, disgusting, or grossly obscene in their main effect. His dialogue is hostile, unpleasant, and abrupt, designed not to persuade but to label or denounce. He views himself not as a modest learner (like Horace) or a struggling out-of-date Roman (like Juvenal), but as a wise man safely arrived at rational perfection among the rare Stoic sages such as Cornutus. He devotes little or no effort to make his perfection appealing to our imaginations or senses, with images that would counter the disgusting ones he has employed to dismiss the usual world. There is, of course, a poetic and Stoic logic in Persius' procedure. For him, the perfect Stoic existence is nonsensuous, utterly rational, totally indistinguishable down the ages from the first Stoic to Cornutus and now himself. He needs no particular physical conditions to aid his pursuit of rationality, unlike Horace with his Sabine farm. Persius starts satire 6 as though he were enjoying escape to the country, but he soon reveals himself as utterly indifferent to his setting and far more interested in attacking materialism. The natural world that other poets find colorful Persius distorts with his images and labels "discolored" (5.52).

There are thousands of sensational and disgusting pursuits that lure men to destruction; against them, Persius proposes a single difficult way of wisdom, the way he has successfully taken, it seems, but has no intention of describing for our benefit. Perhaps, if we respond to this world with the same revulsion that animates his negative pictures, then we shall sternly take the way of austerity, too.

Persius' 660 lines are the most difficult Latin poetry that has come down to us from antiquity. They are also some of the most brilliant. His compact, image-clustered language was unique, without effect on later writers, admired but not imitated. In the twentieth century such poetic diction has once again appeared, and Persius has acquired new admirers. Similarly, his uncompromising austerity stirs affectionate response from people who are utterly ignorant of Stoicism, but are familiar with the absolute claims of religion and political programs. While Seneca may be dismissed by some as a Stoic who compromised away his ideals and finally his life, perhaps even his art, and Paetus Thrasea may be scorned for his futile and ultimately fatal engagement with Neronian politics, Persius' ability to ignore political and social issues and to devote his art to lurid, ingeniously created, hostile pictures of general ethical corruption makes his an extraordinarily interesting talent in a time of amazing talents.

JUVENAL

Juvenal was born late in Persius' short life (possibly even after his death—we really have no reliable information). Persius wrote his work during his twenties and died before he was twenty-eight; Juvenal seems to have begun writing in his thirties and continued over a period of thirty years or more. Persius composed during the flamboyant and murderous years of Nero, yet utterly ignored political and social issues; Juvenal grew up under the Flavians, reacted violently (as did most upper-class Romans) to the excesses of Domitian, and then enjoyed the relative tranquility of the benevolent autocrats Trajan and Hadrian. Persius was independently wealthy; he owned an estate on the Via Appia in Rome, a seaside resort at Luna in northern Etruria, and presumably a family home at his native Volterra. Juvenal talks like a man who is familiar with financial difficulties, projects himself into the role of a desperate client, and waxes indignant over the selfish indifference of the rich or the success of those who have recently gained riches by (he claims) un-Roman unscrupulousness. Persius ignores the daily struggle to get food and clothing, whereas for Juvenal that is a vivid issue. Although Persius manages to turn his back on financial, social, and political problems, an amazing ploy for a satirist in Nero's lurid era, Juvenal plunges himself and his audience into the Roman scene: its murders, criminal trials, sexual enormities, high prices, building booms, and so on. Thus, while Persius forces us to view moral issues from a Stoic position and see the way the rational soul is corrupted by its sensual and materialistic tastes, Juvenal rages like an ordinary Roman against everyday problems, ignoring such technical ethical insights as might emerge from the Stoics or any particular philosophical creed. Persius restricts his attention to self-improvement, no doubt assuming that the ills of society will only be corrected when individuals have changed their ways. Juvenal chooses as his original theme the tragic corruption of Rome and implies that it is hopeless: a good Roman would either be destroyed by Rome or be obliged to flee for survival. Finally, Persius works out a unique and brilliant style for presenting his contemptuous dismissal of the asses, slaves, madmen, and fools he observed in the world: an abrupt, crabbed, image-studded style that defies all the rules, violates the mellifluous contemporary manner, and violently assaults the ears and the reason. Juvenal aims at the emotions with a pyrotechnical rhetorical manner so masterful that often one is lost in admiration of the rhetorical technique and forgets the subject. Poets admired but did not follow Persius; Juvenal was admired and imitated, then and now, and the Juvenalian manner remains the most common choice for satirists.

General Background

Fortune was kind in preserving the useful biography of Persius; but for Juvenal she has left us a late, unreliable, and nearly worthless set of chitchat, almost all of it derived from sensational or stupid distortions of what Juvenal himself wrote, not always about himself or with genuine conviction, in the satires. Whoever put the material together did not know when or where Juvenal was born and could only sweep over the first half of his life by saying that he "declaimed" up to middle age. Those who attempt to convert such statements to scholarly use then deduce that Juvenal was a rhetorician, but that is only a wild and hopeful guess. If we turn to the satires for autobiographical data, we have to admit that we are never sure whether the speaker is acting a part or whether we can trust him, when he says something about himself, to be referring to Juvenal. It is generally assumed that Juvenal was born in Aquinum on the basis of 3.319–320, where a partner refers to the satirist's occasional visits to his native Aquinum. Aquinum, later the home of St. Thomas Aquinas, lay on the Via Latina about seventy miles southeast of Rome. The name Juvenal, not a common one, has been found in an inscription at Aquinum and seems to offer independent confirmation for the presence of the family there.

I have called Juvenal middle-class. The reasoning of scholars on this matter goes this way: he cannot be upper-class, because he would probably not be a poet, surely not a bitter satirist attacking his own class; he cannot be of the lower classes, whether free plebeian or slave or ex-slave, because he would not possess the literary background, the polished style, and the poetic ambitions that he exhibits. It remains, then, to place him in the middle class and to accept as validly personal the statements in 1.15

that the satirist (Juvenal) had been given good training from a rhetorician. We are not sure when he was born, but it seems evident that he shared the reaction of others to Domitian (81–96), and we assume that he shared their experience and so lived through much of that reign in Rome. Two poems of Martial's, written in 91–92, address a friend Juvenal in Rome (7.24 and 91), and one calls him "eloquent": it seems likely that Martial's Juvenal is our Juvenal, and so the two epigrams are judged to confirm the presence of our Juvenal in Rome, his rhetorical talent, and his complete lack of poetic achievement at this date—for Martial would have said something about it.

That is not much to go on. Not one of the many active writers during the 90's or thereafter mentions Juvenal; nobody refers to his satires until long after his death. We can set a general date around the five books of satires that Juvenal published over a period early in the second century. Book 1 contains strong reactions to Domitian, as no later book does, and presumes work within a few years of the hated ruler's assassination in 96. Both Pliny and Tacitus were actively assessing Domitian during the first decade of the century. A third poem of Martial's, written to Juvenal in 101, who is pictured as restlessly roaming through the poorer parts of the city and climbing the hills to seek patronage (12.18), is often thought to allude to the contents of satire 3. In short, after coming to Rome from Aquinum and spending an indefinite number of years in the Domitianic period acquiring rhetorical and poetic skills, Juvenal began writing satire early in the second century and published book 1 between 110 and 115. The four books that follow show definite changes in satiric manner and tone, thus implying a period of time; and two satires in book 5 (13.16–17 and 15.27) refer to the year 127. Thus, some time after 127 Juvenal's last book was published; it seems no exaggeration to assign him some thirty years of activity as a satirist.

Although nobody hailed the satires upon publication or praised or criticized them during his lifetime—none of our surviving writers, that is—it is perhaps not unreasonable to suppose that Juvenal scored some success. We may point to his more urbane, confident, less indignant tone as a clue; we may consider a reference in 11.65 to a productive field near Tibur as evidence that Juvenal had begun to prosper a bit; or it may suffice us merely to argue from the existence of the five books of satires, consistently high-quality work that Juvenal continued over so long a period. Had he failed and found no patronage for his poetry, it is not likely that he would have persisted courting misery in the *same* poetic form.

We cannot follow the obscure trail long after 127, whenever Juvenal published book 5—if he ever did. The manuscript tradition that emerged from the Middle Ages bequeathes us a book that ends with an incomplete satire 16. That probably indicates corruption in the tradition long after publication, but some have conjectured that Juvenal died without finishing satire 16 and that an editor published everything he left, even the unfinished poem. The late chitchat that masquerades as biography dreams up the story that Juvenal aroused ill-will at the court (because of something he had written years ago in 7.90-92), and so at age eighty was exiled to the most remote point of Egypt and there languished and died. Much effort has gone into rescuing that fantastic exile and transforming it into a possible fact, notably by removing it from Juvenal's last years and dating it in Domitian's reign. That would then give Juvenal a very personal reason to vent his indignation on Domitian in book 1. The trouble is, there is no evidence that Juvenal was ever exiled, in the 90's or the 130's, and there is no need to suppose that he needed a personal grievance against Domitian in order to be inspired to write angry satire against the most obvious target of the era. Let us leave Juvenal's death undated, unromanticized with a miserable Egyptian exile; and let us ignore all attempts to turn the storybook exile into a fact for any part of Juvenal's career.

The Indignant Satirist

One of Juvenal's most famous lines comes from satire 1.79: *si natura negat, facit indignatio versum* ("If natural talent denies it, indignation does create my verse"). This statement, which in itself is a superb example (in the Latin) of Juvenal's rhetorical art, with its elegant arrangement of elements and its biased antithesis between cold talent and hot passion, implies that the satires of book 1 spring directly from indignation, that poetic art and talent dwindle to minor concerns. In such an assertion and the build-up to it in previous lines, Juvenal proclaims the dominant mood of the book. To start with, he imagines himself faced with the choice of an ideal genre of poetry, and so he reviews the standard poetry of the era. It is either tragedy or narrative epic working with Greek myths, trite stuff that the poets desperately try to vitalize by excited rhetoric. Persius had rejected contemporary poetry mainly for its empty sensuality; Juvenal rejects it for its empty, irrelevant content. Whereas Persius had turned his back on the exciting, dangerous events surrounding Nero, Juvenal directly faces the sensational world of contemporary Rome and finds in it the content and inspiration for his satire. Who cares about a mythical monster like the Minotaur or a fantastic feat like Daedalus' flight (1.52–54) when one can see on the streets of Rome monstrous *living* types who have ruined the once noble city?

They are a motley series of people he cites, but cumulatively they symbolize the utter decadence of Rome. We start with two women, one who marries a eunuch and another who performs a hunt in Amazon fashion, bare-breasted, at the Colosseum (1.22–23). Next comes an ex-barber who is now a millionaire and an Egyptian immigrant who flaunts his wealth, flashing a gigantic gem in his ring (24–29). There are sadistic informers, gigolos, defrauders of minors, husbands who prostitute their compliant wives, wives who poison husbands, spendthrift young nobles, and so on. In the angry satirist's view, Rome pulses with perversions, and all he can do is watch, indignantly but helplessly, and record in fury what he sees. Unlike Persius, he cannot insulate himself from such evil by retiring to an ivory tower, the creation of wealth and Stoic indifference: he is an outsider in his own Rome, not by choice, but through bitter impotence. From the street corner where he stands and records the corrupt passersby (1.63), he moves to the home of a wealthy snob and besieges it along with a crowd of other needy hangers-on (1.100–101), but unsuccessfully. As he presents himself in satire 1, then, the satirist is a bitter failure, the victim of an unjust and corrupt society, the indignant witness to the success of others' dishonesty and criminality.

Juvenal also wishes in this opening poem to place himself precisely in the satiric tradition. I have already indicated some of his principal differences from Persius; he himself does not mention Persius or include Persius in the tradition that he expressly recognizes. So, like Persius, he looks back to Horace and Lucilius. Persius felt considerable closeness to Horace and painstakingly adapted Horatian phrases and topics to Stoic satire. The characteristic tolerant laughter of Horace, however, does not fit book 1 of Juvenal, and he briefly refers to Horace's "Venusine lamp" (1.51) only as part of the genre. On the other hand, Lucilius emerges as an ideal prototype for defining the special Juvenalian poetry. He cites Lucilius alone when first talking about his chosen field (1.19–30) and presents an image of the "great" son of Campanian Aurunca magnificently steering a chariot and horses. At the end, he again invokes Lucilius in another heroic image "with drawn sword, blazing with passion and roaring" against various malefactors (1.165–167). So Lucilius functions as a grand figure, the embodiment of that old-time direct honesty that wrote whatever it wanted, with complete freedom of speech, under the surge of its burning passion (1.151–153). Alas, although Juvenal would fully imitate the master, the times will not permit such freedom. To name names and directly attack criminals would only result in the rapid death of the satirist. It is, then, a final blot on Rome that the indignant satirist of the early second century, unlike the outspoken and unscathed Lucilius, must veil his attacks and shape his rage to fit the dead. The anticlimax of this unheroic close, which taints both Rome and the prudent satirist, brings us down from the heady wave of passion on which Juvenal has been carrying us and enables us to pause and assess this indignant satirist.

I have described the Juvenalian satirist as helpless and impotent. He lacks economic, political, and social prestige, so his rage can only express itself in words, and now even those words are robbed of their power by being redirected against the dead. When we approach book 1 from that perspective, we are likely to sympathize with the furious poet and accept his vision of decadent Rome. However, there are other possible responses that might be better clues to the purposes and true genius of Juvenal. Those who are familiar with the historical and social conditions in which Juvenal actually composed during the early second century question the validity of his indignant vision: the era of Trajan was on the whole a good one, and it seems to have become conventional—Pliny's *Panegyric* is our best example— to contrast it favorably on all counts with the era of the hated Domitian. No doubt there are immoral men and women at all times, and fraud or undeserved wealth is perennial; but the political crimes and the sense of menace to which Juvenal also refers do not fit Trajan. Thus, Juvenal seems to be evoking a fictitious atmosphere, using a fictional satirist, a Lucilius *manqué*, and deliberately ignoring the relatively good times in which he actually writes: he is, we might conclude, projecting himself and his audience quite safely back into the vanished Domitianic period of the 90's. That is rather different from what he pretends, when he claims that he speaks of the dead only to avoid the murderous reprisals of the powerful and corrupt living.

Juvenal talks to us, evoking our sympathy, but expressing fear of a second audience, the outraged targets of his wrath. His actual audience in 110 or 115 was neither: it consisted of a group of wealthy and sophisticated Romans who originally attended a recitation of the satirist's poetry, then later bought his manuscript from a bookseller. There may have been some practicing poets in the audience; there certainly were many who ranked as acute connoisseurs of poetry, who knew all the strategies open to poets; and everyone knew what the times were like, although their interpretation might vary from conservative to radical. Poetry readings today are social events, enhanced regularly by drinks and food and gossip. I believe that it helps to imagine Juvenal reading satire 1 under similar conditions, conditions that patently dispute the indignant scene of crime and deprivation that he skillfully evokes. He is not attacking or shaming his cultured, comfortable audience, quite unlike Persius. He is creating a clever fiction of outrage and even danger, to which the sophisticated may respond in several delicious ways. They may savor and share the indignation against the past; they may comfortably reflect on the better times in which they live and indeed feel particularly immune to criticism; they may so admire the dramatic fiction and the way Juvenal plays on their emotions that they even smile or laugh or applaud over a particularly effective and affective rhetorical device. What I would emphasize, then, is the ability of Juvenal's own audience to *enjoy* his satires, thanks to their true experience of the times, their affluence, and their literary sophistication. Psychologically speaking, we know that another's anger, so long as it does not threaten us, often works to clarify our attitudes and relieve our emotions. When a skillful poet produces a fictional anger against a dead past, we are free to enjoy and admire it, especially since he never acts except with helpless words and never suffers for his slanders, and none of his targets ever appear to protest, threaten, or avenge the insult. Juvenal has perfectly shaped and circumscribed the dramatic scene to confront us with an obviously fictional mood of indignation that brilliantly challenges and then yields to our sophisticated experience.

Book 1 consists of five excellent satires. In addition to satire 1, where Juvenal presents his indignant satire to his public, he wrote four poems on particular social problems of his fictional Rome. Satire 2 deals with homosexual Rome, angrily and intolerantly, as many conservatives today rant against homosexual San Francisco or New York. Satire 4 dramatizes sardonically a supposed meeting of Domitian's secret council in the early 90's, to decide on the disposition of an item of supreme importance, an oversize turbot. Juvenal manages to hit a note of contemptuous superiority to Domitian and his advisers, who were so menacing in their day, but are made so ridiculous by the gourmet "problem" with which the artful satirist is confronting them in this fiction. Satire 5 takes up the predicament of the poor client who is abused by, and for the amusement of, the cruel, humiliating, rich would-be patron; but Juvenal chooses a client who asks to be humiliated, who lacks the essential standards and indignation that the satirist himself loudly expresses, and we end up hating the patron, but despising the client. Those who accept indignities deserve them; the craven client provides entertainment, as does the professional fool. Juvenal's neat pairing of opposite types, his equally awarded indignation, and his system of clever contrasts combine in a very successful fiction.

The acknowledged masterpiece of book 1, satire 3, occupies a key position in the center and dominates by its size and significance: each of the other poems ends in 170 lines or less, whereas satire 3 extends over 322 spectacular verses. Its target is Rome, not a particular social problem but the general degradation of the city and the quality of its life. In a little drama, the satirist encounters his friend Umbricius, a native-born Roman, at the southern gate, just as he is about to give up in despair and forever abandon his once-beloved home. We are to assume that questions arose and that Umbricius then launched into a venomous denunciation of

Rome that "explains" why it has become intolerable for him, why he says somewhat hysterically that he plans to fix his abode in "empty" Cumae, a venerable seaside town slightly north of Naples, "and to make the Sibyl there a present of one citizen" (3.2–3). Umbricius takes over the satirist's usual function and rages indignantly, and he demonstrates his uncompromising hatred by taking the drastic step at the end of the satire and leaving. However, the satirist, for all his tacit sympathy, does not entirely agree with Umbricius: he watches his friend leave, then turns back into the city. Umbricius points up the distinction, as he notes that occasionally the satirist does temporarily hurry off to his native Aquinum for relief. It is apparent that the satirist is trapped in a love-hate relationship with Rome that prevents him from making a drastic, heroic, but rather unrealistic move like Umbricius'. When we reread Umbricius' complaints, we perceive that the man is an inflexible bigot who has failed to compete successfully with other clients, that his rage exhibits some of the comic qualities of the ultra conservative type.

The Art of Rhetorical Satire

When I have suggested that the indignant Umbricius emerges finally as a prototype ultraconservative; when I have noted the anticlimactic way the satirist descends in satire 1 from a pose of immediate reaction against living examples of Roman vice who parade down the street before his bitter gaze, and safely attacks the dead of a previous generation; when I have claimed that Juvenal's audience enjoyed his indignation more than it vibrated and raged *with* it I have been circling around a key quality of Juvenal's satire and a difficult problem for many readers. There are strong signs that Juvenal does *not* identify closely with his indignant satirist, that he manipulates him as a dramatic character and manipulates the situations into which he plunges him and the details, words, and meter with which he gives the satirist life, that he plays a game with an assenting audience that is regaled with a hell-fire-and-brimstone tirade over a Rome that has little correspondence to reality. These signs all indicate a basic rhetorical quality of Juvenalian satire. This rhetorical element is an essential component of Juvenal's success and of the reputation he has earned over the centuries. But some critics, especially those who preferred to believe romantic notions that a true poet should sincerely voice passions from the heart and never act a role, have attacked Juvenal's dishonesty and dismissed him as a mere declaimer.

Juvenal hardly disguises the fact of his use of rhetoric. Satire 1 begins in a rhetorical context, a scene of poetic recitations or readings. Impatient with the suffering that he has persistently experienced as a member of the audience, the speaker or satirist longs for vengeance (1.3–4). He has, after all, the same credentials as the other poets: he has been punished with the teacher's rod and has practiced some of the standard school speeches (15–17). So, he continues, "It is a foolish kind of mercy, when you meet so-called poets everywhere, to spare the paper, which will perish anyway [from others' dismal poems]" (17–18). What this seems to promise is poetry of the same technical finesse, namely rhetorical skill, as that of other poets. Where Juvenal distinguishes himself is in the genre: he rejects mythological tragedy, epic, and lyric for Roman satire.

The choice of Greek mythological topics automatically excludes engagement with contemporary events and prevents or frees one from—the difference in perspective is significant—direct personal utterance. In the speeches that the dramatist or epic poet writes for his characters, a realistic impression must be conveyed, but writer and audience have a contract for dealing with dramatic realism. The fiction allows emotions to *play*, to be expressed and exploited within artistic limits. Angry Achilles, passionate Turnus, crazed Orestes speak their wild emotions, and the audience responds but remains partly insulated, objective, and critical. The same phenomenon operates in most first-person poetry, and we can claim that Lucilius, Horace, and Persius should not be fully identified with the speaker in their satires. Nevertheless Juvenal made the most outstanding use of a dramatic fiction for the indignant speaker and the conditions surrounding him. In fact, it might help us recognize the analogy between the other poets and Juvenal if we emphasize the "Roman myth" used as dramatic setting for the angry satirist. And indeed the satirist blatantly mythologizes the very data he offers us. For example, by the device of antonomasia a spoiled nobleman—an early "hot-rodder"—who wildly steers a chariot down the Flaminian Way as he shows off to his girl friend is not named but called "an Automedon" in allusion to a famous charioteer in the *Iliad* (1.61). A fire that menaces a Roman garret becomes ironically rendered as the conflagration that threatened Aeneas' rich home during the fall of Troy (*Iliad* 3.198 ff.). This new myth works cleverly two ways: it implies that Juvenal's mythical material is far superior and more "real" than that of his rivals, and simultaneously it keeps reminding the sophisticated audience that it remains in a fictional, dramatic context.

If the basic setting and main speaker are dramatic, then we should not be surprised—as past critics have been—over the manifest unevenness of the speaker's anger and his constantly abrupt modulations of mood by means of wit and art. Here is another short passage from satire 3, where the satirist voices his strong approval of Umbricius' decision to forsake Rome:

For my part, I prefer Prochyta [a tiny island used by emperors as a place of exile for political enemies] to the Subura [the crowded region in central Rome where the down and out, like the satirist, live]. After all, what place have we ever seen so wretched and lonely that is not vastly surpassed in horror by the fires, the continuously collapsing buildings, the thousand dangers of our cruel city, and the poets reciting in the month of August?

(3.5–9)

866

The satirist starts with wild hyperbole in the Prochyta-Subura antithesis. Although the exaggeration would seem to fit his wild indignation, it is undercut first by the audience's own more balanced reaction to the actual Subura and secondly by the obvious fact that the satirist does not immediately charge off to that lonely island, but hears out Umbricius and then goes back into the city, presumably to his residence in the Subura. In support of his hyperbole, the satirist develops a powerful rhetorical question, which ostensibly forces us to answer, "No place is so awful as Rome." The buildup sweeps us along, captivated by the very exaggeration of "continuously collapsing buildings" and "thousand dangers"; for the plurality and frequency of these perils seem to emphasize by contrast the allure of the lonely wretchedness of Prochyta. However, the list of outrageous dangers rises toward a climax and then suddenly plummets in a hilarious anticlimax of poets reciting their verse in the torrid month of August. I can imagine Juvenal reading this passage to his Roman audience: he has been projecting the outrage of the satirist with a stern expression and violent voice, and then he pauses, looks at the audience, winks, and smiles, before ending with the detail of the reciting poets. The ultimate effect would have been achieved if Juvenal himself were reciting in August: then, the potential self-irony, as in satire 1, would be patent, and the audience's laughing, applauding response would be guaranteed.

Juvenal might have been a pupil of the great rhetorician Quintilian: his age and time in Rome would fit the period of Quintilian. Although no firm data prove such a connection, we can at least confidently assert that Juvenal had thoroughly mastered the rhetorical art and adapted it superbly to the special conditions of satire. The principal adaptation lay in rejecting the doctrine of propriety and creating a special method of *impropriety* by which to shock and delight the audience and convey the artful mixture of anger and wit that is Juvenal's hallmark. We have already commented on the devices of anticlimax and antonomasia. Here is the way Juvenal works with apostrophe, as he invokes Mars:

> O father of Rome, how did this terrible degradation come to the shepherds of Latium? How did this vile lust [homosexuality] affect your descendants? Look, a man of distinguished family and possessions is being married to—a man; and you don't shake your helmet or pound the earth with your spear or complain to your father [Jupiter]. Beat it, then, and take off from the acres of the stern field [of Mars], which you are neglecting.
>
> (2.126–132)

It is entirely conventional to apostrophize a god under the stress of passion, and the satirist launches into his appeal to Mars with seeming conviction, for Mars, founder of Rome's virile martial tradition, should be fiercely opposed to what is now going on in homosexual Rome. The satirist selects one of many enormities to illustrate the reason for indignation, a "marriage" between two males, and then he proceeds to abandon the usual serious treatment of apostrophe that belongs to the righteous anger of his grand style. Instead, he starts to belabor the god with insults, for indifference and neglect of duty, and finally sends him packing—out of Rome and, for all he cares, away from the pantheon. When Mars fails to oversee the military exercises of the Campus Martius, then he has ceased to be Mars. The apostrophe has been wittily and meaningfully changed, and then broken off abruptly, as the satirist has become disgusted. Although that is not the "proper" way to treat a god or to develop an apostrophe, no reader can deny that Juvenal's improprieties prove remarkably effective and apt for his context.

Juvenal sweeps his audience along with his rhetorical style. It is a magniloquent style, full, emphatic, favoring figures of speech that help to bring out its articulation. His stylistic techniques include using two or more rhetorical questions, each beginning with the same interrogative, as in the passage just quoted; anaphora (repetition of an initial word); exclamation and apostrophe; well-organized periods; long sentences followed by a short pungent one; meter that duplicates the flow of epic and then abruptly plants a monosyllable where it shatters the smooth rhythm; grand epic diction and then suddenly a plebeian or obscene word. There is no need to apologize for them: Juvenal's poems are magnificent declamations put to the service of a unique kind of satire, undoubtedly the finest rhetoric to have survived from the opening decades of the second century.

Book 2: Satire on Women

A few years after the publication of the five satires of book 1, Juvenal brought out a second book, considerably slimmer than the nearly 1,000 verses of the first, consisting of a single brilliant denunciation of women and marriage in Rome. This was obviously a subject as old as male chauvinism, as ridiculous a target for a serious satirist to choose as for modern legislators and moralists. A great senator named Metellus had long ago summarized the situation in wry resignation, much as is done by the patronizing witticism, "Women, you can't do with them, and you can't do without them." He had admitted the difficulties of being married to a woman, but recognized the necessity—for those days. There are no social merits in attacking the institution of marriage or denying the possibility of chastity in women. But what alternative does the satirist offer? He cannot preach total celibacy, withdrawal to the monastery or nunnery, as later Christian preachers might. Indeed, for the greater part of his inordinately long tirade, the satirist has no perceptible alternative, no positive recommendations at all: he seems exclusively concerned to paint the negative picture in as lurid and passionate and biased a manner as possible.

At the beginning, the satirist imagines that he is responding to the decision of a friend, Postumus, to get married, trying to reason with him about the absurdity of the idea. His basic premise is that adultery is the original sin and that hence there is no way of keeping a wife chaste (6.21–24). But against that he hysterically offers completely unacceptable options.

> Surely you used to be sane. Are you planning to take a wife, Postumus? Tell me, by what spirit of madness, by what poisonous snakes [of hell] are you being harried? Can you endure any woman's domination when there are so many sturdy ropes, when so many high, dark windows stand open, when the Aemilian Bridge offers itself to you nearby [all as means for suicide]? If none of many deaths appeals to you, don't you at least consider it a better alternative to have a boy sleep with you? After all, a boy does not argue with you at night, demands no precious presents from you as he lies there, and doesn't complain that you are saving your energy and are not breathless enough [in sexual intercourse].
>
> (3.27–37)

In satire 2, the argument had raged ferociously against all homosexual behavior; now the argument runs its extreme course and produces the sensational claim that even keeping a boy is preferable to having a wife.

There is nothing new in the charges mounted against wives: they have wild sexual appetites that make them not only vulnerable to predatory adulterers but even aggressive in seeking satisfaction of their lusts. They have various ways of dominating husband and household. They fill their days with vapid, expensive, dangerous pastimes, in pursuit of exotic things, sensations, superstitions. And finally, for the ultimate sensation or pastime, wives turn against their children and hated husbands, no longer content to tyrannize them, and poison them or openly attack them with knives. But what about their victim-husbands? Juvenal refuses to depict them with sympathy, to create a black-and-white situation of a noble, hard-working, trusting, affectionate man who is "tragically" betrayed by a vicious woman. Men are as bad in their way as women, husbands as wives. After all, in satire 1, he had balanced the item of women poisoning husbands (1.69–72) with facts about husbands who prostitute their wives (55–57); debauch their not altogether reluctant daughters-in-law (77); marry for various vicious reasons, easily imaginable (78); or have already been adulterers since their teens (78). Postumus, we have seen, is merely "crazy." Ursidius, who is about to marry and start a family, has the reputation of being the most notorious of Rome's adulterers (6.42). Caesennia's nameless husband has married her for her money and agreed to praise her highly but allow her complete freedom to pursue her various sexual affairs (6.136 ff.). Sertorius concerns himself only with the physical beauty of his wife, Bibula, ready to divorce her as soon as he discovers a few wrinkles or a discolored tooth, sure to pursue another brainless beauty queen (6.142 ff.).

Once again, then, as in satire 5, the satirist has placed himself between two extremes, this time the impossible female and the worthless, gutless male, and rants wildly against the union of these two caricatures. However, there is one important difference, which points to some potential changes in Juvenal's satiric techniques. Whereas the relationship between patron and client was a real social-political issue at the time Juvenal wrote satire 5 and impinged directly on the experience of the audience (many of them involved in patronage) to which he, a poet-client, read the poem, in his denunciation of women and marriage he has chosen an issue that has no political relevance and affects the audience as timeless, even (as the satirist argues it) "unreal" (meaning contrived or fictional), and his examples hark further and further away from the present into the past. He could easily have cited Domitian. In Suetonius, we read that Domitian fell so corruptly and passionately in love with Domitia Longa that he persuaded her to divorce her husband and marry him; that, when she had borne him two children, she fell in love with an actor and he divorced her; that his passion remained so strong that he soon remarried her. Ideal details for satire 6 and for a satirist who poses as loathing the monstrous era of Domitian. Now, however, our satirist seems nonpolitical, no longer

seething with fury against Domitian, and his most vivid historical illustration, the magnificent presentation of Messalina, the whore-empress (6.115 ff.), comes from the reign of Claudius some seventy years earlier.

The widened, less immediate historical perspective receives emphasis in several other ways. Opening the poem, the satirist ranges back to mythical times, somewhat after the era of cavewomen, when the goddess Chastity forsook mankind and adultery became normal. Halfway through his tirade, he pauses to catch his breath and offer another perspective on unchastity (6.286 ff.). Rome had its analogue to primitive cave-dwelling conditions down to the end of the third century B.C., and hence marriages remained viable, so long as husbands were rigidly involved in work or defense of Italy and even Rome, so long as wives labored in the home and had no soft luxuries and sexual pleasures as alternatives. That may sound like history, but it is more a familiar myth for the Romans, and it is certainly so remote, more than three hundred years ago, that it cannot possibly function like the fresh memory of Domitian. Finally, at the end of the satire we encounter a careful comparison between the satirist's material and manner and those of tragedy. It starts from a supposed protest in the audience to the exaggeration involved in citing a stepmother who murders her stepchildren:

> I suppose you think that I am just making this all up, as my satire puts on the high buskin [the elevated shoe worn by tragic actors], as, in violation of the generic limits and conventions established by my predecessors, I rave with mouth spread wide like Sophocles, pouring forth powerful poetry on topics unknown to the Rutulian mountains or the Latin skies. Oh, if only I were inventing it!
> (6.634 ff.)

The satirist then rises to his climax: not only do stepmothers murder stepchildren, but mothers kill their own children and wives their husbands. All the fantastic plots of Greek tragedy are then true. But even mythical tragedy cannot quite equal the horror of modern tragedy. The

Greek tragedians operated with the stereotype of hysterical females, so all the tragic crimes associated with Medea or Procne were crimes of passion. Nowadays, though, wives murder calmly and in cold blood, resorting to poison rather than such crude and silly devices as the axe of Clytemnestra.

It was latent in the argument of satire 1 that indignant satire replaced mythical tragedy because it was "more tragic." However, the true emphasis of that first programmatic satire was on the greater immediacy of the Roman material, on the direct personal involvement of the satirist in the events he reports. In satire 6, the satirist does not explain his anger: although the illustrations are Roman and the tirade can be viewed as summarizing the decadent state of Roman women, Juvenal avoids details that bear mainly upon political and nondomestic social conditions. In order to give the satire immediacy and personal relevance, one critic has suggested that its indignation springs from Juvenal's bitter experiences with a vile wife resembling one or the other of his examples. That, however, is the counsel of desperation: Juvenal eliminates *all* personal connections here, and whether the hypothesis about the disastrous marriage is correct or not—probably *not*—Juvenal has made sure that the audience cannot use it. His satirist's anger is impersonal, his judgment undistorted by unhappiness—but it surely is distorted. More than the satires of book 1, satire 6 exposes the irrational qualities of the satirist's indignation, for he argues an impossibly chauvinistic case and makes hysterical claims for his fiery ranting by appealing to the tragic analogy. The audience, male and female aristocrats, should have greeted this work with fascinated attention and frequent applause, struck, as modern readers are, primarily by its spectacular sensationalism and brilliant stylistic techniques.

Book 3: Experiments

It seems likely that both books 1 and 2 were written during the long reign of Trajan (98–117),

the second book reflecting the greater distance from the monster Domitian and Juvenal's new tactics of indignation. Book 3 contains three satires whose total number of lines approximates that of satire 6, whose indignation has become muted and finally transformed, and it refers in its opening poem to a Caesar interested in literature, hence almost surely Hadrian. If, as seems likely, Juvenal published these poems in the early 120's, it was a quarter-century after Domitian's death, and the necessity to modify his manner was apparent. We of course do not know how Juvenal himself had fared in those years, but it is not unreasonable to assume that as he approached his sixties and enjoyed some success, his own subjective motivations altered.

Satire 7 deals with the miserable plight of the practitioners of the literary arts at the present, just as some slight signs of hope appear with Hadrian. The satirist does not talk as a fellow poet, makes no reference to satire, and the topic itself does not support a powerfully indignant mood. The literary profession has been enduring "toil that is unworthy or indignant" (7.17), but that does not include censorship, prosecution, execution, or prison, circumstances that would fit Domitian's era and a truly outraged denunciation of the *political* enviroment of literature. What he means by "unworthy toil" is profitless work: poets, writers, and teachers are not earning enough. They "work" at their literary craft and expect to be paid, but experience only misery, no pay, or too little. But when the satirist concentrates his sights on the financial aspect of the arts, he robs them of their dignity. We are not told of anything valuable that the poets compose, the writers write, the speakers say, or the teachers inculcate: it is as if they have no real interest in their respective area of the arts except as a job. The themes of "work" and "pay" kill our sympathy for these people. We may not dislike them, as Alexander Pope makes us dislike the writers of London's Grub Street in the *Dunciad*, but Juvenal sees to it that we view with scorn both the ill-paying public *and* the unremunerated purveyors of the arts.

The basically ironic strategy of satire 7 may

be perceived in this passage about the greatest Latin poet and his poem, the *Aeneid:*

> It requires a great spirit, one not anxious about buying a blanket, to visualize the chariots, horses, and forms of the gods and the way the Fury confuses Turnus. For if Vergil had not had his boyfriend and respectable living conditions, all the snakes would have fallen from the hair [of the Fury], and her trumpet would have been silent, not sounded its grim and lugubrious call [to war].
> (7.66–71)

Although nobody would deny that there is some truth in linking poetic productivity with freedom from material worries, the satirist has selected details here that complicate our sympathy. Vergil's finest achievement is hardly the scene in *Aeneid* 7 where the Fury possesses Turnus (though it is an excellently devised situation), and the satirist picks out some of its more fantastic features, such as the snaky tresses of the monster and her subsequent blast on the war-trumpet that is heard throughout Italy. On the other hand, he did not have to describe the basic needs of the poet in terms of pederasty and some kind of free lodging: for lack of a boy to fondle, Vergil would have been unable to give poetic power to his Fury! By means of questionable assertions of this sort, the satirist keeps us amused and distanced from the so-called misery, really the crass materialism, of the intellectuals. The strategy of placement between vice and so-called victim resembles that in satires 5 and 6, but the effect has changed, in that the satirist himself does not even pretend to be indignant.

In satire 8 the satirist addresses an aristocrat, presumably young, whose name is Ponticus, and argues, with rhetorical brilliance but little passion, that aristocracy cannot be inherited, it must be earned by each individual, for virtue is the only real kind of aristocracy (8.20). "Who will call a man high-born," he asks, "who is unworthy [*indignus*] of his birth and outstanding only in the possession of a distinguished name?" (30–32). The adjective *indignus* does not trigger indignation, because most of the aristocratic degenerates whom the satirist selects for illustration are contemptible or ridiculous, not a serious threat and certainly not a contemporary one. The most vivid come from the era of Nero, sixty to seventy years in the past: Rubellius Blandus (39 ff.), Lateranus (146 ff.), and finally Nero himself (211 ff.). After Nero, the satirist falls back on the trite antithesis between noble, corrupt Catiline and nonpatrician, patriotic Cicero; and then he proceeds backward through the centuries to the beginning of the Republic in the early fifth century B.C. and beyond that to the very beginnings of Rome in the time of Romulus, all in order to arrive at a reductio ad absurdum: the oldest Roman families derive their origins from shepherds, criminals, or escaped slaves (272 ff.). The satire, then, starts from a thesis that would win moral assent from anyone. On that thesis Juvenal has hung a series of brilliantly worked illustrations that have an almost independent existence. Ponticus has not done anything wrong yet, but the satirist treats him ironically, even sardonically, in a section on provincial governors (87 ff.), so that his pose as adviser and the extremism of his argument remind us of earlier satires, but the indignation and seemingly personal venom have disappeared.

Satire 9 is the most original of the book, and it shows one striking solution to Juvenal's search for a new, non-indignant manner. Again he considers the perversions of homosexual Rome and the corruptions of the client-patron relationship. We hear the old note of satire 2, namely, that Rome is filled with degenerates, who threaten to persist as long as the city itself (9.130 ff.), but that potentially irate theme is practically drowned out by the voice of a guileless, shameless male whore and gigolo, who dominates the discussion and insists on viewing everything from the perspective of an abused "client," an "honest workman" who has not received his "fair pay." The scene resembles that of satire 3, for the satirist encounters Naevolus in an obvious condition of miserable neglect, asks him the reason for his appearance, and then mainly listens, with brief encouraging comments, to the tirade that Naevolus unleashes on the patrons who have exploited and abused him. Naevolus has sexually served them and their wives, saving their social status, and he feels entitled to a suitable retirement income. Juvenal's innovation here has been to transfer the mood of indignation to a patently corrupt speaker, a professional bisexual who will do anything for a price and complains with naive outrage about being cheated. The satirist remains virtually invisible and silent in the satire, and the art of the poem, the fun for the audience, lies in the increasingly patent discrepancy between the indignation of Naevolus and its causes. Naevolus is an Umbricius whose sexual perversions clearly alienate our sympathy, and he is a Trebius (see satire 5) whose indignation against a cheating patron, Virro, leaves us sardonically amused and receives no encouragement from the now urbane, uninvolved satirist.

Book 4: The Sardonic Satirist

Book 4 consists of three satires totaling about 700 lines; satire 10, longer and more ample than the combined totals for satires 11 and 12, is also generally regarded as a close rival of satire 3 for the title of Juvenal's masterpiece. The rivalry holds considerable interest for criticism, since the two satires operate quite differently: satire 3 is an indignant denunciation of life in Rome for a true Roman, whereas satire 10 shows little interest in Rome, rejects indignation and personal outrage, and adopts a general moral topic, human ambition the world over, on which the satirist can mockingly declaim. In fact, Juvenal takes pains to offer some clear programmatic announcements of his mocking tone. Pausing early in his development (10.28 ff.), he reminds his audience of two opposing Greek thinkers who were often paired in legend: Heraclitus (unnamed and quickly rejected), who wept over human folly, and Democritus, who laughed whenever he set foot outside his home and viewed the ridiculous behavior of people. We may think of Democritus as the counterpart of

the satirist in satire 1: he wanders through his town; encounters various people, including the politicians and criminals; notes each vagary; and then, instead of raging (or weeping, like Heraclitus), laughs sardonically at human turmoil and proves himself totally immune to Fortune's malevolent games (10.52–53). The new satirist in satire 10 spends so much time on Democritus in order to emphasize his appropriateness for the subjects and manner of the book. What Juvenal had been seeking by various means in the three quite different satires of book 3 is elegantly achieved in satire 10: a Democritean satirist mockingly reviewing the follies of human ambition.

Satire 2 of Persius studied prayers and ambitions, too, but it focused on the hypocrisy of those who, while publicly pretending to value high ethical goals, secretly under their breath voiced their real desires for wealth, power, and status—crass, materialistic goals. What concerned Persius, then, was the spiritual corruption behind this hypocrisy and the debased conception of the gods that it entailed. Aloud they would pray for an honorable mind, reputation, and character (2.8), and Persius would advocate precisely that kind of integrity. Similarly, Juvenal in satire 10 ends by recommending a sound mind in a sound body (mens sana in corpore sano: 356), but he reaches that conclusion by very different strategy. For his argument, what disqualifies the prevailing wishes of people for wealth, power, eloquence, military glory, longevity, and physical beauty is not the essential materialism of the ambition, but rather its paradoxical self-destructiveness. Instead of describing people who devote their lives to the vain pursuit of a goal like power or wealth, noting, as Persius does, the irony of the situation when a fool exhausts his possessions in expensive and futile prayers for prosperity or sabotages a wish for long life by overeating, Juvenal adopts the tactic of assuming that we all can gain our wishes and then shows us the fatal results of a foolish ambition granted.

The method Juvenal had used sporadically in earlier books, citation and incisive narration of historical examples, now becomes the main technique of demonstration. Some of the most striking illustrations are drawn from Roman events, but no more recent than the Neronian era (possibly inspired by the contemporary work of Tacitus on that period): the victims of the purge after the failure of Piso's conspiracy (10.15 ff.), Silius (329 ff., under Claudius), Sejanus (58 ff., under Tiberius). But the satirist proceeds back past Cicero (120 ff.), the triumvirs of 59 B.C. (109 ff.), and Marius (276 ff.), to equally brilliant vignettes of Greeks like Demosthenes (126 ff.), the Persian Xerxes (173 ff.), the Carthaginian Hannibal (147 ff.), and even mythical figures like Nestor and Priam (246 ff.). The wide temporal and geographical span of the examples implies the general application of the thesis, the objectivity and distance behind the sardonic argument of the satirist. Juvenal is using his rhetorical mastery in a new and successful manner, to support now not indignation but an extreme vision of malicious Fortune and the sardonic tone that goes well with it.

The other two satires of the book attempt to make the character of the satirist more relevant to the sardonic argument than it was in satire 10, where the satirist is a mere voice. In satire 11 we seem to be starting on a general disquisition about the need for adjusting one's appetite and expense for food to one's means, when suddenly the satirist intrudes with a strong affirmation and places us in a specifically personal dramatic context: he is inviting a friend, Persicus, to dinner (60). By describing the circumstances of his meal, its modest but ample foods, its simple local wine, his unaffected servants, and his useful literary entertainment, by suggesting the favorable analogy of honest old-time Republican simplicity and proposing a number of invidious antitheses in contemporary extravagance, the satirist establishes himself as a positive model. The satire ends almost on a Horatian note of attractive Epicureanism, as the satirist urges Persicus to dismiss his cares, no matter what their origin, to escape the holiday crowd in the Circus Maximus and come enjoy rational pleasure with him. Indeed

the positive emphasis of satire 11 appears so strong that it overwhelms the sardonic element by the end.

Satire 12 also exploits a celebration for its dramatic occasion, but this time the sardonic satirist persists. He proclaims at the start a special holiday that surpasses in importance his own birthday, and only at line 15 does he explain the occasion: his friend Catullus has been miraculously saved from shipwreck and drowning. Now the caustic satirist takes control and comments rather sharply on the circumstances behind Catullus' danger. It would appear that this so-called friend has been sailing back to Italy from Spain, where he has bought up exotic items for import and overloaded his ship; thus, Catullus is the proverbial greedy merchant whom all satirists take as an easy target. Although Catullus himself narrowly escaped death at sea, it seems evident that the satirist's friendly feelings have been "drowned" by his disapproval of the merchant. But once we have heard of the near-disaster, we return to the heartfelt celebration, briefly (83 ff.). Then the satirist attributes to a companion the suspicion that all this ceremony of thanksgiving is a sham, intended to impress rich Catullus and thereby help the satirist earn a good share of his estate. But the suspicion is baseless, for Catullus already has three children who will be his heirs, and the satirist acts from no financial expectations. Here, again, the sardonic satirist takes over and dominates until the end; Catullus, no longer his target, disappears from the scene while our attention focuses mockingly on the grubby class of will-hunters in Rome. They are false friends, whereas implicitly the satirist is true. But in this poem the satirist finds it much easier to express his sardonic nature, and so he concentrates on the devious ways of false friendship and ends with a curse on these people, that they be totally cut off from friends (130). On the whole, the "friendly" satirist does not square with the sardonic one, and the uneven tone of satire 12, as well as the sacrifice of sharp mockery in satire 11, seems to have obliged Juvenal to make changes in book 5.

Book 5: New Developments

In book 5 Juvenal inserts four satires and, even without the lost portion of satire 16, approaches closer to the length of book 1 than in all his other books. Satire 16, which breaks off in midsentence at line 60 just as it launches into an abortive anaphora, would almost surely have been at least 100 lines longer, and that would give the book a total of over 900 verses. In itself, the length is not especially important. But, combined with the versatility of manner, it indicates that Juvenal's satiric genius was far from exhausted when he reached his seventies. As I noted earlier, both satires 13 and 15 contain datable allusions to A.D. 127 and thus guarantee that the book was published no earlier than that year and presumably later. Roughly thirty years of activity writing satire close on a proud note.

Satire 13 employs a technique that combines features seen in satires 5 and 9: the satirist advises a foolish companion (as in satire 5) who is ridiculously irate (as in satire 9). The satirist dominates and clearly expresses his sardonic insight. What has occasioned the fury of the companion, Calvinus, a man who should know better after sixty years of experience, is the loss of money that he loaned trustfully to a man who has now denied his oath and the debt. Calvinus has built this loss up into a major crime, even though he has plenty of wealth left. As he rants and rages, the satirist appeals to him to act his age and face the facts realistically. Such a temper tantrum belongs to a child (33) or, worse still in the chauvinistic world of the Romans, to a hysterical female (191 ff.). Since the satirist does not respect Calvinus, he offers him a mock-consolation for his "tragedy" (120 ff.); and, when that does not work and Calvinus still indignantly demands vengeance, he sardonically reviews various dire penalties. It is particularly interesting that the sardonic satirist pits himself against an indignant "victim of injustice" and rejects indignation as naive: the scorn meted out to Calvinus shows us how far Juvenal

has traveled since book 1 and his period of indignant satire.

Satire 14, the longest of the book, announces its topic as the negative results produced in children by bad parental examples. After running through several typical faults in fathers— excessive passion for food, a craze for building, and superstition—the satirist introduces a distinction (107 ff.). Children instinctively copy their fathers in most follies, but in the case of avarice they must be forced. Avarice proves such an ideal target for mockery because of the basic paradox—the child learns it reluctantly and under considerable duress, disliking it naturally, but all the more so since it is drilled into him as a virtue—that the satirist devotes exclusive attention to it for the remaining 220 lines of the poem. The details of his argument against the sordidness and frenetic efforts of the miser are familiar from traditional ethical disquisitions, but the rhetorical manner lends some freshness to the work. The miserly father, who has insisted on the merits of profit regardless of methods, sees with dismay that his son seeks wealth by criminal devices, and then the ironic situation runs its logical course when the son murderously applies these devices against the father himself, who has been slow to die and leave his inheritance (246 ff.). In reviewing the crazy life of the merchant, its continuously experienced perils at sea, the satirist openly becomes sardonic—and more appropriately than he had done in satire 12. "You can ignore all the drama presented at the festivals of Flora, Ceres, and Cybele," he declares. "The business activities of men provide far more amusement" (262–264). Thus he treats the drowning merchant as a prize actor in the human comedy.

If we were to form our expectations on the basis of satires 13 and 14, where the sardonic satirist has chosen a general moral topic, mocked the folly of all people everywhere, and maintained a cool distance between himself and the selected vice, we would expect satires 15 and 16 to continue in this vein. Juvenal, however, pleasantly surprises us. In satire 15 he loses his mocking objectivity and rages at a crime committed by distant Egyptians, pitting himself angrily as the spokesman for humane behavior against people who have behaved inhumanely as cannibals, worse than beasts. And in satire 16 he focuses frankly on a serious and aggravating social problem in the Roman world: the preference given to the military over the civilian. Although he definitely does not voice outright indignation in the sixty surviving lines, he does take the position of the civilian and records first of all the way soldiers get away with criminal assaults on helpless Romans, then how they receive special attention from the law while civilians must wait in frustration. Juvenal has almost returned to the satirist of book 1, the helpless victim of injustice in Rome who rages impotently. He does not rage now, but the bitter details and the insistence on personal involvement undermine the mocking pose that he starts to assume. We are not enjoying rhetorical variations on a familiar ethical topic in satire 16; the illegal advantages of soldiers provide a new subject for satire. Thus, when we reach the break at line 60, we regret the sudden end of a satire that promised both originality and new developments in Juvenal's ever-changing satirist.

Retrospect

From his earliest satires, Juvenal displayed a thorough mastery of rhetoric and an ingenious rapport with his audience. The early second century fostered an indignation and a reaction to the tyranny perceived in the reign of Domitian, but it also savored its freedom, comforts, and current prosperity. Juvenal devised an indignant satirist for book 1 in order to capture the tension of the decade, to give his audience the pleasure of hearing pyrotechnical anger under utterly safe and comfortable conditions. However, as the years passed, Juvenal realized that he could not continue to exploit that same tone or point to political and social outrages that were no longer vivid in memory. Moving to more general topics, abandoning after satire 6 his patriotic indignation, he explored various options in book 3, some highly ingenious, but settled finally at the beginning of book 4, in satire 10, on a satirist modeled on Democritus, who laughed mockingly at human folly and gave the obscene finger to Lady Fortune. Five satires, 10 through 14, work in versatile ways with the sardonic satirist. Then, refusing to settle down finally with any manner, no matter how well received, Juvenal set himself new poetic and satiric tasks in satires 15 and 16. For many of his admirers and imitators, his reputation rests on the indignant satirist of the early books: tradition has considered "Juvenalian" to mean "indignant." Although I, too, admire and enjoy the indignant satires, I have also chosen to stress in this essay Juvenal's capacity to grow, develop, and interestingly alter his methods. He was a highly talented poet who never rested on his achievements.

Selected Bibliography

TEXTS

PERSIUS AND JUVENAL

A. Persi Flacci et D. Iuni Iuvenalis Saturae, edited by W. V. Clausen. Oxford, 1959.

TRANSLATIONS

PERSIUS

Merwin, W. S., trans. Aulus Persius Flaccus. Satires. Bloomington, Ind., 1961; London, 1981. Introduction and notes by William S. Anderson. The best translation.

Rudd, Niall, trans. The Satires of Horace and Persius. London, 1973.

JUVENAL

Green, Peter, trans. Juvenal; The Sixteen Satires. Harmondsworth, 1979. Penguin Classics. Includes a bibliography.

CRITICAL STUDIES

PERSIUS

Anderson, William S. "Recent Work in Roman Satire: Persius." *Classical World* 50:37–38; 57:344–346; and 63:191–199. The articles cover the periods 1956–1957, 1963–1964, and 1969–1970, respectively.

Bramble, J. C. *Persius and the Programmatic Satire.* Cambridge, 1974.

Dessen, Cynthia S. *Iunctura callidus acri: A Study of Persius' Satires.* Urbana, Ill., 1968.

JUVENAL

Anderson, William S. "Recent Work in Roman Satire: Juvenal." *Classical World* 50:38–39; 57:346–348; and 63:217–222. The articles cover the periods 1956–1957, 1963–1964, and 1969–1970, respectively.

Highet, Gilbert. *Juvenal the Satirist.* Oxford, 1954.

Scott, Inez G. *The Grand Style in the Satires of Juvenal.* Northampton, Mass., 1927.

WILLIAM S. ANDERSON

JOSEPHUS

(ca. A.D. 37–ca. 100)

IN JULY A.D. 67 Jotapata, the main stronghold of the Jewish rebels in the Galilee, was stormed and taken by Vespasian and Titus, as recounted in the *Bellum Judaicum* (*History of the Jewish War* 3.339). The defenders, after forty-seven days of seige, worn out with fatigue and asleep, succumbed to a surprise attack at night. Vespasian ordered the city to be razed and all of its forts burned to the ground. His soldiers massacred the male population, but spared infants and women, who were taken prisoner. The Jewish commander in chief, Josephus, escaped by leaping into "a deep pit." There he found "forty persons of distinction in hiding, with a supply of provisions sufficient to last for a considerable time" (342).

The hiding place, however, was discovered by the Romans within three days. Vespasian sent two of his tribunes to Josephus and urged him to surrender. The Romans offered safe conduct, and Josephus, after some hesitation, decided to accept the Roman terms. According to his own testimony, he took God as his witness that he went over to the Romans "not as a traitor, but as [God's] minister" (354). When he disclosed his decision to his forty companions in the cave, they were outraged and threatened to kill him: "If you meet death willingly, you will have died as general of the Jews; if unwillingly, as a traitor" (354). Josephus was horrified.

He decided first to argue rationally, hoping to convince them that suicide was not only repugnant to human nature but also an act of impiety toward God. Moreover, he agreed with his companions that it was honorable to die for liberty, but on condition that one died fighting. However, this was not the situation. The fight was over, and the Romans no longer threatened their lives. "It is equally cowardly," Josephus argued, "not to wish to die when one ought to do so, and to wish to die when one ought not" (366).

Although the Jewish freedom fighters were not convinced by these arguments, they revered their general and were unable to kill him in cold blood. At this moment Josephus decided to risk his life. He convinced his companions, who had long since committed themselves to die, to draw lots to decide the order in which they would kill themselves. His proposal inspired confidence, but by chance or providence or both, Josephus was left alone with one other man. He persuaded his companion to surrender to the Romans, and so both of them survived (391).

It is precisely this improbable escape that haunted Josephus for the rest of his life. His account of the drawing of lots in the cave met with skepticism, and his survival was attributed to strategy rather than fate; his defection to the Romans was interpreted as a cowardly act of treason. Josephus was aware of his reputation and admitted in his *History of the Jewish War* (3.432–439) that some looked on him as a traitor, others as a coward, and that "throughout the city there was general indignation" over his behavior and "curses were heaped upon [my] devoted head." In most of his writings Josephus tried to justify his behavior in the Galilee. Jewish rebels who fought till the fall of Jerusalem and the burning of the Temple were not the only ones who vilified him. Another Jewish historian, Justus of Tiberias (whose writings do not survive), attacked him too, but from a completely different perspective. According to Justus, Josephus was not as peace-loving as he portrayed himself. On the contrary, he cooperated with the zealots, did not disarm them, and incited obedient people to rebel against their Roman rulers.

It was against these contradictory accusations that Josephus had to defend himself later in life. He did so in the form of an autobiography that may be more unreliable than most, but that still gives us an insight into the author's complex personality. In describing some major milestones in his life he helps us understand his historical writings better.

In many cases little is known about the lives of historians. For example, in order to understand Tacitus better one tries to guess his birthplace and to reconstruct the date of his birth from his senatorial career. As no such guesswork is necessary in the case of Josephus, it is appropriate to begin this essay with a brief sketch of his life.

Josephus, son of Matthias, was born into an eminent priestly family in A.D. 37, one year after Pontius Pilate returned from Judea to Rome and Caligula succeeded Tiberius in the principate (Life 1). He received a traditional Jewish education. Even though modesty was never one of his virtues, Josephus can be believed when he claims that as a youth he distinguished himself in his studies owing to an excellent memory and thorough understanding of problems. Theory alone, however, did not satisfy him. In order to choose among the various sects prevailing in Judea (Essenes, Sadducees, and Pharisees), he lived for some time in the wilderness with the Essenes and studied under the guidance of the Sadducees; only at the age of nineteen did he decide in favor of the Pharisees

(9–12). At the age of twenty-six (A.D. 61) he visited Rome. The journey was rather adventurous. When the ship foundered in the Adriatic, Josephus had to swim to safety; eventually he landed safely in Puteoli. In Rome he was in touch with Aliturus, an actor of Jewish origin who introduced him to Nero's wife, Poppaea (Life 16). Despite modern conjecture, there is no real evidence that she was Jewish (Antiquities 20.195).

When he returned home, Josephus found Judea in a state of sedition and revolt against Rome. It is not certain that in A.D. 66 he was as judicious as he was in the late 70's, when he wrote his History. In his autobiography, however, he emphasizes (on the basis of his knowledge of Rome) that he had warned his compatriots not to start a hopeless war against a great and invincible empire. Josephus failed. The passion of the desperate rebels was not given to reason and understanding (Life 19). It became even more intense after the defeat of Cestius Gallus on the slopes of Beth Horon. Josephus knew that this Jewish victory was a lucky but rather insignificant accident, and that the legion of Cestius Gallus was not representative of Rome's real strength. Many others in Judea believed that the defeat of Cestius Gallus was a testimony to Rome's weakness and that they eventually could defeat the Romans.

The question remains: If Josephus was really convinced of the futility of the war, why did he accept an official position in the Galilee at all? According to him, he was simply afraid that his warnings against war would bring him into odium and incur the suspicion of siding with the enemy. He might even be arrested and put to death. This is how he justified most of his behavior: to be afraid of irrational extremists appears natural and human. Josephus wanted his readers to understand his mission to the Galilee in this context.

This is where the problem begins. Josephus gives two contradictory accounts of the issue: one in his History, written sometime between A.D. 75 and 79, and the other in his autobiography, written sometime between 94 and 100 (and published perhaps as an appendix to the *Antiquities of the Jews*). While minor discrepancies between these two books in proper names and numbers may be ignored, the major contradiction as to the nature of his mission remains.

In the *History* (2.562–568) Josephus tells us that after the defeat of Cestius Gallus, a reshuffling of the Judean high command took place and he was among the new appointees. He was given the Galilee with the addition of Gamala, the strongest city on the Golan Heights (a site only recently excavated by the Israeli archaeologist S. Gutman). Josephus' duty was to recruit a large army and prepare the Galilee for war against the Romans. In his autobiography, however, he does not appear as the commander in chief of the Galilee. According to the latter version, the leading men in Jerusalem found out that only a small portion of the Galilee had rebelled. Of course there were some rebels, but there were also brigands who harassed the civilian population. Most of the Galilee was tranquil. In order to save what could still be saved, the leading men in Jerusalem dispatched a delegation to the north, consisting of Josephus, Joazer, and Judas,

> to induce the disaffected to lay down their arms and to impress upon them the desirability of . . . reserving these for the picked men of the nation. The latter . . . were to have their weapons constantly in readiness for future contingencies, but should wait and see what actions the Romans would take.
>
> (*Life* 28–30)

The whole truth will never be known, but the contradiction is crystal clear. According to the *Life*, Josephus was not sent out as commander in chief of the Galilee. It appears that he was in charge of a fact-finding committee, or perhaps was a supervisor of law and order on behalf of the authorities in Jerusalem. It is also possible that the terms of reference had not been clearly defined and the friction that eventually emerged between Josephus and many Galilean leaders was due to the fact that the latter believed Josephus had usurped his authority. It is also not clear whether the authorities in Jerusalem had already decided to start an all-out war against the Romans. The *Life* indicates only that the Jerusalemites were opposed to anarchy. They believed that if a general rebellion started, it should be controlled by a central command and not by groups of dissidents. Only one order is clear: "Wait and see what actions the Romans will take."

In the *History*, on the other hand, the picture is different: the authorities in Jerusalem had decided to fight. They appointed Josephus as commander in chief and he executed orders. The responsibility was not his. This was the only way to justify his position in Rome after the destruction of the Temple in A.D. 70.

Contradictions of this kind are not unusual and do not occur only in the writings of ancient historians. Scholars of contemporary history who depend a great deal on oral testimony encounter such contradictions only too often. In 1946 a distinguished Zionist leader wrote a report on the attitude of some British cabinet members to the Palestinian crisis. Fifteen years later, when interviewed by a modern historian, he produced an altogether different version of the same issue. Confronted with his written report from 1946, the respectable Zionist leader was shocked. He had not lied, he said, but zeitgeist, the "spirit of the times," had affected his version in both cases.

Nevertheless, one may say that the discrepancies between the *History* and the *Life* teach us more about the attitudes of Josephus to Rome and Judea after the fall of the Flavian dynasty and the death of Agrippa II than about the real role played by Josephus in the Galilee in A.D. 67. Bearing in mind this difficulty, one may now turn back to the autobiography.

There were pro-Roman elements in the Galilee (like the people in Sephoris and Gamala), there were revolutionaries (some more moderate than others), and there were cities (like Tiberias) divided into different factions. One faction consisted of "respectable" citizens; it was pro-Roman and was led by Julius Capellus.

There was also a war party that consisted, according to Josephus, of "insignificant persons"; and there was a third party headed by Justus, son of Pistus, "who feigned hesitation" but in fact supported war (*Life* 32–37). It is against Justus that Josephus points all his poisonous arrows (88; 279; 336–367; 390–393; 410). Josephus would like us to believe that Justus was a scoundrel, a liar, and a hypocrite; that he did not act out of patriotic convictions; and that Justus hated Sephoris more than anything else only because Sephoris, not Tiberias, became the capital of the Galilee. The truth is that as long as Justus lived under the protection of Agrippa II he kept quiet. After Agrippa's death he decided to disclose to the world the "real role" of Josephus in the Galilee: he accused him of being a warmonger. It is against these charges that Josephus had to defend himself.

On the other hand, Josephus attacked John of Gischala, the leader of the war party, and insisted that he acted against John only in accordance with instructions from the Sanhedrin, the supreme rabbinic court in Jerusalem. Rumors were spread against Josephus that he intended to betray his country to the Romans (*Life* 130), despite the fact that he had fought Romans whenever necessary (*Life* 114). These false rumors had their root in Josephus' balanced and judicious policy. His difficult position is shown in Sephoris: as the population of Sephoris was pro-Roman, they hated Josephus because they considered him to have sided with the rebels.

Josephus would like us to believe that all his enemies envied him because of his popularity in the Galilee. Not once did his enemies intend to kill him, nor did he have to flee for his life (95–96). But Josephus overwhelmed everybody with his clemency; he forgave the rebels and pardoned traitors. Above all he tried to avoid civil war, knowing that the Romans were waiting to see rival Jewish factions ruin each other (100). Josephus tries to convince his readers that he was also a very tolerant leader. For example, he prevented forcible circumcision of refugees who wished to live among Jews. Josephus declared that everyone should worship God in accordance with the dictates of his own conscience, and not under constraint (113).

Eventually the jealousy and ingratitude of Josephus' fellow citizens won the day. They could not stand his success. He had fortified cities like Tarichaea, Tiberias, Sephoris, and many villages, stocked them with arms and supplies for their own security (188), and prepared the whole area for a long war. Nevertheless, John of Gischala, a man of mean character (72–76), wanted Josephus removed from the Galilee and convinced even Simon, the son of Gamliel and a leading Pharisee in Jerusalem, to side against him (190).

At first the priests Ananus and Jesus supported Josephus, but eventually they were bribed and consented to send a delegation from Jerusalem to investigate Josephus' competence. Josephus asserts that they had orders to bring him alive to Jerusalem if he would lay down his arms voluntarily, or to kill him otherwise (202–203). Josephus was informed about this plot and decided to quit his post, but the Galileans were shocked when they discovered that he was going to leave them in the hands of brigands, and they rallied in the thousands to induce him to stay (207). Such is Josephus' version of events.

The rest of the autobiography consists of rather tedious stories about how Josephus outwitted his enemies, how eventually Ananus and Simon, the son of Gamliel, lost their case in the general assembly in Jerusalem, and how Josephus was reconfirmed in his command of the Galilee (310). The details are not essential to the understanding of his later writings; mention must be made, however, of what occurred to Josephus after his surrender to the Romans (414). He married a woman taken captive in Caesarea who later left him. He accompanied Vespasian to Egypt, met another woman in Alexandria, and married again. Then he accompanied Titus back to Judea and participated in the siege of Jerusalem. He was considered a traitor not only by Jews; Titus' aides did not trust him either. Josephus went through difficult times. He was tormented by the sufferings of his fellow citizens and tried to help Jews whenever and wherever he could. He freed some of the countrymen he knew personally who had fallen into Roman captivity. On his way from Tekoah he saw many prisoners crucified and, recognizing three of them, managed to have them released, brought to a doctor, and receive some treatment. Two died and one survived.

Back in Rome his privileged position exposed him to envy and danger (424–425). Although he became a Roman citizen exempt from taxes and lived in a palace, he was always haunted and persecuted by what he called "false accusations." Later in life he divorced his second wife and married a distinguished Jewess from Crete, who gave birth to two sons, Justus and Simonides. Away from public life, he dedicated all his time to literary activity. In A.D. 79 he published his *History of the Jewish War*. Although Josephus' attitude to the war is best reproduced in a speech attributed to Agrippa II (*History* 2.345 404), it is doubtful whether its pro-Roman bias reflected his views in A.D. 66. It explains how great an empire Rome was, how easy it may have appeared to defeat weak neighbors such as the Egyptians and the Arabs, but how hopeless and futile it was to tackle an empire of the size and greatness of Rome. Stronger nations than that of the Jews had tried to destroy it and failed. The fact remains that Josephus took up an important position in the Galilee and fought bitterly against all those who tried to depose him.

It is not difficult to explain the main theme and content of the *History* against the background of Josephus' complex personality, but it would be erroneous to discount all his historical writings as personal apology and/or as works of propaganda intended to endear himself to the Romans. Many a scholar has done so, and it is against this trend that Josephus must be defended. True, suspicions cannot easily be discounted. Josephus wrote his books in the for-

mer palace of Vespasian in Rome. Roman official records were put at his disposal. Two young Greeks, students of a school of rhetoric, were to help him correct style and vocabulary. The *History* was originally written in Aramaic, but the original version is lost. The Greek title in fact indicates the Roman point of view: it is translated as "The War of the Romans Against the Jews"—like the Punic war ("The War of the Romans Against the Carthaginians"), the Gallic war ("The War Against the Gauls"), and so on.

Josephus worked at leisure and published his work when it was already clear that Titus was to succeed Vespasian in the principate. He himself admitted: "so anxious was the Emperor Titus that my volumes should be the sole authority from which the world should learn the facts that he affixed his own signature to them and gave orders for their publication" (*Life* 363). One should therefore take with a grain of salt his opening statement in the *History* that he wrote the book to provide the subjects of the Roman Empire with a narrative of the facts to discredit existing writings that lacked historical accuracy. Elsewhere Josephus declares that his historical work had a different purpose altogether. He wanted to console those who were conquered by the Romans (the Jews) and to deter others who might be tempted to revolt. By "others" he could have had in mind not only other Jews but also gentiles in Asia Minor who might have hoped for Parthian help (*History* 3.108; see also 1.6; 2.388).

But the real undercurrent throughout his work is that Jews and Romans were two great nations, that war between these two nations was not inevitable, and that peaceful coexistence was a real possibility if wild extremists on both sides—zealots on one hand, and greedy procurators on the other—had not dragged the two nations into an unnecessary clash. There were good and bad people on both sides (*History* 3.335; 4.60). But the strongest strictures are reserved for those Jews who insisted on fighting the Romans to the bitter end. Jews were plagued by war, tyranny, and factionalism (*His-*

tory 4.397). Titus himself asserted that the Jewish people owed their ruin to civil strife, and that the Jewish tyrants brought down upon the holy Temple the unwilling hand of the Romans. The real enemy of the Jews was within the walls of besieged Jerusalem (*History* 4.184). Civil war paved the way to famine. The city was converted into a desolate no man's land, and almost all the corn that might have sufficed for many years of siege was destroyed (5.25–26). Jews suffered nothing worse at the hands of the Romans than what they inflicted upon each other. It was sedition that subdued the city, and all the tragedy could be ascribed to her own people (5.527). No wonder that a modern historian depicted the zealots as "national Bolsheviks."

Of course, not all Jews were seditious. There were some reasonable people too, but they were not allowed to handle the difficult situation. Such a man was Ananus, the senior chief of the priests, a man of profound sanity who might have saved the city of Jerusalem had he escaped the hands of the extremists (*History* 4.151). Josephus would have liked to appear in Jewish history as another Ananus, but one who unfortunately recognized the hopeless circumstances at an early stage. He knew that no one would listen to his advice, that had he remained in Jerusalem and fought for his ideas his fate could have been similar to that of Ananus (who was killed). (For a different characterization of Ananus see the *Life*.) This is another way of apologizing for his own defection. Josephus had to resign himself to the hatred of his own people but tried to explain to them in his writings that had people like himself and Ananus been allowed to act according to reason, an understanding between Jews and Romans would certainly have been reached. They would have found a congenial counterpart in the Roman camp, namely Titus.

In the *History*, Titus' political astuteness, his diplomatic skill, his organizational talent, and his distinction in military operations are continuously emphasized. Moreover, Titus should be extolled for his unusual clemency, magnanimity, and love for people *(philanthropia)*. Even the burning of the Temple—an act that earned him the epithet *harasha,* or villain, among the Jews—was not his fault. According to Josephus (*History* 6.165), the Jews, not Titus, started the fire that burned the Temple. In a war council Titus explicitly opposed the idea of burning the sanctuary (236–243). But things got out of control when an impatient soldier moved by some supernatural impulse snatched a branch from the burning timber and flung the fiery missile through the door without orders. After victory and before returning to Italy, Titus revisited Jerusalem. He contrasted the scene of desolation before his eyes with the former splendor of the city and, calling to mind the grandeur of its ruined buildings, he bewailed its destruction (7.111). There is, however, a different version in Sulpicius Severus: some members of Titus' staff suggested sparing the Temple, but Titus himself ordered it to be burned to the ground (*Chronica* 2.30.6).

To sum up, the passages in the *History* that deal with Josephus' role in the Galilee, those that depict Titus' personality, and those that vilify Jewish rebels as brigands and robbers should be read with great care. In all other respects, however, Josephus produced a classic that should be rated very high in comparison to other history books written in antiquity. His chronology and geography are impeccable, and recent excavations support the accuracy of his descriptions. From a literary point of view the book is a masterpiece as well. This may be due to the expertise of his Greek assistants, students of a school of rhetoric who knew all the tricks of the trade. But this does not change the fact that the style is smooth and spellbinding and that the story is fascinating and dramatic. The descriptions of the misery of the civil population during the siege of Jerusalem, the burning of the Temple, and the story of the exile could be set as models to what was called in antiquity "pathetic historiography." This historiographical school believed that a history book should influence the reader in the same way as a beautiful sculpture or an impressive picture.

The *Jewish Antiquities* belongs to a different category altogether. Josephus dedicated twenty years of his life to this masterwork. He had improved his Greek during his years in Rome, although he never mastered the pronunciation (*Antiquities* 20.263), and this time he wrote his book without the help of Greek stylists. The language is poor and artificial, and connoisseurs could easily detect that Greek was not the author's mother tongue. But it was not Josephus' purpose to produce a beautiful book. He intended to tell the gentiles something about the Jewish people and their history. Titus was dead, and since Domitian did not care for Josephus at all, he withdrew from the limelight of the Flavians without attracting attention. Only Epaphroditus, an imperial freedman, supported his work.

Josephus' model was Dionysius of Halicarnassus, who produced his *Antiquities of the Roman People* in 7 B.C., also in twenty books. This was quite customary in ancient times. Nations that sought to become part of the civilized world had to tell the Greeks something about their own origin and antiquity. This is what Manetho did for Egypt, and Berossus for Syria and Mesopotamia. The first Roman history was written in Greek, by Pictor Fabius in the third century B.C. Josephus hoped that in recounting to the gentiles something about the antiquity of the Jewish people, their dedication to the tradition of their forefathers, and their high morality, the reputation of the Jews would be enhanced among other nations.

The books are extremely uneven; the first eleven books deal with biblical times, and tell us the history of the Jewish people down to the destruction of the first Temple and the Babylonian exile. In many cases Josephus merely paraphrased the Hebrew Bible, and in order to make his task easier he used to a great extent its Greek translation. Josephus considered it his duty to narrate events as they were recorded in the sacred books (*Antiquities* 3.81) but did not try to impose a particular view on his readers. Incidents of a miraculous or mythical character are followed by such statements as: "but concerning these things let everyone think as he pleases" (1.108). In this respect Josephus followed the customary method of Greek and Latin historians. Livy wrote in his preface that it was the privilege of antiquity to mingle divine things with human, and so to add dignity to the founding of cities: "the historian should neither affirm nor refute these stories" (preface 6–7). Dionysius of Halicarnassus occasionally wrote: "let everyone judge as he will" (*Antiquities of the Romans* 1.48), a formula that might be traced back to Herotodus (7.152).

The weakest part of Josephus' *Antiquities* is his description of the Persian domination and the beginning of the Hellenistic period in Judea. With no serious historical records at his disposal he treated the story of Esther as fact, and never seriously scrutinized the legendary parts of the story of the Tobiades (the first Jewish Hellenizers) or those in the letter of Aristeas, which gives the story of the translation of the Bible from Hebrew into Greek. This is why the last ten books of the *Antiquities* are evaluated as a patchwork compiled from miscellaneous sources that were used uncritically.

For the period of Antiochus Epiphanes down to the rise of Herodes, Josephus used the first *Book of the Maccabees*, Nicolaus of Damascus, Strabo, and some Polybius. From the downfall of the Hasmoneans to the beginning of the administration of the Roman procurators (books 14–18), Josephus mainly followed Nicolaus (just as in the *History*), but some major differences are obvious. The description in the *History* is brief and artistic; that in the *Antiquities*, full and in chronological order. In the *History* Herodes is extolled as a great king; the killings that took place at the court are depicted as tragic events. In the *Antiquities*, Josephus does not hesitate to condemn Herodes' cruelty and to criticize some of Nicolaus' statements as sheer flattery. He states explicitly that Nicolaus did not write a history book but a work meant to help the king. "I however being of a family closely related to the kings descended from the Hasmoneans and therefore having the priesthood together with other honors have considered it unfitting to tell any falsehoods" (*Antiquities* 16.186–187). In books 18–20 Josephus used Roman official records that must have been at his disposal (Suetonius, *Lives of the Caesars*, Vespasian 8) and he also read some Latin historians, perhaps M. Cluvius Rufus.

No wonder that a book as uneven as the *Antiquities of the Jews* became an ideal hunting ground for scholars interested in *Quellenkritik* (source criticism). The authenticity of the *testimonium Flavianum* (*Antiquities* 18.63–64), in which Jesus Christ is mentioned, was already suspect in the sixteenth century by Scaliger. An enumeration of articles and books written about these two passages would fill many pages; a full *Forschungsbericht* (survey of modern research) could easily develop into a big book. An analysis of the authenticity of official documents reproduced in the *Antiquities* has become the topic of many dissertations, and there is hardly a study in *Urkundenfälschung* (falsification of evidence) that does not draw a lesson from them.

Josephus' last and perhaps most brilliant book is *Contra Apionem*, or *Against Apion*, a polemical book in two parts with a subtitle, "on the antiquity of the Jews." The exact date of publication is unknown, but it is certainly later than *Antiquities*, to which it makes reference (*Apion* 1.54; 2.87). Some scholars date its publication as late as the second century A.D. Just as his autobiography is considered to be an apology for his life, so is *Against Apion* an apology for his people. In it Josephus not only makes an effort to demonstrate the antiquity of the Jewish race, he also tries to refute prejudices that prevailed in the Greek and Roman world concerning the origin and religion of the Jews.

Apion was one of the most zealous antisemites of the first century A.D., and three of his slanderous stories may be cited as examples. In one passage Apion repeats the apocryphal charge that Jews were expelled from Egypt as the result of a contagious disease or some similar affliction. He knew that Moses led the Jews through the desert and says:

> after six days of march the Jews developed tumors in the groin and that was why after safely reaching the country now called Judea they rested on the seventh day, and called that day Sabbaton preserving Egyptian terminology: for disease in the groin in Egypt is called *sabbatosis*.
>
> (*Apion* 2.15–20)

In a second story Apion says that in the sanctuary of the Temple the Jews kept an ass's head, worshiping that animal and deeming it worthy of the deepest reverence (2.79–80). The third story is even more bizarre. The king Antiochus found a man in the Temple who fell at his knees and implored him to be set free. The man was a Greek who told the king that he had been kidnaped by Jews and conveyed to the Temple. There he had been shut up and fattened on food of the most lavish description. Eventually he found out their real purpose: Jews would kidnap a Greek, fatten him up for a year, and convey him to a wood. There they slew him, sacrificed his body with their customary ritual, partook of his flesh, and ... swore an oath of hostility to the Greeks (2.89–96).

Apion was not an ignoramus. He was a well-known Homeric scholar who was dubbed by Tiberius Caesar the "cymbal of the universe" (*cymbalum mundi*: Pliny, preface to *Natural History* 25); he wrote a history of Egypt; and he represented the Greeks of Alexandria before Caligula as counterpart to Philo, who represented the Jews. He might have used this kind of argumentation in front of the emperor, but an infuriated Josephus, who understood the damage that might be caused by a man of Apion's international reputation, exclaimed: "I am doubtful whether the shameless remarks of Apion deserve serious refutation ... most of them are pure buffoonery and display the gross ignorance of their author." Nevertheless, Josephus argued in earnest and tried to expose Apion as a totally untrustworthy historian and an impudent liar.

Josephus' polemic was not directed against Apion only, and from this point of view the title of the book is ill chosen. Josephus proved that he was extremely well acquainted with Greek philosophy, history, and poetry, and defended Judaism with great zeal against many other antisemitic writers. He also quoted some nonantisemitic writers who had good things to say about the Jews (for instance, Clearchus and Hecataeus). Hence the great importance of the book. It contains numerous quotations from writings that have not survived, and it is mainly due to the *Against Apion* that scholars of the nineteenth and twentieth centuries were able to produce indispensable anthologies of Greek and Latin texts on Jews and Judaism.

Despite Josephus' literary success he was a tragic figure. It is, of course, true that Rome perpetuated his memory. His statue was erected in the city and his works were placed in public libraries (Eusebius, *Historia Ecclesiatica* 3.9). But it is doubtful whether the Roman emperors considered friendship with Josephus to be an asset. He was never awarded the official title of *amicus Caesaris* (friend of Caesar). He was not among the *comites* (the imperial entourage). He must have been a member of the lower entourages, in the same category as doctors and magicians, philosophers and buffoons. In spite of his victory, Titus never became a Judaicus (as a general who was victorious over the Germans became a Germanicus), perhaps because of the religious connotation of the term. Tacitus, in sketching the history of the Jews, preferred other sources to Josephus. He might have read him, but he never quoted him.

In Jewish tradition the fate of Josephus was even more tragic. It had always been his ideal to appear as a second Jeremiah (*History* 5.391), but to no avail. Jews were never prepared to compare a renegade who acted as an adviser of moderation in Titus' headquarters with a Jeremiah who preached peace and moderation from within the besieged walls of Jerusalem. Josephus' name was never mentioned by the Jewish sages (the Tananim or the Amoraim). Only Christian historians enhanced his reputation. For St. Jerome he was a Graecus Livius; for Cassiodorus, a *paene secundus Livius*. (*Secundus Dionysius* would have been more appropriate.) For his Jewish redemption he had to wait for the Middle Ages. In spite of his efforts Josephus must have been a very lonely man in his old age.

Selected Bibliography

TEXTS

Josephus. 9 vols. Cambridge, Mass., and London, 1956. Loeb Classical Library. Latin with English translation.

CRITICAL STUDIES

Cohen, Shay. *Josephus in Galilee and Rome.* Leiden, 1979.

Naquet, P. Vidal. *Flavius Josèphe ou du bon usage de la trahison.* Paris, 1979.

Rajak, T. "Justus of Tiberias." *Classical Quarterly* 23:345 (1973).

Schalit, A., ed. *Zur Josephus Forschung.* Darmstadt, 1973.

Stern, M., ed. *Greek and Latin Authors on Jews and Judaism.* 3 vols. Jerusalem, 1974–1980.

Thackery, H. St. John. *Josephus the Man and the Historian.* New York, 1929.

Yavetz, Z. "Reflections on Titus and Josephus." *Greek, Roman and Byzantine Studies* 16:411 (1975).

ZVI YAVETZ

MARTIAL

(ca. A.D. 38–ca. 104)

[1]The text by W. M. Lindsay, *M. Val. Martialis Epigrammata*, 2nd. ed. (Oxford, 1929), has been followed in this essay. His numbering, sometimes reflecting his arrangement of poems, especially in books 10 and 12, has also been followed. Where his number differs from that of the order in the manuscripts and in L. Friedlaender's edition, the traditional number is set in brackets.

LIFE

LIKE ALMOST ALL outstanding men of Latin letters, Marcus Valerius Martialis was not a Roman by birth or ancestry. Although his three common names reflect a Roman background, the poet acknowledges his Celtiberian blood (see *Epigrams* 7.52; see also 1.49; 10.13[20]; 12.18).[1] His ancestors would have been among the first Spaniards to confront the Italian invaders of eastern Spain in the later third century B.C. Sometime in the reign of the emperor Caligula, between A.D. 38 and 41, Martial was born at the mountain town of Bilbilis on the Salo River in the Roman province of Tarraconensian Spain (modern Calatayud on the Jalon River in the Spanish province of Zaragoza). The town strategically commanded the valley of Salo, a tributary of the Ebro River, and its high Iberic Mountain terrain yielded gold and iron. The latter was worked and also made into weapons at Bilbilis. Consequently, by Martial's time some natives of the place could boast the equestrian census, the next to highest property rating of Roman citizens (see 1.49; 1.61; 4.55; 10.13[20]; 10.103; 12.2[3]; 12.18; 14.33).

Martial himself enjoyed the census of a Roman knight which he doubtless derived from the wealth of his father. Indeed, Martial's education, all apparently acquired in Spain, reflects the ambitions of the provincial well-to-do (see 3.95; 5.13; 9.49; 9.73; 12.29[26]). The obvious cleverness of the future poet suggested to father or son that he seek a career on the larger stage of the Roman world empire, and in A.D. 64 he arrived in Rome. The moment seemed propitious for a clever and ambitious Spaniard. Yet Martial reached the capital as the last in a short line of Iberians illustrious in learning and literature and powerful in society. In the year 64, the younger Seneca of Corduba was approaching the end of his career both in writing and in governing the empire of Nero. Seneca's nephew Lucan, also engaged in politics, had brought forth his epic, *The Civil War*. Quintilian, the great teacher of rhetoric, was looking forward to a career of considerable influence and eminence. He hailed from Calagurris (today Calahorra in the Spanish province of Logroño), a town not too far from Bilbilis. These Spaniards had undergone an education at the center of empire; Martial had not.

Seneca and his family, along with the Calpurnii Pisones, served to promote Martial's political career (4.40; see also 12.36). He climbed that first rung on the ladder of political and governmental office with the military tribunate (3.95), an office that need not imply any military function at all. Since Augustus' reign, political preferment was accorded those aspirants who had three legitimate children. But even the innovator of this standard, Augustus himself, granted a privilege of three children to the favored of the court whether they were married or not. Martial tells us that he had received this grant of privilege from two Caesars (3.95; 9.97). These two Caesars have been identified as two of the three Flavian emperors, either Vespasian and Titus or Titus and Domitian. It is more likely that the grant was first made by Nero when Martial enjoyed important political patronage and still sought political advancement and that it was subsequently confirmed by Vespasian after the civil war of 69–70. In A.D. 65, an information of conspiracy was lodged against one of the Calpurnii Pisones. Consequently, Nero destroyed the family of Seneca and diminished the authority of the surviving Pisones, who never appear again in Martial's poems as his patron. Of Martial's public career no more is heard. Now in his mid-twenties, the Spaniard took to writing poems that he was to blush at some twenty years later and wistfully regret were still available in book stalls (1.113). Calm and normal government did not return to the empire until 70, when Vespasian secured his regime after three more years of Nero's rule and another of civil war born of rivalry for the vacancy in the government Augustus had established nearly a century earlier.

Martial and others give no clue as to his activities under Vespasian (d. 79). Perhaps he attempted in vain to resume a career hardly begun in 65. More likely, he turned to the writing of the poetry he later regretted. We can safely surmise that his political failure hardly enhanced his financial situation. A frequent refrain of his poems cries poor: poor in money and poor in housing. But poverty then as now was relative. He kept company with important and powerful men, but men not so famous as a Seneca or a Piso. He owned land; he owned slaves. Evidently he went through his share of his patrimony, for when he returned to end his days in Bilbilis he lived on land given to him. Rome was a costly city and its social habits even costlier. When Martial's personal life

emerges through his poems, he is living on the Quirinal Hill close to the place where Spanish metals were handled (1.117; 5.22; 9.18; 10.58; 12.57). Also neighbors were the new dynasty whose private houses were located on the Quirinal, just north of which lay the Gardens of Sallust where Vespasian was the first to establish an imperial residence.

Martial maintained friendly ties with several prominent Spaniards also living in Rome. He counted the widow of Lucan a patroness (7.21; 7.23; 10.64). From Bilbilis he knew the pleader Licinianus (1.49; 1.61; see also 4.55), who was perhaps Valerius Licinianus (Pliny, *Epistles* 4.11) and a relative. Also, a fellow townsman, Maternus, is celebrated by Martial for his great name as a jurist and master of pleading (1.96; 2.74; 10.37). To the barely known writer Decianus of Spanish Emerita (modern Merida) Martial dedicated his second book of epigrams (1.8; 1.24; 1.39; 1.61; book 2, proem; 2.5). From Martial we have a better knowledge of Canius Rufus of Gades (modern Cadiz), who tried his hand at writing historical epic, fable, and tragedy (1.61; 3.20; 3.63; 7.69). Only once does Martial address the great Quintilian of Calagurris in his verses (2.90).

While Martial may represent the acme of Spanish Latin literature, he is more truly admired for his representation of the city of Rome and its inhabitants. His poetry serves as a peculiar, not to say unique, window on the ancient city. Few ancient authors even pretended to an interest in the life and character of inhabitants of any city. Among the few, Martial stands out for the rich variety of his treatment of urban life. He realized success in this endeavor through his choice of genre, the epigram.

THE EPIGRAM

To set us upon familiar ground, an epigram by a contemporary American may be given as an example of the genre. In Ogden Nash's *The*

Old Dog Barks Backwards (1972), we have "Which the Chicken, Which the Egg":

> He drinks because she scolds, he thinks;
> She thinks she scolds because he drinks
> And neither will admit what's true.
> That he's a sot and she's a shrew.

All of Martial's poems are classed as epigrams, although many of them were not cast in the standard epigrammatic meter, and many do not conform to the epigrammatic composition Martial himself made virtually canonical. Two characteristics define Martial's epigram: shortness and subject matter. The subjects, admittedly varied and heterogeneous overall, suggested themselves for the most part because they amused, entertained, and satirized through their own reflection of human nature and through their author's endowment of ready wit. Few of Martial's poems are immediately apprehended today, so that a reader must often labor long over what the poet expressed with pithiness in brief compass.

Normally the epigram had been cast in one or a few elegiac couplets consisting of a dactylic hexameter followed by a dactylic pentameter. The very name "epigram" recalls its Greek beginnings as an inscription on a tombstone or as some other kind of label. Among the Greeks the epigram kept to its couplet form but broadened its scope. Some epigrammatic pieces, that is, epitaphs and other labels, were composed solely for exhibition of the Greek poets' capacity to compose on such subjects and were not intended for use in their proper circumstances. Epitaphs, for instance, might be written for a long-dead man of fame, or a label might be composed to identify a well-known masterwork of art wanting no label. Thence the epigram developed into a short poem marking many occasions in life or commemorating real and imagined lives and social entertainments. The Greeks also chose the epigram to inveigh against personal enemies.

Although Romans were writing epigrams in Greek and Latin by the late second century B.C., we possess no Latin collection of epigrammatic poems before that of Catullus (*d.* 54 B.C.). The Latin epigram took on two aspects borrowed from other literary genres. From satire came attention to the peculiarities of human nature. From the rhetoric of oratory the epigrammatist took the Roman love of vituperation. Sometimes obscene, often merciless, very witty and even funny, the epigram became as much a weapon in Martial's hand as a steel dagger made in Bilbilis.

The epigram had already become a political weapon. Martial himself quotes one of Augustus' directed against Antony's wife, Fulvia:

> Because Antony fucked Glaphyra, Fulvia fixed this fine on me that I fuck her. I should fuck Fulvia? What should I do if Manlius would ask me to fuck him? No, I think, if I'm smart. She replied, "Either fuck or fight." What if I value my life more than my prick? Let them sound the trumpets of war!
>
> (11.20)

Regardless of station, Romans clearly enjoyed expressing themselves with the bluntest vocabulary in epigrammatic form. Catullus so attacked Caesar; Augustus, Fulvia.

Martial found himself heir to both a Greek and Latin legacy of epigram. His Greek predecessors, especially the Neronian favorite Lucillius, are best known to us through the *Greek Anthology*. Martial does not acknowledge directly the popular tradition of epigram at Rome. Instead he names his Latin literary predecessors: Catullus, Domitius Marsus, Albinovanus Pedo, and Cn. Cornelius Lentulus Gaetulicus (book 1, proem; 2.77; 5.5). Marsus, like Vergil and Horace, enjoyed the patronage of Maecenas. Pedo was an active military officer under Tiberius and wrote both epigram and historical epic. Gaetulicus belonged to one of Rome's most splendid patrician families; after a consulship in A.D. 26, he served as a provincial governor for ten years and thereafter was put to death by Caligula. Gaetulicus' reputation rested on love poetry. Attention is here drawn to Gaetulicus, and to Pedo for that matter, because they and others like them earned a reputation for literary production while serving in responsible positions of government. Martial may have hoped to imitate them by combining public and literary careers. Instead we know Martial as an epigrammatic poet following in the footsteps of Catullus.

THE COLLECTION OF MARTIAL'S POETRY

Aside from three lesser books written and published between 80 and 86, Martial's poetic output is concentrated in the twelve books of epigrams written and published over a period of eighteen years (A.D. 85–102). These are the books for which he wished to be, and is, remembered. Most of them were written in Rome and about Rome. For a short while in 87 and 88 Martial sojourned in the north Italian town of Forum Cornelii (modern Imola), whence he launched his third book (3.4; and see 3.1; 3.56; 3.57; and 3.59 for references to other parts of northern Italy). Returning to Rome before the end of 88, Martial lived there until 98, when he re-emigrated to Bilbilis forever. His tenth (a second edition) and twelfth books contain poems written on his native soil as well as pieces looking back to his days in Rome. The twelfth and last book was apparently issued in 102. In A.D. 104 Pliny the Younger mourned the death of the "brilliant, clever, sharp man whose writings exhibit much wit and spleen and sincerity." Pliny also tells us that he had given Martial the money for his journey home out of friendship and in return for the lines Martial had written on him (Pliny, *Epistles* 3.21.1; see also Martial 5.80; 10.20[19]).

Besides the twelve books of epigrams, there survive three earlier books, also epigrammatic, which go by different titles. The oldest is the *Book of Public Entertainments (Liber spectaculorum)*, a modern but convenient title, also called *Book of Epigrams (Epigrammaton liber)*

outside the standard numeration. Next in time are two books of labels: *Xenia (Gifts)* and *Apophoreta (Party Favors)*. In defiance of chronology these books are named and numbered in the surviving corpus *Epigrammaton liber 13* and 14, respectively.

The chronology of the extant books of Martial is based on modern scholars' interpretations of the internal evidence:

Liber spectaculorum	A.D. 80
Xenia and *Apophoreta*	
(*Epigrammaton libri 13, 14*)	83–86
Epigrammaton libri 1, 2	85–86
Epigrammaton liber 3	87–88
Epigrammaton liber 4	December 88
Epigrammaton liber 5	fall 89
Epigrammaton liber 6	summer or fall 90
Epigrammaton liber 7	December 92
Epigrammaton liber 8	mid-93
Epigrammaton liber 9	late 94
Epigrammaton liber 11	December 96
Epigrammaton liber 10	
(*2nd ed.*)	mid-98
Epigrammaton liber 12	101–102

In addition to the poems of his salad days, Martial's first edition of book 10 in, we think, December 95 and a one-book anthology of books 10–11, published in 97, have not descended to us, although stray poems attributed in other sources to Martial may be assigned to the lost books (see 1.113; 10.2; 12.4[5]; 12.11).

MARTIAL'S POETRY

Ancient poetry—and Martial's is no exception—depends on several technical and stylistic devices for literary appreciation. The principal technical device is the choice and treatment of meter, from which follows the subsidiary consideration of metrical pause and the like. Nearly 80 percent of Martial's 1,561 collected poems are in elegiac couplets, distichs comprised of a dactylic hexameter and dactylic pentameter, often repeated, though single couplets are by no means rare. After the elegiac verse the hendecasyllabic meter is the most frequent, 238 poems. The third, and last, frequent meter is the choliambic, found in seventy-seven cases. Other metrical forms are very rare in this poet. In spite of the modest variety in choice of meters, Martial considered all his poems epigrammatic.

Martial, a student of rhetoric as well as verse, utilized many and various tricks of style. Basic, it seems, to most Latin poets was alliteration. Most important for Martial was syntax. As an inflected language, Latin permitted great flexibility in word position so long as the metrical requirements and the poet's sense of word accent/metrical accent were not violated. Within this frame Martial developed the two-liner, where the very last word makes the whole point. Here are two examples:

Quid mihi reddat ager quaeris, Line, Nomentanus?
hoc mihi reddit ager: te, Line, non video.

(2.38)

You ask, Linus, what my Nomentan farm yields? This is what the farm yields: the absence of you.

Compare for idea, not for length, Dorothy Parker's "Sanctuary" in *Death and Taxes* (1931):

My land is bare of chattering folk;
The clouds are low along the ridges,
And sweet's the air with curly smoke
From all my burning bridges.

The following epigram implies an indecency Martial expects the reader to supply:

Zoile, quid solium subluto podice perdis?
spurcius ut fiat, Zoile, merge caput.

(2.42)

Zoilus, why do you ruin the bathwater by dunking your ass? To make it fouler, Zoilus, dunk your head.

The two epigrams are representative. Both put a question in the first line. In the former the second line answers the question with the last word after stating the proposition. In the latter epigram, laded with alliteration, the question is left unanswered while the situation is improved by carrying it to the comparative degree and advising worse with the last word. Here Zoilus' head meant to Martial's reader that he engaged in oral, not anal, sex (compare 11.95).

Wordplay, too, belongs to Martial's style. The word *Gallus* was originally the ethnic noun/adjective "Gaul" that might be used as a man's or woman's proper name (Gallus/Galla). As a descriptive substantive the word also served Latin for "rooster" or, in the same capacity, for a castrated priest of the Great Mother Cybele.

Here is a "Gift" label from the *Xenia* that was to accompany a capon:

Ne nimis exhausto macresceret inguine gallus,
amisit testes. Nunc mihi Gallus erit.

(13.63)

So that the rooster [*gallus*] wouldn't grow skinny in tiring his groin, he gave up his testicles. Now he will be a eunuch priest of Cybele to me.

This epigram plays on the ethnic senses:

Curandum penem commisit Baccara Raetus
rivali medico. Baccara Gallus erit.

(11.74)

Baccara the Raetian has entrusted the treatment of his penis to a physician who is his rival. Baccara will be a Gaul/eunuch-priest-of-Cybele [*Gallus*].

To reinforce the play on nationality Martial also employs the outlandish personal name Baccara. Martial apparently invented the name after *baccar*, a spikenard of the valerian family that had wide medicinal applications. Also, the poet could employ Gallus to heighten the humor of a religious sequence since the word had the sense of the eunuch priest of Cybele. For instance, a long (fourteen-line) epigram on a sacrifice to Bacchus describes an Etruscan gutgazer who orders a dull-witted farmer to castrate the goat victim. The hayseed mistakes a bulge in the gutgazer's clothing and excises it. The poem ends:

Sic, modo qui Tuscus fueras, nunc Gallus aruspex,
dum iugulas hircum, factus es ipse caper.

(3.24)

In this wise you who had just been an Etruscan gutgazer are now a Gaulish [*Gallus*] gutgazer, [for] while slitting the goat's throat, you yourself became a wether.

A similar religious context is created in this epigram:

Drauci Natta sui vocat pipinnam
collatus cui Gallus est Priapus.

(11.72; compare 1.35)

Natta calls teeny peeper the thing of his boyfriend in comparison with whom Priapus is a eunuch priest of Cybele [*Gallus*].

The joke is not limited to the notion of a castrated Priapus and its sexual implications. Martial seems to have invented the word *pipinnam* from the verb "to peep, chirp" to suggest a bird (a *pipio* was a baby bird) and thus to contrast "rooster" (*gallus*) with "teeny peeper" and to set up the emphatic alliteration *pipinnam/Priapus.* Several poems on Priapus are to be found in Martial; they belong to his received genre.

Nowhere does Martial employ the personal name *Gallus* to play with the word in another sense. That would have been too easy. The foregoing four examples contain quite simple wordplay for the poet. None can be rendered simply into another language because the punnings on the word *Gallus* are peculiar to the native language of the poet and his public.

THE TONE OF MARTIAL'S EPIGRAMS

Even the most tolerant of modern readers will sometimes recoil from the blunt terms of Martial's explicit sexual and scatological obscenity. Different times, different readers. In 1701, Vincent Collesso prepared an edition of Martial for the French dauphin at the behest of Louis XIV in which he set apart 150 of 1,172 epigrams of books 1–12 because of their scabrousness. (The king would more likely have been affronted by Martial's poems on bathing.) In the great commentary in his text of Martial, Ludwig Friedlaender, who would dwell long on a metrical deviant and not at all on a man's teeny peeper, cited the number of 150 to show that Martial did not merit the accusation of emphasizing the "dirty side" of Roman life (vol. 1, p. 15). English translations of the poems sometimes render them whole or in part into Italian to spare the English mind contamination. (These Italian versions exhibit such literary taste that an Italian reader may not be scandalized.) In his Loeb Classical Library translation (1919–1920), W. C. A. Ker made this choice inconsistently, because he was capable of rendering *fellator* (cocksucker) as "foul rascal," a rendition leaving much to be desired linguistically and nothing to be desired otherwise. The Loeb edition was revised, without naming the supplementary translator, in 1968 and now contains English translations of all the corpus. Martial did not write for French crown princes of tender years, nor for novices in a nunnery for that matter. He was not attempting to represent social norms, socially acceptable or unacceptable behavior, or "vistas down by-lanes of hideous vice." However, he can be made to speak for himself on this topic. In fine, his indecent poems were intended to serve neither eroticism nor pornography.

Martial's views on the epigram and on his epigrams should be considered together. In his three early books no statement of poetics is to be found. He wrote prose or prose and verse proems to books 1 (for 1 and 2), 2, 8, 9, and 12, as well as verse dedications. From these and epigrams in like vein can be pieced together his aesthetics of the genre. He tries to strike a balance so that no self-respecting person may take offense. Even readers of low station are not hurt by his mockery. Anyway, the names of real persons, let alone of the great, are not uttered. His pleasantries leave no room for misconstruction. Indeed, his poetic models, Catullus and the other Romans mentioned above, had bequeathed him a license to employ the frank and risqué language proper to epigram. The prefatory statement, or even just the scroll's tag, can be the beginning and end of a prude's reading. Epigrams are meant for those who watch the Floral Games, but Cato should not enter Martial's theater unless he intends to stay and watch. Without restraints his poems are the games and popular diversions of both holiday and holyday (see book 1, proem). Martial often returns to the allusion to the Floral Games, a public religious festival held every April and May and marked by much bawdiness. As aedile in charge of those games, Cato the Younger had put in only a ceremonial appearance and then withdrawn so that no spectator would feel inhibited by his curmudgeonly and self-righteous presence. (Even prudish and skittish Romans, especially if politicians, knew when to preach and when to keep silent.) So in answer (1.35) to complaint, Martial likens his book's desire to entertain the reader to a husband's desire to entertain his wife: no prick, no pleasure. Who wants to put clothes on the Floralia and garb the performing whores in a gentlewoman's gown? Funny verse enjoys a privilege. It cannot give enjoyment unless it is randy. Otherwise the book is castrated. What is fouler than a *Gallus Priapus* (1.35)?

Martial had already experienced, or at least anticipated, criticism from every quarter. The emperor Domitian, who had made himself censor for life and thus was empowered to control the private lives of the senatorial and equestrian classes, read Martial's defense. "The ceremony of the triumph is accustomed to badinage that is fit for the 'leader's' ear. Your censorship can allow harmless play. Our writings are playful; our way of living, upright" (1.4). In restating this commonplace of the scabrous poet, Martial alludes to the doggerel soldiers hurled at their generals. Julius Caesar heard, "Residents, lock up your wives. We are bringing home the bald seducer. You fucked away in Gaul the gold you borrowed here at home" (Suetonius, *Life of Caesar* 51). And, with reference to Caesar's sexual submission to the king of Bithynia, "Caesar dominated the Gauls; Nicomedes, Caesar. Look here's the triumph of the Caesar who enthralled the Gauls. No triumph for the Nicomedes who enthralled Caesar" (*Life of Caesar* 49).

In the proem to his second book, Martial states that the epigram takes satisfaction only in its proper—that is, bad—language. Here *mala lingua* may also mean "naughty talk." Pursuing the contrast of good and bad in his works, Martial lists three good points (*bona*) about his books: short pages, short trifles or jests, and the reader can reckon them "bad," not hateful (2.1). Often Martial calls trifles (*nugae*), what we may call light verse. His poetry is addressed to adults. "I told you, chaste lady, not to read on, and you did. My poems are no more reprehensible than the mimes you attend at the theater. So, read on" (3.86). After dinner and over wine is the time of day for his funny songs (4.8; see also 4.82; 10.20[19]).

To the emperor Domitian, Martial addresses his fifth book and prescribes its reading in country retreats (5.1). But the book is also addressed to gentlewomen, to boys, to girls. His first four books have been written for those who like the wanton and the impudent couched in naked wit. His fifth plays for our master, the emperor (5.2). Again, to Domitian: no one complains of Martial's poetry working harm; indeed it bestows fame on those he mentions. Do the poems have a market value? No, they just give the poet pleasure (5.15).

Three years later Martial returns to this matter, again with Domitian in mind.

With heavenly brow untroubled let my master read me and hear my jests as he usually does, since my writings have hurt not even those whom I rightly hated. My renown justifies me because none is made ill at ease.... Our antics hurt no one. You know this well. I swear by the god of powerful Renown and by your ears, for me like unto a mighty deity, oh reader free from impolite jealousy!

(7.12)

Here, and again in 7.72, Martial rejects poetry drenched by the poisoned pen of poets who detest life itself and hound their enemies to death. In his proem to book 8, Martial resumes what he had set forth in book 1 by telling Domitian that he has modulated the pleasantries of his miscellany. Epigrams have been written by men of the strictest morals and of the highest station, who yet approached the abandon of the mimes (see book 8, proem). If Martial's poems please schoolteachers, all well and good. But he writes not for their praise, but so that his poems may live on without the help of schoolteachers (10.21). Jealousy afflicts the poems that speak of moral fault and not of immoral persons (10.33).

Many an epigram in Martial revolves around the merrymaking, partying, and loose behavior of the December festival of Saturnalia. This was a time also for the exchange of gifts and reversal of social positions. Masters waited on slaves. Norms of personal conduct were relaxed. In these circumstances Martial considered his poems Saturnalian (11.2). Old-fashioned ladies can read some of his work, but the present book is full of laughter and more wanton than its predecessors: besotted with wine, drenched with perfume, sporting with boys, dallying with girls, and bluntly calling on that sire of mankind that even reverent King Numa called his prick. The book has none of the poet's morality, just the songs for "Saturnality" (see 11.15).

Read, if you must, the laborious and age-encrusted poets of the good old days. Don't ask me to take them for models. I would go out of business if you did not know what your prick liked.

(11.90)

Prudish reader, quit this book. I wrote it for the sophisticated. It plays to the wanton song of Priapus; it dances to Spanish castanets. Even men of the olden times had erections. Though you, maid, come from the most staid of backgrounds, you too will read the impudent entertainments here when you are having a cup of wine—or two. Lucretia blushed and put down my book. But then she was reading it in front of Brutus. Withdraw, Brutus. She will read on.

(11.16)

Martial wished his poems to be taken only as seriously as any entertainment should be taken. Content and language of the genre required acceptance of holiday mood, a mood elsewhere engendered by some Roman religious festivals. A Numa, a Cato, a Lucretia, too, acknowledged the scope of epigram even if they took no pleasure from it. Martial's audience has come to the theater to watch the mime or the whores' striptease. No one is hurt and most are amused. Those susceptible to sexual shock or prone to expression of moral outrage are advised to read the work of others. While it is a mistake to play down Martial's treatment of the sexually obscene, especially since in nearly every discussion of his epigrams Martial articulates the rules of entertainment among which the sexual joke is paramount, still, there are many other facets of Martial's poetry.

BOOK OF PUBLIC ENTERTAINMENTS

In A.D. 80 the emperor Titus formally dedicated the Flavian Amphitheater on the site of a natural pond that Nero had turned into a private lake ringed with miniature luxury houses within the entry of his Golden House. Vespasian and Titus had engaged in the initial efforts to efface the physical and moral blemish of the Neronian fire of 64. These efforts included the razing of the Golden House. The colossal statue of Nero that had marked the entryway was converted by a change of head into the sun god. But it still towered majestically by the new amphitheater and gave its name at last to what we still call today the Colosseum. An amphitheater was a structure of two inward-facing theaters, which in this case the Flavians intended for gladiatorial combats, wild beast hunts, and mock sea battles. The oldest surviving poetry of Martial commemorates Titus' grand opening of this marvelous place of peculiarly Roman entertainment.

The *Book of Public Entertainments* contains twenty-nine epigrams, to which stray poems are often added by modern editors. But it lacks poems of dedication and farewell. The present small compass of the book suggests that what we possess today is but a lesser part. The new amphitheater is likened to, and made to surpass, the Seven Wonders of the World (1). It marks with its colossus the restoration to Romans of the delights reserved to the tyrant Nero (2). Titus is universally acclaimed father of the fatherland (3). Deadly public informers are suppressed (4). Other poems celebrate the program pieces of the amphitheater: reenactment of the bull mounting Pasiphae; Mars and Venus making obeisance to Caesar; a woman hunting a lion; the crucifixion and mauling by wild beasts of a criminal; Daedalus attacked by a bear; a pregnant sow subjected to Cesarean section by arrows (hymned in three epigrams); an elephant kneeling to worship Titus; Orpheus' re-creation of his taming of nature; Leander or Nereids in the flooded arena; a sea battle in which Thetis, Galatea, Triton, and Nereus vie; a doe spared by hounds who watched her pray to the prince (5-8, 12-14, 17, 21, 24-26, 30). These are epigrams written for occasions that magnify the emperor. The arena themes recur in the poet's later books.

THE BOOKS OF GIFTS AND PARTY FAVORS

Next Martial published his *Xenia (Gifts)* and *Apophoreta (Party Favors).* The former book (now book 13) holds 127 labels, nearly all single distichs, for gifts of food and drink. That for a capon was quoted above. The *Party Favors* (now book 14) holds 228 labels, again nearly all single couplets, for domestic entertainments at the Saturnalia (14.1). Many are pairs of epigrams on a cheap and an expensive gift. Some examples are: hunting spear, hunting knife, belt and sword, dagger (from Bilbilis), sickle, hatchet, barber implements (14.30-36), a couch of citruswood veined like a peacock's plumage, hunter's saddle, curved couch with tortoiseshell inlay, sideboard, citruswood table, maple table (14.85-90), marble hermaphrodite, portrait of Danae in golden shower, clay mask of a German, bronze Hercules strangling snakes, ceramic Hercules, silver Minerva, painting of Europa, marble Leander (14.174-181); editions of Homer, Vergil, Menander, Cicero, Propertius, Livy, Sallust, Ovid, Tibullus, Lucan, Catullus, and Calvus (14.183-196); a monkey, girl from Gades who could make Hippolytus randy, smooth boy, dwarf, idiot, and a pastry cook (14.202-203, 205, 210, 212, 222). Undistinguished as these epigrammatic labels are as poems, they convey something of the delights of luxury in Martial's day. Indeed, whether the subject was a baited rhinoceros tossing a dummy in the amphitheater or a suckling pig, it belonged to the genre of epigram as Martial had received it. Moreover, in the subsequent sixteen or seventeen years after publishing these first three books, Martial continued to write true epigrams: tombstones, labels, and other poems celebrating occasions.

THE BOOKS OF EPIGRAMS: INSCRIPTIONS AND OTHER LABELS

Whether Martial ever realized material return for writing epitaphs or any other such pieces we do not know. We do know that there was a large market for epitaphs, for many in verse have survived with their stone. Sometimes Martial made several efforts on the same late-lamented (for example, 1.114, 116, on Faenius; 6.28, 29, on Melior; 5.34, 37, and 10.61, on Erotion). Martial composed epitaphs for celebrities in public entertainment. For an actor named Paris he wrote:

> Whoever you are, traveler, trudging along the Flaminian Way, don't pass by this noble marble. Buried in this tomb with Paris are the city's delights, the Nile's wit, skill and charm, play and pleasure, the grandeur and grief of the Roman stage and all the world's Venuses and Cupids.
>
> (11.13)

To one of the day's great charioteers Martial gave this sentiment: "I am that famous Scorpus, glory of the Circus' roar. Your acclaim and your delight, Rome, were all too short. Out of spite for my wins Lachesis believed me old at 27 and carried me off" (10.53). Even in composing epitaphs, Martial could not withstand his wit's urging:

> Little, to be sure, is the marble you are reading, traveler, but not surpassed by Mausoleum or Pyramids. My life was twice over remarked at the Tarentine Games and lost nothing until I was cremated. Juno gave me five boys and five girls. The hands of all closed my eyes. I happened to enjoy an unusual bedchamber: my chasteness knew only one prick.
>
> (10.63)

Martial mocks slightly the requirements of childbearing for gentlewomen who sang in chorus at the Tarentine Games (in A.D. 47 and 88), exaggerates the commonplace of children surviving the parent when twenty hands closed two eyes, and finally cheapens the boast many a Roman husband had had carved on his wife's tombstone, "I was chaste and had one husband." Martial loved such ambiguities: "Criminal Chloe carved on the tombs of seven husbands that they were her doing. What could be simpler?" (9.15).

Some of Martial's labels for artistic representation might serve also as epitaphs.

> Gentle glory of the stage and star of the games, I am that Latinus your favorite for acclaim who could make Cato keep his seat and the Curii and

Fabricii lay aside their seriousness. But by our theater my life was not at all changed, and I am considered a player only by virtue of my art. Nor could I have pleased my master without morality. That god looks deep into man's heart. Number me among the parasites of Phoebus so long as Rome knows that I am slave of its own Jupiter.

> (9.28)

Here Martial takes the occasion to dissociate the actor from the low reputation of the actor's calling by pointing to the god-emperor's divine discernment. The point of the epigram is made by contrasting a parasite of Apollo, that is, a member of a professional guild, with a slave of Jupiter, the deity that Martial often invoked in Domitian's person. Much more in the earlier style of epigram is "renowned by branch of Jupiter, glory of the Roman buskin, Memor is restored and breathes through the art of an Apelles" (11.9). Again, Martial flatters Domitian by referring to a branch or wreath bestowed in the Capitoline Games (hence the ambiguities as to this Jupiter's identity) and flatters the anonymous painter by likening his art to that of a famous painter of the fourth century B.C.

Domitian, Suetonius tells us (*Life of Domitian* 13), contrived to build so many arches in the city that some wag wrote on one of them *arcei*, the Greek for "Enough!" Martial composed an inscription for such an arch:

> Here where the far-gleaming precinct of Fortune the Homebringer glitters was recently only a happy square. Here stood Caesar handsome with the grime of the northern war and radiating crimson brilliance from his face. It was here the leader stopped and was greeted by shouts and waves from Romans with locks garlanded in bay and clad in shining white. And yet other gifts bear witness to the great importance of the site. An awe-inspiring arch rises and revels in the taming of foreign tribes. Here two triumphal cars are displayed drawn by elephants, and *his* golden image befits the enormous beams. This gateway, oh Germanicus, is worthy of your triumphs, this avenue of approach gives proper adornment to the city of Mars.
>
> (8.65)

Martial also tried his hand at an inscription for a statue group of Domitian's beloved niece Julia as Venus with Cupid (6.13), but he was apparently more at ease in variations on the epigrammatist's theme of inscriptions for statues of Priapus (6.16; 6.49; 6.73; 8.40).

THE BOOKS OF EPIGRAMS: OCCASIONAL POEMS

Personal and formal occasions invited Martial's poetic effort: marriage, condolence, sightseeing, recovery of health, and, of course, various anniversaries (see, for example, 4.13; 4.44; 7.21–23; 7.47; 7.74; 8.38; 9.39; 9.52–53; 10.23–24; 10.38; 10.87; 11.65; 12.67). Such pieces also belonged to the genre.

THE BOOKS OF EPIGRAMS: ROMAN CHARACTERS

The epigram that has earned Martial his fame was not the formal piece but rather the pungent mirror of Roman life and society.

You want, Cotta, to seem both pretty and grand:
but a man who is pretty, Cotta, is a petty man.

(1.9)

Gemellus wants to marry Maronilla and urges it and begs for it and showers gifts for it. Then she's beautiful? No, the ugliest ever. What then is so pleasing and desirable? She's not long for this world.

(1.10)

If I remember, Aelia, you once had four teeth. One cough launched a pair and another a pair. Now you can safely cough all day long. There's nothing a third cough can do for you.

(1.19)

The slave trader asked me a million for the boy. I laughed. But straightaway Phoebus paid it out. My prick grieves at this and mumbles complaints about me and praises Phoebus to make me jealous. But Phoebus' prick earned him twenty millions. Listen, prick, earn me that amount and I'll buy boys at higher prices.

(1.58)

Charinus is in fine health, yet he's pale.
Charinus drinks little, yet he's pale.
Charinus has good digestion, yet he's pale.
Charinus takes sun baths, yet he's pale.
Charinus tints his skin, yet he's pale.
Charinus licks cunt, yet he's pale.

(1.77)

Why don't I kiss you, Philaenis?   Baldness.
Why don't I kiss you, Philaenis?   Blotchiness.
Why don't I kiss you, Philaenis?   Purblindness.
Whoever kisses these, Philaenis, sucks.

(2.33)

Among the nomads of Libya, Gallus, your wife has the reputation of the base crime of insatiable greediness. But pure lies are told. She usually takes nothing at all. What does she usually do then? Puts out.

(2.56)

And your face I could do without and your neck and your hands and your hips and your breasts and your buttocks and your rump and, not to go into detail, Chloe, I could do without the whole of you.

(3.53)

Your Bassa, Fabullus, always sets a baby beside her and calls it her pet plaything and, more's the wonder, she's no baby-sitter. What's the reason then? Bassa is a chronic farter.

(4.87)

You have never seen a more pitiable creature than Sabellus who was the happiest when he fucked boys. His afflictions are thefts, runaway and dying slaves, fires, dying relatives. Now he is wretched and fucks women.

(6.33)

The court unwillingly grants your booming voice its request for six water clocks of pleading, Caecilianus. But you talk on and on and on and you quaff warm water from flasks at ease in your chair. So that you may at last quench voice and thirst we ask you now, Caecilianus, to drink from the water clock.

(6.35)

That fellow who has the place of honor, the one who had carefully arranged the three hairs of his scalp in three rows with pomade, the one who is drilling his gaping mouth with toothpicks, he's a liar, Aefulanus. He has no teeth.

(6.74)

"Quintus loves Thais." "Which Thais?" "The one-eyed Thais." "Thais does not have one eye; Quintus has two."

(3.8)

And in reply to complaints about the foregoing:

If your girl, Quintus, is not Thais and is not one-eyed, why do you think the distich addressed to you? But there is a similarity. I said Thais for Lais. Tell me how are Thais and Hermione similar? Yet you are Quintus. Let us change the lover's name. If you don't want to be Quintus, let Sextus love Thais.

(3.11)

Thais has black teeth, Laecania white. What's the reason? Thais has her own, Laecania bought hers.

(5.43)

I sent you, Lesbia, hair from some northern tribe so that you might know how much blonder is yours.

(5.68)

Fabulla swears the hair she bought is her own. Paulus, does she ever swear falsely?

(6.12)

Of a morning you always tell me nothing but your nightmares about myself, and that disturbs and upsets my mind. I've spent not just last year's, but this year's vintage, too, to have a witch exorcise your night's work. I have used up heaps of sacrificial meal and incense. My flocks decline with endless lambs as victims. Gone are my pigs, my

fowl, my eggs! Nasidianus, either stay awake or dream about yourself.

(7.54)

Since Galla can be fucked for two bits and can be more than fucked for twice that amount, why did she get ten times that amount from you, Aeschylus? Galla doesn't charge that much for sucking. What then? She keeps her mouth shut.

(9.4)

So long as one bears in mind that the foregoing epigrams require little or no explanation, they may stand as representative of a type. They were so chosen for illustration here because they run to at least four lines.

The epigrams contained within a couplet's limit offer greater difficulty to understanding because of their compression.

Whoever believes Acerra stinks of last night's wine is wrong. Acerra always drinks till dawn.

(1.28)

Diaulus had been a surgeon, now he is a mortician. He has begun again where he left off.

(1.30)

I do not love you, Sabidius, and cannot tell you why. Only this I can tell you. I do not love you.

(1.32)

Diaulus was recently a physician, now he is a mortician. What the mortician practices the physician practiced, too.

(1.47)

You have a prick, Papylus, as large as your nose so that whenever it rises you can smell it.

(6.36)

Titus, our friend Caecilianus never dines without wild pig. Caecilianus keeps fine company.

(7.59)

Oppianus, the one and only time you saw me I was ill. Ill will I ever be, seeing you often.

(8.25)

Whoever says you are full of faults, Zoilus, is lying. You are not a man full of faults, Zoilus; you are a fault.

(11.92)

Even the shortest of Martial's witticisms usually require explanation; some are even beyond our understanding. "If you call your cook Mistyllos, Aemilianus, why shouldn't I call mine Taratalla?" (1.50) supposes the reader's knowledge of a familiar Homeric formula of banquet scenes, *mistyllon t' ara talla* (and at once they carved up the rest [of the meat]: *Iliad* 1.465). Aemilianus has given his chef the fancy name of *Tranchèrent*; and Martial quips that his cook should be called *D'Autres-parts.*

Knowledge of both Greek and Latin classics was expected of readers of all genres of literature. Homer, especially, was known by heart. Martial dubbed boxer Pollux *pux agathos* (good with the fist) and his twin Castor *hippodamos* (horsetamer). "Gabinia turned Achillas from a Pollux into a Castor: he had been *pux agathos* and will now be *hippodamos*" (7.57). Achillas, apparently a professional boxer, used to serve Gabinia sexually in a manner appropriate to his calling. She has changed their roles and now rides his penis. In this case the reader must think in terms of the Latin verb *equitare* in its sexual sense.

Greek punning also occurred with words Latin had borrowed: "Now you are an *oplomachus* who had been an *opthalmicus* before. What you do as an *oplomachus* you did as a physician" (8.74). The *(h)oplomachus* was a very heavily armored gladiator who evidently tried to put out his opponent's eyes. This epigram belongs to the "Diaulus" series selected above and lends emphasis to the fact that Martial tried several times over to write epigrams on the same subject with only the subtlest differences that his keen readers would appreciate.

Cinna was a good Roman name; Cinnamus, a foreign name. "Cinnamus, you ask to be called Cinna. I ask you, Cinna, isn't this a barbarism? If you had formerly been called Furius,

would you be called *Fur* (thief) by that method?" (6.17).

More often than not, appreciation of Martial's pithy barbs rests on acquaintance with Latin colloquialisms and Roman social customs. The latter are readily apprehended, but the former sometimes elude us because the overwhelming bulk of Latin literature is composed in an elevated, not to say artificial, literary language. Here is a poem on a social-climbing nouveau riche. "At your birthday party, Diodorus, a senator reclines at your table and some knights are present and your cash handout is a generous three hundred. No one, however, thinks you have birth [literally, were born], Diodorus" (10.27). "To be not born" is a Roman snobbism for being a "nobody." Diodorus counts himself arrived because of his high-born guests, but their contempt for the parvenu denies the fact of his birth at his own birthday party. Naturally, jokes such as these and many others even more elaborate lose wit in their explication. On the other hand, a full recasting of the epigrams into a different and modern milieu while trying to make a like point robs them of most, if not all, of their Roman savor. A comparable subject is treated in an American epigram that also continues the tradition of the literary epitaph. From "Tombstones in the Starlight" in Dorothy Parker's *Death and Taxes* (1931), here is the epitaph of "A Very Rich Man":

He'd have the best, and that was none too good,
  no barrier could hold, before his terms.
He lies below, correct in cypress wood,
  and entertains the most exclusive worms.

Two other twentieth-century American pieces in a Martialic vein suffice to illustrate several points.

I'd rather flunk my Wasserman test
Than read the poems of Edgar Guest.

We are here today to do honor to a modern
  madonner

899

who stands in the hall in a niche.
For who could adore the world's biggest whore
but the world's biggest son of a bitch?

The first poem, perhaps already requiring explanation to some readers today, could not be rendered into Latin intelligible to a Roman. The second poem, apocryphally attributed to Parker, is a kind of "label" for a statue like that of Julia as Venus and could be rendered into intelligible Latin. But the poem defies appreciation unless the reader knows that the subject is said to be the movie star Marion Davies as the Virgin Mary, that the hall and niche belonged to San Simeon Ranch, and that the owner of madonna and ranch was William Randolph Hearst, a man of great account especially in California, though Martial would have said that he was never born.

THE BOOKS OF EPIGRAMS: THE ENVOIS

One of Martial's happier achievements is the envoi. Besides writing the common dedication of his small book (libellus or parvus liber), well-known in Latin letters from the first poem of Catullus where he, too, describes his epigrams as trifles (nugae), Martial sent his books on explicit errands. He consigned the first to the book dealers of the Argiletum in Rome, because it playfully wanted to leave the safety of his study for a sneering, captious, critical audience (1.3; for similar epigrams on the book trade in Rome, see 1.2; 1.117; 4.72). Although his third book came from northern Italy, the poet concludes it with four lines to Canius Rufus in which he tells the hour of his runner's departure and advises that he will have arrived sodden with downpours of rain. Such were ideal conditions for sending his poems (3.100).

The fourth book is sent to the discerning Faustinus, who has earned possession of these trifles. But the slave is not to hurry off without a Carthaginian sponge. Many erasures could not improve the jests, but one alone could

(4.10). The fifth book was intended for Domitian (see 5.1; 5.2). In 5.6 Martial asks the Muses to intervene with the emperor's chamberlain Parthenius that he might grant an audience to his shy little writings within the threshold of the holy halls and to introduce them to his (Parthenius') calm and receptive Jupiter. At 7.26 Martial bids his limping iambs approach the critic Apollinaris when he is at leisure and, if they would find a warm reception, request his support to make them proof from ill will. The same book has an envoi to Faustinus in retreat at Tibur (modern Tivoli) and expects him to commend the poet to another. The epigram is rendered pleasant by playful allusion to the origin of the slave boy who bears the book (7.80).

Martial dedicated his eighth book to Domitian by means of an epistle followed at once by an epigrammatic envoi (8.1) reminding the book to master a tone of humble respect in the presence of a lord victorious. Naked Venus is ordered to withdraw, for the book belongs to the emperor's Minerva, a deity we otherwise know Domitian much venerated.

Another kind of envoi gives instructions to the book on how to find its way through tortuous Rome so that it may substitute for its author in his service as client. Even without Martial's poems on the irksome toil a client suffered to give many a patron a morning greeting and to carry away, so the client hoped, a handout, we have ample familiarity with the Roman social custom of the morning greetings. Most Romans knew a station in life that required attendance at the morning levee of several men arrayed above them by rank and wealth. The client—and who was not a client to somebody?—was expected to scurry from house to house and to dance attendance upon a patron barely risen or not yet risen from bed.

To Proculus' gleaming house Martial sends his first book on this errand. It knows not the route. Pass, writes Martial, the temple of Castor and its neighbor the house of virginal Vesta, head up the slope of the Palatine where many statues of the most high Leader glitter, turn where drunken Bacchus is housed and Cybele lives in the round shrine adorned with painted Corybantes, look for the lofty halls of the senator on your left, fear not the threshold of the haughty. Should Proculus ask, "Why has not the author come?" the book may reply, "A man who makes a profession of attending levees cannot write what is to be read in me" (1.70). A variation on the type from the same book (1.108) begins with the wish that Gallus' beautiful mansion enjoy a long life of expansion. Yet the house is across the Tiber while the aging Martial's digs look out on Agrippa's bay trees. To greet Gallus in the morning is comparable to moving house. Besides one more man in formal morning clothes makes no difference to him. Martial will greet him many times over in the afternoon. In the morning his book will say hello.

In one of the four envois in the book sent from northern Italy, the book asks for a letter of recommendation since it travels to the city without its poet. One or several? One is enough. Go to Julius whose name is ever on my tongue. You will find him at the beginning of Covered Street at the former mansion of Daphnis. His wife will give a warm welcome though you are covered with road dust. To Julius or his wife, whoever is first met, say, "Marcus sends greetings." That's enough. Other men need letters of recommendation. Not a man with a friend (3.5).

The most famous envoi of this type Martial composed for Pliny the Younger, who, though eloquent, will receive a book of little learning and seriousness. It's a quick job to scramble up the slope of the Subura where you will see the theatrical fountain of Orpheus with its awestruck beasts and the royal bird that carried off the Phrygian boy to the Lord of Thunder and the small exquisite house with its smaller eagle. Be careful not to knock on the door of learning when you are drunk. He spends his entire day in serious business, and so his fame at pleading will rival Cicero's. It's safe to enter when lamps are lit. That's your time of day when Bacchus loses control, when the garland rules, when the hair is perfumed. Then even curmudgeons like Cato may read Martial (10.20[19]).

The times changed with Domitian's assassination and Nerva's elevation. To open his eleventh book Martial again appealed to Parthenius, who had arranged the fall of his former master and is now promoted from chamberlain to chief of the bureau of petitions (*libelli*, allowing Martial's wordplay). Are you going out for a stroll in your finery, book? Are you headed for Parthenius? Of course, go and come back unrolled. He reads not books but petitions. He has no time for poetry, and if he did, he would write his own. Will you settle for less? Go to the colonnade of Quirinus' temple here in our neighborhood. It is thronged with more idlers than the colonnade of Pompey, or of Europa, or of the Argonauts. There are always one or two who might unroll the bookworms of my antic verse but only after they have done talking of and betting on the charioteers (11.1). Here is a Martial weary of the search for discriminating, and generous, readers. His book is destined to find men willing to put out money only on chariot races.

Martial had yielded to the weariness of Roman life nearly ten years earlier and packed himself off to northern Italy. The book he produced there asked to be given as a gift to Faustinus (3.2; see also 4.10) as well as recommended to Julius (3.5). But Martial did not resist employing the envoi to explain himself. If anyone were to inquire of the third book whence it came, the answer is the country of the Via Aemilia (today the region Emilia); and to what place or city, Forum Cornelii. Why has he gone away? He could not bear the unprofitable boredom of formal attire. When is he coming back? He left a poet; he will come back when he has learned to be a harpist (3.4). Poetry lacked even the acclaim and income of a popular musician.

Returned and resigned to Rome, Martial's books traveled to the mouth of the Danube on the Black Sea where Caecilius Secundus soldiered and wished for the poet's portrait (7.84). The same scroll went to Caesius Sabinus in Italian Umbria, where he would recite this, his second favorite poet, to dinner parties, to law courts, to the gods, to the crossroads, to the colonnades, to the shops; the book has been sent to one man and will be read to all (7.97). A copy of the eighth book without its decoration hurries to loveliest Narbo, home of the learned, whither Martial's friend Arcanus has returned to take up public office. Martial wishes he might be this little book (8.72). To another city in Gaul, Tolosa (modern Toulouse), the next book bears Martial's greeting to M. Antonius (Primus), friend and admirer of Martial's and the glory of his hometown (9.99). Primus had been an early military supporter of Vespasian and his new dynasty. Martial's fame also spread to lively Vienna (modern Vienne), where his books delighted young and old, boy and girl (7.88). The last envoi from Rome was addressed to a townsman of Bilbilis with greetings to those childhood companions who yet remembered their fellow townsman departed thirty-four years before. The poem, the last of the tenth book (10.104), must hasten to take ship so that it can beg in good time the purchase of a haven of retirement in Bilbilis by the Salo where Martial may grow lazy. And so he does.

The last book's farewell starts from the tribes of the Tagus and the dourly earnest Salo and reaches Rome a foreigner where once it was at home. But it is no stranger to the lofty mansions of Romulus and Remus. Just seek the home of the Muses or enter the Subura and find the halls of Martial's very own consul Arruntius Stella, whose fountain gives refreshment like the Castalian Springs. Indeed, story has it that the Muses once drank of it. Stella will share this book with his fellow senators, with the knights and the entire people. Stella shall read it with tear-stained cheeks. "Why do you ask for a label? Let two or three lines be read and all will shout, book, that you are mine" (12.2[3]).

To be sure, the envois disingenuously invite favor and patronage, beg for the poet his excuses, and praise men and their home countries. In the same moment, they express the poet's friendship and affection with a winning grace. Pliny the Younger paid Martial's passage home to Spain. That envoi had presumably found Cicero's rival happy in his cups. In this

century Dorothy Parker entitled three epigrams "L'envoi" but to a different end:

> Oh, beggar or prince, no more, no more!
>   Be off and away with your struts and show.
> The sweeter the apple, the blacker the core.
>   Scratch a lover, and find a foe.
>   ("Ballade of a Great Weariness," *Enough Rope*, 1926)

> Prince, a precept I'd leave for you,
>   Coined in Eden, existing yet:
> Skirt the parlor, and shun the zoo—
>   Women and elephants never forget.
>   ("Ballade of Unfortunate Mammals,"
>   *Death and Taxes*, 1931)

> Prince or commoner, tenor or bass,
>   Painter or plumber or never-do-well,
> Do me a favor and shut your face—
>   Poets alone should kiss and tell.
>   ("Ballade of a Talked-off Ear,"
>   *Death and Taxes*, 1931)

THE BOOKS OF EPIGRAMS: SOME PATRONS

Martial addressed himself to many he reckoned actual or potential patrons, men of substance from whom he might draw an income, irregular and uncertain. Most of his addressees have a precarious place in our knowledge; some exist for us only through Martial. Pliny the Younger, of course, enjoys renown by virtue of the survival of his letters and a panegyrical speech addressed to the emperor Trajan. To his peers he was known as a forceful advocate in the law court and a capable senatorial administrator who reached the consulship in A.D. 100. If one wishes to belittle Martial for his eternal mendicancy—and Pliny was to prove a one-way ticket to Bilbilis—one must bear in mind that Pliny called Martial friend and wit.

L. Arruntius Stella, consul a year or two after Pliny, appears in seventeen of Martial's poems, besides the last envoi, and sometimes he is in the company of his wife, who appears twice apart from her husband. This couple can illustrate the patron for whom Martial hoped. In Martial, Stella found himself in the company of Catullus, Vergil, Ovid, the Senecas, and Lucan; he contributed to Patavium's (modern Padua) renown (1.61). His poetry glittered like jewels in finger rings (5.11; 5.12); his house hosted literary recitals (4.6).

In 90, Stella married. Martial introduced his marriage and his bride in a poem. To her he gave the Greek name *Ianthis* (Violet) to conceal the real and brutal Violentilla. The marriage poem exhibits Martialic wit (6.21). The contemporary poet Statius dedicated his first book of *Silvae* to Stella and wrote Stella and Violentilla an epithalamion (*Silvae* 1.2). That and Martial's poem are as chalk and cheese. Martial's is the palatable poem. The fountain of Stella's house worked a cure on Martial and was rewarded with a poem to his Muse-like nymph (6.47, perhaps for inscription). The fountain came under Ianthis' protection (7.15). Its epithets become indistinguishable from those to Ianthis, the queen of the place: glory and pleasure of an outstanding house (7.50). Stella had long ago written a poem on a dove; Martial likened author and bird to Catullus and the sparrow (1.7). Catullus' Lesbia had mourned her dead sparrow; Stella's Ianthis, her dead dove. What pleasant plaything, Martial wrote years later, had Martial's girl to mourn? A slave boy not yet twelve years old whose prick had not yet grown to eighteen inches (7.14)! (Martial was more the birdwatcher than the ornithologist.) In 93, Stella was in charge of Domitian's triumphal games for victory over the Sarmatians. They surpassed the display of the gods; the gifts to the public were extravagant; the chariot races outnumbered those normally given by the consuls. (Stella appears to be filling the office of praetor, just below that of consul.) Stella's games, however, exceed all else because the bay-bedecked Domitian watches them (8.78).

The next year Martial has Apollo ask the kindly emperor to make Stella consul. Then will Martial be obligated to sacrifice in thanks to Apollo. The victim is ready. Hurry, Apollo

(9.42)! Martial's last envoi, that from Bilbilis, acknowledges the outcome of Martial's vow to Apollo, for Stella, weeping over Martial's latest book, is now Martial's consul. For all these poems and others where Stella is merely mentioned (9.55; 10.48; 11.52) or casually addressed (1.44; 5.59; 9.89), what do we know Martial received in turn? A load of roof tiles for his leaking farmhouse. "Stella, you cover the farmhouse and not its farmer" (7.36). Stella had neglected to clothe his poet friend.

THE BOOKS OF EPIGRAMS: MARTIAL AND THE EMPERORS

Naturally enough, Martial aimed at the highest patron. His link to the palace was Domitian's chamberlain Parthenius. Parthenius, a freedman of Nero (less likely of Claudius), served Domitian as chamberlain and traitor (Suetonius, *Life of Domitian* 16–17) and, as we we have seen, Nerva as chief of the bureau of petitions. For Parthenius, Martial wrote a dedicatory inscription to Apollo for offerings on the occasion of the fifth birthday of Parthenius' son (4.45). A year later, in A.D. 89, he asked Parthenius to give the emperor his fifth book (5.6). That there existed some understanding between freedman chamberlain and shivering poet is proven by an extravaganza of twenty-two lines on a toga Martial had received as a gift from Parthenius' hands (8.28). A year later this resplendent pride of his equestrian rank was deemed threadbare by its indigent owner (9.49), who very probably wanted another. One tie between the two men seems to have been an interest in writing epigrams (12.11; see also 9.49; 11.1). After the hesitation in the envoi of the eleventh book (Parthenius was too busy; 11.1), Martial sent his Muse with the twelfth to ask Parthenius to give the "shy little book" to the emperor: "Your Rome is reading this scroll" (12.11). Both in 89 and in 101 or 102 Parthenius acted the intermediary.

In the intervening twelve years or so, Martial's poems had grown no bolder, for his book was shy in 89. Since Parthenius had been slain in 97, this epigram (12.11) was left over from the condensed one-book edition of books 10 and 11 (see 12.4[5]). Martial was either proud of the poem or too tired to compose anew to fill his twelfth book, or in the safety of remote Bilbilis, he vaunted his friendship with the dead minister. By the time the epigram was published in book 12 the empire had passed again to a new prince. Martial still sought a prince's recognition and, what's more, the generosity of a prince's purse.

No doubt, the poet's oldest extant book celebrated Titus' games inaugurating the amphitheater, because that easygoing, jolly monarch might show a readiness to patronize him. Domitian did not appear such an easy mark, though his pretensions of literary talent were broadcast far and wide.

Martial's adulation, if such it be, of Domitian has come in for much undeserved condemnation. This is not the place to weigh Domitian's reign upon some scales of historical or moral judgment. At least one poet (Statius) did not lag behind in praise of Domitian. Tacitus, who outlived the prince and whose condemnatory accounts inform the history of his reign, won advancement under him, a proof of Domitian's poor judgment. Indeed, most of Domitian's survivors are incriminated by virtue of their very survival when his deeds were so foul. Martial could hope to better his lot under Domitian's successors simply because others who had served Domitian later advanced in rank. Stella is one, Pliny another, and Tacitus, too.

Domitian made himself odious to many by enjoining address as "lord god." A tendency to this manner of address had been experienced and squelched decades earlier by Augustus and his successor, Tiberius. Domitian accepted what had emerged from his subjects' loyalty. Moreover, Domitian's attitude fitted, or expressed, his conception of the ruler cult. Horace, for instance, comes in for little blame in writing of Augustus in quite extravagant terms. Yet Augustus' hands were no cleaner than Do-

mitian's when it came to disposing of his political enemies.

On 16 September 96 Domitian lay dead. Martial's eleventh book appeared in December without mention of Domitian. The tenth, issued a year before, was supplanted by a second edition in 98. The bulk of Martial's extant poetry was written and published under Domitian. The emperor had been Martial's lord god since A.D. 88 (4.1; 5.3; 5.8; 7.5; 8.4; 9.79), and his attributes were heavenly, holy, and sacred (8.4), as befitted a deity. Martial had begun likening him to Jupiter (1.6; 4.1; 4.3; 5.1), but by A.D. 90 Domitian had become Jupiter the Thunderer (6.10; 6.83; 7.56; 7.60; 7.99; 9.3; 9.65; 9.91) as well as mere Jupiter (8.15; 8.24; 9.24). In respect to the type, Martial's poems on Domitian's military victories seem extravagant but not tasteless (for example, 7.2; 7.6–8; 8.15).

In A.D. 86 Martial had merely asked the emperor to read his work (2.91). Two years later he opened a book with a birthday poem to his prince who was a god (4.1). In the next year Martial tentatively addressed himself and his fifth book to Domitian with proper wit (5.1; see also 5.6, the earlier envoi to Parthenius, and 5.15). In 90, his newest book "will dare to rest in Caesar's mighty hands though with less anxiety and trembling" (6.1). Some of Martial's "shyness" had worn off the year before when he closed a laudatory piece on Domitian's incomparable reign with a bid for the friendship of the emperor, who laughs at the poet for advice on gift giving and friendship that will profit only the poet himself (5.19).

Issued in 93, the eighth book bears a dedicatory epistle to Domitian and contains some nine poems worthy of remark on the relation between prince and poet. One, an inscription for a triumphal arch with elephant-drawn chariots (8.65), has already been discussed. Here is the prose epistle dedicatory:

All my little books, to which you have given renown, that is life, my lord, go down to you on bended knee. And on this account, I think, they will be read. Yet this, our eighth book, profits more often from the opportunity of loyal devotion. Consequently my talent has toiled less where there had come naturally the material that I have tried to vary with a miscellany of jests so that not every line would heap upon your heavenly modesty their praises that might more easily bore you than they would suffice us. Moreover, although epigrams have been written by the most moral and highest born men in such a manner that they seem to take on the verbal license of the mime, nevertheless I have not allowed these epigrams to speak out so playfully as they are wont. Since the larger and better part of this book is bound up with the majesty of your holy name, it will remember that none but men purified by ceremonial cleanliness should approach the precincts. . . .

(book 8, proem)

True to his word, Martial publishes here no poem that invites "Englishing" into Italian. Consequently, the fifth and the eighth books of epigrams may be read safely even today by those striving to avoid Martial's "prick."

Domitian declined a formal triumph for his war against the Sarmatians, but Martial treated the emperor's achievement as triumphal:

> While the fresh glory of the Balkan war is reckoned and while every altar succeeds in sacrificing to our Jupiter Homebringer, the people offer, the thankful knights offer, the senators offer incense, and a third donation enriches the peoples of Latium. Rome, too, had recalled the triumph concealed, and the bay crown marking your peace was no slighter because you trusted yourself to rely on the reverent loyalty of your subjects. A prince's highest virtue is to know his own subject.
> (8.15)

The games and public gifts for his nontriumphant festival were those put in Stella's charge (8.78).

Martial deferentially seeks personal generosity from Domitian:

> If perchance I ask through my thin, shy book, if my writings have not been wicked, give. And if

you have not given in the past, Caesar, allow the request today. Never do prayers and sacrifice harm a Jupiter. Whoever represents the holy visages with gold and marble does not make the gods. Whoever makes a request of the gods does make the gods.
> (8.24)

Martial cannot be convicted of importunity because a god exists to be the very object of man's prayers.

Martial imitates the first line of the first extant poem in his own *Book of Public Entertainments* with the first two lines of a poem on Domitian's new Palatine palace.

> Laugh, Caesar, at the royal wonder of the pyramids; barbarous Memphis boasts no more of its oriental monuments. How small a fraction of the Parrhasian hall is the Mareotic work? Nothing more splendid is seen by the Day in its full course. One would think the Seven Hills were rising up in unison. The smaller Ossa carried the Thessalian Pelion. It penetrates the fiery heaven just as, set among the shining stars, the stormless peak thunders in the clouds below, and it is imbued with Phoebus' hidden force before Circe looks upon her father's face. And yet, Augustus, this house whose roofs knock at the doors of the planets matches the firmament but falls short of its master.
> (8.36)

Evidently Martial received at least an invitation to dine with his lord:

> Never before did place exist that could hold the parties of the Palatine table and its banquets of ambrosia. Here man can drain cups of holy nectar mixed by a Ganymede's hand. I pray that it may be long before you consent to be a dinner guest of the Thunderer. But, Jupiter, if you hurry, come yourself to dinner.
> (8.39)

Later, Martial will hymn the praises of Domitian's cupbearer Earinos, whom he likens to

Jupiter's Ganymede (9.11–13; 9.36). But the divine banquets were not limited to the palace:

> We are told how great was the banquet at the triumph over the Giants. How great was that night for all the heavenly gods when the good father reclined at table with his subject gods, and Fauns might ask wine of Jupiter. The banquets that celebrate your bay crown, Caesar, are as great as those. Our rejoicings entertain the gods themselves. All the people, knights and senators eat with you and in the Leader's presence. Rome dines on ambrosial dinners. How much greater your gifts than even your promises! We were promised a handout and were given a formal dinner.
>
> (8.49[50])

Emperor Domitian had long engaged in Rome's rebuilding, but he aimed at maintaining the old with the new, the primitive with the sophisticated:

> You restore to us the wonders of our saintly ancestors and let not the old times die when the old ceremonies of the Latin arena are renewed and courage battled with a humbler sword. Just so honor to the old temples is observed by your rule and [Romulus'] hut keeps its divinity in the shadow of the cultured Jupiter. Just so while you found the new, Augustus, you bring back the old. Whatever is and whatever was are owed to you.
>
> (8.80)

With a poem on the honors due to poets Martial concluded this book dedicated to Domitian:

> Augustus, amid a throng of petitioning plaintiffs and poets tendering small poems to their lord, we know a god can find time for business and for literature and even these wreaths do please you. Suffer, Augustus, your bards, for we are your sweet glory, we are your earlier concern, we are your delight. Not the wreath of oak leaves alone nor that of Phoebus' bay leaves becomes you. From us may you wear a civil decoration of ivy wreath.
>
> (8.82)

For his pains Martial took from the emperor's hand no grand gift insofar as the poet himself tells us. Perhaps the emperor looked for an epic poet for the court. Martial looked for a man or god to play Maecenas, but he himself declined to play Vergil (8.55[56]). While Rome's prince embodied divinity and lordship, Martial did not hesitate to address him as a mere leader (8.21; see also 5.19). After the emperor's death, Martial expressed himself freely on Domitian: "Flavian dynasty, how much your third heir has robbed you! The price of the first two was almost too great to pay for the price of the third!" This couplet is not in our extant corpus of Martial, but is recovered from a scholiast on Juvenal (*Satire* 4.38), where Martial's younger contemporary calls Domitian the bald Nero. Presumably Martial's epigram was included in the now lost anthology he made from poems on books 10 and 11. In book 11, Martial mildly refers to Domitian as Nero (11.33). But no biting piece savages the fallen prince.

In addressing Nerva, who briefly ruled after Domitian, Martial acknowledges that Fear has been routed by Trust, Mercy, and circumscribed Power. Nerva had dared to be good under a harsh prince in evil times. This epigram further defines the prince's role of generous donor and patron on a scale rarely met among the gods (12.6). Still Martial had hoped to find his Maecenas in Nerva (11.3), whom he had known before his summons to "circumscribed" Power (8.70; 9.26) and to whom he gave the Saturnalian songs of his eleventh book (11.2).

Under Trajan, Martial says farewell at last to Dame Flattery, who had made him call Domitian lord god. She must migrate to the Orient to abase herself. This new man is not a lord, but a general and the fairest of all fair senators (see also 11.4, to Nerva), who has released unadorned Truth from Hell to preserve Rome from using its earlier language (10.72). Trajan is but a mighty soldier in the Roman tradition (12.8). Gentlest of princes, he embodies the morality of his native Spain (12.9). This last poem is more a compliment to Trajan's new governor of Martial's province than to the new emperor. Perhaps, on his home soil Martial saw a patron in him.

In Nerva and Trajan the poet found old-fashioned virtues to praise. Men of old-fashioned virtues, the Catones, the Curii, the Fabricii, had served him as foils and butts of jest (1.24; 6.19; 7.58; 7.68; 9.27-28; 11.2; 11.5; 11.16; 11.104). Truly Martial had no truck with the much-vaunted simplicity of the past. He recognized the unbridgeable distance between the nostalgia of fancy and the uncouthness of fact. Martial lived in his present, and his wit throve on the foibles of his own age. But his own age had now been relegated to the past while he lived far from the city whose heartthrob had filled his ears.

THE BOOKS OF EPIGRAMS: LOVELIEST ROME

In A.D. 90 Martial had written:

> Greatest of censors and prince of princes, although today Rome owes you so many triumphs, so many temples aborning and born again, so many entertainments, so many gods, so many cities, Rome owes you more because she is chaste.
>
> (6.4)

The poet was marking the occasion of Domitian's new legislation on morals. But the city he celebrated was in a very real sense Domitian's creation and remains so today.

Nero partially reclaimed the wasteland made by the fire in A.D. 64 with his Golden House, which only seemed to engulf the city. Vespasian built and rebuilt as he whittled away at Nero's complex. In 79 another great fire marred Titus' waning regime. Domitian found a city of rubble. His grandiose plan for the new city embraced, as Martial said, restoration of the old and foundation of the new (5.7; 8.80). Much of the new was directed toward public

entertainment: Music Hall, Stadium, and gladiatorial barracks and training schools. Like the rebuilt temple to Jupiter Tonans and the freshly founded temples to the old divinity Minerva and to the new divinity Flavian Dynasty, these new places of public entertainments and the very entertainments themselves echo in Martial's work.

Domitian was a promoter of literary contests and chariot races, but above all he was an enthusiastic fan. The prince's diversions themselves reflected a general taste in the city. While it is true that gladiatorial games and beast hunts traced their beginnings to sand spread on Roman streets, it is also true that cities and towns of the Greek-speaking East as well as the Latin-speaking West now resounded with the applause for favorite gladiators, dancers, actors, and drivers. A reading public in the Gaulish provinces, even in Britain, awaited Martial's newest book. His work was steeped in the capital's ferment. Few knew, or would ever know, the city at first hand. The empire looked at Rome through a window pierced by the poet's eye and framed by his epigrams.

Domitian, in Martial's pardonable exaggeration, turned Rome back into itself from being one large shop where the importunate tradesman had hogged the streets and where thresholds made easement on threshold. Gone were the days of pillars festooned with large jars, of flashing barber's razors endangering passers-by, and of streets choked with dust and cooking smells (7.61). So it had been when Martial lived in Peartree Street on the fourth floor overlooking a grove of bays planted by Agrippa (1.180; 1.117). Thence he sent out his early envois with their street directions (1.70) until he moved to Travertine Pillar Street, also on the Quirinal. No home could truly enjoy a central location:

> If I did not wish and deserve to see you in the morning, Paulus, I would wish your Esquiline abode were farther from me. But I am neighbor to Travertine Pillar where Flora looks out on Olden Jupiter. I have to toil up the track of the Suburan

slope whose stone is always slippery with filth, and I can barely make my way through the mule teams hauling up the marble with their ropes. What's even worse, when I get there after a thousand inconveniences, Paulus, your doorman tells my weary frame you are not at home. This is the outcome of sweat and frustration: It is hardly worthwhile to see Paulus in the morning. A stickler for protocol always has impolite friends. Unless you are still abed, you cannot be my king.

(5.22; compare 10.58)

After quitting the city for good, Martial describes the circumstances of his living there. A poor man has not a moment of repose day or night because of the din: schoolteachers, bakers, bronzesmiths' hammers, money changers taking their time clinking coin on a filthy table, the pounding of Spanish gold, unending ecstatic cries of Bellona's worshipers, a bandaged shipwreck, a mother-taught Jew begging coin, a half-blind hawker of sulphur (12.57). When you walk down the street, you are assailed by the kisses of farmers with foul breath, weavers, fullers, cobblers who have just kissed the cowhide, men with chin ailments, the blind, cocksuckers, cuntlickers (12.59; Ker translated the last two as "many a rascal with the foulest lips," which was rendered "many a sucker and fresh licker" in the revised edition). Martial longed for rest and quiet, and so explains his return to Spain (12.68; compare 12.57). Of course, others lived in worse conditions. The proverbial whores, for instance, who literally lived in holes in the Wall—the aging eastern Rampart of the city walls (1.34; 3.82; 11.61; 12.32).

Some retreated across the Tiber, but Martial found such houses too isolated for morning levees and dispatched a book in his stead (1.108). His friend Julius Martialis kept a country house on the Janiculum overlooking all of Rome and the towns beyond (4.64) that held a library offering a panorama (7.17). Even more fortunate was a man with three town houses:

You have a house on the Esquiline, you have a house on Diana's hill, and on Patrician Street your roof rises. From here you look out on Cybele's shrine, from there on Vesta's, and the old Jupiter, and the new Jupiter. Tell me where to meet you; tell me in what direction to look. Maximus, whoever lives all over, lives nowhere.

(7.73)

No sector of Rome could boast solely elegant residences. Yet any "city man" was a sophisticate in contrast to a bumpkin. Hence in Latin *rusticus* bore pejorative connotations and *urbanus* meant witty, sophisticated, cultured, and, in a word, all that Martial and his audience strove for (see 11.16). A delightful early epigram plays on the word *urbanus* by starting with the word *verna* (home-reared slave), that is, one who took liberties, and ending with reference to professional jesters, Augustus' Gabba and an unknown Tettius Caballus. The latter's second name was colloquial Latin for horse or nag.

Caecilius, you think yourself a city wit. You're not, believe me. What then? An uppity slave, that is, a traveling huckster who trades yellowish sulphur for chipped glass, that is, a seller of soaked chick-peas to a circle of loiterers, that is, the keeper and charmer of snakes, that is, a whole gang of cheap slaves belonging to salt-dealers, that is, a hoarse cook selling steaming sausages from hot shop to hot shop, that is, a poetaster who happens to live in the city, that is, a disreputable dance teacher from Gades, that is, the age-withered mouth of a gossipy faggot. Caecilius, why not stop thinking yourself what only you think yourself, a man to surpass in wit Gabba and Tettius Hack himself? Clever brains have been given to few. The man who jokes with a dullard's wantonness is no Tettius, but a hack.

(1.41)

This epigram exemplifies Martial's wit by listing some denizens of Roman street life, including a versifier who fails to embody *urbanitas*. Naturally enough, Martial scorned the failed poet and, worse, the plagiarist. Writing for friends who prized the verbal originality of wit, he often pillories these versifiers.

To reach Paulus or Pliny one climbed up the Subura, a street and quarter Martial favors in his poems. The following epigrams yield a good sample of Martial's Rome and are selected on the basis of the Subura's occurrence.

A female barber is located at the jaws of the Subura where the bloodied flails of torturers hang and many a cobbler blocks the Argiletum. But that barber, Ammianus, doesn't cut hair. Does not cut, I say. What does she do? She gives a very slick shave.

(2.17)

A little while ago Gellianus was selling at auction a girl of none too good repute like those who are located midway up the Subura. When the low bidding dragged on, he wanted to show everyone that she was pure and drew her close though she was reluctant, and kissed her once, twice, thrice. You ask what he accomplished with his kisses. The man who had just bid six hundred withdrew.

(6.66)

Clucking fowl and eggs and yellow figs and goat cheese and olives and cabbages, you think, Regulus, these were sent from my country place. How scrupulously wrong you are. My land yields nothing but me. Whatever your Umbrian foreman or tenant or country place at the three-milestone or Tuscan or Tusculum farms send you is raised for me along the length of the Subura.

(7.31)

Although you are at home midway up the Subura and outfitted like a manikin, and your own hair left you, and you stow away your teeth at night as if they were Chinese silks, and you lay yourself down like a treasure stored in a hundred boxes, and your face and you do not sleep together, yet you wink with that eyelash that is unboxed in the morning and you show no respect for your hoary cunt, which you can already reckon among your forebears. You promise me six hundred times. But my prick is deaf and although it has only one eye it can still see you.

(9.37)

No Massylian snake guards my orchards; no royal land of Alcinous is at my service. But the garden blooms amid the Nomentan woods and my dark apples fear no thief. Therefore, I send these waxy fruit of my autumn harvest that were just picked right in the middle of the Subura.

(10.94)

Nanneius plays husband with his tongue, adulterer with his mouth. He's fouler than the lips of Lower Rampart Street. When dirty Leda saw him naked from her Suburan window, she closed her whorehouse and preferred to kiss his middle than his top. He, who used to rummage through a belly's plumbing and state with a knowledgeable certainty whether a mother was carrying a boy or a girl in there, could not erect his fucking tongue. Rejoice, oh cunts! for your business has been done. While he was mired in a throbbing vulva and heard babies crying inside, an unseemly sickness paralyzed his throat. Today he can be neither clean nor unclean.

(11.61)

Get some experience of women, Victor, get some experience. Let your prick teach itself that unfamiliar job. A wedding dress is being woven for your fiancée; today the maiden is being readied. Soon your bride will give your boys slick shaves. She will put out that way once to a husband who likes to fuck boys so long as she dreads the first wound of that unfamiliar tool. Her nursemaid and her mother will often forbid its happening and will say, "She, not your boy, is your wife." What anxieties, what troubles you will suffer if the cunt remains for you an outlandish thing. Therefore, hand over your greenhorn to a Suburan schoolmarm. She will make a man of you. Maidens make poor teachers.

(11.78)

After writing such epigrams as these Martial retired on land given him by a lady of Bilbilis named Marcella (12.31). From the poet she received the strangest of compliments:

Who would think you a townsman of the straitlaced Salo, a native of our town? Your smartness is an endearing rarity. The Palatine Hill will call you its child if it shall but hear you once. No daughter of the middle Subura or girl of the Capitoline will contend with you. Nor will any who boast of foreign birth laugh at your qualities of a Roman daughter-in-law. You bid my longing for

Lady Rome to abate. By yourself you make a Rome for me.

(12.21)

One can legitimately wonder whether Marcella had ever read her Martial. To be sure, some of the high and mighty inhabited the upper Subura, but no one of good family since Julius Caesar moved away lived in middle Subura. Was not this epigram meant for discerning friends in Rome?

THE BOOKS OF EPIGRAMS: SOME CITY TYPES

A favorite city type of Martial's was the man who idled away his time in pursuit of a free meal or the like. Spongers frequently appear in the epigrams. Four poems of the second book may serve as illustration and are chosen because Martial employs the same personal name in all four. Sometimes, but not always, he builds characters by merely attaching a name to a type. Occasionally, he puts a Greek name to the person, which can be understood as a *nom parlant,* for example, *Charinus,* "Mr. Gratification." This sponging idler, however, has a plain Roman name.

> Because you see, Rufus, Selius' brow furrowed with care, because he strolls at eventide wearing out the pavement of colonnades, because his lazy face wordlessly considers something sad, because his nose indecorously almost touches the ground, because he beats his breast and pulls out his hair, it does not mean that he mourns the loss of friend or brother. Both his sons live, and long, I pray, may they live. His wife and household goods and slaves are all right; his tenants and foreman have not embezzled the profits of his land. What then prompts his sorrow? Tonight he dines at home.
>
> (2.11)

Whenever Selius beholds the prospect of dining at home he leaves nothing untried, nothing not ventured. He runs to [the colonnade of] Europa and praises your feet, Paulinus, unceasingly comparing them to Achilles'. If Europa does not bring success, he heads for the Enclosures to see whether [the statue of] Chiron or [the mural of] Jason have aught to offer. Disappointed here, he also visits the precincts of the gods of Memphis and plops down on your chair, sorrowful heifer. Then off to the Hundred Columns and thence to Pompey's theater and its two parks. He doesn't turn up his nose at the baths of Fortunatus or those of Faustus or that black hole of Gryllus or Lupus' Cave of the Winds. For in the baths he bathes again and again and again. Even when he has done all the baths and still he finds the gods niggardly, he runs back to the boxwood of warm Europa—at least he's washed out—to grasp at some friend taking an evening stroll. By your leave and by the leave of your lady, O bearer of burdens, I ask you, bull, to invite Selius to dinner.

(2.14)

Listen to Selius hymning praises when spreading his nets for dinner. Listen, you, whether you are a reader or a pleader. "Indeed! seriously! in a minute! too bad! bravo! happily! I meant this!" "Shut up! Your dinner's already made."

(2.27)

You say you're dining out unwillingly, Classicus. I hope to choke if you're telling the truth, Classicus; even Apicius used to enjoy, too, going out to dinner. He was sadder when he dined at home. Why are you going, Classicus, if you go unwillingly? "I'm forced to," you say. It's true. Selius is also forced to. Melior, I see, invites you, Classicus, to a formal supper party. Where are your big words now? Look here, if you are man enough, just say no.

(2.69)

In the last epigram Martial expects his readers to recall Selius as a type that now also includes Classicus. The epigram's point relies on Classicus' having the courage to decline a dinner invitation he has really angled, after he has protested to the poet his preference for dining at home. Why does he protest that he would really prefer to dine at home? Presumably, in response to the poet who has been himself angling for a dinner at Classicus' table.

910

Beside the later envoi to Parthenius already mentioned (11.1) and these wanderings of Selius may be set like epigrams that incidentally provide details of city buildings where men whiled away the daytime. Many Romans loitered with a purpose because they depended on the handouts of their well-to-do lords. Although Domitian himself attempted to diminish, if not abolish, the handouts, the social convention amounted to a national institution pervading the life of cities and towns. Clients could expect regular cash distributions at their patrons' "at homes" or at their afternoon ablutions in the great bathing establishments.

The handout went by the slightly euphemistic name of *sportula* (little basket) that reflected both its origin and the occasional actual practice of bestowing delicacies and superior trinkets in a small receptacle. The ordinary client expended much time and effort stalking his patron and even cadging what he believed he had coming to him. Often the client met disappointment in the size of his *sportula* or in failing altogether to catch up with the patron or his open hand. Martial's mirth at, or ridicule of, the fictitious situations he contrived underscores the inherent uncertainties of the Roman social fabric. An element of the institution, of course, was the client's pose of indigence vis-à-vis the patron's public show of generosity.

The same social relationship underlying the regular handout appears in the many poems on dinner parties. Grandees were supposed to flaunt their rank with lavish banquets where guests of lower station rubbed elbows with the host's peers. Martial obviously considered his quick and ready wit a welcome adornment to another's board. Again, however, disappointment vented its chagrin through epigrams on the paltriness of hosts who served inferior food to the inferior guests or, worse, scanted all for the sake of a mere display of luxurious furnishings (see, for example, 1.43; 3.12; 3.82; 4.68; 4.85; 7.79).

Yet another aspect of the Roman's pursuit of an income attracted Martial's caustic pen. A frequent theme emerges from the witticisms on fortune hunting, on the aged and the ugly men who would dance attendance if only they could be made the heir. The open secret was the hunter's appearance of insouciance, not to say of feigning his own means. Martial handled the subject much as he handled that of dinner invitations or handouts: irony of disappointment following expense of time and money.

Handouts, entertainments, legacies, and similar customs fomented the deeply ingrained Roman belief in social obligation. Award of a boon established, nay required, reciprocity. Romans enmeshed themselves in the elaboration of social credits and debts. *Beneficia* and *officia* they called them. Much of life was passed in exhibiting oneself. The clean and ample toga, a most cumbersome and not usual dress, was supposed to express the client's respect and respectability in his patron's eyes. Much of life was passed in public places: colonnades, halls of justice, parks, cavernous bathing establishments, on the streets. A grandee without a retinue was naked. Ill-matched or ugly litter bearers betokened a man's lack of taste or, worse, of wealth. At the peak of the relationship based on social debts and credits towered the emperor, whose display of himself and outlay of money had to excel the efforts of all the wealthy senators and knights. The wealthy and not so wealthy streamed into that sump that was the city. In their train followed the fortune hunter, the hedonist, the dandy, the jade, and the witty poet. Martial observed them jostling each other in public, sunup to sundown, and captured their gargantuan foibles in verse where we see them as clearly as the bee or ant nature has embedded in amber (4.32; 6.15; see also 4.59).

THE BOOKS OF EPIGRAMS: BEING ELSEWHERE

Like all Roman residents of the upper classes, Martial possessed a country retreat that he claimed gave him no produce, only repose. He had already acquired this land near the town of Nomentum in A.D. 85 but seems to have either sold or planned to sell it by about 98, in anticipation of his return to Spain. Besides acknowledging its use for country holidays, Martial poetically worked his land to make contrasts with the hectic city, the fashionable resort towns, and the quiet backwater towns of Italy (see 1.105; 2.38; 6.43; 7.93; 9.60; 10.48; 10.61; 10.94; 12.57).

An epigrammatic theme traditionally derived from praise of rural living turned especially on the contrast with urban living. Martial might employ the theme for wit, as he does in the poem about the man caught at the outskirts of Rome in a carriage laden with fruits and vegetables who is not entering the city with his country estate's produce but heading out to his barren estate with the food bought in Rome (3.47; see also 7.31). Except for a few poems devoted to the loveliness of villas of close friends (3.58; 4.64; 7.17; 10.30; this type yields the longest of Martial's poems), Martial appears to have had no real poetic interest in the pastoral life (see, for instance, 10.51; 10.96). Indeed, the generic theme served mainly to point up the frenzy of city dwelling (for instance, 12.18, addressed to Juvenal; and 12.57).

Likewise, when Martial glances sidewise at places of resort, he evinces no fondness for, say, Tibur (modern Tivoli) or Baiae on the Bay of Naples, two of the most fashionable. Sometimes they merely set the stage for a brief jest. Perhaps the poet tried resort holidays in 88 after returning from northern Italy. In any case, four epigrams on the subject appear in the fourth book. Martial succinctly dismisses resort life by remarking that one can die in Tibur as well as on Sardinia, a province notorious for its foul climate.

Some allure must have enticed Martial about A.D. 87 to move to Forum Cornelii. But the towns of the north brought out the snob in the outsider. Cobblers, fullers, and innkeepers constituted the local gentry (3.16; 3.56–57; 3.59) and set Martial to singing of Faustinus' villa at Baiae at great length (3.58 in 51 lines). Back in Rome in late 88, the restless Spaniard dreamt of retiring in his old age to the countryside of Aquileia, a large Roman city in the Veneto (4.25). Italian small towns normally appear in the context of compliments to some friend of the poet's (7.93; 10.12). Small-town Italy could not hold a candle to Martial's homeland spattered with outlandish names (4.55). Yet when Martial had gone back to Bilbilis for good, his nostalgia shifted focus to Rome (12.2[3]). Men of his hometown were like inhabitants of all backwaters (see 5.13): minds small, eyes covetous, tongues cutting. Martial wanted libraries, theaters, parties (book 12, proem).

Bilbilis had been able to boast of Martial among its natives who had achieved fame— that is, gone to Rome (1.49; 1.61). The Spanish town hardly recurs in his thoughts until Martial sets his mind to re-emigrating or has indeed gone home again. But Bilbilis and Spain might serve as foils to the pretentious Roman (10.65), much as an emigré Idahoan might deflate a native New Yorker. World-weary, Martial was looking back on a life spent (12.18).

THE BOOKS OF EPIGRAMS: MARTIAL'S SELF-ESTIMATION

Poets by nature enjoyed immortality (1.1; 6.61[60]; 10.2). Better: Martial was read in his lifetime throughout the civilized world. He says so in his first epigram of book 1 and thereafter (1.1; 5.13; 6.61[60]; 8.3; 10.9). He is read in Vienne, in Britain, on the Black Sea (7.88; 11.3). His renown attracted jealousy (9.97; 10.3). It was the epigram that made Martial's name. He had no truck with old-fashioned and dead poets. If dead poets alone win fame, forget it! (5.10). A man might read and imitate the early tragedians Accius and Pacuvius, but that man's prick had better taste and read Martial (11.90). Earlier, Martial would have written an epic if the right Maecenas had supported him (1.107). Content with what the epigram had won for him, including a bust in a grandee's library (book 9, proem), Martial declined to write gentlemen's lofty poetry, epic, and tragedy. The consequence would be a greater humiliation:

Martial's poetry would become the stuff of teachers' lessons (8.3). A fate worse than mortality!

For that bust Martial composed a label:

> *Ille ego sum nulli nugarum laude secundus,*
> *quem non miraris sed puto, lector, amas.*
> *Maiores maiora sonent: mihi parva locuto*
> *sufficit in vestras saepe redire manus.*
>
> (book 9, proem)

He I be who takes first prize for epigram, and makes you, reader, love, I think, and not revere. Greater men may orchestrate greater poems. I am content that you read me often even though I have made only small talk.

This is the closest Martial came to writing his own epitaph.

CONCLUSION

Little did Martial know that in broadcasting his wit and worldly wisdom to sergeants in Thrace, to retired grandees in Tolosa, and to all Vienne, and in lighting these corners of empire with antic vignettes of the capital *purcherrima Roma*—he was laying the footings of the literary bridge that would lead to such truly provincial literature as that of the fourth-century Ausonius of Bordeaux and the fifth-century Sidonius Apollinaris, born at Lyons and bishop of Auvergne. By inadvertence Martial may be said to have fathered the last of antique Latin literature in Gaul. Wittingly, however, he sang not for Rome alone, but of Rome for the civilized world. No poet of lofty epic on how the Romans won the world's greatest empire, the wry epigrammatist wrote for all in the outposts of empire who savored urbanity. Martial took pride in a readership that included persons of both sexes and of all ages, and a greater pride that a poet from the provinces wrote also for the provincials about and with *urbanitas*.

Martial's poems became the stuff of anthology. The flower pickers avoided his scabrous thorns. Before 1600 no vernacular translation of the whole of Martial appeared except in Italian; otherwise there were translations of selections that were chosen on the principle followed by Frusius, who prepared an expurgated Latin school text for novice Jesuits on commission from Ignatius Loyola (1558). This latent censorship continued. The one complete commentary on Martial's Latin by Friedlaender touches only a portion of the matter. English commentators address themselves to no epigram of obscene wit.

Martial has never been fully integrated into the classical curriculum. He is denied to the neophyte and left to the initiate. Yet writers of wit, wittingly or no, often modeled their epigrams on the genre Martial perfected. Here is one of Dorothy Parker's, "A Pig's-eye View of Literature," from *Sunset Gun* (1928):

OSCAR WILDE

> If with the literate, I am
> Impelled to try an epigram,
> I never seek to take the credit,
> We all assume that Oscar said it.

Selected Bibliography

TEXTS

M. Valerii Martialis Epigrammaton Libri, edited by L. Friedlaender. 2 vols. Leipzig, 1886.

M. Valerii Martialis Epigrammaton Libri, edited by W. Heraeus. Leipzig, 1925. Reissued by J. Borovskij. Leipzig, 1976.

M. Val. Martialis Epigrammata, edited by W. M. Lindsay. 2nd ed. Oxford, 1929.

TRANSLATIONS

No translation into English, however complete, is satisfactory. Omission of poems, retention of the Latin, or publication of Italian versions blight the translations.

B(ohn), H. G., comp. *The Epigrams of Martial.* London, 1897. Bohn Library. An interesting melange that preserves the older Italian versions by Graglia "where an English translation would not be tolerable."

Humphreys, R., trans. *Selected Epigrams of Martial*. Bloomington, Ind., 1963.

Ker, W. C. A., trans. *Martial, Epigrams*. 2 vols. London and New York, 1919–1920. Rev. ed., 1968. Loeb Classical Library. Includes all the Latin, most of which is adequately rendered.

Pott, J. A., and F. A. Wright, trans. *Martial: The Twelve Books of Epigrams*. London and New York, 1924. Offers a translation of books 1–12 only, but it substitutes the Latin original for the prudish in some cases.

COMMENTARIES

There exists no complete commentary on all of Martial's poems, although Friedlaender's text is the nearest to a complete commentary (in German). His text also contains a full index of the text and full lexicon of Martial's Latin. The following works are in English.

Bridge, R. T., and E. D. Lake. *Select Epigrams of Martial*. 2 vols. Oxford, 1924. Largest edition, with helpful notes.

Stephenson, H. M. *Selected Epigrams of Martial*. London, 1929.

GENERAL WORKS AND SPECIAL STUDIES

Allen, W., et al. "Martial, Knight, Publisher and Poet." *Classical Journal* 65:345–357 (1970).

Anderson, W. S. "*Lascivia* vs. *Ira*: Martial and Juvenal." *California Studies in Classical Antiquity* 3: 1–34 (1970).

Bellinger, A. R. "Martial, the Suburbanite." *Classical Journal* 23:425–435 (1928).

Best, E. E. "Martial's Readers in the Roman World." *Classical Journal* 64:208–212 (1969).

Buecheler, F., and E. Lommatzsch. *Carmina Latina Epigraphica*. Leipzig, 1895–1926. Collection of Latin verse epigrams inscribed on stone.

Carcopino, J. *Daily Life in Ancient Rome*. New Haven, 1940.

Castagnoli, F. "Roma nei versi di Marziale." *Athenaeum* 28:67–78 (1950).

Colton, R. E. "Traces of Martial's Vocabulary in Sidonius Apollinaris." *Classical Bulletin* 53:12–16 (1976).

Duff, J. W., and A. M. Duff. *A Literary History of Rome in the Silver Age*. 3rd ed. London, 1964. Useful survey. Pp. 397–421.

Friedlaender, L. *Roman Life and Manners Under the Empire*. 4 vols. London, 1913. Informed by Martial on Roman life.

Helm, R. "M. Valerius Martialis." In A. F. Pauly and G. Wissowa, *Realencyclopädie der classischen Altertumswissenschaft*, 2nd ser., vol 15 (8A1, 1955): cols. 55–85.

Johnson, S. "The Obituary Epigrams of Martial." *Classical Journal* 49:265–272 (1953–1954).

Kruuse, J. "L'originalité artistique de Martial: Son style, sa composition, sa technique." *Classica et Mediaevalia* 4:248–300 (1941).

Lattimore, R. "Themes in Greek and Latin Epitaphs." *Illinois Studies in Language and Literature* 28:1–2 (1942). Reprinted Urbana, 1962.

Laurens, P. "Martial et l'épigramme grecque du 1er siècle ap. J. C." *Revue des Études Latines* 43:315–341 (1965).

Mendell, C. W. "Martial and the Satiric Epigram." *Classical Philology* 17:1–20 (1922).

Mohler, S. L. "The *Cliens* in the Time of Martial." In *Classical Studies in Honor of J. C. Rolfe*. Pp. 239–264. Philadelphia, 1931.

Nixon, P. *Martial and the Modern Epigram*. New York, 1927. Reprinted 1963.

Schanz, M., and C. Hosius. *Geschichte der roemischen Literatur*. Pt. 2. 4th ed. Munich, 1935. Pp. 546–560.

Scott, K. *The Imperial Cult Under the Flavians*. Stuttgart, 1936. Reprinted New York, 1975.

Semple, W. H. "The Poet Martial." *Bulletin of the John Rylands Library* 42:432–452 (1959–1960).

Smith, K. F. *Martial the Epigrammatist and Other Essays*. Baltimore, 1920.

Spaeth, J. W., Jr. "Martial and the Pasquinade." *Transactions of the American Philological Association* 70:242–255 (1939).

———. "Martial and the Roman Crowd." *Classical Journal* 27:244–254 (1931–1932).

———. "Martial Looks at His World." *Classical Journal* 24:361–374 (1929).

Weinrich. O. *Studien zu Martial: Literarhistorische und religionsgeschichtliche Untersuchungen*. Tuebinger Beitraege zur Altertumswissenschaft. Vol. 4. Stuttgart, 1928.

Whipple, T. K. *Martial and the English Epigram*

from Sir Thomas Wyatt to Ben Jonson. Berkeley. 1925. Reprinted New York, 1970.

White, P. "The Friends of Martial, Statius and Pliny, and the Dispersal of Patronage." *Harvard Studies in Classical Philology* 79:265–300 (1975).

———. "The Presentation and Dedication of the *Silvae* and the Epigrams." *Journal of Roman Studies* 64:40–61 (1974).

BIBLIOGRAPHIES

Harrison, G. W. M. *Lustrum* 18:300–337, 352–355 (1975).

Helm, R. *Lustrum* 1:299–318 (1956) and 2:187–206 (1957). In German.

ROBERT E. A. PALMER

LUCAN

(A.D. 39–65)

STATIUS

(A.D. 45?–96?)

LUCAN AND STATIUS were born within a few years of one another; and each is best known for his epic of civil war. Yet their poetry, family backgrounds, and the political conditions prevailing when they wrote are remarkably different. Lucan was an aristocrat, Statius the son of a poet and schoolteacher. Statius had not even begun any of his extant works when Lucan died. Indeed, between the composition of Lucan's *Pharsalia* and Statius' *Thebaid*, Rome was shaken by civil wars that ended the Julio-Claudian dynasty of emperors and established the Flavians.

To Lucan, civil war was a distant historical event. As he wrote, Rome had been at peace for a century. Appropriately he treats the subject in a historical setting: the struggles between Caesar and his opponents that destroyed what remained of the Roman Republic. To Statius, civil war was a recent and bloody experience. Yet he treated it in a mythical, not a historical, setting: the archetypal civil war of Greek tradition between the sons of Oedipus. The *Pharsalia* is a call to revolution; the *Thebaid*, a searing commentary on man's brutality and ambitions. Lucan's anger is directed against the unjust peace that followed Caesar's victory. His cry is: "For-

tune, if you were going to give those of us who were born after the battle [of Pharsalia] a master, as you did, you should have given us a chance to fight" (*Pharsalia* 7.645–646).

Statius had seen Lucan's desire for renewed fighting realized; and he had seen the consequences. The civil wars in his own lifetime did not bring restoration of political freedom (*libertas*), as Lucan hoped, but a new dynasty of masters and horrendous carnage. His cry, then, is rather different: "Only one day should have witnessed this crime in all lands and in all ages. This terrible portent should come to nothing in future generations, and only kings should relive these battles" (*Thebaid* 11.577–579).

Lucan's vision in the *Pharsalia* is quite widely understood. The chief scholarly disagreements arise from uncertainty as to where the epic would have ended, for Lucan's death prevented him from completing it. There is also some dispute as to whether the work's primary thrust is philosophical or political. But no critic has ever said of the *Pharsalia* what R. M. Ogilvie recently observed of the *Thebaid*, that it "cannot be said to be *about* anything." The *Thebaid*, like the other Flavian epics, has been little understood.

Our task with Lucan is to examine some of the means by which he builds his vision in the *Pharsalia* and to clarify the nature of that vision. Because he wrote first, and because Statius clearly had the *Pharsalia* in mind as he wrote his *Thebaid,* we will begin with Lucan. Our task with Statius is more complicated. Unlike Lucan, whose only surviving work is the *Pharsalia,* Statius has two surviving works in addition to the *Thebaid:* the *Silvae* and the *Achilleid.* Given the extreme complexity of Statius' vision and the restrictions of space in this article, I have limited my discussion to the *Thebaid,* his most famous and influential poem. All quotations are given in English. The translations are my own.

LUCAN'S LIFE

Marcus Annaeus Lucanus, a nephew of Seneca, was born in Corduba, Spain (modern Cordoba), in November A.D. 39. He came to Rome at an early age and found favor in the highest imperial and senatorial circles. He was regarded as a friend by the emperor Nero, who was only two years his senior, and held a quaestorship before he was twenty-five, a mark of exceptional imperial favor. Sometime after A.D. 62 his relationship with Nero soured, and his uncle, Seneca, also fell from favor. Ancient sources suggest that Lucan began attacking Nero in his writing and that he may even have accused the emperor of burning Rome in 64. Publication of three books of the *Pharsalia* must have damaged his friendship with Nero, for in 64 the emperor banned Lucan from appearances in the law courts and from poetic recitations. The ban on recitation must surely have been Nero's attempt to stop further publication of the *Pharsalia.*

Around the same time, Lucan became virtually the standard-bearer for Piso's plot to murder Nero. When the conspiracy was detected, Lucan, Seneca, Piso, and many others were arrested and charged. Lucan, with no hope of acquittal, committed suicide in April 65, at the age of twenty-five.

The ten books of the *Pharsalia* were probably composed between 62 and 65. Comparisons with Vergil, Statius, and Silius are unhelpful in determining how quickly he wrote, for Lucan is unique among Latin epicists in producing a major work while still very young and while engaged in an active political career. Quintilian describes him as a fiery young man of prodigious energy, a judgment well substantiated by Lucan's career and by his *Pharsalia.*

CAESAR AND THE FAILURE OF THE REPUBLIC

The *Pharsalia* is the epic of Rome's fall, of the civil wars of 49–45 B.C., which destroyed the republic and brought Julius Caesar to supreme power. The ten books Lucan wrote narrate the events of 49–47, reaching their climax with the battle of Pharsalia in book 7, where, Lucan tells us, Rome lost her freedom forever: "We have been cast down until the end of time" (7.640).

Lucan's Caesar is the beneficiary, rather than the cause, of the state's decline. He delivers the deathblow to a political system already corrupt, already shattered by internal conflict. Lucan makes it plain that many of Caesar's opponents are little more than caricatures of their great names and of the great traditions they embody. Their weakness and petty self-interest leave them helpless against Caesar, whose will, arrogance, and ambition would pose a threat even to a healthy state. Caesar is contemptuous of his opposition, indeed contemptuous of everything but himself. Unlike most epic protagonists, he is more interested in power than in honor, glory, even life itself. Odysseus and Aeneas weep at the thought of inglorious death at sea. But Caesar, when threatened by the waves, admits only to some disappointment, then exclaims:

Gods, I do not need a funeral. Keep my shredded body in mid-ocean, deprive me of pyre and cremation so long as I am always feared [*dum metuar*] and people expect me to appear from every corner of the world.

(5.668–671)

Caesar echoes a famous line from Accius' tragedy *Atreus*: "Let them hate, so long as they fear (*oderint dum metuant*)," a phrase that had found new life in imperial Rome. Caligula liked it; Tiberius gave it a more practical twist: Let them hate provided they go along with what I want.

Caesar grasps, as no one before him in epic does, the possibility of *controlling* the world after he is dead, not just being remembered by it. And his means of control is the fear he inspires, for he knows that Rome is not going to be destroyed physically by the civil war as Troy was destroyed by the Greeks. The struggle is to decide *what* Rome will be (*Roma quid esset:* 7.132), not whether Rome will continue to be. He neither dissimulates his ambition nor uses terror as a disguise for inner cowardice. Until his meeting with Cleopatra in book 10 he is consistently fearless. His arrogance increases rather than diminishes in the face of danger, as his address to his mutinous troops shows:

Do you think you have ever provided me a forward push that made any difference? The gods will never be so pressed to rule the world that what is decreed will depend on your collective lives or deaths. Everything that happens follows the motions the leaders make. The human race lives for the benefit of a few.

(5.339–343)

History gives Caesar's words the ring of truth, however ugly. In having Caesar proclaim this credo in a situation where one sword-stroke could put an end to his boasts, Lucan shows the weakmindedness of people when confronted by a fearless and domineering leader. The army's acquiescence under these insults and its cooperation when Caesar then orders the ringleaders executed affirms that he is essentially right in his assessment: men live for their rulers, not for themselves.

It is not just Caesar's ruthless willpower and energy or even the infirmity of his opposition that grant him victory. There are many who want him to rule for their own personal reasons. When Caesar hesitates briefly on arrival in Ariminum, the tribune Scribonius Curio bolsters his resolution: "Once you've fought a few battles—and their outcome will be quite manageable—Rome will have mastered the world for you" (1.284–285). Curio stands to gain by Caesar's victory. He and his friends are outlaws now, but, he declares, "Your victory will make us citizens" (1.279). Similarly, when Caesar's criticisms of Pompey and the Senate, some of which seem justified, fail to stir his troops, the centurion Laelius springs to the rescue. The soldiers' complaint is that Caesar is too cautious: "If you ordered me to stab my brother's chest, cut my father's throat, or plunge my sword into my pregnant wife's womb, I'd do it all, however reluctant my hand" (1.376–378). Laelius goes on to affirm he would destroy any temple or city, including Rome, that Caesar wants him to destroy. And this is what elicits thunderous applause from the army. The troops are indifferent to political reasoning. They want the chance to kill and pillage. They want a leader to die for. If Caesar provides that leadership, they will follow him anywhere, Laelius declares.

War, Lucan notes, is useful to many (1.182). Caesar, like Curio, knows that in practical terms victory and defeat are the measures of guilt and innocence (7.269). Might determines right. Lucan himself puts the matter thus: when criminals win, they "restructure" justice to suit themselves (1.2). Thereafter, national traditions of legality and justice must exist apart from the structure of the state if they are to exist at all.

Lucan's description of this crisis in the Roman state has an ominously familiar ring. When revolution undermines traditional laws and values, the individual must either conform to the new order or fall back on his own spiritual resources, as Cato does.

ROME AS FREEDOM

Caesar wishes to make Rome synonymous and coextensive with himself. To Cato, Rome is *libertas*, freedom. When war breaks out, Cato compares himself to a father at his sons' funeral:

> Grief bids me guide the long procession to the grave as it bids a bereaved parent when he has lost his sons. . . . I shall not be torn away from you, Rome, before I embrace your lifeless body. Your name is freedom, and I shall persist in following its hollow ghost.
>
> (2.297–299, 301–303)

In Cato's terms, Rome is dead because it is no longer free. But this does not deter him from following the ghost of Rome, the ghost of freedom. Cato knows that the only way to embrace a ghost is to die oneself. Lucan develops this notion in one of the epic's most famous scenes: the remarriage of Cato and Marcia.

Marcia, Cato's former wife, returns to Cato after her second husband's death, still dressed in mourning. Her desire is to have the "hollow name of marriage" (2.323–324) and the inscription "Cato's Marcia" on her tomb. She describes herself as old, tired, no longer productive. Cato consents to remarriage, though he too is in mourning: for Rome. With only Marcus Brutus as witness, the ceremony is performed. Lucan describes the scene in terms of all that is missing from a usual wedding: no flowers, no crossing of the threshold, no richly blanketed bed (2.350–364). Their reunion is to be ascetic and sexless, a marriage for death, not life.

As Lucan concludes the scene, he declares Cato to be "a father to the city and a husband to the city" (2.388), blending the images of Cato the father grieving for Rome and Cato the husband remarrying Marcia. In doing so, he makes Marcia symbolic of Rome; he shapes an allegory: the reunion of the free Roman state, now ready to die, with the man who embodies the ideals on which the state was founded. As Marcia embraces Cato the shadow of her funeral robe eclipses the senatorial purple of Cato's toga (2.367). For this moment Brutus, descendant of the republic's founder, is the only appropriate witness.

Cato, like Caesar, has a profound yearning for greatness. He believes he is born not for himself but for the whole world (2.383); he wishes his blood may "redeem the peoples fighting in the war and atone for whatever the Roman way of life has done to deserve this suffering" (2.312–313). Cato's yearning to die for man, like Caesar's desire for power after death, is remarkably Christ-like. Indeed Lucan himself elevates Cato to divine stature:

> If a great reputation is gained by genuine goodness, if we strip a man's real nature bare, removing the ornaments of success, we see that what is praised in any of our great ancestors was really the work of Fortune. For who has earned so great a name as Cato, whatever his victories, whatever peoples he annihilated? I myself would rather lead his triumphal march through the remote regions of Syrte and Libya than ride three times up to the Capitol in Pompey's chariot, or break Jugurtha's neck. Here was a real father of his country, a man, Rome, who really deserves an altar in your city. No one will ever be ashamed to swear on his name as a guarantee of truth. If ever you stand again with neck unchained, one day you will make this man a god.
>
> (9.593–604)

Lucan does not mean that Cato will be an equal of the Olympians, however. The traditional gods play little part in the *Pharsalia*, and they are described as supporting Caesar, not Cato. The gods, in contrast to Cato, have no interest in man. Their passivity proves that "things that die are of concern to no god" (7.454–455); divine approval amounts to no more than acquiescence in the amoral, even criminal, verdict of history. Hence Lucan's observation, cited previously, that fortune, rather than anything in man's individual nature *(virtus)*, accounts for most famous achievements, and his contention that it is worse to win than lose the war (7.706). Civil war, as Horace observes in *Odes* 2.1, is the game of fortune, which tamed everything but the fierce soul of Cato. Cato's approval, then, is a better moral guide than Olympian approval. When Lucan observes, "The conquering cause pleased the gods, but the conquered cause pleased Cato" (1.128), he is telling us that Cato's support made the losers better than the winners.

Cato epitomizes man's struggle to rise above the nexus of events to become master of his own life, resisting thereby the tyranny of the determined world order as well as the tyranny of Caesar and Caesarism. He, like Caesar, perceives man's weaknesses, but, instead of exploiting them to make men his minions, he tries to draw men up to his own level. Cato's reaction to mutiny among the troops can be contrasted with Caesar's:

> You too were fighting for tyranny. You were Pompey's soldiers, not Rome's, weren't you? You are giving up the struggle because you're not living and dying for your generals, because you're not conquering the world for someone, because it's safe now to fight for yourselves. You were looking for a slave's collar since your necks were free. . . . Are you going to deny your country your lives and swords when freedom is so near? . . . You deserve a life with Caesar as your judge. . . . As soon as your lord and master is dead, you run to his successor.
>
> (9.257-261, 264-265, 272-275)

The human race does not *have* to live for the few, Cato explains. Men can fight for their individual freedom and in doing so keep their country free.

Cato can lead only by his personal example and by the forcefulness of his reasoning, by giving himself and his troops a goal neither Caesar nor fortune can deny them. When he speaks to his troops as they cross the Libyan desert he cries: "You men who have joined my forces, men who know only one form of safety you can tolerate: death, free from the shackles of slavery" (9.379-380). Caesar, in contrast, identifies his men with his own ambitions: "Master of the world, guiding genius of my success: my soldiers. . . .You have in your hands the power to

decide how great Caesar will be" (7.250-251; 253). His words, ironically, betray how much his greatness depends on the behavior of others, on fortune, not *virtus*. He is not simply flattering his troops; he is stating, in Lucan's terms, the truth.

Cato demonstrates the validity of the *Pharsalia*'s central paradox: that freedom can be attained by dedication to death, and by death itself. Vergil's Aeneas must *live* to preserve the remains of Troy; Lucan's Cato must *die* to preserve the ideal of freedom. For the ideal does not require physical transmission through the ages as does Aeneas' Trojan blood; it demands an example to inspire others. Thus Cato may embrace Marcia and the ghost of freedom, but Aeneas may not embrace the ghosts of Creusa and Anchises. Aeneas must tear himself away, must sacrifice his soul to save his body for destiny to use.

We cannot be sure how Lucan would have resolved the conflict between Caesar and Cato, since the epic breaks off before Caesar's victory at Thapsus and Cato's suicide at Utica. But Lucan clearly tells us that the struggle between the principles they represent will continue indefinitely. Their conflict is never a physical one; there are no grand duels between the protagonists in the *Pharsalia* as there are in other epics. But, Lucan assures us after Pompey's departure from the battle of Pharsalia, henceforth "the matched pair will be the same as we always have: freedom and Caesar" (7.695-696).

The divine honors accorded Cato offer an ironic comment on the consequences of ideological opposition to the Caesars. Absolutism of one kind produces, as a backlash, absolutism of another kind. Although Lucan constantly ridicules the deification of Caesars (6.809; 8.835, 861-862), he deifies Cato. Further, he declares heaven will be punished for letting Caesar win, since "the civil wars will create gods to match those above . . . and Rome will swear oaths on the names of ghosts in the gods' temples" (7.455-459). Yet this is precisely what he says will be done if Rome is ever free again. Instead of denying man's pretense to divinity, Lucan replaces the Caesars with Cato: the exemplar of *virtus* in place of the champions of fortune. This notion, that the virtuous man is divine, remained in Roman thought and helps in part explain the appeal of Christ, who also promised a spiritual victory in the teeth of apparent defeat.

CAESAR, CATO, AND THE GODS

Caesar and Cato are above the level of ordinary humanity, and both are accorded divine status of a sort in the *Pharsalia*. Although Lucan dismisses Rome's subsequent deification of Caesar, he nevertheless confers on him superhuman energy, willpower, and courage. In 1.151–157, he compares him to a thunderbolt, a massive, destructive force, but very suggestive of Jupiter. Cato is constantly treated as oracular and godlike. Brutus compares Cato's detached serenity to that of the stars far above the air, for the air, being closer to earth, is scorched by thunderbolts. Although Cato abandons this detachment and descends into the regions dominated by Caesar, he remains impregnable to Caesar's power (2.266–273, 286–297).

Had Lucan employed conventional epic deities he would have clouded the moral issues of his work. A comparison with the *Aeneid* illustrates this. In *Aeneid* 2.610–620, Aeneas tells Dido how his mother, Venus, revealed to him that Troy's fall was caused by the inclemency of the gods. This reasoning exonerates not only Helen and Paris, as Venus notes, but all human agents, including Aeneas himself, from responsibility for what happened. Aeneas' account is subtly self-serving. Man, it is implied, is powerless to resist the gods, and resistance would be impious (doubly so if the god is your parent). Thus Aeneas' declared awareness of divine ruthlessness, directly revealed to him by a god, in no way diminishes his quest for divine guidance and instruction, or his claim to *pietas*. By removing the Olympians from the structure, Lucan leaves his characters responsible for their actions and decisions, and removes the argument that one must acquiesce in history's verdict because it is the will of the gods.

What Caesar represents is not at all ambiguous in the *Pharsalia*. There are no Olympians onto whom responsibility is displaced, and Lucan has Caesar declare the doctrine that might is right quite clearly and loudly. Historical events are seen in terms of human actions, ideals, ambitions, and folly; natural phenomena are given meteorological and other natural causation. When Lucan and his characters wish to refer to supernatural causality, they talk in terms of "fate" and "fortune" rather than of Olympians. Nor is there any suggestion that within fate or fortune lies any notion of cosmic or human justice. Lucan has substituted the terminology of contemporary literary and philosophical parlance for the usual gods, and he has even modified that, for in Stoicism there is a general belief in some beneficent divine providence; in Lucan there is not. Fate is merely the appointed and necessary end of all living things, and fortune is the goddess supreme of history (*Fortuna*) and of the individual's role in history.

The duty of the wise man, Seneca and others point out, is to resist rather than to follow fortune. Thus Lucan, by having Caesar follow fortune, as he does throughout the epic, maneuvers Caesar into a position where he is acting in a manner most Stoics would reject: he is allowing history to determine morality. This done, he aligns Cato solidly with those Stoics who would affirm the propriety of the wise man's involvement in politics. Lucan's justification of this politicized Stoicism is unique in first-century literature (2.286–323). Seneca promises he will argue the case but never does.

Lucan's Caesar would be morally unacceptable not only to Stoics but to almost all ancient schools of philosophy. And to make the doctrine that might is right totally repugnant, Lucan has given us a Caesar who is virtually without normal weaknesses. He is a far remove from the tyrant figure of the rhetorical schools. There is, I suspect, a deadly purpose in all this. Lucan not only shapes recent history into epic for the express purpose of attacking the justice of history's verdict, but seeks to persuade the reader

922

that the Caesars gained power by exploiting the weaknesses of the state and confirmed their power by legalizing their crimes. The wise man should take Cato as his example and engage himself in politics, not withdraw. Indeed the attempt to murder Caesar—any Caesar—is not an act of national disloyalty but a patriotic duty; it is the rightful punishment of a tyrant, the only punishment possible, since the tyrant has restructured the laws so as to make conventional legal procedures impossible.

ROME AS LOVE: ROMA AND AMOR

The third major character of the *Pharsalia,* Pompey, is contrasted with Caesar early in book 1. Like the lightning to which he is compared, Caesar has a restless nature that does not know how to stand in one place (1.144–145). Pompey "stands, the ghost of a great name" (1.135). He is like an ancient and infirm oak, sustained by its own weight, extending naked, leafless boughs and casting a shadow with its trunk, not its leaves; it is doomed to topple at the first breath of the east wind (1.136–142). The static Pompey and the static oak have no chance against the darting thunderbolt. So the outcome is predictable. But Lucan's point is more elaborate than this. The oak stands in fertile ground (1.136) and is the sole object of veneration although many forested areas grow vigorously around it (1.142–143). Neither the east wind nor the thunderbolt can destroy every tree in all the forests. Rome is vulnerable to Caesar because it has loaded all its honors on one decrepit oak, instead of distributing them among the vigorous trees around.

Lucan ventures here a comment not just on Rome, Pompey, and Caesar, but on mankind in general. Fear of lightning is common, and weather gods like Jupiter stand at the head of many ancient pantheons. Ironically, man's venerated objects tend to be precisely those fixed, traditional shrines, the sacred oaks most vulnerable to the thunderbolt. More significance is attached to the storm's destruction of such a cult object than to the survival of countless similar objects not so venerated. Hence the danger that the destruction of the symbol will be tantamount to the destruction of everything, even though it alone has perished.

Once Pompey is gone, so too is the old order that he symbolizes in the *Pharsalia.* However absurd it is that Pompey should be the sole cult figure of the republic, with his passing Rome will be Caesar's. Lucan's Pompey, then, represents something more complex than Caesar or Cato. He is loved by Rome, and he identifies Rome with love. As Rome, to Cato, means freedom, to Pompey it is the anagram of *Roma: amor.* When Caesar faces death, he is content as long as he is feared. But when Pompey is murdered, he suppresses his cries of pain and utters his final words: "If my son and wife watch with admiration as I die, they love me" (8.634–635).

The desire to be loved is the core of Pompey's being, as we see in his relationship to his wife, Cornelia—a relationship that tries to be as warm, personal, and sexual as Cato's relationship with Marcia is ascetic and asexual. As Pompey prepares to meet Caesar's army in Greece, he sends Cornelia away to safety. "Love," Lucan observes, "made even you doubtful and hesitant about battle, great Pompey. The one thing you did not wish to stand beneath the blow of Fortune threatening the world and Rome's destiny was your wife. Only your wife" (5.728–731). When told she must leave, Cornelia is lying in her husband's arms (5.734–798); and her desolation the following night is seen in her awareness of the empty place beside her as she sleeps alone, burning with love for her absent husband (5.811).

The joy of love usually eludes Pompey in the *Pharsalia.* Cornelia's abrupt departure robs the couple of a lovers' farewell: "Their last chance to enjoy so long a love passes away" (5.794). Pompey often fails to recognize the affection of others for him because he equates love with applause and success. When reunited with Cornelia after Pharsalia, for example, he finds her weeping. Instead of consoling her, he berates her, insinuating that she loved him for his fame, not for himself: "What you are weeping for is what you loved" (8.84–85). In the past she had rivals for his affection; now she has him for herself (8.79–83). "Love me for myself *because* I have been conquered" (8.77–78). Cornelia reacts not with anger but with apologies, taking the blame for his defeat on herself (8.88–105); then Pompey takes her in his arms and weeps. The shift of guilt from himself to Cornelia gives us a rare moment of close, warm human contact in Latin epic. But it also shows Pompey more ready to respond to Cornelia's sorrow than to national catastrophe: his eyes had been dry at Pharsalia (8.107–108). He wept for what he loved.

Pompey thanks the people of Lesbos, where Cornelia has been staying, and he declares: "This is where my sacred home and beloved household gods have been: this is where Rome has been for me" (8.132–133). Pompey, who had sought the love of Rome as well as of Cornelia in the past, believes he is no longer loved by either. When Cornelia and the islanders respond with love despite his defeat, they become his Rome.

The touching and pathetic beauty of Pompey's vanity transcends his faults and moves Lucan to some of his greatest poetry. At the beginning of book 7, Pompey's dreaming mind returns him to his theater at Rome and the days when he was the adored champion of the city. If only, Lucan adds, Rome too had had the chance to enjoy such a vision of her Pompey: "If only the powers above had granted to your country and to you, great Pompey, one day in mutual, full awareness of impending doom, so you could snatch your last chance to enjoy a love so great" (7.28–32).

The last line is almost an exact repetition of Lucan's comment at 5.794 when Cornelia parts from Pompey. It reminds us that, though Pompey does not understand it, his country's love for him is just as accepting as is Cornelia's. Why it is felt and why it endures may be a mystery; but that it is a force in the *Pharsalia*, as it was in Roman history, is beyond question. Cicero expresses his disillusionment with Pompey as that of a lover whose mistress' conduct has been unworthy. But once he is away: "My love is surfacing again; I can do nothing to allay my longing for him" (*To Atticus* 9.10).

Lucan himself delivers an encomium of Pompey after his death (8.793–872). In it he declares he would be "blessed and more than blessed" if it fell to his lot to "exhume Pompey's remains and bring them to Italy" (8.843–845). Yet it may "one day prove a blessing, Pompey, that you have no proper monument to mark your grave. For your tomb will disintegrate, and with it will perish the proof that you really are dead" (8.868–869). Lucan's reasoning here is precisely, and ironically, the same as Caesar's during the storm in book 5. The absence of plausible proof that someone is dead may lead people to conclude that he is still alive; thus his power may endure beyond the grave. The Cretans, he notes, are considered liars when they point to Jupiter the Thunderer's tomb (8.872); the grave, presumably, is unworthy of its alleged contents. But Caesar's temple and cult are, paradoxically, evidence that he is dead. Perhaps, then, Pompey's lack of burial will enable the love he inspired to endure when fear of Caesar has perished.

CONCLUSION

The numerous minor characters of the *Pharsalia* are as carefully and subtly individualized as the protagonists. At every level of his work, Lucan seems eager to avoid the conventional, the stereotype, the cliché. He is as revolutionary in his poetics as in his political thought. Lucan's modifications of epic tradition are always purposeful. He had to take a different approach to poetry and history than, say, an advocate of Caesarism. When Augustus consolidated his position after Actium, his task was to calm tempers and hostilities that had been seething during prolonged civil war. His ends were best achieved by minimizing the changes he had made in the Roman state, by emphasizing his victory over the Egyptians and Cleopatra rather than his activities during the conflict with Brutus and Cassius. He had acquired power illegally and exercised it ruthlessly. In short, his power was all too real: it needed not historical statement but mythic and ideological reinforcement. It had a body, but it needed a soul. The opponents of the Caesars had exactly the opposite problem. All they had salvaged from the civil wars was a handful of abstract notions, such as *libertas*, or freedom. They needed the past, facts, history, anything that would give the semblance of reality to what no longer had any form. They had a soul but no body. Only history could provide the body, and only epic could present that history in a visionary and vatic way. Unlike Augustus, they sought to revive passions, not to quell them.

Lucan recognized this need. He not only records the past in historical, epic form but looks toward the future as no other ancient epicist really does. He tantalizes his reader with visions of Cato deified and liberty restored, and with personal dreams of bringing Pompey's remains back to Rome. He even "prays" for Caesar's safety during the fighting in Alexandria, fearing that if he is killed by the Egyptians the example of tyrannicide will be lost (10.344). The standard-bearer of the Pisonian conspiracy is clearly recognizable in the *Pharsalia*. The epic shows that Lucan's animosity to Nero was much more than purely personal or literary. It also casts considerable doubt on the common contention that the conspiracy's goal was to make Piso, Seneca, or anyone else emperor. For the *Pharsalia* had given the conspirators a manifesto of *libertas* it would have been hard to put aside. Lucan's *Pharsalia*, alone among ancient epics, is not just a mirror of political power; it is an exercise *in* political power.

STATIUS' LIFE

Most of what we know of Statius' life derives from his five books of occasional poetry, the *Silvae*. His father, himself a poet, ran a Greek school in Naples at which Statius studied, and he was at least as well known in Greek-speaking as in Latin-speaking circles. The elder Statius won prizes at the Pythian, Nemean, and Isthmian games, his son tells us; and a recently published version of an Eleusinian inscription tells of special honors paid by the Areopagus at Athens to a P. Papinius St[atius], who must have been either Statius or his father. Statius compares his father to Homer, a citizen of many lands; and when he mentions his schooling, he emphasizes the Greek rather than the Latin poets he read. It is quite probable that Statius was bilingual, given his father's background and his family's residence in Greek-speaking Naples, which Statius refers to as his *patria*, his homeland.

Statius' Hellenic background is important. Although he wrote in Latin, his themes and his approach to epic are very Greek. Indeed, he often looks on the Roman world with the eyes of an outsider, as Apuleius does a century or so later.

When Statius came to Rome is not clear. His father recited, in Rome, a poem about the fire on the Capitol (A.D. 69), and Statius won the prize at Domitian's Alban games in 89. The elder Statius seems to have died around 80, after he had taken pride in his son's recitations before the senators of Rome but before Statius' victories at Roman poetic competitions. Father and son must have made their first impressions on the Roman literati during Vespasian's principate (A.D. 69–79), but all of Statius' surviving works date to Domitian's reign (A.D. 81–96). Statius left Rome in 94 for his native Naples, after failing to win the Capitoline games, and probably died in 96. There is no reason to believe he survived Domitian.

The poet's date of birth is a matter of guesswork. Most scholars agree he was probably born between 40 and 50.

The *Thebaid*, earliest of Statius' surviving works, was twelve years in the making. It was published in 91 or 92. The first three books of the *Silvae* appeared in 94 and the fourth in 95.

His *Achilleid*, begun probably in early 95, was incomplete when he died, and the final book of his *Silvae* was published posthumously. The *Silvae*, together with Martial's epigrams, provide a fascinating glimpse of the people and places frequented by the Roman literary elite. Statius obviously knew many prominent members of the aristocracy and Domitian's palace bureaucracy. The emperor himself appears as a distant and rather forbidding figure. Although the poet tells us he dined at the palace, the setting was hardly intimate; Statius talks of the armies (*agmina*) of guests being ordered to recline at a thousand tables (*Silvae* 4.2, 32–33).

PREAMBLE TO THE THEBAID

The *Thebaid* tells the saga of the Seven against Thebes, the struggle between Oedipus' sons, Eteocles and Polynices, which sweeps the cities of Argos and Thebes into a mutually destructive war. The tale was well known in antiquity and is familiar to the modern reader chiefly from the Theban plays of Sophocles, Aeschylus' *Seven Against Thebes*, and Euripides' *Phoenician Women*. Statius follows the traditional story in general outline, but his treatment of it differs radically from that found in the Greek tragedians. Although myth is, to Statius no less than Euripides, a means of treating contemporary issues in a traditional narrative framework, the realities of Statius' world were far different from those of fifth-century Athens.

The complexity of the *Thebaid* is such that we cannot do more than treat a few of the issues raised. But since the work is very carefully structured and was revised and published during the author's lifetime, we may be fairly confident that what is true of the parts may to some extent be true of the whole. We cannot fall back on the argument so often adduced by the critic of Vergil or Lucan: "He would have changed it if he'd had the chance." The test of any critique of the *Thebaid* must be whether it makes sense of the work as a whole. My assumption in examining the poet is that Statius' poetic skill and intellectual force may be matched, but they are not surpassed by any Roman writer. He knew what he was trying to say; and what he says is quite unique in ancient literature.

Before offering more general observations, however, we must examine some details, directing attention first to the *Thebaid*'s opening, where the groundwork is laid for everything that follows.

The *Thebaid*'s opening lines are striking and unusual, setting Statius apart from other Greek and Roman epicists. He does not call upon the Muses to help in an enterprise already chosen and defined. Rather he says that the Muses' fire has fallen upon him (*incidit*). He *must* write. And he asks the Muses to tell him not where he should *direct* his epic, but where he should *begin* it:

> Lines drawn between brothers, the alternating right to rule fought to the end with inhuman hatred, the guilt of Thebes: the Muses' Thessalian fire sweeps suddenly upon my mind, and I must spin the tale. You bid me go, goddesses; but where must I go *from*?

> (1.1–4)

His tale has no obvious starting point. He could trace it back to Cadmus or to any of the numerous legends of Thebes. But in lines 16–17 he settles on some boundaries: *limes mihi carminis esto / Oedipodae confusa domus*. The sense is hard to translate: "Let the house of Oedipus, which is 'confused' [for all normal family distinctions and bounds of conduct are transgressed], be the boundary of my song." Statius speaks like a geometrician establishing a theorem in full knowledge that his lines are arbitrary. The *limes*, or boundary of the epic, is arbitrary, because the story of Oedipus' family is part of a much larger network of external causes and is internally a confusion of all the normally prescribed relationships among kin.

As the beginning is arbitrary, so too must be

the end. Statius offers the theme of Oedipus' house because he is not yet ready to sing of Domitian:

> Let the disordered house of Oedipus give shape and definition to my song, since I would not yet dare breathe life into images and banners of Italy, or northern victories: the Rhine bridged twice by your yoke, the Danube twice brought under the rule of law, the Dacians hurled down from their conspiratorial heights. I dare not tell how, earlier, when you were still little more than a child, Domitian, you held at bay the wars of Jupiter; nor dare I sing of you yourself, new symbol of what Latium means to the world. You took up opportunely the new beginnings your father made; and Rome, selfishly, desires eternity for you.
>
> The stars, of course, are confined by stricter boundaries—and the gleaming heavenly zones that go untouched by constellations bringing rain or by the cold north wind trouble you. True, he who holds the reins on the sun's horses shod with fire might personally press down upon your hair his bow that radiates its shafts to the far distance; and Jupiter might cede to you a justly equal portion of the heavens. This I admit. Yet I hope you remain content, restrained by those reins you hold on mortal men. You have the power over elements of land and sea. Make the stars a present to others.
>
> There will come a time (when the Muses' lash of inspiration gives me more courage) when I will sing of your deeds. But now I string my lyre taut enough if I recount the wars in the Muses' homeland, a royal scepter that destroyed a pair of tyrants, a limit to madness even death could not set, flames upon a funeral pyre that started the seditious war anew. I tell of kings' bodies ready for the tomb but lacking burial, of cities worn down to desolation by the fighting, as man for man is killed. Blue Dirce blushed with blood for swampy Lerna's men, and Thetis shuddered as the Ismenos, usually barely able to touch its parched banks, approached her, swollen with heaps of dead.
>
> (1.16–40)

The tale of parricide, incest, and civil war begins before Oedipus, and it continues afterward. Statius has, as yet, the capacity only to narrate the tale of Thebes, which he summarizes in a sequence of bloody and savage images from the war. The suggestion that Domitian's deeds are beyond Statius' narrative capacities, then, is ambiguous. Domitian's deeds may not be "greater" than those of the Seven but are more horrendous. The *Thebaid* confirms this possibility: as Statius explains the causes of war between Oedipus' sons, he wonders how things would have been if the stakes had been greater:

> Naked power armed the brothers. The fight was for a beggar's kingdom. While the dispute goes on as to which will turn the parched soil near Dirce's petty fountain and who will sit in modest exaltation on the throne of a Tyrian exile, all that is good, laws human and divine, and any scruples about the way one lives and dies perish. How far do you stretch your anger, evil men? How would it be if criminal desire set as its goal the sky's boundaries, from the Sun's morning threshold of the East to his Spanish port of rest, from remote lands far off his path that receive only his slanting rays: lands frozen by the north winds, or made hot and humid by the fire of southern breezes? What if the combined wealth of Trojan and Tyrian lands were someday to be brought under the control of one person?
>
> (1.150–162)

No state but Rome ever ruled the kind of empire contrasted here to impoverished Thebes. Indeed Rome's wealth might aptly be described as the combined resources of Phrygian Troy and Tyrian Carthage. If all good perishes in the struggle for Thebes, how can one describe the losses in Rome's dynastic struggles? Only in myth's *inability* to provide an adequate parallel can we grasp the extent of the horror.

Oedipus' story, then, belongs in a continuum extending from the mythic past to the poet's own day. There is no definable beginning or end to the tale of human strife. Statius, like the modern anthropologist, perhaps, feels that there is a better chance of understanding man if one turns to a "simpler" society where motivation may be less complicated and thus more visible than it is in his contemporary "civilized" order. The closer to man's beginnings one gets, the more manageable the presentation of man's behavior; hence, no doubt, the attractiveness of myth.

In alerting his reader to the complexities of causality, Statius is not simply restating something that would have been self-evident to a contemporary Roman; he is telling us how we should read his epic. Any attempt to isolate an individual person or action from context will lead to misunderstanding of that person or event, and of the epic as a whole. Hence his acknowledgment of the arbitrary nature of his specific focus on the house of Oedipus, his admission that his defined boundaries are themselves indistinct. This insistence on the interrelationship of all things in a continuum carries over into every element of his poetry. Words do not carry "absolute" meanings. They carry all the significance that their context imparts to them, as do the events and characters themselves. And Statius exploits the natural ambiguity of Latin to the full. He imparts to his poetry the oracular quality we find in most Latin poets, and indeed describes himself as a *vates*, a singer of oracular songs. The reader, then, must be careful not to project his own hopes and expectations onto the *Thebaid's* "oracular" text. If he does, he will be brought to grief by the oracular utterances, as are so many of the epic's characters, not least Oedipus himself.

Hardly any statement in the epic is not susceptible of more than one interpretation. Consideration of some double meanings in lines 16–40 (cited previously) illustrate the point. Does Statius' remark that Domitian *twice* conquered the Danube and the Rhine intensify or diminish the imperial victories? If a second victory was necessary, the first may not have been an unqualified success; indeed Tacitus and Suetonius considered Domitian's victories "shams." "Rome selfishly desires eternity for you" suggests that Rome (a) wants to claim

Domitian forever and (b) would be happy to see him pass on into eternity. But would that eternity accord the emperor more or less freedom of movement? The stellar world Statius sketches has boundaries and definitions more restrictive than those of earth. And the peaceful, orderly tranquillity of the universe *troubles* Domitian. The suggestion that Apollo might press his crown on Domitian's hair is rich in multiple meanings. Domitian was bald, and the radiant diadem of Apollo could be very fiery. Further, *arcus*, the word Statius uses for diadem, suggests Apollo's traditional weapon, the bow, as well as the rainbow or some burning halo of divinity: Apollo's arrows, no less than his shafts of light, could be directed toward Domitian's head.

Apollo is described as *frenator* of the sun's horses, the one who keeps them under control. According to Suetonius (*Domitian* 19), Domitian hardly ever rode a horse when on campaign, but was carried in a litter. And Statius himself in *Silvae* 1.1, "The Great Equestrian Statue of Domitian," works endless changes on the statue's blatant artistic misrepresentation of the emperor as a military man. The fact that Domitian's statue is bigger than Caesar's does not make him greater than Caesar; it simply makes his pretense to military honors more preposterous.

The imagery of horsemanship carries over into Jupiter's possible offer of equal heavenly power to Domitian. Don't accept it, Statius urges, remain *hominum contentus habenis*: either Domitian should be content with the reins he holds on man or he should be restrained by the reins that control mankind; *contentus* is ambiguous. Jupiter's willingness to give Domitian half his kingdom is also disconcerting, for the *Thebaid* is the tale of two claimants and one throne, and Jupiter's role in the epic is not altogether flattering. Domitian should more properly confine himself to ruling land and sea, Statius says, and make a present of the stars to others. The emperor had, in fact, used his powers to bestow godhood on members of the imperial family. As Martial, Statius' contemporary, observes: "He has given temples for the gods, morality for the people, leisure for the sword, constellations for his family, stars for the sky, and wreaths for Jupiter" (*Epigrams* 9.101.21–22).

Domitian's father, Vespasian, made a famous jest on his deathbed: "Alas, I think I'm becoming a god" (Suetonius, *Vespasian* 23.4). Statius is surely no more serious about imperial divine pretensions. Indeed the limits placed upon the stars were, as Vespasian and Statius recognized, more confining than those placed on the mortal but still living.

One could argue that the intrigues of Domitian's house might well evoke in Statius' contemporaries memories of the tale of Thebes: the emperor's rivalry with his brother Titus, who he believed had deprived him of his rightful share in power after Vespasian's death (Suetonius, *Titus* 3.2; *Domitian* 2.3); his incestuous relationship with his niece (Suetonius, *Domitian* 22). Statius does seem to hint at Domitian in some of his references to Eteocles and Polynices, but these hints are only part of Statius' commentary on power and the powerful. The epic is no precise political allegory of Flavian Rome. These hints should remind us, however, that the *Thebaid* addresses not only the world of myth but also Statius' contemporary Rome, and they should warn us not to see his theme in narrowly restrictive terms. That, presumably, is why he talks so much of boundaries, of limits and their arbitrariness, at the epic's beginning.

THE CONSEQUENCES OF A PRAYER

After the preamble, Statius turns to the war and its immediate cause: a prayer to the Fury Tisiphone by Oedipus, which begins in a tone of ironic bitterness and self-recrimination. Oedipus narrates the results of his quest for knowledge:

> I sought the ancient springs of Cirrha that flow between two horned peaks. I could have lived on, content in the false belief that Polybus was my father. But in a narrow pass of Phocis, where three roads meet, I tangled with a king advanced in years; I cut into the face of a trembling old man. And I was looking for my father! Shrewd man, I solved the riddle of the unjust Sphinx. You showed me the way. How happy I was when I went into marriage with my mother. It was madness and passion, bringing ecstasy, then tears. Many a night of sin it produced for me—and sons, as you well know, I made for you. Soon, greedy for punishment, I pressed down hard upon my eyes. My fingers tore into them, as I wanted them to do; and I left them on my mother.
>
> (1.62–72)

Oedipus, while searching for his father, struck in the face and killed an old man: a rudimentary intellectual error, given the prophecy that he would kill his father. In searching out the mystery of his birth, his eyes had been useless to him. They saw, but did not recognize, his father and his mother. Hence Oedipus' assault upon his vision. Statius, in fact, introduces Oedipus into the epic with the words: "He had already sought out [*scrutatus*] his sinful eyes; his right hand had earned that privilege" (1.46). Oedipus the inquirer, the examiner, the *scrutator* turned the hand that killed his father on the eyes that had failed to examine. Like Appius Claudius, Lucan's *inquirer* into the boundaries of fate (*Pharsalia* 5.122), Oedipus is brought to grief by his own inquiries. Similarly Cadmus, whose search for Europa led him to examine the seas (*Thebaid* 1.6), began a process culminating not in his foundation of Thebes but in a chain of events marked by subhuman savagery and destruction. There is, in Statius, as in Lucan, a close link between examining something (*scrutari*) and destroying it.

Oedipus committed the crimes he sought to avoid *because* he sought to avoid them. Without foreknowledge and the spirit of inquiry, he might not have done so at all. Disillusioned now, he rejects what is reasoned and human and resigns himself completely to the forces of darkness and evil: blindness and the Fury Tisiphone. He asks the Fury to punish his sons, who have not treated him as a father should be treated:

> I was orphaned by my sight and of it [orbum visu] and of my ability to rule and direct anything. They approached their father—and I was their father, regardless of where they were conceived—not to rule and direct me, or even to comfort me with words. What pain they gave me! The moment that I died, they became proud rulers and pounced outrageously upon my deathlike blindness. They hated their father's cries of pain. Was I the blight of death upon them too? And does the spiritless father of the gods see this?
>
> (1.74–80)

I have translated *orbum visu* twice to underscore Statius' point: Oedipus is made an orphan by his eyes, by what they failed to see; he has also deprived himself of his sight. In his mind there persists the connection between his lost sight and his lost father.

Oedipus seems oblivious of the irony in his expectation that his sons should respect him, when he himself has actually killed his own father. He is aware only of the difference between himself and his sons: they knew he was their father; their actions were deliberate. His attack on his sight is legitimate; theirs is not. For they pounced upon his eyes, or, as Jupiter puts it, "they ground them, as they fell, beneath their heels" (238–239). In revenge, Oedipus asks Tisiphone to bring down on his sons *and their descendants* a terrible curse: "Go stand between the brothers, and let their kinship, which should bring them together, make them spring apart" (1.84–85).

The man whose unknowing crime caused his father's death and marriage with his mother now precipitates events that will destroy his sons; his wife, Jocasta; and countless ordinary citizens in generations to come. He acknowledges to Tisiphone that his prayers are twisted (1.59) and that their goal is inhuman sin (1.86). The once unconscious criminal now becomes a conscious force of evil. Oedipus, who solved the Sphinx's riddle, inflicts as much damage on Thebes as did the Sphinx herself. By reverting to primitive instincts of hatred and vengeance he abandons the understanding of man that enabled him to solve the riddle. He becomes the beast he destroyed.

Oedipus' prayer brings immediate results: the Fury induces Oedipus' sons to rule in alternate years, an arrangement that, Statius points out, is bound to have disastrous consequences (1.139–141, 173–196). Further, the prayer is overheard by Jupiter, who declares that Oedipus' self-inflicted punishment entitles him to hope for Jupiter as his avenger (1.240–241). Now Oedipus' only reference to Jupiter is a sarcastic question offered as an aside in his prayer to Tisiphone (1.79–80, cited previously). But it is all that is needed to attract Jupiter's attention.

Jupiter discerns an opportunity to punish the cities of Argos and Thebes, not just Oedipus' sons. He has not forgotten Tantalus' crimes in an earlier generation (1.246–247). Oedipus frankly admitted his request was criminal, but Jupiter passes off his much more sweeping proposals as divine justice. Juno alone voices objections: "How far back in time does one have to go to correct the madness of the earth?" (1.268–270). Her complaint is brushed aside, for Jupiter cannot answer without ultimately condemning himself. He is, by his own admission, founder of the royal houses of both Thebes and Argos (1.224–226). His rape of Danaë started the house of Argos; his rape of Europa sent Cadmus across the sea to Thebes. Like other gods in the *Thebaid*, he holds humanity responsible for events whose initial causes are his own crimes.

Attacks upon parents, the eating of children, rape, and incest have been more crudely practiced by the gods, who judge men, than by men themselves. The *Thebaid* could indeed have begun with Hesiod's *Theogony* as its preamble, for the tale extends back into the violence of creation itself.

Having spoken, Jupiter dispatches Mercury to the underworld in quest of Laius, Oedipus' dead father. The intent of this bizarre move is to persuade Eteocles to retain power after his year of rule. Heaven, like Oedipus, needs hell's resources. But Oedipus and the Fury have simply created the framework for conflict. Jupiter wants to ensure that it occurs.

THE INNOCENT AND WELL-INTENTIONED

As Mercury departs, Oedipus' exiled son, Polynices, arrives in Argos, haunted by dreams of power and vengeance. Wearied by a storm, he slumps exhausted against the door of King Adrastus' palace. His attempted slumber is interrupted by the arrival of Tydeus, exiled from Calydon for killing his brother. Instead of sharing his shelter, Polynices fights Tydeus until Adrastus is awakened and intervenes. Tydeus complains: "Who was he to deprive me of shelter? Was it just because he happened to arrive here first?" (1.454–457). Eteocles will not share the throne of Thebes with Polynices. On a smaller but no less illustrative scale, Polynices will not share his shelter with Tydeus.

Adrastus recognizes from Polynices' and Tydeus' attire the arrival of his destined sons-in-law. For they are, as Apollo had prophesied, wearing the "deceptive appearance of wild beasts" (1.496): Polynices wears a lion skin, Tydeus that of a boar. And the previous day Adrastus had been celebrating a festival commemorating Apollo's visit to Argos. After introducing his daughters and reviving the feast, Adrastus explains the festival's origin (1.557–668).

Apollo came to Argos seeking from King Crotopus ritual purification for his killing of Pytho, the monstrous snake guarding Delphi. While a guest in the palace, Apollo raped Crotopus' daughter. The girl, fearing her father's anger when she became pregnant, fled. Her child, when born, she entrusted to a shepherd, but it was subsequently killed by wild dogs. The daughter, repentant, confessed everything to her father and begged for death, a request her father speedily granted. At this late point, Apollo remembered his affair. In retribution for his child's death, he sent as punishment to Argos a monster "conceived in the hideous bedchamber of the Furies," which had "the face and breasts of a virgin" (1.597–599)—a subtle symbol of Apollo's guilt as well as of his vengeful anger. This creature consumed all the newborn children in Argos until the hero Coroebus, with a band of helpers, killed it (1.605–626). But the horror still does not end.

Apollo, determined to avenge this rather sphinx-like monster, sends a plague upon the city. When asked how the plague may be ended, the god responds that the youths who had killed the monster must die (1.637). Without hesitation Coroebus presents himself at the very shrine Apollo had liberated from the Pytho, and addresses the god:

> I come to your house and shrine, lord of Thymbra, not because I've been sent. And I'm not begging for mercy. My sense of proper duty and my awareness of what it is to be a man forced me down this path. Phoebus, I am the one who subdued and cut down your hideous creation, more worthy of man than god, and no less vulnerable. I am the one you hunt in your injustice with this dark pestilence from a threatening sky. So be it, if inhuman monsters mean so much to the great powers above, and human death is something cheaper, to be thrown away. So be it, if heaven is so brutal and ruthless. But what have the Argives done to deserve this? I, noblest of the gods, yes I have forfeited my life to the decrees of fate.... I've earned what's coming; don't feel the urge to spare me.... But while I'm dying, drive off the sickly mist that hangs down over Inachus' Argos.
> (1.643–652, 657, 659–661)

It is Apollo, not Coroebus, who stands accused. It is the individuals responsible for the crime, not the entire nation, that should suffer. The problem is, of course, that ultimate responsibility lies with Apollo anyway. The god who seeks vengeance and stands in judgment is himself the original cause of the situation, as Jupiter is earlier in book 1. Punishment of others is substituted for self-punishment. Perhaps this is why Jupiter admires Oedipus, and Apollo Coroebus—for Coroebus is spared, much to his surprise. For both Oedipus and Coroebus admit responsibility for their part in the causal nexus and provide an opportunity for divine "justice" and "clemency."

Adrastus' narrative recalls the tale of Oedipus and Thebes in many details: the exposed child, the sphinx-like monster, the plague. We are seeing a pattern in Statius' narrative that occurs in many variations throughout the epic, but what is so odd about this version is the way in which it ends.

Adrastus seems to infer that Apollo is somehow changed after his confrontation with Coroebus. For when, after the story is over, Polynices reluctantly introduces himself, Adrastus lightheartedly dismisses the significance of his past. Polynices should not be ashamed that Oedipus is his father, he declares, because: "Respect for family ties has had many lapses among my ancestors too; *but their sins do not get in the way of their descendants.* Just make sure you are different. Earn with your own success the chance to free yourself of your past" (1.689–692). Adrastus clearly thinks Apollo, in sparing Coroebus, has conceded the justice of Coroebus' arguments. This, presumably, is why he tells the company to offer the god a libation as "savior of our parents" (1.694), a title unwarranted by the narrative. He even asks Apollo to be present with the Argives, "remembering the hospitality they had shown him" (1.716). Argos could surely forgo another such visitation. In Adrastus' mind, however, Apollo has passed beyond the limits of the Hellenic deity; the king prays to him as Titan, Osiris, and Mithra, supreme god of light.

But Adrastus is wrong. Before him as he prays are Tydeus and Polynices, whom a less forgiving monarch would simply have expelled once their names were known. The nature of the universe and of the god is not changed simply by worshiping divine power as something beneficent rather than whimsical. Indeed Adrastus' conviction that heaven has changed binds him and his daughters to the prophecies of Apollo, who had devastated Argos in the past, and to the house of Oedipus, who was himself abandoned by his mother and whose quest for knowledge generated the horror that is now to envelop Argos and Thebes. Adrastus' innocent naiveté is as instrumental in the fulfillment of a criminal destiny as is Oedipus' guilt. If he had not intervened in the fight between Polynices and Tydeus, Tydeus would have killed the Theban. For all Jupiter's plans, the war would not have occurred.

HYPSIPYLE AND THESEUS

Throughout the *Thebaid* Statius shows how entire peoples are held accountable for the actions of a few. Ordinary men, women, and children suffer dreadfully for the misdeeds of warriors, kings, and gods. Yet Statius is careful neither to idealize the downtrodden nor to suggest that they would use power more wisely if they held it.

One of the epic's longest episodes, that of Hypsipyle, shows what happens when the tables are turned, when the individually weak develop a sense of collective identity and sweep away those they perceive as their oppressors with terrible violence and fury.

As the Argive army marches to Thebes to assert Polynices' claim to power, it is afflicted by drought, caused by the god Bacchus, who wants to divert the Argives from his native city. Hypsipyle, nurse to Opheltes, the son of Lycurgus, king of Nemea, shows the army to water (4.652–843). While the troops refresh themselves, Hypsipyle narrates her life's story: how she arrived at Nemea after once being queen of Lemnos (5.1–498).

The women of Lemnos had been separated from their husbands, who were campaigning in Thrace, for almost three years. One of the women, Polyxo, inspired by Venus, declared she had a solution to their loveless and childless isolation: they must kill the men when they returned. It is, of course, ironic that this bizarre remedy derives, ultimately, from Venus, whose infidelity to her own husband, Vulcan—a god especially associated with Lemnos—was notorious. And it is odd that no one detects the elementary flaw in Polyxo's reasoning. She wins the day. The women, Hypsipyle excepted, kill their menfolk. This is the "Lemnian crime" condemned by the female chorus in Aeschylus' *Libation Bearers* as the worst of all crimes (635–638).

Hypsipyle becomes queen, succeeding her father, Thoas, who she pretends is dead. To protect her life she disguises her innocence. Her secret is in greater danger of discovery than that of a private citizen living under a tyrant, for she is constantly before the people's eyes, the blameless ruler of a guilty people. Then the Argonauts arrive. Since there are no men to defend them, the women, willingly or unwillingly, mate with the sailors. Hypsipyle is raped by Jason and bears him twin sons. *Despite* her innocence, she suffers the consequences of others' guilt.

When the Argonauts leave, it is discovered that Thoas is still alive. Now Hypsipyle must suffer *because* she is innocent. On attempting to flee, she is abducted by pirates and sold as a slave to Lycurgus, king of Nemea, who makes her nursemaid to his child.

Yet as Hypsipyle tells her story, Lycurgus' child is unintentionally killed by a divine monster, a snake sacred to Jupiter. This unfortunate death almost leads to wholesale carnage before Adrastus finally calms tempers and holds funeral games for the dead child (5.499–6.946). Capaneus kills the lethal snake; Jupiter almost proves Coroebus right by hurling a warning bolt over Capaneus' head—are monsters dearer to the gods? Lycurgus threatens to kill Hypsipyle; the Argives reply with threats to Lycurgus and Nemea. All this impends because a child was accidentally killed while his talkative nurse was telling her story.

Ironies abound. The well-intentioned Hypsipyle enables the Argives to continue their murderous errand by saving them from drought; the funeral games so piously held over a child's grave offer a preview of the leaders in an impious war. Personal tragedy for Lycurgus and his wife ultimately brings happiness to Hypsipyle, for in the uproar, her sons—born because she was raped by Jason—recognize and are reunited with their mother. Thus the one time Hypsipyle *is* partially to blame—at least by negligence—she is rewarded with the only happiness to emerge from her previous pain. Without the uproar, she and her sons would never have met again.

The story of Hypsipyle is far from irrelevant to the *Thebaid*'s theme. On the contrary, in its significance as well as its location, it is the very heart of the epic. Everything that occurs in the *Thebaid* is undertaken, in the final analysis, so that two brothers may kill each other, something they could as easily have done, as the fight between Polynices and Tydeus shows, outside the royal palace. In Statius' ideal world this is the way it would be: "Only kings should relive these battles. Such would be my wish" (11.579). But this is not the way things happen in myth or history. The rivalry of the powerful sucks everything into its destructive vortex, not only those who seek glory but those who would more happily be bystanders, like Hypsipyle. The moment she makes contact with the army neither she nor Nemea lie outside the epic's sweep, however far removed they might wish to be. Her good intentions no more isolate her from the passions of kings than they did in the past from those of the murderous women whose queen she once was.

The relationship between Hypsipyle's Lemnian story and the main narrative of the *Thebaid* may be simply illustrated: Polyxo's justification of the massacre of men is obviously illogical; the massacre, therefore, is virtually unique in history or myth—only the Danaids come close to rivaling it; the result is a land without menfolk. The result of the main narrative is *two* lands without menfolk because men fail to recognize the absurdity of slaughtering one another for two self-destructive and unlovely princes, or a dead child. This latter scenario has been repeated *ad infinitum* throughout history and myth. Mankind's failure to perceive the stupidity of war paradoxically adds a certain logic to Polyxo's argument. If the

Argive women had all murdered their husbands the consequences would have been less brutal than they become in the *Thebaid,* for then the men of only one city would have died. The attempt to assert the "just claims" of an exiled brother lead to a result more devastating than that of myth's most obvious tale of criminal massacre.

THESEUS AND CLEMENTIA

The total effect of a scene in the *Thebaid* may be quite different from the sum of its constituent parts. For Statius scrupulously avoids "isolating" characters and events. He has no use for the clear-cut distinctions of good and evil Lucan employs in the *Pharsalia.* Although he offers two examples of self-sacrifice, those of Maeon and Menoeceus, which seem at first reminiscent of Lucan's Cato, in the larger context of the epic each illustrates the negative as well as the positive aspects of such behavior. In *Thebaid* 3, the prophet Maeon returns to Thebes as the sole survivor of Tydeus' slaughter of the men sent to ambush him. He enters Eteocles' presence sword in hand. Scholars long ago noted the uncertainty in Statius' narrative as to what is actually happening or what is going to happen in this passage (3.79–91). Is Maeon going to kill Eteocles, are Eteocles' henchmen going to kill him, or is he going to kill himself? The prophet obviously recognizes that Eteocles is to blame for the calamity. But his final action is to commit suicide, not to kill Eteocles. The uncertainty Statius injects into his narrative underscores the incongruity: someone recognizes a problem but attacks himself rather than the problem.

In *Thebaid* 10 we see a different perspective on suicide. Creon's son Menoeceus makes the ultimate gesture of self-sacrifice for Thebes (10.756–782). And he, like Maeon, is praised by Statius for the nobility of his action. But the results of Menoeceus' self-sacrifice are not altogether beneficial. The god-defying Capaneus chooses the very spot where Menoeceus died for his attack on Thebes and heaven, wreaking such havoc on the battlements that Thebes is subsequently without defense against the Athenian army under Theseus. Further, Menoeceus' father is puzzled and embittered by his son's death (10.802–806); Creon's anger and despair prompt him to insist that Eteocles and Polynices fight to the death (11.282–296). In giving up his life for Thebes, Menoeceus is, like Thebes' well-intentioned Boeotian allies in 4.345–362, sacrificing himself to maintain in power the tyrant who rules the city, as well as the city itself. For the city and its ruler cannot be so readily dissociated in practice as in theory. Ironically, once Eteocles is dead, it is Menoeceus' embittered father who assumes the reins of power and imposes a tyranny as unholy as Eteocles'.

Statius never questions the sincerity of Menoeceus' conviction and dedication any more than he questions Adrastus'. But he will not allow us to separate the virtuous man or virtuous act from the nexus of events as Lucan does. Only the ideal itself stands apart. And perhaps the noblest ideal he presents us is that of clemency, in *Thebaid* 12.

When the main fighting is over and Eteocles and Polynices are dead, along with the chief warriors of Argos and Thebes, the women of Argos flock north to claim their dead. Because Creon, now ruler of Thebes, refuses burial to the Argive dead, the women converge on Athens (12.464–480), where they are directed by the common people to the altar of clemency (12.512). This shrine, unlike that of Juno in *Aeneid* 1.441–493 or that of Dido in Silius, *Punica* 1.81–100, is not dedicated to any powerful deity or vengeful spirit, even though the opening phrase describing its site is reminiscent of these other shrines: "There was in the city's center ..." (12.481). This is the altar of those who have lost everything, or almost everything, an altar whose suppliants the goddess hears and answers (12.481–518). It is the altar to which Orestes later comes, driven by the Furies of his dead mother (12.511). In short, it is the shrine that Aeschylus identifies with the Athenian council and court held on the hill known as the Areopagus (*Eumenides* 681–705).

Statius' clemency has nothing in common with the notorious clemency of monarchs. It stands outside the power structure of the state and is explicitly dissociated from any particular god as well as from any monarch. Unfortunately, critics of the *Thebaid* have frequently missed this point, and establish a false connection between the altar and Athens' king, Theseus. They are, of course, juxtaposed in the narrative. The moment Statius completes his description of the Argive women at the altar, he introduces Theseus, returning from victory over the Amazons, accompanied by Amazon captives (12.519–539). Again there is an echo of Aeschylus (*Eumenides* 685–690). For it was on the Areopagus that the Amazons camped and set up their rival city because they hated Theseus. The Areopagus, then, evokes memories of the Amazons as well as of a shrine of justice.

Theseus enters the *Thebaid* in two different capacities: as potential ally to the Argive women and as conqueror and enslaver of the Amazons. In fact, the Amazon queen, Hippolyte, is already pregnant with Theseus' child (12.535–539). This juxtaposition of contrasting relationships between Theseus and women should warn us not to assume that Theseus himself embodies the principles of justice expressed in the altar of clemency. Indeed the Amazon women have no use for the altar of clemency at all, but seek, appropriately, the protection of Minerva, the virgin warrior goddess (12.529–531). For Theseus is a most unlikely champion of women in distress. He had abducted Helen even before Paris made the attempt; he had aided Pirithous in his attempted abduction of Proserpina, queen of the underworld (8.53–54). On his shield is depicted Ariadne, who had helped him survive his encounter with the Minotaur, but whom he abandoned on Naxos (12.676). Although Statius makes no direct reference to Theseus' marriage with Phaedra and her passion for Hippolytus, Theseus' son by Hippolyte, he twice mentions Hippolyte's pregnancy (12.535–539, 635–638). In Hippolyte's womb lie the beginnings of catastrophe for Theseus' own house. Like Oedipus, he will one day place a destructive curse upon his own offspring.

Theseus' heroism is founded to a remarkable extent on the need women feel for him—Ariadne, for example—or on his triumphs over women. Statius studiedly balances Theseus' chivalry toward the Argive women with reminders of the shameful treatment he has accorded others, particularly the Amazons. We must not, then, exaggerate Theseus' stature in the *Thebaid*. Quite apart from his treatment of women, his other credentials as a moral hero in the epic are hardly solid. His accession to power in Athens was clouded by uncertainty. In 12.625–626 Statius mentions Theseus' failure to change the black sails on his ship when he returned from Crete, thereby prompting his father to despair and suicide. There are more ways of killing one's father than striking him down at the crossroads. And we know Oedipus' act was unintentional; with Theseus' we cannot be sure.

Theseus' heroism in the *Thebaid* is the essence of simplicity. By the time he enters, the war (and the epic) are essentially over. Thebes, her manpower, and her opposition lie shattered. The remaining issue is the burial of the Argive dead, and the obstacle to their burial is one, obvious, and old. Creon is no Tydeus or Capaneus, no warrior at the height of his powers. And neither is Theseus, whom Statius also depicts as old; his battle with Creon is a one-sided contest of the elderly. At an earlier stage, victory would probably have proved harder even for Theseus. The issues were more complex, the opponents more formidable; nor is it self-evident that either side would have welcomed his arbitration any more than they welcomed that of the aging Adrastus.

The difference between Theseus and the other warriors of the epic is that he has a straightforward solution to what is now a straightforward problem. Like Maeon, he confronts a tyrant, weapon in hand; unlike Maeon, he uses his weapon on the tyrant, not on himself. Theseus' victory provides a chance for tears rather than a cessation from tears; the *Thebaid* ends with lamentation for the dead, not with paeans celebrating Theseus' victory. Like Hypsipyle's Lemnos, Thebes and Argos are now communities of wives without husbands, and their savior, Theseus, was one of the Argonauts who found Lemnos' lack of men to his advantage (5.431–432). Theseus completes a cycle in the *Thebaid*. Government of Thebes passes first from the old Oedipus to his young sons; with Theseus it reverts to the old. In the future lie other avengers, as Jupiter notes (7.220–221): the sons of the Seven, and the age of Alexander, perhaps, when the city will perish utterly.

CONCLUSION

Every character and action in the *Thebaid* is subjected to changing perspectives. What is seen depends on who is looking, when he is looking, and from what vantage point. In even the tiniest details Statius shows how people misconstrue what is happening because they make elementary errors of reasoning. They establish general rules and interpret specific actions as manifestations of those rules. When the chariot race at Opheltes' games is about to begin, Statius remarks: "The same desire to compete burns in driver and horse alike" (6.396). Yet when Adrastus' horse, Arion, drawing Polynices' chariot, "burns more fiercely" (6.427), his agitation is the result not, as the spectators presume, of excitement at the applause, but of his efforts to escape his charioteer (6.428–429). What was generally true at the beginning of the race is now wrong in this one instance. The exception eludes the onlookers because they presume that what has once been true must continue to be true.

All the protagonists of the epic, both human and divine, view themselves and the world from perspectives that have become fixed at some time or level. Polynices, for example, declares as he dies that he will pursue his right to kingship at Thebes even after his death (11.570–572). His delusion is, of course, pathetic. But such delusions are often the shaping forces of human destiny.

When the warrior-priest Amphiaraus' chariot crashes into the underworld (8.1–126), Pluto assumes he is being attacked by the Olympians or that this intruder is another mortal intent on stealing something from his realm. The reader knows neither of these assumptions is correct, and so would Pluto if he took the time to ask. But he does not. He retaliates immediately, vowing retribution against the warriors of Argos and against Eteocles and Polynices, who, regardless of their other crimes, are hardly directly responsible for Amphiaraus' appearance as a living being among the dead. Indeed Pluto decrees that the Argive dead will be left in the world of the living to rot, a gruesomely ironic vengeance; doubly so, in fact. For Apollo appears to have had Amphiaraus buried alive in order to prevent his dead body from lying unburied (7.775–777). Not only might one question the "blessing" Apollo has bestowed, but the nagging fear lurks that Apollo's foreknowledge of Creon's decree was ultimately the *cause* of that decree, given Pluto's reaction.

Pluto's assumption that he is being wronged is based on memories of what he had experienced not only in previous generations, but before the beginnings of the human race, experiences that have no obvious relationship to the events now occurring. The farther up the hierarchy of power one goes, the more bizarre and terrible are the consequences of such fixed and paranoid perspectives. Appeals to Jupiter and other deities invite the extension of present troubles in a remoter and no less blinkered eternal perspective. To Jupiter, Eteocles and Polynices are typically *human*, rather than typical of the Theban royal family (1.214–217) or separate entities unto themselves, as Adrastus imagines. And it is of *human* crime and his exhaustion with punishing it that Jupiter complains when he addresses the gods. The notions of a world at peace and of beneficent deities are fabrications of well-meaning mortals. To

Jupiter the notion of universal peace occurs only once in the epic: as a means of punishing Mars for his failure to start the Theban war on time (7.29–33). And he modifies the threat before the end of the same line. In no single instance in the *Thebaid* is the exercise of power based on an understanding of the complexity of events and their causes, even when part of that complex is known or knowable.

This dissociation of power from reason is the central theme of the *Thebaid*. Hierarchies of power are based on superior ability and desire to assert oneself at the expense of others: the ability to destroy. The similes of bestial strength common in the *Thebaid* illustrate the proximity of the world of power to that of the wild beast, ruled by instincts unchanged since before the dawn of civilization. Little separates the values of man the warrior and man the hunter. Atalanta decorates oaks with the captured "weapons" of boars and stags (9.585–601); Tydeus assumes the ferocity of the beasts he kills and becomes a predator himself. Theseus, killer of bulls, is more civilized and civilizing than wild animals, but brute force is still his means of civilizing. Even the Arcadian hunter Parthenopaeus, though hitherto innocent of human blood, has been nourished, like a lion cub, on bloodied food (9.739–740). He comes to war because his life as a hunter is unchallenging, because he regards his innocence as shameful. Among hunters the killing of the most dangerous prey brings most honor; and man himself is that most dangerous prey.

Parthenopaeus' Arcadians, Statius explains, are descendants of those who, when the human race was new, lived in such terror of darkness that they followed the setting sun in their despair (4.282–284). But as the Arcadians set out for war, the inhabitants of civilized Mycenae hold back, though not to preserve their innocence. They have warring brothers of their own, involved now in a cannibalistic feast of human flesh that prompts the sun to withdraw from them (4.306–308). As man's civilization develops, so does his notion of what it is honorable to kill. He progresses from killing beasts

to killing men of other communities to killing his fellow citizens, his kin, and finally himself. Man's *virtus* is still, Statius suggests, a measure of his ability to destroy. And this ability is shared by all the male protagonists of the *Thebaid*, whether they excel on the battlefield or, like Maeon and Menoeceus, turn their swords on themselves. A Caesar and a Cato, in Statius' view, have much in common.

Although the development of civilization has afforded man the chance to acquire some sense of the causal nexus in which he lives, it has, simultaneously, enhanced the growth of those destructive tendencies that link him to his primitive past. The availability of larger intellectual horizons is no guarantee they will triumph over primitive instinct or that they will even be known to, much less accepted by, the vast majority of people. For the relationship between political power and the ability to inflict death remains unchanged. Statius' Pluto and Jupiter clearly demonstrate that even the limitless horizons of eternity will not necessarily improve those who enjoy them. And these larger horizons are themselves only a partial perception of the cosmos, as Apollo, god of foreknowledge and of poetry, suggests to the Muses:

> Apollo had a sense of duty, and had often sung the very beginnings, the tales spun of the gods: of Jupiter, Phlegra, and his own achievement with the snake. . . . This time he reveals the energy that drives the thunderbolt and guides the stars, the source of power in flowing water, and what winds feed on. He reveals the wellspring from which the endless ocean drinks, the paths the sun follows when the nights are short and when they're long. He reveals the answer to the question as to whether the earth is the bedrock of the universe, or whether it is at the center, encircled from beneath by another world we cannot see.
>
> (6.358–364)

Of course Statius never gives us the answers to these questions Apollo answers for the Muses. The energy for the thunderbolt could come from Jupiter, and the answer to the final enigma could be: "It is the bedrock." But Apollo is possibly conceding that the gods themselves are simply explanations of phenomena that exist in endless interrelationships and that he himself is but a fiction, a name that has emerged in an attempt to define the indefinable. The more profoundly one pursues one's inquiries, the more hopeless one realizes it is to seek solutions and definitions. The investigator becomes the victim of his own investigations, as Apollo, in a way, does here. For knowledge involves an assault on existing definitions; it too is destructive, as man's more primitive instincts are.

The tale of the house of Oedipus, which knows no boundaries, and which Statius, with magnificent irony, takes as the boundary of his work, is, as Freud recognized many centuries later, the tale of man himself. Man's quest for larger horizons yields only an increasingly intense awareness of his own finiteness; it does not remedy it. He is still governed both internally and socially by irrational, instinctive powers. And the danger lurks that he will do what Oedipus does, discover his origins not intellectually and consciously, but physically and unconsciously. Then, in frustration at the ugly paradox, he may close his eyes to all he has learned and commit himself to the control of those rudimentary forces against which he struggles in vain. If he cannot define life intellectually, he can employ the power he knows ultimately defines him as an individual: the power of death. As Amphiaraus notes, Pluto, god of death, is the great *definer* of things (*finitor rerum*: 8.91). Those who can inflict death define human endeavors not because they are right or even rational, but because they can set the limits on men and cities if only by threatening or achieving their destruction. Paradoxically, then, as Amphiaraus adds, the great destroyer is thus the great creator too (8.92), if only in the sense that Theseus, Jupiter, Apollo, or even Pluto himself can rape as well as kill. From the violent attack upon women is born the new generation.

Between instinct and the inevitability of death, the two coercive forces of existence, lies the knowledge that the government of man's cities can embody those rational principles, those ideals of justice that emerge in man's mind as he reflects. Fleetingly and incompletely they had flourished at Athens, Statius suggests. But he never alludes to their existence at Rome. And here is the force of Statius' Hellenic wrath at the Roman world, as expressed by an old man, Aletes, in book 3: to accept the irrational madness of nature and the gods is one thing; to accept government along the same lines is harder, because alternatives do exist. At the heart of civilization there should be a shrine to Clementia, a goddess who listens rather than punishes.

The world of power and the powerful is grim and forbidding, a world in which innocence and beauty are almost inevitably destroyed. All that prevents that inevitability from becoming absolute is the art that he and other artists practice. Though Statius shows the naiveté of Adrastus' belief in man, he also shows us that belief and challenges us to find a way to make it work. Similarly, though the *Thebaid* tells of the infant Opheltes' death, it also preserves a sense of how beautiful Opheltes was. And it is with precisely such a recollection of human beauty destroyed in war that the *Thebaid* ends: a threefold lamentation for the young Arcadian Parthenopaeus (12.805–807). Parthenopaeus is mankind in its youth, poised between hunting and civilization, between boyhood and manhood. Despite Parthenopaeus' shame at his own innocence and lack of pride in his own beauty, not even death can rob him of his attractiveness. When he tries to contort his face into a grimace of ferocity in sad imitation of adult behavior, he remains a child, and anger simply enhances his beauty (9.705 ff.).

The *Thebaid* is one of the profoundest works of Latin literature and one of the most skillfully executed. Unlike other Roman heroic epics, it has no use for any of the values of heroic or political conflict. There are no winners in the *Thebaid*. Rather, Statius declares the folly of war—whatever the circumstances—in an epic that is the tale of man's progress toward self-annihilation. It is a story that, he feels, should have been told only once. We should have learned "to let kings alone relive these battles." It is not hard to see why Dante chose the author of the *Thebaid* as his guide to paradise.

Selected Bibliography

PRELIMINARY NOTE

The reader of the *Pharsalia* or the *Thebaid* faces numerous problems. No modern commentaries cover the whole of either epic; most of the best critical scholarship is in languages other than English; there are no really adequate translations into English. Worst of all, most criticism of the two works begins with the assumption, whether tacit or overt, that these epics are second-rate products of a period of literary decadence and decline: a Silver Age, not a Golden Age.

Of the four English translations listed in the bibliography, three are prepared by writers who treat their originals with condescension, sometimes contempt. Robert Graves remarks, "Lucan may be called the father of yellow journalism" (p. 13). He spent six months translating him "because the book is a historical phenomenon that cannot be argued away, and because like other prodigiously vital writers with hysterical tendencies . . . Lucan exerts a strange fascination on even the reluctant reader; and because . . . he anticipated so many of the literary genres dominant today that it would be unfair not to put him in modern dress for the admiration of the great majority whose tastes differ from mine" (p. 24). Graves, like many others, insinuates that there must be something wrong with the taste or judgment of someone who likes the *Pharsalia*. J. D. Duff in the preface to his version of the epic comments (p. 12): "*No reasonable judgement* can rank Lucan among the world's great epic poets. He does not tell his story well: the successive episodes are neither skilfully connected nor *well-proportioned*" (the italics in this note are added). J. H. Mozley contends in his preface to the *Thebaid* (p. xiv), "To be the author of a great epic poem is to count as one of the few great poets of the world, and *it need hardly be said* that Statius can make no claim to that honour." These attitudes affect the translations in a very negative way, and the reader who must rely on them is bound to find his own impressions shaped by the dislikes and prejudices of the translator.

The translators of Lucan and Statius, and the commentators, too often follow the mode of criticism that Aristotle, quoting Glaucon, censures in the *Poetics*:

> Critics, he says, jump at certain groundless conclusions; *they pass adverse judgment and then proceed to reason on it*; and, assuming that the poet has said whatever they happen to think, find fault if a thing is inconsistent with their own fancy.
>
> (1461b.1; S. H. Butcher trans.)

This sort of procedure is law-court rhetoric at its worst; and it has, in effect, condemned these once-admired authors to what the German scholar Friedländer described as "the graveyard of literary history." Ironically, it is most frequently used by those critics who express disdain for rhetorical literature. H. E. Butler, in his *Post-Augustan Poetry* (Oxford, 1909), notes in his preamble to a discussion of the *Thebaid*: "The Theban legend is *unsuitable for epic treatment* for more reasons than one. In the first place the story is unpleasant from beginning to end" (p. 208). Statius, presumably, ought to have known better than to choose the subject. Of Statius' battles, Butler remarks: "Homer knew what fighting was from personal experience, or at least from being in touch with warriors who had killed their man. Vergil had come no nearer these things than 'in the pages of a book.' Statius is yet one remove further from the truth than Vergil" (p. 221). Whether Homer fought in or saw battles (or anything else for that matter) is pure speculation. Some would even question his existence. But both Vergil and Statius *had known* civil war in their lives; and killing was never farther away than the arena. Butler's remarks tell us a lot about what he liked but little about Statius.

Similarly, Gordon Williams in *Change and Decline: Roman Literature in the Early Empire* (Berkeley, 1978) contends, "A basic *lack of proportion* pervades Statius' whole work and *renders nugatory the laborious schemes devised* to show its symmetrical structure" (p. 252). Williams, like many scholars, has a fixed idea about the way Latin literature should be. When styles and views shift from what he takes to be the Augustan ideal, one could think of this process as progress or as the exploration of new perspectives.

But for him change is decline. I would concur that most efforts to show the *Thebaid's* structure and symmetry have been unsuccessful. But this does not mean that there *is* no symmetry or structure. Rather it means that the structuring principles are different from those he thinks ought to be present.

The purpose, then, of much work on Lucan and Statius is to show the inferiority of these writers to their Augustan predecessors and to discourage any mode of scholarship that might suggest that Chaucer, Dante, and the many others who were profoundly influenced by the *Pharsalia* and the *Thebaid* were right in their high opinions of Lucan and Statius. Aside from the translators, the majority of those listed in the bibliography here are scholars who believe that Lucan and Statius have something important to say. I frequently disagree with their conclusions, but not at all with their intent. They have significantly advanced our understanding of the *Pharsalia* and the *Thebaid*.

TEXTS

LUCAN

Lucan, De Bello Civili 7, edited by O. A. W. Dilke. Cambridge, 1970. Introduction and commentary in English.

M. Annaei Lucani Belli Civilis, Libri 10, edited by A. E. Housman. 4th ed. Oxford, 1958.

M. Annaei Lucani De Bello Civili, Liber 1, edited by R. J. Getty. Cambridge, 1940. Introduction and commentary in English.

M. Annaei Lucani De Bello Civili, Liber 1, edited by P. Wuilleumier and H. Le Bonniec. Paris, 1962. Introduction and commentary in French.

M. Annaei Lucani Pharsalia, edited by C. E. Haskins. London, 1887. Introduction by W. E. Heitland; commentary on all ten books, in English.

STATIUS

P. Papini Stati Silvae, edited by A. Marastoni. 2nd ed. Leipzig, 1970.

P. Papini Stati Thebaidos, Liber 10, edited by R. D. Williams. Leiden, 1972. Introduction and commentary in English.

P. Papini Stati Thebaidos, Liber 11, edited by P. Venini. Florence, 1970. Introduction and commentary in Italian.

P. Papinius Statius, Thebaid: A Commentary on Book 3, edited by Harry Snijder. Amsterdam, 1968. Introduction and commentary in English.

Publii Papinii Statii Thebaidos, Liber 2, edited by H. M. Mulder. Groningen, 1954. Introduction and commentary in Latin.

Statii Thebais, edited by A. Klotz. Revised edition by T. C. Klinnert. Leipzig, 1973.

Statius: Achilleid, edited by O. A. W. Dilke. Cambridge, 1954.

TRANSLATIONS

LUCAN

Lucan. Translated by J. D. Duff. Cambridge, Mass., 1969. English translation. Loeb Classical Library.

Pharsalia, Dramatic Episodes of the Civil Wars. Translated by R. Graves. Baltimore, 1957. In English. Penguin Classics.

STATIUS

La Tebaide, libro 1. Translated by F. Caviglia. Rome, 1973. Italian translation, commentary, and introduction.

Publii Papinii Statii Thebaidos, Liber 1. Translated by H. Heuvel. Zutphen, Neth., 1932. Dutch translation, introduction, and commentary.

Stace: Achilléide. Translated by Jean Méheust. Paris, 1971. French translation and commentary.

Statius. Translated by J. H. Mozley. 2 vols. Cambridge, Mass., 1928. English translation. Loeb Classical Library.

Statius' Thebaid. Translated by J. B. Poynton. 3 vols. Oxford, 1971–1975. English translation.

CRITICAL STUDIES

GENERAL

Ahl, F. M. "Towards a New Reading of Neronian and Flavian Poetry." *Aufstieg und Niedergang der römischen Welt* 2.32.1 (forthcoming). With appendix on *Silvae* 3.4 by J. Garthwaite.

Cizek, E. *L'Époque de Neron et ses controverses idéologiques*. Leiden, 1972.

Ogilvie, R. M. *Roman Literature and Society*. New York, 1980.

LUCAN

Ahl, F. M. *Lucan: an Introduction*. Cornell Studies in Classical Philology 39. Ithaca, N. Y., 1976.

Brisset, Jacqueline. *Les Idées politiques de Lucain*. Paris, 1964.

Burck, E., and W. Rutz. "Die *Pharsalia* Lucans." In *Das römische Epos*, edited by E. Burck. Darmstadt, 1979.

Durry, M., ed. *Lucain*. Entretiens sur l'antiquité classique 15. Vandoeuvres-Genève, 1968. Essays.

Lebek, W. D. *Lucans Pharsalia*. Hypomnemata Heft 44. Göttingen, 1976.

Marti, Berthe. "The Meaning of the *Pharsalia*." *American Journal of Philology* 66:352–376 (1945).

Morford, M. P. O. *The Poet Lucan*. Oxford, 1967.

Narducci, E. *La provvidenza crudele: Lucano e la distruzione dei miti augustei*. Pisa, 1979.

Rutz, Werner, ed. *Lucan*. Wege der Forschung 235. Darmstadt, 1970. Essays.

STATIUS

Ahl, F. M. "Statius' *Thebaid*: A Reconsideration." *Aufstieg und Niedergang der römischen Welt* 2.32.2 (forthcoming).

Arico, G. "L'Achilleide di Stazio." *Aufstieg und Niedergang der römischen Welt* 2.32.2 (forthcoming).

——. *Ricerche Staziane*. Palermo, 1972.

Burck, E. "Die *Thebais* des Statius" and "Die *Achilleis* des Statius." In *Das römische Epos*, edited by E. Burck. Darmstadt, 1979.

Burgess, J. F. "Statius' Altar of Mercy." *Classical Quarterly* 22:339–349 (1972).

Juhnke, H. *Homerisches in römischer Epik flavischer Zeit*. Munich, 1972.

Kytzler, B. "Zum Aufbau der statianischen Thebais. Pius Coroebus, Thebais 1.557–692." *Aufstieg und Niedergang der römischen Welt* 2.32.2 (forthcoming).

Legras, L. *Étude sur la Thébaide de Stace*. Paris, 1905.

Newmyer, S. T. *The Silvae of Statius: Structure and Theme*. Leiden, 1979.

Vessey, David. *Statius and the Thebaid*. Cambridge, 1973.

White, P. "The Friends of Statius." *Harvard Studies in Classical Philology* 79:265–300 (1975).

BIBLIOGRAPHIES

Frassinetti, P. "Stazio epico e la critica recente." *Rendiconti dell'Istituto Lombardo* 107:243–258 (1973).

Rutz, W. "Lucan 1943–1963." *Lustrum* 9:243–334 (1964).

——. "Zweiter Nachtrag zum Lucan-Bericht Lustrum 9, 1964." *Lustrum* 10:246–256 (1965).

——. "Lucan. Ein Forschungsbericht." *Aufstieg und Niedergang der römischen Welt* 2.32.2 (forthcoming).

FREDERICK M. AHL

QUINTILIAN

(*ca.* A.D. 40–*ca.* 96)

MARCUS FABIUS QUINTILIANUS was a great Roman educator, becoming the first professor of any subject to hold an official appointment in Rome. For twenty years he trained young men destined for positions of leadership in the Roman Empire. He was the author of a Latin treatise, *Institutio oratoria* ("The Education of an Orator"), which describes in detail the training of a citizen and a political leader. This work became the authoritative statement on the subject throughout antiquity. Portions of it were studied in the Middle Ages; for example, by John of Salisbury, who drew on it extensively for his work at the Cathedral School of Chartres in the twelfth century. In 1416 the Italian scholar Poggio Bracciolini found a complete text of the work in a manuscript in Switzerland. Quintilian immediately became very influential in Italian education and ideas of literary composition, and was soon known throughout western Europe. He was widely studied again in England and America in the eighteenth and early nineteenth centuries for his theories of public address and eloquence. For example, John Quincy Adams' Boylston Lectures on oratory at Harvard between 1806 and 1809 owe much to him. Thus a familiarity with his work is important in understanding the history of education and rhetoric throughout much of history.

We know some facts about Quintilian's life from what he says himself and from references in letters of Pliny the Younger, in writings of Suetonius, and in other Roman works. He was born at Calagurris (now Calahorra), a Roman town in north-central Spain, which was then one of the most important Roman provinces. The date was probably between A.D. 35 and 40, in the reign of Tiberius or Caligula, when Rome had already instituted orderly legal procedure, efficient administration, and classical culture in the western Mediterranean. Quintilian's father may have been a teacher in Rome, then moving to Spain, because Seneca the Elder mentions a teacher by that name. Quintilian himself was sent back to the capital to complete his education. Among his teachers in Rome was Domitius Afer, who also practiced as an advocate in the Roman courts. This was around A.D. 55–60, when Nero was emperor and Seneca the philosopher was a leading political and literary influence. Quintilian developed a dislike for Seneca's style in speech and writing, and Nero's court was moving toward oppression and tyranny. He returned to Spain around A.D. 60, although we do not know what he did there. Probably he too became an advocate in the courts, and he may have begun to teach in a school of his own.

In A.D. 68, Galba, the elderly governor of Spain, was proclaimed emperor and led a revolution against Nero. Quintilian accompanied Galba on his long march to Rome, in some unspecified capacity. With Nero overthrown, Galba soon fell victim to those who resented his personal and financial austerity; Rome was plunged into a year of bloody civil war with a succession of short-lived emperors. Vespasian ultimately emerged the victor and was emperor from A.D. 69 to 79. He was succeeded by his elder son, Titus (79 to 81), and by his younger son, Domitian (81 to 96). These three emperors, known as the Flavian Dynasty, brought an end to the extravagance of Nero's court and attempted a more general reform of Roman society. Vespasian named Quintilian as professor of rhetoric, probably in 71. Although some Greek city-states had paid schoolmasters, education until this time had been largely a family or private matter, so that Quintilian's appointment represents an important step in the history of education.

Quintilian tells us in his preface that he held this position for twenty years, that is, from about A.D. 71 to 91. During this period he taught a large number of young men who were preparing for careers in the law courts and Senate or as administrators. He also pleaded cases in the courts. Although he never held political office, after his retirement he was given the *ornamenta consularia,* the honorary insignia for a former consul.

In the years after his retirement, Quintilian revised the lectures that he had given to students and published them around A.D. 95 as *Institutio oratoria.* This is his only surviving work. He had earlier written a treatise, *De causis corruptae eloquentiae* ("On the Causes of the Corruption of Eloquence"), which has not survived. Two collections of declamations attributed to him are probably not genuine.

During his retirement Quintilian was asked by Domitian to take charge of the education of the emperor's two grandnephews, who were heirs to the throne. He mentions this in the preface to book 4 of the *Institutio.* Although Domitian became increasingly cruel and arbitrary, Quintilian, indebted to the Flavian Dynasty, always speaks well of Domitian, even praising his youthful poems as though they were great literature. He may have liked Domitian personally; he certainly respected the position of emperor. Unlike other Romans of his time—the historian Tacitus, for example—he took a positive and optimistic view of the imperial government and the direction of Roman society. Indeed, it is typical of him to look forward, to see the good in people and their actions, and to avoid unpleasantness.

Quintilian was married at about forty to a much younger woman, and they had two sons; his wife and both sons died within a few years. In the preface to book 6 of the *Institutio* he gives a pathetic account of this loss.

Domitian was assassinated in A.D. 96. We do not know what happened to his young heirs or to Quintilian. They simply disappear from history. Domitian's memory was condemned. Quintilian, though, seems to have suffered no disgrace and is spoken of in favorable terms by writers of the early second century, such as Pliny the Younger, who had studied with him. It seems likely that Quintilian quietly withdrew from the court on Domitian's death and died soon afterward of natural causes.

The subject that Quintilian taught for twenty years and to which he devotes most of the *Institutio oratoria* was rhetoric. Rhetoric, the basic curriculum of secondary education in Greece beginning in the fourth century B.C., was taken up by the Romans in the second century B.C. From the Middle Ages to the early modern period it survived as one of the seven liberal arts; and it was an important subject in secondary schools and in the early years at a university. It is the precursor to modern courses in composition (sometimes still called "rhetoric") and in speech for college freshmen. But rhetoric meant more in ancient education and occupied a much more dominant position than it does today. It thus may be helpful to give a brief picture of its content. We know much about the teaching of rhetoric from Quintilian, from Cicero, and from other Roman writers, all of whom were trained in it.

Citizenship was the central fact of life in the Greek city-state as in the Roman Republic, and education prepared one for civic life. Elementary education came in the school of the grammarian, the ancestor of the grammar school of today, and was devoted almost entirely to learning how to read and write. Quintilian recommends that Roman students learn first to read and write Greek, and then to read and write Latin, which of course was spoken at home. This is analogous to the way students in Europe and America, until the eighteenth century, were taught to read and write Latin before having formal instruction in their native tongue.

Although writing was important, political life was largely oral, and the ability to speak effectively was essential for anyone who expected to play an influential role in society. A member of the Roman ruling class was assumed to own property, largely managed by slaves or freedmen, which would provide him an adequate income, and he should not have to earn money. He thus could spend his time in government administration, politics, service to his friends and family, and leisure. Romans of good family did not enter the professions, with one exception (to which we will come shortly). Commerce was not regarded as dignified; and though many Romans did engage in it, they often preferred to do so through intermediaries. Medicine was left to Greeks, sometimes to slaves. The priesthoods and other religious posts were not full-time positions for men and paid no salaries.

The one profession open to Romans was the law; yet even there, before Quintilian's time it was not legal to accept a fee. This was changed by the emperor Claudius, and Quintilian probably made money from practice in the law courts. Even in the law there was nothing in Rome corresponding exactly to a modern American lawyer. There were a few jurisconsults, highly trained legal advisers who gave opinions but rarely appeared in court. Most legal business was conducted by educated citizens whose technical knowledge of the subject was acquired by experience and whose only formal training was in rhetoric. They were called "patrons," and they undertook to speak in court for "clients" who had not studied rhetoric or who were unsure of their ability to speak

on their own behalf. Cicero devoted much of his time to this activity and secured his fame through it.

In a three-book dialogue entitled *De oratore*, written in 55 B.C., Cicero gave an idealized picture of the functions of the orator, who emerges as the highest type of human being, spreading civilization through his persuasive speech and setting an example for enlightened, moral action. This ideal was to some extent intended as a counterpart to the ideal of Hellenistic philosophers, in which wisdom and reasoning powers were more important than eloquence or a willingness to become involved in practical affairs. Since the time of Plato and Isocrates in fourth-century Greece, there had been a debate between teachers of philosophy and teachers of rhetoric, centering on the questions of how much knowledge of the subject under dispute an orator should have and what was the appropriate training for him. Competition for Roman students sharpened this debate, but in general the Romans distrusted abstract philosophy and preferred the ideal of the statesman-orator. Until the time of Cicero the teaching of rhetoric had rarely concerned itself with the moral choices an orator must make and the rightness of the causes he would undertake. Cicero added a strong ethical note to rhetoric, and Quintilian continued this. He greatly admired Cicero, both as a man and as an orator, and he made direct use of On the Orator and other rhetorical writings of Cicero. Conversely, he had little sympathy with philosophical theories and disliked the philosophers of his own time.

Learning to read in grammar school introduced the student to the classics of Greek and Latin literature, especially to poets such as Homer and, by Quintilian's time, Vergil and Horace. Through poetry the student acquired some incidental knowledge of other subjects, such as mythology and history. He also had practice in simple composition, such as retelling fables of Aesop, describing something, or narrating a historical incident. "He" is the correct pronoun, since education was intended almost entirely for boys. Girls learned to read and write at home, or perhaps occasionally in grammar school, but rarely received further formal education, because they were not expected to have any life as active citizens. They would be provided for by their fathers, husbands, or male relatives. Quintilian is unusual in urging the education of women (1.1.6).

Some Roman boys ended their education with grammar; but many, at the age of twelve to fourteen, went on to a rhetorical school. These were private schools run by teachers who were paid directly by parents, until Vespasian appointed Quintilian to a state professorship. Even so, Quintilian could not teach all the young men in Rome, and many other schools continued to exist. He probably attracted the sons of the influential and wealthy, and perhaps some poor students of special ability.

The curriculum of the rhetorical school, like that of the grammar school, was restricted to the verbal arts, with emphasis on the art of speech. In reading and composing speeches the student acquired knowledge of other subjects, including the Roman constitution, law, and legal procedure. He listened to lectures or studied handbooks in Greek or Latin that set out the theory of public address; and he composed and practiced delivery of his own speeches on assigned subjects.

Rhetorical theory, as taught in Greek and Roman schools and described by Cicero and Quintilian, was divided into five parts. These parts reflect five separate acts or stages in the preparation and delivery of a speech: invention, or the planning of the argument; arrangement, or the division of the speech into separate, orderly parts and the disposition of the argument in those parts; style, or the choice and arrangement of words that give expression to the ideas; memory, or the technique of remembering the speech as planned or written out; and delivery, the effective use of voice and gestures before an audience. It was generally expected that the speech would appear to be more or less extempore even if every word had been chosen in advance.

The most common setting for oratory in Rome was the courts, and Roman rhetoric emphasizes judicial oratory. There were, however, two other kinds of oratory in which the student was instructed. If he should have an opportunity to speak in one of the assemblies of the citizens or in the Senate, or to give advice to the emperor, he would need a knowledge of deliberative oratory. A third form, called epideictic, includes all forms in which an orator is not seeking to persuade a jury to come to a just decision or an assembly to take an appropriate action. In epideictic oratory the audience is asked not to make any decision or take any action, but to come to agreement with the orator in his stated view. In Rome the most common type of epideictic oratory was the funeral oration. At the time of the empire, however, speeches in praise of the emperor or members of his family were common, and were an important way to strengthen public support of the state or to win the favor of the emperor. The best example of such a speech is one by Pliny the Younger, who studied with Quintilian and whose *Panegyric*, or speech in praise of the emperor Trajan in A.D. 100, has been preserved.

The principal exercise of the rhetorical schools was what is called declamation. Quintilian has much to say about declamation, and we also have a detailed picture of it, written about the time Quintilian was born, by Seneca the Elder, father of the philosopher. There were two kinds of declamation; the more elementary was called a suasoria, which approximated to the form of a deliberative address. The student was given a situation from mythology or history and asked to write a speech urging some specified action. He might, for example, be assigned to write a speech urging Orestes not to kill his mother, or urging Alexander the Great to turn back from India, or urging Hannibal not to attack Rome. In the more subtle variety of the exercise, one composed a speech for a well-known fictitious person or historical character and sought to portray the character in a convincing way. This was called prosopopoeia.

The more advanced, and by far the more common, exercise was a speech for an imaginary trial in court. This exercise in judicial rhetoric, the controversia, was expected to reflect all that the student had learned about invention, arrangement, and style, as well as to exercise him in memory and delivery before an audience. The teacher usually specifed the law that was to apply to the imagined situation. Often the laws were not actual but imaginary ones designed to test the student's ability. One commonly used law in the rhetorical schools specified that a woman who had been raped was entitled to decide if the convicted rapist should marry her or be put to death. The situation is then imagined that a man rapes two different women within a few hours. He is caught, and one woman demands that he be put to death; the other, that he marry her. The student is asked to compose a speech on behalf of one of the participants, the rapist or a patron for either of the women.

Declamation was not debate. It was not the custom, as in modern debate, to assign opposing sides of a case to different students and expect them to answer each other's argument. Each speech was composed in isolation, and, to judge from the surviving examples, the students were allowed to use quite improbable arguments. Indeed, the argument was regarded as less important than the interpretation of character, motive, or the ornaments of style, such as figures of speech that the student was able to work into his speech. The subjects often involved pirates, ravished maidens, tyrants, and cruel stepmothers, probably because the teachers found that violence and sex aroused the interest of the students. Quintilian considered declamation a practical training for the courts; he avoided the more bizarre subjects and discouraged affected language and artificiality.

Although declamation in some form had been practiced in schools since the fourth century B.C., the exercises just described are largely a development of the later first century B.C., at the time when the empire replaced the Roman Republic and opportunities for significant political oratory, both in assemblies and in the courts, declined significantly. This trend, instead of discouraging the practice of declamation, reduced its practical application and encouraged its artificiality as a mental and verbal exercise. It became fashionable for adults to declaim as a kind of sport, and many teachers of rhetoric encouraged outsiders to come into their schools and participate in declamation before the students. Even some influential, busy people did so occasionally. The opening scene of Petronius' novel the Satyricon, written at the time of Quintilian, is set in a rhetorical school where outsiders have been invited to declaim and where a group of enthusiasts has crowded in to hear them. We do not know whether Quintilian allowed outsiders to participate in declamation at his school.

Quintilian's Institutio oratoria, the treatise based on his teaching of rhetoric for twenty years, is divided into twelve books. Modern editions subdivide the books into chapters, which often reflect natural divisions of the subject matter, but the chapter divisions were made by editors in the Renaissance and not by Quintilian himself. The work was first printed in 1470 and has been reprinted many times in Latin and translated into most modern languages. The printed versions are based on various medieval manuscripts, of which the oldest dates from the tenth century. As with all classical authors, since we do not have Quintilian's own manuscript, there are a number of places where copyists through the centuries did not understand the text they were copying, or made careless mistakes, and where modern editors have to make emendations in order to make sense of the text. These problems, however, affect only occasional details in what Quintilian is saying. His Latin is generally clear, even in the technical discussion.

Prefixed to the Institutio is a short letter from Quintilian to his publisher, Trypho. He says that he had planned to delay publication, since he wanted to revise the work, but has been very busy with other affairs, presumably his responsibilities in overseeing the education of Domitian's heirs. He agrees to publication now because Trypho is to get the work out in response to public demand. He trusts that Trypho will see that the published version is as correct as possible. A Roman publisher had multiple copies made by hand. The author could hardly proofread each copy, and he was at the mercy of the accuracy of the scribes. Publishers had stalls near the Forum where copies of books were sold. Since no copyright existed, any buyer of a book could have additional copies made to sell or give away, and these might introduce additional errors.

Books 1, 4, 5, 6, 7, 8, and 12 begin with prefaces, and that to book 1 is prefatory to the entire work. It pays special attention to the understanding of Quintilian's goals. He begins by saying that he has been urged to write the *Institutio* by friends who found the numerous earlier treatises on rhetoric filled with contradictory opinions. His friends doubtless did say this, but it is also a literary convention among Roman writers to start in this way. In meeting a need for judgment, Quintilian repeatedly reviews earlier opinions on almost all aspects of rhetoric and then gives his own views. The result is very useful to modern students of ancient rhetoric and education, who can find in Quintilian a survey of opinions of writers whose works often do not survive, and thus get a sense of the controversies that raged among ancient authorities at different times. Quintilian notes that earlier writers have assumed that their readers have a good education, and thus have dealt only with rhetoric. He suspects that they have scorned the earlier stages of education, but is convinced that a good rhetorical education can be built only on a good elementary education. An unusual feature of his work is that it deals with all of education, starting with a child's first training in speech and going through studies in grammar school as well as in rhetorical school. It provides us with unparalleled information on early childhood and elementary education in Rome. It is not until well into book 2 that he reaches the subject of rhetoric. After discussing rhetorical education and the theory of rhetoric in books 3 through 11, he adds an unusual discussion in book 12 that traces the career of an orator up to the time of retirement. He thus provides a complete though idealized account of the citizen and statesman, from cradle to old age.

Quintilian seems to have worked on the various parts of the *Institutio* in the order in which they now stand, and to have published the whole without revision. The prefaces reflect stages in the composition. If he had undertaken the work later, when teaching Domitian's heirs, he would almost certainly have dedicated the treatise to the emperor, and the preface to book 4 may be read as a correction of this omission. As it is, the preface to book 1 dedicates the work to a certain Vitorius Marcellus, a friend and an enthusiast of literature, in the hope that it will be useful in the education of Marcellus' young son, Geta. The Latin poet Statius, a contemporary of Quintilian, also dedicated one of his works to Marcellus, who seems to have been a patron of writers of the time.

The central part of the preface to book 1 describes in general terms the perfect orator at which Quintilian aims. He must, first of all, be a good man—good not only in his ability to speak but also in his moral character. As we have noted, this is a Roman view found also in Cicero. It raises the question of the relationship between rhetoric and philosophy, since the latter discipline claimed to teach moral excellence; but Quintilian reveals his contempt for the philosophers of his age. The true philosopher is the orator who has a thorough knowledge of the subjects on which he speaks. This ideal, he thinks, can be reached, and even those who fail to achieve perfection will be better for having tried. He then gives an outline of the twelve books that follow, book by book, and concludes with observations about natural talent. It was a commonplace of the rhetorical schools that a student had to have some natural talent to begin with but that talent could be improved by study and constant practice. Quintilian accepts the concept of nature, theory, and practice combined as the basis for a perfect orator.

Book 1 provides an account of early childhood and elementary education. Quintilian says that a father should have the highest hopes for his son from birth and should employ a nurse who will speak good Latin, so that the child will be accustomed to correct language. Children owe much to their mothers, and women should be educated too, so that they can help to educate their sons. Roman boys whose parents could afford it were attended by pedagogues, or slaves who took them back and forth to school and generally looked after them. They too needed to have a good education to be able to help teach their charges.

Quintilian thought that formal education should begin with Greek, soon followed by Latin. A controversy evidently existed as to whether children should be taught to read before the age of seven. Quintilian believed they should, and that, without unduly pressing the child, all possible advantage should be taken of the ability of the young to learn easily and to retain what they have learned. He wanted early education to be amusing and to encourage an interest in study. Another controversy was about whether the child should learn to recite the alphabet first and then learn the shapes of the letters. The two should be done together, in Quintilian's view. To help the child learn to write, he recommends cutting the letters into a board and having the child trace the forms. From the letters the child moves on to syllables, which he learns to pronounce and to memorize, then on to entire words. Quintilian did not see any point in having students practice on words familiar to them. They should learn less common words, in order to improve their vocabularies. When words are put together in sentences, the thought should convey a moral. Students at this age should start to memorize poetry, since memory will be important for the adult orator.

The second chapter of the book is devoted to the question of whether the child is better off being educated by a private tutor or going to a school. Quintilian discusses the arguments for each but strongly favors a school with a good teacher. The future orator must be accustomed to moving in society, and the rivalries of a school are an incentive to learning. The students will learn there not only from the teacher but also from each other.

The desire to make education pleasurable should not be restricted to its earliest stages but be carried on in the school. There should be play periods, and games should be used for their educational value. In ancient schools fear of physical punishment was a strong deterrent. Quintilian, almost alone among ancient writers, disapproves of it: "It is disgraceful and servile and insulting" (1.3.14). If a child is insensitive to criticism, he will also become hardened to blows, and a teacher should have no need to whip students if he is a good disciplinarian.

The first three chapters deal with the child's primary education. The fourth chapter goes on to the grammar school, where he learns to read and write and studies and learns to interpret the poets and other classical writers. In the long fifth chapter Quintilian goes into considerable detail about Latin morphology and syntax, which the child must learn. The sixth chapter discusses the bases of language, which Quintilian describes as reason, antiquity, authority, and usage. Much of this material is addressed to the teacher, and would not necessarily be taught to students at this stage. In class the teacher is to take lines of verse, perhaps from the Aeneid, one by one; read them out loud; identify all the parts of speech, the grammatical forms, and the figures and ornaments of style; and explain the meaning of the passage, including its mythological or historical references. But he should not become bogged down in pedantic details: "In my opinion, it will be a virtue in a grammarian not to know everything" (1.8.21).

Chapter nine deals with exercises in composition. In the most elementary of these, the student is given a fable by Aesop and asked to paraphrase it closely; subsequently he is allowed to tell it in his own words, with his own embellishment. Another form of exercise, called *chria,* was based on the sayings or actions of a famous person. The student was expected to restate the *chria* in different grammatical forms—for example, employing the name of the person in each of the six cases of the Latin noun—and to give an explanation or draw a moral from the story. The Greeks and Romans eventually established a sequence of fourteen such exercises, including narratives, characterizations, comparisons of two people, encomiums, invective, and descriptions of a place. Since most later writers were trained in these exercises, they tended to think of composition in these forms; and it is possible to analyze Greek and Latin literature, or at least its more ornamental passages, according to the forms taught in such exercises. Ovid's *Metamorphoses,* for example, is made up of fables, narratives, characterizations, and descriptions. These forms of composition were also practiced in schools in the Middle Ages and Renaissance, and were part of the education of writers like William Shakespeare and John Milton, so that they continued to influence English literature until the eighteenth century.

In the three concluding chapters of book 1, Quintilian considers other subjects that should be studied in addition to grammar, reading, and composition. The grammar school will not take up the student's entire day, and he can go to other teachers to learn something about music, geometry, and acting, which will be useful to him in learning how to deliver a speech. Quintilian does not object to training in gymnastics to achieve grace of movement and poise, but the many hours spent by Greeks in the gymnasium were not approved of in Rome.

The first ten chapters of book 2 are Quintilian's proposal for teaching in the rhetorical school. He thinks that parents send their sons to the rhetorician too late and proposes that students start studying rhetoric while still in grammar school, as was the custom in Greece. The

qualities he would like to see in a teacher of rhetoric are described at some length:

> Let him adopt the attitude of a parent toward his student. . . . He himself should neither have vices nor tolerate them. His strictness should not be oppressive, his friendliness not unrestrained. . . . He should answer questions willingly and should himself ask questions of those who do not question him. In praising the speeches of students he should be neither stingy nor effusive. . . . In correcting faults he should not be sarcastic and certainly not quarrelsome. . . .
>
> (2.2.5–7)

Quintilian did not wish exercises in the rhetorical school to be limited to the two common forms of declamation, and recommends that students be required to continue the writing of compositions, as they had with the grammarian, but in a form adaptable to parts of the orations that they would eventually be expected to compose. The exercises he mentions are the writing of narratives, practice in arguing for or against a point, praise of famous men and denunciation of wickedness, elaboration of theses, especially those of a comparative sort (such as "Which is more pleasant, town or country life?"), and arguments for or against proposed laws. Furthermore, the teacher should read the works of historians and orators with the students, subjecting the text to a careful rhetorical analysis. All of this is addressed to the teacher, but one short chapter (2.9) gives advice to the students: they should love their teacher, come cheerfully to school, take criticism well, and show devotion to their studies: "For as it is the duty of teachers to teach, so it is the duty of students to make themselves teachable." Finally the student is ready for declamation, which Quintilian feels has degenerated: the subjects should be closer to real life than those commonly practiced. They should be more specific in the use of real names, should be longer, should use ordinary language, and should show some sense of humor. To judge from Seneca the Elder and other writers, declaimers took themselves very seriously, and cultivated pomposity and affectation.

At this point Quintilian is ready to begin his account of the theory of rhetoric, which the teacher will expound to his students. As an introduction to it, he devotes three chapters to a general consideration of why such instruction is necessary and what it should be like. The untrained speaker seems sometimes to have a natural vigor, but lacks restraint and does not know when to stop. He may be admired for his force, but can lose his case. The system of rhetoric that Quintilian will teach is a matter not of learning absolute rules, but of learning to adapt to the circumstances of the case and the time and place of speaking.

The second part of book 2 (chapters 14–21) deals with the definition of rhetoric. This subject was important not much so for the teaching of rhetoric as for its place in an overall system of human knowledge. Philosophers and rhetoricians of antiquity, the Middle Ages, and the Renaissance regularly attempted to determine it with some precision. In the fifth century B.C. it had been assumed that rhetoric was an art of persuasion useful in the law courts and political assemblies; but Plato in the *Gorgias* raised difficult logical and moral questions about the nature of rhetoric, and later definitions varied considerably. As he had promised he would in the preface, Quintilian reviews many of these definitions and indicates which he prefers. The questions are whether rhetoric is a form of knowledge, like politics; an art, like painting and poetry; a logical faculty, as Aristotle had regarded it, applicable to a variety of subjects; a virtue, or personal excellence, as the Stoics taught; or a skill acquired chiefly by practice. To what extent was it useful? Could it be used only for good ends? Was it morally neutral, or was it essentially a form of flattery? Was it restricted to the use of words, or did it involve other factors, such as the authority of a speaker, the use of bribery or threats, and visual images or gestures? What was its subject matter? Anything at all? Or was it limited to the subjects discussed in law courts and political assemblies? Was its objective persuasion, or did it seek to change, instruct, and inform?

Quintilian's preferred definition is that rhetoric is the knowledge of speaking well (2.15.34). He uses the standard Latin word for knowledge, *scientia*, which is the source of the English word "science"; but he does not mean, as he has explained in a previous chapter, that it has absolute rules in which a given action produces a necessary effect. He means that it is systematic, and can be studied and understood. Calling it a science emphasizes logical and intellectual qualities of the theory in contrast with the art of its execution. Quintilian limits the subject of rhetoric to speaking, but not necessarily to speaking on legal or political matters. The most important word in his definition is "well," (*bene* in Latin). This is the adverb related to the adjective *bonus* (good), and is intended to have a strong moral, as well as some aesthetic, force: the orator should be eloquent; but above all he must be a good man (*bonus orator*), and the objective of his speech must be a morally justifiable one. An unscrupulous politician or shyster lawyer is not, in Quintilian's view, practicing rhetoric. Rhetoric is not only a science; it is also an art (2.17), primarily of the practical sort, though it has elements of the theoretical and productive, and it is a virtue (2.20), for it is a quality of a good man. Its material is everything that comes to the orator for treatment; but Quintilian conceives these materials as falling into the classes of judicial, deliberative, and epideictic discourse (2.21). Thus, in practice he limits rhetoric to public address in the form of a continuous speech.

Book 3 launches into the technicalities of rhetoric. Quintilian is apologetic, both for the dryness of the topics he must discuss and for his general lack of originality here (3.1.5). After a survey of earlier writing on rhetoric and a brief chapter on why rhetoric originated (3.2) —he derives it from human ability to speak rather than from specific historical needs in society—he divides the discipline into the traditional five parts of invention, arrangement, style, memory, and delivery (3.3.1); but, as he has promised to do, he considers divergent opinions that make a smaller or larger number of classifications. Similarly, with the species of oratory he accepts the view, standard since Aristotle, that there are three kinds: deliberative, judicial, and epideictic, but he notes other classifications as well (3.4).

Chapter 5 begins with a series of traditional views: that a speech consists of subject and words; that skill in speaking is a natural endowment, art, and practice; and that the three aims of the orator are to teach, to move, and to charm. Quintilian then moves into the more complicated matter of the classification of the questions on which an orator speaks: some involve a point that is written in the law; some, a point not written but a question of fact. Some questions are definite, involving specific persons, places, and actions; others are indefinite or general, involving a philosophical issue. The orator needs a knowledge of the latter: for example, he cannot deliberate whether Cato should marry unless the issue of whether marriage is desirable has been agreed to first.

The most technical part is the sixth chapter, which is Quintilian's preliminary discussion of "stasis" theory. It is appropriate here, since the function of stasis (status) is to enable a speaker to define the basic issue of the question before planning his argumentation and detailed treatment.

For example, if a defendant accused of murder denies killing the victim, the stasis is one of fact. The defendant may then offer evidence showing that he was elsewhere at the time, or that it is improbable that he could have overpowered the victim, or that he had no motive to kill him. But possibly the evidence that the defendant actually killed the victim is strong; perhaps the attack was witnessed. In this case the defense need not despair if it can fall back on stasis of definition and allege that the action does not fit the legal definition of murder but is a lesser degree of homicide. The act may, for example, have been done in self-defense, as Cicero claimed for Milo in the death of Clodius. If definition will not work either, a third possi-

ble stasis is quality, in which the defendant admits the illegal action but puts criminal responsibility on another person who forced him to do it, or argues that there was great provocation or some mitigating circumstance. There were many different forms of classification of stasis and many subdivisions of the three main headings of fact, definition, and quality.

Quintilian's chapter includes a lengthy historical survey of the classifications that had been suggested by earlier writers, a brief account of the system that Quintilian had taught in his school, and a revised account of his present views. Quintilian is not really at his best in this kind of abstruse theoretical discussion, but the chapter well illustrates the sharp differences between rhetoricians on matters of definition and division, and Quintilian's own desire to find a system that students can understand and apply.

Stasis theory applies chiefly to defining the issues that came before a court of law, but most rhetoricians applied it also to deliberative cases, and some to epideictic as well. Quintilian therefore inserts here chapters on epideictic and deliberative oratory, which are of considerable interest for ancient oratory. By epideictic (3.7) he understands the oratory of praise or blame, which he says had a more practical use in Rome than it had had in Greece. This is primarily because of the Roman custom of funeral eulogies. In the classical period the Greeks, by contrast, had not eulogized individuals. The Roman custom reflects the greater sense of individualism at Rome, as well as the public role of noble families over many generations. In addition, Quintilian says that witnesses were praised or blamed in speeches in Roman courts; there was some campaign oratory for public office; and personal attacks were tolerated in the Senate —none of which was true of Greece. But he does not note the fact, evident to a modern historian, that epideictic grew in importance under the empire, particularly in the case of panegyrics of the reigning emperors, reflecting the growth of flattery in an absolute state and the attempts by orators to gain influence from the emperors for themselves and, sometimes, to hold up ideal models to an emperor in hopes of influencing his future conduct. In later centuries panegyric oratory was encouraged by the court as a way of expressing national solidarity and loyalty to the rulers.

Quintilian suggests that one should begin with events before the subject's birth, celebrate his country, his parents, and his ancestors, and refer to any omens or prophecies of his coming birth and greatness (3.7.10). This should be followed by praise of the individual himself, including his character, his physical endowments, and his employment of the gifts of fortune, such as wealth, power, and influence. Both his words and his deeds should be included. Or sometimes it is more effective to deal topically with separate virtues, such as courage, justice, and temperance. If the person being praised is dead, it is then possible to conclude with posthumous honors accorded him. These topics of panegyric, developed in oratory, were subsequently applied to the writing of biography, including some of the more elaborate lives of Christian saints. Men and women are not the only possible subjects of praise; Quintilian mentions celebrations of the gods; cities and countries; buildings; noble sayings or deeds; and things like sleep, death, or the value of certain foods.

In contrast with panegyric, deliberative oratory declined significantly under the empire. Quintilian's discussion of it (3.8) is two and a half times as long as what he has to say about panegyric, and initially seems an anachronism. But an attentive reader soon discovers that what he is talking about here is not true deliberative oratory in the Roman assemblies, which no longer met, or in the Senate, in which the emperors allowed only limited opportunities for deliberation; rather, it is about suasoriae, the exercises in deliberative form that were still extensively practiced in the rhetorical schools. Moral as always, Quintilian would like the basis of deliberation to be what is honorable rather than political expediency, as it tends to be in true political debate. He says that what

carries greatest weight in deliberation is the authority of the speaker (3.8.12). This is a point not found in Greek rhetoricians, and reflects Roman attitudes and the example of Cicero, who made good rhetorical use of his authority as consul. As we have said, one of the forms of suasoria was the prosopopoeia, in which a speaker tries to impersonate a character from mythology or history, or a type of character appearing in exercises of declamation: sons or parents, rich men or poor men, the gentle or the harsh, the cowardly or the brave, and so on; these are considered in the second half of the chapter. At the end the practical opportunities for deliberative speech are given a passing glance. Students will learn from practice what they may not learn from the schools if they are called "to the councils of their friends, or to speak in the Senate, or to advise the emperor if he should consult them." Deliberation, of course, did not cease to exist in the empire; it went backstage and took place among the emperor's advisers or the heads of the bureaucracy or the army.

The remainder of book 3 returns to judicial oratory, which was the major emphasis in all rhetorical teaching, and outlines the parts of a judicial oration (3.9); the difference between simple, complex, and comparative questions (3.10); and the steps by which the stasis of the case can be determined (3.11). Quintilian gives a full account of the latter but says that it is unnecessary for a teacher to destroy the coherence of his teaching by attention to such minute detail (3.11.21). All the material in book 3 is regarded as part of the topic of invention, but in fact it reflects an advanced stage of invention in which the speaker plans his general approach to the material. Once this is done, he works out the various parts in the order in which they will actually be presented (3.9.8).

The account of these parts is the subject of books 4, 5, and 6. Quintilian recognizes five basic parts: exordium (4.1), narration (4.2), proof (all of 5), refutation (4.5 and 4.13), and peroration (6.1); but he discusses other possible parts recognized by some authorities, including digression (4.3), proposition (4.4), and partition (4.5). In each case he reviews the opinions of other rhetoricians, as he had promised to do in his preface; gives his own judgment; and indicates the special qualities, the parts, and the topic of the particular part of the speech. Much of the theory covered is traditional and is to be found in Cicero, Quintilian's favorite authority, and other rhetoricians; but he occasionally adds something of his own—for example, when discussing the treatment of character in the exordium, he points out that not only the plaintiff, defendant, and judges, as had been the case in Greek courts, but also the patrons or advocates on both sides should be considered. Here he adjusts traditional Greek theory to the conditions of Roman courts. As always, he is not only a theorist about rhetoric but also a teacher of it with his students' needs in mind. Thus, having expounded the theory of the exordium at some length, he adds practical advice for composing one (4.1.52–71). All of the discussions are thoroughly illustrated with examples from Greek and Latin orators, or from historians and other kinds of writers, and occasionally from his own experience (for instance, 4.1.19).

The most technical discussion in these books involves the construction of proofs, to which book 5 is devoted. Quintilian follows the lead of Aristotle in distinguishing between artistic and inartistic proof. The latter is the evidence that the orator uses but does not invent by his art; it includes legal precedents, documentary evidence, and the testimony of witnesses. The seventh chapter is an interesting discussion of how witnesses should be presented and examined in court. Artistic proof consists of the logical arguments actually constructed by the speaker to prove his case or refute his opponent. In formal logic, science, or philosophy, as contrasted with oratory, argument takes the form of the syllogism, a concept developed by Aristotle. An example of a syllogism cited by Quintilian is: "Whatever can be put to a bad use is not good. Money can be put to a bad use. Therefore, money is not good" (5.14.25). Even if he were to have occasion to use this argument,

an orator would probably not say it in this form. Instead, he would say something like, "Can money be a good thing when it is possible to put it to a bad use?" This form of syllogism, in which one step in the argument is omitted, is called an enthymeme. As an example of an enthymeme in a judicial context, Quintilian cites Cicero's words in defense of Milo's attack on Clodius: "Are you sitting there as avengers of the death of a man whose life you would not restore if you could?" (5.14.2). When an orator does have to use full syllogistic form, it is usually because the premises involved are not credible without some supporting reason. An argument in a speech in which various statements are made and supported by reasons, and then a conclusion is drawn, is called an epicheirema.

In contrast with book 5, book 6 is considerably less technical and contains much of general interest about Roman life and literature. The subject is the peroration, or conclusion, of a speech. One of the functions of the peroration is to arouse the emotions of the judges; Quintilian discusses in chapter 2 the bases of emotion in character and in chapter 3 the use of laughter, wit, and humor, which can be effective weapons in court. He advances a theory of humor, based on that found in Cicero's *On the Orator* and traceable back to Aristotle, and cites a number of incidents or remarks that the Romans found highly amusing. Some may appear funny to modern readers, some not. Book 6 also includes a discussion of debate in law courts, something we see little of in preserved speeches, and a brief concluding chapter on good judgment, which he feels some may criticize him for omitting in a discussion of invention.

Quintilian's discussion of invention, the first of the five parts of rhetoric, is now complete. The second part, arrangement, is disposed of much more briefly in book 7. By arrangement Quintilian does not mean the structural parts of the oration—exordium, narration, and the like, which tend to follow a more or less fixed order already discussed. He means the effective arrangement of the argument: what point to start with and what sequence to follow. This he treats in terms of stasis theory, as outlined in book 3, taking up each of the headings of stasis in turn and showing how it may be handled. The basic principle that he follows—indeed the basic principle in all of Quintilian's treatment of education and rhetoric—is to seek a natural order of development rather than to adopt rigid rules or to pursue a complex artificiality that may obscure the inherent strength of what the speaker has to say.

Books 8, 9, 10, and the first chapter of 11 are devoted to the third part of rhetoric, style or expression. The fundamental framework of the discussion is the concept of the virtues of style, originally developed by Aristotle's student Theophrastus and found also in Cicero's works on rhetoric. This framework is described in the first chapter of book 8, where we are told that style (Latin, *elocutio*) is a matter of the choice of single words (diction) or words joined together (composition). Single words must be good Latin, clear, elegant, and suitable—in other words, they must have the "virtues" of correctness, clarity, ornamentation, and propriety. In composition they must be in accordance with grammatical rules, well placed, and well figured. Book 8 then discusses diction; book 9, composition. Correctness (8.17) is largely passed over as a matter of grammar, though it is here that Quintilian quotes the famous statement of Asinius Pollio that Livy's language showed traces of the dialect of his native Padua. Chapter 2 is devoted to clarity and its opposite, the fault of obscurity.

Most of book 8 is devoted to forms of ornamentation found in single words, of which the most important are the tropes described in chapter 6. A trope is defined as the artistic alteration of a word from its "proper" meaning to another. Of such alterations by far the most common is metaphor (8.6.4–18), but other tropes are discussed: synecdoche, metonymy, antonomasia, onomatopoeia, catachresis, metalepsis, epithet, allegory, irony, periphrasis, hyperbaton, and hyperbole. Each is illustrated with ex-

amples, chiefly from Vergil. Book 9 deals with forms of ornamentation to be found in composition: figures of thought (9.2), figures of speech (9.3), and periodic sentences and rhythm (9.4). More than one hundred figures are identified, named, and classified, but as usual Quintilian avoids rigidity. He stresses the practical utility of figures in making arguments believable, in appealing to judges, and in avoiding monotony. The discussion of prose rhythm is a good introduction to a complex subject, both theory and practice, that deserves to be studied by every careful student of Latin. It again illustrates Quintilian's preference for natural language and the avoidance of arbitrary artificiality.

The fourth "virtue" of style, appropriateness, is not discussed until the first chapter of book 11. In between is inserted the most famous and most read part of Quintilian's work, book 10, devoted to the ways by which an orator can gain facility. These include careful study of Greek and Latin writers, from which he can derive a *copia*, or abundance of words and thoughts (10.1); imitation of classical modes (10.2); writing, correction, exercises in written or oral composition, premeditation, and extempore speaking (9.3–7). The chapter on *copia*, which influenced Erasmus and other writers of the Renaissance, contains a discussion of literary genres and a survey of both Greek and Latin literature from the point of view of what a young orator can learn from study of the major writers in each genre. The chapter is not profound literary criticism and is not intended to be, but is of great value in coming to understand how the Romans viewed literature from the perspective of their rhetorical education and how they thought Latin literature compared with Greek. Quintilian sums up the major qualities of the Latin writers in particular in pithy statements that have echoed in classrooms ever since and are still found in surveys of Latin literature.

The chapter falls into three parts. The first contains a general discussion of what an orator can gain from the study of literature (10.1.1–45). Actual oratory will, of course, be the major study; but poets can contribute inspiration in subject matter, sublimity in language, pathos, and an understanding of characterization (10.1.27). Quintilian, like Cicero, thinks of poetry primarily as a form of recreation, and says that it aims "only at pleasure" (10.1.28). As a result it has a freedom of language and in the use of figures that goes beyond anything an orator should imitate. History falls somewhere between poetry and prose: it is written for narrative and not for proof, records events for posterity, and seeks to win glory for its author. The "milky richness" of Livy will not satisfy a reader who is looking for credibility (10.1.32), but the orator can borrow from the historians to embellish his digressions. Philosophers need to be read largely because the orators have abandoned to them subjects they ought to have treated. Quintilian thus regards literature as having four major divisions: poetry, and three forms of prose—history, oratory, and philosophy (chiefly the philosophical dialogue).

In the second part of the chapter (10.1.46–84) Quintilian surveys Greek literature in terms of these four divisions. Poetry is treated in the sequence epic, elegy, iambic, lyric, Old Comedy, tragedy, and New Comedy, followed by the prose forms of history, oratory, and philosophy. In most genres Quintilian appears to be familiar with canons, or approved lists of classical models, which he attributes to the Alexandrian grammarians Aristarchus of Samothrace and Aristophanes of Byzantium (10.1.54; 59). There are, for example, three classical models of iambic poetry and nine of lyric. Quintilian is also familiar with the canon of ten Attic orators (10.1.76), but he does not specifically attribute that to the same source, and it may be a later development. In the discussion one can see that a classicism movement was well developed. No Greek author later than the third century B.C. is recommended.

Quintilian's familiarity with Greek literature does not seem to be very great; he has largely taken over the lists and the judgments of Greek critics. But in the third section (10.1.85–131), on

Latin literature, he may have composed his own list, following the same generic order; he certainly expresses his personal views, and he extends his survey down to his own time, though he names no living author except for a flattering reference to the youthful efforts at epic of the emperor Domitian (10.1.91–92). Vergil is given pride of place among the poets, excelling all Greek or Roman poets except Homer; among prose writers Cicero is first, equaling Demosthenes. Among the most famous judgments are the following: "We worship Ennius like a grove, sacred for its antiquity, in which great ancient trunks do not so much have beauty as give a sense of religious awe" (10.1.88); "We lost much recently in the death of Valerius Flaccus" (10.1.90); "Lucan is fiery and violent and epigrammatic, but to say what I feel, more to be imitated by orators than by poets" (10.1.90); Tibullus is "terse and elegant," but "there are those who prefer Propertius" (10.1.93); Varro is "the most learned of the Romans" (10.1.95); Horace is "most happily bold in his choice of words" (10.1.96).

Quintilian thinks the Roman historians are as good as the Greek, and especially admires "the immortal rapidity of Sallust" (10.1.102); in contrast, "in comedy we most limp" in comparison with the Greeks (10.1.99). He is optimistic about the future of Latin literature, praising (without naming) several writers still alive. The one inimical force in Latin literature that he recognizes is Seneca, for whom he reserves a special place at the end of the discussion (10.1.125–131), explaining that his hostility is not so much against Seneca's own works as against Seneca's influence and the misguided attempts of younger writers to imitate him. His vices are attractive, and he should be read by those with mature judgment. Anthony Trollope in his autobiography surveys Victorian novelists in a similar mood: Dickens was a great writer, but his influence has destroyed many who have sought to imitate him.

Imitation is, of course, the objective of critical reading as outlined by Quintilian, and he devotes the second chapter of book 10 to an explanation of his understanding of it. He shows here the influence of the discussion of the subject by Dionysius of Halicarnassus. The student is to assess his own powers and not to imitate qualities that are beyond him. Cicero is the greatest model, and it is almost enough to imitate only him (10.2.25); but sometimes a young orator can improve his style by taking another writer whose qualities are the ones he most needs to develop: he might, for example, learn vigor from Caesar. The remaining chapters of the book deal with exercises in composition and speech that will perfect the orator's facility.

Book 11 first completes the subject of style by considering its fourth virtue, appropriateness, though actually much of what Quintilian has to say relates as much to subject matter and invention as to style. A speech should, he thinks, be appropriate to the case, the audience, the speaker and his client, and the situation. Some special problems are considered, such as addressing a hostile judge, where flattery may be used to appeal to the judge's sense of honor in giving a just decision even at the expense of his personal antagonism.

Memory was the fourth part of rhetoric; it is best discussed in the third book of the *Rhetorica ad Herennium,* written in the early first century B.C., which outlines a system of visual backgrounds against which images of words or thoughts are imposed on the speaker's mind. When giving the speech, he can then recall the images and their sequence. Quintilian knows this system and describes it briefly in the second chapter of book 11, but he thinks it is easier to divide a speech into separate parts, each to be memorized, and to use mnemonic devices chiefly for remembering names. The real secret of developing the memory, he says, is practice.

In contrast with the brief treatment of memory, the account of delivery (11.3) is extensive, the best in any ancient writer, and a vivid introduction to what it was like to hear a skilled Roman orator. The subject was traditionally divided into voice and gesture; and it is in description of the appropriate gestures of head and arm, the use of the eyes, the stance, and the arrangement of the toga that Quintilian gives the greatest detail.

At the beginning of his discussion of rhetorical theory (2.14.5), Quintilian had said that he would speak of art, of the artist, and of the work of art. The division was a common one in Hellenistic critical treatises. As it turns out, art is given by far the most extensive treatment in the *Institutio,* extending from book 2 to the end of book 11. Most of book 12 discusses the artist— that is, the professional life of the adult orator— but chapter 10 is devoted to the work of art.

Quintilian's picture of the adult orator in book 12 is idealized: he describes his vision of what he calls the good, perfect, or consummate orator, who will be a statesman, an adviser of the great, a defender of the poor and weak, and an inspiration to all. Historically Cicero came closest to fulfilling this ideal; but Cicero lived in the Roman Republic, nominally a free state with freedom of speech and political opportunities for those of ability. Quintilian wrote the *Institutio* under the empire and in the later years of the reign of Domitian, which was in many ways a tyranny. Yet he insists that his ideal remains feasible and, indeed, presents contemporary society as one open to merit. The ideal orator is a goal at which all teachers and all speakers should aim, and he is optimistic that someday a greater than Cicero will come. His views are a valuable counterbalance to the pessimism of Tacitus and Juvenal.

This ideal orator needs various "instruments," and chapters 2 through 4 describe them: knowledge of moral and ethical philosophy, avoiding the inane subtleties of that discipline as Quintilian saw it taught in his time; knowledge of law, which he regards as not difficult to acquire; knowledge of history, from which the orator will draw examples and precedents. Then the orator's career is briefly surveyed: he should develop his natural talents (12.5); he should begin to speak in the law courts when he is still reasonably young, perhaps in his twenties (12.6); he must be careful in the choice of his cases (12.7) and must study them thoroughly (12.8); he must not aim at applause, and though he should write out his speeches in advance, he should be ready to speak extempore if the occasion demands (12.9); he should retire from active practice while he will still be missed and devote himself to other study (12.11).

The chapter on the work of art (12.10) contains an extended analogy between oratory and the arts of painting and sculpture, which have also undergone historical development and have a variety of styles. The passage is of some importance for our knowledge of art criticism in antiquity. It then proceeds to consider the history of prose style in Greece, which was regarded as moving from a chaste and effective Atticism in the classical period to a bombastic and empty Asianism in the Hellenistic period. These concepts had been applied to Latin in the mid-first century B.C., often in a rigid way that limited Atticism to the plain style of a writer like Lysias. Cicero had protested against this view in *Brutus* and *Orator*, insisting that there was a great variety of Atticism and that Demosthenes (and by implication Cicero himself) was as Attic as Lysias. Quintilian agrees, and goes on to discuss the harshness of Latin and the limitations of its vocabulary as he perceives it. Under these circumstances it is absurd to impose rules that will further render Latin expression austere. He also touches on the theory of the three kinds of style—plain, middle, and grand—though he thinks that in fact there are many gradations. The great orator should use all styles as they are appropriate to his subject. This view was in fact gaining ground, especially among Greek rhetoricians, and reaches its fullest expression in Hermogenes of Tarsus' *On Ideas of Style* about a hundred years later. Yet the theory of three styles remained strong in Rome and was the basis of the discussion of Christian eloquence in book 4 of St. Augustine's *De doctrina Christiana (On Christian Doctrine)*.

Most critics have felt that book 12 shows signs of hasty composition, and have pointed to the remark in the introductory epistle that Quintilian was being pushed by his publisher. Yet the book rounds out the work; it contains a number of eloquent passages; and it fulfills Quintilian's promise to treat the subject with a fullness and breadth rarely found elsewhere. Although largely ignored by later Roman writers, who concentrate on abstracting the more technical parts of the treatise, book 12 contributed to the ideal of the union of wisdom and eloquence that was a major theme of humanists of the Italian Renaissance, such as Lorenzo Valla.

Quintilian has often been praised for the eloquence with which he writes about eloquence; but the greatness of his work is not as a piece of literature, nor in the originality of its thought, though the contents are often of great use to scholars because of the fullness of the account and because many of the sources to which Quintilian refers have been lost. His greatest qualities are personal ones: dedication to good teaching; kindly affection toward the young and all who do their best; a faith in Roman culture and an optimism about its future; a preference for a natural order and a natural style as the soundest principles for excellence in writing and speech; clarity, discipline, and patience; good judgment; reasonableness. He is a fine example of Tacitus' dictum that there can be good men even under bad emperors.

Selected Bibliography

TEXT

M. Fabi Quintiliani Institutionis oratoriae libri duodecim. Scriptorum Classicorum Bibliotheca Oxoniensis, edited by Michael Winterbottom. 2 vols. Oxford, 1970. Latin text.

TRANSLATIONS

Butler, H. E., trans. *The Institutio oratoria of Quintilian*. 4 vols. Cambridge, Mass., and London, 1920–1922. Loeb Classical Library. Latin text with English translation.

QUINTILIAN

Cousin, Jean, trans. *Quintilien, Institution oratoire.* 7 vols. Paris, 1975–1980. Latin text and French translation, with extensive introductory material and valuable notes.

COMMENTARIES

Austin, R. G., ed. *Quintiliani Institutionis oratoriae Liber XII.* Oxford, 1948.

Colson, F. H., ed. *M. Fabii Quintiliani Institutionis oratoriae Liber I.* Cambridge, 1924.

Peterson, W., ed. *M. Fabii Quintiliani Institutionis oratoriae Liber X.* Oxford, 1891. 2nd ed., 1939. Latin text with English commentary.

GENERAL AND CRITICAL STUDIES

Cousin, Jean. *Études sur Quintilien.* 2 vols. Paris, 1936.

Kennedy, George. *Quintilian.* New York, 1969. Twayne World Authors series.

GEORGE KENNEDY

PLUTARCH

(ca. A.D. 40–ca. 120)

BACKGROUND AND LIFE

IT IS REMARKABLE that of an author so familiar as Plutarch . . . no accurate memoir of his life, not even the dates of his birth and death, should have come down to us. Strange that the writer of so many illustrious biographics should wait so long for his own." So wrote Ralph Waldo Emerson in 1874, and despite the research and discoveries of another century his remark is still true. Plutarch was born about A.D. 40 in the small town of Chaeronea, in the region of central Greece known as Boeotia. As is usual with ancient authors, practically nothing is known about his family and childhood, so that the early experiences that are often crucial for creative development are lost to sight. Chaeronea had a historic past, having been the site of the great battle at which Philip of Macedon decisively crushed the Greek resistance in 338 B.C.; it also saw a less famous but also decisive battle 250 years later, when the Roman general Sulla defeated the forces of the self-proclaimed liberator of Greece, the Pontic king Mithridates. With the history of his city so closely linked to the loss of Greek liberty and the consolidation of Roman power over Greece, Plutarch's background must have contributed to a noticeable feature of his thought, the tendency to see Greeks and Romans as two peoples equally balanced in the scales of history.

By the time of his birth well over a century had passed since Sulla's battle. Rome was now ruled as a republic not by a senatorial oligarchy, but by the disguised monarchy of the emperors, or "Caesars." The struggles that buried the republic and gave birth to the rule of the Caesars had been cruel to Greek pride and prosperity, but when Plutarch was born his country, now a province of the Roman empire, was beginning to revive. Boeotia is one of the most fertile regions of Greece, and landholding was probably the economic basis for his comparatively wealthy family. This comfortable material background influenced him in several ways. The many dialogues into which he introduces his family and friends suggest a well-informed, well-traveled society, in which dinner talk might readily involve rarely read historians, abstruse questions of philosophy, or the social habits of the Romans and other distant peoples. Plutarch's wide interests certainly owe much to this favorable atmosphere. At the same time, because wealth and politics were closely associated in his as in most societies, his birth put him in a social class that considered city politics its natural preserve. One of the few things Plutarch mentions about his father is some political advice he received from him, and his political interests are reflected not only in certain of his shorter essays but by the interest he shows in the statesmanship of the heroes of his best-known work, the *Parallel Lives*.

Plutarch no doubt received his early education in his own city. The groundwork would have been in literature, with other subjects added in adolescence. One subject, rhetoric, was thought indispensable for every well-educated man, especially one who expected to follow his ancestors' role in local politics. In his mature works Plutarch is ironic at the expense of rhetoric, but it had a marked influence on some of his early writings and never completely let him go.

Chaeronea was the matrix of Plutarch's early education and development, but three other cities were to mean as much to him in mature life. The first was Athens. This was still the spiritual capital of Hellenism, and retained something of its old intellectual ferment; it was in Plutarch's lifetime that the apostle Paul visited it and found the streets full of people "seeing or hearing something new." The young Plutarch moved to Athens to complete his education and met there the only person whom he names as a teacher, a philosopher called Ammonius, of whom scarcely anything is known outside the pages of his pupil. He belonged to the Academy, the philosophic school derived from Plato, and it must be from Ammonius that Plutarch learned the devotion to Plato that marks so many of his works, including the *Parallel Lives*. Ammonius was also active in the politics of Athens, and held for three terms the high office of "hoplite general," responsible for the city's grain supply and the general peace. This combination of the active and the academic life is another example that he set for his brilliant pupil. Plutarch made many friends in Athens, some of them Ammonius' students and of high social status, and in due course he was made an honorary citizen there. He maintained his contacts with the city for the rest of his life, and even though he mainly lived and worked elsewhere, managing without the scholarly facilities of large cities like Athens, still it remained for him a hearth to which he could always go for intellectual and artistic fire.

The religious center of Plutarch's life was in another city, or more precisely in the sanctuary around which the city had developed: Delphi.

Like Greece itself, the great oracle of Apollo had declined in importance but still enjoyed an unrivaled prestige. Even under ancient conditions of transport, it was comparatively near to both Chaeronea and Athens, and in his last period Plutarch became one of the two priests of Apollo there and made Delphi his second home. Apollo was the philosopher god par excellence, and for a Platonist he was the god who had declared at Delphi that Socrates was the wisest of men. Here Plutarch discussed philosophy with students and eminent visitors, and he made Delphi the scene and subject of some of his best dialogues. His religious conviction was as prominent a characteristic of him as his commitment to politics and was translated into his priesthood at Delphi just as his political interests were expressed in his role as magistrate and diplomat.

Plutarch lived in a world dominated by Rome, or rather by the imperial system of which the emperors based there were the head. Rome was the seat of the Caesars and the center of government, and though it had long since made contact with the Greek world and adapted to Greek culture, it was still alien in language, customs, and history. The political advice mentioned above, given to Plutarch by his father, concerned an embassy on which he had gone to the Roman proconsul of Greece, probably on behalf of Chaeronea. The other ambassador fell ill, and though Plutarch successfully completed the mission alone, his father advised him to claim only half the credit. With his keen observation of human nature, his wide interests, his charm and persuasiveness, Plutarch must have made an excellent diplomat. Inevitably these talents brought him more and more into contact with Roman power. At first employed on local missions to provincial proconsuls, he seems later to have gone several times to Italy, probably to represent the whole province. Here he visited famous monuments and made influential friends. One of these, Mestrius Florus, took him on a tour that included Milan and the Po Valley and also obtained Roman citizenship for him, so that in gratitude he took the names "Lucius Mestrius Plutarchus."

Plutarch's last years, from about A.D. 100 to 120, coincided with a period that is traditionally regarded as the zenith of Roman stability and power. The beginning of this period, the reigns of Nerva, Trajan, and Hadrian, also saw the last great flowering of classical literature, with Tacitus, Juvenal, and Suetonius among its chief exponents. Trajan and Hadrian appear to have given public recognition to Plutarch, and this was the period in which he wrote most of his works, including the *Parallel Lives*, in which Greeks and Romans enter an immortal partnership. The assurance and abundance of his major writings is in part a reflection of the circumstances under which they were written.

THE NONBIOGRAPHICAL WORKS

Boswell called Plutarch "the prince of ancient biographers." The *Parallel Lives* were thought his finest work in antiquity, and he is still known best for them. "Philosopher," however, is what he would have called himself and what he was always called by others, and to neglect this side of him is to miss much of the point of the biographies. In some ways he anticipates not so much the objective biography of the eighteenth and nineteenth centuries as the psychological biography of the twentieth.

Even by ancient standards Plutarch was enormously prolific. He is known to have written about 250 works in 300 volumes, though the ancient volume is roughly the length of the modern chapter. About two-thirds of his production is lost. What survives is traditionally and conveniently divided into two groups. The larger group, which will be treated first here, consists of the so-called *Moralia* ("moral writings"), which take their name from the fact that the unknown editor who arranged the collection in its surviving form placed the educational and moral essays first. Works placed later are on widely divergent topics, such as "The

Generation of the Psyche in Plato's *Timaeus*" and "Whether Land or Sea Animals Are More Intelligent." Though the *Moralia* in total length now surpass the *Parallel Lives* by a proportion of about four to three, there is evidence that originally the proportion was more like three to one; in other words, time has been much kinder to the *Lives*, an index of their greater popularity. Moreover, from a surviving though incomplete catalog of Plutarch's output, it is known that the more ambitious of his nonbiographical works are lost. These were mainly philosophical ones, such as the influential treatise in four books "On the Psyche." Had his full production survived, it would be clearer than it is why antiquity regarded him primarily as a philosopher. As often happens, Plutarch's most popular and enduring works were ones that he may have written almost as a relaxation.

It would be impossible to summarize all the works in the *Moralia*, since they are so diverse. It is better to look for certain general tendencies or concerns in them, and thus try to delineate Plutarch's personality and to give background to the *Parallel Lives*.

COMPARISON, CONTRAST, AND JUXTAPOSITION

The most striking feature of Plutarch's biographies is their arrangement "in parallel," with Greeks and Romans side by side. A conspicuous feature of the *Moralia* too is the way in which he uses juxtapositions of various kinds and for various purposes.

An example probably from his youth is the speech "On the Romans' Luck" (*Moralia* 316c–326c). The title is misleading, since this seems to be only the first part of a longer speech in which Plutarch tries to assess whether the success of the Romans was due to luck or to their "goodness" or "courage" (*aretē*). This and similar controversies were a staple of the schools of rhetoric, and two features of the surviving fragment can be directly connected with Plutarch's rhetorical training. One is the way he frames the issue in terms of a comparison. As the preface shows, in the full work he first illustrated Rome's debt to its own luck and then, in the part now lost, did the same for Rome's goodness. From the fact that goodness comes second it probably follows that he gave it the prize. The other rhetorical feature is his use of example. A speaker was trained to argue his case by the accumulation of instances, the more the better. So here Plutarch conducts the argument by recounting a series of anecdotes about luck in Roman history; one of these concerns the luck of Caesar, which carried him safely across the Adriatic at a crucial moment in the Roman civil wars, a story Plutarch was to use again in his Life of Caesar. If this really is an early work, it shows Plutarch already well acquainted with Roman history and able to cite incidents covering a span of about 700 years, some of them to recur in the *Parallel Lives*. Another of the examples is the luck of the general Sulla, which Plutarch illustrates from the inscriptions on Sulla's "trophies" (dedications made by a victorious commander) "in my town of Chaeronea" (*Moralia* 318d): such childhood images may well have set him in the directions he was to follow in his maturity. Plutarch's rhetorical training, then, both contributed to the system of comparisons used in the *Parallel Lives* and encouraged his tendency to read history for the moral lessons that could be drawn from it.

The work "On the Romans' Luck" has a brash vigor absent from the later works, but still shows an author who has not yet fused various influences into a personality of his own. That these influences remained even in his maturity is shown by a work neglected until recently, "On Courage in Women" (243e–263c). Here the problem again turns on the word *aretē*. The usual ancient view that women were naturally timid implied that they could not have complete *aretē*, or at least that in them it was a quality essentially different from that found in men. Plutarch's belief, which is fundamental to the *Lives*, is that *aretē* is unchanging, and if it appears different in different persons, that is only

because of the different natures through which it is expressed. Here he argues the point by a series of historical examples designed to show that in the right circumstances women can be as courageous as men. Just as in the speech "On the Romans' Luck," therefore, the argument is implicitly framed in terms of a comparison, and conducted by example. Even more than in the earlier work, Plutarch shows his intimate knowledge of Greek and Roman history. He deliberately takes his instances from lesser-known historians, and much of the interest of the essay comes from the recent demonstration that he drew on an enormous range of historical reading, not merely handbooks.

The greatest interest of this essay, however, lies in the preface (242e–243e), in which he enunciates several ideas relevant to the *Parallel Lives*. One of these is that the work "treats the historic as demonstrative." At the same time, it "does not shun charm that contributes to demonstration"; this is the principle epitomized by Horace as "mixing the useful and the pleasant" (*utile dulci*). Especially interesting is Plutarch's justification of the comparative method:

> There is no better way of finding out the similarity and difference of women's and men's goodness than by juxtaposing lives with lives, deeds with deeds, . . . though types of goodness have certain differences, as it were colors of their own, because of our natures, and grow to resemble the underlying dispositions, bodily constitutions, upbringing, and way of life.
>
> (243b–c)

Plutarch now uses this justification not merely to score points in a rhetorical contest but to probe human nature. The rhetor has become a philosopher.

LITERATURE, MORALITY, AND EDUCATION

In the *Republic* Plato discusses at length the influence of poetry on the character of the hearer, and finally banishes it from his community. As a Platonist who was also a lover of literature, Plutarch is keenly interested in its moral influence, and certain of the essays in the *Moralia* reveal much about how he read earlier authors and how he expected others to read him.

His essay "On How to Listen to Poetry" (13d–37b) was written for a father whose son is an adolescent and so about the age to study poetry. Plutarch is entirely concerned with its moral effects on the young. To make it acceptable he proposes various stratagems: a teacher should especially emphasize edifying passages, omit offensive ones, or even alter the text to make it acceptable. Though this attitude seems uncharacteristically intolerant for Plutarch, it is in fact typical of him in several ways. Inasmuch as his stand is less harsh than Plato's, it shows him modifying what was almost a sacred text to suit his own liking for literature. It also shows the principle of "mixing the useful and the pleasant," since in Plutarch's scheme poetry, if properly taught, could be a positive stimulus to right action. Above all, it again shows his moral approach to literary texts and the boldness with which he is prepared to handle them when he feels justified. Since for him history was above all literature and not documents, this boldness must be taken into account in order to assess his conversion of history into biography.

This tendency clarifies one of Plutarch's most controversial essays, "On the Ill-nature of Herodotus" (854e–874c). His thesis here is that the great historian of the Greek wars with Persia is actuated by ill nature *(kakoetheia)*, a tendency to belittle the great and extol the unworthy, particularly by means of insinuation. Herodotus had said of the Athenian Isagoras, for instance, that "he was of a well-reputed family, but I do not know about the earlier generations; his relatives sacrifice to Carian Zeus," that is, they worshiped Zeus with the same rites as did the Carians of southwestern Asia Minor, and so were perhaps not Athenian in origin. For Plutarch, Herodotus is not setting out what he knows and leaving conclusions to his readers: he is subtly trying to belittle a noble Athe-

nian, "mixing in a little praise with his malice in order to gain credence."

Characteristically, Plutarch has decided from his knowledge of Herodotus' *History* that its author belongs to a familiar moral type, the *kolax* (parasite, insinuator). For Plutarch this sort of activity was particularly abhorrent since it perverted his principle of "mixing the useful and the pleasant." Here, then, is a clear case in which the assurance of his moral views predominates over his historical sense. For Plutarch history ought to be a stimulus to conduct, and the great figures of the past were models on whom modern readers ought to pattern themselves.

SCIENCE

Though Plutarch's philosophical concern is chiefly with morals, he is also interested in natural science. In fact, he does not distinguish sharply between the two, since it will be seen that as a moralist he always seeks to determine the effect of human nature on conduct. One of the problems he discusses, for example, "Why Do Older People Read More Easily at a Distance than Close Up?" has its moral counterpart in his biographies of Galba and Marius, in which he portrays the effect of old age on behavior.

Plutarch's characteristic method is inductive: he starts with the empirical data and works backward to their causes. This method underlies the longest of his surviving works, the nine books of "Dinner Questions" (612c–748d), in which he uses his favorite literary form, the dialogue, to discuss a variety of questions, such as the one about old people's vision. Many of the questions he poses involve social behavior, for example, the Roman habit of not allowing the dinner table to be removed without food on it. This interest in social customs is also expressed in the two works "On the Reasons for Roman Customs" (263d–291c) and "On the Reasons for Greek Customs" (291d–304f). In the *Parallel Lives* this scientific habit of inquiry is revealed in digressions into the discussion of curious phenomena, such as the shout of joy of the Greeks liberated by Flamininus that stunned the birds flying overhead ("Flamininus" 10.6).

RELIGION

Plutarch was an amateur scientist and yet also intensely religious. Two currents are observable in his religious thought, a theoretical one derived from Plato and a functional one connected with his priestly duties at Delphi, and the two do not always blend.

From Plato he derived a transcendental view of godhead that comes close to monotheism. One of Plutarch's purely philosophical treatises concerns Plato's *Timaeus*, and particularly the account there given of the origin of the universal *psyche*, often but misleadingly translated "soul." With typical willfulness, Plutarch reads into Plato the view that this *psyche* was brought into being when god imposed order on a preexistent principle of disorder, and to this principle he attributes the existence of evil in the world.

The same desire to absolve god of responsibility for evil also explains the great prominence that Plutarch everywhere gives to *daimones*, beings intermediate between gods and men. Evil *daimones* are to blame for apparent miscarriages of divine justice; one of these beings makes a memorable appearance in the *Parallel Lives* as the "strange and monstrous phantom" that appeared to Brutus before Philippi and told him, "I am your evil *daimon*, Brutus" ("Brutus" 36.4). Plutarch conversely makes the good *daimones* the messengers whom god employs in his dealings with mortals, and this concept again saves god from worldly pollution.

The good *daimones* are also Plutarch's way of reconciling his Platonism with his priesthood. He could not have been a priest at Delphi without a firm belief in prophecy: yet god could not talk directly to mortals and, moreover, could not abandon oracles, as he sometimes appeared to do. Plutarch's answer is to suppose that the *daimones* are the immediate source of prophetic inspiration, and that the decline of oracles is due to their death. As proof that *daimones* can die, he tells the famous tale of a man living in the reign of Tiberius who had received a mysterious order to announce the death of Pan (*Moralia* 419b–d). While this theory reconciled Plutarch's priesthood and his Platonism, it brought him dangerously close to making the god he served inferior to the Platonic creator.

ETHICS AND PSYCHOLOGY

This account of Plutarch's religious views reveals a double interest: in the operations of the *psyche* and in the problem of good and evil. These interests take up more space in the *Moralia* than any others and are also basic to the *Parallel Lives*. Most of the theoretical works that they produced, notably the essay "On the Psyche," are lost, and it is better to reserve discussion of Plutarch's psychological system for the *Parallel Lives*. In the *Moralia* posterity has always preferred the essays in which he applies his theories to actual circumstances, and they still make delightful reading. The essay "On the Control of Anger" (452f–464d), for example, is quintessential Plutarch. Rather than using an expository form, as Seneca does in his treatise on the same subject, Plutarch writes a dialogue. The main speaker is Minicius Fundanus, an eminent Roman of the day and also a friend of the younger Pliny, who is made to describe the course of self-criticism whereby he won control over his own temper; incidentally, it is a measure of Plutarch's easy standing with influential Romans that he could discuss their characters in this way.

The liveliness of the presentation is enhanced by two of Plutarch's favorite stylistic devices. One is the vivid use of imagery:

> Those who expect a siege gather in and store up necessities, despairing of outside help; in the same way, we must take especial care to get from philosophy our reinforcements against anger and

import them into the *psyche*, knowing that when the critical time has arrived we will not easily be able to smuggle them in.

(454a)

The other device is the use of quotation to vary the texture and add to the richness of imagery. Thus to make the point that anger is often provoked by a slight remark, Plutarch quotes (454d) a bitter exchange between Helen and Electra from Euripides' *Orestes*; with typical freedom he in fact juxtaposes two widely separate lines from the scene. By this exchange he gives drama and concreteness to what might otherwise have been a disembodied generalization.

Another very characteristic device of this work is the lavish use of historical examples. One of the ways Fundanus has learned to control his anger is by collecting "not only stories about philosophers, who fools say have no bile, but even more of kings and tyrants" (457d). Kings and tyrants are used not merely because of the human tendency to imitate the famous, but for a more important reason. There was a Greek proverb, "Power will show the man," that implied that often only high station will reveal a person's inner nature, since there he is exposed simultaneously to great external pressures and to the inner temptations that come from power. This is another idea fundamental to the *Parallel Lives*.

POLITICS

Plutarch's moral treatises are usually written as guides for conduct: "How to Tell a Flatterer From a Friend" (48e–75a); "How to Praise Oneself Without Giving Offense" (539a–548a); and so on. Because of his belief in the influence of high station on action, he is naturally concerned with the behavior of politicians. From his writings and from other sources it is clear that the city *(polis)* of his day, though greatly changed from that of classical Greece, was still full of vitality. He and others of his class regarded the leadership of their cities as a natural duty, and the pressures of politics were strong

enough to make moral guidance highly necessary.

Plutarch's political treatises are among the most topical of his essays. The chief one is his "Political Precepts" (798a–825f), written to help a young man just entering public life in the Asian city of Sardis. The advice is typical of the author: choose an elder statesman on whom to model your conduct, maintain diplomatic friendships with the Roman governors, above all avoid dissension in the ruling class and preserve its concord. It is also typical that every lesson is illustrated by historical examples drawn almost as often from Roman as from Greek history. On the use of witticisms in politics, for example, he advises:

> Such things are most approved when used in repartee and replies; employing them on purpose and unprovoked is to be like a comedian, and gives an impression of ill-nature too, as the humor of Cicero, Cato the Elder, and Euxitheos the follower of Aristotle did to them.

(803c)

For Plutarch the great men of history were not inert objects of academic study, but could be made to live again by their example, good and bad. In the *Moralia* he draws on history to illustrate a diversity of moral questions: in the *Parallel Lives* the difference is that the material is organized not around problems but around persons.

THE LIVES OF THE CAESARS

The *Parallel Lives* are not Plutarch's only biographies. He wrote a number of individual Lives, of which two are extant, the *Aratus* and the *Artaxerxes*. There was also a series of biographies of Roman emperors from Augustus to Vitellius, of which there remain only the Lives of Galba and Otho, two of the ephemeral emperors of the years 68 and 69.

The scheme of the whole work immediately recalls the more famous *Lives of the Caesars* by Plutarch's younger contemporary Suetonius. The fact that Plutarch, unlike Suetonius, does not include the Flavian dynasty, which ended in 96, suggests that he wrote before that date, and he certainly wrote before Suetonius. Before Plutarch there had been serial biographies of rulers; the Roman Cornelius Nepos, for example, probably included in his work *On Illustrious Men* most or all of the kings of Rome. Individual emperors had also been given biographies in Greek, such as the *Life of Augustus* by Nicolaus of Damascus. Plutarch is nevertheless the first author in Greek or Latin known to have written a series of imperial lives. It may well be from him that Suetonius drew his immediate inspiration, even though he was to fulfill it on a much larger scale and in a completely different manner. It is characteristic that in these biographies Plutarch should appear particularly interested in Roman history and write in a style similar to Roman biography.

As in the *Parallel Lives*, Plutarch distinguishes between his aim and the aim of history proper: "to report every event in detail is the business of formal history, but I too ought not to pass over noteworthy events which are bound up with the things done by or done to the Caesars" ("Galba" 2.3). In the "Alexander," Plutarch claims to be seeking "the expressions of the *psyche*," whereas here he expresses a more neutral interest in the Caesars' personal history. This difference is connected with the difference of subject. For the *Parallel Lives* Plutarch could pick and choose among the great men of the past and select those whose lives showed virtue, or sometimes vice, projected by circumstances onto the screen of history. With the Caesars he was obliged to treat subjects who would never have gained admittance to the *Parallel Lives*, such as the weak Galba and the corrupted Otho. Despite the differences, however, the *Lives of the Caesars* anticipate the *Parallel Lives* in several ways. One is the concentration on the moral characteristics of the subjects, the weakness and meanness of Galba or the mixture of debauchery and decisiveness in Otho. Another is the tendency to raise the moral tone of the work by probably unconscious flattery of the subjects: thus Galba's errors are largely ascribed to the evil influence of his councillor Vinius, and both Galba and Otho are given edifying death scenes.

The chief interest of the two Lives, however, is due to certain incidental features. They are the only narratives in which Plutarch describes events through which he himself had lived. Some of his information came from Roman friends who had been directly involved, such as Mestrius Florus, who later showed him the battlefield of Bedriacum. Moreover, in certain passages these two Lives resemble, down to details of wording, the narrative of the same events given by Plutarch's contemporary Tacitus in the *Histories*. Plutarch reports Galba's last moments thus: "offering his throat, he said, 'Do your work, if this is better for the Roman people'" ("Galba" 27.1). According to Tacitus:

> His last words are variously given according to the hostility or admiration of the reporter. Some say that he pleaded, asking what wrong he deserved and begging a few days to pay off his public gift. Most state that he voluntarily offered his throat to his executioners, telling them to do their work and strike, if that seemed in the public interest. It made no difference to his killers what he said.
>
> (*Histories* 1.41)

It is disputed whether these similarities are due to a source common to both authors: what is clear is the contrast in approach. Tacitus reports two versions, and implies that neither is likely to be based on fact. Plutarch, from either ignorance or bias, gives only the version of the majority, which happens also to be the more edifying one. Tacitus is a historian and a realist; Plutarch is a biographer and an optimist.

THE PARALLEL LIVES: PLAN AND FORM

The *Parallel Lives* were probably always the most admired of Plutarch's works, and correspondingly are the best preserved. Only one pair is known to have been lost, the "Epaminondas and Scipio," which may well have been the first of the series. The remaining twenty-two pairs comprise forty-six Lives, because one of the pairs concerns two sets of persons, the Spartans Agis and Cleomenes and the Romans Tiberius and Gaius Gracchus. Plutarch seems not to have planned the series, but to have added one set of Lives after another as he felt inclined. The whole work is dedicated to a very prominent personage of the reign of Trajan called Sosius Senecio, a citizen, senator, and consul of Rome, though, like Plutarch, he may have come from a Greek-speaking province.

Within each pair, the chronologically earlier of the two heroes comes first, so that Greeks almost always precede Romans. However, Coriolanus is correctly put before Alcibiades, while Aemilius Paulus is incorrectly but deliberately put before Timoleon: this pair also happens to have an unusually full preface. In its complete form, the Plutarchean pair begins with a preface, which may do one or both of two things: discuss general points connected with those particular heroes, and justify the choice of subject. In the often-quoted preface to the "Alexander" Plutarch does only the first and explains why he has not included all the famous deeds of his two heroes, Alexander and Caesar, the most celebrated in their respective histories. In the "Theseus and Romulus" he does only the second, and justifies his choosing the founder of Athens to balance against the founder of Rome. He does both in the "Demosthenes and Cicero," first discussing the difficulties caused by his lack of books and unfamiliarity with Latin, and then the similarities in his two heroes' lives.

Similarly, in its fullest form the Plutarchean pair ends with a brief essay contrasting the two heroes. Ostensibly Plutarch's purpose is to judge which is better or, as he puts it, to award "the prize of virtue," but in practice he never makes a clear judgment and seems concerned to show not the imbalance of the heroes but their equipoise. Though these comparisons (synkriseis) delighted readers in the Renaissance and later, nowadays they are usually dismissed or even omitted. This is wrong, since they are not mere appendices to the Lives but vital to understanding their moral purpose. Moreover, they have their part in the architecture of the Parallel Lives and are designed to show the differences between the heroes just as the prefaces show their similarities. However, while Plutarch sometimes omits one or both of the preface and the comparison, he omits the preface much more often; and of the two the comparison is often longer.

The individual Life is usually narrated in chronological order. The only subject that Plutarch habitually treats by grouping instances is that of his heroes' sayings: he therefore contrasts sharply with Suetonius, who tends to arrange his subjects' lives by topics. Another great difference in which Plutarch resembles a historian more than does Suetonius is his use of speeches and other set pieces such as battle scenes or topographical descriptions.

Yet another feature that recalls ancient historians is the use of digression. Plutarch will sometimes linger over an incidental topic that takes his interest and then move on, often with an apology. For example, in his "Pericles" he has to introduce his hero's mistress, Aspasia, who interested Plutarch because of the tribute paid to her in Plato's Menexenus. After a long discussion he concludes: "all this came into my head as I was writing, and perhaps it would have been unkind to reject it and pass it by" ("Pericles" 24.7). At other times it is not something peripheral that he lingers over, but some event in the narrative. Much of the "Crassus," for instance, is devoted to an almost historical narrative of Crassus' defeat and death at the great battle of Carrhae in 53 B.C. The younger Cato's last hours take up a good fraction of his biography.

It would be wrong to conclude from his delays and digressions that Plutarch could not control his pen. The Parallel Lives are generally written in a form designed to attract the cultivated amateur, not to inform the specialist. As a strong believer in the principle of "mixing the useful and the pleasant," Plutarch varies his narrative with material that interests him as a means of interesting his reader.

PURPOSE

Not every writer writes with a purpose in mind, or, if he does, he may try to conceal it from his readers or even from himself. Plutarch, however, mentions his purpose so often, and his achievement corresponds with it so closely, that his sincerity can hardly be doubted. At the same time he naturally has subsidiary motives, and even the chief one of these is fairly complex.

"We will be all the keener both as spectators and as imitators of the lives of better men, if we do not remain uninstructed in lives that are bad and reprehensible" ("Demetrius" 1.6). Contemplation (theoria) and imitation (mimesis) are the two cylinders that propel the Parallel Lives. In Plutarch's moral theory, which is largely borrowed from Aristotle, to see what is good is to be drawn toward it: the word kalos, often translated "beautiful," has in Greek a nuance of attractiveness or desirability that the English equivalent lacks.

Whenever Plutarch discusses the purpose of the Parallel Lives, one or more of the three notions of contemplation, imitation, and beauty always occurs. The most instructive passage is in the preface to the "Aemilius." Plutarch claims that in writing his biographies he tries

> using history as if it were a mirror, somehow or other to arrange my life and make it resemble my heroes' virtues. For the experience is really like nothing so much as staying and living together, when I receive and entertain each of them in turn in my narrative [historia] and contemplate "how great and of what aspect" each of them is, deriving from their actions what is most important and most beautiful to know.
>
> (1.1)

Similarly in the "Pericles" Plutarch disparages the representational arts because of the moral inferiority of the artists: "no well-bred youth after seeing the Zeus at Olympia wants to be Phidias," whereas "virtue by its actions immediately disposes us to admire its deeds and imitate their authors" (2.1).

To be visible, character had to be writ large, and greatness is another key concept in the Parallel Lives. This is of two kinds. Externally it implies that Plutarch's heroes must be involved in great actions. He apologizes in the "Nicias" for including events already better described by others, but adds that "they above all show the man's character as it was revealed by many, great misfortunes" (1.1). So also in the "Pompey" he hurries over his hero's youth in order to arrive at "the great matters and those that show his character best" (8.7).

External greatness was not sufficient for inclusion in the Parallel Lives, however; the heroes had also to be great of soul, not merely small men like Galba caught up in the currents of history. This insistence on spiritual grandeur justifies the inclusion of some men who were heroic in their vices, such as Demetrius and Antony, since "great natures produce great vices as they do great virtues" ("Demetrius" 1.7). It also justifies the claim Plutarch makes in the preface to the "Alexander" that he must be allowed to "penetrate to the tokens of the psyche," since "often a little thing, a remark, some joke, reveals character better than battles with myriad corpses, huge confrontations, or sieges of cities" (1).

Plutarch's moral purpose has many consequences for his method. A general one is connected with his emphasis on "the beautiful." Because he wishes to hold up examples for imitation, he does not like to dwell on his heroes' faults. A long preface is necessary to justify the inclusion of Demetrius and Antony. In the "Cimon" Plutarch holds that when describing the beautiful things in a man's life "we should give a full and true account," whereas we should not be eager to dwell on "faults and blemishes due to some misfortune or political necessity" (2.3–4). On the other hand, his optimism never becomes adulation, and even those he admires, such as Nicias and Alexander, are all the more real for their faults.

THE PARALLEL METHOD

The arrangement of the *Parallel Lives* in pairs is their most striking feature, and yet the reason for it is not immediately obvious. Here, too, the moral purpose provides much of the explanation.

In the essay "On Courage in Women" Plutarch argued that the bravery of men and the bravery of women were one and the same; the differences were due to the different material provided by women's nature and circumstances. So also in the *Parallel Lives* the basic intention is to show two persons both possessed of the same qualities and in roughly similar circumstances, and thus to understand more exactly what those qualities are:

> I compare [Phocion and Cato] not only because of common similarities, as good and statesmanlike men; . . . for except for the least, irreducible differences these two men's virtues exhibit a single stamp, form, and common color mixed with their characters, . . . so that it requires a very subtle discussion as a sort of implement to distinguish and discover their differences.
>
> ("Phocion" 3.4–5)

Etymologically the word "parallel" only means "side by side," and for Plutarch it refers in the first place to a principle of arrangement. After determining to write about Romulus, for example, he says, "I decided to confront and contrast (*parabalein*) the founder of beautiful and famous Athens with the father of great and invincible Rome" ("Theseus" 1.2). The two lives are parallel because Plutarch chooses to place them side by side, not because of some mysterious affinity between them. In this case the reasons seem almost frivolous: for example, "both were born under uncertain and obscure circumstances and were believed to be the sons of gods" and "both are associated with the sei-

zure of women" ("Theseus" 2.2). Usually, however, the reasons given are of a moral kind, as in the "Phocion," or are a mixture of moral and accidental, as in the "Demosthenes."

The fact that Plutarch chooses to compare Greeks with Romans does not follow necessarily from his moral purpose: he could have compared men of the same nation who lived in different times and cities. The best explanation for this system is also the simplest one, that the device is merely aesthetic, or as Plutarch would say, it mixed "the useful and the pleasant." It recalls such equivalents in the representational arts as the grotesque two-faced sculpture in Berlin, which shows Socrates on one side and Seneca on the other. Here too there are similarities in external circumstances, and also (at least in the eyes of Seneca and his admirers) in inner character. It is not accidental that when talking about the *Parallel Lives* Plutarch constantly makes analogies to painting and sometimes to sculpture, as when he speaks of the "common color" in the characters of Phocion and Cato.

In a larger sense the placing of Greeks and Romans side by side also reflects their status in Plutarch's world, in which Greeks like himself, and perhaps also Sosius Senecio, could become Roman citizens and mix with men like Minicius Fundanus on equal terms. To draw subtle political or cultural inferences—for example, to suppose that Plutarch wished to show the Greeks that the Romans had men of culture or the Romans that the Greeks had statesmen and generals—is to ascribe to his society an anachronistic ignorance.

BIOGRAPHY AND HISTORY

In the "Nicias" Plutarch apologizes for retelling events already better told by Thucydides and the Sicilian historian Philistos: he did not wish to vie with the inimitable, but his moral purpose made it impossible to omit events that revealed his subject's character (1.4). He lived in a stable age and could not anticipate that a time might come in which classics like Philistos would perish while he himself survived. His high tone and his reduction of lengthy sources into readable abridgments, though they ensured his survival, in a sense also did him a disservice: by accident he became a witness to history, especially for ill-attested periods like the Hellenistic age. Modern source books and readers tend to treat him as if he was a moralizing historian, when in fact he is a historical moralist.

In the preface to the "Alexander," Plutarch similarly apologizes for not including all the well-known deeds of his two heroes, but adds, "I am not writing histories, but lives" (1). In this, as in other respects, the preface is only a partial statement of his aims, made with reference to that particular pair. The kind of history he is thinking of here is what he elsewhere calls "formal history" (pragmatike historia), which gives "an exact account of the details of events" ("Galba" 2.3). By contrast, Plutarch abbreviates formal histories in order to emphasize transactions that reveal character, the "evidences of the psyche" ("Alexander" 1): "the most important things and those most beautiful to learn" ("Aemilius" 1.12), and the "things worth remembering" (comparison of "Theseus" and "Romulus" 1.1).

Elsewhere Plutarch makes it clear that he regards his work as a kind of history. In the "Aemilius," for example, he talks of entertaining each of the heroes "in my history" (1.1); in the "Demetrius" he justifies the inclusion of bad men on the ground that "we should not lack a history" of them (1). In the same passage of the "Nicias" in which he declines to emulate Thucydides and Philistos, he claims even so to have included certain details that have escaped others, "not assembling a history that has no use, but offering one that helps to observe character and manner" (1.5). He means here to claim some historical value for the Parallel Lives, in that the reader of the usual sources will find in his work scraps of new or unexpected information. In practice he is ready to cite inscriptions or variant traditions, to settle not only

questions relevant to morality like the poverty of Aristides (1.1), but such antiquarian ones as the names of Aristides' descendants (27.1–3). The history that he implicitly dismisses as "useless" is not all history, since he has just praised the classic writers whose accounts revealed the character of Nicias: it is rather the antiquarian compilators from whom the reader derives no moral profit at all. Basically historia means "inquiry" or the results of inquiry, and inasmuch as his Lives are the fruit of research, they are historia.

There is another sense of history inherent in Plutarch's view of his task, and that is history as the antonym of myth. The distinction between myth (mythos) and history, and the cognate distinction between falsity and truth, were fundamental to the emergence of Greek history and are basic to Plutarch. Prefacing the Lives of Theseus and Romulus he expresses dismay at leaving "a period accessible to considerations of probability and able to support an inquiry (historia) that holds on to events. . . . Let us hope that the mythical will be purged and submissive to reason, and will take the form of history" ("Theseus" 1.1; 1.3).

Plutarch had more than one reason for his misgivings about myth. As Plato had complained already, it was amoral and ascribed reprehensible acts to gods and heroes: it is instructive to compare Plutarch's gingerly, "rational" account of Romulus slaying Remus with the dramatic gusto of Livy on the same subject. Another problem was that the world of myth tended to involve divine beings in human affairs to a degree distressing for a man of Plutarch's piety. The tradition that the Roman king Numa had been the lover of the nymph Egeria prompts a long discussion as to whether "a god or daimon can have union and pleasure with the body and the beauty of a human." Plutarch prefers to think that Numa made the story up in order to gain divine sanction for his legislation ("Numa" 4.8). This is precisely making "the mythical submissive to reason." Another difficulty of myth was that the word suggested falsity. Plutarch wished to provide models for conduct, and they were not likely to be effective if the reader saw them as creatures in a world remote from reality. Though he wrote individual Lives of such figures as Heracles and the centaur Chiron, in the *Parallel Lives* he stays closer to history.

Plutarch's statement in the "Alexander," therefore, is only a part of the truth. Plutarch was not writing formal history or histories in the plural, but he was engaged in *historia*, which imposed on him many of the duties and obligations of the historian. Above all, he had to tell the truth and avoid "a false and fictitious narrative" ("Cimon" 2.3). As well as abhorring deliberate falsehood, he has evidently taken care "not to be thought careless and lazy" ("Nicias" 1.5), and has something of the historian's concern for factual accuracy. Essentially, however, the *Lives* are not history, but a study of history conducive "to the observation of character and manner," and the way in which Plutarch conducts his inquiry is different from the historian's way.

THE COLLECTION OF INFORMATION

The *Parallel Lives* are a comparatively late work, probably not begun until the author was fifty or older. Already in the fifth pair, the "Demosthenes and Cicero," he talks of his stays in Rome, his political duties, and his many pupils there as things of the past (2.2). The composition of the work had therefore already been preceded by a lifetime of culture: not only travel and teaching, but wide reading in literature of every kind and incessant learned discussion like that described in the "Dinner Questions." A feature of Plutarch's life that is antecedent to the *Parallel Lives* in a different way is a practical one. He wrote in the small city of Chaeronea, remote from the great libraries he had seen at Rome. Though he must have had notes and extracts, he often relied on his memory. He should probably also be envisaged working largely with the aid of cultivated slaves or freedmen as researchers, readers, and aman-

uenses. These may have read to him those works or extracts that he had to hand, and he would have dictated the *Lives*, so here too memory was paramount.

To understand Plutarch's relation to his authorities, it is not enough to think of the flat rearrangement on his page of extracts from earlier writers, reduced or expanded and then pasted in. It is better to imagine him working in three dimensions, with some authors at hand or fully retained in the memory, others remembered from notes or incidental reading, others not read at all but known by hearsay or from reference in subsequent works; in addition, there is the contribution of things heard firsthand by himself and his friends. The great Greek classics, Herodotus, Thucydides, and the like, were no doubt known to him from school days, and were at hand even in Chaeronea; his detailed knowledge of Herodotus at least is shown from the extracts that he cites to prove the historian's malevolence. The same intimate knowledge can also be presumed for many nonhistorical authors, for example, the letters of Plato used in the "Dion" and the speeches of Demosthenes.

It is impossible to tell exactly how much of the *Parallel Lives* Plutarch could have written from his prior knowledge and how much of them required special research. In the "Alexander," for example, he cites twenty-four authorities, not only all the famous ones, such as Aristobulus and Callisthenes, but some so obscure that they are known only through him. In addition, he relies much on letters written by or to Alexander, the authenticity of which he did not doubt, even if modern scholars have. He had probably known the main authors before conceiving the Life, and some at least of the obscure ones may be the fruit of casual reading rather than planned research. He seems to have read the letters, however, because of the belief articulated in the preface to this Life that a man's sayings are important for understanding his character. Yet he makes almost no use of one of the most important authorities, Ptolemy, who was one of Alexander's marshals and later the first Macedonian king of Egypt. In the generation after Plutarch the historian Arrian makes much of Ptolemy as one "who, as he was a king, would have found it more disgraceful to tell lies than anyone else." This marks the difference between the historian and the biographer. Plutarch wished to write the truth and not a "false and fictitious narrative" ("Cimon" 2.3), but he was not concerned with being "exhaustive" ("Alexander" 1). He read enough to form a definite impression of each hero's character, but did not feel obliged to read everything relevant. Scholarship is a dividend drawn from his knowledge and gladly passed on to the reader, but is a mere bonus when compared with the real profit of the *Parallel Lives*.

The same tendency to make do with the sufficient is even more marked when Plutarch writes about Romans. How much Latin he knew is uncertain, and in need he could always have relied on friends or bilingual assistants. In practice he cites many fewer Latin authors than Greek and is more prone in Roman Lives than in Greek to follow a single authority, sometimes Latin but preferably Greek. The "Coriolanus" is almost exclusively based on a rhetorical Greek writer whose work happens to have survived, Dionysius of Halicarnassus. Plutarch knew the classic historian of early Rome, Livy, but Dionysius was fuller and easier to read, and for his purposes that was good enough.

Similarly when he uses the evidence of his own eyes or ears, he does so again as a bonus extraneous to the real matter of the *Parallel Lives*, like the many digressions in which such evidence often occurs. The "Aristides" begins with a long discussion in which he uses an inscription he has seen to contradict the historian Demetrius of Phalerum (1.2), but even this is only one item among several, most of which are drawn from his reading. The journey that he took in northern Italy with his friend Mestrius Rufus provided him with several details later used in the *Parallel Lives*, such as the charming story picked up in Milan that closes the "Brutus." There is no sign, however, that Plutarch traveled in order to collect materials, and,

again, these reminiscences are mere curios added for adornment.

Nevertheless, Plutarch was not indifferent to questions of accuracy. He knew that contemporary evidence could be distorted by bias, while later evidence lacked the value of immediacy ("Pericles" 13.11). Where his sources differed, he would sometimes justify his choice between them. He cautions the reader, for example, "I am aware that according to Theophrastus, Hyperbolus was ostracized when Phaeax, not Nicias, was the opponent of Alcibiades, but I follow the majority" ("Nicias" 11.7). When describing Themistocles' desertion to the king of Persia, he found that more sources named the king as Xerxes than as his successor, Artaxerxes. There was more dramatic irony in the former view, but Plutarch accepts the latter because it was supported by Thucydides and chronological tables, "even though they are not entirely settled" ("Themistocles" 27.1). No doubt he was influenced not only by the fact that Thucydides was close to the event in time, but by an instinctive feeling that he could be trusted. Just as he felt that he could discern the characters of great men from the pages of history, so he could sometimes discern the characters of historians: Herodotus was given to malevolence ("Alcibiades" 32), Duris of Samos to excessive pathos ("Eumenes" 1.1–2). The psychologist in Plutarch is never far away.

If he seems to resemble a historian, that is because he liked history and had an amateur's knowledge of its techniques; it is not because he was a professional. His wide knowledge and diplomatic nature enabled him to adopt the mannerisms of those with whom he consorted without losing sight of his own mission, and his mission is best judged by the message he conveys.

THE BIOGRAPHER AND HIS HEROES

The aspects of the *Parallel Lives* considered so far are ones in which Plutarch resembles the historian: digressions, speeches, and the collection and weighing of evidence. It is time to consider the aspects that mark his divergence from historiography.

When toying with the idea of writing history, his contemporary Pliny could contemplate an almost unlimited choice between periods "ancient and written about by others ... or untouched and new" (*Epistles* 5.8). Plutarch's biographical aims limited his selection. Chronologically, just as there was an upper limit prescribed by myth, so there was a lower one for which the reasons are less clear. The latest Greek whom he treats is the Achaean general Philopoemen, whom he calls "a child born to Greece in her old age" and whom a Roman had called "the last of the Greeks" (1.4). His last Roman is Antony. Just as Philopoemen tried to slow the irreversible movement of Greece into the Roman sphere of influence, so Antony was the last opponent of Augustus and the Principate. Plutarch may have felt that the loss of liberty that both heroes witnessed prevented the "great deeds" that showed virtue and vice. His comment on Philopoemen shows that, along with many others, he also held a theory of natural decline whereby later generations were inherently inferior to earlier.

The biographical approach also limited his choice in other ways. There are no women. Plutarch believed that women had potentially the virtue of men, but he also shared the common view of the time that their sex was usually an impediment and subjected them to faults, such as timorousness and gossipiness. For similar reasons his heroes are almost always represented in decline if they live to old age, since this too impeded the full play of virtue and encouraged vice.

Another way in which Plutarch's biographical approach works against history is that the focus on a central figure makes for distortion of the periphery. Because a hero is an example, he tends to appear to better advantage in his own life than in someone else's. In the "Lucullus," for instance, the supporters of Pompey instigate an informer called Vettius to say that Lucullus had bribed him to assassinate Pompey, and when the plot goes awry they have Vettius killed (42.7–8). In the "Pompey" such an incident would have blemished the hero's virtues, and it is entirely omitted. Another form of biographical distortion is that apparent sins of the hero are ascribed to the machinations of small villains. When Pompey betrays his old friend Cicero and allows him to be sent into exile, it is because of the "utterly loathsome and outrageous Clodius, who had picked Pompey up and thrown him under the people's feet" (46.7). Similarly, minor figures who oppose a hero receive no mercy: thus the democrat Cleon, who opposed Nicias, is described, exactly like Clodius, as "loathsome and rash" ("Nicias" 2.2). It has recently been observed that this principle of distortion also affects Plutarch's system of parallels. The great emphasis that he gives to the attacks on Pericles' conduct of the Peloponnesian War is due to his desire to make Pericles more like Fabius Maximus, the great "delayer" in the second Roman war against the Carthaginians.

The most obvious and criticized of Plutarch's distorting tendencies concerns context. He more than once asks his reader's indulgence for abbreviating history. In fact, as the historian Polybius observed, biography differs from history not only because of its different emphases but because of its lack of "demonstration," the context of background, chronology, and causation (*Histories* 10.21). Plutarch very rarely orients his readers as Tacitus does at the beginning of the first books of the *Histories* and *Annals*. Similarly, though Plutarch is aware of the differences wrought by time and place, they seem to have little effect. The reader has the impression that life, above all political life, was not far different in the Athens of Theseus and of Pericles than in the Rome of Romulus and of Caesar. This indifference to context is perhaps an illusion fostered by the concentration on individuals: from the assumption that human nature remains the same it is an easy step to the same assumption about human environment.

To some extent Plutarch can be excused by his intention. His biographies are written as a study of history, not as a substitute for it. Nevertheless, even his admirers may feel that a different approach might have produced a more convincing picture. Plutarch's heroes have the vividness of characters in drama or fiction, but like such characters their lives remain an illusion contrived by their creator: they do not have the unexpected, autonomous qualities of Tacitus' Tiberius or Boswell's Johnson. In a sense Plutarch's portraits are all details of an unconscious self-portrait, and the character that draws the reader to them is the author's own.

BIOGRAPHY AND PSYCHOLOGY

The language of ancient moral philosophy occurs on almost every page of the *Parallel Lives*: psyche, aretē (virtue), physis (nature), ethos (character). Yet Plutarch never explains how these concepts are related to one another, probably because he considers the connections self-evident.

The *psyche* is the vital principle that leaves the body at death ("Romulus" 28.8) and hence, as already remarked, is conventionally translated "soul." However, it also has a sense close to that of "mind"; thus when Plutarch says that Marius' "*psyche* trembled at the thought of a new war" ("Marius" 45.4), the effect is what would now be called "going out of one's mind." This mental aspect of *psyche* explains its connection with virtue, since the virtues—not only the intellectual ones but also the ethical ones like temperance and justice—are arts that involve choice between good and evil ("Demetrius" 1.4). Plutarch can thus talk of "virtues and *psychai*" ascending to heaven together after death ("Romulus" 28.8).

Though the *psyche* is basic to Plutarch's moral scheme, the two terms that he uses most often in this context are *physis* and *ethos*. The word "nature" indicates not the constitution that we are born with, but the form we realize when our growth is complete, even though our constitution at birth inevitably affects our final one. For Plutarch nature applies equally to body and mind, and physical and psychological nature are closely connected. Alexander, for example, had a naturally fiery constitution, which was expressed physically in his red skin and sweet smell, mentally in his being "given to drink and fury" ("Alexander" 4); Plutarch seems to think that Sulla's savage and variable nature was expressed in his blotchy face ("Sulla" 2). Mental, like physical, nature is announced early, but not always brought to fruition. Marius was "naturally manly and warlike," and the effect of military practice was to emphasize his fierce temper ("Marius" 2.1); Caesar, on the other hand, because of his ambition in other fields "did not reach the degree of oratorical skill to which his nature was leading him" ("Caesar" 3).

Nature is therefore the developed set of bodily and mental attributes whereby we are what we are; it is the basis of character, not character itself. Plutarch rarely if ever talks of persons as "having a kind nature," for example, though he can talk of nature as having moral qualities. Pompey, for example, "had an ambitiousness that was not malevolent or ignoble" ("Pompey" 49.14). More frequently he talks of someone as having a characteristic "by nature," as Sulla was "fun-loving by nature" but also "naturally harsh and vengeful" ("Sulla" 2, 6).

Like nature, character can be concealed by inner or exterior circumstances. Sulla's unpredictable behavior made it impossible to tell if he was "arrogant or servile by nature" ("Sulla" 6); Cicero was the first person to see beneath Caesar's easygoing manners "to the hidden cleverness of his character" ("Caesar" 4). Character cannot, however, be changed, even though it sometimes appears to be. Comparing the effect of power on Marius and Sulla, Plutarch finds that "Marius was harsh from the start, and in power he augmented but did not change his nature," whereas in Sulla the difference between his early and later behavior

of course created a suspicion that great power does not allow characters to retain their original dispositions [*tropoi*], but makes them crazy, vain, and unfeeling. It would take a different kind of work to determine whether this is the movement and alteration of nature by external circumstances [tyche] or rather the revelation by power of underlying vice.

("Sulla" 30)

Plutarch clearly inclines to the second solution, since it better suits his idea of nature, and therefore of character, as something essentially fixed after a certain age.

Character is therefore practically moral nature, what we become as the result of natural endowments, training, and habitual circumstances. It has been seen that Plutarch believed strongly in the immutability of the virtues, and character is essential for him in explaining their different manifestations: thus "the virtues of [Phocion and Cato] exhibit a single stamp, form, and common color mixed with their characters, as if affability were blended in equal proportion to sternness, and caution to courage" ("Phocion" 3.5). Once again Plutarch resorts to the visual arts to convey his meaning: virtue is the fixed outline, character is the color that fills it.

Plutarch's moral scheme might be thought only to obtrude occasionally in the *Parallel Lives*, but the reader can never afford to forget it. In effect, his method is less to determine a man's true character than to justify the determination he has already made. Positively, this means highlighting all the aspects of his subject's life that seem to Plutarch to confirm his judgment: thus actions that show Alexander impulsive or prone to persuasion receive more emphasis than those that show him calculating or ruthless. Negatively, actions that go against Plutarch's analysis are variously explained as being due to compulsion (ananke) or circumstances (tyche), or being simply "against nature." Thus he thinks that Pompey was "compelled" by his political adversaries to ally himself with Clodius in 60 B.C., since his view of Pompey made him unwilling to see the insincerity that was plain to Cicero and Tacitus. So far does the exaltation of character go that Plutarch sometimes puts it even above chronology. A well-established tradition made the Athenian Solon converse with the Lydian king Croesus; Plutarch knew that there were difficulties of chronology but was "not going to sacrifice to mere so-called chronological tables so famous a story, one so well attested and, what matters more, one that suits Solon's character and is worthy of his magnanimity and wisdom" ("Solon" 27.1). Nowhere is the priority of biography over history so evident in Plutarch as in his treatment of character.

RELIGION IN THE PARALLEL LIVES

Since the *Parallel Lives* are so concerned with morals, they naturally show the stamp of Plutarch's religious views. The conventional gods appear in the narrative, but only as the objects of conventional worship, as when Sulla plunders Apollo's shrine at Delphi ("Sulla" 12) or Aphrodite appears to Lucullus in a dream ("Lucullus" 12.1). Plutarch seems to ascribe positive influence on human affairs only to a single, nameless power, which he calls "god" (theos) or more generally the "divine" (theion). God decides to remove Brutus from the path of Julius Caesar, and so prevents a certain conjunction of circumstances (tyche) that would have saved him from defeat at Philippi ("Brutus" 47.3). When Demetrius Poliorcetes' portrait is impiously woven into the sacred robe of Athena, the divine shows its displeasure by causing the robe to be torn in a high wind ("Demetrius" 12.3).

In such passages god is envisaged as a kind of general manager responsible for overall policy, of which the execution is delegated to his agents. The chief of these are naturally the *daimones*, but tyche, which can be translated according to context as "luck," "chance," "fortune," or "circumstances," is scarcely less important. Plutarch's notion of the "demonic" is closely linked to that of chance. It is the "demonic" to which he ascribes the fact that Cicero's son was consul when public vengeance was taken on the memory of Antony, Cicero's enemy ("Cicero" 49.6). A similar coincidence, the fact that Caesar was assassinated at the very foot of Pompey's statue, is due to "some *daimon* bringing and summoning the act to that spot" ("Caesar" 66).

Daimones are also imagined as attached to particular persons, a belief in which Plutarch was encouraged by Socrates' belief in his *daimonion*. An incident adapted by Shakespeare in *Julius Caesar* concerns the vision seen by Brutus before Philippi, which was said to have had "a monstrous and hideous shape" and announced itself as his "evil *daimon*" ("Brutus" 36.3). Another incident, also found in Shakespeare, occurs when an Egyptian seer explains to Antony why he always loses to the young Caesar at gambling: "he said that [Antony's] *tyche*, though most brilliant and great, was dimmed by Caesar's. . . . , 'For your *daimon*,' he said, 'fears his'" ("Antony" 33.3). Here *tyche* is virtually identical with the personal *daimon*; so again when Julius Caesar assures the captain of a ship taking him across the Adriatic, "You convey Caesar and Caesar's *tyche*" ("Caesar" 38).

Tyche can also be a set of circumstances that has a decisive effect on human affairs, like the *tyche* that god "cut off" from Brutus at Philippi ("Brutus" 47.3). Plutarch several times uses the phrase "divine *tyche*" to express the idea that god guides the world through the remote control of apparent chance.

Like Plutarch's psychology, his religion might appear to a casual reader of the *Parallel Lives* to impinge on them only as stage effects and not to affect the actual course of the narrative. Apart from the abundant use of omens and portents, however, there are two topics in which his religious views regularly bias his presentation. One is superstition, a vice that Plutarch much disliked since it ascribed to the gods a meddlesome ill will toward humanity. His view of the Athenian general Nicias is largely a portrait of superstition in action that flaws his character as avarice flaws that of the companion hero, Crassus. Plutarch preserves other heroes from the taint of superstition by supposing

that they were only using religion for political ends. We have already seen how he thinks it possible that Numa made up the story of his intercourse with the nymph Egeria in order to win acceptance for his legislation ("Numa" 4.8).

The other topic in the *Parallel Lives* that brings out Plutarch's religious bias is that of the deification of human beings. He does not deny that mortals can become gods, since virtue is divine and the souls of outstandingly virtuous men may pass through the ranks of heroes and *daimones* to join the gods. What he vehemently denounces is the deification of the living, since that implies the divinity of the human body, which is perishable and therefore not divine ("Aristides" 6.4; "Romulus" 28.7). Yet, as a biographer, Plutarch is confronted by the problem that certain of his heroes, notably Alexander and Caesar, appeared to have sought divinity in their lifetimes. He has several ways of dealing with the difficulty, all of them presumably adopted unconsciously. One is to ascribe these claims to the machinations of lesser men. Thus the divine honors voted by Athens to Demetrius are blamed entirely on Athenians, and especially on the demagogue Stratocles, "who was generally outrageous and a dissolute liver" ("Demetrius" 11). Similarly, the excessive honors voted to Caesar were the work of his enemies as much as of his flatterers, since they wanted as many excuses as possible for killing him ("Caesar" 57).

Plutarch sometimes appears to be led by his dislike of divine claims to alter or conceal the evidence for them. Arguing that Alexander did not really believe in his own divinity, he contrasts a letter of his that does imply this belief with a later remark that does not, and infers that the second represents Alexander's mature view. In fact, the letter, even if spurious, refers to the last year of Alexander's life, so that Plutarch has juggled the evidence to suit his belief ("Alexander" 28). By a similar unconscious subterfuge, he calls "inflated and bizarre" the honors voted to the living Caesar, but stops short of saying that they implied his divinity, which he says only of the honors voted after Caesar's death ("Caesar" 57, 67). Plutarch should have known that the living Caesar had his own priest, since it is mentioned in a work he cites elsewhere, Cicero's second *Philippic* ("Antony" 6.1). Modern historians have sometimes had motives similar to Plutarch's for denying that Alexander or Caesar made divine claims, and have cited him as a witness. This is a clear case in which the *Parallel Lives* mislead when they are read as history.

POLITICS

"It is admitted that man possesses no virtue more complete than the political kind" ("Cato the Elder" 30). From his early youth Plutarch was involved in politics, as in various ways were all the heroes of his Lives; the *Parallel Lives* have even been seen as a sort of political textbook. But Plutarch's interest in statesmen and generals is more easily explained by his belief that greatness was necessary to reveal virtue and vice. Nonetheless, his strong political views, like his moral and religious ones, are another of the forces that shape the work.

It has already been seen that the Greek city of his day was still a living organism. The old view that it was a lifeless mime in comparison with the city of the classical period is mistaken; the truth is rather that the language of politics remained the same, but now corresponded to a different reality. "Freedom" was not what it had been in classical or even Hellenistic Greece, but that of a world in which the ultimate power lay with Rome. Externally, there could no longer be war or foreign policy; internally, discord might lead not to self-administered remedies like ostracism (the expulsion of a citizen by popular vote) but to the drastic intervention of Roman might. Rome had also altered the meaning of "democracy." The assembly still met and voted but lacked an articulate voice; it was reduced to a pressure group kept content with largesse and able to express its will only by shouting and the threat of violence. Policy was devised, articulated, and executed by a small group of rich notables like Plutarch himself, the "first men" or "politicians."

Plutarch takes no notice of this shift in the meaning of political language, and just as he imposes his moral and religious views on his biographies, so also he interprets the heroes' politics in the terms of his own. Even those who are kings, like Theseus and Romulus, have political opponents. The majority, however, are "politicians" with the same duties as those in Plutarch's day. Pericles exemplifies the ideal in a politician's dealings with the people: he secures their goodwill, "training his oratory like an instrument" ("Pericles" 8.1), but also withstands their pressure when his policies are unpopular. Poplicola had his house demolished when it gave offense, and thus "showed what a good thing it is for one in power and high position to have ears that admit free speech rather than flattery" ("Poplicola" 10.2). Caesar is the type of the politician who uses the popularity gained by largesse to overthrow his rivals. Sulla and Marius, Pompey and Caesar are the leaders respectively of the aristocratic and popular parties of their day. Plutarch's own sentiments have a conservative bias, as is shown by his admiring "Pompey" and by his execration of demagogues such as Cleon, Stratocles, and Clodius. The closest he comes to a sympathetic view of popular politicians is in the Lives of Agis and Cleomenes and of the Gracchi; but the Gracchi at least are an example of excess, "which is always dangerous, and is ruinous when accompanied by political ambition" ("Agis and Cleomenes" 2.3).

Like Plutarch's views on the deification of human beings, his political opinions have not only shaped the *Parallel Lives* but have appealed to those with kindred sentiments. "Periclean Athens," a city raised by one man's will to its cultural and military zenith, is a concept that owes much of its vitality to Plutarch. Visitors to the Acropolis Museum in Athens can see his encomium on Pericles' buildings ("Pericles" 13.3) carved in stone. In Roman history, too, Plutarch has had great influence with his view of late republican politics as a struggle between popular and aristocratic parties, with an irresponsible Thersites like Clodius in the first, and a high-minded crusader like Pompey in the second. Once more, it is fatal to treat Plutarch's biographies as history merely divided up another way.

THE BIOGRAPHICAL TRADITION

Personal as Plutarch's biographies are, they were not created out of nothing. The history of ancient biography is obscure, largely because of the almost total loss of Greek prose literature between the fourth and first centuries B.C. Nevertheless, enough survives to show that Plutarchean biography has at least some formal antecedents.

The first two classics in the field, and probably the first real biographies, are the extant *Evagoras* of Isocrates and *Agesilaus* of Xenophon. The *Evagoras* is close in form to a funeral oration and is frankly encomiastic. Isocrates sets out to "praise [Evagoras'] virtue," and gives a leisured and ornate account of his life from which the personality of the deceased scarcely emerges. Two contrasts used by Isocrates were to enjoy a great success. Evagoras is favorably compared with his adversary, the king of Persia, and the verbal portrait of an encomium is declared far superior to the perishable ones of the figurative arts. Plutarch probably knew the *Evagoras*, since the close of it is echoed in the preface of his own "Aratus." Though he no doubt found the style sophistic, he would have approved of the emphasis on virtue and of Isocrates' view that a man's life should be made exemplary to others through the medium of words.

Xenophon, as a historian and a pupil of Socrates, appealed to Plutarch more, and the *Agesilaus* is a primary source for his own Life of the king. Like Isocrates, Xenophon praises his hero's virtue to make it an example to others, but his presentation is much more plausible and direct: Agesilaus is allowed to speak in his own voice, and is not muffled in a cocoon of rhetoric. Xenophon, too, compares his hero favorably with the king of Persia and depreciates physical portraits in comparison to "the memorials of the *psyche.*" He and Isocrates therefore anticipate several of Plutarch's basic ideas: the power of virtue described to inspire virtue in action, the notion of biography as verbal portraiture, and the use of comparison. Plutarch does not, however, take over the idea that biography is praise. Even if in practice he favors his heroes, his aim is a true depiction of their virtues, and his picture of Agesilaus is considerably more shaded than Xenophon's.

Another biography also used by Plutarch as a major source is lost, but it too seems to have affected his conception of his task. When Polybius compares his *Life of Philopoemen* with his treatment of him in the *Histories*, he expresses several ideas similar to Plutarch's. The lives of great men are important for the "correction" of the reader; biography has different aims than history; it may narrate personal matters more fully and the "most conspicuous acts" more summarily (*Histories* 10.21). Like Isocrates and Xenophon, Polybius talks of his biography as "encomiastic" in contrast to the "true account" of his history, while Plutarch—in intention at least—eliminates the gap between biography and truth.

Though no known biographer anticipated Plutarch in writing a series of paired lives, his system of parallels also has antecedents. It has been seen that praise by the use of contrast was a rhetorical device favored by Isocrates and Xenophon, though Plutarch employs it to show not the imbalance of his heroes but their equipoise. This approach is again anticipated by Polybius, who weighs Lycurgus with the elder Scipio, to the advantage of both (*Histories* 10.2); the effect is similar when Cicero implicitly compares himself with Demosthenes in the "Brutus."

The introduction of this device into biography is—on the basis of present evidence—a

PLUTARCH

Roman innovation. The scholar Varro composed a work entitled *Hebdomades* ("Groups of Seven"), in which sets of famous Greeks and Romans were shown by means of pictures with epigrams beneath; this recalls the connection between Plutarch's pairs and the visual arts. About the same time as Varro, Cornelius Nepos wrote brief Lives of distinguished Greeks and Romans and judged them against each other, but it is uncertain whether individually or in groups. This work Plutarch certainly knew, and the form of his biographies must have been influenced by it. It is typical of Plutarch's sympathies that just as his are the first biographies of Roman emperors known to have been written in a series, so the *Parallel Lives* took their most striking formal feature from Roman authors. In form, and to some degree in moral interest, therefore, Plutarch is indebted to earlier biographers.

The content of the *Parallel Lives* comes from quite different sources, however. The greatest influence is philosophy, above all Plato, but also Aristotle. Plutarch must also have known the *Characters* of Aristotle's pupil Theophrastus, which sketch behavior typical of such persons as the "superstitious Man" and sometimes recall Plutarch's habit of seeing people as embodied characteristics. The influence of poetry is also strong. Like every educated Greek, Plutarch knew Homer intimately, and some of his more dashing heroes, like Dion of Syracuse or Antony, have a trace of Homeric vigor. Plutarch had an evident affection for drama, especially the comic poet Menander (incidentally, a pupil of Theophrastus), whose plays he had seen at Athens and on whom he wrote an admiring essay. Again it is possible to be reminded of some of Menander's characters by Plutarch's, for example, the infatuated soldier Polemon in the *Perikeiromene* by Plutarch's Antony. For most English speakers his heroes are familiar from the plays of Shakespeare rather than from his own biographies. That his characters should end up on stage or screen is perhaps only a realization of their true potential.

PLUTARCH'S REPUTATION

The history of Plutarch's reputation is a very fertile subject connected to the whole history of classical culture. It has already been the theme of one general study and several partial ones, especially on his reception in France; but much remains to be done, notably on the Byzantine period, for which only his textual tradition has been investigated. Here will be noted some high points in his fortunes since the Renaissance.

The first of these is the late sixteenth century. Though the first printings had appeared in Italy in the early decades of the century, the edition that laid the foundation for all subsequent ones was produced in Geneva in 1572 by Henri Estienne II (Henricus Stephanus). Plutarch's literary fortunes received a more important impetus from the translations of Jacques Amyot, the *Parallel Lives* in 1559 and the *Moralia* in 1572. Amyot's translations inspired his contemporary Montaigne. Through the translation of the *Parallel Lives* from French by Sir Thomas North in 1579 Amyot also gave Shakespeare the material for several of the historical plays, notably *Coriolanus*, *Julius Caesar*, and *Antony and Cleopatra*.

Though Plutarch remained immensely popular throughout the seventeenth and eighteenth centuries, his reputation rose to another peak during the Enlightenment and the revolutionary period that followed it, from 1775 to 1815. By a curious and yet understandable transformation, he had come to be thought of as a champion of heroism and liberty. Benjamin Franklin says of his father's library, "Plutarch there was in which I read abundantly, and I still think that time spent to great advantage." Plutarch was one of Beethoven's favorite authors. In a letter of 1800 he writes, "I have often cursed my existence; Plutarch taught me resignation." In France, where he had long been established as a classic by Amyot, Plutarch received new honor from Napoleon, and in the series of sculptured panels around the emperor's tomb in the Invalides the one representing Education gives him pride of place. Once more, general and scholarly interest went together. This was the era of several notable editions, by the German Johann Jakob Reiske, the Greek patriot Adamantios Koraïs (printed at Paris), and the Swiss Daniel Wyttenbach, who did more for Plutarch than anyone since Estienne and who was decorated by Napoleon.

However, the scientific age that had already opened was to be unfavorable to Plutarch. He was thought to belong to an age of Greek decadence, and with the exaltation of scientific method his amiable amateurism sank. Once again scholarly study followed the trend of opinion, and its modern revival was begun only toward the end of the nineteenth century by a Hellenist whose interests were not confined to a narrow classicism: Ulrich von Wilamowitz-Moellendorff. Wilamowitz encouraged and aided the editors of the now standard Teubner text, especially of the *Moralia*, of which two volumes are dedicated to him. The scholarly basis for work on Plutarch was further strengthened by the monograph published in 1949 by the editor of the Teubner *Lives*, Konrat Ziegler.

Since World War II both professional and general interest in Plutarch has grown steadily. The underlying reason is perhaps a renewed feeling of kinship with a man who lived in an international world, felt the flow of political and cultural currents, and yet held firm to what he believed.

Selected Bibliography

TEXTS

MORALIA

Moralia, edited by R. Flacelière et al. Paris, 1974– . 3 vols. in 5. The Budé edition, which has Greek text with facing French translation and very full introduction and notes.

Plutarchi Moralia, edited by W. R. Paton et al. Leipzig, 1925–1978. 7 vols. in 12. Vols. 1–4 reprinted 1971, 1972, and 1974. The Teubner text; the standard.

Plutarch's Moralia, edited by F. C. Babbitt et al. Cambridge, Mass., and London, 1927– . 15 vols. in 16. The Loeb Classical Library, which contains Greek text and facing English translation. It is now almost complete, and only the index is lacking. Later volumes, notably vol. 13 by H. Cherniss, constitute full critical texts and commentaries.

VITAE PARALLELAE

Plutarchi Vitae Parallelae, edited by K. Ziegler. Leipzig, 1964–1980. 4 vols. in 7. The standard Teubner text, first edited by C. Lindskog and K. Ziegler and reissued with a very useful index, which has been revised by H. Gärtner.

Vies, edited by R. Flacelière et al. Paris, 1957–1979. 15 vols. The Budé edition, with facing French translation; now complete.

Vitae parallelae, edited by B. Perrin, with index by J. W. Cohoon. Cambridge, Mass., and London, 1914–1926. 11 vols. The Loeb Classical Library, which has only a derivative text and few notes.

TRANSLATIONS

MORALIA

Babbitt, F. C. et al. See above under "Texts."

Goodwin, W. W. *Plutarch's Morals*. Boston, 1874. 5 vols. A revision of the London translation of 1684–1694, with a remarkable introduction by Ralph Waldo Emerson.

Hadas, M. *On Love, the Family and the Good Life: Selected Essays of Plutarch*. New York, 1957.

Warner, R. *Plutarch: Moral Essays*. Harmondsworth, 1971. Five of the most characteristic essays, with notes by D. A. Russell.

PARALLEL LIVES

Clough, A. H. *Plutarch's Lives*. London, 1910. 3 vols. Revision of the so-called Dryden translation in the Everyman Library.

North, T. *Plutarch's Lives*. New York, 1967. 6 vols. Sir Thomas North's classic translation has often been reprinted, most recently in the Tudor Translations, first series, vols. 7–12, a reprint of the 1895 edition.

There are now translations of thirty of the *Lives* in the Penguin Classics.

PLUTARCH

GREEKS

Scott-Kilvert, I. *The Age of Alexander.* Harmondsworth and Baltimore, 1973

——. *The Rise and Fall of Athens.* Harmondsworth and Baltimore, 1960.

ROMANS

Scott-Kilvert, I. *Makers of Rome.* Harmondsworth and Baltimore, 1965.

Warner, R. *Fall of the Roman Republic.* Harmondsworth and Baltimore, 1958.

COMMENTARIES

Apart from the Loeb and Budé texts, there are many modern commentaries on individual works. *L'Année Philologique* is the best guide to commentaries on individual works.

Frost, F. *Themistocles.* Princeton, N. J., 1980.

Manfredini, M., and L. Piccirilli. *Solon.* Verona, 1977. Both this and Frost's commentary above are noteworthy.

Russell, D. A. *Plutarch.* Oxford, 1971. Pp. 164–174 provide a summary but useful list of further works.

INDEXES

For subject indexes see above under "Texts."

Helmbold, W. C., and E. N. O'Neil. *Plutarch's Quotations.* Baltimore and Oxford, 1959. Indexes works quoted directly or cited.

Wyttenbach, D., ed. *Moralia.* 2 vols. Oxford, 1829–1830. Reprinted Hildesheim, 1962. Corrected ed., 2 vols. Leipzig, 1843. This antiquated edition provides the only extant word index.

PRINCIPAL CRITICAL STUDIES

Babut, D. *Plutarque et le Stoicisme.* Paris, 1969. A discussion of much of Plutarch's philosophy.

Hirzel, R. *Plutarch.* Leipzig, 1912. Mainly on Plutarch's later influence.

Jones, C. P. *Plutarch and Rome.* Oxford, 1971. On Plutarch's own historical background.

Jones, R. M. *The Platonism of Plutarch.* Menasha, Wisc., 1916.

Russell, D. A. *Plutarch.* London, 1973. A general guide to Plutarch and to ways of reading him.

——. "Plutarch's Life of Coriolanus." *Journal of Roman Studies* 53:21–28 (1963).

Stadter, P. A. *Plutarch's Historical Methods: An Analysis of the Mulierum Virtutes.* Cambridge, Mass., 1965. Important for Plutarch's reading and historical judgment.

Ziegler, K. *Plutarchos von Chaironeia.* Stuttgart, 1949. The basic work of reference, also published as an article in A. F. Pauly and G. Wissowa, eds., *Realencyclopädie der classischen Altertumswissenschaft,* vol. 21, part 1. Stuttgart, 1951.

C. P. JONES

EPICTETUS

(*ca.* A.D. 50–*ca.* 120)

MARCUS AURELIUS

(A.D. 121–180)

INTRODUCTION

EPICTETUS AND MARCUS Aurelius were described in an essay by Matthew Arnold as "the great masters of morals." The expression has an old-fashioned ring, but there was nothing odd in using it a hundred years ago. By the time Arnold wrote, Epictetus and Marcus Aurelius, through innumerable translations, were little less familiar to many Western readers than the New Testament. Wrongly supposing (as many have done) that Marcus Aurelius was more hostile to the early church than his predecessors, Arnold wrote, "What an affinity for Christianity had this persecutor of the Christians!" Much of his essay consists of an eloquent appreciation of Marcus Aurelius, colored by Arnold's own conviction that the emperor's "melancholy" was in part due to his lacking the "gladness" and "elation" Christianity could have offered him.

A culture whose official religion is Christianity naturally invites comparison between Christian teaching and secular or pagan ideas about morality. This point is made, explicitly at times, by Sir Kenneth Dover in *Greek Popular Morality* (1974). But it was far more common in Ar-nold's day, just as it was easier then to write "masters of morals"; and for very obvious reasons. The contemporary Western world, speaking quite generally, is neither profoundly Christian nor morally coherent. "Masters of morals" is a fine-sounding phrase, but who will now lay claim to it? In certain respects Arnold's England was closer to the Roman Empire (or was so regarded by prominent persons) than it is to our own time. Through Christianity and the enormous influence of Immanuel Kant (1724–1804), the prevailing moral tradition among philosophers has continued to view right actions in ways that often resemble the Stoic ethics of Epictetus and Marcus Aurelius. Contemporary moral philosophy tends to be a rare-fied activity, however, and in its work there are many signs of dissatisfaction with such assumptions as the pure moral (or rational) grounds that supposedly determine a good person's will. Psychology and sociology, new political systems, communal living, drug stimulation, the experience of modern warfare: these are only some of the factors that distance us from Arnold's style of writing. Confidence in divine providence and the perfectibility of rational human beings is not a characteristic of the late twentieth century. The sermon and the moral precept cannot claim to be popular.

In a historical perspective this is new. William Congreve could start the play *Love for Love* with a penniless young man reading Epictetus in his garret, and his fashionable audience would have recognized the name. If, in absolute terms, it was only a tiny minority of Europeans or new Americans who read Epictetus in all seriousness, some of those who did so were influenced by him and influenced their times. There is much that a modern reader may and probably should find implausible or even uncongenial in Epictetus and Marcus Aurelius. Neither of them, it may seem, adequately perceived the creative power of human emotions, the charm of spontaneous behavior, or the delight of aesthetic experience. The Stoic psychology that they accepted can be faulted for being incompatible with ordinary experience. Many will say that Epictetus was just wrong to claim that no one who has seen the good will fail to choose it (*Discourses* 3.3.2–4). Surely Medea was right in Euripides' play when she said, "I know what kind of evils I intend to do, but my anger is stronger than my principles" (1078–1079). Her point against Epictetus seems convincing, but can moral understanding and action really diverge so sharply? In order to answer that question one must try to attend, without modern prejudices, to the reasons Epictetus offers for his view and only then make a judgment. For the purpose of a short essay, it seems best to try to view Epictetus and Marcus Aurelius on their terms, having issued the proviso that their assumptions on many questions will differ from modern attitudes. An evaluation of relative merits would be neither possible nor appropriate.

BIOGRAPHICAL AND INTELLECTUAL CONTEXT

Neither of the subjects of this chapter was a writer in the ordinary sense. Epictetus worked as a Stoic preacher and teacher, communicating, like the Socrates he so admired, solely through oral discourse and dialogue. Marcus Aurelius, emperor of Rome from A.D. 161 to 180, composed nothing for publication during his lifetime. Yet substantial records of their thoughts have survived, and these are justly regarded as a notable part of classical literature in the early Christian period. The peculiar nature of the literary form in which they are expressed requires extended discussion. It can be taken up after Epictetus and Marcus Aurelius themselves have been introduced, the one a slave by birth, the other adopted by Antoninus Pius (Roman emperor, A.D. 138–161) as his imperial successor.

Epictetus and Marcus Aurelius never met. It was from his philosophy teacher and friend Rusticus that Marcus Aurelius borrowed a copy of "the works of Epictetus" (*Meditations* 1.7), books that were greatly to influence his attitudes and the organization of his thoughts. This first encounter with Epictetus was in the 140's, when the philosopher himself was already dead. Epictetus was born during the reign of Nero (A.D. 57–68) in the Greek-speaking city of Hierapolis, in Phrygia (modern Turkey). As the slave of Epaphroditus, a freedman and powerful civil servant of Nero's, he came to Rome. The chronology and other details of much of his life are uncertain; but as a fairly young man he became the friend and disciple of Musonius Rufus, a Stoic teacher and a resolute opponent of imperial tyranny. During this period philosophy often came under suspicion of being subversive, and in about A.D. 92 the emperor Domitian (81–96), whose paranoia increased with age, expelled philosophers from Rome. Epictetus withdrew to Nicopolis, in northern Greece, and seems to have stayed there for the rest of his life (Aulus Gellius, *Attic Nights* 15.11.4–5).

Nicopolis, a city founded by Augustus, was a busy and accessible center. The pupils Epictetus attracted there provided him with an audience to spread the word of his teaching. One of these pupils was the historian of Alexander the

EPICTETUS AND MARCUS AURELIUS

Great, Arrian (Flavius Arrianus), who had a distinguished public career under the emperor Hadrian (117–138). It is to Arrian that we owe our record of Epictetus' discourses, though as early as the time of Marcus Aurelius these could pass under the philosopher's own name.

Epictetus was a philosopher by profession. For the emperor Marcus Aurelius philosophy provided the foundation for his own behavior and inner life. He did not claim any expertise in the subject or capacity to instruct other people. In spite of the enormous differences between the fortunes and careers of these men, however, no figures from antiquity agree more closely in their convictions and in the moral tone of their thoughts. Their mutual sympathy is not simply due to the fact that both were committed to the same philosophy, Stoicism. This explains common themes and doctrines, but Epictetus and Marcus Aurelius are marked off from other Stoic writers like Seneca by their palpable sincerity, commitment, and urgency and by the largely unacademic expression of their thoughts. In their memorable phrases and vivid metaphors they both reflect the rhetorical taste of their times. But they speak a living language in which stylistic excellence is the thought itself and not a contrivance that strains for effect. It is the Greek of the New Testament, not the literary language. Epictetus and Marcus Aurelius were neither Christians nor influenced by Christianity, but no one can fail to recognize common ground between them and the authors of the gospels and epistles.

Stoicism was a Greek philosophical movement that developed after the conquests of Alexander the Great and the expansion of Greek culture throughout the Mediterranean world. Its roots, like those of its rivals Epicureanism and Skepticism, lie in the extensive field of earlier Greek philosophy that had been permanently enriched by the colossal achievements of Plato and Aristotle. For about two hundred years, from 300 to 100 B.C., the post-Aristotelian philosophers debated unceasingly with one another and shaped the systems of

thought that are recorded in the philosophical writings of Cicero. Physical speculation, theory of knowledge, and logic formed a prominent part of their inquiries. But all or most philosophers of the time were agreed that their activity had one fundamental goal—to provide a foundation for happiness, living well, and tranquillity of mind. Traditional Greek and Roman religion, with its emphasis on domestic and civic rituals, offered little to guide moral choice or to relieve emotional and mental distress. Stoicism and Epicureanism, by providing complete explanations of the world that incorporated theology, succeeded in satisfying many people's religious aspirations as well as their more intellectual demands.

By the time of Cicero the creative period of the new Hellenistic philosophies was over. But this did not diminish their cultural importance as established systems of belief. Not only Lucretius and Cicero, but also Vergil and Horace reflect their dissemination, especially that of Stoicism. A Roman did not need to be a Greek speaker to sense the relevance of that philosophy to his own concerns. When Cato ended his opposition to Julius Caesar at Utica by taking his own life (46 B.C.), his patriotic suicide united Roman ideals with the Stoic doctrine that the truly rational man is always free to decide the time of his end. For republican-minded Romans of the early empire Cato became a paradigm of traditional rectitude and Stoic virtue. What Stoicism lost in innovation and intellectual edge at this time, it gained in practical and political significance and influence. The victims of Nero's and Domitian's purges included many aristocratic Romans who professed themselves Stoics. It is all the more remarkable that a Stoic was to sit on the imperial throne in the next century.

If Stoicism was a threat to tyrannical rulers, this stemmed from its general principles rather than a doctrinal opposition to autocracy. Taking the world as a whole to be like a well-ordered state, the Stoics taught that nothing is of ultimate value to a man except his moral integrity.

All external contingencies are part of the divine economy and indifferent with respect to virtue. Yet if a Stoic's moral purpose is endangered by outward things, he will not compromise. Epictetus constantly insists that a man's ultimate allegiance is to god or to his own moral character, and in ways that do not ignore the possibility of civil disobedience:

> god is within and so is your own divine spirit . . . to this god you also should swear the oath just as soldiers do to Caesar. . . . And what will you swear? Never to disobey, never to criticize or complain at anything given by god, never to go against your own purpose when you have to do or suffer something. Can this oath resemble that of the soldiers? There they swear to honor no man above Caesar; but here we swear to honor ourselves above all!
>
> (*Moral Discourses* 1.14.14–17)

It was this philosophy, expressed in this form, that caught the imagination of the young Marcus Aurelius. As a patrician Roman he had the customary early education in grammar and rhetoric. His tutor in the latter subject, which embraced literary studies quite generally, was Marcus Cornelius Fronto, whose reputation for eloquence was second to none. In the early nineteenth century, Italian manuscripts were discovered containing considerable parts of Fronto's correspondence with Marcus Aurelius, a correspondence that was maintained up to the older man's death. These letters cast a warm light on the characters of both men and the affection of their relationship. But they also show how Fronto and Marcus Aurelius differed in their assessments of the value of rhetoric and philosophy. Fronto's literary interests were antiquarian and lexical to a point that strikes the modern reader as pedantic. He could write a letter urging Marcus Aurelius to strike out the word *dictio* from a speech, telling him never to use it in place of *oratio* (*Epistolae*, Haines ed., vol. 1, p. 189), and he would plead the need for philosophers to use literary artifice (p. 101). Marcus Aurelius did his best to cultivate the rhetorical skills that Fronto advocated. But in

one letter he makes it plain that his choice is philosophy:

> As for what you gave me to write, I haven't given even a moment to the work, though I was quite free. Ariston's books [one of the earliest Stoic philosophers] are treating me well just now, and badly too, at the same time. When they teach me how to improve then of course they treat me well. But when they show how far my character falls short of this improvement, your pupil keeps blushing and is angry with himself that at twenty-five my mind has still not drunk fine attitudes and purer principles. . . . But now I will put something together; and as an Athenian orator advised his fellow-countrymen that the laws must sometimes be allowed to sleep, I will make up with Ariston's books and let them rest for a while, and after reading Tully's [Cicero's] short speeches I will turn all my attention to that dramatic poet of yours. But I will write on only one of the two sides [of a question], for Ariston will surely never stay asleep to allow me to defend both of them.
>
> (pp. 217 ff.)

This letter nicely reveals Marcus Aurelius' sense of humor and lack of pomposity, but it shows in its final sentence that he declines the orator's stock in trade—the ability to speak for and against the same issue. Fronto's literary tasks for him are gently mocked, just as his tutor could jest at Marcus Aurelius' philosophy, "I thank the gods that they have kept you safe and unharmed. I am sure that you were not disturbed since I know your principles. But I was utterly shocked, however much you sages laugh at me" (pp. 197 ff.).

Looking back on his benefactors toward the end of his life (*Meditations* 1), Marcus Aurelius turns repeatedly to those who convinced him of the value of philosophy. He saw this manifested in the lives of his adoptive father and many others, but in expressing his indebtedness to Rusticus he emphasizes this philosopher's effect in diverting him from the models esteemed by Fronto, "giving up rhetoric and poetry and elegant style . . . writing letters unaffectedly" (*Meditations* 1.7). He also thanks the gods for his lack of progress in literary pursuits (1.17.23). Marcus Aurelius was not being disingenuous, but his *Meditations* are actually a remarkable combination of philosophy and literary facility.

Through the teaching and example of others and through their belief in its essential truth and humanity, Epictetus and Marcus Aurelius wholeheartedly embraced the doctrines of Stoicism. Each in his own way, however, was an interpreter and creative exponent of the system he had adopted, not an orthodox exegete or learned essayist in the tradition of Seneca or Plutarch. Epictetus and Marcus Aurelius compel our attention as much by how they address us as by what they say; and how they address us is unlike the manner of other moralists. Ancient literature has its own styles of sermonizing; much of what passes there for edification has a dull ring of literary models windily repeated. Epictetus and Marcus Aurelius are repetitious but never tedious, sanctimonious, or posturing. These rare qualities cannot be easily explained, but have much to do with the circumstances of their lives as well as indefinable characteristics of personality. Bound up with these is the quite unusual nature of the literary form of their work. Following this introduction we may now look more closely at the *Moral Discourses* of Epictetus and then pass on to Marcus Aurelius' *Meditations*.

EPICTETUS AND ARRIAN

Arrian explained his role as Epictetus' publicist in a letter to an otherwise unknown Lucius Gellius that appears at the beginning of our manuscripts of the *Discourses:*

> I have not composed the discourses of Epictetus in the way that such compositions might be made, nor did I myself give them out to the public; in fact composition is not how I describe them. But whatever I heard him say I wrote down verbatim, as far as I could, trying to keep it as records, for my own future use, of his way of thought and un-

inhibited speech. So they are what you would expect one man to say to another spontaneously and not compositions intended for posterity to read. Such being their character they have somehow or other passed out into the public without my knowledge or intention. But it matters little to me if I shall be regarded as incapable of composition; and to Epictetus it doesn't matter in the slightest if anyone should despise his discourses, since in uttering them he was clearly desiring nothing except to set his hearers' minds on the best things. So if these discourses achieve that at least, they would have the effect, I think, which the discourses of philosophers ought to have. But if not, those who read them should realize that when Epictetus spoke them the hearer could not fail to experience just what Epictetus intended him to. If the discourses by themselves do not achieve this, I may be to blame, or perhaps it is unavoidable.

What does this elaborate apology mean? It has generally been taken quite literally, but that begs too many questions. In theory Arrian could have taken down Epictetus' words in shorthand, but for a variety of reasons he is unlikely to have done so. Writers of his time (or of any other) were not obliged to tell the whole truth about their methods of composition. His self-effacement cannot be understood quite as simply as he professes. While the majority of the *Discourses* take the form of sermons spoken by Epictetus in his own person, some are presented as dialogues between him and a pupil or a visitor, with Arrian discreetly setting the scene. "When someone consulted him about how he could persuade his brother to stop resenting him he said . . ." (1.15.1; compare 1.11, 1.14). It is implausible to suppose that Arrian was always present during such encounters, though Epictetus may have reported the gist of them to his class.

For all their impression of spontaneity the *Discourses* show some evidence of literary organization. They also vary greatly in length and complexity from a simple moral message occupying one page to an elaborate lecture on freedom that is thirty times as long. None of this tallies well with the idea that Arrian has merely recorded what he heard. But apart from the actual form of the *Discourses* Arrian clearly conceived of himself as working within a familiar tradition. He was far from being the first ancient writer to record the words of a great teacher. In the *Discourses*, as in all his writings, he wanted himself to be regarded as the Xenophon of his time. Xenophon had written books purporting to give Socrates' conversations with various people, and Epictetus, as he emerges through Arrian, was not only an admirer of Socrates but someone whom Arrian could expect to be taken for the modern Socrates. Arrian's interest in modeling himself on Xenophon went so far that he actually took the older writer's name.

On the basis of such considerations it has been argued that we should not speak of the "works of Epictetus" at all. Rather, we possess compositions by Arrian himself, *literary* works written to give the appearance of being Epictetus' own words. According to this view, Arrian was genuinely concerned to publicize the teaching of Epictetus, but he did so in a form that admits of his own invention and idealization and that also derives as much from earlier literary models as it does from anything Epictetus actually said.

Such an interpretation strains credulity little less than a purely factual reading of Arrian's preface. He had no reason to declare his purpose as he did unless it genuinely reflected his belief that the real speaker in his writings is the real man Epictetus. He could have employed scribes to take down Epictetus' words, but more likely he made notes at the time himself and used his memory to fill them out. No doubt he worked up his material into a more finished form. Here and there he will have composed more freely. In some cases he may have relied on reports by fellow pupils. But the repetitious style, the brilliance of the dialogue, the philosophical command and moral earnestness—these are not the voice of Arrian, whose other writings seem to betray little or no commitment to Stoicism. The point need not be labored. For Arrian Epictetus was indeed the Socrates of his

day, and he could think of himself as a Roman Xenophon; but that does not prevent us from continuing to read Epictetus as we read Arrian.

EPICTETUS' DISCOURSES: *CRITICAL ANALYSIS*

One discourse by Epictetus is much like another. The same moral themes are constantly repeated no matter what may be the particular question of each discourse or the circumstances of his real or imagined interlocutor. Such repetitions and the absence of any arguments progressively developed in the sequence of discourses would be a blemish in a literary work. Epictetus, however, is speaking and teaching for the occasion. The work Arrian compiled should not be read from cover to cover like a normal book. Epictetus is better approached by sampling, by a close study of one or two discourses that can be picked almost at random. Although his themes are relatively static and unlikely to surprise the reader who knows him well, Epictetus has an imagination and power of illustration that offer something new in every discourse. His repetitiousness as a teacher, moreover, is quite deliberate: "Have you not been told time and again that you ought to eradicate desire completely?" (4.4.33). Regarding his lecture room as a hospital (3.23.30), he was no more concerned than a doctor would be with novel cures. Tireless insistence on his pupils' need to practice and train themselves was vital to his conception of the philosopher's task.

Here, then, is one short discourse in its entirety to exemplify his thought and style. It has the title (probably provided by Arrian) "What Should Be Exchanged for What?"

(1) Have this at hand, whenever you lose an external possession, "What are you getting in its place?" And if it's worth more, never say, "I've been deprived." No deprivation in getting a horse for a donkey, an ox for a sheep, a noble action for a tiny sum of money, genuine peace for pointless conversation, and decency for foul language. (2)

If you bear this in mind you will everywhere keep your character in the right state. If not, realize that you are wasting your time and that you are going to spill and overturn everything that matters to you now. It takes little to destroy and overturn everything, just a slight deviation from reason. (3) To overturn the ship the helmsman doesn't need the same degree of preparation as he does to keep it safe; but if he turns into the wind a little he is done for. Done for, even if he does nothing deliberately but happens to let his attention slip.

That's what it's like here too. You've only got to nod off and everything acquired up to now is gone. (4) So pay attention to your states of mind, keep a watchful eye on them. It's no little thing that you are guarding, but decency, integrity, consistency, equanimity, the absence of pain, fear, and disturbance—to sum it up, freedom. (5) For what are you about to sell these things? Look at the value of what you are getting in exchange. "But I shall not get anything like that for what I am selling." When you have got something, look at what you are taking in place of what you are giving up. "I take modesty, he a tribunate; he takes a praetorship, I decency. But I don't make a big noise where it's out of place. I will not stand up where I shouldn't. For I am free and a friend of god so as to obey him willingly. I shouldn't lay claim to anything else, not body, or property, or public position, or reputation—quite simply, nothing. For he does not want me to claim them. If he had wanted me to, he would have made them good for me. But he has not done so. I cannot therefore disobey his instructions."

(6) Guard your own good in everything; and for the rest be satisfied with just what you have been given so long as you can exercise good judgment in it. If not, you will have an unhappy life; you will be thwarted and frustrated. (7) These are the laws dispatched from god; these are his commandments. It is in these that you should become an expert; make yourself subordinate to these, and not the laws of Masurius and Cassius.

(4.3)

Arrian has four ways of beginning a discourse: an imperative in the second-person singular (as here), a question raised by or put to Epictetus, a narrative generally introducing discussion between Epictetus and a pupil or visitor, and a moral statement that is to be proved or examined. The last of these is his most common practice, especially in books 1 and 2, but in the two later books he most frequently gives Epictetus an imperatival opening (for example, 4.2, 4.4, 4.12: "whenever you slightly let your attention go, don't imagine ..."; 3.17: "whenever you blame providence, consider ..."). The "you" whom he addresses, even when identified with an individual or type of person, is everyman, so to speak, and does not exclude himself. Epictetus uses dialogue as a teaching device, not as a way of indicating that he is holier than thou.

The first section of 4.3 (the discourse translated above) takes up a Stoic theme of central importance. "External" possessions are morally indifferent; they do not belong to a man or contribute to his true happiness or unhappiness. How we use such things is not morally indifferent, however (see 2.6.1–2). A man shows his moral character in his judgments and actions concerning external possessions. Epictetus connects this standard doctrine with one of his favorite psychological points, which may be called his theory of descriptions. "If you lose a possession don't say you've been deprived." The concept of deprivation implies impoverishment, losing something of real value. If you believe you have been deprived, your state of mind will be that of someone who really has been deprived; but, Epictetus maintains, the belief is false. By misdescribing your condition in regard to what you no longer have, you suffer needless emotional distress and exercise incorrect moral judgment. In his examples, "a horse for a donkey" and the rest, he moves from mundane barter to exchanges in which we lose something that might incorrectly be judged worthwhile (telling a joke) and gain moral integrity. Actions and passions, as he repeatedly maintains, depend on the judgments we make (1.11.33): it was not the death of Patroclus itself that made Achilles grieve but the fact that he wanted to grieve. The description we give of things makes all the difference to our peace of mind; call a crowd of people a mob or a nuisance and you will be ill-tempered. You can be content if you call it a festival (1.12.20–21).

In the second section of our passage Epictetus applies his thesis concerning external possessions to his principal concern throughout all the discourses, the maintenance of moral character in the right state. All his teaching seeks to give instruction on this fundamental Stoic doctrine. Moral judgments are the only sphere in which every man enjoys complete freedom (see 1.1.7 ff.). Men differ in their innate propensities (1.2.5 ff.), but all of us by instruction and practice are capable of founding our lives on rational judgments that accord with the proper nature of man. Crucial to these is Epictetus' first point in this discourse, the understanding that every man should value moral integrity above external possessions. Now he affirms the foundation of moral integrity on correctness of judgment, indicating that only small misjudgments are sufficient to misdirect a life and wreck all that it represents. The Christian notion of temptation looks similar, but as a Stoic Epictetus is not invoking any principle of cosmic evil or original sin. We are perfectible by our own efforts if only we keep our judgments straight by the standard of what is truly valuable.

In order to make his point more vividly Epictetus draws on a familiar image (section 3). Similes and metaphors taken from everyday life pervade his work and lighten, just as they reinforce, the moral message. Athletics, political life, mythology, commerce: these are only some of the dominant fields from which he gathered his images. Many of them, but not all, have a long tradition both in poetry and in popular preaching. Here the picture of the helmsman challenges us to regard life itself as a journey that demands the most watchful attention. The kinds of false judgments that can overturn the unwary traveler are exemplified in nearly all Epictetus' discourses.

The fourth section opens with a further imperative, "pay attention to your *phantasiai*," translated here as "states of mind." This too is a way in which Epictetus repeatedly expresses the essence of the moral life. Translators generally render *phantasiai* as "sense impressions," but this is misleading in two ways. A *phantasia* is any mental state or state of awareness, not confined to objects that we perceive with the senses. Secondly, "sense impressions" suggests sounds, colors, and so forth, which are the supposedly uninterpreted evidence of the sense organs; but in Epictetus' usage here, and frequently elsewhere, *phantasiai* stand for our view of things, which will include the judgments and values we set on them. That is why he stresses the need for watchfulness. All men can recognize a precious stone. The moral questions are "What use do we make of this perception?" "What value do we set on it?"; reason is our faculty for making proper use of *phantasiai* (1.20.5). The proper use of reason is the only human good. It is summed up in the word "freedom," which Epictetus uses in an exclusively moral sense. To be free is to be a man and not a slave, where enslavement refers not to social position but to absence of moral autonomy. Only in our judgments are we always and unequivocally free, and it is incumbent on us to choose this freedom. Yet we typically reject it in favor of subservience to unfulfillable desires and external possessions (see 1.1.14 ff.). Freedom in Epictetus' conception is both a positive state of wanting to act well at all times and the absence of the emotional disturbance that accompanies misdirected fears and desires.

Returning to his main theme in the fifth section, Epictetus shifts from the second-person singular to the first-person, but he is almost certainly not speaking of himself. He is imagining how someone should speak who knows that moral virtue is to be preferred to high rank in society and is contrasting him with the average man who would think otherwise. Such abrupt changes in his dialogue style can be difficult to interpret, and their difficulty is evidence of Arrian's accurate reporting. In oral delivery, gesture and tone of voice would have helped to clarify the progression of such sections. Epictetus' key word is again "freedom," which derives its particular force from the difference between choosing to act well (obedience to god) and being controlled by desires for nothing truly worthwhile: a man driven by worldly ambition to "make a big noise" to gain recognition is slavish. We may take wealth or high rank if it comes our way; to claim it as ours is to err fundamentally in our conception of the good for man.

Happiness and moral freedom, then, are one (section 6). "It is impossible for that which is by nature free to be disturbed or impeded by anything except itself" (1.19.7). Epictetus calls such principles divine commandments (section 7), contrasting them with human legislation, just as he contrasted high human office (being tribune or praetor) with moral excellence. Again the tone can remind us of the New Testament, but Epictetus' conception is ethical or an appeal to natural religion rather than the Christian notion of a transcendent deity. In his philosophy a man is "a fragment of god"; "you carry god within yourself" (2.8.11 ff.). To be obedient to human reason, to one's own proper nature, is to obey god.

This study of one short discourse will serve as an introduction to Epictetus as Stoic philosopher. His methods of argument and compelling manner need further illustration. How does he regard his audience and himself? What does he hope to teach them? Where does he stand in relation to intellectual and literary tradition?

THE PHILOSOPHY OF EPICTETUS

The Epictetus whom Arrian encountered regarded himself as an old man (1.10.13); but though self-deprecating (2.6.24), he was clearly renowned as a teacher and visited or consulted by many prominent people. Recent studies have shown that his pupils were largely upper-class young men who would expect to succeed, like Arrian, in public life; and this helps to explain the treatment of moral themes in terms that would have more practical relevance to potential senators than to slaves or tradesmen. Examples of how one should evaluate a consul-

ship, for instance, or threats of imprisonment or execution recur time and again. They would be otiose if Epictetus were addressing a low-born audience. "Today a man was chatting to me about a priesthood of Augustus" (1.19.26); someone says, "I am a senator and friend of Caesar; I have been consul and I have many slaves" (4.1.8).

The starting point of Epictetus' teaching was very likely the reading and exposition of a passage from a famous Stoic philosopher (1.26.1; 2.14.1; 2.21.11), but he constantly warns against mistaking academic knowledge for moral expertise. A man should pride himself not on solving the "Master" argument (a notorious problem in logic) but on resisting sexual desire (2.18.18). The meaning of "education" is understanding that we are answerable for our moral purpose but not for our bodies, our relations, or our country (1.22.9). Facility in formal argument is necessary only insofar as it contributes to the moral life (1.27). If someone tells us that death is an evil, we must have at hand the argument that real evil should be avoided, but death is simply something inevitable.

Open-ended inquiry or theoretical questions such as the basis of sense perception (1.27.17) did not belong to Epictetus' conception of philosophy. In many of his discourses he simply assumes knowledge of basic Stoic principles and exhorts his hearers to apply them in their lives. But the exhortation can properly be called philosophical because it is always based on reasons and inferences from propositions that, he assumes, any reasonable man must grant to be true and perspicuous. All men have conceptions of good and evil (2.11.3), but they differ in their opinions about what things are good and the opposite. The task of philosophy is to examine and confirm the criteria for settling such disputes (2.11.23-24). That rationality, as conceived by the Stoics, must be this criterion follows from the fact that we are men and not beasts. If Epicurus claims that bodily pleasure is the good, we have only to point out that his doctrine fails to square with his own behavior—a life devoted to reasoning and seeking to improve the human condition (1.20.17; 2.20.6 ff.).

Early Stoics had divided the subject matter of philosophy into three fields—logic, physics, and ethics—all of which, they insisted, were blended together in a well-ordered whole. Epictetus, we have seen, declined interest or expertise in technicalities of the first two subjects, but their general importance to him seems to be shown not only in isolated remarks but also in a three-part scheme of moral training that he mentions several times (1.4.11; 3.2.1; 3.12.12–15). In order to make progress: (1) we need to train ourselves emotionally, so that we never fail to get what we want, or get what we do not want; (2) we need to base our conduct on correct reasoning, so that we always aim at the right things; and (3) we need to train our faculty of judgment so that we avoid error in our acceptance or interpretation of evidence, propositions, or arguments. Clearly all three of these fields of training or study are ethical and reinforce each other, but it is probably right to interpret them by reference to the early Stoic division into logic, physics, and ethics. Epictetus makes it plain that his third topic (the most advanced, in his view) corresponds to logic and is mistakenly limited by contemporary philosophers to technical problems (3.2.6). The second topic fits ethics in the strict sense, which leaves physics as the subject that would match his first topic, emotional training. That will seem curious only if we regard physics in its modern scope. For a Stoic, physics embraced the study of nature quite generally, including theology, psychology, and anthropology. Epictetus frequently introduces general principles of Stoic physics, and in contexts where they do indeed give support to his conception of the proper emotional training.

"A man is only a tiny part of the whole" (1.12.26; 2.5.25). "The universe has been organized by god in the best possible way" (1.6.1). "Nothing is in our own power except our reasoning faculty" (1.1.7). Principles such as these lend theoretical backing to Epictetus' con-

stantly repeated insistence that we can be content and always achieve what we desire if only we submit ourselves willingly to the unavoidable and right course of events and desire only what it is within our power to have. Marcus Aurelius enunciates the physical laws on almost every page of his *Meditations*. Epictetus does so less readily, but both men see the closest of connections between cosmic order and human values.

In his methods of teaching Epictetus is at his most effective as a shock psychologist. His *Discourses* abound in acute analysis of mental states and problems. Suppose a man wants to change his mode of life but fears that old drinking companions will think badly of him for avoiding their company. Well, says Epictetus, he must make a choice. He can't have it both ways. "If you don't drink with those you used to drink with you can't be liked by them as much as before; so choose whether you want to be a boozer and likeable to them or sober and not likeable" (4.2.7). In presenting the demands of the moral life he uses metaphors and examples that may alternate between hyperbole and bathos but rarely fail to seize attention and banish complacency. A man is really making moral progress if he bathes "as someone who keeps his word" and eats "as a man of integrity" (1.4.20). An adulterer is as useless as a *man* as a cracked saucepan, and deserves to be thrown on the dung hill (2.4.4). A "coward and weakling" is really only a "corpse" (1.9.33). Life itself is a game, or a military command, or an athletic contest: Socrates played the ball well, though it consisted of imprisonment, exile, drinking poison (2.5.19). "This man has won the first round. What will he do in the second? What if it's blazing hot? What if he's at Olympia?" (1.18.21).

Following the model of Cynic philosophers, who strongly influenced him, Epictetus uses the word "man" as what we should strive to be but most of us are not. We tend to act as if we were "runaway slaves" (1.29.62); but we should consider "who we are" (2.10.1). Of himself and his pupils he says: "when we can't even fulfill the profession of man we take on that of the philosopher besides; that's a load like someone unable to lift ten pounds wanting to hold the stone of Atlas" (2.9.22). Yet as our models and heroes we should take Socrates or the Cynic Diogenes. The tone of admonition can be caustic, the standard of excellence is utterly uncompromising, but those who are to be judged by it are ourselves and not others. As one interlocutor says:

> They are thieves and robbers. What is being a thief and a robber? They have gone astray regarding good and evil. Should one get angry with them or pity them? Point out the error and you will see how they give up their mistakes. But if they don't see, they have nothing better than their own opinion.
>
> (1.18.3–4)

That is the Socratic thesis that no one does wrong deliberately. Perhaps it seems naive only if one has a naive view of moral knowledge.

Matthew Arnold—and he is by no means alone—observed that "it is impossible to rise from reading Epictetus or Marcus Aurelius without a sense of constraint and melancholy, without feeling that the burden laid upon man is well-nigh greater than he can bear" (*Essays in Criticism*, p. 346). The reader must judge for himself. Epictetus does not stretch out a helping hand, perhaps. He gives us reasons for thinking we have the means to help ourselves. His strength as a moralist lies in the fact that he tells us what those reasons are. He pays us the great compliment of presenting an image of humanity that is intelligible in the light of reason. Courtesy demands that we offer him reasons if we reject it.

EPICTETUS AND THE GREEK DIATRIBE

The ancient moralist par excellence was Socrates, as Arrian and Epictetus acknowl-

edged. In doing so they were also defining their own activities as contributions to the diatribe tradition that derived much of its original character from Xenophon's portrayal of Socratic discourses. Nearly 500 years separate Xenophon from Arrian. During this time, especially among Cynics (followers of Diogenes), it became common practice for philosophers to give public lectures or sermons on moral themes, known in Greek as "diatribes." Popular preaching was the special province of the Cynics, who strongly influenced Stoic ethics both in the earliest phase of Stoicism and at the time of Epictetus. As a Stoic who admired the moral radicalism of the Cynics (though he deprecated their more extravagant external gestures), Epictetus in his discourses exemplifies a tradition that was completely familiar to his audience.

Enough is known at second hand to form some impression of earlier diatribes. The philosopher took a theme, such as exile or pleasure, and sought to convince the audience by the force and liveliness of his style. Vivid examples, anecdotes, quotations from well-known poets, sardonic humor, and caustic attack were typical of the genre. All of these are to be found in Epictetus.

Here for comparison is one of the few surviving sayings of Bion of Borysthenes (third century B.C.), the most influential exponent of the early diatribe:

> Just as we leave a house whenever the landlord, having failed to collect the rent, removes the door, removes the roof tiles, blocks up the well, so we also leave the body whenever nature, who has rented it to us, removes eyes, ears, hands, and feet. I will not stay behind, but I will leave life just as I leave a drinking party, with no complaints.
>
> (*Bion of Borysthenes* F68, Kindstrand ed.)

The theme of this diatribe is self-sufficiency. Contrast with Bion's style this extract from Epictetus' elder contemporary and teacher, Musonius Rufus:

> When an exile was distressed at his plight, he comforted him in this way. "How could someone with any sense be distressed at exile? It doesn't deprive us at all of water or earth or air, nor of the sun and the other stars. Nor does it deprive us of human society, for one can share in that anywhere and everywhere. If we are deprived of some portion of earth and human society, what's terrible about that?"
> (*C. Musonius Rufus, Reliquiae* 9.4.11, Hense ed.)

The style is flat, the thought sincere but commonplace. Here is Epictetus saying the same thing, but in a very different way:

> My little body is nothing to me. Its parts are nothing to me. Death? Let it come when it wants. . . . Exile? And where can anyone expel me to? Outside the universe he cannot. Wherever I go away, the sun's there, the moon's there, stars are there, dreams, omens, fellowship with the gods.
> (3.22.21)

Exile was a stock moral theme. Musonius and Epictetus drew upon a common tradition for their demonstration of its indifference. Yet Epictetus' voice recalls the urgent personal manner of Bion, quite different from the mild but unimpressive Musonius.

Should we conclude, then, that Epictetus harked back to an older style of diatribe? That would go beyond our evidence. The passage quoted from Musonius is certainly a typical one, and to that extent it is easy to see why his work has been neglected in contrast with that of Epictetus. Musonius' teaching also comes to us largely through the writings of a pupil named Lucius. This man quite clearly has not attempted to retain the manner of oral delivery. So Musonius may have influenced Epictetus more directly than the present form of both their works suggests. But subjective impressions as well as contemporaries' judgments (Arrian and Marcus Aurelius) justify us in regarding Epictetus as the outstanding pagan moralist of the Roman Empire. If he was not strikingly original in his thought or in his style, the combination of them appears to be entirely his own.

MARCUS AURELIUS' MEDITATIONS
Textual History and Form

The books commonly called the *Meditations* of Marcus Aurelius are unlike any other classical text. Their authenticity has never been doubted, but it is virtually certain that the emperor wrote them for himself alone without any thought of their being copied by scribes and made available as published works. *Meditations* is a title based upon the phrase "The emperor Marcus Antoninus' books 'to himself,'" which was included in the Greek manuscript, now lost, that Xylander edited for Andreas Gesner in the first printed edition (Zurich, 1558). "To himself" or "meditations" is an apt description of the work, but Marcus Aurelius is no more likely to have given the books a title than a modern diarist. In origin the *Meditations* appear to be thoughts and memoranda that the emperor wrote in his own hand for his self-improvement and guidance.

Many considerations support this assessment. First, scarcely anything seems to be known of the work before the ninth century A.D. The orator Themistius probably refers to it in A.D. 364 under the description "The Precepts of Marcus"; and that is all until the bishop Arethas tells a correspondent that he has "an old copy of the emperor Marcus' invaluable book." This obscurity would be extraordinary if Marcus Aurelius were known to have been writing a book in the ordinary sense. Secondly, his own remarks in the *Meditations* strongly imply that he had no aspirations to compose a work of philosophy designed for the instruction of others. Finally, and most important, the form of the *Meditations* belies any systematic treatment of themes or literary plan. In Xylander's lost manuscript they were organized into twelve books of numbered sections, but there is no means of knowing how exactly this corresponds to Marcus Aurelius' own arrangements or stages of writing. It is likely that the *Meditations* were mainly written down during the last years of his life and that they were found among his papers when he died. We do not know whether they are complete, but their present form almost certainly owes something to one or more editorial hands.

Theories that the *Meditations* are fragmentary remains of a would-be moral treatise have been adequately refuted by modern scholars. Parts of the work have coherence and literary finish; some pages seem to contain mere jottings. The more polished and unified passages can be perfectly well explained in terms of the emperor's personal circumstances. Sometimes he had the leisure or inclination to develop a train of thought; at other times he wrote more briefly and obscurely. Many of the *Meditations* are as memorable for their style as their thought; but that occasions no surprise in a "man thoroughly trained in the art of verbal expression."

Here is a summary of the first meditations of the fifth book, selected without omissions as an illustration of the way Marcus Aurelius addresses himself. He begins in the manner of Epictetus by telling himself to "have at hand" the thought, "I get up to do a man's work." He is tempted to linger in bed, but a sluggish life is not what his nature as a man demands. Self-reproach, contrasting his sleepy inclinations with animals' behavior and with men who give up food and sleep for petty pursuits, leads to the question, "Do you think public affairs are more trivial and less deserving of attention?"

These thoughts are developed in a full page of Greek. They are followed by a single sentence: "How easy it is to drive out and erase every disturbing or uncongenial state of mind and at once enjoy perfect peace" (5.2). Plainly a change of mood and circumstances explains the difference of this bland serenity from the previous reflections. In the next two meditations the emperor dwells again on nature, associating his own essence as a rational man with "universal nature" conceived, in Stoic terms, as the necessary and providential course of events. Following nature in these two senses, he tells himself to ignore critical remarks of other people that could pervert his moral judgments (5.3). He will travel on through nature, which has sustained his life, until he draws his final breath (5.4). Self-admonition returns in the more personal tone of the next meditation. Nature has not endowed him with a sharp mind, but that is no excuse for him to complain. Nor does his slow wit prevent him from displaying all manner of fine moral qualities; yet, he tells himself, "You are still willing to stay below them" (5.5).

Concern with the performance of good actions continues in his following reflections (5.6), but the tone is now more reflective and detached. He has been asking himself, as a moral philosopher might, whether the doer of a good act should chalk it up as a credit mark. He replies by means of analogy, a favorite method of his thought. A good act should be unselfconscious, like the due fulfillment of its nature by a plant or an animal. His next remark can be given in full: "A prayer of the Athenians: 'rain, rain, dear Zeus, upon the crops and fields of the Athenians.' Either one should pray thus simply and freely, or not at all" (5.7). Marcus Aurelius liked the quotation and penned it as a model for himself.

The following meditations are more elaborate and philosophically complex. One of his favorite themes is the willing acceptance of everything that happens. He develops this in a medical analogy (5.8): as a doctor gives different prescriptions for different people's health, so Marcus Aurelius tells himself to regard all events as contributions to the health or harmony of the whole world order. Perhaps the medical image stayed in his mind, for the next meditation is an injunction to regard philosophy as a medical treatment rather than as a schoolmaster (5.9). His thought has returned to his earlier sense of fallibility, yet less harshly than sometimes. He should not despair over his lapses but remind himself that the moral virtues are more delightful than pleasure.

Such confidence gives way to an utterly pessimistic assessment of the world, ameliorated only by courageous resignation (5.10). Our judgments are unstable, and the things we encounter are as disgusting as they are transient. He can see nothing to rouse his enthusiasm. All a man can do is await his end patiently, comforted with two thoughts only: "Nothing will happen to me that is not in accord with the nature of the universe"; and "It is in my power to do nothing contrary to my own divine spirit." It appears likely that the Stoic emperor's moods veered sharply between contentment, self-criticism, and world-weariness. In the next meditation his more positive tone of moral admonition returns: "For what purpose am I now using my soul?" (5.11). Is he living as a child, a tyrant, or a beast? The impersonal, reflective philosopher reappears in the following meditation, where he contrasts moral goods with wealth and conventional values (5.12). Then (clearly on a different occasion) he comments quite unemotionally on his own mortality, setting this within the context of Stoic physics. The universe is a sequence of changes of imperishable material. Out of those changes he came to be, and his own parts will be changed into other parts of the universe (5.13). Next, he impersonally asserts the identity of reason and right action (5.14).

Themes and Style

In all of these meditations Marcus Aurelius writes as a would-be Stoic. He recalls Epictetus in tone and doctrine. But Epictetus was addressing a variety of men. Marcus Aurelius is concerned with himself. This does not make the *Meditations* egotistical in any discreditable sense. Marcus Aurelius constantly has his mind on the needs of other men, the tolerance he should show toward them, and the supreme importance of benevolence and justice; but the great interest and effectiveness of his work lie in its private character. The moral themes he selects are those that mattered most deeply to

him. His repetitiveness is indicative of his prevailing states of mind. The way in which he writes provides remarkable knowledge of a man who was unusually sensitive and who also possessed greater political power than anyone else alive at his time.

Many of his characteristic thoughts have already appeared in the passages summarized above. He repeatedly represents himself as the mutable part of a harmonious whole, directs himself to consider the providential ordering of things, and sets his own nature as a man within the context of a divinely structured cosmic nature. Such emphasis on the relationship between the individual self and the world at large is entirely Stoic. Among Stoic writers Marcus Aurelius dwells upon it far more than Epictetus and others. Its importance to him seems a sure reflection of his role as a ruler and of the need to buttress himself against disappointments and frustrations.

Related to this physical definition of himself is his obsession with time and its passage. "Don't waste what's left of your life in thinking about others, except when you can connect them with some common good" (3.4). "Continue to bear in mind that each man lives only this present, a mere moment" (3.10). "Consider, by way of example, the times of Vespasian, and you will see all these [or "the same"] things: men marrying, rearing children, being ill, dying, fighting, celebrating, trading, farming, flattering . . . loving, hoarding, longing for consulships. . . . That life of theirs no longer exists anywhere" (4.32). "He who sees the present has seen everything that has ever been from time everlasting and that shall be forever. Everything is of the same kind and form" (6.37). "Soon you will have forgotten everything; and soon everything will have forgotten you" (7.21).

As these passages show, Marcus Aurelius' preoccupation with time has many aspects. It can be an urgent reminder to act here and now, but time is also a measure of the impermanence of ordinary life and especially of the shortness of fame. Time provides him with grounds for resignation or tranquillity. Yet, even as time passes, each moment is completely real and demands emotional strength and moral decision.

The theme of time and mutability in the *Meditations* seems an authentic instance of Marcus Aurelius' patterns of thought, but it also provides an important clue to the literary form of the *Meditations*. The most famous utterance on time and change in Greek thought was the dictum of Heraclitus: "It is not possible to step twice into the same river." What Heraclitus actually intended by this statement is controversial, but in antiquity it was universally interpreted as an image of flux for the general condition of things. Heraclitus was believed to have held that "all things flow" (like a river). As a Stoic, Marcus Aurelius was bound to be familiar with Heraclitus, whose doctrines were an important formative influence on Stoicism. Yet his interest in Heraclitus was much more than doctrinal allegiance. Next to Socrates he names Heraclitus more often than any other historical person. For several of Heraclitus' statements Marcus Aurelius is the only source (4.46), but his implicit allusions to the older writer are pervasive. "Time is a river of what comes to be, and a powerful flow" (4.43). The image is recurrent in his work.

Nor was it just the philosophy of Heraclitus that helped to shape Marcus Aurelius' thoughts. The emperor's epigrammatic style and singular imagery are strikingly similar to those of Heraclitus. Compare the following. First, Heraclitus: "God is day night, winter summer, war peace, surfeit famine; but he changes just as fire, when mixed with incense, is named after the scent of each spice" (frag. 67, Diels-Kranz, *Die Fragmente der Vorsokratiker*); and "connections— wholes and not wholes, joining separating, consonant dissonant, from all things one and from one all things" (frag. 10). Then Marcus Aurelius: "The nature of the whole, out of the substance of the whole, now molded a horse as out of wax, then broke it up and used its matter for a tree. There's nothing terrible for the box to be broken any more than for it to be assembled"

(7.23); and "The rotations of the universe are the same, upwards downwards, from period to period" (9.28). Heraclitus had written, "A road upwards downwards one and the same" (frag. 60). It is surprising that Marcus Aurelius' stylistic affinity to Heraclitus has not been regularly noticed. He was influenced by many other writers too, and Heraclitus had little to teach him in moral outlook. What particularly appealed in Heraclitus, however, was the memorability of his sayings. The Roman emperor wanted to imprint his own reflections on his memory no less indelibly.

So it comes about that the *Meditations*, in spite of their privacy, possess striking literary qualities. Many of the emperor's images turn his thoughts into poetry—or so we should call it—with word balance and skillful rhythm assisting. Repeatedly he steels himself against passions that would manipulate him like a puppet (2.2; 3.16; etc.). Life is a ball tossed in the air, a bubble, the light of a lamp (8.20). He should end his life "like a ripe olive that falls, praising the earth that gave birth to it and thanking the tree that made it grow" (4.48). "Whatever anyone does or says, I must be good. So might the gold or the emerald or the purple keep saying, 'whatever anyone says or does, I must be an emerald and keep my color'" (7.15). The mind free from passions is a "fortified city" (8.48). "A man who is straightforward and good should be like someone who smells as strong as a goat"; thus everyone must be aware of him (11.15).

There is literary distinction in the *Meditations*. Notwithstanding his disclaimers, Marcus Aurelius had a creative writer's imagination and control. But the singular qualities of his work are attributable neither to the philosophy nor to the style nor even, in the final analysis, to their joint product. Other men might have said these things, and said them in similar ways. The amazing fact is that a Roman emperor said them, and said them to himself. For the last twelve years of his life he was continuously engaged in defending the northern frontiers of the empire against tribal attacks. Many of the *Meditations* were probably written when he was encamped far from Rome. His health and temperament did not equip him to be a great general or administrator. He lacked an autocrat's ambition and a planner's vision. As an emperor he was dutiful but only moderately effective. Physical weakness, chronic insomnia, family troubles, and the loss of nearly all his children in infancy cannot have given him much conventional happiness. About such circumstances of his life the *Meditations* are completely silent. Yet in writings to Fronto his ordinary human concerns are constantly evident: his anxiety for Fronto's health, his joy in one of his own children.

So, in a sense, the *Meditations* are highly selective of Marcus Aurelius' experience and of himself. They do not reveal what he was doing when he wrote them, nor all that he must have been feeling. But if they lack the spontaneity of a normal diary they seem to be no less genuine as the chronicle of a person. Marcus Aurelius was someone very unusual; for Matthew Arnold, "perhaps the most beautiful figure in history." What he chose to write down was only rarely a stream of consciousness, an outflow of feeling. He strove rather to give shape to his thoughts, to present himself with images and models of life and excellence that could direct and control his moods and aspirations. Thus the *Meditations* are both articulate and personal, objective and autodidactic. This is another way of stating their author's Stoicism, but it also helps to explain why the *Meditations* belong to the history of literature.

Selected Bibliography

TEXTS

EPICTETUS
Four books of *Discourses* survive out of the eight published by Arrian. The *Manual (Encheiridion)* is also preserved, comprising fifty-three short extracts from the *Discourses* selected by Arrian; Simplicius' commentary on this survives in *Epicteti disserta-*

tionum ab Arriano digestarum libri iv, edited by J. Schweighaeuser (Leipzig, 1799–1800).

Epictetus. Entretiens, edited by J. Souilhé. Société d'édition "Les belles lettres." 4 vols. Paris, 1948–1965.
Epicteti Dissertationes ab Arriano digestae, edited by H. Shenkl. 2nd ed. Leipzig, 1916.
Epictetus, edited by W. A. Oldfather. 2 vols. London and Cambridge, Mass., 1925. The Loeb Classical Library.

MARCUS AURELIUS
The surviving writings are *Meditations*, in twelve books composed in Greek, and *Letters* in Latin, preserved as parts of the correspondence of his former tutor, M. Cornelius Fronto. Further evidence on Marcus Aurelius' life is given in Dio Cassius, *Historia Romana*, books 71–72, and in the *Historia Augusta* 4.1.

MEDITATIONS
The Communings with Himself of Marcus Aurelius Antoninus, Emperor of Rome, edited by C. R. Haines. New York and London, 1916. The Loeb Classical Library.
Marci Antonini imperatoris In semetipsum libri XII, edited by H. Schenkl. Leipzig, 1913.
Marcus Aurelius Antoninus Wege zu sich selbst, edited by W. Theiler. Zurich, 1951. With German translation.

LETTERS
Epistolae, edited by C. R. Haines. 2 vols. Cambridge, Mass., and London, 1919–1920. The Loeb Classical Library, with English translation.
Epistolae, edited by M. P. J. van der Hout. Leiden, 1954.

TRANSLATIONS

EPICTETUS
Long, G. *The Discourses of Epictetus; with the Encheiridion and Fragments*. London, 1877. With notes, a biography, and a study of Epictetus' philosophy.
Matheson, P. E. *Epictetus. The Discourses and Manual*. Oxford, 1916.
Saunders, J. *Greek and Roman Philosophy After Aristotle*. New York and London, 1966. Contains an edition of the *Manual*.

EPICTETUS AND MARCUS AURELIUS

MARCUS AURELIUS

Grube, G. M. A. *Meditations.* Indianapolis and New York, 1963.

Staniforth, M. *Marcus Aurelius: Meditations.* Baltimore and Harmondsworth, 1964.

COMMENTARIES

EPICTETUS

Most of the *Discourses* lack any modern commentary. "On Cynicism" (3.22) is studied in depth by M. Billerbeck (Leiden, 1978).

MARCUS AURELIUS

Farquharson, A. S. L. *Meditations of Marcus Aurelius.* 2nd ed. 2 vols. Oxford, 1952. With text and English translation.

GENERAL WORKS AND SPECIAL STUDIES

EPICTETUS

Bonhöffer, A. *Epiktet und die Stoa.* Stuttgart, 1890.

———. *Die Ethik des Stoikers Epiktet.* Stuttgart, 1894.

———. *Epiktet und das Neue Testament.* Giessen, 1911.

Brunt, P. A. "From Epictetus to Arrian." *Athenaeum* 55:19–48 (1977).

Colardeau, Th. *Étude sur Épictète.* Paris, 1903.

Döring, K. *Exemplum Socratis.* Wiesbaden, 1979.

Hadot, P. "Une Clé des *Pensées* de Marc Aurèle: Les trois *topoi* philosophiques selon Épictète." *Les Études philosophiques* 1:65–83 (1978).

Millar, F. "Epictetus and the Imperial Court." *Journal of Roman Studies* 55:140–148 (1965).

Stadter, P. A. *Arrian of Nicomedia.* Chapel Hill, N.C., 1980.

Wirth, Th. "Arrians Errinerungen an Epiktet." *Museum Helveticum,* 24:149–189; 197–216 (1967).

Xenakis, J. *Epictetus, Philosopher-Therapist.* The Hague, 1969.

MARCUS AURELIUS

Arnold, M. *Essays in Criticism.* New York, 1883.

Birley, A. *Marcus Aurelius.* London, 1966.

Brunt, P. A. "Marcus Aurelius and the Christians." In *Studies in Latin Literature and Roman History,* edited by C. Deroux. Collection Latomus, vol. 64, pp. 483–520. Brussels, 1979.

———. "Marcus Aurelius in His *Meditations.*" *Journal of Roman Studies* 64:1–20 (1974).

Farquharson, A. S. L. *Marcus Aurelius. His Life and His World.* Edited by D. A. Rees. Oxford, 1951.

Stanton, G. R. "Marcus Aurelius, Emperor and Philosopher." *Historia* 18:570–587 (1969). With response by B. Hendrickx, *Historia* 23:254–256 (1974).

BIBLIOGRAPHIES

EPICTETUS

Oldfather, W. A. *Contributions Toward a Bibliography of Epictetus.* Urbana, 1927. Supplementary edition, *With a Preliminary List of Epictetus' Manuscripts,* by W. II. Friedrich and C. U. Faye. Urbana, Ill., 1952.

MARCUS AURELIUS

Klein, R. *Marc Aurel.* Wege der Forschung, 550. Darmstadt, 1979. Contains a series of recent articles by different scholars.

LITERARY BACKGROUND

THE GREEK DIATRIBE

TEXTS

Bion of Borysthenes, edited by J. F. Kindstrand. Uppsala, 1976.

C. Musonius Rufus. Reliquiae, edited by O. Hense. Leipzig, 1905.

Teletis Reliquiae, edited by O. Hense. 2nd ed. Leipzig, 1909. Reprinted New York and Hildesheim, 1969.

STUDIES

Most of the books listed here contain detailed bibliographies.

Brown, P. *The World of Late Antiquity, from Marcus Aurelius to Muhammad.* London, 1971.

Brunt, P. A. "Stoicism and the Principate." *Papers of the British School of Rome* 43:7–35 (1975).

Cary, M., and H. H. Scullard. *A History of Rome.* London, 1975.

Dill, S. *Roman Society from Nero to Marcus Aurelius.* 2nd ed. London, 1905.

Guthrie, W. K. C. *A History of Greek Philosophy.* Vol. 1. Cambridge, 1962.

Hodson, A. *La Morale sociale des derniers stoïciens, Sénèque, Épictète et Marc Aurèle.* Paris, 1967.

Kahn, C. H. *The Art and Thought of Heraclitus.* Cambridge, 1980.

Long, A. A. *Hellenistic Philosophy.* London, 1974.

MacMullen, R. *Enemies of the Roman Order.* Cambridge, Mass., 1966.

Millar, F. *The Emperor in the Roman World.* London, 1977.

Nock, A. D. *Conversion.* Oxford, 1933.

Oltramare, O. *Les Origines de la diatribe romaine.* Lausanne, 1926.

Pohlenz, M. *Die Stoa. Geschichte einer geistigen Bewegung.* 2nd ed. Göttingen, 1959.

Rist, J. M. *Stoic Philosophy.* Cambridge, 1969.

Sandbach, F. H. *The Stoics.* London, 1975.

van Geytenbeek, A. C. *Musonius Rufus and Greek Diatribe.* Assen, 1962.

Wendland, P. *Die Hellenistisch-römische Kultur in ihrem Beziehungen zu Judentum und Christentum.* 3rd ed. Tübingen, 1912.

Wilkinson, L. P. *The Roman Experience.* London, 1975.

A. A. LONG

TACITUS

(*ca.* A.D. 55–after 117)

"TACITUS I CONSIDER the first writer in the world without a single exception." So wrote Thomas Jefferson in a letter to his granddaughter in 1808. The verdict at first sight seems surprising. What could a champion of colonial independence find to admire in the historian of imperial Rome, the chronicler of the triumph of despotism over freedom and the rout of virtue before the murderous forces of corruption and decadence? Yet precisely these subjects engaged Jefferson; the Rome of Tacitus illustrated the fate that could befall a young republic that was not vigilant in maintaining its virtue, a virtue arising from the independence of a life lived on the soil, such as that which the soldier-farmers of the early Roman Republic once enjoyed. Imperial Rome was thus a grim example of the perversion of freedom, and Tacitus, for Jefferson, was its prime exponent: "His book is a compound of history and morality of which we have no other example." At almost the same time Jefferson was expressing these thoughts, Emperor Napoleon Bonaparte understandably took a different view: "Tacitus! Don't talk to me about that sensation-monger! He has libeled the emperors."

Another theme in Tacitus' writing, closely linked to the first, and one that also engaged Jefferson's special interest, was the contrast between barbarian peoples living in such backward areas as Britain and Germany, and "civilized" Romans in the heart of the empire. Jefferson considered the former in Tacitus'

writings to be simple and upright, vigorously expressing and defending their freedom by frequent warfare; the latter to be the effete products of a supposedly higher culture, prepared to forfeit freedom for luxury and self-indulgence. For example, Tacitus recounts in his *Life of Agricola* how the sons of British chieftains became attracted to the amenities of Roman life: "Our way of dress thus came to be admired and the toga became popular. Gradually they were drawn to the blandishments of vice: porticoes, baths, and elaborate banquets. This among the inexperienced was called 'civilization,' when it was part of their enslavement" (21).

Jefferson thus found in Tacitus an expression of what he took to be native Teutonic freedom, which had subsequently been stifled by the medieval institutions of church, nobility, and divine right of kings, a freedom he believed resurgent in the New World. The fate that befell many of those vigorous frontier peoples stood as a warning to young America, as did the conditions in the heart of the Roman Empire, where subjects bent before the will of corrupted and corrupting princes.

HIS CAREER

Cornelius Tacitus—both Gaius and Publius are attested as a first name—was born about A.D. 55: that is, shortly after the young Nero (A.D. 54–68), last of the Julio-Claudian dynasty, became emperor. Tacitus' origin was probably provincial, his family equestrian in status. The equestrians, or knights, formed a social class just below the senatorial order; wealthy, cultured, distinguished by dress and privilege from the vast bulk of the population below them, they comprised roughly one-tenth of one percent of the population (the senatorial order being something like two-hundredths of one percent).

Under the Roman Republic, which ended with the victory of Augustus over the forces of Antony and Cleopatra at the Battle of Actium in 31 B.C., the equestrians were the nonpolitical element of the upper class; the emperors, of whom Augustus was the first, gave the equestrians new employment in the administration of empire. In time a course of equestrian offices developed, parallel to and slightly inferior in prestige (but often not in power) to the offices reserved for senators. We hear of a Cornelius Tacitus serving, probably during the 50's A.D., in the equestrian office of procurator of the province of Gallia Belgica, a financial post of importance. The man is almost certainly a relative; there is a good chance that he was the historian's father.

Tacitus was thus born into a family with a tradition of government service, and he lived his early years under Nero. The excesses of that emperor doubtless made a strong impression on his mind, as did the period of civil war that engulfed the Roman world after Nero's enforced suicide in June 68. The aged Servius Sulpicius Galba seized the vacant throne by arms, but lasted only six months. He was toppled in January 69 by Salvius Otho, disgruntled at not receiving higher promotion. Otho, who owed his elevation to the Praetorian Guard in Rome, at once had to meet an uprising by legions on the Rhine led by their commander, Vitellius. Within three months Otho had fallen; by December Vitellius had followed him. The winner was Flavius Vespasianus, coming with his troops from the East, the fourth emperor in "the one long year" of A.D. 69. Vespasian brought the civil upheaval to a close and founded the Fla-

vian dynasty; he was succeeded by his elder son, Titus (79–81), and his younger son, Domitian (81–96). Tacitus was in his early teens when these momentous and bloody actions were taking place; he may well have witnessed some of them firsthand, whether in Gaul, northern Italy, or Rome itself.

At the start of his *Histories* (1.1) Tacitus says that his career began under the emperor Vespasian, and was carried further by Titus and still further by Domitian. That is, he was admitted to the senatorial order and proceeded to fill the regular senatorial course of offices: military tribune, quaestor (in 81 or 82), aedile or tribune of the plebs, and praetor (88). In the year after the assassination of Domitian, Tacitus attained the highest office: under Nerva he was suffect consul[1] in 97.

All the signs point to a career of distinction and steady promotion: admission into the senatorial order at a young age; marriage to the daughter of Julius Agricola in 77, the year of Agricola's consulship; early admittance—by 88—to one of the four chief priestly colleges (the fifteen-man board that kept the oracular Sybilline books). For four years after his praetorship, during which his father-in-law died and Domitian began a savage purge of the Senate in reaction to an unsuccessful coup against him, Tacitus was absent from Rome in one or more provinces on unspecified assignment. His elevation to the consulship in 97 may have been due to the favor of the dead Domitian: consuls were often designated in advance, and even nominations by emperors whose memories were execrated could be honored by their successors.

Nerva, like Galba, was an old man at his accession. Since he had no heirs, he adopted as his successor a successful military man then in Upper Germany, Ulpius Traianus (Trajan), and providentially died. It was under Trajan (98–117) that the capstone to Tacitus' career was added: proconsul of the province of Asia in

[1]One who was chosen for and served in office after 1 January.

112–113. He probably lived on into the reign of Hadrian (117–138), dying perhaps around 117.

In addition to his official career, Tacitus was the leading orator of his age: his friend the younger Pliny acknowledges the fact, while flattering himself that many, in the same breath, customarily couple his name with that of Tacitus when speaking of those of preeminent literary attainment (*Epistles* 7.20.6; 9.23.3). Tacitus was chosen to deliver the funeral eulogy in 97 for the aged and venerable Verginius Rufus, the man who in the year 68 had refused the purple in favor of Galba, when offered it by his soldiers: "He claimed the empire not for himself but for his country" went his proud epitaph. In 100 Tacitus and Pliny jointly undertook a celebrated prosecution: that of Marius Priscus, former governor of Africa, before the Senate with Trajan presiding. Tacitus, according to Pliny, "spoke with great eloquence, and, what is most characteristic of his oratory, with majesty" (*Epistles* 2.11.17).

Tacitus clearly was one of the great men of his age: orator, senator, and consul. He was active in most phases of political life; he knew the workings of government as both participant and close observer. Given his equestrian birth and the fact that he did not make his mark as a military man, his senatorial career was outstanding; only a few outstripped him, those who held second or third consulships, for example, or who served as prefect of the city. The facts of his career are vital for understanding his historical works: Tacitus came to history as one who had been deeply involved in events of great moment, whose career flourished even under emperors whom he privately loathed, who knew firsthand the effects that absolute power has on its holders and on those who stand nearest them.

THE AGRICOLA

Between the years 98 and about 105, before the appearance of his major historical works,

Tacitus wrote three short essays: the *Agricola*, the *Germania*, and the *Dialogus*.

The first dates to 98, and is a biography of his father-in-law, Gnaeus Iulius Agricola. It is a compelling but curious work. Parts concern topics found in standard biographies, such as Agricola's career, parentage and death, character and achievements. But large sections are devoted to quite different matters: for example, an excursus on the geography and ethnography of Britain (10–11), the island that Tacitus exaggeratedly claims Agricola wholly conquered (10.1; see also *Histories* 1.2.1). In addition, he gives a brief history of the island from Julius Caesar's first landing in the 50's B.C. to Agricola's tenure as governor (13–17); Agricola's achievements are then recounted at considerable length (18–38), with all the trappings of a standard historical narrative, including a set of paired speeches by the British chieftain Calgacus and Agricola, each exhorting his troops before the decisive battle of the Grampian Mountain. These parts of the *Agricola* thus look to be a first experiment in straight historical writing. Yet the work also has many features of a funeral eulogy, a standard form of oratory among the Romans. Tacitus and his wife were absent from Rome when Agricola died under the watchful eye of the emperor Domitian, who, claims Tacitus, was jealous of Agricola's preeminent military fame. The last few sections of the work are couched in the form of the final tribute that Tacitus might have delivered over the bier itself: the intensity of the emotion and the control under which that emotion is held create a passage of solemnity and power.

The *Agricola* is thus a blend of biography, history, ethnography, geography, and eulogy. Scholars have been much exercised in attempting to define the genre, but in vain: the *Agricola* is unique, and it succeeds. The transitions among its parts are easy and the total effect is one of mastery.

The *Agricola* is also programmatic of all that follows, for in it are expressed Tacitus' fundamental views about the nature of autocracy and the precarious middle course that a senator who wishes to serve the state must take, avoiding servility and unworthy self-seeking on the one hand, demotion and danger through a willful display of independence on the other. The style and techniques of Tacitus' mature writing are also here: strong characterization, vivid narrative, and the use of rumor and innuendo to urge a view that sometimes the facts themselves tend to undercut.

The opening three sections set the tone. The oppressive tyranny of Domitian's reign had cut off even simple interchange of speech and hearing; in those fifteen years ("a great part out of a human life"), the young in silence reached old age, the old the end of their lives. Philosophers and the wise were driven into exile, men of goodness ordered to die, and even works commemorating their goodness burned in the forum: so hostile was the age to virtue. Hence Tacitus craves an indulgence from his readers for writing something almost unknown to the age: the record of a good man who had served his country well. He can do so because a new and happier era has begun under Trajan and his adoptive father, Nerva, who "blended two things hitherto irreconcilable, liberty and the principate" (res olim dissociabiles miscuerit, principatum et libertatem).

Agricola is depicted in glowing terms, with all the standard attributes of the prudent and successful general. The portrait therefore is idealized, his most prominent characteristic being—somewhat unexpectedly—"moderation" (4; see also 8): that is, self-effacing behavior in order not to provoke the displeasure and jealousy of his superiors. The emperor himself was the most sensitive. His own campaign in Germany had been a failure, Tacitus unfairly claims, and the triumph he celebrated a ludicrous sham (39): sensible men could see that Agricola's achievements in Britain far eclipsed the deeds of Domitian. Agricola therefore had to proceed with caution in order not to provoke further an already envious prince. On his return to Rome he slipped into the city by night and went directly to the palace, where he received a perfunctory kiss but no word of greeting; he then melted into the mass of courtiers (40). Henceforth he cultivated retirement and quietude; he was not called upon again for government service, and when the customary time came for him to take up the governorship of Asia or Africa, the emperor's advisers—first by insinuation and then by threats—forced Agricola to request to be excused from the post, which Domitian in an interview granted with sinister condescension (42). Agricola's sudden death in 93 at the age of fifty-six, moreover, was rumored to have been the result of poison (43); whatever the truth, says Tacitus, the reports to the emperor by his agents were so frequent as to betoken more than ordinary interest in the agonies of Agricola's last hours.

Agricola's anxiousness to comply with the wishes of his superiors could, on an ungenerous estimate, be attributed to a want of principle or of courage. Tacitus sweeps the imputation aside in a vigorous rebuttal:

> It was Domitian's nature to be quick to anger, which, the more he concealed it, the less could it be assuaged; he was, nevertheless, mollified by the moderation and good sense of Agricola, who did not endanger his reputation or his life by obstinacy or an empty show of freedom. Let those whose habit it is to admire the flouting of authority know that there can be great men even under bad emperors, and that obedience and self-control, if combined with diligence and energy, can win the same measure of fame as many have achieved by dangerous courses, of no use to the state, and suffering a martyr's death at the end.
>
> (42)

Tacitus' animus here seems in part to be directed against a specific group, the so-called Stoic opposition. These were men, often devoted to Stoic philosophy, who pointedly flouted the imperial will by public displays of independence and who, when ordered to die, did so in imitation of Socrates, with disciples about to record their words and actions for posterity. But Tacitus' defense of Agricola is also directed more generally to the widespread attacks that were made against Domitian's favorites immediately after his assassination. The heat of Tacitus' remarks suggests that some of the criticism touched Agricola.

One may also wonder about Tacitus himself. Most of *his* offices were owed to Domitian: aedileship or tribunate, lifetime priesthood, praetorship, a four-year period of service abroad after the praetorship, and perhaps the consulate. His words can therefore be seen as being much a defense of his own career as of the career of his father-in-law. Some have wondered whether he may not have been suffering from a bad conscience: certainly he was the recipient of Domitian's evident favor. While a member of the Senate, he and his fellow senators voted to condemn their friends during Domitian's reign of terror: "*Our* hands dragged Helvidius off to prison; we withered under the looks that Mauricus and Rusticus gave us; we were covered in Senecio's innocent blood." "We set a remarkable endurance record," he says with crushing irony of himself and his fellow senators (2: *dedimus profecto grande patientiae documentum*).

However we assess Tacitus' own psychology, the defense in the *Agricola* is powerfully urged. The Roman noble was born to a tradition of service to the state. Men of talent who turned their backs on a career of public service were not admired; they contributed nothing to their country or to their reputations, and they laid themselves open variously to charges of frivolousness, timidity, selfish pride, or secret vice. Tacitus was aware of the attraction of inactivity and soft living: "The pleasure of idleness itself steals over us, and the inaction we at first dislike we come to love"(3). He felt it *was* possible, however, even under the worst of emperors, for a man to serve the state with energy and to preserve his self-respect. He makes a special point of singling out such individuals when they appear in his history: Marcus Lepidus in the reign of Tiberius (*Annals* 4.20; 6.27), Cassius Longinus under Claudius (12.12), Memmius Regulus under Nero (14.47). Of Lepidus he says:

I am convinced that for those times Marcus Lepidus was a principled and wise man, for he often diverted the cruel proposals of flatterers to a better course. He also exercised self-restraint, since he enjoyed equal influence and favor with Tiberius. Hence I must wonder whether it is the chance of birth, as in other matters, that causes princes to like some men and dislike others, or whether something within our control allows us to steer a course between dangerous obstinacy and unseemly obsequiousness, untouched by self-seeking and peril.

(*Annals* 4.20)

The question of how men of prominence were to conduct themselves is a persistent theme in Tacitus' writings. For example, after the aged Tiberius suddenly toppled Sejanus, his powerful praetorian prefect, the relatives, associates, and friends of the fallen minister were prosecuted with unremitting fury. The knight Marcus Terentius at his trial is made to assert:

I will admit that I was a friend of Sejanus, that I sought to be so, and that I was delighted when I succeeded. . . . Intimacy with Sejanus brought one closer to friendship with the emperor, while those whom he disliked were set about with fear and humiliation. I will name no names, but I will, at the cost of the danger that threatens only myself, defend all of us who had no part in his attempted coup. . . . Caesar, we honored the man who was your son-in-law, your colleague in the consulship, your chief minister in running the state. It is not for us to question your choice for the highest honors, or your motives: the gods have given you absolute power; to us is left the high privilege of compliance.

(*Annals* 6.8)

In book 4 of the *Histories* Tacitus records a debate in the Senate between two bitter enemies. On one side was Helvidius Priscus, praetor-elect in the year 70, who had devoted himself to the study of Stoic philosophy, "not in order to conceal a life of inaction under an imposing credo, as many do, but to undertake an active public career steeled against the vagaries of fortune" (*Histories* 4.5). Helvidius' opponent was the notorious and influential informer

Eprius Marcellus, who had urged in Nero's Senate that Thrasea Paetus, another prominent Stoic and Helvidius' father-in-law, be condemned to die. Tacitus' description of Thrasea's suicide is the last episode that survives from his pen (*Annals* 16.34–35). Now, in the aftermath of Nero's death, when his favorites were vulnerable to attack, the son-in-law attempts to bring down his father-in-law's persecutor:

> Why should Marcellus be afraid? . . . "He possesses wealth and power, by virtue of which he would excel many men were he not stricken by consciousness of his misdeeds. . . . It is enough for Marcellus that he urged Nero to destroy so many innocent men; let him enjoy his rewards and his impunity, but let him leave Vespasian to enjoy better advisers."
>
> (*Histories* 4.7)

As powerfully as this speech is urged, Tacitus gives Marcellus an equally compelling defense:

> We must particularly be on our guard that the zealotry of certain people does not provoke one who is just beginning his reign in watchfulness and who is still scrutinizing the looks and words of everyone. I am aware of the times into which I have been born and of the form of government that our fathers and grandfathers have instituted. I admire the past but go along with the present, and although in my prayers I ask for good emperors, I acquiesce in those we get. Thrasea was no more condemned by what I said than by how the Senate voted: the savagery of Nero delighted in such games, and I was made no less anxious because of my friendship with him than others were in their exile.
>
> (4.8)

The similarities with the situation in the *Agricola* are instructive: a son-in-law defends the memory of his father-in-law, who fell victim to a tyrant; a prescription is given for serving and surviving under such an emperor; and allusion is made to the deaths of the proud individualists who were his victims. But the similarities do not combine to form parallel situations. Quite the contrary. In one case the victim (Thrasea) did not shrink from offending the emperor and was ordered to die; in the other the "victim" (Agricola) was a complaisant servant of the regime, to whose death the emperor is linked by only the most tenuous of rumors. Thrasea is a Stoic martyr, Agricola a man whose achievements, we are told, far excel those of men who pursue courses of willful independence and die ostentatious deaths. In the *Agricola* the one who gives a prescription for serving under bad emperors is Tacitus himself; in the *Histories* the spokesman is a notorious informer. Many of the same features are thus present, but their recombination, like the twist of a kaleidescope, creates a new picture from the old elements. The procedure is wholly in the manner of Tacitus. History is not so pliant or so tame as to lend itself to simple answers or comfortable analogies. On the contrary, most historical situations and persons are compounded of the good and the bad, in a highly complex way. Tacitus looks at them all with an eye that delights in permutation and paradox: the blackguard mouthing the purist sentiment, the low-born who dies a noble death, the noble who betrays his own mother, the man of principle who sets an example of firm independence amid groveling flatterers, the zealot who glories in provoking those in power and in his own death.

Tacitus thus does not follow single points of view or formulate balanced syntheses. Often he is content to let the "facts" speak for themselves, his special aim being to emphasize anomaly and inconcinnity, his method being to select the facts carefully with an eye to such effects. The conclusion the reader is left to draw is therefore not obvious or easy. For example, in the clash between Helvidius and Marcellus, Helvidius is for the most part presented sympathetically: a man of courage, a lover of freedom, a loyal son-in-law. Yet adverse opinions of certain unnamed critics are recorded (*Histories* 4.6): that he was too eager for glory, that when the wind shifted he would trim his sails. Then again, his desire to embarrass Marcellus involved changing the rules of the Senate, which that body refused to do, and when Helvidius proposed that the Senate without consulting the emperor restore the ruined Capitol on its own initiative, "senators of moderation let the motion pass in silence" (4.9: *eam sententiam modestissimus quisque silentio . . . transmisit*). This last remark is a good example of the difficulty in making clear-cut value judgments. Is Helvidius to be admired for urging the Senate to take an independent course, or criticized because the action would be a calculated slight to the emperor? The answer must be that both considerations are involved: it is a mirror of the uneasy marriage of autocracy and the tradition of senatorial liberty. Tacitus asserts that Nerva had united these two irreconcilable elements, liberty and the principate (*Agricola* 3). It is possible but unlikely that he actually believed this. One was expected, after all, to make such auspicious noises at the start of a new reign. Note, too, that Tacitus appends at once a marked reservation: "Yet given the frailty of human nature, remedies are slower than the evils they are meant to cure." Then again, nowhere else in his writings does he endorse the notion that personal freedom and autocracy can coexist. In fact, Marcellus ends his speech by saying, "Just as the worst emperors love unlimited tyranny, the best of them want some check to be put upon freedom" (*Histories* 4.8).

The *Agricola* also exhibits another characteristic device of Tacitus': the use of rumor and innuendo to create an adverse impression that the facts he himself gives either do not support or even subvert. His portrait of Domitian is a clear example. In the first three chapters he characterizes all fifteen years of the reign as a period of unrelenting tyranny, which is not true; he also disingenuously affects to believe the age to be so hostile to virtue that he must seek permission from his readers to write a laudatory work, which he would not have had to do were it his intention to denounce someone.

Toward the end of the essay the emperor is painted in still darker colors. After spectacular victories in Britain, Agricola was recalled, Domitian being all too conscious of his own ineffectual German campaign and sham triumph, and of the axiom that "one could more easily pretend to overlook other qualities, but military success was plainly an imperial virtue" (39). Tacitus also suggests that Domitian's fear of Agricola as a rival caused him to hint that Syria would be Agricola's next command: this in order to induce Agricola to leave the island, thereby separating him from his troops. He records the rumor ("believed by many": 40) that Domitian dispatched one of his freedmen with a letter promising the post, but with the proviso that the freedman not hand it over if Agricola had already left the island; the messenger, on sighting Agricola's boat in the middle of the English Channel, promptly turned about without a word of greeting. On returning to Rome, Agricola was frequently the target of accusation (41); Tacitus gives no particulars, noting only that he was "absolved in his absence." Then comes the story, already referred to, of how Agricola was forced to request Domitian to be excused from the governorship of Africa or Asia, Tacitus adding that the salary customarily given in such instances was withheld (42). Finally, Tacitus reports the "prevalent rumor" (43) that Agricola died from poison; he himself refuses to state it as a fact, but notes that important freedmen and doctors intimate with Domitian paid more frequent visits to Agricola than one would expect, and that couriers kept up constant reports in Agricola's last hours, "nobody believing that news brought so swiftly would be heard with a sad face" (43).

It is important to note that the offer of the Syrian command, the story about the freedman dispatched to Britain, and the poisoning are all represented as rumors. Tacitus does not personally vouch for them, going so far in the second case to suggest that, if it were not true, it was probably a fiction "made up to fit the emperor's character" (40). The statement reveals the biographer's prejudice and method: Domitian is throughout depicted as a cruel and jealous tyrant, and although rumors are recorded as such, their inclusion blackens the emperor still further because those that fit in with the emperor's character as Tacitus describes it are the ones he chooses to include.

Agricola, in fact, enjoyed an unprecedented length of tenure as governor of Britain (A.D. 78–84). He was recalled after he had reported to Domitian the subjugation of the island (10; see also 39) and when troops were needed to meet a serious crisis on the Danube (see also 41). Moreover, the prospect of the Syrian command was most unlikely, given his already long tenure in Britain. The rumor is therefore a fiction, especially the anecdote of the journey of Domitian's freedman. On Agricola's return his victories were suitably recognized by the awarding of triumphal insignia and a statue in the forum (40). In addition, the disasters on the Danube and Rhine prompted the common people, according to Tacitus (ore vulgi: 41), to ask for Agricola as commander. This may be doubted; besides the fact that Agricola had no experience in the region, Tacitus nowhere else credits the masses with an interest in foreign affairs, but only in feeding their bellies (see also Histories 1.4; 4.38). Finally, the notion that Domitian had Agricola poisoned is inherently and circumstantially implausible.

On the other hand, it should not be doubted, as some have, that Domitian was jealous of Agricola. The emperor's reception of him on returning to Rome was perfunctory, Agricola's request to be excused from the governorship of Asia or Africa was enforced, and he was not employed in any capacity in the nine years between returning from Britain and his death. These items point to a coolness on Domitian's part, and probably jealousy as well, but they do not amount to much. Tacitus' effort to paint Agricola as one of the fallen victims of the tyrant fails to convince; in fact, a surface friendship between the two must have subsisted, as the frequent visits by the emperor's ministers to the dying Agricola suggest.

THE GERMANIA

Tacitus' essay on the tribes and customs of the Germans was, like the Agricola, written in 98, probably immediately after the biography (Germania 37). It divides into two parts, the first concerning the customs and institutions of the Germans as a whole (1–27), the second the separate tribes (28–45). The writing of such geographical and ethnographical treatises, whether as separate works or as digressions within historical works, had a long pedigree in Greco-Roman literature, reaching back to Herodotus, the father of history, and beyond. Livy discussed both the Gauls and the Germans, Sallust the tribes and terrain of Numidia, and Tacitus himself Britain in the Agricola.

The information in the Germania appears to derive wholly from written sources; we find no sign that Tacitus reports any of it from firsthand knowledge. There is nothing surprising in this; working up in new form information gathered by others was common practice in classical antiquity, as in other ages. What is surprising, however, is Tacitus' use of one or more out-of-date sources. For example, a few passages appear to reflect conditions in Augustus' reign a hundred years before, such as the boundaries of Germany (1). Puzzling, too, is the failure to incorporate recent information known to everybody, such as the new frontier created by Domitian's campaigns in the 80's (see also 29 on the decumates agri).

What was Tacitus' aim in writing the Germania? Since it clearly was not to add new information or to correct old errors, many have thought that he wanted to bring out the contrast between the upright, freedom-loving barbarians and the corrupt, servile practices of contemporary Romans. Certainly this viewpoint is strongly emphasized both explicitly and by implication. For example:

Adultery is very rare among such a numerous people, the penalty for which is swift and entrusted to the husband: after his wife's hair has been cut off he ejects her naked from the home in the presence of relatives and drives her with lashes through the entire village. Adultery meets with no indulgence; she will not find another husband for all her beauty, youth, and wealth. No one *there* laughs at vice, nor is it the fashion to corrupt or be corrupted.

(19)

The Germanic form of government also makes an obvious contrast with the Roman; the chiefs do not possess absolute power (11), and no one accounts it shameful to be in a chieftain's entourage (13). Women, too, are respected, and even worshiped: "In the days of the deified Vespasian we saw Veleda, who had long been held to be a deity by many people; earlier, too, they venerated Albruna and many other women. Not, however, out of flattery or with sham deification" (8). The excellence of German customs derives from their simple life, untouched by the enervating amenities of "civilized" living, and from their love of freedom. Tacitus had emphasized the same traits among the inhabitants of Britain in the *Agricola* (for example, 11; 21; 30–31). Such peoples preserved their independence through constant warfare; extended periods of peace blunted their ferocity and made them prey to more powerful neighbors (see also *Germania* 36; 40). Hence Tacitus throughout his writings often describes peace as debilitating, sterile, and even cruel (see *Germania* 14). For example, during the civil war of A.D. 69 the civilian population of Italy did not care who was the victor because "a long period of peace had broken them to endure any kind of servitude, ready as they were to submit to the first comer and indifferent to which side had the better cause" (*Histories* 2.17). In the *Agricola* he compares the Gauls, who had been under Roman influence for some time, with the newly encountered peoples of Britain: "The Britons are more aggressive because they have not become enervated by a long peace. Indeed, we have heard that the Gauls too were once great warriors, but when inaction and leisure supervened, they lost their fighting spirit along with their freedom" (11).

Yet despite Tacitus' praise for the Germans, it is implausible that he wrote the essay primarily to exalt their virtues. The second half of the work, concerning the individual tribes, has little to do with the subject, and even in the first he puts on record many German failings: their drunkenness (23), living in squalor and filth (20), refusal to produce by work what they can steal by war or plunder (14), addiction to gambling such that a man will stake his personal freedom on a throw of the dice (24). No doubt the opportunity to contrast German and Roman ways of life was a strong inducement to write the *Germania*, but it is difficult to believe that this was the chief or only reason.

Some have speculated that Tacitus wanted to warn the Romans and particularly Trajan (who was in Germany at the time the essay was written) of the danger to the empire that the Germans posed:

Rome was in her 640th year when she first heard of the invasion of the Cimbri in the consulship of Caecilius Metellus and Papirius Carbo. If we reckon from that time to the second consulship of the emperor Trajan, almost 210 years have passed. So long have we been subduing Germany. In the long interval great defeats have been suffered by both sides. Not the Samnites, not the Carthaginians, not the Spanish, not the Gauls, not even the Parthians have given us more frequent warnings: indeed, German liberty is a more serious threat than Parthian monarchy.

(37)

In perhaps the most famous passage of the *Germania* he records how the tribe of the Bructeri had lately been annihilated by their fellow Germans:

More than 60,000 fell, not by Roman arms but, what is far grander, before our delighted eyes. I pray that, if not love for us, at least mutual hatred may persist among them, since fortune can give us no greater gift than discord among our foes, as the destinies of empire urge us ever onward.

(33)

Thus the German nation constituted a serious threat to the empire in Tacitus' eyes; he seems long before the event to have anticipated the invasions from the north that would threaten the fabric of the western part of the empire and ultimately overwhelm it. The fact that Trajan himself was on the Rhine at the time of the essay's composition also may have been an inducement to its writing. Admittedly Tacitus nowhere suggests that the emperor should undertake the conquest of Germany; such a proposal would have been unseasonable and without weight, coming at the start of a new reign and from one who had no military reputation himself. Yet the suggestion that the Romans would do well to consider the conquest of Germany seems palpable though unexpressed in the *Germania*.

It is a mistaken belief that because Tacitus lauds much of German life and especially admires the determination of the Germans to enjoy freedom and independence, he believed they should be let alone or that Romans should become like them. *Libertas* in Roman eyes was not freedom to do simply as one liked; it was a collection of privileges that involved corresponding obligations and restrictions and that varied among social classes. For example, in writing about emancipated slaves in Germany, he says:

> The status of freedmen is not much above that of slaves; they rarely carry weight in the home, never in the state. The exceptions are those tribes ruled by kings, where freedmen enjoy a higher place than the freeborn and nobles. Among the rest of the Germans the inequality of the freedmen is proof of their liberty.
>
> (25)

(He is alluding to the high place of some freedmen in the Roman world, particularly of the emperor's freedmen.) The complete freedom enjoyed by the Germans, moreover, entailed disadvantages: for example, when summoned to a meeting, the participants came when they liked, sometimes arriving two or three days late

(11). Moreover, the only opinion that Tacitus explicitly attributes to his father-in-law in the *Agricola* is this: "I often heard him say that Ireland could be conquered and held by a single legion and a few auxiliary units, and that it would be helpful in the fighting against Britain if Roman armies were to be seen everywhere and liberty, so to speak, were removed from its sight" (23). In short, Tacitus approved of and admired Roman imperialism: Rome's efforts to conquer these people ensured its *own* military prowess and national vigor. His attitude is clearly shown in the *Annals*, where the campaigns in Germany of Germanicus under Tiberius and of Corbulo under Claudius are depicted in a most favorable light. Tiberius, jealous of the young Germanicus, was "a prince indifferent to the extension of empire" (4.32) who recalled him when it was "held for certain" (2.26) that one more year's campaigning would have ensured the conquest of Germany. Domitius Corbulo, who held the command in Germany under Claudius, was deemed a threat "to a timid emperor" (11.19), and when ordered to quit Germany altogether he exclaimed, "Fortunate Rome's commanders of old!" (11.20).

As for the question of why Tacitus wrote the *Germania*, the assumption that there was one overriding motive is misguided. He wrote it because he was interested in Germany (which interest continued, as his subsequent writings show) and believed that the empire would face a formidable foe if the tribes should unite in a single effort; because many German customs and institutions were admirable, contrasting sharply with the Roman; because he wished to unite in one short essay and in his own arresting language information scattered in the works of earlier writers who were more prolix and less gifted stylists. No one motive predominates, but together they explain the *Germania*.

DIALOGUS DE ORATORIBUS

The *Dialogue on Orators* was long believed not to be by Tacitus because the style is so unlike that of his other writings; instead of swift, concentrated prose marked by inconcinnity and abruptness, a full-bodied style in the manner of Cicero characterizes the work. Later, when belief in Tacitean authorship gained ground, the date of composition was put in the early 80's: Tacitus must have begun, it was posited, as a disciple of Ciceronianism, steadily working away from it in the next fifteen years, until, with the writing of the *Agricola* and the *Germania*, his Latin was the antithesis of what it once had been. Nowadays this view is rejected by most scholars on the ground that genre determines style: that is, since it was Cicero who introduced into Latin the dialogue on an oratorical subject (conducted by eminent persons and set in the historical past; for example, his *De Oratore*), Ciceronian Latin was the appropriate medium of expression. Accordingly, they would date the *Dialogus* somewhere in the decade 98 to 108.

The work is dedicated to Fabius Justus, consul in 102, whose question about the causes of the decline of contemporary oratory has prompted Tacitus to record a conversation on the subject he claims to have heard in his youth. The scene is put in the year 74 or 75. Although present at the supposed conversation, Tacitus himself takes no part. Instead, the interlocutors are Curatius Maternus (at whose home the dialogue takes place), Marcus Aper, and Julius Secundus (Secundus playing only a minor role); partway through, the well-born Vipstanus Messala arrives and joins the conversation.

The work divides into three sections; in each section, a point of view is developed in a set speech, then refuted in another set speech. In the first, the question whether poetry is a better thing than oratory is debated. Maternus—although a great orator himself—declares at the opening that he has abandoned oratory for poetry. We learn, in fact, that Maternus has offended those in power by writing a free-spoken tragedy on the younger Cato, the republican hero who committed suicide rather than live under the dictatorship of Julius Caesar; Maternus, nothing daunted, says he plans to continue

with a *Thyestes*, a new play in which whatever he had failed to say in the *Cato* will find expression (3). After the introduction Aper gives the first main speech (5-10), in which he chides Maternus for his decision, arguing energetically that oratory is a more honorable and more useful pursuit than poetry. Maternus then refutes him mildly but firmly (11-13). The arrival of Messala marks the second section, in which he and Aper debate whether the orators of old or those of the present day are the better: Aper advocates the cause of the moderns (15-23), Messala the ancients (24-27). The third section begins with Maternus interrupting to bring the discussion back to the original question; he himself doesn't doubt for a moment that the orators of old were indeed better: the question before them is why. Messala takes up the challenge at once by arguing that inferior education is the cause (27-35): his chief point is that whereas the young used to learn by attending upon the great speakers of their age and did so under a strict regimen—the very method by which Tacitus says he learned from Aper and Secundus (2)—modern children do not learn from direct experience. They are brought up by slaves and are taught in schools by rhetoricians who require them to speak on fanciful subjects unrelated to life.

At this point a break in the manuscript occurs. Scholars have long debated the important question of its length, but the hiatus is probably short, since when the text resumes we find an unnamed speaker (clearly Maternus) refuting Messala. Neither education nor moral decline explains the change, he says. Great oratory requires great subject matter, in which issues of the highest moment are debated. When the republic was collapsing in the midst of partisan strife and civil war, the issues were indeed most critical. He contrasts these conditions (37) with those of the contemporary court and Senate, with their staid issues and controlled proceedings:

> We are not speaking of a retiring or quiet accomplishment that delights in goodness and modera-

tion; the great and notable eloquence of old is the child of license, which fools call freedom: the companion of sedition, the spur to an excitable rabble, without restraint, without control, a rebellious, destructive, arrogant thing that has no place in a well-ordered state.

(40)

No one, declares Maternus, would prefer to live in that terrible time for all its eloquence; just as physicians prosper when men are ill, so orators flourish in the midst of wrongdoing and upheaval. The empire, with its peace, its restraint on license, and its unanimity, forbids great eloquence: "What need for lengthy speeches in the Senate when the best men quickly reach agreement? What need of public meetings, when no ignorant mob deliberates about the state's welfare, but a single man—and one preeminently wise?" (41: *sapientissimus et unus*).

Maternus' argument is powerfully urged, for the most part, and by ending the dialogue it makes a doubly strong impression. It is often taken—reasonably enough—to represent the view of the author. But there are disquieting hints that it may not be a full reflection of Tacitean opinion. Certainly Maternus' confidence in the excellence of the imperial dispensation raises doubts, particularly when the emperor is described as a man "preeminently wise," whose "perfect discipline has pacified eloquence along with everything else" (38). Indeed, in rebutting Messala's argument, Maternus of necessity assumes a one-sided position, which he maintains by taking up all the weapons of the oratorical arsenal; a line of irony thereby appears along the cutting edge of the argument. A further irony emerges when one remembers that it is Maternus who, however secluded "midst the groves and glades" of poesy (9: *inter nemora et lucos*; see also 12), has offended those in power by praising Cato, who refused to live under an autocrat, and by planning an equally outspoken drama on the subject of Thyestes, an archetypal tyrant.

But the true significance of Maternus' argument and the reason that it probably represents

Tacitus' own opinion is its grounding in history. Moral or aesthetic reasons do not explain the decline of oratory; historical circumstances do. The speakers of the late republic flourished because they had momentous subjects to discuss. Be assured, says Maternus to his listeners, that had you by some quirk of fate been living in those days, you would have risen to the greatest heights of oratory; and had men of that time been transported to contemporary Rome, moderation and self-restraint would have been their lot (41). Simultaneous enjoyment of great personal fame and great personal security is impossible in history.

The question of decline in artistic endeavor was debated widely by writers of the early empire, among them the author of "On the Sublime," Seneca, and Quintilian. Moral decline, loss of incentive, "fate," and the failure of education (as Messala argues) were variously advanced. Tacitus' answer, at once political and social, is original and convincing: oratorical genius requires a compatible environment in which to flourish, one in which crises arise and free speech is the chief means in reaching a solution. No one would prefer to live in such crisis situations, however; certainly what modern courts lacked in freedom to indulge in unchecked rhetorical pyrotechnics they made up in justice and expeditious verdicts (38–39). However much Tacitus disliked the empire, he was not deluded into believing the republic better than it was. Freedom and justice, like freedom and the principate, were at bottom irreconcilable.

THE HISTORIAE

Tacitus wrote the first of his two major historical works in the decade 100–110. Pliny, in two letters dating to 106 (6.16 and 20), supplies his friend with an eyewitness account of the eruption of Mount Vesuvius in the year 79 that buried the cities of Pompeii and Herculaneum and in which his uncle, Pliny the Elder, was killed. Tacitus had requested the information for a historical work on which he was then engaged; it is thus likely that the writing of the *Histories* was already under way by 106. In the next year Pliny sent another letter (7.33), concerning his role in an event of the year 93, that he hoped Tacitus would include, adding the confident prediction that Tacitus' history would be immortal.

The work begins on 1 January 69, in accordance with the tradition of Roman annalistic history, which followed a strict year-by-year format. The emperor Galba, who had succeeded Nero six months before, is in the last days of his reign; "the one long year" of A.D. 69 will see four emperors on the throne, of whom the last, Vespasian, founded the Flavian dynasty. The first part of the work thus traced the destructive course of the civil war. The middle section was doubtless painted in brighter, more hopeful colors, covering the reigns of Vespasian, Titus, and possibly the early years of Domitian: Vespasian had brought an end to the civil war and was the only emperor whom Tacitus considered changed for the better in holding supreme power (*Histories* 1.50). In the final part the shadows of Domitian's despotism lengthened steadily, until the state was plunged into the darkness of his last years, "when no longer at intervals or between breathing spaces but with one continuing blow he drained our life-blood away" (*Agricola* 44). Possibly a brief epilogue testifying to the happiness of the present regime was added, contrasting the civil war that followed Nero's death with the peaceful transition under Nerva and Trajan after Domitian's assassination.

Unfortunately, only the first part of the *Histories* has survived to us by a single manuscript tradition (which also includes books 11 through 16 of the *Annals*). Our text breaks off early in book 5 in the year 70: Tacitus thus takes more than four books to describe less than two years, perhaps the most detailed account of any period in ancient historiography that survives to us.

The historical actions of the years 69–70 were numerous, the events themselves complex, spread over the whole of the Roman world, often occurring simultaneously. The major and minor clashes among the many groups of Romans in arms were further complicated by serious revolts in the provinces of Gaul and Judea. Tacitus' handling of this complex material is masterful. After three sections of general introduction, he surveys rapidly the mood and resources of each part of the empire (4–11). At the start of this review he explains the long-range historical significance of the upheaval. For a hundred years the family of Augustus, the Julio-Claudians, had ruled the Roman world in dynastic succession; the emperor and the Senate shared the duties of ruling the empire, sometimes amicably, sometimes in a climate of tension and danger; but for the most part the world enjoyed a remarkable measure of peace and well-being. The suicide of Nero, however, stripped away this happy façade to reveal the basis on which the empire truly rested: the army. For in the absence of a clear-cut choice for the throne, only the armies had the power to enforce their choices, which were usually the men who commanded them. The Senate, the ostensible source of authority, found itself powerless to do anything but ratify the decisions of others. "The secret of empire had leaked out: an emperor could be made elsewhere than at Rome" (1.4: *evolgato imperii arcano, posse principem alibi quam Romae fieri*). Even though the Roman world was lucky to escape a catastrophe similar to that of 69 for many years to come, the "secret" remained; a century after Tacitus died the empire was nearly done in by fifty years of civil strife, at the end of which it emerged so shaken and changed that we reckon the start of the Middle Ages to have been the result.

In the opening section of the *Histories*, Tacitus states his reasons for writing. After the Battle of Actium in 31 B.C., when it became essential to peace for all power to be centered in one man, good history ceased to be written. Truth was impaired by men's lack of experience in governing, since effective power was in the hands of another (1.1). Then again, writers either were eager to flatter those in power or came to hate them. Tacitus believes that he can surmount these obstacles despite the fact that his career was fostered by Vespasian, Titus, and Domitian: "Every person must be spoken of without partiality or hatred by those who claim to write the plain truth" (*incorruptam fidem professis neque amore quisquam et sine odio dicendus est*). He adds that in the new age of Nerva and Trajan one may at last think what one likes and say what one thinks.

This passage should be compared with the opening of his next historical work, the *Annals* (1.1), where he makes the same claim in slightly different language. Under Augustus, he says, the growing habit of flattering those in power frightened away writers of talent from composing history, while works concerning the reigns of Tiberius, Gaius, Claudius, and Nero were falsified out of fear in their lifetimes and out of hatred after their deaths: "Accordingly I intend to write briefly about the last days of Augustus, then about the principate of Tiberius and those that followed, without anger or partiality, since the reasons men felt such emotions then do not reach to me in this age" (*Annals* 1.1: *sine ira et studio quorum causas procul habeo*).

Most commentators speak of Tacitus' claim to objectivity in these passages as if he were a modern historian brought up in the tradition of nineteenth-century or twentieth-century science. Yet he is not advocating the suppression of personal or moral judgments. All ancient historians were expected to pronounce on the goodness and badness of men and events; failure to do so would have been a serious breach of the historian's duty. Tacitus is simply saying that the cause of distortion in history is the good or bad treatment one has received from those in power: so he is careful to point out at the start of the *Histories* (1.1) that he himself had no personal knowledge of Galba, Otho, and Vitellius, while he recognizes the special need to be on guard when discussing their successors, whom he did know. He says at *Annals* 1.1 that since he himself never knew Tiberius, Gaius, Clau-

dius, and Nero, he can and will write of them without hatred or favoritism. The implication seems to be that one will not feel partial or hostile to a historical character if one has not had some personal, immediate experience of that character. It is true that at *Annals* 4.33 he says such feelings may occasionally be passed down to one's descendants and that a reader whose character is evil may resent historical personages because of too sharp a contrast between himself and good men or too close a similarity between himself and bad men. But this is not a significant qualification either of his belief that the historian must be on his guard against partiality and dislike when discussing men whom he has known or of his assumption that these emotions will be absent when speaking of men whom he has not known. It is thus peculiar and ironic that his portrait of Tiberius, the emperor furthest removed from him in time, is the most biased of all those in his historical works.

The remaining days of Galba's reign are described in thirty-eight chapters. The aged, parsimonious emperor looks about for an heir to adopt as a prop to an insecure throne. His unfortunate choice is Piso Licinianus, a reserved young aristocrat; in passing over Salvius Otho, who had hoped to be the choice, Galba prompts Otho at once to intrigue with the Praetorian Guard to topple the emperor and place himself on the throne. At the moment of adoption, Tacitus puts in Galba's mouth a set speech on the Roman principate. It is a noble, even majestic, oration, penetrating in its commentary on the nature of imperial power. The dangers of flattery and of the lack of sound advice are especially stressed:

> "Adulation forces its way in, together with flattery and self-seeking, that worst poison of sincere feeling. And even though you and I speak frankly between ourselves today, others will address themselves more to our position than to ourselves: for it is a difficult task indeed to persuade a prince of his duty, while to flatter him, whatever manner of man he may be, is unfeeling and routine."
>
> (*Histories* 1.15)

Galba goes on to laud the principle of adoption rather than dynastic succession, for it alone will discover the worthiest successor and can substitute for liberty *(loco libertatis)*, since the huge fabric of the empire is unable to cohere without one man's moderating rule. Galba laments the fact that he was a man who would have been worthy to inaugurate a republic; even so, he cautions Piso, Rome is not a state in which one family rules and all others are subjects: "You will be ruling over men who can endure neither complete servitude nor complete freedom," he concludes.

The speech is not wholly in the grand manner, however. Galba's justification of his seizure of power is self-serving, the appraisal of his present position culpably blind (in four days he and his new son will be dead). Moreover, his past record (especially his bloody entrance into Rome) and his unprepossessing character undercut somewhat the nobility and pertinence of his utterance here. Then, too, there is the parallel with the situation in the year 97: the aged Nerva sought by his adoption of Trajan to secure his throne in the midst of unrest and uncertainty. Tacitus' love of paradox is therefore apparent in even some of the noblest utterances he places in the mouths of his historical characters. Seldom is the character of the speaker commensurate with the splendor of what he says. Such speeches serve an ironic double function: to express general historical truths and to point up the fact that these truths seldom are translated into unalloyed good effect.

Tacitus' graphic description of Galba's murder and the accession of Otho illustrates at once some of his major historical concerns in the *Histories* and his power as a narrative artist. Greatest emphasis is placed upon men's hypocrisy and fickleness in the midst of civil strife. The populace at large loudly demands of Galba that he kill the usurper Otho,

behaving like spectators in the circus or amphitheater, possessing neither judgment nor sincerity, particularly in view of the fact that on the same day they would be demanding the reverse with equal insistence. It was their habit to flatter whatever ruler was in power with reckless shouting and empty demonstration of partiality.

(1.32)

Immediately after Galba's murder everyone, including the senators, rushed to the praetorian camp to denounce Galba and to worry Otho's hand with kisses. The scene recalls an earlier occasion on the same spot when Otho, in order to ingratiate himself with the soldiers, "blew kisses to the crowd, acting the slave in order to become the master" (1.36). As the day comes to a close we see Otho's litter being carried through the forum over heaps of corpses, while the senators in the Senate house rival each other in flattery, striving to wipe out any thought of the abuse that they had just been heaping upon him (1.47). Otho's accession presented them with a peculiarly delicate problem: the emperor had lately been one of them and carried with him a particularly lively appreciation of what they were up to (1.85).

Thus the breakdown of all loyalties save to the self operates at all levels of society and in all situations: city mob, soldiery, senators, knights, and provincials. Tacitus, by taking pains to note the few examples of noble conduct in all of this, causes them to stand out the more nakedly in their isolation (for example, 1.43, 45).

Tacitus' summing up of the murdered Galba is one of the most celebrated passages in his writings. Emphasis is placed on Galba's good fortune in the reigns of others rather than in his own, his noble lineage, and his wealth. But his character was of an average sort, more free of vices than distinguished by virtues:

His noble ancestry and the parlous times caused what was indolence to be dubbed wisdom. In his prime he proved an excellent military leader in Germany, governed Africa as proconsul with moderation, and in his old age ruled Nearer Spain with equal justice, seeming to be greater than a private citizen while yet a private citizen, and by common consent one who would have been equal to empire had he never been emperor. (1.49)

The last phrase *(capax imperii, nisi imperasset)* is particularly striking and is an example of one of Tacitus' favorite stylistic devices: the *sententia,* or striking aphorism, couched in few and memorable words. One translator has rendered it this way: "a man with a great future behind him."

The course of events during Otho's brief reign is described in the last half of book 1 and the first part of book 2 (1.50–2.50). His victorious rival is Vitellius, a description of whose revolt in Germany ominously inaugurates Otho's reign (1.51 ff.). Vitellius himself is painted in contemptible colors. Fat, indolent, prone to self-indulgence (1.62), he is manipulated by the ambitions of those more energetic and cunning than he, such as his lieutenants Fabius Valens and Alienus Caecinus. The narrative drives forward with remarkable energy as Tacitus describes the two-pronged invasion of Italy from the north and Otho's march up the peninsula to meet the Vitellians at Bedriacum, where he is defeated and commits suicide.

Otho owed his elevation to the dissatisfied praetorian guard, which in numbers and discipline proved an unreliable prop. At the end of the first book, for example, Tacitus describes a sudden tumult among the soldiery at Rome, sparked by some trivial cause but carried to extremes because of the lack of military discipline and the many recent examples of insubordination. The soldiers, fancying that the senators were attempting to undermine Otho's position, burst into the palace while Otho is entertaining in lavish style the most distinguished men of the state; as the panic-stricken senators and their wives attempt to slip out the doors, Otho finds he is able to quell the disturbance only by standing on a dining couch and pleading tearfully with them to desist. A large donative is promptly given; the way having been prepared, Otho ventures to enter the praetorian camp to address the soldiers.

The speech is a noble defense of and panegyric on the Senate, while Vitellius is branded an inferior renegade with slight support:

"We have the Senate, *we* the Republic. On the other side are the enemies of the state. Do you think that the magnificence of this city consists of houses, buildings, and edifices of stone? These are mute and lifeless things that can be destroyed and rebuilt at will. No, it is the security of the Senate that ensures world peace and the safety of myself and of all of you. The Senate was established by the founding father of our country, and from the kings to the emperors has survived unbroken, imperishable. Let us hand it on to our descendants as we received it from our ancestors. For just as the senators come from your ranks, so the emperors come from the ranks of the Senate." (1.84)

Noble sentiments, indeed, but in no way answering to the real situation (or to the facts of history). The senators and the Roman people had been reduced to spectators in a struggle carried on by others more powerful than they, although the military regularly invoked their names to cloak disloyalty and greed with the fair mantle of legitimacy. Two legions in Germany on the first day of the year 69, for example, overthrew the images of Galba, "but, so as not to seem to have discarded all reverence for the empire, invoked the now obsolete names of Senate and Roman people" (1.55), a meaningless oath, as Tacitus reemphasizes a few lines later.

The remainder of book 2 describes the aftermath of the defeat of Otho and his troops, Vitellius' increasing lapses into self-indulgence as he moves upon Rome with his victorious army, and the revolt of Vespasian and his supporters in the East. Mucianus, the shrewd governor of Syria, prompts Vespasian, who had been sent to Judea by Nero to quash a rebellion of the Jews and hence commanded a large number of loyal troops, to seek the purple for himself. Vespasian accepts; his lieutenants at once energetically push forward, especially Antonius Primus and Mucianus himself. Vespasian hangs back

1018

to secure Egypt, thereby cutting off the chief source of grain to the city and preparing for the possibility of lengthy struggle by attrition. But because Tacitus' main focus is on events in Italy and because the king-maker Mucianus is initially the prime mover, Vespasian in the extant narrative only slowly moves into our range of vision: an effective and suspenseful technique.

Book 3 of the *Histories* is perhaps the finest Tacitus ever wrote: scenes of unexampled horror and irony fill a narrative of nervous, brilliant energy. The book opens with the daring and unauthorized invasion of north Italy by Antonius Primus. Mucianus, unable to stop Primus or to control him, follows rapidly in jealous frustration. The enterprising and lucky Primus meets and defeats the Vitellian forces, commanded by the traitorous Alienus Caecina, near the colony of Cremona, which had sided with Otho and was not far from the site where Otho had lately fallen. The sack of Cremona by Vespasian's forces follows: for four days forty thousand men were permitted to have their way with the population and its possessions. So complete was the pillage and burning that only a single temple outside the walls survived the catastrophe.

Vitellius, who had stayed behind in Rome, was paralyzed by the news of the defeat. In order to avoid thinking about the situation or taking steps to counteract it, "he hid himself away in his shady gardens and lay there like a torpid beast stuffed from the food heaped up before it" (3.36). So unwilling was he to face up to the worsening situation that a strange silence would fall whenever he came upon those discussing the war. Then all talk about it was forbidden (3.54).

Mucianus had by now caught up with Antonius Primus, and ill feeling was openly displayed on both sides. Primus, quick in responding to immediate crises and sudden opportunities, was no match for the wily Mucianus when the time came for political solutions. Both men indeed offered to guarantee Vitellius' personal safety and a retirement home if he would abdicate. Vitellius in his naiveté tended to trust these overtures, and even discussed possible sites for his seaside estate and how many servants he would require: "He was so benumbed that he would have forgotten that he was emperor had not others reminded him." Shortly afterward he made a tearful attempt to abdicate. The supporters of Vespasian then began to gather openly, but upon hearing that Vitellius had returned to the palace and that his German troops were roaming menacingly about the city, they took refuge on the Capitoline Hill and threw up barricades. The Vitellian troops launched an attack, in the course of which the Capitol was burned to the ground. Gone in an instant were all the temples, shrines, and holy places, including the temple of Jupiter Optimus Maximus, the most visible and venerable symbol of Rome's greatness and worldwide supremacy. "The most grievous, most disgraceful event in the history of Rome," writes Tacitus. "What were the reasons for the conflict? What was the justification for such a disaster? Ah, yes! 'We were fighting for our country!'" During the conflict Vespasian's younger son, Domitian, escaped by disguising himself as a priest, while Vespasian's elder brother was brought before Vitellius and cut down to please the bloodthirsty crowd, the emperor being powerless to save him.

The final scenes depict the street fighting that followed the entrance of Vespasian's troops into the city. The Roman mob looked on as if watching a mock battle in an amphitheater, cheering on the combatants and applauding the slaughter below. Near the heaps of corpses and pools of blood stood pimps, prostitutes, and male whores plying their trade. The baths and taverns were filled with revelers, while all exulted in the carnage, as if an extra spectacle had been added to the festivities of a national holiday: "They didn't care which side won and enjoyed thoroughly the public catastrophe" (3.83). When one group of combatants would retreat and take refuge in the shops or houses, the crowd would shout out to their pursuers where they were hidden. They then had the pleasure of witnessing the slaughter of the ones dragged from their hiding places, after which they rushed to strip the corpses as the fighting moved on down the street.

Vitellius, in the meantime, fled the palace to his wife's home on the Aventine Hill. But not knowing what to do next or where to turn, he retraced his steps to the now deserted palace. Numb with fear, he wandered through the empty, echoing corridors, and tried to hide himself. When discovered, he was dragged out and hurried into the forum, where a sword's point under his chin forced him to raise his head and see his statues falling all about and to suffer the taunts of the heartless crowd. "Yet I *was* your emperor," he said to a tribune as he fell under a rain of blows.

Much of the fourth book is taken up with the revolt of Claudius Civilis in Gaul and Germany, a rebellion that spread so widely and quickly that many believed the empire to be on the verge of extinction. The themes of freedom and servility, of exploitation and imperialism, are especially prominent. An experienced military leader, Petilius Cerialis, is sent to quell the insurgents, and in his mouth Tacitus puts a particularly fine speech (4.73–74). In addressing the natives of Trier, in northern Gaul, Cerialis asserts that Roman motives for the initial conquest of Gaul were free from self-seeking; the Romans were invited in by the ancestors of those present to end incessant civil strife among the warring tribes. Now, after many years of internal peace and prosperity, the empire protects them from attacks by hostile German tribes across the Rhine. Moreover, they are now full participants in the running of the empire, furnishing military commanders and provincial governors. They enjoy all the blessings of imperial rule under worthy emperors, although living far away. Under bad princes they suffer less because those nearest perforce receive the brunt of their excesses. "Just as you endure barren crops, floods, and other natural disasters, so you should put up with the passions and avarice of your rulers. There will be vices as long as there are men, but they do not

continue indefinitely and are balanced out by the coming of better times." He particularly warns against believing in appeals to native liberty, especially on the part of the Germans, whose only aim is to cross the Rhine and seize the wealth of Gaul: "Liberty and such fair-sounding names are but pretexts; no man ever desired domination over others and rule for himself without invoking the same catchwords" (4.73).

The speech is the finest defense of empire in Tacitus' extant writings. Doubtless it reflects in large part his own views, for he clearly espoused the vigorous defense and extension of Roman territory. But the speech, as one would expect in Tacitus, is not to be taken wholly at face value. Cerialis' claim that Roman motives for the initial conquest were free of self-interest is disingenuous, to say the least, while the attribution of hypocrisy to those who seek to justify their domination of others is the central argument of just such a justification.

The fifth book is brief, the lone manuscript tradition breaking off abruptly in mid-sentence; what survives is at most a third of the whole book. It opens with an introduction to the Jewish war carried on by Vespasian and his son Titus. The survey of the Jewish state and its religion (2–8) is one of the sorriest passages in Tacitus, marred by prejudice, distortion, and plain error. The narrative then returns to the revolt of Civilis, shortly after which the text breaks off.

THE ANNALES

Tacitus' last work in its completed form covered the reigns of Tiberius, Gaius (nicknamed Caligula), Claudius, and Nero (A.D. 14–68). It survives in two parts, each by a single, mutilated manuscript tradition: books 1–6, concerning the reign of Tiberius (A.D. 14–37), with most of the fifth book missing; and books 11–16, covering the last half of Claudius' reign (books 11–12: A.D. 47–54), and much of Nero's (books 13–16: A.D. 54–66). Whether the *Annals* ended with

Nero's suicide in June 68 or continued to the end of the year (thereby linking up with the completed *Histories*) is unknown. To this writer the latter seems more likely. There is a chance, of course, that Tacitus died suddenly, writing nothing beyond the incomplete sentence that ends our text partway through book 16.

It is interesting to contemplate how Tacitus came to history and how he proceeded once he arrived. The *Agricola*, as noted above, has a considerable amount of straight historical writing in respect to both subject matter and technique. In the essay he declares his intention to write sometime in the future "the story of our prior servitude and a testimonial to the present happiness" (3), referring to an account of Domitian's reign and the start of Nerva's. When he came to the task in the *Histories*, however, he shifted his starting point back in time to 1 January 69, and the last days of Galba's reign. After he had finished the *Histories*, and as if something were yet missing or unexplained, he moved back again, beginning this time with the accession of Tiberius in August A.D. 14 and bringing the narrative up to the point (or near the point) where the *Histories* had begun (that the *Histories* were written first is clear from a number of passages, especially *Annals* 11.11). Even so, after having completed only two and a half books of the *Annals*, he says that he hopes he will live long enough to narrate the lengthy principate of Augustus once he has finished the present work (3.24). Some have supposed that he realized shortly after beginning the *Annals* that for a variety of reasons August A.D. 14 was an infelicitous point of departure. This may be so, but the plan to move further back in time is part of a long-standing pattern in his pursuit of history. Some scholars also believe that the chief aim of the *Histories* and *Annals* was to explain how and why the principate began and became entrenched as an institution. Yet it seems unlikely that he made so many false plans and starts before realizing that Augustus was where these questions could be elucidated. Moreover, at the start of Tiberius' reign the principate is an accomplished fact:

the rush into slavery was immediate and total (*Annals* 1.7), the arts of flattery fully matured (1.8), while Tiberius' protestation of doubt about his capacities and his hesitation in ruling were to the senators an embarrassing charade (1.10). It does not seem, therefore, that Tacitus' intention (except perhaps at the last, when he planned to write on Augustus) was to explain the reasons why the principate came into being and took on its characteristic features. His concentration was rather fixed on working out the consequences of what in its essential aspects had been already established.

The question of how Tacitus viewed historical change is complex and has been little discussed. Within reigns change is frequently (but by no means wholly) due to the deterioration of the emperor's character (as with Tiberius and Nero) and once to an improvement (Vespasian: *Histories* 1.50). But what of changes between reigns? He stresses such subjects as the gradual growth of the emperor's power (and the corresponding weakening of the Senate), the increase in delation and of trials for treason, and the vicissitudes in morality and moral legislation (for example, *Annals* 3.52–55). These and like topics combine to form a *developmental* view of history, and his repeated shifting further back in time may be seen in part as an effort to comprehend more fully what was basically a slow, almost imperceptible process. In a remarkable passage in book 4 he breaks into the narrative to protest that his readers should not compare his efforts with those of historians who wrote of the old-time republic (he has Livy particularly in mind):

They described great wars, the sack of cities, kings captured or put to flight, and, when turning to internal affairs, expatiated at length on discord between consuls and tribunes, agrarian and grain laws, conflict between the nobility and common people. My task, however, is circumscribed and inglorious: peace undisturbed or slightly broken, depressing events in the city, an emperor indifferent to the extension of empire. Still, it will not be without value to examine those at first sight trivial events from which great changes often take their rise.

(*Annals* 4.32)

It is not clear precisely what "great changes" he has in mind. Among them may be the civil war that followed the collapse of the Julio-Claudian line, the beginning of which would form the end and climax of the *Annals*.

Tacitus' account of Tiberius' reign is generally conceded to show the historian at the height of his powers. His style has fully matured: arresting, rapid, rejecting parallelism and symmetry for inconcinnity and the unexpected. Unfortunately, no translation can do justice to the highly charged and idiosyncratic qualities of his prose; often, indeed, how things are expressed is more significant than what is said. One scholar has written that describing the style to one who has not read the Latin is like trying to describe the taste of peppermint to a man who has never tasted it. Nevertheless, such translations as those of Church and Brodribb give some sense of the irony, concentration, and power of the original.

The portrait of Tiberius himself is unforgettable: austere, reclusive, cunning, he strives to conceal his shameful desires and enjoyment of power, but yields step by step in his advancing years to ever more open revelation of his inmost soul. Tacitus is fascinated by the man, his fascination compounded in unequal parts of puzzlement, loathing, and grudging admiration. The obituary at the end (6.51) asserts that Tiberius went through four stages, each caused by the removal of a friend's or relative's restraining influence. As a private citizen or while acting in positions of authority under Augustus, his manner of life and reputation were commendable. Such virtues were assumed, however, and they continued into his reign as long as his stepson, the noble Germanicus, and his natural son, the less admirable Drusus, were alive. From then until the death of his aged mother, Livia, widow of Augustus, his character was a compound of good and bad; later, even Sejanus, his praetorian prefect, whom he both loved and feared, kept some check on his cruelty and sex-

ual appetites. But when Sejanus fell, Tiberius erupted into acts of savagery and lust: "Shame and fear were gone; he could indulge in his own inclinations at will" (*postquam remoto pudore et metu suo tantum ingenio utebatur*).

This striking formulation comes as something of a surprise, however, for the four stages enunciated here are by no means clearly marked or obvious in the preceding narrative. And there are other oddities. At the start of book 4 Tacitus marks the emergence of Sejanus to full power as the turning point both in the reign and in Tiberius' character. We are told (4.6) that hitherto Tiberius' principate had been for the most part exemplary and marked by restraint, which is not the impression Tacitus has so far given. Sejanus plotted to seduce the wife of Tiberius' son, Drusus, and then to poison him; Sejanus succeeded in both. Later, when he asked for the widow's hand in marriage and received a cryptic rejection, he decided to urge upon Tiberius the advantages of retirement to the island of Capri, away from annoyance and offense (4.41). Yet when the time comes for the emperor's departure, Tacitus changes his mind (4.57). Earlier he had followed majority opinion among historians by attributing it to the prompting of Sejanus, but since the emperor continued to live in seclusion on Capri for the six years remaining of his life, Tacitus is now inclined to attribute the withdrawal to Tiberius' personal impulse; and he notes that during the reign of Augustus, Tiberius had on his own initiative acted similarly, retiring to the island of Rhodes for six years.

The retirements to Rhodes and Capri were due to Tiberius' desire to give vent to his cruelty and unnatural sexual appetites away from the eyes of the curious and disapproving. But in going to Capri, Tacitus adds, he may also have wanted to hide the repellent physical appearance of his old age. The historian seldom tells us how his historical characters looked in life. The description here is unexpected and done with multiple effect: tall, bent, and very thin, the emperor had a bald head, his face an eruption of pustules that he tried to hide by the application of medicinal plasters. A description of the breathtaking beauty of Tiberius' chosen retreat comes a few chapters later (4.67). Note, too, that the last item in the description is symptomatic of Tiberius' whole person and personality: the attempt to hide his real self from the gaze of the world. Hypocrisy is the form the impulse commonly takes; the unforgettable scene in the Senate at the start of the *Annals* (1.7–8, 11–14) emphasizes it above all else. When asked what powers he wished voted him, Tiberius replied that he really wanted none and would prefer to be excused wholly. Nonplussed, the senators attempt to persuade him to declare his wishes. In doing so, several offend him, to their eventual cost: "Later men came to realize that he assumed an air of hesitation in order to divine the true feelings of the nobility, for he would twist their words and expressions into a crime and treasure up the remembrance in his heart" (1.7). The reluctance to assume power, Tacitus is convinced, was wholly feigned: he wanted not only to test the feelings of the senators but to appear to have been freely chosen. Then, too, everyone had to maintain the pretense that Rome was still a republic and that the discussion was about matters in which there was free choice. But there was not. With Augustus' last breath Tiberius had assumed command of all military forces; an escort of soldiers attended him everywhere. The scenes in the Senate were thus an excruciating, ludicrous charade. They all knew Tiberius wanted power, but could see no way of gracefully making him admit and accept it:

> Tiberius' speech, even in matters that he didn't care to conceal, was wavering and obscure, whether by nature or habit. But now that he was struggling to hide his inmost feelings it was even more entangled in uncertainty and ambiguity. The senators poured forth tears, cries of distress, and prayers to heaven, for their one fear was that they might seem to understand him.
>
> (1.11)

In the last years, when his true character emerged like a beast from its lair, Tiberius could not shake off his habits of concealment and of testing the attitudes of others. Even at the end, when his strength was failing him, he perceived the attempt of a doctor to take his pulse surreptitiously, whereupon he continued to feast late into the evening in order to hide his weakened condition. When he was believed dead and Caligula was stepping forth to receive the congratulations of those in attendance, the old emperor did not let go: he revived and called for food; the panicked throng dispersed, leaving Caligula stunned and silent. The emperor was dispatched by being smothered under his bedclothes. *Sic Tiberius finivit* is Tacitus' striking phrase (6.50): "Thus Tiberius ended."

Tacitus is fascinated by those moments in which the mask that the emperor assumed slipped to reveal his true self. For with all his cunning Tiberius could not conceal it; and his suppressed feelings, when they did appear, would erupt suddenly and savagely, but with a quick attempt at recovery. Tacitus considered Tiberius basically an intelligent man who saw through to others' hypocrisy and false sentiment (which he particularly loathed, perhaps because he himself was such an adept), but who failed to realize that others could perceive the same insincerity in him. But as he retired from public view and as the restraining influence of his sons, mother, and finally even Sejanus fell away, he allowed more frequent and fuller glimpses of his real nature. In a letter written to the Senate shortly after Sejanus' death, he began: "What I should write to you senators, or how to write, or what to leave unsaid—may the gods and goddesses punish me more terribly than the misery I feel crushing me daily, if I know." This was the cry, Tacitus affirms, of a guilty soul in torment, and he mentions Plato's belief that if the minds of tyrants could be laid bare, bruises and wounds would appear, for just as the body is disfigured by lashes, so is the spirit by savagery, lust, and evil thoughts: "Neither position nor solitude prevented Tiberius from confessing the torment of his soul and his self-inflicted punishment." Later, after he had persecuted and killed the widow and two eldest sons of his adopted son, Germanicus, Tacitus records how Tiberius in a letter to the Senate described the death of the younger boy, Drusus, who had been imprisoned, whipped by his guards, and denied food to the point that he ate the stuffing of his mattress. Tiberius published the diary Drusus had kept during his torment for all to read, accusing the young man of treason and perversion: "The senators cried out in affected horror. Secretly they felt fear and amazement that a cunning prince who had hitherto covered up his crimes should so expose himself that the prison walls had, so to speak, been pulled back to reveal his grandson under the lash of the centurion, whipped by slaves, begging in vain for the last sustenance of life" (6.34).

Though Tacitus conceived of Tiberius' character as developing in a series of stages, "developing" is perhaps misleading; "revealing itself" might be more accurate, for it reflects Tacitus' apparent belief that character was set from birth: Tiberius was always a bad man, but was restrained by various persons and circumstances in his life from expressing his true self. R. G. Collingwood in *The Idea of History* therefore concludes that for Tacitus, "Power does not alter a man's character; it only shows what kind of man he already was." Yet there are passages in Tacitus showing that he was familiar with the idea of the corruption of character by power and of character change in general. For example, only a few pages before Tiberius' obituary the emperor's friend Arruntius declares that the prince "despite his long years of experience was utterly changed and perverted by holding power" (6.41: *post tantam experientiam vi dominationis convulsus et mutatus sit*).

But Tacitus' chief concern in history is not with character but with events. For much of his life Tiberius led a commendable existence because of the restraining influence of Augustus, his mother, and others. In Aristotelian terms he was at that time potentially evil, not actually so. And since the subject matter of history is what

men do, not what they are capable of doing (although some find "might-have-been" history a powerful attraction), the implication is clear: circumstances and environment are paramount, since only they allow a man's character to affect events. Had Tiberius never become emperor, had he died earlier in his reign, or had people like his mother or sons continued to live, men could only guess at how he might have turned out. What it was that made Tiberius evil is not a question history can satisfactorily answer; but it can explain how and why a man's character, if given the opportunity, will express itself.

A review of Tiberius' reign shows that little of real substance occurred in terms of major events or marked changes. The emperor discouraged military conquest in favor of negotiated settlements, retained the same men in office for years on end, added little to the city by way of buildings or physical improvements, and spent the last ten years of his life as a recluse on Capri. Tacitus is frank about the often petty material he must record, as he confesses at *Annals* 4.32–33, quoted previously. The *Annals*, being a political history, have as their abiding theme the nature and development of imperial power and of its growth over time. This nature and development are revealed in a myriad of episodes at first sight trifling, yet pregnant with meaning for the historian who sees to their deeper significance. An example concerns the praetor's courts in Rome (1.75). When he learned that powerful men sometimes exerted undue influence on the decisions of the praetors, Tiberius effectively stopped the practice by taking a seat at the end of the tribunal and merely looking on. "This, while serving the interests of justice, compromised freedom" is Tacitus' comment. Here we see summed up in the briefest of notices (some five lines) the dilemma of the principate and liberty, those "irreconcilable elements" that Tacitus affects to believe Nerva reconciled (*Agricola* 3).

This same approach on a larger scale can be seen in the military revolts in Germany and

Pannonia at the start of Tiberius' reign, which take up the bulk of the first book (16–71). Narrated with great vigor and much detail, these revolts have been criticized as blown up far beyond their historical importance. Tacitus succumbed, it is averred, to the opportunity to indulge in vivid writing: crowd scenes, set speeches, acts of heroism and folly. Especially inviting, it is said, was the chance to feature Germanicus, the nephew of Tiberius whom Augustus had required him to adopt; affable, handsome, and enterprising (foolishly so on occasion), the young man in the first two books is a foil to the morose, cautious, jealous old emperor. No doubt Tacitus was indeed attracted by all these possibilities. But the historical issues raised by the events far transcend their immediate effects: the ever-present threat of an unruly military, the relation of the soldiery to the emperor and the whole of the Julio-Claudian house, the forces and impulses that motivated both soldiers and commanders; these and many other issues are illustrated in these episodes, for all their lively narration and artistic merit. The army was the basis upon which the principate rested (mark, for example, the emperor's crushing response to an attempt to tamper with military arrangements at 6.3). Moreover, the *Annals* began with a great revolt and would end with a far greater one at the death of Nero. Tacitus was clearly looking to the end of the *Annals* when writing the first book.

Tacitus has been criticized for being too Rome-centered, for excessive concentration on the emperor and those nearest him, for neglecting the social and economic conditions under which the vast bulk of the empire's population lived. Such criticisms are misdirected: his aim was not to write a history of the Roman world, but to reveal the nature of autocracy as seen in the Roman principate. Hence his preoccupation with Rome, with subjects such as character and dynastic intrigue, two of the most powerful elements in the syndrome created by the existence of the principate. By "syndrome" is meant the complex series of relationships that obtain among those who exercise or aim to exercise a measure of political power: the emperor, his ministers, members of his family, heirs apparent, administrators (including senators, knights, imperial slaves, and freedmen), and the armies with their officers and commanders. The aim of most individuals is to seek power, whether indirectly as advisers and confidants or directly as administrators and officers. The top prize, of course, is the throne itself, whether for oneself or as king-maker. The will to power, the passion to play the master (for example, 15.53: *cupido libido dominandi*), is for Tacitus one of the strongest drives in men. It is not universal, however; a few, such as Agricola or Germanicus, have the self-control to fulfill the role that falls to their lot. But such individuals are rare. Recurring situations are to be expected under such conditions: flattery of the emperor to obtain favor, flattery of his favorites for the same end, attempts to manipulate the emperor by exploiting his secret fears and desires, denouncing one's enemies by playing upon these fears, and so forth. So, too, the appearance of "character types": the despised informer, the intriguing wife, the treacherous stepmother, the oily confidant, the noble victim. In all of this the temperament of the emperor is a decisive variable, of course, for neither situations nor characters are ever alike. One of Tacitus' particular pleasures in writing was to observe the ever-changing interplay between similarity and novelty: a new twist in adulation, whether fatuous or clever; an accused man in peril who contrives to turn the tables on his accuser; the one who divines what the emperor secretly desires and advances spectacularly because of it, yet falls victim to the very passions he has roused.

The portrait of Tiberius, particularly in books 1–3, suffers from marked distortion. Tacitus often impugns the emperor's motives and blackens his character, although the evidence that he himself supplies sometimes fails to support his interpretations. For example, the trials for treason *(maiestas)* that for the historian were such a hallmark of the reign are represented at their very inception as a villainous novelty devised by a malevolent prince:

> It will not be without point to record the first attempts at such charges that were made against Falanius and Rubrius, Roman knights, so that the reader may know how this terrible scourge first crept in among us, with what cunning Tiberius initiated it, how it was repressed but in the end burst into flame and consumed everything.
>
> (1.73)

A few lines later we find, however, that both men were promptly acquitted at Tiberius' insistence. Granius Marcellus is then arraigned by Caepio Crispinus and Romanius Hispo. The latter is singled out as an archetypal informer,

> who entered on a way of life later made infamous by the miseries of the age and men's brazenness. Poor, low-born, and restless, he pandered to the emperor's vindictive nature by making secret incriminations, quickly proved a threat to the most distinguished citizens, and in gaining one man's favor and the hatred of everyone else set an example whereby paupers became wealthy and the contemptible terrifying, bringing ruin to others and in the end themselves.
>
> (1.74)

Marcellus was accused of traducing Tiberius, which Tacitus describes as "a charge not to be evaded" *(inevitabile crimen)*, since Hispo based his case on the worst features of the emperor's character: what was said about Tiberius was true, and thus the charge was believed to be true. Yet almost immediately we learn that Tiberius allowed the accusation of treason to be dropped. Tacitus has narrated the episode so adroitly, however, that without checking back we may not remember that this particular charge was one "not to be evaded." Such discrepancies between fact and impression have been well discussed by B. Walker in her perceptive book *The Annals of Tacitus.*

The reasons for such distortion are not simple or immediately obvious. In the case of treason trials, Tacitus tells us that he wishes to emphasize the initial steps of a process that was to grow to alarming proportions. Certainly the last book devoted to Tiberius' reign is mostly a numbing concatenation of accusation, suicide, and execution. Then again, his belief that Tiberius' character was always the same would prompt him to see discreditable motives early in the reign when the emperor was still inhibited by the existence of those to whom he feared to reveal his true self. The rhetorical schools may also have had some influence on his thinking, for one of the stock characters of declamation and drama was the tyrant, whom the practitioners of rhetoric (almost the whole of the educated elite) fitted out with a full panoply of deadly sins. Very influential as well must have been the historical sources Tacitus used. Parallel accounts of Tiberius' reign in authors such as Suetonius and Dio Cassius suggest that they and Tacitus share one or more common sources that put a similarly unfavorable construction upon the emperor's character and motives.

Perhaps the most curious aspect of the problem is that the greatest distortion comes in the period most distant from Tacitus' own time. Tacitus believed that a historian's prejudice toward his historical characters came largely if not wholly from personal experience (*Annals* 1.1; *Histories* 1.1); it was suggested earlier that perhaps he was least on his guard the further removed he found himself from the period he was writing about. Yet none of these reasons individually is enough to explain the distortion, and collectively they do not consort together comfortably or offer a completely satisfying answer. The problem remains and is perhaps not fully soluble.

The text of the *Annals* resumes in the middle of book 11. The emperor Claudius is on the throne, a man whom Tacitus represents as weak-willed and weak-minded, easily manipulated by freedmen secretaries such as Pallas and Narcissus and by his beautiful, willful, and lascivious wife, Messalina. The passive verbs that appear when Claudius comes into view are indicative of his role in Tacitus' narrative, as also is the comment at *Annals* 3.18, where the senator Valerius Messalinus, in proposing a decree of thanksgiving to the imperial family in the days of Tiberius, forgets to include Claudius. The omission is quickly remedied, Tacitus adding, "The more I study past and present history, the more I perceive the mockery of all human plans and aspirations [*ludibria rerum mortalium*], for in reputation, expectation, and general respect anybody was a more likely candidate for the purple than the man whom Fortune was hiding in reserve as emperor of the future."

The surviving portion of book 11 opens with Messalina at the height of her power; at the end of the book she meets her death, having concocted the mad scheme of marrying another man while Claudius was a few miles away attending to official duties at Ostia, Rome's port city. Book 12 brings Agrippina, Claudius' niece and last wife, to center stage. She is selected after a contest among three of Claudius' freedmen, each promoting the charms of different ladies (of whom Agrippina is one) and despite the fact that, to the Romans, marriage to a niece was incestuous. Agrippina's beauty and hard-willed ambition prevail. She immediately begins to promote the interests of Nero, her son by a previous marriage, first by betrothing him to Octavia, Claudius' daughter, and later by having Claudius adopt him as his son, thereby making him an older coequal of Claudius' natural son, Britannicus. At the end of the book, disquieted by signs that Claudius is tiring of her and her son, she poisons the emperor, but not before making plans to keep Britannicus in the palace while Nero steps forth to receive the acclamation of the crowd as emperor: "Some are said to have hesitated by looking back and asking where Britannicus was; but soon, when no one championed a different candidate, they went along with what was offered" (12.69).

An episode in Claudius' reign reveals the methods and aims of the historian: the debate in the Senate whether to admit men of central and northern Gaul to membership in that body (11.23–25). Tacitus gives the emperor a speech in support of the motion (11.24), impressive in its language and argument. By chance we possess the original that Claudius actually gave, preserved on a bronze tablet found in Lyons (ancient Lugdunum). Comparison shows that Tacitus has preserved the chief thrust of the original, although he omits some points, adds others, and thoroughly rearranges the whole. More striking is the elimination of the emperor's clumsiness and gaucherie, together with his abrupt shifts in mood and idea. Had Tacitus wished to belittle Claudius, he had every opportunity and justification here. The rejoinder might be made that speeches in ancient historiography were the original compositions of the author and should therefore reflect and display his artistic powers: it would be unthinkable for Tacitus deliberately to commit solecisms or cultivate ineptitude. The rejoinder is true. But what is striking here is Tacitus' refusal to let his poor opinion of the speaker come through or to echo by significant word or phrase any utterance of the original (such character touches and echoes seem to be present in the speeches he gives to Tiberius). The reason must be that the importance of the subject itself forbids compromising it by demeaning idiosyncrasy or allusion to the known, accessible original. The oration is concerned with nothing less than the extension of Rome's power and the romanization of the empire: the basis of its power rests and has always rested upon the willingness to change past practice by extending to others rights and political privilege. Tacitus has Claudius conclude with these words: "All things, senators, now considered hallowed by time were once new; plebeians followed patricians in holding office, Latins the plebeians, the rest of Italy the Latins. This, too, will be part of the past, and what we are justifying today by citing precedent will itself become precedent." A noble theme is thus enhanced by the historian's considerable rhetorical powers. At the same time we are meant to be struck by the contrast between the nobility of the utterance and the character of the person into whose mouth the speech is put. The orations in the *Histories* of Galba (1.15–16) and Otho (1.83–84), discussed previously, are meant to make the same sort of ironic contrast. One might surmise that one of Tacitus' motives in composing such speeches was to show what the speaker might have said had he been equal to the grandeur of his theme; but Tacitus' ghost-writing was not at bottom invention: certainly he preserves in this speech the basic line of argument that Claudius used on the occasion in question.

After briefly describing the last days of Augustus at the start of the *Annals*, Tacitus selects the following episode to introduce Tiberius' principate: "The first murder of the new reign was that of Postumus Agrippa, who, surprised and defenseless, was dispatched with difficulty by a most determined centurion" (1.6). He uses the same damning technique to inaugurate Nero's principate: "The first death of the new reign was that of Junius Silanus, the proconsul of Asia, the result of Agrippina's contrivance and without Nero's knowledge" (13.1). The similar circumstances under which each emperor succeeded to the throne doubtless prompted Tacitus to reinforce the parallel as he did: despite great disparity in their ages at accession, Tiberius and Nero were stepsons, promoted by their mothers over the interests of those related to the emperor by blood, and in each case the news of the death of the old emperor was concealed until the ladies had prepared the way for their sons' full assumption of power.

The young Nero at the start was very much under the influence and guidance of his mother, as well as of Seneca, his tutor, and Burrus, the prefect of the praetorian guard. Hence the reign begins with Agrippina as the dominant personality, and it is she who engineers the "first death of the new reign." The first years, however, were by and large exemplary, the young prince deferring to the Senate and his advisers with becoming modesty and sensitivity to constitutional niceties. But, unlike Claudius, who throughout his reign remained under the thumb of others, Nero did not long prove docile. His development thus parallels that of Tiberius, for gradually his base character emerges as he sheds himself of those who would restrain it, until in the end it has free scope to indulge itself at will. Yet the differences between Nero and Tiberius are as great as the similarities, if not greater. Perhaps most significant is the manner in which their characters are revealed. Tiberius tried to conceal his thoughts and feelings in a long retreat from public view; in the end he withdrew his very person to the seclusion of Capri. Nero, on the other hand, displayed himself before the public with increasing frequency, first as promoter of games and theatrical spectacles, then as a performer himself, whether in artistic pursuits, such as playing the lyre and singing, or in athletics, as charioteer. A claque of supporters kept up constant, rhythmic applause on these occasions lest silence or uneven clapping should suggest less than full enthusiasm. Some spectators were crushed to death in the throng, Tacitus affirms (16.5; see also 14.15), others stayed in their seats day and night fearing to be seen to leave, while a few sickly souls actually expired in their places. The future emperor Vespasian barely escaped death when he was roused by one of his freedmen as he began to nod off.

That a man of the upper class, to say nothing of the emperor himself, should show himself on the public stage or in the circus was disgraceful:

> He long had the desire to race a four-horse chariot, and the no less demeaning passion to sing to the accompaniment of a lyre under the conditions of a public contest. . . . When resistance was no longer possible, it seemed wisest to Seneca and Burrus to grant him one wish lest he have his way in both. An area in the Vatican valley was fenced off so that he might race his horses away from the public eye. But soon the Roman people were summoned, and exalted him with their praises, as is the habit of a pleasure-loving crowd that delights in a prince who shares the same inclinations. But

the shame of public self-display did not satisfy him, as they had thought it would, but proved only a stimulus to further acts.

(14.14)

Nero thus emerges as the darling of the public, giver of lavish entertainments in which he increasingly is the star attraction. Public tours in Italy are then arranged (15.33–36), and a still grander tour of all Greece is projected (which we know, from other sources, he took in the period after the text of Tacitus breaks off). Even during the great fire of A.D. 66, in which much of Rome was destroyed, a pervasive rumor had it that "at the very time the city was in flames Nero stepped out on a private stage and sang of the fall of Troy, comparing the present misfortune to disasters of old" (15.39). That Nero had deliberately set the fire in order to found the city anew and name it after himself was another rumor so widely bruited about that the emperor decided to fix the charge of arson on the Christian sect. His method was characteristic of the showman: he opened his private gardens to the spectacle of the Christians, covered in the hides of wild animals, being torn apart by dogs; or being crucified; or, when night fell, set on fire to provide illumination. In the same period he gave public games in which he appeared costumed as a charioteer and mingled with the common people (15.44). The adulation of the public and his courtiers became in the end so unstinting that he had the greatest difficulty in comprehending why anyone would conspire against him. Such a plot (the so-called Pisonian Conspiracy) was mounted shortly after the great fire; it was a shoddy affair, not least because most motives of the several conspirators were personal and petty. Nero's initial incredulity is revealed when he personally interrogates some of the conspirators as to why they would ever have wanted to harm him. Nothing in the whole affair shocked him so much as when some told him the truth, declares Tacitus, "unaccustomed as he was to hear of the crimes he had committed, however ready he

was to commit them" (15.67). It is clear that to the end Nero was captive to the public's applause, blind to much that was going on about him, and paralyzed when a crisis confronted him. Suetonius credibly reports in his biography of the emperor (Nero 49) that his last words before committing suicide were "Qualis artifex pereo!" ("What an artist they are losing in me!").

Getting rid of those who tried to guide and restrain him, as well as those who were merely an annoyance or who were fancied as rivals, was a necessary preliminary to self-indulgence and self-display. So his younger brother by adoption, Britannicus, the natural son of Claudius, was poisoned at the dinner table while Nero and his guests looked on, the emperor idly remarking that the boy's agony was probably only an epileptic fit. "So the festivites resumed after a brief lull. The same night witnessed both his death and funeral, since the funeral preparations had been made ahead of time" (13.16–17).

Nero's mother, Agrippina, was naturally worried by this development. As she sat at the dining table, "Fear and consternation flashed out, though she tried to control her expression. . . . She well understood what the example of a kinsman's murder could mean for herself." Almost at once, Nero, tired of her domineering ways, removed her living quarters to a separate establishment, where she was visited by only a few ladies, "whether out of affection or malice is hard to say" (13.19). Yet she survived an attempt shortly thereafter to bring her down by boldly confronting her accuser and carrying the day. But when Nero became enamoured of the beautiful and scheming Poppaea, she induced him to get rid of Agrippina, who championed the cause of Octavia, Nero's wife and the daughter of Claudius. Various schemes were canvassed. Poison was ruled out because one could not plausibly ascribe Agrippina's death to accident after what had happened to Britannicus; then again, the lady regularly fortified herself with antidotes as a preventive against such contingencies. Suborning her household slaves was risky when the mistress was herself an adept in crime and on guard against treachery (14.3). Anicetus, commander of the fleet stationed in the Bay of Naples, came up with the clever scheme of drowning her in a collapsible boat:

> Nothing was so prone to the vagaries of chance as the sea; if she perished in a shipwreck who would be so unkind as to believe that the actions of wind and wave were prearranged? Besides, the prince would build a temple and altars to the deceased lady and add other displays of filial devotion.
>
> (14.3)

So Nero invited her for a visit to his seaside estate; there she was treated with all solicitude, and, when she rose to leave, "Nero followed, clinging to her and kissing her, whether as the crowning touch to his performance or because the sight of his mother in her final moments had its effect even on that brutal heart."

She set out on a calm sea, the night brilliant with stars. The boat indeed collapsed, but faultily. Agrippina and her maidservant were thrown into the water. The maid, thinking to save herself, called out that she was the emperor's mother and was promptly dispatched by oars and punting poles. Agrippina, wounded in the shoulder but silent, succeeded in swimming ashore. She was under no illusion as to what had happened, and decided her only course was to put the best face on it. She sent a messenger to Nero to report that by the will of heaven and his own good fortune she had escaped a terrible mishap, and to request that he delay paying a visit until she might compose herself. She then ordered a search be made for the maid's will and had her property sealed, "in this alone acting without pretense" (14.6). Nero in the meantime was paralyzed by the news of the abortive attempt. Again Anicetus came to the rescue: a dagger was thrown at the feet of Agrippina's messenger, and he and his mistress were accused of making an attempt on the emperor's life. In the meantime Anicetus and his henchmen went to Agrippina's villa, where they cut her down; as they did so she thrust her body forward, crying, "Strike my womb!" Tacitus reports that in earlier days, when consulting astrologers about Nero's future, she was told that he was destined to rule but kill his mother: "Let him kill her," she replied, "so long as he is emperor" (14.9).

Few sequences are as instructive for Tacitus' view of autocracy as the aftermath of Nero's murder of his mother. The first night was terrible for the emperor, who at one moment sat mute, the next leaped up in fear and distress. Burrus then bade the soldiers congratulate him for having escaped the danger of Agrippina's plotting. They did so, and his spirits began to lift. When his friends next visited the temples to give thanks for his deliverance, the towns in the area followed their example by instituting public sacrifices and sending delegations to testify to their joy. Cheered, Nero traveled to Naples and from there sent a message to the Senate concerning Agrippina's plot and her past excesses. It was a clumsy, even embarrassing communication (though composed by Seneca), in which even the story of the shipwreck was related. The senators, undeterred, decreed a thanksgiving to the gods and that annual games be added to the festival of Minerva, as the day on which the plot had been discovered. An image of Minerva in gold, with a statue of Nero at her side, was set up in the Senate house, while the day of Agrippina's birth was classed as ill-omened ever after (14.10-11). Even so, Nero was reluctant to come to Rome because he was unsure how he would be received. His friends scoffed at his hesitation, assuring him that everyone had detested Agrippina and that her death had only increased the people's affection. The decision was made to return to the city, but it was thought prudent for the friends to go on ahead to prepare the way. Yet there was no need: they found everyone even more enthusiastic than they had claimed. The city tribunes streamed out to meet Nero; the Senate came in festival attire; women and children, grouped by sex and age, did the same. Bleachers were set up along the road for the spectators, as if a general were celebrating a triumph over a foreign enemy; Nero passed through the happy throng and, like a *triumphator,* proceeded to the temple of Jupiter on the Capitol to give his thanks to the god for the successful murder of his mother: *superbus ac publici servitii victor* ("exulting in his victory and his people's enslavement").

At *Annals* 3.65, after recording a minor contretemps in the Senate, Tacitus writes: "it is my intention to register only those senatorial opinions that were notably excellent or shameful, for I consider this to be history's special function: to let no act of goodness go unrecorded...." At first sight this remark seems tame enough. That history should commemorate greatness went back to Herodotus, the father of history, and beyond him to Homer, who had sung of "the glorious deeds of men" *(klea andrôn).* History was thus in part a record of greatness for such diverse historians as Herodotus, Polybius, and Livy. Naturally they stigmatized bad conduct when now and then it manifested itself. A negative viewpoint might even predominate, as it did for Theopompus, who in writing of Philip II of Macedon held up that monarch as a pattern of evil incarnate. But Theopompus' approach was exceptional. Dionysius of Halicarnassus, a Greek historian who was a contemporary of Livy's, contrasted Herodotus with Thucydides in an essay entitled "A Letter to Pompeius," in which Thucydides is criticized for deciding to write about the Peloponnesian War. It was a dismal subject that marked the incipient decline of the Greek world, one that best of all should not have happened, but since it did, should have been forgotten by historians. Yet even allowing Thucydides his subject, he did it badly, for he was critical of his native Athens, whereas he might have pinned the blame for the outbreak of the war solely on Sparta. Dionysius proceeds to show how Thucydides should have written his first book by giving free play to feelings of patriotism and deeds of moral uplift. Dionysius'

canons for good history are remarkable because he does not regard them as controversial. "These desiderata are ones we all look for in history," he says.

Now, while Tacitus subscribed to the tradition of recording noble words and deeds, such memorials are scarce in his history. One reason is his often trifling and inglorious subject matter. At *Annals* 4.32–33, discussed previously, he asks the reader not to compare his history with those that described the stirring wars and great upheavals of the republic. In the same passage he nevertheless affirms that his history will have its uses. One reason is that even from petty occurrences "vast changes often take their rise." Another is this:

> Now that the Roman state has been revolutionized and is nothing but the rule of a single man, a record of these events will have its value, since few possess the foresight to distinguish right from wrong or the useful from the harmful, while most learn from what has happened to others. Still, however beneficial my history may be, it will not make pleasurable reading.
>
> (4.32–33)

The allusion to Thucydides is clear, for the Greek historian had made a similar disclaimer (but went on to assert that *his* history would be "a possession for all time").

Tacitus thus distinguishes, as had most of his predecessors, two chief values in the study of history. The first is utilitarian: to instruct the reader in the nature of government (as in Polybius) and to set forth examples of base and noble conduct that readers can use in their own lives, whether for imitation or avoidance (as in Livy). The second is commemorative: to record instances of noble conduct (as in Herodotus) and occasionally even of base actions (as in Theopompus) so that the memory of them will live on.

Although there are passages in Tacitus that both commemorate goodness and make a claim to usefulness, they are far outnumbered by instances of baseness and evil. What is the reason? Some have supposed that Tacitus, despite his disclaimer, rather fancied his material. Yet his was not the temperament, say, of Alice Roosevelt Longworth, whose embroidered couch pillow read, "If you haven't got anything good to say about anyone, come and sit by me." Detraction is easy and shallow, as Tacitus well knew: "People give a ready ear to disparagement and spite, and while to flatter may be interpreted as demeaning subservice, malice can have the false appearance of honest speech" (*Histories* 1.1). Nor will any reader long imagine Tacitus to have liked most of the actions and persons that crowd his pages. Sometimes his repugnance is palpable, intensified by the tension between the strong emotion he feels and the effort to keep that emotion under control. This intensity makes him the powerful writer he is; it is embodied both in the concentrated energy of his style and in the vigorous, sometimes fierce thrust of the narrative as it drives forward. These qualities are a mirror of the man himself and especially of his commitment to the writing of history.

Of all his motives in writing, the most powerful doubtless was "to make the fear of infamy among posterity a deterrent to evil words and deeds" (3.65: *utque pravis dictis factisque ex posteritate et infamia metus sit*). He is thinking chiefly, of course, of the emperors. For they were all-powerful, whatever republican trappings were draped about them. If they could escape assassination and serious military revolt, whatever they wanted to do they did, and whatever they did was praised. Nero's triumphal entry into Rome after the murder of his mother is in many respects the culmination in the *Annals* of the progress of autocracy since the days of Tiberius. Even writings that offended the emperor were destroyed or burned, as happened during the reign of terror under Domitian that Tacitus personally witnessed and about which he writes so scathingly in the *Agricola* (1–3).

One thing, however, and perhaps one thing only, is beyond the autocrat's control: men's memory of what he has done. And that memory, translated into a historical narrative, becomes permanent. This the autocrat cannot prevent, cannot control, cannot destroy. Tacitus thus undertook what for him was a solemn and urgent mission: the autocrat must not be allowed to escape the judgment of history; he must come to realize that he cannot ensure what men will think of him after death. The truth will out.

In the days of Tiberius, Tacitus records the trial of Cremutius Cordus, who was accused of having praised in his history Cassius and Brutus, the assassins of Julius Caesar. The conclusion of the trial is as follows:

"Are Cassius and Brutus now in arms on the field of Philippi or am I inciting the people to civil war by my harangues? Did they not die more than seventy years ago? Do we not know how they looked in life by their statues, which even the victor did not destroy, just as we know something of what they did through what men have written? To each man posterity gives his due. If I should be condemned, there will be those who will remember me, just as they do Cassius and Brutus." He then left the Senate and ended his life by starvation. The senators ordered that the aediles burn his writings, but they survived, hidden and republished. And so I am all the more inclined to laugh at the stupidity of those who suppose that the autocracy of the present can extinguish the memory of those in the next generation. On the contrary, repression ensures the survival of works of genius, nor will foreign tyrants or those who ape them ever win anything but infamy for themselves and glory for their victims.

(*Annals* 4.35)

Selected Bibliography

TEXTS

Cornelii Taciti Annalium ab Excessu Divi Augusti, edited by C. D. Fisher. Oxford, 1906. Oxford Classical Texts.

Cornelii Taciti Historiarum Libri, edited by C. D. Fisher. Oxford, 1910. Oxford Classical Texts.

Cornelii Taciti Opera Minora, edited by M. Winterbottom and R. M. Ogilvie. Oxford, 1975. Oxford Classical Texts.

TACITUS

Cornelius Tacitus. Annales, edited by E. Koestermann. Leipzig, 1965.

Cornelius Tacitus. Germania, Agricola, Dialogus de Oratoribus, edited by E. Koestermann. Leipzig, 1970.

Cornelius Tacitus. Historiae, edited by E. Koestermann. Leipzig, 1969.

TEXTS AND COMMENTARIES

The Annals of Tacitus, edited by F. R. D. Goodyear. Cambridge, 1972 and 1981. Vol. 1: *Annals* 1.1-54. Vol. 2: *Annals* 1.55 to 2.

The Annals of Tacitus, edited by H. Furneaux, vol. 1, books 1-6. Oxford, 1896. Vol. 2, books 11-16, revised by H. F. Pelham and C. D. Fisher. Oxford, 1907.

Cornelii Taciti De Vita Agricolae, edited by R. M. Ogilvie and I. Richmond. Oxford, 1967.

Germania, edited by J. G. C. Anderson. Oxford, 1938.

The Histories—Book 3, edited by K. Wellesley. Sydney, 1972.

COMMENTARIES WITHOUT TEXTS

Chilver, G. E. F. *A Historical Commentary on Tacitus' Histories 1 and 2.* Oxford, 1979.

Heubner, H. P. *Cornelius Tacitus Die Historien.* 4 vols. Heidelberg, 1963–1976. In German.

Koestermann, E. *Cornelius Tacitus Annalen.* 4 vols. Heidelberg, 1963–1968. In German.

TRANSLATIONS

The Annals of Imperial Rome. Translated by M. Grant. Baltimore, 1956. Penguin Classics.

The Annals of Tacitus. Translated by D. R. Dudley. New York, 1966. Mentor Books.

The Complete Works of Tacitus, edited by M. Hadas. Translated by A. J. Church and W. J. Brodribb. New York, 1942. Modern Library.

The Histories. Translated by K. Wellesley. Baltimore, 1964. Penguin Classics.

Tacitus on Britain and Germany. Translated by H. Mattingly. Harmondsworth, 1951.

Tacitus. Agricola, Germany, Dialogue on Orators. Translated by H. W. Benario. New York, 1967.

CRITICAL STUDIES

Benario, H. W. *An Introduction to Tacitus.* Athens, Ga., 1975.

Boissier, G. *Tacitus and Other Roman Studies.* New York, 1906.

Dorey, T. A., ed. *Tacitus.* New York, 1968.

Dudley, D. R. *The World of Tacitus.* London, 1968.

Goodyear, F. R. D. *Tacitus.* In *Greece and Rome Surveys* 4 (1970).

Martin, R. *Tacitus.* Berkeley and Los Angeles, 1981.

Syme, R. *Tacitus.* 2 vols. Oxford, 1958.

———. *Ten Studies in Tacitus.* Oxford, 1970.

Walker, B. *The Annals of Tacitus.* Manchester, 1952.

T. JAMES LUCE

PLINY THE YOUNGER

(*ca.* A.D. 61–*ca.* 112)

PLINY THE YOUNGER occupies a unique niche in the pantheon of Latin literature as the undisputed master of a minor but vigorous genre, the composition of literary epistles. His letters were not the diverse daily correspondence of a master of prose style, as were those of Cicero, nor were they disguised essays on topics of intellectual interest, as were those of Seneca. They were true literary epistles, that is, they were real letters to his friends that were composed with unusual care and then, with even greater care, polished up for publication and presented to the world in nine artfully arranged books at intervals in the first decade of the second century.

This unusual tension between life and art imparts a rare character to the correspondence. Pliny is most often, and rightly, seen primarily as the mirror of a prosperous, stable, and somewhat dull society in the days of the high empire, the successor of Statius and Martial as social commentator, and a model of upper-class conformity in thought and expression. Yet he is also just as much of an artist as his poet contemporaries, and his art colors real life every bit as much as does theirs, and far less obviously. At a glance, Pliny's letters offer a detailed landscape of Roman society, a full record of the affairs and concerns of a decent, conventional, and highly educated gentleman viewed through a nicely applied literary varnish. But on closer inspection they reform themselves into a complex and calculated self-portrait of the artist, the autobiography in fragments of an individual who was in many ways rather untypical of his age. Repeatedly this latter picture reveals the artistry of the former. Pliny was a man profoundly concerned with winning eternal fame, and the literary epistle was his carefully chosen vehicle.

CAREER

Gaius Plinius Caecilius Secundus was born either in A.D. 61 or 62, being (as he himself tells us) in his eighteenth year when he was an eyewitness to the great eruption of Mt. Vesuvius on 24 August 79. Both his father (a Caecilius) and his mother (a Plinia) came from leading families in the flourishing municipality of Comum (modern Como), in the delightful lake region of northern Italy, a vigorous area on the cultural frontier between Italy and Gaul that had long supplied Rome with a succession of its greatest writers and that was now beginning to produce a series of statesmen. Pliny was thus born into the right class, the right place, and the right time; and this conjunction of circumstances was little affected by the early death of his father: his education was undertaken by a loving mother; he was at some point adopted by his famous uncle the elder Pliny, an omnivorous polymath and a tireless servant of the emperors; and his career was energetically promoted by a band of powerful senior senators.

There can have been little doubt that a youth with Pliny's background and connections was destined for a career as a Roman senator. Sometime in the early 80's he filled two essential preliminary posts, serving as a minor magistrate *(decemvir stlitibus iudicandis)* in charge of the centumviral court that was to be so important to him as the scene of his greatest forensic triumphs, and as a junior officer *(tribunus militum)* of a legion stationed in Syria, where he first demonstrated his financial skills and where he made useful contacts with the world of Greek intellectuals. In the late 80's he held the first office that admitted him to the Senate, the quaestorship, serving in fact as one of the emperor's assistants, a good sign of Domitian's favor. Then, after another necessary junior office (the tribunate of the people) and at about the time of his emergence as one of the leading advocates at Rome, Pliny held his first senior magistracy, the praetorship, in 93.

Now came the crucial years between praetorship and the height of a man's ambition, the consulship. For those lucky enough to make the transition there were several possible routes, usually involving command of one of the emperor's legions and one of his provinces. Pliny, however, took a highly unusual route, serving in succession as prefect of the military treasury and prefect of the public treasury *(aerarium Saturni)* at Rome, and then acceding before his fortieth birthday to a suffect (substitute) consulship in the autumn of 100. After the consulship there was a pause in his career, with none of the great provincial commands, but rather the important if unexciting curatorship of the Tiber's banks and riverbed and of the city of Rome's sewers, and after some delay he won an eminent priesthood, an augurship. Finally, about ten years after his consulship, there came a special appointment by the emperor Trajan to the governorship of the eastern province of Pontus and Bithynia, which extended over at least three calendar years (109–111, 110–112, or 111–113). Then all record of him in his lifetime ceases, and it is commonly assumed that Pliny died while in the East. He was certainly dead before the death of Trajan in 117.

Even in its bare bones Pliny's public career supplies essential background to the stylized world of the correspondence. For a start, he immediately stands out as an unusually talented senator who rose swiftly to the top by very unorthodox means, without ever leaving Rome to govern a province. More important, the career acts as a corrective. The Pliny presented in the letters is above all the man of culture who begrudges any moments not spent in learned intercourse or in retreat with his books and his writing tablets. Nevertheless, it has been pointed out that to the world at large his image would have been as much that of the lawyer who had risen to the top through his outstanding oratorical skills and that of a financial expert who checked the accounts of local troops while a young military tribune, who passed through both state treasuries en route to the consulship and who died while struggling valiantly with the chaotic finances of a large oriental province. That was the image he set out to correct with the publication of his letters. Similarly, the Pliny of the letters is a brave and decent man who narrowly avoids destruction in the bloody final years of the tyrant Domitian (81–96) and who thereafter loses few opportunities to praise the new golden age of Trajan. Yet only by subtle misrepresentation or repression of facts can he disguise a career that flourished under Domitian, and it is only the occasional sigh for better days or the unsuccessful bid for patronage that reveals a certain dissatisfaction with life under Trajan. We must always, then, be wary of accepting any of Pliny's assertions as the unvarnished truth.

WORKS

From a lifetime spent in writing, three of Pliny's works have survived, of which only nine books of the letters have any claim to literary value. Of the other two, one is the so-called *Panegyricus* of Trajan, which is in fact a speech of thanks *(gratiarum actio)* to the emperor delivered in the Senate by Pliny during his consulship in September 100. This massive and tedious text, which is a much expanded version of the oration actually delivered, will tire the most tireless student. Dealing with the crimes of Domitian and the glories of Trajan, the orator abandons himself to an orgy of technical virtuosity, unleashing a host of repetitive platitudes, reveling in the flood and variety of words, triumphantly deploying all the devices of formal rhetoric. As literature the piece has little attraction for modern taste, but for the historian it presents nuggets of considerable importance buried within the mass of verbiage: precise and valuable references to events and attitudes of the early years of Trajan's reign. The oration is above all a superb piece of propaganda, showing off the virtues of the new golden age, particularly in contrast with the Domitianic terror, and it coincides remarkably in its themes and its emphases with those exhibited on coins and public inscriptions. Equally important, it is a good reflection of what people wanted in a good ruler and feared in a bad one, for, as Pliny pointed out early on (4.1), it was through such speeches of thanks that good princes recognized their own deeds and evil ones learned what they ought to do. As such it became a model for all such productions, and it survives today not in any manuscript of Pliny's letters but as the first of *XII panegyrici latini*, the remainder of which date from the days of the later Roman Empire.

The letters themselves are presented in ten books, nine of them containing those elegant occasional pieces that Pliny carefully revised for publication. The tenth book is substantially different, comprising primarily the official correspondence between Pliny and Trajan while Pliny was serving as the emperor's legate in the East, although a few stray exchanges from an earlier period have been added to them. They were surely published after Pliny's death. The

style of these official communications—some seventy-four letters from Pliny with fifty-one of the emperor's replies—is attractively clear and simple, literate yet without the careful polish that distinguishes the other nine books. Their historical value is immense, full of detail about the workings of imperial government and the rich social and economic life of a turbulent eastern province. To take but a sample run of ten exchanges in the middle of the book, we hear in turn about the problems of moving an ancient temple to accommodate a new forum at Nicomedia, about Pliny's gratitude for the transfer of a relative by marriage to his province, about loyal celebrations of the anniversary of the emperor's accession, about the feasibility of lowering interest rates to encourage borrowing of excess public monies, about local feuds and the recognition of annulled acts by previous governors, about a philosopher's claim for exemption from jury duty (supported by a sheaf of documents), about the problems of building a canal between lake and river at Nicomedia, about the reception of an embassy from the king of the Bosporus and his feud with an imperial servant, about the public maintenance of those exposed at birth and subsequently rescued, about the moving of mortal remains, and about the siting of a new public bath at Prusa on the ruins of a house willed to a former emperor. The aggregate of such detail is priceless, the gem of the collection being undoubtedly the famous exchange (10.96–97) on how to deal with the Christians, which constitutes one of the very few major documents on the history of the early church. And, most pleasantly, a picture accumulates throughout book 10 of Pliny as a hard-working, conscientious, intelligent, and humane administrator.

It is, however, on the first nine books of letters that Pliny's reputation rests. It has long been realized that these 247 letters represent an innovation in Latin literature, with no real antecedents in either prose or verse epistolography, and equally that their true predecessors are in the collections of short poems by Statius (his *Silvae*) and by Martial. They are truly occasional pieces in the strict sense of the word and thus admirably suited to the letter form of daily life, as each epistle deals with a particular topic of interest and each book displays a pleasing variety of subjects.

The broad characteristics of the correspondence have been well set out by A. N. Sherwin-White in the indispensable introduction to his commentary on the correspondence. One cardinal rule is that whenever possible each letter should deal with one theme only. When more than one is included there is almost always some attempt, however artificial, to link them, and extraneous material beyond standard inquiries after health and the like has generally been excised. Furthermore, brevity is an important consideration, a quality, like the unity of each letter, that Pliny shares with the poets. There are certainly exceptions, such as the long set-piece descriptions of his villas, or the historical narrations of his uncle's death and the eruption of Vesuvius, but by and large each epistle is neatly developed without an excess of unnecessary detail and rounded off with an aphorism or an opinion—though Pliny was of course delighted when a correspondent requested longer letters. Moreover, while he is not bound by meter and the conventions of poetry, he does impose a certain amount of form on the letters beyond the customary. Thus (again to follow Sherwin-White) there are several standardized openings, along the lines of "You ask that," "I am delighted that," "An amazing thing has happened," or "I have received your delightful letter and . . . ," or else he plunges into his subject without introduction beyond a general remark or an aphorism. All of this goes to underline the very literary nature of this particular correspondence.

Pliny's prose style is clear, graceful, and elegant, and it is obvious that he took considerable trouble over it. Surprisingly in a man who had so much to say about the writing of poetry and orations, he expresses few opinions on the art of epistolography; but then of course the letters would speak for themselves. Just once, in a letter of advice to a young friend (7.9.8), does he allude to the style demanded by an epistle: it must be *pressus purusque,* concise and unadorned. There is certainly much effective writing in the letters that obeys this injunction with clear vocabulary and simple syntax, but usually (as with so much of ancient literature) the constriction of form is taken as a challenge to virtuosity. Pliny reacts with elaborate and highly effective devices, employing a colorful variety of vocabulary, syntax, and subject matter, and keeping a careful observance of prose rhythm with an eye to the elegant balance of words, phrases, and clauses.

Moreover, style and its variations are a great deal determined by what kind of epistle is intended, and again Sherwin-White has defined the different categories, eight in number, most of which had been developed by previous classical authors: narratives of public affairs, both contemporary and historical, anecdotal or from personal involvement; character sketches of both living and dead; matters of patronage, particularly *litterae commendaticiae* (letters of recommendation); advice, including praise and blame; domestic affairs; literary matters; description; and courtesy. Each automatically entails certain stylistic requirements. Thus, historical narratives call for a rhythm alternating concise assertion with more elegant reflection and comment. Scenic pieces carry more than a touch of poetic vocabulary and elaborate description of detail. Conversely, the form and content of the letter of recommendation are so rigidly circumscribed by conventions of praise for the subject's abilities, family, wealth, and so forth that Pliny can do little to vary them, however warm his feelings; while letters on literary subjects (and particularly on the writing of poetry) tend to be didactic and argumentative, and therefore full of special pleading and elaborate dissections of individual themes. On the whole, such a rich mixture of style and theme achieves the intended effect of constantly diverting the reader, alternately amusing and instructing, juxtaposing scandal with erudite disquisition or high politics with remarks on the grape harvest, each subject carefully treated in the appropriate fashion.

HERO AND VILLAIN: TWO CHARACTER SKETCHES

To comprehend the world presented by Pliny's letters, which span the period A.D. 96–108, it is necessary first to look briefly at its past. Naturally the writer cannot avoid reference to history, be it in the guise of formal historical narrative on the death of his uncle or his own involvement in senatorial trials, or be it in set homilies on the arrogance of imperial freedmen or the decline of oratory. Yet the immediate past has a special urgency. The correspondence begins in the reign of a weak old man, the emperor Nerva (96–98), and it continues through the first decade of an imperial general, Trajan (98–117). Before then the world had been governed for fifteen years by the emperor Domitian who, after his assassination in September 96, was branded at once and for all time as a bloodthirsty tyrant. Within months the first letters of book 1 were written, and Pliny naturally joined in excoriation of the late "reign of terror." The bad old days crop up regularly in later books, even in the last one, where Pliny recalls enthusiastically and at length his hounding of a wicked man who had flourished under the tyrant (9.13).

That his actions and opinions did not reflect the prevailing climate Pliny himself admits. Many would have preferred to forget the past and their own part in it: *Salvi sumus qui supersumus* (Let us be safe, we who survive) was their watchword. In fact there was little danger, and Pliny's efforts came to naught. He realized, without bitterness, that despite the fall and rise of monarchs, the ruling class carried on. When the emperor Nerva wondered what one of Domitian's more vicious cronies would be doing now if he were still alive, a fellow banqueter replied without hesitation, "He would be dining with us" (4.22.6). Pliny succinctly stated the reward for writing the history of recent times:

grave displeasure and little thanks. So he refrained from such composition, and he stopped short of prosecution. His comments on Domitian in the letters and the panegyric accordingly stick to general attacks. When the emperor's associates are named, they are all but one conveniently dead. However genuine his outrage may have been, behind it lay a strong element of self-preservation.

The proper presentation of the author's own past actions was a matter of great delicacy. The present could be carefully shaped and presented in the letters, but for those who had acquiesced and flourished under a regime that had sent braver men to death or exile, there was a problem of justification. Pliny's friend Tacitus affected bluff indifference, confessing that his own career had been much advanced by Domitian and then saying no more about it: his history of the times would be unprejudiced by either love or hatred. In fact, he had already submitted his own apologia in the guise of a life of his father-in-law, Agricola, a highly tendentious biography purporting to demonstrate that good men could flourish even under bad emperors. Pliny tried to reshape his own past more directly, relying on the twin arts of insinuation and omission. According to him, it was a miracle that he survived at all, as bolts of lightning hurled by that robber and butcher Domitian struck down so many of his friends around him (3.11.3, an image repeated from *Panegyricus* 90.5). He daringly lent money and comfort to a philosopher who had been banished from the city, his forensic activities kept him in peril, his successful rise to high office was voluntarily delayed in silent protest. In short, he came to be hated by the worst of tyrants, and there were clear signs of his impending doom; indeed he was close to being prosecuted, for an informer had lodged an accusation against him. All of this is an artistic retouching of the past: the only legal brief that might have injured him had been pressed upon him by the Senate; the friends who were killed—the so-called Stoic opposition to Domitian—turn out rather to have been acquaintances whose relatives were cultivated after their martyrdom; and the signs of impending doom visible in 93 were no more tangible three years later.

Pliny was not killed, nor did he suffer in any way; indeed Domitian did not hate him at all, and here the art of omission enters. In 93 Pliny was praetor, and in that year he courted danger by prosecuting a powerful senator and protecting an expelled philosopher; in 98 he was appointed prefect of the treasury of Saturn after attacking his predecessor, a creature of Domitian's, and from there he passed quickly to the consulship. His career suffered under Domitian, he tells us, and he was in great danger: this can refer only to the years between his praetorship and Domitian's death, 93–96. Yet during this period he held (as we know from an honorific inscription) the triennial prefecture of the military treasury; that is, he prospered in the last years of Domitian. Every other office from the quaestorship upward is recalled with pleasure in the letters, usually more than once: this is the one office he never mentions. The past has been carefully rewritten. Pliny is the sole hero of the correspondence, and his smooth self-portrait must always be examined with care.

Similarly, there is only one villain, and it is not Domitian: he is brought in only for standard abuse and then not too frequently, for detailed personal reminiscence might arouse the reader's curiosity about Pliny's relations with the dead butcher. The real villain, the only man who is dragged in (often on the flimsiest pretexts) for unmitigated vituperation is Marcus Aquillius Regulus. This monster was, in Pliny's memorable phrase, "a rich intriguer, cultivated by many, feared by more" (*locuples factiosus, curatur a multis, timetur a pluribus*). This characterization appears in one of the earlier letters (1.5.15), wherein Pliny recalls a passage at arms with Regulus in the first months after Domitian's murder. Regulus, whose crimes (we are told) were no less under Domitian than they had been under Nero, only better concealed, had helped to prosecute Arulenus Rusticus and had attacked Herennius Senecio, both of

them victims of Domitian's and friends of Pliny's. Moreover, during a court battle in which they had appeared on opposite sides under Domitian, Regulus had attempted to betray Pliny into a choice between abusing a friend and flirting with treason, while on another occasion he had sneered at Pliny in court for emulating the eloquence of Cicero without great success. For all these past iniquities Regulus tried to make amends under the new regime, and he was careful not to invite Pliny to a recitation of his speech against Arulenus. In another famous letter (2.20.7), Pliny pillories Regulus as the master of *captatio*, the art of hunting inheritances and legacies. In one case Regulus won the favor of a dying woman by persuading her that she was going to live, in another he urged the doctors to keep a man alive long enough to sign the will and then upbraided them for prolonging his agony, and in a third he pressured a lady into bequeathing to him the clothes on her back.

By such shameful deeds, Pliny adds, Regulus raised himself from a poor and mean background to an eminence of amazing wealth, and so Pliny goes on with never a good word. Regulus it was who induced others to propose a light sentence for a rascally former proconsul of Africa prosecuted by Tacitus and Pliny; Regulus who spoiled his son in life and mourned him in death so excessively, and who sought to marry again at an indecently advanced age; Regulus who offended propriety by reciting the story of his son's life before a packed auditorium and who arranged for public readings in the town halls of Italy and the provinces. As to his oratorical skill, it was negligible: the man's talent was crazy, his eulogy of his son so inept that it was more likely to raise laughter than tears.

Pliny's attack on Regulus is so unusual in the correspondence—unusual in its passion, its uniformity, and its continuation until the man's death—that it deserves closer inspection. None of this portrait will stand; that is, our conception of this man as one of the worst informers (*delatores*) is due almost entirely to Pliny's art.

Whatever his misdeeds under Nero and soon after, Regulus' record under Domitian is (to us) unblemished: no crimes are attributed to him in an age when several wicked informers of the highest rank are firmly attested. Much of his abuse of Pliny and his friends was perfectly normal courtroom practice, and in two cases at least it was in fact a rejoinder against men who had attacked him first. What is more, Pliny lets slip on two occasions that he and Regulus had actually worked together as allies in court battles, and he records snatches of conversation that betray no signs of animosity; indeed, the fact that Regulus made a point of not inviting Pliny to the recitation of his speech against Arulenus must imply that Pliny was normally present on such occasions. The eulogy of a dead child is held up to ridicule, yet Pliny had likewise praised the son of a distinguished friend. Again and again Pliny grossly distorts Regulus' words and deeds.

Why does Pliny for once lose control? Moral outrage may contribute, but it is overdone. More suggestive are Pliny's comments on Regulus' style as an orator. In a reflective mood, after the man's death, Pliny admits at last that, whatever his faults may have been, Regulus' one virtue was that he truly loved oratory and took great pains over the preparation and delivery of his speeches (6.1.1–2). Earlier, however, he had vehemently attacked Regulus for his atrocious delivery, his slow-witted inventiveness, his poor memory: impudence and passion alone had earned him the title of orator. In the Roman mind, talent and character were closely connected, and Cato's definition of the orator was often repeated, that he was a good man skilled in speaking. Thus Pliny quoted with approval another's jibe at Regulus, that he was a bad man unskilled in speaking (4.7). In a most revealing passage Pliny recalls a conversation with Regulus on the differences between their styles. Pliny's speeches were long and circuitous, working out each point separately, overwhelming his opponent, whereas Regulus went immediately for his opponent's weakness and hung on terrierlike—in his own inimitable

words, "As soon as I see the throat I pounce on it" (1.20.14). Regulus was all energy, and Pliny comments unfavorably in other places on his *vim* and his *vigor*; he himself loved to pursue his quarry at length, talking sometimes for several days.

In short, he and Regulus were rivals, and not only in oratory but specifically in law. It is as a trial lawyer that Regulus appears most often in the letters. The major civil law court of the day was that of the *centumviri*, the place that Pliny could call "my arena" and where his greatest triumphs occurred. Yet if we listen to Martial in the more than a dozen poems praising Regulus—Pliny received one—Regulus was the great orator of the day, and the centumviral court rang with his praises; Regulus was famous, Regulus was courted by a crowd of clients, Regulus was fabulously wealthy. Thus Regulus posed the greatest single threat to the image that Pliny sought to project; hence the campaign against him that vilified his past and ceased abruptly when the older man died. The villain of the correspondence reveals a good deal of its artist hero.

PLINY'S WORLD

Pliny's greatest value lies, of course, in his portrait of Trajanic society, in the revelation of his own opinions and emotions, and (equally significant) in what he omits. For him, as for tens of millions of inhabitants of the Roman Empire, the center of the world was unquestionably the emperor. Inevitably a prominent Roman senator spent much of his life dealing with him or thinking about him, but most of Pliny's thoughts on the facts of empire are monumentally banal: Trajan, in whose reign both the letters and the panegyric were published, naturally appears as the Good Emperor with all the conventional attributes, while Domitian must of course be the very sum of all imperial vices. Consequently most of Pliny's views on monarchy, good and bad, are superficial and unoriginal. Only occasionally does a heartfelt sentiment slip out, as when he laments a real lack of subject matter for his pen (3.20.10). Letters, he thinks, should contain more than petty news and personal affairs, but, alas, there is really nothing noteworthy done in contemporary politics now that everything is under the sway of one man, who has alone undertaken the cares and toil of everyone for the common good. It is only by his benevolence (velut rivi ex illo benignissimo fonte) that there is ever anything to discuss at all. Sometimes indeed, despite the horror of Domitian's tyranny and despite the present peace, Pliny will allow himself to glance back with nostalgia, even to regret the passing of Aquillius Regulus.

The truth is that Pliny was not very close to the emperor or to his court, and the picture he offers is a very narrow one. Of the traditional wielders of power within the imperial staff and entourage there is little trace in the letters. The empress is mentioned once, no more than an acquaintance, while other imperial relatives are absent, most notably the ascendant cousin and eventual successor, Hadrian. Similarly the great freedmen of the emperor are not there, with the exception of one involved in a hearing that Pliny happened to attend. Such men could be major brokers of power and sellers of honor. For instance, Epictetus suggests that Valerius Maximus, a friend of Pliny's, won an imperial post by courting the freedmen with presents and flattery; Pliny saw in it only a reward for the man's past services; that is, either he was ignorant of such dealings or he turned a blind eye to anything sordid or dangerous. Furthermore, the civil servants from the equestrian class, who are his social equals, do not move in Pliny's world. Only two men of the highest rank, that of prefect, intrude, one because of his love of literature, the other only to receive a note of recommendation that shows no sign of familiarity; no prefect of the emperor's guard (the senior post) appears as friend or acquaintance. And at the lower levels there is but one procurator, a protégé of Pliny's own mentor who has been long since retired from active service.

Pliny does, however, have some contact with the emperor through a less formal though no less important channel, the emperor's council (consilium principis). This body, composed of whomever the emperor chose to summon, deliberated on any matter he chose to submit to them, and Pliny proudly records three separate occasions on which he was summoned. Yet again his position must be closely defined. The consilium could discuss matters of high policy, questions about taxes, the army, foreign affairs, and the like: none of this appears in Pliny. His attendance as councillor is limited strictly to the other function of the council, the administration of justice, playing assessors to the emperor's judge. This is the closest we find Pliny to the center of power: the litigants are of high rank, the charges are serious and have serious social repercussions, each case offers a fine opportunity for the display of imperial virtue on wider fronts. Pliny is, of course, in his natural element as one of the leading trial lawyers of the day. Yet there is one thing missing. Pliny, who lost no opportunity to record his own apt words on any occasion, nowhere recalls a single opinion on any subject offered by him to the emperor. However this silence may be explained, it is very curious.

The extent of Pliny's power or influence is quite clear. He fails almost as often as he succeeds in obtaining offices and honors for his friends from the emperor (though failure is skimmed over or ignored), and his own pursuit of a priesthood was painfully slow. This gulf between Pliny and the emperor is firmly bridged by a handful of great patrons who are as important to his success as are his native talents. Dozens of amici principis (friends of Caesar's) parade through the correspondence, several of them are claimed by Pliny as friends, but a small group clearly stands out as crucial to his well-being, all of them new men like himself, all of them senior ex-consuls, and all of them powerful figures at court: Corellius Rufus, Iulius Ursus Servianus, Iulius Frontinus, Verginius Rufus, and perhaps Vestricius Spurinna. These are the men who promote Pliny at every opportunity, praising him to the emperor Nerva as "a good youth," obtaining privileges for him, canvassing for him at elections, nominating him for priesthoods. In them lay Pliny's influence, hence whenever they appear in the letters they are praised wholeheartedly.

Pliny's natural sphere of activity lay rather in the Senate of Rome, and the activities of the Senate form one of the major subjects of the correspondence; indeed Pliny is perhaps our greatest source for its various day-to-day activities. Through him we learn a vast amount about who attended the Senate and why, about the busy round of elections, trials, great ceremonies of state, and about the complex routine with its impassioned but orderly debates. Much of its business seems distressingly trivial, for always in the background, often present in person, is the towering figure of the emperor. Thus, a vast amount of the Senate's time is taken up with simple, almost ritualized, praise of the monarch, of which Pliny's panegyric is but one example; while a distressing amount of effort is saved by the sad expedient—Pliny records several occasions—of referring any controversial matter to the emperor's decision. A great deal of the Senate's time is also spent in voting honors to individuals: a public funeral to Verginius Rufus, for instance; a triumphal statue to Vestricius Spurinna. Elections to senatorial offices are often reduced to a farce, as the emperor's general approval is needed by all candidates and his specific favor guarantees sure success, while electoral battles tend to be struggles between the candidates' senior patrons (suffragatores): several of Pliny's letters concern such wheeling and dealing for friends and friends of friends (he says that his own reputation is at stake). In one outraged letter protesting the use of secret ballots he tells of an anonymous cynic who wrote down the names not of the candidates but of their suffragatores. Nevertheless, Pliny fully justifies the continued existence of the Senate as a major administrative, diplomatic, legislative, and judicial body, particularly in its supervision of the state treasury (headed by Pliny for three years), of the maintenance of public order, and of the welfare of the provinces (if only in the curbing of its own errant governors).

He is, moreover, especially illuminating on the subject of the senatorial class, allowing us from numerous hints to build up a complex mosaic of its customs and opinions that is remarkably clear in its outlines. Ancestry is all-important. Again and again Pliny recommends a man because his father or grandfather or other relative was a consul or a senator or a leader of the equestrian order. It is crucial in contracting marriage alliances to go into the partner's pedigree, for proper ancestors would assure the glory of their posterity: as Pliny writes to his wife's grandfather—the sentiment is echoed in other forms elsewhere—their joint descendants would enjoy a clear path to high honors, a name widely famed, and distinguished ancestors (8.10.3).

Along with family went character. The senator, as befitted one of such distinguished family, had an exceptional character, and exceptional ignominy was his if he lapsed; accordingly a man's morals play a major part in Pliny's recommendation of him. A closed club was thus formed, in theory, of families of good birth, high character, and achievement: for a senator to attack a senator was bad form (Pliny was more than once reluctant to prosecute, despite the seriousness of the crimes involved); for an outsider to oppose a senator was an affront to the entire body that demanded exceptional justification. Needless to say, parvenus were abhorred. Pliny cannot forget that the father of a brutally murdered senator had been a slave, and he laments with an ex-praetor fallen on hard times that professors have become senators and senators professors. Within the club elaborate attention is paid to hierarchy as Pliny carefully records the precise rank (and office, if one is held) of each senator whom he discusses in any detail, and often that of his family as well. The important point is that while the correspondence clearly (if unwittingly) reflects the weakness of the Senate itself, it equally clearly reveals the unquestioned power of individual members of the senatorial class, a power ultimately wielded in the form of *gratia* (influence). Offices and favors won from the emperor demonstrate the influence of the recipient; rivalry between senators is seen as a struggle in influence; patronage or oppression of lower orders rests initially on the exercise or perception of influence. Here, at least, Pliny's views expressed in the letters to or about senators surely coincide with contemporary opinion.

Pliny's original road to prominence as a young senator was through the law courts, and forensic matters hold an enduring interest for him as the topics of letters. Ignoring the many other possible motives for entering upon a career as a lawyer, he quotes with approval a senior friend's list of the cases one should undertake as a matter of course: those of friends, those that others have abandoned, and those that will serve as precedents. To these he would only add one more category, those that will bring the speaker glory and fame, subjects in which he himself took a passionate interest (6.29.1–3). In fact Pliny's own cases are almost completely confined to the first type, for by far the majority were *causae amicorum,* that is, affairs directly involving his friends or, in very many instances, affairs of other folk in which a friend of Pliny's has begged him to intercede. Quite different from these are the three major trials in the Senate of former governors and their colleagues wherein Pliny represented the aggrieved provinces: they all receive massive coverage in the correspondence; but it is clear in each that Pliny, who was of course reluctant to prosecute fellow senators, was persuaded by the Senate to take up the matter and that he had no close ties with the provinces either then or subsequently.

Pliny the lawyer must be carefully defined by the courts in which he appeared. Of the cases that he recalls, none was pleaded before the emperor himself, and only one before judges appointed by the emperor; then the charges were serious, but Pliny makes no mention of the outcome of the case, and his sole recorded action in it is a strategic silence. Much more play is given to his appearance before the Senate meeting as a court, in each case to conduct the trial of former provincial governors. In three of these he acted as a reluctant prosecutor, in two as the defender of friends, but, it should be emphasized, in all of them Pliny was but one of a number of lawyers on both sides, and it is by no means clear that his arguments or opinions had any great effect. (Certainly on one of these occasions, when he had talked on for almost five hours, the emperor Trajan very delicately, in the form of concern for Pliny's health, suggested that he should stop.)

In contrast with all of this, Pliny's heart lay in his true arena, the centumviral court, a court concerned particularly with inheritance disputes. There vast audiences hung on his every word, there he could speak for seven hours on end, there he could fix adjournments for friends behind the scenes. The course of these trials—many are hinted at, and details are given of some eight of them—is usually obscure, for Pliny only draws on them as background to introduce some other topic for discussion (a good sign of how they pervaded his daily life and his thoughts). The one element common to them all is that they involve highly important people (*potentissimi*), both as lawyers and as litigants, which is not surprising if large sums were at issue. Thus Pliny was not a great leader of the criminal bar, nor did he particularly shine in the courts that heard important political cases—despite his long narratives of the Senate trials. Rather he was the lawyer of high society, as indeed was only fitting for a man so interested in recording its history.

His forensic career had been launched by a successful centumviral case at a very early age against some exceedingly powerful citizens. Later, however, he was to express outrage at modern youths bursting into his court fresh from the bloodless battles of the rhetorical schools and careless of the decorous ways of their ancestors. Those ancestors had been properly introduced into court life by their own seniors in a form of apprenticeship, which Pliny—who was genuinely concerned about the future of forensic oratory—both applauded and practiced. His complaint was not merely a legal one; it was literary as well. He felt the tolerant contempt of a trial lawyer for the fictional practice cases of the schoolroom, but he was truly upset at some of the teachings. At one point in his diatribe against modern youth he sneers at the *fracta pronuntiatio* ("mincing accents," as one translation has it) of these youngsters, thus revealing a deeper prejudice: he simply did not like the elaborate, inflated style of the "Asianist" school of rhetoric.

This touches on the question: Why did Pliny win his cases? The question is a matter of oratory, and Pliny's two supreme qualities stand out. First, and rather surprisingly for the calm Pliny of the letters, the orator must be "pugnacious," and forensic oratory demanded "a pugnacious and rather warlike style." Hence he approves the ferocity of others and attributes his own success to pugnacity. Here the anecdote about his rival Regulus going for his opponent's metaphorical throat is relevant and easy to misunderstand: Pliny disapproved not of Regulus' method but of his impatience. Where Regulus went for the throat at once, Pliny carefully looked everything over, made sure that he had actually located the neck (not the knee or the heel, as Regulus tended to), and then he too—the gentle Pliny—sprang.

In this patience lay Pliny's second claim to supremacy, *copia* (fullness). He demanded time to make his points and to drive them home by repetition and rephrasing, and thus he praises fullness in others and scorns certain Asians who mistake volubility for copiousness. Moreover he closely ties this treatment at length with its ferocity, in the vivid comparison of a successful courtroom attack, to a sword repeatedly striking a body (1.20.3; and note for that matter his image of the court as his "arena" at 6.12.2). Pliny paints one grand picture of just such a speech (full of *copia* and *pugnacia*) before a packed court, in which he set sail on a sea of rhetoric, full of indignation, anger, sorrow, and the whole baggage of the practiced orator (6.33.8–9).

Above all, Pliny wished to be remembered as a man of letters; that is, for what he himself wrote and for his encouragement of other writers. Culture accordingly predominates over all other possible topics in the letters, to the point even of obscuring other activities equally important to Pliny's life. Certain areas of literature interest him not at all. Technical writings and writers, be they concerned with law or natural science, receive almost no attention. Philosophy is equally uninteresting as a subject of correspondence and is reduced to a matter of personalities: certain philosophers are socially acceptable (one is recommended for his ability to "polish" a man of culture), others are figures of satire. However, three arts do engross Pliny's full attention: oratory, poetry, and history.

Oratory in court or Senate or public hall played a large part in Pliny's life, to which must be added the long hours passed in revision, criticism, recitation, and finally publication of what must have been scores of speeches: all phases of the process reappear constantly throughout the letters. Although no friend to the Asianist theories, Pliny tried nevertheless to steer a middle course, avoiding equally the terse, dry style of the "Atticists." The keynote of his speeches—as he saw it—was a controlled fullness of treatment set off by a refreshing variety of style and topic. He often, therefore, defended his own practices and attacked the theories of others, but there was no question that he was a master orator and renowned as such.

Nevertheless, where Pliny really yearned to achieve recognition was in the world of poetry, and poetry edges out oratory as a subject for discourse. The letters disclose a constant round of recitations by himself and his cronies, mutual praise, and incessant encouragement. The scraps that survive are the embodiment of conscientious mediocrity. Despite desperate application and immense versatility in the forms, the dominating traits both in Pliny's theories and in his surviving scraps are those twin banes of talent: slavish imitation of earlier and better poets and the crushing display of erudition. Repeatedly Pliny shows himself to be on the defensive for writing poetry, elaborately justifying to his friends both the composition and the recitation, particularly as a form of relaxation from the cares and business of the day. Poet after poet parades through his letters, each of them praised or discussed, all of them now lost and forgotten; of those who are still remembered, Martial appears only once, posthumously and in a condescending sketch, Statius and Juvenal not at all.

As for the writing of history, Pliny's attitude is curious. He admires its concern with deep truths and great examples, and he takes a constant interest in those of his contemporaries who dabble in historiography and biography. Many of them urged him to indulge as well, but despite some flirtation with the muse he never did. In part this was perhaps because with his letters he was already in effect writing contemporary history while avoiding many of its problems. In part it was undoubtedly also because he was shrewd enough to see that his generation had produced a truly great historian, his friend Tacitus. Hence he did a great deal to aid Tacitus, not merely encouraging him in his work but sending him considerable material for inclusion, most of which mentioned Pliny himself. For him history held a special interest: it was not just the recorder of truth, it was the bestower of immortality.

As important to Pliny as the creation of literature was its promotion at all levels and in all surroundings. Proper education is a repeated concern of the correspondence as he searches out tutors for the children of his friends, endows a public teaching post, and follows with interest the careers of professors. Privately Pliny encourages friends, especially his juniors, to work and study with him, and the art of general conversation on literary matters is highly developed. Two major activities stand out. First, the dissemination of literature. Many of Pliny's shorter notes deal with the circulation of new compositions for critical comment. The standard form is to send the work with a polite request that the recipient read and emend it with an eye to publication. Much of this criticism was undoubtedly mere flattery, but it should be noted that the practice was not Pliny's particular self-delusion, for Tacitus apparently valued his opinion, sending him material more than once. Much more dubious was the practice of recitation before invited audiences, then at its height and very much attacked by contemporaries. Pliny indulged in it with a vengeance, both as performer and auditor, and he replied at length to those who disapproved of it. The second form of literary promotion was simple patronage of men of letters. This encompassed not merely teachers, poets, and retiring amateurs, but almost everyone Pliny wanted to help for whatever reason. That is to say, literary talent or erudition was taken for granted in the genteel world of Pliny's society, so that whether recommending a man for political office, for a marriage alliance, or for legal assistance, Pliny's standard practice was to include praise either of the man's talent or at least of his appreciation of it in others. Thus, for better or worse, literature was directly or indirectly protected and standards of good taste ensured for the future.

The emperor and the Senate, the practice of law, and literary culture: these are the main subjects of Pliny's correspondence and the central interests of his life. Brief mention must also be made of two other elements that are no less important to him, but that are left in the background of the letters. First, of course, there is money, the fundamental thread in the whole fabric of Pliny's society. Pliny was a very wealthy man, and, as he states bluntly, almost all of his money was in land, the rest lent out at interest.

Land, in particular country estates and farms, was indeed the main source of most aristocratic wealth and power, but Pliny betrays some attitudes to it that are not typical of his class. True, one of his often repeated themes is that of retreat to the countryside (secessus) whenever he can tear himself away from work, there to relax, to take exercise, and above all to read and write in peace—a peace all too often broken by the problems of his farms and the complaints of his tenants. Yet this rural idyll of literary seclusion is something of a pose, part of the carefully cultivated image of the man of letters. In fact, Pliny takes a rather close proprietary interest in all aspects of real country life: the leasing of farms, the supervision of tenants, the problems of sowing and harvesting, weather conditions good and bad, and above all the fluctuation of prices. He took as well a keen interest in various aspects of the property market.

His general attitude to money matters is of a piece with this. He was, in fact, the largest known private benefactor in Italy in imperial times—his childlessness was doubtless important here—and his actions were genuinely prompted by the public good and his own love of renown, as were those of most of his class. But he stands out as being particularly canny in these expenditures: he would for instance subsidize only part of the salary of a public teacher in order to ensure that the town took an active interest, and he carefully recommended to a friend the most responsible and least risky method of spending money for the public good. Pliny assiduously cultivated the image of a man of letters, but he was undoubtedly known to his contemporaries as something of a financial expert, a talent more clearly reflected in his official career. None of this is exploited in the letters; it is simply there.

The converse is true of the social world—its structure and its opinions—within which Pliny operated, for that is the subject that gives the correspondence its eternal fascination. Pliny is delighted to share his highly conventional ideas on marriage and the role of the wife, on the upbringing of children, on the proper relationships with various family members, with friends, and with acquaintances, and his fashionably humane views on slaves and freedmen. Similarly there is much to be gathered on the depth of his local roots in his native Comum, "my delight," as he called it, his visits there, his patronage of the place, his many close friends there and in the surrounding region. The functioning of this world is as well defined as its structure: ritual morning salutations, dinner parties, visits in the country, recitations in the city, meetings with friends for advice on literary matters or financial affairs, the duties of friends affectionate and friends politic, the highly ritualized act of recommending a client to a prospective patron (an art that demands a separate letter form to itself), the etiquette of giving gifts in life and legacies in death, everywhere the maintenance of good relations, the constant granting of favors and rendering of thanks. All of this Pliny deftly portrays in a large and convincing landscape of a particular society at a particular time, and he does it through the unusual medium of a mosaic of letters: in both subject and execution he was a great innovator, and he deserves considerable praise for that.

In searching for his motives we soon discover that Pliny is both more honest and more dishonest than other writers. Nowhere does he actually say why he chose to make a high art of epistolography, merely that friends encouraged him to collect his more carefully written letters. Nevertheless his motive is clear throughout. Much that is not immediately obvious can be coaxed from the letters to form an estimate of Pliny's own mental landscape, his emotions and his self-perception, his views of nature and supernature, his attitudes to pain, disease, and death. One obsession stands out from them all, running as a connecting theme from the first book to the last: immortality. As Pliny himself allowed, "the prize of eternity" was before his eyes, yet only when one looks out for this obsession does one realize how pervasive it is. For example, a writer friend is urged to publish, for he is mortal, his works will be an eternal monument to him; the panegyric of the emperor is a light for posterity; death came cruelly and prematurely for another author who was composing an immortal work—causing Pliny to reflect on his own mortality and his own writings; he believes that Tacitus' histories will be immortal and frankly confesses that he wants to be in them; Verginius Rufus, a great man and Pliny's friend, will live forever in the memory and conversation of men; nothing so excites Pliny as the love and desire for a long-enduring fame. In the end, he offers a definition of the most fortunate of men as one who could delight in the prospect of a good and lasting reputation, and who, being assured of posterity, could enjoy his future glory now (9.3.1). He therefore set out carefully to build his own monument, choosing an unusual medium and working in it better than anyone had done before. It is impossible to resist applying to him his own words on the death of the poet Martial (3.21.6): "What he wrote will not last forever, you say. Perhaps not, but he wrote it as if it would."

Selected Bibliography

TEXTS

XII panegyrici latini, edited by R. A. B. Mynors. Oxford, 1964. This Oxford Classical Texts volume is the best edition available.

C. Plinii Caecilii Secundi Epistularum libri decem, edited by R. A. B. Mynors. Oxford, 1963. Likewise the best edition, in the Oxford Classical Texts.

Pliny. Letters and Panegyricus, edited by B. Radice. Cambridge, Mass., 1969. This Loeb Classical Library edition offers Mynors' Latin text with Radice's extremely good translations on facing pages.

TRANSLATIONS

Radice, B. *The Letters of the Younger Pliny.* Harmondsworth and Baltimore, 1963. This Penguin edition reprints Radice's Loeb Classical Library translation.

COMMENTARIES AND INDEX

Durry, M. *Pline le Jeune: Panégyrique de Trajan.* Paris, 1938. Highly recommended.

Jacques, X., and van Ooteghem, J. *Index de Pline le Jeune.* Académie royale de Belgique. Classe des Lettres. Mémoires. Sér. 2, 58, fasc. 3. Brussels, 1965. This word index is essential to any serious study.

Sherwin-White, A. N. *The Letters of Pliny. A Historical and Social Commentary.* Oxford, 1966. Despite the many flaws that were pounced upon by reviewers, this is indispensable; its general introduction (pp. 1–84) is the best introduction to Pliny in any language, and its remarks on the tenth book (pp. 525–555) are very useful.

GENERAL WORKS AND SPECIAL STUDIES

There is no good modern book on Pliny either as a literary or a historical figure, and very few articles of broad scope. However, the general reader may find the following useful:

Guillemin, A. M. *Pline et la vie littéraire de son temps.* Paris, 1929. An important study on the literary life of the day.

Radice, B. "A Fresh Approach to Pliny's Letters." *Greece and Rome* 9:160–168 (1962).

———. "The Letters of Pliny." In *Empire and Aftermath. Silver Latin II*, edited by T. A. Dorey. London, 1975. Pp. 119–142.

———. "Pliny and the Panegyric." *Greece and Rome* 15:166–172 (1968). All three of these essays are highly recommended to the general reader.

Syme, R. "People in Pliny." *Journal of Roman Studies* 58:138–151 (1968). Reprinted in his *Roman Papers.* Oxford, 1979. Pp. 694–723.

———. "Pliny's Less Successful Friends." *Historia* 9:362–379 (1960). Reprinted in his *Roman Papers.* Oxford, 1979. Pp. 477–495. Both useful on Pliny's society.

———. *Tacitus.* Oxford, 1958. Chapters 7 and 8 provide the advanced reader with the best introduction to many aspects of Pliny's life.

White, P. "The Friends of Martial, Statius, and Pliny and the Dispersal of Patronage." *Harvard Studies in Classical Philology* 79:265–300 (1975). Also useful on the literary society of the day.

EDWARD CHAMPLIN

SUETONIUS

(*ca.* A.D. 69–after 122)

THE CIVIL SERVANT

THE SECOND CENTURY after the birth of Christ, generally regarded as the period of the greatest prosperity and tranquility in the history of the Greco-Roman world, is also marked as an age of increasing bureaucracy, an age when benevolent emperors attempted to ensure the well-being of their people by increasing the supervisory role of the central administration, in both the capital and the provinces. This tendency is associated especially with the emperor Hadrian (A.D. 117–138), that restless traveler and inspector of cities and provinces who wanted always to see for himself what was going on and to supervise his own measures: he personally initiated the consolidation of the northern frontier of Britain by constructing the wall that still bears his name. Neither then nor during succeeding reigns did people have reason to suppose that this paternalism and the bureaucracy that it involved would lead to the mass of red tape that strangled enterprise during the last centuries of the Western Empire and was perhaps largely responsible for the final collapse of Roman civil and military power. But there is no doubt that by Hadrian's time a distinct type of imperial officer was emerging, which we can recognize as the civil servant.

One of the best known of this class is Gaius Suetonius Tranquillus. He was born probably about A.D. 69, when the suicide of Nero, the last of the original family of the Caesars, led to a year's fierce civil war and to the rise to power of the Flavian family as the second imperial dynasty. Suetonius' father was an army officer of the equestrian order (*equites*), the wealthy upper middle class that played an important part in the army and the administration, ranking immediately below the senatorial class, for which it provided an increasingly large proportion of recruits. The origin of the family was perhaps on the north coast of Africa, already strongly Romanized; but, after fighting in the civil wars, the elder Suetonius seems to have settled in Rome. Several references in the son's biographies describe incidents that he had witnessed there during his early years. Toward the end of the century, the young Suetonius was already thinking of playing some part in the law courts, as a promising field of activity for an ambitious man; then, just after A.D. 100, we hear of him applying for a commission in a legion serving in Britain, a normal step in an equestrian's career, but deciding against it as soon as it was offered. He very likely became a member of a standing panel of jurors that had some characteristics of present-day court magistrates. At some time he returned to his hometown in Africa to hold local office as a priest (not a religious appointment in our sense, but a normal mark of honor for a young man with a future) and probably visited the province of Bithynia, in northwestern Turkey, in the retinue of the younger Pliny, governor there in about 111–112. Otherwise his career seems to have been spent in Rome, where in due course he held three successive posts in the emperor's personal service, posts that under the early emperors had normally been held by ex-slaves but were now regularly entrusted to equestrians. It was probably under Trajan (A.D. 98–117), one of Rome's most successful military leaders, that Suetonius held the post called a *studiis*, evidently a sort of research-assistant providing the emperor with references and reading matter for administrative purposes or relaxation. After that or possibly at the same time, he became responsible for the imperial libraries, both within the palace and at various points in the city, with a staff of subordinate librarians. Finally, after Trajan's death in the East, he moved into one of the top administrative posts under Hadrian, in charge of official correspondence; the nature of the preceding offices throws some light on the qualifications required for this position. Scholars have attempted, with little success, to ascertain whether this position involved any scope for genuine initiative: whether Suetonius would personally draft letters and documents, including those marking military and civil appointments, or simply ensure that whatever the emperor dictated to a secretary was properly dispatched and filed. It was likely in any case to have been a more arduous post than the other two; for Trajan's intellectual interests were limited, and under him Suetonius normally may have had plenty of opportunity to pursue his own scholarly work while the emperor was campaigning in Armenia and Mesopotamia. Hadrian was away from Rome even more than his predecessor, once he began his imperial tours in A.D. 121; but it is probable that his chief secretary would accompany him as a key member of the administrative headquarters.

It seems to have been in 121 or 122 that Suetonius, together with Septicius Clarus, one of the joint commanders of the praetorian guards, was dismissed from office as a result of treating the empress with lack of proper respect. The fact that Hadrian did not care for Sabina was no excuse for his subordinates to neglect her official dignity. We cannot tell whether both empress and officers were with Hadrian in Britain at this time—it is possible that the event took place in northern Africa several years later—but it certainly marked the end of imperial service for both men. Moreover, if Suetonius had enjoyed a somewhat privileged position with access to imperial records and letter files, he was now reduced to the library facilities available to the ordinary public. In view of the large number of literary, or scholarly, works that he is known to have produced, he may well have lived on for a long time in retirement. He would have been barely seventy when Hadrian died in A.D. 138, but we know nothing whatever about his life after his loss of place at court. It should be noted that the biographer was never the subject of a biography himself and that our knowledge of him has to be pieced together from very scattered sources: references in letters written by his friend and patron, the younger Pliny, during the years 96–111; a rather incoherent mention in the highly dubious Augustan Life of Hadrian written some 250 years after his death; a remark in John the Lydian, a scholar writing in Constantinople in the sixth century, concerning the dedication of the major work, the *Lives of the Twelve Caesars,* to Septicius as commander of the guard; and a number of quotations from and references to his various writings by later Greek and Latin grammarians and scholars. The one relatively solid piece of evidence is an inscription from Bône, in Algeria, giving a summary of Suetonius' career down to the final secretaryship; but the inscribed stone is so fragmentary that certainty is impossible on many details. However, its discovery in 1952 was gratifying in that it confirmed what we already supposed about its subject's career. The only real problem was its presence in Bône, since it clearly mentioned no benefit done to the citizens of the place (Hippo Regius, it was then called), and so could hardly be accounted for except on the grounds that

Suetonius was a local boy who had recently made good and might indeed be expected to show some gratitude to his hometown. Many points in interpretation are still, like this, subject to debate.

MINOR WORKS

What is beyond dispute is the nature of Suetonius' main works. Late Roman grammarians and Byzantine authorities report (not necessarily from direct acquaintance) treatises on Greek games, Roman shows and spectacles, the Roman calendar, symbols used in books, names of articles of clothing, abusive expressions, Roman customs, bodily faults, the institution of official posts, kings, and "various things"—this last, perhaps some of the others as well, apparently included in the books entitled *Prata*, "the meadows." With the exception of the works on Greek games and abusive expressions, which have been partially preserved in Greek manuscripts and were probably written in Greek in the first place, these works are completely lost or survive only in scanty fragments. From what we can tell of them, they seem largely to have been comprehensive catalogs of names or words, with careful explanations. Among these lost works the one that has aroused some interested conjecture is on the institution of offices; it has been thought to comprise a discussion of the reorganization of the Roman civil service by Hadrian, of which Suetonius might be expected to have had personal and first-hand knowledge. All the clues there are, however, point to a purely antiquarian study, attempting to trace various imperial posts back to vaguely similar institutions under the early republic. The general impression we gather is of painstaking pedantry and a careful concern for the precise meaning of words. Not too much regret need be expressed at the almost total disappearance of so much of Suetonius' scholarship.

But after what appears to have been a phase when the term "scholastic" sums him up all too comprehensively, Suetonius evidently took the decisive step into the branch of writing in which he was to achieve lasting success. The *Caesars* could hardly have followed immediately the encyclopedic works that exhibit so little interest in real life. First must have come the tentative experiment in writing biographies, growing perhaps out of such inquiries into the institution of offices or Roman customs. His interest turned to those teachers who had introduced and perfected the intellectual activities in which he himself had been engaged. First, in the *Grammarians* he tackled the question: How did the study of language and literature begin at Rome? Who were the main scholars who established this as a major branch of education? After a preliminary discussion of the derivation of the study from the Greeks and its beginnings at Rome, we have short chapters devoted to nineteen practitioners, down to the great Valerius Probus, who appears to have flourished during the reign of Nero. Some of these Lives are sketches of no more than five lines, and none is of more than thirty. They contain a surprisingly large number of relevant and enlightening quotations from authorities of all sorts; the section on the poet and critic Valerius Cato contains no less than five extracts from short poems by his friends and disciples, such as Cinna (Shakespeare's "Cinna the poet") and Furius Bibaculus. But despite this interesting documentation, Cato receives very scanty treatment for such a prominent figure in literary history. In particular, no indications are given of the period when he lived, apart from an incidental remark that he lost his property in the troubles connected with Sulla. The nearest thing to a firm date anywhere in the *Grammarians* is the statement about Verrius Flaccus (17) that he died at an advanced age "under Tiberius," that is, at any time between A.D. 14 and 37. Nor in any way does Suetonius attempt to follow up the respects in which the study of "grammar" changed or to view it as a chronological development. The same limitations are to be seen in the *Rhetoricians*, which is introduced with a summary of the history of the teaching of oratory. This work now breaks off with the fifth rhetorician, Albucius Silus, although we know from the table of contents that eleven more Lives were to follow, down to the great Quintilian in the reign of Domitian, but they have simply been lost through damage to the book at some later date. While the work was still complete it was drawn on by St. Jerome, the scholarly Christian writer of the latter part of the fourth century, who borrowed details from these Lives, including some now lost, to add to a chronological table of world history that he was adapting from an earlier Greek work by Eusebius. In addition, St. Jerome indicates that Suetonius' complete work was called On Famous Men (de viris illustribus) and also that it included at least three further categories of more distinctively literary figures—orators, historians, and poets. The lack of dates evidently made the Grammarians and Rhetoricians a highly inconvenient source for Jerome to exploit for his particular purposes; for while he inserts the figures under discussion reasonably aptly in his chronology, he can attach them to only the vaguest sort of floruit ("is accounted distinguished"), rather than to anything as positive as a date of birth or death. Some at least of the orators, who most probably followed the rhetoricians since they practiced the skill taught by rhetoricians, have dates for both birth and death; whereas Cicero (who might have been included among the rhetoricians but was evidently reserved for the orators, among whom he achieved real preeminence) has in addition the dates of his early withdrawal to Rhodes and his exile in 58 B.C., but curiously not the date of his famous consulship and successful overthrow of Catiline in 63. Of the historians, the other main group of prose writers, Sallust and Livy have birth and death dates recorded; others, less distinguished, either had no dates in Suetonius or were not considered worth this sort of detail by St. Jerome.

We are best informed about the poets, not because their section of the work has been preserved as a whole but because extensive parts of several Lives (Terence, Vergil, Horace, Lucan) were transcribed by editors of their works, probably in the fourth century, when the book was still complete, at the beginning either of copies of their works or of commentaries on them. Evidently much more material was available on these four writers than on many of the others; we should give a great deal to know what biographical data Suetonius, with his rapidly increasing zeal and efficiency, could have discovered concerning Lucretius or Catullus. But what is most striking here is the improvement in scholarship and biographical technique. The number of quotations from early authorities in the Terence has given rise to suspicions that the greater part of this material had previously been assembled by the great scholar Marcus Varro, writing his treatise on comedy toward the close of the republic. He may indeed have opened Suetonius' eyes at this stage in his career as a biographer to the possibilities offered by this sort of historico-literary investigation. At all events, the Life of Terence includes such matters as the poet's origin and social class, the occasion of his introduction to literary circles in Rome, his reliance on patrons for assistance in writing plays, the place and date of his death (his undistinguished birth seems never to have been recorded), together with critical opinions (in verse) from Cicero and Caesar: a pattern quite unlike that of the much shorter Lives in Grammarians and Rhetoricians. The Vergil and Horace, on the other hand, contain something much more striking: quotations from the personal correspondence of Augustus. These are less abundant in the Vergil, where indeed only one letter is quoted (31) and that not verbatim. It is curious that an answer to this very letter, in which Augustus had requested an extract from the still unfinished Aeneid, has been preserved for us by the fifth-century scholar Macrobius (Saturnalia 1.24.11). Since Macrobius notoriously draws his material without acknowledgment from earlier writers, it is likely that this Vergilian letter had already reached the public in some way before Suetonius compiled his biography, which may explain his reluctance to incorporate it, preferring as he always does to quote material not easily accessible elsewhere.

The most significant feature of these four Lives, however, is that by this time Suetonius has developed from being the compiler of disconnected notes on a series of people who do not really interest either him or us into something we can recognize as a biographer; and the four Lives already possess many of the more striking peculiarities of the *Caesars*. If we possessed more of the *Orators* or *Historians* than the scanty extracts on Passienus and the elder Pliny that chance has preserved to us, we might be able to observe with confidence the gradual development of Suetonius' technique. These two categories, with their much greater involvement in public life than the two groups of teachers, would have made a truly historical perspective almost inevitable. In any case, we have enough evidence to be reasonably certain that the order of composition of the different groups of Lives was as suggested here.

We cannot indeed tell whether *On Famous Men* is the work about whose publication the younger Pliny teases Suetonius in a letter (5.10) in about A.D. 105 or 106. This may well have been one of the purely scholarly treatises already listed. What is clear is that the *Famous Men* was not originally planned as a single continuous work. Apart from the considerable difference of scale, the preface to the *Grammarians* (4.6), as well as the table of contents, includes a definite link with the *Rhetoricians*, which follows, whereas the preface to the *Rhetoricians* (25.1) makes it grow naturally from the *Grammarians* but gives no hint of any further series to follow. It is hard not to conclude that the subsequent sets of Lives were inspired by the success of the original two, perhaps after a considerable interval of time.

PLAN OF LIVES OF THE TWELVE CAESARS

At all events, the latest and finest of the *Famous Men*, the *Poets*, seems to lead almost directly into the more substantial work for which Suetonius is mainly known, the *Lives of the Twelve Caesars*. Like the *Famous Men*, the *Lives* appears to have developed in the course of composition, with single books devoted to Julius and each of the five Julio-Claudian emperors, who still used the name Caesar because of some claim to kinship with the great Julius; and then, perhaps as an afterthought and on a considerably smaller scale, a seventh book on the three emperors who met their deaths in the course of A.D. 69, and an eighth on the three Flavians, Vespasian and his sons Titus and Domitian, covering the period down to 96, perhaps little more than a score of years before Suetonius started work on the project. Exactly like Tacitus, who began his history of the events of 69 onward not long after the turn of the century, Suetonius did not attempt to take in the reign of the elderly emperor Nerva (96–98), founder of the new adoptive dynasty that both writers regarded as presiding over an age of freedom and prosperity, nor his successor, Trajan. Suetonius concludes his final Life with a reference to "the restraint and moderation of the following emperors" (*Domitian* 23.2). Unlike Tacitus, whose later work, the *Annals*, begins with the death of Augustus in A.D. 14 and surveys the reigns of Tiberius, Caligula, Claudius, and Nero, Suetonius did not merely include Augustus as the first true emperor, but in addition went right back to the man who so nearly established permanent monarchical rule in Rome and was able indirectly to hand down supreme power to his great-nephew and adoptive son, power that became institutionalized during his forty-five years of supremacy. Thus there is some ambiguity in Suetonius' title: Is it the history of a dynasty, from which the last six should properly be excluded, or a list of emperors, as understood in the writer's own day, among whom Julius had no real claim to be counted? The former is probably correct for Suetonius' original plan; but he seems to have revised and extended it when he realized that the next six emperors were no less interesting and could be described frankly without any fear of causing offense.

If Suetonius moved on fairly directly from

such Lives as those of Vergil and Horace to those of Julius and Augustus, we still cannot be certain when this was. We know that the dedication of the *Caesars* was to Septicius Clarus while he was praetorian prefect. An attempt has recently been made, on the strength of a military discharge document found in Rumania, to argue that Septicius, with his colleague Turbo, was appointed only in A.D. 123 and may not have been dismissed, and Suetonius with him, until about 128; but a more careful analysis of the document has shown that this argument is almost certainly invalid. Thus, if the traditional dates are still reliable, the dedication belongs about A.D. 120 to 122, within the first five years of Hadrian's reign. But, just as Pliny had addressed the first book of his *Letters* to the same Septicius about twenty years earlier and published the following eight books without further dedication over the next ten years or so, in the same way Suetonius appears to have followed the pattern of the *Famous Men* in issuing the first one or two *Caesars* under the dedication to Septicius (now lost, together with the opening to the *Julius*) and continuing with the others over a period of perhaps ten years. The date of 130 or later for the last two of these Lives depends on the interpretation of a passage in *Titus* (10.2), where the dowager empress Domitia, attested as still alive about 129, is apparently referred to as a figure of the past.

Evidence for the composition of the *Caesars* piecemeal depends largely on considerations in some respects diametrically opposite to those determining the writing of the *Famous Men*. There can be little dispute that the *Julius* and *Augustus* are superior to the remainder; and those after *Nero* are both brief and slipshod compared with the Julio-Claudian sequence. Again, all the Lives after *Augustus* contain what seems to be a deliberate affectation of vagueness, as the writer withholds names (often known to us from other sources and thus patently available for Suetonius to use had he wished) or actually replaces named individuals with plural expressions: as the "provincial governors" in *Tiberius* 32.2 refers simply to Rectus,

the prefect of Egypt; and the "certain people" and "some" specified among the conspirators in *Nero* 36.2 are without question the officers Subrius Flavus and Sulpicius Asper, respectively. More striking is the way in which quotations from the correspondence of Augustus, already marked in the *Horace* and *Vergil*, continue in the *Augustus, Tiberius, Caligula,* and *Claudius* (after which they would admittedly cease to be relevant); but no letters of any other emperor are quoted in these Lives or elsewhere. The explanation for this phenomenon seems to be that having discovered the files of Augustus' letters while working in one of the palatine offices and having used them for the *Poets*, Suetonius copied out extensive sections throwing light on various matters of interest concerning not only Augustus himself but the next three emperors as well; then, before he was able to work through whatever imperial letters were contained in other files, he was dismissed from his post as secretary and immediately lost his privileged access to those invaluable documents that he would have known so well how to exploit.

Two other features of the *Caesars* point toward a change in attitude after the publication of the *Augustus*. One is that in several passages Suetonius seems to be going out of his way to correct errors that he may have detected in the *Annals* of Tacitus, generally thought to have been produced during the latter part of Trajan's reign (112–117) and perhaps in the next few years. Thus in the first book Tacitus reports, without actually asserting, the idea that Augustus chose Tiberius as his successor in order to gain credit from the comparisons that people were bound to draw (10.7). Suetonius (*Tiberius* 21.2) includes this suggestion among several of the same sort, but goes on to refute it by quoting verbatim a series of passages from Augustus' letters to establish the genuine affection he felt for Tiberius. Again, in the same book (41.2) Tacitus refers in passing to the future emperor Caligula as "born in the camp." When Suetonius comes to the question of Caligula's birth (*Caligula* 8), he devotes an unexpectedly long chapter of detailed argument to the conflicting versions: at Tivoli; in a village near Coblenz on the Rhine; actually in a legionary camp; or, as the official records make clear (" so I find," asserts Suetonius, as he does nowhere else in relation to these records), at Anzio, on the coast near Rome. He caps this with a letter from Augustus himself; but his final appeal is to "the authority of a public document," a typical example of his scholarly, or bureaucratic, approach. This is indeed the most elaborate of any of his discussions (including as it does the philological note, matched by several in the minor works, that the word *puerperium,* which he found in a relevant inscription from near Coblenz, can refer to the birth of a child of either sex). The pains he takes over the whole question are best accounted for if they were provoked by something in an earlier historical work. Likewise Suetonius indulges in further documented argument in his rejection of the supposed poisoning of Claudius' father, Drusus (*Claudius* 1.5), using the same word, "cut off" *(interceptus),* that Tacitus employs in his report of prevalent suspicions of poison (*Annals* 2.82.2). One is tempted to wonder whether the page and a half of quotations from Augustus' letters (*Claudius* 4), establishing the emperor's attitude to his stepgrandson, were inspired by something asserted by Tacitus in the lost book of the *Annals* (9), in which he must have formally introduced Claudius on his accession as emperor. It certainly looks as if Suetonius, while working through Augustus' unpublished correspondence for points to illustrate that emperor's Life, was struck by useful passages concerning the next three emperors and copied them out for use when he came to compose the later three Julio-Claudian Lives. The same may be true of the rough draft of some of Nero's verses, which he mentions as "having come into my hands" (*Nero* 52), and uses to correct the view expressed by Tacitus (*Annals* 14.16.1) that Nero incorporated other poets' ideas in his own compositions. Whether or not Suetonius found the draft in the palace files, he is careful not to refer directly to Tacitus' argument.

The other feature is perhaps more indicative of a more critical attitude on the biographer's part. This is a group of passages that look as if they have a bearing on the situation shortly after Hadrian's accession and are hard to account for completely in terms of the contexts where they occur. One of them describes the sudden execution by Titus of Alienus Caecina at the very end of Vespasian's reign (*Titus* 6.1), "by which means, while taking due care for his future safety, he incurred a great deal of unpopularity at the time, so that it would be hard to find any emperor who came to the throne with so much hostile talk and such widespread unwillingness." Whether true or not of Titus (and he very soon established himself as "the darling and delight of the Roman people," as Suetonius tells us), the expression is very odd, especially as no emperor at all seems to have started off with any degree of unpopularity, except perhaps Tiberius. But when Hadrian reached Rome from the East at the start of his reign, he was already in very bad odor, thanks largely to the summary execution of four ex-consuls, men of the same high rank as Caecina. Second, in *Nero* 18 Suetonius relates how that emperor "even considered withdrawing the army from Britain, and abandoned the idea only out of shame, in case he should appear to be finding fault with his parent's glory." He uses the word *parens,* rather than *pater,* as perhaps slightly more appropriate to an adoptive father, as Claudius was to Nero and Trajan to Hadrian. Nero may indeed have been reluctant to criticize Claudius too openly, since his adoption by Claudius was the whole basis of his claim to the throne, and the abandonment of Claudius' one major conquest would have amounted to a serious devaluation of his memory; although in fact the picture given by Suetonius (*Nero* 33.1) of Nero's attitude toward his predecessor reveals little but a succession of jibes. Hadrian was notoriously prompt to cancel Trajan's conquests in Armenia and Mesopotamia within the first months of his reign; and the description of Nero's hesitation is very curiously worded in view of the situation at the time when Suetonius was writing. Third, within a short time of Trajan's death there appears to have been a great deal of doubt as to whether he had really, on his deathbed, adopted Hadrian as son and successor or left the matter open to be organized after his death by his widow, Plotina. Similarly, both Tacitus (*Annals* 1.5.5), writing some time before Trajan's death, and Dio Cassius (56.31.1), writing about a century later, claim that there was some doubt whether Augustus died before Tiberius could arrive from the Balkans and receive his last instructions as heir to the Principate. Suetonius, writing this second of the Lives while still a loyal imperial employee, is remarkably silent about this controversy, including the suspicion that Augustus' widow, Livia, concealed her husband's death until Tiberius had time to join her: he simply states (*Augustus* 98.5; *Tiberius* 21.2) that Tiberius enjoyed a long, last, secret meeting with the dying emperor—just as Hadrian was currently supposed to have done with Trajan. Yet when Suetonius comes to the death of Claudius (*Claudius* 44.2), he has no hesitation in reproducing a version that throws discredit on the dowager empress Agrippina: "his death was concealed until all the arrangements should be made for the succession." If rumors were really rife about double-dealing at Trajan's deathbed, the imperial secretary's discretion in ignoring similar talk about the death of Augustus was only to be expected: what is striking is that in the later Lives, written (as I have suggested) after Suetonius' dismissal from court, the language invites the reader to enjoy the reference to yet another weak point in Hadrian's position, as obviously as the writer could without obvious libel. But neither here nor in relation to Tacitus does Suetonius venture on anything like an open criticism.

BIOGRAPHICAL TECHNIQUE

If, then, the *Caesars* contains something of the history of the author's personal misfortune, he does not for that reason cease to be essentially a civil servant, never the historian proper,

as he approaches his subject. History was one of the grandest of literary forms, handled at Rome by such great names as Livy and Tacitus. But Tacitus had already dealt with the six later Caesars in his own *Histories*, written probably before A.D. 110, and had evidently published at least the earlier books of his *Annals*, covering Tiberius, Caligula, and Claudius. Biography had no such status. It was hardly ever featured among the major branches of literature and was all too often regarded as the proper activity of a scholar rather than of a true man of letters. The *Famous Men* is not far removed from the tradition of writers of scholarly commentaries. On the other hand, there had been a long tradition of panegyric, whether posthumous or not: the Greeks Xenophon and Isocrates had written in this way about Agesilaus of Sparta and Evagoras of Cyprus, and it had become the practice for a great Roman to be praised in a funeral speech. Tacitus as early as A.D. 97 had written the life of his father-in-law, Agricola, in a manner that evidently owes a good deal more to panegyric than it does to history. Much in the biographies of the Greek Plutarch, writing about the same time as Suetonius, inclines to a similar approach. Suetonius is well aware of both techniques, and on the whole he continues in the objective manner employed in the *Famous Men*. But with the much greater scale possible concerning such public figures as emperors, with so much material available, both favorable and hostile, and with such an amount of traditional historical writing already in existence, for the earlier Caesars in particular, he was almost obliged to react as strongly as possible in the direction of bureaucratic composition.

In particular he takes as the basis of his biographical scheme a method, already traceable in Greek panegyric, of dividing his material by topics so that both actions and qualities are set out not chronologically but under a series of rubrics. Thus in the *Julius* the subject's early career (a much larger proportion of the Life than in most of the others) is dealt with in a more or less chronological manner; yet even here one can observe the emergence of distinct topics, such as "occasions of civil war" (29) and "real reasons for civil war" (30.2), or "triumphs and shows" (39), and note how prominently this last topic appears in Life after Life. In 44.1–3 comes a very characteristic statement of topics to be covered, followed in due order by examples of the various types. "As time passed, he entertained more and greater plans for [1] adorning, [2] equipping, likewise [3] protecting, [4] extending the empire." (I have inserted the numbers for clarity, and the arrangement would be a great deal easier to follow if Suetonius had provided them for us.) There follow in succession illustrations of each project, from the building of a great temple to Mars to the defeat of the Dacians on the lower Danube and the conquest of the Parthians beyond the Euphrates. Only if we have carefully noted the introductory divisio (the setting-out of items) do we appreciate that the defeat of the Dacians was simply defense, whereas that of the Parthians was to involve their incorporation into the empire, a rational enough scheme, since the area from the Euphrates to the Indus had formed part of Alexander the Great's empire, whereas Dacia (Rumania) was wild and uncivilized, hardly meriting the expense of acquisition. Trajan, it might be observed, had conquered both, and Hadrian had given up the Parthian provinces while retaining the barbaric Dacians.

Suetonius goes straight on with a much more extensive division: "As he acted and planned in this way, he was cut short by death. Before I describe this, it will not be irrelevant to set forth in outline details concerning [1] his appearance, and [2] bearing, [3] his personal habits and [4] character, and also his practices in [5] civil and [6] military life" (44.4; numbers added). Sure enough, each of these six topics is taken up in turn with a series of illustrative anecdotes and other details. But the writer seldom bothers to spell out the subject of each section as it comes up, so that it is all too easy to miss the transition from one section of the index to the next.

Having ostentatiously announced this program for arranging material, he goes on in the Augustus (9) simply to announce that he is going to describe the emperor's life not chronologically but by topics. What the divisions are to be, we have to work out for ourselves from what follows as civil wars (9–18), risings and conspiracies (19), foreign wars (20–23), followed by military reforms (24–25), then a similar series on civil affairs. After a series of complex subsections on these, he comes to a further major division: "Since I have set out what he was like in military and civil power and in establishing the republic in peace and war throughout the world, I shall now relate his private and family life and his character and fortune" (61). He goes on with chapters on a wide range of such topics, ranging from personal relationships to literary style and idiosyncrasies in letter writing (87–88), a matter in which the imperial secretary displays particular interest. But again, he provides no clear signposting to enable the reader to grasp at once what the theme of each paragraph is going to be.

Once this pattern is established in the first two Lives, Suetonius tends to incorporate it without any further definite acknowledgment, as if the reader should now be able to sort things out for himself. Thus in Tiberius 42.1 he does indeed promise to describe the emergence of Tiberius' vices one by one; but it takes careful attention to observe the succession of drunkenness and gluttony (42), sexual perversions (43–45), avarice (46–49), and cruelty (50–62), the last of these introduced only with the words "hatred towards his relatives . . . ," to be followed by a widening circle of victims under a number of subheadings, culminating in a special section on sadistic punishments inflicted (60–62). The parallel treatment of Nero's vices is introduced with a proper division (26.1), listing the five main topics, which is fairly easy to follow. The last section, however, on cruelty, is curiously twisted by the incorporation of a paragraph on wives as victims (35), which includes Poppaea's baby, Claudia, who died in infancy of natural causes, and halfheartedly introduces the third wife, Statilia, who in fact survived Nero unscathed; then, from general hostility to the Senate, Suetonius goes on (38) to the fire of Rome as a deliberate act (otherwise it could not stand in this section at all), and finally (39) to three disasters that in no way illustrate Nero's cruelty, if indeed they reflect on him at all: a plague, the sufferings caused by Boudicca's rebellion in Britain, and the ignominious surrender of Paetus' legions in Armenia, the last two of which were in reality fully counterbalanced by the campaigns of Suetonius Paulinus and of Corbulo, respectively. It should be noted that these last two items illustrate a further trick that becomes more noticeable as Suetonius proceeds—total concentration on the central figure of the biography, so that other characters central to such incidents play no part at all. Passages like this, mentioning neither the British queen nor the Roman generals, emphasize the line drawn between biography and history. The reader is clearly expected to be familiar with the main outlines of the reign, so that he does not need to be told specifically about Boudicca and Corbulo. What Suetonius is doing is to focus his account of the period closely on the personality of the subject, hardly admitting anything that does not have an immediate bearing on the emperor. When he does not wish to give the emperor credit for the good administration of a reign, he undercuts a list of useful reforms by saying, as he does of Claudius, "But these and other things and, to a great extent, his whole reign he administered not so much by his own choice as by that of his wives and freedmen" (25.5). Or he relates his list with all the verbs in the passive, as "A limit was applied to extravagance ... the Christians were punished ... charioteers' games were banned ..." (Nero 16.2–17), as if Nero were not personally responsible for such salutary measures. Normally the emperor is the subject of the great majority of sentences, since he is what the Life is about.

Not only the pattern of the biographies but also the content would for the most part have been regarded with scorn by a historian proper.

Much of what Suetonius reports with circumstantial exactitude is sordid and trivial. One has only to compare his detailed account of the last hours of Vitellius, putting on a money-belt full of gold coins, hiding in a porter's cubicle, and protecting the door with a watchdog, a bed, and a mattress (Vitellius 16–17), with the dramatic and dignified version in Tacitus (Histories 3.84.4–5), where no explicit details are mentioned beyond "a shameful hiding-place." Suetonius is continually criticized for his addiction to "scandal." Of course, for his portrayal of character, incidents revealing cruelty or lust or absentmindedness are vitally relevant, adverse though they may be to "the dignity of the Roman people" invoked by Tacitus (Annals 13.31.1), as determining the suitability of material for true historical writing. Again, all too much of this material reads like libelous pasquinade, and sometimes Suetonius does not believe it himself. So at least one judges from the way in which he cites hostile witnesses to the debauching of the young Julius Caesar by King Nicomedes of Bithynia (Julius 49): "I say nothing of the notorious verses of Calvus" (which he then quotes); "I pass over the speeches of Dolabella and Curio" (though he selects key phrases from them); "I also reject the edicts of Bibulus" (of which he gives a juicy extract). Whether or not the original story of seduction was true, what is significant is that it was certainly made the excuse for a whole series of savage and jocular attacks by political opponents and others; and thus it is of curious importance in Caesar's life. Similarly, introducing his account of Tiberius' unnatural lusts, he remarks, "It is scarcely right for these things to be reported and listened to, let alone believed, as if he really did..." (Tiberius 44.1). The lubricious stories follow, as essential parts of the Tiberius legend. The danger is, of course, that we forget the initial warning and assume that Suetonius is giving some warrant to the stories. Tacitus, we should note, hinting at the same horrors but omitting everything specific (Annals 6.1), fails to provide any qualifying remark. On the other hand, Suetonius is sometimes more positive in his assertions than Tacitus simply because his biographical pattern requires it. The fire of Rome is blamed on Nero because it comes as an appendage to the topic of cruelty (*Nero* 38), whereas Tacitus admits (*Annals* 15. 38.1) that the cause was doubtful; and the same emperor's incestuous passion for his mother is included without reservation among instances of his lusts (28.1–2), whereas Tacitus, hesitating between versions that respectively blamed Nero and his mother for taking the initiative, relates in somewhat lurid terms the advances made by Agrippina to her son and indicates that he accepts this version as the more plausible because the empress had always made free of her favors in order to advance her power. This latter consideration can carry no weight with Suetonius, since he has chosen to devote the whole context to Nero's lusts, as the second of his major vices, and there can be no place for him in this paragraph as the relatively innocent victim of his unscrupulous mother.

If the Lives represent in many respects the ingenious shuffling of a card index, it is still remarkable how readable they are; how vividly they present the character of the subjects; and how varied they contrive to be within the limitations of the framework of topics. This is largely because the civil servant has not allowed himself to be stereotyped by a standard formula. The pattern of headings is carefully adapted to suit each emperor: vices and virtues differ from man to man, according to suitability; sometimes there is a decisive change from fairly good to bad (as with Tiberius and Domitian), sometimes from an unpromising youth to a fine and popular maturity (as with Augustus and Titus); sometimes a topic such as wives will be included under personal relationships (*Augustus*), sometimes under victims (*Nero*), sometimes under lack of independence (*Claudius*), while in the *Julius* the wives are introduced as they occur in the chronological narrative of the early life, their importance being mainly political. Mistresses, on the other hand, rate a section of some length among Caesar's personal characteristics (*Julius* 50–52), as they do in Au-

gustus 69, *Caligula* 36 (along with male lovers), and *Domitian* 22. Objectivity may be questioned when fires and plagues count among the vices of Nero (38–39) but among occasions for the generosity of Titus (8.3–4). This is to be explained by the extent to which Suetonius has initially made up his mind about the character of each emperor. The fact that both the disasters in Titus' short reign, together with the eruption of Vesuvius, seem to have left the emperor more popular than before is implicitly contrasted, perhaps rightly, with the contribution made by quite fortuitous misfortunes to Nero's complete loss of popular support during the last months of his life.

But Suetonius is not a moralizer, as so many Roman writers are. For the most part, on the surface at least, he presents his material with impartiality, not pausing to comment as the greater historians constantly do. He was bound to be at the mercy of earlier writers, who had already established many features of the imperial portraits down to Vitellius at least; and although there is no indication that he made direct use of the *Histories* of Tacitus, their authority must have contributed greatly to the portrayal of the three Flavians (especially Domitian, as represented in the *Agricola*) by all subsequent writers. Almost all the allegations of depravity given by Suetonius are traceable, though not always explicit, in the accounts of Tacitus and Dio Cassius, who evidently drew on much the same primary sources. The one emperor to whom Suetonius may have made a major original contribution is Titus, whose treatment by Tacitus is hard to infer from his brief appearance in the surviving early books of the *Histories*. Certainly Suetonius' position with regard to Titus is in many ways unique, coming closer to panegyric than in any of the other *Caesars*. From the start, he is "darling and delight of the human race" (1); he is compared continually with other emperors, being more unpopular than any on his accession (6.2) though swiftly redeeming himself by his behavior, abstemious in demands on other people's property if anyone ever was (7.3); gaining gratitude and praise on his death surpassing that accorded to any living emperor (11): even the plague during his reign would be hard to match (8.3). Yet the true characteristics of panegyric are hardly to be found: even an imperial secretary would not have regarded the skills of a superlative forger (3.2) as part of the model prince. Most probably, what we observe here is simply the traces of some earlier comparison between the two brother-emperors, Titus and Domitian, building up the excellence of the former in order to blacken the latter. Yet even here Suetonius does not abandon objectivity but allows plenty of minor human weaknesses to temper the general approval.

Apart from a few minor slips, Suetonius seems to be amazingly accurate in reproducing his sources, dubious though those sources may often have been. His accuracy is largely due to his lack of stylistic obsessions, beyond the determination to write lucidly and simply. His Latin is strangely lacking in any positive elements of style: it tends to be difficult only because, in addition to assuming the reader's familiarity with the history of the period, he continually uses ordinary everyday words for ordinary everyday things, such as a turnip, a mattress, or a box-tree, which dignified historians would normally avoid mentioning. Moreover, unlike any serious Latin writer, he has no objection to quoting other works verbatim and extensively in prose or verse, and even in Greek, a practice that Sallust, Livy, Tacitus, or Cicero (except in informal letters) would regard as intolerable. His refusal to shun the commonplace and the low means that his Lives provide a picture of imperial Rome by no means limited to the interior of the palace and bring the reality before our eyes more vividly yet with less exaggeration than do the works of virtually any other Latin writer.

INFLUENCE OF THE LIVES OF THE TWELVE CAESARS

The combination of straightforward Latin and interesting anecdotes, together with a certain amount of satisfaction among the Christians at the moral shortcomings of the pagan empire, made Suetonius an undeservedly popular source for historical writers of later centuries, who wanted the essence of an emperor's reign compressed within the limits of a brief Life rather than in the six books on Tiberius or four or more on Nero in Tacitus' Annals. Much of the material we find in later writers seems therefore to have been borrowed straight from the Caesars. In the actual composition of biography Suetonius seems to have set a fashion, followed about a century later by Marius Maximus, with a second set of twelve imperial biographies. This work has not survived; but Maximus was evidently exploited, as a source if not as a model, by the author(s) of that strange collection the Augustan History, written in the late fourth century and based in certain respects on a knowledge of Suetonius and a determination to imitate his biographical technique, even to the extent of inserting totally spurious documents to obtain an air of authenticity, yet lacking any understanding of the basis of his arrangement of material. The work contrives to be simultaneously salacious and tedious, and demonstrates remarkably the mastery of Suetonius, to whom a telling tribute is made at one point (Probus 2.7), where the author rejects the eloquence of the great Roman historians in favor of Suetonius and his imitators, "whose aim was accuracy rather than style." For the most part, however, biography, whether civil or ecclesiastical, becomes more and more a matter of uncritical eulogy, with the striking exception of the Life of Charlemagne written by Einhard in good Suetonian Latin during the early ninth century. Despite a more marked partiality for Charlemagne than Suetonius displays toward any of his subjects, Einhard has learned much from his Roman model; and the result is a biography that stands out in the genre until modern Europe, with the invention of printing, became capable of producing Lives that the economical and orderly Suetonius would have regarded as intolerably garrulous and lacking in focus.

1060

Selected Bibliography

TEXTS

De vita Caesarum, edited by Maximilian Ihm. Leipzig, 1907.

Grammatici e retori, edited by F. della Corte. Rome, 1954. Revised ed. Turin, 1968.

Praeter Caesarum libros reliquiae. Pars 1: De Grammaticis et Rhetoribus, edited by Georgio Brugnoli. Leipzig, 1960.

Praeter Caesarum libros reliquiae, edited by A. Reifferscheid. Leipzig, 1960. Reprinted Hildesheim, 1971. Does not include the *Caesars*.

Quae supersunt omnia, edited by Carl L. Roth. Leipzig, 1958.

TRANSLATIONS

Ailloud, Henri, trans. *Vies des douze Césars*. 3 vols. Paris, 1931–1932. 4th ed., 2 vols. Paris, 1967. French translation.

Graves, Robert, trans. *The Twelve Caesars*. Harmondsworth, 1957. Penguin Classics.

Holland, Philemon, trans. *The Historie of Twelve Caesars*. London, 1906. Reprinted 1931.

Rolfe, John C., trans. *Suetonius*. Cambridge, Mass., and London, 1914. Reprinted 1964. Loeb Classical Library. Includes Latin text.

COMMENTARIES

Augustus, edited by E. S. Shuckburgh. Cambridge, 1896.

Augustus, edited by M. Adams. London, 1918.

Augustus, edited by M. A. Levi. Florence, 1951.

Caligula, 1–21, edited by J. A. Maurer. Philadelphia, 1949.

Claudius, edited by H. Smilda. Groningen, 1896.

De Poetis, e biografi minori, edited by A. Rostagni. Turin, 1944.

Galba-Vitellius, edited by P. Venini. Turin, 1977.

Galba-Domitian, edited by G. W. Mooney. Dublin, 1930. With translation.

Julius, edited by H. E. Butler and M. Cary. Oxford, 1927. Revised by G. B. Townend. In progress.

Julius and Augustus, edited by J. H. Westcott and E. M. Rankin. Boston, 1918.

Nero, edited by B. H. Warmington, Bristol, 1977.

Nero, edited by K. R. Bradley. Brussels, 1978.

Tiberius, 1–23, edited by M. J. du Four. Philadelphia, 1941.

Tiberius, 24–40, edited by J. H. Rietra. Amsterdam, 1927.

Tiberius, edited by W. Vogt. Ph.D. dissertation. Wurzburg, 1975.

Titus, edited by H. Price. Menasha, 1919.

Vespasian, edited by A. W. Braithwaite. Oxford, 1927.

CRITICAL STUDIES

Alföldy, G. "Marcius Turbo, Septicius Clarus, Sueton und die Historia Augusta." *Zeitschrift für Papyrologie und Epigraphie* 36:233–253 (1979).

Cizek, Eugen. *Structures et idéologie dans les "Vies des douze Césars" de Suéton*. Paris, 1977.

della Corte, F. *Svetonio, eques Romanus*. 2nd. ed. Milan, 1967.

Funaioli, G. C. *Suetonius Tranquillus*. In A. S. Pauly and G. Wissowa, eds., *Realencyclopädie* 4.A. 593–641 (1932).

Gascou, J. "Nouvelles Données chronologiques sur la carrière de Suétone." *Latomus* 37:436 (1978).

Gugel, Helmut. *Studien zur biographischen Technik Suetons*. Vienna, 1977.

Howard, A. A., and C. N. Jackson. *Index verborum C. Suetoni Tranquilli*. Cambridge, Mass., 1922. Reprinted Hildesheim, 1963.

Macé, A. *Essai sur Suétone*. Paris, 1900.

Mouchova, Bohumila. *Studie zu Kaiserbiographien Suetons*. Prague, 1968.

Steidel, Wolf. *Sueton und die antike Biographie*. Munich, 1951.

Syme, R. *Tacitus*. Oxford, 1958. Pp. 778–782.

Townend, G. B. "Suetonius and His Influence." In T. A. Dorrey, *Latin Biography*. London, 1967.

Wallace-Hadrill, A. F. *Suetonius on the Emperor*. Ph.D. dissertation. Oxford, 1980.

G. B. TOWNEND

LONGINUS

(*fl.* First Century A.D.)

IN 1554 THE French poet and scholar Marc-Antoine Muret referred with delight to an "excellent Greek work" he had undertaken to translate. "When," he says, "I was beginning to translate into Latin the treatise of Dionysus Longinus, *On the Sublime*, which no one has edited ... I discovered in it indeed not only many things of sufficient value to make all cultivated men eagerly await the book itself, but a most voluptuous ode by the poet Sappho, of which Catullus has translated the greatest part." This first critical evaluation of a work that had been virtually unknown foreshadows many appreciations it has received since 1554: a good deal of justified enthusiasm and a certain number of questionable statements. As it happens, the treatise had been edited a few months earlier by the Italian humanist Francesco Robortello; Muret's translation has never been found; and the work, although excellent and Greek, is not by Dionysius Longinus.

These are but some of the difficulties the work presents. A few others may be worth mentioning. The treatise exists in eleven manuscripts, of which the oldest and best is grievously mutilated: twenty-one of the fifty-two leaves devoted to *On the Sublime* are missing. Many passages are exceedingly difficult to unravel. Not only is the real author unknown; the date of composition remains a mystery and a matter of considerable controversy. The work is addressed to one Postumius Terentianus, about whom we know almost nothing. Furthermore,

the fame *On the Sublime* has enjoyed since 1674, when Nicolas Boileau published his elegant translation, equals and often obscures the complexities of the original. From the seventeenth century on, interpretations of the text have enriched and colored it to such an extent that it is sometimes unrecognizable. The "sublime" that Boileau made available differs from the concept that Edmund Burke discusses in *A Philosophic Enquiry into the Origins of Our Ideas of the Sublime and Beautiful* (1757). Both Boileau and Burke would be surprised and puzzled by the connotations the word had acquired by the middle of the nineteenth century. Longinus has spoken deeply, and in deeply different accents, to such twentieth-century critics as Elder Olson, R. P. Blackmur, and Harold Bloom.

Despite the mysteries surrounding the date and the authorship of the treatise, the great gaps in the manuscripts that have come down to us, and the distortions that the work has suffered, recent scholarship has done much to situate it in time, clarify some of the questions concerning its composition, identify its author's sympathies in terms of ancient literary theory and practice, and elucidate its fundamental principles and organization. It is now generally believed that the treatise was written during the first century after Christ, perhaps during Nero's reign (A.D. 54–68). The table of contents of the best manuscript gives Dionysius or Longinus as the author; these names probably represent a

Byzantine scholar's educated guess that the work was by either Dionysius of Halicarnassus or Cassius Longinus. Neither now seems a likely candidate. It does seem likely or at least possible that the author was a Hellenized Jew, and it is probable that he was a follower of Theodorus of Gadara—which is to say, an opponent of Apollodorus of Pergamum.

The differences between Apollodorus and his younger rival Theodorus can be stated fairly simply, for they are differences that any student of any period of literature or art will recognize. According to Apollodorus and his followers, the Apollodorei, rhetoric is a science (epistēmē); that being so, poetry, in the largest sense, is a matter of fixed rules. To know the rules is to be able to make a speech, an ode, anything that can be made with words. On the contrary, according to Theodorus and the Theodorei, rhetoric is an art (technē), and the rules, although important, are not sovereign. The poet's task and study are to discover, by training and by taste, what works and what does not in specific circumstances. A science suggests timelessness and rigidity; an art, timeliness and suppleness. We shall return to these distinctions shortly. For the time being, it is worth remarking that the opposition between the Apollodorei and the Theodorei does not take, in Longinus' treatise, the stark form it might have taken and sometimes takes elsewhere. It is not a question of rules or no rules; it is rather a question of certain kinds of rules and how and when they should be observed by the writer and applied by the critic.

In Longinus' treatise, the Apollodorei are represented by Cecilius, the Theodorei by Longinus himself and, no doubt, his young friend Postumius Terentianus. The brilliant opening section of *On the Sublime* not only states but illustrates the differences between the two ways of defining rhetoric:

> You know, my dear Postumius Terentianus, that when we were studying together Cecilius' little treatise on the sublime we found it was too trivial to satisfy the full demands of the subject and

omitted altogether to touch upon the main points, and that consequently it does not render to its readers very much of that assistance which should be an author's chief aim. Moreover, in every systematic treatise there are two requisites: the author must first define his subject, and secondly, although this is really more important, he must show us how and by what means of study we may reach the goal ourselves. Cecilius, however, while assuming our ignorance and endeavoring by a thousand instances to demonstrate the nature of the sublime, apparently thought it unnecessary to deal with the means by which we may be enabled to educate our natures to the proper pitch of elevation. Still, so far as Cecilius is concerned, we ought perhaps rather to praise him for the mere conception of such a treatise and the trouble spent upon it than to blame him for his omissions. But since you have now required me in my turn to prepare some notes on the sublime purely for your own sake, let us then see whether our views have any real value for public speakers; and in the details of our enquiry you yourself, my friend, will, I am sure, do what duty and your heart alike dictate and give me the benefit of your unbiased judgment.[1]

(1.1–2)

From the beginning, Longinus reduces Cecilius to something like insignificance: his "little treatise" is not only trivial, low, and unworthy in thought; it does not even do, however imperfectly, what a systematic treatise should do. Cecilius' text, which we see only through Longinus' eyes, is thus useful only insofar as it shows how not to go about the job, that is, insofar as it provides a valid pretext. What Postumius Terentianus and we are about to read is neither a "little treatise" nor a "systematic treatise," it appears, but a letter a man writes to a friend in response to a request for "some notes on the

---

[1] "Longinus," *On the Sublime*, edited and translated by W. Hamilton Fyfe, in *Aristotle, The Poetics; "Longinus," On the Sublime; Demetrius, On Style*, rev. ed. (New York, 1932; reprinted Cambridge, Mass., and London, 1960), the Loeb Classical Library. All subsequent quotations from *On the Sublime* are from this translation and are identified by chapter and section number in parentheses or square brackets. I have made a few minor changes in the interests of clarity.

sublime." In place of an ostentatious formal dedication of the sort one might expect to encounter at the beginning of a formal treatise, we find, casually inscribed in the third line of the first page, a friend's name, a name that is always generously associated with the author's project and with his undogmatic tone. And that project, from the very beginning, eschews the formalities of systematic exposition, delights to do something different from what has been done, something better, more useful, and worthier of both subject and audience.

To be sure, Cicero had long since discovered the possibilities of the familiar letter. Longinus' decision to write a letter rather than a treatise is hardly original; but it is a clever and effective strategy. His references in *On the Sublime* to other works—"my book on Xenophon" (8.1), "two treatises" on "the arrangement of words" (39.1)—are tantalizing, for the three works are lost. But they usefully invite us to consider *On the Sublime* as something different from them, a kind of discourse in which the matter and perhaps the manner of the other works would seem pedantic and inappropriate. A familiar letter cannot comfortably bear the weight of evidence that a scholarly treatise can; a scholarly treatise can scarcely leap from point to point as a letter can.

I have used the word "strategy" for strategic reasons of my own. What can be said about Postumius Terentianus, for whom and to whom *On the Sublime* was apparently written? He is young (15.1), presumably a Roman (12.5); he studied with Longinus (1.1) and is now well versed in literary studies (1.3), so much so that he could suggest on his own the reflections with which Longinus concludes the first chapter of his work. He is a lover of knowledge (44.1). We know nothing else about Postumius Terentianus. I suspect that his identity is rhetorical rather than historical. Let us consider what Longinus himself says about changes of grammatical person. They produce, he says, an effect as vivid as that produced by change of tense, "and often [make] the audience feel themselves set in the thick of the danger" (26.1). Commenting upon a passage in which Herodotus suddenly switches from first-person narration to a discourse in the fictional second-person singular, Longinus asks, "Do you see, my friend, how he takes you along with him through the country and turns hearing into sight?" (26.2). He goes on to generalize:

> All such passages with a direct personal application set the hearer in the centre of the action. By appearing to address not the whole audience but a single individual—"but you could not have told on which side Tydeus' son was fighting" [*Iliad* 5.85, R. A. Lattimore trans.]—you will move him more and make him more attentive and full of active interest, if you rouse him by these personal appeals
>
> (26.2–3)

These comments, and the passages that elicit and illustrate them, deserve attention for several reasons. For one, Longinus is the only ancient writer on style and rhetoric who discusses this special use of the second-person singular. The passage from Herodotus gives an account of the Nile beyond Elephantine; as Herodotus is careful to say, it is an account based not on his own travel and experience but on question and hearsay. In Longinus' text, the passage from Herodotus reads as follows: "You will sail up from the city of Elephantine and there come to a smooth plain. And when you have passed through that place you will board again another ship and sail two days and then you will come to a great city, the name of which is Meroë" (26.2). To give the account some of the liveliness and plausibility it might otherwise lack, Herodotus uses the fictional second-person singular. Since the account is based on hearsay, as Herodotus admits and as Longinus surely knows, it might well be fiction, but it is not dull. Far from being put off by it, the reader is drawn into it; the vividness of the account even makes you forget Herodotus' careful distinction between what he saw for himself and what he relates at second or third hand. His writing has an energy that destroys some of the barriers between fiction and fact, barriers that are often mere fictions or simple conveniences, as students of history know. Just so, the energy in battle of Tydeus' son, Diomedes, makes it impossible for the spectator to distinguish Trojan from Achaian. And for us it is a wonderful coincidence that Homer should go on to describe Diomedes as

... storming up the plain like a winter-swollen
river in spate that scatters the dikes in its running
   current,
one that strong-compacted dikes can contain no
   longer.
(*Iliad* 5.87–89, R. A. Lattimore trans.)

As far as Longinus is concerned, the coincidence is probably deliberate: two quotations, two rivers, two examples of the obliteration of ordinary distinctions (I/you; truth/fiction; Trojan/Achaian; and so on). As is almost always true, the closer you look at Longinus' text the more it yields.

Deliberate, too, it would seem, is his use of the second-person-singular pronoun in this discussion of the fictional second-person-singular: "do you see . . . he takes you . . . you will move him . . . if you rouse him." This coincidence invites us to entertain even more happily than we might otherwise the hypothesis that Postumius Terentianus is a fiction, "a mere device," a fictional friend and disciple whose existence makes it possible for Longinus to create and maintain, without apparent effort, the impression of immediacy and vividness he savors in Herodotus' account of the Nile beyond Elephantine, a Nile that he never saw but that his discourse allows us to see. In *On the Sublime*, Postumius Terentianus helps Longinus overcome various obstacles in his quest for an unpedantic and urbane discussion of the sublime.

Speaking of metaphors, Longinus notes that "the vulgar phrase sometimes proves far more enlightening than elegant language. Being taken from our common life it is immediately recognized, and what is familiar is halfway to conviction" (31.1). This statement applies to all figures that are "taken from our common life," including of course the figure by which Herod-

otus makes his account more convincing than it might otherwise be, and by which Longinus makes his appreciation of Herodotus more energetic than it might otherwise be.

In general, the form Longinus chooses for his work—the familiar letter—allows him to exploit the possibilities of certain figures without drawing attention to what he is doing, without arousing mistrust or suspicion in his reader. He can assume, unlike Cecilius, that other readers will be only too happy to substitute themselves for Postumius Terentianus and join in the civilized conspiracy of good taste and flawless judgment that is celebrated in *On the Sublime*. To sum up these observations on Postumius Terentianus, we might say that although he is probably a fiction and the second-person pronoun is merely a figure of speech, both fiction and figure become opaque and problematic only when the discourse as a whole is subjected to rigorous analysis. And even then it remains impossible to decide one way or the other, for the distinctions have blurred. To say that is only to rephrase a remark Longinus makes himself: "a figure is always most effective when it conceals the very fact of its being a figure" (17.1–2).

So much for the form, at least for the time being. What about the subject of this familiar letter? In the first chapter, wasting no time on what others have said, acknowledging and exploiting the presence of Postumius Terentianus, Longinus marks out his territory:

... writing for a man of such learning and culture as yourself, dear friend, I almost feel freed from the need of a lengthy preface showing how the sublime consists in a consummate excellence and distinction of language, and that this alone gave to the greatest poets and historians their preeminence and clothed them with immortal fame.
(1.3–4)

He then proceeds to make three oppositions that illuminate the specific quality he is interested in:

... the effect of the sublime is not to persuade the audience but rather to transport them out of themselves. Inevitably what inspires wonder casts a spell upon us and is always superior to what is merely convincing and pleasing. For our convictions are usually under our own control, while such passages exercise an irresistible power of mastery and get the upper hand with every member of the audience.

(1.4)

From these oppositions alone it is clear that for Longinus the sublime has little or nothing to do with what is conventionally called the sublime or grand style; as we shall see, the sublime is a quality, a force, that may well be present in the simplest kind of discourse. In any event, he goes on in the preface to assert that our perception of it differs from our perception of the overall shape of an argument or a work:

Again inventive skill and the due disposal and marshaling of facts do not show themselves in one or two touches: they gradually emerge from the whole tissue of the composition, while a well-timed flash of sublimity scatters everything before it like a bolt of lightning and reveals the full power of the speaker at a single stroke.

(1.4)

Having made that lofty comparison, Longinus deftly turns his preface back to the person to whom it is ostensibly addressed: "But, as I say, my dear Terentianus, these and other such hints you with your experience could supply yourself" (1.4). No need, in a letter to an intelligent friend, to adduce a multitude of instances, to belabor the point; better to pass on to other matters, specific questions, representative examples, close analyses.

Ecstasy, wonder, or, more precisely, the kind of fear or surprise that knocks you out, mastery: these are strong words. The bolt of lightning epitomizes the sublime in its awesome power, its brightness, and its irresistibility. All of these characteristics are further explored and illustrated in On the Sublime.

Another point, however, requires particular emphasis before we continue. Longinus speaks of a "well-timed" flash of sublimity; it has the true effect only if it flashes forth at the right moment. The concept of the right moment, the opportune moment, is fundamental to Longinus' theory of the sublime, and the word kairos[2] and its derivatives are among the key words of the treatise. In referring constantly to this concept and in exploiting the diverse meanings of kairos, Longinus differs most radically from formalistic critics such as Apollodorus and Cecilius. Formalistic critics build systems and develop methods that by their very nature are hostile to the concept of kairos. For Longinus, the concept is indispensable, and the use he makes of it in his art reflects his desire to avoid the extremes he mentions in the introductory section that follows the preface: "Some think those are wholly at fault who try to bring such matters [as sublimity and profundity] under systematic rules" (2.1). The concept also reflects the open spirit in which he conducts his inquiry: what is appropriate and timely in one kind of discourse might well be inappropriate and untimely in another; rules alone will not explain why. Still less will they guide a writer or an orator infallibly. But that is not to say that there are no rules or explanations. Natural ability—genius—accounts for much, but by no means for all: "In all productions Nature is the prime cause, the great exemplar; but as to all questions of degree, of the happy moment in each case, and again of the safest rules of practice and use, such prescriptions are the proper contribution of an art or system" (2.2). Furthermore, "the very fact that in literature some effects come of natural genius alone can only be learnt from art" (2.3). This sentence, which is part of a passage some scholars think spurious, usefully broadens the scope of the inquiry. It is no longer necessarily limited to composition; there is an art of criticism too. And we may be sure that in Longinus' eyes, kairos is a secret of

[2]In Greek, "the right moment" is ho Kairos. The word kairos has many other meanings: "appropriateness," "fitness," "ripeness," "opportunity," "critical moment." Kairos also was personified and had an altar at Olympia; he was depicted as a bald-headed man with a long forelock. Because no single word in English suggests the range of meanings, I shall use the Greek throughout this essay.

good criticism as well as of good poetry. So, returning to the charge with which these introductory remarks begin, Longinus courteously but firmly dismisses those who might be tempted to consider his critical enterprise "superfluous and useless" (2.3).

Whether those words mark the end of the introductory remarks we cannot tell, for the next two leaves of the manuscript are missing. The text resumes with a quotation, probably from a lost play of Sophocles, and a commentary that criticizes the lines for their turgidity and tumidity. Generalizing from this example and others, Longinus says that tumidity "seems one of the hardest faults to guard against." Bad in tragedy, "which is essentially a majestic matter and admits of bombast," it is obviously worse in "discourse that deals with facts." Here, at the beginning of chapter 3, the empirical and relativistic nature of Longinus' method is remarkable, as is the appropriateness of the analogy that follows and sums up the discussion of tumidity: In texts as in living bodies, swellings can be good and bad; a bad swelling, as of a tumor, means weakness and emptiness; a good one, as of a muscle, means strength and solidity.

This chapter isolates three manifestations of a fault Longinus might have named in the missing leaves of the manuscript. We might name it disrespect of *kairos*. Tumidity is one manifestation; another is puerility, which comes from "trying to be uncommon and exquisite" (3.4); a third is *parenthyrson*, a term Longinus borrowed from Theodorus to denote "emotion misplaced and pointless where none is needed, or unrestrained where restraint is required" (3.5). As for the emotions, they constitute a distinct subject, which he says he will treat in another place.

Manifestations of a second fault, here called frigidity, are discussed in chapter 4. As elsewhere, quotations illustrate the point being made, and the comments elicited by the quotations illustrate the difference between dogmatic criticism, which is bound by the rules, and Longinian criticism, which is informed by the principle of *kairos*. After quoting a "frigid conceit" from Plato ("let the walls lie slumbering on the ground and never rise again"), Longinus turns to Herodotus:

Herodotus' phrase for fair women is not much better [than Plato's slumbering walls]: "eye torture" he calls them. Yet he has some excuse, for in Herodotus this is said by the barbarians, who are, moreover, in their cups. Yet even in the mouths of such characters as these it is not right to display an unseemly triviality before an audience of all the ages.

(4.7)

Longinus finds Plato's metaphor inappropriate by any standard. The conventional rules of rhetoric hold that barbarians, especially drunken ones, should speak like barbarians, and so it is possible to justify Herodotus' metaphor. But Longinus goes beyond the rules and criticizes the metaphor. His sense of what is fitting and timely tells him that the metaphor is trivial and unworthy of the author, if not of the character. As D. A. Russell puts it, "to make an exhibition of oneself to all eternity is too high a price to pay for realism." The appeal to posterity foreshadows a major test for the sublime, which will be proposed as soon as the chief cause of frigidity has been identified.

The cause is "that passion for novel ideas which is the prevalent craze of the present day" (5.1). To the same cause or craze, of course, we owe much that is worthwhile, "for our virtues and vices spring from much the same sources." In reaching for the sublime, we make mistakes. How can we avoid them? In chapter 6, Longinus says that one requirement is a "clear knowledge and appreciation of what is truly sublime": no easy matter, to be sure, but not impossible, even though "judgement in literature is the last fruit of ripe experience" (6).

Chapter 7 proposes first a comparison, then a statement of effect, then a test. The comparison, which recalls the discussion of tumidity in 3.4, concerns greatness. Some great things are despicable, and it is a mark of greatness to despise them; other things are admirable. So with the sublime. "The true sublime, by some virtue of its nature, elevates us: uplifted with a sense of proud possession, we are filled with joyful pride, as if we had ourselves produced the very thing we heard" (7.2). The contrary follows as a matter of course:

> If, then, a man of sense, well-versed in literature, after hearing a passage several times finds that it does not affect him with a sense of sublimity, and does not leave behind in his mind more food for thought than the mere words at first suggest, but rather that on careful consideration it sinks in his esteem, then it cannot really be the true sublime, if its effect does not outlast the moment of utterance.
>
> (7.3)

The true sublime sticks in the mind: "It is [difficult], nay impossible, to resist its effect: the memory of it is stubborn and indelible" (7.3). What Longinus does not say, although it seems obvious, is that the memory of the sublime makes us desire further experiences of it.

So much for the comparison and the statement of effect, both positive and negative. The test, already suggested in connection with the drunken barbarians in Herodotus, is the judgment of posterity:

> To speak generally, you should consider that to be truly beautiful and sublime which pleases all people at all times. For when men who differ in their habits, their lives, their tastes, their ages, their dates, all agree together in holding one and the same view about the same writings, then the unanimous verdict, as it were, of such discordant judges makes our faith in the admired passage strong and indisputable.
>
> (7.4)

The obvious implication that writers should write for posterity is developed toward the end of the next main section of the treatise (14.3).

The richness and allusiveness of *On the Sublime*, which the foregoing quotations and analyses suggest, increase as Longinus explores further examples of the mysterious force that he

defines in the preface, circumscribes in the discussion of two principal faults, and redefines at the end of chapter 7. In the thirty-six chapters that follow, we can discern something like a plan, but for three reasons any attempt to reduce the chapters to a diagram is more than a little ridiculous. First, as we have noted, there are substantial gaps even in the best manuscript. Second, the conventional divisions into chapter and section are not due to Longinus or even to the scribe of the tenth-century Paris manuscript, but to Franciscus Portus, who introduced them into his edition of Longinus (Geneva, 1569). To some, these divisions seem "perverse and unpractical," and in a sense they are. But their very perversity has its uses, for it reminds us—this is the third reason—that the informal, digressive, discursive, and above all allusive character of the text scarcely lends itself to systematic divisions and neat outlines.

Yet Longinus himself sketches out what appears to be a plan for the rest of his book, at the beginning of chapter 8. "There are, one may say, some five genuine sources of the sublime in literature, the common groundwork, as it were, of all five being a natural faculty of expression, without which nothing can be done" (8.1). Two of these sources are primarily innate: "the first and most powerful is the command of full-blooded ideas"; and "the second is the inspiration of vehement emotion" (8.1). The remaining three come primarily from art: first, proper construction of figures of thought and speech; second, nobility of diction, which includes choice of words, use of tropes, and elaboration of style; third, composition, or the dignified and elevated arrangement of words. (Longinus does not specify or need to specify here that he will conclude with a brief discussion of the causes of the current decline in literature.)

As far as the three sources that come primarily from art are concerned, the working out of the plan is fairly straightforward: chapters 16 through 29 treat figures of thought and speech, 30 through 38 nobility of diction, and 39 through 43 composition. The conclusion, which is incomplete, occupies all that remains of chapter 44. But there is a complicated textual problem in connection with the first two sources of the sublime and the topics under consideration in chapters 9 through 15. The textual problem is a great lacuna—longest of them all—in chapter 9. Eight leaves are missing from the tenth-century Paris manuscript; only the first and the last can be supplied from later copies.

At the end of chapter 15, we read this sentence: "This must suffice for our treatment of sublimity in ideas, as produced by nobility of mind [or] imitation or imagination." Nothing apparently about the emotions here. Finally, we read at the very end of the book, "'Tis best to leave this to a guess' and pass on to the next question, which is that of the emotions, a topic on which I previously undertook to write a separate treatise" (44.12). What conclusion do these remarks point to?

Many scholars contend that these statements must mean that, contrary to what he writes in the sketch of the plan in chapter 8, Longinus does not treat the emotions. It seems to me, however, that in all probability Longinus does discuss, in chapters 9 through 15, precisely what he proposes to discuss. Since he specifies that both full-blooded ideas and vehement emotions are innate sources of sublimity (8.1), and since he observes that "sublimity is the true ring of a noble mind" (9.2), it seems reasonable to suppose that early in the lacuna he noted that it is often difficult, at times impossible, to discern which of these two sources is responsible for a given instance of sublimity. To put it another way, the two sources have a common source, namely greatness of mind. Lest the conclusion to chapter 15 and the last lines of the treatise be adduced as evidence against this simple solution, I join Jacques Bompaire in observing that the sentence at the end of chapter 15 does not constitute a formal conclusion to the whole section; instead, it loosely summarizes the matter of the three preceding chapters. I would prefer, in fact, to delete the first "or"— which is in any event not in the manuscripts—

and read: "This must suffice for our treatment of sublimity in ideas as produced by great-mindedness of imitation or imagination." As Bompaire reminds us, too, the last lines of the treatise are a late addition to the manuscript, in a different hand, that simply makes the best of a puzzling situation by promising another work. Thus there is reason to suppose that in the original conclusion Longinus treated the emotions aroused by the second great love that enslaves us and may account in part for the decline of literature in his day, namely, love of pleasure (see 44.6: The first great love, which *is* discussed in the conclusion, is love of money).

I assume in any event that chapters 9 through 15 concern the kinds of sublimity that are due to greatness of mind, without which there can be no full-blooded thoughts or vehement emotions. That Cecilius should have omitted emotion as a source of the sublime is not surprising, for we know from the beginning of Longinus' treatise that Cecilius' treatment in general is low and unworthy of the subject. A small-minded critic is not likely to understand the complex connections between emotion and sublimity. Nor would he be likely to discover the sublimity found in silence. But Longinus is not that kind of critic. He knows that although sublimity and emotion are not necessarily the same thing (8.2), "nothing makes so much for grandeur as genuine emotion in the right place" (8.4). Silence can be as expressive of emotion and conducive to sublimity as words: "even without being spoken the bare idea often of itself wins admiration for its inherent genius," he says. He then proceeds, in a brilliant touch, to praise the silence of Ajax in the *Odyssey* (543–567), a silence "more sublime than any speech" (9.2–3), that is, than any speech could be in such circumstances.

Whether or not Longinus is, in Pope's words, "himself the great Sublime he draws," this part of the treatise contains his most famous judgments. It has provoked acrimonious controversy and evoked fervent admiration. In his journal for 3 October 1762, Gibbon recorded the happy discovery many readers have made for themselves:

> The 9th chapter . . . is one of the finest monuments of Antiquity. Till now, I was acquainted only with two ways of criticizing a beautiful passage; The one, to shew, by an exact anatomy of it, the distinct beauties of it, and from whence they sprung; the other, an idle exclamation, or a general encomium, which leaves nothing behind it. Longinus has shewn me that there is a third. He tells me his own feelings upon reading it; and tells them with such energy, that he communicates them. I almost doubt which is more sublime, Homer's Battle of the Gods, or *Longinus's* apostrophe to *Terentianus* upon it.[3]

Chapter 9 and the six that follow constitute a veritable pantheon. Celebrated in these pages are gods, poets, heroes, statesmen—Homer, Ajax, Moses, Zeus, Sappho, Archilochus, Cicero, Plato, the Pythian priestess, Herodotus, Stesichorus, Thucydides, Euripides, Orestes, Helios, Phaëthon, Aeschylus, Dionysius, Oedipus, Achilles, Hyperides—and this is not the whole list. It is entirely characteristic of Longinus that the distinctions between gods and men, heroes and poets, are blurred. Only a few passages that are less than sublime are admitted into this sacred precinct, which is guarded by the sublimely silent ghost of Telemonian Ajax (9.2–3) and the two great orators of Athens, Demosthenes and Hyperides (15.9–10).

Let us consider for a moment the lines from Homer that Gibbon refers to in his journal:

> . . . the huge sky sounded as with trumpets. . . .
> Aïdoneus, lord of the dead below, was in terror
> and sprang from his throne and screamed aloud, for fear that above him
> he who circles the land, Poseidon, might break the earth open
> and the houses of the dead lie open to men and immortals,

[3]D. M. Low, ed., *Gibbon's Journal* (London, 1929), pp. 155–156.

ghastly and mouldering, so the very gods shudder before them.

> (*Iliad* 21.388; 20.61–65, R. A. Lattimore trans.)

Longinus' commentary addresses itself to two very different matters. He first asks Terentianus whether he does not see "how the earth is split to its foundations, hell itself laid bare, the whole universe sundered and turned upside down; and meanwhile everything, heaven and hell, mortal and immortal alike, shares in the conflict and danger of that battle" (9.6). Here we feel acutely the disorder and excitement that a great danger entails. But Longinus quickly passes on to another danger. The passage he has just quoted poses a great threat to orthodox thinking:

> Terrible as these passages are, all the same, unless one takes them allegorically, they are utterly irreligious and show no sense of what is fitting. I feel indeed that in recording as he does the wounding of the gods, their quarrels, vengeance, tears, imprisonment, and all their manifold passions, Homer has done his best to make the men in the *Iliad* gods and the gods men.
>
> (9.7)

Longinus finds the sublime is itself, then, as dangerous as the dangers that—evoked by a great mind—engender it.

Great as that passage is, it is, says Longinus, "far surpassed by those passages which represent the divine nature in its true attributes, pure, majestic, and unique" (9.8). The lines that illustrate his observation (*Iliad* 13.18; 20.60; 13.19; and 13.27–29) celebrate Poseidon, the protector of the Achaeans. In the most extraordinary moment of this extraordinary treatise, he offers yet another example of the proper representation of the divine nature:

> So, too, the lawgiver of the Jews [Moses], no ordinary man, having formed a worthy conception of divine power, gave expression to it at the very threshold of his *Laws* where he says: "God

said"—what? "'Let there be light,' and there was light. 'Let there be earth,' and there was earth."

(9.9)

As D. A. Russell has rightly said, "hardly anything in L[onginus] has so caught the fancy of readers as this passage." Without dwelling on the controversy that erupted in the seventeenth century between Boileau and Pierre-Daniel Huet because of this passage, we might stop to remark that Boileau and others are on the right track when they emphasize the extent to which the true Longinian sublime and great simplicity of expression are linked. The greatness of biblical style is often due to its simplicity, as Saint Augustine discovered (*Confessions* 3.5). In the important and influential preface to his translation of Longinus, Boileau devotes a substantial paragraph to this matter:

> You must know that Longinus does not mean by the word sublime what orators call the sublime style, but rather that which, being extraordinary and marvellous, strikes us in a discourse, and accounts for the ability of a work to uplift, ravish, transport. The sublime style always requires great words; but the sublime can be found in a single thought, a single figure, a single turn of phrase. A thing can be in the sublime style yet not be sublime, that is to say, be neither extraordinary nor surprising. For example, *The sovereign Arbiter of Nature with a single word formed the light.* That is in the sublime style; it is nevertheless not sublime, because there is nothing very marvellous in it, nothing one couldn't easily come up with. But, *God said, Let there be light; and there was light.* This extraordinary turn of phrase, which so well marks the obedience of the creature to the orders of the creator, is truly sublime, and has something of the divine about it.
>
> (*Traité du sublime, ou du Merveilleux dans le discours,* 1674)

A few additional observations before we return, as Longinus does, to Homer: The praise of this quotation from Genesis suggests, once again, that the sublime often comprises a perfect coincidence of ethics and aesthetics; it also suggests that a critic may examine holy writ with the same eye he casts upon profane works, that the word of God is not exempt from being inscribed in human systems of discourse. A text is a text.

Longinus does return to Homer and Ajax:

Father Zeus, draw free from the mist the sons of
  the Achaians,
make bright the air, and give sight back to our eyes;
  in shining
daylight destroy us, if to destroy us be now your
  pleasure.

(*Iliad* 17.645–647, R. A. Lattimore trans.)

In Genesis, God calls for light, and thereby creation begins. In Homer, Ajax prays for light, and thereby the death of Patroklos will be avenged, the destruction of Troy assured, and the action of the *Iliad* completed. The prayer to Zeus for light should remind us of one of Zeus's attributes, the lightning bolt, which illuminates and destroys; and that attribute should remind us of Longinus' comparison in chapter 1: "a well-timed flash of sublimity scatters everything before it like a bolt of lightning" (1.4). Brilliance and destruction—we have only to think of what happens to Ajax in later texts: Odysseus' humiliation of him, related in book 11 of the *Odyssey*, which explains the silence Longinus praises at the beginning of chapter 9; his madness and his suicide, represented by Sophocles. To call for light is worthy of a hero, but it is to risk destruction.

Ajax and the theme of light reappear in the next section of *On the Sublime*, which Longinus disingenuously calls a "digression" (9.14) and in which he compares the *Iliad* and the *Odyssey*. In his view, the *Odyssey* is a kind of epilogue to the *Iliad*. Hence Nestor's response to Telemachos' question about the fate of those who fought at Troy:

there Aias lies, a man of battles, there lies
  Achilleus,
there lies Patroklos, one who was like the gods for
  counsel,
and there lies my own beloved son.

(*Odyssey* 3.109–111, R. A. Lattimore trans.)

Longinus notes that action predominates in the *Iliad*, narration in the *Odyssey*. He compares Homer in the *Odyssey* to the setting sun: "the grandeur remains but not the intensity" (9.13). Further on he associates not only garrulity but interest in character-study with the decline of emotional power in great poets and writers (9.14 and 9.15). One last remark he makes about the *Odyssey* brilliantly illuminates a central fact concerning that poem: "in every one of these passages reality is worsted by romance" (9.14). The sublime, too, has a way of convincing us that we see what we hear, a way of making us believe in the reality of what is, in the end, only a tissue of words and figures. We shall return to this matter in our discussion of the central pages of *On the Sublime*.

Having concluded his so-called digression, Longinus turns in chapter 10 to the importance of careful selection and ordering of material. The chief ornament of the chapter is the Sapphic ode that Muret discovered to his surprise and delight when he undertook to translate Longinus in 1554. "Sappho," writes Longinus, "never fails to take the emotions incident to the passion of love from the symptoms which accompany it in real life. And wherein does she show her excellence? In the skill with which she selects and combines the most striking and intense of those symptoms" (10.1). He then quotes the ode:

Like the very gods in my sight is he who
sits where he can look in your eyes, who listens
close to you, to hear the soft voice, its sweetness
     murmur in love and
laughter, all for him. But it breaks my spirit;
underneath my breast all the heart is shaken.
Let me only glance where you are, the voice dies,
     I can say nothing,
but my lips are stricken to silence, underneath my skin the tenuous flame suffuses;
nothing shows in front of my eyes, my ears are
     muted in thunder.
And the sweat breaks running upon me, fever
shakes my body, paler I turn than grass is;
I can feel that I have been changed, I feel that
     death has come near me.
  (Sappho 2, *Greek Lyrics*, R. A. Lattimore trans.)

It is noteworthy that this poem, which was famous in antiquity, is preserved only in *On the Sublime* and thus remained a tantalizing mystery—referred to, paraphrased, translated (by Catullus), celebrated, but never quoted in full—until the middle of the sixteenth century. Since then it has been adapted, imitated, translated, and annotated; and even in the least inspired of the translations something of Sappho's special magic can be felt. Trying to communicate his own sense of that magic and succeeding better than most critics, Longinus asks:

Is it not wonderful how she summons at the same time, soul, body, hearing, tongue, sight, color, all as though they had wandered off apart from herself? She feels contradictory sensations, freezes, burns, raves, reasons—for one that is at the point of death is clearly beside herself. She wants to display not a single emotion, but a whole congress of emotions. Lovers all show such symptoms as these, but what gives supreme merit to her art is, as I said, the skill with which she chooses the most striking and combines them into a single whole.
                        (10.3)

He goes on to say without a pause, "It is, I fancy, much in the same way that the poet [Homer] in describing storms picks out the most alarming circumstances" (10.3). Some readers of Longinus find it puzzling that Sappho's ode should appear in *On the Sublime*. To Gibbon, "It may be beautifull, it may be passionate; but surely there is nothing in it which elevates the mind: Longinus's own characteristic of the sublime" (*Journal*, 4 October 1762). But the presence of the ode serves to broaden the inquiry and to show that the sublime is not limited to oratory, history, epic, and tragedy. Furthermore what Longinus says of a storm that Homer describes in the *Iliad* (15.624–628) applies perfectly to Sappho's ode and suggests precisely how it does elevate the mind: "instead of defining the danger once and for all, [he] depicts the sailors as being all the time, again and again, with every wave on the brink of death" (10.6). Like Homer, Sappho has made a poem that brings us continually to the brink of annihilation, a poem that combines into a single whole the signs of the most powerful and destructive of forces. The bolt of lightning scatters, but it also illuminates; the sublime leaves us speechless, paralyzed, feeling as if death had come near us. There is absolutely no loss of continuity in the discussion. War, madness, love, death: keenly imagined by great-minded poets, these are the subjects that involve the greatest passions and that are naturally conducive to the sublime.

We can look more rapidly at the remaining chapters of this part. In chapter 11, Longinus discusses amplification. He then compares Cicero and Demosthenes in chapter 12. In comparing the two orators he uses almost exactly the same comparison as in the first chapter: "Our countryman [Demosthenes], with his violence, yes, and his speed, his force, his terrific power of rhetoric, burns, as it were, and scatters everything before him, and may therefore be compared to a flash of lightning or a thunderbolt" (12.4).

In chapter 13, Longinus' praise of Plato leads to an incisive treatment of imitation and emulation, particularly of Homer, as goads to sublimity:

> Plato would never have reared so many of these flowers to bloom among his philosophic tenets, never have wandered so often with Homer into the regions and phrases of poetry, had he not striven, yea with heart and soul, to contest the prize with Homer like a young antagonist with one who had already won his spurs, perhaps in too keen emulation, longing as it were to break a spear, and yet always to good purpose.
>
> (13.4)

Longinus' visualization of this rivalry is impressive; even more impressive is his brilliant insight into what makes Plato the great writer he is.[4]

In chapter 14, Longinus proposes that a writer should ask how Homer or Plato or Demosthenes or Thucydides would have said something "that demands sublimity of thought and expression" (14.1–2); that a writer should imagine how Homer or Demosthenes would listen to a passage he has composed and how it would affect him (14.2–3). Finally, and most important: "Even more stimulating would it be to add, 'If I write this, how would all posterity receive it?'" (14.3). It is at this point that the connection between greatness of mind in emulation and greatness of creation coincide in the ideal time and space of posterity: "But if a man shrinks at the very thought of saying anything that exceeds the comprehension of his own time, then must all the conceptions of that man's nature be like some blind, half-formed embryo, all too abortive for the life of posthumous fame" (14.3).

The vividness of this metaphor might well be the most interesting link between chapter 14 and chapter 15, which concludes this section of the treatise, and which is devoted to *phantasia*—imagination or, more precisely, visualization. "The word [imagination] has now come to be used predominantly of passages where, inspired by strong emotion, you seem to see what you describe and bring it vividly before the eyes of your audience" (15.1–2). Euripides furnishes several illustrations, partly because he "spends his fondest efforts in presenting these two emotions, madness and love" (15.3). Aeschylus and Sophocles furnish other examples. Counterexamples come from "our wonderful modern orators" (15.8), who borrow recklessly and inappropriately from the poets. Not so Demosthenes and Hyperides: "our attention is

---

[4]In "The Criticism of Harold Bloom: Judgment and History," *Centrum* 6:1 (Spring 1979), pp. 39–42, Jonathan Arac points out Bloom's debts to Longinus: "Men become gods

to one another, as the 'effluences' of past greatness fill the young writer. To achieve full power, however, one must leave such passivity and emulatively combat one's predecessor, as Plato did Homer, 'entering the lists like a young champion matched against the man whom all admire.'" Likewise another of Bloom's important, apparently idiosyncratic, notions: the Scene of Instruction. "To achieve the sublime, one may conjure up the great past writers as judges and exemplars; the 'ordeal' of this ghostly 'tribunal' will yield us the power to immortalize ourselves, or quell us if our spirits are inadequate."

drawn from the reasoning to the enthralling effect of the imagination, and the technique is concealed in a halo of brilliance" (15.11). In the Greek text, the word for "enthralling" here echoes "what inspires wonder" at the beginning of the treatise (1.4) and "the object of poetry is to enthrall" earlier in this chapter (15.2). It reappears at the end of another discussion of Demosthenes (22.4). Each instance emphasizes the difference between persuasion and astonishment. Longinus soon returns to the matter of the concealed figure; and later, in his discussion of nobility of diction, he returns to the comparison and explains why Hyperides, for all his qualities, is greatly inferior to Demosthenes. A brief conclusion (15.12), which we have already examined, summarizes the last three or four chapters on imitation and visualization. Thus, this part of the treatise devoted to the innate sources of the sublime comes to an end.

The next part treats the first of the three artificial sources, figures of thought and speech. Longinus does not distinguish rigorously between the two. By "figure" he seems to mean an abnormal arrangement of words or expression of thought that has a pleasant or elevated effect. On the whole, the exposition is fairly straightforward. As we shall see, however, particularly in chapter 17, a few surprises await even a wary reader.

He considers the following twelve figures:

1. *adjuration* (chapter 16): using an oath. Example from Demosthenes: "It cannot be that you were wrong; no, by those who bore the brunt at Marathon" (16.2; *De corona* 208).

2. *rhetorical questions* (chapter 18). Examples from Herodotus.

3. *asyndeton* (chapter 19): suppressing conjunctions. Examples from Xenophon and Homer.

4. *asyndeton combined with anaphora* (chapter 20): suppressing conjunctions combined with the repetition of words at the beginning of successive clauses. Examples from Demosthenes.

5. *polysyndeton* (chapter 21): repeating con-junctions. Hypothetical example illustrates the effectiveness of Demosthenes' asyndeta.

6. *hyperbaton* (chapter 22): "This figure consists in arranging words and thoughts out of the natural sequence and bears, so to speak, the genuine stamp of vehement emotion" (22.1). Example from Herodotus, references to Demosthenes and Thucydides, and a spectacular example in Longinus' own discourse:

> For he [Thucydides] often hangs up the sense which he has begun to express and meanwhile manages to wheel on to the empty stage one extraneous idea after another in a strange and unlikely order, making the audience terrified for the total collapse of the sentence and compelling them from sheer excitement to share the speaker's risk: then unexpectedly, after a great interval, the long-lost phrase turns up pat at the end, so that he astounds them all the more by the mere reckless audacity of his inversions *(hyperbata).*
>
> (22.4)

7. *polyptoton* (chapter 23): Longinus seems to mean changes of case, tense, person, number, gender. Examples from unknown authors, Sophocles, and Plato.

8. *singular for plural* (chapter 24). Examples from Demosthenes.

9. *vivid present tense* (chapter 25). Example from Xenophon.

10. *imaginary second person* (chapter 26). Examples from Homer and Herodotus.

11. *sudden shifts into direct speech* (chapter 27). Examples from Homer, Hecataeus, Demosthenes.

12. *periphrasis* (chapters 28–29.1): using a longer phrasing in place of a possible shorter form. Examples from Plato, Xenophon, Herodotus. "It is a risky business, periphrasis, more so than any of the other figures, unless used with a due sense of proportion" (29.1).

A short conclusion (29.2) brings this section to an end. Before we go on to consider the next section, we must return to chapter 17, which I passed over, and which is of much greater importance than one might at first suspect. He states: "While on this topic [adjuration] I must not omit to mention a view of my own, dear friend, which I will state, however, quite concisely" (17.1). It is characteristic of Longinus that this view, which he states at the exact center of the treatise, should be presented as if it were an afterthought. It is, in fact, of central significance. "Figures," he goes on to say, "seem to be natural allies of the sublime and to draw in turn marvellous reinforcement from the alliance" (17.1). Then he addresses the important question: "There is an inevitable suspicion attaching to the unconscionable use of figures. It gives a suggestion of treachery, craft, fallacy, especially when your speech is addressed to a judge with absolute authority, or still more to a despot, a king, or a ruler in high place" (17.1). There is danger in any figure that arouses suspicion or hostility when those reactions are not what the orator wants. Consequently, as we have already seen in connection with the fictional second-person-singular pronoun, "we find that a figure is always most effective when it conceals the very fact of its being a figure. The sublimity and the effect on the emotions are a wonderfully helpful antidote against the suspicion that accompanies the use of figures" (17.1–2). So it is that Demosthenes can get away with his extraordinary oath "no, by those who bore the brunt at Marathon," by which he hopes to strengthen his attempt to prove that although his policy had led to the terrible defeat at Chaeronea (338 B.C.), it was still the right policy. That oath again mixes up men and gods, what happened and what might have happened, history and poetry; and it completely conquers the audience. As Longinus explains in his analysis of the passage:

> He has transformed his argument into a passage of transcendent sublimity and emotion, giving it the power of conviction that lies in so strange and startling an oath: and at the same time his words have administered to his hearers a remedy and an antidote, with the result that, relieved by his eulogy, they come to feel as proud of the war with Philip as of their victories at Marathon and Sal-

amis. In all this by the use of the figure he is enabled to carry the audience away with him.

(16.2)

The medical imagery here is particularly remarkable. "Remedy," "antidote," "relieved"—these expressions foreshadow the images in chapter 17—"a wonderfully helpful antidote" (17.2); in chapter 32—"the proper antidote for a multitude of daring metaphors is strong and timely emotion and genuine sublimity. These by their very nature sweep everything along in the forward surge of their current" (32.4); and in chapter 38—"As I am never tired of saying, to atone for a daring phrase the universal specific is found in actions and feelings that almost carry one away" (38.5). A timely figure serves as a timely remedy: it purges mistrust and discomfort; it creates a feeling of well-being. And it does so discreetly, secretly, almost naturally. Thus there is, at the center of Longinus' treatise, a secret that we may call dirty or clean according to our lights: the sublime is that by means of which an orator or poet can put something over on us, by means of which he can make something pass, can do something without our noticing or objecting.

The precise nature of this central secret is perhaps best revealed by a statement Longinus makes later on about unseemly things, matters that are sordid and contemptible but necessary:

> . . . the proper course is to suit the words to the dignity of the subject and in this imitate nature, the artist that created man. Nature did not place in full view our dishonorable parts nor the drains that purge our whole frame, but as far as possible concealed them and, as Xenophon says, thrust their channels into the furthest background, for fear of spoiling the beauty of the whole figure.

(43.5–6)

The principle of organic unity is often invoked in literary criticism. It is seldom invoked and understood as rigorously as it is in *On the Sublime* (see, for example, 40.1). The human body is beautiful in part because its necessary but "dishonorable" parts are hidden (significantly, hidden at the center); sublime discourse is beautiful in part because its necessary but dishonorable parts—figures are necessary but, being akin to lies, are dishonorable—are hidden, too, and the better they are hidden, the better they work.

Much more could be said about this central secret and the way it radiates throughout the work. But we must pass on to the second artificial source of sublimity, nobility of diction, in chapter 30. The discussion opens with a graceful acknowledgment of shared wisdom: "It is probably superfluous to explain at length to those who know, how the choice of the right word and the fine word has a marvellously moving and seductive effect upon an audience and how all orators and historians make this their supreme effort" (30.1). After a lacuna the text centers on metaphors and certain judgments of Cecilius. Longinus observes that the passages from Plato's *Timaeus* depicting the human body in a sustained series of metaphors "suffice to show that figurative writing has a natural grandeur and that metaphors make for sublimity: also that emotional and descriptive passages are most glad of them." The dangers associated with metaphors need little emphasis: "that the use of metaphor, like all the other beauties of style, always tempts writers to excess is obvious without my stating it" (32.6–7). Even Plato—especially Plato, in fact—does not escape censure on this point.

Are we then to contend with Cecilius that Lysias, whose style is immaculate and flawless, is preferable to Plato, whose style is sometimes too metaphorical? Longinus responds that generally "great excellence, even if it is not sustained throughout at the same level, should always be voted the first place, if for nothing else, for its inherent nobility" (33.4), an opinion that echoes a sentence from the discussion of emulation, specifically Plato's emulation of Homer: "Fair indeed is the crown, and the fight for fame well worth the winning, where even to be worsted by our forerunners is not without glory" (13.4). It follows then that Hyperides, for

all his virtues, is not superior to Demosthenes; and Plato so outshines Lysias that the comparison is ridiculous. To explain why we admire greatness, Longinus makes several remarks that became immensely important in modern theories of the sublime, particularly in the mid-eighteenth century:

> Within the scope of human enterprise there lie such powers of contemplation and thought that even the whole universe cannot satisfy them, but our ideas often pass beyond the limits that enring us. Look at life from all sides and see how in all things the extraordinary, the great, the beautiful stand supreme, and you will soon realize the object of our creation. So it is by some natural instinct that we admire, surely not the small streams, clear and useful as they are, but the Nile, the Danube, the Rhine, and far above all, the sea.
> (35.3–4)

Developing these thoughts, he refers to the stars and to the craters of Etna in eruption: "It is always the unusual that wins our wonder" (35.5). And, as we learned earlier, what finally puts the seal on greatness is the judgment of all ages (36.2).

Plato's excess in metaphor has led to a digression on correctness as contrasted with greatness. Now Longinus picks up the thread he left at the end of chapter 32 in order to treat similes, but a lacuna intervenes almost immediately. Suddenly we find ourselves in the midst of his comments on hyperbole, which lead to a pointed criticism of Isocrates (38.2), who, unlike Demosthenes, does not hide his game but boldly announces it at the beginning of his speech. As one would expect by now, Longinus says that "the best hyperbole is the one that conceals the very fact of its being a hyperbole. And this happens when it is uttered under stress of emotion and to suit the circumstances of a great crisis" (38.3). In yet another extension of the ground being surveyed, Longinus concludes this chapter, and this part of his treatise, with comments on comic expressions and on satire (38.5–6).

The last part of the treatise (chapters 39

through 43) deals with composition—the arrangement of words—third and last of the artificial sources of sublimity. It is the shortest section, probably because Longinus has, as he states, already written two treatises on this subject. Here, comparing composition to melody, he maintains that "it casts a spell upon us and always turns our thoughts toward what is majestic and dignified and sublime and all else that it embraces, winning a complete mastery over our minds" (39.3). An example from Demosthenes illustrates the point. The concept of organic unity informs the rest of the analysis. It is taken for granted, for example, that the parts constitute a whole that is greater than their sum. Composition can make even vulgar words sublime. Weaknesses in this regard are "weak and agitated rhythm" (41.1), "extreme conciseness" (42.1), prolixity (42.2), and "trivial words" (43.1). This last weakness is illustrated by a long passage from Theopompus, who "runs away from the sublime to the trivial, where he needs rather a crescendo. As it is, by introducing bags and spices and sacks in the middle of the whole equipage he has almost given the effect of a cook-shop" (43.3): here as always Longinus is acutely, almost morbidly, aware how one false step can destroy a whole text, how a writer must sometimes be silent and hide rather than reveal the secrets of his art. It is no accident that he should object to the presence of "bags and spices and sacks in the middle of the whole equipage" of Artaxerxes Ochus' expedition against Egypt; are not spices the means by which a skillful cook transforms ordinary victuals into food fit for a king?

This chapter and the part of the treatise devoted to composition conclude with the observations concerning the drains of the human body that we dealt with previously: "There is, however, no immediate need for enumerating and classifying all the factors of mean style. As we have already laid down all the qualities that make our utterance noble and sublime, it obviously follows that the opposite of these will generally make it trivial and ungainly" (43.6). This summary is exemplary; it makes a useful generalization, and it does so tactfully. It quietly draws our attention away from what is, as it were, dishonorable. The critic owes it not only to himself and his reader, but to the writers whose work he admires, to keep his own discourse as free as possible from what does not bear scrutiny, especially toward the end. And we should not disregard the graceful limitation that the word "generally" provides. No rule is without exceptions.

Longinus' remarks in 43.6 echo what he says concerning faults with respect to *kairos* and frigidity in chapters 3 through 5. The last pages of the treatise put us back in mind of the first. "One problem now remains for solution, my dear Terentianus, and knowing your love of learning I will not hesitate to append it—a problem which a certain philosopher recently put to me" (44.1). We have many "shrewd and versatile" men, but no great ones; literature is in decline. Longinus' philosopher wonders whether the lack of greatness can be explained by political realities: democracy stimulates, despotism withers "the spirit of mutual rivalry and eager competition for the foremost place" (44.2–3). Longinus records his response: "it is easy . . . to find fault with things as they are at the moment" (44.6); the true reason lies not in the peace the world enjoys but in our vicious habits. "It is the love of money, that insatiable sickness from which we all now suffer, and the love of pleasure that enslave us, or rather, as one might say, sink our lives, soul and all, into the depths" (44.7). And the first evil, love of money, is the subject of an allegorical development (44.7–10). At the end as at the beginning of the treatise, the connections between greatness of soul and sublimity of discourse are explicitly stated. *On the Sublime* concludes with a fragment that might, as we remarked earlier, have introduced a second allegorical development, on the love of pleasure, but the actual substance of the last—and lost—two pages remains a mystery.

The treatise was unknown until 1554, when it was edited by Robortello and praised by

Muret. Another edition of the Greek text was published by Paulus Manutius in 1555. A third edition appeared in 1569. The first Latin translation was published in 1566, the second in 1572. With the exception of scattered references to the treatise as the source of one of Sappho's odes, one finds few traces of the work in other printed books. It is possible, even probable, that Montaigne knew Longinus, and that some of his reflections on great poetry are Longinian in spirit as well as vocabulary, as in the essay on Cato the Younger (book 1, chapter 37) and the essay "On some verses of Vergil" (book 3, chapter 5). Perhaps the overwhelming authority of Aristotle's *Poetics* and Horace's *Ars Poetica* overshadowed Longinus in the Renaissance.

On the Sublime begins to come into view in the seventeenth century. The first printed translation, by John Hall, appeared at London in 1652 but seems to have attracted little attention. Boileau's French translation, published along with his *Art poétique* in 1674, was immediately and immensely successful. It put Longinus squarely into the mainstream of European literary theory and poetic practice.

From 1674 until 1740 or so, Longinus' fame increased; soon after 1674, the sublime became a complex and multivalent concept that was nothing short of phenomenal. As time went on, there was a gradual movement away from the treatise itself and toward interest in terror (as in Burke) and the aesthetic experience of literature, nature, and art. Even before the eighteenth century ended, Longinus' star had begun to dim.

That it should have been Boileau who brought Longinus fully to life for Europe and England is less paradoxical than Boileau's detractors like to believe; French classicism and Boileau's situation in it have been grossly misunderstood until recently. It is time to reject the traditional view of Boileau as an implacable, rule-bound pedant trying to reign over Parnassus, time to see him as he was, a poet of verve and fantasy. To read Longinus is, by no paradox at all, to discover what makes Boileau a poet rather than a mere versifier, a critic rather than a tiresome censor. Most of all, it is to discover a text that understands and cherishes the relations between poetry and criticism, art and nature, literature and life.[5]

Selected Bibliography

TEXT

"Longinus," On the Sublime, edited by D. A. Russell. Oxford, 1964. With introduction and commentary. Includes bibliography. Best modern text and commentary.

TEXTS WITH TRANSLATION AND COMMENTARY

Du Sublime, edited and translated by Henri Lebègue. Paris, 1939. Reprinted Paris, 1965. Greek text and French translation.

"Longinus," On the Sublime, edited and translated by W. Hamilton Fyfe. In *Aristotle, The Poetics; "Longinus," On the Sublime; Demetrius, On Style*. Rev. ed. New York, 1932. Reprinted Cambridge, Mass., and London, 1960. Loeb Classical Library. Most accessible modern text and translation.

Longinus, On the Sublime, edited and translated by W. Rhys Roberts. 2nd ed. Cambridge, 1907.

TRANSLATIONS

Dorsch, T. S, trans. *Longinus: On the Sublime*. In *Classical Literary Criticism*. Harmondsworth, 1965. Reprinted 1977. Penguin Classics.

Grube, G. M. A., trans. *Longinus on Great Writing (On the Sublime)*. New York, 1957.

Russell, D. A., trans. *Longinus, On Sublimity*. In *Ancient Literary Criticism: The Principal Texts in New Translations*, edited by D. A. Russell and M. Winterbottom. Oxford, 1972.

CRITICAL STUDIES

Atkins, J. W. H. *Literary Criticism in Antiquity: A Sketch of Its Development*. 2 vols. Cambridge, 1934. See especially vol. 2, pp. 210–253.

[5] I would like to thank Professor David Armstrong, of the University of Texas at Austin, and Professors John Keaney, John Arthur Hanson, and David Quint, all of Princeton University, for valuable criticism and advice.

Bompaire, Jacques. "Le Pathos dans le *Traité du sublime*." *Revue des Études Grecques* 86:323–343 (1973).

Brody, Jules. *Boileau and Longinus*. Geneva, 1958.

Crossett, John M., and James A. Arieti. *The Dating of Longinus*. University Park, Pa., 1975.

E [lse], G [erald] F. "Sublime." In *The Princeton Encyclopedia of Poetry and Poetics*, edited by Alex Preminger. Princeton, 1965. Pp. 819–820.

Gilmartin, Kristine. "A Rhetorical Figure in Latin Historical Style: The Imaginary Second Person Singular." *Transactions of the American Philological Association* 105:99–121 (1975).

Hertz, Neil. "Lecture de Longin." *Poétique* 15:292–306 (1973).

Monk, Samuel H. "'A Grace Beyond the Reach of Art.'" *Journal of the History of Ideas* 5:131–150 (1944).

———. *The Sublime: A Study of Critical Theories in XVIII-Century England*. New York, 1935. Reprinted Ann Arbor, Mich., 1960.

Mutschmann, Hermann. *Tendenz, Aufbau und Quellen der Schrift vom Erhabenen*. Berlin, 1913.

Olson, Elder. "The Argument of Longinus' *On the Sublime*." *Modern Philology* 39:225–258 (1941–1942).

R [ose], H [erbert] J [ennings]. "Kairos." In *The Oxford Classical Dictionary*, edited by M. Cary et al. Oxford, 1949.

J. L. LOGAN

LUCIAN

(*ca.* A.D. 120–after 181)

OF LUCIAN'S LIFE and career little is known. There is no external testimony to his existence from his contemporaries and very little from later antiquity: a highly unreliable entry in the *Suda* and brief, unenlightening comments in Lactantius, Eunapius, Isidore of Pelusium, Photius, Arethas, and the Byzantine scholiasts. Lucian was evidently born in Samosata, former capital of the kingdom of Commagene, a mountainous area north of Syria. Commagene possessed a distinct national tradition, deriving in part from a certain superficial Hellenization, evident as early as the first century B.C., and in part from Iranian and Semitic ethnic connections. Roman occupation of Commagene in A.D. 72 left little trace. It was mostly a policing exercise aimed at protecting the borders against the Parthians. Material alterations, in the shape of bridges and roads, were made, but social institutions remained Greco-Persian. With its adequate roads to Cilicia and Cappadocia and better ones to Syria, its water and land routes connecting with Mesopotamia and India, the province cannot, by the start of the second century A.D., be described as having been physically or culturally cut off. Yet it was undoubtedly a backwater, a typical example of a small border kingdom synthesizing the influences of the cultural forces around it. If Lucian left home permanently in his youth, it would hardly have been surprising. He could not have made much of a career for himself in Samosata.

The date of his birth is uncertain, though it is usually thought to have been in the early years of the reign of the emperor Hadrian (soon after A.D. 117). He evidently died after Marcus Aurelius (A.D. 181), who is mentioned in *Alexander* 48. Between these approximate chronological limits a few historical references can be traced in his works: to Rutilianus, a provincial administrator, and Alexander of Abonoteichus, a fashionable mystic, in *Alexander*; to the Cynic philosopher Peregrinus Proteus and the Olympic Games of A.D. 165 in *Peregrinus*; to Lucius Verus (co-emperor with Marcus Aurelius) and his mistress Panthea in *On Portraits*. Apart from indicating that these works were all written fairly well on in Lucian's career, these references tell us nothing. A little more can be gleaned from the apparently autobiographical works, *Lucian's Career*, *The Double Indictment*, and *Apology for "On Salaried Posts."* The first presents him as having been unsuccessfully apprenticed to his uncle as a sculptor; the second suggests that he trained as a public speaker and became an entertainer only around the age of forty; the third indicates that in later life he held a civil service post in Egypt. To these one can add the mention in *Alexander* 56 of his taking his family and father to Amastris, and in *The Eunuch* 13 of his having a young son, and the various references to "lecture tours" in Italy (*Amber* 2; *Herodotus* 5) and Gaul (*Hercules* 7). It is difficult to make a substantial portrait out of these scraps, let alone to deduce a sensible chronological account of the writer's life from them. It is not even clear, as we shall see shortly, that we can take the evidence as true, in a strict historical sense. All that the works show us of importance is that Lucian was a public performer of sorts whose career seems to have been principally occupied with touring in what seem, for a Greek speaker, to be surprising parts of the empire.

It is more important, in fact, to understand the period into which Lucian was born than to know the details of his life. He was growing up as the Roman Empire approached the height of its material prosperity, a prosperity dependent on social injustice and an economic and political system that carried the seeds of its own destruction. Hadrian consolidated the bulk of the imperial expansion achieved under Trajan, though he withdrew to slightly smaller frontiers. Relative peace encouraged the expansion of trade; the civil service was put on a more professional basis; an artistic revival of an imitative "neoclassical" sort was fostered in Rome itself. Lucian's middle years, under Antoninus Pius (138–161), coincided with a period of improved communications and greater commercial activity in the provinces. Only in later years would he have seen a gradual decline on all fronts. During the reign of Marcus Aurelius (161–180), there were long and expensive wars on the eastern and northern frontiers; plague and famine reduced the population; taxation became more burdensome. Only then did communal and individual liberty begin to be eroded. Most of Lucian's life thus coincided with an age that, for the Romans, was one of contented exploitation of the benefits of past achievements. But Lucian was not a Roman, and neither, in all probability, were most of his audiences. The Greek and Hellenized upper classes of the Eastern provinces, the Greek-speaking émigré communities of the Western ones, all wealthy but all politically impotent, had to find solace more and more in harking back to the cultural glories of the Greek past.

The determination of second-century-A.D. Greek society to reassert its cultural identity as a counterbalance to the erosion of its political identity turned respect for tradition into an almost political stance. History and archaeology were the passions of the age, not from a purely antiquarian point of view (even if at worst the literature is artificial and pedantic) but because these were channels through which antique values could be reabsorbed into the modern world. It is interesting in this context to note how many of the great sophists (public speakers) of the age were, like Lucian, Hellenized Asiatics—Herodes Atticus, Polemon, Philagros. It is as if by choosing the most ostentatiously traditional of all contemporary literary activities, they were seeking to give themselves an intellectual pedigree that legitimized their Hellenic status. This is not to say that no writers of the period were interested in Rome. The historian Appian concerned himself with the Roman conquests; the sophist Aelius Aristides wrote an extensive panegyric, *On Rome*. But they were exceptions. In general, intellectual life was geared to the ideas and forms of a Hellenic world that had vanished six centuries earlier.

The most important mode of access that the second century had to its past lay through literature. It saw the principles of life as encapsulated in books. The function of education was to train people in the selection of authors to study and in how to read critically, because, in the words of Dionysius of Halicarnassus, "the reader's spirit absorbs a similarity of character [with what he reads] by the act of continuous concentration on it" (*On Imitation* frag. 6). Furthermore, the schools taught how to transfer what one read into one's own writings. The manuals of the grammarians demonstrated how to analyze great works of art; the study of rhetoric prepared one for the trial reproduction of the elements analyzed into new forms consonant with the old models. This process does not exclude the concept of imagination. "Longinus" speaks lyrically, in *On the Sublime* (13.2–14), of the inspirational element necessary for creative imitation. But imagination is not used in the invention of material and form. It is what guides their selection and combination. This theory of *imitation* is difficult for the modern reader to accept, yet it formed the basis of European literature from Vergil to Racine, and was only formally overthrown by the romantics' insistence on the paramountcy of originality. Its philosophical justification could be found in Platonic philosophy (the second century was fertile in Neoplatonic doctrines), its rhetorical principles in Isocrates. Yet there lies the rub. The program of Isocrates was designed as an "art of persuasion" to be used in political oratory. And the Macedonian victories that coincided with the death of Isocrates marked the end of the practical function of political oratory in Greece. In the world of Lucian, the art of rhetoric had to have a function other than that for which it had been designed. That function was, primarily, to entertain.

Foremost among the entertainers were the sophists, public speakers who gave lecture tours of a sort. Other writers in other genres showed the same predilection for putting cleverness before profundity—Maximus of Tyre in his philosophical pieces, Arrian in his *Anabasis*. But the sophists were exclusively concerned with virtuoso performance. The main contemporary source for our knowledge of them, Philostratus' *Lives of the Sophists*, is unfortunately itself a piece of literature of entertainment, emphasizing, like a gossip column, the social and political activities of its subjects rather than their literary principles and concentrating on amusing anecdotes at the expense of historical perspective. Nonetheless, we know that they were men of considerable learning who earned themselves pop-star adulation by public displays of verbal skill (usually extemporized) on topics of historical interest. Typical examples are the two surviving speeches of Polemon, which elaborate on the idea that the funeral oration at Marathon is to be delivered by the father of the man who has died the most glorious death. Taking the deaths of Cynegirus and Callimachus from Herodotus (book 4), Polemon proceeds to a long antithesis, ingenious but fantastical and tasteless in its excesses, in which the historical "facts" are left far behind. This is a style intended to impress the ear; on the page it becomes preposterous.

What had happened to rhetoric was, quite simply, that its two main branches, political oratory and legal oratory, ceased to have a basis in real life and were subordinated to the third branch, occasional oratory. Polemon's speeches take the historical matter of political oratory and the structural manner of legal oratory, but they had neither a political nor a legal function. In this context, the assertion in *The Double Indictment* that Lucian was, in his early career, a conventional sophist receives some support from works like *Phalaris* 1 and 2. In the former, the tyrant's ambassador makes an attempt to persuade the assembly at Delphi to accept the offering of his infamous bronze bull (an instrument of torture); in the latter, a citizen of Delphi speaks in favor of Phalaris' case. The format is technically one of legal oratory, but the processes of "proof" are replaced by persuasive arguments more appropriate to the political style. At the same time the speeches are designed to offer merely a clever defense of the indefensible, on a topic of no relevance to the second-century context. On a more modest level Lucian is reproducing the tricks of the fashionable rhetoricians.

Lucian was not, however, a sophist in the conventional sense. Perhaps that is why Philostratus did not include any reference to him in his *Lives* (unless he had never heard of him, which is equally probable). He resembled the sophists in that the nature of his writing suggests that it was designed for live performance and that the audience needed a considerable literary knowledge to appreciate its intricacies. He seems to have been another sort of traveling entertainer, using his rhetorical training and the general principles of imitation to create, in many of his works, new literary forms from entirely conventional material.

A total of eighty-two works has been commonly attributed to him. Of these, four are certainly not by his hand. *Philopatris* is a Byzantine imitation, possibly of the mid-eleventh century, obscurely reflecting the political and religious troubles of the period. *Charidemus, or On Beauty*, a work not found in the better manuscripts of Lucian, on linguistic grounds can also be assigned to the Byzantine period. *Nero*, attributed to Lucian in three manuscripts, is probably by the eldest of the Philostrati (father of the writer of the *Lives of the Sophists*). And fifty-three epigrams included in the *Greek Anthology* are variously assigned to Lucian for no good reason; they are not included in the manuscripts of his own works. A further four works, *Octogenarians*, *The Sham Sophist*, *In Praise of Demosthenes*, and *The Cynic*, are thought to be spurious on linguistic and stylistic grounds. More positive evidence condemns *Affairs of the Heart*, which contains apparent internal reference to the material decline of the cities of Lycia in the third century A.D.; *Halcyon*, also included among the spurious works of Plato but attributable on the evidence of Diogenes Laertius and Athenaeus to an otherwise unknown first-century writer, Leon; and *Swift o'Foot*, which may be a comedy by Acacius, friend of Libanius' and a leading literary figure of Athens in the fourth century A.D. Speculation on whether other works, such as *Astrology* or *On the Dance*, are not by Lucian depends on unjustified assumptions about Lucian's world view and unrealistic attempts to define a single, unified Lucianic manner. It is wiser to accept that the rest of the works form a coherent literary corpus, for reasons that will shortly become obvious, and may therefore reasonably be attributed to one writer.

At the simplest level, Lucian composed formal exercises that can be assigned directly to one or another of the traditional branches of oratory. Thus *The Tyrannicide* and *Disowned* are examples of fictitious legal rhetoric. In the first a man claims the reward for killing a tyrant on the grounds that by killing the tyrant's son he caused the tyrant himself to commit suicide from grief. The second repeats the theme of one of Seneca the Elder's *Controversies* (4.5). A son, who has been disowned by his father, trains as a doctor. When his father goes mad, he cures him and is taken back into the family. But on refusing to treat his stepmother for an apparently similar disease he is disowned again. The speech constitutes the son's complaint against his father's action. Both works are structured along strictly conventional lines. In *Disowned*, for example, an exordium sets out the essence of the argument, that since medical science cannot deal with all illnesses, it is unjust "to disown a man who will not promise the impossible." There follows a narrative of events relevant to the case, sketching in the speaker's history and family relationships and setting out the proofs on which the plaintiff's case relies. The greater part of the speech, however, is given over to an interpretation of the relevant law and its application to the case in hand (8–31), into which are worked both the refutation of the possible arguments of the defense and a digression (27–30) on the limits of medical science, all harping on the initial theme—that it is impossible to cure people to order. If the consequent summing-up of the case is irregular, it is only in the dramatic warning that the father's conduct is likely to bring back the illness of which his son has so recently cured him.

In similar fashion *The Fly* and *In Praise of My Country* adhere to the rather looser rules for occasional oratory in its strict original form of a speech apportioning praise or blame. Thus in *The Fly* the references prescribed by theoreticians (such as Hermogenes, probably a younger contemporary of Lucian's) for the praise of animals—to birth, diet, physical and moral qualities, accomplishments, and death—are all there, suitably decked out with comparisons and rounded off with a little joke: "Though I have a lot left to say, I shall stop, for I do not want to seem, as the saying goes, to be making an elephant out of a fly [a mountain out of a mole-hill]." *The Fly* follows the conventions of paradoxical praise for the apparently unpraiseworthy. *In Praise of My Country* attempts a degree of originality by refusing to develop the aspects normally thought appropriate to this sort of topic and substituting sentimental arguments of a general sort. Yet this is a procedure no less governed by the rules; it merely inverts them by emphasizing what is not being done. In these works, as in *The Tyrannicide* and *Disowned*, Lucian is confining himself to rhetorical exercises of a sophistic kind, in which verbal skill and ingenuity of argument are the only criteria of merit.

The interest of these works is limited to their ingenuity. Elsewhere, Lucian's proficiency in basic rhetorical exercises led him to more original variations. In the construction of a piece of formal oratory, he uses a range of techniques to vary the literary texture—such as narrative, formal description, and comparison. Lucian sometimes develops one of these exercises, which were normally used simply for training practice in school, into a literary form in itself. *Hippias, or The Bath*, is almost exclusively a description; *Demonax* is compounded largely out of characteristic sayings, usually with a moral import though not so here. More significantly, he combined several of the exercises into a special literary genre, the introduction, a short piece used in performance as a curtain raiser to the main rhetorical display.

It is worth looking more closely at the introductions, because they give some indication of the direction in which Lucian's literary skill developed. There are eleven of them in the Lucianic corpus: *Amber, Bacchus, The Dipsads, The Hall, Harmonides, Hercules, Herodotus, Lucian's Career, A Prometheus in Words, The Scythian*, and *Zeuxis*. Each is designed to establish a relaxed relationship between speaker and audience. Hence the final note has a self-deprecatory air about it, an assumption of modesty as in *Amber* and *Hercules*, a flattering appeal to the critical perception of audience or patron as in *The Hall* and *The Scythian*.

A typical example is the end of *Zeuxis*, where, having prepared the audience for the novelty of his work while purporting to play down the value of novelty as such, Lucian observes that, of course, his more solid qualities will not be overlooked by an audience of such discernment: "But no, it won't go unappreciated, for you are artists yourselves and look at each aspect in a professional way. I only hope

it is up to the standards of its audience!" (12). Apart from the similarity of the endings, however, there is nothing about the introductions to suggest that they follow a common rhetorical recipe. Some, like *The Hall, Zeuxis*, and *Herodotus*, give great importance to formal description; others, *Amber* and *Harmonides* for example, rely on a single narrative for their interest. *Lucian's Career* presents a comparison (between sculpture and education) that borrows from legal oratory in its structure. *The Scythian* follows the traditions of formal encomium. They do not even have clear-cut rhetorical developments. Yet if these pieces lack a rhetorical structure, in the sense of patterns prescribed as predicted by the manuals (indeed, the manuals themselves stress the absence of formal composition in the introductions), they are for the most part very neatly organized in a literary sense.

Herodotus, one of several works apparently written for a tour in Macedonia, is a good example of this literary cohesion. It is built around a *diegema* (narrative), the story of how Herodotus found a short cut to fame and fortune by reading his histories aloud at the Olympic Games. Into this is inserted an *ekphrasis* (description) of the picture *The Wedding of Roxana and Alexander* by the painter Aetion, who similarly chose Olympia to launch his work on the public. This structure is used to present, first, a comparison of Lucian with a great writer of the past (covered by the modesty formula "How I wish it were possible to imitate the qualities of Herodotus"); second, the theme of displaying your works before an audience assembled from a wide area; and third (by implication), the glorious past of Macedonia as embodied in the figure of Alexander the Great. These themes are then brought together (7–8) in an encomium of the Macedonian audience Lucian is addressing. The theater is Lucian's Olympia, but with a much more discerning public than Herodotus'. And thus the piece returns to the comparison and modesty formula on which it started, made more striking by the image of Lucian as an athletic competitor waiting to be mentally stripped and appraised by his critical audience.

The comparable, if more elaborate, structure in *Zeuxis* seems more perfectly executed, because the painting described there, of a female centaur, is thematically central to the argument of the piece. However, one suspects that Lucian's insistence on how Aetion's "reward for the marriage he had portrayed" was a real-life marriage to the daughter of a top Olympic judge hides an allusion to the circumstances of the performance for which *Herodotus* was written (a complimentary reference to a patron's marriageable daughter perhaps), which would have tied it in neatly with the general encomium of his audience. Even without that evidence it can fairly be said that what he has done is to apply the devices he has learned in his formal rhetorical training to the creation of something whose literary unity raises it well above the level of a technical exercise.

It is, then, as an innovator within the sophistic tradition that Lucian stands out. Not content, like an Aristides or a Polemon, to disguise one genre as another, he deliberately creates a series of new forms by combining dialogue, modeled in the main on Plato and on the dramatic techniques of Old Comedy, with elements from the rhetorical repertoire. The phrase "new forms" cannot, however, be taken to indicate new genres as such, for though it is possible to draw up an exhaustive list of the possible formal ingredients that Lucian may use, this tells one little about the final products. How well could one predict the flavor and appearance of a cake on the strength of the information that cakes are usually made from flour, butter, eggs, and sugar, may contain dried fruit, are sometimes iced? The Lucianic repertoire is at least as varied as that of a master pastry cook.

Nonetheless, a review of the literary ingredients in relation to the customary labels attached to Lucian's works is a good starting point for any reassessment of them. These customary labels are confusing in that they randomly adopt function or form as the criterion for grouping certain works together. Function is only a limited indicator. We have seen how the introductions, though identical in function, are quite different in rhetorical form. Similarly the pamphlets *Alexander*, *The Ignorant Book Collector*, *The Mistaken Critic*, *Peregrinus*, *A Professor of Public Speaking*, and *On Salaried Posts*, though alike in apparent satirical purpose, have as many features in common with many nonpamphlets as with each other. Beyond these two categories it is in any case difficult to find convincing functions for most of Lucian's work. "Satire" will not do, for not all of it is even superficially satirical. At best it could be described as intended for entertainment, which is hardly a useful categorization.

Form is less helpful than function. There are no obvious ways to classify a corpus of works in which some are wholly narrative (*A True Story*, *The Ass*, *The Ignorant Book Collector*), some principally narrative within a barely characterized framework of dialogue (*The Lover of Lies*), others narrative disguised as letters (*Alexander*, *Peregrinus*); or in which dialogue may be entirely dramatic (*Timon*, *The Dead Come to Life*), entirely philosophical (*Hermotimus*), subordinated to techniques of occasional oratory (*Anacharsis*, *The Parasite*), or used as a vehicle for short narratives (*The Ship*).

Starting from the criteria of function or form, one might therefore be tempted by the conclusion that there is no unifying feature in Lucian's work. Yet the content is strangely repetitive. The "message" underlines the vanity of human endeavor, the arbitrariness of human value scales, and that mutability of fortune that makes a mockery of human pretensions to power, virtue, and knowledge. Sometimes the approach is general: a Charon or a Menippus sermonizes on the shortcomings of mankind as a whole. More often an attack is specifically directed to a single vice (calumny, pride, charlatanism) or to a single class of human activity (philosophical speculation, religious beliefs and practices, political and military power). But whether the comment is authorial, as with the ridicule of beliefs about death in *On Funerals*, or is embodied in an ironical observer, as with

Lycinus' dry deflation of the pretensions of philosophers in *The Banquet*, the view expressed is always that summed up by Charon in the dialogue of the same name: "Men are all bubbles of air of varying sizes. For some the inflation is short-lived and soon over; others break as soon as they are formed. But all are destined to burst" (19).

This rather negative, if indisputable, moral stand is matched by a positive appeal to the virtues of the common man and the simple life. Micyllus the cobbler, in *The Cock*, is judged a happier man than the rich and powerful; Menippus, in *Menippus*, is swiftly convinced by what he sees of philosophers that "the way ordinary men live is the golden one." This contrast is not just a question of life-styles. It represents an ethical principle. Customarily, wealth, power, and fame are considered preferable to mediocrity. In demonstrating the inadequacies of the way men think about themselves, Lucian is stressing the gap between the world as it ought to be and the world as it is shown in the text. As the standard by which that gap is judged, he takes the very neutral principle of common sense and assimilates his audience to it. Characters like Lycinus, whether in the bantering mood of *The Eunuch* or the apparently more serious one of *Hermotimus*, take the view that if all pretensions are deflated, all that is left is the basic philosophy that life is for living. It is a standpoint the audience is assumed to accept.

If the content of Lucian's pieces is as uniform as this account suggests, then was the Renaissance perhaps right to regard him as a moralist? The first indicator that this view is inadequate is that, though the same moral standpoint is repeated from work to work, it is in each case merely touched upon. No attempt is made to convince the audience; they are simply reminded. For the fact is that though the content of many of the pieces embodies the same basic moral, their focus is not on the content at all. The audience's attention is precisely directed to the variations in the surface of the text.

By the surface of the text I mean the motifs and literary techniques out of which the text is structured. Though Lucian's writings draw on stock types and situations, these are arranged, like the colored shapes in a kaleidoscope, to give different patterns in different combinations. Let us look, for example, at what are loosely called his satirical works, a heading that covers pamphlets, treatises, and dialogues. In the pamphlets, the target of the moral criticism, the man who is revealed to be other than what he pretends, is always characterized by the same set of vices—dishonesty, immorality, and ignorance—in varying proportions. The charges of low birth, male prostitution, pederasty, adultery, and murder leveled against both named and unnamed characters are the same as those in the speeches of Aeschines and Demosthenes (we find them again in Philostratus' *Lives*). They are commonplaces of character blackening, made by Lucian into a negative character-type, the villain. This type can be compared with the parvenu, such as is described by Wealth in *Timon* (21–23): an ex-slave, stupid and vulgar, who gains his fortune as a reward for sexual favors to his master and lavishes his newfound wealth on prostitutes and low entertainments. The characteristics of the type can equally be distributed among a number of representatives of a particular class of man, extended by a vice or vices peculiarly appropriate to that class's pretensions. So in *The Banquet* the representatives of the philosophical sects are freely charged with pederasty (15, 26), adultery (32), pandering (32), attempted rape (46), greed (passim), and ignorance (particularly in Ion's absurd speech, 39). As Lycinus sums it up, "The intelligentsia were behaving in a thoroughly immoral way; they were insulting each other and stuffing themselves full of food and drink; they made a hullabaloo, and ended with a punch-up" (35).

In most of the realistic dialogues, the pretentious ones are philosophers, different aspects of human failing being featured in different works: for example, sexual indulgence in *The Eunuch*, intellectual dishonesty in *Menippus* and *The Lover of Lies*, greed in *The Dead*

Come to Life. But it makes little difference if the object of attack is a king or a rhetorician; the technique is the same. What is odder is that this narrow range of vices and its puppet representatives is echoed in the comic treatment of the gods, for they are portrayed as possessing most of the vices of the humanity they castigate. Here Lucian is not drawing a particular type or types, but taking the Homeric traditions to their logical absurdity. Powerless to influence the affairs of men, the gods are no more than the embodiments of conventional epithets—Zeus the lecher, Hera the scold, Hermes the thief. Whereas the gap between doctrine and behavior in the case of the philosophers gives off the semblance of satire, the gods, like characters in an Offenbach operetta, provide pure amusement by the contrast between the divine status to which they lay claim and the human conduct and attitudes they reveal.

In presenting these villains and buffoons, Lucian has the choice of a real or a fantastic setting. Within each there is plenty of scope for further variety. The fantasy dialogues, for example, are of two types, *ingénu* satires and works where the action takes place in heaven or in which gods or personified abstractions intervene in human affairs. I use "*ingénu* satires" somewhat loosely to cover both works in which the human world is seen from an unusual perspective and works in which an outsider visits another society that he compares with his own. In *Charon* the boatman of the dead comes up from the river Styx to observe mankind; in *Menippus* the central character of that name visits Hades and compares it with the world above; in *Icaromenippus* Menippus' journey to the moon gives him a total view of human activity as seen from the outside. None of these types offers a strict comparison between societies of the sort we associate with Montesquieu's *Lettres persanes* or Swift's *Gulliver's Travels.* In *Icaromenippus* the hero is an outsider in a purely physical sense; in the other two, hell is a consequence of the human world rather than an ideal contrast with it. Further variation is offered by the narrative form. In *Charon,* *The Downward Journey,* and *Dialogues of the Dead* 20 the form is dramatic: criticism of the world arises from the action and the comments of the characters on that action. In *Menippus* and *Icaromenippus* events are presented through retrospective narrative, with Menippus formulating the criticism for us as he recounts his adventure.

The other class of fantasy dialogues is more disparate. *Zeus Catechized* takes place entirely out of time and space; the *Dialogues of the Gods* and *The Parliament of the Gods* are set in heaven; *Zeus Rants* has a double setting, both in heaven and on earth, as the gods observe the debate about their very existence, which Damis and Timocles are conducting in the Stoa at Athens. By contrast, in pieces like *The Dead Come to Life,* *The Runaways,* and *The Double Indictment,* the action takes place exclusively on earth, but various gods or personifications (Philosophy, Truth, Justice) appear among the human characters. The action of these works is consistently dramatic, but it is varied by, for example, the courtroom procedures of *The Double Indictment.* Thus, within the fantasy presentation alone, Lucian contrives a substantial number of variations, each of which can be developed in different directions according to the subsidiary techniques employed.

Once the selection of a real or fantastic setting has been made, a further dimension of variation is added in the choice and combination of three satirical manners—invective, verbal irony, and burlesque. Invective is the open denunciation of vices. Burlesque is reductive ridicule, relying on the exaggeration of a few major traits (thus a form of caricature). Irony ranges from the simple inversion of the author's meaning (sarcasm) to the unintentional self-revelation of the pretentious, and relies on the audience's ability to spot the gap between apparent and actual meaning.

The treatises *On Funerals* and *On Sacrifices* rely largely on sarcasm; the pamphlets rely on invective, relieved by the vivid detail of the frequently obscene anecdotes that illustrate the vices attacked. Both sarcasm and invective are potentially monotonous devices. Accordingly Lucian ornaments them in various ways. In *On Funerals* the criticism is illustrated by the conduct of a father at his son's funeral and the sarcastic criticism of it by the corpse of the boy himself. A more subtle transfer is made in *The Mistaken Critic* and *A Professor of Public Speaking*: in the first case the attack is delivered by the victim's own tongue, and in the second it is incorporated into the rhetorician's encomium of his own vices. In the realistic dialogues, the sustained medium is irony coupled with burlesque. The philosophers of *The Banquet* reveal their own inadequacies in the course of the action; the comments of Lycinus merely emphasize the obvious. A Zenothemis or a Cleodemus may lay claim to superior status; their words and actions reveal them as no more than the sum of their shortcomings, hence morally inferior to the average man. The fantasy dialogues show less concern with variation, since the burlesque context automatically provides a contrast in tone. In *The Runaways*, for example, Philosophy delivers what is in effect a long speech of invective against false philosophers (4–21), punctuated by helpful comments from Zeus. In *Philosophers for Sale*, by contrast, almost all the philosophers unintentionally prove their own absurdity by the mishmash of doctrines that they are made to display to their prospective buyers; the exception is the Cynic, who delivers a mock encomium of his own vices (10). Whatever the general form of the dialogue, the shifts of satirical manner do not correspond to any variation in the content: they are motivated entirely by considerations of literary interest.

The jigsawing of conventional material should not be taken as a way of disguising its conventionality. On the contrary, it is the skill with which recognizable borrowings are blended together into something new that confers the seal of artistry on these works. Lucian's sources are clearly defined. Not, that is, by any theoretical statements; for the discussions of rhetorical models in *The Ignorant Book Collector*, *Lexiphanes*, and *A Professor of Public Speaking* are all suspect as examples of rhetoric themselves, taking their color from the context of puritanical invective in the first instance, parody in the second, and irony in the third. More credence might be given to the words of Dialogue, in the comic courtroom scene of *The Double Indictment*, when he accuses Lucian of dragging him down from his lofty role as a vehicle for philosophy, of giving him a comic function instead, and associating him with satirical techniques culled from epigram, Old Comedy, and Menippean satire.[1] But Lucian's sources are really defined by the evidence of the texts themselves.

The first type of borrowing is from handbooks, various compendia of philosophical commonplaces, rhetorical examples, and the like. Lucianic morality is drawn from Cynic diatribe, as are many of the illustrative motifs, such as the absurdity of fearing death, the ludicrous demands men make upon the gods, the folly of prizing physical beauty, the fearless freedom of speech that marks the true sage. Many of the characters chosen to embody these themes come from the rhetorical repertoire: a ruler will be Alexander, Philip, Croesus, or Xerxes; a tyrant Phalaris, Dionysios, Peisistratus; a philosopher Socrates, Diogenes, Menippus; and so on. Associated with each figure are a small number of characteristics and anecdotes selected according to the requirements of the context. Alexander is a typical case. His portrait is limited to a few references about his military career, his supposed divine birth, his love for Hephaestion, his education by Aristotle, his marriage to Roxane; and to two main qualities, vanity and bravery. There are two quite distinct traditions at work here: the criticism of the worldly ambition of Alexander by the Stoics and Cynics and the praise of Alexander as a model general and ruler by such writers as Plutarch. Lucian does not "believe"

[1]So little is known about this genre that it is impossible to make fruitful conjecture as to Lucian's debt to it. The old view, developed by Helm, that Lucian merely copied and extended the work of Menippus has long been shown to be quite untenable.

in either; he uses whichever suits the occasion. In *Dialogues of the Dead* 25—a comparison of the virtues of Alexander, Hannibal, and Scipio—Alexander's bravery is not in doubt; in the twelfth dialogue of the same series, his victories are trivialized as part of the attack on his vanity. Similarly in *Slander* 17-19, his vanity makes him the fool of flatterers; whereas in *How to Write History* 12 and 40, he is specifically shown to have contempt for such men. For a performer who, as we saw with reference to *Herodotus*, evidently toured in Macedonia, Lucian shows very little historical knowledge of the greatest Macedonian of all time and equally little interest in the rights and wrongs of the facts he does adduce. Alexander, like all the other historical characters, is merely a literary device.

The second type of borrowing is from a specific writer or literary tradition, although the borrowing itself is of a general kind. Plato, for example, is the source of the dialogue form in *The Parasite*, where the Socratic method is used for a parodic encomium of the art of the parasite, and in *Hermotimus*, where the hero, persuaded by the apparently well-meaning Lycinus to explain what he expects to get from the study of philosophy, finds his position systematically undercut by the same Socratic question-and-answer technique. In *Anacharsis* the imitation does not lie in the manner of the discussion, which is a purely rhetorical comparison of two points of view about physical education. Here it is the conventions of presentation that are familiar. The description of the setting and the characterization of the speakers follow the pattern of Plato's *Euthydemus* or *Phaedrus*. Elsewhere the imitation is a general parody of a specific work, as with the implied parallel between *The Banquet* and *The Symposium*, and the comic version of the same work in *Lexiphanes*. The borrowings from Old Comedy offer a comparable range. Side by side with very different material, there are Aristophanic types and motifs. For example, Demeas in *Timon* combines the functions of the decree-maker and the flatterer from *The Birds*, while

the mock decree itself is a device found in *Knights* (654-662) and *Parliament of Women* (408-426; 1015-1020). Some borrowed motifs play a more structural role. Both *Timon* and *The Dead Come to Life* feature a succession of types who come to plague the hero or heroes and are dealt with in the same way, as happens in *Acharnians* and *The Birds*. Both dialogues also use the device of the violent expulsion of the villain found in *Acharnians* and *Clouds*. In a more complex way, the interrelation of gods, personified abstractions, and human characters in the fantasy dialogues—indeed the whole machinery of the supernatural in works as various as *Timon*, *Zeus Rants*, and *The Runaways*—follows the pattern of plays like *Peace*. One notices in particular the same kind of shifts of scene from heaven to earth, and even, in *The Runaways*, a comparable use of the full-blown journey. None of these elements is closely modeled upon a specific text; they are done in the manner of a recognizable literary tradition.

The third type of borrowing depends upon precise reference to a particular text, often in the form of a quotation. Setting aside, for the moment, the extended parody of Homer and the historians in *A True Story*, there are two main types of quotation in Lucian. The *ornamental* restates an idea in a more elegant or striking way or uses someone else's words to further the exposition of the narrative; the *authoritative* gives backing to a point of style or content by illustrating it from another source. There are many ways of varying the effect of a quotation. It can be disguised by paraphrase, as with the version of the description of the valley of the Illisos from Plato's *Phaedrus* that is incorporated into *The Hall* 4. It can be modified grammatically to fit a new context. In particular it can be altered for comic effect, especially when part of a *cento* (a passage entirely jigsawed together from snippets of the same author). The extreme effects of this last kind of quoting can be seen in *Zeus Rants*. In theory this dialogue has a serious theme: the existence of divine forces is thrown into doubt by their apparent inability to control evil in the world.

The satirical function of the first part, set in heaven, is to show the gods in precisely that state of helplessness that Damis uses as a proof of their nonexistence in the second part. The irony of a divine power that is unable to punish even sacrilege is touched on (25) but not strongly brought out. Instead the focus of the dialogue is on the comic possibilities of literary reference. It opens with seventeen lines of metrical dialogue that include a loose parody of Homer, a precise parody of the opening lines of Euripides' *Orestes*, and a quotation from Euripides' *Heracleidae*. It goes on to feature a proclamation patched together from Homeric lines, a peroration borrowed from the first Olynthiac of Demosthenes, and further scattered echoes of Homer and Euripides. The characters even draw attention to what they are doing. Hera complains (1) that unlike Zeus she has not swallowed the complete works of Euripides; Zeus tells Hermes (6) to put lots of verses from Homer into his proclamation; Hermes advises Zeus (14) to adapt a speech of Demosthenes. The result is that the debate between Damis and Timocles, which also draws heavily on Homer and is similarly decked out with quotations, becomes an extension of the literary game rather than a serious discussion. Quotation is not so much a comic technique as the reason for the dialogue's existence.

Once we see that even the superficially satirical works of the Lucianic corpus are all variations on the same purely literary material, then the division between these works and others that are clearly parody and pastiche disappears. *A True Story*, *The Syrian Goddess*, perhaps even *The Ass* are different from *Zeus Rants* or *Timon* only in the degree to which they openly admit to being bravura exercises in reproducing the mannerisms of a certain sort of literature for comic effect. The *Dialogues of the Sea Gods* and *Dialogues of the Courtesans* are a further variant in that they are lighthearted transpositions of the conventions of one genre into another. Transposition is an extension of the rhetorical exercise of paraphrase (reproduction of a prose passage in verse or vice versa)—enlarging an extract or episode from a longer work, or abridging such a work into a single short piece. It is difficult to be certain about Lucian's models, for we know too little about satyr plays or even New Comedy. However, the *Dialogues of the Courtesans* are almost certainly based in large part on episodes of the latter: numbers 3, 6, 7, and 8, for example, all show an older and more cynical woman explaining to a young girl how to behave, and numbers 9 and 13 are built round the character of a boasting soldier, both motifs that, to judge from the comedies of Plautus, must have been featured widely in New Comedy. The humor in these works is thus inherent in the types and situations of the originals; the literary interest derives from the skill with which familiar theatrical material is expanded or contracted into armchair dialogue.

The *Dialogues of the Gods* and of the *Sea Gods* are transpositions of elements from Homer, the *Homeric Hymns*, and Alexandrian poetry. A typical example is *Dialogues of the Sea Gods* 10. Lucian takes the episode in *Iliad* 21.211–382, where the river Xanthus attacks Achilles and is punished by the scalding fire of Hephaestos. This incident he develops into a dialogue of complaint between the scalded river and the sea (personified as an unsympathetic goddess, Achilles' grandmother). The idea of a dialogue involving the river in person is already sketched in for Lucian in three places in the *Iliad* account. The first is:

> Indeed the swift Achilles would have killed more Paeonians, had not the swirling river in its indignation taken on the shape of a man and addressed him, its voice issuing forth from a deep whirlpool. "Achilles [. . .] my lovely stream is full of corpses. I am so choked with them that I cannot pour my waters into the divine sea, but you continue the slaughter."
>
> (11.211–220)

The second is 11.356–360, where the river begs Hephaestos in vain to draw off his fierce heat, and the third is 11.369–376, where it asks Hera to intercede with Hephaestos. Characteristically, Lucian alters the focus of the incident by making it retrospective and placing it at the point of confluence between the Xanthus and the "divine sea" (note how the conventional epithet has been made real by the personification of the sea as goddess).

The details of Lucian's version are all drawn from the *Iliad* description. Compare, for example, the river's address to Achilles (above) with its report of that conversation in the dialogue: "The son of Thetis here [Achilles] is responsible for it. While he was massacring the Trojans I entreated him to stop, but he did not relent from his anger. He simply kept blocking up my stream with corpses" (1). There follows an account of the river's attack on Achilles in an attempt to frighten him and of the retribution from Hephaestos. Colorful details are taken from the original: elms and tamarisks burned, eels and fish cooked alive, the river bubbling and nearly drying up. The essence of a longish epic scene is thus caught in a mere eight brief interchanges. Yet not merely the compass but the tone too has changed. The majestic force of the river, the horror of the slaughter, the catastrophic nature of Hephaestos' intervention are all deliberately reduced in importance. The effect is more whimsical: the river is a little petulant, the sea decidedly unhelpful. A little Alexandrian fantasy has been wrought out of an incident of epic brutality.

The transpositions, then, are exhibitions of skill in miniaturizing well-known passages of the classics, in which the comic element is either inherent in the material or is a by-product of the process of reducing the scale of the episodes transposed. The parodies are more conscious exercises in the humorous treatment of sources. *The Syrian Goddess* is a pastiche of the language and narrative manner of Herodotus, particularly with reference to his account of Egypt in book 2. By making the description of the temple and cult overflow with both verbal tricks and a credulity and amazement that are characteristically Herodotean, Lucian achieves that close balance between the technical skill of pure pastiche and the comic effects of parody that is the essence of the genre. Works like *The Ass* and *A True Story* range much wider. It is somewhat difficult to judge *The Ass*, which we probably have in only an abridged form. It would seem to take the subjects of the Greek novella (adventure, magic, and love), together with the contemporary taste in mysticism, and reduce them to a set of comic, largely erotic incidents. With *A True Story* we can judge rather more closely. According to the Byzantine patriarch Photius (ca. A.D. 820–891), the source for Lucian's work was a novella by Antonius Diogenes called *The Wonders beyond Thule*. Into this framework of a traveler's tale Lucian has inserted a vast number of short pastiches and parodies, using such writers as Herodotus, Thucydides, and especially Homer for his material. The combination is intended both to amuse and to keep the audience alert for allusions to the style and themes of well-known works. It is an art that could only be fully appreciated by a very well-read minority.

What we have, then, in Lucian's works, whether superficially didactic, satirical, clever, or purely lighthearted, is an elaborate series of literary cocktails in which what is said is less important than not only Lucian's own compositional skill but also the recognizable references to previous literary classics worked into the new form. Creative imitation is the end in itself. The subject of a dialogue is therefore not "the vanity of human wishes" or "the incoherence of the Olympian religious traditions"; it is the treatment of those themes in diatribe, comedy, tragedy, or epic. What Lucian is doing is in fact only an extension of a natural artistic process. In Northrop Frye's words, "literature shapes itself and is not shaped externally." All art refers implicitly to the forms and conventions of the art that precedes it. Some art, like Prokofiev's *Classical* Symphony and Tom Stoppard's *Rosencrantz and Guildenstern Are Dead*, overtly refers to a style or an example in previous tradition. Lucian, like the other writers of his period but with more self-conscious inventiveness, develops this principle into a very acute form of art for art's sake.

Does this mean that Lucian's works do not reflect the world in which they were written and that they cannot be said to express an attitude to life? At one level this is clearly untrue. Any writer is conditioned by his environment in his choice of material and form. We have already seen that the whole doctrine of imitation as developed in the second century A.D. is in part a response to a political and social situation. But can we detect in Lucian more specific echoes of the preoccupations of his times? In a fragmented form such echoes seem to exist. Not in social terms, for there the picture of both Greece and Rome is completely stylized. With intellectual currents the picture is different. Although it is not possible to derive from the works a sustained critique of philosophical doctrines or religious beliefs in the second century, let alone any coherent statement of personal views, the recurrence of certain features in many Lucianic pieces is significant. In general, of course, his review of the gods is distinctly Homeric. Even when he discusses new deities, he ignores the recent fashionable imports Isis, Osiris, and Sarapis, and barely mentions Mithras. Instead his targets are Dionysus, Anubis, Apis: gods who were barely new six centuries earlier. The key features of second-century religion—the updating of the old cults by new ceremonials, the influence of new cults, the interest in astrology, the rise of new oracles—are all passed over in silence. Yet one has to admit that if the subjects of certain works are treated in terms of literary tradition, they are nonetheless burning issues of the day: for example, the credentials of interloping cults (*Parliament of the Gods*), the relationship between gods and fate (*Zeus Rants, Zeus Catechized*), the fashion for superstition and magic among intellectuals (*The Lover of Lies*).

In the same way, though there is no serious presentation of philosophical doctrines nor any evidence that the typical features attributed to the various sects in a work like *Philosophers for Sale* were in fact the principal features of those sects in Lucian's day, the portrait of Lucian himself in *Nigrinus* and of Menippus in *Men-ippus* reflects closely what we may call the pattern of philosophical aspirations characteristic of the period. In *Menippus*, the hero is seeking a single truth in philosophy, and, failing to get it from any of the traditional sects, he looks to a magician for instant revelation. In *Nigrinus*, the speaker presents Nigrinus as a man of evangelistic charisma whose philosophy works instant revelation upon him. In both cases, of course, the doctrinal center of the work is null, with the implication that there is no such solution to fundamental problems. The two dialogues thus offer a commentary of sorts on the contemporary thirst for metaphysical certainties. But the commentary is a very incidental one; it can be seen as a literary device, building up a contrast between the hollow content and the extravagant claims made for it. All we can really deduce from this sort of evidence is that Lucian's own religious and philosophical beliefs were nonexistent and that he did not share in the contemporary taste for the irrational. For, even with the best of literary precedent, nobody of strong metaphysical convictions would choose consistently to use for comic purposes motifs that bear upon comparable problems.

The same subservience of contemporary detail to literary effect can be found in *Alexander* and *Peregrinus*, which both undeniably deal with contemporary figures, though conveniently dead ones. (Tradition has it that the butt of *A Professor of Public Speaking* is the orator Pollux, but beyond the gossip of scholiasts there is not a shred of hard evidence to support this.) Peregrinus was a Cynic philosopher who burned himself alive at the Olympic Games in A.D. 165. In the portrait of him in Lucian's pamphlet, there are certain historically corroborated facts—the hostility between Peregrinus and Herodes Atticus, the existence of a disciple of Peregrinus called Theagenes, the reference to a rebellion in the province of Achaea. There are also the famous and not unsympathetic references to the Christians that were to get Lucian into trouble with the Catholic church centuries later but that merely emphasize trivial aspects of their life-style that must have seemed amusing at the time. In every other respect the "biography" is a stylized vilification of a villain in terms identical to those used everywhere in the rhetorical tradition. We do not take Demosthenes literally when he says that Aeschines' father was a slave and that his mother officiated, with her son's help, at dubiously respectable religious rites (in fact they were probably orgies). Nor do we instantly believe Aeschines when he accuses Demosthenes of seducing a young man, tricking him out of his fortune, and encouraging him to murder one of Demosthenes' own political enemies. It would be unwise therefore to accept on Lucian's word that Peregrinus was a pederast, adulterer, and parricide.

What is not clear is why Lucian wrote such a piece. The Kronios to whom it is addressed may have been a real person, but there is no indication why he should have wished to commission a scandalous attack on a dead man. The problem is apparently clearer with *Alexander,* which seems to have been written at the behest of an Epicurean. The central figure of the pamphlet, who founded the cult and oracle of Glycon at Abonuteichos in Paphlagonia, would certainly have been on bad terms with the Epicureans, who were the main opponents of the mystical revival that made such cults so successful. Like *Peregrinus,* the work is full of historical, or at least historically plausible, material, particularly in the account of the neo-Pythagorean doctrines and magical practices that characterize the cult. But when it comes to the account of Alexander's early history, the detailed "revelation" of malpractice at the oracle, the attempted murder of Lucian himself, one is back in the world of the *psogos* (exercise in denigration). Where could Lucian have gotten most of his information from anyway? The fact is that this highly colorful and skillfully contrived piece of invective, unlikely though it is to have been featured prominently on the bookstalls of Abonuteichos, is in essence a conventional literary construct decked out with just enough genuine local color to give it credibility for the unwary modern reader.

What we seem to have here are two cases of special commission of a kind that can be paralleled elsewhere in Lucian's writings. The panegyric of the mistress of Lucius Verus in *Essays in Portraiture* and its companion piece *Essays in Portraiture Defended* is another example, this time of *encomium* (praise) instead of *psogos* (blame). The pieces written with a special venue in mind—*Hercules* for Gaul, *Amber* for northern Italy, *Herodotus* for Macedonia—are another variant on the same principle. These purpose-written works raise again the question of what kind of performance Lucian is writing for, what kind of audiences he has in mind. I said earlier that it was clear that his works were intended for live performance and that the audience needed a considerable knowledge of the literary classics to appreciate his full skill. The "feel" of Lucian's performance is there in the introductions, works that openly acknowledge the audience. It is the time-honored patter of the one-man show, "How wonderful to be here with all you very wonderful people in this very wonderful place, which is so much nicer than where I've just come from." Take *Herodotus* for example: "So you've all come along here tonight, the top people of every town, everyone who is anyone in Macedonia, and here we are in this marvelous city. It's so different from Pisa, thank heavens! The lack of space there, the tents, the huts, the stifling heat!" (8).

Once we see Lucian as an intellectually sophisticated cabaret artist, a lot of things about his work fall into place. Many of the apparent structural faults disappear when you take into account that the audience would be listening to the cumulative literary or rhetorical effect, not analyzing a logical progression upon the page. Oral situations impose a certain repetition or emphasis of key elements and permit a certain negligence in the details of plotting or characterization, which are balanced by histrionic virtues in the actual delivery of the piece. This is particularly true if the audience is principally concerned with appreciating the skill of the literary references and the interplay of different strands of tradition. Perhaps one can hypothesize beyond this that Lucian's repertoire consisted of a number of very general items, which could be appreciated anywhere from Marseilles to Samosata because built on solid traditional material (Homer, Euripides, Old and New Comedy), together with a number of specially commissioned pieces, sometimes as specific as *Alexander*, more often generally appropriate to a locality, as with the Thracian associations of *Anacharsis* or *Toxaris*. It is even possible that the character-types of the pamphlets or of dialogues like *The Eunuch* would acquire a certain topicality by association with local scandal in certain areas in which Lucian performed, whereas they would simply be appreciated as virtuoso literary exercises elsewhere. *The Eunuch*, with its picture of undignified wrangling for a well-paid "chair" in philosophy, could certainly sound near-the-bone in Athens, where such imperial sinecures existed. A thousand miles away the same dialogue would be just another cleverly written blue anecdote.

The very special nature of the literature of Lucian's age in general and of his own work in particular led to the total misreading of his works for eighteen hundred years. Yet there was hardly a classical author more influential in Europe from the beginning of the fourteenth century in Italy to the end of the eighteenth in France, Germany, and England. Almost consistently he was read as a moralist, sometimes with a positve message, sometimes an entirely negative one. His very name became a term of abuse during the Renaissance, and his works were placed on the *Index* (though surprisingly late in the sixteenth century). Yet he was imitated by Catholics, Protestants, and atheists alike. Major writers of quite different virtues, such as Erasmus, Ben Jonson, and Henry Fielding, were closely influenced by him, and his work was an indispensable spur to the development of three minor literary genres—satirical dialogue, the imaginary voyage, and the dialogue of the dead. What is, perhaps, most interesting is that although the admirers of Lucian thought they had borrowed his supposed critical spirit, what they had in fact adopted were more often his literary techniques: how to construct a vivid dialogue; how to use burlesque, parody, and pastiche; how to build anecdote, mock encomium, and comic quotation into a coherent narrative. In this respect there is no more typically Lucianic work than the dialogue of the dead, *Les Heros du roman*, by the seventeenth-century French satirist and critic Nicolas Boileau, for its subject matter is literature, and its humor is built from parody and burlesque. Though Lucian's literary function was misinterpreted for so long, the machinery of his art managed to impose itself by stealth on five centuries of European polemicists, satirists, and comic writers.

Selected Bibliography

The following works are probably by Lucian and are arranged in alphabetical order. The English titles, for the most part those given in the Loeb translation, are as used by me in the text. Works attributed to Lucian by the manuscripts but generally considered spurious have been omitted. In parentheses I give a transliteration of the Greek title, except where this is virtually identical with the English.

Alexander (Alexander ē pseudomantis)
Amber (Peri tou ēlektrou ē tōn kuknōn)
Anacharsis (Anacharsis ē peri gumnasiōn)
Apology for "On Salaried Posts" (Apologia)
The Ass (Loukios ē onos)
Astrology (Peri tēs astrologias)
Bacchus (Dionusos)
The Banquet (Sumposion ē Lapithai)
Charon (Charōn ē episkopountes)
The Cock (Oneiros ē alektruōn)
The Consonants at Law (Dikē phōnēentōn)
A Conversation with Hesiod (Dialogos pros Hēsiodon)
The Dead Come to Life (Anabiountes ē halieus)
Demonax (Dēmōnaktos bios)
Dialogues of the Courtesans (Hetairikoi dialogoi)
Dialogues of the Dead (Nekrikoi dialogoi)
Dialogues of the Gods (Theōn dialogoi)
Dialogues of the Sea Gods (Enalioi dialogoi)
The Dipsads (Peri tōn dipsadōn)
Disowned (Apokēruttomenos)

LUCIAN

The Double Indictment (Dis katēgoroumenos)
The Downward Journey (Kataplous ē turannos)
Essays in Portraiture (Eikones)
Essays in Portraiture Defended (Huper tōn eikonōn)
The Eunuch
The Fly (Muias enkōmion)
Gout (Podagra)
The Hall (Peri tou oikou)
Harmonides
Hercules (Hēraklēs)
Hermotimus (Hermotimos ē peri haireseōn)
Herodotus (Hērodotos ē Aetiōn)
Hippias (Hippias ē balaneion)
How to Write History (Pōs dei historian sungraphein)
Icaromenippus (Ikaromenippos ē hupernephelos)
The Ignorant Book Collector (Pros ton apaideuton kai polla biblia ōnoumenon)
In Praise of My Country (Patridos enkōmion)
The Judgment of the Goddesses (Theōn krisis)
Lexiphanes
The Lover of Lies (Philopseudēs ē Apistōn)
Lucian's Career (Peri tou enupniou ētoi bios Loukianou)
Menippus (Menippos ē nekuomanteia)
The Mistaken Critic (Pseudologistēs ē peri tēs apophrados)
Nigrinus
On Funerals (Peri penthous)
On Sacrifices (Peri thusiōn)
On Salaried Posts (Peri tōn epi misthōi sunountōn)
On the Dance (Peri orchēseōs)
The Parasite (Peri parasitou)
The Parliament of the Gods (Theōn ekklēsia)
Peregrinus (Peri tēs Peregrinou teleutēs)
Phalaris I and II
Philosophers for Sale (Biōn prasis)
A Professor of Public Speaking (Rhētorōn didaskalos)
Prometheus
A Prometheus in Words (Pros ton eiponta Promētheus ei en logois)
The Runaways (Drapetai)
Saturnalia (in Greek there are individual titles for the three sections of this work: Ta pros Kronon, Kronosolōn, and Epistolai Kronikai)
The Scythian (Skuthēs ē proxenos)
The Ship (Ploion ē euchai)
Slander (Peri tou mē radiōs pisteuein diabolēi)
A Slip of the Tongue in Greeting (Huper toy en tēi prosagoreusei ptaismatos)
The Syrian Goddess (Peri tēs Suriēs theou)

Timon (Timōn ē misanthropos)
Toxaris (Toxaris ē philia)
A True Story I and II (Alēthōn diēgēmatōn)
The Tyrannicide (Turannoktonos)
Zeus Catechized (Zeus elenchomenos)
Zeus Rants (Zeus tragōdos)
Zeuxis (Zeuxis ē Antiochos)

TEXTS

Lucian. Collected Works, edited by C. Jacobitz. Leipzig, 1887–1904.
Lucianus Samosatensis. Opera, edited by M. D. Macleod. 2 vols. Oxford, 1972–1974.

TRANSLATIONS

Fowler, H. W., and F. G. Fowler, trans. *The Works of Lucian of Samosata*. Oxford, 1905. Stylish, if old-fashioned.
Harmon, A. D., K. Kilburn, and M. D. Macleod. *Lucian. Collected Works*. 8 vols. New York and London, 1913–1967. Loeb Classical Library. The standard version.
Reardon, B. P., trans. *Lucian: Selected Works*. New York, 1965.
Turner, Paul, trans. *Lucian. Satirical Sketches*. Baltimore, 1961. Penguin Classics.

INDEX

Reitz, C., ed. *Index Lucianicus*. Utrecht, 1746. Reprinted Amsterdam, 1965.

BACKGROUND STUDIES

Bowersock, G. W. *Greek Sophists in the Roman Empire*. Oxford, 1969.
Bowie, E. L. "Greeks and Their Past in the Second Sophistic." *Past and Present* 46:3–41 (1970).
Reardon, B. P. *Courants littéraires grecs des IIe et IIIe siècles après Jésus Christ*. Paris, 1971.

BIOGRAPHICAL AND CRITICAL STUDIES

Allinson, F. G. *Lucian: Satirist and Artist*. New York, 1927.
Andò, V. *Luciano critico d'arte*. Palermo, 1975.
Baldwin, B. *Studies in Lucian*. Toronto, 1973.
Bellinger, A. "Lucian's Dramatic Technique." *Yale Classical Studies* 1:3–40 (1928).
Betz, H. *Lukian von Samosata und Das Neue Testament*. Berlin, 1961.

Bompaire, J. *Lucien écrivain: imitation et création.* Paris, 1958.

Caster, M. *Lucien et la pensée religieuse de son temps.* Paris, 1937.

———. *Études sur Alexandre ou le faux prophète de Lucien.* Paris, 1938.

Coenen, J. *Lukian: Zeus tragodos.* Meisenheim am Glan, 1977.

Homeyer, H. *Lukian: Wie man Geschichte schreiben soll.* Munich, 1965.

Householder, F. W. *Literary Quotation and Allusion in Lucian.* New York, 1941.

Peretti, A. *Luciano: Un intellettuale greco contra Roma.* Florence, 1946.

Robinson, C. *Lucian and His Influence in Europe.* London and Chapel Hill, N.C., 1979.

Schwartz, J. *Biographie de Lucien de Samosate.* Brussels, 1965.

CHRISTOPHER ROBINSON

APULEIUS

(b. ca. A.D. 120)

INTRODUCTION: THE MUSE IN AFRICA

APULEIUS WAS BORN in the North African city of Madauros, in the generation after Pliny and Tacitus. Like most major Latin authors he did not come from Rome; unlike many of them he did not aspire to make a career there. This was a new development in Latin literature. From the time of Ennius and Plautus, generations of Greek and Roman authors had been drawn to the capital as it grew to be the center of the empire. In the second century A.D., there was still a lively intellectual and literary world in Rome, but genius was now as likely to flourish contentedly in great provincial cities like Smyrna or Carthage. For Apuleius, the most important city of all was his native town in southern Numidia (today eastern Algeria); he was proud to be known as the Madauran (Madaurensis). We have a biographical sketch in a speech he delivered at Sabratha (near present-day Tripoli) in 158 or 159:

> As for my native land, you have declared that I have said in my own writings that it lies on the very borders of Numidia and Gaetulia and that I described myself as "half-Numidian," "half-Gaetulian" in a public discourse delivered in the presence of the proconsul Lollianus Avitus. I see no more reason to be ashamed of this than Cyrus the Great of Persia should be ashamed of being half-Mede and half-Persian by descent.
>
> (Apology 24)

His extended education in rhetoric and philosophy carried him to Rome and Athens, but he never forgot to remind his public of his corner of the world. He had nothing to be ashamed of. Madauros had been in good standing with Rome since 204 B.C., late in the Second Punic War:

> I need not apologize for my country, since even in the time of Syphax we were a township. When he was conquered we were transferred as a gift from the Roman people to King Masinissa. Then, after veterans from the Roman army settled there—a second founding of the city—we became a settlement of the highest distinction.
>
> (Apology 24)

If Madauros was respectable, so was Apuleius' family. Both he and his father held important offices in the town's government:

> In this settlement my father rose to the post of chief magistrate and became the foremost citizen of the place after he had served in all the municipal offices. Immediately after my own admission to the town senate, I succeeded to my father's position in the community, and, so I hope, I am in no way an unworthy successor but one who maintains the same standards in personal honor and reputation.
>
> (Apology 24)

After Madauros, the city that claimed his greatest loyalty was Carthage, the metropolis of the region. Statues were set up in his honor there and elsewhere in the empire. His effusive gratitude is preserved in a speech delivered before the senate of Carthage:

> What greater pride could one merit, what more substantial, than in speaking well of Carthage, where you, an entire city, are the most cultivated of men, who have in your possession all learning, which your children learn, your young men display, your old ones teach? Carthage, the venerable schoolmistress of our province, Carthage, the heavenly Muse of Africa, Carthage, Camena [Muse] to the people who wear the toga.
>
> (*Florida* 20)

This Africa is a different place from the one depicted in earlier Roman literature. Long departed was the enemy nation of Livy, Vergil, or Sallust: those were all portraits of a world that in Apuleius' time had ceased to be.

Dedicated as he was to his career as an orator and philosopher in Madauros and other cities in Africa, however, Apuleius is best known today for his novel *The Golden Ass* or *Metamorphoses*, a work that in many ways sums up a tradition in classical literature that begins with Homer's *Odyssey*. It is a delightful work, and very difficult. This essay atempts to explain what is important and original in that novel and in its author's literary career.

THE STORY AND THE STRUCTURE OF THE GOLDEN ASS

The Golden Ass is a novel in eleven books about an insouciant young Greek named Lucius who has a fatal curiosity about magic and metamorphosis. When he visits the strange city of Hypata in northern Thessaly, he stays at the house of a family friend, Milo. There, learning that his host's wife, Pamphile, is skilled in the practice of magic, he decides to enlist the aid of her beautiful serving maid, Fotis, to help him discover her secret arts. One night, with Fotis' aid, he spies on Pamphile and sees her apply a magic ointment that transforms her into an owl. He hopes to try the same thing. Unfortunately

for him, Fotis confuses the jars of her mistress' ointments, and Lucius, to his horror, is transformed into an ass and stolen by bandits before he can eat roses, the only antidote to the spell. In his ass form he serves under several masters and has many adventures, some of them comical and many more quite dangerous; he recounts them all for his readers' entertainment. He also tells tales about other people, one of which, the tale of Cupid and Psyche, is the most famous passage in *The Golden Ass*. At last, with the aid of the goddess Isis, he succeeds in eating a wreath of roses and is transformed once again into a human being. Out of gratitude to her, Lucius joyfully enrolls in her service and starts out in a new life, reborn in the religion of Isis.

Delightful as these adventures may be, the history of Apuleian criticism shows that this is no work for those with a traditionalist's taste in classical literature. By comparison with more common genres, Apuleius' novel may seem wildly undisciplined and self-indulgent. Yet *The Golden Ass* in fact marked a momentary renaissance in a literature and language passing out of its silver age and declining into something bronze, if not worse. In writing the novel, Apuleius freed himself from the kind of burdens that inevitably came with more prestigious genres. As the late epic poets Valerius Flaccus (*d.* A.D. 93) or Silius Italicus (*d.* A.D. 101) discovered, to write an epic in the traditional style invited comparison with Vergil and Homer, and the contest was not an equal one. By contrast, although Greek and Roman novelists were largely ignored by ancient critics, none of them ever faced that kind of comparison. Apuleius was able to be exciting and vital at a time when the mainstream of classical literature was distinguished by neither of those qualities.

Another reason for the originality of Apuleius' work lies in its powerful spiritual inspiration. At this point in the ancient world, the balance of creative power was shifting to Christian writers, as we can see in the works of Apuleius' fellow Africans Tertullian and Augustine. Compared to them, the later celebrations by pagan authors of the glories of a (largely) passé

Greco-Roman culture seem pallid and tame. Isis, however, gave Apuleius an inspiration fully comparable to Christianity, or so at least the last book would suggest. As we shall see later, aside from the *Apology*, his other works expound only the received values of Greco-Roman culture, and we feel that we are reading book reports, digests, and very little else. But *The Golden Ass* is a work of genius, of an author in touch with the great issues of his age. Here he reveals his power to seize on his world, to respond to its absurdities, and to transform his perceptions into what proved to be the last great work of pagan literature. His themes are those of the greatest writers: What does it mean to live a life? What is this world we live in? How should we conduct ourselves in such a world? The picture of the world he creates, the problems he perceives, and his own solutions to them are still a powerful challenge to his reader.

The alternate title for these adventures is *Metamorphoses*, "transformations," and it is an uncommonly appropriate one. This is not only a novel about metamorphoses; it is itself, as a narrative, in a constant state of metamorphosis. In the three-sided relationship of Apuleius the author, Lucius the narrator, and the reader, the rules of the game are subject to constant change. The narrative reflects Apuleius' religious and philosophical scruples. As a Platonist he is concerned with transcendent values, the nature of the divine, and individual salvation. The belief in the eternal and the unseen necessarily entails doubts about the reality of the visible world around us. Since Apuleius as Platonist naturally questions the reality of what everyone thinks is the real world, it is natural to see the Platonist turned novelist writing about a world that is subject to constant change, a world filled with illusions and misunderstandings. The fictive and the unreal can and do turn into reality, and what Lucius the narrator and perforce his reader assume to be real and permanent just as easily turns into mere illusion.

Although this is a novel about a world in apparent chaos, underneath that seeming chaos a powerful intelligence has shaped a coherence and an order that become visible and real only in book 11. No better instance of Apuleius' astonishing preoccupation with the occult and the divine could be found than the simple fact that the novel is divided into eleven books. At first glance this seems an odd division. The first ten books of Lucius' adventures are as different from book 11 as night from day. This sharp contrast will impress every reader who comes to the novel for the first time, and that fact in itself has led some critics to question the novel's unity and coherence. But the contrast, like the asymmetry of eleven books, is basic to Apuleius' design, because a symbolic significance underlies this scheme of ten "bad" books plus one "good" one.

In Pythagorean numerology the number ten possessed special significance because it constituted the sacred *tetractys* or "fourness," a perfect number that is the sum of the first four digits $(1 + 2 + 3 + 4)$. In book 11, for example, Lucius is instructed to abstain from meat and drink for exactly ten days by the priest Asinius Marcellus in order to prepare himself for induction into the mysteries of Osiris (11.28). The first ten books of *The Golden Ass* are as imperfect and disturbing a picture of this world as any artist has ever created. They are the very antithesis of the ten *Eclogues* of Vergil or the ten books of Plato's *Republic*; they show the way the world ought not to be, a place in which no sensible person would wish to live. Book 11 marks the start of a new life and a new world for Lucius; in terms of numerology, it also marks a beginning of a new series of ten, a tetractys: that is, $1 + \dots$. Some readers have preferred to think that the novel was cast into its form purely by accident rather than by design. But the scheme of an inferior tetractys followed by the first unit of a genuinely sacred tetractys reflects in numerology and in structure the ever-changing character of the narrative itself. One book is devoted to establishing Lucius' identity (book 1); two books reveal the real purpose of his journey, to learn about magic (books 2–3); three books are set in the robbers' cave, the locus for the tale of Psyche's ascent, fall, and reunion (books 4–6); and four books are an episodic patchwork with no order and with more and more realization by Lucius of Fortune's power (books 7–10). Isis, the Queen of Heaven of the last book, reestablishes Lucius' true identity and puts him on the course of a new life (book 11). She reveals to him an enduring reality and delivers him from an otherwise illusory world. The last book of *The Golden Ass* is the first book of Lucius' new life.

THE PROLOGUE

Reading Apuleius entails a constant questioning of our perceptions of reality and illusion. Real people and events become the stuff of fiction; and, conversely, made-up characters and illusory experiences become actual fact. This is what the narrator of the novel—not necessarily Apuleius himself—has to say about it:

> However, in this Milesian discourse I shall weave together varied tales and win over your welcoming ears with a charming whisper—that is, if you will not disdain to look over an Egyptian papyrus inscribed with the sharpness of a Nilotic reed—so that you'll marvel at the forms and fortunes of men transformed into other images, then one with the other back again into their former selves. Now to begin.
>
> "Who is this man?" you ask. A few words will suffice. Mt. Hymettus, in Attica, and the Isthmus of Corinth and Mt. Taenarus, in Sparta—all famous lands immortalized in even more eternally famous books—these are my old family roots. There in the first campaign of boyhood I won the Attic tongue. Soon after, a stranger in the Latin city, with painful effort and with no master to guide me, I learned the native speech of the Romans.
>
> Behold then, I ask for pardon if I, a rude speaker, annoy you with unfamiliar or strange constructions in this foreign tongue. As a matter of fact this very change in language corresponds to the acrobatic science we are about to explore. We begin a Grecian tale: attend, reader, and you shall find delight.

> (*The Golden Ass* 1.1)

The prologue of *The Golden Ass* does not summarize the novel, but in retrospect this brief preface becomes more and more eloquent. It is in effect the novel in microcosm, and for that reason it repays close attention.

The first word is so unusual that critics have attempted to emend it to something more conventional. The conjunction *at* ("however," "on the other hand") has strong adversative force; it is as if we were in the middle of a conversation that had been going on before the novel started and the narrator were replying to something we, his readers, had said. We are even given what is in effect a rhetorical question that prompts the narrator to tell us something about his background: "Who is this man?" Only part of the answer to the question is here. We do not learn his actual name until the end of book 1, where it emerges in the words of Pythias, Lucius' friend from student days in Athens (1.24). For most of book 1, in short, we are not quite sure who this narrator is. At the end of the prologue, like an actor introducing a comedy by Plautus or Terence, he says to us, "Attend, reader, and you shall find delight." An easy familiarity is established, and we are thus launched into the "conversation" or "language" of the novel.

But establishing a conversational tone is only one achievement of this opening chapter. If we were to leave our reading of Apuleius at this point, we would have reached only the level of understanding that cursory readers of Apuleius sometimes betray. The fourth-century Platonist Macrobius, for example, seems to have taken *The Golden Ass* to be literally what this prologue says it is, a medley of Milesian tales: that is, a work of no serious import, since the Greek city of Miletus was notorious in literature, if not in fact, for its luxurious and wanton ways. The Milesian tale was a kind of ancient short story of modest reputation and epitomized the tastes and morality of that city. But it would be unwise to take the narrator in the prologue at face value, because even at this point he is not what he seems to be.

The first hint that we are not getting the

whole truth is his cryptic aside in the opening sentence: "that is, if you will not disdain to look over an Egyptian papyrus inscribed with the sharpness of a Nilotic reed." This pious hope can make little sense at this point, unless we wish to believe that the narrator is literally apologizing for his writing materials. The implications of this cloudy apology become absolutely clear only when we reach book 11, where the narrator is inducted into the mysteries of Isis. The author's duplicity is reflected in his ambiguous language. The "sharpness" (argutia) of the Nilotic reed could also be translated as its "cleverness," and no word could better describe the sharpness, wit, even outright trickery that Apuleius practices on his reader from the opening sentence onward.

There is one other apology in the prologue that reveals something important about the language and style of Apuleius' novel. The narrator says he is a Greek who learned Latin only with the greatest difficulty: "Behold then, I ask for pardon if I, a rude speaker, annoy you with unfamiliar or strange constructions in this foreign tongue." (One is reminded of Othello's "rude am I in my speech," in Shakespeare.) We do not need to wait until book 11 to see how preposterous a disclaimer this is. Not only is this little apology itself elegantly phrased; it constitutes a third and concluding section to the other parts of a three-part prologue that is filled with one tricolon (a threefold rhetorical pattern) after another. The opening sentence is in three sections, the description of the narrator's background and education is in three parts, and even his ancestral background comes in threes: "Mt. Hymettus, in Attica, and the Isthmus of Corinth and Mt. Taenarus, in Sparta."

Far from being the scribblings of a romanized Greek, the language everywhere reflects a writer in total control of his style. Translation inevitably destroys most of the artifices of this language and thus obscures much of the irony of the apology. To grasp fully how disingenuous this passage really is, we need to consider the artistry of only two clauses in the opening sentence: "in this Milesian discourse I shall weave together varied tales and win over your welcoming ears with a charming whisper" (sermone isto Milesio varias fabulas conseram auresque tuas benivolas lepido susurro permulceam). The two clauses have the same grammatical pattern of nouns (sermone, aures: "discourse," "ears"); pronominal adjectives (isto, tuas: "this," "your"); descriptive adjectives (Milesio, benivolas: "Milesian," "welcoming"); characterizing adjectives (varias, lepido: "varied," "charming"); nouns (fabulas, susurro: "tales," "whisper"); and verbs (conseram, permulceam: "I shall weave," "I shall win"). There is also a chiasmus, or pattern of A B B A, in the cases or word endings of the nouns and adjectives: sermone isto Milesio, "in this Milesian discourse" (A); varias fabulas, "varied tales" (B); aures tuas benivolas, "your welcoming ears" (B); lepido susurro, "with a charming whisper" (A). The parallelism of the two clauses even extends to the same number of words (six) and to the number of syllables in each word: sermone and auresque (three); isto and tuas (two); Milesio and benivolas (four); varias and lepido (three); fabulas and susurro (three); with variation only in conseram (three) and permulceam (four). Very typical of Apuleius is the most obvious effect of all, the rhyming jingle of the verbs conseram and permulceam ("I shall weave together," "I shall win over").

The elegance of the prologue brings to mind the exordium, or opening section, of a classical oration, which is designed to win over the orator's listeners by removing their anxiety, disarming their envy, and turning them to the speaker's favor even before a word has been said about the actual issues that the speech addresses. Nor is that all. By striving after every kind of acoustical conceit, the narrator reveals himself to be a writer living in the age of Marcus Cornelius Fronto (A.D. 100–166), tutor to Marcus Aurelius and other members of the imperial family, and doyen of a new school of rhetoric that departed sharply from the example and precepts of Cicero and Quintilian. Apuleius' "rude speaker" is up-to-date in the latest fashions of Roman literary tastes. His prose abounds with rhymes, puns, alliteration, elaborately constructed parallels, archaic Latin, and neologisms crowded side by side on a single page. The prologue alone amply demonstrates that he is an ancient writer whose sharp wit demands equal wit in his reader.

BOOKS 1–3: THESSALY AND THE HOUSE OF MILO

As the narrator begins his story, he turns from the present and future tenses of the prologue and recounts what happened in the past in his Grecian tales. This shift in tenses is important. From the moment Lucius enters Thessaly until his conversion to Isis in book 11, he is not identical with the person who speaks in the prologue, and this creates a complex perspective for the reader. Apuleius combines two characters in one: a "narrating I" and an "experiencing I." The first is the voice of a person recalling past events and shaping his story in the same artful, self-conscious manner we have observed in the prologue. But the second "I" is very different. Lucius the character is actually experiencing these fantastic adventures for the first time. Usually he does not grasp what is happening to him, nor can he perceive the deeper meanings that often lie beneath the surface of things.

This double perspective accounts for the comic obtuseness of Lucius. Even though he well knows that Thessaly is a province notorious for its witches and magicians (2.1), he never understands the forces at work there. His adventures are a comedy of errors and misunderstandings. He hears about the dangers of *curiositas* ("curiosity" with a sinister meaning), the desire to know not simply things, but things human beings are not meant to know. He hears several people complain about the power of a *Fortuna* who rules their lives in a capricious and often brutal way. He hears tales about the dangers of magic from Aristomenes (1.5–19) and Thelyphron (2.21–30). He sees a sculpture of the metamorphosis of Actaeon, a transformation explicitly interpreted as a punishment of curiosity (2.4). Throughout books 1–3, Lucius remains oblivious to what the reader realizes are increasingly obvious warnings about a dangerous world.

But the irony of *The Golden Ass* is not simply the dramatic irony of the comic stage. Our sense of superiority to Lucius is no less illusory than his understanding of his world. Even though we understand more than he does, and even though his adventures ultimately culminate in his salvation in Isis, we must realize that our perception is as limited as his. We know at most that something is dreadfully wrong with the world that the narrator describes. What is wrong and why remain as opaque to us as to the "experiencing" character Lucius, and all does not come clear until the end of the novel. In this sense, any critical explanation or summary distorts Apuleius' purposes, since for the first ten books of the novel, the essence of his fiction is that neither Lucius nor his readers can quite grasp the full import of what the devious narrator is telling. This disorienting perspective may be compared to that of Roman satire, to the two-edged irony of the kind Horace speaks of: "What are you laughing at? Change the name and the tale is told about *you*" (*Satires* 1.69–70).

The first person Lucius meets on his way to Hypata perfectly illustrates Horace's moral. In the tale of Aristomenes (1.5–19), Aristomenes not only tells his own adventures but also picks up on some details of Lucius' credulous character and uses them in his story about an encounter with his friend Socrates and the witch Meroe. In Lucius' first words, he claims he is "not curious," "not a prying fellow" (1.3), yet he proceeds to act in precisely the opposite way. He is disposed to believe anything he hears, even though Aristomenes' skeptical companion laughs at the tale from beginning to end. And he is also perfectly content to let Fortune work her way with mortals (1.20), even though in the tale of Aristomenes he hears Socrates described quite explicitly as a victim of Fortune (1.6). Aristomenes also says that Meroe vowed to punish him for his curiosity, even though he seems to have stumbled into the disasters of Socrates quite by accident (1.12). Very little of what Aristomenes has to say seems to register with Lucius, though his story reveals a world ruled by magic and a Fortune menacing and unpredictable. His tale is in effect an overture to what follows, with leitmotifs and themes whose true meaning Lucius does not even begin to comprehend.

In book 2, the minatory tone becomes still stronger after Lucius has settled himself in the house of his miserly family friend Milo. He wants to learn what he can about magic and metamorphosis. At the home of his mother's friend Byrrhena, he sees a sculpture of Diana and Actaeon. Actaeon is punished by metamorphosis for his curiosity (2.4). "Everything you see here belongs to you," says Byrrhena (2.5); while Lucius evidently thinks this refers to her house, the reader will recognize the ambiguity of her words. Later at Milo's house Lucius tells his host about the predictions a Chaldean prophet named Diophanes (God's Revelation) had made about Lucius' future fame and fortune: "He told me that I would have quite a flourishing reputation, that I would be the subject of a great history and an incredible story and many books" (2.12). Milo at once tells of his own experience with Diophanes, who lost a valuable fee from the businessman Cerdo (Mr. Profit) because he could not keep his wits and refrain from telling a tale about his own incompetence. Lucius once again hears the truth, only this time he is telling the story on himself. The prophecy of Diophanes will come true in a way Lucius cannot imagine.

When Lucius is at a dinner at Byrrhena's house, he hears another tale that is told as much about him as about the man who tells it (2.19–20). Thelyphron's story about guarding the corpse of a dead man from witches seems to proceed straightforwardly enough and is just the kind of tale that would appeal to Lucius. But the story contains many loose threads that puzzle the reader, if not Lucius. After Thelyphron has been discharged for presumably doing his job well, the father of the dead man accuses the widow of murder, and suddenly there appears "Zatchlas, an Egyptian prophet of the first rank" (2.28), a priest with shaved head, a man who can call the dead back to life and learn the truth of the matter. The father of the dead man addresses Zatchlas in language that we shall not hear again until book 11:

> "Take pity, priest, take pity by the heavenly stars, by the powers of the underworld, by the natural elements, by the nocturnal silences, and the enclosures of Coptos, and the flood of the Nile, and the mysteries of Memphis and the sistrum of Pharos."
>
> (2.28)

This may look like mere verbosity, but it is not. The old man is pronouncing a series of Egyptian names and places clearly associated with the mysteries of Isis. With his shaved head, Zatchlas also looks like a priest of Isis, even though he is not explicitly identified as such. Like the apology for the papyrus and Nilotic reed in the prologue, he is a glimmer of what lies ahead for Lucius and his readers.

Thelyphron's tale ends with his horrifying revelation of the mutilation and humiliation that he suffered instead of the corpse. Yet the drunken company at Byrrhena's party laughs at Thelyphron's story (2.31), and Lucius simply thanks his hostess for a charming evening and stumbles home drunk. After battling with what he takes to be three bandits trying to break into Milo's house, he slays them and collapses in bed. Of course the bandits turn out not to be bandits at all, but wineskins that had been enchanted by Lucius' hostess, Pamphile. Fotis explains the mix-up to Lucius (3.15–19). She was instructed to steal some locks of hair from a young man Pamphile (Lady All-Love) wanted, but she substituted tufts of bristle instead; hence the wineskins rather than the young man had answered the call of Pamphile's magic spell. At the end of book 3, genuine bandits break into the house of Milo and use Lucius to carry off their spoils (3.28). Now what was only a joke has become reality, and Lucius is a real victim. He is dragged before the whole town for a murder trial, yet the "trial" explodes into laughter as the "corpses" are revealed.

The mock trial scene (3.2-10) is Apuleius' commentary on the nature of this comedy, for the reader of Lucius' story is in the same position as the audience that laughs at his humiliation. The trial is a perfect instance of the self-conscious and deceptive fictions Apuleius perpetrates on his readers. The narrative keeps calling attention to itself and to the reader's tenuous hold on what is real and what is unreal. The joke of the wineskin bandits is revised, as it were, into anything but a joke. It should come as no surprise that these genuine bandits will eventually be transformed into figures of pure jest and harmlessness.

BOOKS 4-8: CHARITE, PSYCHE, AND CHARITE AGAIN

The central books of The Golden Ass constitute a complex panel of tales and episodes that constantly shift from one perspective of reality to another. It is not simply the case that the books deal with the illusions that fiction can create, though that is a substantial part of what these books are about; the characters themselves are also constantly engaged in the enterprise of masking their identities, and in the process, they deceive themselves as much as others. Lucius is now plunged into a world in which he is largely the observer of people acting out their deceptions and fictions on others, so that the jokes they play with one another in what they take to be real life nicely complement the game of fiction that has already begun.

The focal character of this part of the novel is a beautiful captive maiden abducted by the bandits on her wedding day. She and her husband are very much like the hero and heroine of such Greek romances as Chariton's *Chaereas and Callirhoe* or Achilles Tatius' *Clitophon and Leucippe*; in those novels, the young couple is typically separated and spends the balance of the novel trying to be restored to one another and to their homeland. That seems to be the type of fiction Apuleius is writing in books 4-8, but in fact the conventional, pleasing sentimentality so typical of Greek romance is subjected to wrenching distortions in *The Golden Ass*.

The captive maiden who dominates this part of the novel is named Charite, "Grace," as in the three Graces; but she is not named until book 7, so that for much of the story she is simply "the girl," the type of the innocent heroine of the Greek romance. Although Charite is ostensibly the focal point of books 4-8, much of the story is in fact devoted to the famous tale of Cupid and Psyche, which is supposed to console her and help pass the time. But events show that "Cupid and Psyche" in reality has no bearing whatever on Charite or her husband, Tlepolemus, since they are destroyed by a jealous suitor named Thrasyllus, as we learn in a subsequent tale in book 8. Because of her curiosity and her suffering under Fortune, Psyche is more apt a parallel to Lucius than Charite. And the tale of Psyche has still wider relevance. Because she and her husband are allegorical figures (Psyche is Greek for "soul" and Cupid is Latin for "love"), the full import of their tale can apply to any person, including the reader.

To understand books 4-8, it helps to step back from the novel and take this cast of characters in their ensemble as they appear throughout these five books. This will be no substitute for reading Apuleius' artful arrangement of things. But our aim here is to understand Apuleius, and that calls for pulling together widely separated events, tales, and characters from books 4-8 and even anticipating to some extent what happens to Lucius in book 11.

The first gallery of characters to understand is Apuleius' bandits. They are responsible for bringing Lucius to his present state. Like Charite they are stock figures in the Greek romances, since it is usually bandits or pirates who are given the task of abducting the hero or heroine in Greek fiction. Apuleius also treats these stock figures in a special way. It will be remembered that, in books 2 and 3, the idea of brigands started out as a joke: Lucius killed what he thought were bandits, who proved to be only wineskins. Then in book 3 the joke turned into a reality, as bandits really did invade Milo's house and did carry Lucius off. What happens in the course of books 4 and 7 is that the bandits are essentially turned back into a joke. They are exposed as being as gullible as any other characters, and although they occasionally succeed in duping others, they are themselves the victims of an ingenious fraud perpetrated by the disguised husband of Charite, Tlepolemus, who passes himself off as Haemus, a bandit who wishes to join the gang (7.5–8).

For all their menacing remarks to Lucius and Charite, this gullible bunch of cutthroats enjoys only limited success. One of their number tells the story of the deaths of three of their fellows: Lamachus, Alcimus, and Thrasyleon (4.9–21). The heroic exploits of the third robber deserve special attention, because he is the only one of the three who actually achieves something. Thrasyleon (Bold Lion) disguises himself as a bear and is so effective in this hoax that he enables his fellow bandits to rob the house of the wealthy Demochares. The feat costs him his life, but he maintains the disguise to the death and does not call out in a human voice even when he is set upon by dogs and men with weapons (4.21).

The bandits of these tales are elaborate jokes on the basic themes of metamorphoses in form and fortune. They try to steal the fortunes (wealth) of others and suffer particularly bad fortunes (luck) in the process. For Lucius and the evil boy under whom he suffers in book 7, there will be a particularly nasty return of the theme of bears. A real bear, not a man in disguise, devours the wicked boy who delights in tormenting Lucius (7.24–26).

The disguise of Tlepolemus works very well with this crowd. In the process of explaining who he is and what he lives for, he reveals that he once passed himself off as a young woman in disguise, and that this ruse worked perfectly well (7.6–8). The captive maiden unaccountably warms to this fellow, and Lucius is indignant at

her seeming lechery; but then Tlepolemus reveals himself and Charite's name at the same instant (7.12), and all falls into place—or so it seems at the time. Haemus (in reality the disguised Tlepolemus) gets the bandits drunk and disposes of the same crew that had once included Thrasyleon and other bold criminals skilled in disguise. But the last joke is not on the bandits, after all, as we shall see when we consider the entire career of Charite and her husband.

Next we turn to the story of Cupid and Psyche. If the central books are far and away the most difficult part of *The Golden Ass* to describe adequately, the central creation within them, the tale of Cupid and Psyche, is more challenging still. Remember that it begins quite modestly, with the old woman who serves the bandits recounting a story she characterizes as a charming tale, an old woman's story (4.27). The old woman's tale begins with a plot very similar to what has happened to Charite and her husband; in the course of the story, however, her tale expands to all kinds of details and incidents that have more bearing on Lucius' experiences than on Charite's. Only at the end of the story, when we hear of the joyous reunion of a husband and wife, do we perhaps imagine that the tale offers a consoling vision for Charite.

The basic outline of the tale of Cupid and Psyche is as follows: A beautiful young woman so earns the admiration of men everywhere that the worship of Venus, goddess of love, is neglected. For this Venus becomes enraged at the girl, Psyche, and in the course of the story becomes in effect the vindictive, implacable goddess Fortune, who torments Lucius and everyone he meets (book 4). Psyche is supposed to be destroyed by Cupid, whom Venus recruits for the task, but instead he falls in love with her and makes her his wife. His only condition is that Psyche never look upon him. He warns her of Fortune's threat to their happiness and tries to keep Psyche's jealous sisters from stirring up her curiosity. Although Psyche tries to obey, she is eventually persuaded to look on her husband, and when she does so and recognizes him as Cupid, she violates his trust and he flies away. Psyche attempts to hold on to him but falls away: literally, the fall of the soul as depicted by Plato in the *Phaedrus* (book 5). The balance of the tale tells how Psyche wanders in search of Cupid and eventually falls into the hands of her bitter enemy, Venus. She must submit to a series of cruel tests, each of which she passes, thanks to the supernatural intervention of creatures and objects in the world around her. Her final labor is to bring back Proserpina's jar. Although she succeeds in this task, her inveterate curiosity again leads her astray; she opens the lid and instantly falls into a deathlike sleep. Cupid intervenes and restores her to life. He then asks Jove to intercede and bestow immortality on Psyche. Jove does so, and, after Psyche is admitted into the company of the Olympian gods, she in time gives birth to her child by Cupid, named Voluptas or Joy (book 6).

The happy ending of the tale seems to promise good things to Charite, but it cannot be fully grasped for the religious-philosophical allegory it really is until we reach book 11, with its account of Lucius' conversion to Isis and his personal discovery of the way to individual salvation. For these reasons, to make the story clear at this point we must anticipate the conclusion of the novel, where Lucius will be restored to his human form and saved from Fortune by the divine intervention of Isis. It will become very clear by then that no one can reliably save himself from Fortune. Consequently, if salvation is to be found, it will have to come from without. Psyche's tale is a crystallization of the novel's world view. Although the tale is ostensibly about the eventual happy reunion of husband and wife, it is in its deepest meaning a story that transcends Charite and reaches beyond Lucius to us. When Cupid saves Psyche and makes her immortal, he does precisely the same thing that Isis will do for Lucius. Both Psyche and Lucius are victims of their own curiosity; both are victims of Fortune; and both are saved not by their own efforts but by the interventions of a divine being.

Nowhere else does Apuleius better reveal how well he deserves the epithet of Platonist than here. For him, as for Diotima in the *Symposium*, divine love is the answer to the problems of human life: that love offers the only way for humanity to transcend its mortality and strive for the transcendent and the permanent. Isis enables Lucius to escape the world of the first ten books of the novel. He—and we—realize the precariousness of the human condition and the utterly unjust and unforeseen way events can turn out. The birth of Psyche's daughter, Joy (6.24), suggests that genuine happiness can come into being only when such a union with the divine is achieved.

Finally we return to Charite. She is crucial to the dynamics of the plot, which eventually brings Lucius to Isis. The happy ending of the tale of Cupid and Psyche, Tlepolemus' rescue of his wife, and the punishment of the bandits would seem to be a perfect conclusion to Lucius' perils. *The Golden Ass* would be exactly like one of the Greek romances if it concluded in this way, with the wicked punished and the good saved. Instead Charite and Tlepolemus are brutally destroyed. The whole complex of books 4 through 8 blows sky-high the illusory logic of events and also gives the reader the disquieting idea that nowhere in this world of Lucius' travels is any place surely stable and reliable. Tlepolemus, for all his manliness and the clever lies by which he easily duped the bandits, is in the end undone by the treacherous suitor Thrasyllus. Thrasyllus (Rashness) insinuates himself into the affections of the young couple, then lures Tlepolemus out on a boar hunt and kills him. He is eventually punished for his crime, but in effect he also destroys Charite, who kills herself after revealing his crime.

Books 4–8 in sum present readers of *The Golden Ass* with glorious entertainment but also create a contradiction that they cannot resolve. At this point, as Lucius and the household of Charite flee to new masters and other adventures, neither he nor we can understand what the old woman's tale means. The celestial vision of the reunion of Cupid and Psyche seems wildly inappropriate, since every person who told a tale in books 4–8 is now dead: the bandits, Tlepolemus, and the old woman who told the tale of Cupid and Psyche.

BOOKS 9–10: LEPIDAE FABULAE

To leave the central books of *The Golden Ass* is to leave behind a complex of tales that have depicted two women who embody ideals of femininity at two levels: Psyche, raised to the divine by her husband, Cupid; and Charite, who follows her husband, Tlepolemus, to her own death rather than submit to the adulterous suitor Thrasyllus. In short, this world, at least as Lucius has experienced it, proves to be a place in which neither Charite nor Psyche could survive.

Now we take up yet another complex of related stories, and they center around the themes of adultery and revenge rather than any single character. Here is a world in which women, if they survive, do so by being faithless and even murderous. Lucius now moves from one master to the next. Each of them proves to be more humane than the last, so that by the tenth book he enjoys first the favor of an opportunistic pair of brothers, the cook and the baker, and then of his last master of all, Thiasus (Mr. Revel), who organizes the festivals in Corinth. But there is an increasing savagery in these books, and it is not so much in Lucius' own experiences (as in books 4–8) as it is the "charming tales" *(lepidae fabulae)* with which he regales us. Furthermore there is a curious monotony about all of them. Books 9 and 10 are a series of variations on one theme: the destruction of the family.

The plots of the "charming tales" are restricted to a few simple types. In book 9, in the tale of the tub (9.5–7) and the three tales-within-tales concerning the young adulterer Philesitherus (9.14–31), the basic plot for all the tales is in three parts: (a) an adulterous wife and her lover are interrupted by the unforeseen return of the husband; (b) the lover is hidden away in some large container, either a large tub (9.5), a basket (9.24), or a bin (9.26); and (c) the lover is discovered by the husband, with astonishingly varied results. In the tale of the tub, the wife and her lover boldly bluff their way out of the situation by persuading her husband that the lover is really a customer inspecting the tub (9.5). They consummate their passion on top of the tub, while the cuckold is inside cleaning it. In the second tale, which the baker's wife hears from an old woman, the clever adulterer Philesitherus uses his wits to escape from being caught by accusing the accomplice slave of stealing the shoes he had left behind; even the quick-witted husband, Myrmex, is fooled, and the adultery is never punished (9.21). This happy ending encourages the baker's wife to try the same young man; unhappily he is discovered and, just like the adulterer whom the baker tells about next door, is punished by sexual abuse and a beating. In this fourth and last tale about adultery in book 9 the scandalized Lucius himself intervenes. On the way to his stable with other animals, he treads heavily on Philesitherus' fingers, and the young man's cries reveal him to the baker (9.27). But Lucius' intervention does not produce quite the happy ending those earlier tales would lead us to expect. The adulterous wife of the baker first tries to win back his affections, and when she fails, she enlists the aid of magic to kill him (9.30). Lucius than passes into the service of a gardener, though not for long. Book 9 concludes with the story of a cruel landlord who brought about his own death and the deaths of a father and three sons (9.38): yet another instance of the vulnerability of the family in the face of Fortune and the evil people are capable of. Shortly thereafter the gardener runs afoul of a brutal Roman soldier, and Lucius is turned over to another master.

The tales of the wicked stepmother (10.21) and the jealous wife (10.23–28) in book 10 have remarkably similar plots: (a) a disruption of family ties, with attempted incest or the murder of a relative as outcome. In the first tale, the adulterous stepmother tries to seduce her innocent stepson, and when he rejects her, she plots to murder him. In the second tale, the wife quite unjustly suspects that her sister-in-law is committing adultery with her husband. Then, (b) the wives enlist the aid of doctors and poison to take revenge. In the first tale, the wife attempts to poison her stepson, but her own child takes the drink by mistake and collapses in a deathlike sleep. In the second, the wife poisons not only her husband but also the doctor, his wife, and her own child, in order to acquire the entire inheritance of the family. The conclusions (c) to both tales are dramatically different. In the alleged "tragedy" (10.2) of the first story, the doctor who supplied the poison reveals the wife's plot and declares that he furnished only a sleeping potion. In the second tale the doctor cannot even save himself, and the evil wife's complete triumph is blocked only by the dying confession of the doctor's wife before the governor of the province.

Lucius' last master proves to be his kindest. One of Thiasus' servants, however, has contracted with a certain matron to let her sleep with the ass (10.21–22), and although Lucius is afraid of harming the woman and worried that he might be condemned to the wild beasts if he does so, the matron proves to be more than adequate as a partner: "Nor did I think," confesses Lucius, "that the mother of the Minotaur was so wrong to take delight in a mooing adulterer" (10.22). But Lucius' dalliance in fact earns him the very fate that he feared would happen. Because he has shown such unexpected prowess, his master, Thiasus, hires him out for a public show in the arena at Corinth: he will mate with the very woman whose exploits were the subject of the second tale in book 10. The magistrate, so Lucius reports, condemned her to the arena and the wild beasts simply because he could not think of anything worse to do with her (10.28). And now Lucius is about to become part of her punishment.

The "charming stories" of books 9 and 10 combine the arts of the stories and adventures in the two earlier sections we have divided for present purposes into "Thessaly and the House of Milo" (books 1–3) and "Charite, Psyche, and Charite Again" (books 4–8). That is, Lucius' "charming stories" entail constant retelling and reworking of similar plots in books 9 and 10, because they involve that same process of "revision" that we noticed in the complex of stories around Charite, the bandits, and Psyche. The instability and illusion that characterize the world of Fortune are perfectly reflected in the bewildering contradictions the tales act out. Secondly, the tales are minatory and threatening to Lucius himself once again, just as the earlier stories of Aristomenes and Thelyphron proved to be for Lucius. The fiction and entertainment of those tales, like the lifelike sculpture of Actaeon, proved to contain germs of reality for Lucius himself. Books 9 and 10 turn fiction into reality.

Lucius' journey ends in the arena at Corinth, where he sees a pantomime of the Judgment of Paris (10.29–32). The Judgment of Paris reminds him of other infamous decisions: the contest between Ajax and Odysseus for the arms of Achilles, the slanderous condemnation of the innocent Palamedes, and worst of all, the execution of Socrates by the Athenians (10.33). He stops with a typical piece of self-mockery: "But so that no one will take offense at my outbreak of indignation, and say to himself, 'See now, we've got to endure an ass philosophizing to us,' I'll go back to the story where I left off" (10.33). But the philosophizing ass has made an excellent point, and it is, not surprisingly, the point that a philosophically trained mind would turn to. The crucial failing in Paris, Psyche, Lucius, and all other characters in the novel lies in their judgment, their capacity to make the right decision; in short, in their perceptions of the realities of the world. They have been beguiled by the "earthly" or "common" Venus, about whom Plato wrote in his *Symposium* (180 D). Apuleius describes her in his *Apology*:

> But I will not enlarge here upon those lofty and divine teachings of Plato that few or none among the pious do not know, but about which all the

profane are ignorant: that Venus is a twin goddess, with each of the pair producing her own passion in different kinds of lovers. One of them is the earthly Venus, who is aroused by the ordinary passion of love to stimulate lust not only in human souls but even in those of cattle and wild beasts; she drives the enslaved bodies of creatures so stricken by her to immoderate and savage embraces.

(12)

To see the celestial Venus (Plato's Aphrodite Urania) we must wait until book 11.

The pantomime of Venus and Paris in the arena of Corinth is a devastating comment on the nature of human life and the possibility for happiness. A thoughtful reader will feel the need to go on to book 11, since only one character in the whole of books 1–10 has come to an unambiguously happy ending: Psyche.

BOOK 11: THE QUEEN OF HEAVEN

In fleeing Corinth, Lucius has turned at last from the domain of the "earthly" Venus, whom Apuleius describes in the *Apology*. Here is his account of Plato's Venus:

> Heavenly Venus is endowed with the purest love; she cares for human beings and but few of them. She strikes her followers with no stimulants or allurements to shameful desire. For her love is not a pleasing or lascivious one; on the contrary, it is plain and serious in its intrinsic beauty. And if her love ever graces lovely bodies, it wards off any slander against them.

(12)

This celestial Venus is like the transformed Venus at the end of the tale of Cupid and Psyche, who, it will be recalled, turns from being Psyche's worst enemy to a friend. She is also the new Fortune, in whom, as the priest of Isis says to Lucius after his retransformation into human form, one can rejoice: "You have been taken into the care of Fortune, but a Fortune

who sees, who illuminates even other gods, with the splendor of her light" (11.15).

Like Lucius himself, the evil Fortune of books 1–10 has been metamorphosed into something new. The final book of *The Golden Ass* reveals Apuleius' religious and philosophical dualism. In the course of his journeys, Lucius has moved between two poles: at one end stand the forces of magic and evil Fortune, and at the other stands Isis, the Queen of Heaven, who now delivers him from the world of the first ten books. The tone of book 11 is markedly different from the tone of the preceding ten books. Where all was indirect, deliberately misleading, or downright puzzling, there is now clarity, joy, and light. Isis tells Lucius and us the real significance of the asinine form:

> At once, then, when the crowd has been pushed aside, join the procession and trust in my good will; and when you draw near as though to kiss the hand of the priest, gently pluck the roses, and free yourself at once from the hide of that beast that I have so long loathed.

(11.6)

The beast so long detested by Isis is the demon god Typhon (or Seth), who had murdered Isis' brother-consort, the god Osiris. We thus learn only now the true significance of Lucius' metamorphosis into an ass: he was in effect ensnared by the black magic of witches, Typhon, Fortune, and all else opposed to the forces of good. To be delivered from that form is, in short, to be delivered from a symbol of Typhon and Fortune.

Lucius addresses Isis as Queen of Heaven, and as the name *Regina Caeli* itself would suggest, his fervor is near to what the Christians would later feel for Mary. His prayers to Isis (11.2, 11.25), together with his threefold initiation into the cults of Isis at Corinth and Rome and the cult of Osiris, and the genuinely sincere evangelical tone of the whole book, are the most extensive and powerful account of conversion in pagan literature. Book 11 is near in spirit and tone to the *Confessions* of Augustine, Apuleius' fellow African.

Here is Lucius' prayer to Isis:

> You, holy and perpetual savior of the human race, ever generous in your care of mortals, you bestow the sweet affection of a mother on the misfortunes of wretched people. Nor does a day or night nor even a brief moment pass without your kindnesses. . . .
>
> (11.25)

Here is Augustine:

> O Lord, I am your servant, I am your servant and the son of your handmaid. You have broken my bonds; I will sacrifice to you the sacrifice of praise. Let my heart and my tongue praise you, let all my bones say, "Lord who is like unto you?" Let them speak, and answer me and say to my soul: "I am your salvation."
>
> (*Confessions* 9.1)

The tone of book 11 is commonly taken to be so markedly different from the rest of *The Golden Ass* that it has come to acquire a separate life of its own, as the "Isis Book." But this book, like those containing the tale of Cupid and Psyche, is an integral part of Apuleius' novel of transformations and by no means a detachable monograph about religious experience. A closer look at the final chapters of book 11 reveals far more than religious exercises at work.

Lucius tells how a certain priest of Osiris named Asinius Marcellus came to aid him in his induction into the mysteries of Osiris. Asinius' name, as Lucius remarks, is not without some reference to his own transformation into an ass *(asinus)* (11.27). Asinius tells Lucius that on the night before, as he was placing chaplets on the statue of Osiris,

> he dreamed that he had also heard from the mouth of the god through which Osiris pronounces the fate of all individuals that a man from Madauros would be sent to him, and that even though this man was quite poor, he must at once teach him the sacraments; for by the god's providence glory would come to that man for his

religious zeal and a grand reward for Asinius himself.

(11.27)

The clear perspective of truth in book 11 is as subject to Apuleius' art as any other part of the novel. From Apuleius' report of Lucius' report of Asinius' report of what Osiris said to Asinius—a report at *fourth* hand, exactly like the narrative technique of Plato's *Symposium*—we learn that the person who is to be admitted to Osiris' mysteries is from Apuleius' native city. Does this mean that Lucius has really become Apuleius himself? No clear answer is possible, but the kind of career and rewards that Lucius says he will enjoy come very close to sounding like what Apuleius himself said he experienced in his *Florida* and *Apology*. For Lucius' new life is not purely ascetic, as he says he learned from no less a god than Osiris himself:

> Finally, after only a few days had passed, the god Osiris, greater god of the great gods and highest god of the greater gods and greatest god of the highest gods and ruler of the greatest gods, not now transforming himself into some other figure but addressing me in his own person and divine words, seemed in my sleep to say that I should at once be famous for pleading causes in the forum and that I should not fear unduly the slanders of the malevolent, to which my hard-won learning had rendered me so liable.
>
> (11.30)

Apuleius has remained a trickster to the end. Lucius reports that Osiris appeared to him not transformed into another shape *(non in alienam quempiam personam reformatus)*, in the language of the prologue, not as one of the *figurae in alias imagines conversae* ("shapes turned into other appearances"). Yet this clear vision only comes to him (and his reader) in a dream. Is it any more substantial than the dream of Asinius Marcellus? In *The City of God*, St. Augustine says that Apuleius may well have written *The Golden Ass* about himself, as if he had experienced all of Lucius' adventures (18.18). The suggestive yet enigmatic breaks in the fabric of fiction at the end of the novel more than justify Augustine's suspicions.

Book 11 solves at least one puzzle. The true significance of the old woman's tale of the reunion of Cupid and Psyche and the birth of Voluptas or Joy is now clear. By joining with the divine, in the manifestation first of Isis and then Osiris, Lucius has discovered true joy at last. As he describes his initiation into the mysteries, he warns his readers against that same curiosity to which he was prey throughout his journeys: "Perhaps, zealous reader, you would like to know what was then said and done. I would tell you were it permitted me to tell you; you would know if it were permitted you to hear. But both your ears and my tongue would suffer equally for that rash curiosity" (11.23). He goes on to tell us of his descent into Hades, a journey prefigured, we now realize, by the descent of Psyche in her last and most difficult labor for Venus (6.16–21). Lucius then declares that we cannot understand what we have just heard: "Behold, I have told you things which, even though you have heard them, you must nonetheless not know" (11.23). So much for clarity, even in this clearest of books. In the end, the narrator of book 11 turns out to be as enigmatic as the narrator of the prologue. Lucius (or the man from Madauros) is as elusive as the mysteries he describes. His tale ends as it begins, with riddles and jokes played on the reader.

Although book 11 is often treated as a great source book in the history of religions, it is as infected with wit and deceptive comedy as any other part of *The Golden Ass*. Books 1–10 promise us an "entertainment," but everywhere there is a deeper meaning than Lucius allows. In the same way, as readers reach the end of what may seem to be a surprisingly religious conclusion to the novel, they must realize that this allegedly sincere religious experience is shaped by the same writer of fiction as the first ten books; only now comedy and irony ripple beneath the surface of what professes to be a deeply serious religious document.

CONCLUSION: APULEIUS AS PHILOSOPHER AND NOVELIST

Like most writers who succeed in writing one great book, Apuleius left works that easily divide into that one masterpiece and such minor writings as survive the arbitrary transmission to which every author in the ancient world was subject. His lesser-known works include treatises that break down the complexities of Greek philosophy (chiefly Plato) into easily digestible bits. An untutored person could follow them and learn something of profit without undue exertion. *On the God of Socrates* is a discourse about the *daimonion* or "divine sign" by which Socrates claims to live in Plato's *Apology*. *On Plato and His Doctrine* explains some basic ideas from Plato, all apprehended at the literary level. This kind of writing once served a useful purpose: it was addressed to a special audience, one knowing Latin and the major authors of the Latin language, but evidently with little knowledge of Greek. Somewhat like the philosophical works of Cicero, albeit on a notably more modest level, Apuleius' philosophy is today of interest chiefly to historians of philosophy, specifically of the Middle Platonists in the period before Plotinus. Such digests are typical of literary efforts in the second century A.D.

Also typical of the times is an anthology of selections from his orations, the *Florida*, consisting of occasional speeches in which Apuleius can be seen acting out his role as transmitter of Greek wisdom to a Roman world evidently unacquainted with it. Here, for example, is an oratorical travelogue that begins with information for the untraveled natives of Roman Africa on the wonders of the Greek world:

Samos is an island in the Icarian Sea of moderate size; it is opposite Miletus, situated to the west and separated by only a small expanse of sea. Under easy sail one can go from one place to the other within two days; it is unfit for the plough, more fertile for olives, nor is it dug by the vinegrower or the gardener. Its entire nature as country lies in light hoeing and trees growing [*ruratio omnis in sarculo et surculo*] from which activity the island is more fructiferous than frugiferous [*magis fructuosa insula est quam frugifera*].

(*Florida* 15)

His *Apology* was delivered in either A.D. 158 or 159 in a court at Sabratha (near modern Tripoli, in Libya). We depend entirely on Apuleius' version of the story and pass over here any attempt to unravel the formidably complex issues. The speech in essence reveals that Apuleius was dedicated to a life at once religious and philosophical: "But we the family of Plato know nothing but what is festive and joyous, solemn and divine and heavenly. Why, in its zeal for loftiness, this school has explored regions higher than heaven itself and stood on the outer edge of the universe" (*Apology* 64).

If Apuleius the philosopher thought about any problem, it was the nature of reality and the means whereby we perceive it rightly or wrongly, and also how we can live in it. The novel transformed the philosopher Apuleius into the novelist who created Lucius. The ironic mode of the Socratic thereby became the dramatic irony of the novelist. The professed but fake ignorance of the Socratic became the literal ignorance of the hero Lucius, to whom anything and everything could happen.

Life as Apuleius portrays it in the *Apology* and in *The Golden Ass* is not only a journey of the body through time or space but also a journey of the mind and soul toward enlightenment. Good Platonist that he is, he much prefers the second kind of journey to the first. Readers who come to *The Golden Ass* for the first time thus confront an otherworldliness quite without parallel in ancient novelists like Petronius, Longus, Lucian, or Chariton. If Apuleius' profession of faith resembles anything, it is the faith of such early fathers of the Christian church as Tertullian (A.D. 160–240), the earliest

and most vociferous apologist for the new religion.

The Golden Ass has a happy ending, but it is not the happy ending so typical of the Greek novels. It is one contrived by a novelist with a pronounced philosophical detachment about the human comedy. This is one ancient novel— in fact, the only one—that attempts to make a universal statement. Of course, we do not read Apuleius today for all the reasons he and his ancient readers mention; for example, that he was from Madauros, a flourishing city of Roman Africa, or that he was a "noble Platonist," in St. Augustine's phrase. We read him because of *The Golden Ass*, a work of prime importance to many later writers of fiction, like Boccaccio, Rabelais, the anonymous author of *Lazarillo de Tormes*, and Cervantes. In terms of the classical world, Lucius' Grecian tale is the domestic comedy of the Hellenistic romance raised to a universal statement through the religious and philosophical disposition of Apuleius. He had the power to do what every other ancient novelist could do and, as the tale of Cupid and Psyche and the final book about Lucius and Isis both show, considerably more besides.

Selected Bibliography

TEXTS

Apulée Apologie, Florides, edited by P. Vallette. 2nd ed. Paris, 1960.

Apulée. Opuscules Philosophiques, edited by J. Beaujeu. Paris, 1973.

Apulei Opera Quae Supersunt, edited by R. Helm. Vol. 1: *Metamorphoseon Libri 11*. 3rd ed. Leipzig, 1955. Vol. 2.1: *Apologia (De Magia)*. Rev. ed. Leipzig, 1959. Vol. 2.2: *Florida*. Leipzig, 1910.

De Philosophia Libri, edited by P. Thomas. Leipzig, 1908. Reprinted Stuttgart, 1970.

Metamorphoseon Libri 11, edited by C. Giarrantano and P. Frassinetti. 2nd ed. Turin, 1960.

Les Métamorphoses, edited by D. S. Robertson. 3 vols. Paris, 1940–1945. Translated and with an introduction by P. Vallette.

APULEIUS

TRANSLATIONS

Adlington, William, trans. *The Eleven Books of the Golden Asse.* London, 1566. Revised by Stephen Gaselee. London, 1915. Reprinted Cambridge, Mass., 1965. Loeb Classical Library.

Graves, Robert, trans. *The Golden Ass.* New York, 1952.

Lindsay, J., trans. *The Golden Ass of Apuleius.* New York, 1932. Best English translation currently available.

COMMENTARIES

Butler, H. E., and A. S. Owen *Apulei Apologia sive Pro se de Magia Liber.* Oxford, 1914.

Fernhout, J. M. H. *Ad Apulei Madaurensis Metamorphoseon Librum Quintum Commentarius Exegeticus.* Dissertation. Groningen, 1949.

Fredouille, J. C. *Apulée. Metamorphoses Livre 11.* Paris, 1975.

Grimal, Pierre. *Apulei Metamorphoseis 4.28–6.24.* Paris, 1963.

Hijmans, B. L., Jr.; R. T. van der Paardt; et al. *Apuleius Madaurensis, Metamorphoses, Book 4.1–27.* Groningen, 1977.

Hildebrand, G. F. *Lucii Apulei Opera Omnia.* Leipzig, 1842.

Jonge, B. J. de. *Ad Apulei Madaurensis Metamorphoseon Librum Secundum Commentarius Exegeticus.* Dissertation. Groningen, 1941.

Molt, M. *Ad Apulei Madaurensis Metamorphoseon Librum Primum Commentarius Exegeticus.* Groningen, 1938.

Scobie, Alexander. *Apuleius Metamorphoses (Asinus Aureus), 1.* Meisenheim am Glan, 1975.

INDEX

Oldfather, W. A.; H. V. Canter; and B. E. Perry. *Index Apuleianus.* Middletown, Conn., 1934

STUDIES IN LANGUAGE AND STYLE

Bernhard, B. *Der Stil des Apuleius von Madaura.* Stuttgart, 1927.

Calebat, L. *Sermo Cotidianus dans les "Métamorphoses" d'Apulée.* Caen, 1968.

Schober, E. *De Apulei "Metamorphoseon" compositione numerosa.* Dissertation. Halle, 1904.

STUDIES IN SOURCES AND COMPOSITION

Bianco, G. *La fonte greca delle "Metamorfosi" di Apuleio.* Brescia, 1971.

Fehling, D. *Amor und Pysche. Die Schöpfung des Apuleius und ihre Einwirkung auf das Märchen, eine Kritik der romantischen Märchentheorie.* Mainz and Wiesbaden, 1977.

Junghanns, P. *Die Erzählungstechnik von Apuleius' "Metamorphosen" und ihrer Vorlage. Philologus.* Supplement 24, Heft 1 (1932).

Lesky, A. "Apuleius von Madaura und Lukios von Patrai." *Hermes* 76:43–74 (1949).

Thiel, H. Van. *Der Eselsroman 1. Zetemata.* Heft 54.1. Munich, 1971.

BIOGRAPHICAL AND CRITICAL STUDIES

Binder, G., and R. Merkelbach. *Amor und Psyche.* Darmstadt, 1968.

Drake, G. "Candidus: A Unifying Theme in Apuleius' *Metamorphoses.*" *Classical Journal* 64:102–109 (1968–1969).

Haight, E. H. *Apuleius and His Influence.* New York, 1927.

Heine, R. *Untersuchungen zur Romanform des Apuleius von Madaura.* Dissertation. Göttingen, 1962.

Hijmans, B. L., Jr., and R. T. van der Paardt. *Aspects of Apuleius' "Golden Ass."* Groningen, 1978.

Neumann, E. *Amor and Psyche: The Psychic Development of the Feminine: A Commentary on the Tale by Apuleius.* New York, 1956.

Penwill, J. L. "Slavish Pleasures and Profitless Curiosity: Fall and Redemption in Apuleius' *Metamorphoses.*" *Ramus* 4:49–82 (1973).

Regen, F. *Apuleius Philosophus Platonicus.* Berlin and New York, 1971.

Riefstahl, H. *Der Roman des Apuleius: Ein Beitrag zur Romantheorie.* Frankfurt am Main, 1938.

Schlam, C. C. *Cupid and Psyche: Apuleius and the Monuments.* University Park, Pa., 1976.

———. "Platonica in the *Metamorphoses* of Apuleius." *Transactions and Proceedings of the American Philological Association* 101:477–487 (1970).

Scholes, R., and R. Kellogg. *The Nature of Narrative.* New York, 1966.

Tatum, J. *Apuleius and the "Golden Ass."* Ithaca, N.Y., and London, 1979.

———. "The Tales in Apuleius' *Metamorphoses.*"

Transactions and Proceedings of the American Philological Association 100:487–527 (1969).

Walsh, P. G. *The Roman Novel. The "Satyricon" of Petronius and the "Metamorphoses" of Apuleius.* Cambridge, 1970.

Wlosok, A. "Zur Einheit der 'Metamorphosen' des Apuleius." *Philologus* 113:68–84 (1969).

STUDIES OF OTHER ANCIENT NOVELISTS

Hägg, T. *Narrative Technique in Ancient Greek Romances.* Stockholm, 1971.

Heiserman, *The Novel Before the Novel.* Chicago, 1977.

Merkelbach, R. *Roman und Mysterium in der Antike.* Munich, 1962.

Perry, B. E. *The Ancient Romances. A Literary-Historical Account of their Origins.* Berkeley and Los Angeles, 1967.

Reardon, B. P. "The Greek Novel." *Phoenix* 23:291–309 (1969).

Sullivan, J. P. *The Satyricon of Petronius. A Literary Study.* London, 1968.

Trenkner, S. *The Greek Novella in the Classical Period.* Cambridge, 1958.

HISTORICAL, CULTURAL, AND SOCIAL BACKGROUND

Abt, A. *Die Apologie des Apuleius von Madaura und die antike.* Giessen, 1907.

Birley, A. *Marcus Aurelius.* London, 1966.

———. *Septimius Severus. The African Emperor.* New York, 1972.

Bowersock, G. W. *Greek Sophists in the Roman Empire.* Oxford, 1969.

Bonner, S. F. *Roman Declamation in the Late Republic and Early Empire.* Liverpool, 1949.

Brock, M. D. *Studies in Fronto and His Age.* Cambridge, 1911.

Broughton, T. R. S. *The Romanization of Africa Proconsularis.* Baltimore and London, 1929.

Champlin, Edward. *Fronto and Antonine Rome.* Cambridge, Mass., 1980.

Dillon, John. *The Middle Platonists.* Ithaca, N. Y., and London, 1977.

Kennedy, G. *The Art of Rhetoric in the Roman World.* Princeton, 1972.

Millar, Fergus. "The World of the *Golden Ass.*" *Journal of Roman Studies* 71:63–75 (1981).

Reardon, B. P. *Courants littéraires grecs des IIe et IIIe siècles après Jesus Christ.* Paris, 1971.

STUDIES OF ISIS AND THE ISIS CULT

Griffiths, J. G. *Apuleius of Madauros. The Isis Book.* Leiden, 1975.

Nock, A. D. *Conversion.* Oxford, 1933.

Plutarch's De Iside et Osiride, edited by J. G. Griffiths. University of Wales, 1970. Translation, introduction, and commentary.

Solmsen, F. *Isis Among the Greeks and Romans.* Cambridge, Mass., and London, 1979.

Wittman, W. *Das Isisbuch des Apuleius.* Stuttgart, 1938.

BIBLIOGRAPHIES

Molt, M. *Ad Apulei Madaurensis Metamorphoseon Librum Primum Commentarius Exegeticus.* Dissertation. Groningen, 1938.

Schlam, C. C. "The Scholarship on Apuleius since 1938." *The Classical World* 64:285–308 (1971).

JAMES TATUM

AMMIANUS MARCELLINUS

(*ca.* A.D. 330–*ca.* 395)

I

IN THE SUMMER of A.D. 363 a demoralized Roman army lay in camp below the city of Nisibis in northern Mesopotamia (modern Nisaybin, on the Syrian-Turkish border). The army also played an unwilling role as funeral cortège, for it escorted the body of its commander, the emperor Julian, who had led its disastrous invasion of Persia and been killed in a skirmish during its retreat. To add to its miseries, the army was compelled to watch while the Persian standard was run up on the citadel of Nisibis, the city evacuated by its inhabitants and occupied by a Persian garrison. The surrender of Nisibis, three other cities in Mesopotamia, fifteen fortified places, and five satrapies along the upper Tigris was the price exacted from Julian's successor, Jovian, for the safe departure of the Romans from Assyria.

Ammianus Marcellinus, at the age of thirty an almost exact contemporary of Julian's, was an officer in the army and witnessed the surrender of Nisibis, which he later described in his history in highly wrought emotional language (26.9.1–11). The Persian campaign of Julian forms the centerpiece of the books of his history that still survive—books 14–31, covering the history of Ammianus' active lifetime. In a brief epilogue, Ammianus notes that his work had begun with the reign of Nerva (31.16.9). If the entire period from A.D. 96 to 353 was described in the first thirteen books, the description was

evidently on a much smaller scale than what now survives. Irrespective of the lost books, however, Ammianus' work was the first major history of Rome written in Latin for almost three hundred years. That it was written by a Syrian Greek from Antioch lends the work a historiographical, and its author a sheer human, interest that, one may say without disparaging much excellent recent research, is not yet matched by any general appreciation of their qualities.

No one can measure what may be the most important facet of Ammianus' attitude toward the times in which he lived, the sense of disappointment that he and others of his mind felt at the failure and death of Julian the Apostate— a disappointment that may have become less acute but was hardly less profound when he was completing his history at Rome in or very near the year 390. Julian had turned against the Christian religion of his family, that of Constantine the Great, and in 361, on succeeding Constantine's son Constantius after a civil war that Constantius' death saved him from having to fight to a finish, devoted himself to reversing the policies of the house of Constantine and to a restoration of the traditional religious practices of the Roman Empire. The period after the death of Julian saw a reassertion of the links of the emperors with Christianity and the Christian church, a process much intensified by the aggressive legislation of Theodosius in the decade immediately preceding the completion of

Ammianus' history. The development of Ammianus' view of Julian and his reign, over years that saw his own advance into late middle age and the rejection by Julian's successors of all he stood for, is surely as important in the understanding of Ammianus Marcellinus as it is inaccessible to his student.

For the late Roman historian, Ammianus is inescapable. He is the central source for the political, diplomatic, and administrative history of his age, its frontier wars and provincial rebellions. He has much to say on the urban social life of the empire, especially of Antioch, his birthplace, and of Rome. He offers perceptive, circumstantial descriptions, often based on his own observation, of parts of the empire and its eastern neighbor extending from Babylonia to Mauretania, from Gaul to Kurdestan. He undoubtedly pays less attention than he should to the religious controversies that absorbed so many of the energies of his age, but even here on individual issues Ammianus can offer concise and often devastating judgments. He remarks, for instance, on the strain placed upon the imperial transport service by the bishops hurrying to the various church councils supported by the emperor Constantius (21.16.18); gives a refreshingly secular account of the character of Bishop Athanasius of Alexandria (15.7.7 ff.); explains the growth of the cult of martyrs (22.11.10); and describes the life-style of metropolitan bishops lording it in spectacular processions and eating dinners fit for kings—in contrast with the modest manners of provincial clergy, whose behavior commended them to "true lovers of the Divinity" (27.3.14–15). As this last reference implies, Ammianus was not indiscriminately hostile to the new religion. He defends the bishop of Bezabde, on the Tigris, unjustly suspected of betraying his city to the Persians in the siege of 360 (20.7.9).

Had Ammianus been a writer of the classical age, there would be a mountain of modern literature on a whole range of interesting (and many less interesting) subjects about him, from his view of the law of treason to his use of the participial gerund. But it is obvious, apart from his subject matter, that Ammianus could in no way have been a writer of the classical age. Gibbon, taking leave with regret of Ammianus as an "accurate and faithful guide," had nevertheless criticized in a footnote the "vices of his style, the disorder and perplexity of his narrative" (*Decline and Fall* 3.26.122, Bury ed.). This extreme judgment reflects above all the classicism of Gibbon's own tastes; it was with similar admiration for the literature of an earlier age that he praised the poet Claudian, who "soared above his feeble contemporaries and placed himself, after an interval of three hundred years, among the poets of ancient Rome" (3.30.284).

For Gibbon the greatest of Roman historians was Tacitus, the first who "applied the science of philosophy to the study of facts"; yet, for the German critic Ernst Stein, Tacitus was surpassed by Ammianus in his objectivity and in the breadth of his geographical sympathy—a judgment one can share without necessarily endorsing Stein's view that Ammianus was the greatest literary genius between Tacitus and Dante, unmatched in his capacity to stir the emotions. Possibly the most appreciative assessment of Ammianus' style is offered by Erich Auerbach, emphasizing above all the visual quality of Ammianus' writing, the sense of theatrical movement and color sometimes touching the grotesque that Auerbach saw as characteristic of late Roman society itself (*Mimesis*, pp. 50–76). These judgments would have thrilled the writer who, in occasional asides, allows himself to wonder whether he will ever have any readers and refers to the inadequacies of his talent to meet the challenge of his subject. I would add one facet of Ammianus' gifts that will strike the reader, his ability to seize the moment and present it in terms of dramatic vividness—as in the case of the general Marcellus, who, accused of failure to assist the caesar Julian when besieged at Sens, in Gaul, went to court and defended himself. He spoke, says Ammianus, with immense movements of his body that matched his turbulent and almost crazy temperament (*ita enim "cum motu quo-*

dam corporis loquebatur ingenti": 16.7.2; emphasis added).

In some ways Ammianus' standpoint is full of irony, as of a man living outside his time. He was born in about 330, after the conquest of the eastern empire by Constantine the Great and after the Council of Nicaea, the first attempt by an emperor to impose doctrinal unity on the Christian church, but an attempt that, as he grew up in the Greek east, Ammianus saw repeated many times. Writing at Rome in 390, he was living, still a believer in the old gods, under that "most Christian" of emperors, Theodosius I. The possible year of Ammianus' arrival at Rome, 384, also saw the arrival there from Carthage of the young Augustine. Converted in 386, while serving as public orator at Milan, to a life of Christian philosophy and asceticism, Augustine returned, before Ammianus' history was complete, to become a monk in north Africa and, before long, a bishop. In 385 a Dalmatian monk and former government official, Jerome, who had come to Rome after a spell in the Syrian wilderness not far from Ammianus' Antioch, sailed from Ostia for Bethlehem, having offended the ecclesiastical establishment by his outspokenness, by the excessively rigorous ascetic regime that he imposed on his religious protégées, and by his driving ambition. Jerome left on record, in a letter to one of these protégées, his conviction that he had been thought worthy "in the judgment of all" to succeed Damasus as bishop of Rome (Epistle 45.3). Damasus' own accession to the pontificate in 366 is described by Ammianus in two passages in book 27 of his history. It had been marred by riots in which no less than 137 corpses were left on the floor of one of the basilicas of Rome, and which were finally suppressed by the disciplinary action of the prefect of Rome, Vettius Agorius Praetextatus, a famous pagan senator (27.3.12–13; 9.9). Praetextatus' death in 384, inspiring remarkable public demonstrations of grief, was another event in this extraordinary decade of Roman history. It shortly followed the rejection by the emperor Valentinian II of the pagan senator Symmachus' petition for the restoration of the ancestral privileges recently taken from the Vestal Virgins and priestly colleges, and of the altar of Victory to the senate house. Symmachus' *Third Relatio*, in which he presented the case for the ancient cults of Rome, is not only a memorable document of paganism in its last days but a timeless assertion of the principles of the state religion of Rome.

It is not at all surprising that Ammianus should fail to mention such men as Augustine and Jerome, not so much for the obvious reason that their activities fell outside the terminal point of his history (Ammianus does allow himself in digressions and asides to mention events after 378), but for other reasons. Augustine, despite the recommendation by Symmachus that secured him the post of public orator at Milan, was only one of those gifted and ambitious literary men produced by the Roman world in such proliferation. Jerome's activities as patron and guide of a group of religious *dévotes* might have fueled Ammianus' outrage at what he would have seen as the unworthy eccentricities of Roman aristocrats. Yet Rome was a great city in which all sorts of interesting and disreputable activities might pass unnoticed, and Jerome was perhaps not sufficiently notorious to attract the interest of an outsider. This brings up another consideration: Ammianus was writing history in a specific and ancient tradition, a selective account of great events worthy of public note—wars, high politics, court intrigue, heroic deeds, and the fortunes of the Roman state, with such digressions as seemed necessary for their full illumination. The relations of Christian priests with their female admirers, the plotting of ecclesiastical advancement on the fringes of the papal court—these were no proper matters for authentic Roman history.

Ammianus' failure to mention Symmachus, great senator, orator, and literary grandee of his day, is more surprising. Ammianus does mention Symmachus' father, in an episode from which he does not emerge with credit. He was rumored—falsely, Ammianus believed—to have said during a shortage of wine that he would use the surplus produce from his estates to make concrete rather than sell it cheaply to the people (he was referring to a technique for the manufacture of a form of waterproof cement used in constructing pools). In retaliation, an enraged mob set fire to his fine house beyond the Tiber (27.3.4). Ammianus also records the elder Symmachus' dedication of a bridge at Rome, "to the great joy of the citizens" (27.3.3). As for the orator Symmachus, his consulship, in 391, falls just after the date of completion of Ammianus' history; the latest event that he anticipates beyond the range of his narrative is the consulship of Neoterius, which fell precisely in 390 (26.5.14), and other such references converge on the period just before that (21.10.6; 27.6.2; 27.11.2). Yet there were earlier opportunities. As senatorial ambassador to the imperial court in 369–370, Symmachus had delivered panegyrics to the emperor Valentinian and his sons, describing in them works of fortification also mentioned by Ammianus (28.2.1 ff.). He had been proconsul of Africa in 373 and by the mid-380's was the greatest orator of his day, prefect of Rome, and leader of the Senate. Ammianus must have known of Symmachus and could evidently have provided himself with an opportunity to mention him had he wished to do so.

Symmachus' absence from the history argues against the once common assumption that Ammianus, as a cultivated visitor to Rome, must have been a member of the "circle of Symmachus," a society of like-minded men interested in the culture, religion, and traditions of ancient Rome. The assumption was partly based on the correspondence of Symmachus, a collection of letters addressed to about 150 named correspondents, ranging widely from members of his own family and senatorial colleagues to politicians, bureaucrats, generals, even a bishop (Ambrose of Milan). Most of the letters are "business" correspondence—the exchange of favors of patronage—or exchanges of courtesy. Although there are letters on literary subjects and matters to do with the pagan cults of Rome, the extrapolation from the letters of a

"circle" of men of similar religious and literary tastes to which Ammianus must have belonged is unjustified, a consequence in part of the historian's tendency to make every aspect of the relations within a society conform to what happens to be best known about it. Further, the only letter in Symmachus' correspondence thought to be addressed to Ammianus has been cogently argued by Alan Cameron in the *Journal of Roman Studies* to have been written to someone else. The letter in question (9.110) is addressed to an anonymous senatorial correspondent and contains a simple explanation of a Greek expression—hardly apt if Symmachus were actually writing to a Greek. Nor is there any likelihood at all that Ammianus ever became a senator.

If Ammianus' active career shows him as an energetic, rather sociable figure with strong personal commitments to other individuals, as a historian he begins to appear independent and isolated, not bound to any particular influential figure or group of his time. Indeed, his own account of the typical reception of a visitor to Rome by its great families implies that he was rejected, not accepted, by high society there (14.6.12–13). It is no less difficult to assess his impact as a historian upon his contemporaries and on posterity. There is, however, one precious item provided by the aged Libanius, a famous rhetorician from Ammianus' own city of Antioch. A letter from Libanius, addressed to a compatriot named Marcellinus, reports the writer's pleasure at hearing of the success won by his historical work in recitations at Rome. Though the letter was written late in 392, the recitations in question probably took place two or three years earlier. In 389 the emperor Theodosius came to Rome on one of the rare state visits then made by the emperors to the ancient capital, before returning to the East in 391—an opportunity surely not to be missed by an ambitious historian looking for an appreciative public. The men returning from Rome to Antioch who announced Ammianus' success to Libanius can plausibly be seen as courtiers of

Theodosius returning from the West, with news of events and people seen there.

After Libanius, there is little evidence of the reception enjoyed by Ammianus' history. In the early sixth century the grammarian Priscian, writing at Constantinople, cites Ammianus for a linguistic usage. The reference says something for the diffusion of Ammianus' text in early Byzantine Latin-speaking circles. On the other hand, the usage in question (*indultum* written for *indulsum*) is not particularly striking; and the fact that Priscian's example is taken from book 14, the first surviving book of the history, might suggest that the first thirteen books were already lost by the time of Priscian. It would be pleasant to imagine that Ammianus was as successful as he had hoped to be in seeking admirers among the Latin-speaking courtiers of Theodosius on the point of their return to the East; but if the oldest manuscript, a ninth-century text originally from the monastery of Fulda, in Germany, represents a western tradition of descent, then the loss here, too, of the first thirteen books suggests that the text of Ammianus was transmitted to the East only during the fifth or early sixth century.

II

In a brief epilogue, concluding his history with the aftermath of the battle of Hadrianople and death of Valens in 378, Ammianus entrusts its continuation to historians of the new generation, men with youth and learning on their side: but, if they do attempt it, warns Ammianus, they must strive to achieve the "higher style" appropriate for the history of the present age. As Gibbon sharply noted, the rising generation was not disposed to accept the challenge, and Ammianus, the first great Latin historian of the Roman Empire since Tacitus, is also the last.

Ammianus had written, he explains in the epilogue, as "a former soldier and a Greek" (*ut miles quondam et Graecus:* 31.16.9). Now, that he meant this in a concessive sense—"although a soldier and a Greek"—is suggested by his accompanying remark that he had written "as well as my talents allowed" (*pro virium explicavi mensura*). We need not assume that Ammianus was really so diffident about his gifts; his modesty belongs with those other phrases, in which he refers to the "mediocrity" of his talent (16.1.2), allows himself to question whether he will ever have many readers (14.6.2), and refers to his own "humble opinion" (*iudicioli nostri*) in passing judgment (27.11.1). They are expressions of formal or rhetorical diffidence; yet Ammianus is inviting his readers to feel surprise that a "soldier" and a "Greek" should write history, and it is worth asking briefly why this should be so.

The first part of Ammianus' expression is not so difficult to understand. Even the superior soldiers in Ammianus' history are not notable for their literary or emotional sophistication. Often of rustic, if not barbarian background and culture, they sometimes rise, like one of their number, Agilo, "by immoderate leaps" to high commands, in which they conduct themselves with insensitive brutality (20.2.5). Ammianus' own patron, Ursicinus, was, in the historian's opinion, a loyal and energetic servant of the emperors. Yet he, too, caught up in the subtleties of treason trials at Antioch, is described as a plain, straightforward figure, "warlike, always a soldier and a leader of men" (*bellicosus sane milesque semper et militum ductor*), out of his depth in courtroom intrigues (14.9.1). These were the most able of their class; it is not impossible, of course, but it would be paradoxical to find such a soldier writing history.

Ammianus' admission that he wrote as a Greek is in one sense easier to interpret, if he meant to refer to his choice of the Latin language in which to write history. For an easterner in the Roman Empire to choose Latin as a literary medium is indeed cause for surprise. Ammianus' example, ignored by historians, was followed by a poetic successor of the "rising generation," Claudian of Alexandria; more typical is Ammianus' compatriot, Libanius, who never learned but resisted Latin, seeing (and fearing) it as the language of bureaucrats and lawyers, threatening outsiders in Libanius' world of Greek literary culture.

At the same time, the combination *miles et Graecus*, considered more closely, does involve certain definite advantages. Ammianus was far from being an ordinary soldier of the ranks, stolidly tramping about the empire and standing shoulder to shoulder in the line of battle. As a *protector domesticus*, he belonged to an officer elite. Promotion to the ranks of *protector* involved the ceremony of *adoratio purpurae*, conceded to those favored officials "thought worthy," as one law in the *Codex Theodosianus* of A.D. 387 put it, "to touch Our purple (6.24.4)." His position with Ursicinus is an example of the arrangement known as *deputatio*, by which a *protector* might be assigned by the emperor to serve under a general in the field. Ammianus' attachment to Ursicinus and later to Julian's Persian campaign means that he was on hand for some of the most significant events of the day; while his dashing and adventurous personal exploits under Ursicinus' command mark him as very unlike a regular soldier of the ranks.

Ammianus' age when he first appears in the history, already a *protector domesticus* in 354 (14.9.1), also marks him as out of the ordinary. The few parallel cases hardly amount to proof but rather suggest that, for a man to be *protector domesticus*, as Ammianus was, at the age of twenty-five or less, he must enjoy certain initial advantages. One such youthful officer was Jovian (made emperor in 364), who owed to his father's virtues his own modest claim for consideration (25.5.4). He was the son of Varronianus, a well-known general. As head of the corps of *protectores* at thirty-three "he can hardly," as A. H. M. Jones put it, "have had time to serve in the ranks" (*The Later Roman Empire*, vol. 2, p. 638).

This introduces the second part of Ammianus' self-identification, *ut miles . . . et Graecus*. Ammianus' home city of Antioch was in the fourth century not only a great Greek metropolis but also the main Roman administrative center of the East. Especially under Constantius, it was an imperial residence and the focal point of imperial campaigns against the Persians (as in Julian's campaign of 363). Antioch was the seat of the praetorian prefecture and of the *magister militum* (master of the soldiery) of the East. A man of the generation of Ammianus' father, the praetorian prefect Musonianus, was there in the late 350's; in days gone by he had helped Constantine in his "inquiries" into the heretical sect of the Manichees and now initiated negotiations with the Persians on behalf of Constantius. According to Ammianus, Musonianus was "distinguished for his eloquence in both languages"—that is, in Latin and Greek (15.13.1).

To combine these hints: if Ammianus owed his early entry into the ranks of *protector domesticus* to family influence (perhaps a father who knew Ursicinus), then his relationship to the imperial administration began with the previous generation and would have brought early contact with Latin-speaking government circles at Antioch. It seems at least possible that Ammianus' knowledge of Latin, far from being acquired in adult years or even during his eighteen-month stay in Gaul between 355 and 357, derives from his family background and childhood upbringing.

"Ammianus the Greek" thus turns out to be as deceptively simple a definition as "Ammianus the soldier." Now, the history itself must be understood in terms of an alliance of the two elements, the Greek and the Latin. To take the Greek first: Ammianus sometimes cites Greek words, particularly in scientific digressions, referring to them as words of his own language. "Horizons," he writes in one passage, "as we call them" (18.6.22); "*syringes*"—cavities in the earth in which earthquakes are said to originate—"as we call them in Greek" (17.7.11); and there are several other such references (22.8.33; 25.2.5, for example). Of course, the affinity goes much deeper than this, and one passage, in which Ammianus mentions his source for a digression on the origins of Gaul, is particularly telling. This was a matter, says Ammianus, left incomplete by other writers until it was taken up by Timagenes, *et diligentia Graecus et lingua* ("in diligence and in language a Greek": 15.9.2).

In the same passage, Ammianus justifies his digression. He wishes to avoid the situation of a sailor who finds that he has to make running repairs in a storm when he could have prepared himself at leisure and in safety. The digression itself goes far beyond what is needed to make military and geographical sense of the Gallic campaigns of Julian, extending as it does to the mythological origins and early history of Gaul. In its expansiveness it resembles the still longer digression with which Ammianus introduces the Persian campaign of Julian (23.6.1–88, concluding with a comparison between the pearls produced by Persia and by Britain). Ammianus admits at the outset of this digression that, while his text might seem lengthy (*prolixior*), this will be in the interests of "complete knowledge" (*ad scientiam proficiet plenam*: 23.6.1). Writers on Gaul before the Greek Timagenes had left "incomplete knowledge" (*notitiam . . . semiplenam*: 15.9.2).

There is nothing more "Greek" in Ammianus' conception than his use of digressions on this scale, and nothing more Greek (or Herodotean) than his notion of the "complete knowledge" required to explain a historical narrative. *Scientia plena* might be taken as Ammianus' motto: he means by it the full cultural, geographical, and historical context of the events described. It was not what Ammianus' Latin contemporaries, the epitomizing historians Aurelius Victor, Eutropius, and Festus, were doing; in fact, no Latin Roman historian had done it for centuries.

Similarly, the "Roman" elements in Ammianus' writing come out on different levels. There is a single linguistic allusion to set against those mentioned above, in which Ammianus refers to the city of Pessinus as deriving its name from a Greek word meaning "to fall," which he then translates to Latin: *quod "cadere" nos dicimus* (22.9.6); and he quite often refers to Greek words in a way that implies no personal interest (21.1.8; 26.1.8; 22.15.14). Of far more positive significance is a reference to the annexation of the province of Arabia, which according to Ammianus was "compelled" by the emperor Trajan to obey "our" laws (*obtemperare legibus nostris Traianus compulit imperator*: 14.8.13). The identification of Ammianus the Greek with the ideals of Roman imperialism could not have been more explicit, or less self-conscious.

Ammianus' commitment to Roman attitudes is persistent and obvious to his reader, particularly in his admiration of Rome itself, "which will live as long as there are men" (14.6.3). His denunciations of the debased behavior of some citizens of Rome, two of his best-known passages, spring from his outrage that the ancient assemblies of the eternal city are so betrayed by a minority of men "who do not reflect where they were born" (14.6.7). The description preceding this of the process by which Rome, growing from infancy to youth and maturity and now in serene old age, has secured her eternity by conveying her inheritance to the caesars, "as to her children," is not only from the point of view of Ammianus' political attitudes one of the most interesting passages in the history; it is also profoundly Roman (14.6.5).

Also worth noting is Ammianus' "Romanization" of Julian's Persian campaign, from the emperor's speech at the outset (23.5.16–23) to its final, tragic conclusion. The campaign is attended by hostile omens, interpreted by haruspices, the priests who divined the future in the entrails of sacrificed animals and birds. The presence of haruspices was of course Julian's doing, for all that he actually preferred the advice of the Greek philosophers of whom Ammianus was critical. Ammianus' heavy emphasis on the ominous aspects of the campaign, as well as on Julian's rejection of the advice of the haruspices and others who opposed the campaign (23.5.4), is his own, however, as is his measurement of Julian's personal heroism in the campaign by reference to exemplary Roman deeds of which the emperor "had read"

(23.12.16–17; see also 3.5). This aspect of Ammianus' account of the campaign is all the more striking since, as is now widely agreed, he used a Greek source, probably the history of Eunapius, at least to clear up certain details in his narrative of the campaign.

III

If the Greek and the Roman elements in Ammianus provide the cultural framework of his writing, it is still necessary to ask the more fundamental questions: Why did Ammianus take to writing history at all? And why did he write history on the scale and in the manner in which he chose to do it?

The first impulse was surely provided by his personal experiences, through which his narrative moves from the East and Antioch to Milan, on for nearly two years (355–357) to Gaul, and then back to the eastern frontier, all under the command of the general Ursicinus (books 14–19). Ammianus' loyalty to Ursicinus is rightly seen as influencing his view of the emperor Constantius II, under whom Ursicinus performed his services and by whom he was finally cashiered for his outspoken criticism after the capture of Amida in 359 (20.2.1–5). Summoned to Antioch to supervise the treason trials conducted there by Constantius' deputy, the caesar Gallus, Ursicinus was himself suspected of involvement in conspiracy and, after Gallus' dismissal and execution (14.11.1–34), was called to the western court of Constantius and there held in suspense while his enemies plotted against him and his fate hung in the balance (15.2.1–6). The opportunity for Ursicinus to redeem his reputation came in 355 with a usurpation at Cologne, where a Frankish general, Silvanus, was proclaimed emperor. Ursicinus, with Ammianus on his selected staff of ten *protectores*, was sent to suppress Silvanus, which he accomplished through hired assassins after initial displays of friendship and sympathy. Ammianus describes these events with a matter-of-fact unconcern for the morality of the methods used by Ursicinus. As E. A.

Thompson points out (*The Historical Work of Ammianus Marcellinus*, pp. 45, 52), most of his commentators have been far more squeamish—"sordid," "underhand," and "dishonorable" are some of the words used—but all agree on the vividness with which Ammianus expresses the uncertainty in the minds of the party as they set out, none of them expecting to return (15.5.23).

Ursicinus stayed in Gaul while Julian was appointed caesar by Constantius and won his first victories (15.8–16.7); but by the time of the battle of Strasbourg, in which the Alamannic confederation of King Chonodomarius was defeated by Julian (16.12.1–70), he had already been transferred to the eastern front to meet the threat of Persian invasion. The Persian invasion of 359 and the siege of Amida, with which it culminated, show Ammianus' involvement at its most circumstantial, as he is pursued by Persians, fights them on the Tigris banks, and escapes into Amida with the refugees crowding into the city (18.7–9). Ammianus' description of his entry into Amida, with the bodies so tightly crammed together that dead men had no room to fall and were carried along upright, while the defensive artillery thundered away on the walls, is one of the most memorably vivid passages in all of Roman history (18.8.11–14). His escape from Amida at the point of its collapse and his return to Antioch bring to an end this period of intense involvement in the events of his times (19.8.5–12).

These are fascinating books that contain descriptive and narrative writing of a very high order. But they are unusual in their concentration on Ammianus himself and his experiences. It is a narrowing of view that in some ways can prove unreliable. Ammianus saw events through his own eyes and those of a superior resentful of his treatment by Constantius. During most of the events described, Constantius was very far away, needing to maintain his position in the East until he could go there himself. His instructions to Sabinianus, the general of the eastern field armies, were to avoid a major engagement with the Persians and to preserve his troops. To the impatient Ursicinus, this policy looked like contemptible inactivity, and Ammianus reflects this attitude as he describes Sabinianus' pious slumbers by the "tombs," or martyrs' graves, of Edessa (18.7.7); this is one of Ammianus' more indirect, though possibly one of his most biting, references to Christianity. Yet Ursicinus' opinion, reported by Ammianus, that Sabinianus should have sent "all his light-armed troops" to the relief of Amida (19.3.1) seems ludicrous in relation to the colossal forces that Sapor loosed against the place, as Ammianus himself describes in brilliantly evocative language (19.1.2 ff.).

Ammianus' criticism of Constantius and Sabinianus is on this occasion personal and ill-balanced. As for the account of his own involvement, it sometimes develops into personal memoir that seems out of place amid the implied claims of a Roman history covering two-and-a-half centuries. The crucial transition in Ammianus' development as a historian is provided by the second of the two basic influences in his evolution, the figure of Julian the Apostate.

That Julian was at the center of Ammianus' historical conception is easy to show, not from anything so subjective as the attitudes that he expresses, but from the rhetorical framework and the devices employed in presenting him. Describing the elevation of Julian to junior emperor in 355, Ammianus breaks into verse to evoke the greater theme now in store, in a reference to Vergil's introduction of the wars fought by Aeneas after the landing of the Trojans in Italy: *maius opus moveo, maiorque mihi nascitur ordo* ("a greater theme I now begin, a greater order lies before me": 15.9.1; compare *Aeneid* 7.44). Julian himself, a few sentences earlier, quotes Homer in a prophetic allusion to "death in the purple, and the mastery of fate" (15.8.17; compare *Iliad* 5.83).

Julian's arrival at Vienne inspires a prophecy from a blind old woman who, when told that it is Julianus Caesar who enters the city, declares that "this man will restore the temples of the gods" (15.8.22). Then follows Ammianus'

long digression, mentioned earlier, on the history, geography, and culture of the Gallic provinces. The effect is to enlarge the scale of treatment, and the actual exploits of Julian are introduced with the assertion that what Ammianus writes will be more like panegyric than history, though based on the best evidence. The narrative will tax to the full the writer's modest talents, which may be insufficient: *instrumenta omnia mediocris ingenii, si suffecerint, commoturus* (16.1.2).

To pass immediately to the end of Ammianus' account of Julian, his obituary (25.4.1–27) has a structure unlike that of any of his other obituaries, in which virtues and shortcomings are contrasted, usually with rhetorical illustration that has the effect of making the latter appear more substantial than they really are; this is particularly noticeable in the obituary of Constantius (21.16.1–21), where after seven sections on the virtues, the vices are expanded to eleven sections, largely by the help of rhetorical allusions to historical precedents for Constantius' cruelty, and to philosophers' opinions. Julian's obituary is constructed around the four cardinal virtues of the philosophers (*sapientes*): *temperantia* (moderation), *prudentia* (wisdom), *iustitia* (justice), *fortitudo* (courage); with the addition of four others: *scientia rei militaris* (knowledge of the art of war), *auctoritas* (authority), *felicitas* (good fortune), *liberalitas* (liberality). With this introduction, the obituary cannot be other than a panegyric. The structure of the section in praise of Julian follows this pattern, each virtue being illustrated with examples. The shortcomings, briefly listed, follow in six short sections, with the addition of a further five in rather unpersuasive support against its critics of Julian's Persian campaign.

These two elements, personal memoir and admiration for Julian, are in their respective ways fundamental in considering the broader of two ways of putting the question, Why did Ammianus turn to the writing of history? Ammianus' own experiences were linked to the course of Roman history at large, not only by their intrinsic importance but through the figure of Julian. The more precise question of why Ammianus chose the particular form of writing that he did—a large-scale history, in Latin, reaching back to the reign of Nerva—remains.

In considering this question, it is important to realize that, despite initial impressions, Ammianus' personal experiences and the figure of Julian do not coincide very closely. Julian, of course, dominates a large part of the surviving books. Introduced as caesar at the end of book 15 in the passage with the Vergilian echo mentioned above, he is throughout the next ten books a leading protagonist and a foil to Constantius. Books 22–25, after the death of Constantius, are dominated by the immense and ultimately tragic momentum of the Persian campaign.

Yet for much of this time Ammianus knew little of Julian at close hand. He was in Gaul for the first phase of Julian's regime as caesar but not for its climax, the battle of Strasbourg; for by then he and Ursicinus had been recalled to Sirmium and transferred to the eastern frontier (16.10.21). The next phase, that of Ammianus' most intense personal involvement in events, saw him fighting on Constantius' behalf when the emperor's relations with Julian were becoming increasingly strained.

Between 360 and 363, Ammianus, like Ursicinus, was out of the public eye. It has been argued that he was given some minor administrative duties, but it seems equally probable that he simply lapsed from service and lived quietly at Antioch as a "nonassigned officer." By the time of Julian's arrival at Antioch in late 362, he and his future historian had been separated for more than five years by many provinces and, at times, by the entire width of the Roman world. The separation may indeed have lasted even longer, if it is a correct inference that Ammianus joined the Persian campaign at Circesium, on the Euphrates. It is shortly after the departure of the army from there that Ammianus begins again to speak in the first person (23.5.7).

Except for the first period of Julian's regime as caesar, Ammianus' personal experiences and the figure of Julian do not, therefore, coincide very closely. Nor was Ammianus' relationship with Julian one of simple hero worship, whether at close hand or from a distance. He criticizes Julian on a number of fundamental issues, in observations made in the text as the occasion arose and repeated in his obituary of the emperor (25.4.16–21).

In some respects, the shortcomings are personal and trivial: Julian talked too much and was excessively fond of popularity, affecting sometimes to speak with unworthy men. In this, Julian was setting himself against the pomp and ceremony of the imperial office sustained by the emperors of the fourth century and approved by Ammianus in Constantius. Further, Julian inclined to superstition in his religious observances and indulged so lavishly in animal sacrifices that, had he returned victorious from the Persian campaign, cattle would have become extinct (25.4.17)! Under Julian, continues Ammianus, Justice herself descended from heaven; although there were occasions when Julian behaved arbitrarily, he was then "unlike himself." Ammianus notes elsewhere that Julian sometimes asked those appearing in courts of law what their religious beliefs were (22.10.2). This was untimely (*intempestivus*).

In two respects in particular Ammianus offers severe criticism of Julian's policies. He issued a law forbidding professors of rhetoric and literature to practice unless they returned to the worship of the old gods. This, says Ammianus, was inhuman (*inclemens*), adding in an earlier, still stronger, passage, that Julian's action should be "buried in perennial silence" (*obruendum perenni silentio*: 22.10.7). Equally intolerable was Julian's overstrict enforcement of membership in city councils, with the attendant financial and administrative burdens, on foreigners (*peregrini*) and men who possessed valid exemptions. Ammianus makes this criticism more than once in his text (21.12.23; 22.9.8), adding as a general comment that under Julian no curial candidate, once sought by his council, was able to escape, whether on grounds of origin, privilege, or imperial service (22.9.12).

It is difficult to be sure whether in making these criticisms Ammianus really appreciated how fundamental they are. In effect they undermine the entire basis of Julian's attempt to restore traditional beliefs and practices. His policy involved the renewal of the civic life and traditional culture as well as the religious integrity of the Roman Empire, and the restoration of the imperial office from the suspicious despotism that it had become under Constantius to something more like the "civil magistracy" one could at least pretend it to have been in the days of Marcus Aurelius. Despite his admiration, therefore, Ammianus' view of Julian is marked by quite fundamental criticisms and ambiguities that make his final judgment extremely difficult to determine. Ammianus' criticisms are precise in matters crucial to Julian's policies and aims, and they can only show that in the historian's final opinion Julian's behavior as emperor was at least badly flawed. But he had seen the early regime of Julian at close quarters in Gaul, from Julian's arrival there at the end of 355 to Ammianus' own departure in 357. It was this early phase that Ammianus thought especially noteworthy, especially since it was the most unexpected (16.1.5); in this section, too, Ammianus records his most unreserved praise of Julian's abilities as ruler (16.5.1–17).

Ammianus' personal experiences and the figure of Julian may therefore be seen to interrelate on two levels. First, in relation to Ammianus' personal experiences (which essentially began with the suppression of Silvanus and the early regime of Julian in Gaul) the person and activities of Julian established these as part of a much broader historical context, broader even than the Persian campaign of 359 and the siege and capture of Amida. This was the young man who would "restore the temples of the gods," put the barbarians to flight, and restore old standards of modesty and integrity to the imperial office and to imperial government. This sense of the convergence of Ammianus' experiences and the broad stream of Roman history was confirmed, for all its tragic

outcome, by the Persian campaign. Second, on a more general level, the reign of Julian developed disconcertingly. Julian's view of the nature of the imperial office, his culture (religious and literary), his civic and military policies—all this challenged comparison with Julian's predecessors, the Christian emperors of the fourth century; with Diocletian and the tetrarchs; and, still more distantly, with Julian's admired model, the philosopher-emperor Marcus Aurelius. At the opening of his account of Julian's regime as caesar, which Ammianus says will resemble panegyric rather than authentic history, the historian compares him to various emperors of the past. In prudence he was a second Titus, in martial glory he was like Trajan, in clemency he resembled Antoninus Pius. In the pursuit of correct and true reason, he was the counterpart of Marcus Aurelius, after whom he modeled his actions and character: *ad cuius aemulationem actus suos effingebat et mores* (16.1.4).

To conceive of Ammianus' admiration of Julian as the link between his own experiences and the broader course of Roman history has the advantage that it takes criticisms of Julian as much into account as praise; both embody those respects in which Julian challenged comparison with the emperors of earlier times, a challenge that stood, whether or not Julian succeeded. This conception also fixes Ammianus' original inspiration to write history in his experience of contemporary events, an emphasis that seems to be required by the actual content of the history as we have it. It remains to define Ammianus' evolution as a historian in terms of the historiographical and literary traditions that may have influenced him, and this can best begin with Ammianus' own description of his methods and procedure as a historian.

IV

In a preface to book 15 of the history, Ammianus announces his method for the part to follow and summarizes that of recent books. In them he has narrated those events the truth of which he could discover, either being of an age to witness them himself or by closely questioning (*perplexe interrogando*) those who had taken part. The rest he will set out with as much care as his ability permits, not being deterred by critics who may object to the length of his work. Brevity, writes Ammianus, is a laudable virtue only when it avoids untimely delays without detracting from the knowledge of what is done (15.1.1).

The preface certainly describes Ammianus' historical method as far back as the first half of the reign of Constantius (337–353). There is no change of scale between books 14 and 15, and his back-references in these books, as to the battle of Singara in 348 (18.5.7; 9.3) and the usurpation of Magnentius (15.6.4; 16.6.2), clearly show that events of those years were narrated on a scale comparable to what survives. His statement of method may be assumed also to reach back to the later years of the reign of Constantine the Great (324–337), for there were many still living—and many who appear in the pages of Ammianus—who had personal knowledge of the time of Constantine. Ammianus' own patron, Ursicinus, was one of them: a *magister militum* in 353 must surely have seen service as a young officer in the later years of Constantine; indeed Ammianus says as much himself (15.5.19).

It has been argued that the preface to book 15 describes Ammianus' method in all the lost thirteen books of the history and inferred from this that these books in their entirety covered the period that could be described after consultation with eyewitnesses. According to this theory, the history of the second and third centuries was narrated in an entirely separate work, which could evidently, in this case, be very extensive in scope. But the assumption is arbitrary: it is equally possible that a preface to an earlier book, say, book 10 or 11, announced a change from a more summary method to that declared at the beginning of book 15. Ammianus does not write of the earlier part of his history as if it formed part of an entirely separate work; in referring to it he uses quite plain expressions like "as I explained above," or "as I mentioned earlier" (16.10.16; 23.6.24). To judge by such back-references, certain rather important matters one would have thought might merit detailed attention in a full-scale history seem in fact to have been dealt with quite briefly, as for example, the execution of Crispus Caesar (14.1.8) and the reigns of Maximus and Gordian III (23.5.7). One particularly interesting and important subject, the introduction of the late Roman ceremony of "adoration of the purple," was evidently not described at all in its proper place but is mentioned for the first time under the year 355 (15.5.18)—hardly suggesting a very detailed account even of the relatively recent reign of Diocletian.

As to his future procedure, Ammianus explains that he will describe what follows with care, to the best of his ability: *residua ... pro virium captu limatius absolvemus* (15.1.1). The word *limatius* does not necessarily imply a promise to describe with *greater* care than before; Ammianus regularly uses the comparative form of epithets as a sort of emphatic positive. Yet his defense against those who may consider his work too long does suggest a certain expansion of scale in the treatment of the events of Ammianus' active lifetime—an expansion not necessarily beginning suddenly at any particular point but becoming progressively more apparent in the later books.

In a subsequent preface at the beginning of book 26, Ammianus makes a somewhat different claim. He there asserts the claims of history to cover high affairs (*negotiorum celsitudines*) and not to waste time ferreting out unworthy details—the building of unimportant forts, the names of those who pay court to the urban praetor, and so on. A man who wished to record such things might as well try to "count the atoms" (26.1.1). Ammianus' declaration here does not contradict his preface to book 15. What will be included or left out even of a full history will require the exercise of judgment. Ammianus may be thinking of those contemporaries who would object because they were not personally mentioned in some trivial event in which they took part, or he may be making an implicit criticism of the biographical genre of historical writing, which tended to confuse the significant with the trivial.

Ammianus' concern, as expressed in these prefaces, was the accurate recording of the history of his own age, and it is in the context of this concern that we should interpret his travels in the years after his retirement from active service following the failure of Julian's Persian campaign. He had certainly visited Egypt. He had seen Alexandria (26.10.19), looked at obelisks standing and lying around at Egyptian Thebes (17.4.6), and heard from the natives an account of the habits of the hippopotamus (22.15.24) and many other things. In the preface to the digression in which he reports some of these matters, he refers back to earlier treatments in his now lost discussions of the reigns of Hadrian and Septimius Severus, *visa pleraque narrantes* (22.15.1). He had passed by the coast of southern Greece, seeing there the hulk of a ship cast two miles inland by the great tidal wave of 358 and now gaping apart "after long decay": "telling of many things that I myself had seen" (26.10.19). How much time—presumably some years—had elapsed since the tidal wave and where Ammianus was going when he "passed by" Mothone he does not say. He had visited the Black Sea, for his digression on that area is derived from what he had "seen or read" (22.8.1); and a Vergilian reference to the bones still "whitening the fields" (*Aeneid* 12.35) after one of the Gothic battles with the Romans in 376-378 may, but need not, reflect his presence there (31.7.16). The site in question, Ad Salices, in the Dobrudja, is rather remote, and it is possible that Ammianus here conveys the vividness of someone else's impression. It would be agreeable to suppose that behind his reference to the funeral at Constantinople of the Gothic king Athanaric lies a personal recollection of the event (27.5.10). A visit to Constantinople in the early 380's (the death and funeral of Athanaric were in 381) would form part of a convincing biography of Ammianus, but this suggestion remains entirely conjectural. It is hard to see, however, how Ammianus can have avoided visiting the eastern capital at some stage.

Adding these journeys to what he had seen in active service, it is evident that when he packed his bags for Rome sometime in the early 380's, Ammianus was an extremely well-traveled man. He had seen Cologne and Ctesiphon, passed with Ursicinus through Illyricum, and now seen Egypt as well as the Black Sea and southern Greece. If these travels had any purpose, it must be evident that when he came to Rome his plans as a historian were already far advanced. How much was already written in a final form is a different matter, though it would have been advisable for an aspiring historian aiming to find a niche in Roman society to have some examples of his work available for inspection or recitation. By the same token, eyewitnesses of events whom Ammianus wished to interview might well need some reassurance that their trouble was going to be worthwhile; perhaps Ammianus had the unreasonable expectations of such men in mind when he disclaimed the need for excessive detail in an ambitious Roman history that devoted itself to *negotiorum celsitudines*.

Yet there was much information still to gather. Whatever their source, Ammianus' accounts of the administrations of successive prefects of Rome, beginning with the prefecture of Orfitus in book 14 (6.1), assume his presence at Rome, as do his denunciations of the moral decadence of the Senate and the people of the ancient capital (14.6.7-26; 28.4.6-35). Ammianus' complaint in the first of these digressions—that on one occasion foreign visitors of literary tastes had been sent from the city during a shortage of corn, while 5,000 dancing girls and their attendants were allowed to stay—conveys a resentment that has fairly been taken to reflect his own expulsion at that time. Ammianus states that the event had taken place "not so long ago" (14.6.19). If the expulsion is rightly interpreted as that recorded for the year 384, then this passage, in the earliest surviving book, cannot have been written until the late 380's.

It is clear that substantial parts of Ammianus' later books on the reigns of Valentinian and Valens must have been composed after Ammianus had come to Rome and had access to western information. Such are his narrative of the trials for adultery and magic arts conducted by Valentinian's agents in the 370's, where Ammianus reflects senatorial opinion (28.1.1–57); his account of Valentinian's frontier works (28.2.1–3); the complaints of the citizens of Lepcis Magna to the imperial court over the conduct of the *comes Africae Romanus* (28.6.1–29); the campaigns of Theodosius in Mauretania (29.5.1–56); and many other passages. This point can be pursued in a more precisely relevant way: first, as we have seen, such passages occur not only in these latest, but also in the earliest of the surviving books; and second, it was not only information about the more recent past that Ammianus was able to gather at Rome in the 380's. During his stay, there also lived in the city a former adviser of Julian's as caesar in Gaul, the eunuch Eutherius. Ammianus gives his biography. Born of free parents in Armenia, Eutherius had come as a boy slave to the court of Constantine the Great and there advanced through his culture, his intelligence, and his "immense memory." He had served the emperor Constans and then Julian and, now living in old age at Rome, was admired by those of all social ranks (16.7.4–7). Ammianus surely means to say that he, too, was acquainted with Eutherius. If so, it would, to say the least, be negligent of him, given Eutherius' powers of memory, to limit his inquiries to the more recent past. Even after his arrival in Rome in the 380's, therefore, Ammianus was able to gather first-hand information on Constantine and his court, and to incorporate it into his history.

If Ammianus could still add information on substantial issues, not all of them very recent, after he came to Rome, it is fair to ask whether his historical conception itself was still open to influence and modification; in particular, what new literary and historiographical influences might still exert themselves on him. Although it became more formalized after Ammianus' day, the Greek tradition of historical writing, with which Ammianus had many affinities, had produced a chain of works that, in effect and often in intention, constituted a continuous history. So Herodotus was continued by Thucydides, Thucydides by Xenophon, and, in the Roman period, Cassius Dio by Dexippus and he by Eunapius of Sardis, Ammianus' contemporary, whose work may well have been known to him. If we were to apply this Greek tradition of continuous historiography to Latin historical composition we would be bound, of course, to link Ammianus with Tacitus. In his epilogue, Ammianus appealed to others, if they were confident, to cover the history of their own generations. We do not possess the preface to his work, in which Ammianus would have announced in what tradition he saw himself in relation to his predecessors, but the epilogue directs us firmly to the reign of Nerva, where Tacitus had left off.

This was also, of course, the terminal point of Suetonius' *Caesars*. Ammianus certainly knew of Suetonius' successor, the biographer Marius Maximus, whose writing comes under Ammianus' fire in a well-known passage where he denounces Roman senators for reading nothing better, in their profound distaste for culture, than Juvenal and Marius Maximus (28.4.14). Disapproval of Juvenal comes oddly from a historian whose own writing, in just such passages as these, shows so many satirical traces. As for Marius Maximus, it is conceivable that Ammianus viewed him as an unworthy successor to Suetonius, whom he admired; more likely, however, he thought poorly of both Marius Maximus and the historiographical tradition to which he belonged. The distinction between "annalistic" and "biographical" history was certainly becoming blurred by Ammianus' day. Jerome actually said that Tacitus wrote "lives of the Caesars" in thirty books, which is by the strictest standards a rather confused way of referring to the *Historiae* and *Annales*. The fundamental differences of style and method between Suetonius and Tacitus remained at all times plain to see. For Ammianus, biography, as represented by Suetonius and Marius Maximus, may have seemed to efface precisely that distinction between trivial details and *negotiorum celsitudines* that he asserted so forcibly in his preface to book 26.

It is generally assumed that Ammianus was a conscious successor to Tacitus as Latin historian of the Roman Empire, and it is difficult to see how, in general terms, this can fail to be true. But it is worth asking, in view of what has been argued above about the origins of Ammianus' historical conception in his own experience and its affinities with Greek models, how profound the influence of Tacitus might have been.

First, on the assumption that the second, third, and early fourth centuries were described in the lost thirteen books, it is unlikely that the earliest part of the history, in which Ammianus succeeded Tacitus with the reign of Nerva, would have much resembled his predecessor in the impression it made on the reader. Although Ammianus could improve on the pitiful later Latin tradition of historiography of that period by drawing on Greek sources, his account of those centuries would still have been much briefer than the later books of the *Historiae* and (for the additional reason that Greek sources would be used) in style as well as content very unlike his predecessor's.

Second, Ammianus arrived in Rome in about 384, having traveled widely in the empire, with information still to gather for his history but with much material already assembled, some of it even written up and, one would assume, the main outlines of its structure clear in his mind. If I am right in arguing that the "Greek" in Ammianus is the dominant influence on his historical writing, in its scale of treatment and in its lavish use of digressions, it is hard to see how the influence of Tacitus can be much more than formal. Tacitus may have determined the starting point of Ammianus' history in the absence of any worthy successor during the intervening centuries, but, I suggest, this was a late influence and one without profound effect on the manner and style of Ammianus' presentation. This conclusion is intrinsic to the view, outlined above, of the origins and development of Ammianus' interest in historical writing and leaves aside such questions as the likelihood of his being able to acquire a copy of Tacitus in Antioch or elsewhere in the East in the later 360's or 370's, and the difficulty of establishing any linguistic influence of Tacitus on Ammianus. In such passages as that describing Valentinian's trials for adultery and magic at Rome, conducted under the law of *maiestas* (28.1.11), some well-chosen Tacitean echoes would have enriched the allusive depth of Ammianus' writing had he wished his readers to make the connection: but they cannot be found.

I have also argued that the Latin language itself was far deeper in Ammianus' experience than is usually assumed. As a Greek, but a Greek from a great Roman administrative capital at a time when the language of imperial administration was Latin, Ammianus' affinity with this language and with Roman ideals (compare his remark on the annexation of Arabia) was already implicit in his viewpoint as a young man.

Primarily, however, I have suggested that the transition between Ammianus' personal experiences and the writing of Roman history on a large scale is provided by the figure of Julian the Apostate, in the challenge that he posed to the Christian establishment of the fourth century and the comparison he invited with the emperors of an earlier period. The implications of my arguments are that Ammianus' emergence as a Roman historian is an integral expression of his own background and intellectual evolution. As for Tacitus, the end of the *Historiae* provides an appropriate point at which to start a history that is in an obvious sense its continuator; but even this may have been a relatively late and not really profound influence on the way in which Ammianus wrote history. For the purpose of a summary account in a few books of Roman history of the second and third centuries, it would not much matter precisely where one began (so long as Marcus Aurelius was included). The reign of Nerva was suggested by the double influence of Tacitus and Suetonius, a suggestion possibly hardened by the inadequacy of Marius Maximus as Suetonius' successor; but Ammianus' original notion of writing history and his emergence as Latin historian of the Roman Empire were developments integral to himself.

V

It is dangerous in the case of an observer so comprehensively alert as Ammianus to define his view of Roman history in terms of a central attitude or preoccupation. If one is to be sought, I would suggest that it lies in his view of law and justice and in the obligation of Roman emperors to respect the public institutions by which law and justice and individual rights are defended. For Ammianus, the emperors had inherited the protection of law and settled life from the senatorial government of the republic. His most explicit statement on the origins of the imperial system links it by organic development with the institutions of the city of Rome. Ammianus introduces the topic in order to explain why it should be that whenever his narrative turns to Rome there is nothing to tell of but "riots, drunkenness, and other such trivialities" (*nihil praeter seditiones narratur et tabernas et vilitates harum similis alias*: 14.6.2). The dignity and grandeur of Rome, symbolized in the glory of its ancient assemblies, Senate, and people, was betrayed by the frivolity of a few unworthy members. Ammianus shows the "splendor of the assemblies" by describing the growth to power and maturity of Rome as a life span. From birth to the end of youth, a period of three hundred years, Rome suffered and triumphed in local wars, and in early adulthood and maturity it spread influence over the world, bringing home laurels and triumphs. In present times Rome, now approaching old age and con-

quering "by name alone" (14.6.4), has withdrawn to a quieter life, everywhere respected as mistress and queen, the white hair of the senators and the name of the *populus Romanus* being revered and honored.

It is too easy to read this passage as a statement on the mortality of empire, a premonition that Roman power is coming to an end; this is not at all what Ammianus means. His metaphor is applied not to the empire at large, but to the city of Rome and its institutions. Rome, having achieved in maturity the mastery of the world, has in old age yielded the exercise of power to the emperors, having "like a careful parent, wise and wealthy, left her inheritance to the Caesars, as to her children" (14.6.5). This is not an image of decline; as Rome the city enters old age, her children the emperors carry on the mission. Ammianus saw Senate and emperor as integrally linked with each other in a relationship of mutual respect. This respect could of course be undermined by circumstances, as during the trials conducted at Rome by the agents of Valentinian (28.1.1–57), but even here without the connotations of profound ideological conflict between the two which had been the central theme of the writings of Tacitus.

Ammianus was no abstract political theorist; his views on the duties of the imperial office were straightforward and serviceable rather than elaborately sophisticated. The proper end of imperial power, as he put it in his obituary of the emperor Valentinian, was to preserve the interests and security of loyal men: *finis enim iusti imperii, ut sapientes docent, utilitas obuedientium et salus* (30.8.14). He set it out in very similar terms elsewhere, while criticizing the emperor Valens' abuse of his position; the purpose of empire was to preserve the safety of others, and a good emperor would to this end restrain his exercise of power. This, too, was the opinion of philosophers (29.2.18).

Ammianus' conception is sharply brought out in his descriptions of occasions on which its principles were violated. In the prosecutions conducted by Gallus Caesar at Antioch in 354, men were executed, exiled, forced to live on the charity of others; no resources were left them but "grievances and tears." Rich houses were closed as the empire was turned to the bloody whim of one man: *civili iustoque imperio ad voluntatem converso cruentam* (14.1.4). Not even were suborned prosecutors heard in court to preserve a pretense of legal procedure, a formality that even notoriously cruel emperors had sometimes allowed. Whatever Gallus himself decided was treated as right and lawful and immediately put into effect: *id velut fas iusque perpensum, confestim urgebatur impleri* (14.1.5). There was no attempt to examine the truth of claims made in court or to distinguish the guilty from the innocent. The rule of law was driven from the courts: *e iudiciis fas omne discessit* (14.7.21). At one point, two men were accused before Gallus. One, a philosopher "in name only, as became apparent," when put to the torture and threatened with death, confessed complicity in treason that had never existed. He was in addition, said Ammianus, totally ignorant of legal procedure. His fellow victim, who knew the law, proclaimed that the affair was an act of brigandage, not a court of law; he demanded a proper accuser and the regular formalities. But it did him no good. He was dreadfully tortured for his insolence and dragged out for execution (14.9.5–6).

Ammianus did not deny the necessity for a law of treason. He discussed the matter in narrating inquiries made by Constantius in 359, when an affair came to light involving the consultation of oracles, exaggerated by Constantius' suspicion and the pressure of his courtiers into a great affair of state (19.12.1 ff.). Matters reached such a pitch of tension that to wear an amulet against the quartan fever or walk by a grave at night might be turned into a charge of black magic, and execution ensue (19.12.13). Ammianus agreed that strict inquiries were in order; anyone in his right mind, he wrote, would agree to that (19.12.17). A lawful emperor, the protector and defender of men of good will (*propugnator bonorum et defensor*), was in turn entitled to the full protection of all men. To this end the Cornelian laws had permitted torture and even execution, as near-contemporary legislation confirms (*Codex Theodosianus* of A.D. 358, 9.16.6; of A.D. 369, 9.35.1). But it was wrong for an emperor to take pleasure in such affairs, so that his subjects appeared to be under despotism rather than lawful power. Cicero had written that excuses should be sought to pardon rather than punish; or, as Julian put it in the same spirit, an emperor should always seek to increase the number of his friends by clemency (22.14.5). Constantius, on the other hand, whose inquisitions into cases of treason led him to greater cruelty even than Caligula, Domitian, and Commodus, was roused by fear of treason to actions more severe than were compatible with what was lawful or humane (*acrius exsurgens quam civiliter*). He, like Valens in such cases, appointed judges especially chosen for their harshness (21.16.8–9; compare 31.14.6). This was a violation of all proper procedure, for it was in the observance of this humanity and in respect for the courts of law that the essence lay of what Ammianus called a "civil and just empire" (*civile iustumque imperium*: 14.1.4).

If there was a single concept at the heart of Ammianus' attitudes to imperial government, it was perhaps this notion of *civilitas*, conveying a sense of the moral and institutional restraints that an emperor ought to observe. Ammianus mocked Constantius for his ambition to model his rule on that of the *civiles principes* of earlier times while styling himself in dictated correspondence as *Aeternitas Mea* ("My Eternity") and in letters written with his own hand designating himself "Master of the Entire World." This was a departure from justice indulged in by Constantius after the execution of Gallus, when his courtiers persuaded him that his virtue and fortune were without limit, and that he was free from the usual inconveniences of mortality (15.1.2–3).

Ammianus' objection here is little more than a debating point and curious in itself, for he must have known that this use of abstract terminology—*Aeternitas Mea, Serenitas Nostra* ("Our Serenity"), and other such expressions—

was a regular feature of the official language of his age; the Theodosian Code is full of examples of it. In other contexts Ammianus shows himself aware of the need for a certain ceremonial deportment on the part of the emperors. It is the first of the points listed in his obituary in favor of Constantius that this emperor regarded the imperial position with the dignity due it. In an allusion to the raised shoe used by dramatic actors on the stage, he remarked that Constantius always kept on the trappings of imperial authority and proudly disdained the pursuit of mere popularity: *imperatoriae auctoritatis cothurnum ubique custodiens popularitatem elato animo contemnebat et magno* (21.16.1). This contrasts sharply with Ammianus' judgment of Julian, that he fed on the applause of the multitude, seeking praise without restraint, affecting in his thirst for popularity to converse with the unworthy: *vulgi plausibus laetus, laudum etiam ex minimis rebus intemperans adpetitor, popularitatis cupiditate cum indignis loqui saepe adfectans* (25.4.18). On one occasion Julian was sitting with the Senate in session at Constantinople when the arrival of the philosopher Maximus was announced. Julian leapt up unceremoniously and went charging out of the Senate to meet his friend, kissed him in greeting, received him with reverence (that is, as an equal or superior and not as an emperor receives a subject), and escorted him into the Senate. The incident seems to show Julian as an ostentatious seeker for praise and glory—like those philosophers who, according to Cicero, wrote books denouncing fame and ambition and yet put their names to them (22.7.3–4)! More curtly, Julian simply "forgot who he was" (*qui esset, oblitus:* 7.3).

Ammianus recognized the complexity of the relationship between the character of an emperor and the nature of the imperial office. He quotes Valentinian's opinion that the office tended to provoke envy and misinterpretation; the emperor used to remark that imputations of severity always attended the correct exercise of power (30.8.10). Introducing his obituary of Valentinian, Ammianus notes how the possession of power is liable to lay bare the intimate reaches of the soul, revealing good and bad alike: *vitiorum ... vel bonorum, quae potestatis amplitudo monstravit, nudare solita semper animorum interna* (30.7.1). The emperor Jovian, mentioned in a brief obituary notice, ate and drank excessively and indulged in unrestrained sexual relations—faults which, had he lived, respect for the imperial office would perhaps have led him to correct (25.10.15). Ammianus' emperors are indeed notable for the sobriety of their private and sexual lives: it is remarked on in his obituaries of all except for Valens, of whom nothing is said in this respect, for good or ill.

The subtlety and precision of Ammianus' conception of the imperial office emerge particularly well in his famous description of the arrival of Constantius II on a state visit to Rome in 357. The passage is a classic illustration of Ammianus' technique and power of visual evocation. Constantius sat in a golden carriage amid the glitter of precious stones. He was attended by the figured standards of his army, dragon ensigns fluttering in the breeze, their mouths gaping open as if actually hissing; on either side were mailed infantrymen, their armor fitting their bodies as closely as if they had been bronze statues. The emperor sat immobile, not moving to the right or left, holding his neck rigid even when the carriage jolted, his hands quite still (16.10.7–10). Ammianus' remark that Constantius neither spat nor wiped his face or nose with his hands may seem a shade bizarre to the modern reader; but this would be a mistaken reaction. Such behavior was meant to indicate superhuman self-control, regarded by Xenophon in a remarkably similar passage (*Cyropaedia* 8.1.40 ff.) as a visible proof of kingly stature. It is mentioned in Ammianus' obituary notice of Constantius among the virtues of the emperor (21.16.7).

Ammianus' criticism of Constantius' behavior is precisely expressed. He was offended by the "triumphal" aspects of the procession, conducted after victories in civil war by an emperor whose record in foreign wars did not merit the celebration. Constantius wished to demonstrate imperial power to the Roman people, who lived in peace and quiet, neither expecting nor wanting to see anything like it (16.10.2). The emperor carried himself as if he were off to "intimidate Euphrates or Rhine with a show of arms" (10.6), and his remote, imperturbable posture was such as was commonly seen in the provinces (10.9). A triumph in all but name (absque nomine . . . triumphaturus: 16.10.1), the procession to Rome was inappropriate to the shrine of empire and all the virtues, the residence of peace, civility, and freedom. Once he was inside the city Constantius' behavior changed. He addressed the Senate in the senate house, the people from the tribunal in the forum; he held equestrian games and took pleasure in the friendly shouts of the people, who respected both due modesty and their traditional liberty. The emperor, too, preserved proper decorum and, as an interesting concession to the ancient liberties of Rome, even allowed the horse races to find their own outcome. In other cities, it is implied, he used his own discretion to control the results (16.10.13–14). It was in general, adapted for different social classes, the behavior that Theodosius' panegyrist of 389, the orator Pacatus, did in fact describe as *civilis*.

The notion of *civilitas*, applied to the proper behavior of a Roman emperor, thus covers a broad but coherent range of applications: avoidance of excessive expressions of despotism, respect for such existing legal and political institutions as courts of law, a sense of the appropriate comportment of an emperor on formal and informal occasions. If, for Ammianus, the emperors should operate within the framework of the institutions and rules by which individual rights as well as the emperors' interests were protected, it may be possible in conclusion to use this notion to illuminate his view of one particularly important issue, the religious views of Julian the Apostate. Ammianus' summary of Julian's religious attitudes, which he classifies among the shortcomings briefly set out in the obituary of the emperor, was that he was "superstitious rather than a legitimate observer of divine affairs": *superstitiosus, magis quam sacrorum legitimus observator* (25.4.17). "Superstition" is a notoriously difficult word to define; Ammianus also uses it to describe the emperor Constantius' "old woman's superstition" in his obsessive treatment of the disputes of the Christian religion (21.16.18). It might be possible to make more progress with the word *legitimus*, as applied to Julian's religious conduct.

It was partly a matter of degree. Julian's religiosity was excessive, like that of Hadrian. He drenched the altars with the sacrifice of hundreds of animals; Ammianus cites as parallel a mock petition of the "white cattle" to Marcus Aurelius, protesting that if he went on winning victories, they, the white cattle, would be exterminated (25.4.17)! Julian's sacrifices at Antioch were so lavish, and the meat provided by them so plentiful, that his soldiers had sometimes to be carried home to their billets, incapacitated by food and drink (22.12.6).

A more precise sense of what Ammianus meant by *legitimus* may be provided by a group of episodes taken from the Persian campaign itself. On the second day of the march into Persia, a military detachment brought to Julian the body of a huge lion that had been shot down as it attacked the army (23.5.8 ff.). Then a soldier, with the symbolic name Jovianus, was killed by lightning while watering horses by the Euphrates (23.5.12). The official seers (haruspices) accompanying the army were asked to interpret the omens. Getting out their books, whose titles Ammianus gives as the *Libri exercituales* and *Libri fulgurales*, the seers pronounced that the omens were adverse; the gods were advising against the campaign. The opinions of the seers, however, were "trodden underfoot" by "philosophers," whose authority was "at that time revered." These philosophers, "persisting in matters they little understood," declared that the omens were either neutral, the expressions of natural phenomena, or were actually in favor of the campaign (23.5.10 ff.). Later, on the morning of Julian's death, a shooting star was seen.

The seers, again consulting their books, the *Tarquitiani libri, in titulo de rebus divinis,* advised that nothing must be done that day or that at the very least there must be a delay (25.2.7–8). Their advice was again overridden by the philosophers, with the consequence that within a few hours they found themselves acting in another capacity, sharing Julian's deathbed reflections on the immortality of the soul (25.3.23).

These philosophers, Julian's old friends Maximus and Priscus, were actually theurgists—men skilled in magical arts that were believed to evoke animation in statues, and to bring oracles from the lips of these statues, and in other techniques whose object, as Maximus had once put it to his colleague Chrysanthius, was "forcing the heavenly powers to yield to their servant." Ammianus was openly critical of what he regarded as their spontaneous inventions in "matters they little understood," as against the predictions of the seers based on the ancient books. It was Ammianus' privilege as a historian to be proved right by the outcome, but the basis in principle of his objections to Julian's conduct remains important; he believed that, for a Roman emperor leading a Roman army on a campaign, the official seers and not the philosophers were the proper interpreters of the information provided to men by the gods. It was on their understanding of the signs and not on that of the philosophers that the "conjectures of men," as Cicero had put it (21.1.14), were more securely based. In religion as in politics, correct behavior was enshrined in respect for regular institutions and procedures, symbolized in this case by the books in which they were written.

This essay has begun and ended with the Persian campaign of Julian, and more particularly with its failure and the death of the emperor who led it. If a single moment that turned Ammianus to the writing of history had to be chosen, it would, I think, be this one. It would set on yet another and very immediate level Ammianus' description of himself in his epilogue as a "soldier and a Greek," but there is nothing more broadly fundamental in his attitudes toward the political life—and, I have argued, to the religious life of the empire—than his respect for its established institutions. These are what stand between the emperors and willful self-indulgence and despotism, and there is nothing more Roman in Ammianus than his conviction that this was so. It is this, despite his affinities with Greek historiography and rather than any specific debt to Tacitus, that marks Ammianus as the last of the great Roman historians.

Selected Bibliography

TEXTS AND TRANSLATIONS

Ammianus Marcellini rerum gestarum libri qui supersunt, edited by C. U. Clark. 2 vols. Berlin, 1910–1915. Only volume to present clearly the essential work of early editors of Ammianus, as well as manuscript evidence; unlikely to be superseded.

Ammianus Marcellinus, edited by J. C. Rolfe. 3 vols. Cambridge, Mass., 1933–1939. Loeb Classical Library. Latin with English translation.

Rerum gestarum libri qui supersunt, edited by V. Gardthausen. Stuttgart, 1874–1875. Reprinted 1967. Teubner edition; remains convenient and serviceable.

COMMENTARIES

Brok, M. F. A., ed. *Die Perzische Expeditie van Keizer Julianus volgens Ammianus Marcellinus.* Groningen, 1959. Comprises books 23–25.

De Jonge, P., ed. *Philological and Historical Commentary on Ammianus Marcellinus.* Groningen, 1935–1980. So far covers books 14–18; still in progress.

Galletier, E., G. Sabbah, et al., eds. *Histoire.* Paris, 1977. Vol. 4 on books 23–25, edited by J. Fontaine, is particularly full and useful.

Szidat, J., ed. *Historische Kommentar zu Ammianus Marcellinus Buch XX–XXI.* Historia, Einzelschriften 31. Wiesbaden, 1977.

AMMIANUS MARCELLINUS

CRITICAL STUDIES

Auerbach, Erich. "The Arrest of Peter Valvomeres." In *Mimesis: The Representation of Reality in Western Literature.* Princeton, 1953. Reprinted 1968. Pp. 50-76. A brilliant discussion of Ammianus' style as reflecting the temper of his age.

Austin, N. J. E. "In Support of Ammianus' Veracity." *Historia* 22:331-335 (1973). Authenticates a detail of Ammianus' trip to Corduene (Kurdistan) in 359.

———. *Ammianus on Warfare: An Investigation into Ammianus' Military Knowledge.* Collection Latomus 165. Brussels, 1979.

Blockley, R. C. *Ammianus Marcellinus. A Study of His Historiography and Political Thought.* Collection Latomus 141. Brussels, 1975. A most persuasive presentation of this aspect.

Cameron, Alan. "The Roman Friends of Ammianus." *Journal of Roman Studies* 54:15-28 (1964).

Camus, P.-M. *Ammien Marcellin: Témoin des courants culturels et réligieux à la fin de IVᵉ siècle.* Paris, 1967. Relatively slight, though perceptive and helpful.

Chalmers, W. R. "Eunapius, Ammianus Marcellinus, and Zosimus on Julian's Persian Expedition." *Classical Quarterly* n.s. 10:152-160 (1960). On the complex problem of Ammianus' relationship with Greek sources on the campaign.

Charlesworth, M. P. "Imperial Deportment: Two Texts and Some Questions." *Journal of Roman Studies* 37:34-38 (1947).

Crump, G. A. *Ammianus Marcellinus as a Military Historian.* Historia, Einzelschriften 27. Wiesbaden, 1975.

Demandt, W. "Zeitkritik und Geschichtsbild im Werk Ammians." Ph.D. dissertation. Marburg, 1965.

Dillemann, L. "Ammien Marcellin et les pays de l'Euphrate et du Tigre." *Syria* 38:87-158 (1961). Establishes Ammianus' independence of other sources as an eyewitness of Julian's Persian campaign.

Drexler, D. *Ammianstudien.* Spudasmata 31. New York and Hildesheim, 1974.

Ensslin, W. *Zur Geschichtsschreibung und Weltanschauung des Ammianus Marcellinus.* Klio, Beiheft 16. Leipzig, 1923. The foundation of much more recent work.

Flach, D. "Von Tacitus zu Ammian." *Historia* 21:330-350 (1972).

Jeep, L. "Die verlorenen Bücher des Ammianus." *Rheinisches Museum* 43:60-72 (1888). Criticizes the work of Michael, below.

Klein, W. *Studien zu Ammianus Marcellinus.* Klio, Beiheft 13. Leipzig, 1914.

MacMullen, R. "Some Pictures in Ammianus Marcellinus." *Art Bulletin* 46:435-455 (1964). On the "visual" and ceremonial aspects of Roman life.

Matthews, J. F. "Mauretania in Ammianus and the Notitia." In R. Goodburn and P. Bartholomew, eds., *Aspects of the Notitia Dignitatum.* Oxford, 1976. Pp. 157-186. Shows the richness and accuracy of Ammianus' account in the context of other evidence, including archaeological.

Michael, H. *Die verlorenen Bücher des Ammianus Marcellinus.* Breslau, 1880.

Monigliano, A. "The Lonely Historian Ammianus Marcellinus." *Annali della Scuola Normale Superiore di Pisa, Classe di Lettere e Filosofia.* 3rd ser. Vol. 4, 4. Pisa, 1974. Pp. 1393-1407.

Pack, R. "Ammianus Marcellinus and the 'Curia' of Antioch." *Classical Philology* 43:80-85 (1953).

———. "The Roman Digressions of Ammianus Marcellinus." *Transactions and Proceedings of the American Philological Association* 84:184-189 (1953).

Paschoud, F. *Roma aeterna: Études sur le patriotisme romain dans l'occident latin à l'époque des grandes invasions.* Rome, 1967. Pp. 33-70.

Rosen, K. "Studien zu Darstellungskunst und Glaubwürdigkeit des Ammianus Marcellinus." Ph.D. dissertation. Heidelberg, 1970. Emphasizes the influence of rhetorical models on Ammianus, but at times understating his circumstantial accuracy.

Rougé, J. "Une Émeute à Rome au IVᵉ siècle. Ammien Marcellin XXVII 3.3-4: Essai d'interprétation." *Revue des études anciennes* 63:59-77 (1961).

Rowell, H. T. *Ammianus Marcellinus, Soldier-Historian of the Late Roman Empire.* Sample Lectures, ser. 1. Princeton, 1967. Pp. 265-313.

Sabbah, G. *La Méthode d'Ammien Marcellin: Recherches sur la construction du discours historique dans les Res Gestae.* Paris, 1978. A discussion of Ammianus' historical principles rather than his method as a historian.

Seeck, O. "Die Reihe des Stadtpräfecten bei Ammianus Marcellinus." *Hermes* 18:289-303 (1883).

Syme, R. *Ammianus and the Historia Augusta.* Oxford, 1968. A characteristically vivid and challenging study, ranging widely in the literary and cultural life of the fourth century.

Thompson, E. A. *The Historical Work of Ammianus Marcellinus.* Cambridge, 1947. Reprinted Hildesheim, 1969. The most accessible and broadest account for English readers.

POLITICAL AND CULTURAL BACKGROUND

Alföldi, A. *A Conflict of Ideas in the Late Roman Empire: The Clash Between the Senate and Valentinian I.* Oxford, 1952.

Alonso-Nunez, J. M. *La vision historiografica de Ammiano Marcelino.* Valladolid, 1975.

Barnes, T. D. *The Sources of the Historia Augusta.* Collection Latomus 155. Brussels, 1978.

Bidez, J. *La Vie de l'Empereur Julian.* Paris, 1930.

Bowersock, G. W. *Julian the Apostate.* London, 1978.

Cameron, Alan and Averil Cameron. "Christianity and Tradition in the Historiography of the Late Empire." *Classical Quarterly* n.s. 14:3, 6–328 (1964).

Cameron, Averil. *Agathias.* Oxford, 1970.

Chastagnol, A. *La Préfecture urbaine à Rome sous le Bas-Empire.* Paris, 1960.

———. *Les Fastes de la préfecture de Rome au Bas-Empire.* Paris, 1962.

Codex Theodosianus. *Theodosiani Libri XVI, cum constitutionibus Sirmondianis,* edited by T. Mommsen and P. Meyer. Berlin, 1905. Translated and commentary, glossary, and bibliography by Clyde Pharr. Princeton, 1952.

Dill, S. *Roman Society in the Last Century of the Western Empire.* London, 1899. Reprinted New York, 1958.

Dodds, E. R. "Theurgy and Its Relationship to Neoplatonism." *Journal of Roman Studies* 37:55–69 (1947). Reprinted as appendix II ("Theurgy") in his *The Greeks and the Irrational.* Berkeley, Calif., and London, 1951.

Downey, G. *A History of Antioch in Syria.* Princeton, 1961.

Ensslin, W. *Die Religionspolitik des Kaisers Theodosius der Gr. Sitzungsberichte der Bayerischen Akademie der Wissenschaften.* Heft 2. Munich, 1953.

Eunapius. *Lives of the Philosophers and Sophists.* Translated by W. C. Wright in *Philostratus and Eunapius, The Lives of the Sophists.* Cambridge, Mass., and London, 1921. Reprinted 1961. Loeb Classical Library.

Fridh, A. J. *Terminologie et Formules dans les Variae de Cassiodore.* Stockholm, 1956.

Jones, A. H. M. *The Later Roman Empire: A Social, Economic and Administrative Survey.* Oxford, 1964.

———, J. M. Martindale, and J. Morris. *The Prosopography of the Later Roman Empire.* Vol. 1: A.D. 260–395. Cambridge, 1971.

King, N. W. *The Emperor Theodosius and the Establishment of Christianity.* London, 1961.

Liebeschuetz, J. H. W. G. *Antioch: City and Imperial Administration in the Later Roman Empire.* Oxford, 1972.

Lippold, A. *Theodosius der Grosse und seine Zeit.* Stuttgart, 1968.

MacMullen, R. "Roman Bureaucratese." *Traditio* 18:364–378 (1962).

Matthews, J. F. "Gallic Supporters of Theodosius." *Latomus* 30:1073–1099 (1971).

———. "The Letters of Symmachus." In J. W. Binns, ed., *Latin Literature of the Fourth Century.* Boston and London, 1974.

Paschoud, F. "Quand parut la première édition de l'histoire d'Eunape?" *Bonner Historia-Augusta-Colloquium 1977–1978.* Bonn, 1980. Pp. 149–162.

Petit, P. *Libanius et la vie municipale à Antioche au IVe siècle après J.-C.* Paris, 1955.

Seeck, O. *Die Briefe des Libanios.* Texte und Untersuchungen, N. F. XV.1–2. Leipzig, 1906. Reprinted Hildesheim, 1966.

Segal, J. B. *Edessa: The "Blessed City."* Oxford, 1970.

Stein, E. *Histoire du Bas-Empire.* Translated by J.-R. Palanque. Paris and Bruges, 1959.

Wiesen, D. S. *St. Jerome as a Satirist.* Cornell Studies in Classical Philology 37. Ithaca, N.Y., 1964.

J. F. MATTHEWS

INDEX

Arabic numbers printed in boldface type refer to extended treatment of a subject. References to footnotes are indicated by the letter n.